ISBN 978-1-331-45025-2
PIBN 10191818

NOTES AND QUERIES:

ser. 3, v. 7

A

Medium of Inter-Communication

FOR

LITERARY MEN, GENERAL READERS, ETC.

"When found, make a note of."— CAPTAIN CUTTLE.

THIRD SERIES. — VOLUME SEVENTH.

JANUARY — JUNE 1865.

LONDON:

PUBLISHED AT THE

OFFICE, 32 WELLINGTON STREET, STRAND, W.C.

1865.

LONDON, SATURDAY, JANUARY 7, 1865.

CONTENTS.—N° 158.

Notes.

THE YOUNG PRETENDER'S CONFORMING TO THE CHURCH OF ENGLAND AND VISIT TO LONDON IN 1750.

Some peculiarly interesting documents illustrative of the history of the time having been discovered among the *Stuart Papers*, which are now in the process of arrangement at Windsor, under the superintendence of Mr. Woodward, the Queen's Librarian, Her Majesty "was pleased to command him to make them publicly known, considering them to be too valuable a contribution to the exact knowledge of our history at that time to wait until the Calendar of the Stuart Papers should be published." Acting upon this command, Mr. Woodward has printed them in *The Times*, in a communication which appeared in that Journal on the 27th ult., and I venture to hope you will transfer to "N. & Q." the following interesting extract from it, and will consider its interest a sufficient excuse for its length. Let me first observe (which Mr. Woodward has not considered it necessary to notice), that the first of these documents, the "Remarks" on the Commission, were obviously added to it at a subsequent period.

"The first of these papers is a copy of a ' Manifesto,' dated 1745, and addressed by the Prince to Scotland. It

is appended to a ' commission ' from his father, dated in 1743. At the end of it we find some ' remarks,' one of which is this : —

"8ly. To mention my religion (which is) of the Church of England as by law established, as I have declared myself when in London the year 1750."

"The next three are memoranda for letters or reports in the Prince's handwriting— the first two written on torn scraps of paper ; the third, on a thin card.

"Parted ye 2d Sept. Arrived to A[ntwerp] ye 6th, parted from thence ye 12th Sept. E[ngland] ye 14th, and at L[ondon] ye 16th. Parted from L[ondon] ye 22d, and arrived at P[aris] ye 24th. From P[aris] parted ye 28th, arrived here ye 30th Sept. If she dos not come, and yr M. agreed on to send bac for yr Letter and Procuration ; ye House here of P. C. and her being either a tretor or a hour, to chuse which, not to send to P. even after her coming, unless in absolute necessity, or her requiring it then at her dor."

Verso. "The letter to Godie retarded a post, ye Lady being arrived or her retard to be Little if she is true stille."

" Ye 5th Sept., O. S., 1750, arrived ; ye 11th, parted to D[over] ; ye 12, in ye morning, parted and arrived at B[oulogne] ; and ye 13th at P[aris]. N.*S., ye 16th Sept., ye 22d, 23d, and 24th.

" Either ill counsiled or She has made a Confidence. Mr. Lorain's being here ye 12th Sept. Mr. Duran his discorces to amuse not having to do with anybody but ye Lady, and Mr. Lisle's not marrieeng, or appearing ; to go ye same day with ye King, speking to W. ye last day.

" Md. H. here this six weeks."

Verso. "The Vignion for W., and letters K and L, the money and *adresses*. (*In pencil*, " The money for Dormer.")

" Je ne puis pas envoie pour ne pas doner du subson et si jenvoi pas je done encore."

"The last sentence, notwithstanding its bad French, is clearly indicative of the Prince's growing hopelessness in his own cause : —

" Lux. Novemr. ye 26th. Mrs. Tomson. Ye P.M. is the best time for me to go. Rue Verneuil, visavi La Rue Ste. Marie faug. St. Germin, Ju. Waters. . . . ' ye Ordonances ; ye Lady ; my being a Republican ; Sr. J. Grems [*Graham's*] being sent ; Sr. J. Stuard ; ye Envoy of P.[*russia?*] at Lu. ; Charles Smit ; Mr. Heborn [*Hepburn*] ; my resons of Declaring myself a Protestant at ye age of 30ty. my being at London ye yr. 50ty. K. of P[*russia's?*] uniform for to go Lu. ye 50 Louidors for Ca : Kely ; Wm. Murray," &c.

* In *The Times* this was erroneously printed R. S., which gave rise to an opinion that there was a discrepancy in the dates. But it will be seen that the difference is only that of eleven days, the difference between the Old and New Styles.

" On the *verso* of the card are some memoranda of money matters, and the date ' ye 21rst March, 1754.'

" The letter now to be given contains neither date nor signature; but I think the name of the writer (evidently a Scotchman) will be ascertained from a comparison of the writing and with other papers of the same period. The date is approximately determinable as 1769 or 1770, from the references to the death of the Chevalier de St. George (the Old Pretender) and to the flight of Miss Walkinshaw with their child. The proposal to repudiate the National Debt is very curious and amusing : —

" It was most certainly a very great affront and Injury done to the Prince to carry from him his Daughter, that behoved to be a fine amusement to Him in his solitary way of liveing, while still expecting better Times.

" When He Discovers Him that acted it, or had a share in the Crime, He or they should be punised, tho' with much goodness, to imitate our great Creator.   In the meantime it should not be resented to His own Disadvantage, or that of his most sincere Weal Wishers, but a proper time waited when it can be done more effectualy. If his Majesty had any share in it, It can be imputed to nothing else than a wrong principle in his Religion, and ought therefore to be heartyly forgiven, and a good Understanding fully reestablish'd.   It must be a great Loss to His Royal Highness and all true subjects to have the intercourse betwixt Him and them intirely cutt off by his Resolution of so strict a Retirement which they most earnestly wish and beg He would change to their Vast Comfort; and it is the greatest Glory of a man to forgive ane Injury. I hear'd more than three years ago, That the Prince (upon the King's Death) was resolved to goe to Rome, of which I took no notice, haveing hear'd long before, That he said That He would never return to Rome. It is most earnestly Wished That He would be so good as Change his intention of goeing there, if He ever had it.   It may happen That his Affairs in Britain might be at the Crisis in his favours at the time he was there, which could not faill to make a very bad turn, even with his friends upon hearing it.   But hou would his Enemies Triumph and be Overjoyed. Yea, his best Wishers might justly belive.   That he was not fully settled in his principles of religion, which being the same with their Own, gave them the best grounds to believe, That they would get Him safely settled on the Throne of his Fathers, as there was no other possible objection against Him But upon his being there, they might suspect; That He was resolved at the bottom to continue in his Father's Principles of Religion. Besides if· He should go there and retain his present Opinion He might be exposed to great Hazards amidst a People so bigotted to a different way of thinking, and Its not to be Doubted but they would contrive something against Him, at least to disappoint Him of the

Desine he had for goeing, and whatever View He has, It is not to be compared with the gaining the Crowns of Scotland, England, and Ireland ; But not to pry into what the Desine of his Journey may be He is sure to Obtain it more easiely when he is possessed of these Crowns.   [turn over

" The Present State of Britain is in a very Unsettled way, Their Vast Load of Debt must Ruin them, And they have no other way to get Clear of it but by settleing the Royal Family on the Throne, When One Act of Parliament will Discharge It, As haveing been contracted to Exclude and keep them from their Just Right, and Those who suffer will have themselves only to blame, tho' These who shall be reduced to great Indigence by this Act, can from time to time, be provided so as to live, they and their Familys in a Comfortable Way.   Every Reasonable Man would aprove of this Conduct, as the most effectual Beacon against new Usurpation; But If the Debts should be annulled dureing the Present Usurpation, It would bring ane Indelible Ignominy upon the whole Nation.

" I most sincerely wish his Royal Highness would frequently correspond with his Friends in Britain ; And if He would allow me to his Prescence I would Begg on my Knees That He would never goe to Rome on any Account Whatever.

" This is from a faithfull Subject who does not want five months, of being seventy two years of age Compleat."

" I append the following fragments, which are of the class which Lord Stanhope has printed, as ' Lays of the Last Stuart.' If they do not illustrate the poetical genius of the Prince, they show, I think, that he was *negatively* sincere in his profession of Protestantism.   They occur among the numerous scraps of paper on which he was accustomed to scribble memoranda of every conceivable kind : —

" Papish, Irish, such is fools,
" Such as them Cant be my Tools."

" I hete all prists, and the regions they rein in,
" from the pope at Rome to the papists of Britain."

" And to this he has added a conplet from Rochester's well-known poem, which similarly illustrates his being a ' Republican' : —

" I hete all Kings and the Throns they sit on,
" From the H[ector] of France to the Culia [Cully] of B[ritain]."

" ' *Vice versa* at present,' he adds, which seems to show that he appreciated the difference between the wretched Louis XV. and our valorous George II., who certainly were ' *vice versa*' to Louis XIV. and Charles II. in Rochester's time."

Thus far Mr. Woodward. Let me add that this visit to London is confirmed by Dr. King, in his well-known *Anecdotes of his Own Time*, and in a very striking manner by the interesting *Diaries of a Lady of Quality*, recently published under the editorship of Mr. Hayward, where we read, on the authority of the lady's brother, Mr. Charles W. W. Wynn, not only that the Young Pretender was in England in 1750, and then conformed to the Church of England, but that such conforming took place at St. James's, Piccadilly. ·

"My grandmother often repeated to me the account which she had herself received from Lady Primrose of Charles Edward's visit to London in 1750 (a letter from the historian Hume to Sir J. Pringle, published in the *Gentleman's Magazine*, May 1788, relating the same incident, assigns to this visit the date 1753).[*] She described her consternation when Mr. Browne (the name under which he was to-go) was announced to her in the midst of a card party, among whom were many who she felt might have seen him abroad and would very probably recognise him. Her cards almost dropped from her hands, but she recovered herself, and got him out of the room as quickly as she could. He slept at her house that night only, and afterwards went to that of a merchant in the city. The impression he left on the mind of Lady Primrose, a warm and attached partisan, was by no means favourable. I have read myself among the Stuart papers a minute of the heads of a manifesto in Charles Edward's own handwriting, among which appeared, '*My having in the year 1750 conformed to the Church of England in St. James's Church.*' Some idea may be formed of the extent of the panic felt at the time of his advance to Derby from the account given by an old workman at Wotton, of his having at that period assisted in burying by night all the family plate in the garden.—C. W. W. W."

One word more. Would the books of *St. James's Church* record the "conforming" of "Mr. Browne?" As the search would necessarily be limited to five days, namely, between the 16th and 22nd Sept., 1750, Old Style, it is to be hoped some reader of "N. & Q.," who may have the opportunity of examining the Registers at St. James's, will do so, and give us the result of his inquiries.   T. P.

SCOTTISH HISTORICAL GOSSIP.

I do not know that the Dalkeith portrait of Claverhouse has ever been copied, engraved, or photographed; but I cannot agree with F. M. S. (3rd S. vi. 472) that it is the only one that does Dundee justice, when I recollect those at the Lee and Milton-Lockhart. At the latter place, Claverhouse's most interesting portrait hangs over

---

"[*] Hume speaks of a second visit on the authority of Lord Holderness, and adds, 'You see this story is so near traced from the fountain-head as to wear a great trace of probability. Query, what if the Pretender had taken up Dymock's gauntlet?' Miss Strickland, in her *Life of Mary II.*, says, 'This incident has been told as a gossip's tale pertaining to every coronation of the last century which took place while an heir of James II. existed. If it ever took place, it must have been at the coronation of William and Mary. That there was a pause at this part of the ceremony of above two hours, and that when the champion appeared the gauntlet was heard to be thrown, but nothing that was done could be seen on account of the darkness of the evening, all this rests upon the authority of Lamberty, the historian and diplomatist.'"

Allan's picture of the Murder of Archbishop Sharp, which arrangement led to the following lines being written:—

" On Graham the Avenger.
" What, tho' the bigots of our own more peaceful times
May paint thee still a monster stained with crimes,
Breathes there a man unwarped by party lore,
Could hear that struggling orphan pour
To deafened ears her agonizing prayers
For mercy on that old man's silver hairs,
Nor feel they had earned the avenging rod,
Who sold their king, and slew the priests of God ? "

This allusion to the sale of the king by the Scotch army reminds me to call attention to the extraordinary blunders in regard to its constitution, and the appointment of its officers, published by Mr. Bisset in his *Omitted Chapters in the History of England*, especially his confounding Lord Loudon, Chancellor of Scotland, with the Laird of Lawers, who commanded a regiment. Mr. Bisset tells us, that the appointment of these officers is "a subject somewhat dark, but after much digging in the *rubish heaps and fossil remains of the Scottish Records*, and Scotch peerages and baronages, we obtain some glimpses of light."

Although I could not conceive why our admirably kept records (almost perfect, except where they were taken away from us by Edward I. and Cromwell), should be called "rubish heaps, and fossil remains" more than those in the English Record Office, still I did hope that on reading further I should have received some new information as to the officers of the Scottish army at the period. Guess my astonishment when I found that the extent of the *diggings* of this would-be Macaulay was the Douglas *Peerage* and *Baronage*, with Sir Walter Scott's *Tales of a Grandfather*, the latter originally being merely a hasty set of sketches, dashed off to amuse an invalid child, and hurriedly got up as a publication, under the pressure of pecuniary circumstances.

The extent of Mr. Bisset's digging (I should call it *scratching*) may be estimated by the fact, that he has never consulted such an obvious source of information as "The Books of Reference in the Reading Room of the British Museum." He would there have found a collection entitled *The Acts of the Parliaments of Scotland*, published by the Record Commission. Had he done so, he would probably have dropt upon such an entry as this—showing that, although the Earl of Loudon was a Campbell of Lawers, he had nothing to do with the regiment of the Laird Lawers (vol. vi. p. 415):—

" At Edinburgh, the 9th day of March, in the year of God 1649. The which day was presented and produced in face of Parliament, in name and behalf of Colonel James Campbell, son to the late Colonel Sir Mungo Campbell of Laweris, ane particular list and roll of persons from whom money is to be borrowed; which, being heard read, the Estates ordain the same to be submitted by the Lord Chancellor, and have remitted the same to the Committee to be appointed for borrowed monies."

This document is endorsed: "Produced by the Laird of Laweris, and remitted to the Committee." Signed, "LOUDOUN CANCEL. I.P.D.P."

In fact, there are numerous entries in this volume of the *Acts of Scotland;* as for instance, the Petition of Colonel James Campbell of Laweris, p. 366. The List of Colonels, p. 389, contains the name of Col. Colline Campbell, of Laweris, as commander of the Foot, raised in Linlithgowshire. But it would be endless to continue; suffice it to say, that these *Acts of Parliament* contain the most complete information as to officers in command of regiments in the Scottish service.

I would further ask, on what authority Mr. Bisset founds his assertion, that any one of our Scotch families sets up a pedigree, commencing at the flood?

My old Milton-Lockhart recollections lead me also to take this opportunity of correcting an error in another book, which I approach in a totally different spirit than the senseless and coarse abuse of Scotland contained in the *Omitted Chapters of the History of England.* To Mrs. Gordon all Scotchmen, and especially those who, like myself, had the good fortune to be pupils of her father, owe a deep debt of gratitude for her admirable *Memoir of Professor Wilson.* There are, however, spots in the sun; as the following passage in her work (vol. ii. p. 94, note) is calculated to give an erroneous idea of the character of my old friend John Gibson Lockhart, and is an instance how a literary anecdote may lose its point in passing from hand to hand.

"On a later occasion Mr. Lockhart amused himself, in a similar manner, by appending to a paper on Lord Robertson's *Poems,* in the *Quarterly Review,* the following epitaph: —

' Here lies the peerless paper Peer, Lord Peter,
Who broke the laws of God and man, and metre.'

These lines were, however, only in one copy, which was sent to the Senator [of the College of Justice]; but the joke lay in Lord Robertson imagining *that it was in the whole edition.*"

The article in the *Quarterly Review* on Lord Robertson's *Poems* (vol. lxxvi. p. 424), commences: —

" This is a very pleasing, as well as a beautiful little volume;" and concludes, "we should ill-discharge, even our critical duty, if we omitted the praise so justly due to the amiable tone which in the little volume before us is constantly perceived. The sound good sense and purely moral feeling of the learned and ingenious author is not more remarkable than the tenderness of heart which everywhere shines through his verses."

Into an article with such a heading and such a conclusion it is of course needless to say that a sarcastic epitaph like the above could not be

dovetailed with any chance of a successful hoax. The real facts of the case were as follows: — Lord Robertson and John Lockhart met in the autumn of 1845 at the hospitable table of William Lockhart of Milton-Lockhart, the brother of the editor of the *Quarterly.* His lordship, better known as Peter Robertson, had, as is not unusual, under the mass of jocularity and even buffoonery which attaches to his memory, a deep underlying current of sentiment, which first broke out in the conclusion of his well-known speech in defence of the Glasgow cotton spinners. On being raised to the Bench, he published a small book of sentimental poems entitled *Leaves from a Journal and other Fragments in Verse.* When on this occasion he visited Milton-Lockhart, he had become aware that this brochure was to be reviewed in the December Number of the *Quarterly* for 1845, and tried all he could to get out of Lockhart the nature of the forthcoming critique, but without success. The next morning after breakfast, Lord Robertson renewed the attack, when J. G. Lockhart, after tantalising him for some time, walked over to the table in the oriel window, where there were always writing materials, scribbled a few words, and returning said, "Peter, you have been trying all you can to find out what the *Quarterly* is going to say about your poems. You know that it is against all rule for me to tell you; but as you are an old friend, I will give you the epitaph with which it concludes, from which you may judge of the general tone."

Of course Robertson was too shrewd a man not to know that the critique was favourable, and after lunch he and John Lockhart started in the highest spirits to dine with another old friend and distinguished literary character, at whose house the *Quarterly* having come of age . . . . " Every thing would be on the scale of the greatest magnificence, and an author roasted whole." (See *Quarterly Review,* vol. lxxvi. p. 247.)

GEORGE VERE IRVING.

REGIMENTAL BADGES.

Many years since my lamented friend, the late Colonel Thomas Sidney Powell, C.B., 53rd regiment, placed in my hands the following letter, which must interest your numerous military readers. The author holds the rank of Major-General in the British army, and served with Colonel Powell in the 6th, or Royal 1st Warwickshire Regiment of Infantry. I feel certain that he shares with me my sorrow at the murder of Colonel Powell by the mutinous sepoys, in India, on the first of November, 1857: —

. "Mr. Cannon, in his *Records of the Sixth Regiment of Infantry,* states that, 'Tradition has connected the badge of the Antelope with the services of the regiment in Spain, in the year 1710; and, as several stands of colours were taken by the regiment at Saragossa, and presented by Colonel Thomas Harrison to Queen Anne, it has been considered probable that one colour taken from an African regiment in the service of Philip, which bore on it the Antelope, was among the number, and that Colonel Harrison obtained the Queen's permission to adopt the Antelope for a regimental badge.'

"Mr. Cannon, however, admits that no documentary evidence has as yet been found which would substantiate the tradition.

"The late Colonel Hugh Maurice Scott, of the sixth regiment, told me, when I was an ensign in the corps, that his father, who had been lieutenant-colonel of the sixth regiment for very many years, and had been born in the corps, believed that the badge of the Antelope was as old as the time of Queen Elizabeth; and that the regiment, then in the service of the States of Holland, adopted the badge owing to the Antelope being the crest of its colonel, Sir William Russell. For many years I thought this the most probable of all the conjectures which I had heard.

"Some years since I suggested to the editor of a military journal my opinion, that the badges of the first nine old regiments of infantry had one and the same origin, and that they all obtained their badges in the reign of King William the Third, or, at least, that the badges were *then* confirmed to these regiments. Let us now see how the matter stands.

"All persons will have noticed that most of the badges have been derived from parts of the arms of the English crown. The following may suggest sources of investigation to those persons who have time for examining military documents and histories:—

"The Royal Regiment Badge, 'The Royal cypher, within the collar of Saint Andrew, and the crown over it.' This badge is manifestly derived from the Scottish crown, 'The King's cypher, within Saint Andrew's collar, and the crown over it.'

"The Queen's Royal Regiment Badge, 'The Paschal Lamb,' from the royal arms of Portugal; the regiment being raised for service in Tangiers, part of the dower of Catherina, Queen of King Charles the Second, and who was previous to her marriage, Infanta of Portugal.

"Third Regiment Badge, 'The Dragon,' one of the supporters of the royal arms in the times of the Tudors I believe.

"Fourth Regiment Badge, 'The Lion of England,' a supporter of the royal arms.

"Fifth Regiment Badges, 'Saint George and the Dragon,' and the 'Rose and Crown,' part of the royal insignia.

"Sixth Regiment Badges, 'The Antelope,' and the 'Rose and Crown.' The Antelope was one of the supporters of the royal arms before the Unicorn was assumed.

"Seventh Regiment Badges, 'The Rose within the Garter, and the Crown over it,' and the 'White Horse.' The 'Rose within the Garter and the Crown over it,' come from the royal arms, and the 'White Horse' comes from the Saxon dynasty.

"Eighth Regiment Badge, 'The White Horse.' This corps bore the badge of the 'White Horse' before any Hanoverian sovereign ascended the throne of England.

"The Ninth Regiment Badge, 'The Figure of Britannia.' This badge was borne by the regiment long before it served as a marine corps, and was confirmed to the regiment by the commander-in-chief, on July 30th, 1799.

"Now, the common origin of these badges leads me to infer that they were not conferred for any particular service, but that they were granted as crests to each of 'the nine old corps,' as they used to be called. In after times,

King William the Third gave 'The Lion of Nassau' to the Eighteenth, or Royal Irish, regiment; and the Twenty-first and Twenty-seventh Regiments received appropriate badges as national corps. This seems to be the principle, as far as I can judge.—J. ff. C."

This letter was written in 1851.   Juverna.

PEMBROKE COLLEGE, OXFORD.

Wishing to test the current accounts of a certain *incomparable pair of brethren*, successively lords chamberlain of the royal household, and chancellors of the university of Oxford, I had recourse to a semi-official periodical work in high repute—whence I transcribe the paragraph which follows:—

"PEMBROKE COLLEGE. This college, originally Broadgates Hall, was founded in the year 1624, by king James the first, at the costs and charges of Thomas Tesdale, esquire, of Glympton in Oxfordshire, and Richard Wightwick, B.D., rector of Ilsley, Berks, for a master, ten fellows, and ten scholars, or more or fewer; and *obtained its name from Philip Herbert, earl of Pembroke, who was chancellor of the university when it was founded.*"

More than suspicious of this accredited guide, with regard to one part of the information which he gives, I consulted a guide who wrote two centuries before him, and published his curious volume with academic sanction. It is entitled *Academiæ Oxoniensis notitia. Oxoniæ, typis W. H. Impensis R. Davis*, 1665.—and calls for another extract:—

"COLLEGIUM PEMBROCHIANUM. Collegium quod hodie *Pembrochianum* audit, olim *Latarum Portarum Aula* dicta est. Cum vero Thomas Tisdale, etc.* * *Collegium ibi loci instituendum concessit *Jacobus* rex; quod in honorem D. *Guilielmi Herbert, Penbrochiæ* comitis, Academiæ tunc temporis cancellarii, *Penbrochianum* appellari visum est."

The author of this anonymous tract was William Fulman; ob. 1688. The copy in my hands was formerly in the collection of Alexander Chalmers, and subsequently in that of the learned and estimable Philip Bliss—who records an edition of 1675.

Now, as to the modern guide, I presume to make two observations. 1. William Herbert, earl of Pembroke, was chancellor of the university of Oxford from 1616-17 to 1630; 2. Philip Herbert, who was created earl of Montgomery in 1605, was elected *steward* of the university in 1615; but he did not become earl of Pembroke till the death of his brother in 1630, nor did he obtain the chancellorship before the resignation of archbishop Laud in 1641. (Camden, *Annales Jacobi I.*; Antony Wood, *History, etc.* by Gutch; Laud, *Autobiography.*)

Do the members of Pembroke ever condescend to examine *The Oxford university calendar?* Seldom, I conceive—for the error now pointed out has been in existence for twice-seven years!

    BOLTON CORNEY.

Barnes, S.W.

ROPE-TYING.—There is a passage in the life of Apollonius of Tyana which has a curious bearing on the performances of the Brothers Davenport. Apollonius, according to Lucian, was a skilful magician, and made a profession of it; but his biographer, Philostratus, portrays him as a philosopher, with the power of performing miracles. I have not access to the original; but, in Tillemont's *Life of Apollonius Tyaneus*, which is compiled from Philostratus, it is stated that, being imprisoned by the Emperor Domitian —

"whilst he was in chains he assured Damis, his pupil, who followed him into prison, that Domitian could do him no hurt. And, to show him what he could do, he freed his leg from the chain which was fastened about it, and then put his leg into the chain again."

Tillemont quotes this from *Philostratus, Vita Apoll. Thyan.*, c. xv. pp. 366, 367. Apollonius had visited India, and professed to have acquired much of his skill amongst the Brahmans.

J. EMERSON TENNENT.

"COOPER."—The following passage from *Every Day Papers* by Andrew Halliday, Lond. 1864, ii. 257, explains the origin of this mixture of stout and porter: —

"Some brewers, who are jealous for the reputation of their beer, employ a traveller, who visits the houses periodically, and tastes the various beers, to see that they are not reduced too much. This functionary is called the Broad Cooper. When the Broad Cooper looks in upon Mr. Noggins, and wants to taste the porter, and the porter is below the mark, Mr. Noggins slyly draws a dash of stout into it. And this trick is so common and so well known, that a mixture of stout and porter has come to be known to the public and asked for by the name of 'Cooper.'"

T. C.

DUCHESS OF QUEENSBURY. — Walpole, in his Letter to Montagu of May 18, 1749, describing an entertainment given by the Duke and Duchess of Richmond, speaks of this eccentric lady "in her forlorn trim—a white apron and a white hood; and would make the Duke swallow all her undress." Upon which the editor has the following note: —

"There is a good caricature of the Duchess in this costume fencing with Soubise, the black; whom she educated and indulged in extravagance, till he got so much in debt, that she was obliged to send him to India. The first Marquis of Townshend made the drawings, aided by one Austen a drawing master."

As this note is not reproduced in the last edition, I may give it a corner in "N. & Q." for the use of caricature collectors and future Walpoleans.

D. O.

A LONDON BOOK-AUCTION, 1698.—The following extract, from *A Journey to London in the Year 1698*, "written originally in French by Monsieur Sorbiere, and newly translated into English," London, 1699, p. 23, may prove interesting and suggestive:—

"I was at an auction of books, at Tom's Coffee House, near Ludgate, where were above fifty people. Books were sold with a great deal of trifling and delay, as with us, but very cheap; those excellent authors, Mounsieur Maimbourg, Mounsieur Varillas, and Mounsieur le Grand, tho' they were all guilt [*sic*] on the back, and would have made a very considerable figure in a gentleman's study, yet after much tediousness were sold for such trifling sums, that I am asham'd to name 'em."

The book from which I quote, is rather curious, being "after the ingenuous method" of Dr. Martin Lister's *Journey to Paris in* 1698, of which, as I understand, an excellent notice may be found in the *Retrospective Review*, xiii. 95—100.

ABHBA.

JOHNSONIANA. — There are many phrases and peculiar expressions in current use in this present nineteenth century, which, we flatter ourselves, are of recent invention; but which may, nevertheless, be traced back to the sturdy old lexicographer. One of these comes across me as I turn over some of Boswell's "magnetic" pages. The Doctor is writing to console his friend Dr. Lawrence on the loss of his wife, and uses the following magnificent language: —

"He that outlives a wife whom he has long loved, sees himself disjoined from the only mind that has the same hopes, and fears, and interest; from the only companion with whom he has shared much good or evil: and with whom he could set his mind at liberty to retrace the past, or anticipate the future. *The continuity of being is lacerated*," &c.

My remark applies to the phrase "continuity of anything." I apprehend this to have been perfectly new at the time it was used: one, in fact, of Johnson's own creating. It is of great force and elegance; but, if I mistake not, nine out of ten would look on it as a Gallicism of our own day. In French physical works, we continually read of a "solution of continuity" instead of a *break*, &c. This query, therefore, arises: Has any French author so used the word *continuity* before Johnson? Or, can any French author be supposed indebted to Johnson for it?

PHILOLOGUS.

AMERICAN DEPRECIATION OF CURRENCY. — In December, 1779, and in the state of Maryland, an English officer (one of the convention troops) received an innkeeper's bill which, in his *Travels* (Aubury, ii. 492), he has printed in full length, amounting in *paper* money to 732l.; and this bill he paid *in gold* with four guineas and a half (Mahon's *England*, vi. 416). In other words, the Englishman paid a debt of 155l. to an American with the value of one sovereign. At this time General Washington said, "A waggon-load of money will now scarcely purchase a waggon-load of provisions." It is just now an interesting question to Americans, "Who lost the difference between 732l. and 4l. 14s. 6d.?"

T. J. BUCKTON.

"TURNING THE TABLES."—Instead of considering this proverb, or saying, as a metaphor taken from the vicissitudes of fortune between two opponents at a gaming-table, or backgammon (as suggested to MIRGLIP in the Notice to Correspondents, 3rd S. vi. 140), its origin, I am disposed to believe, may be traced' to a passage in Pliny. During the Augustan age, the Romans expended inordinate sums of money on tables made of the most costly materials: of ivory, gold, silver, marble, and highly-prized woods. The citrus-wood, the produce of the forests of Mount Atlas (Plin. xiii. c. 29) became at one period the most valued and attractive material for the purpose. These tables were denominated Tigrine, or Pantherine, from the spots of the grain—the lines of which also resembled, at times, the eyes of a peacock's tail: "pavonum caudæ oculos" (Plin. *loc. cit.* c. 31). The price of a single table equalled a Senator's income (Seneca, *De Benef.*, vii. 9, p. 136). Cicero, notwithstanding his comparatively moderate means, gave no less than one million sesterces—about 9,000*l.* sterling (Plin. *loc. cit.* c. 29). And the sale for its weight in gold, of one belonging to Ptolemæus, King of Mauretania, proves Martial's Epigram to be no exaggeration :—

" Accipe felices, Atlantica munera, sylvas :
  Aurea si dederit dona, minora dabit."—xiv. 89.

" This citrus table Mount Atlas sends to thee,
  Were it of pure gold, the gift far less would be."

"Mensarum insaniæ," observes Pliny, "quas fœminæ viris contra margaritas regerunt." Wives, when reproached for extravagance in pearls, retort the table-mania (that is, turn the tables,) on their husbands.*   W. PLATT.
Conservative Club.

RICHARD SACKVILLE, EARL OF DORSET.

This somewhat celebrated lord appears to have included in his great extravagance the buying of costly books, and he had in his library some in very expensive binding, one of which is in my possession, and I am desirous of ascertaining where seven of its early companions are ? It is a large folio, —

" Works of Seneca. Printed by Wm. Stansby, dwelling in Thames-Streete, by Paul's-Wharfe, next to St. Peter's Church. 1620."

containing about 950 pages, spotless as new, gilt edges, bound in red silk velvet, impressed on both sides of the cover with the letters R E D about an inch long, stamped in solid gilding. On a fly-leaf is written the following note : —

[* This explanation of the saying was suggested in our 1st S. iii. 276.—ED.]

" R E D stand for Richarde Earle of Dorset, whose Book this formerly was, and by his daughter, Margaret Countess Dowager of Thanet (together with seaven other books, all of the same binding), was since left as part of her legacy to me. 1676."

(Signed with a monogram formed of the letters C and H, surmounted with a Viscount's coronet, neatly outlined.)

The date refers to the year when the Dowager Countess of Thanet died, Christopher Lord Hatton not being created a Viscount until 1682.

Richard Earl of Dorset died 1624. He was the first husband of the more celebrated Anne Clifford, Countess of Dorset, Pembroke, and Montgomery. Their daughter, Lady Margaret Sackville, married, 1629, John Tufton, Earl of Thanet, and died his widow August 14, 1676. Her daughter, Lady Cecilia Tufton, was the first wife of Christopher, second Baron Hatton, and afterwards Viscount Hatton. Margaret, Countess Dowager of Thanet, by her will, dated June 20, 1676, proved at Doctors' Commons (Bence, 106), gives to her daughter, the Lady Anne Grimstone, her jewels, pictures, coins, china, and books of what sort soever, —

"except only my eight books, bound with red velvett, and marked with the letters R. E. D., which were formerly my father's, Richard Earl of Dorset."

She afterwards says, —

" I give to my son-in-law, the Lord Hatton, 100*l.* ; and also my said eight books, covered with red velvett, and marked with the letters R. E. D."

The death of her daughter, Lady Cecilia Hatton, was a dreadful event. Her husband and his family were residing, when he was governor of Guernsey, 1672, at Cornet Castle, in Guernsey. The magazine of powder was fired in the night by lightning; the lady and several of her women were blown into the sea and killed. Lord Hatton was blown through the window of his bedroom upon the ramparts of the castle, but he and his children received little injury. One of the children, an infant, was found the next day alive, sleeping in its cradle under a beam. Aubrey, the antiquary, tells a remarkable story, how "the Countess of Thanet saw, as she was in bed in London (the candle then burning in her chamber), the apparition of her daughter, my Lady Hatton," ... "who was then in Northamptonshire," so that it must have been sometime before this catastrophe.

It is probable that on the death of Viscount Hatton, 1706, the eight volumes went to the Finch family, Anne Hatton, only surviving child of Cecilia Lady Hatton, having married Daniel Finch, Earl of Nottingham, from whom descended the Earls of Nottingham and Winchelsea.
RICHD. ALMACK.
Melford, Suffolk.

THE BLUE COAT SCHOOL.

From a letter in the State Paper Office (now the Record Office) it would appear probable that that celebrated and excellent foundation, the " Blue Coat School," owes its preferment to Dudley, Duke of Northumberland — a fact that I have not seen stated by any writer. The letter runs thus : —

John Dudley, Earl of Warwick, to Mr. (afterwards Sir William) Cecil, 1st Feby. 1547-8.

" After my right harty commendacions thies may be to require you to gyve credyte to this berer, my servunt ; who shall at length shew you th' affect of this my send-ing at this tyme, which ys at the instant sute and request of certeyn of my neybors concerning the preferment of a certeyn free scole, wherin sondry poore folkes hath allso theyr fynding, that they may opteyn my Lorde's grace* good favor for the preferment therof, which they wold styll kepe in the same foundacion. Wherin his grace shall do (in myn opynyon) a right charitable act, and your furderunce herin shalbe by theym honestly con-syderyd.

" So I byde you for this tyme hartely farewell. At Ely Place this fyrste of February, An° 1547. [1547-8.]

" Your Loving ffrend,   J. WARWYK.

" To my loving freende, Mr. Cicell."

Holinshed speaks of the " Earl of Warwick's lodging, which was then at Ely Place, in Hol-born." Stow, in his *Survey of London*, speaks of the " Bishop of Ely's Inn, commonly called Ely Place, as it pertaineth to the Bishops of Ely." Dudley's letters, while he was Earl of Warwick, were dated from Ely Place. The Serjeants-at-Law held their feasts in this house. At one of them, held in 1531, Henry VIII. and Queen Katherine dined there with the foreign ambassa-dors, Lord Mayor, judges, aldermen, citizens, mer-chants, and the "Crafts of London." Stow re-lates that this feast continued for five days.

At the same time that Christ's Hospital was founded, St. Thomas's Hospital was established for the relief of the sick. Bridewell also, built by Henry VIII., was appropriated "for the correc-tion and amendment of the vagabond and lewd ; provision also being made that the decayed house-keeper should receive weekly parochial relief."

In connection with this is a very curious letter from Ridley, Bishop of London, preserved among the Lansdowne MSS., in the British Museum:† —

" *To the righte Woourshipfull Sr William Cicill, Knighte, One of the Principall Secretaries unto the Kinges Maiestie.*

" Good Mr Cicill, I muste be a suter unto you in our Master Christe's cause, I beseache you, be good unto him. The matter is, Syr, Alas, he hath lyen to too long abrode (as you do knowe) wthout Lodginge, in the Stretes of London, both hungrie, naked, and colde. Now thankes be unto all mightie God, the Citizens are willinge to re-freashe him and to geave him, both meate, drinke, cloth-inge, and fyreinge. But Alas, Sr, they lacke Lodginge

* Protector Somerset.
† Lansdowne MSS., vol. iii.

for him ; for in some one howse, I dare saie, they are faine to lodge Thre families under one Roffe.

" Sr, there is a wide Large emptie howse of the Kinge's Majesties, called BRIDEWELL, that would wonderfullie well serve to lodge Christe in, if he mighte finde suche good Freindes in the Courte, to procure in his cause. Suerlie I have suche a good opinion in the Kinges Matie, that if Christe had suche faithefull and hartie freindes, that would hartely speake for him, he should undoubtedlie spede at the Kinge's Maties handes. Syr, I have pro-mised my Brethren the Citizens in this matter to move you, because I doo take you for one that feareth God, and would that Christe should lye no more abrode in the Strete. There is a Rumor, that one goeth aboute to buy that howse of the Kinge's Matie, and to pull it downe, if there be any suche thinge, for Gode's sake, speake you in or Master's cause. I have written unto Mr Gates more at large in this matter. I joynne you wth him, and all that love and looke for Christe's finall Benediccon on the latter daie. If Mr Cheke (in whose recoverie God be blessed) were amonges you, I would suerlie make him in this be-haulf, one of Christe's speciall Advocates, or rather one of his principall Proctor, and suerlie I would not be saide nay. And thus I wishe you in Christe evr well to Fare.

" From my howse at Fulham, this presente Sondaie, beinge the xxixth daie of Maij, 1553.

" Yours in Christ,   NIC. LONDON."

" I pra yow suffer the beror hearof to talk ij or iij wordes wth yow in this cause."

Nicholas Ridley was translated, by Edw. VI., from the Bishopric of Rochester to that of London, April 1, 1550. Edward died July 6, 1553, only five weeks after Ridley's letter was written. On the accession of Mary, Ridley was deprived and burnt to death by her orders, October 16, 1555.

Can any of the readers of " N. & Q." furnish any further light on the subject ?   G. A.
Barnsbury.

[The letter of the Earl of Warwick, we are inclined to think, does not relate to the foundation of Christ's Hos-pital ; but may refer to a projected school at the Charter House, at this time the property of the Earl (afterwards created Duke of Northumberland). In 1542 the Charter-House was granted by Henry VIII. to John Brydges and Thomas Hale for their joint lives ; and, in 1545, to Sir Edward, afterwards Lord North. This nobleman sold it to the Earl of Warwick, who being afterwards attainted of treason, it reverted again to the Crown. On a copy of the Letters Patent of Queen Mary, granting for the second time the Charter-House to Lord North, is the following memorandum : — " There is enrolled a grant from the Queene [Mary] unto Sir Edward Northe, of the scite of the House or Priory of the Carthuse, within men-cōned to be granted by these Lres patentes of 36 Henry VIII., and of the gardens, gates, conduyts, and other things within mencōned, and in the said Lres patents of 1 Mariæ specyfyed to come to the Crowne by the attayn-der of John, Duke of Northumberland. Soe it seemeth that Sir Edward North, after the grant thereof to him, 36 Henr. VIII., did sele or conveye the same unto the Duke of Northumberland ; who afterwards being attaynted of treason for rebellion, the p̄misses thereby came to the Crowne agayn at the begynning of Queene Maryis reigne, who granted the same agayn to Sir Edward Northe, with the same libertyes as are mencōned in this of 36 Henr. VIII."

In 1550 Ridley was translated from Rochester to Lon-don ; and both in the council-chamber and the pulpit, he boldly resisted the sacrilegious spirit of his day. Although the young king [Edward VI.] was but partially able to stem the torrent of corruption, he yet founded (according to Carlisle) at the suggestion of Ridley, no less than sixteen grammar-schools, and designed, had his life been spared, to erect twelve colleges for the education of youth. It was shortly before the death of Edward, that Ridley preached his famous Sermon, in which he so strongly pressed the duty of providing for the poverty and ignorance of the lower classes, and which eventually led to the foundation of Christ's Hospital, Bridewell, and St. Thomas's. The greater portion of the Bishop's letter furnished by our correspondent has already appeared in Glocester Ridley's *Life of Bishop Ridley*, p. 377, 4to, 1763 ; in Strype's *Stow*, p. 169 ; and in Trollope's *History of Christ's Hospital*, p. 37.]

Mr. Baskett. — One of the persons to whom the authorship of *The Whole Duty of Man* has been attributed, was a Mr. Baskett, who, I believe, was the clergyman of some place in Worcestershire.* Is there any biographical or other notice of him to be met with in any magazine or other publication ?   Llallawg.

Bedstead Superstition. — Having ordered a neatly constructed single bedstead, with somewhat high and ornamented sides, I was surprised when it was brought home to find that the ornamentation of one side of the bedstead was not repeated on the opposite side, it being in fact quite plain. I expressed my surprise and dissatisfaction to the maker ; saying that, when the bedstead was placed with its head against the wall of a room, the sides then showing will appear quite unlike—one ornamented, and the other plain. At this, the maker expressed his surprise that I should be ignorant of a German custom and prejudice : "for," says he, "in Germany single bedsteads are only placed sidewise against a wall, or partition ; and only removed from this position, and placed with its head against the wall, to receive a dead body." And the worthy maker assured me that nowhere in Germany could a native be induced to sleep on a single bedstead which had not its side placed against a wall, or partition. The same objection does not hold against placing two single bedsteads side by side, with their heads against a wall. It is possible that this German custom has already a place in "N. & Q. ;" although, in a hasty looking over of my set, I did not find it. Does the custom, with prejudice, obtain in other countries ? The custom I think does, but not the prejudice— at least, not in England or America.   W.
Frankfurt-am-Main.

Bernardino.—In the preface to *Specimens and Notes on Living English Authors*, Boston, 1846, the author says that the early English poets were indifferent about originality : —

[A clergyman of *Somersetshire*, according to Nichols's *Literary Anecdotes*, ii. 604.—Ed.]

" Chaucer invented little or nothing ; Shakspere borrowed nearly all his plots, and helped himself freely to all the language which was worth taking ; and Ben Jonson took two-thirds of his *Catiline and Sejanus* from Sallust and Tacitus, and his *Alchemist* and *Volpone* from Bernardino."—P. vi.

I shall be obliged by information as to Bernardino and his works, which have been so named.   E. S.

Sir Richard Braham.—Can any of your correspondents give me the exact date of the death of Sir Richard Braham, M.P. for Windsor in the reign of Charles II. ? He was created a baronet 1662, and described of New Windsor ; but dying without issue, his title became extinct. Tighe and Davis, in their *Annals of Windsor*, mention a payment toward his funeral expences ; but they entirely omit, in their list of M.P.'s for that borough, the election that was caused by his decease. I find, from a MS. document in his handwriting, Sir Francis Winnington, then Solicitor-General, was returned M.P. for Windsor, Feb. 19, 1676 ; and sat during the remainder of the then existing Parliament. Browne Willis also, in his *Notitia Parliamentaria*, omits this return.
Thos. E. Winnington.
Stanford Court, Worcester.

Caryll Family. — Did any member of the Caryll family of Harting settle in South Brent, Devon ? If so, when ? Did he leave any descendants ? What are the armorial bearings of this family ?   Carilford.
Cape Town, S. A.

The Princess Charlotte of Brunswick.— I lately read one of the most fascinating and delightful works I ever had the good fortune to meet with, in which genius, goodness, and beauty meet together in the happiest combination, showing the additional charm of an historical basis— *Too Strange not to be True*, by Lady G. Fullerton : who, by the way, also wrote, many years ago, one of the most disagreeable books I ever read, at once clever and repulsive, viz. *Ellen Middleton*. Lady Fullerton mentions that the germ of her strange romance of history was a sketch published by the late Lord Dover, in the *Keepsake* of 1833, entitled "Vicissitudes in the Life of a Princess of the House of Brunswick." I was speaking of Lady Fullerton's book, the other day, to a lady who had just read it ; and she told me she read the strange story of the Princess Charlotte, worked up into a romance in two volumes, between the years 1810—1820. My informant could not remember the title, nor the author's name distinctly ; but she said it was a name like Holcroft, Hoffmann, or Holford, and added that the same writer had published some German tales. I observed, that Mrs. Hofland had written a book called *Czarina*, in 3 vols. ; but my friend replied, that the book she read was written before Mrs. Hofland's publications, to the best of her belief. Can you identify the work referred to ?

EIRIONNACH.

COMETS.—In the opening chapter of Mr. Hind's work on *The Comets*, there is this passage : —

"The Chinese astronomers, though they looked upon comets without any fears of their malignant agencies, had a very *fanciful opinion* respecting them, which, nevertheless, led to the frequent observation of the position of these bodies," &c. •

What was the fanciful opinion alluded to ? and where can I find detailed information on this point ? E. V. H.

Derby.

"DEADLY MANCHINEEL" TREE.—In *A Naturalist's Sojourn in Jamaica* (Longmans, 1851), the above reference is made to a handsome tree which has acquired, throughout the West Indies, a very repulsive reputation. Suspecting exaggeration in the statements afloat, I plucked a few of the freshest and youngest leaves, and rubbed them with some force over the pulse of my wrist, and against the earnest remonstrance of some friends; but there was no result whatever, much to the surprise of the latter. Was this simply an *exceptional* case ? S. Q.

GUILING. — In an article in the *Quarterly Review*, on "Workmen's Benefit Societies," occurs the following extract from the Rules of an old Society in Gloucestershire : —

"No member on the feast day shall provoke another by calling him nicknames, or by *guiling* at him, or casting meat or bones at another, or about the room ; neither shall any member feed another by way of fun, and wasting the victuals, to the shame of the company."

What is the meaning of "guiling" ? And I don't quite see the fun of feeding another.

H. FISHWICK.

WHO OR WHAT WERE HENGIST AND HORSA ? — It is generally supposed that Hengist and Horsa were two men, who led the Danes and Jutes; but there is every reason to believe that they were simply two poles surmounted by horses heads, and were carried in advance of the army as tutelary deities. At this day, the houses in Jutland are all built with the gable rafters projecting in the form of a V, each limb being surmounted by a horse's head. On inquiring of any of the inhabitants the meaning of this, the answer invariably is—"Oh, those are Hengist and Horsa; they are put up for good luck."

Hengist in the Danish means a stallion; and *Horsa*, a mare. There is a tradition in the country that these were formerly worshipped as gods. Jutland, from time immemorial, has been celebrated for its breed of horses, which no doubt were brought with them in their migration from Asia; and, to this day, they pay great attention

to the rearing of horses. The Saxons were composed of Danes and Jutes. From these grounds, I think I have shown that there are good grounds for believing, that Hengist and Horsa were merely a stallion's and a mare's head, carried on poles at the head of the army. Another instance to be added to the many, showing the proneness of Pagan nations to deify animals that are useful to them. The analogy to the Roman eagles will not escape observation.• S. C. SEWELL, M.D.

Ottawa.

IRISH POOR LAW.—In Swift's Sermon on the wretched Condition of Ireland (*Works*, vii. 30), it is said that by the ancient law of that country, and still in force when he wrote, every parish was bound to maintain its own poor. What law was that ? In the debates in 1840, on the introduction of the present Irish poor law, it was always treated as a measure wholly new in principle and detail; and especially it was assumed that there was no existing law of *settlement*, as the above extract would seem to imply.

LYTTELTON.

IRISH SONG.—Above forty years ago I heard a song, part of which and the chorus I recollect, viz. : —

"There's the childer stark naked, all covered wid' rags,
  Who eat no honest bit, but the morsel they steal ;
At home there is nothing but three empty bags,
  And the devil a skirret to fill them wid' meal.
    To your kill me now, arrah! dow, wid' your cold
      water now ;
    Water's a drink only fit for a whale.
    Boney got beat at the poor game of Waterloo,
    Whiskey had brought him off clean as a nail.
" ' Is it me you disparage,' said Phelim, ' you devil ?
  A tight Dublin lad, and so handsomely cast ;
And you, faith and troth, the curst Spirit of Evil,
  Auld wadlin' Peg Shambles, the sport of Belfast :
A short leg and a shorter, a head wid' one eye in't ;
  A mouth wid'out teeth, that you better might bawl ;
A nose cocking up, to behold your eye squint ;
  And a hump on your back, like the huge linen hall.' •
    To your kill me now," &c., &c.

Was this song ever published ? If so, when and where ? I never saw it in print or manuscript. When I heard it, it was attributed to the Marquis Wellesley ; and said to have been written by him during the first time he was Lord-Lieutenant of Ireland. C. D.

PATRICK KEIR, M.D., published —.

"An Enquiry into the Nature and Virtue of the Medicinal Waters of Bristol, and their Use in the Cure of Chronical Distempers. London. 8vo. 1739."

He was buried at St. Mark's, Bristol; and his epitaph is printed in Barrett's *History of Bristol*, p. 348. It thereby appears that he died December 17, æt. thirty-seven. Unfortunately, the *year*

[* Four articles on the historical existence of Hengist and Horsa appeared in "N. & Q." 2nd S. i. 439, 517 ; ii. 76 ; iii. 170.—ED.]

of his death is not stated. If any correspondent can supply it, I shall be obliged.   S. Y. R.

LADIES OF THE ORDER OF THE GARTER. — In the *Memorials of the Order of the Garter* by Mr. Beltz, at p. ccxxi. a list is given of the Ladies of the Order; *i. e.* of ladies for whom robes of the order were provided : —

"The favour was not limited to the consorts and relicts of the Knights of the Order, but extended to others of their families; and where such connection does not appear, there is room for the conjecture that the distinction was an especial homage to eminent personal or mental endowments, spontaneously paid by the Sovereign himself, or at the suggestion of a Knight who by some martial act had acquired a claim to the nomination."—(*Ib.* pp. 246-7.)

Had such ladies the right to encircle their shields with the Garter? One of the ladies, the Countess of Warwick, was named in the 10 Henry VI. 1432. Her figure on her tomb in Ewelme church is represented with the Garter around the left arm. (*Ib.* ccxxiii.)   EDMUND WATERTON.
Athenæum Club.

OMAR CHEYAM, ABOULHASSAN KUSCHIAR, AND JAMAL'U-DIN.—The first of these three is said to have been one of the eight astronomers Jelal'u-din Malek Shah employed to regulate the Persian State Calendar about A.D. 1075; the second is mentioned in Herschel's *Outlines of Astronomy* (3rd ed. p. 635); and the third is said to have regulated the Chinese Calendar in the thirteenth century. Fuller information respecting them and their works, with references to authorities, would greatly oblige   J. B.
Bombay.

HERBERT PALMER'S BURIAL.—Your notice of Mr. Grosart's book (3rd S. vi. 525) puts into my mind to ask you whether some of your Westminster correspondents (of whom you seem to have many and good ones), cannot tell us in your pages where Herbert Palmer was buried? He died, it appears, on 13th August, 1647, and was buried at "the New Church, Westminster," says one authority, "New Chapel, Westminster," says another. Was this the New Chapel, Broadway, Westminster, built, according to Peter Cunningham—(how glad I am to see him again appearing as a correspondent to "N. & Q.")—as a chapel-of-ease to St. Margaret's, about the beginning of the reign of Charles I. and replaced in 1843 by a new church called Christ Church? Burials in this chapel-yard seem to have been entered in the register of burials at St. Margaret's. Is there any entry there relating to Herbert Palmer?
JOHN BRUCE.

QUOTATION.—Where are the words to be found, "perfervidum ingenium Scotorum," or, as the *Saturday Review* says, "prefervidum"? They are generally ascribed to George Buchanan, and he is said to have quoted from an older author.
SCOTUS.

ROMNEY'S PORTRAIT OF WESLEY.—
"Monday (Jan.) 5 (1789). At the earnest desire of Mrs. T——, I once more sat for my picture. Mr. Romney is a painter indeed. He struck off an exact likeness at once, and did more in one hour than Sir Joshua in ten."—Wesley's *Journal.*

Is anything known of Romney's portrait of Wesley, or Sir Joshua's, which I suppose is implied?   QUIVIS.

TOMBSTONE INSCRIPTIONS, ST. JOHN'S, HORSLY-DOWN.—I should feel much obliged if any reader of "N. & Q." can inform me if there are any MS., or printed copies, of the inscriptions which were on the tombstones that were removed from the churchyard of St. John's, Horslydown, South-wark, Surrey, a few years ago, when the vaults under the church were closed? I believe a great many of the headstones were used to pave the footpaths of the churchyard.   W. D.

HYMN TO THE VIRGIN. — Where can I find a hymn, one verse of which runs thus?—
"Our Lady sings Magnificat,
In tones surpassing sweet ;
And all the choirs of virgins
Sitting around her feet."
IS. STEVENSON.

THE UNIVERSAL ACCOMMODATION OFFICE, ESTA-BLISHED IN 1778. — Is anything known of the origin, career, or fate of "The Universal Accommodation Office, No. 100, Long Acre," which, it was announced, "will be elegantly finished and opened for business on Monday, the 13th of April, 1778"? It was intended for two objects: 1. The letting of shops, houses, chambers, lodgings, &c., in London, and all the villages within ten miles. And 2. The registration and hiring of servants; which, it was proposed, might be much better managed at *one* such office than at the many register offices, "or rather *hovels*," which were then in existence, and whose shameful frauds, and other malpractices, were reprobated with the utmost severity. The Prospectus of this scheme, a sheet of four closely-printed foolscap pages, is now before me; and I shall contribute it to the interesting collection of Broadsides, and other papers of the kind, preserved in the Library of the Society of Antiquaries.   J. G. N.

WASHINGTON ARMS. — In the work of Sir Bernard Burke, which contains the coat armour of all the English families, that of Washington of Lancashire and four other counties, is given as, Argent, two bars gules in chief, three mullets of the second. As its chief is usually of a "different" tincture in arms generally, could any of your readers inform me if such is ever the case with those of Washington? The stars and stripes are not such legitimate descendants of the first bearing as they would be, provided its chief was different in tincture.   H. P.

Queries with Answers.

CIVITAS LUCRONII. — What city is termed in Latin Lucronium ? In the Prolegomena to Dressel's *Prudentius*, in the list of the editions of that author one is mentioned (p. xxviii.), of which the subscription is —

" Impressum præsens opus in civitate Lucronii per Arnaldum Guillermum de Brocario, et finitum die secunda mensis Septembris anno a nativitate Christi millesimo quingentesimo duodecimo."

As this printer was the same who executed the Complutensian Polyglott, I want to ascertain where Lucronium is, where he exercised his art before he took the charge of the printing office of Cardinal Ximenes at Alcalà. From the date of his edition of Prudentius, it is clear that he *could* not have removed to Alcalà for more than about five months before the accession of Leo X. to the Popedom. The importance of this is, that it has been thought that the writers of the Polyglott have not spoken accurately when they express their thanks to that Pope for his aid in having sent Greek MSS. for the New Testament. The volume containing the New Testament was completed January 10, 1514, and it has been asserted that it *must* have been begun long before the accession of Leo; but it is clear that the printer had not taken up his abode at Alcalà a year and four months before that volume was completed : so that at all events it may be quickly printed; and why not in less than a year? The locality of Lucronium may throw some light on this, and it may lead to a further knowledge when the printer settled at Alcalà.   S. P. TREGELLES.

Plymouth.

P.S. Since sending my query as to the modern name of this place, I felt persuaded that it must be Logroño; and, on examining Sprüner's *Historical Atlas*, I find this to be the case. This elucidates one point in the life of Brocario the printer; and it is so far a contribution to the history of the Complutensian Polyglott, that we can say that it *could not* have been commenced at press before September, 1512; and as much later as was needful for Brocario to change his abode, and remove his whole establishment to Alcalà.

MARRIAGE RINGS. — I am anxious to know how, when, where, and why the custom originated of employing a plain gold ring in matrimony ; and whether a priest or Sir James Wilde could interfere with the fantastic taste of anybody who chose to prefer a wedding-ring of any other fashion. The Rubric of the Church Service only orders that "The man shall give unto the woman a ring."

On this same subject of rings, there are, I believe, several legends connected with good King Solomon. Will some one of your readers tell me where I can find these ?   R. C. L.

The Temple.

[The legend of King Solomon's ring will be found in Josephus (*Antiq.* lib. viii. ch. 2), which, however, has been considered an interpolation. It is there stated that Josephus had witnessed the healing of many demoniacs by one Eleazar, a Jew, in the presence of the Emperor Vespasian, by the application of a medicated ring to the nostrils of the parties ; and that on this Jew's reciting several verses connected with the name of Solomon, the devils were extracted through the noses of the parties.

It is not improbable that this story, for which Josephus is made responsible, is nothing more than an allusion to the celebrated Magic Ring of Solomon, said to have been found in the belly of a fish, and concerning which a great many idle fictions have been created by the Arabian writers. The Arabians have a book called *Scalcuthal*, expressly on the subject of Magic Rings ; and they trace this ring of Solomon, in a regular succession, from Jared the father of Enoch to Solomon. More concerning it may be seen in Licetus, cap. xxii., and in D'Herbelot, *Biblioth. Orient.* pp. 478, 819, folio edition. (*Archæologia*, xxi. 123.)

With respect to the style and material of the marriage ring, the pattern of those used among the Romans appears to have been one which has gone out of use, namely, right hands joined, such as is often observed on ancient coins. According to Swinburne, that oracle of canon law, " the ring at first was not of gold, but of iron [*i. e.* among the Romans], adorned with an adamant ; the metal hard and durable, signifying the durance and perpetuity of the contract. Howbeit (he adds) it skilleth not at this day, what metal the ring be of ; the form of it being round, and without end, doth import that their love should circulate and flow continually." (*Matr. Contr.* sect. xv.) As substitutes for the usual wedding ring, it is said that curtain rings, and even the church key, and one made of glove leather, have been used in the celebration of marriage. ("N. & Q." 2nd S. x. 290.) The plain gold ring at present used as a visible pledge, appears to have descended to us, in the mere course of traditionary practice, from the time of the Saxons, without any impulse from written authority or rubric.]

HOSPITALS FOR THE SICK. — When was the first hospital of this kind founded ? So far as I am aware, there is no trace of any such institution in the classical writers. I shall feel thankful for reference to any works bearing on the subject.   CPL.

[We have never met with any work containing a connected historical account of these beneficent establishments. Bearing some resemblance to our present hospitals was the bath of Asclepius, a temple of the gods called Epidotæ, erected by Antoninus Pius at Epidaurus—a temple dedicated to Hygieïa, Asclepius, and Apollo surnamed the Ægyptian, and a building beyond the sacred enclosure for the reception of the dying, and of women in labour (*Paus.*

11. 27.) Epidaurus is also described by Strabo (viii. p. 374) as a place renowned for the cure of all diseases, always full of invalids, and containing votive tablets descriptive of the cures, as at Cos and Tricca. (Smith's *Dict. of Geography*, i. 841.)

Hospitals for the poor and sick, however, are pre-eminently characteristic of Christianity. In the first ages of the Church, the Bishop had immediate charge of all the poor, both sound and diseased. When the churches came to have fixed revenues allotted them, it was decreed, that at least one-fourth part thereof should go to the relief of the poor; and to provide for them the more commodiously, houses of charity were specially erected for the sick. So early as the Council of Nice, A.D. 325, hospitals for the sick are spoken of as commonly known. The first celebrated one was that of Cæsarea, A.D. 370-380, richly endowed by the Emperor Valens. After it followed the hospital of Chrysostom at Constantinople.

We learn from Jerome, that Fabiola, a wealthy Christian widow of a noble Roman family, who died in his time, first erected a public infirmary: "Prima omnium νοσοχομεῖον instituit, in quo ægrotantes colligeret de plateis, et consumpta languoribus atque inedia miserorum membra foveret." (*Epist.* lxxvii. ed. Migne. Paris, 1845, tom. xxii. 694.) And Gregory the Presbyter, in his Life of Nazianzen, says, that Basil, who lived in the same age with Jerome, built a large hospital for lepers with charity money, which he collected for that purpose. (Secker's *Sermon*, preached before the Governors of the London Hospital, Feb. 20, 1754.)

In early times no convent was without its tenement for the sick poor; but the first order which we find exclusively founded for hospitals are the Hospitalières, who follow the rule of St. Augustine, and were appointed to the care of the Hôtel Dieu at Paris. For an account of the Religious Orders in the Roman Catholic Church consult the *Encyclopédie Théologique*, par M. l'Abbaye Migne, and the *Histoire des Ordres Réligieux* par M. Herion.

Connected with this subject is the history of the various 'Spitals, such as St. Mary's 'Spital, near Bishopsgate; St. Bartholomew's 'Spital, Smithfield; St. Thomas's 'Spital, Southwark, and the New Abbey of Tower Hill, called "Our Lady of Grace." *Vide* Stow, Newcourt, and the numerous 'Spital Sermons. A list of works on the Hospitals of London is printed in the Catalogue of the Library of the Corporation of London, 1859, pp. 69-72. Mr. Murray, in 1850, published a useful little work on this subject, entitled *Hospitals and Sisterhoods*, 12mo. Consult also a valuable article in Rees's *Cyclopædia*, vol. xviii.]

Old Inns of Southwark.—Observing that the Catherine Wheel Inn, High Street, Southwark, Surrey, is to be closed in the course of a few days for the purpose of making alterations, I should feel much obliged if any reader of "N. & Q." can refer me to any historical account which will inform me when it was built; and also of the other old inns of Southwark—namely, the Talbot,

King's Head, Queen's Head, George Inn, Horse Shoe, &c.

I am also very anxious to know if there is any water-colour drawing of the Catherine Wheel, and of the other old inns I have mentioned; if not, I should advise that some one equally interested in the matter should take a water-colour drawing before the alterations commenced, it being a very ancient building. I observe that at the Talbot Inn there is an old painting over the outside of the door of the booking-office, which is now very defaced. I should feel obliged if any reader is able to tell me what it represents.   D. R. J.

Streatham Hill, Surrey.

[An interesting paper on the Inns of Southwark from the pen of the late Mr. George R. Corner is printed in the *Collections of the Surrey Archæological Society*, vol. ii. pp. 50-81. Some historical notices are given of the following Inns:—The Tabard, or Talbot; the George (with an illustration); the White Hart (with an illustration); the Bear's Head; the Bear at the Bridge Foot; and the White Lion, afterwards called the Crown and Chequers, The Three Brushes, or Holy Water Sprinklers. A continuation of Mr. Corner's paper will shortly appear in the *Proceedings of the London and Middlesex and Surrey Archæological Societies*. Among some water-colour drawings by Mr. J. C. Buckler, to illustrate Pennant's *London*, in the Library of the Corporation of London, are the following Southwark Inns:—The Ship, taken down in 1831; The George; The Spur, on the east side of High Street; The Tabard, now the Talbot; The White Hart; The King's Head; The Queen's Head; The Boar's Head Place, formerly an inn on the east side of High Street, pulled down in 1830; The Dog and Bear Inn, and old Croydon House, on the west side of High Street; The Catherine Wheel Inn; and the Green Man Inn, Old Kent Road.]

Hagbush Lane.—Where is, or was, this lane? I fancy somewhere in the northern suburbs of London. About forty years ago, I more than once saw in the Royal Academy Exhibition views of "the Cottage in Hagbush Lane"; a picturesque old "bit," evidently dear to the artists of those days. Has it been swallowed up among the new streets of "enlarged, and still increasing, London?"   J.

[Many a sexagenarian now living can remember his rural rambles in summer time from the metropolis over the green fields between Pentonville and Highgate—more especially to that sequestered and shady retreat, Hagbush Lane, the favourite suburban haunt of every botanizing perambulator. But the spoilers have been abroad—

"Bricks and mortar! bricks and mortar!
Give green fields a little quarter:
As sworn foes to Nature's beauty,
You've already done your duty!"

So sang one, lately removed from among us, who always delighted to take an interest in the topography and antiquities of his "Merrie Islington."]

Hagbush Lane extended from the northern end of the present Liverpool Road, Islington, in a winding direction westerly to the fields by Copenhagen House, from whence it proceeded northerly in a zig-zag course to Crouch End and Hornsey. The upper part of this Lane, now divided by the Camden Town Road, pursued a winding course northerly to the road leading from Kentish Town to Upper Holloway. It then made another zig-zag or elbow, and was continued by a passage into the great North Road at Upper Holloway by the sign of the Mother Red Cap—a public-house celebrated by Drunken Barnaby in his amusing Itinerary —

> "Thence to Hollowell, Mother Red Cap,
> In a troup of trulls I did hap ;
> Whores of Babylon me impalled,
> And me their Adonis called ;
> With me toy'd they, buss'd me, cull'd me,
> But being needy, out they pull'd me."

The late Mr. George Daniel, of Canonbury, had in his possession a token, on the right side of which is engraved "Mother Red Cap" holding a Black Jack, with the initials of the proprietor "J. B. his Half Peny ;" and on the reverse, "John Backster, at the Mother Read Capp in holloway, 1667." It was sold among his Miscellaneous Objects of Art (lot 2223), where it is said to be unique ; but we know of at least four others in the collections of numismatic antiquaries.

Hone, in his *Every-Day Book*, i. 870-879, has given a graphic description of Hagbush Lane, with an engraving of a cottage formerly in it. A plan of the lane is faithfully delineated, from a survey made by Mr. Dent in 1820, in Tomline's *Perambulation of Islington*, royal 8vo, 1858, p. 26.]

LEYCESTER'S PROGRESS IN HOLLAND.—I once read in a monthly periodical or some other magazine, an account of Leycester's Progress and Reception in Holland, written by a contemporary of the earl. I cannot remember in what periodical it was. It must have been before 1854, since that was the date when I read it. Poole does not give any reference to it. Could possibly any of your numerous correspondents kindly oblige me with this information ? .Q.

[There is "A Journal of my Lord of Leicester's Proceeding in the Low Countries, by Mr. Stephen Burrogh, Admiral of the Fleet," printed in the *Correspondence of Robert Dudley, Earl of Leycester, during his Government of the Low Countries*, edited by John Bruce, Esq., for the Camden Society, 4to, 1844. Is it possible that our correspondent has met with a review of this work in some periodical ? Mr. Motley, in his *History of the United Netherlands*, 2 vols: 8vo, 1860, has given numerous quotations from it ; but has not even alluded to any subsequent article on Leycester's Progress in Holland.]

Replies.

GREEK DRAMA : EZECHIEL'S "EXAGOGE."

(3rd S. vi. 388, 447.)

A correspondent inquired if certain fragments of a Greek drama, by a Jewish poet, named Ezechiel, which are preserved by St. Clement of Alexandria and Eusebius, are rendered into English in any of the translations of their writings. Another correspondent answered, that there has been no English translation. There was, however, a work published about twenty years ago, called *Leaves from Eusebius*, being an English translation of select portions of his *Præparatio Evangelica*, in which was given a stiff and obscure version of a very small part of the extracts from Ezechiel. I have therefore made a complete translation of the whole of these fragments, expressly for the pages of "N. & Q.," and to gratify the correspondent who wished to see such a translation. It may be well to premise, that the introductory and intermediate sentences in prose are in the words of the respective writers, St. Clement and Eusebius. I have translated from the Greek of the Wurtzburg edition of St. Clement of Alexandria, 1778, and from the Paris edition of Eusebius, 1628.

"On the education of Moses, Ezechiel will agree with us, who was a writer of tragedies; who in the drama, which is entitled the *Exagoge*, thus writes in the person of Moses : —

> " When Jacob had deserted Chanaan's land,
> With seventy souls around him, chosen band,
> To Pharao's realm he came, and numerous were
> His progeny in after years begotten there.
> Long did they bear a wicked nation's yoke,
> And groan beneath increased oppression's stroke.
> Pharao the King beheld our race increase,
> And by deceitful arts destroyed their peace.
> No respite to their cruel toils he gave,
> Forced them to furnish bricks, to work and slave
> Building high towers, and cities stretching wide,
> With fruitless toil, through tyranny and pride :
> And to the Hebrews gave the dire command
> To drown each infant-male throughout their land.
> Then, as my honoured mother would relate,
> Three months she hid me from that cruel fate ;
> Then bore me to the river rolling wide,
> And laid me wrapt where sedges fringe its side ;
> While my sweet sister Mary, stationed there,
> Watched me with all a sister's anxious care.
> Not long did I all helpless thus remain ;
> For Pharao's daughter, with her numerous train
> Of beauteous handmaids came beside the wave,
> In the refreshing stream at morn to lave.
> There she observed the unconscious floating child,
> Saved me from threatening death, and on me smiled.
> Knew 'twas a Hebrew babe ; while Mary ran
> With joy and eagerness, and thus began
> The princess to accost : ' Dost thou desire
> That I should find the nurse thou wilt require,
> A Hebrew woman, fit for such employ ? '
> She gave assent ; and Mary flew with joy,
> To bid her mother quiet her alarms,
> And come :—she came, and pressed me in her arms.

Then spoke the princess: 'Nurse this child for me,
Well for thy care shalt thou rewarded be.'
She named me Moses, having deigned to save
Me from the danger of a watery grave.
    " When infancy had passed, the princely dome
Thenceforth became my rich and happy home;
Thither my mother led me; but before,
Oft had she carefully repeated o'er
All that concerned my origin and race,
My nation, and God's wondrous gifts and grace.
There, till my years of boyhood all were spent,
I lived in ease and luxury content,
As if I'd been of royal birth, supplied
With rich profusion, and no wish denied.
But when I reached the fulness of my days,
My splendid home I left for arduous ways.*
    " I saw my race afflicted, and assailed,
Where the King's wanton tyranny prevailed;
And shortly I beheld in savage feud,
A brother Hebrew beaten and subdued
By an Egyptian: and as none was near,
No witness of my deed had I to fear;
So to avenge my countryman, I slew
The fell Egyptian, and concealed from view
His body buried in the sand; that so
None might betray me, or the murder know.
The next day I beheld two more engage
Egyptians both, in fight with mutual rage:
To one I said: 'Why, coward, dost thou strike
One to thy strength unequal and unlike?'
But he replied: 'And who appointed thee,
Our judge and master here supreme to be?
Wilt thou kill me, as thou didst yesterday
My countryman, the poor Egyptian, slay?'
Hearing these words I feared, and full of dread,
'Who can have made this known?' I trembling said.
'Will not this deed soon reach King Pharao's ear?'
It quickly did: his threats pursued me near,
He sought to kill me; but I quickly fled;
And since in foreign lands my life I've led."

"Then he speaks thus of the daughters of Raguel:—

    'Before me seven fair virgins I behold.'

He enquires whose daughters these virgins are,
and Sephora answers:—

    "'Stranger! the land thou seest from afar,
Is Libya called, there Ethiopians are,
Thousands of dark skinned people; o'er whose lands
And in whose wars one Emperor commands.
But here o'er all things human and divine
The priest holds rule, who is their sire and mine.'

"Then after mentioning the watering of the
flocks, he inserts the nuptials of Sephora, and introduces Chumus thus addressing Sephora:—

"As it behoves thee, Sephora, make known
To this our guest thou'rt given, and made his own."

Thus far Eusebius quotes from the drama of
Ezechiel. In his next chapter, he gives passages
from the same as quoted by Demetrius, who relates the early history of Moses, as it is found in
the Bible. Then he observes that the poet Ezechiel recounts the same in his *Exagoge*, adding

---

* Thus far is taken from St. Clement of Alexandria: the
rest is from Eusebius.

also the dream of Moses, interpreted by his father-in-law. Thus he introduces Moses discoursing
alternately with his father-in-law:—

"A large and splendid throne do I descry,
Raised on the radiant summit of the sky:
Seated thereon of noblest form is seen
A monarch crowned, and of majestic mien.
His left a rich and ponderous sceptre wields,
His right to me a gracious summons yields.
I fly in haste, and quickly reach the throne:
At once he yields it; it becomes my own.
He hands the sceptre, and enthrones me there,
And binds his glittering diadem round my hair.
Then as I view the world's immense extent,
The earth below, the heavenly firmament,
From all the sky departing, and through all,
A multitude of stars before me fall.
All these I number separate on their way,
Moving like warlike legions in array.
Fear seizes me, and trembling at the sight,
With sudden start I chase the dream of night."

"Which dream the father-in-law thus interprets:—

"Stranger! what joyful things has God foretold
To thee. And shall I see them,—I so old?
Take courage, son, thou shalt erect a throne,
And thou shalt rule whole nations as thine own.
For all thou then didst see,—all earth contained,
And all that heaven's vast firmament sustained,
All that exists at present thou shalt see,
All that has been, and all that is to be."

"Then of the burning bush, and how he was
sent to Pharao, he again represents Moses conversing with God. Moses says:—

"This burning bush, this sign, what can it mean?
What monster this, which none will think I've seen?
The bush was suddenly suffused with flame,
Yet though on fire, all green it stands the same.
Why is this so? I'll go, and view it near,
This wonder none will credit when they hear."

"Then God answers him.

"'Moses! no nearer dare to come, but stay,
Put off thy shoes, ere thou may'st tread this way;
The place beneath thy feet is holy ground.'
Then from the bush came words of solemn sound:
'Take courage, son, hear in this awful place
My words: no eye of man could bear my face;
But thou art privileged to hear my voice,
Thou, favoured man, the object of my choice.
I am the God thy honoured sires adored,
Of Abraham, Isaac, Jacob,—God and Lord:
And mindful of my ancient mercies, now
I come, myself the parent to avow,
And the avenger of the Hebrew race,
Whose wrongs cry out for vengeance to my face.
Then go thou, Moses, in my awful name,
Tell Pharao, and the Hebrew race the same,
All it shall please me to make known to thee,
To aid thee to lead forth my people free.'"

"Then after some further alternate converse,
Moses speaks:—

"But I am slow of speech, how shall I bring,
My tongue thus boldly to address the King?"'

"But God answers:

"Send then thy brother Aaron; let him know
My words, as thou hast heard them: he shall go

And speak instead of thee, and every thing
   Fearless shall he declare before the King."

"Then they converse concerning the rod, and the
other prodigies.

"'Say what is that thou holdest in thy hand?'
'A rod, o'er flocks and men a potent wand.'
'Cast it upon the ground, but quickly fly,
For a huge serpent shall its place supply.'
It is cast down : 'O save me thou, I pray,.
How frightful is this monster in my way!
Help, I entreat thee : for I sorely fear.'
'Fear not the serpent, confident draw near,
And seize its tail, all danger will be o'er,
It shall become the rod it was before.—
Into thy bosom put thy hand, and lo!
Dost thou not bring it forth as white as snow?
Place there thy hand again ; it shall be seen,
When taken out, as it had ever been.'"

"Then, after a few other matters, he (Demetrius)
goes on to say : 'These same things Ezechiel
commemorates in his *Exagoge.*' And of the prodigies, he introduces God speaking thus : —

"With this same rod shalt thou work every woe.
The river first with blood alone shall flow ;
In every fountain, every pond and flood,
The water shall be hideously changed to blood ;
Frogs shall abound, sciniphs shall fill the air,
And dust, like ashes, I will scatter there.
Foul sores and ulcers it shall cause : and then
Large stinging flies shall torture Egypt's men.
After these plagues, a pestilence shall rise,
Beneath its rage, the stoutest sinks and dies.
The heavens shall frown, and shower down hail and fire
On sinful mortals, with avenging ire.
The fields shall be laid waste, the beasts shall die.
Three days in darkness Egypt's land shall lie.
Locusts, all food devouring, shall be seen,
The corn shall perish in the fields yet green ;
Each first-born son I'll slay of every age,
And thus at last shall cease proud Egypt's rage.
For hardened Pharao I command in vain,
Till he shall see his first-born son lie slain.
Then seized with dread, he'll set my people free.—
Thus then instruct them, as I speak to thee.
This month shall be the first of all the year,
When you shall go forth free from bonds and fear,
And shall possess the long since promised land,
Proclaim again unto them this command,—
That month I bid you, when her fullest light
The moon shall reach, offer, the previous night,
The Paschal lamb to God, and with its blood
Sprinkle your door-posts, as you hope for good.
The angel sent to slay, shall see, and spare
Your dwellings, while the rest no mercy share.
The lamb's flesh roasted you shall eat that night.
Quickly shall Pharao, trembling with affright,
Urge you to fly : my favour you shall find,
Woman to woman goods of every kind
Shall freely give, their vessels, garments, gold,
And silver for your wants, unweighed, untold.
Then when your feet at length secure shall stand
In your own long desired, and promised land,
Seven days from that, on which was first begun
Your march from Egypt, then shall every one
Each year eat bread unleavened, and shall bow
To God, and first-born animals shall vow
And sacrifice ; and with each first-born son
Of woman also shall the like be done."

"And then he observes that God gave more minute
directions respecting the same festival : —

"In all your families of Hebrew race,
This month, which as the first of months has place,
Take sheep and calves, without a spot or stain,
And let them till the fourteenth day remain.
Then offer them in sacrifice that eve,
And eat with entrails roasted ; nothing leave,
Having your loins, while eating, girded round,
Staves in your hands, and on your feet shoes bound.
Let all thus offer, and thus eat that night ;
For hastily the King shall urge your flight.
This for your sacrifice, is my command :
Take each a bunch of hyssop in your hand,
Dipped in the blood, your door-posts on each side,
Sprinkle, and so escape destruction wide,
Keep to the Lord this feast : seven days complete,
No leavened bread shall any dare to eat :
God freed you in this month from woes accursed,
This then of months and times shall be the first."

"Ezechiel also,' he says, 'in the drama entitled *The Exagoge,* introduces a messenger describing the position of the Hebrews, and the defeat of the Egyptians, thus : '—

"When the King Pharao, with a mighty.host,
Went forth full armed, with proud insulting boast,
With horses, chariots, generals trained to war,
His numerous army terror spread afar.
Infantry in the midst, in proud array,
Marched on, but leaving clear a chariot way :
The cavalry protected either side
Of the Egyptian army, flushed with pride.
I ask the number of the imposing band ;
Ten thousand thousand own the King's command,
Outspread the Hebrews lie, all Egypt's foes.
Some stretched along the Red Sea's shores repose,
Others their babes, and older children feed,
And aid the faint and weary in their need.
Their numerous flocks and herds are feeding round,
And household vessels everywhere abound.—
When these defenceless saw our army near,
They filled the air with shrieks, and cries of fear,
With trembling limbs, bewildered and amazed,
Their hands and voices to their God they raised.
A city near them we encamped before ;
Beelsephon the name that city bore.
But when the sun was set, we took repose,
Waiting for morning, to assault our foes,
Confiding in our veteran troops, and arms,
Men to subdue, half-dead with dire alarms.
But lo! a wondrous prodigy was seen ;—
There stood, the Hebrews' and our camp between,
A pillar formed of clouds : and Moses brought
The rod, with which such wonders he had wrought,
Such prodigies and plagues in Egypt's land ;
And raising it he struck with mighty hand
The great Red Sea ; and at his stroke the tide
Obeys, the waters instantly divide,
And all the Hebrews safely tread their way
Through the deep bed, untouched by salt-waves' spray.
We quickly followed, marching boldly on,
And loudly shouting, where they first had gone.—
And now 'twas night ; our noiseless wheels sunk deep,
Our men no footing in the mire could keep.
Suddenly, to our wondering eyes, a light,
Like fire from heaven appeared, intensely bright.
And then we knew, appalled and sore afraid,
That God was their protector, strength, and aid.

And when the Hebrews safely reached the shore,
Down came the impetuous waters rolling o'er,
And gathering round us: then arose the cry:
'O from this great Avenger let us fly!
These he protects, on us his angry frown
Sends only evil and destruction down.'
The whelming waters of the deep Red Sea
Closed over all : our army ceased to be."

"Again, a little after, they went a journey of three days, as Demetrius commemorates ; and this the Holy Bible also testifies. But as they had no sweet water, but only what was bitter, by the command of God, he cast a certain kind of wood into the spring, and the water was made sweet. Thence they came to Elim, and there they found twelve fountains of water, and seventy palm trees. Of these, and of a certain bird which they saw, Ezechiel introduces a person addressing Moses ; and on the subject of the palm trees and the twelve fountains, he speaks thus : —

"Attend, great Moses ! we a spot have found,
Where breezes through the valley softly sound.
Here in this charming place, this sweet retreat,
Thou mayest wisely choose to fix thy seat.
Here there appeared a light of heaven divine,
A fiery column, of great joy the sign.
And then a wide, well-shaded space we found,
Where watered meadows spread luxuriant round.
For in the valley's bosom wide, but low,
Twelve fountains from one rock are seen to flow.
There, firmly rooted, seventy palm trees stand ;
And flocks feed richly on the fertile land."

"He then goes on to describe the appearance of the bird : —

"'Soon after this, we saw a living thing,
A strange and novel bird upon the wing.
Equal he was to twice the eagle's size ;
His wings were beautiful with changing dies.
His purple breast great admiration won,
His legs with bright vermillion colour shone.
Around his graceful neck, like fleece, there grew
Rich plumage of a golden yellow hue.
Pale yellow round the pupil of his eye
Was seen : the pupil was of scarlet die,
His voice the most melodious ever heard,
He was in truth the king of every bird.
All others followed him in silent dread,
While he, like Taurus, proudly reared his head."

F. C. H.

FISHER'S "GARLANDS."

(3rd S. vi. 286.)

The query of J. M. scarcely admits of a concise and ready reply ; there has also been some evident mystification practised on this subject, which makes it rather difficult to get at the truth ; but from a notice lately published in the *Fisherman's Magazine* (No. VII.) of a work entitled *A Collection of Right Merrie Garlands for North Country Anglers,* Newcastle-on-Tyne, 1864 ; from Mr. T. Westwood's very excellent and interesting *Bibliotheca Piscatoria,* a book seemingly not so well known as it deserves to be ; and from my own

collection of angling literature, I am enabled to give the information required.

The first Garland was published in 1821, in form of a single-sheet broadside ; it commences, " Auld Nature now revived seems," and was the joint production of Robert Roxby and Thomas Doubleday. It was annually succeeded by similar pieces, principally by the same writers, till 1832, when the series terminated. It is impossible to say how many editions of these single sheet broadsides were issued, or how many of each ; but it may be set down as a significant hint, that some of them, published at Newcastle for a halfpenny, were bought by collectors in London for sixpence, and even one shilling, and we may conclude that demand found its usual supply. There was a kind of mania at the time for angling works, and many dodges were the consequent result ; one of these may be mentioned here as a curious, if not amusing, piece of literary history. A person named Lathy one day called upon Gosden, the well-known bookbinder, publisher, and collector, with an original poem on angling. Gosden purchased the manuscript for 30*l.*, and had it published,[*] with a whole length engraved portrait of himself, in a fishing dress, armed with rod and landing-net, leaning sentimentally against a votive altar, dedicated to the manes of Walton and Cotton, as a frontispiece. A number of copies were printed on royal paper, and one on vellum, the vellum alone costing Gosden 10*l.*, before it was discovered that the whole was a plagiaristic swindle, the manuscript being very little more than a copy of a rather rare poem, entitled *The Anglers. Eight Dialogues in Verse.* London, 1758.[†]

To return, however, to the *Fisher's Garlands.* In 1836, the set of Garlands from 1821 to 1832 inclusive, were published in a collected form, octavo, by Charnley of Newcastle, their original publisher. There were fourteen garlands in this collection, two being placed to the credit of 1824, and the well-known *Angler's Progress* of Boaz, written and published in the previous century, being interpolated as the " Fisher's Garland " for 1820. How many editions were published of this collection, or what were their dates, is now unknown. In 1842, after a lapse of ten years, an attempt was made to resuscitate the annual series of garlands, but without success ; they only continued till 1845, and then completely and finally ceased. But in 1842, Mr. Charnley published *A*

---

[*] Under the title of *The Angler ; a Poem in Ten Cantos, with Notes, &c.* By T. P. Lathy, Esq. Subsequently, when the fraud was discovered, the last words were altered to " By Piscator."

[†] Correctly ascribed to Dr. Scott, a dissenting minister at Ipswich. The poem was afterwards published by Ruddiman, in his *Collection of Scarce, Curious, and Valuable Pieces, &c.,* Edinburgh, 1773. See also *Gentleman's Magazine,* vol. lxxxix. p. 407.

Collection of Right Merrie Garlands for North Country Anglers, 8vo, Newcastle; and, as the writer in the *Fisherman's Magazine* observes, " with an ingenuity worthy of a better cause," raked a number of fishing songs together, to supply the vacant years when no garlands were published. How many editions of this collection were published is also unknown; nor is it clear, whether we should class with it an edition published by the Newcastle Typographical Society, including the *Fisher's Garlands* from 1821 to 1845, with the *Angler's Progress* and *Tyne Fisher's Farewell*. Again, in this present year of Grace, we have, published at Newcastle, *A Collection of Right Merrie Garlands for North Country Anglers*. Edited by Joseph Crawhall and continued to this present Year." Here, as before, a number of poems are collected from all quarters, to represent the garlands of years when none were published. Thus we have them selected from Chatto's *Angler's Souvenir, Scenes and Recollections of Fly-fishing*, Watts' *Annual Souvenir*, Richardson's *Borderer's Table Book*, and other sources. Mr. Crawhall contributes some of his own compositions, and the very best of the whole are written by Mr. Westwood.

I may add that the choice of the Roxby and Doubleday Garlands were published, in a collected form, as *The Coquet-Dale Fishing Songs*, by the Blackwoods in 1852. And I should not conclude this unpleasant notice of *crambe repetita* of the worst kind, without observing that Allan Cunningham actually published one of the Roxby and Doubleday garlands, *The Auld Fisher's Welcome to Coquet-Side*, in the strange *omnium gatherum*, which he had the boldness to term *The Songs of Scotland*; though, at the same time, he had, or could have easily found, at least fifty genuine Scottish songs to take its place, any one of them fifty times superior to the Northumbrian doggrel garland aforesaid.

WILLIAM PINKERTON.

"COUSINS," A SONG: PRAED'S POEMS.

(3rd S. vi. 414.)

W. M. F. inquires if Praed were the author of this song; and though an answer will probably be given ere this reaches England, this query and several like it may serve as an excuse for a note on Praed's poems. This poem was in the American edition, and is not in the authorised collection. The American book was necessarily composed of such poems as were found in print and were signed by Praed; and it contained also poems supposed to be written by the same author. As editor, I have had occasion to examine many of the Annuals and Magazines to which Praed contributed, and the result of the search is as follows:

The poems reprinted from the *Etonian* and the Annuals are, with two exceptions, said there to be by W. M. Praed, or by " the Author of *Lillian*."

Those contributed to Knight's *Quarterly Magazine* have also been easily recognised; but in 1828, when Mr. Knight edited the *London Magazine*, Praed sent him four poems, all published over the signature Σ. These were, " School and Schoolfellows," " Arrivals at a Watering Place," " April Fools," and " Our Ball."

In the *New Monthly Magazine* a series of poems appeared, all signed Φ. In 1826, without a signature, "Josephine " was printed, which is confessedly Praed's.

In 1827, with the signature were " Utopia," " A Year of Impossibilities * ", " A Song for the Fourteenth of February," " To —— by an Exquisite *," and " Goodnight to the Season."

In 1828, " My Partner," " A Chapter of Ifs *," " The Fancy Ball," " A Letter of Advice," and " The Light o' Love *."

In 1829, " Twenty-eight and Twenty-nine," " Chivalry at a Discount *," " Quince," " Song to a Serenader in February*," " Sybil's Letter," " The Vicar," and " Cousins *."

Of these poems all but seven, marked with a star in the preceding list, are reprinted in Mr. Coleridge's most interesting edition. As all the poems appeared over the same signature, it seems difficult to decide upon the authorship, unless the poet left some list of his publications.

Six other short poems in the *London Magazine* signed ξ were printed in the American book, and are doubtless not the work of Praed. One of these, signed Φ, " Chivalry at a Discount," was especially noticed in the London *Times*, Oct. 7, 1864, with an expressed wish from the critic to know who wrote it, if Praed did not. In the *Literary Souvenir* for 1830, another poem on the same subject, and one called " An Invitation," signed φ, were printed; the same volume contained two poems by the " Author of *Lillian*," and one, " Where is Miss Myrtle," unsigned, but written by Praed.

It seems hardly possible that two writers would use the same signature in the same volume, and yet if Praed was φ of the *New Monthly* in 1827, 1828, and 1829, would he have been apt to yield the name in 1830 in a volume to which he contributed, especially if he had already written a poem on the same subject?

It has been repeatedly said that some of these poems were written by a Mr. Fitz-Gerald. Surely it cannot be too late to learn something about him. In 1834, two songs, " I remember," and " The Runaway," were published by Dannely, London, the words by Praed, the music by Mrs. E. Fitz-Gerald. Could this lady's husband have been so intimate a friend that Praed joined with him in his enterprises, and shared the signature φ with him?

The question is interesting because in 1839 and 1841 certain Charades appeared in the *New Monthly*, which were the production of no inferior poet. These are numbered 1, 2, 21, 22, 25—30, in the American work. Two of them, "Sir Geoffrey lay in his cushioned chair," and "There kneels in holy St. Cuthbert's aisles," are certainly worthy of Praed's genius. If we are yet to have the collected works of one who belonged to Praed's school, and who has so successfully studied his style, it is time the enterprise were announced.

Lastly, may we not hope that, in view of these repeated inquiries, Mr. Coleridge will inform us if the edition contains all the poems which Praed acknowledged, and in what form the declaration was made; or whether it contains only such poems as the surviving friends of the poet can identify positively. If the latter, it is not unreasonable to hope that an author will be found for these poems, which so nearly approach the perfection of one who must rank as chief of the minor poets of England for the present century.

W. H. WHITMORE.

Boston, U.S.A.

THE GROTTO OF THE NATIVITY AND OTHER CHRISTMAS MATTERS.

(3rd S. vi. 493, 519.)

The readers of "N. & Q." are much indebted to Dr. RIMBAULT for his interesting article on the Pifferari in Rome, at the same time it contains some remarkable mythological speculations after the manner of Conyers Middleton, upon which I would fain offer a few remarks.

The Pifferari speak of our Saviour having been born in a Grotto: Dr. RIMBAULT is pleased to consider this a "popular corruption of the Scriptural text," and adds, "I am not aware that any attempt has been made to trace the origin of it." He undertakes the task himself, and traces it mediately to the false gospels forged by some of the ancient heretics, and ultimately to "the great Mithraic mysteries, the Sibyl's Cave, the Cave of Trophonius." On his way to these primæval antiquities, Dr. R. picks up "the celebrated religious poet Sannazarius of Naples," who has "unequivocally adopted" this corruption of Scripture, and who, I fear, helped on Dr. R. to his Pagan conclusions. M. l'Abbé Gaume, a good Catholic, thus disposes of this "religious poet," notwithstanding his having founded a church:—

"Sannazaro, in his poem entitled *De Partu Virginis*, makes a medley, which we should call ridiculous, were it not indecent, of the most august truths of the Faith, and the absurdities of mythology. The whole poem is filled with gods and goddesses, while the name of our Lord

does not occur once."—*Le Ver Rongeur des Sociétés Modernes*, ch. xi.*

I am at loss to conceive how the allusion in the Pifferari Hymn could in any sense be called "a corruption of the Scriptural text." It is a tradition of universal Christendom, which comes under the conditions of the golden rule of St. Vincent of Lerins, *Quod ubique, quod semper, et ab omnibus creditum*. The Eastern Church refers to it in her services, and the early Greek writers and painters commemorate it; moreover, the local tradition is clear and steadfast. It would be easy to quote a host of authorities, I shall however quote but a few, and those readily accessible. The learned patristic theologian, Mr. Isaac Williams, says of our Lord's birthplace:—

"It was a cave in the native city of David according to the testimony of Justin Martyr, Origen, and others; for such the stables in that country often are. And thus as He was buried, so also was He born in a cave in the rock."—*Comm. on the Nativity*, 1852, p. 83.

Bp. Taylor says in his *Life of Christ*:—

"She that was Mother to the King of all creatures, could find no other place but a stable, a cave of a rock, whither she retired."

And in a note to this passage he refers to the Septuagint Version of Isaiah, xxxiii. 16, which some ancient writers consider to be a prophecy of this birth-place.†

We have not only good testimony to show that our Saviour was born in a cave of a rock at Bethlehem, but we have also good reason to believe that the very cave can be identified, the record of it having been preserved by an uninterrupted tradition. Mr. Chester, in his admirable little work entitled *Three Weeks in Palestine and Lebanon*, which, I believe, the S. P. C. K. has stereotyped, thus writes of "the lowly scene of the Messiah's birth, upon entering which," he says, "I sank instinctively upon my knees . . ."

"Buckingham treats the idea of the Grotto of the Nativity being really the scene of that event as an absurdity, chiefly on account of its being underground: while Clarke, though generally so sceptical with regard to the identity of the Holy Places, says that the tradition respecting this cave seems so well authenticated as hardly

* The poet's tomb was quite in keeping with his pagan predilections. We are told in an account quoted by Hone that—"His superb tomb in the church of St. Mark is decorated with two figures originally executed for, and meant to represent Apollo and Minerva; but as it appeared indecorous to admit heathen divinities into a Christian church, and the figures were thought too excellent to be removed, the person who shows the church is instructed to call them David and Judith.

† The note is curious and worth quoting here: "Juxta propheticum illud, Esai. xxxiii. 16, Ὄυτος οἰκήσει ἐν ὑψηλῷ σπηλαίῳ πέτρας ἰσχυρᾶς· Ἄρτος δοθήσεται αὐτῷ, apud lxx., sed hanc periodum Judæi eraserunt ex Hebræo textu; sic et Symmachus. [*Hexapl.* Montf. vol. ii. p. 146], ἄρτος δοθήσεται, mystice Bethlehem, sive *Domus panis*, indigitatur."—*Eden's* ed. vol. ii. 64.

to admit of dispute. Whatsoever the truth may be, I do not think Buckingham's objection a valid one, as it is by no means uncommon in these countries to use similar *souterrains* as habitations both for man and beast; and the adherence to ancient customs in the 'never-changing East,' argues the probability of similar usage in our Saviour's time."—Ed. 1838, p. 57.

DR. RIMBAULT looks askance at "the winter wild," and other accessaries to the Nativity; but these are trifles, let us pass on to a graver matter. Granting that in the conversion of Heathendom, new converts clung to some of their old superstitions, which in some cases the Church was unable to eradicate, and in others unwisely permitted, "christening the ceremonies of pagan superstition, and adapting their fables to the mysteries of Christian worship, which will undoubtedly account for much of the ceremonies and superstitions of the modern Church of Rome:"[*] Granting that the old image of Jupiter at Rome does duty for the Jew Peter, and that the Mariolatry of Rome is a most deplorable heresy—still, surely DR. RIMBAULT might have found a truer and a fairer origin for this last than the foul worship, and abominable rites of Cybele![†] Surely if he had reflected a little, he would have shrunk from such an association with the Blessed Virgin Mother of our LORD. It is true that the accomplished and lamented authoress of *Legends of the Madonna* gravely refers us [‡] to the Egyptian group of Isis and Horus as the prototype of the Blessed Virgin and Child of Catholic Art, and the inspiring Idea of Cyril and the Council of Ephesus! But the instincts of her heart were truer than the teaching of her creed, and elsewhere she does more justice to the subject. Devout celibates, poring with love and wonder upon that abyss of mystery the INCARNATION, became dazzled by "the matchless dignity of Mary," and loved not wisely but too well: not preserving "the proportion of faith," their fond imaginings at length condensed into new articles of faith, and they came at last to receive as sober truth and revelation what they had long wished might be true— *Populus vult decipi, et decipitur.* From S. Bernard to Pio Nono we may trace the successive stages of Mariolatry.[§] This is illustrated by an

* See Polydore Virgil, *De Rerum Inventoribus,* and Jones of Nayland's *Reflexions on the Growth of Heathenism among Modern Christians.*

† Middleton quotes the following passage from a congenial writer, "the describer of Modern Rome" (who is he?):—

"If in converting the profane worship of the Gentiles to the pure and sacred worship of the Church, the faithful desire to follow some use and proportion, they have certainly hit upon it here, in dedicating to the Madonna, or Holy Virgin, the temple formerly sacred to the Bona Dea, or good goddess."—*Letter from Rome.*

‡ Ed. 1852, p. xxii.

§ For the earlier history of it, the reader can refer to Mr. Tyler's valuable work, and to Bp. Hall, *The Old Religion,* ch. xiv.

anecdote related by the late Rev. H. J. Rose in a very instructive article on "Catholicism in Silesia," published in the first volume of the *Foreign Quarterly Review:*—

"A friend of ours, long resident in the south of Italy, was in the habit of talking to a very devout old woman in the neighbourhood. One day the old lady, in the course of conversation, said that there was but one thing she wanted to be perfectly happy. On being asked what was this one requisite for the *vita beata,* she said, 'If the Virgin could but be made God—for *He* was so severe, but the Virgin was always kind, and gentle, and compassionate.'"—P. 552.

The French beggars referred to by DR. RIMBAULT, who asked alms *au nom de la* BONNE DEESSE, seem to have reached that happy height of imagination to which the Italian devotee in the above story only aspired, wistfully and despondingly.[*]

In Hone's *Ancient Mysteries* and *Every-Day Book,* he describes a very interesting edition of Sannazaro's curious Poem, a quarto volume printed at Florence in 1740, with engravings of the Nativity, from sculptures on an ancient sarcophagi at Rome. Hone also describes a very curious sheet of Carols, printed in London in 1701, price one penny. The description is as follows:—

"It is headed 'CHRISTUS NATUS EST: *Christ is born*;' with a woodcut 10 inches high by 8½ inches wide, representing the stable of Bethlehem; Christ in the crib, watched by the Virgin and Joseph; shepherds kneeling; angels attending; a man playing on the bagpipes; a woman with a basket of fruit on her head; a sheep bleating, and an ox lowing on the ground; a raven croaking, and a crow cawing on the hay-rack; a cock crowing above them; and angels singing in the sky. The animals have labels from their mouths bearing Latin inscriptions. Down the side of the woodcut is the following account and explanation: 'A religious man inventing the conceits of both birds and beasts drawn in the picture of our Saviour's birth, doth thus express them: the cock croweth, *Christus natus est,* Christ is born. The raven asked, *Quando?* where? The crow replied, *Hac nocte,* This night. The ox crieth out, *Ubi? Ubi?* Where? where? The sheep bleated out, *Bethlehem.* A voice from heaven sounded, *Gloria in Excelsis,* Glory be on high.'"

This was, when Hone wrote, in the possession of Mr. Upcott. Where is it now? I have quoted the above description of this curious carol that I may give an instance of the same treatment of the subject existing in fresco in this country. Dr. J. M. Neale, who refers to it in *The Unseen World,* seems not to be aware of the existence of the broadside. He says:—

* See Bp. Hall's Apostrophe to the B. V. M.: "O Blessed Virgin, if in that heavenly glory wherein thou art, thou canst take notice of these earthly things, with what indignation dost thou look upon the presumptuous superstition of vain men, whose suits make thee more than a solicitor of Divine favours! Thy humanity is not lost in thy motherhood, nor in thy glory. It is far from thee to abide this honour, which is stolen from thy Redeemer."—*Cont. N. T.* lib. II. p. 50, folio ed.

"An example, which in modern times would be considered ludicrous, of the manner in which our ancestors made external Nature bear witness to our LORD, occurs in what is called the Prior's Chamber in the small Augustinian house of Shulbrede, in the parish of Linchmere, in Sussex. On the wall is a fresco of the Nativity; and certain animals are made to give their testimony to that event in words which somewhat resemble, or may be supposed to resemble, their natural sounds. A cock, in the act of crowing stands at the top, and a label issuing from his mouth bears the words, *Christus natus est*. A duck inquires, *Quando, quando?* A raven hoarsely answers, *In hac nocte*. A cow asks, *Ubi, ubi?* And a lamb bleats out *Bethlehem*."—P. 27.

What is the earliest date at which this curious design first appears, and where else is it found? The whole design is stamped with the quaint and *naif* character of the Middle Ages, and the introduction of the bagpipes points to an Italian origin.

In which of the old English versions of the Bible does the word *cratch* occur in St. Luke's Gospel?—

"And this shall be a sign unto you; you shall finde the Childe swadled, and layd in a cratch . . . . So they came with haste, and found both Mary and Joseph with the Babe layd in the cratch."

It is quoted in a devotional work of the seventeenth century now before me, and I have not Bagster's *Hexapla* or any such book to refer to. Our old divines, Bp. Taylor, Bp. Hall, &c., use this word *Cratch* instead of that in our Authorised Version.   EIRIONNACH.

P.S. It may be well to mention that the above (intended as a Christmas paper) was written and despatched to the Editor on Dec. 20, and consequently before the appearance of F. C. H.'s valuable communication (vol. vi. p. 519).

PASSAGE IN "HAMLET."

(3rd S. vi. 410.)

Your correspondent, DR. F. A. LEO, proposes two emendations of the text of Shakspeare in *Hamlet*, Act I. Sc. 1.

Now, with regard to the first passage, I am unable to appreciate the objection to the reading "sleaded" or "sledded," that "it must have been a ridiculous position," an unkingly action "to smite down a man sitting in a sledge." For, in the first place, the sledge would be to the "Polack on the ice," as a chariot or horse to the combatant on less slippery ground; and, in the second place, I believe Shakspeare to have intended by "the Polack" an army or nation, and not a single man. Indeed, Malone considers it probable that he wrote "Polacks," which is confirmed by the Quarto, "Pollax."

Again, that "it was not a remarkable—not a memorable fact that in the cold Scandinavian country in winter-time, people were found sitting in a sledge," seems to me to be an argument for rather than against the reading, "sledded." Shakspeare did not mean to convey anything remarkable by the epithet. If he had, would "sturdie" have better answered his intention? I conceive the epithet "sledded" used of the Polack to be akin to those *constant* epithets, as they are called, which are so common in epic and ballad poetry: to possess, that is, this property of a constant epithet, that the Polack need not *at the time* have been in a sledge at all, and yet Shakspeare might call him with perfect poetical propriety "The sledded Polack."

Once more: I do not quite see how "sturdie" "should express a provoking manner;" but I am entirely at a loss to discover how the emendation "sturdie" follows as much as possible the form "sledded" or "sleaded."

With regard to the second reading. Instead of "Disasters in the sun," Malone would read "Disasters dimmed the sun;" and he certainly has much to adduce in support of his conjecture. He remarks on "the disagreeable recurrence of the word stars" in the next line, and thinks Shakspeare may have written —

"Astres with trains of fire and dews of blood
Disastrous dimmed the sun . . . ."

Perhaps we might read —

As stars (*i. e.* while stars—) . . *or* "And stars . . .
Disastrous dimmed the sun."

Malone's emendation seems to me to be preferable to those proposed by your correspondent.

May I be allowed to question whether

" . . . . stars
Did *enter in the sun* . . ."

is Shakspearian English?

I certainly think that the words "disaster" or "disastrous" (cf. Homer's ούλιος άστηρ), and "dews of blood" (cf. Virgil's "sanguinei rores," and Statius' "rores cruenti") must not be sacrificed to any emendation.

FABIUS OXONIENSIS.

THOMAS SYDSERF, BISHOP OF BRECHIN.

(3rd S. vi. 206.)

"Tho. Brechin" was certainly *Thomas Sydserf*, who was consecrated Bishop of Brechin, in Scotland, on July 29, 1634, at Edinburgh, by the Primate, Archbishop John Spottiswoode. His name is omitted by Keith, among the occupants of that see; although afterwards he correctly states, under the Bishops of Galloway, that he was "translated from Brechin to Galloway," and hence the difficulty of I. B. E. Dr. Sydserf, who was then Rector of St. Giles's church, Edinburgh, and Dean of the cathedral of that diocese, was consecrated on the same day that his predecessor in the see of Brechin, Dr. David Lindsay, was installed as Bishop of Edinburgh; and his successor there, Dr. Walter Whitford, Rector of Moffat, co. Dumfries, and Sub-dean of Glasgow, was nominated in June, 1635—and not "in September, 1634," as erroneously stated by Keith; but his consecration had not taken place up to September 19, 1635, though it must have occurred shortly after that date. Dr. Sydserf consequently held the see of Brechin for at least one year till translated to that of Galloway, in June, 1635; and he sat in the latter till December 13, 1638, when he was deprived of his temporalities, as well as "deposed and excommunicated," by the Glasgow Assembly. He survived, however, until the Restoration, being then the sole remaining member of the Scotish Hierarchy of the "Spottiswoode succession," as it was termed; and, during his long exile, of twenty-two years from his native land, he appears to have resided partly in England, but the greater part of the time in France. He was in Paris in 1644-5; and is recorded as having, on June 12, 1650, conferred the orders of both deacon and priest in the English Ambassador's chapel there—after a sermon by Dr. Cosin (then Dean of Peterborough, and afterwards Bishop of Durham,)—upon Messrs. John Durell and Daniel Brevint: of whom the former became Dean of Windsor, and the latter Dean of Lincoln, at subsequent periods. In 1658, he appears to have been again in England; since, in that year, he superintended the printing at London of *Considerationes Modestæ et Pacificæ*—the valuable and learned work of Dr. William Forbes, first Bishop of Edinburgh. The initials "T. G.," subscribed to the "Præfatio ad Lectorem," showing that he had never abandoned, even in name, his right to the see of Galloway. Among those ordained by him was, also, Dr. John Tillotson (afterwards Archbishop of Canterbury), about the year 1660; though there were doubts, for a long time, whether that prelate ever had received episcopal ordination; and it is said that Bishop Sydserf incurred the dislike of the bishops in England for conferring holy orders within that kingdom in an irregular manner, and without requiring either oaths or subscriptions from the candidates.* Other accounts, however, give a different description of his proceedings in England; and state that, being desired and allowed by the English bishops, he ordained, according to the Scots form, several hundreds of the English Nonconformists who had some scruples and objections against the English ordinal. One of these was the famous Dr. Thomas Manton, who had been admitted to deacon's orders

[* It was Bishop Sydserf who conferred orders in Westminster on the notorious Richard Kingston, preacher of St. James's, Clerkenwell, which being so contrary to ecclesiastical rule, we felt inclined to call it in question. See "N. & Q." 3rd S. ii. 471.—Ed.]

only by Bishop Hall of Exeter, but still officiated as a parish minister both at Stoke Newington and Covent Garden, London; but, being sensible of his error, he applied to the Bishop of Galloway for the order of Presbyter, and received it from his hands. He relapsed, however, to Nonconformity.

On the re-establishment of Episcopacy in Scotland in 1661, instead of being raised to the Primacy as he fully expected, and should have been, Dr. Sydserf was translated to the Bishopric of Orkney and Zeatland—one of the best endowed of the Scotish sees; and he was installed in the cathedral church of St. Magnus, at Kirkwall, on November 14, 1662; but it is believed by proxy, for it is doubtful whether he ever personally visited his remote diocese, owing to his advanced age.

He died at Edinburgh, September 29, 1663, in the thirtieth year of his episcopate; and was interred on the 4th October following, in the aisle of St. Giles's cathedral there. On which occasion, funeral sermons were preached by Dr. George Wishart and William Annand, the Bishop and Dean of Edinburgh; and commemoration made of his life and learning, and of his labours and sufferings.

The character of this prelate fully merited the commendations of his contemporaries. During the worst of times, he had never shrunk from the open profession of his principles; and, when restored to power and station, he practised those lessons of moderation which he had learnt in poverty and adversity.

Among the Bishop's children, one son, *David-Andrew Fairful*, who was born in 1648 (probably in France), entered the Society of Jesus in 1678, and was a priest on the Scotish Mission for a considerable period, during which he was twice apprehended, and suffered long imprisonment. On Feb. 2, 1697, he was promoted to the rank of a professed Father, and was famed as a preacher. In 1708, he appears to have been Rector of the Scots College at Douay, in Flanders; and, in 1716, he was at Paris; but the period of his death I have not ascertained, though it cannot have been long subsequently to the latter date, when he was nearly seventy years of age.

A daughter, Margaret Sydserf, married Alexander Fergusson, Baron of Kilkerran, co. Ayrshire; and had two sons, viz. 1, Alexander; and 2, James, who became a clergyman in England. The elder son, Alexander, married Catharine, daughter of Sir William Weir of Stoneybyres, by whom he had three sons: 1. John, who married Margaret, daughter of David Crawford of Kerse; and died without male issue, leaving only one daughter; in conjunction with his father, he sold the ancestral lands of Kilkerran in 1700. 2. William, married Agnes, eldest daughter and co-heir of John Kennedy of Auchinblain; and joined his father

and elder brother in the renunciation of his right
to the family estates. And 3. Alexander, who
perished during the unfortunate Darien expedition of 1699—1700.

The name of Sydserf is said to be derived from
St. Serf—an ancient Scotish bishop, "Apostle of
the Orkneys," and a disciple of St. Palladius: of
his history little is known, but he has ever been
highly venerated by the Church of Scotland, and
died A.D. 443. Nisbet, in his *Heraldry*, however,
states that the name came originally from France;
and he gives, from "Pont's MS." the following
arms of this family: "Argent, a flower-de-luce,
azure."

The above account of Bishop Thomas Sydserf—
which has, I fear, exceeded the proper limits of a
reply, and expanded into a note—is abridged from
my "MS. Fasti Ecclesiæ Scoticanæ:" a work
which I have been occupied in compiling for
many years, though it is still far from completion.
Indeed, the ancient records of the Church of Scotland, especially from the thirteenth to the sixteenth century, are so very scanty as regards the
episcopal succession in the different sees, that,
even the *names* of the bishops who occupied them
cannot be ascertained, in many instances, with
any approach to accuracy. Considerable light
has been thrown upon this subject, of late years,
by the publication of many of the Scotish chartu-
laries; but much remains still to be done in this
almost untrodden field, before a work like Stubbs's
Registrum Sacrum Anglicanum can be expected
from the sister kingdom. Bishop Keith, in his
Historical Catalogue of the Scottish Bishops, with
Bishop Russell's continuation to 1824, is almost
the only work which attempts to give anything
of the kind; though Grub's *Ecclesiastical History
of Scotland* (4 vols. 1861) adds considerably to it,
and is the best work we have on the subject; but
" an attempt to exhibit the course of the Episcopal Succession *in Scotland*, from the Records and
Chronicles of the Church," is still a desideratum
in Scotish literature.

My authorities for this article are : —

Keith's "Historical Catalogue of Scottish Bishops,"
edit. 1824.
Grub's "Ecclesiastical History of Scotland," 1861.
Row's "History of the Kirk of Scotland," 1842.
Gordon's "History of Scots Affairs," 1841.
Garden's "Life of Dr. John Forbes."
Tytler's "Life of Sir Thomas Craig."
"Diary of Alexander Jaffray."
Hailes' "Memorials and Letters of the Reign of
Charles I."
Evelyn's "Diary and Correspondence," 1850.
Baillie, Wodrow, Kirkton, Lamont, Law (*passim*).
Burnet's "History of his own Time," 1839.
Pepys's "Diary"; Forbes's "Considerationes." 1850-56.
Birch's "Life of Tillotson."
Rose's "Biographical Dictionary."
Symson's "Present State of Scotland," 1738.
Playfair's "Baronetage of Great Britain," 1811.
Nicolls's "Diary of Public Transactions," 1836.

Lawson's "Episcopal Church of Scotland," 1844.
Stephen's "History of the Church of Scotland," 1848.
Spalding's "Memorials of the Troubles in Scotland,"
1850-1.
Anderson's "Scottish Nation," 1863.
Cunningham's "Church History of Scotland," 1859.
Dalzel's "History of the University of Edinburgh," 1862.
Peterkin's "Rentals of Earldom and Bishoprick of
Orkney," 1820.
Oliver's "Collections towards Biography of Scotch
Members of the Society of Jesus," 1848, &c., &c.
                                                A. S. A.

Banks of the Ganges, Cawnpore, E. I.

CHRISTMAS WAITS (3rd S. vi. 487.) — As Mr.
CHAPPELL has done me the honour to refer to
some observations of mine (with a slight defect
in the orthography of my name) in the *Archæological Journal*, printed some twenty years ago,
he will allow me to advert to a correction or two
that ought to be applied to those observations, or
to his quotation from them.

The word *Wayternesse* ought to have been
printed *Waytern-fee;* the word in the original
roll had been misread by the transcriber of the
copy seen by me. In the original record, now in
the Public Repertory, the last syllable is clearly
fee; i. e., feodum, or fief. I am speaking, of
course, of the Launceston Castle document, and
not of the Winton Domesday.

In the words " *Curia de Gayte,*" also quoted by
MR. CHAPPELL, he has either inadvertently, or
from misconception, introduced an accent on the
last letter, as if the word had been synonymous
with *yaieté*, whereas it is the Low Latin *gaita*, or
wacta (*hodie*, guet) of the Glossaries, and is no
otherwise connected with music or minstrelsy
than a watchman is with his rattle, and certainly
is quite unconnected with the idea of carols. Essentially and originally the word implies the duty
of keeping watch, and nothing more. The mode
of awakening the garrison, or sounding the alarm,
whether by horn, drum, or gun-shot, is only an
incident of the duty. Of course I quite agree with
MR. CHAPPELL that the modern waits are the
legitimate descendants of these watchmen of old,
the incidental music having become the substantial meaning and essence.

                                        EDWARD SMIRKE.

I have a faint recollection (brought to my
mind whilst reading the first portion of MR.
WILLIAM CHAPPELL's interesting article on this
subject), of seeing a woodcut in the *Illustrated
London News*, some number of years ago, which
represented a farmhouse—it and the surroundings
being covered with snow — in Saxony, I believe,
in front of which were assembled two or three of
the peasantry, playing on their "oaten reeds," and
several children, who sang a carol favoured with
the aforesaid musical accompaniment. To the
best of my remembrance it was stated in the text

descriptive of the scene, that it was an ancient custom, among the poorer class of people, to go round to the various farmhouses in their vicinity on Christmas eve or day, playing and singing of the approach or arrival of the anniversary of the birthday of our blessed Saviour, and crying out, after the finish of their simple carol, " Wassail ! Wassail !" and that it was the practice of the farmers to give them something to drink; and of the husbandmen's wives to bestow upon them the articles wherewithal to make their Christmas dinner. Thus the well-to-do classes in the agricultural districts had the satisfaction of knowing that their needier brethren were possessed of the means for enjoying themselves upon this most auspicious day. I trust, therefore, you will pardon me for any error in this description, as I quote entirely from memory, having only seen the engraving at the time of the publication of the number it appeared in. Some of your readers who have access to the " back" volumes of the *Illustrated London News*, may be able to refer to the paper and verify, rectify, or abnegate my account hereof. If I am correct, the usage may date to an ancient custom imported into England by the Saxons from the " Vaterland." I dare say you are aware it is the custom in some parts of England at the present day for the children of the poor to sing a simple carol at the principal houses in the village on the Christmas morning. Perhaps the idea sprang from the Song of the Angels when they announced the birth of Jesus to the shepherds of Bethlehem: "Glory to God in the highest, on earth peace, goodwill toward men."
                                                GEO. RANKIN.

VIEL-LIEBCHEN (3rd S. vi. 458, 501.)—CHITTABOB, in a recent number of " N. & Q.," from close resemblance in pronunciation, has for the German term *Viel-Liebchen* substituted *Philippine*, and thus induced annotations foreign to the former.

Twin almonds or other nuts in one shell are designated in Germany *Viel-Liebchen*,—a term not susceptible in our language of strictly literal translation, but which may be rendered true-love, or less unliterally, much-love, with the final diminutive of endearment, *chen*. The origin of the custom associated with the *Viel-Liebchen* I have never heard explained. The usage is, however, universal among, probably peculiar to, the Germans. In the family circle it is a mark of affection, among friends of kindness and courtesy, when a *Viel-Liebchen* is found, to address to one of them the question, " *Wollen Sie ein Viel-Liebchen mit mir essen?*" The invitation is of course accepted, and the twin nuts are eaten. At the first meeting of the partakers on any subsequent day, each of them seeks to anticipate the other with the greeting, " *Guten Morgen, Viel-Liebchen!*"—the person speaking first being entitled to a present from the other. The

custom is the source of entertainment amongst all classes in the *Vaterland*, more especially among more refined and courtly circles. Ingenuity is taxed in devising expedients and stratagems for securing the first greeting. Children conceal themselves and lie *perdus* behind curtains, screens, and under tables, for the opportunity of unexpectedly pronouncing the " *Guten Morgen, Viel-Liebchen*," which ensures their gift,—devices often connived at for the pleasure of conferring it. Frequently also the custom is taken advantage of as affording the means of generously bestowing a present which could not otherwise be so gracefully granted or received.

Some of the readers of " N. & Q." may probably be able to indicate the origin of this national custom. The word denoting it is not to be found in German dictionaries, and several years ago I failed to meet with it in a *Conversations Lexicon*. The compound word *Viel-Liebchen* occurs in old German Volkslieder, and in these I have remarked that the affectionate meaning of the term *liebchen* is generally enhanced by the addition of *treu*, or *fein*, or *viel*. The following, which I quote from memory from Volkslieder, may be cited in illustration : —

" *Viel-Liebchen* ich muss scheiden,
    Viel-Lieb es muss geschehn," &c.

" Schwimm hin, schwimm her, Gold Ringelein,
    Schwimm bis in den tiefen See ;
Mein *Feinslieb* das ist gestorben —
    Jetzt hab' ich kein *Feinslieb* meh'."

" Gestern bin ich geritten durch eine Stadt,
    Da dein *Feinslieb* hat Hochzeit gehabt."

" Ich hatt ein *Treulieb* auserkoren," &c. &c.
                                                JOHN HUGHES.

STREET MELODY (3rd S. vi. 274.) — In glad compliance with MR. ROFFE's suggestion I send you the *notation* of three London cries that still dwell in my memory after the lapse of many years. I also have *inveigled* a brother, not in the flesh, but in the love of music in all its varieties, Mr. Pickard Hall of this city, to note down these few primitive cries, which melodiously warbled to the following words : —

  1. Two bunches a penny, sweet lavender ;
     Two bunches a penny.

I think wall-flower was occasionally substituted for lavender.

  2. Hot-cross buns,
     One a penny, buns ;
     One a penny, two a penny,
     Hot-cross buns.

  3. Young lambs to sell !
     Young lambs to sell !
     If I'd as much money as I could tell,
     I never would cry
     Young lambs to sell.

The lavender and wall-flower were carried about

by young girls neatly dressed, and as bright and fresh-looking as the flowers themselves. The young lambs were the property of an old man, also very neat and clean; and the hot-cross buns seemed to be offered by the goodwill of the whole street population, emblematic of the good news to all mankind conveyed by the bun.

J. MACRAY.

Oxford.

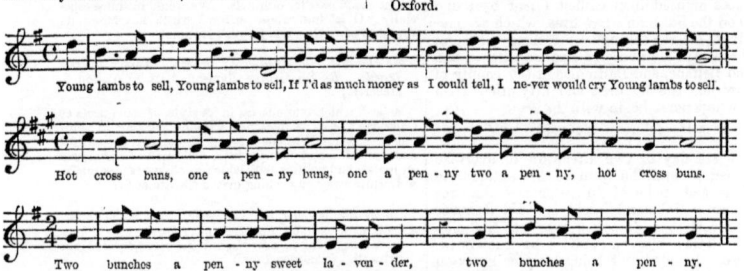

Young lambs to sell, Young lambs to sell, If I'd as much money as I could tell, I ne-ver would cry Young lambs to sell.

Hot cross buns, one a pen - ny buns, one a pen - ny two a pen - ny, hot cross buns.

Two bunches a pen - ny sweet la - ven - der, two bunches a pen - ny.

PASSAGE IN "DON QUIXOTE" (3rd S. vi. 473.) The Spanish *mil*, as well as the English word *thousand*, denotes a great number, quantity, or distance indefinitely. "He finds a thousand occasions for generosity," writes Addison in *The Spectator*, and "a thousand chances to one" is an every day expression. The example, "Viva V. M. muchos años!" quoted by MR. THOS. KEIGHTLEY is the only one given for the usage of *mil*, in an indefinite sense by Aldrete in his *Dictionary*: "Mil años—esto es, *Muchos* años."

The translation, therefore, of the passage is "On a lofty throne was seated a nymph clad in *many* (or several) veils," &c.

In Marmol's *Robelion y Castigo de los Moriscos* (lib. iii. c. 9) occurs a sentence in which *mil* is employed indefinitely in relation to distance:—

"Y cualquiera que alaba à Dios por su lengua, no puede escaparse de ser perdido, y al que hallan una ocasion, envian tras dél un adalid, que, *aunque estè á mil léguas*, lo halla y preso."—Aribau. *Biblioth. de Autores Españoles*, vol. xxi. p. 180, col. 1.

W. PLATT.

Conservative Club.

In answer to MR. KEIGHTLEY's query, I wish to observe that the Spanish word *mil* is constantly used in an indefinite sense, like the corresponding word in French and Latin, &c. But *mil velos*, in the passage referred to in *Don Quixote* (part II. cap. xxxv.) cannot, I think, mean "an immense large veil," but simply that the nymph was clad in several robes of cloth of silver—which were probably very light. Wilmott, in his *English Translation of Don Quixote* (vol. ii. part II. p. 186), gives a free translation in these words: "Upon an elevated throne sat a nymph, habited *in robes of silver tissue*," &c. *Velos* may mean robes as well as veils.

In the Spanish we have the words—a few lines lower down the page (275, ed. Salisbury, par Juan Bowle, 1781, tom. iv.)—"Traya el rostro cubierto con un transparente y delicado cendal," &c. It seems evident, therefore, that the *mil velos* must refer to her dress of cloth of silver, as her *countenance* was covered with something else named *un delicado cendal*. J. DALTON.

Norwich.

MASTMAKER (3rd S. vi. 439.) — Your correspondent should have stated the connection in which he met with the word *mastmaker*, to obtain a categorical reply. Nevertheless, the word *mast* in German, Anglo-Saxon, and English meaning *pigs' food*, the mastmaker may be the person who selects and mixes the acorns, and other such edibles suitable for pigs, and excluding what may be pernicious or not tending to fat. The word *mast* appears to be confined in this sense to the productions of the forest: hence the mast of a ship may be so named from its being also a product of the forest. T. J. BUCKTON.

A TAILOR BY TRADE (3rd S. vi. 26, 76, 484.)— *Vide* the old ballad of "Edward IV. and the Tanner of Tamworth," in Bp. Percy's Collection:—

"'What craftsman art thou?' said the King,
    'I pray thee tell me trowe.'
'I am a barker, Sir, by my trade;
    Now tell me what art thou?'"

E. H. A.

ORDER OF THE LION AND SUN (3rd S. vi. 107, 156, 482.)—This order was instituted in honour of Sir John Malcolm, whose predecessor, Sir Harford Jones, refused the order of the Sun on account of its origin, as it had been created for the ambassador of Buonaparte. (Malcolm's *Sketches of Persia*.) E. H. A.

GENERAL VALLANCEY (3rd S. vi. 482.)—EIRION-NACH's note of this renowned archaist brings back on my conscience a prank which I played him nearly threescore and ten years ago. I had been more amused than edified I fear by a discussion on the St. John's Eve fires, which are memorially set a-light throughout Ireland; wherein he had talked as familiarly of Baal and Belus, and Bëal and Beltane, and Baltinglas in the county of Wicklow, and the hundred and fifty other Irish places, whose name begin with Bal—

" As maids of thirteen do of puppy dogs."

Happening a day or two afterward to overtake the learned general, he resumed his antiquarian prolusions, and spoke of Zoroaster and the fire-worshippers. "General," said I, "did it never occur to you that Zoroaster was an Irishman born?" "God bless me no!" he exclaimed. "Because," I added, "Z being, as you know on Shakspeare's authority, an 'unnecessary' letter, his family name must have been O'Roaster."

Off I turned into a lucky cross street, and kept out of the etymologist's way for some days. A friend lectured me sharply on my impertinence, assuring me that, but for my juvenility, he would have had me into the fifteen acres.   E. L. S.

Miscellaneous.

NOTES ON BOOKS.

Heraldry, Historical and Popular. By Charles Boutell, M.A. *With 975 Illustrations. Third Edition revised and enlarged.* (Bentley.)

That the favourable opinion of Mr. Boutell's endeavour to furnish Heraldic Students with a practical and useful guide, was one to which the work was fairly entitled was at once made manifest by the fact that a second edition of it was called for in less than two months. That second edition has been for some time out of print; and We have now to direct the attention of our readers to a *third edition* entirely revised, and greatly enlarged. Thus, the chapters entitled "Marshalling" and "Cadency" now appear enlarged, and re-arranged, severally bearing the titles of "Marshalling and Inheritance," and "Cadency and Differencing." A chapter has been devoted exclusively to "Royal Cadency." The chapter on the "Royal Heraldry of England" has been in part re-written, and that on "Foreign Heraldry" has been considerably extended. Lists of Plates and Illustrations and a very copious Index, give completeness to a work which is clearly destined to supplant the excellent Introduction, which the best heralds have hitherto regarded as the most complete—we mean Porny's well known *Elements*—and to become for the future the recognised Text-Book for Students of this interesting branch of historical learning.

Hymns from the German; translated by Frances E. Cox. *Second Edition, revised and enlarged.* (Rivingtons.)

It is hardly necessary to do more than announce the second edition of a work, so long before the public, and the first attempt to make the German Hymns familiar to English readers. The German and English are printed on opposite pages, as though our practised authoress were not afraid to challenge criticism on her power of exact translation. Yet some of them flow so smoothly, that they might easily pass for originals. We would instance especially " O let him whose sorrow," which has found its way into more than one English Hymnal.

The Moralist and Politician; or many Things in few Words. By Sir George Ramsay, Bart. (Walton & Maberly.)

A book which reminds us, in its style, of some parts of Coleridge's *Aids to Reflection*, without affecting to emulate its power. Without being profound, it is thoughtful and sensible; and forms a little collection of aphorisms on morals and politics, with which a solitary reader might well while away an evening over a Christmas fire.

Familiar Words: an Index Verborum, or Quotation Handbook, with parallel Passages, of Phrases which have become imbedded in our English Tongue. By J. Hain Friswell. (Sampson Low.)   .

This is not only the most extensive Dictionary of Quotations which we have yet met with, but it has, moreover, this additional merit, that in all cases an exact reference is given to every chapter, act, scene, book, and number of the line. Parallel passages are moreover added in the notes; and the nearly seven thousand quotations, to be found in the volume, have been made readily available by an index so copious, that in some cases the same quotation has been indexed four or five times under its most remembered phrases. Need we add one word more in commendation of this useful little volume, which must have cost Mr. Friswell a vast amount of time and labour?

The History of Playing Cards, with Anecdotes of their Use in Conjuring, Fortune-telling, and Card-Sharping. Edited by the late Rev. E. S. Taylor, B.A., and others. (Hotten.)

Such of our readers as remember the zeal and perseverance with which the late Rev. E. S. Taylor pursued in these columns his investigations into the History of Playing Cards, will feel assured that the work in which he should give to the world the result of those researches would be one of considerable interest. Such is the work before us. Long delayed by the illness and subsequent death of that lamented gentleman, and now completed by other hands, it forms a volume in which will be found concentrated the labours of English and Foreign Antiquaries; and if not a substitute for, certainly a necessary companion to the works of Singer and Chatto upon the same subject. Many of the illustrations of the present volume are extremely curious. We shall be glad to see the curious "Chapters on Card Conjuring, Fortune-telling, and Card-Sharping," enlarged into a separate little volume. The subjects would be much better kept distinct. One does not expect to find "Boxiana" appended to Bell *On the Hand*.

Furioso, or Passages from the Life of Ludwig van Beethoven. From the German. (Deighton & Bell.)

This is a most valuable contribution to our knowledge of the great musician, furnishing details of his boyhood, which was very superficially treated by Spindler. The book is rich too in pictures of the olden time, gives us pleasant glimpses of bygone manners, and furnishes an interesting account of Beethoven's introduction to the

Emperor Joseph II. and Haydn. It is a book which must interest all who admire the genius of Ludwig van Beethoven.

SERIALS AND PERIODICALS.—We have to bid welcome to a new magazine, *The Englishman's*, published by Messrs. Rivingtons, whose name is a guarantee that, though the bulk of the magazine will be devoted to matters purely secular, the assertion of the truth, as it is held by the Church of England, will never be lost sight of. *The Autographic Mirror*, of which we have already spoken with high commendation, goes on with undiminished spirit—the twenty-third Part, which is just issued, being as varied and interesting as any of its predecessors. *The Orator* furnishes us, at very small price, with the most celebrated speeches in the English tongue; and deserves the attention of all admirers of English oratory. *The Graves and Epitaphs of our Fallen Heroes in the Crimea and Scutari*, by Capt. the Hon. J. Colborne and F. Brine, is a work of more melancholy and touching interest, with its lithographic views and literal copies of inscriptions. *The Astronomical Register* refers with pride to the increased success with which it enters on the third year of its useful existence.

DEATH OF JAMES HEYWOOD MARKLAND, ESQ. — It is with great regret that We announce the death, on the 28th ult., of this much respected scholar, to whom the readers of "N. & Q." have been so frequently indebted. MR. MARKLAND was as benevolent as he was accomplished, and his loss will be mourned by a wide circle of friends; including many of the dignitaries and most eminent members of the Church of England, of which he was indeed a faithful son.

Notices to Correspondents.

FAMILY QUERIES. *The increasing number of these Queries compels us to inform our Correspondents, that where such Queries relate to Persons and Families not of general interest, the Querist must in all cases state in his communication where the Replies will reach him; as, though willing, as far as possible, to give facilities for such inquiries, We cannot give up our space for Replies which are worse than useless to the majority of our Readers.*

To our Correspondents generally let us here suggest, though We do not insist upon it —
1. That Contributors to "N. & Q." append their name and address.
2. That, in writing anonymously, they give the same guarantee privately to the Editor.
3. That quotations be certified by naming edition, and chapter or page, references to "N. & Q." by series, volume, and page.
4. That in all cases Proper Names, at least, be clearly and distinctly written.

H. INGALL. *The volume of "Marston's Works" was published in 1633; Shakspeare died in 1616.*

F. M. S. *The "Delicate Investigation" was into the conduct of the Princess of Wales. See our 1st S. V. 201, 354.*

HERMENTRUDE asks, What are they ? *The answer is gross forgeries.*

T. B. *The remarkable quotation from Col. Hanger on the subject of America appeared in "N. & Q." of the 26th July last. Had the journal, from which you extracted it, acknowledged that it was copied from "N. & Q." your goodnature would not have been taxed in vain.*

F. M. W. *A Life of John Carpenter, Town Clerk of London, was published by Mr. Thomas Brewer in 1856.*

R. I. O. *The book you mention is De Foe's well-known History of the Devil.*

OXONIENSIS. *Some particulars of the mysterious autographs, or the Devil's handwriting, said to have been formerly in Queen's College library, Oxford, will be found in our 1st S. xi. 146, 189.——In excellent digest of the various speculations respecting the Mandrake and its properties is given in Dr. Harris's Dictionary of the Natural History of the Bible.*

M. A. *The lines commencing —*
"*I hear a Voice you cannot hear,*" &c.,
occur in Tickell's ballad of " Colin and Lucy.".

A Reading Case for holding the weekly Nos. of "N. & Q." is now ready, and may be had of all Booksellers and Newsmen, price 1s. 8d.; or, free by post, direct from the publisher, for 1s. 8d.

⁂ Cases for binding the volumes of "N. & Q." may be had of the Publisher, and of all Booksellers and Newsmen.

"NOTES AND QUERIES" is published at noon on Friday, and is also issued in MONTHLY PARTS. The Subscription for STAMPED COPIES for Six Months forwarded direct from the Publisher (including the Half-yearly INDEX) is 11s. 4d., which may be paid by Post Office Order, payable at the Strand Post Office, in favour of WILLIAM G. SMITH, 32, WELLINGTON STREET, STRAND, W.C., to whom all COMMUNICATIONS FOR THE EDITOR should be addressed.

"NOTES & QUERIES" is registered for transmission abroad.

LONDON, SATURDAY, JANUARY 14, 1865.

CONTENTS.— N° 159.

Notes on Books, &c.

Notes.

MONTFAUCON AND ENGUERRAND DE MARIGNY.

In his preface to the romance of *Berthe aux grands pieds*, M. Paulin Paris says: "Je ne crains pas de le dire, pour bien connaitre l'histoire du moyen âge . . . . il faut l'avoir étudiée dans les romans." Without, perhaps, endorsing absolutely this opinion, we have no hesitation to say that many a passage in the old metrical romances of the middle ages can be adduced as illustrating important historical facts, clearing up difficulties of either chronology or archæology, and even refuting errors which have been handed down from time immemorial by writers more anxious for *ad captandum* paragraphs than for truth. An instance of this suggested itself to me a short time ago as I was perusing the well known work of Adenès, composed in 1270 or 1274. Speaking of a certain Tybert, who had been condemned to capital punishment, the author goes on to say:—

"Quant la vielle fu arse, Tybert font ateler,
Tout parmi la grant rue le firent trainer,
· à Montfaucon le firent sus au vent encrouer."

Now, the general opinion has long been current that Enguerrand de Marigny ordered the construction of the hanging establishment at Montfaucon; but, if we admit 1260 as the date of his birth, we see at once that the popular story must be dis-carded. It was evidently put into circulation for the sake of drawing an ingenious and moral parallel between the supposed cruelty of the unfortunate Marigny and his melancholy fate: it was set forth as an act of retributive justice, a *dignus vindice nodus*, just as Cardinal la Balue's iron cages, and the more expeditious instrument of Doctor Guillotin. Pierre Rémy is another person to whom the *édification* of Montfaucon has been ascribed, though with as little probability. In point of fact, the real originator of the celebrated gibbet is not known, and the name of Pierre de Brosse, or la Brosse, adduced by some, must be considered, in the present state of historical investigation, as simply hypothetical.

Under the sweeping measures of Baron Haussman all the remains of old Paris are quickly disappearing; the rue du *Puits-qui-parle*, and the *Place Maubert*, the *Collegium Bajocassense*, and the numerous glories of the *Quartier Latin* have departed, whilst the few reminiscences of days gone by that are left standing (such as the Hôtel de Cluny, and the tower of Saint Jacques la Boucherie), scraped, furbished up, and decorated after the newest fashion, seem to us wretchedly bereft of their character and their beauty.

Such being the case, we should cordially welcome every attempt to preserve for future ages a memorial of Paris as it used to be. We are glad as we walk through London not to see grim-looking skeletons dangling in the breeze from the *actual* gallows at Tyburn; we rejoice that our more humanised civilisation is inconsistent with the exhibition of traitors' heads from every "coign of vantage;" but at the same time we like to know where the utmost sentence of the law was wont to be inflicted, and as we read in memoirs, diaries, and correspondences, pages full of tragic interest, we feel a most legitimate desire to identify the locality, the exact spot of those scenes.

Such is the interest belonging to M. Firmin Maillard's little volume, *Le Gibet de Montfaucon*, to which I naturally turned in quest of the particulars I wanted about Enguerrand de Marigny—his career, and his deplorable end; and, as I am thus brought to mention it incidentally here, let me be allowed to recommend it for the valuable information it contains on the subject of capital punishment during the middle ages.[*] With its help we can mark on a map of Paris all the spots where either justice or (too frequently, alas!) despotism and revenge brought wretches to the brink of eternity: the Abbot of Saint-Germain des Prés had his pillory at the Place Sainte Marguerite; the Bishop of Paris kept his immediately in front of the cathedral, and it was there that Pope Clement V.'s bull was read, condemning to death all

---

[*] *Le Gibet de Montfaucon, étude sur le vieux Paris,* par Firmin Maillard, 12°. Paris: Aubry.

the Knights Templars. The Metropolitan Chapter, the Prior of the Abbey of Saint Martin des Champs, the Grand Prior of France, the Abbot of Sainte-Geneviève, in fact, every individual or body corporate exercising any authority, had a privileged corner reserved for the punishment of culprits who fell within their respective jurisdictions.

Montfaucon, the most celebrated of all these dismal places, situated on the road to Meaux, between the *Enclos Saint Lazare* and the *Butte Saint Chaumont*, was a parallelogram of solid masonry, surmounted by sixteen pillars joined by beams, from each of which a ghastly row of skeletons might constantly be seen, testifying to the *lenient* style of mediæval justice. Pierre de Brosse, favourite of Philip the Bold, and accused of having poisoned Prince Louis of France, was the first man (at least the first person *of consequence*) who died at Montfaucon. He inaugurated a long list, in which we find amongst many others, Enguerrand de Marigny, Henry Tapperel, Provost of Paris; Jourdain de l'Isle, who was accused of no less than *forty-eight crimes*, each punishable by death; Olivier le Daim, Jacques de Beaune de Semblançay, and the illustrious Admiral de Coligny. If the poet Villon did not enjoy the pleasure of *going backwards to heaven* (*aller au ciel à reculons*, as the Slang Dictionary has it), it was only thanks to the kindness of Louis XI. The last tragedy enacted at Montfaucon appears to have taken place in 1617. On account of the extension given to the fauxbourgs du Temple and Saint Martin, the gallows themselves were moved in 1760 from their original locality to some distance beyond the walls of the city; and on Jan. 21, 1790, the last remaining pillars of the building fell never to rise again. Henceforward those who wish to be acquainted with Montfaucon must study it in M. Maillard's instructive little volume, and the ominous woodcut prefixed to the title-page.　Gustave Masson.

Harrow-on-the-Hill.

PURCELL PAPERS, No. III.*—"THE CONJUROR'S SONG."

Amongst the music to the Third Act of the *Indian Queen*, will be found one of Purcell's finest efforts, known as "The Conjuror's Song;" and consisting of the recitative, "Ye twice ten hundred Deities," and the air "By the croaking of the toad," written for Ismeron, the "prophet and conjuror." This recitative and air may well stand a comparison with any incantation music since produced. Nothing, surely, can be more solid and severe than is the treatment of the subject by Purcell, who has here shown himself able to take

---

* *Vide* 3rd S. vi. 105.

his place by the side of Gluck. In that memoir of Mr. Bartleman, to which I have already referred, is an interesting notice of his performance of Ismeron's song at the Ancient Concerts. Professor Taylor had been treating of the preponderance of Handel's music at the Ancient Concerts, and of Mr. Bartleman's desire to bring forward the compositions of Purcell. These are the Professor's own words:—

"In 1796, Bartleman resumed his place at the Ancient Concerts; but the season had half expired ere he was allowed to venture on the novel and perilous experiment of reviving Purcell. At the sixth concert he sung the Magician's song from the *Indian Queen*—'Ye twice ten hundred Deities;' and his auditors were soon made to feel the truth of Burney's remark, that this song opens with the finest piece of recitative in our language. But who will ever forget his delivery of the passage:—

"From thy sleepy mansion rise,
And open thy unwilling eyes."

The gradual crescendo, from the first bar of this expressive passage, until the full power of his splendid voice pealed in at its close, took the audience by surprise. Accustomed to the chaste simplicity and quiet excellence of Harrison, the fire and animation of the new English singer, and the bold originality of the music on which he was engaged, woke them as from a dream."

That minute particularity in editing, which is so justly bestowed upon Shakspeare, should not be withheld from Purcell; whose whole secular works, it is to be hoped, will one day be edited in the style of that portion which has been done for the Musical Antiquarian Society. In the meanwhile, with the wish to aid a little in gathering materials for any future editions of Purcell's *Works*, it is proposed to note down the nature of the circumstances under which the Conjuror's song occurs. All dramatic music ought, for those who wish fully to enter into the composer's intentions, to have its surroundings indicated; and, therefore, not only when the time and the editors have come, for a complete National Edition of Purcell, but even when a new edition of this particular song appears, it will be desirable to have it signified that the scene of the incantation is the Conjuror's cave; where, while lying asleep, he is roused by the Indian queen Zempoalla, who, stamping on the ground and calling thrice upon the Conjuror's name "Ismeron," awakes him up. Then follows the grand recitative—"Ye twice ten hundred Deities;" but, on the stage, before the air ensues, is the following piece of dialogue between the queen and Ismeron:—

"*Zempoalla.* How slow these Spirits are! Call, make them rise,
Or they shall fast from Flame and Sacrifice.
"*Ismeron.* Great Empress!
Let not your Rage offend what we adore,
And vainly threaten, when we must implore;
Sit, and silently attend—
While my powerful charms I end."

Now follows the air: "By the croaking of the toad," at the end of which air, rises up the God of Dreams. All these circumstances known, will help to paint to the imaginative singer what sort of images he must strive to set before his audience. The *Indian Queen* itself is one of those plays which we must think is for ever vanished from the stage; and, therefore, it becomes still the more necessary that the right editor should give us a little argument, as it were, to the song; embodying all the information which is now brought together.

The original singer of the Conjuror's song is stated, by Sir John Hawkins, to have been Richard Leveridge; and, although I am not at present able to verify that statement—as neither in the old editions of the song, nor in the play itself, is any name given to us—yet I will assume it to be so; and we shall thus be led to consider the correctness of certain notions put forth by Sir John as to Leveridge, of whom he affirms that—

"Though he had been a performer in the Opera at the same time with Nicolini and Valentini, he had no notion of grace or elegance in singing—it was all strength and compass."

Now, notwithstanding the confidence with which the historian has here expressed himself, it is really very difficult to receive his dictum in this case. Leveridge showed marked talent as a composer; and it seems hardly philosophical to think that a man, who could produce such a melody as "Black-ey'd Susan," and who had heard two of the best singers of Italy, should make "strength and compass" his chief measures of the vocal art. As to Ismeron's incantation, and the peculiar *romantic* style required to produce effect with it, we may be as certain as we can well be of anything, that, whoever was the original singer, he must have had the benefit of receiving Purcell's conception of the style in which that incantation should be given from Purcell himself. This would also, most surely, be true as to the original singers of Purcell's songs in general; and, as it would seem, involves a point altogether overlooked by those who are so prone to think that Purcell's singers could not at all adequately execute his music. Considering the unquestionable talents of Leveridge, and the advantages he possessed, it really seems to follow that, if he were the original Ismeron, the audiences of the *Indian Queen* might have enjoyed a striking performance of that very remarkable composition, "The Conjuror's Song."

ALFRED ROFFE.

Somers Town.

A LINCOLNSHIRE DIALOGUE.

Scene: *Inside of a Cottage. Old Woman and a little Boy. Knock heard at the door. Enter another Woman.*

1st Wom. A-deary me, Mrs. Cox, who'd ha' thowt of seeing thee! Why thou'rt quite a sthranger.

Mrs. Cox. Well, I thowt I'd joust coom and see t'now t'hast flitted; its a sthrange nice't house, Mrs. Davy.

Mrs. Davy. Oh, its nice't enouf; but t'would ha' beean a deal nice'ter if they had beean cha'ambers i'steed o' parlours. When I'm a sitting here o' wi'indy da'ays there's sich an a draft. Lor' it is some cowd!

Mrs. Cox. Well I can't say as thou hast got a very good roo'ad up to it, and this howry da'ay maes it clattier still. As I was a-crossing the beck t'was so slape, down I coomed with sich a belk; I'm quite wetchard, and I could hardlins get out. But who's that bairn?

Mrs. Davy. Why my maister's uncle to him; his poor father was sla'ain lastPag-rag Da'ay; * he was remmeling a sta'ay when it fell right-a-ways upov his yead and killed him. He left two poor bairns, a little boy and a little gel; and my maister sees, "Well, missus," says he, "we mun ta'ak toner—which is't to be?" Now I beant noways fond o' bairns, they're allost a-tewing and a-taving about, and making sich an a clat; but I sees, well then we'll hev t'little boy, he can addle a penny now and then wi' tenting craws, and he is a gallace't little chap, I'll apaud; when he's grawn up he'll ma'ak a wakkenish bla'ade, though now it offens caps me what to do wi' him; and t' little lass is but a poor wanckle creetur. She has joust hed sich a bout wi' the fever.

Mrs. Cox. Well, I mun be a-going whoam, but what hes got t'gardin?

Mrs. Davy. Thou may well ast. T'other da'ay I heerd sich an a bealing, and when I looked, some beast had brok out o' Mr. Ward's crew, and there they was a-ramping about the gardin. I was flinging some sto'ans at 'em to get 'em out, when one of the sto'ans fell right into a cletch of young gibs, and killed one on 'em. Well, there was Mr. Ward down upov me in a moment, a-telling me I mun pa'ay for killing t'gib. "Pa'ay thee," I sees, "it's t'other-way-on; it's thou as ought to pa'ay me. Joust look where them there beast hev been trampling up the tonhups and yeating the pays, and breaking down the pipricks, and not a rasp nor a berry shall I hev t'year wi 'em." "Ma'aking sich an a blather about it," he sees, "why t'gardin has ta'aken no payment; look at them ta'ates and

* "Pag-Rag Day is the day in May when all the farm servants leave their places and *pag* (Lincolnshire for pack or carry) away their rags."

the marquery." * Aye, I ses, them's the only things they've left, and I'd a deal sooner they'd ta'en the marquery; for we've had sich a vast sight on it, I'm clear stalled.

Mrs. Cox. Well, ni'bour, I really mun go; but I can't get this door opened no ways.

Mrs. Davy. Why thou'rt sthrange and unheppen. What meagrims art thee up to? Thou mo'an't pull i' that how; thou nobbut hes to pull the sneck. That's reight, good da'ay to thee.

C. P. T.

TRANSLATIONS OF HOMER.

Lord Derby's translation, great in itself and in its circumstance, has done all that the ten syllables of our heroic metre, under its restrictions of Syntax and Prosody, can do with the seventeen of the classic hexameter; wherein abides, I think, so much of the expression of Homer's several characteristics. As nearly as possible Chapman's version approached this plenary power, but failed under the *rhyme* which induced his many additions and omissions. Cowper shook off this incumbrance; but the assumption of Milton's manner with his form set him yet further away from the manner of Homer. The divinities of the Olympian Bard are merely human; the humanities of the Uranian are almost divine. Milton's is dialogic, Homer is dramatic. It were an anachronism to say that he is Shakspearean! but Lord Derby has shown us what neither Pope nor Cowper showed our fathers —that Shakspeare is Homeric; that his variety, his energy, his directness, his raciness, have descended on him from his Attic precursor. We may now dismiss the regret of our college days— that Dryden had not left Virgil to Pope, and taken Homer into his own hands.

Had Mr. Newman, when disrhyming Chapman's metre of its eight-and-six jingle forborne his own trochaic terminals, the old Elizabeth fourteens might have escaped Professor Arnold's censure of Balladism. I cannot resign my notion of their being the metre most congenial with Homer's dactylic freedom, and most expressive of his several moods. Thus thinking, I venture a translation of the well known Ὣς δ' ὅτ' ἐν οὐρανῷ, wherein is studiously noted every word of the original in its separate and relative meanings. This I have endeavoured to do *linea pro lineâ*, the surest mode of transfusing a poet's spirit in a metre as, or nearly as, *numerous* as his own: —

"As when the firmamental† stars around the shining moon
Show excellently beautiful, and stirless in the air;

---

* Marquery is a vegetable that seems peculiar to Lincolnshire. It resembles spinach.
† Dryden.

When all the sea-marks rise to view, the foreland's lofty range,
And woodland dells; then the broad heavens unfold their topless height,
And all the stars come out, and glad the shepherd is at heart: —
So thickly o'er the plain between the ships and Xanthus' streams
By Trojan hands the fires were lit before the walls of Troy;—
A thousand fires, and round the blaze of each sate fifty men;
While hungerly * their horses champed the barley and the rye,
And, tethered at the chariots, stood, waiting the brightthroned dawn."

O mihi præteritos!—were I half a century younger (I arrived at man's age a year before Lord Derby was born), I might have attempted the whole *Iliad* in this fashion.

E. L. S.

LONGEVITY OF CLERGYMEN. — The following cutting from a newspaper will show that the Roman Catholic *clericos* of Canada have as good reason to boast of their longevity as their clerical Protestant brethren in the British isles: —

"Nearly all the Roman Catholic Bishops of the Province will be present at the celebration in Three Rivers to-morrow of the fiftieth anniversary of the ordination to Priesthood of the Right Rev. Msgr. Cooke. The Roman Catholic Bishops of the Lower Province, we may say in this connection, have on the whole been singularly long lived. Mgr. de Laval, the first Bishop of Quebec, was ordained in Paris on the 23rd Sept., 1645, and died on the 6th May, 1708, in the 63rd year and 7th month of his priesthood. Mgr. de St. Vallier, the second Bishop of Quebec, had also passed the fiftieth year of his priesthood, as he died at the advanced age of 74 years. Mgr. Duplessis de Mornay, third Bishop of Quebec, his successor, expired at the age of 78 years, and Mgr. Dosquet, the fourth Bishop of Quebec, at 86, having filled the See during the long space of 52 years. The seventh Bishop of the same Diocese, Mgr. Briand, lived to the age of 79 years and 5 months. The eighth, Mgr. Mariaucheu d'Esgly, witnessed the 53rd anniversary of his ordination to the priesthood, and Mgr. Panet, the twelfth Bishop, the 55th anniversary of the same proceeding. Mgr. Turgeon, the present Archbishop of Quebec, is also in the 55th year of his priesthood. It would thus appear that of the fourteen Bishops who have successively filled the See of Quebec, eight lived to witness the fiftieth anniversary of their ordination. A correspondent of the French Press, to whom we are indebted for the foregoing particulars, further states Mgr. McDonell, the first Bishop of Kingston, had at his death on the 13th January, 1840, been 52 years and 11 months in the priesthood. We hope and trust that, advanced as Mgr. Cooke's age seems to be, he will live to witness, if that be possible, the 75th anniversary of his affiliation to the Church."—*Montreal Gazette*, Sept. 17, 1864.

And *l'âge mûr* of Canadian bishops of the Church of England has, probably, not fallen much behindhand. The first Bishop of Quebec, Mountain (descended from a French Protestant family),

---

* Shakspeare.

and his son, the third bishop, died at the respective ages of 75 and 72 years; and the present Bishop of Toronto, Strahan, is in the 60th year of his priesthood, and 87th year of his age, with a constitution that bids fair to carry him through to the end of *his* century.   ERIC.

Ville-Marie, Canada.

BAPTISM FOR THE DEAD.—The passage in 1 Cor. xv. 29, may be illustrated from a Jewish legend; where one person was to risk his life to save the community of Jews from the vengeance of a Pasha of Jerusalem, as recorded by Dr. Frankl:—

" The lot fell upon one of the servants of the synagogue, a man of distinguished piety. ' I am the servant of God,' he said; and prepared his soul *to meet death by bathing, and by immersing himself three times in water.*"

Baptism with the Jews was symbolic of entering on a new course of life: the baptism of John was distinct from the baptism of Jesus, because a different life was contemplated and entered on by that act. The baptism for the dead was symbolic of the entrance into a new and future state, for which preparation was made when death approached. St. Paul intimates to the Corinthians that, as Christians, they were liable constantly to death; or, as he expresses it, " we stand in jeopardy every hour," and then by a strong metaphor, he asserts that he "died daily."

T. J. BUCKTON.

Lichfield.

SPENSER AND THE DAISY. — I find these words printed in a book intituled, *Dreamthorp; a Book of Essays written in the Country,* by Alexander Smith, London, 1863, namely:—

" Spenser's genius was countryless as Ariel; search ever so diligently, you will not find an English daisy in all his enchanted forests."

Mr. A. Smith's reading of Spenser's *Works* must have been confined to the *Faery Queene,* for I cannot find that I noted any lines with the word *daisy* in them in that poem; but if your readers will turn to Spenser's poem, headed " Prothalamion," they will find these words:—

" Of every sort which in that meadow grew
They gather'd some: the violet, pallid blue,
The little dazie, that at evening closes,
The virgin lillie, and the primrose true,
With store of vermeil roses,
To deck their bridegroom's posies
Against the bridal-day, which was not long;
Sweet Thames! run soft till I end my song."

EDWIN ARMISTEAD.

Leeds.

DR. JOHNSON AND MACAULAY. — In *Boswell's Johnson* (vol. iii. p. 353, A.D. 1778), occurs the following passage:—

" Looking at Messrs. Dilly's splendid edition of Lord Chesterfield's *Miscellaneous Works,* he (Johnson) laughed, and said: ' Here are now two speeches ascribed to him, both of which were written by me; and the best of it is,

they have found out that one is like Demosthenes, and the other like Cicero.' "

Johnson wrote the Parliamentary Debates at that time for the *Gentleman's Magazine,* &c.; hence the statement as to authorship. In Macaulay's review of Thackeray's *History of Lord Chatham,* we observe the following:—

" A contemporary historian," says Mr. Thackeray, " describes Mr. Pitt's first speech as superior even to the models of ancient eloquence. According to Tindal, it was more ornamental than the speeches of Demosthenes and less diffuse than those of Cicero."

This parallelism is curious; and gives rise to the question, whether it was Tindal who applied the same simile to Chesterfield's supposed oratory mentioned by Johnson? Upon whom should the simile be fathered? Macaulay's favourite phrase about a man's eloquence being as durable as the English language, is well known.

PHILOLOGUS.

THE VICTORIA CROSS.—The following is an extract of the rules and ordinances of the above-named naval and military decoration:—

" Firstly, it is ordained that the distinction should be styled and designated ' The Victoria Cross,' and shall consist of a *Maltese Cross* of bronze," &c. &c.

How has it happened that the decoration is in the form of *Cross patée,* and *not* in the form of a " Maltese Cross," as prescribed by Her Majesty's command?   J. S. R.

Queries.

BARONETESS. — I have always understood that the legal designation of a baronet's wife was Dame. But Chamberlain (*Mag. Brit. Not.,* ii. 47) states that Sir Cornelius Speelman, General in the service of Holland, was created a baronet Sept. 9, 1686, with a special clause of precedency for his mother, who was to take the rank and title of a Baronetess of England.   S. P. V.

THE BELL INN AND BROADHURST. — The notice of the " Old Inns of Southwark," in the New Year's number of " N. & Q.," reminds me of a query I have long intended making relative to the scenes of Archbishop Leighton's retirement and death. I am anxious to know whether there are any representations extant of the Bell Inn, Warwick Lane, and of the mansion of Broadhurst in Sussex. The Bell Inn, at the time of Leighton's death in 1684, was but some sixteen years old, its predecessor having been destroyed in the Great Fire. In Mr. Chambers's *Book of Days,* there is a woodcut of the modern Bell Inn as it now stands. How far it resembles the inn of 1668, I know not. The mansion of Broadhurst, the property of Mr. Lightmaker, has long since disappeared. I shall be much obliged to any one who will kindly give me the required information, either privately or through the medium of " N. & Q."

EIRIONNACH.

CARICATURE: SYR MITCHIL BRUCE.—A print collector would be glad of any information about a curious caricature, entitled "Syr Mitchil Bruce, Stowkiller, 1742; W. Stukeley, *inv. et delin.*" It represents a naked man with weights round his neck, pursued into a fiery lake by a demon, from whose lips issue the words " Arthurs Oon." The following Latin words are at the bottom : " Furias, ignemque severum Cocyti metuet tortosque Ixionis angues." J. B. D.

CHALMERS OF CULTS: NOVA SCOTIAN BARONETCY.—It is presumed that this Aberdeenshire family were concerned in the Rebellion, and the title of "Sir" forfeited. The last that enjoyed the title was Sir Charles Chalmers of Cults, Captain in H. M. Royal Regiment of Artillery. I am anxious to find particulars of a pedigree that will connect this Sir Charles Chalmers with other members of the Cults family, viz. Rev. James Chalmers, D.D., Rector of Little Waltham and Wickham St. Paul, both being in the county of Essex. His son was the Rev. Henry Chalmers, D.D., also Rector of Little Waltham.

JOHN RICHARDSON.

12, St. Helen's Place, London.

COINAGE. — In the *Sunday Magazine* for Nov. 1864 (p. 139), it is stated that, "in round numbers, two millions of sovereigns may be manufactured from a cubic yard of metal." Is this a correct statement? It is further stated, that if we were converting into gold all the silver and copper coinage in the world, and melting the whole into a solid lump, it would not make a block of more than seven yards broad, and long and high. It is immediately afterwards assumed that the solid cube condensed would amount in value to 600 millions of sterling pounds.

Are these statements accurate, or is there any means of ascertaining the value of all the silver and copper coinage in the world?

There was the model of a pyramid of gold at the Great Exhibition of 1862 to indicate the bulk which all the gold of Australia would assume if put into a pyramidal shape. Was such model accurate? What amount of gold did it represent, and what has become of it? J. B. G.

DWIGHT FAMILY.—Can you put me in the way of tracing the pedigree of the Dwight family?

J. L. B.

12, Canning Street, Liverpool.

FRASER EPITAPHS. — William Fraser, Esq., Under-Secretary of State in 1760, was buried at or near Bath; where there is, I understand, a monument to his memory. His son Charles, minister successively at Madrid and the Hague, lies buried at Hove, near Brighton. I shall be very greatly obliged to any one who will kindly copy the inscriptions, and send them to me.

F. M. S.

229, Clarendon Villas, Plumstead.

THE INVENTOR OF GUNPOWDER.—Maitre Guérin in the new play of that name, is made to say : —

" L'inventeur de la poudre est mort de son invention. Avis aux inventeurs."

Is this a French tradition? If so, what are its details? H. C. C.

HARRISON FAMILY (3rd S. vi. 274.)—I shall feel much obliged if your correspondent CADET will have the kindness to inform me (a Norfolk man) in what village the Harrisons mentioned by him lived? And where an account of their motto—"Humus sumus "—can be found.

FRED. HARRISON.

London : 15, Carlton Villas, Maida Vale.

LEIGH HUNT'S DESCRIPTION OF A CLASSICAL WASHERWOMAN.—

" There is a rock from whose deep base
　　The bubbling fountains flow ;
　　And from the top we sink the vase
　　To reach the stream below.

" I have a friend who thither brought
　　Rich vests with radiant purple wrought,
　　To bathe them in the crystal dews,
　　Then on the rock's steep ridge display,
　　To the warm sun's etherial ray,
　　The gaily tinctured hues."—P. 151.

(*Specimens and Notes on Living English Authors,* Boston, 1845, 12mo, pp. 204.)

I cannot find the above among Leigh Hunt's poems, and he was careful that none should be lost. Is it a stray, or a burlesque? The author of the above-mentioned work treats him with half-contemptuous praise. E. S.

JACK-STONES. — In Ireland, as in almost every country of Europe, a domestic game is played with five pebbles, or five small bones, which are thrown up into the air, and caught as they fall on the back of the hand. The Greeks called these πεντέλιθοι, and they seem to have been the original of our dice, when numbers were marked on the several sides. In its primitive form, the pastime is called by the modern Italians, *mano in cielo;* by the Spaniards, *juega de tahas;* by the French, *jeu des osselets;* and by the Irish, *jack-stones.* What is the origin of the latter word? Ought it to be spelled *jact-stones,* from the act of throwing them into the air previously to catching them on the back of the hand in their fall? Is the term common in England, as it is in Ireland?

J. EMERSON TENNENT.

MODERN LATIN PRONUNCIATION. — Many years have elapsed since I acquired a tolerable knowledge of Latin, and perhaps new discoveries have been made in this progressive age as to the pronunciation of words. Can any of your correspondents give me a satisfactory reason for what is taught, in the Edinburgh Academy, as to the proper pronunciation of the genitives of *domus* and *fructus?* I am now told that *do-muse* and *fruc-tuse* have superseded *domus* and *fructus*.   J. M.

LELAND'S "ITINERARY," AND ST. SARIK. — In Leland's notice of Sonning, or Sunning-on-Thames, near Reading, is the following : —

"There is an old chappelle at the est end of the church of St. Sarik, whither of late tyme resortid in pilgrimage many folkes for the disease of madness."

I am very much interested in the detection of the worthy canonized under the name as above, and should heartily thank any one who enabled me to lay hold of him. I have searched in vain in the library of the British Museum. There is no trace of the saint in Sonning church of the present day, though the fabric in Leland's time must have been mainly as it is now, excepting the embellishments, which were added a few years ago.
HEVED.

"LIMEHOUSE," *unde deriv.?*—The three following extracts occur in Cunningham's *Handbook of London*, 1850 : —

"Lime-hurst or Lime-host, corruptly called Lime-house." *Stow*, p. 157.

"At last they left Greenwich ; the tide being at great low fall, the watermen get afraid of the crosse cables by the Lime-house."—Tarlton's *Jests*, 1611.

"9th Oct. 1661. By coach to Captain Marshe's at Lime-house, to a house that hath been their ancestors' for this 250 years, close by the Lime-house, which gives the name to the place."—*Pepys*.

Tarlton, Stow's contemporary, it will be observed, adopts the usual spelling of the word, and Pepys actually mentions the "house" as still existing in his time. Stow's etymologies are not always to be trusted. "Lime-hurst" would mean a grove of lime trees ; but what would *host* mean ?
JAYDEE.

"MEMOIRS OF THE LIFE OF LORD LOVAT," London, printed for M. Cooper, at the Globe, in Paternoster Row, 1746, sm. 8vo, pp. 88. No author's name. Who was the author of this pamphlet ? He states on p. 1, that he had a personal acquaintance with his lordship for many years.   F. M. S.

MILTON AND CHARLES II. — In Mr. Mark Lemon's *Jest Book*, No. 879, there is a statement to the effect, that Charles II. and his brother James called on Milton and insulted him in a most cowardly manner with reference to his blindness. I am anxious to know if there be any foundation for this statement, and where it is to be found.
E. S.

Edinburgh.

EARLY MSS. ON ENGLISH LAW AND GOVERNMENT.—Can any reader of "N. & Q." give the names of any private libraries likely to contain the MS. *works* of any celebrated writers of the fifteenth century on the Principles of Law and Government in England, most of our public libraries having been searched already ?   KAPPA.

GENERAL PAOLI'S RESIDENCE IN LONDON. — It is stated in *Boswell's Johnson* (vol. iii. p. 390, A.D. 1779) : —

"On that morning Johnson came to me from Streatham, and, after drinking chocolate at General Paoli's in South Audley Street, we proceeded to Lord Marchmont's in Curzon Street."

We also find, from the *Annual Register*, that Paoli lived in Oxford Street,* near the corner of the Edgware Road. Can the number, or the exact position of these houses be given ?
H. L. J.

ST. DONAT'S CASTLE. — Can any of your correspondents furnish any information relating to a book entitled *Venustum Poema*, by D. Thos. Leyson, a native of Neath, and afterwards a physician at Bath ? It was published in 1569. A transcript of such parts of the poem as describes the castle of St. Donat's, in Glamorganshire, is desired. Is there any foundation for a tradition that Wesley once preached from the fountain, in the centre of the court, at St. Donat's castle ? And also, explain why its owners, the Stradlings, who were ultra-royalists, are not in the list of persons who compounded for their estates during the Commonwealth ?   S. A.

SOCIETY OF INDUSTRY. — I should be much obliged by information as to the nature, and whether still in existence, of a Society who struck a medal of which I give particulars :—Round the edge (face)—"Peace and Plenty are the fruits of industry and subordination." On face : Two female figures ; one holding a horn of plenty, and the other an olive branch, with a beehive between them. On reverse of medal is the name of holder, "Mr. Peel, Trustee, 1792." Surrounding the name : "Society of Industry, founded 29 Nov., 1783."†   S. C.

WHITBREAD FAMILY IN SUSSEX.—In the *Memoirs of the Rev. John James Weitbrecht*, 1854, p. 2, I find the following passage : —

"Mr. W.'s family have resided for several centuries in Schorndorf, and one branch of it is believed to have come to England about the period of the Norman Conquest, who are supposed to have been the ancestors of the family now known in this county as the Whitbreads. An old churchyard in Sussex, not very far from Brighton, contains several tombstones of considerable antiquity erected over members of this family, where the orthography of the

[* Gen. Paoli's letter, dated "Londra, 10 Dec. 1796," is signed "Oxford Street, No. 200."—ED.]

[† This Society appears to have been connected with the county of Lincoln. *Vide* the *Gent. Mag.*, lxi. (ii.) p. 843.—ED.]

name approximates very nearly to the German mode of spelling it."

The immigration of an untitled German family into England about the period of the Norman Conquest would be very difficult to verify. The name of Weitbrecht does not appear in Riet-stap's *Armorial Général.* It means "far-shining," and has, therefore, no connection with Whit-bread so far as its meaning is concerned. Can any reader of "N. & Q." inform me what "old churchyard in Sussex" is alluded to in the above extract? As for the "tombstones of considerable antiquity," very few stones in open churchyards can show inscriptions more than two centuries old.

JAYDEE.

Queries with Answers.

REREDOS.—I shall feel obliged by one of your architectural correspondents informing me what is the Latin equivalent to *reredos, rerdos, reredosse, arrière dos,* Fr. Does the *Architectural Dictionary* contain any philological or etymological matter?

A CORRESPONDENT OF FIFTEEN YEARS.

[The Mediæval Latin equivalent for this term is given variously by Du Cange *sub voce* as *dorsale, dossale, doxale, dorsile pallium,* and *dorsuale.* It is a term applied to the back of a throne, or other seat of state, as well as to the hangings behind an altar. *Reredos* is also similarly applied, and sometimes means the iron back to an old-fashioned fireplace, where the wood is burnt on the old andirons. Some very valuable information is given in Viollet-le-Duc, *Dictionnaire de Mobillier, sub voce* "Dorsal."

As to the work of which our correspondent inquires, it is the Dictionary published by the Architectural Publication Society. The articles are written by various members of a Committee, to whom they are allotted, or by whom chosen, as seems best. These articles are then put into type in "slip proofs," and circulated through the whole Committee, each member of which sends his corrections or emendations, or further information, as the case may be. The whole is then referred back to the original writer, so that the article may be made as complete and correct as possible. Every statement, authority, quotation, or other similar matter, *must* be verified with the original: and it is very curious to see that, even in such books of the highest authority as Bingham's *Origines,* or Liddell and Scott's *Dictionary,* slips of the pen have been discovered.

As to our correspondent's query we can only say, not only is the philology and etymology of every word carefully given in all the ancient and modern languages, but the chemistry, botany, geology, natural history, and everything connected with any material used in architecture, is fully entered into. The literature of the subject, from Homer downwards—including all incidental remarks in the Greek tragic poets—or in Aristophanes, in Herodotus, in Strabo, or Pausanias—in the Roman writers, particularly Vitruvius and Pliny—in the lexicographers and in the mediæval chroniclers—is also given as fully as possible, and every article illustrated by engravings. The work is rather more than half completed, and bids fair to be the most comprehensive yet published on any branch of art or science. Among the writers, the following names may be recorded : the late Professor Cockerell, Professors Donaldson and Kerr, Messrs. Angell, Ashpitel, Burnell, Gosling, I'Anson, Knowles, Lewis, Lockyer, Nelson, J. W. Papworth, Wyatt Papworth (the active secretary), Smirke, Tite, &c., &c.]

RELICK SUNDAY, ETC. — In the churchwardens' books of St. Martin's Outwich, the following entries occur : —

" *Relihe Sonday,* 1524. Payde for red wyne on Relykys Sondaye, 1d.

" *Paschall, or Hallowed Taper,* anno 1525. Payde to Thomas Vance, Waxechandeler, for makyng & renewyng of the beme lyght, and for makyng of the Paskall, wt the tenabur candell and crosse candell, xxs."

Can you give me any information about "Relic Sunday," which, according to Halliwell, is the third Sunday after Midsummer Day? Can you also explain what the "beme light" and the "tenabur candell" were? The extracts are given in Godwin and Britton's *Churches of London.*

R. B. PROSSER.

[In the Harl. MS. 2247, is a curious collection of Postills, or Homilies, written in the reigns of King Edward IV. and King Henry VII. At fol. 168 b is one entitled "In festo Reliquarum," commencing "Worshipful friends, on Sunday next coming shall be the holy feast of all relicks (called Relick Sunday), that be left here in earth to the great magnificence, honour, and worship of God and profit to man, both bodily and ghostly, for inasmuch as we be insufficient to worship and reverence singularly all reverent relicks of all saints left here in earth, for it passeth man's power. Wherefore holy church, in especial the Church of England, hath ordained this holy feast to be worshipped the next Sunday after the translation of St. Thomas of Canterbury, yearly to be hallowed and had in reverence."

For some notices of the Tenebræ office of Wednesday, Holy Thursday, and Good Friday, consult "N. & Q." 2nd S. viii. 32.]

"THE CHURCH OF ENGLAND AND IRELAND."— When was this designation first used? See Procter's *Book on the Common Prayer.* O. T. D.

[That unmeaning clause, "The United Church of England and Ireland," which occurs on the title-page of *The Book of Common Prayer,* was first used at the commencement of the present century. The authority for this phrase is the fifth article of the Union of 1800 : "That the Churches of England and Ireland be united into one *Protestant* (!) episcopal Church, to be called 'The United Church of England and Ireland.'" Of course, churchmen are not responsible for the theology of Acts of Parliament, especially those passed during the dark ages of the Georgian era. We cannot see that in reality the Church of Ireland has been in any respect more united with the English since the Union than before it. It is still perfectly independent as to jurisdiction. It still has its own proper Book of Common Prayer, its own Convocation, and its own peculiar customs. The Irish service book contains a prayer for the Lord-Lieutenant; an Office for Visiting Prisoners; and a Rubric concerning the time of publishing banns, which are not found in the English Prayer Book. The late Archbishop Magee, in one of his published Charges, very distinctly asserted the authority of the Irish Prayer Book. As regards doctrine and general discipline, it has *always* been united with the Church of England.]

TITLE OF MAJESTY. — When was the title of Majesty appropriated to English sovereigns. It was occasionally used at an early period; but was at first almost confined, as a title, to the Emperor.
HISTORICUS.

[We believe Henry VIII. was the first English sovereign who was styled "His Majesty." The titles of English sovereigns have undergone many changes: Henry IV. was "His Grace;" Henry VI., "His Excellent Grace;" Edward IV., "High and Mighty Prince;" Henry VII., "His Grace," and "His Highness;" Henry VIII., first "His Highness," and then "His Majesty." "His Sacred Majesty" was the title assumed by subsequent sovereigns, which was afterwards changed to "Most Excellent Majesty."]

HILPA AND SHALLUM. — In *Frazer's Magazine* for January, 1865 (p. 95), occurs the following sentence in an article on Richardson, the novelist: —

"In strong contrast to these boisterous lovers is the gentle and prolix Sir Charles, who woos her in sentences a page long, and by slow approaches, which remind one of Hilpah and Shallum."

What is the allusion here? If it refer to anything biblical—and I know my Bible passably well—I cannot recall it. O. P.

[Addison's charming legend of Hilpa and Shallum will be found in the eighth volume of *The Spectator*, Nos. 584, 585. Hilpa, the Chinese antediluvian princess, was one of the hundred and fifty daughters of Zilpah, of the race of Cohu, by whom some of the learned think is meant Cain. Shallum, her lover, "of a gentle disposition, beloved both by God and man," was lord of a manor consisting of a long chain of rocks and mountains, which goes under the name of Tirzah.]

MR. BENTLEY'S HARLEQUINADE "THE WISHES." Was this piece, which Bentley's quondam friend Walpole speaks of as very witty and humorous, till maimed for party purposes, ever played or printed? And if so, is any copy to be got of it? (See Walpole's *Letters*, Cunningham's edit. iii. 407, 491, 512; viii. 196.) QUIVIS.

[Richard Bentley's comedy, *Wishes, or Harlequin's Mouth Opened*, was acted at Drury Lane on July 27, 28,

and 30, 1761, and at Covent Garden on Oct. 3, 1761. After being circulated in manuscript, admired and applauded by those who had perused it, it was first privately rehearsed at Lord Melcombe's villa, afterwards Brandenburgh House. It was never printed. See Baker's *Biog. Dramatica*, ed. 1812, and Geneste's *Hist. of the Stage*, iv. 617. Consult also *A Letter to R— B—, Esq., author of the new Comedy, called The Wishes*. Lond. 8vo, 1761.]

Replies.

"THE REFORMED MONASTERY."

(3rd S. vi. 456.)

That a copy of this work, dated 1677, exists in the Bodleian Library, may be seen by a reference to the Catalogue under the Initials B. (L.). Watt gives it, with the date 1678, under the name *Jesus*, and makes no mention of the author. In order to facilitate the discovery of the author, it seems desirable to give the whole of the title, which I here transcribe from a copy in the public library of this University, the frontispiece to which has been torn out.

"*Claustrum Animæ*: The Reformed Monastery; OR, THE LOVE OF JESUS. A sure and short, pleasant and easie way to HEAVEN. In Meditations, Directions, and Resolutions to Love and Obey JESUS unto Death. In two Parts. LONDON, Printed for *Henry Brome*, at the Gun in *S. Paul's* Church-Yard, the West-End. MDCLXXVII."

The second part, which has a shorter title, is dated MDCLXXVI. The Imprimatur is dated "Ex Æd. Lambeth. Febr. 16, 1675-6. The work is dedicated to John [Fell], Bishop of Oxford, who was also Dean of Christ-Church, to whom the author expresses himself under obligations. In the preface to the first part he represents his aim to be "to have every Christian to be really devout and precise, without entering the cloister or the conventicle." In the preface to the second part he says: —

"Not that I would deny that places for Religious Retirement might afford many great advantages, in order to greater devotion and heavenly mindedness; for I bewail their loss, and heartily wish that the piety and charity of the present age might restore to this nation the useful conveniency of them. Necessary Reformations might have repurg'd Monasteries as well as the Church, without abolishing of them: and they might have been still houses of Religion without having any dependance upon Rome: " — and more to the same effect, which he concludes thus: "*Bene vixit qui bene latuit*—he lives best and most safe, who is least acquainted with the world and lives farthest from it."

The Epistle Dedicatory is signed "Your Lordship's most dutiful Son and most humble Servant, L.B." Now I am very strongly of opinion that the author was *Luke Beaulieu*. We learn from Wood (*Athenæ Oxon.*, iv. 668), that he was a native of France, educated at the University of Saumur, came into England on account of religion about the year 1667; was made divinity reader in the Chapel of St. George at Windsor; was admitted at Christ-Church, Oxford, where he took the degree of B.D.; was a prebendary of Gloucester, and chaplain to Chief Justice Jeffries. He was the acknowledged author of the following works:—

"Take heed of both Extreams; or, plain and useful Cautions against Popery and Presbytery, in two parts. Lond. 1675."

"The Holy Inquisition; wherein is represented what is the religion of the Church of Rome. Lond. 1681."

"A Discourse showing that Protestants are on the safer side, and that their religion is the surest way to heaven. Lond. 1687."

As neither of these works is in our University Library, I am unable to compare their style with that of *The Reformed Monastery*; but many parts of the preface to the first part of the latter work might well have done the same duty for the first of the three preceding works, "Take heed of both extreams." In one place he writes:—

"Must we retire into *Thebais*, with the fathers of the desert? Must we confine ourselves to the solitude of a *Monastick Cell?* Or shall we become Quakers, and profess the sullenness of Melancholy Fanaticks? Why, truly in Popish Countreys, the Cloister hath ingross'd the name of Religion, and they that would be, or be thought to be, devout beyond others, do usually put on a Fryer's hood, and embrace the Rule of some *Religious Order:* and, amongst us, Puritanism hath usurp'd the name of *Godliness.*"

This is so like a caution against "both extremes," that the presumption is thereby greatly strengthened that Beaulieu is the author. E. V.

Cambridge.

[We have since discovered a copy of *The Reformed Monastery* in the British Museum entered under the initials B. (L.) The work no doubt is from the pen of Luke Beaulieu, as it was issued by the publisher of his other works. Beaulieu also translated Bishop Cosin's *History of Popish Transubstantiation*, Lond. 8vo, 1676. In addition to the few particulars given by Wood, we may add, that Beaulieu was Rector of Whitchurch in Oxfordshire, and Prebendary of St. Paul's. He died in 1723, and was buried at Whitchurch.]

JAMES I. AND MARSTON.

(3rd S. v. 451.)

"Consider for pity's sake what must be the state and condition of a prince whom the preachers publicly from the pulpit assail,—*whom the comedians of the metropolis bring upon the stage,—whose wife attends these representations to enjoy the laugh against her husband,—*whom the Parliament braves and despises,— and *who is universally hated by the whole people.*"—De Beaumont, 1604, quoted by Von Raumer, ii. 206.

In illustration of the italicised portions, take the following from Marston's *What you Will*, in the prologue to which the author, who had already been imprisoned for ridiculing the Scots in his *Eastward Hoe!* says, he —

"Nor once dreads or cares
What envious hand his guiltless muse hath struck.

(1). *Quadratus.* Why hark, good Phylus (O that thy narrow sense
Could but contain me now). All that exists
Takes valuation from opinion.
A giddy minion now.—Pish, thy taste is dull
And cannot relish me. (Act I. Sc. 1.)

(2). *Jacomo.* Hark! Lorenzo. Celso, the loose Venice Duke,
Is going to bed; 'tis now a forward morn
'Fore he take rest. O strange transformed sight,
When princes make night day, the day their night.
Andr. Come, we'll petition him.
Jaco. Away, away.
He scorns all plaints; makes jest of serious suit.
[Enter the Duke coupled with a lady; two couples more with them, *the men having tobacco-pipes in their hands.* The women sit; they dance a round. The petition is delivered up by Randolfo; *the Duke lights his tobacco pipe with it, and goes out dancing.*
Rand. St. Mark, St. Mark!
Jaco. Did not I tell you, lose no more rich time;
What can one get but mire from a swine?" (Act I.)

Here the proof that the loose Venice Duke was he whom scandal called Rizzio's son, lies chiefly in the disproof; and the audience are directed to the true aim of the satire by the attribution of acts of marked unlikeliness. The prince is ostentatiously made a smoker and a dancer,—habits which, if need were, would be adduced to show that the tobacco-hating and ungainly monarch was not alluded to.

(3). Lampatho, *apropos* of nothing, says—

"The Venice state is *young, loose*, and *unknit*;
Can relish naught but luscious vanities.
Go, fit his tooth. O glavering flattery,
How potent art thou! Front, look brisk and sleek,
That such base dirt as you should dare to reek
In princes' nostrils. (Act II.)

(4). *Ran.* Cease, the Duke approacheth: 'tis almost night,
For the Duke's up: now begins his day.
Duke. What sport for night?
Lamp. A comedy entitled Temperance.
Duke. What sot elects that subject for the Court?
What should dame Temperance do here? Away!
The *itch* on Temperance, your moral play!
Quadr. Duke, Prince, Royal blood!—thou hast the best means to be damned of any Lord in Venice—thou great man. . . . . I will do that which few of thy subjects do,—love thee: but I will never do that which all thy subjects do,—flatter thee. (Act V.)

(5). *Duke.* How shall we spend the night?
Quadr. Gulp Rhenish wine, my liege; let our paunch rent;
Suck merry jellies; preview, but not prevent,
No mortal can, the miseries of life. (Act V.)

It should be remembered that there is nothing in the plot which necessitates the introduction of so loose-living a prince, or of such marked satire. The cause, therefore, must be sought in well-known external circumstances. Again, as De Beaumont wrote in 1604, and as *Eastwood Hoe!* was published in 1605 (in three different editions) it is not unlikely that the suppressed passages of this play contained allusions not only to

Scotchmen but to the king. This supposition is strengthened by the cutting of ears and slitting of noses with which Marston, Chapman, and Jonson were all threatened, and by the story of the poison which Jonson's mother had prepared for herself and her son if sentence had been pronounced against him. It is not likely that punishments deserving of avoidance by poison would have been inflicted on the satirists of Scotchmen merely.

As to Queen Anna's attendance on these representations, *Eastward Hoe!* was played by "the Children of Her Majesty's Revels," the "little eyases who were then the fashion," and that *What you, Will* was played by the same, is shown by the stage direction at the close of the second Act, where "the sweet gallants" are represented by a "company of boys within." If the Queen did not really attend such representations, the fact that they were played by her company of boy actors might have led to the misapprehension, but if Charles I. and his Queen could be praised for their virtue, and the virtuous changes made in the Court, and could yet listen to the *Cœlum Britannicum* in which they were thus praised, Queen Anna could not outrage the manners of the times by enjoying a laugh against James. In the *Cœlum Britannicum* not only is the language most gross, but the immoralities of James and his Court are typified by all the worst details of the Jovian mythology.

I would add that, as the players changed the Scotch lord in the *Merchant of Venice*, into "that other lord," so we can now understand why the folio, printed as it was from an acting copy, omitted in Act I. Sc. 4, Hamlet's long speech beginning "This heavy-headed revel." It is not probable that they were purposely levelled at James; but no words could be more pointedly applicable.   B. NICHOLSON.
New Zealand.

PRETENDED SON OF LOUIS XVI.

(3rd S. vi. 473.)

Besides the work translated from the French by the Hon. and Rev. C. G. Perceval, Rector of Calverton, Bucks, 1838, there is a work by A. De Beauchesne, translated by W. Hazlitt, under the title—

"Louis XVII., his Life, Sufferings, and Death: the Captivity of the Royal Family in the Temple," 1853.

This prince was born in 1785, and died June 8, 1795; and his titular sovereignty lasted not quite seventeen months, his father Louis XVI. being beheaded January 21, 1793 (Walter Scott's *Life of Napoleon*, c. xiii.) His uncle, the Count of Provence, born 1755, succeeded to the title in 1795, but not to the sovereignty as Louis XVIII.

till 1814. I cannot adopt the epithet "pretended" son, given by your correspondent M. A., as the existence of this son is an historical fact, verified by the title Louis XVIII., as the existence of a titular Napoleon II. is verified by the present title of Napoleon III. I have not seen Perceval's translation; but if it be similar to Hazlitt's, it must be treated as historical, although like all history, errors may be detected in it.

T. J. BUCKTON.
Lichfield.

The following extract from *The Times* of Dec. 22 furnishes an answer to A. M.'s query,—if the statement it contains, that the pretended Dauphin "went to Java in 1853, and died there," be correct:—

"A Paris journal publishes the following strange history of an old Gothic arm-chair, which was sold a few days since at the public auction-rooms in the Rue Drouot. The article in question, at first richly ornamented, was presented by the maker to Maria Theresa, and figured in her boudoir. After the death of the Empress of Austria it was sent, in conformity with her desire, to Queen Marie Antoinette of France, and was subsequently used by Louis XVI. during his imprisonment in the Temple. After the King's tragical death Cléry, his valet-de-chambre, became its owner, and took it to England; where it successively became the property of the Prince Regent, and afterwards of the Duke of Cumberland. The latter took it with him to Berlin, and there sent it to an upholsterer for repair. The workman to whom it was intrusted found in the stuffing of the seat a diamond pin, the portrait of a boy, and several sheets of very closely written manuscript. The man sold the pin, and gave the portrait and papers to a watchmaker of his acquaintance. Some years later the watchmaker, whose name was Naundorff, endeavoured to pass himself off as Louis XVII., and produced the papers and portrait in support of his pretensions. After making some noise in France, and then in Belgium, where he lost his son, who called himself the Duke of Normandy, he went to Java in 1853, and died there. The workman who found the portrait and documents kept his secret till just before his death, when he revealed the whole to his family. One of his relatives, having ascertained that the chair was still at Berlin, purchased it, and sold it to a French traveller, who carried it to Paris; where it ultimately came into possession of an old woman, the inmate of an asylum for the aged, lately deceased. It has now been sold by auction with the rest of her effects."

The cutting, at all events, deserves to be preserved in "N. & Q." It has since been stated that this chair fetched a high price, and is now gone "into a Gallery in Piccadilly."   P. S.

TOURNAMENTS.

(3rd S. vi. 440, 477.)

In Favyn's *Théâtre d'Honneur et de Chevalerie* (Paris, 1620), tom. ii. 1752-1798, will be found a list of the thirty-six great German tournaments, with the arms in each case of the nobles or princes at whose expense they were held, as well as of the "Quatre Rois du Tournoy."

Favyn professes to correct the errors of Modius, whose book, entitled —

"Pandectæ triumphales, sive Pomparum et Festorum ac Solennium Apparatuum, Conviviorum Spectaculorum Simulacrorum Bellicorum equestrium et pedestrium, Naumachiarum ludorumque, denique omnium nobiliorum tomi duo,"

was printed at Frankfort in 1586. As there are many discrepancies between the dates in Favyn and those given by your correspondent on p. 477, I have made a list of the first twelve tournaments. Favyn says : —

"La première assemblée fut tenue par l'Empereur Henry surnommé l'Oiseleur Premier du nom, Duc de Saxe, le Premier Dimanche d'apres les Roys, l'an de Grace Neuf cents trente huit, en la Ville de Magdebourg," &c. &c.

1. Magdebourg	. . . .	938
2. Rotenbourg	. . . .	942
3. Constance	. . . .	948
4. Mertspourg	. . . .	969
5. Braunschweig	. . .	996
6. Treves	. . . .	1019
7. Halle	. . . .	1042
8. Augsbourg	. . . .	1080
9. Gottingen	. . . .	1119
10. Zurich	. . . .	1165
11. Cologne	. . . .	1179
12. Nürnberg	. . . .	1198

The others agree with the list already given, with the exception of the three following : —

19. Bamberg .	. . . .	1362
28. Würtzburg	. . .	1474
34. Bamberg	. . .	1486

It will be seen that the list above also supplies the omissions in the one given at p. 477, and that it fixes the date of the first tournament eight years later.

Although Favyn professes to correct Modius, the descriptions given by both of them of the arms borne at the earlier tournaments must be received with a good deal of caution. Arms had probably not become hereditary distinctions in those days, and Favyn and Modius appear to have assigned to those who took part in these tournaments the arms which were afterwards borne by their descendants. For example, at p. 1770, the arms of the Counts Palatine of the Rhine in the year 1337, are made to include the golden orb, or Reichs-Apfel, which was not granted until the year 1544. (*Vide* Spener, *Operis Heraldici pars Specialis*, Frankfort-on-the-Main, 1717, p. 678.)

The list given by your correspondent appears to be taken from Rüxner's *Thurnier Buch*, published at Siemern about 1530, a copy of which very curious book I met with some years ago ; a second edition was published later at Frankfort.

                      JOHN WOODWARD.

New Shoreham.

QUENTIN MATSYS (3ʳᵈ S. vi. 374, 421, 476.)— Your correspondent under the signature of W. H. JAMES WEALE, has shorn Quentin Matsys of some of his most towering plumes derived from the anvil and the pencil. It is, however, to be regretted some works of this great artist were not named, and where they are to be found, and whether " relaid " or retouched. Of the merit of the iron font-crane in the church of St. Peter at Louvain, but little can be said, excepting upon the finial, which certainly is well designed and ingeniously executed.

There is an exceedingly fine piece of ironwork in the beautiful church of Aerschot, a few leagues from Louvain : it is the only iron chandelier in mediæval design worthy of the age. While standing beneath it in fixed admiration, the gruff and busy Swiss growled in my ear, " That, sir, was made by Quentin-Matsys, and designed to hang over the tomb of his wife. It was lately found buried beneath a mass of rubbish, and much damaged ; but has just been restored, and placed as you now see it." This is in substance engraved upon the hoop, which forms the basis of the design. Heigh, in his *Continental Interiors*, in his view of the magnificent screen, has given only a portion of this chandelier.

A tombstone, said on the same authority to have been discovered amongst the wrecks caused by the havoc of the French Revolution, and placed as it now remains, by the south door of the church, is inscribed to a female of the Matsys family.

If your correspondent would furnish a few remarks on this chandelier, on the artist (under whatever name he may be found), or on the tombstone, it is probable he would afford valuable information to your readers.   H. D'AVENEY.

GENERAL HUGH MERCER (3ʳᵈ S. vi. 473, 537.) From MR. EDWARDS's reply to C. W. B., General Mercer appears to have been of the family of Mercers of Knockbally Style, or of Lodge, both in the county of Carlow, one of whom (*circa* 1725) married a Vigors of Burgage. Both these families I suppose to have descended from Colonel William Mercer, a poet and parliamentary officer under the Earl of Essex, who was the son of Mr. James Mercer, parson of Slaines, Aberdeenshire, and was settled at Dublin in 1784. He was five times married. I have always considered General Hugh to have been the great-grandson of John Mercer, whose *Chronicle* was published some thirty years since by the Spalding Club. He was born in 1721, educated as a medical man, served in that capacity, at the battle of Culloden, and probably finding the climate of Scotland too warm, emigrated shortly after that disastrous event to America.

                            M.

THE MICKLETON HOOTER (3ʳᵈ S. vi. 464.) — The following facts may tend to throw light on this Gloucestershire mystery. About a year back sounds closely resembling those described by H., kept the neighbourhood of Bringsty Common, near Bromyard, in Herefordshire, in nightly fear. The noise, as respectable persons who frequently heard it assured inquirers, was "an awful wailing sort of sound," appearing "to rise and fall," sometimes "quite close," and "the next instant dying away in the distance," and resembling nothing remembered in those parts. It was attributed variously to unheard-of beasts, escaped lunatics, foxes, owls, plovers, &c., while supporters of a supernatural theory were not wanting. I believe that some intelligent champions of a fox-origin are not yet satisfied; and it may be conceded that at a time when the good folks were, each night, in painful expectation of a hideous outbreak, a fox's cry may occasionally have been taken for that of the monster. But this much is certain: First, that several well-informed individuals came to the conclusion, after much sifting of evidence, that the sounds must proceed from a bird, and that bird a *bittern*. Secondly, that after a few weeks, a bittern, a bird very rarely seen in those parts, was shot by a farmer within a short distance of the chief scene of the alarms. Thirdly, that thereupon the reign of terror ended. I may add, that gamekeepers and others, well acquainted with the night music of foxes, were at a loss to account for the noise, until a bittern was suggested as its author, some time before the lucky shot (*i. e.* lucky for the alarmed rustics, though not lucky as slaying a rare and beautiful bird) was fired.   Ω.

HOLLANDS: CHEERS (2nd S. iii. 169.) — I have just stumbled upon an early allusion to *Hollands*, which, as I do not find the query asking for any such references has been answered, you may perhaps like to insert.

In a *Letter from the Facetious Doctor Andrew Tripe at Bath*, 8vo, 1714, p. 27 (a pamphlet which has excited some notice in "N. & Q.") the writer says: —

"But by all means, you must renounce *Holland, Geneva,* and *Brunswick Mum.* For one corrupts your *Lungs,* and the other stupifies your *Intellects.*"

Let me add an instance of the use of "cheers" in our modern sense, — a question debated in "N. &. Q." some time since, though I cannot find the reference to it. The *Scots Magazine* for 1789, p. 356, describing an archery meeting at Hatfield, says, that Miss Harcourt was saluted "with three cheers" as Queen of the Target.   H. T.

THE YOUNG PRETENDER (3rd S. vii. 1.) — I am nearly certain that Horace Walpole says that it was in the church of St. Martin-in-the-Fields that the Young Pretender conformed to our Church. I have read that a Book of Common Prayer was always at hand wherever he went.   W. H.

OLD INNS OF SOUTHWARK (3rd S. vii. 13.) — A question is asked by D. R. J. respecting the old inns of Southwark, and especially the Catherine Wheel Inn, High Street. I would refer D. R. J. to a paper which I am now printing in the forthcoming part of the *Surrey Archæological Society's Transactions,* and which I anticipate will very shortly be published. It is a continuation of, or rather a supplement to, Mr. Corner's paper on the same subject, and will contain much additional information relative to the *White Lion* Inn; but I have not met with anything about the Catherine Wheel Inn.   WILLIAM HENRY HART.
Roupell Park, Streatham.

MUM (3rd S. vi. 434, 503.) — This was a strong sort of beer introduced from Germany at the beginning of the last century. It is sometimes called *Hamburgh Mum*; sometimes *Brunswick Mum*. In Playford's *Second Book of the Musical Companion,* W. Pearson, 1715, is the following —

> " *Catch in Praise of Mum.*
> "There's an odd sort of liquor
>   New come from Hamborough,
> 'Twill stick a whole wapentake
>   Thorough and thorough ;
> 'Tis yellow, and likewise
>   As bitter as gall,
> And as strong as six horses,
>   Coach and all.
> As I told you 'twill make you
>   As drunk as a drum ;
> You'd fain know the name on't,
>   But for that, my friend, *mum.*"

In the curious little book, *Political Merriment; or, Truths told to some Tune,* 1714, is a short poem, "In Praise of Brunswick Mum" (p. 96); and at p. 3 of the same work, "An Excellent Ballad," concluding with the following stanza: —

> "Now, now true Protestants rejoice,
>   Stand by your laws and King,
> Now you've proclaim'd the Nation's choice,
>   Let traitorous rebels swing ;
> Let royal George, the Papists' scourge,
>   To England quickly come :
> His health till then, let honest men,
>   Drink all in *Brunswick Mum.*"

Pope also has an allusion to this popular liquor, in the following couplet: —

> " The clamorous crowd is hush'd with mugs of *mum,*
>   Till all, tun'd equal, send a general hum."
>   EDWARD F. RIMBAULT.

Some late articles relating to *Mum* bring to my remembrance a witty saying of Henry Erskine's, which you may possibly think worthy of notice. There used to be an Act of Parliament annually relative to the duties on "malt, mum, cyder, and perry." Mr. Perry, editor of the *Morning Chronicle,* being indicted by the Attorney-General for an alleged political libel, conducted his own defence, made an able speech to the jury, and had a verdict of "Not guilty." Not long afterwards Cobbett was indicted for a seditious passage in his *Register*, and, prompted by the success of the *Chronicle's* editor, resolved to follow the same course. He did so, but failed; being convicted and sentenced to a heavy fine and imprisonment. Henry Erskine's observation on this was, that Cobbett tried to be *Perry*, when he should have been *Mum*.

J. R. B.

JOHNSONIANA: SOLUTION OF CONTINUITY (3rd S. vii. 6.) — In the *Dictionnaire de l'Académie* the phrase "*solution de continuité*" is given as an established one in medical and philosophical works. This is in the *fourth* edition of the *Dictionary*, and is therefore nearly sufficient to disprove the notion that this phrase was taken from Johnson, though it is true that the said edition was published in 1762, and Johnson's letter was written in 1720. It can hardly have been *publici juris* till Boswell printed it. But it is immaterial. The phrase is also found in Cotgrave's old *Dictionary*, 1611.

LYTTELTON.

Hagley, Stourbridge. .

PHILOLOGUS may be assured that this expression is far older than the time of Johnson. It will be found in Rabelais, I cannot give the exact reference. The application will not bear explanation in your columns.

A. F. B.

ENGLISH TUNES "ANNEXED" BY THE YANKEES (3rd S. vi. 430.)—The quotation, "Hearts of Oak," &c., is not from Garrick; but is part of Smollett's well-known song, "Come, cheer up my lads, 'tis to glory we steer."

C. B.

[The words of the still popular song, "Hearts of Oak," are by David Garrick (as stated by MR. PINKERTON). The song was sung by Mr. Champnes in *Harlequin's Invasion*, in 1759. The tune is by Dr. Boyce. *Vide* Chappell's *Popular Music of Olden Time*, ii. 715.—ED.]

Dr. Boyce was the composer of this fine old patriotic song. I have two broadside copies now before me. One is entitled "A Loyal Song, sung by Mr. Champnes in *Harlequin's Invasion*;" the other "A Loyal Song set by Dr. Boyce." *Harlequin's Invasion* was a pantomime produced at Drury Lane, Dec. 31, 1759. The dialogue was written by David Garrick, and the plot and machinery were of his invention.

EDWARD F. RIMBAULT.

NOLO EPISCOPARI (3rd S. vi. 48, 189.) — Dr. Farmer, it is said, twice refused a bishoprick. The following instance deserves notice from the curiousness of the reply. My authority is Dibdin's *Reminiscences* (vol. i. p. 173) : —

"He (Dr. Andrews, Dean of Canterbury), had a full, strong voice, and is said never to have used it more sonorously and effectively than when, to the Prime Minister's question (I think it was Lord Liverpool's, though Mr. Perceval gave him the deanery), 'whether he would be a bishop,' he answered 'Nolo.'"

P. W. TREPOLPEN.

COMPOSITION AT HABERDASHER'S HALL (3rd S. vi. 266.) — After the royalist party had been subdued, commissioners were appointed by the parliament to compound their estates. These commissioners sat at Haberdashers' Hall. In Cary's *Memorial of the Great Civil War*, vol. ii. p. 277, will be found a letter from Francis Rous to Sir Harry Vane relative to this commission. Amongst other matters he complains "that there is little hope of despatch at Haberdashers' Hall, they having before them, as a lawyer of the counsel of the trustees told me, fourscore causes when a motion was to be made for this business."

P. W. TREPOLPEN.

MUMMY (3rd S. vi. 267.) — There is in the Museum of the College of Surgeons, Dublin, the body of a woman, which was accidentally discovered in the Bog of Ardee, co. Louth, in 1849. The skin is completely tanned, forming an integument like leather in colour and texture, and thus preserving unaltered the form and proportion of body and limbs, and there is no perceptible smell, or other sign of decay. The tradition amongst the neighbouring peasantry was, that about seventy years previously, a girl named Mary Carcha had poisoned herself (? with arsenic) in a fit of jealousy; and as the peasantry would not permit the body to be interred in consecrated ground, it was buried in the Bog; and now, after a lapse of eighty-five years — seventy beneath the peat, and fifteen exposed to atmospheric influences — the body lies in a glass case in the Museum, having been completely mummied, or rather converted into adipocire, by the tannin and other antiseptic constituents of the peat, which seem to have penetrated every part of the structure; for the bones were at first so soft as to be easily penetrable by any sharp instrument: but after exposure to the air gradually resumed their normal hardness.

J. L.

Dublin.

BYRON'S " DON JUAN " (3rd S. vi. 513.) — MR. WARREN doubtless refers to the stanzas issued from the Great Totham press, under the following title : —

"Some Rejected Stanzas of *Don Juan*, with Byron's own curious Notes. The whole written in Double Rhymes, after Casti's manner, an Italian Author from whom Byron is said to have plagiarized many of his Beauties. From an unpublished Manuscript in the possession of Captain Medwin. A very limited number printed. Great Totham, Essex: Printed at Charles Clarke's private Press, 1845."

The pamphlet is a quarto, and contains *twenty* stanzas complete, except the third, which has the last couplet omitted. The stanzas occupy five pages, but printed only on one side, and the notes (eleven in number) fill two pages. With all my respect for the genius of Byron, I do not find these stanzas at all worthy of him; but keep my copy of them as a curiosity, never having seen this publication elsewhere.

ESTE.

Angus M'Diarmid (3rd vi. 507.) — The book-seller at Aberfeldy, who issued the edition of M'Diarmid's pamphlet in 1841, appears to have no feeling for the rough eloquence of the author, and equally little disposition to make allowance for the difficulty he may have felt in the use of what to him must be regarded as a foreign lan-guage. On the contrary, the motto chosen for the titlepage indicates a desire to draw down contempt upon the work. I have now before me a copy, of which the title runs thus : —

"Striking and Picturesque Delineations of the grand, beautiful, wonderful, and interesting Scenery around Loch-Earn. By Angus M'Diarmid, Ground-officer on the Earl of Breadalbane's Estate of Edinample. *Superas se tollens in auras, in astra surgens.* Edinburgh : printed for the Author by John Moir, 1815."

The dedication to the Earl bears the same date, which seems to mark this as the first edition. In the year now referred to I was myself at Loch-Earnhead, where I saw the book at the inn, and was also introduced to the author, then a fine athletic young man, who, though manifesting abundantly the enthusiasm which prompted him to compose his *Delineations*, conducted himself with a degree of modesty which, in the society of Saxons, a Gaul of that day could hardly have been expected to maintain. Whatever may be thought of M'Diarmid's style as a writer of English, every candid reader will give him credit for a keen per-ception of the beauties of natural scenery, and will admire the generous ardour which he displays when describing any act of heroism, or feat of manhood. He may even be commended on the score of his charity; for so unwilling does he ap-pear to judge harshly of his neighbours, that his strongest expression for a robber goes no further than calling him "a man of incoherent transac-tions." If my recollection serves me, I was in-formed that the gentleman who put M'Diarmid's work to press was a Colonel Riley, or O'Reilly. I am not certain, after the lapse of so many years, whether the name assumed the English or the Irish form ; and as in 1815 " N. & Q." were only *in posse*, the inducement to record that class of facts, and even the means of doing so, were want-ing. It may be presumed that the Colonel, and and not the author, is responsible for the Latin motto which appears on the titlepage.

R. S. A.

Scarlett Family (2nd S. ix. 197.) — A Gene-alogist is mistaken in regard to Christiana Scarlett's marriage into the family of the Gordons of Earls-ton. Sir John Gordon's *first* wife was Juliana J. Scarlett. By her he had no family, and Sir Wil-liam Gordon's mother was an Irving of Gribton.

Gamma.

English Soldiers at the Battle of Leipzig (2nd S. viii. 537.) — I spoke on this subject a few days ago to an old soldier in this parish, who was at the battle of Leipzig. He tells me that the only English there were a troop of artillery armed with rockets, which were then a new invention. He thinks that there were in all about one hun-dred men under Captain Bogue, and attached to Bernadotte's army. He describes the rockets as most effective, and as, from their novelty, causing great confusion in the French army. The troop remained for some time attached to Bernadotte's army.

Gamma.

Disclaiming (3rd S. vi. 392, 461.) —

"He was born at Wakefield, in Yorkshire, in the year 1653, and notwithstanding the heralds, as appears by their books, thought fit to disclaim his father's pretensions to bear arms as a descendant from the Radcliffes of Dilston, in the county of Northumberland, the chiefs of which family had been knights, barons, and earls from Henry IVth's time to this very day, yet the late Earl of Der-wentwater, Sir Francis Radcliffe, acknowledged him for a kinsman, and suffered the son to wear a bend in graile sable, field argent, on his coach, which none of the College belonging to the Earl Marshall thought fit to animadvert on during his life, though they have admonished the University of Oxford not to erect any such escutcheon over or upon his monument."—*Life of Dr. Radcliffe* (1715) p. 3.

E. H. A.

Sarsen Stones (3rd S. vi. 456, 523.) — I am obliged by the replies I have received, and beg to observe that, though Stukeley was a great anti-quary, he was nevertheless a visionary one, and I should be sorry to rely on him as an authority in points of archæological obscurity. There are very few Phœnician words known, and I question very much whether *Sarsen* be one of them. It has been too much the custom to attribute to the Phœnicians the origin of things for which no reasonable explanation could be suggested; but I have known the Phœnician hypothesis so com-pletely blown to the winds in one remarkable instance of ancient relics, that I have no great faith in the solution of any antiquarian problem founded upon such an assumption. With regard to the *Sarsen* stones of Stonehenge, they are not *un-hewn*, and moreover they afford rude examples of the tenon and mortice joint, therefore the pro-hibition in Deut. xxvii. 5, 6, and Jos. viii. 30, 31, will not apply to that and similar temples, how-ever it may be thought applicable to such temples as Abury.

W. W. S.

A Poem having only One Vowel (3rd S. v. 526.) — Ein Frager's desire for one-vowelled pa-ragraphs may, perhaps, be stayed for awhile by the following poem, which, though probably not of Canadian origin, I have cut from a Canadian newspaper : —

"In the following only one vowel is used, and a very peculiar verse we have in consequence. We do not know who took the trouble to write the lines, but they are curious now they are done : —

'No monk too good to rob, or plot,
No fool so gross to bolt Scotch collops hot.
From Donjon tops no Oronooko rolls.
Logwood, not lotos, floods Oporto's bowls.
Troops of old tosspots oft to sot consort.
Box-tops schoolboys, too, oft do flog for sport.
No cool monsoons blow oft on Oxford dons,
Orthodox, jog-trot, book-worm Solomons!
Bold Ostrogoths of ghosts no horror show,
On London shop-fronts no hop-blossoms grow.
To crocks of gold no dodo looks for food,
On soft cloth footstools no old fox doth brood.
Long storm-tost sloops forlorn do work to port.
Rooks do not roost on spoons, nor woodcocks snort,
Nor dog on snowdrop or on coltsfoot rolls, .
Nor common frog concocts long protocols.' ''

          Eric.

Ville-Marie, Canada.

John Ralston (3rd S. vi. 455.) — John Ralston was a teacher of drawing about forty years ago in Manchester, and the neighbourhood. He was a man of some talent, and of a social disposition. His pictures consist principally of boat pieces, river and coast scenery. The colouring somewhat warm. There must be persons living in Manchester and the neighbourhood to whom he was known, and who could give further information concerning him. I merely speak from the knowledge and impressions of a boy. One of his pictures adorned the walls of " the nursery."

          Crowdown.

"Take my Cap" (3rd S. vi. 498.) — I have always understood this phrase to mean : " You have surpassed me, you may wear the cap"—as in fighting, the victor wins the belt. .

We have the saying quite common : " You have *capped me* "—gone beyond me. Also, "That caps all."   J. A. G.

Islington.

Portrait of Oliver (3rd S. vi. 444.) — The Goodwood portrait was brought to the notice of your readers some years ago (2nd S. ii. 468 ; iii. 410). On that occasion (iii. 514) I mentioned a portrait of Cromwell that I had seen, many years before, in the Duke D'Aremberg's collection at Brussels ; which, to the best of my recollection, answered the description given of the one at Goodwood. And I now beg to repeat the wish that I then expressed, that some correspondent of yours at Brussels would be kind enough to communicate an account of it.   Meletes.

The Virginia Company (3rd S. vi. 515.) — Much information respecting this Company is given in Mr. Sainsbury's *Calendar of Colonial State Papers.* Reference may also be made to Smith's *History of Virginia;* Stith's *History of Virginia;* Bancroft's *History of the United States;* Anderson's *Colonial Church;* and *Lives of Nic. Ferrar,* edited by the Rev. J. E. B. Mayor.

         C. H. & Thompson Cooper.

Cambridge.

"The Tickler " (3rd S. vi. 514.)—Abhba will find, on further inquiry, that *The Tickler* is ascribed to Paul Hifferman, an Irish writer, whose name comes to us heaped with obloquy. Your correspondent's query has set me looking over a lot of Irish tracts, mostly political squibs in verse ; among which, I find one of those he inquires about, say :

" The Marrow of the Tickler's Works, or Three Shillings' worth of Wit for a Penny, in a Ballad. (To the tune of 'Derry Down.') There is more liquor in a Quart of Small-Beer for an Halfpenny, than in a Pint of Wine for a Shilling. 8 pp. 16mo. Printed in the year 1748."

The burthen of its prose and verse is to ridicule the truisms of the paper in question, which will no doubt be more intelligible to the initiated in the original *Ticklers*. In the " Dedication to the learned and celebrated Paul Hifferman, M.D., author of the inimitable *Ticklers*," signed " Scriblerus," we have a confirmation of the correct ascription of the work. If your correspondent is looking up the satirical squibs "in opposition to the well-known Charles Lucas," I could show him the following if he was on this side the water :

" The Horse and the Monkey : a Fable humbly inscribed to Mr. C——s L——s, Freeman."
" A Scourge for the Incendiary."
" The Chymerical Patriot : or, Lucas Awake."

All in verse, published at Dublin in 1749. There are no names of authors ; but in some poetical satires of the same period, "B——t B——n," figure on the titles. Perhaps Abhba can interpret these for me.   A. G.

Circumstantial Evidence (3rd S. vi. 471.) — Your correspondent T.'B. will, I doubt not, find the particulars of the case he refers to by looking for the name " Waterhouse " in the index to the *Annual Register* for 1830, and a year or two before and after that date.

I have not the means myself of referring to the *Register*, but the particulars, which are incorrectly given in *The Examiner*, made a lively impression on my mind at the time of the occurrence. The victim of the murder was not a farmer but a clergyman, the Rev. Mr. Waterhouse, incumbent of Stukely, in the county of Huntingdon, and the trial took place at the assizes for that county. He was a very old man with white hair, and the circumstantial evidence which hanged the prisoner was the finding in his cottage of a hatchet or bill-hook, with recent blood clotted on it mixed with a few white hairs. The medical witness at the trial declared that he had examined these hairs microscopically, and that he knew them to be hairs from the head of a human being.

The wounds which produced death were evidently made on the head with a sharp instrument, and the man, who was a very bad character, was convicted, and sentenced to death. Shortly before execution, not hoping to save his life, as supposed, but in order to revenge himself on the medical witness, he confessed the murder, and pointed out the place in which he had buried the instrument with which it was done, and that instrument was accordingly found. The blood and hairs on the hatchet found in the cottage were accounted for by his having killed a sheep with it by a blow on the head a short time before.

No doubt was entertained of the man's guilt before his confession; but, as in Müller's case, it was thought very strange that he had kept by him the evidence of his guilt, and so procured his own conviction.

The moral, however, deducible from this case is not so much the danger of convicting on circumstantial evidence, as the danger of relying upon opinions, on material points, authoritatively given by medical witnesses.   A. P.
Dublin.

I think I can give you a clue to the case of circumstantial evidence here referred to, as taken from a statement in *The Examiner*.

I have no doubt it refers to the case of Joshua Slade tried at the Summer Assizes at Huntingdon in the year 1827, and reported briefly in the *Annual Register* for that year at pp. 122 and 140. He was tried and convicted of the murder of the Rev. J. J. Waterhouse, a clergyman of recluse and miserly habits. The proof appears to have been that he murdered the unfortunate man with a hatchet or bill-hook. The judge was not satisfied with the conviction, and the criminal was twice respited.

In his confession he said that he had committed the murder with a sword which he had stolen a few weeks before from a public-house at Huntingdon. In all probability this is the case referred to by your correspondent T. B.
                                   C. R. LITTLEDALE.
U. U. C., Suffolk Street, Pall-Mall, E.

HEREFORDSHIRE QUERIES (3rd S. vi. 498.) — It will be interesting to MR. ROBINSON to know that in Sir G. C. Lewis's *Provincial Words of Herefordshire* (a volume, by the way, out of print), TUMP, s. a mound or hillock, is derived from the Welsh, *twmp*. In the same glossary "to tump" is said to be a provincialism for "to put into small heaps." It is, of course, not improbable that the substantive is from the Welsh. *Tomen*, or *twmen*, and *twt*, are synonyms for *tump* apparently in this border county. There is a Castle Twt hard by Kington, and a Tomen Castle a mile or two beyond Radnor. *Twt* would seem to be akin to *tot*, as mentioned in your correspondent's letter. Passing over the Carey question, as to which I can offer no light, I would just remark, *à propos* of the last part of your correspondent's note, that there is no end to the names of places in this district

which seem to have an Anglo-Saxon derivation. In the parish of Pembridge (the *peneg*, "penny," and *brygg*, "bridge") is a farm called *Leen*, which is probably derived from *lean*, A. S. for a reward. The parish of Knill suggests the origin of its name in *cnyll*, A. S. for "knell," the sound of a bell. Spon, or Spond, a hamlet of Almeley (which may itself be derived from *almes*, A. S. for "alms") is not improbably to be referred to *spon*, A. S. for "span." The Rodd, the name of a farm, suggests the A. S. for rood or cross, and so on *ad infinitum*. The meadow adjoining my lawn is called the Dumnercroft, meaning, I suppose, *domne-croft*, "prædiolum domini." Any Anglo-Saxon scholar might do a great deal hereabouts in this matter of names and places. I regret my own ignorance and inability to do more than call to my aid and handle very unskilfully Bosworth's *Anglo-Saxon Dictionary*. I have two fields, I should perhaps add, called "Great" and "Little Roman Hill," I know not from what antiquity.   J. DAVIES.
Moor Court, Kington.

MOUTRE (3rd S. vi. 267, 316, 357.) —
" On appelle droit de *moute*, ce que payent les Vassaux pour moudre leurs blez au moulin bannal du Seigneur."— *Dictionnaire de Furetière*, voc. MOUTE.
                                   MELETES.

SUPERSTITION OR SYMPATHY, WHICH? (3rd S. vi. 496.) — Nothing is more common than for a man, whose leg or arm has been amputated, to complain of pain in a toe or finger long after the limb is removed. May this not account for the marvels related under the above head? Speaking medically, it might be termed "sympathy."
                                   A. W. D.

Sympathy.—When an arm or leg is amputated, of course the nerves which supply the hands and feet are cut across. This also, and its attendant consequences, keeps up an amount of irritation along those cut nerves, and causes pain; which pain is referred to the parts which beforetime were supplied by them, as nerves refer their sensations to their extremities.   PHYSICIAN.

JUVENAL (3rd S. vi. 386.)—
" Eripient somnum Druso, *vitulisque marinis*."
                                   Sat. III. v. 238.
I cannot agree with H. C. C. in thinking that there is, in this line, any allusion that the commentators have failed to catch. *Ruperti* (whose name your correspondent appears to have inadvertently curtailed into " Rupert ") after referring to Pliny for another purpose, proceeds thus: " qui etiam, lib. ix. 13, s. 15, docet, *nullum animal graviore somno premi* phocis."

A little lower down he goes on to say: " Sententia itaque h. l. est, strepitus curruum auriga-rumque tantus est, ut vel animalia somniculosa expergescere queat."

No doubt Juvenal is alluding to seals. But why specially to the seals of Proteus? Sound sleep was a recognised characteristic of the whole race; and surely the object the satirist had in view was not to show himself off as a well-read scholar, but to put his meaning in a strong light by adverting to a fact in natural history well known to the readers of his day. MELETES.

BEAG-BHEUL: MODERN BELIEF IN THE BROWNIE (3rd S. vi. 511.)—The communication of F. A. M. corroborates and supplements my statements relative to the Carskey Brownie (*Beag-bheul,* or "Little-mouth"), in *The White Wife* (pp. 250-2). I there showed that the Cantire belief in the Brownie existed in 1863; although Sir Walter Scott had stated that—

" the last place in the south of Scotland, supposed to have been honoured or benefited by the residence of a Brownie, was Bodsbeck in Moffatshire, which has been the subject of an entertaining tale by Mr. James Hogg."

Since the publication of *The White Wife,* a valued correspondent, dating his letter Dec. 22, 1864, writes as follows:—

" In confirmation of what you say, there is no doubt whatever as to the belief in 'Little-mouth' existing at the present day. The people also believe in the evil-eye, and use charms to destroy the influence. Our friend Miss —— has just returned from Carskey, where she occupied a bedroom next to *Beag-bheul's* room, much to the wonder of the servants, one of whom said to her: ' Eh, Miss! are ye no frichtet to sleep so near *Beag-bheul?* I wadna do it for a thoosan' poonds!' The Laird has had many narrow escapes from accidents when riding, which the country people put down to the credit of 'Little-mouth.' "

This note, coupled with the communication of F. A. M., shows that the belief in the Brownie exists up to the present time in that very interesting Western Highland district, which Sir Walter Scott himself dubbed as "*wild* Cantire."
CUTHBERT BEDE.

HENRY PIMPERNEL AND JOHN NAPS (3rd S. vi. 110.)—The meaning of the allusion to these names, by ELIA, was asked for in "N. & Q." some months since, but has not been given [see p. 199]. Moxon & Co. announce a perfect edition of Lamb's *Works,* to console English readers for the exclusion (through the copyright law) of a forthcoming American edition; said to contain many pieces by Lamb, hitherto uncollected. I should have supposed, but for this, that the copyright of all Lamb's writings had already expired. But I would suggest that Messrs. Moxon's editor should enlighten his edition with notes explanatory of the many allusions and quotations scattered through Lamb's *Works,* that are too recondite for the attainments of "work-a-day" readers. C. B.

GRACE MACAULAY (2nd S. ix. 198.)—Mr. William Smith, ordained minister of Cranston in the Presbytery of Dalkeith, on October 31, 1733, was married on July 3, 1735, to ——, Macaulay, daughter of Mr. Robert Macaulay, minister at Stirling. They had one daughter, named Beatrix, born March 29, 1736. Mr. Smith married again in Feb. 26, 1742, Joan Baird, daughter of Mr. Baird of Chesterhall. By her he had five sons; one of whom was minister of Gulston—a son of whom is Dr. George Smith, now one of the ministers of Edinburgh. T. G.

THOMAS BARTON (3rd S. vi. 470.) — Edmund Marmion discharged the first fruits of the living of Eynesbury, in Huntingdonshire, on January 3, 1615 (First-fruits Registers, quoted in Gorham's *History of Eynesbury,* p. 119), and occurs rector, in the parish vestry records, in 1643. Will MESSRS. C. H. & THOMSON COOPER give the authority for their statement that Thomas Barton was presented to that living in 1629? JOSEPH RIX, M.D.
St. Neot's.

REV. DR. CHARLES LLOYD (3rd S. vi. 473.) — Dr. Lloyd was minister of the Unitarian Chapel at Palgrave in Suffolk, and kept a boarding school in the house formerly occupied by Mr. and Mrs. Barbauld. The Doctor lost his wife at Palgrave, Dec. 11, 1808 (*Gent. Mag.,* Suppl., 1808, vol. lxxviii. pt. ii. p. 1101), and removed to Highgate about 1811. JOSEPH RIX, M.D.
St. Neot's.

HARRISON'S CASE (3rd S. vi. 388, 423.) — Mr. George Lilly Craik prefaces the narrative of this trial, copied by him into the English Causes Célèbres (Knight's *Miscellanies,* vol. i. p. 255), by this account of his authority:—

" This is the famous case to which we have alluded in a preceding page (p. 129) in speaking of Sir Robert Hyde, the judge by whom it was tried. We will here give it as it is detailed, with considerable minuteness, and with such accompanying evidences as apparently to remove all doubt as to the facts, in an account first printed in 1676, probably under the direction of Dr. Thomas Shirley, or Sherley, physician to King Charles II., to whom the narrative seems to have been transmitted by his friend, Sir T. Overbury, a magistrate resident in the neighbourhood of Campden."

Mr. Craik here adds Sir T. Overbury's letter, but unfortunately does not mention where he met with the original of the epistle and the narrative.
ARCHIMEDES.

ARMS OF A CONQUERED KNIGHT (3rd S. vi. 483, 540.)—My note at p. 483 purported (as clearly as inverted commas, different type, and reference to volume, edition, and page could make it), to be an extract, without a word of comment, from Burke's *Extinct Peerage.* MR. ROBERT DYMOND, JUNIOR, is therefore not justified in supposing I have fallen " into a prevalent error." Whether what he alleges to be a mistake is so or not, could have been better judged had he conformed to the rules of "N. & Q.," and cited some authority for his statement. WALTER RYE.

THE ATHENIAN MISOGYNIST (3rd S. v. 450, 496.) I cannot find the passage mentioned by MR. MI-ALL, in the *Hippolytus*, though in that play Euripides has certainly said enough against women to deserve the title of " the Athenian Misogynist." Aristophanes, though not complimentary to the sex, was not a woman-hater, but I think he is the person so called by the French Essayist.

Χρήματα πορίζειν εὐπορώτατον γυνή,
Ἀρχουσά τ' οὐκ ἂν ἐξαπατηθείη ποτέ·
Αὐταὶ γάρ εἰσιν ἐξαπατᾶν εἰθισμέναι.
Ecclesiazusæ, vv. 236-8.
H. B. C.

U. U. Club.

RESTORATION OF ANCIENT BUILDINGS (3rd S. vi. 424, 538.) — The pleasing intelligence communicated by P. of Her Majesty's desire to restore Holyrood Chapel is what might be expected from the well-known patriotic sentiments of our beloved Queen, and so much the more pleasing that I have no doubt it will some day be carried into effect. The appeal to MR. FERREY is made in the right place; and I should suppose, with all deference, that to no one could the work of restoration be more confidently confided. As to St. Giles's church, I fear that one work of restoration at a time is enough for Scotland; but Her Majesty's example will work wonders. I am ashamed to own that the mass of my countrymen are sunk in utter apathy with regard to the Fine Arts in general, and look, in particular, on the splendid remains of ecclesiastical art that still abound on the historic soil of their native land, with a sort of pious horror, as of so many memorials, not of the Christian religion, but of some depraved form of pagan abominations. It is deplorable that such ignorance, combined with fanaticism, should exist in a country celebrated for the general good sense and information diffused among its people. Scotland was long cut off, both by prejudice and local barriers, from much intercourse with her more civilised neighbour, England, and took a delight in cherishing feelings and practices utterly alien to all sound and rational views. I speak of the common people, not of the nobility and gentry, whose minds were in general highly cultivated by education and foreign travel. The same better influences are now at work to improve *the million*; and a new leaven is permeating the old and stagnant body, and raising it to a higher, more refined, and more dignified condition. One remarkable symptom of this spirit of improvement is the strong desire expressed in many quarters for a more seemly celebration of divine worship in the manner of the Church of England. IONA.

UNHISTORICAL (3rd S. vi. 532.)—This word will be found in the dictionaries of Webster and of Worcester. No quotation is given, but *Park* is the authority cited by both. EDWARD VILES.
15, Carlton Road, Kentish Town, N.W.

Miscellaneous.

NOTES ON BOOKS, ETC.

The Music of the most Ancient Nations, particularly of the Assyrians, Egyptians, and Hebrews; with Special Reference to recent Discoveries in Western Asia and in Egypt. By Carl Engel. *With Numerous Illustrations.* (Murray.)

The author of this very curious contribution to the history of music, and who very unnecessarily requests indulgence for disadvantages which he fears he may labour under, in expressing himself in a language which is not his mother tongue, tells us that, having for years taken every opportunity of ascertaining the distinctive characteristics of the music both of civilised and uncivilised nations, he soon saw that the latter was as capable of yielding important suggestions, for the science and history of music, as the languages of savage nations in philological and ethnological inquiries. Being more and more convinced, as he proceeded, that in order to understand clearly the music of various modern nations, it was necessary to extend his researches to the music of ancient nations, he directed his attention to the Assyrian monuments in the British Museum. The facts which Mr. Engel has gathered from these studies form an entirely new addition to the history of music, and are put forth in the present volume, which must find favour with musical antiquaries. It is beautifully illustrated; many of the woodcuts, illustrative of Assyrian and Egyptian music, have been copied from the antiquities in the British Museum; while many of the Egyptian musical instruments are derived from Sir Gardner Wilkinson's well-known work.

Ballads and Songs of Britanny. By Tom Taylor. *Translated from the " Barsaz Breiz" of* Vicomte Hersart de la Villemarque, *with some of the Original Melodies harmonised by* Mrs. Tom Taylor. *With Illustrations by* J. Tisson, J. E. Millais, R.A., J. Tenniel, C. Keene, E. Corbould, *and* H. K. Browne. (Macmillan.)

Who but takes any interest in the study of Folk Lore but knows the *Barsaz Breiz* of Villemarque, and their great value in illustrating the history and connection of popular fictions? These records of the Celtic races of Brittany are of special interest to English antiquaries, and it was with no small pleasure that we heard of Mr. Tom Taylor having undertaken to make them better known to English readers. What he so undertook he has very successfully accomplished; and his version of *Astrou Nann Hag ar Goorigan*—"The Lord Nann and the Fairy"—has all the ring and pathos of an old ballad—of any one of the many similar ballads current throughout Europe. This indeed may be very justly said of all his translations. The book is beautifully got up; and the illustrations are every way worthy of the racy old songs which they are intended to glorify, and of the reputation of the respective artists. We hope Mr. Taylor will be encouraged to give us more of these Ballads of Brittany.

A Selection from the Works of Alfred Tennyson, D.C.L., Poet Laureate. (Moxon.)

This little volume, which is a perfect gem in typography, paper, and ornamentation, is the first of a series of volumes which are about to appear under the title of *Moxon's Miniature Poets.* It contains upwards of sixty of the Laureate's poems. Could such a series be more worthily inaugurated?

Letters from Sir Robert Cecil to Sir George Carew. Edited by John Maclean, F.S.A. (Printed for the Camden Society.)

We must content ourselves with announcing this volume as one of great value for its illustration of the state of Ireland during the time when Carew was Governor of Munster, and of the personal character of Sir Robert Cecil.

The Public Schools Calendar, 1865. Edited by a Graduate of the University of Oxford. (Rivingtons.)

The utility of a Public School Calendar is obvious. We are glad to see that its preparation has been undertaken by one who, knowing the information which would be sought for in such a work, has obtained it from the best sources, namely, the Reports of the Public Schools Commissioners, and in most cases the authorities of the different schools.

The Berlin Society for the Promotion of the Study of Modern Languages offers two prizes to English, French, and German Scholars. The first prize of 100 Fredericks d'or (85*l.*) is for an Essay on Shakspeare's Influence on the Development of the English Language. The essay is expected to contain—1. An account of the stage of the development which poetic diction had attained in England in the period immediately preceding Shakspeare. 2. Illustrations of the progressive development of the language in the works of Shakspeare. 3. An exposition of the relation in which the peculiarities of Shakspeare stand to those of his contemporaries. 4. Illustrations of the influence of Shakspeare on the poetic diction of England. The subject of the second essay, the prize for which is to be 34*l.*, is the History of the Criticism of the Shakspearian Drama among the Germans, as also among the Nations speaking the Romance Languages. The essays may be written in German, French, or English, and are to be forwarded to Professor Herrig, the President of the Society (Neue Friedrichsstrasse, 16, Berlin), on or before July 1, 1866. Each essay is to be accompanied by a sealed letter containing the author's name and address, and superscribed with a motto, which is also to be annexed to the essay.

A very interesting Shakspearian discovery has been made in Germany. A copy of the *Hundred Mery Tales* has been found, which is said to be not only of an earlier date than the edition lately reprinted by Mr. Hazlitt, but also perfect, which unfortunately is not the case with that used by Mr. Hazlitt.

English Philologists will be glad to learn that Mr. Way's valuable edition of the *Promptorium Parvulorum* is all but completed; and that the Third Portion, which concludes the work, will probably be issued to the Members of the Camden Society as one of the books for the subscription of 1864-5.

In England we have journals devoted to the *spelling* as well as to the *reading* public; but they beat us in France. A journal has just been started in Paris under the title of *Le Baby*, "destiné a des abonnés qui la plupart ne savent pas lire."

BOOKS AND ODD VOLUMES
WANTED TO PURCHASE.

Particulars of Price, &c., of the following Books to be sent direct to the gentlemen by whom they are required, and whose names and addresses are given for that purpose:—

Apollinarii Interpartatio Psalmorum, Versibus Heroicis. Parisiis, 1552. 8vo.
Patterson's (Dr. Wm.) Observations on the Climate of Ireland, etc. Dublin, 1801. 8vo.
Procès des Trois Anglais, MM. Wilson, Hutchinson, Bruce, &c. Paris, 1816. 8vo.
Miller's (George, D.D.) Second Letter to the Rev. E. B. Pusey, D.D. London, 1841. 8vo.

Wanted by *Rev. B. H. Blacker*, Rokeby, Blackrock, Dublin.

Rouse's Doctrine of Chances.
Browne's Guide to the Turf.
Denison's Philosophy of the Turf.
Kentfield on Billiards.
Green's Book of the Odds.
Any other Works on the History of the Turf, and the Theory of Chances.

Wanted by *Mr. Henry Moody*, Low Pavement, Nottingham.

Notes and Queries. First Series. Vol. II.
Percy Society Publications. Nos. 1, 5, and 17.
Ossian's Poems. Perth, 1795. Vol. I.
Scottish Antiquarian Society Proceedings. Sm. 4to. Vol. I. Part 1. Vol. III. Parts 2 and 3.
Edinburgh Royal Society Transactions. Vols. III. IV. VI. and VII. Boards.

Wanted by *Mr. Thomas G. Stevenson*, 22, Frederick Street, Edinburgh.

Notices to Correspondents.

THE INDEX to our last volume will be issued with "N. & Q." of Saturday next.

HISTORICUS *will find the information which he desires respecting the title "Reverend" in our* 1st S. vi. p. 245.

CAUTION TO OUR BOOK-BUYING FRIENDS. — *We think it advisable to print the following letter:—*

"Rokeby, Blackrock, Dublin, Jan. 6th, 1865.
"The Rev. B. H. Blacker, presents his compliments to the Editor of " N. & Q." and thinks it well to mention the following particulars:—
"Three or four weeks since a list of books wanted by Mr. B. was kindly inserted by the Editor; and two or three days after a letter came headed ' 53, Drummond St., Euston Square, London,' in which the writer proposed to supply an excellent copy of one of the works—*Liber Munerum Publicorum Hibernici*, &c.—for 11. 5s., and specified a Post Office in the neighbourhood, in case Mr. B. would send an order for the amount. As the writer did not appear to be a regular bookseller, Mr. B. wrote at once to a clerical friend in London, asking him to call on the writer, and to arrange about the payment for, and the transmission of, the books. Mr. B.'s friend went without delay, but could find no such person. The owner of the house stated that many inquiries of the same kind had been made.
"As Mr. B. has reason to think that other Correspondents of ' N. & Q.' have been written to in like manner, he has been induced to trouble the Editor upon the subject."

N. J. H. *The conception of the New Zealander sitting on the ruins of Westminster Bridge was no doubt suggested to Lord Macaulay by the poet Shelley, in a passage which occurs in the dedicatory letter of his poem, Peter Bell the Third to T. Brown*, i. e. *Moore. See "*N. & Q.*" 1st S. ix. 361.

WM. DAVIS. *For the bibliography of Alban Butler's Lives of the Saints, consult "*N. & Q.*" 1st S. ix. 360.

T. T. W. *There is so much that is conjectural in Dr. Borlase's account of the Rock Basins being connected with the sacrifices of the Druids, that our Correspondent must consult the work itself. The only authority quoted by the Doctor in support of his opinion is La Rel. de Gaul.

A. McNIVEN. *Hicks's Hall is on Clerkenwell Green, and is the Sessions House of the County of Middlesex.

R. I. *We cannot find in the British Museum an Eclogue on the marriage of Charles I. by Adam Abernethy. There is one in French (4to. 1627) signed J. D. B., and written as a dialogue between Jacquet, Robin, and Andriot.—Mr. Patmore's dramatic MSS. will not be available for some weeks.

J. C. H. F. *Some remarks on the passage in Milton's* Lycidas (lines 158—163) *occur in "*N. & Q.*" 1st S. vi. 143. — The poem "The spacious firmament on high," is by Addison. Vide our* 1st S. v. 513, 548, 597.

"NOTES AND QUERIES" *is published at noon on Friday, and is also issued in MONTHLY PARTS. The Subscription for* STAMPED COPIES *for Six Months forwarded direct from the Publisher (including the Half-yearly INDEX) is 11s. 4d., which may be paid by Post Office Order, payable at the Strand Post Office, in favour of* WILLIAM G. SMITH, 32, WELLINGTON STREET, STRAND, W.C., *to whom all* COMMUNICATIONS FOR THE EDITOR *should be addressed.*

"NOTES & QUERIES" *is registered for transmission abroad.*

LONDON, SATURDAY, JANUARY 21, 1865.

Notes.

SOBRIQUETS OF REGIMENTS.

Encouraged by the Editor's kindness in giving insertion to "The Regimental Badges," I send a list of the "Sobriquets of Regiments" as given some time since in a country newspaper, with such additions as I have deemed necessary.

Royal Horse Guards—*Oxford Blues.*

First, or King's Dragoon Guards—*The Trades' Union.*

5th Dragoon Guards—*The Green Horse.* So named from their green facings. At the battle of Salamanca, this corps, when in General le Marchant's Brigade, was particularly noted as "The Green Horse."

2nd Dragoons — *Scots Greys*, and *Second to None.* The latter words were for many years on their appointments.

7th Hussars—*The Black Horse,* so called from their Regimental Facings.

8th Hussars—*St. George's,* from their Colonel, Richard St. George, 1740-1755.

11th Hussars—*Cherubims* and *Cherry Pickers,* having had some men taken while on out-post duty in a fruit garden in Spain.

14th Hussars—It is a curious circumstance that the 14th Hussars had very many years ago the name of *Hamilton's Runaways.* In India this was

brought up against them and made much mischief.

On Sept. 20, 1745, the King's troops, under Sir John Cope, confronted the Scottish insurgents near Preston Pans, and the night was passed in the field. The 14th Dragoons, commanded by Lt.-Colonel Wm. Wright, furnished videttes and patrols on the flanks of the army. Before daybreak of Sept. 21, a chosen band of Highlanders advanced through the fog, and attacked the right of the King's troops. Their sudden advance in the dark, their superior numbers, and peculiar mode of fighting, struck with consternation the few men who guarded our artillery, and who faced about and fled. The Dragoons advanced to charge the Highlanders; but seeing the very superior numbers of their opponents, and being discouraged by the loss of their artillery, they made but a feeble effort to stem the torrent of battle, and afterwards retired from the field. Several officers, and a few private soldiers, however, behaved with great gallantry, and among others, Major Richard Bowles, 14th Dragoons, particularly distinguished himself; the few troopers who rallied round him had been cut down and his own horse killed; but he continued to fight on foot: he was surrounded, and had received eleven wounds, when a rebel leader interposed, and saved his life." (Cannon's *Record of the Fourteenth Dragoons,* page 6.) Thus it will be seen that only a part of this gallant regiment was engaged on this disastrous occasion; and it is most unfair to stigmatise a glorious regiment as cowards because a small portion of the corps was surprised and overpowered in a fog in the Highlands, before the break of day. There is not a braver or more justly honoured regiment in the British army than the 14th Hussars.

17th Lancers—*Bingham's Dandies.* The Earl of Lucan, when Lord Bingham, was Lieutenant-Colonel of this corps, which was remarkable for the well-fitting uniforms both of the officers and men of the corps.

Grenadier Guards—*The Sand Bags.* "Sand Bags" is the designation of all Grenadiers, and, *par excellence,* of the Grenadier Guards.

1st Foot—*Pontius Pilate's Body Guard.* From a fictitious anecdote of a dispute between Le Regiment de Douglas (now our 1st Foot) in the French service, and the Picardy Regiment, in 1637, as to the antiquity of the Corps; the Regiment of Picardy claimed to have been on duty the night of the Crucifixion, to which Douglas's Regiment rejoined, that "had *they* been on guard, they would not have slept on their post."

2nd—*Kirke's Lambs.* From having on their colours the "Paschal Lamb," granted for having been a guard of honour to the queen of Charles II. on her progress to London, and from having been commanded by Colonel Piercy Kirke from April, 1682, to Oct. 1691; it is said that this regiment was employed in enforcing the cruelties devised by the infamous Judge Jeffries, who died in April, 1689; hence (referring to the colours of the Regiment) the ironical title of "Kirke's Lambs."— See Cannon's *History of the 2nd Foot.* And *Sleepy Queen's.* At Almeida, by their carelessness, Gen. Brennier effected his escape (after blowing up his works) by Barba del Puerco, May 10, 1811.

3rd—*The Nutcrackers* and *The Resurrectionists.* Obtained at Albuera, where the regiment was dispersed by the Polish Lancers, and reappeared shortly after. An officer present at a conversation, among officers of various corps, respecting regimental mottos, on hearing some one ask what motto was borne by the "Buffs," and learning that none appeared, at least in the "Army List," he suggested that the 85th, which bore "aucto splendore resurgo," might present the Buffs with "resurgo," as appropriate to the corps, and retain the "aucto splendore" for itself. The officer was called out for his wit by a captain of the Buffs, but a sensible second made up the matter without a duel. These *sobriquets* were undeserved. "The Buffs" is a gallant veteran regiment, bearing on its colours the names of ten general engagements where it covered itself with glory. The corps *has* a well-deserved motto — "Veteri frondescit honore."

4th Foot—*Barrell's Blues,* from William Barrell, Colonel of the regiment from August, 1734, to August, 1749.

5th—*The Fighting Fifth.* Although no regiment in the British Army could better deserve the appellation of "The Fighting Regiment" than the gallant "Fifth," still it is well-known that this designation was justly conferred on the "Fifth Division" during the Peninsular War, and not on any particular corps. In fact, where every British regiment behaved itself nobly in face of the enemy at all times, it would be alike invidious and unjust to designate any single regiment as "The Fighting Corps."

6th—*The Saucy Sixth,* or *The Warwickshire Lads,* or *Guise's Geese.* Alliteration is the cause of two of these *sobriquets.* "Saucy Sixth," is one; "Guise's Geese," another. Colonel John Guise (pronounced "Gees") was Colonel of this distinguished corps from November 1, 1738, to the period of his death in June 1765.

9th—*The Holy Boys,* from their selling their Bibles, for drink, in the Peninsula, and passion for sacking Convents.

10th—*The Springers.* So called from their readiness for action, whenever their services were required—a character which the corps will, we are certain, always deserve This title has also been given to the 62nd Regiment.

11th—Was styled "bloody," from being nearly annihilated in action on several occasions, owing to its distinguished bravery; witness Alamanza, Fontenoy, Roucoux, Ostend, and Salamanca.

14th—*The Old and Bold,* and *Calvert's Entire* (having had three battalions kept up, for the good of the then Adjutant-General, Sir Harry Calvert, their Colonel, from February 8th, 1806, to the date of his sudden death, September 3, 1826. The family name is now changed to "Verney."

17th—*The Bengal Tigers,* from the badge on the regimental colours. As the badge here referred to happens to represent a *green* tiger, I leave it to persons more experienced in Indian affairs than I can boast of being, to decide where a green tiger has been discovered in the Bengalee Presidency.

19th—*The Green Howards.* Styled "The *Green* Howards" (or "Howard's Garbage"), in order to distinguish it from the 24th regiment, known at that time as "Howard's Greens;" the Hon. Charles Howard being Colonel of the 19th Regiment from Nov. 1738 to March 1748, and Thomas Howard being Colonel of the 24th Regiment about the same period, viz., from September 1717, to June 1737.

20th—*The Two Tens* and *The Minden Boys,* and *Kingsley's Stand*; the last-named honorable title was given to the regiment in consideration of its conspicuous bravery at Minden, August 1, 1759, where it repulsed every charge of the enemy. It formed part of the brigade commanded on that occasion by Major-General Wm. Kingsley, who was Colonel of this distinguished regiment from April 9, 1746, to the period of his decease in October, 1769.   JUVERNA.

(*To be concluded in our next.*)

JOHN RICHARDSON.

In the recent biographical sketch of the life of this esteemed gentleman, in the *North British Review* for November, it is asserted that, in 1811, he married Miss Elizabeth Hill, a *cousin* of the author of *The Pleasures of Hope.* That the poet may have been connected with the young lady is possible enough; but it must have been through her mother, for it could not have been through her father.

Miss Hill was the only surviving daughter of Lawrence Hill, Esq., Writer to the Signet in Edinburgh. Her brother, Lawrence Hill, Esq., of Barlanark, is still living; but has, it is understood now retired from business. Their parent, a man of great energy and talent, about the end of last and commencement of this century, managed the Whig interest in North Britain. At that time the voters for Members of Parliament held their feudal estate directly of the crown or prince; and although not so numerous as since the alteration of the franchise, still collectively through Scotland, they presented a pretty formidable front. Now this indefatigable gentleman had what was ordinarily designated in his office as "the book," or the "books,"—mysterious volumes, carefully excluded from the prying eyes of the clerks; but which contained a regular list of the voters, from one end of the northern kingdom to the other, with their political predilections; and suggesting means, or inducements, by which their votes might be influenced. What became of these singular volumes—for I have always understood there were many of them—I have never been able to trace; but it is most probable, they ultimately were consigned to the purchasers of waste paper: for when the business, which had been continued by his brother Robert, was finally given up, boxes of papers and books, with which the place of business were literally crammed, were disposed of in this way. Mr. Lawrence Hill had also been engaged in the great contest between the sixteen peers at the end of last century; and had collected and bound up his searches into the pedigrees of those interested in a great number of volumes. These were kept perhaps by the family, as they were not included in the catalogue of Mr. Robert Hill's books which were sold by auction.

Mr. Lawrence Hill died prematurely in the beginning of the present century, at a time when there was every prospect of his making a large fortune: for, unlike many of his profession now-a-days, he was a careful and industrious man. His demise was deeply regretted by all who knew him; and it may be added, that his daughter was not a tocherless bride.   J. M.

Shakspeariana.

"Hamlet," Act III. Sc. 2 (Quarto, 1604).—

> "For thou doost know, oh Damon deere,
> This Realme dismantled was
> Of Joue himselfe, and now raignes heere
> A very very paiock."

If one of the commentators had showed himself *contented* with the different readings (paiock, paiocke, pajock, paddock, peacock, bajocco), I would not add a new word to the rather sufficient number; but since the question is yet an open one, a new combination will not be out of place.

What I give is only a possibility, without the least support of an authoritative character, and I would not even mind it if one of the other readings would "suit the word to the action."

Hamlet means "ass," and does not intend to weaken what he means by supplying it by such an innocent word as "peacock," "paddock," &c. He says, "A very, very . . . . .," and then he says *nothing more*, but *hems* only in a rather characteristic way; and so gives to the hearer the opportunity to supply by rhyming what he has left unsaid.

And so I suppose the word in question did not belong to the verse, but was a stage direction, which I should like to understand as — "hiccup" (hiccough.)

"A very, very . . . . [hiccups."
    F. A. Leo.
4, Hafenplatz, Berlin.

The Hundred Merry Tales.—I am happily able to lay before the readers of "N. & Q." a few further particulars of the recently discovered copy of this curious Shakspearian volume. It was found in the Royal Library at Gottingen, and consists of twenty-eight leaves in folio, of which, however, only twenty-six are numbered, the title-page and the last of the tales being without numbers. It contains four tales more than are to be found in the later editions.

On the back of the last leaf there is the following colophon: —

> " § Thus endeth the booke of a. C. mery
> talys. Empryntyd at London at the sygne of
>   the Merymayd At Fowlys gate next
>   to chepe syde. § The yere
>   of our Lorde. M. v. C.
>   . XXVI. § The . XXII.
>   day of Noveber.
>
> Johannes Rastell.
>
>   § Cum priuilegio
>   Regali."

The name of John Rastell forms a portion of his woodcut device (which is copied in Mr. Hazlitt's reprint).

I am glad to add that this earliest edition of the " C. Mery Tales," is about to be reprinted under the editorship of Dr. H. Oesterley.
    T. H. M.

" Stung like a Tench " (3rd S. vi. 324.) — In the revised issue of the Pictorial Edition of the *Works of Shakspeare*, edited by Charles Knight, I find the following note on this subject: —

" The second carrier appears to have had some popular knowledge of the natural history of fishes. The tench which is stung, and the loach which breeds fleas, appear to be allusions to the fact that fish at particular seasons are infested with vermin. The particular charge against fleas of troubling fish as they do lodgers ' within victualling houses and inns,' is gravely set forth in Philemon Holland's translation of Pliny " (vol. i. of " Historical Plays," p. 196).

The above does not appear to me to be a very satisfactory explanation; but perhaps a reference to Pliny might throw further light on the subject.
    H. Fishwick.

Passage in Macbeth: " Blanket of the Dark." — It has occurred to me that the much-vexed question of the meaning of the expression used by Lady Macbeth in her speech after reading her husband's letter—" . . . nor heaven peep through the *blanket* of the dark," &c.—might be set at rest by substituting *blankest* for *blanket.* I believe that the *s* was omitted through the carelessness of a transcriber, or an error of the press. The word *blankest* conveys the idea of the most intense darkness, is a word such as Shakspeare would use, and adds to the power of the passage. The correction is a very simple one, and does away with all necessity for ingenious speculations upon the unhappy *blanket.*

JOHN JESSOPP,
Chaplain of Surrey County Gaol.

[This suggestion has never, We believe, been made. Coleridge proposed *blank height.* Mr. Collier's MS. Corrector, *blankness.*—ED. "N. & Q."]

LINE IN HAMLET: "HE IS FAT AND SCANT OF BREATH."—In these days of Shakspeare-worship, every line the poet ever wrote, good, bad, and indifferent, is undergoing such rigid scrutiny, that one hardly dares to propose the most trifling verbal emendation, for fear of suggesting something which has been already published. I would, therefore, humbly deprecate the wrath of critics, while noticing the line in *Hamlet,* where the Queen says of her son, " He is fat, and scant of breath."

Commentators have been struck with this ludicrous description of one who is elsewhere spoken of as " the glass of fashion, and the mould of form," and they have got up a very improbable story about a certain corpulent performer who used to act the part of Hamlet. Can we suppose that Shakspeare was so short-sighted as to have written his plays with an especial eye to the bodily peculiarities of his contemporaries?

May not "fat" be a misprint for *faint?* If the latter word were written in the original MS. in the contracted form of *fait,* with a stroke above the letters, the mistake might easily occur.

Have I been anticipated in this suggestion?

J. DIXON.

[Mr. Dixon's proposed emendation is not, we think, to be found in any commentator.—ED. " N. & Q."]

TYPE MNEMONICS.

Last St. Valentine's week the New York correspondent of *The Standard* sent over for the amusement of his readers here the following score of " typographical symbols." He copied it from the pages of the Philadelphian *Advertiser*—a paper which contains typefounder's advertisements of all sorts. As it is ingeniously arranged, and many of the associations cleverly hit off, I think it should have a niche in "N. & Q." Some of these types are essentially American however! —

" The type of a Glazier should be *Diamond.*
The type of an Oyster should be *Pearl.*
The type of a Jeweller should be *Agate.*
The type of an Honest Man should be *Nonpareil.*
The type of a Citizen should be *Bourgeois.*
The type of a Schoolmaster should be *Primer.*
The type of a Bull should be *English.*
The type of Freedom should be *Columbian.*
The type of a Maiden should be *Paragon.*
The type of a Mother should be *Double Paragon.*
The type of a Soldier should be *Canon.*
The type of an Author should be *Script.*
The type of a Preacher should be *Text.*
The type of Aristocracy should be *Title.*
The type of a Baby should be *Small Caps.*
The type of a Hussy should be *Boldface.*
The type of an Alderman should be *Extended.*
The type of a Drunkard should be *Backslope.*
The type of a Barber should be *Hairline.*
The type of our Foundry should be *Excelsior.*"

With a view of making the series more complete, I have added a score of lines embracing some of our more common English founts. I believe even a couple of readings of the two will benefit many of your readers, who have hitherto been unable to master the trade names of our typefounders and printers. The *Memoria technica* here used will not help one to the relative sizes of the types, but that is soon learnt afterwards :—

The type of a Book-keeper should be *Contra.*
The type of an Artist should be *Ornamental.*
The type of a Ploughboy should be *Rustic.*
The type of a Servant should be *Minion.*
The type of a Clown should be *Grotesque.*
The type of a Freemason should be *Relief.*
The type of a Mummy should be *Egyptian.*
The type of a Painter should be *Perspective.*
The type of an Engraver, should be *Outline.*
The type of a Beadle should be *Church.*
The type of an Antiquary should be *Grecian.*
The type of a Penny-a-liner should be *Condensed.*
The type of a Wineseller should be *Body.*
The type of a Poet should be *Elizabethan.*
The type of a Fool should be *Reversed.*
The type of a Gentleman should be *Open.*
The type of a Tomb-writer should be *Skeleton.*
The type of a Roman should be *Italic.*
The type of a Lady's lips should be *Ruby.*
The type of Notes and Queries should be *Brilliant.*

W. E.

"BIBLIOTHECA HIBERNICA." — Being engaged in compiling a "Bibliotheca Hibernica" on a very comprehensive scale, on which work I have been occupied many years, I would feel very much obliged to any of your readers for notices of rare books, pamphlets, broad-sheets, &c., written by Irishmen; or of works published in that country on any subject. Also, for notices of works by Irishmen, or relating to Ireland, published abroad. Biographical notices of authors, and bibliographical notes of their works, will be also very acceptable, and thankfully received by

JOHN POWER.

3, Grove Terrace, St. John's Wood, N.W. .

THE OGILVIES OF BANFF AND FINDLATER.—
There can be no doubt that, at least as regards the
Barony of Banff, the patent extends to the next
heir-male; and the only question is, who that
heir-male may be ?   .

The writer of this note has in his possession the
original case for the late Baronet in MS.; which
would have been lodged, had the further prosecution of the claim, in the absence of sufficient pecuniary means, been considered advisable.

The earldom of Findlater went in a different
line; and it is believed, in consequence of a second
patent, that this peerage may not be extinct.

The father of the baronet took both the titles
of Earl of Findlater and Baron of Banff. He
procured a loan in London to enable him to prosecute his claims; but in place of applying it for
that purpose, he threw it away, and lost the opportunity of putting himself on a proper footing
in the House of Lords. He died in absolute
penury.   J. M.

CUDDY: MAN, BIRD, AND BEAST.—In the north
of England, where Cuthbert is a tolerably common
Christian name, it is familiarly abbreviated to
"Cuddy." Perhaps the most illustrious possessor
of the name in modern times was the grand old
admiral, Cuthbert, Lord Collingwood, who was
affectionately known in the navy as "Old Cuddie."
Now we know that "Neddy" or "Edward"
(teste Dickens in Our Mutual Friend), is, in the
midland and southern counties, the popular name
for a donkey—or, rather, for an ass : for the word
"donkey" is not to be found in a dictionary, unless it be that of Mr. Hotten. Why an ass should
be called "Edward" or "Neddy," appears to be a
query equally as hard to be satisfactorily answered as the inquiry that I now make : Why
should an ass be called Cuddy? for, in northern
counties, "Cuddy the ass" is a household word.

    " Hast got thy breakfast, brother Cuddy ? "

is the first line of "The Address to an Ass," in
David Wingate's Poems (1862). And yet, although "cuddy" is an ass in Northumberland and
the North Country, yet, in Yorkshire, "cuddy"
appears as a hedge-sparrow (the "cuddy" or
"cuddy hedge-creeper"); and elsewhere, "cuddy"
becomes a moor-hen. I am not aware if the
"St. Cuthbert's ducks," that visit the Northumbrian seaboard, are ever called "cuddies;" but
the above-mentioned widespread application of
the familiar word "cuddy" to man, bird, and
beast, seems to me somewhat remarkable.

                                 CUTHBERT BEDE.

TACQUET'S "ARITHMETIC."—The first edition
of this book appears to be Lovanii, 1656. There
is an edition of Antv., 1665; again, 1680, 1682,
1683, 1704, and Naples, 1732; and, lastly, Venice

1740. . The "Cylindricorum" (lib. iv.) was Antwerp, 1651; and "Liber Quintus" added 1659.
I cannot find anything of 1655, as given in Cyclopædia of Biography, article "Tacquet."
                                           W. DAVIS.

LAURENCE STERNE.

It is stated, both by Sir Walter Scott and by
Mr. Fitzgerald in his Life of Sterne (vol. i. p. 188),
that the illustrations to Wodhull's Poems—bearing in the corner the name of "L. Stern del.
Romæ "—were designed by the author of Tristram Shandy. Some confirmation of this statement would be very satisfactory. If the sketches
were really drawn by Sterne, it must have been
when he was at Rome, in the spring of 1766.
Where was Mr. Wodhull at that time ? What
authority is there for supposing that he ever was—
as Mr. Fitzgerald styles him—a friend of Sterne's?
I am not aware that any Life of Mr. Wodhull has
ever been published. But have none of his papers
been preserved at Thenford? If they have, I
should think they could hardly fail to clear up
these points.* If it could be ascertained, that in
the year 1766 Sterne really employed his pencil
in drawing illustrations, the question naturally
suggests itself: How came it that he drew none
for any of his own works? The two frontispieces
to Tristram Shandy were by Hogarth. What
then were the relations between Sterne and Hogarth? This is a point that is of more interest
than may be at first apparent. The portrait of
Mrs. Sterne, signed "Pigrich, f."—to which I
drew the attention of your readers in a former
communication (2nd S. xii. 369)—would, as I conceive, require no further authentication if the
artist could be identified. In character of execution, the sketch of Mrs. Sterne is very like Hogarth's "Politician." Is it possible that, under
the assumed name of Pigrich, Hogarth may lurk
in disguise? The conjecture derives confirmation
from a comparison of the signature with those
annexed to some of Hogarth's etchings. The
similarity in the character of the letters is striking,
and such as in my mind to leave little doubt upon
the point.

One word more respecting the Wodhull illustrations : —

  " Dr. Johnson told Sir John Hawkins that on the only
occasion he had been in Sterne's society, the latter (i. e.
Sterne) had exhibited a very indecent print."

  [* May not the artist have been Lewis Stern, a Roman
painter, born in 1708, and died in 1777 ? He painted
game and other birds, flowers, fruit, and scriptural subjects, in admirable style. Wodhull's three illustrated
poems, although not published until 1772, are dated 1760
and 1762.—ED.]

In commenting on this statement (vol. ii. p. 393), Mr. Fitzgerald says: —

"Even one of the pictures with which Sterne illustrated his friend Woodhall's (sic) Poems—conceived as it was in a classical taste — might deserve Johnson's severe censure."

I have looked through the three illustrations from first to last, and back again from last to first, and as Mr. Fitzgerald is a contributor to "N. & Q.," I hope he will have no objection to state which of the three he alludes to in the passage that I have quoted.   P. S. C.

JACOBITE SONG.

Can any of your readers give a more correct version of the accompanying song? I copied it from the dictation of a friend many years ago, and have never met with it in print. There is another verse as my friend sang it; but as the whole of the stanzas relate to the 1745 rebellion, and this verse mentions the names of those who figured in the former rebellion of 1715, I give it separate: —

" The Earl of Mar rode in the front,
    With the Lords Kilmarnock and the brave Glengarry,
    Glen Grigor, Glen Gyle, and the brave Lochiel,
    Fought manfully to keep the Plaidie."

I shall be glad to receive any further information.

" THE TARTAN PLAIDIE.

" Our brave young Prince rode through the North,
    With the manly looks of a Highland Laddie;
  Gart* a' our Scottish hearts for to warm,
    And to love the lad wi' the Tartan Plaidie.
" Its when we came to bonnie Aberdeen,
    Where ilka ane was making ready,
  For to overthrow our brave young Prince,
    And to catch the lad wi' the Tartan Plaidie.
" When Geordie heard the news was come,
    And he was come to heir his daddie,
  He says ' I'll give you the plunder of bonnie Edinbro',
    If you'll catch the lad wi' the Tartan Plaidie.'
" Then Charlie said to encourage his men,
    ' Your hearts of gold be true and steady;
  If you this day will fight for me,
    I'll make you a nation free, and keep the Plaidie.'.
" We were a' drawn up at Preston Pans,
    Where mony a babbie lost its daddie;
  We made them to fly like the wind in the sky,
    Every shake that we gave the Tartan Plaidie.
" We all fought on with might and main,
    Regarding neither man nor bodie;
  Our brave young Prince rode on the right,
    For he thought it no shame to wear the Plaidie.
" There were feather beds and carpeted rooms,
    They could na please a Hanover Geordie;
  But a far better Prince than ever he was,
    Could lie on the ground wi' his Tartan Plaidie."
               JAMES GIBSON.

23, Spring Gardens, Bradford.

* I am not sure whether this is the correct spelling for the Scotch word gart, or gar'd; it means in English made, only more expressive in Scotch.

AZIZA: AZAZEL. — Captain Burton describes a fabulous inhabitant of the woods in Dahome in these terms: —

" The Aziza, for instance, is a sylvan beast—erect, man-like, and loud-voiced: it teaches the hunter fetish, and makes him wondrous brave."—A Mission to the King of Dahome, vol. ii. p. 296.

To me the passage at once suggests the Azazel of Leviticus xvi. 8. Aziza is a supernatural being in the mythology of the Dahomans, and the scape-goat has been considered by some as a sacrifice to the Devil, under the name of Azazel. In fact, no one knows what Azazel means. It can do no harm to ventilate the question.   A. B.

COCKADES.—Wanted, some information on the subject of the origin of cockades: —
1. When were they first used?
2. Is there any duty payable on the use of them?
3. What regulates the pattern for individual use?
4. To what books can I refer, or to whom apply, to find an ultimate authority on the subject?
5. What is the correct manner of discovering the diplomatic cockade suitable for, or belonging to, any given county?
6. Is the Heralds' College a likely place to obtain information?*
     ROBT. W. ARTHUR GORDON-JERNINGHAM.
5, Belgrave Square.

CORONETS.—Will any correspondent state the period when coronets were first adopted to denote different ranks in the peerage? For a long time fancy coronets were worn.   HISTORICUS.

FITZWARYN, WILTS AND DORSET.—I am desirous of proving the descent of the Fitzwaryns of Wilts and Dorset from the baronial house of Whittington; but have not met with anything to help me in the British Museum, or elsewhere. As there is no pedigree of this branch in any published work or MS., I append a short sketch.

Nicholas Fitzwaryn and Agnes his wife, occur 12 Edw. III.; Sir William Fitzwaryn (his son), and Matilda his wife, 21 & 23 Edw. III. " Magister Peter Fitzwaryn" (brother of this William), and a Reginald Fitzwaryn and Margery his wife; deeds of all these parties concerning lands in Bratton, &c., are recited in the Cartulary of Edington (Brit. Mus.) Sir Philip Fitzwaryn (probably son of Sir William), and Constance his wife, also occur 1360. Harl. MS. 5184 (fol. 1.) says he was "borne at Bratton by Edynton," and Constance his wife was cousin of Bishop Wyvill, widow (1.) of Sir Henry Percy, Kut., of Great

[* Several articles on the origin and use of the cockade appeared in our 1st S. iii. 7, 42, 71, 196, 293; vii. 329, 434, 618; xi. 186, 231; and for those in servants' hats, 2nd S. vols. vii. viii. ix.—ED.]

Chalfield, who left her a life interest in his estates; and (2.) of John Percekay, of Little Chalfield, Esq. By Sir Philip she had two daughters and co-heirs: Isolda, wife of John Rous, lord of a moiety of the manor of Immer; and Joan, wife of Thomas Bewshin of Cotels Atworth, co. Wilts, and Bewshyns-hayes, co. Dorset. In 1404, Sir Philip was not only dead, but his wife, the widow of a fourth husband, Sir Henry de la Ryver, Knt.; and she presented to the living of Great Chalfield in 1419, about which time she must have died very aged. This clears up the confusion of the account of the manors of Folke and Upcerne in Gough's Hutchins's *Dorset*, where for Philip *Fitzpayne*, should be read *Fitzwaryn*. William Rous, Esq., son and heir of John Rous and Isolda, conveyed his moiety of the manor of Folke to Walter, Lord Hungerford, by fine, 16 Hen. VI. Ralph Bushe, who held the manor of Upcerne of Walter Hungerford and Thos. Bewshyn, was the second husband of Alianor, daughter and heiress of Ivo Fitzwaryn. Sir William Fitzwaryn, the father of Ivo, was a baron by writ, and styled "le frère;" from which, we may presume, he had another and elder brother of the same name. This brother was, doubtless, Sir William, the father of Sir Philip. According to a MS., *penes* Sir Tho. Phillipps, transcribed in *Coll. Top. et Gen.* (i. 247), the baron had "John, Philip, Eve (Ivo?), and Johanna, wiff of Edmund Cheney."
Brompton.   A. S. ELLIS.

GARRICK AND DR. HILL.—I have a letter, dated March 20, 1759, from Garrick to Dr. Hawkesworth, in which he says, referring to the notorious Dr. Hill:—

"Such a villain sure never existed: his scheme now is abuse, and he talks of a paper call'd yᵉ *Theatre*, in which his Pen will be as free as my crabstick whenever I meet his worship."

Did Hill ever carry out his threat of publishing *The Theatre?*   BEARLEY.

GOODWYN OF BLACKHEATH. — It is well known that this gentleman left at his death an enormous mass of arithmetical calculations, which were purchased by the Royal Society. I call the attention of the members of the Decimal Association that Mr. Goodwyn says he was not a *decimalist*, though engaged in calculation, and on the very subject of the comparison of the yard and metre. Goodwyn published a Centenary Table in 4to, which is in the Museum fortunately; and an 8vo tract on *Circulators* as far as 1000, which is not. Now, at the end of Gauss's *Disq. Arithmet.*, there is a similar table as far as 100; and Gauss says that he has himself carried this particular matter as far as 1000. Now, can any of your readers connect in any way the labours of Gauss and Goodwyn? It would have saved the more learned of these mathematicians a good deal of labour, had

he known of the work of the latter, and they were working contemporaneously. Again, it is a well known problem of the higher arithmetic to detect whether a given number is prime or not; and Gauss, after Euler, has given two solutions of the problem. And on this matter, Mr. Goodwyn also has furnished some criteria.   WM. DAVIS.

HACKNEY HORSES: AFFRI. —Much has been said of the antiquity of the term *hackney*. The following is extracted from the "Status Domus" of Jarrow Monastery, anno 1313, in vol. xxix. of the Surtees Society's publications, p. 11:—

"¶ Item in stabulo sunt ij palefridi, de domo Dunolm, et j hakenay."

And in p. 15, anno 1326—

"In stabulo j equus pro monachis, j hakenney, iiij affri pro carectis."

What English word shall be used for *affri?*
                                             J. M. ON.

HAMILTON'S "GAZETTEER OF INDIA."—Can any one of your readers give me any particulars about the author of the above work, or his family, or the addresses of any of them?   K. M. N.

"HODEGUS CONFUTED," ETC. — Can you oblige me with the name of the author of an octavo pamphlet, published in reply to Mr. Toland, and entitled *Hodegus Confuted, &c.*, London, 1721?
                                             ABHBA.

OLD ALMANAC. — This is one of that rare and interesting class of books: English books printed abroad — *Almynack and Pronosticatio* of Gaspar Laet the younger, for 1530, printed at Antwerpe. It is on a large single sheet:—

"The declaratiō of this Almynack. The Golden Number XI. Iniitio iii. The cicle of the Sunne XXVII. The Sunday letter B. Moreover ye shall finde, after oure old custum, upon what Day that the Sun changed her Syne. And also what sine and degree that the Mone is from day to day *at none*. Ye shall also find the newe Mone and full Mone, with her quarters written all along uppon what day, houre, and minute that they shall be, with *her* effectes. This yere we shall have an Eclipse of the Sun, which shall be the 29 day of March, 6 hours and 49ᵐ before none. And the beginning shall be uppon the same day 5ʰ and 51ᵐ, the end thereof the 7ᵗʰ hour and 47ᵐ before none. We shall likewise have an Eclipse of the Mone 6 October, 12ʰ 6ᵐ after none: *begins* 6ʰ 14ᵐ after none, *ends* 7ᵗʰ day 1ʰ 54ᵐ before none."

After describing the meaning of the various columns in the Almanac, he says: "ye shall find the number of dayes of every month, with the correspondant to the same number." Will any of your learned readers tell me what is a "correspondant?"   WM. DAVIS.

PISCIS FLOTANS. — Among the Records in the custody of the Master of the Rolls is an inquisition of the 32nd year of the reign of King Henry III., setting forth the ancient customs of the island of Guernsey and the laws instituted by King John.

In the latter part of the inquisition the following passage occurs : —

"Constitutum similiter fuit quòd omne batellum dictæ Insulæ portans *piscem flotantem* in Normanniam pro quolibet turno daret duodecem solidos."

What was *piscis flotans?*   P. S. C.

"PLAIN SERMONS BY CONTRIBUTORS TO TRACTS FOR THE TIMES." — In vol. x. of the above work, there is an appendix which states that the Sermons were contributed by seven writers in various proportions : A. was, I believe, John Keble ; B., Isaac Williams ; C., Dr. Pusey ; D., J. H. Newman ; E., Thomas Keble. Can any of your correspondents tell me who F. and G. were ? Was F. Dr. Manning ?   GAMMA.

QUOTATIONS. — Where can I find the following lines, quoted by Tennyson in his "Sea Dreams," a poem included in the same volume with *Enoch Arden* (p. 106) ? —

" With all his conscience and one eye askew,
  So false, he partly took himself for true ;
  Whose pious talk, when most his heart was dry,
  Made wet the crafty crowsfoot round his eye."
    [And eleven following lines.]

Also, who is the author of a beautiful hymn, beginning thus ? —

" In the hour of trial,
    Jesus, pray for me ;
  Lest, by base denial,
    I depart from thee," &c.

It is to be found at length in Mercer's Hymn-book, No. 265.   T. J. G.

Can any of your correspondents tell me where the following beautiful lines occur ? —

" I never see a castle old,
    Which time has changed to iron grey,
  Whose high crenelles o'ergrown with mould,
    Are crumbling silently away,
  But comes the thought that years before,
    Now hid by Time's obscuring pall,
  Some tiny foot hath tripped the floor,
    Some silver voice hath filled the hall."

In what song, which I lately heard sung, do the following lines occur ? —

" O why wer'n't you cunning, O why wer'n't you 'cute ?
  Why didn't you run away from the Frenchman's shoot ?
  O how did it happen, at all and at all,
  That you didn't run away from the big cannon ball ?
  An open war I will proclaim,
  Against Bonaparte and the King of Spain :
  And dearly I'll make them to rue the time,
  That they shot away the shins of a son of mine."
                     GAMMA.

" Ocean of Time ! thy waters of deep woe,
  Are brackish with the salt of human tears."
                     A. H.
Digby.

" When just as the clock on the turret struck one,
  He jumps up and cries, 'There, you Devil, you're
    done !' "
                     J. H.

THOMAS GEORGE STREET was author of —
1. "Aura, or, the Slave ; a Poem in Two Cantos. 4to. London, 1788."
2. " The History and Reign of Louis XVI., King of France. London. 8vo. 1795." [One volume only published.]
3. " Vindication of the Duke of Bedford's Attack on Mr. Burke's Pension, in reply to a Letter from Edmund Burke to a Noble Lord. London. 8vo. 1796."

In the *Biographical Dictionary of Living Authors*, 1816, he is termed one of the proprietors of *The Courier* newspaper. Dr. Parr made the following note on Street's *History of the Reign of Louis XVI.* : —

" The 2nd and 3rd vols. were never published. Street, after being a republican, became an apostate ; and by defending the opinions he formerly opposed, he made a large fortune,"—*Bibliotheca Parriana*, 388.

Street, proprietor and editor of *The Courier*, 1799—1822, is mentioned in Mr. Alexander Andrews's *History of British Journalism* (ii. 3, 63, 64, 113), but in the Index he is called *James* Street.

According to Mr. Jerdan (*Autobiography*, i. 92), Street, who had led a sumptuous and gay life, ultimately died in poverty ; the date or place of his death being unknown to those his former bounty fed. It is perhaps, therefore, hardly probable that the date of his death can now be recovered ; but should any of your correspondents be able to give information on the subject, I shall be obliged.   S. Y. R.

SWEDISH AUTHORS. — 1. Hans Olffsen, author of *The Three Wise Men*, a drama, 1635. Is anything known of this author's history ?
2. Prytz, Bishop of Linkoping, about 1650—1660, a Swedish dramatist. What are the titles of his dramas ?
3. Hjarn, Beronius, Kolmodin, Wellander : these four Swedish dramatists belong to the middle, or end of the seventeenth century. I would like to know the titles of their dramatic works, or any particulars regarding the authors.
4. *King Lear*, a tragedy ; translated from Shakspeare, 1818, Upsala, Anon. *The Tempest ;* translated from Shakspeare ; Stockholm, 1836. Anon. Who are the authors of these translations ?
                     R. I.

TRANSLATIONS OF VIRGIL. — Will MR. DAVIES, or any other correspondent of " N. & Q.," kindly give me the date of the publication of Miller's translation of Virgil ; accompanied with a reference to any critiques on the same which may have appeared in papers, reviews, or magazines ? Also the date and general description of a version of Virgil, formed upon the same principle as Mr. Ring's, and published, if I recollect rightly, in Edinburgh some thirty years ago ; with the publishers' names of both works ?   W. J. B.

Queries with Answers.

WHO WAS HE ?—In Trapp, the Puritan's *Commentary on 1 Peter*, iii. 20, he commemorates —

"The Prior of St. Bartholomew's in London, who upon a vain prediction of an idle astrologer, went and built him a house at Harrow-on-the-Hill, to secure himself from a supposed flood, foretold by the astrologer."

Has the name of this worthy descended to posterity ?
X. Y. Z.

[An amusing story is related by Hall and Speed, but doubted by the worthy John Stow, of William Bolton, Prior of St. Bartholomew, who on the 23rd of September, 1522, succeeded Cuthbert Tonstal as Rector of Harrow. It is related that Prior Bolton, with all the brethren of the priory, with wagons full of provisions as well as boats, fled to a house built by the Prior at Harrow, that being the highest ground in Middlesex, for the purpose of obtaining an asylum during the prevalence of a great flood, which was expected to happen in the year 1524. This story was probably fabricated at the time, as a joke on the presumed credulity of cloistered ecclesiastics, though gravely repeated by several chroniclers. The relators of it do not seem to have been aware, that Prior Bolton, who was a great builder, had the rectory of Harrow as early as 1522, and was very likely to rebuild the parsonage-house, called by Stow a *dove-house*, whether a flood was prognosticated or not.

Stow informs us that William Bolton "builded of new the manor of Canonbury at Islington, which belonged to the canons of St. Bartholomew ;" and the old brick tower which still remains was doubtless erected by him, as his rebus (a bolt in a tun) was some years ago visible in several parts of the wall * originally connected with the tower, and which is evidently of the same materials and workmanship. The priory of St. Bartholomew, also, and the parish church adjoining (now about to be restored) with the lodgings belonging to the priory, were all either rebuilt or completely repaired by him. Camden, in his *Remaines*, remarks, "It may seeme doubtfull whether Bolton was wiser when he invented for his name a bird-bolte through a tunne, or when he built him an house upon Harrow-hill, for feare of an inundation after a great conjunction of planets in the watery triplicate." Bolton, who luckily escaped the predominance of Aquarius, died at his parsonage at Harrow on April 15, 1532, and was there interred. Both Stow and Weever mistake in calling him the last prior of St. Bartholomew's; for it appears, he had a successor, Robert Fuller, abbot of Waltham Holy Cross, who was elected in 1532, and held the priory with his abbacy.] .

GEORGE MORE.—There was printed at London, 1629, small quarto,—

, " Principles for Yong Princes collected out of Sundry Authors, by George More, Esquire. Prov. 19., ' Heare

* " On the outside of that wall which faces Wells' Row, the bolt in tun is cut in stone in two places. The tun lies in fees, and the bolt runs through it." (Nichols's *History of Canonbury*, 1788, p. 3.) This part of the wall has been long pulled down.

counsell and receive instruction, that thou mayst be wise in the latter end."

An address "To the Reader," of eleven lines, follows the title. It mentions that the author had no intention originally of publishing "this collection;" but that, upon reconsideration, he had changed his mind, thinking it "fit for yong noblemen and gentlemen to read." There is no dedication, and no notice is taken of the publisher or printer. The anecdotes are numerous, and indicate a vast extent of reading.

Who was George More? And was this work ever published ?
J. M.

[Two editions of this work were published; the first with the imprint "London, Printed by Nicholas Okes, dwelling neare Holborne Bridge, 1611," 18mo. To this edition is prefixed a Dedication "To the Most Noble, Mightie, and Hopefull Prince, Henry, Prince of Great Britaine," in which he reminds the Prince, that " it is more than thirty yeares ago that I dedicated my poore service to your Highnesse Grandmother, which by my best endeavours I have ever continued to His Majesty, and will never faile to yourself." This Dedication is omitted in the second edition, "Printed at London, 1629," 4to. At first we were inclined to attribute this work to the celebrated Sir George More of Loseley House, in Surrey, who was from 1604 to 1610 Treasurer or Receiver-General of Prince Henry's revenues, but he received the order of knighthood as early as 1597. Consult Wood's *Athenæ* (Bliss), ii. 364 ; Birch's *Life of Prince Henry*, p. 229 ; and Manning and Bray's *Surrey*, i. 95.]

COLTHEART.—There is a work mentioned by a person of this name, entitled *The Quacks unmasked*, London, 1727, 8vo. It would be very obliging if a full copy of the title of this book could be furnished, or a very brief notice of what it is about. .
J. M.

[The title-page gives the contents of this work : " *The Quacks Unmask'd :* which detects, and sets in a true Light their Pernicious and Destructive Practice, with some Reasons why it ought to be entirely abolished. By P. Coltheart, Surgeon. 'Sine me, liber, ibis in urbem.'. *Ovid.* .London, Printed for the Author, and sold by the Booksellers of London and Westminster, 1717." The author's protest will not be considered inapposite even at the present time. He says, " The fruits of encouraging such pretenders, whose advertisements fill the daily papers, may be observed from the wretched condition of those patients who have escaped out of their hands with life, and are a sad memento to those who look upon those subjects of their experiments, to be seen in the streets, like so many walking spectres, and whose looks seem to cry aloud, *Beware of Quacks!*"]

DR. CHAPLIN AND "THE WHOLE DUTY OF MAN."—One of the persons to whom the authorship of *The Whole Duty of Man* has been attributed was Dr. Chaplin, of University College, Oxford. What are the reasons for supposing that he was the author? Is the subject mentioned by any contemporary writer? The examination of the numerous claims which have been made to the authorship of that work has not yet been thoroughly instituted. LLALLAWG.

[The authorship of *The Whole Duty of Man* was attributed to Dr. Chaplin by Evelyn. In his *Diary*, under the date July 26, 1692, he says, " I went to visit the Bishop of Lincoln [Dr. Tenison], when, amongst other things, he told me that one Dr. Chaplin, of University College in Oxford, was the person who wrote *The Whole Duty of Man*; that he used to read it to his pupils, and communicated it to Dr. Sterne, afterwards Archbishop of York, but would never suffer any of his pupils to have a copy of it." In Pickering's edition [1842] is a valuable Preface on the authorship of this work by the Rev. Wm. Bentinck Hawkins, M.A., F.R.S. of Exeter College, Oxford. Consult also "N. & Q." 1st S. ii. 292 ; v. 229 ; vi. 537 ; viii. 564 ; ix. 551 ; 2nd S. i. 135.]

FATHER RICHARD AUGUSTUS HAY.—Mr. Chambers (*History of Peeblesshire*, p. 321) cites *Genealogie of the Hayes of Tweeddale*, by Father Richard Augustus Hay ; printed from MSS. belonging to the Faculty of Advocates: Stevenson, Edinburgh, 1835. I have not been able to meet with a copy of this work, and shall therefore be thankful for any account of the author. S. Y. R.

[Of Father Richard Augustine Hay some account will be found prefixed to the *Genealogie of the Hayes of Tweeddale*, 4to, 1835, a copy of which is in the British Museum. Being himself a descendant of that family, and in direct succession to a part of the honours, his Memoir down to the year 1700, in the latter portion of the *Genealogie*, is, from its minuteness, of considerable importance. Mr. Hay was Canon Regular of St. Genovefs of Paris, and Prior of St. Pieremont. He died in reduced circumstances in the year 1735 or 1736.]

VENUS DE MEDICI.—Can you tell me the exact height of the Venus de Medici ?
A. M'NIVEN.

[The height of the figure itself is 4 feet 11 7/10 in. English measure ; if the figure stood erect it would be 5 feet 2 in.]

Replies.

DANIEL DEFOE AND "THE LONDON REVIEW."
(3rd S. vi. 527.)

The absence of all party spirit in the consideration of historical subjects is a peculiar characteristic of " N. & Q." Supported by a large body of unconcerted contributors, differing in religion and politics " wide as the poles," its columns rarely contain even an expression capable of giving offence to any reader. So may it ever be! The whole surface of society is more than sufficient for daily agitation by " unstable wind." Beneath, where lie scattered " the multitudinous relics of

the past," there is rest; and the gatherers up of " buried treasures" should be reverential, sober men.

This reflection has been induced by the contrast between the introduction of the recently discovered letters of Daniel Defoe to the readers of " N. & Q.," and the objectionable manner of their earlier introduction in the *London Review*.

The following was written before I knew that the letters would be reprinted in " N. & Q. ;" and I have to thank the Editor for allowing me since to revise.

I propose at present to condense, into as small space as I can, the " history " contained in these letters of Defoe, and to make some remarks on the criticism of the *London Reviewer*.

What Defoe did, under his engagement with the government, and the morality or otherwise of his conduct, I reserve for another, and I hope shorter communication.

The letters were all written within the space of two months (in 1718), and clearly disprove the statements of his biographers, that his political life closed in 1715. They also point to the materials for an entirely new chapter of the *History of Defoe's Life and Times*.

In 1716, Lord Chief Justice Parker urged upon Lord Townshend (then in the ministry) the misrepresentations under which Defoe had suffered ; the claims he had upon the government, to which he was sincerely attached ; and the valuable services the administration might derive from his pen. They were then much harassed, internally by symptoms of dissension, and externally by attacks from the Tories in public journals, which had become so virulent that not even the king escaped. Lord Townshend sent for Defoe, and proposed to him to write as if still under displeasure, so that he might be more serviceable than by appearing openly in support of the Government. A weekly journal (in opposition to a scandalous paper called *Shift Shifted*) was first intended, but laid aside ; and Defoe engaged himself in *Mercurius Politicus*. Dyer, the news-letter writer, dying about the same time, Defoe had an offer of a share in the property and its management. Lord Townshend, being made acquainted with the proposal, strongly approved of it, as the publication had been " very prejudicial to the public" (i. e. the ministry). Defoe therefore completed the arrangements, and was still conducting the journal, as part owner and sole manager, at the time of writing these letters in 1718. The style of the paper continued Tory, but furious attacks on government, by correspondents, were suppressed ; the sting was taken out ; the party was amused, and did not set up another paper, which would have destroyed the design.

It does not appear that, in the first instance, Defoe received anything more from the government, than a promise that his services should be considered. After a year's employment, however, in thus moderating party rancour (without compromise or change of the political principles he had always firmly held), he was rewarded by the noble lord with an "appointment" (probably some small sinecure), "with promise of further allowance as service presented." Shortly afterwards (1717) occurred the defection of Walpole and Townshend from the ministry, and the appointments of Lords Stanhope and Sunderland as their successors. The latter knew Defoe thoroughly, having, when in office many years before, secretly commissioned him to Scotland on government business. Both these noble lords, therefore, approving the "appointment," continued his services. With Lord Sunderland's approbation, Defoe now similarly introduced himself into the management of *Mist's Journal*, but without any share in the property. Mr. Mist was fully aware that he was liable to government prosecution for the violent Tory articles that had appeared in his paper; and convinced that abstention from treason and libel, under Defoe's advice, saved him from ruin.

Defoe states the abhorrence he feels at all the "traitorous expressions and outrageous words" he has to hear "against his Majesty's person and government," and "the scandalous and villanous papers" that come to him for insertion; but by suppression and moderation, he says —

"Upon the whole the weekly *Journal* and *Dormer's Letter*, as also the *Mercurius Politicus*, will be always kept (mistakes excepted) to pass as Tory papers, and yet be disabled and enervated, so as to do no mischief or give any offence to the government."

It is a curious fact, that in the letter of May 23, he wishes the government to know that he had no hand in a paragraph inserted in *Mercurius Politicus*, from another printed paper, of a person hanged at York for three halfpence. The offensive words were, that *it was a piece of justice unmixed with mercy*. For reprinting this, Morphew, the publisher, was committed to prison.

In the prefatory remarks of the *London Reviewer*, Defoe is assailed on account of these letters with the epithets, "baseness and dishonesty" — "if he had any principles" — "rascality" — "dirty and disreputable work" — "a traitor on all sides" — "his death, in 1731 in a spunging-house, *or something like it*" — "dishonest," — "corrupt writer" — "contrived to insinuate himself" — "prostitute." I leave for others to determine the competency of such a writer—in respect of temper—to deal with a subject of historical interest.

The scope of the *London Reviewer* is, that Defoe was always universally unpopular with his contemporaries; that he was so because he was utterly dishonest, and worse; that his modern biographers have been unable to offer anything

more than speculation and ingenious apologies for him; and that upon this anonymous reviewer (with the key of the letters "now first published"), has devolved the duty of opening the arcanum of Defoe's inner man, and consigning his memory henceforth to the *limbo* of perpetual execration.

The reviewer says of Defoe, "As a party-writer he had done much to deserve it, not an iota of favour fell to his lot." Defoe stood high in the personal favour of King William III., and of Queen Mary, and was both employed and rewarded immediately after the publication of *The True born Englishman* until the death of the king. He stood high in the favour of Queen Anne and of her ministers, Harley and Sunderland, and was employed and rewarded, from early in 1706 to 1709, when his *History of the Union* was dedicated to the Queen. The letters, "now first published," show him to have been employed and rewarded by the government of King George I. Other occasions of his employment and favour might be mentioned, but these will suffice.

The reviewer goes on: —

"His modern admirers, wiser than his contemporary, have discovered that what the latter took for serious was banter; and Defoe's political writings must be interpreted by the rule of contrary," &c. "We are inclined to think that his contemporaries were not wrong in their estimate of his character,—that what they took to be serious was serious in Defoe's primary intentions, though it afterward suited his purpose, when parties changed, to avoid the charge of tergiversation and political apostacy, to represent his meaning as irony and banter. Gross as this conduct may appear," &c.

It is scarcely necessary to inform the readers of "N. & Q." that the above has reference to the celebrated tract, *The Shortest Way with the Dissenters*: considered by many accurate critics, contemporary and modern (including Sir Walter Scott and Charles Lamb), to be the most exquisite piece of irony in the English language.

The above quotation contains a remarkable example of debased criticism : — 1. The suggestive : "We are inclined to think." 2. The assertive: "When parties changed." 3. The conclusive : "Gross as this conduct may appear."

The answer is short. There was no delay or change of parties. The Sacheverellites immediately adopted the pamphlet, as expressing their own views ; and this being the mark Defoe aimed at, he as quickly published, to their great consternation, *A Brief Explanation of a late Pamphlet, entituled The Shortest Way with the Dissenters*—showing that it was only a satire on their persecuting principles. Both the *Shortest Way* and the *Explanation* were published in the year 1702.

In order to make Defoe appear "a traitor on all sides," the *London Reviewer* proceeds to say : —

"Walpole and Townshend, by one of those intrigues which prevailed in the time of the first George, were ousted from favour, and Stanhope and Sunderland took their places. To the latter Defoe now addressed himself, avowing his base connection with their rivals, and claiming his promised reward."

The logical inferences are, that there was a change of government from one great party in the state to its *rivals*—the opposite. And that Defoe, who had before prostituted his pen for money, in proving that black was white, hastened to offer himself to the new ministry to write for pay that white was black.

Again, the answer is short. Walpole and Townshend (differing from their colleagues as to an appointment) seceded from the government; and Lords Stanhope and Sunderland took the vacant places. It was the same Whig government as before. Its principles remained entirely unchanged, and no alteration was made with respect to the services of Defoe.

A Mr. Buckley appears to have been the medium through whom the government communicated its instructions to Defoe; and in the fifth letter, Defoe writes: —

"The liberties Mr. Buckley mentioned, viz, to seem on the same side as before, to rally *The Flying Post*, the Whig writers," &c., &c.

In the very same column, the *London Reviewer* thus comments: —

"For fear his meaning should not be clearly understood, or his services duly valued, Defoe explains his plan of operations more fully. It was 'to seem to be on the same side as before (that is, the Tories), to rally *The Flying Post* (a Whig journal, honoured with a place in the *Dunciad*), the Whig writers,'" &c., &c.

Having so distorted the instructions received from his employers into Defoe's own plan of operations, the reviewer concludes: —

"How much credit is to be attached to the statements of a writer in his other works against his political and religious opponents, when he could thus prostitute his honour and his talents?"

The premises do not warrant the conclusion. But, as Defoe would have said, " of this in its place."

Everybody conversant with the history of the reign of Queen Anne, knows that George Lockhart, of Carnwath, is the reputed author of a book called —

"Memoirs concerning the Affairs of Scotland, from Queen Anne's Accession to the Throne to the Commencement of the Union," &c., &c. 8vo. London, 1714.

It is right to say that the author's name does not appear on the title-page; but the internal and circumstantial evidence is so complete, that it would not have been strengthened by the subscription of his name in full. I affirm that no other man could have written it, for the following reasons:—The Preface states that the book was not intended by its author to be made public until the "obstacle" (the queen) should have been removed (devoutly adding, "and I pray God it may

be soon,") and the king (the Pretender) restored. He was so conscious of its treasonable character, that he adds: —

"Common Prudence requires these Memoirs should lie dormant 'till such be out of a capacity to resent the same, either on Myself or Posterity."

The Preface goes on to "declare solemnly" the origin of the *Memoirs*: —

"I'm now to tell you, having had the Honour to represent one of the Chief Shires in Scotland during the Four last Sessions, I did apply myself to become as useful as I could to my Country. . . . I used, for the most part, to make my remarks on what I thought observable, as they occurred either in or out of the Parliament House. . . . Having followed this method for Four Years (1703 to 1707), I liv'd thereafter some time privately at my House in the Country, and thought I could not divert myself to better purpose than by ranging my Notes into Order."

He states that he knew the rise of the transactions, and was "trusted by the Chief of the Cavaliers and Country Parties" (meaning the Jacobites and Rebels); and that, in the *Memoirs*: —

"I have not spar'd my *near Relations, particular Friends*, and *intimate Comrades*, when I thought them Faulty."

Throughout the whole book the treasonable sentiments of the writer and those of Lockhart are identical.[*] What the latter said and did, in privacy, is related in full. Whenever Lockhart was present, at the most secret meetings of the traitors, the proceedings are carefully narrated in the *Memoirs*. The same of his correspondence with St. Germains, preparatory to the Pretender's invasion in 1707. On one occasion, during the opposition to the Union, Lockhart (as a Commissioner) stood perfectly alone; but the *Memoir-writer* not only endorses his conduct, but *explains his motives*, and approves. What people told to Lockhart in his own house in the utmost secrecy, and his replies, are contained, apparently verbatim, in the *Memoirs*. The same may be said of the secret conversations (whilst travelling) between the Duke of Hamilton and Lockhart; and also, between the latter and Captain Straton. Before closing his book, I must quote its author's opinion of a man, in political principles and conduct as in genius, his antipod: —a man who wrote nearly twenty works favouring the Union of England and Scotland; and almost as many against Jacobitism and the Pretender, and in favour of the Revolution, and the succession of the House of Hanover.

At p. 229 of these *Memoirs*, Lockhart says: —

"That vile Monster and Wretch Daniel De Foe, and other mercenary Fools and Trumpeters of Rebellion, have often asserted that these Addresses, and other Instances of the Nation's Aversion to the Union, proceeded from the false Glosses and underhand Dealings of those that opposed it in Parliament."

* In this I except the Introduction, as being written by another.—W. L.

I now return for the last time to the *London Reviewer*, who, in a further long paragraph asserts—without even the slightest pretence of evidence—that Defoe himself was the author of these same treasonable *Memoirs concerning the Affairs of Scotland*; that he collected his observations for the work while employed in Scotland by the Government (in 1706-7), to *promote* the Union; that the book contains Defoe's real opinions; that it was not ready for publication until 1714, when the Whigs were in power; and that, therefore—"with a baseness, happily singular in the annals of literature, Defoe printed his work and published it anonymously; but to make his peace with the Whigs, he prefaced it with an introduction, written in the spirit and tone of a Whig."

The reviewer afterwards, in the same paragraph, quotes from the Introduction; and thereby identifies the book, beyond all question.

The readers of "N. & Q." will form their own conclusions on this, the first part of my self-imposed task.   W. LEE.

BABYLON.

(3rd S. vi. 533.)

Though many writers suppose that Baltassar (in Authorised Version, Belshazzar) is "the king of Babylon" against whom the prophecy of Isaiah (chap. xiv.) is directed; yet the point is difficult to ascertain with certainty. As Bishop Lowth observes (*Notes on Isaiah*, vol. ii., ed. Glasgow, 1822), the preceding chapter (xiii.) should be joined with chapter xiv., because thereby the unity of the prophecy is preserved. The words of Isaiah, in the 16th and 17th verses of chap. xiv., seem to be *more* applicable to Nabuchodonosor, or as rendered in the Authorised Version, *Nebuchadnezzar*, than to Baltassar, who, it is supposed, only reigned about four years. As Nabuchodonosor conquered Syria, Judea, Phœnicia, and Egypt, the words of the prophet seem very applicable to *him* :—"Is this the man that troubled the earth, that shook kingdoms?" (ver. 16)—"That made the world a wilderness, and destroyed the cities thereof, that opened not the prison to his prisoners?" (ver. 17, Doway Version). After his wars were ended, history tells us how he beautified, enlarged, and adorned Babylon, in such a wonderful manner, that he exulted in its magnificence, and exclaimed, when walking in his palace, "Is not this the great Babylon, which I have built to be the seat of the kingdom, by the strength of my power, and in the glory of my excellence?" (Daniel, iv. 27, Doway Version.) The terrible punishment with which he was instantly afflicted for his pride, illustrates very clearly the words of Isaiah: "How art thou fallen from heaven, O Lucifer, who didst rise in the morning? How art thou fallen to the earth that didst wound the nations?" (chap. xiv. 12).

Part of the prophecy may, however, refer to Baltassar, the last king of Babylon. Several historical difficulties connected with this king, and the last four kings of Babylon, have been cleared up by the discoveries of Sir W. Rawlinson, who dates the death of Baltassar B.C. 538. Rosenmüller (*Scholia in Vetus Testamentum*, tom. i., Lipsiæ, 1810) makes a plausible remark in his annotations on the fourteenth chapter of Isaiah, viz., that "the King of Babylon" may be poetically used for Babylon itself. These are his words:—

"Qui rex Babylonis hic dicitur, non tam certum aliquem è Babylonis Regem videtur indicare, quam metonymicè et poeticâ sub figurâ *ipsum Babylonium imperium*," &c.

Several important works on Assyria, Babylon, Nineveh, and the ancient history of the Jews, have been published during the last few years; such as Layard's *Nineveh and Babylon*; Rawlinson's *The Five Great Monarchies of the Ancient Eastern World*; Keith's *Evidence of the Prophecies*; *Nineveh and Persepolis*, by Mr. Vaux. Several other works are mentioned in Smith's *Dictionary of the Bible*, under the heading of "Assyria and Babylon." Rollin's *Ancient History* was once considered to be *the* great authority on these subjects; but it is now, though containing much excellent reading, almost useless as a work of reference. Though Milman's *History of the Jews* may be of great service to your correspondent, H. U., yet the learned author's views and opinions on many points are to be received with caution. As proofs of the literal way in which the prophecy of Isaiah has been fulfilled, with respect to the utter destruction of Babylon, the testimonies of Rich, Sir Robert Ker Porter, Ainsworth, Fraser, and Niebuhr, &c., are abundantly conclusive.

J. DALTON.

Norwich.

The king of Babylon, who is the subject of several verses of the fourteenth chapter of Isaias, is understood to be Baltassar (*Belshazzar*, Authorised Version). The denunciations apply to him rather than to Nabuchodonosor, who lived and died gloriously; and, as many are of opinion, was saved. Baltassar, on the contrary, was conquered and slain; and in him the royal race was extinguished, and the city and monarchy of Babylon destroyed.

F. C. H.

EDGAR A. POE AND "THE FIRE FIEND."

(3rd S. vi. 223, 224.)

Unless another correspondent shall, in the meantime, have better performed the task, I ask you, in justice to the memory of Mr. Poe, to insert the following account of the "Fire Fiend," which I condense chiefly from a small pamphlet lately published by C. D. Gardette, Philadelphia, 1864.

In the course of a discussion upon Poe's genius which took place in November, 1859, Mr. Gardette was challenged to produce a successful imitation of the style and rhythm of "The Raven."

"Under this challenge, Mr. Gardette composed the 'Fire Fiend,' and its public success being part of the bargain, he sent it to the editor of *Harper's Magazine* for publication. He, however, while admitting its resemblance to Poe in manner and treatment, considered the magazine an unsuitable medium for its publication, and politely declined it. But, he added, that he had shown it to a literary acquaintance, the editor of the *New York Saturday Press*," who, after communication with the author, published it in that paper on the 19th of November, 1859. It was accompanied with the following letter: —

"Philadelphia, November 6th, 1859.

("To the Editor of the *Saturday Press*.)

"Dear Sir,—The following fantastic poem was written by Mr. Poe, while experimenting towards the production of that wondrous mechanism, 'The Raven ;' but considering it incomplete, he threw it aside. Some time afterwards, finding it among his papers, he enclosed it in a letter to a particular friend, labelled *facetiously*—'To be read by firelight, at midnight, after thirty drops of laudanum.' How it finally came into the possession of the undersigned, he is not at present at liberty to tell. The poem is copied *verbatim, literatim, et punctuatim* from the original MS.

"Yours, &c.

"C. D. GARDETTE."

This was the first time that the "Fire Fiend" ever appeared in print. It was prefaced on that occasion with the following editorial note in brackets: —

"[We postpone several articles this week to make place for the following communication, which we print with the single remar$k$, that we 'don't see it.']"

"The 'Fire Fiend' then," says the pamphlet, "was written as a hoax, published as a hoax, with an editorial remark sufficiently indicating the fact to any reader of fair perspicacity ; and as no money was asked nor received for or by its publication, and no efforts whatever made to disseminate or perpetuate the hoax, either by its publisher or author, I feel no hesitation in pronouncing it, and in believing that my readers will pronounce it, to have been a venial and harmless literary joke."

As it was probably more owing to the direct assertions of the letter above quoted, than to the quality of the piece itself, that the latter has deceived anybody, some readers may be pardoned for not seeing the "joke."

That part of the letter signed M. McCready in the *Morning Star* of Sept. 1 (quoted by T. B. in "N. & Q."), which relates to the "Fire Fiend" is so obviously taken from Mr. Gardette's note to the *Saturday Press*, that it is remarkable that the doubt expressed by the editor of that paper is not also referred to. It may be further observed, that the rest of M. McCready's letter, which relates to her conversations with Mrs. Clem, says nothing (unless by implication) about the "Fire Fiend," or any other poem than "The Raven." I agree with T. B. that "honour compels us to do justice to a man who had little but his genius to recommend him ;" and it is, I believe, as certain that Poe did write "The Raven" as it is that he did not write the rather feeble and unpleasant imitation which has called forth these remarks.

St. T.

SIR ANDREW RAMSAY.

(3rd S. vi. 460.)

In the above article there occur certain mistakes which it will be obliging to correct. They refer to a Scotish judge, and are as follows :—Sir Andrew Ramsay was transferred from the civic chair as Provost of Edinburgh, "to the Judicial Bench, as one of the *Searchers* of the *Courts* of Justices, when he *lost* his seat as Lord Abbotshall," &c. Now it should run thus : That the Lord Provost was placed on the Bench as one of the "Senators" of the "College" of Justice, where he "took" his seat "as Lord Abbotshall."

It sounds strange, that a chief magistrate should be placed on the Bench as a judge ; and, moreover, keep both places, but such was the case with the individual in question. It might, nevertheless, happen again ; for barristers are now eligible to be members of the town council of Edinburgh, and already two of the learned profession have held the civic chair, viz. Sir James Forrest, Bart., of Comeiston, and Francis Brown Douglas, Esq., both advocates : who might either, or both, have been placed on the bench if it had been the pleasure of her Majesty's ministers. A barrister—a baillie, if we remember rightly—was made a judge in Ceylon ; and several counsellors have been converted into sheriffs : that is to say, into supreme judges in the Scotish counties, whose decisions could only be corrected by an appeal to the Court of Session—in other words, to use the ordinary law phraseology, by "suspension" or "advocation." What a sensation it would make in England, if the Lord Mayor of London were made Lord Chancellor, an alderman a Baron of Exchequer, and if the Indian judges were selected from the Common Council !

Sir Andrew Ramsay was a shopkeeper : for there were no merchants in Edinburgh in those days, according to the English meaning of the word. Whether he dealt in whisky or woollens is not now known. He may, like the founder of the Kinlochs, have been a tailor ; but true it is, and of verity, that he knew well on which side his bread was buttered, for having successfully gratified the chief of the Maitlands by getting for him from the town council the enormous price of 5,000*l.* for the superiority of Leith, Lauderdale was so much satisfied of his judicial capabilities, that hé deemed him an uncommonly nice man, and one superlatively qualified from his practical knowledge to be a first-rate Lord of Session.

During the recent discussions on the question of precedence between Edinburgh and Dublin, we rather think the fact has been lost sight of, viz. that Sir Andrew, in 1667, procured a letter from Charles II. declaring that he should have the same precedence as the Lord Mayor of London; and that he, and no other Provost in Scotland, should be called "My Lord."

Lauderdale metamorphosed three other persons not lawyers into Scotch judges, viz. his brother Hatton (afterwards Earl of Lauderdale), Robert Preston, and Richard Maitland. There have been lots of persons not lawyers upon the Bench subsequently; but, so far as we can learn, all contrived to be admitted advocates.   J. M.

CHRISTMAS WAITS.

(3rd S. vi. 487, 509.)

Mr. Chappell's observations on the Early History of Christmas Waits, reminds me of a similar practice universal throughout the East. It is the duty of the municipal police in every town and village of Southern Asia to patrol the streets at each change of the watch, during the night, with drums and horns. This is done under the orders of an officer called the Kotwal. In India he used to be styled Danda-pálaka, and his myrmidons Dandiyas; the latter term is still in use. There are four watches, or pahars, in the night, and on each of these the Kotwal and Dandiyas perambulate every street, beating the tambourine (called tapti in the south, dhamuka in the north), and occasionally winding a long blast on the curved trumpet, known to Englishman as the kallari-horn. The object of this noisy procession is stated to be to arouse the vigilance of the inhabitants, and to deter the evil disposed from deeds of violence by showing them that the guardians of the public safety are on the alert.

The more natural inference would be that the householders, accustomed to the stated noise, would soon cease to notice it, and the thieves would quietly wait until the patrol had passed, and then proceed with their depredations. Singular as such means of affording protection may appear, it seems nevertheless to be identical with the original institution of the Waits of England; for according to the *Liber Niger* of Edward IV. quoted by Mr. Chappell, the duty of the "waytes" is defined to be "to pipe watch four times in winter, and three times in summer for the purpose of being heard by the inmates, and also to keep away thieves." And such appears to have been the practice in all our great towns—London, York, Chester, Norwich, &c. A remnant of the custom

has even descended to our own times before the recent abolition of the time-honoured Charlies, who went their rounds shouting the hour of the night, with an appropriate remark on the weather. It can hardly be doubted, I think, that this curious organisation of a municipal police; exisiting under such precisely similar conditions among the Indo-Germanic communities, has descended to us from our Aryan ancestors.

But besides exercising functions of a police character, the Waits are described as having been minstrels attached to castles, palaces, camps, &c., receiving fees and holding lands on the tenure of keeping watch at the castle gate, under the control of the *Curia Vigiliæ;* and from the mention made of them in Queen Isabella's Household Book, to have pertained to the retinues of great noblemen or persons of distinction.

This description approaches very closely to the Eastern institution of the Naubat. The Naubat is an honorary distinction of the highest order, conferred by the sovereign as a special mark of favour on persons of rank, and consists of the privilege of having music sounded in the gateway of the fort or palace of the grantee, or in camp when he is in the field, at stated hours. To maintain this distinction, a grant of land is conferred in what is called jágír, or service tenure. The minstrels are nine in number, performing five times in the twenty-four hours, and using five kinds of instruments. They are generally paid by subsidiary grants of land in the Naubat jágír.

Although now, as the name (signifying in Persian a time, occasion) infers, a Mohammedan institution, it is of great antiquity, and is found among the titles of Hindu kings in the oldest inscriptions extant. It seems also to have been used in Assyria; and it was probably by the sounding of Nebuchadnezzar's Naubat that the worship of the golden image, in the plain of Dura, was regulated. (Dan. iii. 5.)

The Naubat in former times was only performed three or four times a day, and with fewer instruments than at present. In the Persian dictionary, entitled *Burháni Qatia*, the following account is given of the change:—

"During the reign of Síkandar-Zu'l Karnain [Alexander the Great] the Naubat was played only three times a day, but during his latter years he ordered it to be beaten four times."

"When Sultan Sanjar was expelled by his enemies and driven to great straits, he was attacked by severe illness, and unable to continue his flight. In his extremity he ordered the Naubat to be sounded a fifth time, in the hope that his enemies might suppose he had expired, and that the unusual performance signified the accession of his successor. The ruse succeeded, and he continued the practice during the remainder of his reign. From him it has been adopted by all succeeding sovereigns."

Ferishta, in his *History of the Mussulman Princes of India*, states that the Naubat was first adopted by the second King of the Bahmani dynasty of Calbarga, and that one of his successors increased the number of instruments from five to nine. (Briggs's *Ferishta*, ii. 300; iii. 328.)

The distinction of the Naubat has occasionally been conferred on meritorious native officers of the Indian army by the British government. When the Right Hon. Stephen Rumbold Lushington was Governor of Madras, it was granted to Subahdar-Major Mohammed Ghause, commandant of the body guard, with an appropriate jágír. Part of the ceremony consisted in a pair of silver kettle-drums being fastened to his shoulders, which were beaten by the governor in token of investiture. During seasons of mourning the Naubat is silent. When the news of Sir William H. Mac Naughten's murder reached India, the late Nawáb of the Carnatic wrote to the Governor of Fort St. George, on January 30, 1844, to say that "H. H. has ordered the Circar Naubat to cease for the usual period, according to the Mussulman custom observed in cases of calamity." △.

Johnson does not notice the word, but Burke in his copy of *Johnson's Dictionary*, now in the British Museum, includes it in some MS. addenda at the end of vol. ii. Thus —

"WAIT, n. s. from ye French *guet* (literally a sentinel on outpost duty). 2. Waits, in ye pl. an old word signifying ye night Guard in ye city of London."

BRIGHTLING.

GRACE MACAULAY (3rd S. vii. 46.) — If T. G. will kindly communicate with me, he will confer a favour. F. M. S.

229, Clarendon Villas, Plumstead.

OBJECTIONS TO WHITE PAPER (3rd S. vi. 454.) — As then editor of, and writer of the notes on the above subject in, the *Ophthalmic Hospital Reports* referred to by EIRIONNACH, I am glad to find literary men, *par excellence* (two contributors to "N. & Q." and Mr. Babbage), confirming my opinion; and that of other medical men, including Dr. Aitken. I may here note, that the exact reference to the *Ophthalmic Hospital Report* is vol. ii. pp. 117—120 (1859). I refer to it specially because some other objections to modern printing, so much inferior to that of our ancestors, and so much deteriorating even now, are referred to, and may elicit some valuable *notes*. I wish to observe, that I question if *colour* is wanted in paper. Is not the common fault in paper that it is bleached, or too much bleached? Is it not the secret charm of old print that, besides a more legible *thinner* type, and more space, the paper was unbleached? * A lemon-coloured paper is becoming common;

* I suppose linen rags were more unbleached than they now are.

but to me and some others it is trying to the eyes. "The colour of ripe wheat," is very pleasant. It does not follow, though it may be necessary, that the colour must be added in making the paper; and, therefore, that the paper should be more expensive. Instead of adding colour, I should subtract from the bleaching process of paper-making, and so perhaps cheapen paper, besides making it so much pleasanter in use for readers and writers. I look forward to the day when not only Christmas books, and other splendid publications, but "N. & Q." and other books constantly before our eyes, will be printed on toned (? un-bleached) paper. J. F. S.

HENGIST AND HORSA (3rd S. vii. 10.) — DR. SEWELL's conjecture of horses' heads being carried as standards by the Saxons, is rendered more probable by a passage in the well-known Celtic poem of *Y Gododin*. This lay records the concluding struggle between the Celts of the second immigration, which then occupied the Lowlands of Scotland, against the Saxons of Northumberland, aided by the Scots and Picts of the North. The campaign lasted for seven years, from 642 to 649. The passage to which I refer occurs in the 35th stanza, and is thus translated by the Count de la Villemarqué, the well-known Celtic scholar : —

"Un chef qui tenait [en guise d'étendart] le quartier de devant d'un loup sans tête à la main."

GEORGE VERE IRVING.

SYMBOLIZATION OF COLOURS IN HERALDRY (3rd S. vi. 394, 395, 479.) — I admit that Wlson de la Colombiere's first book was published in 1639, but it must be borne in mind that this work contained seventy-four plates in folio, all engraved by himself, the work doubtless of several years. Wlson expressly declares that he was the inventor of the system, and that Petrasancta had merely adopted and copied his invention :—

"Afin que le Lecteur se satisfasse entierement, ie luy presente les deux metaux, les cinq couleurs, et les deux pennes graués en la page suiuante, et luy fais voir l'inuention de laquelle ie me suis seruy au premier liure de blazon, que ie fis imprimer pour connoistre les metaux et les couleurs par la taille douce, *laquelle a esté imitée et practiquée par le docte Petrasancta, au liure intitulé Tessera gentilitiæ qu'il a composé en Latin, et fait imprimer à Rome.*"—*La Science Héroïque*, chap. iv. p. 30. Paris, 1644.

Now I ask, is it likely that Wlson, who has always borne a most honourable character, would thus deliberately lay claim to the invention if it were not really his? Is it not much more probable that Wlson may have mentioned his invention to his patron, Cardinal Barberini, and that by him it may have been communicated to Petrasancta, who never claimed the invention as his, nor contradicted Wlson's statement that I have quoted? The Jesuits were surely the least likely body at that time to leave such an assertion unrefuted if the invention could have been proved to belong to one of their order.

As I do not possess the Second Series of "N. & Q.," I am not aware whether these facts have appeared therein.

W. H. JAMES WEALE.

SIR THOMAS LUCY: SAXON TYPOGRAPHY (3rd S. vi. 515.) — The two leaves forming the cover of W. P. P.'s copy of the Funeral Sermon on Lady Lucy, are part of Charles Butler's *Principles of Musik in Singing and Setting: with the two-fold Use thereof [Ecclesiasticall and Civil].* 4to, London, 1636. Butler, in 1634, had published at Oxford an *English Grammar,* and also a work entitled, *The Feminin Monarchi, or the Histori of Bees,* both printed from the same types as the *Principles of Musik.* In each of the works on Bees and Music an address from the printer to the reader refers to the *English Grammar* for an explanation of the peculiar orthography used in those works, "and the grounds and reasons thereof." Bagford, in one of the quaintly written notes interspersed throughout his collections, speaking of the three works, says, —

"Yt it is to be noted that a new font of letters was cast at ye cost of the Author as the comon letter would not serve to ye spelling, there being two letters together. And as I have heard by Report from ye learned Mr. Pote it was intended for the printing a bibell with ye same letters."

I presume the intended Bible never appeared. In the attempt made some years ago to introduce a phonetic orthography, was Butler's system ever alluded to?　　W. H. HUSK.

The two leaves, partly in Saxon characters, about which W. P. P. inquires, are from a rare book, of which I have a beautiful copy, entitled *The Principles of Musik, in Singing and Setting: with the two-fold Use thereof, Ecclesiasticall and Civil.* By Charles Butler, Magd., Master of Arts. London: Printed by John Haviland for the author, 1636.

The types, cut expressly for Butler, were first used in the author's *Feminine Monarchy; or, a Treatise on Bees,* 1623; and are known as "Haviland's" types, being occasionally used by him for other works. They were, I believe, the second set of Saxon types cut in England, the first being those of old John Day. Haviland printed *The Paschal Homily of Ælfric,* in 1623, with these types.

EDWARD F. RIMBAULT.

CONFIRMATION OF ARMS (3rd S. vi. 461, 539.) I cannot at the moment refer to my answer to the query of H. S. G., nor do I recall the precise terms employed by me in controverting his idea that arms stated to be borne by his family, confessedly without "legal right," could become the subject of a grant of confirmation by the College of Heralds.

If it be clearly proved that there has been a grant of arms, and neither the original grant nor the record of it can be found, or if there be proof by immemorial usage, "from time whereof the memory of man runneth not to the contrary" — viz. from the reign of Richard I. — of a prescriptive right to arms, proceeding on the legal presumption of an original grant, in either of these cases it is intelligible that a grant of confirmation should be made by the College of Heralds to individuals proving their right by descent. Nor would there be anything inconsonant with principle in an official instrument by the College certifying, as distinguished from confirming, the right of an individual to bear arms, to which he has proved himself by inheritance or grant to be entitled. But that there should be a grant of confirmation of arms to which a person had already a clear right seems irreconcileable with principle. If the right was clear, what need was there of confirmation? *Cui bono?* Assuming that the cases referred to by P. P. do not come within the exception I have suggested, they must be very anomalous or otherwise exceptional, and the contribution of some of them *in extenso,* showing the motive of the grant as set forth in the preamble in each individual case, with a list of others, to "N. & Q." would be interesting to its heraldic and genealogical readers.　　MIDDLE TEMPLAR.

GUILDFORD FAMILY (3rd S. vi. 455, 543.) — I should have stated that there is on the foot of the chalice at Montaigu a second shield charged with four lozenges in pale, and surmounted by a helmet, having for its crest a unicorn. Are these the arms of Thomas Bodenham?

W. H. JAMES WEALE.

The following note of the baptism of Clara Monson may be useful to M. P. and other readers of "N. & Q.:" —

"Clara, the daughter of Anthony monson (sic), baptized April 1, 1681." — *Northorpe Par. Reg.*

EDWARD PEACOCK.

VIOLON: LOCK-UP (3rd S. vi. 496.) — I observe in the number of Dec. 17 a cutting from *Galignani* on the word *violon,* in the sense of lock-up. The following explanation by the late eminent French philologer, Génin, is more to the purpose. I took note of it from a series of papers he furnished some years ago to the *Journal de l'Illustration,* but it is to be found with many other curious things in his *Récréations Philologiques:* —

"*Mettre au Violon.*—Il est constant qu'au moyen âge on disait, au lieu de mettre au violon : *mettre au psaltérion.* (M. Génin en cite plusieurs exemples.) Psaltérion, saltérion, sautérion, ne sont autre chose que le mot latin psaltérium, accommodé à la française. Les sept pseaumes pénitentiaux étaient durant tout la moyen âge une prière d'usage, aussi fréquent que l'oraison dominicale ellemême. C'est au point qu'il en était né une façon de parler proverbiale : le temps de dire *unes sept-pseaumes,* comme on dit encore le temps *de réciter un pater.* Mettre au psaltérion c'était donc mettre au psautier, mettre en pénitence, en lieu où l'on a tout le temps de méditer sur ses sottises, et de s'en répentir, et de réciter *unes sept-pseaumes* sans risquer de se voir interrompu. Mais le psaltérion était aussi un instrument de musique. Le peuple dans son humeur gauloise profita de l'équivoque, et voyant le psaltérion passé de mode y substitua le violon qui était devenu le roi des instruments. Au lieu de dire mettre au psaltérion il dit mettre au violin, et le calembourg fut sauvé."

                           DITCHFIELD.

POEM WANTED: "THE DOG AND THE SHADOW" (3rd S. vi. 534.) — It is by the late James Smith, one of the authors of the *Rejected Addresses,* and will be found in a collection of his minor pieces in two vols. post 8vo, edited I believe by his surviving brother, Horace Smith. The date of publication I am at present unable to supply, having mislaid my copy of the book.   R. S. Q.

DONKEY (3rd S. vi. 432, 544.)—MR. RIX carries back the use of the word Donkey to between the years 1774 and 1785. He omits to mention that Palgrave, where Mrs. Barbauld wrote the mock Eclogue, is in Suffolk. This fact seems to bear out the statement of Pegge and others, that the word Donkey was originally an East Anglian provincialism. MR. RIX's suggestion that the word may have been derived from *donker* (Dutch for gloomy), presupposes either that the East Anglians were in the habit of using a Dutch adjective to express gloominess, or that they had adopted from the Dutch some ready-made name, derived from *donker,* as the equivalent of "ass." The only name, however, by which the animal is known in Holland is *Ezel.*   J. DIXON.

It cannot, I think, be gravely supposed that the name "Dickey" given in Norfolk to an ass can be derived from German, Dutch, or Flemish. It is more likely adopted from "Dick," as in the West of England the animal is called "Neddy," and generally elsewhere a "Jackass." It is also very frequently in Norfolk called "Donkey" by the humbler classes.   F. C. H.

UMBRELLAS: PATTENS (3rd S. vi. 532.)—A correspondent, who remarks upon some expressions in Gay's *Trivia,* wishes to know whether umbrellas were formerly *oiled.* My own recollection goes back to the concluding years of the last century; and I well remember that all umbrellas then in use were made of oiled silk. They were not then used to walk with; that improvement was introduced a few years later; but they had a ring at the top, and a round handle, like that of a hearth-brush. They were usually carried under the arm, but often slung across the back; the ring served to hang them up by, and occasionally for carrying them. Gay was a poet and not a philologist, and his tale of the Lincolnshire yeoman's daughter can only be regarded as a poetical fancy. The *Trivia,*

indeed, is made up of similar conceits. The name of *patten* is, I think, evidently derived from the French name for a skate, *patin;* in each case there is a wooden sole raised upon iron.   F. C. H.

Compare Swift's amusing *Description of a City Shower :* —

   "The tuck'd-up sempstress walks with hasty strides,
     While streams run down her *oil'd* umbrella's sides."
                        P. W. TREPOLPEN.

"THE ROBBER'S GRAVE" (3rd S. vi. 498.) — The writer of the volume bearing this title was the Rev. R. Mostyn Pryce, formerly of Gunley, in Shropshire, or Montgomeryshire. He was a preacher of considerable eloquence, and his little book gives token of literary powers, which it is to be regretted he did not employ on any more important work. His testimony is trustworthy, so far as it goes, and I have heard the story frequently in Shropshire.   J. D.

Your correspondent T. B. will find an interesting account of this in that most amusing book, *The Season Ticket,* published some years ago. Unfortunately I do not possess the book, and cannot refer him to the exact page.   OXONIENSIS.

R. Mostyn Pryce, the author of *The Robber's Grave,* was a clergyman of the Church of England. He was an agreeable and clever but somewhat eccentric man. He committed suicide at Newton, Montgomeryshire, about 1857. I cannot vouch for the fact of the grass not growing on the grave, but I know the circumstance was credited in the neighbourhood.

Particulars of the trial and case are no doubt contained in the *Shrewsbury Chronicle* of 1821, the principal or only chronicle of local intelligence of the district at that date.
     J. E. DAVIS, Stipendiary Magistrate.
Stoke-on-Trent.

MASSYMOR: MAZMORRAS (3rd S. vi. 530.) — This word, as applied to a dungeon, may perhaps be derived from the Arabic, *matmuret,* vulgo, *matmure,* a subterranean granary, a crypt (*fovea subterranea, crypta, in qua frumentum reconditur*), from the Arabic root, *tamr,* to fill (*replere* [*cellam*]). Another word, *muzmer,* a hiding place (*locus occultationis*), approaches more nearly the sound of *massymor,* but the first word is almost identical both in sound and sense with the French term found in the *Dictionnaire de l'Académie,* and I am inclined to consider it as the parent of the expressions referred to by J. R. B. In the warmer countries of Asia, the surplus grain is usually stored in pits, or subterranean granaries, which in India are called *khaus.* The habit was probably introduced by the Saracens into Spain, and so the word may have passed into France. As applied to a dungeon the term may have been brought from Syria by the Crusaders, and may have been very appropriately applied to such a crypt as that in Hermitage Castle, into which Sir Alexander Ramsay was thrust by the Knight of Liddesdale. It was situated immediately under the granary of the castle, and the wretched man, being left without food, prolonged his life for sixteen days by means of the grains which fell through the floor, till death put a period to his sufferings.

Another familiar instance of a word adopted from the Arabic into all the modern languages of Europe, is found in magazine, derived from *makhzán*, a store (*apotheca, cella, horreum*), from the root *khazn* (*recondere in horreo*).   W. E.

I am acquainted with the parish of *Maismore*, in Gloucestershire, a short distance westward of the city of Gloucester. Can there be any connexion between its name and the names above? If so, it would be still more singular to see it in the English language, in addition to the Scotch, French, and Saracenic.   F. C. H.

ANTOINE GODEAU'S PSALMS (3rd S. vi. 497.)— Bishop Godeau's translation of the Psalms into French verse were so highly thought of at the end of the seventeenth century, that they almost superseded the version of Marot in family use.

I have now before me a rare little volume, bearing the following title :—

" Paraphrase des Pseaumes de David, en vers François. Par Mre Antoine Godeau, Evesque de Grasse et Vence. Derniere Editione, reveuë exactément, et les Chants corrigez et rendus propres et justes pour tous les couplets. Par M. Thomas Gobert, Prestre, ancien Maistre de la Musique de la Chapelle du Roy, et Chanoine de la sainte Chapelle de Paris. Suivant la Copie, A Paris, chez Pierre le Petit, Imp. Ord. du Roy. MDCLXXVI."

This work is not mentioned by either Burney or Hawkins ; and is, therefore, deserving of being chronicled in the pages of " N. & Q."

I regret not being able to help my friend MR. HUSK in his inquiries about Jacques de Gouy, and his music to Godeau's Psalms. I have examined numerous Psalm Books, printed by W. Pearson at the beginning of the last century, without finding a single advertisement of his reprint of Gouy's work.

The true date of Bishop Godeau's death is April 21, 1671.   EDWARD F. RIMBAULT.

ROBERT BROWN, THE SEPARATIST (1st S. ix. 572.)—Under this title ANAT. relates that, at the time of the marriage of the last descendant of Robert Brown with George, Lord Pomfret, her servants persisted in ringing the bells of the village church, to the annoyance of the vicar's wife, then recently confined ; and that the vicar's pupils drove the servants out of the church, and removed the clappers of the bells ; and that the circumstance was made the subject of a very scarce mock

heroic poem called the *Brunoniad* (London, 1792, printed by Kearsley), and that the author was Thos. Foster. After ten years' search, I have at last obtained a copy of the poem, but its title-page is " *Brunetta, or the Birthday Battle* : printed in the year 1792." As ANAT. has not been accurate in the description of the poem, nor of the circumstance giving rise to it (for Miss Brown was not married until 1793), I am desirous of knowing what authority he has for attributing the authorship to the Rev. Thomas Foster.   Jos. PHILLIPS, Jun.
Stamford.

Miscellaneous.

NOTES ON BOOKS, ETC.

The Christ of the Gospels and the Christ of Modern Criticism. Lectures on M. Renan's " Vie de Jesus." By John Tulloch, D.D. (Macmillan.)

These Lectures contain a calm, temperate, and closely-argued refutation of the philosophical and critical assumptions, and untenable historical pretensions of M. Renan's book,—a refutation which becomes the more effective from the absence of all personal criticism.

The Chronological Bible : containing the Old and New Testament, according to the Authorised Version, newly divided into Paragraphs and Sections, with the Dates and Places of Transactions ; concise Introduction to the several Books ; and Notes illustrative of the Chronology, History, and Geography of the Sacred Scriptures. By Robert B. Blackader. (Simpkin & Marshall.)

The Chronological New Testament, &c. Second Edition, revised and enlarged. (Simpkin & Marshall.)

Ample as this title is, it is far from doing justice to the various ingenious arrangements by which the editor has endeavoured to throw light upon the Authorised Version of the Holy Scriptures. As little can we hope to do so in the limited space which we can devote to it. The text is printed in paragraphs, and on each page are two columns of illustrative notes, including parallel passages printed in full. Introductory notices are prefixed to the several Books : the poetical books are printed rhythmically ; speeches are printed with inverted commas ; variations of ancient versions are given ; quotations in the New Testament of passages from the Old Testament are printed in capitals ; and many similar means adopted to render the meaning of the Sacred Text more intelligible. Nothing but an examination of the book can show its value, and such an examination ought to secure for it a very general acceptance and a wide circulation.

In the New Testament, which may be purchased separately, a comparison of the received text with the Vatican MS. B., is instituted by means of a different type. Mr. Blackader deserves great credit for the intelligence which he has displayed, as well as for the time and labour he has expended on his " good work."

Mornings of the Recess, 1861-4. A Series of Biographical and Literary Papers reprinted, by Permission, from " The Times," and revised by the Author. Two Vols. (Tinsley.)

Who that has been, during the recess, as agreeably as unexpectedly surprised to find a few columns of *The Times* rescued from the American war, the Müller trial, or the speeches of Members out of Parliament—and devoted to notices of the best books of the season—has not longed to see those masterly sketches preserved in some permanent and available form? That wish has at length been gratified; and to those who remember the articles contained in these volumes, a mere list of them will be their strongest recommendation. They are between twenty and thirty in number, and treat of—Sir John Eliot; Coins of the Ancient Britons; Forsyth's Cicero; Naturalist of the Amazon; English Engineers; Saxon Leechdoms; Dixon's and Stebbing's Bacon; Francatelli's Cook's Guide; Professor Wilson; Female Life in Prison; Ionian Islands in 1863; Mrs. Trench's Journal and Remains; English Cant and Slang; Lord Lyndhurst; Lady Cowper's Diary; Miss Knight's Autobiography; The Dahomey Mission; English Cathedrals; Works of Alexander Neckam; Modern English Caricatures; The Leadbeater Papers; Vacation Tourists; The Napiers; Omitted Chapters in English History; and Kebbel's Essays. It is long since two more able or pleasant volumes have come under our notice.

Studies in Biography. By Lionel James Trotter, late Captain in the 2nd Bengal Fusileers. (Moxon.)

These biographical sketches of Mahomet, Thomas Becket, Frederick II. of Germany, Savonarola, Bacon, Pitt, and Sheridan, reprinted from the *Dublin University Magazine,* and other high class serials, are well worthy reading. Captain Trotter has a ready pen and a keen appreciation of character; and in his endeavour to combine what have been called the sympathetic and judicial forms of criticism, he does not lose sight of that striving after truth which is the first duty of a biographer; whose admiration for Bacon's intellect, to use our author's own words, "should never lead him to slur over his moral failings; his love of truth, his sympathy with the good that everywhere challenges notice, should force him in spite of a hundred prejudices, to acknowledge with equal readiness the pure asceticism of Savonarola, the essential earnestness of Mahomet, the lofty patriotism of Pitt, and the cloudier, if more taking, brilliancy of Sheridan."

The Herald and Genealogist. Edited by J. G. Nichols, F.S.A. Parts X. XI. and XII. (Nichols & Sons.)

These three parts, rich in every variety of heraldic and genealogical information, complete the second volume of Mr. Nichols's most useful serial. "The Heraldic Chronicle" for 1863, and articles on "The Heralds' Visitations of Counties," are among those articles which will be found of more particular interest.

Lord Overston has shown his respect for the late Mr. M'Culloch by a very graceful act, the purchase of that gentleman's well-chosen library—rich alike in fine classics, and works on Political Economy, at the price at which he understood the late owner to have estimated it—five thousand pounds.

The long-expected "Vie de Cæsar," by the Emperor Napoleon, is at length on the eve of publication. An *édition de luxe* of a thousand copies, which, when splendidly bound, are to be presented to the sovereigns, diplomates, and celebrities of Europe will be first issued. There is a question as to who is to translate the work into English. Why should not the Emperor translate it himself? Should his version display a few Gallicisms, they would be readily overlooked in the compliment which England would feel had been paid to her by her great ally.

A General Meeting of the Camden Society was called for Wednesday, for the election of a President in the place of the much-lamented Marquess of Bristol, whose death has been felt as a great loss to the Society. Fortunately the Marquess Camden, who, as President of the Kentish Arch-

æological Society and of the Archæological Institute, has shown great interest in historical and antiquarian pursuits, had consented to be put in nomination, and his Lordship was unanimously elected.

BOOKS AND ODD VOLUMES
WANTED TO PURCHASE.

Spirit of the Public Journals for 1805. Vol. IX. Lond. 1806.

The Redeemed Rose; or, Willie's Rest, by Eliza Rumsey. Hatchard. Wanted by *Rev. J. Maskell,* Tower Hill, London, E.C.

Illustrated London News for 1864. Vol. II.
Gardener's Chronicle Newspapers from June 11 to the end of 1864, in clean and good condition.
Wanted by *M. N.,* 2, St. Leonard's Place, Bishop's Road, Paddington.

Johnson's Thieves and Highwaymen. Original folio edition with plates.
Wanted by *Mr. Percy B. St. John,* Southend, Essex.

Mrs. Trimmer's Fabulous Histories; or, Tale of the Robins.
Wanted by *Dr. Fisher,* 5, Appian Way, Upper Leeson Street, Dublin.

Louis XVII. sa Vie, son Agonie, sa Mort, par M. A. D. Beauchesne.
The Lost Prince, by John H. Hanson, published by Putnam, New York, 1854.
Life of Eleazar Williams, by his Son. Supposed to be also an American publication.
Wanted by *M. Mellands,* Kenton, Exeter.

Notices to Correspondents.

We are compelled to postpone until next week our Notes on many Books—among others of Goderich and Porter's edition of Webster's Dictionary; Dr. Russell's Review of Todleben's Sebastopol; Booth's Reprint of First Folio Shakspeare, &c.

C. L. S. *Full information respecting the City of London School will be found in the Public Schools Calendar.*

Llallawg. *The statement "The blood of the martyrs is the seed of the church," is derived from the expression of Tertullian: "Semen est sanguis Christianorum," which occurs at the conclusion of his "Apologeticus adversus Gentes."—The 7th of July, 1854, fell on Monday.*

A. F. Barlow. *The first six musical notes are said to have been invented by Guy Aretino, a Benedictine monk, about A.D. 1025; but consult Hawkins's History of Music, and "N. & Q." 1st S. xii. 301, 432,—For the origin and literary history of The Arabian Nights, see Mr. Lane's Review at the end of the third volume of his edition (1859), pp. 674—686.—For some articulars of Jacqueline consult Nouvelle Biographie Générale, 8d. 1858, xxvi. 215; and Biographie Universelle, ed. 1858, xx. 478.—For the meaning of the terms Objective and Subjective, see "N. & Q." 1st S. v. 42, 141; ix. 170.*

Carisford (Cape Town.) *The work Fifty Reasons why Anthony Ulrich, Duke of Brunswick and Lunenburg abjured Lutheranism, 1741, appears to be very scarce. We cannot find a copy in the Catalogues of the British Museum or the Bodleian.*

Errata—3rd S. vii. p. 43, col. i. line 27, *for* "Gaul" *read* "Gael." The signature to the article should be "R. S. Q."

A Reading Case for holding the weekly Nos. of "N. & Q." is now ready, and may be had of all Booksellers and Newsmen, price 1s. 6d.; or, free by post, direct from the publisher, for 1s. 8d.

*** Cases for binding the volumes of "N. & Q." may be had of the Publisher, and of all Booksellers and Newsmen.

"Notes and Queries" *is published at noon on Friday, and is also issued in Monthly Parts. The Subscription for Stamped Copies for Six Months forwarded direct from the Publisher (including the Half-yearly Index) is 11s. 4d., which may be paid by Post Office Order, payable at the Strand Post Office, in favour of William G. Smith, 43, Wellington Street, Strand, W.C., to whom all Communications for the Editor should be addressed.*

"Notes & Queries" is registered for transmission abroad.

LONDON, SATURDAY, JANUARY 28, 1865.

CONTENTS.—Nº 161.

Notes.

REFLOWERING QUEEN MARY'S GARDEN.

Queen Mary's Bower or Garden (for it goes by both names), is thus described: —

" At the Port of Menteith, three-and-a-half miles from the Cardross station of the Stirling and Loch Lomond railway, there is a good inn. Taking boat from the tourist may visit two islands, Rest and Talla, or the Earl's Isle. The former, which is the larger and more easterly island, consists of about five acres, and contains the ruins of a priory, where Queen Mary resided during the invasion of the English in 1547, before she was removed to France. The priory was founded about 1238, by Walter Comyn, Lord of Badenoch, who became Earl of Menteith by marriage with the Countess." *

After his death, Walter Stewart, brother of the High Stewart of Scotland, inherited the property and title in right of his wife, the younger sister of the Countess of Menteith. A writ was granted by Robert Bruce at this place, in April, 1310, as recorded in the Chartulary of Arbroath; and at the priory of Inchmartho (Inchmacrome), King David II. and Margaret Logie were married, in 1363.†

The architecture of the monastic buildings is early English. The archæologist will see with delight the extreme beauty of the western door,

* Wyntoun, ii. p. 393.
† For an interesting account of the Earls of Menteith, see Mr. Craik's *Romance of the Peerage*, vol. iii.

richly moulded and sculptured along its deep retiring jambs. In the choir there are crypt, sedilia, a piscina, and other usual adjuncts of a mediæval church; and an ancient tombstone is supposed to mark the grave of the founder. But what will be viewed with most interest is a recumbent monument of two figures, male and female, cut out of one large stone. The knight is in armour, one leg crossed over the other. A triangular shield with the check fesse proves the bearer to have been a Stewart, but the arms on the shield show that the figure is not that of the founder. The arm of the lady is twined round his neck, and while much of the monument has been defaced, this memorial of affection seems to have been respected. The monastery was built for monks of the Augustine order, and was dependent on the great house of Cumbuskenneth. Here you find large Spanish chestnuts, one lying dead, others standing stark and peeled, like gigantic antlers, and others flourishing in their green old age, whilst in a thicket you see the remains of the monastery of great beauty, the design and workmanship exquisite. You wander through the ruins, overgrown with ferns and Spanish filberts, and old fruit-trees, and at the corner of the ancient monastic garden you come upon a strange and most touching sight—an oval space of about 18 feet by 12, with the remains of a double row of boxwood all round, the shrubs of box being 14 feet high, and 8 or 9 inches in diameter, healthy, but plainly of great age. What is this? It is called in the Guide-books, " Queen Mary's Bower."

" It is plainly the child-queen's garden, with her little walk, and its rows of boxwood, left to themselves for three hundred years. Yes, without doubt, ' here is that first garden of her simpleness.' Fancy the little, lovely, royal child, with her four Maries,* her play-fellows, her child-maids of honour, with their little hands and feet, and their innocent and happy eyes, pattering about that garden, laughing and running and gardening as only children do and can. As is well known, Mary was placed by her mother in the Isle of Rest before sailing from the Clyde to France. There is something ' that tirls the heartstrings a' to the life,' in and looking on this unmistakable relic of that strange and pathetic old time."

Supposing as I do the Fotheringhay Missal to be of the age of her father James V., the account of that remarkable volume which I give says, " No part of the writing proper, or illumination, are by the unfortunate Queen; *it is probably earlier than her mature day.*" It gives the illuminations representing several flowers, which would be

* Three of the Queen's Maries are mentioned in a verse of the ballad of " The Lament of the Queen's Marie," in Sir Walter Scott's *Minstrelsy of the Scottish Border* : —

" ' There was Marie Seeton, and Mary Beatoun,
And Marie Carmichael, and me.' "

The fourth " me " was Mary Livingstone.

known in Scotland, at least at the Court of Holy-rood House, and therefore might form such as would be planted in the little queen's garden.

The following is the account given by Professor Charles Piazzi Smyth : —

"Among the objects of interest in Russia of which I was enabled to bring away photographic records during my recent visit was a stereograph of Queen Mary's Fotheringhay Missal, a subject which has perhaps sufficient of national interest about it to justify my requesting you to present a copy in a suitable stereoscope to the Society of Antiquaries in Scotland. Although my visit to the great empire of the North-east was mainly connected with science, still, when I heard in St. Petersburgh of there being in the Imperial Library of that city a very precious manuscript volume that had belonged to Queen Mary, and which had been written in (some also added illuminated by her) during her English captivity, I could not but be anxious to bring back to her own country some veri-facsimile of the handicraft of one as talented as unfortunate, and as much misunderstood by some as admired by others. This was a matter of considerable difficulty, but at length, through the kindness of a Russian lady, the Emperor's permission was asked and obtained. The book proved to be a moderate-sized quarto of between two and three hundred pages vellum, and bound in dark crimson velvet with gilt clasps. On a careful examination, we found the general description given of it by Prince Labanoff in the 7th vol of his *Lettres de Marie Stuart* extremely exact. It is described by able authorities as a superb manuscript in the Gothic character, magnificently enriched with arabesque miniatures in gold and brilliant colours of the first order, and must have been the work of distinguished professional hands. No part of the writing proper, or illumination, are by the unfortunate Queen ; it is probably earlier than her mature day. The 25th page bears the legend, in the Queen's own hand : —

" ' Ce livre est à moi, Marie, Royn, 1554.' "

This was about four years before her marriage with the Dauphin. It is mentioned in the Chartley Catalogue of her belongings in August, 1586, under the name of a *Livre d'Heures*, and again under that of a matins-book in the 'Inventoyre of the Jewells, &c. of the late Queene of Scottes,' in February, 1587, as bound in velvet with corner-pieces, middle-plates, and clasps of gold adorned with diamonds. It appears to have been her companion through all her varied career, and finally during her long imprisonment in England. Here it was thought she began to enter in it her mournful thoughts, always in French, and generally in verse. Every spare portion of page is thus occupied, and one of the pages in the photographic view, the only originally blank page in the book, is covered with verses and memoranda of various dates, filled in at last sideways and cornerways. Professor Smyth then goes on to prove very skilfully that the book was a gift to the Queen from her royal lover ; hence her careful preservation and constant use of it. He also mentions the erasure of numerous coats of arms through the book, and supposes these to have been the arms of *England* blended with her own, which it is well known were used by her as Dauphiness on the death of the English Queen Mary. An example of such a blank and rudely-rubbed shield exists on the right hand of the photograph. It is gathered from certain entries, that the book was kept about the English Court till 1615. It was then lost sight of until the early years of the French Revolution, when, stript of its costly binding, the volume was bought at a cheap rate in Paris amidst a heap of

plunder from the Royal Library there, by M. Dombrousky, then attached to the Russian Embassy in France, and by him transmitted to St. Petersburgh. On the right page is a specimen of the illumination ; on the left the Queen's manuscript. The miniature represents King David with an open book, and a harp before him, Jerusalem in the distance, and beside him a model of the Temple ; in the sky an appearance of the Deity, and underneath the miniature in Gothic character the beginning of the 38th Psalm in Latin. The floral ornamentation is extremely beautiful,—numerous Scottish plants are introduced, the ivy, convolvulus, strawberry, apple blossom, bulrush, &c., and above all the thistle, which the artist has never been tired of reproducing. The Queen's manuscript consists of verses and memoranda, of which the following are specimens near the top of the page : —

" ' Qui jamais davantage aist contraire le sort ;
Si la vie m'est moins utile que la mort !
Et plustot que cha(n)ger de mes maux l'adventure,
Chacun change pour moi d'humeur et de nature.'
                                          "Marie R."

Now we have only to suppose Queen Mary's Fotheringhay Missal to have been made in the time of her father James V. to suppose it possible that some of the flowers there depicted were such as might have formed the decoration of the garden of her childhood.   W. H. C.

SOBRIQUETS OF REGIMENTS.*

21st—*The Earl of Mar's Grey Breeks.* Derives its title from the dress worn by the corps, on its formation, in Sept. 1678, when Charles, fifth Earl of Mar, was appointed its Colonel, which appointment he retained until July, 1686.

22nd—*The Two Twos.*

23rd—*The Nanny Goats* and *The Royal Goats.*

24th—*Howard's Greens.* The 24th has been frequently styled the Bengal Tigers, like the 17th.

25th King's Own — *Borderers*, or *Botherers* (raised 1688-9—David, Earl of Leven's regiment —in Scotland.)

28th—*The Slashers.* This regiment obtained the name of " The Slashers" from their gallantry at the battle of the White Plains, and passage of the Brunx River, Oct. 28, 1777, with the old 35th Regiment.

30th—*Triple Xs.* The 10th Regiment of Infantry used to bear on its forage caps a single X ; the 20th Regiment two XXs, and the 30th Regiment three XXXs, instead of " 10," " 20," and " 30." Hence the *sobriquet* of the 30th Regiment.

31st—*The Young Buffs.* The 31st were styled the " Young Buffs," to distinguish the corps from the 3rd Foot, or " Old Buffs." There exists an anecdote, that on one of the numerous occasions when the 31st Regiment distinguished itself in battle, a General Officer exclaimed, " Well done,

---

* Concluded from p. 50.

Old Buffs." " We are not the Buffs, Sir," replied the officer commanding the regiment. " We are the 31st."—" Well done, *Young Buffs*, then," exclaimed the General.

35th—*The Orange Lilies*, from having orange facings.

36th—*The Saucy Greens*. From the colour of their facings.

38th—*The Pump and Tortoise.*

39th—*The Green Linnets*. From the colour of their facings.

40th—*XLrs (Excellers).*

42nd—*Black Watch.*

43rd—*The Light Bobs.*

44th—*The Two Fours.*

45th—*The Old Stubborns*, and *Sherwood Foresters*. The late Colonel Guard, of the 45th Regiment, unsuccessfully applied to have the corps styled " Sherwood Foresters." Not long after, the 45th was brigaded with the 87th and 88th, and when Cols. Butler and Duff called their corps to " attention " by their titles " Prince's Irish," and " Connaught Rangers," Colonel Guard shouted out to *his* regiment, " Nottingham Hosiers, attention!" to the great amusement of the whole brigade, which burst out into a most unmilitary fit of laughter.

46th—*The Surprisers*. From their conduct in the surprise of Wayne's American brigade, Sept. 20, 1777, after the spirited action of the Brandywine, on the 11th. " Mad 'Antony," as Wayne was called, was " caught out this time," and paid off by Gen. Grey, notwithstanding the rebuff he gave us at Stony Point.

47th—*The Cauliflowers*, and *The Lancashire Lads.*

50th—*The Dirty Half Hundred*. From the men wiping their faces with their black cuffs, after review and drill, in " sweating times." And *The Devil's Royals*. No cleaner, smarter, or braver regiment ever took the field.

51st—*The Kolis*. So called from the initial letters of the Regimental title, " King's Own Light Infantry."

53rd—*The Brickdusts*. From their red facings.

55th—*The Two Fives.*

56th—*The Pompadours*, and *The Saucy Pompeys* (short for Pompadours). From their purple facings, the favourite colour of Madame Pompadour, the mistress of Louis XV., about 1745; she died in 1764, a Marchioness. (Jane Antoinetta Poisson, her proper name). The 56th wore deep crimson facings, and white lace; pink facings were worn in 1761.

57th—*The Die Hards*. Received their honourable title from their gallantry at Albuera, where the 3rd Foot, 29th, 34th, and 48th Regiments also highly distinguished themselves.

58th—*The Steel Backs.*

59th—*The Lilywhites*. The 47th and 59th Regiments, both having white facings, assumed the distinguished titles above given.

62nd—*The Springers*. (In taking open order, the word instead of *March*, was *Spring*.) Named " The Springers," from the rapidity of its pursuit of the American rebels, after the action at Trois Rivières in Canada, 1776.

74th—*The Assaye Regiment*. The 74th and 76th derive their titles from the places where they first distinguished themselves in action.

76th—*The Hindostan Regiment*. Also named *The Seven and Sixpennies*, from the number of the corps.—J.

77th—*The Pot-hooks*, from the figure " 7."

78th—*The King's Men*. So styled from their motto. " Cuidich'n Rhi," help the King. This is the second 78th Regiment raised by the Earl of Seaforth's family. The senior corps so numbered was raised in 1777 by William fifth Earl of Seaforth, and was principally recruited from the class of " Caber Feidh," as the Mackenzies were named, from the stag's horns borne on the armorial bearings of Earl Seaforth. Several senior regiments having been disbanded in 1783, the 78th regiment was numbered on December 20, 1787, " the 72nd " regiment, which number it has borne ever since. The present 78th regiment was raised by a letter of service, dated March 7, 1793, and the first colonel appointed to the corps was Thomas Humberstone Mackenzie, whose commission bears date March 8, 1793. He died in the spring of 1796, and was succeeded by Colonel Alexander Mackenzie Fraser. There are now a Major, two Captains, and a Lieutenant of the Mackenzie Clan serving in this splendid National Regiment.

83rd—*Fitch's Grenadiers*. The first parade of this fine regiment took place in the yard of Dublin Castle, in the Autumn of 1793. The title of " Grenadiers " was originally given in derision, owing to the average smallness of the soldiers who originally belonged to the corps; but the regiment has been for very many years remarkable for the superior height of the men who have been selected as its recruits.

85th—*The Elegant Extracts*. The motto of the 85th was taken on the corps being reformed by " Elegant Extracts " from the officers of other regiments in Colonel Cuyler's time (1813), when so many courts-martial took place as to induce the commander-in-chief to disperse aN the unbroken officers, and form the corps anew.

87th—*The Old Fogs*. The title is a corruption of the war-cry of the corps, " Fag-an-Bealach," pronounced " Faug-a-bollagh," meaning " Clear the way."

88th—*The Devil's Own, Connaught Boys*. The 87th being " The Prince's Own," General Picton named the 88th " The Devil's Own," as a complement to their dauntless bravery in presence of he enemy, and their then uniform irregularity in camp and quarters.

89th—Blayney's Blood-hounds, and the *Rollickers.* This old and excellent regiment received the former *sobriquet* from its unerring certainty in hunting down and nearly exterminating the Irish rebels in the year 1798, when the corps was commanded by the late Lord Blayney, the eleventh lord.

3rd West India Regiment—Buckmaster's Light Infantry. Mr. Buckmaster, tailor, used to issue "Light Infantry uniforms," for some years, to the officers of this corps, without (as is stated) any authority from the Commander-in-Chief.

JUVERNA.

INVOICE OF CARGO, 1803: A BUSINESS COMMUNICATION.

The enclosed photograph is of an invoice of cargo, dated 1803, reflecting the highest possible credit on the business qualities of our respected foregoers, or perhaps *still living grandfathers,* which is worthy of a place in "N. & Q." The charming effrontery of its tone is delicious, "marked and numbered as in the margin," 115 males, 64 females; total, 179 *slaves.* There is no boggling or dodging here, but plain Saxon. "God's grace" has been yoked to strange enterprises, but this I think must be allowed to be about the queerest attachment extant; "and so *God* send the good ship to her desired port in safety." The "t'other party had more to do with it probably." In the words of an ancient merchant of this place, acting as magistrate, trying a she-thief for stealing tea from a ship's side —"What tempted ye to do it?" It was said to be her first offence. — *Prisoner* (in a flood of tears): "It was the deevil temptit me."— *Magistrate:* "The deevil, honest man, had naething to do with it; (*sotto voce*) at least a never kenn'd he was sicna judge o' tea, for it was the best kist in the ship."

The photograph gives of course the *entire* of the document, but I send a written copy in case any word should be difficult of decipherment. The interlineation after "Seas," "Insurectio and Mortality" excepted, is too horribly suggestive to be missed. The date is *blank* Feb., 1803, and the writing is delicate, and evidently that of an elderly man, as the hand shows tremulousness (see word *belonging.*) I think it is written with a *fine crow quill;* the means and the end jar strangely. The cargo was for a West Indian plantation, shipped, as stated by the vessel's owners, in their own ship. Where is "Kissing"? —

"*Shipped* by the grace of God, in good order and well-conditioned, by Mess⁵ Irving & Fraser in and upon the good [ship]* snow called The Ariadne . . . . . . whereof is master, under God, for this present voyage, Captᵈ [Wᵐ]* Wᵐ Mᶜ Bride and now riding at anchor in

* The words in brackets are deleted and corrected, in the original.

the Riopongoes . . . . . and by God's grace, bound to West Indies . . . To say: . . . . One hundred and Seventy-nine Slaves * . . . . . being marked and numbered as in the margin; and are to be delivered in the like good order and well-conditioned, at the aforesaid port of West Indies . . . (the danger of the Seas [Insurectio and Mortality] † only excepted) unto . . Order . . . . or their assigns, ... Freight paid Vessel belonging to the Owners . . . . with primage and average accustomed. — In witness whereof the master and purser of the said ship hath affirmed to three bills of lading, all of this tenor and date; one of which bills being accomplished, the other two to stand void; and so God send the good ship to her desired port in safety. Amen.—Dated Kissing, Feb⁷ʸ, 1803.
(Signed) "Wm. McBride."
C. D. Lamont.
Greenock.

THE COMPLUTENSIAN POLYGLOTT, AND BROCAR THE PRINTER OF IT.

As the Rev. S. P. Tregelles, no doubt, feels a great interest in everything connected with the history of the Complutensian Polyglott, I take the liberty of sending him, through "N. & Q.," a few further observations on the subject.

1. It was in the summer of 1502, when Cardinal Ximenes was residing in Toledo, that he first conceived the plan of his great Polyglott. It was there also that he published his editions of the Mozarabic Missals and Breviaries, the ancient Gothic MSS. having been previously revised by Canon Alfonso Ortiz, who was assisted by three other priests in Toledo. The date of their publication was either 1500, or, according to Gomez, 1504.

2. Who was the printer? Most probably Arnold William *Brocar;* who was invited into Spain about this period, from Germany, by the Cardinal himself — according to the statement of most Spanish writers. It is, I think, incorrect to call him *Brocario,* as if he were an Italian. He had a son named *John Brocar;* who, clad in festal garments, carried the last sheets of the Polyglott to Ximenes, just as he was on the verge of the grave.

3. From Toledo, Brocar and his son John, very probably migrated to Logroño — where the work was printed by the father, referred to by your reverend correspondent (3ʳᵈ S. vii. 12). It would be very interesting to know the *exact* year, when Brocar was invited by Ximenes to reside in Complutum (Alcalà de Henares); and also, in what year the *New Testament* was commenced. We know, indeed, that it was completed January 10, 1514.

* Summed in figures in the margin, thus —
"115 Males
64 Females
---
179 Slaves."
† The words in brackets are interlineated.

4. The Rev. S. P. Tregelles seems to have some difficulty respecting the chronology being reconciled with the date of Pope Leo's election, who, it is supposed, could not have sent any Greek MSS. to Ximenes, because Leo X. was elected Pope in March, 1513, and the New Testament was completed in 1514. In answer to this apparent difficulty, I may be allowed to observe, that several critics—such as Marsh, Hug, Feilmoser, and Dr. Hefele—are of opinion that Leo X. sent the Greek MSS. to Ximenes *before* he had been elected pope, when he was only a cardinal; and that Ximenes gave his Holiness public thanks, in the Preface, for the loan of those MSS. *after* he had been ·chosen pope. (See *Der Cardinal Ximenes*, von Carl Joseph Hefele, zweite Auflage, Tübingen, 1851, xii. Haupt, S. 117.)

5. We cannot, therefore, suppose "that the writers of the Polyglott spoke inaccurately, when they express their thanks to Leo X. for his aid in having sent Greek MSS. for the New Testament." I sincerely hope that the Rev. S. P. Tregelles may one day publish a "History of the Complutensian Polyglott;" and do full justice not only to the illustrious Cardinal, at whose sole expense it was published, but also to the great scholars who assisted him—such as Antonio de Lebrija, Demetrius Ducas, Lopez de Zuniga, Nuñez de Guzman; and the learned Jews, Alfonso of Alcalà, Pablo Coronell de Segovia, and Alfonso de Zamora. (See Gomez, *De Rebus Gestis, &c.*, Compluti, 1569, p. 37.)   J. Dalton.
Norwich.

Note for Spanish Scholars. — While comparing the text of the *first edition* of the Second Part of *Don Quixote*, the proof sheets of which must have been *revised by Cervantes*, with the edition published by Clemencin, I find after the words "por tan poco precio" (p. 241), the following sentence omitted: —

"Y advierta, Sancho, que las obras de caridad que hazen tibia y floxamente, no tienen merito, ni valen nada."

"And know, Sancho, that the works of Charity are not to be done slow and lazily, for they merit nothing, and are of no value."
W. Platt.
Conservative Club.

Queen Anne Boleyn. — Mr. J. B. Heath communicated to the Philobiblon Society in 1863, "An Account of Materials furnished for the use of Queen Anne Boleyn and the Princess Elizabeth, by William Loke, 'the King's Mercer,' between the 20th Jan. 1535 (27 of Henry VIII.) and the 27th April, 1536." This would lead a casual reader to suppose that the account extended over more than a year, but being O. S., it is really for two months only. There is some little confusion or error about the commencement,

.as some items are dated the 14th and 17th of January; but it may be worth mentioning that the total of this ten weeks' bill is 124*l.* 15*s.* 2*d.*— rather a large sum if translated into its equivalent in our present money.   Job J. B. Workard.

Curious Anachronism.—I read in a newspaper lately, an account of the erection of a memorial window in a church at Birmingham. This window is described as "representing David playing before Saul, under the inspiration of St. Cecilia." Surely, after this, we may expect some painter to favour us with a representation of "Henry VIII. consulting George IV. as to the disposal of one of his wives."   W. H. Husk.

Bishop King and Dr. John Rainolds. — Mr. Grosart has just edited for Mr. Nichol's *Series of Commentaries*, the lectures of Dr. King on Jonah, and of Rainolds on Obadiah and Haggai. Biographical notices are prefixed to each. In the first, reference is made to the fiction which was circulated affirming that Dr. King had professed himself a Roman Catholic. Allow me to add a reference to those which Mr. Grosart has given. Some account of the matter may be found in —

"The New Art of Lying covered by Iesuits under the Vaile of Equivocation; discovered and disproved by Henry Mason, Parson of S. Andrew's Vndershaft, London," 12mo, 1634, p. 206, &c.

The same book also contains an interesting anecdote concerning Dr. Rainolds (pp. 199—206). It appears that a stupid report was set afloat about Dr. Rainolds; and to prepare against anything worse, his friends drew up for him a confession of faith, which he was too weak to write himself, but which he signed; and which was witnessed by nine persons, May 20, 1607. You may not wish to have the document, but here are the names: Henrie Airay, Vice-chancellor; Henrie Wilkinson, Edward Rilston, Richard Taylor, Henrie Hindle, Daniel Faireclough, Henrie Mason, Alexander How, and Iohn Dewhurst.

Mr. Mason adds, that he was in possession of the original, from which he makes "a faithful transcript." Of this Henry Mason, I have no further information, except what Wood says in *Athen. Oxon.*, ii. 56, ed. 1691.   B. H. C.

Queries.

MEAT AND MALT: MOROCCO.

I was present some time since at a conversation in Cumberland, when a drink peculiar to a place called Levens Hall, in that county, the seat, I believe, of a branch of the Carlisle family, was mentioned, and described as extremely strong ale, in the brewing of which beef or meat was introduced. Having repeated this to some friends a short time since, considerable doubts were expressed as to the probability or possibility of combining meat with malt and hops, and I consequently wrote to my friends in the north, but have only been able to collect the following accounts. One friend writes: —

"Morocco is the name of the drink; it is brewed at Levens near Milnthorp, from a recipe found wrapped up in lead near an evergreen in the old garden. Flesh is certainly introduced, as I believe it to be in the Durham University strong beer. The exact recipe for brewing Morocco is kept strictly secret. There is a legend that the secret was brought by a Crusader Howard, and during the Civils Wars buried where it was found as above some years ago. Helpless, truly, is the state of that man who stoops to drink inferior liquor after imbibing the mighty Morocco. It is almost dark, pours like oil, and tastes mild as milk in its treachery."

Another gentleman writes to me: —

"Some time ago I walked over with a friend from G——e to Levens Hall, for the express purpose of tasting this Morocco, and after tasting it the conversation turned upon the method of making it. The old gardener who was living at that time (called Forbes) informed us that the receipt was found attached to a bottle, which was found buried under a tree in the grounds; and as far as I can remember, he stated that meat was used in making it, but in what state he did not mention. I fancy the making of it is a family secret. I have been given to understand that the man who brews it is sworn not to divulge the secret. I have heard of raw beef being put into ale, but for what purpose I cannot say."

Another gentleman confirms what I have above quoted with regard to the Durham ale, viz., that flesh is or was used.

The use of meat in brewing is curious and very little known. If you will give the above extracts a place in your valuable publication, I have no doubt we shall soon be well informed on the subject.   C. C. P.

ANONYMOUS.—Who was the author of following?—

"Three Discourses:—1. On the Use of Books. 2. On the Result and Effects of Study. 3. On the Elements of Literary Taste. Delivered at the Anniversary Meetings of the Library Society at Chichester, Jan. 1800, 1801, 1802. By the President. London. 8vo. 1802."

My copy has the book-plate of "R. J. Harper, F.S.A."   WILLIAM BATES.

BELL-RINGING: FINES FOR ITS OMISSION. — In the Churchwardens' Accounts of Bray in Berkshire for 1601-2 we read:

"It payd for not ringing when the Queen dyned at Folly John   .   .   .   .   iijs iiijd."

And in the accounts of St. Lawrence, Reading, for the year ending Michaelmas, 1529:

"It to the qwen's amersmt for that the bells wer not rong at her comyng into the town   .   .   viijd."

And in the accounts of St. Mary, Lambeth, for 1517-18:

"Itm. paid to yem a amyner ffor defawtts off the ryngynge off the bells at the kynges comynge   ijs iiijd."

Query, by what law were these fines imposed? And has it ever been repealed?   A. D. T.
Merton College.

CLAIRVOYANCE AND MESMERISM. — Are clairvoyance and mesmerism recognised and acknowledged as sciences by the Académie des Sciences at Paris?   J. W.

CROMWELL'S IRONSIDES. — It is said that the cuirasses that have been in use in the Household Brigade of Cavalry since the coronation of George IV. up to within a very recent period were those that were worn by Cromwell's celebrated "Ironsides." Can any one of your numerous readers corroborate that report as being a fact, or, on the contrary, prove its incorrectness?   W. B. C.
Florence.

CURLL'S POETRY. — Amongst several Collections of miscellaneous and indifferent poetry, published by Curll about 1727, and bound up in one volume, occurs a collection, 52 pp. in length, without a title-page. The first poem is "The Stamford Toasts." I shall be obliged if any of your correspondents could give me the title-page in full, and the name of the author.
                                JOS. PHILLIPS, Jun.
Stamford.

DANCING UPON SIPPETS.—In Evelyn's Mundus Muliebris, 1690, is this curious expression:—

"They danced the Canarys, Spanish Pavans, and Sellinger's Round upon sippets, with as much grace and loveliness as any Isaac, Monsieur, or Italian of them all can teach with his fop-call, and apish postures."

Can any of your readers explain this phrase? Can it be a corruption of "chopins," or high-heeled slippers?   A. A.
Poets' Corner.

EDGAR AND ELFRIDA.—I should like to ascertain what different places in England have laid claim to having been the scene of the tragedy connected with Queen Elfrida. Local tradition points to Harewood Forest (Herefordshire) as the spot in which Ethelwold concealed Elfrida, and was afterwards himself assassinated, and Mason has followed this account in his once well-known drama. Some vestiges of an ancient castle are still visible in Harewood, and a farm bears the name of Elvaston or Elverston (Elfrid's town).
                                      C. J. R.

FORDS IN ENGLAND: THE CATWATER. — Mr. Taylor, in his work on Names and Places, draws attention to the fact that some inlets from the sea on our coast still retain the name of Ford, derived from the Scandinavian Fiord. He instances, if I recollect right, Helford in Cornwall, Milford in Wales, and Wexford in Ireland. I am curious to know if the Catwater at Plymouth ever bore the name *Ford*, to which it seems well entitled. A house near it has been called Radford since the reign of King John, and the reason is not apparent. •   W. S. R. S.

FOUR-AND-TWENTY· SWORN MEN OF GOOS-NARGH.—A vestry book of the seventeenth and eighteenth centuries, belonging to the parish church of Goosnargh, contains the minutes of the meetings ·of what are called "The fower-and-twentie sworne men of the parish of Goosenerghe." Were ,these the ancient representatives of our modern sidesmen, or *testes synodales?*

From the following minute, it appears that the twenty-four.included in their number the church-wardens: —

"Mar. 31st, 1730. It was ordered that Mr John ffish-wicke be one of the 24 instead of Charles Holmes, and *Churchwarden.*

I should be glad to learn what was the form of oath taken, and what were the duties of these men.   H. FISHWICK.

GAELIC GRAMMAR, ETC.—What is the name of a good Gaelic Grammar, price, &c.? Is Cromek's *Remains of Nithsdale and Galloway Song*, 8vo, 1810, still in print; and its price?   HIGHLANDER.

Manchester.

SIR THOMAS GLOVER.—I have before me —

"A Sermon preached at Constantinople, in the Vines of Pera, at the Funerall of the virtuous and admired *Lady Anne Glover*, sometime Wife to the Honourable Knight, *Sir .Thomas Glover*, and then Ambassador ordinary for his Majesty of Great Britain,'in the Port of the Great Turke. By *William Forde*, Bachelour in Divinity, and lately Preacher to the Right Honourable Ambassadour, and the rest of the English Nation resident there. London : Printed by Edward Griffin, for Francis Constable, &c. Quarto, pp. 82. 1616."

Lady Anne Glover's maiden name was "Lambe;" and such, says the preacher, "was her nature— a Lambe in name, and a Lambe in nature." From the preface, it would appear, that she was brought up under the care of the Lady Wentworth, to whom the *Sermon* is dedicated in terms of exalted commendation. The sermon was delivered, it is said, "instead of a fair Temple, in a pleasant Garden, under a lofty Cypress Tree, in a goodly assembly of divers Nations." "There were present," it is added in a note, persons "of most Nations under the Sunne—English, French, Dutch, German, Italian, Polish, Hungarian, Turkes, Jews, &c." The *Sermon* was printed some years after the death of Lady Anne; but, it is probable, took place in 1608. Can any of your readers oblige me with some account of Sir Thomas Glover? * •   X. A. X.

· [* Some notices of the Glover family will be found in our 3rd S. i. 182; ii. 256.—ED.] •

OLD HORSE AND GROOM INN, STREATHAM, SUR-REY. — Can any reader of "N. & Q." inform me at what period the Old Horse and Groom Inn, Streatham, Surrey, was built; and if there is any historical sketch and illustration of it? A few years ago it was pulled down and rebuilt, when the two old dead trees which stood in front of the house were cut down. I have been informed that, many years ago, it was the principal inn on the road. The original building was very ancient; with a very pretty garden at the side,. now covered with houses. I am not aware that it is mentioned in any history of Surrey. I should also·be glad to know if this inn was older than the Greyhound or Pied Bull Inns, facing Streatham Common, which I believe are the two oldest inns at Streatham.   W. D.

THE INSCRIPTION ON THE CROSS.—Can any of your correspondents inform me how the statement of St. Luke (chap. xxiii. 38), regarding the *order* of the languages in which the inscription on our Saviour's cross was. written, may be recouciled with the parallel statement in St. John's Gospel (chap. xix. 20)? In what order may the·three languages be supposed to have come? CLUTHA.

IS IT A FOSSIL?—In Fairholt's *Up the Nile* (p. 197), I read: —

"St. George is the patron· saint· of the Coptic Christians, and his exploit with the Dragon is delineated in very ancient paintings in these churches, as well as upon the temples they converted into churches, as in Dakke in Nubia. It will be remembered that this legendary history lays the scene of the famous encounter in Egypt, and that the lady freed from the monster by his prowess was the daughter of the Sultan of Egypt. The dragon is merely a winged crocodile; and it is somewhat curious that at Mons, in Hainault, where a local knight, Gilles-de-Chin, is reported to have freed the land from a similar pest, the head of the dragon is preserved as proof positive of the tale; which head is, in reality, the skull of a crocodile."

Can any of the readers of "N. & Q." say whether this relic is the head of a crocodile, mummied and brought from Egypt, or the head of some saurian taken out of the earth in an unscientific age, and never recognised ·in its true relation to earth, and time, and history?

    O. T. D.

ISABEL, ABBESS OF AMESBURY, OR OF ACORN-BURY.—Isabel, daughter of Henry of Lancaster, and granddaughter of Edmund Crouchback, second son of Henry III., is generally stated to have been Abbess of Amesbury in Wiltshire (see "N. & Q." 2nd S. ix. 60); but I find an absolute contradiction to this statement in a MS. quoted in the *Topographer*, vol. i. p. 99, and which I presume to be Harleian MS. 6729. The writer describes some coats of arms which might in his time be traced upon an arch in the Nun's Chapel at Aconbury, co. Hereford, and assigns them to—

" Henry Plantagenet, Lord and Baron of Monmouth, who after his eldest brother's decease, was Earle of Lancaster and Derby, &c., and married Maud, the sole daughter and heire of Patricke de Caducis or Chaworth, Knight. They had a daughter named Isabell, whom many writers call Abbess Almesbury (not Ambesbury), corruptly for this Alcornebury."

" The Chartulary of Aconbury Priory " (printed in the 8th Report of the Dep. Keeper of Public Records), proves that Henry of Lancaster was a benefactor to the house, but at that period (7 Edw. I.), and also as late as 1309 (3 Edw. II.), Catharine de Geniville appears to have been prioress.

In the absence, therefore, of any direct evidence in its favour, I think the anonymous writer's statement must be dismissed, though I should still be glad to obtain some further and more definite information before accepting the counter-statement.   C. J. R.

KNIGHTS BACHELORS.—It is wished to ascertain whether the undermentioned Knights Bachelors are still living, and if not when and where they died :—

Sir Daniel Williams, Chief Magistrate of Lambeth Police Court, knighted in June, 1802.

Sir William Alexander Fletcher, knighted by the Lord Lieutenant of Ireland, Sept. 9, 1811.

Sir Alexander Wilson, M.D., knighted by the Lord Lieutenant of Ireland, May 10, 1813.

Sir Thomas B. Marshal, knighted in 1837.

Sir Francis William Smith, M.D., knighted by the Lord Lieutenant of Ireland, March 8, 1837.

The knighthoods of Sir Daniel Williams and Sir Thomas B. Marshal do not appear to have been gazetted, but their names appeared in the Royal and Imperial Calendars.   L. H.

LANCASHIRE: OLD TIMBER HALLS. — I have lately met with ten etchings of old timber halls, "post and petrels," which were "drawn, engraved, and published by G. N. Philips of Chatham Street, Liverpool." They comprise Garston Hall, Ince Hall, Dinkerley Hall, Clayton Hall, Garrat Hall, and several others. No letterpress accompanies them, nor do I find any reference to these plates in any work I have consulted. Is anything known of them ?   T. T. W.

METRICAL SERMON. — An octogenarian informs me that he has heard his mother, upwards of seventy years since, repeat the following singular lines, which she stated she heard in a Derbyshire church on the occasion of the clergyman having forgotten his sermon : —

" Our ingress to the world is naked and bare,
  Our progress through the world is trouble and care,
  Our egress from the world nobody knows where ;
  But if we do well here, we shall do well there,
  And I can tell you no more if I preach the whole year."

I should feel much obliged if any reader of " N. & Q." can inform me, what the above lines are taken from, and if this is a correct version.
                                                W. D.
Kennington, Surrey.

MISTLETOE. — What is the derivation of this word ? Dr. Bosworth writes it "mistel-ta," and refers it to German, Danish, and Swedish, without further explanation. Richardson derives it from mist (A.-Sax. mixen, dung), and ta or toe, "that part of the foot by which the bird is caught by the viscus, or bird-lime." This does not seem a very satisfactory etymology; what mist has to do with dung, or the latter with bird-lime, does not appear clearly.

The word is but once used in Shakspeare, Titus Andronicus, Act II. Sc. 3 : —

" The trees, though summer, yet forlorn and bare,
  O'ercome with moss, and baleful mistletoe."

Why should the most discerning of all poets, in matters both of natural history and folk lore, give the plant so sad a designation; and why, and at what period, did it begin to take so prominent a part in our Christmas festivities? When we read in The Times that tons upon tons of this parasitical plant are sold every year, the query may not seem out of place. A well known passage in Pliny (Nat. Hist., lib. xvi.) tells us, that nothing was more sacred among the Druids than the misletoe. How came it in Shakspeare's time to be considered "baleful," and in our days the most "mirth-provoking" of all plants ?   A. A.
Poets' Corner.

NUMISMATIC.—A gold coin, about the size of half-a-crown, thin and unmilled, was lately found in the soil at Bexhill, on the coast, about five miles from Hastings. The superscription, in old Celtic letters—" Phillippus Dei Grat: Francorum Rex"—surrounds the king, enthroned and crowned, the drapery behind being covered with fleur-de-lis. On the obverse are a cross, with roses and four crowns between its arms, and the legend, " imperat — regnat — vincit." Three characters, being no doubt the date, are repeated before each of these words. The first character is the Greek chi, somewhat in the form of the fylfot; the second is rho, thus making 1100; but the third character is similar to the c in vincit, the value of which as a numeral I cannot find, and only guess it to stand for 5.

I hope, therefore, to be informed, through " N. & Q.," what is the actual date of this coin ? Is there any reason in the history of this first " Philip, by the grace of God, King of the French," why the date should be repeated before each verb, " He rules, he reigns, he conquers ? " Also, what were the circumstances under which this finely finished and perfectly preserved relic of that king was coined ?   GEO. MOORE.
Hastings.

RELIGIOUS STATISTICS.—What is the proportion, I mean the relative numbers, of the various Christian sects and churches? In one of the leading Quarterly Reviews, I have seen a statement on the subject, which a moment's thought proved to be most erroneous, but I do not know where to obtain correct information. F. H. M.

RICHARD JOHN TETLOW, of Knottingley, attorney-at-law, published *An Historical Account of the Borough of Pontefract*, Leeds, 8vo, 1769. Dr. Miller, in his *History of Doncaster* (published 1804), mentions at p. 34 the late Mr. Richard John Tetlow of Ferrybridge, a celebrated antiquary; and at p. 35, gives a letter from Mr. Tetlow to Thomas Seaton, Esq., the Mayor of Doncaster, dated Ferrybridge, May 21, 1781. In the Addenda (p. xlv.) it is stated that all the charters were translated, and the notes to them written, by the late R. John Tetlow, of Knottingley, Esq., a celebrated antiquary.

I hope, through your columns, to obtain further information respecting this gentleman; at any rate, the time of his decease. S. Y. R.

Queries with Answers.

REV. JOHN BRABANT. — In the churchyard of Bishop Middleham, co. Durham, on an altar-tomb near the south wall of the chancel, is the following inscription : —

> "Johannes Brabant, Vicarius,
>   obiit 28 Junii, Aᵒ Dñi 1683.
>   Nuda Sacerdotis docti bene
>   credere inertem.
>   Verba docent PoPulum,
>   vivere vita docet.
> Elizabeth his wife died the 4th of August, 1684.
> Blessed are the departed which die in the Lord."

Will any correspondent be kind enough to help me to a translation of the first line of the epitaph? Is there any meaning in the second capital P in Populum, or is it simply a freak of the stone-cutter?

John Brabant was at first one of the intruding Puritan divines. The earliest entry in the parish register that can be traced as made by him is the baptism of his son John, Aug. 16, 1653. In 1660, the ejected incumbent, Thomas Bedford, was restored. He did not long enjoy the living, as he died in Sept. 1660, and was buried the eighth day of that month in Middleham church.

Up to the time of the restoration of the church there existed, to the north of the altar, a wooden tablet, on which was the following inscription : —

> "Thomas Bedford, Vicar of Bishop Middleham, departed this life Sept. 1660, aged 72, who married Alice, the daughter of Bryan Frizell, and had by her Aman, Robert, Thomas, and John, Elizabeth, Alice, Mary, and Bridget. Alice, the relict of Thomas Bedford, departed this life in

October, 1680, aged 74 years. She was mother, grandmother, and great grandmother to seventy-four children, besides embrios."

This tablet has disappeared. The inscription is preserved in Surtees' *History of Durham*.

JOHNSON BAILY.

[*Nuda* in the first line agrees with *Verba* in the third. As the four lines taken together are in fact a hexameter followed by a pentameter, it will only be requisite to exhibit them in that character, and to dismiss the full stop improperly inserted after *inertem*; the true sense of the passage will then be manifest.

> "Nuda Sacerdotis docti bene credere inertem
>   Verba docent PoPulum, vivere vita docet."

That is, Nuda verba Sacerdotis docti docent inertem populum bene credere, vita docet vivere; or, The bare words of the learned Priest instruct the people how to *believe*, his life instructs them how to *live*.

With respect to the second capital P, it is by no means impossible that, as the wrong insertion of the full stop would seem to have been due to the stone-cutter, this reduplication also, as our correspondent suggests, may have been due to the same party. If, however, the P P be deemed intentional and significant, the difficulty will then lie in making a selection from the great variety of meanings borne by P P in Latin inscriptions, both old and mediæval. It may have been *populum*; it may have been *populum plebem*; it may have been one of many other words or expressions having a plurality of *ps*.

It may be remarked, however, that P sometimes stood for 7, and that the *age* of John Brabant is *not given*, apparently, elsewhere in the inscription. P P, therefore, may have been meant to convey the information otherwise wanting, and to signify that he died aged 77. This method of indicating numbers, especially dates, by letters larger than the rest of the text, is Jewish, and may be seen repeatedly in Jewish books.]

CHARLES I. AND DONNE'S SERMONS. — I have seen it stated that the king had such a high opinion of the dean as a preacher, that he offered a large reward (3000*l.*) for the publication of his Sermons. What is the foundation for this statement? I recollect nothing of the kind in Walton's *Life of Donne*. CPL.

[From the following Advertisement prefixed to the second volume of Donne's *Sermons* (fol. 1649) it appears that his son, John Donne, LL.D. received a *douceur* of some kind from the government on their publication : —

"For the Right Hon. Bolstred Whitlock, Richard Keeble, and John Leile, Lords Commissioners of the Great Seale.

"The reward that many yeares since was proposed for the publishing these Sermons, having been lately conferred upon me under the authority of the Great Seale, I thought my selfe in gratitude bound to deliver them to the world under your Lordships' protection; both to show, how carefull you are in dispensing that part of the Churches treasure that is committed to your disposing, and to encourage all men to proceed in their industry, when they are sure to find so just and equall Patrons, whose fame and memory must certainly last longer than Bookes can find so noble readers, and whose present favors doe not onely keep the living alive, but the dead from dying.

"Your Lordships' most humble Servant,
"Jo. Donne."

This Advertisement must have been written a few weeks after the martyrdom of Charles I.

Again, in an address "To the Reader," prefixed to the third volume of Donne's *Sermons* (fol. 1661) by his son, we read, that "upon the death of my father, Dr. Donne, Deane of Pauls, I was sent to, by his Majesty of Blessed Memory, to recollect and publish his Sermons: I was encouraged by many of the nobility, both spiritual and temporal, and indeed, by the most eminent men that the kingdom then had, of all professions, telling me, what a publick good I should confer upon the Church. . . . . The first volume that I published, consisting of Fourscore Sermons, I dedicated to his Majesty [Charles I.] then living, by whom it was not only graciously received, but I had fresh incouragements to proceed. For the Second Volume, I was forced to take protection from those that were then in authority."]

MACKENZIE, EARL OF CROMARTY.—I am anxious to know as much as possible of Sir George Mackenzie, of Tarbatt, created Viscount Tarbatt and Earl of Cromarty, *circa* 1700, his private life, opinions, &c. &c. Can any one help me with a reference ? F. M. S.
299, Clarendon Villas, Plumstead.

. [A most ably drawn and full compendium of the principal events in the life of the Earl of Cromarty will be found in Brunton and Haig's *Historical Account of the Senators of the College of Justice*, p. 356, published in 1832 by Clarke of Edinburgh, and Saunders and Benning of London, where all the printed sources of information are referred to. If further details are required, our correspondent must sweep the admirable Indexes of *The Acts of the Parliament of Scotland*, published by the Record Commission, and consult such manuscript collections as the Lauderdale papers in the British Museum, and those of Wodrow and others of the time in the Advocates' Library.]

"COMPLAYNT" OF SIR DAVID LYNDSAY.—I shall be much obliged for an explanation of the following line in "*The Complaynt* of Sir David Lyndsay of the Mount, directed to the King's Grace."

Sir David was reminding the king of the incidents of his childhood when he used to amuse him : he says—

"The first syllabs that thou didst mute,
Was *pa da lyn* upon the lute."

These three words evidently mean, as they appear to me, "Play, David Lyndsay," just as a child might express itself. A better philologist

than I am being of a different opinion, I beg to trouble you with this letter. L.

[Our correspondent's explanation of the phrase is clearly the right one. Although Gawyn Dunbar was preceptor to the young prince [James V.], Lyndsay was in attendance on him as a page of honour, and entrusted with his amusement. Lyndsay himself in his *Complaynt*, after telling that he "lay nichtlie by the king's cheek," goes on to relate pleasingly : —

"How as ane chapman beris his pack,
I bure thy grace upon my back ;
And sumtymes stridlingis on my neck
Dansand with mony bend, and beck ;
The first syllabis, that thou did mute,
Was pa—da—lyn, upon the lute ;
Then playit I twenty springs, perqueir,
Quhilk was great plesour for to heir ;
Fra play, thou leit me never rest,
But, gynkertoun,* thou luffit ay best ;
And av quhen thou come from the scule,
Then I behuffit to play the fule."

Such were Lyndsay's playful occupations with the boyish prince, whereof he delighted to sing.]

TAYNTON (GLOUCESTER) REGISTERS.—I find that the registers of this parish go back to Sept. 1538. Is not this very unusually early ? Perhaps some of your correspondents can tell me. On the inside of the cover of this early register is pasted the following notice : —

"Año Dom. 1606.

"This parchment register was copied out of the ould register in the month of August, in the year of our Lord God one thousand six hundred and six, and in the fourth year of our Sovereign Lord James, by the Grace of God, of Great Britain, France and Ireland King, Defender of the Faith. The said ould Register was for —— (word illegible) years before very ill —— (word illegible) and carelessly kept. As much as was found in 'him' is herein included."

C. G. CRAWLEY.
Taynton Rectory.

[By the Parish Register Abstract of 1830, it appears that there then existed in England no less than 812 registers commencing in 1538, when, as Bishop Prideaux says in his *Directions to Churchwardens*, "Parish registers were first ordered by the Lord Vicegerent Cromwell in the 30th year of King Henry the Eighth, 1538, and from thence all parish registers had their beginning." See upon this subject Mr. Burn's valuable *History of Parish Registers in England*, 2nd ed. 1862.]

. TOKEN : THOMAS JOHNSON.—I met with a copper coin the other day about the size of a penny piece. The obverse presents the bust of a man, with the legend "Thomas Johnson ; " the reverse has the words, in three lines, "Bella ! Horrida Bella ! " surrounded by the legend—"Science and Intrepidity," with the date 1789. It is evidently one of those tokens, of which so many were put into circulation by private individuals about that date ;

---

* The name of a Scotish tune.

but who was Thomas Johnson ? And what particular events do the legends on the reverse refer to ?
E M'C.

[The token is described in Conder's *Provincial Coins,
&c.* ii. 205, among "Coins not local of the penny size."
It is not considered rare ; but who the peace-loving
Thomas Johnson was must remain a query.]

Wm. Dyason, author of *Poetical and Prose
Works,* seven vols. 1804. Can you give me any
account of this author, and the contents of these
volumes.   R. I.

[The copy of William Dyason's *Poetical and Prosaic
Works,* Lond. 12mo, 1804, in the British Museum is in
six volumes. Vol. I. contains Philosophical Remarks
and Essays. II. The Idalia Britannica. III. and IV.
Poetry in Letters relative to Books, Men, and Manners.
V. and VI. Miscellaneous Poems. There are no dramatic
pieces ; nor can we find any biography of the author in
Griswold's *Poets of America,* or in any other work.]

The Rev. Joseph Charles. — This gentleman
was Vicar of Wighton, in Norfolk, and published
a very singular book, entitled —

"The Dispersion of the Men at Babel considered, and
the Principal Cause of it inquired into. London : Whis-
ton and White, at the Boyle's Head in Fleet Street,
1755."

Was he the author of any other works ?
D. Blair.
Melbourne.

[The second edition of this work, corrected and enlarged, was published in 2 vols. 8vo, 1769. We cannot
find any other production of the author's pen.]

Replies.

PRETENDED SON OF LOUIS XVI.
(3rd S. vi. 473 ; vii. 39.)

The following is an extract from one of several letters I received from late chevalier Jean
de Carro of Carlsbad, in the year 1852, with reference to this subject : —

"Josephine's Death.

"During the Congress of Vienna, 1814-5, I often met
with Sir James Wylie, physician to Emperor Alexander.
He told me that, whilst at Paris, he had been sent by
Alexander to Josephine, inhabiting then Malmaison
(where this sovereign and some other princes used to
visit her), on the first information received by his majesty of the sudden and dangerous illness of the ci-devant
Imperatrice des Français. Sir James found her in a
hopeless state, with every symptom of poison. She died
soon after he had left her. He made no observation on
that death as a crime. He merely mentioned it as a fact,
nor did I ever think any more about it *during twenty-two
years.*

"I spent the whole winter of 1836-7 at Dresden ; where
the whole family (Naundorf) of the Duke of Normandy
or Lewis XVII. resided, whilst the Prince was, as you
may perhaps remember, at Camberwell, near London,

occupied with some pyrotechnical invention of his own. His
wife wishing to consult me about Carlsbad, I was called
to her, where I went with the utmost reluctance, after
having attended here the Duchess of Angoulême, in a
most serious illness, and having left her as well satisfied
with me as I was with her Royal Highness. In spite of
all that reluctance, and of the notion I had that I was
going to visit adventurers, that opinion disappeared gradually and completely. By all that I saw, heard, and
read, I do not more firmly believe in my own existence
than I believe in the identity of the late Lewis XVII. ;
who died at Delft, in Holland, on the 10th of August,
1845, after having had with him the most interesting
personal correspondence. All his family are still at
Breda.

"Lewis XVII.'s escape from the Temple, in 1796, was
the work of Josephine (widow Beauharnais), associated
with Pichegru, Hoche, and a Count de Frotte, with a help
of much money from the Vendeans. Some beautiful
medals, called *Les 6 Victimes,* have been coined at Berlin ;
upon one of which the four names of the orphan's libera-
tors are engraved. He was entrusted to a Swiss family
(watchmaker), who was ordered to bring him to Rome ;
and the Vatican Chancery delivered to the Swiss couple
a certificate of having received his royal person. He
passed two years in the Romagna, till at last Lewis
XVIII., then Count of Provence, discovered his place of
refuge, had him seized, and, during no less than sixteen
years, had him thrown into mysterious confinements, and
persecuted him so atrociously, that it would appear fabulous if the truth of it was not so well ascertained. All
this is admirably described and documented by Mons.
Graun[?] de la Barre, formerly Procureur du Roi à Angers,
in his *Intrigues Devoilées, ou Louis XVII dernier Roi
Legitime de France, décédé le 10 Août,* 1845, *etc.,* at Delft,
in Holland ; and to be had at Paris, Bruzelles, and
Leipsic. The only friends he had among crowned heads,
was the late King of Holland, who allowed that he
should be buried at Delft, under all his French names
and titles. An autopsy of his body took place under
eight physicians and surgeons ; who had under their eyes
an old little album, in which Madame de Rambaud, his
governess, had, while still in the cradle, described a singular natural sign which the Prince had on one of his thighs ;
representing, as they then used to say, a flying dove (*La
Colombe du St. Esprit*) ; and the scars left behind one
of his ears by leeches, which Madame de Rambaud had
applied with her own hands ; and the corpse and album
were found to conform.

"The Hon. and Rev. Charles Percival, Rector of Calverton also—who translated some Memoirs written by
Louis XVII. from Delft, with a very flattering preface—
tells, in one of his notes, the following anecdote about
Josephine :—' In one of her *soirées* at Malmaison, a few
days before her death, Emperor Alexander was speaking
of the happiness he felt from the share he had in the Restoration of the Bourbons. Upon which Josephine smartly
replied : ' Quant à la Réstauration vous y êtes ; cela est
vrai, mais quant à la légitimité, Sire, vous n'y êtes
pas. Tous les morts ne sont pas dans le tombeau.'

"Nobody assuredly will doubt that in such a *salon*
Louis XVIII. had his own spies ; and that such an allo-
cution of Josephine to such a sovereign as Alexander
must have been dreadful to the King ; because, to admit
Louis XVII.'s existence, was synonymous to the acknowledgment of his usurpation of the French crown. Whoever knows the prodigality which Louis XVIII. has shown
in the use of poison, gunpowder, and dagger, in the whole
history of his nephew's life, does not find the least difficulty in explaining the *post hoc propter hoc* of Josephine's
sudden death, after her imprudent speech to the Emperor Alexander, in the middle of such a brilliant *salon* as

we may imagine to have been the persons invited with Alexander. Though not mathematically proved, few persons, who know the villanous history, doubt that the Duke of Berri was a victim of his lively sympathy for Louis XVII., in whose favour he spoke warmly to Louis XVIII.—in whose ante-chamber a dreadful scene was once heard between the uncle and the nephew a few days before the Duke was murdered."

GEORGE VERE IRVING.

There have been five persons who, at different times, have put forth claims to be recognised as the Dauphin, long supposed to have died in the Temple.

The first in date was *Hervagault*. He was first heard of in 1802, and died in 1812.

The next was *Naundorff*, who put forth his claim in 1812.

The third was *Bruneau*, who appeared before the public in 1816. His story excited but little attention. The date of his death is uncertain.

The fourth, *Hébert*, was perhaps the best known. He lived for some years in England. He died in 1845.

Finally came *Eleazar Williams*, a dissenting minister in America, who died in 1858. F. M.

DAVISON'S CASE.
(3rd S. v. 399; vi. 539.)

The case referred to by T. B. took place in the Northern Circuit in the last century, and was tried by Lord Mansfield. It is reported from the note book of a deceased lawyer, in a publication named the *Story Teller*. A person, supposed to be a stranger, called one evening at a gentleman's house, and was hospitably entertained. He slept there, and was found dead in his bed in the morning, but without any marks of violence ; so that the coroner's jury returned a verdict of "Died by the visitation of God." Suspicion, however, fell upon the master of the house, in which he kept only a housekeeper, and a man-servant, the latter of whom slept in an outhouse adjoining the stable. The only evidence was that of a man, who happened to pass by the house at about three o'clock in the morning, observed a light moving about the house, and saw a figure holding a light go from the room where the master slept to the housekeeper's room ; and then saw two persons come out of that room, when the light disappeared for a minute. They returned, passing along to the master's room again. In about five minutes the light disappeared. Before it was extinguished, however, he had twice perceived some dark object come between the light and the window, as if a door had been placed before the light. But in the room there was nothing to account for this object : there was neither cupboard nor press in the room. The only other fact adduced was

that there had been found in the house the stopper of a small bottle of a singular description, and apparently of foreign manufacture.

The judge, when the case was closed, thought there was hardly sufficient evidence to call for a defence, and the jury consented that the case should be stopped. A verdict of acquittal was about to be taken, when the prisoner requested to be allowed to call a witness to clear his character, and explain those circumstances which seemed to make against him. Lord Mansfield, though against his inclination and usual habit, consented. The prisoner then gave his own account of the affair— that he had been taken ill in the night, and had gone to call up his housekeeper to make him a fire ; but that after some minutes, finding himself better, he had dismissed her, and gone to bed again. The housekeeper was called, and of course repeated the same story. But the counsel for the prosecution had attached much importance to the statement of the previous witness, that while the two were in the room, something like a door had intervened between the candle and the window, and he suspected some secret closet. He therefore asked her, in a tone and manner not likely to awaken any suspicion, whether while the candle stood in the middle of the room, the closet or cupboard opened once or twice ? To this she gave no answer. He then said he would call it to her recollection, and he asked if, after her master had taken the medicine out of the closet, he shut the door. She answered "Yes."

"Then," said he, "it was opened again for the purpose of replacing the bottle, was it ?"—"It was."

"Do you recollect how long it was open the last time ?"—"Not above a minute."

"The door, when open, would be exactly between the light and the window, would it not ?"—"It would."

"I forget whether you said the closet was on the right or left hand side of the window."—"The left."

"Would the door of the closet make any noise in opening ?"—"None."

"Can you speak positively to that fact ? Have you ever opened it yourself, or only seen Mr. S. open it ?"—"I never opened it myself."

"Did you ever keep the key ?"—"Never."

"Who did ?"—"Mr. S. always."

At this moment she happened to turn her eyes towards the prisoner, who looked pale as death, with a cold sweat upon his brow. The consequences of her answers flashed across her mind; she shrieked and fainted, and the court was adjourned till between four and five o'clock, when the counsel again addressed the housekeeper thus: "I have very few more questions to ask you ; but beware that you answer them truly, for your own life hangs upon a thread.

"Do you know this stopper?" — "I do."
"To whom does it belong?" — "To Mr. S."
"When did you see it last?"—"On the night of Mr. T.'s death." *

At this moment the solicitor for the prosecution entered with a tray, on which were a watch, two money bags, a jewel case, a pocket-book, and a bottle of the same manufacture as the stopper, and closed with a cork. The solicitor had set off on horseback with two sheriff's officers, during the adjournment of the court, to the house, about ten miles distant, and had discovered the secret closet, within which he had found the whole of the property of the deceased, as also the bottle which the medical men pronounced to contain the prussic acid, from which the deceased had been poisoned. The result is obvious: the murderer was convicted and executed.

Without undertaking to reconcile this account with the story of Mr. Davison, I may observe that it differs in some respects from the relation of T. B. The first witness *had* deposed to the door of the closet as a dark object, intervening between the window and the light; and it was the cross-examining counsel, and not the judge, who so cleverly put the questions to the housekeeper, which led to the conviction of the murderer.

F. C. H.

HAGBUSH LANE.

(3rd S. vii. 13.)

In the year 1847, "many a time and oft," I repaired to the remnant of Hagbush Lane, there also to do my "bit" of sketching, as others had done forty years ago. The object of my sketch was a brickmaker's shed, gracefully finished off, in the true "bit" style by an elm tree. The rude roadway in front of this shed I always looked upon as part of the ancient Hagbush Lane; the part I am speaking of being little more than a lusty stone's throw from the north end of the Copenhagen Tunnel, on the Great Northern Railway. Opposite the Caledonian Asylum, in 1847, there was, some small distance back from the Caledonian Road, a very picturesque cottage, *seemingly* at the top of a high bank, owing to the clay in front having been dug away for bricks — oh, word of horror! The back of this cottage — which might easily have been the "Cottage in Hagbush Lane," for it was picturesque enough, and much more than old enough to have been pictured in the Royal Academy Exhibition forty years ago — came pretty level with the field, the greater part of which is now occupied by the "Cattle Market." I was much taken with the appearance of this

cottage, at the time of my frequent visits to that spot in 1847, because there seemed some reason to suppose this cottage might once have been in Hagbush Lane.

Besides the notice of this lane in William Hone's *Every-Day Book*, that entertaining individual, in his *Table Book*, vol. ii. p. 784, has another touch at this ancient way, and the illustration which accompanies it is called "A last look at Hagbush Lane." This otherwise rude illustration is of artistic curiosity, as containing a "bit" of costume : the huge cape-cloak and high stuck-up collar. I just remember the vanishing visions of the last of that kind of cloak. In this paper there is one little touch of the times, 1827, worth being recalled. William Hone says,—

"We proceeded by a stage to the Old Mother Red Cap, Camden Town, and walked from thence along the New Road, leading to Holloway, till we came to the spot at the western corner of Hagbush Lane, on the left-hand side of the Road."

All this comes as sweet music to one, who, like myself, can remember the time, seemingly but yesterday, when the first two bricks were mortared together, for the purpose of forming the Camden Road Villas; to the fields about which I repaired, when a boy, to gather "cock-sorrel."

Gramercy! to think of having to "proceed by a stage" to Camden Town; and yet such things were but a little longer ago than yesterday. Indeed, it appears *only* yesterday I was told, by one on whose face there hung alarmèd looks, that a yellow omnibus had commenced running all the way to Hungerford Market; but not all the way from Camden Town, the starting place being at first only a few yards from the south end of Mornington Crescent. The children of my informant went off one summer evening for an experimental ride to Hungerford Market, and back to the corner of Granby Street, near unto the crescent above named. However, before many days the omnibus distance was extended up to Camden Town, and now how vast a traffic it has become in that quarter.

But to return to Hagbush Lane, the surroundings of which, on the 28th day of November, 1827, the time of William Hone's "Last Look," may be imagined from William Hone's last words thereon :—

"Along the dreary line of road, and the adjacent meadows, rendered cheerless by alternate frosts and rains, there was not a human being within sight."

Alas, how different now!

To those who at this day are whirled through our vast suburbs of bricks, by two, three, and four-penny omnibusses, but who would, nevertheless, like occasionally, in their imaginations, to "merrily hent the stile-a," or "jog on the footpath way" of former times, and so view the suburbs as "*they used to was,*" before London began to sprout out so extensively, Rocque's beautiful

Survey of London and the Country about it, 1748, will enable them pleasantly so to do. By such means and at such a time, to see how near the fields approached to Hyde Park Corner, St. Giles's Pound, Holborn Bars, London Bridge, or even the Standard in Cornhill, is enough to make the most devoted lover of his country feel sad at heart. But there are things worthy of note in Rocque's map. Hagbush Lane, to the north of the present Camden Road, is called "Hague Bush Lane," while the portion nearer London is marked as "Copenhagen Lane," and is, in fact, represented as curving round to Copenhagen House. A lane occupying apparently the present Camden Road from Hague Bush Lane down towards Holloway, is called "Maiden Lane," while the Maiden Lane of my youth — re-christened the York Road — is by Rocque entitled "The Black Lane."

EDWIN ROFFE.

Somers Town.

HOW DID THE ANCIENTS KINDLE THEIR FIRES? (3rd S. vi. 472, 535.) — None of the published replies to this query contained any allusion to the burning glass, which is mentioned as a means of kindling fires in Aristophanes' *Nubes*, line 766.

A. D. T.

Merton College.

CRACCHE (3rd S. vii. 21.) — The word *cracche* is found in Wycliff's translation of the second chapter of St. Luke's Gospel, vv. 12 and 16: —

"And this is a token to 3ou, ye shulen fynde a 3unge child wlappid in clothis, and leide in a cracche; and they hi3yne camen; and founden Mari and Joseph and the 3ung child leid in a cracche."

I think it is in the town of Nottingham that you may find, at the present day, *stables* behind the dwelling houses, hollowed out of the living rock. In Derbyshire it is common enough to see, not only out-houses but dwelling-houses hewn out of the stone; near Buxton and in Dovedale such examples occur.

A. H.

BOSTON HOUSE, MIDDLESEX (3rd S. vi. 247, 542.) — Bordeston, or Burston, commonly called Boston, was part of the possessions of the Prioress of St. Helen's, Bishopsgate. Edward VI., in 1547, granted it to Edward, Duke of Somerset, on whose attainder it reverted to the crown. It successively passed through the hands of Robert, Earl of Leicester; Sir Thomas Gresham; Sir William Reade; and Sir Edward Spenser. One of James Howell's letters, dated Sept. 20, 1647, is addressed to the latter "at his house near Brainford, Middlesex."

A fire took place, about 1665, when the greater part of the old mansion was consumed, destroying all the ancient Court Rolls. It was rebuilt in 1671, as appears by the dates of the pipes, ceilings, &c.

The most remarkable features of the existing mansion have furnished several plates to one of the interesting works on *Ancient Architecture*, published by C. J. Richardson, F.S.A.

The trees about the old mansion are chiefly elms, of a large size; many of which have been considered to have been planted in the time of Charles I. EDWARD F. RIMBAULT.

MURIEL (3rd S. vi. 200, 239, 278.) — With regard to the period at which the word Muriel was used as a Christian name in England, I observed in the Harl. MS. 1500, fol. 63, that Muriel Hastings, married to Sir Ralph Eure, had a son William, created Baron Eure 1544, who named one daughter Muriel. His grandson also named a daughter Muriel. It might be useful to notice the discovery of Seiraphenisia as a Christian name in Harl. MS. 5058, fol. 252. J. W. P.

If your readers will look into the works of the Abbot Trithemius, or into Barrett's *Magus*, they will find this to be the name of the Angel presiding over the sign Cancer. Persons born under this sign were called Muriël, just as those under the sun are named Michaël, or the moon Gabriël. The name is generally supposed to signify "the healing of God," from מור, and to be an auspicious appellation. PHILO-MATHEMATICUS.

THE YOUNG PRETENDER (3rd S. vii. 1.) — The following extract from the *Caledonian Mercury*, 1726, No. 983, is worth preserving in "N. & Q.":—

"Rome, July 13, 1726. The Chevalier de St. George, who has dismissed the major part of his servants, still persists in causing his eldest son to be educated in the persuasion of the Church of England, to the great grief of the Princess Sobieski; who is the more concerned at it, because that the young gentleman begins to profess it publicly: of which they give this one instance, that, as he passed by a church, attended with the Duke of Inverness, as they stile him here, he did not kneel down at the singing of the Ave Maria."

Such scraps are valuable to the future historian. T. P.

SIR RICHARD BRAHAM (3rd S. vii. 9.) — On Feb. 16, 1676-7, the House of Commons ordered the Speaker to issue his warrant for a new writ for the election of a member for New Windsor, in the room of Sir Richard Braham, *Knight*, deceased (*Commons' Journals*, ix. 383). Notwithstanding the terms of this order, it is clear that he was a baronet. He is mentioned in Messrs. Tighe and Davis's *Annals of Windsor*, on pages not specified in the index. Particulars respecting him may also be derived from Ashmole's *Berks*, iii. 61-64; *Lords' Journals*, xi. 299; Green's *Calendar of Domestic State Papers, Charles II.*, i. 113, 250, 526; ii. 326; iii. 253; v. 139, 208.

C. H. & THOMPSON COOPER.

Cambridge.

SURREY BELL-FOUNDERS (3rd S. vi. 389, 443, 544.)—One of the sources of my information regarding the Eldridges is the Churchwardens' Account-Book of Winkfield, in Berkshire, where the following entry occurs:—

· " Anno dni mdlxvto pmo die Maii. Md That Willm. Mountagewe hath delyvered to Thomas Eldruge of Okyngm for castyng of the ij bells the sum of xxxiijs iiijd, for wych money sayd Willm. must have the wood in the churche close at a ćten price tyll he be payd agayn, that ys to saye byllett xxijd the loode and baven xxd, and yf the woode wyll not pay hytt, then the said Willm. Mountagewe shall occupye the sayde close tyll the sayd money be payd to Willm. payng yerely to the churchewardens iijs iiijd."

I know of only one bell, which can be attributed to this founder, and that is the third bell at Yately, a village in the north of Hampshire, a few miles from Wokingham. The inscription of it is—

" LOVE THE LORD THE GOD AND OF EHS (sic) 1577 TE FR."

The inscription is in rough letters, and there is also a rude figure of a man, on the bell, holding a wheel in each hand.

Again, the Churchwardens' accounts of Bray, in Berkshire, show that the foundry continued at Wokingham in Richard Eldridge's time; for the following entries occur among the expenses for the year ending June 25, 1602 :—

" It. payd to the Bellfounder for castyng the
ffourthe bell .   .   .   .   .   .   iijll
It. payd to the Bellfounder of Oakingham for
casting the fourthe bell .   .   .   .   xls
For the carrige and recarrige of the bell to
and from Oakingham and for victuals there .

I believe the Wokingham foundry became extinct on Richard Eldridge's death in about 1623, for Bryan Eldridge, whose name occurs on bells as early as 1618, though never to my knowledge in combination with Richard, describes himself in his will, in 1661, as a bellfounder of Chertsey. A spot in Wokingham parish, about a mile to the north of the church, still known by the name of " Bellfound," marks the probable site of the foundry, but beyond the name, no traces of it exist.

Many bells, bearing the name or initials of Richard Eldridge, are to be found in the neighbouring counties: there are three at Yately, where the following are the inscriptions of the remaining bells :—

" 1. WILLIAM YARE MADE MEE 1613.
2. ✠ Sancta Katerina Ora Pro Nobis.
(There are a lion's face, a coin, and a fleur-de-lis cross on this bell.)
3. (As above.)
4. Our hope is in the lord. R. E. 1617.
5. Lord in thy wrathe reproue mee not. R.E. 1617.
Sanctus bell. 1623. R.E."

A heart occurs in all the spaces between the words on the fourth and fifth bells. The fifth bell is cracked.   A. D. T.
Merton College.

STYLE OF COUSIN BY THE CROWN (3rd S. vi. 308.)—

" In writs, and commissions, and other formal instruments, the king, when he mentions any peer of the degree of an earl, usually styles him, ' trusty and well-beloved Cousin '; an appellation as old as the reign of Henry IV., who being either by his wife, his mother, or his sisters, actually related or allied to every earl in the kingdom, artfully and constantly acknowledged the connexion in all his letters and other public acts; from whence the usage has descended to his successors, though the reason has long ago failed."—Blackstone's Commentaries, i. 398.

The passage that I have here extracted from Blackstone may not give B.S. all the information that he is in search of, but I think it will afford him such a clue as to enable him to solve the problem that has presented itself to his mind; and if he would be at the pains of working out how Henry IV. was related to the several nobles of his day of a rank higher than that of baron, I am sure that by inserting in your columns the result of his labours, he would confer a signal benefit on the students of English history.
                                                            MELETES.

TO TAKE UP ONE'S CROSS (3rd S. vi. 416, 462.)—I beg to refer MR. TRENCH to the late Bishop Maltby's sermon, No. 22 of his Lordship's Collection, which he preached before the University of Cambridge on the 22nd Nov. 1814, for an explanation of the words "Take up thy cross and follow me," used by our Saviour.
                                                            FRA. MEWBURN.
Larchfield.

NEWTON AND VOLTAIRE (3rd S. vi. 533.)—It is quite possible that Voltaire may have said of Newton that, " When he became an old man, and got into his dotage, he began to study that book called the Bible." But if he did say so, it was in direct contradiction of what he has said elsewhere :—

" Newton fut d'abord destiné à l'E'glise. Il commença par être théologien, et il lui en resta des marques toute sa vie."—Dictionnaire Philosophique, art. Newton et Descartes.

I am afraid that the Rev. Mr. Craig, Vicar of Leamington, is one of those careless writers who do not give their authorities. If so, I hope the deficiency will be supplied from some other quarter; for it is but right, either that the charge should be brought home to Voltaire, or that he should be cleared from the imputation.
                                                            MELETES.

KING NIBUS (3rd S. vi. 498, 542.)—Miebidus, or Niebes, sixth king of the first dynasty, reigned twenty-six years. Manetho's History, quoted in

S. Sharpe's *Early History of Egypt*, p. 35. (Lond. 1836, 4to.)   Joseph Rix, M.D.
St. Neot's.

The Bottle Conjuror (3rd S. vi. 531.) — The original advertisement of the celebrated hoax, given by your correspondent O. M., is printed in the *New Foundling Hospital for Wit*, No. 6, 1749. To it is appended, along with other curious matter, an account of what took place at the theatre upon the evening advertised, which we are told was crowded with dukes, duchesses, lords, ladies, &c. I have copied the paragraph as a pendant to the preparatory announcement: —

"Last night, viz., Monday, Jan. 16 (1749), the much expected drama of the Bottle Conjuror of the New Theatre in the Haymarket, ended in the tragi-comical manner following : — Curiosity had drawn together prodigious numbers. About seven, the theatre being lighted up, but without so much as a single fiddle to keep the audience in good humour, many grew impatient. Immediately followed a chorus of catcalls, heightened by loud vociferations, and beating with sticks, when a fellow came from behind the curtain, and bowing, said, that if the performer did not appear the money should be returned. At the same time a wag crying out from the pit, that if the ladies and gentlemen would give double prices, the conjuror would get into a pint bottle. Presently a young gentleman in one of the boxes seized a lighted candle, and threw it on the stage. This served as the charge for sounding to battle. Upon this the greatest part of the audience made the best of their way out of the theatre, some losing a cloak, others a hat, others a wig, and others hat, wig, and swords also. One party however staid in the house, in order to demolish the inside, when the mob, breaking in, they tore up the benches, broke to pieces the scenes, pulled down the boxes, and in short dismantled the theatre entirely, carrying away the particulars above mentioned into the street, where they made a mighty bonfire, the curtain being hoisted on a pole by way of a flag. A large party of guards were sent for, but came time enough only to warm themselves round the fire. We hear of no other disaster than a young nobleman's chin being hurt, occasioned by his fall into the pit, with part of one of the boxes, which he had forced out with his foot. 'Tis thought the conjuror vanished away with the bank. Many enemies to a late celebrated book, concerning the ceasing of miracles, are greatly disappointed by the conjuror's non-appearance in the bottle ; they imagining that his jumping into it would have been the most convincing proof possible that miracles are not yet ceased."

Edward F. Rimbault.

Waking Time (3rd S. vi. 534.) — This word also means *sitting up* with a sick person when death is hourly expected. May the words not then be a corruption of "*watching* time"? "They have *waked* with him for several nights," is a common expression in Lancashire. I have heard the phrase associated with the Irish custom of *waking* with the dead; because in both cases candles, or other lights, are used.   T. T. W.

Barley (3rd S. v. 358; vi. 481.) — The Lancashire use of this word is correctly explained in Halliwell's *Dictionary*. When a boy I used to ramble on the moors with my companions, and

always shouted *Barley* when I found a well-stocked blackberry, or whinberry, bush. After this caution had been pronounced, no one was allowed to share in the find. In our country games, too, we always called out "barley" when we did not wish to continue the play, or desired to avoid payment of forfeits.   T. T. W.

Halliwell is quite right in saying *Barley* means "I bespeak" in Lancashire ; but the phrase is invariably "Barley *me*." Now that I am grown up I say "I bespeak," but when I was a young one I said "Barley me," as other young Lancastrians are wont to do.   P. P.

Irish Song (3rd S. vii. 10.) — I think, from my recollection of the chorus, the song appeared in a worthless serial called *Life in Ireland* (or *Dublin*) : an imitation, or supposed continuation of *Life in London*, wherein Tom, Jerry, and Logic visited the Sister Isle at the time it was honoured with the presence of George IV.   J. H. L.

Perhaps, Mr. Editor, neither C. D. nor your honoured self, ever heard the variation made by a Teetotaller for the latter part of the first verse of the Irish song at the above reference : —

"To your kill me now, Arrah ! dow, wid' your vile
    whiskey now ;
Whiskey's for sots and for fools to regale.
Wellington beat poor old Boney at Waterlow,
Whiskey had killed him as dead as a nail."
    (*Cætera desunt.*)

F. C. H.

Hays of Erroll (3rd S. vi. 545.) — Is the date of the "Tabill" correctly given as "circa DCCCCLXXX," if it were the work of Sir David de Haya, who was slain 1346 ? I beg to call Mr. Davidson's attention to this seeming error.   H.

Latin Puzzle (3rd S. vi. 398, 443, 503.) — My friend Bibliothecarius Chethamensis appears to be quite on a wrong scent, in reference to Lipsius's letter —

    "Aio Locutio tu lita ego fidei strenue,"—

proposed as a puzzle by Scioppius. Its meaning has no relation whatever to Lipsius's Catholicism, nor to his "Diva Hallensis," nor to his "Diva Aspricollis." "Aio Locutio tu lita," is merely speak (or write) ; and "ego fidei (litabo) strenue," — "and I will punctually, and without failing on my part, answer;" or, to paraphrase it in verse : —

Pray break thro' your silence, you bad correspondent ;
And you'll find me a faithful, hardworking respondent.
                    Jas. Crossley.

Amongst the farrago of fun and nonsense dished up by the wits of the day, for the entertainment of Tom Coryate's guests at the Odcombian Banquet, are some verses by Donne which have never been printed in his works. I may be very stupid, but they have puzzled me quite as much as any of those given by your correspondents. Here they are. Will anybody " give me a construe? "—

" *In eundem Macaronicon.*

" Quot dos hæc Linguists perfetti disticha fairont,
Tot cuerdos States-men hic liure fara tuus.
Es sat a my l'honneur estre hic inteso ; Car I leave
L'honra de personne nestre creduto tibi."
       Coryat's *Crudities Hastily gobbled vp*, fol. d 4,
       4to, 1611.
                                        Cpl.

HYMN TO THE VIRGIN (3rd S. vii. 11.) — The hymn inquired after is not a hymn to the Virgin, but one of those commonly called Jerusalem hymns, from their subject and ordinary commencement —

       " Jerusalem, my happy home,"—

or something similar. The verse quoted by your correspondent is one in a Jerusalem hymn, which I find in *Barnes on Revelation* (Cobbin's edition, 8vo, p. 597). The original is said to be in the British Museum (Add. MS. 15,225); and its date the reign of Elizabeth or James I. As given by Barnes the form is :

       " Our Lady sings Magnificat,
           With *tune* surpassing sweet ;
       And all the virgins bear their parts,
           Sitting *above* her feet."

The next verse is :

       " Te Deum doth Saint Ambrose sing,
           Saint Austin doth the like ;
       Old Simeon and Zachary
           Have not their song to seek."
                                        B. H. C.

The verse which MR. STEVENSON inquires about, is contained in the long hymn beginning :

       " O mother dear, Jerusalem !
           When shall I come to thee ?
       When shall my sorrows have an end ?
           Thy joys when shall I see ? "

I have seen it attributed to David Dickson, a Scotch writer early in the seventeenth century; but I do not know on what grounds. In the version I have seen, it stands :

       " There Mary sings Magnificat," &c.
                                        C. B. PEARSON.
Knebworth Rectory.

DODDRIDGE MSS. (3rd S. vi. 472, 541.)—There is something specially painful in the insinuation which has been thrown out in " N. & Q." as to the character of Dr. Doddridge, upon the evidence of letters which were in the possession of his descendants. When a portion of those letters were published, many years since, I recollect a remark made in some review that the editor should have exercised a sounder judgment in their selection ; and that they did not set the Doctor's character before the public in a way calculated to maintain the high reputation he had previously held. One cannot but feel the greatest regret, should the statements thus made be incapable of refutation.

The date of such letters may help us to decide whether the works, which have hitherto identified the name of Doddridge with the most exact and earnest exposition of Christian doctrine and duty were written at a period when the sins and follies of youth were repented of and forgiven; or whether, for the future, we are to read *The Rise and Progress of Religion in the Soul* with a painful suspicion that inconsistency, or, according to the statement in " N. & Q.," some culpable infraction of the purity of the Gospel, lessens the effect, though they do not impair the truth and value of the teaching and exhortation contained in that and in other works of the same writer.   E. W.

IRISH EXPRESSION, "NEGER" (3rd S. vi. 455.)— The origin of this term is given by Miss Edgeworth, in one of her tales. She spells it *negur*. It is from *niggard*, a mean, selfish person.
                                        T. J. B.
Chichester.

HOODS (3rd S. vi. 481.) — It may be as well to add to the information given by H. F. that the hood lined with scarlet and white, worn by St. Begh's men, is a pure assumption. I could mention one bishop who makes it a condition of ordination that this hood should not be worn by candidates who present themselves from St. Begh's. The terms in which he speaks of the affair are strong but deserved.   JOHNSON BAILY.
Bishop Middleham.

Miscellaneous.

NOTES ON BOOKS, ETC.

An Enlarged and Illustrated Edition of Dr. Webster's Complete Dictionary of the English Language. Thoroughly revised and improved. By Chauncy A. Goodrich, D.D., LL.D., *and* Noah Porter. *To be completed in 12 Monthly Parts, Part I.* (Bell & Daldy.)

This is the first part of what promises to be at once the completest and cheapest English Dictionary yet published. Its completeness is shown by the statement that it will contain no less than 140,000 words, being 10,000 more than any other dictionary. It contains scientific and technical terms revised specially by professional men. It claims to be peculiar in the precision and nice discrimination of its definitions ; the pronunciation is believed to be more correctly presented than in any other dictionary. The etymology has received for five years the attention of Dr. C. A. F. Mahn of Berlin ; the spelling has been reduced to a standard of uniformity ; the synonyms have been greatly expanded, and will be found under the words to which they belong ; 3000 pictorial illustrations on subjects of Science and Art are introduced into it, and in addition to various etymological and pronouncing Vocabularies of Names of Places and Persons, and Series of Quotations, this Dictionary will contain an entirely new feature in an *Explanatory and Pronouncing Vocabulary of the Names of noted Fictitious Persons, Places, &c.* Such are the claims to public favour of a Dictionary, which will be completed in twelve monthly Parts at 2s. 6d. each. We surely need not say one word more to secure for the first Number an examination of anyone in search of a good and cheap English Dictionary.

*General Todleben's History of the Defence of Sebastopol,
1854-5. A Review. By* William H. Russell, *late Special Correspondent of "The Times."* (Tinsley.)

As it was obviously desirable that the British public should be made acquainted with the Russian Account of the great War in the Crimea as narrated by the illustrious Defender of Sebastopol, no channel was so fit for disseminating that information as *The Times*; and the conductors of that Journal could not have entrusted the task of analysing, compressing, and reviewing that narrative into better hands than that of their Special Correspondent, who had himself so closely watched and so ably described all the pomp and circumstance of that mighty struggle. When the series of Papers appeared in which Dr. Russell sought rather to give an idea of what the author said than to criticise his statements or controvert his facts, everybody felt a wish to possess the review in a more permanent form. In that form it now appears; somewhat enlarged by extracts from the Russian Narrative, and with some few additional comments intended to correct assertions which its editor knows to be erroneous or unjust, as regards our portion of the Allied armies. As the extraordinary number, size, and consequent costliness of the maps which accompany the original work interpose considerable difficulty in producing that work in English, and even if produced it could only find comparatively few purchasers, the general public are greatly indebted to all who have contributed to the appearance of the present most acceptable volume for an opportunity of studying this great Campaign from the Russian point of view. There is one passage in Dr. Russell's Preface which, in justice to himself and other able representatives of the English Press, who were in the Crimea, deserves special notice, namely, that in which he calls attention to the remarkable corroboration by their then sometimes discredited statements, by this matured history of the siege prepared by General Todleben himself.

The Upper Ward of Lanarkshire Described and Delineated.
The Archæological and Historical Section by George Vere Irving, F.S.A. Scot. The Statistical and Topographical Section by Alexander Murray. Three Volumes. (Murray & Son, Glasgow.)

These three portly volumes are a valuable contribution to the local history of Scotland, and the production of works of this character we trust is a proof of the growing estimation of the utility and value of this department of literature. Pleasant indeed is it to turn aside for a few hours from the many scissors-and-paste compilations of the present day, to a book which reminds us of the works of worthy John Stow, the industrious Camden, and dear old Tom Fuller. It was at the suggestion of that prince of Scottish antiquaries, Adam Sim, of Coulter-Maynes, Esq., that the task of "Describing and Delineating the Upper Ward of Lanarkshire" was undertaken. The work, as stated above, is the joint production of Mr. George Vere Irving and Mr. Alexander Murray. The amount of curious information—topographical, biographical, ecclesiastical, and statistical—concentrated in these volumes, does high credit to the learning, diligence, and vigilant research of the respective Editors. The work too is an admirable specimen of typography, and is not only profusely illustrated with maps, portraits, and mansions of this delightful district; but the numerous facts embodied in its pages are made available by copious Indexes of persons and places. We must, however, refer our readers to the work itself, feeling confident that every lover of Scottish antiquities and Scottish scenery, will be delighted and instructed in conning over its pleasant pages.

*Shakespeare. A Reprint of his Collected Works as put
forth in 1623. Part III., containing the Tragedies.*
(L. Booth.)

At length that consummation, so devoutly wished for by all students of Shakspeare, namely, an accurate and trustworthy reprint of the First Folio at a cost which all such students could afford, has been accomplished. We believe the reprint issued by Mr. Booth, of which the third and concluding Part is now before us, leaves nothing to be desired in the way of a faithful reproduction of the great original. We are sure that the very moderate price at which it is published is such as to justify all concerned in its production in looking for a remunerative sale; and we trust that their just expectation will not be disappointed.

We may add, that Mr. Booth proposes to reprint in the same manner the *Pericles*, and the six Doubtful Plays.

BOOKS RECEIVED.—

The Plays of William Shakespeare. Carefully edited by
Thomas Keightley. *Vol. VI.* (Bell & Daldy.)
This, certainly the most beautifully got-up pocket volume edition of Shakspeare, is completed by the publication of its Sixth Volume.

The Book of Perfumes. By Eugene Rimmel. *With above
250 Illustrations.*

A beautifully printed and handsomely illustrated book, which contains much curious historical matter. The volume seems to resolve itself into its subjects: for its very pages—

"   .   .   .   .   .   .   dispense
Native perfumes, and whisper whence they stole
Those balmy spoils."

*The History of Scotland, from the Accession of Alexander
III. to the Union. By* P. F. Tytler. *Vol. IV.*
(Nimmo.)

Mr. Nimmo's compact reprint of Mr. Tytler's valuable *History* is here brought to a close. The volume contains a biographical sketch of the author, and a capital Index.

We are desirous of calling the attention of our readers to *The Philobiblon, a Monthly Bibliographical Journal*, containing critical notices of, and extracts from, rare, curious, and valuable books. It is published by Philes & Co. of New York, and in this country by Trübner; and in the two volumes already issued will be found a vast amount of matter to interest all lovers of old books. We are glad at the same time to announce that *Le Bibliophile, Revue Mensuelle illustrée*, which is under the editorship of M. Berjeau—whose reproductions of old woodcuts are so happy—still continues its useful career.

Notices to Correspondents.

We are compelled to postpone until next week many Notices to Correspondents, and our List of Books Wanted.

T. W. *Certainly "write to you."*

"NOTES AND QUERIES" *is published at noon on Friday, and is also issued in* MONTHLY PARTS. *The Subscription for* STAMPED COPIES *for Six Months forwarded direct from the Publisher (including the Half-yearly* INDEX) *is* 11s. 4d., *which may be paid by Post Office Order, payable at the Strand Post Office, in favour of* WILLIAM G. SMITH, 32, WELLINGTON STREET, STRAND, W.C., *to whom all* COMMUNICATIONS FOR THE EDITOR *should be addressed.*

"NOTES & QUERIES" *is registered for transmission abroad.*

LONDON, SATURDAY, FEBRUARY 4, 1865.

CONTENTS.—Nº 162.

Notes on Books, &c.

Notes.

LADY COWPER'S DIARY.

The Diary of this lady, published last year, has only a short time ago fallen into my hands, or it would have obtained an earlier notice in your pages. It is of so interesting a character—such a vein of good sense and honest simplicity based upon religious principle pervades the whole of it, that one cannot but regret the loss of any portion of it, that, we are told, once existed. She and her excellent husband, the Lord Chancellor Cowper, were indeed striking examples of wisdom and integrity amidst a corrupt and odious court, and shine to us from afar as bright luminaries in the "naughty world" of their day. She was a widow and he a widower when they married, and though the circumstances that led to their union were by no means romantic, the secrecy that accompanied it has puzzled all those who have discussed the subject, and has never been explained.

The editor of her Diary informs us that "her introduction to her future husband arose out of some law business on which she had occasion to consult him at his chambers, and the marriage, which very speedily followed, was for some time kept secret, as the readers of Lord Campbell will doubtless call to mind. Lord Cowper, in a letter to his wife of December 28, 1706, as quoted by Lord Campbell, says, 'I am going to visit my

mother, and perhaps shall begin to prepare her for what she must, I hope, know in a little time.' Lady Cowper herself alludes to the secrecy which accompanied the marriage, in a passage relating to Lady Harriet Vere, and her designs on the heart of the Chancellor in p. 33 of the present Diary. Yet no sufficient reason is given for the concealment either by Lady Cowper or any other person."

The solution of this mystery is manifestly of no great importance; nor will what I have to produce tend to effect it. Some, indeed, may be of opinion that it involves it in still deeper obscurity. Be this as it may: considering the high character of the parties, and the deliberation with which they formed their several resolutions in the choice of each other, we may fairly give them credit on this head for motives of the most valid kind.

When I read the passage above quoted from the introduction to the *Diary*, it brought to my mind a letter of this lady, which I met with and copied many years ago. It has the advantage of being endorsed by his lordship's own hand. The firmness of thought and delicacy of expression that it exhibits on her side, do justice to the self-gratulatory sentiments expressed by him to whom it was addressed; and the act of endorsing and preserving it are proofs of the deep impression it made upon his mind. He chose her deliberately as a partner fit to accompany him in his meditated retirement, and he was not disappointed. Altogether it appears to me such a favourable exposition of character, that I have thought it a pity it should be suppressed. It is as follows:—

"Sept' 21, 1706.

"My Lᵈ—

"'I'm this minute come to town, and yᵉ first thing I met wᵗʰ was yʳ letter,* wᵗʰ yᵉ welcome good news of yʳ being got safe to yʳ own house. I'm very much concern'd yᵗ you shou'd meet wᵗʰ so bad a journey, but more so at yᵗ having given me a testimony of yʳ affection to me, wᶜʰ might possibly endanger yʳ affairs so much as yᵗ of wednesday wou'd do shou'd it be suspected. I shall take all yᵉ care I can to prevent it, but at yᵉ same time you must give me leave to tell you, yᵗ had I known it before I wou'd have put it out of yʳ power to have made me so dangerous a complimᵗ, however unhappy I had made my Self by it. I can't help taking notice of yᵉ satisfaction yᵗ pᵗ or yʳ letter gave me where you seem to believe yᵗ greatness is no temptation to me: You are very just to me in yᵗ particular, for now I may tell you yᵗ no body but you cou'd ever have tempted me

[* Lord Cowper's Letter, which is dated Sept. 19, 1706, is printed by Lord Campbell in his Life of Lord Chancellor Cowper. (See *Lives of the Chancellors*, vol. v. p. 261, ed. 1857.) It is indorsed, in the handwriting of Lady Cowper, "My Lᵈˢ first letter to me after that we were marry'd."—ED. "N. & Q."]

to break y^t firm resolution (as I thought it) wch I had made of never marrying whilst I liv'd. All ye return I can make to you is to assure you y^t it shall be ye whole business of my life to study w^t will be agreeable to you, and endeavour by an intire obedience to make you as happy as it is in my power to do, since I am wth ye greatest Sincerity

" y^r affectionate wife
and most obedient humble Servt
M. Cowper.

" my Lady Wood thanks you
for y^r letter and is y^r
humble Servt
You dont tell me if you carry'd
Mrs Cowper down wth you."

The writing is in a neat female hand upon gilt letter-paper of a small size, and it had an envelope, which, with the address, is lost. On the upper part of the fourth page, about the middle, is this endorsement: —

"First fre I rec̃d frõ my wife, formerly Mrs Clavering, having been privatly marry'd to her without consum^n by wch it appears I judged rightly of her understanding I hope also of her other good qualitys: j was not induced to the choice by any ungovernable desire: but I very cooly and deliberately thought her ye fittest wife I could have to entertain me and to live as I might when reduced to a private condition wth w^h a pson of great estate would hardly have been contented. W. C."

It is satisfactory to add, more particularly, that in the ensuing period of her life she amply verified the sincerity of her own professions and the accuracy of his anticipations; for, from all that can be learned of her, she proved a very paragon of conjugal duty and affection, the latter of which was so carried out that the decease of her husband was speedily followed by her own.

This morçeau attracted my attention among some papers of the family of Coningsby, formerly of Hampton Court, in the county of Hereford. How it came there I am unable to say, for it had no connection with the rest of the papers. I send it to you for the reasons already stated, in the hope that it may prove as amusing to the readers of "N. & Q." as it did to me. U. U.

LORD DERBY'S ILIAD.

Lord Derby's *Iliad* is a fine piece of typography, to say nothing of its literary merits. Is it not, therefore, matter of regret that its outward appearance should be marred by a recurrence to the practice of eliding the *e* in the preterites and participles?—for instance, "fill'd" and "provok'd," on the first page. The usage of thus writing these

words in verse no doubt arose while there yet lingered about our language a tradition of the time when the *ed*, in this position, formed a distinct syllable, and versifiers wished to save their readers any hesitation at the word, as to how it should be pronounced. But now, when you come to the word *filled* in prose, the question of its being anything but a monosyllable never suggests itself to your ear, and therefore there can be no occasion for presenting it in any other form when you employ it in metre. Mr. Browning, who not unfrequently makes the *ed* an independent syllable, distinguishes it on such occasions by a special notation, "*fillèd;*" thus recognising the popular pronunciation that the word in its ordinary guise is one syllable only. Mr. Tennyson (at least in his later editions) follows the same rule as Lord Derby. In the line —

" The vexed eddies of its wayward brother,"

he leaves the reader to infer from the absence of any indication to the contrary, that *vexed* is to be pronounced as two syllables. He would not, however, have written *provok'd* as Lord Derby does, but *provoked* in all cases, because there is a final *e* in the verb. Consequently, when you come to the line

" So tranced, so rapt in ecstacies,"

you do not know, except from the structure of the metre, whether *tranced* is one syllable or two. Thus, in the "Palace of Art," he writes *stored* as a rhyme to *pour'd*. The older practice would have been to write the former word *stor'd*, and with greater consistency, because in the time when one was a dissyllable the other would have been also.

Lord Derby uses a similar elision in such lines as

" The priest to rev'rence and the ransom take."

I venture to submit that the word ought to have been written in full, *reverence*. The mark of elision ignores the undoubted right of an English versifier to use two short syllables instead of one long one, in certain cases to which his ear will guide him. In Milton's line—

" A multitude such as the populous North,"

Lord Derby, if he were transcribing it, would surely not write *pop'lous*. Yet he ought to do so, in consistency with his *sov'reign*, *vig'rous*, &c.

C. G. Prowett.

Carlton Club.

SIR MATTHEW HALE.

This admirable judge is often gratefully mentioned by Calamy, as relieving the sufferings of persecuted Nonconformists. (*Acc.* 167, 289, 578; *Continuation*, 161, 332.) He was a friend of Stillingfleet's (S.'s *Life*, 21), and executor to Selden (Wilkins, *Vita Seld.* liii. *sq.*) On his MSS. see *Annual Biography* (1823), 130, 131. His

" Origin of Mankind " was translated into German in 1683. " *Der erste Anfang, oder das ursprüng-liche Herkommen des menschlichen Geschlechts. Samt einem Vorrede von dem Atheismo, teutsch herausgegeben von H. Schmettaw.* Cölln. a. d. Spr." fol. A Preface to his tract on the Lord's Prayer (*Fabricii Vita*, 198.) See further, beside Burnet's *Life of Hale* (abridged in Sam. Clarke's *Lives of Eminent Men*, 1683), the biographical works of Welsby and Foss. The following notes may, it is hoped, elicit notices of other annotated copies of Burnet : —

BURNET'S " LIFE OF SIR MATT. HALE." ED. 1682. (Brit. Mus. 1130. e. 15.)

(*Notes by Francis Hargrave.*)

Title page — See further concerning the Life of Lord Hale, *Athen. Oxoniens.* ii. 424. Baxter's Additional Notes on his Life and Death.

Under the Portrait—" Anno 1679." A mistake, for Ld. Hale died Christmas, 1676.

" 1643. Nov. 13. Archbishop Laud broᵗ to his trial. His covnsel, Mʳ. Chute, Mʳ. Herne, and 'Mʳ. Hale, having spoken to the points of law, the Lords adjourned. *Whitel. Memor.* 77. See State Trials.

" 1646. July 12. The eleven members charged by the army to parliament ordered by the Commons to bring in their answers within a week, and Mʳ Chute, Mʳ. Glover, Mʳ Prynn, and Mʳ Hales to be of counsel for them." (Note. Hollis and Glynn were two of the eleven members, and the former at this time had fled abroad. *Whitel. Memor.* 258.)

" 1648. Feb. 13. Earl of Cambridge (*i. e.* Duke of Hamilton) broᵗ to bar of High Coᵗ. of Justice, and required to make good his plea ; and on his desire Mʳ Chute, Mʳ. Hales, and Dʳ A. Walker assigned to him for counsel. Whitel.

" 1648. Feb. 15. *Whitel.* 381.
" 1651. Jan. 20. *Ib.* 253, 256, 258.
" 1651. July 1. *Ib.* 497, 2 *St. Tr.* 159.
" 1660. May 22. *Parl. Hy.* 267, 256. (258 ?).
" —— Aug. *ib.* 417, 424."

On p. 33—" No such thing appears as far as I can find, upon the Journals of the Lords. Mʳ Lane and the then recorder of London were the two counsel, who spoke on matter of law for Lord Strafford. But other counsel appear to have been counselled by him ; tho' their names are not mentioned, and Lord Hale might be one of them."

P. 36. line antepenult. See, however, 2 *State Trials*, 159, where on Mr. Love's trial in 1651, Lord Hale, then counsel for the prisoner, is stated to acknowledge having taken the engagement.

P. 51. Parl. See 22 *Parl. Hist.* 256, 258, 267, 417, 424. Kennet's *Reg.* 130.

P. 190, after 8. " *A Discourse of the Knowledge of God and of ourselves.* I. By the Light of Nature. II. By the Sacred Scriptures. With Brief Abstract of the Christian Religion, and Considerations seasonable at all times for the cleansing of the Heart and Life. Printed in 8vo, in 1688. Note. The Preface to this Book contains some matters relative to Lord Hale deserving of attention."

Among MSS. 2. " In vol. iii. of the Collectⁿ I had from Mʳ Jekyll there is a copy of the chapters of Lord Hale's books de Deo, which I take to be what is here intitled concerning religion. The title seems to be Lord Hale's own title, for it is, ' Capita Librorum meorum de Deo.' "

P. 191. No. 6.—" I have lately boᵗ a fair copy of this volume. My copy is in three volumes. I have given it

to Dr. Parr, and hope that he will find time to publish it."

No. 11. In Mr. Jekyll's *Collect.*
P. 192. No. 13. " Published."
——. Nos. 14-18. " In Mr. Blagden's possession."
No. 19. " Mr. Hardinge's MSS. now mine."
Nos. 20, 21. " Do. and now printed."
23. " Printed."
P. 193, after No. 28.—" A tract on naturalisation, said to be by Lord Hale, and a continuation thoᵗ to be by Sir Wm. Temple. Ex informat. Thom. Astle, Armigeri."
⎰ Cones ⎱ Mr. Jekyll.
⎱ of the am. ⎰
Touching. Printed.
Upon. In Mr. Jekyll's Collⁿ.
P. 202. *Hist. of the Marches.* " I understand this book to be wanting at Lincoln's Inn Library."

JOHN E. B. MAYOR.

St. John's College, Cambridge.

AN ACCOUNT OF THE GREAT BELL OF ST. LAWRENCE, READING, CALLED HARRY KELSALL.

Some time ago a list appeared in the pages of " N. & Q." of bells that have been cracked by attaching the roₑe to the clapper for tolling. This is no modern introduction, for as early as 1594 the practice was forbidden by the parishioners of St. Lawrence, Reading, at which time Joseph Carter, was one of the churchwardens. The great bell had probably been cracked by it, for in the next year it was recast. The actual entries in the churchwardens' account-book are as follows : —

" Michaelmas, 1594.
" Whereas there was through the slothfulness of the sextun in times past a kind of toling ye *Toling* bell by ye clapper rope : yt was now forbidden *by the* and taken awaye : and that the bell should be *clapp.* toled as in times past and not in anni such idle sorte.   J. SMITH " (the Vicar.)

Then at giving in the accounts, at the end of a year, in 1595, we find —

" By this accompt also yt was agreed that our gret Bell should be cast againe, and not so much the Tune of the Bell was cared for, as to have yt a lowd bell and hard ffar, and the churchwarden Joseph Carter consented and agreed to cast yt before midsommer ffollowing, and so he was chosen again churchwarden the second time."

The accounts of recasting the bell were given in on Dec. 29, 1596, by Joseph Carter and Robert Malthus, the latter being the accomptant —

" Kelsall.—*The accompt concerning the gret Bell.*
" The gret bell waied when he was first taken downe, 34ᶜ 38ᵘ.
" The same bell hanged up againe ys increased in mettall to 36ᶜ 49ᵘ.
" So the overplus of metall ys 211ᵘ, for wᶜ ys allowed to Joseph Carter at vijᵈ the pond   .   .   .   .   vⁱᵘ xvijˢ iᵈ
" (N.B., the 211ᵘ should be 2ᶜ 11ᵘ, *i. e.* 235 lb., for which the price is paid).

" Also he ys allowed for the casting of
the bell by the ffirst bargain   .   .   vijᵘ

" And for as much as yt fell out that he
was inforced by misfortune of a fall, in
the first casting, to cast him twise againe.
Therfore there ys allowed in curtesie to
the sayd Joseph being oᵣ neighbour above
his bargain of increase   .   .   .   xlˢ

" So the somme of the whole   .   xvᵘ xvijˢ iᵈ

" Whereof paide by the arreraigies of the
last accompt remaining in his owne hands   iiijᵘ vijˢ iᵈ
" Rest due to him   .   .   .   xjᵘ xˢ."

Other items in the expenses of the year are,

" Paid to Howse the carpenter ffor taking down and having up the gret bell   .   xxˢ
" Geven to the belfounders workmen
that cast the gret bell   .   .   .   xijᵈ
" Paid to those that drew the gret bell
to the church from Joˢ Carter's howse   .   ijˢ."

The debt of xjᵘ xˢ was paid the next year.

The bell is frequently called the Kelsall in the
accounts, having been given by one Harry Kelsall
apparently in 1499. The Churchwardens' Book
begins with the accounts given in on the Feast of
the Annunciation in that year, and one of the items
among the payments is —

" Itm. payed for haloweng of the grete bell
namyd Harry   .   .   .   .   vjˢ viijᵈ
" And mem. that Sir Willm. Symys, Richard Clech, and
maistres Smyth, beyng godfaders and godmoder at the
consecracyon of the same bell and beryng al or costs for
the suffrygan."

This was apparently the usual fee for conse-
crating a bell. A brass in Week church, in Hampshire, erected in memory of William Complyn,
records that he gave 10l. to make new bells for
the church, and vjˢ viijᵈ to the hallowing of the
greatest bell.

It is not stated who cast this bell in 1499, but
it was probably made by William Hasylwood, a
bellfounder then living in the parish. After the
addition of this bell, until 1662, the number of
bells in the tower appears to have been five.

The next interesting entry regarding this bell is
in 1516, when we read —

" Ordinaͣc̄o. Hit is coveñiityd and agreyd by the assent and consent of all the pysshe that what pson wyll
have the greate bell of the gyfte of Harry Kelsall to be
rong at the knyll or any other tm̄ent or obyte, all such
psons to pay for the same bell so ryngyng at eny tyme
xijᵈ to the church wardens for the use of the same church.
And to eny pson that wyll have hym tylled to paye iiijᵈ.
And that the said bell be rong or tyllyd for no pson but
he pay as ys above expssed.
" Pvyded allwey that the said bell to be rong or tylled
at all tymes for the obite or mynde of the said Harry
Kelsall (to be kepte). And also at the obite and mynde'
to be kepte for Mᵣ Thoms Justice Vicar of the pish
church of saynt Lawrence wtout paying eny money therfor but to have the said bell rong and tylled for the seid ij
psons at all tymes free."

The distinction between ringing and tolling here
is important, especially when we compare it with
the order forbidding tolling to be performed by
pulling the clapper. The men that drew up these
orders must have considered that tolling a knell
consisted in chiming single blows. In illustration of this I may mention that the parishioners
of St. John's, Winchester, in 1557, passed a resolution, by which

" It is ordyned at this accompte that no man dwellinge
withowte the pishe shall have any dowble knyll with five
bells, but that there shalbe paid therfore to the Churche
ijˢ, and to stand to the charge of the ryngers."

A " dowble knyll " must mean ringing, in which
the clapper strikes both sides of the bell, as opposed to chiming, in which it strikes only one.

At the time of the reformation, the great bell
narrowly escaped the fate of the candlesticks,
crosses, images, holy-water pots, handbells, and
apparel of the " mores dawncs." The churchwardens for one of the years in which this demoli-
lition was going on, and for which period the
accounts are imperfect and confused, concluded
a bargain for selling the great bell. Fortunately,
however, the parishioners interfered in ~time to
save it; they bought the bell back, and made the
churchwardens pay the costs. In a list of debts
due to the church in about the year 1556, there
occurs —

" It. upon Robt. Sylley and Wᵐ. Lipscombe for redemyng of the great bell sold
by them as appereth uppon their accounts . xxxiijˢ iiijᵈ."

The neighbouring church of St. Mary, Reading,
was less fortunate upon this occasion. Its two
greatest bells, weighing 38 cwt. 14 lb., were sold
for 57l. 3s. 4d., and only replaced seventy years
afterwards at the cost of about 150l.

The parishioners of St. Lawrence, also, though
saved from this wholesale loss, were put to great
expense about their bell, which had to be recast
three times, before the end of the sixteenth century. The first occasion was in 1507, the total
charge being xjᵘ vijˢ vᵈ, which was raised by
subscription in Reading and its neighbourhood.
Among the expenses are —

" Impmis to Willm. Knight for casting
the same bell   .   .   .   .   vijᵘ viˢ viiiᵈ
" Itm. for drinke for thͤ that tooke
paines to take up and downe the same bell   xxᵈ
" For makinge the obligacon wherein
the bellfounder stoode bound to ye pish   .   viijᵈ
" For xlii foote of boorde for ye sowth
window in the steeple where the bell was
taken out and in, and one hondreth and a
halfe of nayles   .   .   .   .   ijˢ vjᵈ."

The second occasion was in 1581. Three of
the other bells were also recast at this time, all by
Joseph Carter; so that the accounts for the years
1579-1585 are full of collections to defray the
expense, and payments to the bellfounder, and for
taking the bells down and putting them up, making

the obligations, and performing other necessary operations about them. One item in 1582 shows that the great bell then put up was inferior in size to its predecessor, viz. : —

"Rec^d. of Joseph Carter, Bellfounder, at severall tymes for the rest of the metall yt was left out in castynge ye fowrth bell and gret bell　.　.　.　.　.　vij^{li}　.　."

It is worth mentioning that the first and third bells had also been recast in 1574 and 1575 by William Knight.

The third occasion on which the great bell was recast before the end of the same century, was in 1596, of which an account has been given already. The bell then made lasted for fifty years, when it broke again and was recast at the expense of 26l. 5s. 6d. But soon after this a great change was made in the bells of St. Lawrence, Reading. Peals of eight had been introduced, of which one of the earliest was put up at Bishop's Cannings in 1602, and their music was found very superior to that of the old peals of five or six. Accordingly at a vestry held on May 29, 1662, it was—

"Agreed that the five bells in the steeple be made into eight tuneable Bells, and that the Churchwardens doe take care to see it done, provided that noe taxe be layd on the parishe towards the charge of altering the said Bells, and provided that the Churchwardens doe bring and secure the said eight Bells in convenient tyme into the said steeple w'hout charge to the pishe."

We see another alteration of practice caused by the introduction of ringing bells in peal, in that "eight tuneable bells," are here required, whereas in 1596 "not so much the tune of the bell was cared for." (Suprà).

The parishioners of St. Mary's, Reading, must have made some similar stipulation on recasting their bells in 1640, viz. that the parish should not be taxed nor put to any charge for it, for there are still three bells in that peal dated 1640, one of which bears the names of "Walter Feilowe and Wilham Gandi, Church Wardens:" but in the accounts for that year, brought in by these very men, there is not one word relating to the bells. The churchwardens of St. Lawrence, however, under similar circumstances, entered in their book a short account of the money they received, and the manner in which they laid it out for the bells. That is to say in 1662,—

"Rec^d of the parishioners of St. Lawrence and others towards the casting of the bells　lxij^{li}　v^s　ij^d
"Whereof payd to Henry Knight, Bellfounder, for casting the five bells into eight bells　.　.　.　.　xliiij^{li}　ij^s　iiij^d
"Item paid to John Stroud, carpenter, for altering the Bells frames, and making the Bells wheeles, and other worke about the Bells　.　.　.　.　xxij^{li}
"Item paid to William White Blacksmith, for Iron and worke about the Bells　xiij^{li}　viij^d."

And in 1663—

"Rec^d of the parishioners of St. Lawrence towards the casting of the Bells　.　xxij^{li} iiij^s
"Payd to Henry Knight, the Bellfounder, for metall added to the great Bell　.　vij^{li}."

If, as is here implied, this amount of metal was added entirely to the great bell, the tenor of this peal of eight must have weighed nearly two tons. But I think it more probable that the tenor then cast was inferior to its predecessor in weight, and that the extra metal was the excess of the whole new eight bells over the old five. Certain it is that the present bell, which may be regarded as the successor of the tenor of the 1662 peal, is very far from weighing two tons; indeed it is probably less than 25 cwt.; for in 1748 the whole peal was recast by Robert Catlin, and made into ten, of which the tenor and first seven bells remain to the present day, but the eighth and ninth have been recast. Altogether, then, the bell given by Harry Kelsall in 1499, has been recast six times since, viz. in 1567, 1581, 1596, 1647, 1662, and 1748.　　　　A. D. TYSSEN.

Merton College.

EPIGRAMS.—The article on this subject in the present number of the *Quarterly Review* will doubtless interest many of the readers and writers of "N. & Q.," to which periodical it makes repeated reference. It suggests to me a few remarks. It seems singular that, among the many specimens of Martial given in this article, a line, perhaps the most remarkable he ever wrote, and certainly expressing the most elevated sentiment to be found in all his epigrams, is not included. Here is this wonderful line : —

"Quas dederis solas semper habebis opes."—V. xliii. 8.

I need hardly say that revelation shows a foundation for this sentiment, of which Martial could have no notion. It has indeed become almost a hackneyed lesson of divines and moralists : that those riches alone which are given in charity, and thus lent to the Lord with a sure promise of repayment, are ours for ever. I may next remark that the reviewer, in his notice of all epigrammatists, old and new, at all eminent, entirely omits Ausonius. Few epigrams are more pointed, and perhaps none is more celebrated than one of his. Two sessions ago, it was quoted in the House of Commons by Lord Palmerston : —

"Balnea, vina, Venus, corrumpunt corpora nostra,
　Sed vitam faciunt balnea, vina, Venus."

The reviewer concludes by counselling such of his readers as remember good epigrams that are falling into oblivion, to embalm them in "N. & Q." I follow his advice as to two. The author of the first, which appeared in the last century, I forget : —

" Says Chloe, ' Though tears it may cost,
    It is time we should part, my dear Sue ;
For your character's totally lost,
    And I've not got sufficient for two ! ' "

Nothing surely can be neater than this other
by Lord Holland, being literally an *epigram* —
that is, an inscription—written by him, and still
to be seen in a summer-house in the grounds of
Holland House; in which the poet of *Memory*
often rested :—

" Here Rogers sat, and here for ever dwell
    To me, those pleasures that he sings so well."
                                                    K.
Paris.

I hope the hint in the last *Quarterly*, that the
many good modern epigrams, now slumbering in
" many a drawer in a scholar's escritoire," should
be communicated to " N. & Q." will not be lost
sight of. Pray call the attention of your readers
to the suggestion ; and in the mean time accept,
what I believe to be an unpublished epigram upon
an epigram : —

" An epigram should, like a pin, conjoint
    In its small compass, show both head and point."

Which describes, however, rather the English than
the Greek epigram.   M. N. S.

THE LATE EMPEROR OF RUSSIA AND THE ACTOR.
The following anecdote has been sent to me from
an undoubted authority, and I forward it as exhibiting a somewhat new feature to us in the
character of the late autocrat of all the Russias ;
and also as recording one of the most happy escapes from an awkward position that wit and
presence of mind might afford. Some years ago
there was a very celebrated comic actor at St.
Petersburg named Martinoff. He had most extraordinary powers of imitation, and was so great a
favourite with the public, as sometimes to venture interpolations of his own, instead of following
the advice of Hamlet to the players to "speak no
more than is set down for them." The emperor
at the same time had a high chamberlain, or personage filling a similar office, named Poloffsky.
Whether for fun or malice, Martinoff while performing contrived to let fly some puns against
this great man, which were warmly received by
the audience. The consequence was, as soon as the
play was over, the actor found himself in the
custody of a guard of soldiers, who took him to
prison, where he was told he was to be confined
for a fortnight. Not contented with this, Poloffsky either told the emperor himself or contrived
that it should come to his ears, that the player
had actually had the presumption to indulge in
imitations of his Imperial Majesty.

On his liberation, Martinoff went to court to
pay his respects as usual, and the emperor told
him of this accusation, which he denied. " Well,"
said the emperor, "if you never did so, let me

have an imitation of myself *now*. We know you
can do so if you choose." This was an awkward
and dangerous position for the poor actor, who felt
he should get into trouble for either falling short
of, or overdoing the character. Still the autocrat
was determined ; there was no escape. Suddenly
a bright thought struck the player, and drawing
himself up, he assumed the exact bearing and
manner of the emperor, and, in a voice so like that
it made every one present start, said " Poloffsky ! give Martinoff [himself] a thousand silver
roubles ! " " Stop," said the emperor, " I have
heard quite enough. The imitation is admirable,
but the entertainment promises to be too expensive. Give him the roubles, Poloffsky ; and now
mind, sir, let this be the last time you ever dare
to mimic me here or elsewhere." It is of course
unnecessary to say Martinoff was too glad to
pocket the money, and escape so well.   A. A.
Poets' Corner.

WILLS PUBLISHED. — I beg to add two to the
lists already noted : —
    " 1558, May 18. Will of Richard *Almoke* of Sand-
hooton, co. York, proved at York, 16 Sep. 1558, by John
Almoke, his son."
    " 1558, March 4. Will of John *Almoche*, the son ' of
Sandhuton,' proved at York, 10 May, 1559, by Thomas
Almoche and Robert Almoche his brothers."

These were published in the *Archæological
Journal*, vol. viii. p. 116, with very elaborate and
learned notes.

The material point as to dates appears to have
been overlooked by the editor. The 16th Sept.
1588, when the son proved his father's will, was
previous to March 4, 1588 (O. S.), when he made
his own will.

The importance of this is shown in the form of
the wills. The testators "died in the days of
strong religious reaction," as the editor of the
wills truly says, and it is on this point that they
are interesting.

The first attesting witness to both is " Sr Bar-
tholmew Smith," and no doubt he was the priest
who made them both. In the father's will he
requests " to be buried within the Pšhe Churche
earth of our Blessed Lady in Thriske ; " and he
gives to " Sr Bartholomew Smithe " a very small
legacy " to pray for my soull, and all Christen
soules." This was very right and lawful in May,
1558, the last year of Queen Mary.

In the following March of the same year
(O. S.) when " Sir Bartilmewe " makes a will for
the son, Queen Mary had been dead about four
months; and, although he repeats the words as to
being "buried in the pishe churche of our Ladye
in Thriske" (Thirske), and the legacy to a somewhat larger amount to "Sr Bartilmewe Smyth,"
he ends there, and does not venture to say a word
about praying for souls. Elizabeth was queen,
and the priest was prudent.

The difference of spelling names of persons and places is remarkable. There are five attesting witnesses to each will, and three are the same to both, and they all spell their names differently in the two wills.   A. K.

An Old Soldier. — The *United Service Gazette* states that the oldest officer now in the army is Adjutant G. Peacocke, on half-pay of the 88th Regiment, whose commission bears date March 31, 1783. His name appears in the same Army List with those of Quartermasters Ranson and Lewis, who were reduced to staff-pay in 1712 and 1713, "so that we have an officer now living who may have conversed with two veterans of the wars in the Low Countries of William III. and Marlborough," it being assumed that all these officers had originally served in the ranks.   S. P. V.

Certificate relative to Royal Touch. — The following extract from the Register of Harewood Chapel, Herefordshire, is curious: —

"1684.

"September 29, '84. That day made a certificate for Alice, the daughter of Christopher Williams of this pish for the King's Evell.

"My name and seale to it as Minister.
"Her Father's as Guardian."

I presume the certificate was to the effect, that the sufferer had not been already touched.

C. J. R.

Protestant. — The original Protest sent by the Convention of the States of Bohemia and Moravia to the Council of Constance, from which the term *Protestant* is derived, is in possession of the College of Edinburgh, who acquired it in 1657. A detail of how they did so, and a copy of the document, will be found in Maitland's *History of Edinburgh*, pp. 371-2.   J. R. B.
Edinburgh.

The Female Franchise. — It is a noteworthy fact that at this moment the female franchise is held and exercised in the colony of Victoria. It happens thus: — By the last Electoral Act all borough ratepayers are entitled to have their names transferred, without question, to the electoral roll. Now it never seems to have struck our legislators that there may be, and are, *female* as well as *male* ratepayers. No clause of exclusion, consequently, against the ladies was inserted in the Act. Here is the result, as attested by an extract from the Melbourne *Argus* of a few days since : —

"The *Mount Alexander Mail* of yesterday says the contest for that district caused an excitement which has not been witnessed in Castlemaine since the defeat of Mr. Ireland. 'Everything, however,' it adds, 'passed off most orderly.' The same paper records the following fact:—'At one of the polling-booths in the Castlemaine district a novel sight was witnessed. A coach filled with ladies drove up, and the fair occupants alighted and recorded their votes, to a man (?), for a bachelor candidate

—Mr. Zeal.' The *Bendigo Independent* mentions that at the Sandhurst election, also, the 'fair sex,' to the number of ten or a dozen, exercised the franchise, and recorded their votes for their favourite candidates."

D. Blair.

Melbourne, Nov. 26, 1864.

Queries.

PEPYS'S DIARY.

I had always been under the impression that this entertaining diary was published *in extenso* by the late Lord Braybrooke, with the sole exception of such portions as were unsuited to the refined tastes of modern readers. I was greatly surprised, therefore, in looking the other day through an anonymous and undated work, entitled *The Excursionist's Guide to Cambridge* (E. Johnson, Cambridge [1864]), to meet with the subjoined passage. The writer is speaking of Magdalene College: —

"The main object of interest in this college is the *Pepysian Library*, erected at the expense of Samuel Pepys, Esq., Secretary of the Admiralty, and the author of the well-known Diary, which gives us so vivid a picture of manners in the reign of Charles II. The original MS. is preserved here. It is in six volumes, containing upwards of 3000 pages, closely written in Rich's system of shorthand. It is to be regretted that the whole of this inimitable journal has not been given to the world, instead of the curtailed extracts published by the late Lord Braybrooke."

At first I was inclined to think that the writer was misinformed on the subject, but on referring to the preface to the second edition of the printed work (London, 1828,) I found the noble editor frankly admitting that, as Pepys was in the habit of recording the most trifling occurrences of his life, it became absolutely necessary to curtail the MS. materially, and in some cases to condense the matter. Again, in the preface to the third edition (London, 1848,) Lord Braybrooke says: —

"A very general notion prevailed that I had used the pruning-knife with too much freedom ; and some persons even assumed that the most entertaining passages had been excluded ; whilst it was suggested from many quarters that, if ever the Diary should be reprinted, the opportunity of bringing it forth as nearly as possible in its integral shape ought not to be neglected. Anxious, however, as I felt to adopt such a course as might satisfy all parties, I found, after once more carefully reading over the whole of the MS., that a literal transcript of the Diary was absolutely inadmissible : I determined, therefore, in preparing the forthcoming edition, to insert in its proper place every passage that had been omitted, with the exception only of such entries as were devoid of the slightest interest, and many others of so indelicate a character that no one with a well-regulated mind will regret their loss."

That the late Lord Braybrooke was by no means an infallible judge of what was interesting in the Diary and what was not, is sufficiently shown by the circumstance of many of the most characteristic passages which occur in the third edition having been omitted from the first and second. Every literary inquirer would, I feel assured, be glad to possess an unmutilated transcript of a work which is alike interesting to the grave historian and the most frivolous "general reader;" and I therefore venture to ask, through your columns, whether there be any prospect of the suppressed passages being made public, excepting, of course, such as are disfigured by indelicacy. The record of the "most trifling occurrence" of Pepys's life would probably cast much light upon the manners and customs of our ancestors who lived under the Merry Monarch.

GAMALIEL EVANS.

APOCRYPHAL WORKS HONOURED BY THE INSTITUTE. — In the *Foreign Quarterly Review*, No. 11, is an article on Caillie's *Travels in Africa* (Paris, 1830). The editor of this work is rather severely handled by the reviewers, and at p. 119 occur the following remarks : —

"After all, we, like M. Caillie's countrymen, may have been imposed upon. . . . . . The Geographical Society of Paris will be no worse off than their brethren of the Institute, who, but a very few years since, bestowed their highest honour upon a work which the philosophers of Europe have ever since regarded as apocryphal; and Charles X. will be much in the same situation as our most gracious sovereign, who, by a barefaced fraud, was led to confer the honour of knighthood upon a pair of most impudent and consummate quacks."

Query 1. What is the work alluded to as having deluded the Institute? 2. What is the story of the "pair of impudent quacks" honoured with knighthood by our own sovereign? Q.

"BAILLER AUX CORNEILLES."—The French Examiner for the Academy at Woolwich, in the contest of which the result is not yet known, asks the question, "What is meant by the phrase *Bailler aux corneilles?*"

Now the best phraseological dictionary to which access to gives no such phrase under *bailler* or *corneille*, but under the latter word, and also under *bayer*, there is *bayer aux corneilles*, with a quotation from Piron. Would the examiner pretend that *bailler* and *bayer* are different forms of the same word; or is he right, and the lexicographer wrong? C. W. BINGHAM.

BANKERS AND GOLDSMITHS.—Sir Josiah Child, in his *Tracts on Trade*, after mentioning the laws by which he considers the Dutch reduced the rate of interest in Holland, and thereby increased their wealth, argues that a legal reduction of interest might be made with good effect in England; "being certain that the goldsmiths in London could have what money they would upon *their servant's notes only*, at 4*l*. and 4*l*. 10*s*. per cent. before the late emergencies of state" (4th edit. p. 65).

I would ask to what practice of the bankers and goldsmiths of the kind does Sir J. Child in this passage refer? ALGERNON BRENT.
Audit Office, Somerset House.

DUKE OF BUCKINGHAM: COUNTESS OF SUFFOLK. What portraits exist in English galleries, and what engraved portraits have we, of the Duke of Buckingham (Steenie)? And who was that Countess of Suffolk, *temp.* Elizabeth, to whom a portrait by Zuccaro could be assigned? X.

"CALEDONIA."—About the middle of the last century the packet-ship "Caledonia" plied between Great Britain and America. Is it possible to ascertain from what port in Great Britain she usually sailed? S. W. P.

COURT OF LOUIS XIV. AND XV.: GRANDEE OF SPAIN: PRIVILEGES, ETC.—Grandees of Spain were divided into first, second, and third classes. How was the honour conferred, or the privilege obtained? St. Simon, in his *Memoires*, informs us, "that the ownership of the smallest portion of land in Castile made you a grandee." I do not find this confirmed by other writers. If any of your correspondents can give me information on this subject, it will oblige IGNORAMUS.

DISSOLUTION OF RELIGIOUS HOUSES.—Where can I obtain full information as to the subsequent fate of the lesser religious houses? At Harewood, in Herefordshire, there was formerly a preceptory of the Knights Templars, which afterwards belonged to the Knights Hospitallers of St. John of Jerusalem. The Grants of monastic property (Inventory of particulars in the Record Office) have perhaps two references to it, from which I gather that it was in some degree subordinate to the preceptory or commandery at Dinmore, and that Robert and Hugh Thornhill applied for information about its lands 26 June, 38 Henry VIII. Whether they became its purchasers I have not been able hitherto to ascertain.

In what respects did a commandery differ from a preceptory? C. J. R.

SIR THOMAS FORTESCUE, KNT. — Elizabeth, daughter of Sir Ferdinando Cary (who died in 1638), married, first, Francis Staunton, of county Salop, Esq.; and second, Sir Thomas Fortescue. Who was the latter? C. J. R.

"HARD CASH:" "O JUPITER AID US."—The author of *Hard Cash*, in giving a translation of a doctor's prescription, in several instances apparently considers the symbol ℞, with which such documents commence, as equivalent to the invocation "O Jupiter aid us." Is this his meaning? And if so, what is the authority for the interpretation? It is generally supposed that ℞ is short for "Recipe." W. B.

HERALDIC.—Will any of your heraldic correspondents kindly elucidate the following coats of arms, which being in old French, are not as clearly translatable as I could wish?—

1st. "Escartelle de gueulles et d'or à une face contre-escartellée, bordé et composé de mesme."

Am I correct in my version?

"Quarterly gu. and or; a fess counter-charged of the field; within a border composed of the same.

2nd. "Party en face et souzicelle vers la pointe, en potences d'azur et d'argent.
"D'aucuns dit bass face. Et d'autre, Champaigne potencée."

Does this mean the potences belonging to the arms of the Comte de Champagne?

EMMA CUNLIFFE.

Pant yr Ochain, Wrexham.

"JONAS REDUX" BY JONAS ANGLICUS.—I have before me a 4to pamphlet, with this title —

"Jonas Redux. or A Divine Warning—Piece Shot from the Fort-Royal of Ninive, to all Cities, Countreys, Kingdoms, and Empires, to Exhort them to be careful how they do Admit of the Dominion of SIN, within their Respective Territories, lest they fall into the like danger. By JONAS ANGLICUS. London : Printed for Henry Brome, at the Gun at the West End of St. Paul's. MDCLXXII."

In the dedication to Sir Joseph Sheldon, Alderman of London, and the whole Honourable Company of Drapers, the author alludes to the signal obligations he had from his childhood received from Sir Joseph's most reverend and honourable uncle, the Archbishop of Canterbury, and says he had the honour to be a Draper by descent. It is a poem in Latin and English on opposite pages. Who was the author?   S. Y. R.

LADY MASHAM. — Can any of the readers of "N. & Q." inform me, if there is an engraved portrait of this supplanter of the Duchess of Marlborough? If there is such a portrait, can any reader state where one is purchaseable?

G. W. J.

INSCRIPTION TO SAMUEL MASON. — I shall be obliged to any one who can give me a copy of the arms and inscription to "Samuel Mason, Esq." on a large monumental stone in the chancel of St. Lawrence church, near Maldon, Essex. The stone is now almost entirely covered over by the altar-rails, &c; hence the difficulty of obtaining a copy. He died I believe in 1730. Perhaps some collector of inscriptions may have visited this church, and copied the inscription before it was made invisible.   SAM. TUCKER.

20, Doughty St., Mecklenburgh Square.

MAYO QUERIES.—1. Who was Sir Peter Mayo, mentioned in Guillim as bearing arms: A woodman between two trees, &c.?
2. Who was Richard Mayow, minister of Kingston-upon-Thames, who wrote the Life of Dr. Stanton, 1673?

3. Who was the Miss Mayo, an heiress, from whom the Capels of the Grove derived their estate by marriage, 1710 (vide Burke)?
4. Who was the Rev. John Mayo, D.D., Rector of Great Wratting, Suffolk, about 1623?
5. Who was Thos. Mayo, Esq., of Beyford Place, Herts, about 1660?
6. Who was the Rev. William Mayo, Rector of Brington, Northamptonshire, during part of the eighteenth century?

Can any one suggest a derivation of the name of Mayo?

Any information respecting the above-named persons, or the families to which they belong, and the armorial bearings of the five last, will greatly oblige.   T. T.

The Union, Oxford.

MORTIMER, EARL OF MARCH.—Can any one tell me if Mortimer, the favourite of Isabella, Queen of Edward II., had any motto? His coat armour is known; but I should be glad to know whether he, or any of his immediate blood relations, had adopted any motto as pertaining to his or their arms?   P. HUTCHINSON.

THE REV. STEPHEN STREET. — This gentleman was of Queen's College, Oxford, B.A., Feb. 1, 1777; M.A. Dec. 17, 1779; and Rector of Treyford, Sussex, 1789 to 1795. He published: —

"A New Literal Translation of the Book of Psalms, with a Preface and Notes. London. 2 vols. 8vo. 1790."

His name occurs in the Biographical Dictionary of Living Authors, 1816; but I have reason to think he had then been dead many years. In that work, 1799 is erroneously given as the year of his M.A. degree. Precise information as to the date of his death is solicited.   S. Y. R.

ST. ANDREW, WOODTHORPE, IN THE CITY OF LONDON. — I should be greatly obliged by being told if the old registers of this church, mentioned by Stowe, are still in existence.   J. O. H.

HISTORY OF THE TURF, ETC.—Wanted names of, and reference to, books or paragraphs relating to the History of the Turf, the Theory of Betting, and the Doctrine of Chances. Replies addressed to 15, Low Pavement, Nottingham.

HENRY MOODY.

TRADITIONS OF AN ANTECEDENT WORLD. — Would some of your correspondents kindly inform me whether there are not some old traditions held by the Jews of an antecedent world, which world was supposed to have been the habitation of the "Angels which kept not their first estate"? Faber, in his Many Mansions, entertains this very

[* Our correspondent will find a list of recent works on the Turf in the Index to the British Catalogue of Books, published during the years 1837 to 1857, compiled by Sampson Low.]

idea from study of the Holy Scriptures; and moreover suggests that this same planet, in which we live, had been originally the kingdom forfeited through the rebellion of Satan; and which, on his expulsion, was resolved into the dark and confused chaos, out of the blasted residue of which chaotic materials our present world was organized by the word of God. It would be very confirmatory of Faber's opinion, if there were ancient traditions held by the Jews to the same effect; and, admitting this supposition as at least suggestive of truth, as founded from long study of God's ancient records, may not our geologists be finding vestiges of an antecedent, not merely the laboratory materials and scaffolding of a present earth? May not the "stones cry out" to corroborate God's written word by His works revealed in nature?   H. B.

LORD WILLOUGHBY. — In Mr. Dineley's *Notitia Cambro-Britannicæ*, recently printed from the Duke of Beaufort's MS. at Badminton, it is stated —

"His Grace's ancestor, then Lord President of Wales, lay at Gwidir, in Carnarvonshire; which place came to Lord Willoughby *of Parham*, in marriage with Sir R. Wynne's daughter and heire—Lord and Lady Willoughby being at that time from home."

Sir B. Burke, in his *Peerage and Baronetage*, informs us, Mary, daughter of Sir Richard Wynne, in 1714, married Bertie, 13th Baron Willoughby of *Eresby*, and Duke of Ancaster—whose descendant, the present Lord Willoughby, is in possession of Gwidir.

Either Sir B. Burke or Mr. Dineley must be incorrect, and perhaps the two baronies of Willoughby may have confused the Duke of Beaufort's chronicler, Mr. Dineley. Some correspondent may perhaps inform me how a Lord Willoughby came to possess the ancient Gwidir property in 1684, when the heiress, according to Burke, was only married in 1714.   THOMAS E. WINNINGTON.

WINTHROPP : LLAMAN : VIZE. — Can any one give me the names and addresses of the representatives of the above families? A Mr. Winthropp was governor of the Bank of England.
                   H. O'D.

YEW TREES CALLED PALMS.—In Hunter's edition of Evelyn's *Silva*, London, 1825 (vol. i. p. 269), in a foot-note, it is said: "the yew trees in the churchyards, in East Kent, are at this day called palms." I have never heard of this designation in West Kent, or the Weald. Is it so used now in East Kent? Perhaps some of your readers can inform us.   A. A.

Poets' Corner.

Queries with Answers.

DUNCANSON FAMILY OF CANTIRE.—That somewhat remote corner of the world, Cantire, has been so often mentioned in your pages lately, in conjunction with the well known name of CUTHBERT BEDE, that I am tempted to put a query relating to some people who formerly dwelt there, with the hope of eliciting from him or some one else, something about them. My query, though strictly speaking a family one, may yet have, I hope, a little general interest. The family I allude to is that of Duncanson. They seem to have been in their day people of no small importance, but I do not know if any descendants now exist. They appear to have been faithful adherents of the great family of Argyle. Thus when Argyle made his unfortunate expedition in 1685, and when everything had failed, just before he was taken prisoner, he sent off Sir Duncan Campbell, and "the Duncansons, father and son," to raise new levies, "persons all three by whom he seemed to have been served with the most exemplary zeal and fidelity." (See Fox's Historical Work.)

Again, I find mention in one of Burke's Genealogical works of a "MS. History of the Family of Campbell of Argyle by James Duncanson of Inverary."

Later, in 1692, Robert Duncanson, "Major to the Regiment of Foot commanded by the Earl of Argyle," is mixed up in the horrible affair of Glencoe. He afterwards fell at Valencia de Alcantara in 1705. His arms (arg. a chev. sable between 2 sheafs of arrows in chief gules, and a bugle in base of the 2nd) are registered in the Lyon Register, Edinburgh, in the former year, as descended of the family of Fassokie, Stirlingshire. I presume this is *Fasoquhie* mentioned in conjunction with a James Duncanson, in the Retours, 1620.

Later still, *cir.* 1750, I find two brothers, James and John Duncanson, the former proprietor of Kiels, near Campbelton, the latter a surgeon at Inverary. They married sisters, Isabel and Barbara Mayne, sisters of William, Viscount Newhaven (created Viscount 1776, o.s.p.; see Boswell's *Johnson*, by Croker), and daughters of Mayne of Powis (see Douglas' *Baronage, voc.* "Mayne of Powis").

James left a son John, a captain in the army, who was killed in a duel at Malta. Perhaps your old correspondent M. S. R. can tell us something about him. He left also other children, as did his brother John. Any information respecting these personages, more especially any information tending to show the connection between them, will be most welcome.   F. M. S.

229, Clarendon Villas, Plumstead.

[Our correspondent's quotations from Douglas's *Baronage* as to this family are not quite accurate; for it is there stated (i. 263), that Barbara, the third daughter of William Mayne of Powis, married James Duncanson Keyles, Esq., collector of His Majesty's customs at Campleton; and Isabel his fourth daughter John Duncanson, surgeon at Inverary. F. M. S. has therefore made each of these brothers marry his sister-in-law, while he has overlooked the peculiar Scotch phraseology of the *Baronage*, which shows that the elder was not proprietor, but only tenant of Keyles. Historically the most remarkable member of the Duncanson family was the Rev. John Duncanson, chaplain to James VI., who along with Mr. Patrick Galloway, received a grant of the *life-rent* of the temporalities of Dunblane, which accounts for the name appearing in a Stirlingshire retour. Among the poor scholars of the county of Argyle, to whom a grant was made by the parliament of 1661, there appears the name of James Duncanson. Major Duncanson escaped examination by the parliament as to his share in the massacre of Glencoe by being engaged in military service in Flanders, and the king refusing to recall him for that purpose. A Robert Duncanson was one of the baillies of Dumbarton from 1689 to 1701.]

SEVENTH-DAY BAPTISTS.—Having recently, by mere accident, stumbled upon the place of worship of this obscure body of Christians, and having heard therein an excellent sermon, I shall be thankful for direction to any sources of information with regard to their history and principles.

JOSEPHUS.

[The Sabbatarians, as they are called, who are distinguished by religiously observing the seventh day of the week as the Sabbath, are a branch of the body of Anabaptists. They object to the arguments which are adduced in proof of the change of the Sabbath to the first day of the week, and say that the change was effected by Constantine. Their views are contained in the three following statements :—1. That God hath required the seventh or last day of the week to be observed by mankind universally for the weekly Sabbath. 2. That this command is perpetually binding on man. 3. That this sacred rest of the seventh day Sabbath is not (by Divine authority) changed from the seventh or last to the first day of the week. As a sect it sprang up about 1670, and is now almost extinct. We have only heard of two congregations in London, one in Mill Yard, Goodman's Fields; the other in Eldon Street, Finsbury; and about nine or ten societies in the West of England, which are kept from dissolution by endowments.]

CEDRENUS. — I have seen it mentioned in a biblical work that Adam had thirty-seven sons and twenty-eight daughters, and the reference given for the statement is Cedrenus. Who was the writer, and what authority is due to his works? I believe he compiled a *Synopsis of History* in Greek.

J. DALTON.

[George Cedrenus, a Grecian monk, lived in the eleventh century, and wrote *Annales, sive historiæ ab exordio mundi ad Isacium Comnenum usque* [A.D. 1057] compendium, Gr.

and Lat.; cum annotationibus et tabulis chronologicis, Gul. Xylandri. Bas. fol. 1566; and again printed at Paris in 1647, 2 vols. fol., with the Latin version of Xylander, and the notes of father Goar, a Dominican. This work, which is not executed with much judgment, is no more than an extract from several historians, and chiefly from Georgius Syncellus, Theophanes, and Thracesius Scylitzes. *Vide* Dupin, Cave, Fabric. Bibl. Græc., and Moreri.]

EPIGRAM AGAINST ARCHITECTS, BY WHOM?—Who is the "ancient writer," stated to have written the following couplet? —

" If of weak parts the stripling you suspect,
A herald make him, or an architect."

This quotation is from a work of the year 1810. The lines sound like one of Martial's ill-natured epigrams, but after an hour's search, I do not discover it in his work.

W. P.

[Our correspondent is correct; the passage is in Martial, lib. v. ep. 56. He is advising his friend Lupus as to the education of his son, and tells him if he wishes to be rich he must neither be grammarian, orator, nor poet :—

" Artes discere vult pecuniosas ?
Fac, discat, citharœdus, aut choraules ;
Si duri puer ingeni videtur,
Præconem facias, vel architectum."

The variorum note says this expression is not meant invidiously against architects, but simply that the occupations alluded to were much better paid than learned men or poets.]

ANDERSON.—The life and times of Anderson of Dumbarton, a fierce northern polemic, attracted considerable attention in " N. & Q." 2nd S. vi. to viii. In vol. viii. 255, he is stated to have been the son of John Anderson, who had fled from Elgin, owing to religious persecution, and settled in Edinburgh. I am anxious to identify this John Anderson with John Anderson, " depute clerk to the Justice Court," *circa* 1690.

F. M. S.

229, Clarendon Villas, Plumstead.

[We are afraid our correspondent will fail in his identification. The statement to which he refers is to the effect that John Anderson, a person of some standing, born and resident in Elgin, was persecuted by *the Presbyterians* as a Nonconformist, and was obliged to leave Elgin for Edinburgh. This could not have occurred later than 1650-1, and as he is said to have been a person of some note at that time, he must have been at least twenty-five years of age when he left Elgin, and sixty-five at the Revolution; an age at which it is by no means probable that he would be appointed to such an office as Depute Clerk to the Justiciary Court.]

" THE LIFE OF CAPTAIN ROBERT BOYLE."—I lately became possessed of a number of old books and papers, and on examining these, I found a small volume, with the above title, on the top of each page. The volume is imperfect, however. It wants the full title-page, and at the end, some leaves are out. The last page remaining is marked

230. The *Life* itself is quite in the style, &c. of *Roderick Random* and other similar romances of the middle of last century. Would some of your correspondents have the kindness to state, first, Who was the author? and, secondly, When, and by whom, this book was printed and published?

B. J.

[This work is entitled *The Voyages and Adventures of Captain Robert Boyle in several Parts of the World, &c.* Lond. 1728, 8vo, and has been frequently reprinted. It is a fictitious narrative, attributed to Benjamin Victor as well as to W. R. Chetwood—most probably by the latter.]

Replies.

A LONDON BOOK AUCTION, 1698.
(3rd S. vii. 6.)

The passage cited will lose much of its value and suggestiveness, when it is known that the *Journey to London*, of which it forms part, was purely imaginary, and in no way a record of actual observation. It was never "written originally in French by Monsieur Sorbiere," or any one else, and consequently never underwent the process of translation; but was the production of the witty Dr. William King, Advocate of Doctors' Commons, in facetious imitation of the *Journey to Paris*, in the same year, by Dr. Martin Lister, whose records of his trip were thought too minute and trifling for a man of his professional and scientific reputation. This had been preceded about thirty years before by the *Journey to London* of M. Sorbiere, which, the fruit of three months' sojourn in this country, is such a dull and dreary farrago of mistakes and misrepresentations, that it was thought fit and politic to deprive him of his office of historiographer of France, for so malicious an attack upon a friendly nation; while he was not less severely censured by his countryman Voltaire, than by Sprat, Bishop of Rochester, here. The volume appeared in this country under the title of—

"A Voyage to England, containing many things relating to the State of Learning, Religion, and other Curiosities of that Kingdom; as also, Observations by Dr. T. Sprat, &c. London, 8vo, 1709."

Thus this author too appeared fair game to Dr. King, who appropriately ascribed his ironical travestie to him, while it is made to accord, paragraph by paragraph, with the *Journey* of Dr. Lister. That relating to book-auctions, which corresponds with the passage cited, is as follows:

"I was at an Auction of Books in the Rue St. Jaques, where were about forty or fifty people, most abbots and monks. The books were sold with a great deal of trifling and delay, as with us, and very dear; for *Hispania Illustrata And. Sciotti*, of the Francfort edition, from 20 livres, at which it was set, they bid up by little and little; to 36 livres; at which it was sold. The next was a *Catalogue of French Books*, in a thin fol. in an old Parchment Cover by De la Croix de Maine, 8 livres. And so I left them to shift it amongst themselves."—*A Journey to Paris, &c.* p. 136.

An excellent edition of the works of Dr. King, including the "Remarks on Varillas," "Journey to London," "Art of Cookery," "Art of Love," "Miscellany Poems, &c." was published in three volumes, small 8vo, 1776, with historical notes and memoirs of the author, by the editor, Mr. John Nichols. With *this* Dr. King, of *Doctors' Commons*, must not be confounded his namesake and contemporary, Dr. William King, *Principal of St. Mary's Hall, Oxford*. This latter, "equally eminent as a wit and tory," was author, *inter alia*, of the celebrated satire against the Countess of Newburgh, entitled *The Toast*, of which an interesting notice will be found in Bentley's *Miscellany*, for June, 1857, p. 616. This caution is not unnecessary, as Lowndes has rolled these two single gentlemen into one, and H. G. Bohn, in his new edition, has failed to detect the error; though both properly ascribe to the latter author the *Political and Literary History of his own Times*, London, 8vo, 1819, thus published half a century after the death of the writer.

It may not be out of place to add that *The Toast*, and the other pieces of Dr. King, were gathered into a quarto volume, under the title of *Opera Gul. King, LL.D., Aulæ B. M. V. apud Oxon: Princip.*, with a curious frontispiece by Gravelot, in which Lord George Granville is represented displaying the youthful charms of the Countess of Newburgh (formerly Lady Francis Brudenel, sister of the Earl of Cardigan) to Apollo, while a Satyr points with derision to her coquettish airs and ghastly appearance in after life. I have seen a copy of this volume in which was inserted a letter from Dr. Bullock, executor of Dr. King, in which he stated that he had reserved only fifty copies for the Doctor's old friends, and had committed the rest to the flames. It has thus become very rare.

Some sixty years ago the ponderous, hot-pressed quartos of Sir John Carr managed to acquire, I suppose in the dearth of better books, a considerable share of public favour, and were productive of no little emolument to author and publisher. One of these, *The Stranger in Ireland*, a tissue of puerile and trivial observations, fell under the notice of the witty Edward Dubois, who travestied it, as Dr. King had previously *Lister's Voyage*, in a volume entitled, *My Pocket Book; or, Hints for a Ryghte Merrie and Conceitede Tour, in quarto, to be called "The Stranger in Ireland,"* in 1805, 3rd ed. 12mo, London, 1808. This piece of happy satire spoilt Sir John's market; the public ceased to buy his books, and the publishers refused to embark in new speculations. Hence an action for libel by the worthy knight against

Hood and Sharpe (London, 8vo, 1808) which resulted, " without a minute's consultation," in a verdict for the defendants. In the same year appeared also, *Old Nick's Pocket-Book; or, Hints for a Ryghte Pedantique, and Mangleinge Publication, to be called " My Pocket Book,"* 12mo. See also *New Monthly Magazine,* vol. lxxxi. p. 84.

WILLIAM BATES.

Birmingham.

The account of this auction appears in a *Journey to London,* in the year 1698, assumed to be " Written originally in French, by Monsieur Sorbiere, and newly translated into English," but in fact written by the humorous Dr. Wm. King, as a quiz on the voyage of Monsieur Sorbiere into England, published in 1664, a work full of scurrility and errors. In the Introduction, Monsieur Sorbiere is made to say, " I might here take the opportunity to beg pardon of the English for my misrepresentation thirty years ago; but it is to be hoped this book will make peace with that nation." This *Journey* is also intended as a satire on Dr. Lister's *Journey to Paris,* which was considered to be of a trifling nature. The whole of this assumed *Journey to London* of Monsieur Sorbiere will be found in the first volume of Dr. King's *Original Works* in 3 vols. 1776. W. S.

THE BLUE-COAT SCHOOL.

(3rd S. vii. 8.)

The original grant of the monastery of the Gray Friars, for the purpose of founding Christ's Hospital, was in the last year of Henry VIII., viz. 1546-7. Dudley's letter, in application to Cecil for the "preferment of a certeyn free scole," was in February of the following year. The coincidence of dates inclines me to the opinion, that Dudley's application was in relation to that grant. It could not refer to the Charter House School, as that was not established till after 1611—nearly seventy years later. The credit of the latter establishment is due *alone* to Thomas Sutton, the founder.[*] In 1609, Sutton obtained an Act of Parliament empowering him to erect a hospital at Hallingbury Bouchers, in Essex. He soon afterwards changed his mind as to the situation of the hospital; and purchasing the then lately dissolved Charter House from the Earl of Suffolk for 13,000*l.,* he petitioned King James, and obtained permission to change the hospital from Hallingbury Bouchers to the Charter House in London, under the name of the "Hospital of King James"—the

[* We were perfectly aware that the Charter House ... was not established till 1611; but as we conjecturally ..., the Earl of Warwick's letter " may refer to a proposed school at the Charter House." The Earl at this time was residing in Ely Place, Holborn.—Ed.]

letters patent for which were duly issued. Sutton died Dec. 12, 1611.

Till that time, I apprehend, there had been no thought of establishing any school at the Charter House. Dudley (while Earl of Warwick) had purchased it from Sir Edward North, merely as a town residence.

Maitland, in his *History of London* (fo. 1739), says of Christ's Hospital: —

" This is a Royal Foundation, which was granted by *Henry* the eighth, anno 1547 : and in the year 1552, confirmed to the Citizens by Charter of *Edward* the sixth, who thereby incorporated the Governors of his several Foundations in the City and Liberties thereof by the name of the *Mayor, Commonalty,* and *Citizens* of the City of London, Governors of the Possessions, Revenues, and Goods of the Hospitals of Edward the sixth, King of England, &c. . . . . So hearty and zealous were the Citizens in the prosecution of this good work, that the Hospital was no sooner fitted up, than they took into the same, in the Month of November of the said year 1552, three hundred and forty children ; which number, before the end of the year, being increased to three hundred and sixty, the charge thereof in the first year amounted to Fourteen hundred and sixty-two pounds eight shillings and eight pence."

Stow, in his *Survey of London* by Strype (fol. 1720), says of Christ's Hospital : —

" The Gray Friars within Newgate, and St. Bartholomew's Hospital, belonging antiently to the Priory of St. Bartholomew's hard by, together with St. *Nicholas* and St. *Ewen,* two neighbouring parishes, were obtained by the City of K. *Henry* the eighth, in the 38th year of his reign : All which that King granted to the City for the relieving and succouring of their Poor ; one of the last good Acts that King did before his Death. . . . . .

" He also then founded two Churches out of those two religious houses : the one to be called *Christ Church,* out of the *Gray Fryars* ; and the other *Little St. Bartholomew's,* out of the Hospital of that name ; with Competent Salaries for the respective Vicars and Ministers.

" And as the King had founded Churches on these places, so according to that, his Grant, it lay upon the City to establish here a standing provision for the poor. And accordingly, some part of the scite of the *Gray Friars* they purposed for a large Hospital for poor Fatherless Children ; here to be decently maintained and piously brought up, and fitted for Trades and Callings. But it was not before 5 or 6 years after the King's Grant, viz. anno 1552, the Lord Mayor and Citizens fell upon the reparation and fitting up of the *Fryars* for the reception of the Children. And they effected it the same year, and called it *Christ Church Hospital.* So that in the month of *September* they took in near 400 Orphans, and clothed them in *Russet*; but ever after they wore Blue Cloth Coats, whence it is commonly called the *Blue Coat Hospital.*"

G. A.

Barnsbury.

" THE IRISH TUTOR" (3rd S. v. 479; vi. 542.) With all respect for the authority mentioned by W. J. F. I cannot but think he is mistaken in saying that the part of the Irish Tutor was written for Tyrone Power.

The farce was performed in London for the

first time at Covent Garden Theatre on 28th October, 1822, when the part of Terry O'Rourke (Dr. O'Toole) was performed by Connor, an actor, who, although he had previously occasionally performed Irish characters, had been principally employed as the representative of such parts as Pizarro, Count Wintersen in *The Stranger*, and Bedamar in *Venice Preserved*. Connor's admirable performance in *The Irish Tutor* led to his becoming the acknowledged representative of Irish characters, to which line of business he was thenceforth almost exclusively confined. He continued at Covent Garden Theatre until the close of the season 1825-26, after which his name is not found in the bills.

I do not know when Power first appeared, but during the season of 1825-26, he was engaged at Covent Garden Theatre, where he performed—not Irishmen, who still continued to be played by Connor, but—a variety of characters of very opposite kinds, and requiring considerable versatility of talent. His name appears to such parts as the Duke Vivaldi in *Clari*, and I myself well remember seeing him play Robin in *No Song, no Supper*,—in which piece, I may mention parenthetically, I on the same occasion saw Mrs. Keeley, then Miss Goward, perform the character of Margaretta, which I have lately seen played by her daughter Louise.

In the following season (1826-7), Power succeeded to the Irish parts, and commenced that successful career which was so suddenly and sadly terminated. I believe his first original part was O'Shocknessy, in the farce of *The £100 Note*, in which Keeley so successfully impersonated Billy Black with his almost endless store of conundrums.

Genest (*Account of the English Stage*), recording the first performance in London of *The Irish Tutor*, says: " This poor piece was written by a nobleman, and consigned to the care of Abbott, the actor; it came out originally at Cheltenham." Can W. J. F. or any other correspondent say when it was performed at Cheltenham, and who then represented the principal character ?

W. H. Husk.

Rev. John Rippon and the Oratorio of the " Crucifixion " (3rd S. vi. 319.)—The Oratio of *The Crucifixion* was not composed by the late Rev. John Rippon, D.D., but by his nephew John Rippon. John Francis.

Gladys: Gwladys (3rd S. vi. 267, 334, 538.)— No doubt that Mr. C. H. E. Carmichael is right in identifying the name Gladys with the Welsh Gwladys, the equivalent of Claudia. Any one who translated it "the Welsh maiden," must, I think, have intended to paraphrase what he supposed to be the etymology, as if from *gwlad*, "country;" he must have treated the name as meaning *his* " fellow countrywoman." Besides

the Claudia of 2 Tim. iv. 21, there is another Gwladys, well known in Cambrian Hagiology, the daughter of Brychan, the wife of Gwynlliw, and mother of Catwg Ddoeth (Catwg the Wise), the same Cadocus to whom two churches in Glamorgan are dedicated, both of which are called in English Cadoxton, in Welsh Llangatwg. This Gwladys is mentioned in the *printed* volume oddly entitled " *Iolo Manuscripts* " (Llandovery, 1848), p. 120 (or in the English translation, p. 520). The short pronunciation of the penultimate in this name is, I think, common in South Wales, though it could hardly have been so enunciated by any one who derived it from *gwlad*, "country," in which the vowel *a* is necessarily long (pronounced *āh*, not *ay*). The natural length of the syllable, according to the best authorities, would be long, and many syllables which are short in South Wales (Dehenbarth and Morganwg) are long in Powys and Gwynedd. In the Vale of Neath two places bear the name of Gwladys: Craig Gwladys, and a beautiful waterfall called Ysgwyd Gwladys. The use of this name in the Herbert family springs no doubt from Wales, the present Herberts, Earls of Pembroke, being descended from the Earls of the former creation (who were themselves of Welsh family), one of whom had an illegitimate son (at least according to English law) by a woman in the west of Glamorgan, to whose son the revived earldom was given by Edward VI. in 1551. When in Wales last year I was glad to find that the elegant Welsh female name, *Enid*, had come into use again since the publication of Tennyson's *Idylls;* it is well to keep up such characteristic names, when they are not harsh or offensive. Though not a Welshman I like Welsh things in their places. Laelius.

Arms of Sir Walter Raleigh (3rd S. iii. 451; iv. 33, 355, &c.)—As the identification of the quarterings on Sir Walter's seal has not been entirely satisfactory, perhaps the following note may be useful. I have now before me a volume of trickings of arms very beautifully executed by William Smith, Rouge Dragon, 1602. The MS. seems to have been dedicated to John Philipott and his friends. The coat of "Sir Walter Rayhley" contains sixteen quarterings, and as they differ somewhat from J. D.'s list (3rd S. iii. 452), and have all the colours displayed, I will repeat them :—

1. Gules, 5 lozenges conjoined in bend, argent.
2. Azure, 7 martlets (2, 3 & 2) or ; on a canton of the second, a mullet sable.
3. Azure, 3 garbs or (or argent), a chief of the second.
4. Argent, a fesse between two chevrons sable.
5. Gules, a bend vair between 6 escallops, argent.
6. Barry nebuly of six, argent and gules.

7. *Or,* three chevrons gules.

8. Azure, a lion rampant *or.*

9. Gules, 5 lozenges conjoined in bend argent (or possibly *or*).

10. Argent, on a chief azure, three crosses formée fitchée. (N.B. These crosses are very indistinct.)

11. Sable, 3 garbs *or.*

12. Azure, an eagle displayed *or.*

13. *Or,* three stags' heads cabossed gules.

14. Azure, 3 garbs argent in bend, argent between two bendlets of the second.

15. *Or,* on a bend cotised, azure, 3 cinquefoils *of* the field.

16. Argent, on a bend sable, 3 horse shoes *or.*

It will be seen that Nos. 1—5 are the same in both lists, as are Nos. 13—16. My No. 6 is different, and my Nos. 7—11 are J. D.'s Nos. 8—12. His No. 7 and my No. 12 are peculiar to their respective shields.

As to crests this tricking has four; viz., 1, a fleur-de-lys *or ;* 2, a stag's head cabossed, gules, between the antlers a fleur-de-lys *or ;* 3, apparently a morion, surmounted with three feathers, all per pale argent and gules; 4, a buck trippant (*not* statant), proper. Motto, "Amore et virtute."

It is very difficult to decide in one or two of these cases whether the metal of some of the charges is argent or gold. I think the ninth quartering is the same as the first, and is Ralegh; the lozenges or fusils are clearly not ermine, and I feel sure they are not different in form from the first quartering. This contemporaneous evidence may enable J. D. to trace out the marriages by which these arms were inherited.

W. H. WHITMORE.

Boston, U. S.

MUM (3rd S. vi. 434, 503; vii. 41.)—Bailey, in his *Dictionary,* states this to be "a strong liquor brought from Brunswick, in Germany." Ash defines it "beer brewed from wheat." I have, however, a curious old dictionary in 18mo, no name, but about 1700, which says : —

"*Mum,* a kind of physical beer made (originally) at Brunswick, in Germany, with *husks of walnuts* infused."

Is this correct ? If so, is the manufacture carried on there now; or is there any record of walnuts being used in brewing; and again, is it the green shell, or what part of the fruit ? Broom tops formerly were employed in England for giving a bitter to beer, and are so to the present day in Italy. Many sorts of bitter have also been tried. This is the first time, however, I have heard of walnut in any form.   A. A.

Poets' Corner.

The following is from a manuscript note-book in my possession, bearing date 1738 : —

"*Mum* is a sort of sweet malt liqr, brewed with **barley** and hops, and a small mixture of wheat; very **thick,**

scarce drinkable till purified at sea. It is transported into other countries. Hides and Mum chief trade of Brunswick Wolfenbuttel."

H. FISHWICK.

PATTENS (3rd S. vi. 532.) — This word is probably from the French *patin,* the sole or cill of a wooden partition, the sole of a shoe, or a skate—"patin de glace." Meige gives *patin,* a *pattin*—evidently meaning *patten.*   A. A.

Poets' Corner.

HEREFORDSHIRE QUERIES (3rd S. vi. 498; vii. 45.) — I am obliged to MR. DAVIES for his desire to assist me in ascertaining the derivation of the word "tump," but I seek to trace it beyond the Welsh form *twmp,* which is but another way of writing the same word. The language of the Celts contained, and contains, many words borrowed immediately from the Latin, and probably still more which are derived from a common origin with it. I suspect that τύμβος, *tumulus, twmp,* and *tomb,* descend from the same ancestor, and that perhaps *toft* and *tot* are also nearly related to them, but the exact course of descent I am unable to trace.

I observe that in the East of England *toft* is a common name for a place, *e. g.,* Toft, near Cambridge ; Monks Toft, in Norfolk, and Toft-Trees, in the same county. If *toft* and *twmp* be identical in meaning, the distribution of the two forms is significant.

I should hesitate about accepting your correspondent's suggestion as to the connection between Rodd and Rood; the former seems to me to be a form of Red.   C. J. ROBINSON.

Harewood, Ross.

PASSAGE IN "DON QUIXOTE" (3rd S. vii. 25.)—I am very much obliged to those gentlemen who have endeavoured to aid me in my difficulty, but am sorry to say it remains unremoved. I think I must give up the notion of *mil* being used in the sense of immense; but I cannot believe that the nymph could have had several *velos,* one over the other; for what would be the use when only the outer one could be seen ? My conception is that she wore a very large *mantilla,* which being fastened, as usual, on the top of the head, descended in front on both sides, covering the forepart of her person as she sat; and from its magnitude and its folds Cervantes used the plural — *of majesty,* as Hebrew grammarians would say. I therefore return to my original supposition that he had written *unos,* of which the printer managed to make *mil.* In the description of Ximena's wedding-dress, in the *Romancero del Cid,* we read that

"De paño de Londres fino
Era el vestido bordado,
Unas garnachas muy justas,
Con un chapin colorado."

("Of fine cloth of London was her embroidered dress, *a gown* very well-fitting, with red chopines.")

Here we have the plural for the singular; for she could not have worn more than one cloth dress, and that a close-fitting one (*justas*) reaching of course from the throat to the feet. Odd enough, in the last line we have the singular for the plural, for she surely had a pair of chopines, or thick-soled shoes. As to the editors taking no notice of *mil*, they did not understand it, and so, as is their wont, they said nothing about it. It is perhaps for the same reason that I have never met with a note on

"Let's briefly put on manly readiness" (*Macbeth*, Act II. Sc. 3),

for the sense is by no means obvious; and most certainly the late Mr. Singer did not understand it. Thos. Keightley.

"Perfervidum," etc. (3rd S. vii. 11.)—The well-known phrase, the paternity of which is sought, did not proceed from Buchanan, though it appears to have been first used with reference to him. It occurs in the *Jesuita Vapulans* of Andreas Rivetus, a Calvinistic minister, and professor of theology at Leyden in the middle of the seventeenth century. The phrase is cited in the following passage : —

"These books I will in some things no otherways commend than Andreas Rivetus, professor of Leyden, did the doctrine of Buchanan and Knox; whose rashness he ascribed *præfervido Scotorum ingenio, et ad audendum prompto*."—Sir T. Urquhart's *Tracts*, Edin. 1774, p. 134:

This was in answer to the recrimination of a Jesuit, who affirmed that Buchanan, Knox, and Goodman, had written "as boldlie for the rebellion of subjects against princes, as any of their order at any time had done." (*Demands concerning the Covenant*, 1638.)

Thus much I gather from Mr. Robertson's entertaining little volume, *Deliciæ Literariæ*, 12mo, 1840, p. 154.

Another work of this same Andreas Rivetus is before me, *Suspiria Pœnitentis Afflicti, Solatia confidentis animi, Meditationes in VII. Psalmos, vulgo dictos Pœnitentiales*, 12mo. Arnhemii, 1638. This scarce little tome appears to me worthy of note, as containing a letter to a friend on the contagiousness of the Plague, in which occurs a "Digressio de sepulturis in Templis, in quâ redarguitur mos cadavera mortuorum in templis sepeliendi," which is interesting from the rational and enlightened views thus early expressed with regard to this most disgusting and abhorrent practice. William Bates.

Birmingham.

Leycester's Progress in Holland (3rd S. vii. 14.) — Q. will find an account of Leycester's progress and reception in Holland in the *Sydney State Papers*, 2 vols. fol. "Life of Robert Dudley;" in the *Biographia Britannica* by Dr. Kippis, article "Dudley, Robert;" and a very full account in *Life of Robert, Earl of Leicester, the Favourite of*

Queen Elizabeth Drawn from Original Writers and Records, 8vo, Lond. 1727, without any author's name, but written by Dr. Samuel Jebb. Geo. Adlard.

Barnsbury.

Princess Charlotte of Brunswick (3rd S. vii. 9.)—Many years ago I read a two-volumed French novel founded on the same fact that Lady G. Fullarton has taken as the groundwork of her interesting work, *Too Strange not to be True*. It was entitled *La Princesse de Wolfenbüttel*, and must, I think, have been published previous to the year 1817, although I only met with it many years later. H.

Colours in Heraldry: Arms of the Family of Ximenes de Cisneros (3rd S. vi. 394, 480.) — Some shading was certainly common in drawing coats of arms before the time when the present system is said to have been invented. In the title-pages of the volumes of the Complutensian Polyglott, the arms of Cardinal Ximenes are given (fifteen squares, three in a row), as if the blazon were alternately *vert* and *argent*. As engraved in the title-page of the cardinal's Life by Robles, the blazon is *sable* and *argent*. What ought the tinctures to be? It appears to me strange *if* the seals on the death-warrant for Charles I. are the first place in which we now find heraldic shading; if so, this mode of designating blazon must have started into general use at once; whereas single instances would be far more likely. Lælius.

"Sedes Stercoraria" (2nd S. xi. 187, 252.)—Without controversy, and as a simple matter of literary curiosity, allow me to add a reference to the list of authorities on this subject. Friar Robert, who wrote in 1291, in the south of France, says he had a vision wherein he was removed to Rome; and, among other things, tells us this : —

"Duxit me Spiritus ad Lateranense Palatium, et posuit me in porticu ante *sedes porphyrii; ubi dicitur probari Papa an sit homo* : et omnia pulvere plena erant, et vivens ibi non videbatur."

The edition from which I quote is the one which appeared at Paris in 1513 (fol. 25 a). The volume is very rare; and contains Hermas, Uguetinus, F. Robertus, Hildegardis, Elizabeth, and Mechtildis. The existence of this book has been doubted, but "possession answers all objections." B. H. C.

Comets (3rd S. vii. 10.)—I would refer E. V. H. to the following passage in Milne's *Life in China* (edit. 1859, p. 144) : —

"*** This [the appearance of a comet in the southwest] created some apprehension in the minds of the peaceably disposed citizens of the city ; as a phenomenon like this is believed to be an infelicitous omen of warlike invasions, from the quarter where it first appears. After their struggle with the British lion, not only a rumour, but any bellicose augury, seemed to strike the public heart with a panic throe."

If this be the "fanciful opinion" to which Mr. Hind alludes, it would appear not to have been confined to the "celestials." Thus an "outer barbarian," one John Milton, speaks of a comet (*Paradise Lost*, ii. 708—710)—

"That fires the length of Ophiuchus huge
    In the Arctic sky, and *from his horrid hair
Shakes pestilence and war*."

And Ammianus Marcellinus (*Hist. Aug.* 1. 30), has the same idea. See also, *Script. φ. Bed.*, 512; *Dec. Scriptor.*, 961; Izacke, *Exeter*, 170, &c.

WYNNE E. BAXTER.

ROMNEY'S PORTRAIT OF WESLEY (3rd S. vii. 11.)—The portrait, three-quarters (bust) size, was painted in 1788 for Mrs. Tighe (? the poetess), and was sent to Ireland. An engraving from it in mezzotint, by J. Spilsbury (9 in. × 12¾ in.) was published in 1789; impressions of which, if not extremely rare are very uncommon. A more recent mezzotint, a little smaller in size, by W. Ward, A.R.A., from the same portrait—although, by an error in the inscription, said to have been "painted in 1790"—was published by the Rev. Thomas Roberts, Bristol, 1825. But in neither instance is it mentioned where the original is treasured.

I trust some account of Sir Joshua's portrait of the same distinguished person may also be elicited by the *query* of QUIVIS. I have never met with the information elsewhere that the great religious reformer of the last century had sat (as from the words in *Wesley's Journal* it may fairly be inferred he had) to the first President of the Royal Academy.

The query as to Mrs. Tighe, hypothetically and parenthetically introduced above, is suggested by the fact that all we know of the *personnel* of the lady of that name—the authoress of *Psyche*, first published, I think, in 1805—comes to us from the picture for which she also sat to Romney; but in what year, I have failed to ascertain.

JOHN BURTON.
Preston.

PORTRAITS OF VISCOUNT DUNDEE: CLAVERHOUSE (3rd S. vi. 472; vii. 3.)—Although the interesting portraits of John Graham of Claverhouse, Viscount of Dundee, which are said to be in the dining-room at Dalkeith Palace, and at Lee and Melton-Lockhart, may never have been copied, engraved, or photographed, yet there will be found illustrating—

"Mr. Mark Napier's Memorials and Letters, illustrative of the Life and Times of John Graham of Claverhouse, Viscount Dundee, Edinburgh, 1859—1862,"—

four very fine portraits of the "gallant Graham" and "Bonnie Dundee," all of which are considered

to be faithful likenesses. The first one is engraved from a mezzotint print by Williams, of which only two copies are known to exist: one of them being in the Bodleian Library, and the other in the possession of Mr. Stirling of Keir. Williams having been an artist contemporary with his subject, considerable reliance may be placed upon the resemblance. The second one is engraved from the original painting now in the possession of William Graham of Airth. The third one is from the painting long in the possession of the noble family of Leven and Melville, and recently inherited by Lady Elizabeth Leslie Melville Cartwright. The fourth one is from the original in the possession of the Earl of Strathmore. The Earl of Stair and Sir George Clerk, of Penicuik, are said to possess copies of the Airth portrait.   T. G. S.
Edinburgh.

MS. ON ENGLISH CONSTITUTION (3rd S. vii. 35.)—There is a MS. copy on vellum of Bracton's *De Legibus Angliæ* in the library at Stanford Court, Worcestershire.

The handwriting is small, but remarkably neat, and contractions frequent; it appears to contain the whole substance of the printed copies, so far as can be ascertained from a cursory examination.

It was once the property of the Leicestershire Antiquary, from an inscription on the fly-leaf:—"Liber Will^mi Burton Lendliaci, Leicestrencis, ex dono Tho^t Disney de Wiken, Com. Leic. 21 Jan. 1633, 9 Car."   THOMAS E. WINNINGTON.

ST. SARIK (3rd S. vii. 35.)—I fear that your correspondent HEVED has been engaged in a search quite hopeless. The learned and venerable Bishop Challoner published in 1761, a more accurate British Martyrology than the one put forth about a hundred and fifty years before it by the Rev. John Wilson, under the title of the *English Martyrologe;* and at the end of his work, entitled *A Memorial of Ancient British Piety; or a British Martyrology*, Bishop Challoner gave an Appendix with the names of other saints honoured by our British ancestors, but whose days he had been unable to make out; nor, it is to be inferred, had he been able to discover any particulars of their history. Among these occurs the following entry: "S. Sarik, in Leland's time, had a church at Sunning: whither of late (says he, vol. ii. p. 3) many folks resorted in pilgrimage for the disease of madness."   F. C. H.

PEWS (3rd S. vi. 414.)—It should be borne in mind that not only did pews in churches often exist, but also that pew rents were enforced before the time of the Long Parliament. Abp. Laud subjected the churchwardens of St. Andrew's, Plymouth (then the only church in the town) to a Star Chamber prosecution to compel them to levy pew rents; with this they were unwillingly forced to comply.   LAELIUS.

To Pluck a Crow (3rd S. vi. 390.)—"I've a crow to pluck with you, and a poke to put the feathers in," is I think the usual North country proverb, the poke for the feathers being rather an important part of the threat, judging from the stress the speaker lays upon it.   P. P.

Thomas Barton, B.D. (3rd S. vi. 470; vii. 46.)—We subjoin an extract from Mr. Bruce's *Calendar of the Domestic State Papers of Charles I.* (iv. 101), which will doubtless satisfy Dr. Rix that we had good authority for our statement:—

"1629, Nov. 20. Westminster: Presentation of Thomas Barton, M.A. to the rectory of Eynesbury, co. Huntingdon, void by simony. Lat."—*Sign. Man. Car. I.* vol. xi. No. 45.

The letters patent presenting Barton to Eynesbury bearing date 7 Dec. in the same year, are abstracted in Rymer's *Fœdera,* xix. 139.

By an error in the Index to the Hague edition of Rymer, Barton's rectory is stated to have been Fillingham in the diocese of Lincoln. The mistake clearly arose from Barton's presentation to Eynesbury immediately following that of Ralph Hollingworth, B.D., to Fillingham.

     C. H. & Thompson Cooper.
Cambridge.

Philippines (3rd S. vi. 501.)—Is "Philippine" exclusively the *English* word used in this game, if such it may be called? It was introduced to my notice in childhood by an Austrian lady, and she never mentioned any other phrase than "Bon jour, Philippe (or Philippine)." Had this amusement been of German origin, I cannot help thinking that she would have used, in preference, the phrase of her own country.   Hermentrude.

Isabel of Gloucester and Hubert de Burgh (2nd S. xi. 491; xii. 35, 153, 197, 212, 297, 403.)—I forward two extracts from the *Chronicle of Dunstaple,* which may perhaps be considered conclusive as to the marriage of these old friends of ours. The chronicler certainly appears to know some particulars about Isabel (the place of her sepulture for instance) which I have not been able to discover in the pages of any other writer, though his curious mistake in calling her "Johanna" a little qualifies the weight which might otherwise be given to his assertions. After speaking of the death of Geoffrey de Mandeville at a tournament, he proceeds:—

"Qui paulo ante guerram Johannam, Comitissam Gloucestriæ, repudiatam à Johanne, Rege Angliæ (Archiepiscopo Burdegalensi divortium celebrante) duxit in uxorem, licet invitus. Pro cujus maritagio cavit Regi de decem milibus marcarum et amplius, quas nunquam solvere potuit: pro quarum solutione, destructa sunt nemora, et maneria nullis temporibus impignorata. Cui sine filiis mortuo, successit Willelmus frater ejus, et relictam ipsius duxit Hubertus de Burgo, Justiciarius Angliæ; *quæ post paucos dies decessit,* et apud Cantuarium sepelitur."—*Chron. Dunst.,* ed. Hearne, i. 74.

The second extract is under the date of 1232:—

"Hubertus de Burgo, Justiciarius Angliæ, conventus super peregrinatione Sanctæ-Crucis, per literas Papæ, per absolutionem Pandulfi Legati tunc Angliæ, se rationabiliter expedivit. Super divortio verò tertiæ uxoris suæ, scilicet filiæ Regis Scotiæ, conventus super eo, *quod erat consanguinea secundæ* * *uxoris suæ, scilicet Comitisse Gloverniæ* . . ."—*Chron. Dunst.,* ed. Hearne, i. 207.

If it really be the case, that Isabel survived her marriage with Hubert a few days only, it would explain why he never assumed her title; but it still leaves unexplained the fact, that no grant nor reference to the marriage appears (so far as I can discover) in the Close Rolls, or the Patent Rolls.

My sole desire is to arrive at the truth in this matter; and if the authority of the *Chronicle of Dunstaple* can be held to be conclusive, I am ready at once to retract my originally expressed opinion that the marriage is "not proven."

While on this subject, I may just remark, in answer to the observation of S. P. V. (3rd S. iv. 255), that "it was this marriage (to Isabelle of Angoulême) that the King of France advised," that this does not appear to be the meaning of the chroniclers. The *Annales de Burton,* nevertheless, expressly say that it was the second marriage, and not the divorce, which was "de consilio Domini sui Philippi Regis Franciæ." (*Annales Monastici,* i. 202.)   Hermentrude.

The Bell Inn and Broadhurst (3rd S. vii. 33.)—In the query on this subject, I was surprised to observe the following statement: "The mansion of Broadhurst, the property of Mr. Lightmaker, has long since disappeared." It is true that nearly thirty "fugacious" years have passed since I spent some very happy months at Horsted-Keynes as its curate, and what sacrilege may have been committed therein this long interval I cannot tell: but I certainly was, at that time, under the strong impression that the gabled old farmhouse at Broadhurst was at least an integral portion of the mansion, in which dear sainted Archbishop Leighton spent his latter days. I copy from a children's periodical, published seventeen years since, a few lines which seem to confirm my impression:—

"We are in the midst of a desert-garden, belonging to an *ancient manor-house, now a farm-house.* . . . A few straggling roses, green walks, raised up one above another, the plots of ground, the piece of water, all mark where once the garden was, though all is now desolate. There is a shady avenue behind us all overgrown with fern, and at the end a group of aged trees; in this avenue and beneath those trees, the good Archbishop Leighton passed many of his last hours on earth: for this was the place where he spent his last years, and the fern-covered avenue is still pointed out as his favourite resort."

Whether distance, and the pleasant memories of youth "lend enchantment to the view," I

* Isabel was Hubert's third wife, not his second.

cannot tell; but Horsted-Keynes is still embalmed in my heart as one of the sweetest nooks I ever saw, and worthiest of its pure and holy denizen.

C. W. Bingham.

Ladies of the Order of the Garter (3rd S. vii. 11.)—The tomb in Ewelme church, called by your correspondent that of the "Countess of Warwick," is that of Alice, *Duchess* of Suffolk, widow of William de la Pole, Duke of Suffolk, who was beheaded at Dover in 1449. The duchess was married three times—first to Sir John Philips, Knt.; then to Thomas Montacute, Earl of Salisbury; and, lastly, to William de la Pole, Duke of Suffolk. She died in 1475. She was the granddaughter of Geoffrey Chaucer. Her father, Sir Thomas Chaucer, is also buried in Ewelme church, and both their monuments are interesting; hers for its great beauty, and both for the many shields, quartering the arms of Roet, Despencer, Burgherst, Beaufort, Earl of Somerset; Richard Plantagenet, Duke of York; Neville; Montacute; Monthermer; Beauchamp; Newburg, Earl of Warwick; Clare; John Lord Mohun of Dunster; De la Pole; and Percy.

A particular account is given in Skelton's *Hist. of Oxfordshire* (Ewelme Hundred), pp. 4, 5, 6. It also contains a good view of the two monuments; and there is a beautiful engraving of the effigy of the duchess in Hollis's *Monumental Effigies of Great Britain*, London, 4to, 1840-1—a work, which I believe, was left incomplete in consequence of Mr. Hollis's early death. I should be glad to know if any of your correspondents can tell me where the Countess of Warwick, mentioned as living in 1432, was buried. Also if she is represented wearing the garter, as it is generally said there are only three female effigies so decorated; viz. Sir Robert Harcourt's lady, in Stanton Harcourt church, Oxon; Constance, daughter of John Holland, Earl of Huntingdon and Duke of Exeter (first married to Thomas Mowbray, Duke of Norfolk; and secondly, to Sir John Guy, Knight of the Garter in the reign of Henry V., and Earl of Tankerville in Normandy; her monument was in the church of St. Catherine, near the Tower of London); and the Duchess of Suffolk in Ewelme church. These particulars are chiefly from Skelton.   L. C. R.

Miscellaneous.

NOTES ON BOOKS, ETC.

A History of Caricature and Grotesque in Literature and Art. By Thomas Wright, M.A. *With Illustrations from various sources, drawn and engraved by F. W. Fairholt, Esq., F.S.A.* (Virtue.)

To those who, understanding Caricature only in its more limited sense, expect in this work an amplification of the curious history of political satire which Mr. Wright furnished in his *England under the House of Hanover*, the present volume may be somewhat disappointing, for such branch of the subject is only treated of in its relation to the whole. The general reader will, on the other hand, find in it an able, though necessarily rapid glance over the whole field of the grotesque in Art, and of so much of the grotesque in literature as is inseparably connected with it. Thus the grotesque in Egypt, the Comic Masks of the Romans, the Satirical Sculptures and Illuminations of the Middle Ages, the Dance of Death, the Romance of Reynard, &c., all pass under Mr. Wright's review, are all illustrated by Mr. Fairholt's faithful pencil and graver—(his illustrations amount to nearly 250), the whole forming a compendious history of literary and pictorial satire which is, at once, learned and amusing.

Le Morte Arthur. Edited from the Harleian MS. 2252 in the British Museum. By F. J. Furnivall, M.A., with a Prefatory Essay on Arthur by the late Herbert Coleridge. (Macmillan.)

Ane Compendious and Breve Tractate Concerning ye Office and Dewtie of Kyngis, Spiritual Pastoris and Temporall Jugis, laitlie compilit by William Lander. Edited by F. Hall, M.A., D.C.L. (Early English Text Society.)

Sir Gawayne and the Green Knight. An alliterative Romance Poem. Re-edited by Richard Morris. (Early English Text Society.)

We owe the very handsome volume, the title of which heads this notice, to the desire on the part of the Publisher and Editor to ascertain whether among the thousands who have been interested in the Laureate's beautiful Arthurian revivals, there exists a sufficient number of admirers of the original "legends old and quaint," yet eminently poetic withal, to justify the publication of the original texts. The step is a judicious one; and as in the present volume we have a highly interesting poem, a learned preface by the editor, and an admirable Essay on this "world famed legend" by the late Herbert Coleridge, we trust that the movement will prove as successful as it is judicious, and that the result will be a large accession of members to the *Early English Text Society.*

Lauder's Tractate and *Sir Gawayne and the Green Knight* are the third and fourth publications which that Society gives this year to the Members in return for their annual subscription of one sovereign. They are both highly curious and well deserving of the attention of students of our language and our Early Literature. *Sir Gawayne* was edited some years since with great care and accuracy by Sir F. Madden, and is re-edited from his edition with the contractions expanded &c. It has been carefully collated, and Sir F. Madden's Glossary has received several additions. All this of course has been done with the full sanction of that gentleman, who as we learn from the Editor, "has most generously placed at the disposal of the Early English Text Society any of his works which it may determine to re-edit." It is clear that Sir Frederick remembers his old favourite, Chaucer's description of the true scholar, that—

"Gladly wolde he lerne and gladly teche."

Brief Notes on the Greek of the New Testament. By the Rev. F. Trench, M.A. (Macmillan.)

A little volume composed with the praiseworthy object of conveying some accurate ideas of the force and meaning of the original Greek Text in the New Testament to intelligent persons who are not acquainted with that language.

Walks and Talks about London. By John Timbs, F.S.A. (Lockwood.)

The Old City and its Highways and Byways. By Aleph. (Collingridge.)

The number of books about London increases as rapidly as London itself. Our old acquaintance Mr. Timbs, who promises by-the-bye a new and enlarged edition of his *Curiosities of London*, gives us a series of pleasant gossiping Essays about everything, from " Sir Richard Phillips " to " Railway London ; " while Aleph's contribution is a reprint of some forty articles about City Haunts and City Worthies contributed by him to the *City Press*.

The Voices of the Year ; or, The Poet's Kalendar, Containing the choicest Pastorals in our Language. Illustrated. (Griffin & Co.)

This is a handsome tribute to that love of rural life which is the innate feeling of all Englishmen. A collection of all the best pastorals in our language (and how many and how fine they are this volume sufficiently proves), beautifully printed and nicely illustrated, can scarcely fail to become a popular book.

At the meeting of *L'Académie des Inscriptions* on the 20th ult., some sharp comments were made on the approaching publication at Berlin of a Monument of the highest interest recently discovered at Abydos by M. Auguste Mariette, and which represents Seti I. accompanied by his son Ramses II. (Sesostris) making an offering to seventy-six kings, several of whom belonged to a period between the sixth and eleventh centuries, and are as yet unidentified. M. Mariette had himself intended to give this to the world, but is said to have been forestalled by this publication, made from a copy surreptitiously obtained, and sent to Germany, where, if this report be true, M. Bismark's axiom, *La force prime le droit*, seems to be extended from the world of politics to that of science.

According to the *Bulletin Bibliographique Espagnol*, the lost books of Tacitus have been found in the ruins of a house at Catania in Sicily. We wonder how often similar reports have been circulated !

BOOKS AND ODD VOLUMES
WANTED TO PURCHASE.

Particulars of Price, &c., of the following Books to be sent direct to the gentlemen by whom they are required, and whose names and addresses are given for that purpose:—

Evans's Catalogue of Engraved Portraits. Second-hand will do.
   Wanted by *F. M. S.* 229, Clarendon Villas, Plumstead.

Plates of Fashion (like Ackermann's) of the last century.
   Wanted by *John Nunn, Esq.*, 23, Euston Square, N.W,

Cudworth on Free Will.
Cudworth's Intellectual System of the Universe.
Whitehead's Life of Sir Walter Raleigh in the *National Illustrated Library*, 1854.
   Wanted by *Rev. J. Maskell*, Tower Hill, London, E.C.

Theobald's Shakspeare Restored. 4to.
History of Bray, Berkshire.
Garrick's Correspondence. 2 Vols. 4to.
Vaughan's Hours with the Mystics. Vol. I.
   Wanted by *Mr. John Wilson*, 93, Great Russell Street, W.C.

A Political and Satyrical History of the Years 1756 to 1759. Two Parts. London ; For E. Morris, near St. Paul's.
   Wanted by *Rev. J. C. Jackson*, 5, Chatham Place East, Hackney, N.E.

Notices to Correspondents.

H. A. W. *The work is of no great value.*

H. W. *The first Marquis of Winchester, who held office during the reign of Henry VIII., Edward VI., Mary, and Elizabeth.*

G. Prideaux. *We presume Duchesne's valuable Historiæ Normannorum Scriptores antiqui, etc., Paris, 1619, folio, is the work alluded to.*

H. B. M. *who writes about* —
   " An Austrian army awfully arrayed,"
is referred to our 2nd S. viii. 412, 460; xii. 173, 279, 336.

Cpl. *Defoe's Letter to Dyer is printed in Wilson's Defoe*, iii. 185.

George Lloyd. *The disputed authorship of* The Whole Duty of Man *has been so frequently discussed by literary antiquaries during the last two centuries, that we feel disinclined to re-open the subject unless some new facts are discovered. Consult Nichols's Literary Anecdotes, the* Gent. Mag., *and "* N. & Q." *Mr. Hawkins, in his Introductory Essay to the edition of 1842, has ably examined the claims of the principal candidates.—The printed sources of information respecting Abraham Woodhead were given in our last volume, p. 475. The following inscription was on his monument in St. Pancras churchyard: "Elegi abjectus esse in domo Domini, et manni in solitudine, non querens quod mihi utile, sed quod multis." In 1782 a new monument was erected with a different inscription.*

P. W. S. (New York.) *The Rev. Samuel Tapper's translation of the seven books of* Milton's Paradise Lost *was never published. Calamy says* " He wrote several things, but printed nothing."

Ignoramus *will find the subject* " Why Moses is represented with horns " *discussed in our* 1st S. i. 419, 420.

C. Booth (Montrose.) *The author of* Maurice and Berghetta *was* Wm. Parnell, M.P. for co. Wicklow. *See* " N. & Q." 2nd S. iii. 56.

D, *thinks it probable that the word, which he read* " mastmaker " (3rd S. vi. 434), *is* " maltmaker." *The Diary is in a very crabbed hand.*

Epsicy. *A solution of the enigma is given in* " N. & Q." 2nd S. xii. 35.

R. W. B. *will also find a solution of the Latin riddle in our* 3rd S. v. 199, 209.

A Reading Case for holding the weekly Nos. of " N. & Q." is now ready, and may be had of all Booksellers and Newsmen, price 1s. 6d.; or, free by post, direct from the publisher, for 1s. 8d.

⁂ *Cases for binding the volumes of* " N. & Q." *may be had of the Publisher, and of all Booksellers and Newsmen.*

"Notes and Queries" *is published at noon on Friday, and is also issued in* Monthly Parts. *The Subscription for Stamped Copies for Six Months forwarded direct from the Publisher (including the Half-yearly* Index) *is* 11s. 4d., *which may be paid by Post Office Order, payable at the Strand Post Office, in favour of* William G. Smith, 32, Wellington Street, Strand, W.C., *to whom all* Communications for the Editor *should be addressed.*

"Notes & Queries" is registered for transmission abroad.

Another Cure of Cough by Dr. Locock's Pulmonic Wafers.—"s, Wilson Terrace, St. Leonard's Street, Bromley, E.—I can myself testify that they have relieved me of a most severe cough, so bad that I was unable to lie down, and I shall do my best to recommend them. Wm. Nicholas." They give instant relief to asthma, consumption, coughs, colds, and all disorders of the breath, throat, and lungs. Price 1s. 1½d., 2s. 9d., and 4s. 6d. per box. Sold by all Druggists.

THE OLD DRAMATISTS.

In royal 8vo volumes, illustrated with Portraits, with Introductions, Memoirs, and Notes, by Gifford, Hartley Coleridge, Dyce, and others.

CAMPBELL'S SHAKSPEARE.   Illustrated by JOHN GILBERT, 12s.

   BEN JONSON, 16s.
   MASSINGER and FORD, 15s.
   WYCHERLY, CONGREVE, VANBRUGH, and FARQUHAR. 15s.
   BEAUMONT AND FLETCHER, 2 Vols. 32s.
   JOHN WEBSTER. 10s. 6d.
   CHRISTOPHER MARLOWE. 12s.
   GREENE and PEELE. 16s.

   ROUTLEDGE, WARNE, & ROUTLEDGE,
      The Broadway, Ludgate Hill.

THE OLD POETS.

In royal 8vo volumes, with Portraits.

CHAUCER, edited by TYRWHITT. 10s. 6d.
   SPENSER, with Memoir and notes by Todd. 10s. 6d.
   DRYDEN, edited by Warton. 10s. 6d.
   POPE, edited by Cary. 10s. 6d.

   ROUTLEDGE, WARNE, & ROUTLEDGE,
      The Broadway, Ludgate Hill.

Just ready, crown 8vo, 6s.

BRIEF NOTES on the GREEK of the NEW TESTAMENT. By the REV. FRANCIS TRENCH, M.A., Rector of Islip, Oxon.

"These Brief Notes have been composed with one single object in view, viz. that of bringing some contribution towards an accurate perception of the force and meaning of the original Greek in the New Testament. It will be found that with a view of making these Brief Notes available to all intelligent persons, whether acquainted with the Greek and Latin languages or not, all Greek and Latin words are excluded from the body of the page, and placed below, as not essential, although helpful, towards the comprehension of the book."

Extract from Author's Preface.

MACMILLAN & CO., London and Cambridge.

LONDON, SATURDAY, FEBRUARY 11, 1865.

CONTENTS.—N° 163.

Notes.

THE BATTLE OF LA PLANTA.

AN ANCIENT HISTORIC BALLAD OF THE VAL D'ANNIVIERS, CANTON DU VALLAIS, SWITZERLAND.

(*From the Romande.*)

The original of the following ballad is in the Romande of the Val d'Anniviers, a wild ravine in the High Vallais, a short distance from Sierre on the Simplon road. It is a favourite folks-song in the Valley of Anniviers, and its popularity is rather on the increase than the decline. It was not known beyond the valley until Baron Charles de Bons, an accomplished Swiss archæologist and scholar produced a traditional copy before the "Suisse Romande Society." It is now printed in the Society's Transactions. M. de Bon's copy is evidently in a very corrupt state. Some of the verses rhyme, others do not. Some of the lines have evidently been transposed, and there are lines where it is pretty clear that the first portion ought to change place with the conclusion. Translations have appeared in German rhyme and French prose. In the following version (the only English one) I have adopted the metre of the original, *ex. gr.* : —

> " A oui allais vos verd conto?
> A oui vos endallaz?
> Yo ouie allai trovar las tchievres—
> Oi las tchievres d' hau Valli."

If the ballad really relate to the battle of *La Planta*, we may presume that it was written shortly after the event, which occurred in 1475. It was one of those numerous skirmishes that took place between the Helvetians and the Savoyards, when the latter had for a leader Charles Duke of Burgundy, known in history as "Charles le Téméraire." But the ballad may be older and relate to another battle. M. le Comte d'Angreville de Beaumont of Epinacy, Canton du Vallais, in a communication to me, writes as follows: —

"C'est bien en 1475 qu'a eu lieu la battaille de la Planta, aux portes de Sion, où plusieurs mille soldats et 300 nobles Savoyards et Bas Vallaissans furent tués. La ballade de M. de Bons doit plutôt se rapporter à la *battaille de St. Léonard*, qui a lieu *un siècle avant*, soit en 1375. Nous appelons cette guerre, la guerre des Châtillons. La Ballade en parlant du *Comte Verd* (Amadeus VI.) et *la Planta* commet un anachronisme. Il est bien vrai que le Comte Verd a eu plusieurs guerres avec les Vallaisans, mais il était mort (1382) lors de la battaille de la Planta (1475)."

I rather lean to the opinion of Count d'Angreville, and am inclined to believe that the ballad is really a minstrel effusion composed on the Battle of St. Leonard, and altered to suit a later event by some one whose historical knowledge was defective, or who was careless though he executed his task. It is only in the last verse that "La Planta" is met with —

> "Il y ha commencia a doze,
> Et a treichi il y ha fenna ;
> Et vingte et mill hommos,
> Sont restas in la Planta."

It is by no means an improbable conjecture, that the last line may have been tampered with, and that we ought to read —

> "Sont in *St Leonard* restas."

Neither La Planta nor St. Leonard are in or near the Val d'Anniviers. The connection of the ballad with Anniviers is for the reason above stated.

> " 'Whither away so fast, Green Count?
> Whither so fast and far?'
> 'I seek the goats of the Vallais land
> That up in the mountains are.'
> " 'By my fay*, my gentle Count,
> You may be baulk'd ere long!
> Instead of finding the goats you seek,
> You may meet with some wild-bucks strong.'
> " 'I rede thou com'st from the High Vallais,
> Thy tongue is so bold and free !
> But let us have less of thy jesting here,
> Or thy head may the forfeit be.'
> " 'Gramercy ! I'll pay down the worth, Green Count,
> Of this lubberly head of mine ;
> Lo ! a hundred chucs to drink my health
> In a bumper of Sion Wine! †

---

* This phrase *Per ma fée* occurs twice. We find it in all the old ballads of Scandinavia, England, Scotland, &c. The Vallais formed a part of *Celtic Switzerland.*

† The meaning of "chuc" is not very clear. There

" 'But what are your wills, my noble Count?
    Speak frankly and out, I pray ; ·
    'Twere better than talking of cutting off heads—
    A game at which two can play.'
" ' I demand Sion, Siérre, Valére,
    And Tourbillon's hall and shrine ;
    And that every village to Simplon's height
    Pay tribute to me and mine.' *
" ' You ask too much, my noble Count,
    Least ! so doth it seem to me ;
    In three days I shall be with my merry men all,
    And it's then shall our answer be.'
" ' I will but give thee one single day —
    Return thou to-morrow noon ;
    Thou wilt find me sat in the capital
    A-taking of my dejeune.' †
" He went alone where the Simplon's snow
    Shone clear in the calm midnight,
    But he was not alone when the towers of Sion
    Bask'd fair in the mid-day light.

" ' Look out, look sharp ! my Nephew bold,
    And tell me what you can see ?
Comes any goat from the High Vallais
    A-bearing response to me ? '
" ' By my fay ! my gentle Count,
    I wish we were far away,
Enjoying the smiles of our loving wives,
    And sharing our children's play.
" ' For lo ! they come, a countless host,
    And seem a right valiant band—
I like not the frown of their angry faces,
    Nor the staffs that they bear in hand.‡
" ' They look like knights of high degree,
    As the forest lion braves ;
    Their heads have helmets, as cauldrons huge,
    Their plumes in the breezes wave.'
" ' He I met was a cunning huntsman,
    Well aim'd was his dart and true ;
He hath broken my glass, and spilt my wine,
    And our parley I sorely rue.'

never was any such money coined by the Prince Bishops
of Sion, as may be seen by consulting Count d'Angreville's work, *La Numismatique Vallaissanne.*" The German
translator renders the word by " Crutz," the common abbreviation of " Creutzer." A crutz was a trifle less in
value than our halfpenny.
    * This is certainly more like the language of Amadeus
VI. than that of Charles the Rash.
    † " Capitala " and " dezunai " are in the original. Sion
was of course not the capital of a republican canton either
in the days of Amadeus VI. or Charles the Rash ; but it
was in those times, and long afterwards, the capital · of a
palatinate presided over by a Prince Bishop. " Dejeune "
was the common name for the mid-day meal, used by all
the northern nations. It is still in use in Scotland. In
one of Hogg's ballads we read, " Taking of her *dejeune.*"
    ‡ In the Breton Ballad of " Tannedik-Flamm," we read
" Do you see any black sheep descending the mountain ? "
The answer is, " I see no troop of black sheep, but I see
an army, who come to besiege Henbont."— Barzaz-
Breiz, *Chants Populaires de la Bretagne,* par Th. Hersert
de la Villemarque. Paris, 1846. The resemblance is
remarkable. In the Vallais ballad, " goats " is a term of
contempt, as " black sheep " is in the Breton ballad. The
replies, too, are very much of the same character. · Is this
accidental ? A friend thinks the author may have been a
priest to whom ballad literature was not unknown.

. . . . ·ː . . . .
" At the hour of twelve the fight began,
    It was over at thirteen,*
When a thousand and twenty foemen fierce
    Lay stretch'd on La Planta's green."
                                                D.

Florence, Jan. 6, 1865.

STAMP OF THE CROSS ON BREAD: AND JOUSTS
AND TOURNAMENTS PROHIBITED BY ROYAL
MANDATE.

I send you two curious articles for your Note
Book, which I hope you will think worthy of insertion : —
        " *Ex Rotulis Clausis, 36 Hen. III.*
    " Mandatum est Vice Comiti Essex et Hertford quod
clamari faciet per totam ballivam suam et firmiter ex
parte Regis prohiberi, ne quis pistor, panem faciens vena-
lem, signum Crucis, vel agni Dei, vel eciam nomen Jesu
Christi, imprimi faciet in pane suo, ne per culpam pis-
toris, vel alia casu inopinato, signa predicta vel nomen
Domini, quod absit, deturpetur.
    " Teste meipso apud Stum. Edmundum primo die
Septembr.
    " Eodem modo mandatum est aliis Vice-comitibus."
    " *De Prohibitione Rotundæ Tabulæ ex Rot. Claus.
        36 Hen. III.*
    " Rex Omnibus ad Rotundam Tabulam faciendam con-
venturis apud Waleden, vel alibi, salutem.
    " Precipimus vobis, quod, in fide qua nobis tenemini,
et sub amissione terrarum et tenementorum vestrorum,
quod nullam Rotundam Tabulam faciatis apud Waleden,
vel alibi in regno nostro, ad torneandum vel ad justas
faciendum sine licencia nostra, scituri quod, si super pre-
missis aliquid attemptaveritis contra hanc prohibitionem
nostram, taliter ad vos, ut bona vestra capiemus, quod
exinde grave dispendium incurretis.
    " In cujus, etc. Teste Rege apud Stum. Edmundum,
vi. die Sept."
                                        T. Phillipps.
Middle Hill.

[The documents, for which we are indebted to the
courtesy of Sir Thomas Phillipps, are certainly very
curious. The prohibition to place the " signum Crucis,"
&c., upon the bread, luckily no longer exists ; or, what
would become of our " Hot cross buns " at Easter ? As
for the prohibition of jousts and tournaments, Royal Man-
dates to that effect are very common in the Close Rolls
and Patent Rolls. The king frequently forbad them for
political reasons. The " Rotunda Tabula " was a joust.
In the *Archæologia Cantiana* (vol. v. p. 159, note 7), there
is a note fully explaining this. At p. 160, there is a pardon
granted to Sir Roger de Leyburn for slaying Ernulph de
Munteny at a " Rotunda Tabula " at Walden, in 36 Hen.
III. The pardon is dated October 19, 36 Hen. III. The
" Rotunda Tabula " at Walden, is dated Sept. 6, in the
same year ; which looks very much as if De Munteny's

    * The *thirteenth* hour gives an old look to the ballad,
and induces me to believe that the ancient mode of com-
puting time by twenty-four hours was in use when the
minstrel author wrote. Even in the Vallais, a border
country to Italy, the present mode of two twelves has
been in use for two centuries, and perhaps longer.

murder had induced the king to issue his prohibition, putting an end to the joust. Matthew Paris gives an account of this joust.—Ed.]

UNPUBLISHED LETTERS OF ANGELICA KAUFFMAN

I have the pleasure of sending to the Editor of "N. & Q." two unpublished German letters, one from Angelica Kauffman to a cousin in Schwartzenbach, in the Austrian Tyrol, her father's native village; the other to the same individual from Johannes Kauffman, also a cousin of Angelica, who, on the death of her second husband Zucchi, resided with her at Rome as the manager of her affairs. Of these letters I send translations as literal as I can render.

The letter of Angelica Kauffman is characteristic of the kindness of heart and piety by which she was no less distinguished than by eminence in art and by varied accomplishments. The earnest interest for the temporal and spiritual welfare of her relatives—humble artisans, in an obscure village of the Bregenzer-Wald, exhibited in this letter, written from the "Eternal City" where she was the object of the flattering homage of the great and eminent—is very touching. It manifests an innate tenderness, deepening the sympathy inspired by the cruel wrong inflicted upon her by the unprincipled adventurer by whom she was inveigled into her first marriage. The letter of Johannes Kauffman is amusingly illustrative of the combined simplicity, worth, and shrewdness—prominent features then, as now—of Tyrolese character. To the cousin to whom Angelica's letter was addressed, she by her will, of which I possess a copy, left her sketches and drawings; and by the son of this individual some of them, with the letters in question, were sold :—

"Rome, 29 June, 1801.
"Much beloved Cousin,—

„ I thank you from my heart for your letter, which I received with pleasure. Your good conduct and diligence in your trade has at all time given me joy. I hope that you will always continue striving to turn to account the years of your youth, applying yourself perseveringly to all matters connected with your business, and that you will especially seek to fulfil to the best of your power your duty towards God (from whom we derive our being, and from whom we receive everything), as also your duty towards your parents. He who turns to good account the years of his youth, will in his old age enjoy the fruits. The present times are unhappily very dangerous for those who have little experience. One must commend oneself to God, and seek association with good and pious men, and avoid idleness as much as possible. The reading of good books is very useful ; but good books, such as serve to educate the heart and intellect, and teach scientifically , and in this matter, the advice of a righteous man is very necessary ; for how many have been deluded by the writings of the philosophers of our day ! I do not doubt that you will strive to attain perfection in your trade as much as possible. Cousin Johann will add some lines : here.

with I conclude, with the assurance that I shall at all times take the greatest interest in your welfare. God give you his blessing.
"I remain your
"Truly devoted Cousin,
Angelica Kauffman.

"P.S. From a letter of your good father, Cousin Casimir, which I have recently received, I learn that he is convalescent, at which I heartily rejoice."

"Rome, July 4, 1801.
"Much beloved Cousin,—

"For the note of 17 May, which you enclosed, and which Cousin [Angelica] gave to me, I thank you. In the meantime I have received letters from your father informing me that his arm is better, at which I rejoice, and that he intends putting off establishing a workshop until the spring, in which, in my opinion, he does wisely ; for between this and the spring so many [political] changes may take place, in conformity with which an unfettered man may set his sail according to the wind. Would to God that brother Joseph Conrad would also wait and look on; but, on the other hand, if he means to marry he certainly has no time to lose. May God give him enlightenment and his blessing in his undertaking.

"An interesting Courier has arrived here from Paris, but up to this date the dispatches he has brought are kept secret. We have no news. As on a former occasion, I send this letter to your father because you have omitted to indicate your address.

"Pray give my greeting to brother Conrad. I assure you all that your letters will be pleasing to me at all times, that I may be informed of your prosperity, which I always heartily wish. With best greeting,
"Your affectionate Cousin,
"Johannes Kauffman."

The Editor will be pleased to exercise his discretion as to printing the original letters, or the translations, or both.

Philippa Swinnerton Hughes.

CONGLETON ACCOUNTS.

Judging that a few extracts from a MS. vol. in my possession from the cash books of the borough of Congleton, in the county of Chester, will not be unacceptable to readers of "N. & Q." I send them. I should indeed be much obliged to any correspondent who could inform me what were the precise duties and office of the Reader mentioned several times in them. I presume that he was not licensed to preach, as that portion of duty was supplied by the curate : —

1588.	£	s.	d.
Paid Wm Tilman, Schoolmaster, his Quarter's wage	2	0	0
Thos. Davenport, the Reader	1	0	0
To Smith tending the Wood, a Yrs. wage	0	10	0
1589.			
Sir Roger, the Curate, his Qtr wage	1	13	4
Pd Mr Trafford's man, the Bearward	0	4	4
To Thos. Ward for going to Holmes' Chapel to fetch Wine to treat the Earl of Derby when here	0	0	9

1590.	£	s.	d.
Boards for the School House . . .	1	0	0
Mr. Tilman, Schoolmaster, towards his Wage .	0	16	0
Do. his Qrs Wage, and part of another .	5	0	0
Remains unpaid to him 1l. 13s. 4d.			
Sir Humphrey Phithion, the Minister, his Quarter's wage	2	10	0
Leading Clods for the Cockpit, and mending it the third time	0	2	0
To Sir John Hollworth's Bearward . . .	0	2	0
Bestowed on Mr Cawdwell, Sc. when he preached at the Chapel	0	7	4

[I now go on to] 1599.

	£	s.	d.
Mr Carr of Middlewich for preaching of 4 Sermons :	0	5	0
Mr Tanington, the Schoolmaster's, wage .	3	6	8
The Reader his Quarter's wage . . .	1	13	4
6 Gallons of Dirt to blend Mortar with at Dane Bridge	0	1	0
To a preacher who preached on Saturday, and on St. Martin's Day . . .	0	5	0
Wine and a Gallon of Sack bestowed on Edwd Fitton, Esq.	0	4	8

1600.

	£	s.	d.
Richd Green, Senr, the Reader, Qrs Wage .	1	13	4
Candles at Morning Prayers this Quarter .	0	1	10
Second Quarter, Mr Shenton, Schoolmaster, Paid Jas. Brooker to fetch Shenton's Books and Apparel from Oxford . . .	1	6	8
Given to the Bearward at the Great Cockfight the 5th, 6th, and 7th May . . .	0	6	8
Clods, 19 Load, to make Butts at the Wakes on the Bearward Green	0	4	0
Spent on Sir John Savage, and Lord Keeper's Sqn	0	8	7
Dressing the School at the Cockfight . .	0	0	4

From these extracts I gather that there were four distinct names given to those who officiated in the chapel at Congleton—viz. *Reader, Minister, Curate,* and *Preacher;* and it would almost seem from the item of *Candles at Morning Prayer* as if there was an early, perhaps a daily, service. Again, I note the prefix *Sir*—a title given in those times to clergymen. It is not, however, assigned to the Reader.

It is almost needless to add, as the Shakspearian illustrations of this prefix, *Sir* Hugh Evans in the *Merry Wives of Windsor,* and *Sir* John Hume in *King Henry the Sixth,* Part II. OXONIENSIS.

REMARKABLE COINCIDENCE. — When I was at Florence in 1835, there occurred an accident so similar in most particulars to that which happened at Westminster on the 26th ult., that one account might almost read for the other. On March 19, 1835, at the festa of San Giuseppe, a great number of persons were collected in the house, No. 2967, Via della Chiesa, in Florence. They had assembled on the second *piano* of the house, to celebrate a religious ceremony styled "La Passione di nostra Signore," when the floor suddenly gave way, and to increase still more the calamity, the first *piano,* inadequate to the superincumbent pressure, also sunk, precipitating the unfortunate congregation to the ground floor. From this catastrophe eight lives were lost, and from sixty to seventy severely wounded. The account of this melancholy accident which I drew up at the time was forwarded to the *Courier* newspaper, and appeared in the impression of April 4, 1835. Φ.

EXTINCTION OF NATIVE RACES.—The gradual, and, alas! apparently inevitable decay of the dark skins before the advance of the white man is affectingly illustrated in the following incident, recorded by the *Hobart Town Mercury* of October 20th, 1864 : —

"At the last ball at Government House, Hobart Town, there appeared the last male aboriginal inhabitant of Tasmania. He was accompanied by three aboriginal females, the sole living representatives of the race besides himself, but not of such an age, or such an appearance, as to justify the expectations of any future addition to their number. The Tasmanian natives, as a race, are now virtually extinct."

In all the Australian continental colonies the aborigines are diminishing in numbers with greater or less rapidity, according as European settlement proceeds. D. BLAIR.
Melbourne.

FAGG: A REMNANT.—In some interesting extracts from the archives of the city of Worcester, now being published in *The Worcester Herald* by Mr. J. Noake (a former correspondent of "N. & Q."), mention is made, in the *Herald* for Jan. 14, 1865, of a bequest of John Chappell, a Worcester clothier, who leaves to his sister-in-law a "fagg" to make her a petticoat; and "to Roger Massye, our Curate, a white fagg to make him a coat." In a note, Mr. Noake says, "This perhaps meant a remnant; we still use the term 'fag-end.'" CUTHBERT BEDE.

PASSAGE IN EUSEBIUS: DR. CURETON AND THE "QUARTERLY REVIEW."—When remarks are made condemnatory of the statements of scholars, sufficient explanation should be given so as to make the strictures intelligible, that we may test their accuracy. In the very interesting and valuable paper on Syriac MSS. in the number of the *Quarterly Review* which has just appeared, the anonymous writer says of Dr. Cureton, p. 168,—

"His critical remarks on Syriac are always valuable, but we cannot accord the same praise to his remarks on Greek, *which occasionally betray very great want of care.*"

In proof of this a foot note is subjoined,—

"*E. g.,* in his *Martyrs of Palestine,* p. 64, he mistakes a neuter plural, ἀδελφά, for a feminine singular, ἀδελφή, Comp. Eus., *De Martyr. Pal.,* c. viii. (p. 114, ed. Heinichen), with his note."

I suppose, from the form of the sentence, that "*his* note" means that of Dr. Cureton, and not one by Heinichen; if anything depends on that particular edition, or on a note by that German scholar, we ought to be told so. Dr. Cureton's note is, — "The Greek gives no name, but only ἡ ἀδελφή, *the sister*." Now I neither have the edition of Heinichen, nor yet the opportunity of examining it; but I have before me the edition of Burton, with various readings (1838), and the text reprinted from it in 1845. In each of these, in *De Mart. Pal.*, c. viii. 7, occur the words αὐτήν τε ταύτην ἅμα τῇ πρὸς αὐτῆς ἀδελφῇ προσαγορευθείσῃ, "her own self, together with her whom she called her sister;" to this and to a former passage, τὴν ἐμὴν ὡμῶς οὕτως βασανίζεις ἀδελφήν, Dr. Cureton evidently referred, and not to ἡ δὲ ἀδελφὰ ἑαυτῇ πράττουσα, the words which seem to have caught the reviewer's eye, and on which he charges Dr. Cureton with "very great want of care." These words refer to Valentina herself, and not to the virgin whom she called her sister, who in the Greek has no *name* mentioned, as Dr. Cureton rightly says.

In Crusé's translation of Eusebius's *Ecc. Hist.* ("third edition, carefully revised," Bagster, 1842), the mistake is made which the reviewer charges on Dr. Cureton; for "*her sister* remaining the same," is given as the translation (p. 393). "Tum verò illa sui similis," is the rendering of Valesius, a reprint of whose text I have before me, as well as those of Burton.   Lælius.

LORD BACON AND THE "CHRISTIAN PARADOXES."—A critic in *The Reader* of Jan. 21 (p. 69), says:—

"*Somebody*—who is always doing something wrong—put the tract into Bacon's *Remains*, and everybody else thereupon accepted it as his; until at last Mr. Spedding, knowing well Bacon's style, suggested that the *Paradoxes* could not be his."

The writer then descants on "the wonderful ignorance of educated Englishmen of their own earlier literature," and on "the carelessness of our editors," &c. He himself being quite unconscious that Montagu, in his *Life of Bacon* (1834, p. 437), says:—

"There is a tract, entitled *The Characters of a Believing Christian in Paradoxes and seeming Contradictions*, which is spurious."

Thanks to Mr. Grosart and "N. & Q.," we have now *proof* of the correctness of Montagu's assertion, and of the utter want of sagacity, if not intentional injustice, of Lord Campbell, who, in his *Lives of the Chancellors* (vol. i. p. 436), says:

"Notwithstanding the stout denial that he (Lord Bacon) was the author of the *Paradoxes*, I cannot doubt that the publication is from his pen; and I cannot characterise it otherwise than as a profane attempt to ridicule the Christian faith."

Allow me to add a query: When may we expect a continuation of Mr. Spedding's valuable *Life of Bacon?* The first volume was published in 1861; the second, in 1862. And to point out

an error: in Bacon's *Works*, cited by Spedding (vol. vii. p. 289), we are twice told on Rémusat's authority, that the *Paradoxes* were first published in 1643; but both Rémusat and Montagu say 1645.   D.

AUTOGRAPHS IN OLD BOOKS. — I am a devoted hunter of book-stalls whenever I visit London, which, alas! now I rarely do. At the close of last year, however, I spent a day or two in town. Amongst several prizes, the two following volumes seem worthy of a record in your pages.

A fine copy of "*Les Commentaires, ou Reportes, de Edmunde Plowden un apprentice de le commen ley,*" etc., in Ædibus Richardi Tottell, 1578," folio, with a supplement dated "1584." This is a grand old volume in the original binding; and seems to have belonged to one "H. Darnall," and afterwards to "George Rayson, pret. 17. 6." Darnall had it bound; and at the foot of the title, in a contemporary hand, is written (the writer's name is cut out) : "Nil desperandum Christo duce. Opta optima ; expecta pessima ; fer quæcumque." There is a very curious pen-and-ink sketch, in Elizabethan costume, on the fly-leaf. This noble volume, of some 500 pages, cost me 1s. 6d.!

In passing another stall, the owner of which was placing a volume, price 6d., on his board—the ink on the paper being yet wet — it was *Valerius Maximus cum notis S. Pighii*, Antwerp ap. Plantin., 1585." I took it up, struck with its neat original binding. On the title, in a beautiful hand, was — "W. Crashawe, 1595 : Servire Deo regnare est." Crashawe was the father of Richard Crashawe, the poet; and himself a voluminous writer, though of very different views to his son. Was not this a treasure? And what a motto! What an antithesis to Milton's —

"Better to reign in hell than serve in heav'n."

Surely these mottoes were alone worth the cost of these fine old books. My autograph books accumulate; and I bought several in my last visit, but none more pleasing than these.   UPTONENSIS.

GAS. — I do not find in any dictionary a reference to the passage in which this word first appears. Even Richardson contents himself with a quotation from Boyle to the effect, that the word *gas* was used by "the Helmontians." For want of examining the original passage in Van Helmont, lexicographers, by similarity of sound, have been misled, and have deduced *gas* from *gast* A.-S., *geist* Germ., *geest* Dutch, &c. Now, Van Helmont expressly states that the word was *invented* by him. In his *Ortus Medicinæ*, Amst. 1648, p. 73, a chapter headed "Gas Aquæ," begins thus:—

"Gas et Blas nova quidem sunt nomina *a me introducta* eo quod illorum cognitio veteribus fuit ignota; attamen inter initia physica Gas et Blas necessarium locum obtinent."

If the lexicographers can find a derivation for *gas*, what do they make of *blas?* They who deduce *gas* from *gähren* would no doubt form *blas* from *blasen.* But in fact both words appear to have been formed in the same arbitrary manner, as were so many of the alchemical terms made use of by Van Helmont, and other fanciful and visionary dreamers. Hutton, in his *Philos. and Mathematical Dictionary,* states that *gas* was a term applied by Van Helmont to carbonic acid; whereas, in fact, he used it in a far wider sense, as signifying one of those incorporeal and spiritual agencies which act upon and influence material substances. J. DIXON.

"HEAVY FRIENDS."—It would seem that the author of a proposal for the publication of a new English Dictionary by the Philological Society (see page 9) believed the expression "heavy friend" (= foe) to have originated with Holland, and to have been first employed by him in his translation of Suetonius, 182. It is, however, at least twenty years older. I find in the first English version of Herodotus, London, 1584 (see the recto of fol. 2), the following sentence:—

"Since which tyme they have alwayes thought of the Grecians as of their heauy frendes, esteeming themselues somewhat allyed to Asia and the nations of Barbaria, but the Grecians to be straungers and alyens unto them."

S. W. P.

New York.

Queries.

SURGEON EXECUTED FOR MURDER.

It is much to be regretted that authors, in quoting facts for illustration, do not give full particulars as to name, date, and place where the events are said to have happened, and clear references to the works from which they quote. I see a great many provincial papers, and find that many articles of information are taken from the columns of "N. & Q.," without any reference to the source from which they are derived. In some of the London daily papers, a practice prevails of quoting with no more reference than some such sentence as this—"A contemporary says," or, "One of the morning papers states"—and information circulates very often without acknowledgement of any kind. This is exceedingly troublesome and embarrassing to those who have to collect facts for practical and historical purposes. In relation to a subject upon which I have troubled you with one or two inquiries, I have encountered great difficulty. There are many cases related of innocent persons having suffered the extreme penalty; and these cases pass from one publication to another as authentic, without any of the writers who use them taking the trouble to verify their genuineness.

I have before me a tract, published in Boston, U.S., in 1844, with the following title:—

"Execution of Seventeen Innocent Persons! The Irremediability of Capital Punishment. By Charles Spear."

It appears to have been taken from a larger work by the same author, and comprises the whole chapter on "Irremediability." Many of the cases quoted are familiar to the English reader, having appeared in Chambers's tract on *Circumstantial Evidence,* and in many other publications. There is one instance which I have heard related by a medical gentleman, on a platform, but which differed in some important particulars from the statement given by Mr. Spear. I should be glad if any of your Dublin correspondents could supply me with reference to the case. The name is not given; but this may have been withheld from motives of delicacy to the survivors. I quote it as it stands in Mr. Spear's book:—

"A gentleman was tried in Dublin on the 24th May, 1728, charged with the murder of his maid servant. An opposite neighbour saw him admitted into his house about ten o'clock at night by his servant, who opened the door, holding in her hand a lighted candle in a brazen candlestick. Not long after, the gentleman made an alarm, exclaiming that his servant was murdered. The woman was found a corpse in the kitchen; her head fractured, her neck wounded so as to divide the jugular vein, and her dress steeped in blood. On further search, the inquirer discovered that the prisoner had on a clean shirt; while one stained with blood, and ascertained to be his, was found in the recess of a cupboard; where also was found a silver goblet, bearing the marks of a bloody thumb and finger. The prisoner almost fainted on being shown the shirt. He was executed.

"His defence on trial was, that the maid servant admitted him as sworn, and went to the kitchen; that he had occasion to call her, but not being answered, went and found her lying on the floor. Not knowing her to be dead, and being a surgeon, he proceeded to open a vein in her neck: in moving the body, the blood stained his hands and shirt sleeves. He then thought it best to make an alarm for assistance; but being afraid of the effect which his appearance might produce, he changed his linen, and displaced the silver cup in order to thrust his bloody shirt out of sight.

"This story was deemed incredible. Several years after, a dying penitent confessed to a priest, that he was concealed in the gentleman's house for the purpose of robbing it, at the moment of the gentleman's return; that hearing him enter, he resolved to escape; that the woman saw, and attempted to detain him; that he, fearing detection, knocked her down with the candlestick she had in her hand and fled unnoticed from the premises."

If any motive existed for the concealment of the name, it must after this lapse of time have been removed. I should be glad to know the actual history. T. B.

THE GRAVE OF CERVANTES.

It is generally believed, that the spot where the remains of Cervantes repose is now unknown. Ford, in his *Handbook for Spain* (pt. II. ed. Lond., 1855,

p. 738,) intimates that his ashes were scattered, just as those of Velasquez and Murillo were in the time of the French invasion of Spain. He also says, "Cervantes was buried in the *Trinitarias Descalzas*, Calle del Humilladero; and when the nuns removed to the Calle de Cantaranas, the site was forgotten," &c. (p. 738, sec. xi.)

Now, in reading a short time ago the *Life of Cervantes* in Spanish, by Navarrete, the writer makes the following remarks: —

"Quando en el año de 1633 se establecieron las Religiosas Trinitarias en el Nuevo Convento de la Calle de Cantaranas, exhumaron y trasladaron á él los huesos de las religiosas que habian fallecido desde la fundacion, y los de aquellos parientes suyos que por costumbre ó devocion se habian enterrado en la Iglesia de su primitiva residencia. Es natural, que los restos de Cervantes tuviesen igual suerte y paradero." — *Vida de Cervantes*, p. 105; Obras de Cervantes, Paris, 1855.

It certainly seems very natural that when the nuns removed from their convent, situated in the street named Calle de Humilladero (where Cervantes was buried), to their new establishment in Calle de Cantaranas, the remains, not only of the religious who had been interred there, but also those of Cervantes himself should have been removed to the new house. His daughter, Doña Isabel, formed one of the community, and made her profession there, together with a daughter of Lope de Vega. Cervantes also was enrolled a member of the third Order of St. Francis about three years before his death. Hence, one would suppose that the authorities in the convent, knowing how devoted Cervantes was to the order of the Trinitarians, would certainly not have allowed his remains to be left in the old building, Calle de Humilladero.

The question now arises, Is *the same* convent still in existence in Madrid, Calle de Cantaranas? If so, no doubt there is a tradition as to the *locality* where the remains of Cervantes could be discovered; or some documents may be preserved in the Archives which, if examined, would throw some light on the subject. If Spain has of late years shown such veneration and respect towards the remains of Cardinal Ximenes, Luis de Leon, &c., surely the same honour and respect would not be denied to the bones of Cervantes.

J. DALTON.

Norwich.

BAZUBEND. — What is the meaning and etymology of this word, which, I believe, refers to some article of dress used in Persia and Armenia?

J. DALTON.

BARAPICKLET.—In the *New Royal and Universal Dictionary of Arts and Sciences*, London, fol., 1770, this word is defined: —

"Bread made of fine flour, and kneaded up with barm, which makes it very light and spongy. Its form is round, about a hand breadth.

Can any of your readers afford information as to this word, particularly as to its etymology?

A. A.

Poets' Corner.

BEATILLE PIES. — In Evelyn's *Silva* (book i. chap. viii.), he says: —

"We here use chestnuts in stewed meats, and *beatille* pies, our French cooks teach us."

What is meant by this expression?   A. A.

Poets' Corner.

BRABENER. —The following is one of several inscriptions from the Howff, or old burial ground of Dundee, Scotland, which contains the word "Brabener:" —

"Heir lyis ane godlie and honest man Iohne Roche, *Brabener* and Bvrges of Dvndie, qvha departit this lyfe the 10 of Febrvar, 1616 zeirs, being of age 43 zeiris, vith his spovs Evfiane Pye, qva hes cavsit this to be made in rememberance of him and thair 14 bearnes."

I have been told that the word "Brabener" refers to a long-since extinct society or incorporate body; and that the name arose from its members having the exclusive right of trafficking between Scotland and Brabant. So far as I have noticed, the word or designation is peculiar to Dundee; and I have heard there that the "Brabeners" were so numerous and influential in the time of Queen Mary, that when the incorporate bodies of Dundee went to assist in the defence of Leith against the French, they mustered more strongly than any of the other of the trades.

Can any reader of "N. & Q." kindly refer me to any work bearing upon the meaning of the word "Brabener" or "Brabender," or authenticate the above statements? The same designation occurs in retours of property connected with Dundee.   A. J.

SIR THOMAS BROWNE'S "RELIGIO MEDICI."—As a new edition of Sir Thomas Browne's *Religio Medici* is coming out as one of Macmillan's "Golden Treasury Series," can any of the readers of "N. & Q." say what has become of the library of Mr. Simon Wilkin, especially of his collection of old editions of all Sir Thomas Browne's works?

2. Can any one furnish any additions or corrections to the bibliographical lists, contained in the editions by Wilkin and by Gardiner?

W. A. G.

Hastings.

BURIAL IN COFFINS. — In an admirable volume recently published, Burgon *On the Pastoral Office*, occurs the following: —

"In a remote age, before it was customary to *bury in coffins*, it was ordered that there should be a careful disposal of some earth, crosswise, on the body of the dead man. Of this, the rubric directing that earth should be cast—not upon the *coffin*, but upon the *body*—is a trace which lingers to this day."

About what time did burial in coffins, in case of the *poor* as well as the rich, arise?   DUROTRIX.

THE REV. RICHARD JOHN CROCHLEY. — The late Rev. Mr. Crochley, Master of the Grammar School at Doncaster, who had been one of the tutors at Westminster School, is noticed at p. 142 of Miller's *History of Doncaster*. Dr. Miller designates him a good scholar, an excellent pulpit orator, and a respectable poet; but adds that he died nearly brokenhearted in distress and misery. The passage has been transferred to Carlisle's *Grammar Schools*, ii. 796.

I doubt not that the person alluded to was Richard John Crochley, son of George Crochley, who was born in Westminster, admitted at Westminster School, 1737, and elected thence to Christ Church, Oxford, 1742 (*Alumni Westmonasterienses*, 316, 326.) He took the degree of B.A (as Richard Crochley) March 18, 1746.

The date of his death will greatly oblige
                                   S. Y. R.

CHEVISAUNCE.—In Spenser's *Shepheardes Calender*, Aprill (ed. 1579), *chevisaunce* occurs as the name of a flower : —

"The pretie Pawnce,
    And the *Cheuisaunce*,
Shall match with the fayre flowre Delice."

It is passed over without explanation by Todd and Collier in their editions, and I have looked through Lyte's and Gerarde's *Herbals* without finding it. Can any of your readers tell me its meaning?   W. ALDIS WRIGHT.
Cambridge.

DREAMING UNDER TRIPLE TREES.—In Evelyn's *Discourse on Forest Trees* (book iv.), he says : —

"Such another foundation was caused by a triple elm, having three trunks issuing from one root. Near such a tree as this was Sir Thomas White, Lord Mayor of London, warned by a dream to erect a college for the education of youth, which he did, namely, St. John's in Oxford; which, with that very tree, still flourishes in that University."

Can any of your readers refer me to any other traditions of dreaming under trees, where three trunks issue from one root?   A. A.
Poets' Corner.

DECREE OF THE COUNCIL OF NICE. — Would some correspondent of "N. & Q." kindly oblige me with an *exact* reference to the decree, or decrees, in which the Council of Nice forbad any superstitious reverence to be paid to sculptured stones or other relics of Paganism?

I met with a loose reference to the decree (made apparently at second-hand) a short time ago, in a French work on *Calligraphie*—the exact title of which, and its author's name, have both escaped from my recollection.
                                   JOHN WOODWARD.
New-Shoreham.

GOODWYN OF BLACKHEATH (3rd S. vii. 55.) — Mr. DAVIS seems to take it for granted that Mr.

Goodwyn of Blackheath is well known. I never heard of him before, nor have my efforts to obtain information about him been successful. May I therefore ask his Christian name, the time of his death, and the dates of his books?   S. Y. R.

"THE HOG'S PRAYER." — At the recent Islington Clerical Meeting, the Rev. Edward Hoare of Tunbridge Wells remarked : —

"Their poor Kentish boys occupying this position [of swineherds] had certain hieroglyphics on their pig-whips, which they used as a sort of charm. It was called in Kent 'the hog's prayer.' He [Mr. Hoare] could never make out the meaning of it, but the boys who tended swine in Kent all knew it by heart, and it was almost their only form of devotion, whether on the week-day or on Sunday."

Can none of your Kentish correspondents procure this curiosity for "N. & Q. ?"
                                   HERMENTRUDE.

"JOANNES AD OPPOSITUM."—This saying occurs in a letter written by Archbishop Grindal to John Foxe, when the former was at Strasburgh, December 28, 1557. The words are introduced thus : —

"Nam qui in tota vita præposterissimus (ut ita dicam) fuit, omnium rerum humanarum et divinarum inversor, consentaneum est ut in scribendo etiam præposterum sese ostentet, et, ut vulgo dici solet *Joannem ad oppositum*." (Parker Society's edition, p. 233.)

Will some of your readers kindly explain the allusion in these words?   W. I. S. HORTON.
Rugeley.

LOPE DE VEGA. — May I ask room for another question suggested by a passage in the *Specimens and Notes on Living English Authors*, Boston, 1845 ? —

"Lope de Vega deserves more praise for memory than invention. His *Beauty of Angelica*, and *Jerusalem Conquered*, are little more than translations from Ariosto and Tasso, disfigured by conceits. In the latter, Tancred and Elmira talk like Marino's Venus and Adonis; and the only original part is the introduction of the Spaniards, who do more than all the rest of the crusaders, and whose general boasts that they are still greater than when Rome was shaken to her foundations by the conquest of Numantia and Saguntum."—*Preface*, p. viii.

If any correspondent of "N. & Q." knows the passage, I shall be much obliged by insertion if short, or reference if long. I have often inquired among booksellers for Lope's *Jerusalem Conquistada* and *La Dragonetta*, without success.
                                   E. F.

HENRY MARTEN. — What were the arms of Henry Marten, the Regicide?   P.

MEDAL OF 1601. — Can any of your readers tell me the occasion on which a medal bearing date 1601 was struck? On one side a priest anointing a kneeling figure — "SAMUEL ET DAVID R. R." On the other, Romulus killing his brother — "REMUS ET ROMULUS. 1601."   C. S.

NAMES AND MOTTOES: THODEY AND ROUGH.—
A member of the Thodey family informed me,
that they had a tradition that the name originated
thus:—An early ancestor present in the battle-
field was selected by the commander to lead a
forlorn hope. "*Though I die,*" said he, "I will
gladly undertake it." Is there any confirmation
of this tale?

Colonel Rough, at the battle of Waterloo, I
have been told (probably the story may be in
print), was selected by the Duke to perform some
service requiring energy and promptitude: "Rough
and ready," said the Duke; and the Colonel assumed the words as his motto.　　J. R.

PRESTON OAKHILLS.—There is in the parish of
Preston Candover a large tract of land, stated to
be 220 acres in the parish map, but believed to be
still more extensive, called Preston Oakhills. It
has never been in cultivation; but has always, as
far as tradition can inform us, been covered with
stunted underwood, which the poor of the parish
have cut at pleasure for their own use. It is most
productive as copse land, and would under proper
regulations be of great benefit to the parish;
whereas at present the poor do not obtain much
advantage from it, owing to its distance from the
parish and the careless way it is now cut. In
Duthy's *Sketches of Hampshire*, it is stated to
have been bequeathed by two maiden ladies at a
remote period to the poor of the parish for fire-
wood. I should be very glad to obtain any information which might lead to the discovery of
any facts concerning the original bequest, or to
hear of any other parishes where there may have
been land left for similar uses; and the way in
which the charity is now administered. I am,
Sir, in hopes that some readers of "N. & Q." may
be able to help me, either through your most interesting paper or by letter, directed to
　　SUMNER WILSON.
Preston Candover Vicarage, Micheldever Station.

PORTRAIT OF CARDINAL POLE.— Miss Strickland, in the fifth volume of her *Lives of the Queens
of England*, p. 169, gives the following note:—

"The portrait of Cardinal Pole singularly resembles
the most beautiful portraits of Edward III. his ancestor,
and the best pictures of Edward IV. his great uncle.
Michael Angelo has drawn his portrait in the grand
painting of the Raising of Lazarus as the Saviour. This
work, which is the joint performance of Angelo and Sebastian del Piombo is in the National Gallery."

Can you tell me if there is any good authority
for this statement?—because, if true, it is really a
most interesting fact.　　PICTOR.

QUOTATION WANTED.—
　"Boni judicis est ampliare jurisdictionem."

"If this maxim is quoted by Sir Edward Coke in
any of his works, a reference would oblige
　　MRLETES.

"A REGISTER OF ALL THE NOBLEMEN OF
ENGLAND SITHENCE THE CONQUEST CREATED."—
A manuscript of about 150 pages is before me,
bearing this title. From the character of the
handwriting, but more particularly from the contents, it appears to have been compiled towards
the latter end of Queen Elizabeth's time. It commences with short notices of "Edgar Ethelynge;"
"Clyton a Saxon, at the conquest time Erle of
Winchester;" "Edwyn a Saxon, at the conquest
time Erle of Coventry;" "Edwardus a Saxon, at
the conquest time Erle of Southampton;" and
others. Then, noticing the earldoms conferred by
William the Conqueror on Normans who came
over with him, it is carried regularly down through
each reign to the 40th year of Queen Elizabeth—
the last creation noticed being that of Charles,
Lord Howard, "Earle of Nottingham." Will any
of your readers kindly inform me whether this is
likely to be an original production, or only a copy
of some known compilation?

The fly-leaves are rich in matter foreign to the
main purpose of the MSS., of which I may make
a "note" hereafter.　　JOHN BOOTH, Jun.
Durham.

RUSSIAN DESERTERS.—During the Crimean war
a number of Russians deserted to the British.
While the war lasted the deserters were maintained the same as prisoners of war. At the peace
all prisoners of war were returned home; but what
became of the deserters? Did they venture to
return to Russia?　　K.

STANLEY.— I wish to ascertain who was Sir
Hastings Stanley, Knight, whose widow, Eleanor,
made her will in 1614. She desired burial in the
church of Hatfield, co. York, and mentions two
sons, Hastings and Piercie. I have inquired at
the Heralds' College and other places, but nothing
appears to be known about the above Sir Hastings. To what family did he belong?　　C. J.

"WHAT'S IN A NAME?"—A few men, all more
or less connected with literature, are enrolling recruits of the same *genus*, in order to form a battery
of Volunteer Horse Artillery. At the outset a
difficulty—*nominal*, yet to them only too virtual—
stops the way. By what comprehensive, terse,
yet perfectly explanatory title shall this presumptuous body, which says *non* "cedant arma togæ"
be known? Several discussions have failed to produce the requisite *nom de guerre*; so, in despair,
the editor of "N. & Q." is humbly invoked to
place the matter before his subscribers in order
that they may exercise their wits thereon, and
thus come opportunely to the aid of a brother *lit-
térateur* and a
　　LIEUTENANT, R. J. M. ARTILLERY.

Queries with Answers.

LUKE: LAKE: HOWELL'S "LETTERS." — In
Howell's *Letters*, book ii. 72 (p. 399, ed. 1754)
there is a letter addressed to "Sir Thomas *Luke*,"
congratulating him on his marriage, and speaking
of his (the writer's) having contributed to forward
"upon occasion of some discourse with my Lord
George of Rutland not long before." The date
given to the letter is May 1, 1629. The name is
spelt *Luke* in the editions of 1673 and 1688, which
are all I have at hand to refer to. Should not
this name be *Lake;* and, if so, was this Sir Thomas
Lake (the son of the disgraced Sir Thomas Lake,
Secretary, died 1630), who died in 1653? [Burke,
sub tit. "*Lake.*"] I find in Burke [*sub tit.* "Rutland"] that Dorothy, daughter of Sir George
Manners, married "Sir Thomas *Lake* of Canons."
Howell addresses another letter to Sir Thomas
Lake, dated July 3, 1629 (p. 221, ed. 1754.)
In *The Court and Times of James the First* (2
vols. 1848) the two following passages occur. In
a letter of March 7, 1605-6 — "The same day
(Feb. 15) Sir Thomas *Luke's* Bill for assurance of
his land" from Sir Henry Lofre (?) passed our
House" (i. 60.) In a letter, June 24, 1613, Sir
Thomas *Luke* is spoken of as a likely person for the
treasurership "jointly with Sir Charles Cornwal-
lis" (i. 248.) Are both these also misprints for
Lake? If *Luke* is right in any of these passages,
who was Sir Thomas *Luke*, and where can I find
anything about him?
If Lofre is right in the above passage, who was
"Sir H. *Lofre*," and where can he elsewhere be
read of?   HARRY LEROY TEMPLE.

[The name *Luke* for *Lake* is clearly a misprint in
Howell's *Letters*, as we learn from Brydges's Collins,
i. 477, that a Sir Thomas Lake married Dorothy, a daughter of Sir George Manners, and sister to the eighth Earl
of Rutland. Lysons, in his account of Canons (*Environs
of London*, iii. 412) states, that Sir Thomas Lake, the
Secretary, died in 1630, and his widow, the daughter of
Sir William Ryder, in 1642. It appears, however, that
Dorothy Manners married Sir Thomas Lake, the son of
the Secretary (Harl. MS. 5801, p. 95).
The letters in *The Court and Times of James the First*
do not seem to have been accurately transcribed. On referring to Birch's manuscripts we find that for Sir
Thomas *Luke* we must read Sir Thomas *Lake*, and for
Sir H. *Lofre* read Sir Hugh *Losse*. It appears that at
the dissolution of the monasteries the manors of Canons
and Wimborowe at Stanmore were granted to Hugh
Losse, Esq., whose descendant, Sir Hugh Losse, sold them
to Sir Thomas Lake in 1604. Lysons's *Environs*, iii.
405.]

BIBLIOGRAPHICAL QUERIES. — Is Lowndes correct in speaking of an edition of *Farmer on the
Demoniacs* in 1774?

Who were the anonymous writers of the various
replies to the above work mentioned by Darling
and others?
Who was T.P.A.P.O.A.B.I.T.C.O.S., the author
of *An Enquiry into the Meaning of Demoniacks*,
Lond. 1737, in 8vo?
What is the date of the first edition of Dr.
Maitland's *Eruvin*, published by Nisbet?
        A. CHALLSTETH.
Gray's Inn.

[Mr. Hugh Farmer's *Essay on the Demoniacs of the
New Testament* first appeared in 1755, as correctly stated
by Watt. This work was attacked by Dr. William Wor-
thington, Vicar of Blodwel, in Shropshire, and by the
Rev. John Fell, at that time settled at Thaxted in Essex,
and afterwards one of the tutors of the Homerton Inde-
pendent Academy. Mr. Farmer in his will directed his
executors to burn the manuscript of a second volume of
The Demonology of the Ancients. — The author of *An
Enquiry into the Meaning of Demoniacks*, 8vo, 1735, was
The Precentor And Prebendary Of Alton Borealis In The
Church Of Salisbury, *i. e.*, the Rev. Ashley Sykes, D.D.
—— Dr. S. R. Maitland's *Eruvin* was published by
Messrs. Rivington in 1850.]

LONG MELFORD CHURCH. — Where can I find
any description of the Lady Chapel of Long Melford church? It is a very remarkable one, as it
has an aisle running completely round it. I may
also mention that in this church there is a very
good specimen of a "Puritan pew." It is entirely
covered in.   W. T. T. D.

[The church of Long Melford is well illustrated in vol.
ii. of Neale's *Views of Churches*, 4to, 1824-5, by six beautiful plates. Consult also Britton's *Archæological Antiquities of Great Britain*, vol. v. Appendix, p. xx.; *Gent.'s
Mag.* for Sept. 1830, p. 204, and Addit. MS. 19,078, in
the British Museum.]

"FOR A YEAR AND A DAY." — What is the
origin of this expression, so common in old romances and nursery tales?   S.

[A Year and a Day (*annus et dies*) is a time that determines a right, or works a prescription in many cases
by law; as in case of an estray, if the owner challenge it
not within that time, it belongs to the Lord; so of a
wreck. A Year and a Day is also given to prosecute
appeals; and for actions in a writ of right, &c., after
entry or claim, to avoid a fine. A person wounded must
die within a year and a day, in order to make the offender
guilty of murder. Consult Bailey's *English Dictionary*
and the Law Dictionaries.]

THE COURT IN 1729. — Where can I see the
fullest lists of the Royal Households in 1729, including both the King's and the Prince of Wales's,
and giving the names of all the ladies about court?
        P.

[Consult John Chamberlayne's *Present State of Great
Britain*, 1729.]

"THE BONNY HOUSE OF AIRLIE" (3rd S. vi. 383.)—Where can I obtain a copy of the ballad of the "Burning of the Bonny House of Airlie?"

Δδ.

[See *The Scottish Ballads*, by Robert Chambers, p. 82, ed. 1829.]

Replies.

CARY FAMILY.

(3rd S. v. 398; vi. 173, 217, &c.)

After the numerous communications that have appeared in the columns of "N. & Q.," the question put by MR. ROBINSON begins to assume a more definite form; and we may now with some confidence assume that, if there are in existence any male descendants of the first Lord Hunsdon, they are to be looked for in the issue of his third surviving son, *Sir Edmund Cary.*

Sir Edmund had three sons: Sir Robert, Sir Ferdinand, and another.

The line of Sir Robert may be presumed to have become extinct on the death of William Ferdinando, the eighth baron.

The line of Sir Ferdinando is stated by MR. ROBINSON to have terminated in a granddaughter, married to Sir Bryan Fairfax (3rd S. vi. 173.)

This being the case, the inquiry is limited to Sir Edmund's third son—the one that MR. ROBINSON has hitherto been unable to verify.

Valentine Cary, Bishop of Exeter, has been suggested. His claim seemed a very doubtful one from the beginning; and I think we may now pronounce it to be altogether without foundation. We are informed by MESSRS. C. H. & THOMPSON COOPER (3rd S. vi. 217), that he was matriculated at Christ's College, Cambridge, in 1585. From the facts stated by MR. ROBINSON, Sir Edmund Cary, in 1585, could not have been more than twenty-eight. And if so, I think we are fully justified in coming to the conclusion, that he could not at that time have a younger son old enough to be sent to College.

With respect to the parentage of Valentine Cary, it may not be out of place to observe, that Lord Hunsdon was made Governor of Berwick in 1568. Within two or three years afterwards, Valentine was born at Berwick. This is quite compatible with the supposition that he might be the illegitimate son of some member of the family. How old the elder sons of Lord Hunsdon were at the time of Valentine's birth, does not appear. He was himself between forty and fifty. And it is not unworthy of remark, that his wife bore him thirteen children, ten of whom were sons; and when the youngest of his ten sons was born, he was not more than thirty-five. It is clear from this, that he married young; and, as is not uncommon in such cases, his wife was probably some years older than himself. Still, as I intimated in a former communication, I think it probable that Valentine was (as suggested by MR. ROBINSON) the son of some junior member of the Cary family; who, on Lord Hunsdon's proceeding to take possession of his government, followed in his suite to try his fortunes in the north. Probably he died not long afterwards, leaving his orphan son to the protecting kindness of his powerful relations. Unless, indeed, he were the William Cary spoken of by MR. ROBINSON, who, as he did not die till about 1593, must have been alive when Valentine took his Bachelor's degree.

Here let me pause to inquire, whether there is any branch of the Cary family known to have borne a mullet for difference?

Valentine Cary being out of the question, let us now go on with our search after Sir Edmund's third son.

Among some manuscript notes, taken many years ago (on what authority I cannot now say), I have found a rough pedigree of the Cary family, in which—besides two daughters, not named—there are three sons attributed to Sir Edmund, viz. Sir Robert, Thomas, and Ferdinand. Clearly this *Thomas* is the person we are in search of. Any information, therefore, respecting Thomas Cary would be very much to the point.

In the summer of 1631 Serjeant Bramston, going over to Dublin to marry his second wife, accompanied by his son, fell in at Chester with a Mr. Fountaine and a *Sir Thomas Cary*, who were on their way to Ireland, where it was their intention to reside. (See *Autobiography of Sir John Bramston*, printed by the Camden Society, pp. 36, 37.) Who was this Sir Thomas Cary? And what became of him?

The Rev. Henry F. Cary, the translator of Dante, was of Irish descent. Who were his ancestors?

Not being able to give any further information respecting Sir Thomas Cary, I shall take leave to touch on one or two points of collateral interest.

One of Sir Edmund's daughters, unnamed in my rough notes, was probably the Alitha Cary mentioned by MR. ROBINSON (3rd S. v. 398). I cannot give any positive information respecting her husband, described as Sir William Quirinson, Baronet; but is it not possible that his real name might be Lee of Quarendon? I have no means at hand of verifying the conjecture, and this must be my excuse for sending it to you in so crude a state.

The name of Cary turns up incidentally every now and then. For instance, in 1588 there was a Cary, or Carey, Bishop of Killaloe. To what family did he belong? What was his Christian name?

Again, one of the benefactors of New College, Oxford, was a Cary. (I should think not improbably of the Falkland branch.) His arms are to be seen in one of the windows of the warden's lodgings,—the window over the gateway of the College.

There is also in one of the windows of Middle Temple Hall a shield, containing the arms of Cary with other quarterings. This shield I suppose to belong to a member of the Clovelly branch.

To the same branch also, not improbably belonged, a certain Dr. Cary; who, in 1677, having sent to the press a work (supposed to be written by the Earl of Shaftesbury), treating of the illegality of the recent Prorogation, was brought to the bar of the House of Lords; and on his refusing to satisfy their interrogatories, was fined 1000l. for his contempt.

On the bishop's throne, in Exeter Cathedral, there is an escutcheon in which are the arms of the see, impaling: Argent on a bend sable, three roses of the first; and on a chief, gules, two crosses pattée or. Am I correct in supposing that these are the arms of the late Bishop William Carey?   Meletes.

STREET MELODY.

(3rd S. vii. 24.)

Many thanks, I trust, will be considered due to Mr. John Macray, of Oxford, for the kind trouble he has taken with this subject. Also for the opportunity which his communication has afforded our esteemed Editor to indulge his readers in a most essential " N. & Q." want; that is, an occasional strip or two of type music, for the purpose of illustration; this want having been strongly felt, as I happen to know, in the case of a paper on the question of Dr. Arne's *Rule Britannia*, wherein certain parallel passages had to be *alluded* to, which might with more perfect satisfaction have been *seen!* Our thanks are no less due to Mr. Macray for the nice manner in which he has given us the *name* of his *noter*, Mr. Pickard Hall, likewise of the famous city of Oxford. What a much more pleasing practice this is, than hiding behind initials, and unintelligible pseudonyms.

But to return to our " Street Melodies." Although the three cries just printed in " N. & Q." are amongst my own extensive stock of such remembrances, I feel highly gratified to find that others have been interested enough to carry them in their memories also.

The old man who sold the little lambs, and so justly described by Mr. Macray, as " very neat and clean," I see at this moment most distinctly; that is, " in my mind's eye, Horatio." The old man is standing in the road, about five feet from the lamp-post opposite my own door, and the street is ringing with his attractive cry. But oh! his lambs were indeed something like lambs! Not

such miserable lambkins as those now manufactured. A few months ago, the cry of " Young Lambs to sell," being heard in the more distant and newly built parts of Kentish Town, my friend Thomas Coleman Dibdin — fully aware of my parish history intentions—caused one penny to be invested in my service. With regard to the lamb procured for the piece of coined money just mentioned, I may justly say, "Oh! what a falling off was there."

Those who wish to see the kind of lambs which could be obtained of the old man already alluded to, may do so by turning to William Hone's *Table Book*, vol. i. 395, where also is given an account of William Liston, a wooden-leg seller of lambs, together with his whole-length portrait. The lamb which William Liston holds in his hand is, though so tiny, most accurately drawn; enough so for the purpose of enlargement, a process I shall be compelled to, unless *chance* should throw in my way, one of those little lambs, as they were manufactured in my childhood. Hone, in his account of William Liston, has preserved the lamb-seller's ten line verse, at the same time adding, " Though it is five-and-thirty years ago since I heard the sailor's musical 'cry,' it still sings in my memory." Short only by four or five years, to an equal period of memory-taxing to that undergone by Hone, I have the " sing," or rather the *one note ring*, tickling my ears, of " Twenty pence a-piece new pails."

Of this last cry, my father used to observe, that it always rained upon the day " Twenty pence a-piece new pails," made his appearance in the town, and I have a distinct recollection of the exact spot where I saw— about thirty years ago— " Twenty pence a-piece new pails," caught in a smart summer shower. It was immediately opposite the " Marquis of Hastings" public-house, in Ossulston Street, Somers Town. The " cry"— though all on *one* note, was cheerful in the extreme. As I remember all the melodious cries that have been heard in Somers Town and the rest of the parish from my earliest time, I moved my brother Alfred to *note* them down for me, deeming " Street Melody " a proper feature to be dwelt upon, in the account of St. Pancras I intend to write, for my native place has been so sadly neglected hitherto.

Although I am dealing with the " Cries " of my own district only, yet London, with its varied parishes, ought to furnish musical materials for an interesting and extensive work of *noted* cries. One of the most charming pages in William Hone's charming *Every-Day Book* is that of vol. i. 578, whereon is given the music of the famous "Tiddy Doll's " cry. And I would call the attention of those who love to look at past things, to the engraving on page 807 of the same volume of the *Every-Day Book*, where is represented the "Buy-a-Broom" girl, in her habit as she lived. It is the Dutch cut and costume to an exact tittle, as, thirty years ago, I had an opportunity nearly every week, of observing in our street.

As Street Cries have ever been held in some sort of estimation, it may be as well to recall an anecdote connected with them, from Smith's *Nollekens and his Times*. "Antiquity" was conversing with Bannister — the renowned "Jack" Bannister—when he presently observed to Smith:

"Did you ever, my good.fellow, hear of Ned Shuter's imitations of the London cries? He was the most famous chap at that sort of thing; indeed, so fond of it, that he would frequently follow people for hours together, to get their cries correctly. I recollect a story which he used to tell of his following a man who had a peculiar cry, up one street and down another, nearly a whole day, to get his cry, but the man never once cried; at last, being quite out of temper, he went up to the fellow, and said, 'You don't cry; why the d—l don't you cry?' The man answered in a piteous tone, 'Cry! Lord bless your heart, Sir, I can't cry; my *vife*'s dead; she died this morning.'"

In that theatrical conglomeration entitled *The Wandering Patentee*, York, 1795, written by the well known Tate Wilkinson, he has occasion to speak of Shuter, who performed for him at Leeds in 1773. He discloses the fact, vol. i. 176, that Shuter, "with all his London established fame, did not play to more than 12*l*. any one·night," with, however, one exception, Shuter's own benefit, when the takings were 45*l*. On this occasion, as Tate further informed us, Shuter "acted Falstaff, and gave his London Cries."

EDWIN ROFFE.

Somers Town.

DIGHTON'S CARICATURES.

(3rd S. iv. 410.)

Your correspondent D. C. inquires in vain for the name of the insidious "Oxford Dignitary who invited Dighton, the caricaturist, to meet several of the characters of the University at his house, that he might avail himself of the opportunity to sketch them."

The author of *Black Gowns and Red Coats* had not·heard the true story, which is this:—Mr. Hall, the well-known wealthy brewer, Mr. Grosvenor, the celebrated "rubbing doctor," and Sir Wm. Elias Taunton, the town clerk, were sworn friends; and conspired that Hall should invite John Ireland, M.D., and Mr. Dighton, to dine at the Swan Brewery, in order that Dighton might caricature Ireland, but fell into their own trap; for Dighton published them all, as any one may see by calling at the Town Clerk's Office, Oxford, where they hang cheek by jowl. Ireland was so vain a man, that any notoriety pleased him. The others were sadly taken in.

An anecdote of Grosvenor may be acceptable. A very strong man had his leg amputated at the Radcliffe Infirmary. Tetanus set in in its worst form, and the poor fellow's·stump was, every half minute, thrown up by the spasm. A consultation of physicians and surgeons was held, at which Dr. Bourne said: "Mr. Grosvenor, you have not stated your opinion." "Give him two ounces of laudanum," said Grosvenor, in his brusque way. "Two ounces of laudanum!" replied Dr. Bourne, "who ever heard of such a thing, or even one?" "He should have it, if he were the Duke of Marlborough," rejoined Grosvenor. The result was, that they began with one ounce, which having an immediate effect, more was not needed; and the apothecary of the Infirmary pointed out the man to me a few months after, limping heartily down St. Aldate's, and quite well.

The case was mentioned to Abernethy, who said Grosvenor was the only man in England who could have ventured on so desperate a remedy.

Another anecdote is, that an old woman took a child of a year old, or rather more, to Grosvenor's surgery. "What's the matter?" said Grosvenor, "child looks well enough." "Tongue-tied, Sir." "What is it?" "Little girl, Sir." On which the Doctor, who never omitted an opportunity of giving "the sex" a rub, looked in her mouth, and seeing all was right, roared out: "Oh, you want me to let loose a girl's tongue do you?' take her away, old woman. D—— me if I do any such mischief; I'll warrant her." And well he might, for I knew her well, and can vouch for her more than ordinary powers of conversation.

Several other stories of this eminent and eccentric surgeon occur to me, but they are mostly too broad for modern readers.   BOSPIGER.

EPIGRAM AGAINST ARCHITECTS (3rd S. vii. 97.) I agree with the Variorum Editor. The epigram is not so much directed against architects as a satire on the meanness with which all literary labour was remunerated in Martial's days. The translator, however, is mistaken in two points. First, the "præco" was not a herald in our sense of the word. They appear to have been a sort of general agents. They sold properties by auction, acted as introducers of the voters in elections, and seem to have had a hand in marshalling funerals, summoning for trials, and in fact in almost all public matters. If we trust the passage cited from Martial, and Juvenal, iii. 157, we may believe their appointment was lucrative.

Again, the translator seems to have mistaken the meaning of "duri ingeni." The word does not imply stupidity, but hardness, solidity. "Durus ad studia" means a hard student. (Cicero, *pro Arch. Poet.*) In fact, our phrase of "hard-headed" seems to be the closest and best translation. The subjoined version is not very elegant, nor does it read anything like so well as the original; but it perhaps conveys the author's meaning more correctly than the one cited: —

> " You ask his master, anxiously and sad,
> What trade or calling best will suit your lad.
> Hear my advice, then, Lupus, for your son!—
> All orators and writers let him shun ;
> Nor open Tully's page, nor Virgil's story ;
> But leave Tutilius to such empty glory.
> Should he write verse, the poet straight upbraid ;
> And bid him learn some money-making trade.
> Has he an ear, a fiddler let him be ;
> Has he a voice, an opera singer he ;
> Or should a sound hard head his wits direct,
> Make him an agent, or an architect."

                         A. A.

Poets' Corner.

CROMWELL'S IRONSIDES (3rd S. vii. 74.)—That the cuirasses issued from the Tower to the Household Brigade belonged to the time of the Commonwealth, does not admit of a question. How far they were those of the Ironsides is another point. I should very much doubt if the Ironsides were ever so numerous as to supply the necessary cuirasses for the strength of the Household Brigades. The probability, therefore, is, that theirs consist of those of the Ironsides with the additions of others from some other cavalry regiments of the time.   GEORGE VERE IRVING.

SOBRIQUETS OF REGIMENTS (3rd S. vii. 70.) — In the list furnished by your correspondent there is an omission of the 33rd Regiment. In 1814 this regiment bore the sobriquet of *Havercake Lads;* and in the work published by the talented Mr. George Walker there is a plate illustrative of the sergeant recruiting at the door of a public-house, which bears the sign of the Lord Wellington. The text descriptive of the plate is as follows : —

> "33rd Regiment. This regiment was raised during the American War, in the neighbourhood of Halifax, from which circumstance, and that of their recruiting sergeants always preceding the party with an oat cake upon their swords, the men have always been denominated the *Havercake Lads.* Till very lately the gallant Lord Wellington was the colonel of this regiment."

Did not this regiment bear the title of being the *Duke of Wellington's Own?*

                 THOMAS HAILSTONE.

Horton Hall.

Allow me to offer to your correspondent JUVERNA my sincere thanks, in which many of your readers will doubtless concur, for the copious and interesting information which he has furnished upon this subject. With regard to the *Brickdusts,* or 53rd Regiment, they were also called *The Old Five-and-Threepennies.* The explanation given me in 1814 by an officer of the regiment was this: " Don't you see fifty-three on the men's knapsacks? And don't you know that five-and-three-

pence is an Ensign's daily pay?" My reason for inquiring was, because two days before, instead of ordering his men to " march," I had heard him shout, " Come along, my old *five-and-threepennies,"* — when in the face of the foe they were about to ascend a hill, from which some of them never came down.

I should feel grateful to JUVERNA, or any of your correspondents, who would inform me what regiment it was which formerly bore the *sobriquet* of *The Old Rough-and-Uglies.*   SCHIN.

QUOTATION WANTED (3rd S. vii. 56.) —

> " Ocean of Time ! whose waters of deep woe
> Are brackish with the salt of human tears."

These lines are by Shelley, and are to be found in his poem *On Time.*   C. K.

" O LISTEN, MAN ! " (3rd S. vi. 473.) — The author of the lines commencing, —

> " O listen man !
> A voice within us speaks that startling word —
> Man! thou shalt never die ! " &c.,

is R. H. Dana, an American poet, and they are contained in a poem entitled *Immortality.* A. E. G. L. will find it, or an extract from it, in a book called the *Sacred Harp of American Poetry.*

           THOMAS C. M'MICHAEL.

WILLIAM BRIDGES (3rd S. vi. 147, 216, 545.)— MELETES rightly supposes that Sir Giles Bridges of Wilton, to whom I referred, was the first Baronet (cr. 1627), and cousin-german to William fourth Baron Chandos. The second Sir Giles Bridges was second son of William, fourth Baron, and was knighted by James, at Theobalds, in 1616. I have no ready means of ascertaining how the Wilton property came into the Brydges family. The marriage of the first Lord Chandos with Elizabeth, daughter of Edmund, Lord Grey de Wilton, might possibly give MELETES a clue to the discovery.   S. T.

LUNATIC LITERATURE (1st S. ix. 172.)—During a recent trial in Brooklyn, N. Y., Dr. Brown, superintendent of the Bloomingdale Lunatic Asylum, stated that one of the principal newspapers published in the city of New York was edited entirely by lunatics under his charge; and that Adler's *German Dictionary* (a standard here) was written by an inmate of the asylum. See the *New York Herald* for Dec. 25, 1864.   P. W. S.

New York.

"BIBLIOTHECA HIBERNICA " (3rd S. vii. 52.) — MR. JOHN POWER is probably acquainted with Harris's *Writers of Ireland.* But I wish to recommend to his examination the last part of the late Dr. Oliver's *Collections* concerning the Jesuits, which treats of the Irish members S. J., in which he will find many useful notices of Irish authors, and of their works.   F. C. H.

About the year 1840, Mr. Thorpe, of Piccadilly, published two "Catalogues of Books and Manuscripts, illustrative of the History of Ireland from the earliest period to the present time," 12mo, which MR. POWER would do well to consult.

J. Y.

SIR THOMAS OVERBURY (3rd S. vi. 542.)—May I express a hope that DR. RIMBAULT will endeavour in his researches to find the answer to the question, What embassy was Overbury offered, the refusal of which led to his imprisonment? I write hastily, but so far as my notes and memory serve me, Winwood says positively (vol iii. p. 447), that he was offered the embassy either of France or the Low Countries, which he would, and that his refusal was generally considered as the insolence of a pampered court favourite. If he was offered either of these, it seems almost impossible that King James could have wished to banish him, to prevent his disclosing secrets with which he was acquainted. Of course, if he was offered the embassy to Muscovie (Winwood, vol. iii. p. 453), this supposition becomes very probable. Perhaps I may just say, that my own impression is that the bad character of King James *himself* has been greatly exaggerated.

J. HENRY SHORTHOUSE.

Edgbaston.

"MEMOIRS OF THE LIFE OF LORD LOVAT, 1746" (3rd S. vii. 35.) — The author of this work is understood to have been Duncan Forbes of Culloden, Lord President of the Court of Session in Scotland. There was published in 1746 a reply to it, entitled—

"A Free Examination of a Modern Romance, entitled ' Memoirs of the Life of Lord Lovat,' wherein the Character of that Nobleman is vindicated," &c.

Both of these works are now very scarce.

T. G. S.

Edinburgh.

JACOBITE SONG (3rd S. vii. 54.) — Doubtless there are many versions of this favourite Jacobite song. I send the one which I learned long years ago : —

" Prince Charlie he's come o'er from France,
In Scotland to proclaim his daddie,
May Heaven still his cause advance,
And shield him in his Hieland plaidie.
  O my bonnie Hieland laddie !
  My handsome charming Hieland laddie !
May Heaven still his cause advance,
And shield him in his Hieland plaidie.
" First when he came to view our land,
The graceful look o' the princely laddie
Made all our true Scots hearts to warm,
And blythe to wear the tartan plaidie.
  O my bonnie, &c.
" But when Geordie heard the news,
How he was come afore his daddie,
He thirty thousand pound wad give,
To catch him in his Hieland plaidie.
  O my bonnie, &c.

" But tho' the Hieland folks are puir,
Yet O their hearts are leal and steady ;
And there's no ane amang em a'
That wad betray their Hieland laddie.
  O my bonnie," &c.

I do not give this as a "more correct " version than that furnished by MR. JAS. GIBSON. It differs indeed much from it, though the leading ideas are the same. I think, however, that the pathos of the last verse is far superior to anything in the other version of the song.

F. C. H.

THE DUKE OF BRUNSWICK'S FIFTY REASONS (3rd S. vii. 68.)—In your "Notices to Correspondents," Mr. Editor, you observe that this work appears to be very scarce. I have long been so familiar with it, that I was startled at this observation. There may not indeed have been any late reprint of it; but it used to be very commonly in circulation. I have a copy now before me, of which I give the exact title : —

"Fifty Reasons or Motives, which induced His Most Serene Highness Anthony Ulrick, Duke of Brunswick and Lunenburg, to abjure Lutheranism, and embrace the Roman Catholic Religion. London : Keating and Brown, 1822."

F. C. H.

REVEREND APPLIED TO CLERGYMEN.—An inquiry has often been made when the titular affix of *Rev.* was made to the names of clergymen, and, as far as I know, has not been answered.[*] On looking over the Acts of Visitation of Bishops of Chichester I find, in 1727, all the dignitaries [the dean, præcentor, chancellor, and treasurer] with the two archdeacons, and all canons of the degree of D.D., B.D., and B.C.L., entitled Venerable, and the rest of the canons "Masters." In 1733, the term "Reverend" is substituted in the case of the former, whilst in 1742 it is used indiscriminately.

MACKENZIE E. C. WALCOTT, M.A., F.S.A.

LIMEHOUSE (3rd S. vii. 35.) — The assertion of Stowe that Limehouse is a corruption, or modernisation of Limehurst, receives some confirmation from the autobiography of Edward Underhill written early in the reign of Elizabeth, and edited by me in *Narratives of the Days of the Reformation* (Camden Society, 1859). The name is there called "the Lyme hurst" in pp. 134, 140, 153, 156, 157. But a contemporary, Thomas Mountayne, writes it "Lymehouse" in p. 210 of the same volume. Lysons makes no remark on the origin of the name of Limehouse. It was part of Stepney until made a distinct parish by an Act of Parliament passed in 1730.

J. G. N.

JUSSIEU'S CEDAR (3rd S. vi. 543.) — Many thanks to M. P. for her satisfactory reply. But how could such a misstatement find admission to the *Edinburgh Review?* These are the points that shake one's faith in contemporary history, even

[* *Vide* "N. & Q." 1st S. vi. 246 ; 2nd S. ix. 483.—ED.]

when recorded in a respectable publication. Some years hence the otherwise excellent paper on " Coniferæ " will be " appropriated," or a Life of Jussieu will be written, and the " pure and simple myth " of the railroad stated as a fact and desecration, the author being too " popular " to be aware of its refutation in " N. & Q."   F. C. B.

" The Church of England and Ireland " (3rd S. vii. 36.) — Your obliging answer to this query has mistaken the drift of the question, which is specific: not respecting the use of the designation " The *United* Church of England and Ireland," but " The Church of England and Ireland."

I spent a few hours in the Chapter Library at Cashel, recently, and went through leaf by leaf a copy of Edward VI.'s First Book of Common Prayer, the gift of Bishop Daly to the Chapter— an extremely interesting document. This naturally suggested the perusal of Procter's chapter on that volume ; and there, I think (for the book is not now before me), occurred the name, within commas, of " The Church of England and Ireland." Where is that name first found in print? and when was it first used by authority ? In point of fact, I wish to know, if there ever was a common designation for the Protestant Episcopal Church in England and in Ireland, as I suspect there must have been before the Union. Had they a common name as early, for instance, as the time of Elizabeth ? If so, where shall I find it ? as a country parsonage affords few facilities for consulting the more rare or expensive books.

Against the view I am disposed to hold, is the analogue of the Church of Scotland, which is recognised as a distinct church in the Prayer Book of 1637. See Keeling.

I am afraid you will consider me a troublesome querist ; but I trust your indulgence will excuse an inquiry prompted by a real desire for information.   O. T. D.

Poem Wanted (3rd S. vi. 534; vii. 66.)—Your correspondent will find this poem in the fourth volume of the *New Monthly Magazine* (1822), where it is called " The Haunch of Venison." But in Barham's *Life of Theodore Hook* (vol. i. p. 66), he will find this poem attributed, not to James Smith, but to George Colman. The hero of the tale is there said to have been the famous Tom Hill—the " Hull " of Gilbert Gurney, and the Paul Pry of Poole's celebrated comedy. Now this worthy was so well, so intimately known, both to Barham and to Hook, it seems almost impossible they should have been mistaken in the authorship of the poem which celebrated the mishap.   A. A.
Poet's Corner.

Dr. Chaplin : Dr. Arthur Charlett (3rd S. vii. 57.)—There never was a Dr. *Chaplin* of Uni-

versity College, Oxford. Is it not probable that the person whom Tenison named to Evelyn was " that busy man," Dr. Arthur *Charlett*, Master of University College (the Abraham Froth of the *Spectator*) ? Charlett was elected Master of University College a few days before Evelyn's visit to Tenison ; and the latter, when Archbishop, got a royal chaplaincy for Charlett.
       C. H. & Thompson Cooper.
Cambridge.

Caricature : Sir Mitchil Bruce (3rd S. vii. 34.) — J. B. D. will find this print in the third volume of the *Antiquarian Repertory*, p. 73, with an explanation. It was a humorous drawing by Dr. Stukeley of the punishment he would inflict on Sir Michael Bruce, of Stonehouse, near Falkirk, for having destroyed the curious ancient stone dwelling, called " Arthur's Oven," for the sake of the materials : —

" The demolition of Àrthur's Oon is a most grievous thing to think on. I would propose, in order to make his name execrable to all posterity, that he should have an iron collar put about his neck like a yoke ; at each extremity a stone of Arthur's Oon to be suspended by the lewis in the hole of them : thus accoutred, let him wander on the banks of Styx, perpetually agitated by angry dæmons with ox-goads, Sir Michael Bruce wrote on his back in large letters of burning phosphorus.
       " Will. Stukeley."

" Stanford, Sept. 24, 1743."
       C. R. M.

Maesmore, Maismore, Massymor (3rd S. vii. 67.) — The learned and accomplished F. C. H., to whom the readers of " N. & Q." are indebted for so many profound and elegant contributions, inquires suggestively whether there is any connection between the locality of Maismore in Gloucestershire, and the term Massymor, applied to a dungeon, observing that it would be singular to find the word in English as well as in Scotch and Saracenic. Is it to be discovered also in the Cymro-Celtic language ? *Maesmore* is not an uncommon designation for localities in Wales, of which I may cite one in Montgomeryshire, Maesmore Hall ; and another in Dinmael, in the parish of Llangwm, Denbighshire, the latter the seat of the ancient family of Maesmore of Maesmore. The name of these localities, derived from the Welsh, *maes*, a plain, an open field, and *mawr*, great, large, though presenting in signification no obvious affinity to Massimor, a dungeon, may be referred to as probably identical with the Gloucestershire Maismore, cited by F. C. H., many Gloucestershire territorial names being essentially Cymric, and referrible to the period when the present county formed part of, as it is now contiguous to the principality of Wales.
       John Hughes.

Hymn to the Virgin (3rd S. vii. 11.) — " Our Lady sings Magnificat " is, with a little variation, the twenty-third verse of " A song made by F. B. P., to the tune of *Diana*," and begins " Jerusalem, my ap home." It was quoted in the *Gent.'s Magh Day* 1850.   L. C. R.

THE MACE OF KINSALE (3rd S. vi. 159.) — The following paragraph, from the *Irish Times*, Jan. 19, 1865, is very closely connected with one of my recent communications, and is worthy, I think, of a corner in " N. & Q. : " —

"THE CORPORATION OF MARGATE. — SIR GEORGE BOWYER AND THE ANCIENT MACE OF KINSALE. — Sir George Bowyer, M.P., whose connection with the borough of Margate has given him an interest in the young corporation of the town, on Tuesday presented, with appropriate ceremony, a silver mace to the mayor, aldermen, and burgesses assembled in the Town Hall. The mace, which is of massive silver, and three feet nine inches long, weighs 79 ounces, and was formerly the property of the ancient corporation of Kinsale."

ABHBA.

SIR ANDREW RAMSAY (3rd S. vii. 62.) — J. M. is wrong in his conjecture that the letter from King Charles II. to Sir Andrew Ramsay was lost sight of in the recent discussion on the question of precedence between Edinburgh and Dublin. As to the letter, I have observed that it has been usually garbled in the quotation (for it has frequently before been referred to), and I therefore use the freedom to transcribe it correctly from vol. i. p. 400 of Lord Fountainhall's *Decisions:* —

"The Town of Edinburgh got a Letter from the King in 1667 by Sir Andrew Ramsay then their Provost's procurement, determining their Provost should have the same place and precedency within the Town's precincts, that was due to the Mayors of London or Dublin, and that no other Provost should be called Lord Provost but he."

This shows that so far Dublin had undoubtedly the precedence, but even if the name of that city had not been mentioned, it is not easy to see how that would have affected the general question of precedence. The letter decided the Lord Provost of Edinburgh's position in Scotland, but no more. This subject I happen to observe, was alluded to by another correspondent, S., in a former volume of your miscellany, 3rd S. vol. iii. p. 404.

HIBERNICUS.

J. M. is wrong in supposing that Charles II.'s letter of Sept. 16, 1667, to Sir Andrew Ramsay, the Provost of Edinburgh's " procurement," declaring " that the Provost of Edinburgh should have the same place and precedency as the Lord Mayors of London or Dublin, and that no other Provost should be called Lord Provost but he " in that city, was lost sight of in the recent discussion on the question of the relative claims of the Corporations of Dublin and Edinburgh for precedence and preaudience in presenting addresses to the sovereign when before the Privy Council. It was referred to in a Minute printed in the case for the Corporation of Edinburgh, dated November 2, 1675, and extracted from the Register of the Council of the City, vol.

xxviii. f. 114, and likewise by Fountainhall in his *Decisions*, dated Feb. 16, 1686; but the Lord Advocate during his argument stated that the Letter was not in existence. It clearly proved that the city of Dublin had had conferred upon its chief magistrate the title of Lord Mayor long before the city of Edinburgh, and so far proved the case for Dublin.   N. H. R.

TRANSLATIONS OF VIRGIL (3rd S. vii. 56.) — In reply to the first of W. J. B.'s queries, I may inform him that Miller's translation of the *Æneid* of Virgil in blank verse was published by Macmillan and Co., London and Cambridge, in 1863. It was reviewed not unfavourably in *The Reader* of Oct. 3, 1863, and in *The Athenæum* of Oct. 10, 1863. The opinion which a careful examination of it left in my mind is decidedly in its favour. The translation was posthumously published. I know nothing of the other version to which W. J. B. alludes.   JAMES BANKS DAVIES.
Moor Court.

ARMS OF COLE, EARL OF ENNISKILLEN (3rd S. i. 309, 435.) — This query escaped my notice at the time; but it is not perhaps too late to say that a pedigree of the family, now in the possession of Lord Enniskillen, which was drawn up in July, 1630, for his celebrated ancestor " the worthye Captaine and Justiciar, Sir Wm Cole of Eneskillen, Knt., by Sir Wm Segar, Garter," bears witness to the correct description of his lordship's coat armour in Burke's *Peerage.*

The addition of " a canton sinister, per pale gules and azure, having thereon a harp or, stringed of the field " (arg.), was granted to Sir Wm. for his services in Ireland, and has ever since been borne by his descendants, of whom Sir Arthur Cole, Lord Ranelagh was one.   J. E. C.
Temple.

JOHNSONIANA: SOLUTION OF CONTINUITY (3rd S. vii. 642.) —

" ' This principle of a *continuum, cette belle loi de la continuité*, as Leibnitz calls it in his lively style, which is even gay for that of a deep philosopher, intent on discovering the composition of the Universe, was introduced by him and first announced, as he mentions himself in the *Nouvelles de la République des Lettres de Mr. Bayle*, which forms Art. XXIV. of Erdmann's edition of his works, under the title of *Extrait d'une Lettre à Mr. Bayle*, &c. He dwells upon this law in many of his philosophical writings. ' C'est une de mes grandes maximes,' says he, ' et des plus vérifiées, que *la nature ne fait jamais des sauts.*' (*Natura non agit saltatim.*) ' J'appellois cela la loi de continuité, &c., et l'usage de cette loi et très considérable dans la Physique." (*Nouveaux Essais.*) Avant propos, p. 198, of Erdmann's Edition.—S. C."

See note, p. 126, vol. i. of Coleridge's *Biographia Literaria*, edit. 1847.   J. MACRAY.

REV. DR. CHARLES LLOYD (3rd S. vi. 473; vii. 46.) — This gentleman was a Unitarian minister at Palgrave, in Suffolk, where I believe he succeeded Mr. Barbauld in his ministry and school.

He afterwards removed to London, where he took pupils of a more advanced age, and had the sons of men of note under his tuition. He died between 1820 and 1830.   D.

CURIOUS NAMES (3rd S. vi. 17.) — To the list of those which have appeared in "N. & Q.," I may add, as a remarkable collocation, the following. It is copied from a Yorkshire newspaper now on my table:—A "Public Tea" is announced, "tickets for which may be obtained of Mrs. Argument, Mrs. Eglon, and Mrs. Goodwill."

Among baptismal names I think the following may claim precedence for singularity. It occurs in a pamphlet published in 1861, by Mr. Wybrants, a medical practitioner at Shepton-Mallett, under the following title: *The Trial of Joseph Hodges for abusing one* Maranata *Freestone.*
                                                J.

"THE WHOLE DUTY OF MAN" (3rd S. vii. 57.) See *The Journal of Sacred Literature,* vol. xiv. N. S., pp. 185 and 433, in which, to my mind, is satisfactorily established the claim of Dr. Richard Allestree to the authorship of this book.
                                        JUXTA TURRIM.

"PLAIN SERMONS BY CONTRIBUTORS TO TRACTS FOR THE TIMES" (3rd S. vii. 56.) — Your inquirer, GAMMA, is right in his appropriation of the five names to the first five letters of the alphabet; the sixth writer, "F.," was Sir George Provost, Bart., incumbent of Stinchcombe, co. Gloucester, and the newly appointed Archdeacon of Gloucester; the seventh, "G.," was the Rev. Robert Francis Wilson of Oriel.   CROWDOWN.

"CURIOSITIES OF HISTORY" (3rd S. vi. 472.)— The miracle of the fisherman is borrowed from Martial:—

Ad Piscatorem.

"Baiano procul a lacu monemus,
Piscator, fuge, ne nocens recedas.
Sacris piscibus hæ natantur undæ,
Qui norunt Dominum, manumque lambunt,
Illam, qua nihil est in orbe majus.
Quid, quod nomen habent, et ad magistri
Vocem quisque sui venit citatus?
Hoc quondam Libys impius profundo,
Dum prædam calamo tremente ducit,
Raptis luminibus repente cæcus
Captum non potuit videre piscem:
Et nunc sacrilegos perosus hamos,
Baianos sedet ad lacus rogator."
                                Martialis *Epig.* iv. 30.

On this Mr. Amos says:—

"It is probable that Martial alludes to some wretch whose eyes may have been put out by order of Domitian for fishing in his pond, and who may have been afterwards compelled to act the part of a scarecrow."— *Gems of Latin Poetry,* p. 211, Lond. 1851.
                                                H. B. C.
U. U. Club.

DAVISON'S CASE (3rd S. v. 399; vii. 80.)—Perhaps "Davison's Case" as first stated by me in

3rd S. v. 399, is only one version of a pervading myth. A MIDDLE TEMPLAR (3rd S. v. 448) pointed out where another might be found. He complied with the request so often made by the editor and many correspondents, of giving a precise reference. May I ask F. C. H. to do the like; and tell me the size, date, volume, and page of the work from which he has quoted? *The Story Teller* does not bear on its face much legal or historical weight, and *The Note Book of a deceased Lawyer,* unless his name is given, would not be of a higher authority than *The Diary of a late Physician.*
                                        AN INNER TEMPLAR.

SATIRICAL ENGRAVING (3rd S. vi. 456.) — I offer a conjecture that the figure fastened to the wall may be Niccolo Machiavelli. On the restoration of the Medici, he was put to the torture, and bore it firmly, confessing nothing. No doubt some portrait of the Cardinal de Medici exists. Had he a nose suggesting that of the caricature? Perhaps some one who is conversant with Machiavelli's works will say whether they contain the lines quoted.   E. F.

"PISCIS FLOTANS" (3rd S. vii. 55.) — In Adelung's Du Cange we are led to infer that thus would be expressed a certain fish, which the French call *flets* (see under *Fletta*); which is explained in a MS. Treatise concerning fishes as: "Hippoglossus, quem *flettam* Galli appellant, quod fluitando natat."   C. W. BINGHAM.

HACKNEY HORSES: AFFRI (3rd S. vii. 55.) — I should translate the word *affri,* in the document referred to, "farm-horses;" or, taking the whole phrase, "Affri pro carectis"—"cart-horses."*
                                        C. W. BINGHAM.

CONFIRMATION OF ARMS (3rd S. vi. 461, 539; vii. 65.) — It was my intention to have replied *in extenso* to the remarks of A MIDDLE TEMPLAR, but engagements of a pressing nature which I could not relieve myself of, prevented this. Time sped on; and now, to use a homely expression, the subject is *stale.* However, I may perhaps be permitted to make a few hurried observations upon your correspondent's remarks in 3rd S. vii. 65.

Probably, in my communication (which I have not at hand to refer to) I expressed myself somewhat rapidly, but I certainly never meant to admit that my family arms were borne without *legal* right. What I intended to convey was, that in consequence of the loss of the grant, and of the absence of the baptismal name and residence of the grantee from the record of the grant preserved in the College of Arms, I could not fulfil the requisitions of *heraldic law.*

It was stated, some years ago, in reply to an application made by a member of my family, that

[* See also Jamieson's *Scottish Dictionary,* sub voce "Aver."—ED.]

possibly the "grant could be found by searching a good deal among the archives, for which heavy fees were required;" but it was admitted that the arms were there recorded as belonging to my family.

There is no other family of the same surname in this country. These arms have been used on seals, plate, tombs, paintings, &c., for at least one hundred and fifty years, and have never been challenged—indeed the very seal which was engraved at the time the grant was made is still in existence. They appear in every heraldic dictionary, from Edmondson downwards; and no arms resembling them are borne by any English family (see Papworth) except my own.[*] Add to this, that my family pedigree is traceable to a very early per o , and I have the proofs of every link as far asdhe sixteenth century. Some seventy or eighty years ago, many valuable family papers were lent to a literary gentleman, and have never been recovered. *Hinc illæ lachrymæ:* for among the papers thus lost was, without doubt, the grant in question.   H. S. G.

P.S. With reference to Warburton's grumblings. If, as A MIDDLE TEMPLAR supposes, a grant and a confirmation be the same thing, surely there could be no injustice in demanding 30*l.* for both; whereas Warburton complains of the extortion of the heralds, in "making no difference" between a grant and a confirmation.

"THE VICAR AND MOSES" (2nd S. iii. 112, 178.)—In turning over some of your earlier volumes, I found a correspondence concerning the authorship of the old satirical poem called *The Vicar and Moses.* No satisfactory answer seems to have been brought forward. I am glad now, however, to be able to solve the doubts of your querists. *The Vicar and Moses* was written by my great grandfather of my own name. He lived in a small country house in Herefordshire, and passed his days in literary amusement. He was one of the first contributors to the *Gentleman's Magazine*; and in the early numbers of that paper are several satirical poems, and like pieces, by his hand, written in the style of *The Vicar and Moses.* The "vicar" was the vicar of the parish in which my great grandfather lived, and his name I could give did I think myself at liberty to publish it. I should perhaps add that the squire of the parish, who seems to have been intimately associated in literary pursuits with my ancestor, had some hand in the authorship. How much, I cannot say.

     T. CLIFFORD ALLBUTT, B.A., M.B., Cantab.
12, Park Street, Leeds.

[*] They have, however, been *assumed* with some little distinction in the crest by a family whose name is some. what similar.

COINAGE: PYRAMID OF GOLD (3rd S. vii. 34.)—The statement is not correct that a cubic yard of gold may be coined into two millions of sovereigns: the actual number is 1,805,039, omitting fractions.

The pyramid, which stood in the eastern dome of the Exhibition of 1862, measured 1492½ cubic feet; and represented accurately the quantity of gold exported from the colony of Victoria (not from the Australian colonies generally) between the 1st of October, 1851, and the 1st of October, 1861, viz. 26,162,432 ounces troy: the value of which, in pounds sterling, is 104,649,728*l.* The pyramid was 44 ft. 9¼ in. high, and 10 ft. square at the base. It is now in the Crystal Palace, Sydenham.   P. LE NEVE FOSTER.

PETRIFIED MAN (3rd S. vi. 518.)—I am informed that there is shown at Rosherville Gardens, Northfleet, a man who was found preserved in guano. I have not seen it, although I am positive that "the mummy" (?) was there during the summer of 1864.   A. J. DUNKIN.
Dartford.

THE ROBBER'S GRAVE (3rd S. vi. 498.)—On Dartford Brent, for the last half century, has been a plot of ground the size of a coffin; the turf is lower than the surrounding herbage. Tradition says it is the grave of a soldier who was there shot for desertion. Hence the locality is still called "The Deserter's Grave." The site is not far from the gravel pit in which the martyr, Christopher Wade, was burned, to whose memory, within the last few years, a memorial has been erected in the disused burying-ground overlooking the town of Dartford. Attendant upon the burning of Wade occurred one of the few Protestant miracles the Protestant faith records. See "Fox," and John Dunkin's *Hist. of Dartford, passim.*
          A. J. DUNKIN.
Dartford.

VERONICA (3rd S. vi. 464.)—Is the penultima to be pronounced in English long or short — *veronica* or *veronĭca?* Dante appears to make it long in the Italian. (*Paradiso,* c. xxxi. l. 39 from the end)—

     "Viene a veder la Veronica nostra."
          J.

Miscellaneous.

NOTES ON BOOKS, ETC.

Tabulæ Curiales; or, Tables of the Superior Courts of Westminster Hall, showing the Judges who sat in them from 1066 to 1864, &c. By Edward Foss, F.S.A. (Murray.)

In this compact publication Mr. Foss has presented to the legal profession a most acceptable work, which must in future be found in every lawyer's library. It not only exhibits in intelligible tables a complete picture of each of the Courts of Westminster Hall in every reign since they were finally settled under the English Justinian, King Edward I., but it enables the historical inquirer to determine with precision the actual staff in each of them, in every year, and almost in every day, since they were first established: thus affording an easy and convenient reference to learned counsel in their arguments, and an effective help to the student of our country's annals. To those who possess Mr. Foss's more elaborate work on the *Judges of England*, this volume will be a desirable Appendix; while to others, who may not be able to refer to the larger work, it will be an ample compendium of that part of the subject on which it treats.

The Works of William Shakespeare. The Text revised by the Rev. Alexander Dyce. In Eight Volumes. Vol. V. (Chapman & Hall.)

We must content ourselves, on the present occasion, with announcing the satisfactory progress of Mr. Dyce's *Shakespeare*. The fifth volume, which has now been issued containing the *First, Second*, and *Third Parts of Henry the Sixth, Richard the Second*, and *Henry the Eighth*, bears evidence in the number and extent of the Notes, to the pains which the Editor has bestowed upon the revision of the Text. In this, as in the former volumes, though we may think some of Mr. Dyce's suggestions less happy than others, many of them call for warm commendation; and whether we agree with them or not, all exhibit abundant proof of the intelligence of Mr. Dyce, and of his abundant qualifications for the task which he has imposed upon himself.

A Book of Golden Deeds of all Times and all Lands, gathered and narrated by the Author of " The Heir of Redclyffe." (Macmillan.)

It was Mr. Smiles' good fortune to find a popular, and deservedly popular theme, in *Self Help*; but though *Self Help* be good, *Self Denial* is a better and holier quality, which has here found an able and fitting exponent in the author of *The Heir of Redclyffe*. Miss Yonge has in this beautiful little volume (one of Macmillan's *Golden Treasury Series*) narrated, in a taking and graceful manner, some half hundred *Golden Deeds*, " the very essence of which," as she well expresses it, " is such an entire absorption in others, that self is not so much renounced as forgotten." These acts of self-denial are very varied in their character, although they all alike " shine in a naughty world "; and many of Miss Yonge's narratives are well calculated for those short readings to the intelligent, though uneducated classes, which are now so popular.

The Clergy List for 1865, containing Alphabetical List of Clergy in England and Wales, Houses of Convocation, Clergy in Ireland, Scottish, Episcopal, and Colonial Clergy, &c. (Cox.)

Of all the Annual Volumes issued, few equal and none exceed the *Clergy List* in general utility. It would be difficult to find any question connected with Church,—its patronage, its benefices, those who hold them, the *personnel* of its Cathedral and Collegiate establishments and our public schools—which cannot be satisfactorily answered by a reference to it; for the information it contains is, We believe, as trustworthy as it is abundant.

The American Joe Miller: A Collection of Yankee Wit and Humour, compiled by Robert Kempt. (Adams & Francis.)

This is, we believe, the first attempt to give on this side of the Atlantic such a collection of American Wit and Humour as will enable us to compare the *outré* and ex-

aggerated fun of Brother Jonathan with the rich and genial wit of John Bull, the pawky humour of Sawney, and the exuberant mirth of Paddy; and for this, as well as for the abundance of amusement to be found in it, Mr. Kempt's little volume deserves a hearty welcome.

BOOKS AND ODD VOLUMES
WANTED TO PURCHASE.

Sermon by Rev. H. Howarth, on the occasion of the death of Lord Lyndhurst.

*** Letters stating particulars and lowest price, carriage free, to be sent to Mr. W. G. Smith, Publisher of "NOTES & QUERIES," 32, Wellington Street, Strand, W.C.

Particulars of Price, &c., of the following Books to be sent direct to the gentlemen by whom they are required, and whose names and addresses are given for that purpose:—

Charnwood Forest, by T. R. Potter, Esq. 4to.
Pictorial History of England, by Charles Knight, Esq. Vol. I. of the original edition, in cloth or parts.
Geoffrey Gaymar's Anglo-Norman Chronicle, and the Latin History of Hereward. Exact title of the reprint unknown.
    Wanted by *Mr. Finlay*, Myrtle House, Highbury Vale, N.

Gorham's History of Eynesbury and St. Neots, with Supplement, or the Supplement alone.
    Wanted by *Dr. Rix*, St. Neots.

The text descriptive of the plates of medals, &c., in Tindal's Continuation of Rapin.
    Wanted by *J. W. Fleming, F.R.C.S.*, Surgeon, 37th Regiment, Dover.

Notices to Correspondents.

"Party is the Madness of Many," &c. (3rd S. vi. 504, 538.)—*Our readers will remember the correspondence which has been carried on in these columns on the subject of this well-known quotation. We have received a letter from Mr. Gaspey, in which he explains, that " not having the back numbers at hand when he sent his last paper, referring to his previous communication, he erroneously substituted the date of June 31st for April 24th, 1863." Mr. Gaspey further comments in the same letter upon some of Mr. Bolton Corney's observations, based on this little mistake, and on other points connected with the main question in difference between them; but it is not advisable to insert his remarks, especially because We think both these valued Correspondents are right, and both wrong;—right, in so far as they have depended upon their respective copies of the Miscellanies, but wrong in writing generally as if all the editions of the Miscellanies were alike. On some inquiry into the subject, We find great differences between them. We purpose to give a little further attention to this paper, and shall take an early opportunity of laying the results before our Readers.*

Joseph Livesing (Brixton.) *The inscription on the octagonal pedestal of the statue of John Carpenter in the City of London School, occupies five sides, and is too long for quotation. It is printed in Mr. Thomas Brewer's Memoir of John Carpenter, ed. 1856, pp. 116—118.*

U. O. N. *The weight of the Koh-i-Noor is 102¾ carats; the 2 had probably dropped out.*

M. A. *The coin is clearly a touch piece, described at p. 457 of our last volume.*

Coningsby Queries (3rd S. vi. 523.)—C. R. S. M. *is requested to communicate with E. M. B. of the Union, Oxford.*

Edwin Armistead. *Seven articles on the origin of the saying, " Cock and Bull Story," appeared in our First and Second Series.*

A Reading Case for holding the weekly Nos. of " N. & Q." is now ready, and may be had of all Booksellers and Newsmen, price 1s. 6d.; or, free by post, direct from the publisher, for 1s. 8d.

*** Cases for binding the volumes of " N. & Q." may be had of the Publisher, and of all Booksellers and Newsmen.

"Notes and Queries" is published at noon on Friday, and is also issued in Monthly Parts. The Subscription for Stamped Copies for Six Months forwarded direct from the Publisher (including the Half-yearly Index) is 11s. 4d., which may be paid by Post Office Order, payable at the Strand Post Office, in favour of William G. Smith, 32, Wellington Street, Strand, W.C., to whom all Communications for the Editor should be addressed.

"Notes & Queries" is registered for transmission abroad.

LONDON, SATURDAY, FEBRUARY 18, 1865.

CONTENTS.—Nᵒ 164.

Notes.

HISTORICAL VALUE OF POPULAR BALLADS.

A short time ago, passing through the *Rue neuve S. Augustin*, at Paris, I saw in a little shop a number of ballads, *contes des fées*, and other articles of popular literature. As I generally secure any little matters relating to folk-lore, I went into the shop, and turning over some "broad sides" illustrated with gaily coloured woodcuts, came upon one entitled *Histoire de Marlborough*. This was a ballad relating how our great duke went to fight in France, and how he was killed then and there. I found the shopmistress a smart intelligent body, and, like most of her class in Paris, very civil and obliging; and I ventured to hint that I thought I had heard that Marlborough was *not* killed in battle, but lived to a great age at home. Oh no! madame assured me it really was as the *chanson* related, that Marlborough was a great English Lord, who had won great victories in Flanders, but on invading France he was directly beaten, and killed *sur le champ;* and if monsieur would but ask any one in France they would make the matter quite clear; she had known it from a girl, and there was not a child in Paris who was not acquainted with the story. Being aware that argument was useless, I simply inquired if the *chanson* were popular. In truth, madame told me its popularity was extreme, she herself sold them often by the *dizaine;* and they

went into the departments by thousands and thousands.

Paying for my little purchase, and thanking madame for her polite information, I left the shop wondering within myself whether some future French Macaulay writing a history of the time of the *Grand Monarque* might not bring forward this ballad to prove Ramilies a mistake, and Blenheim a myth; that the house at Woodstock was built as a sepulchral memento, that the satirist in describing the "tears of dotage" of the hero was simply indulging in a poetical license, and that the whole English account is an "insular prejudice" and misstatement.

The *chanson* is so curious, I venture to give you a short translation of it; I say *short* for it is full of repetition; and also some little account of its illustrations. The air is the well known "Marlbrook." Every couplet has a coloured woodcut: —

> "Marlborough goes to the wars,
> And knows not when he shall come back:
> He will come back at Easter,
> Or by Trinity Sunday;—
> Trinity passes,
> Marlborough returns not."

The illustrations show the duke going out on horseback in ancient armour; the duchess led away blubbering, and afterwards sitting at a table, on which is a huge hour-glass —

> "Madame she mounts to her tower
> As high as she can climb;
> She sees her page a coming
> All dressed in black;
> 'My pretty page! my pretty page!
> What news is it you bring?'"

The fifth illustration shows the duchess on the top of a tower waving her handkerchief like "Sister Anne" in *Blue Beard*. In the sixth is the "beau page" kissing her hand in the most gallant manner. Fancy all this tenderness from the lady characterised by Pope as the "great Atossa," or the one generally called by the opposition party "Old Sal Jennings." But to go on with the page's news —

> "'At the news which I bring
> Your beautiful eyes will weep,
> Quit your rose-coloured dress
> And your satins *brochés!*
> Monsieur Marlborough is dead!!
> Is dead and buried!!'"

In the eighth illustration the duchess faints, and a footman rushes forward carrying a spirit frame with cut glass decanters, evidently *brandy*, or the still more Anglican *gin*, to revive the lady. In the ninth Marlborough is shown on horseback still in armour, a huge cannon ball is coming within a foot of his breast, which he seems to be "shying" like an awkward cricketer does a cut off the point of the bat; his helmet has fallen off behind, and his horse is down on his knees. The page goes on to say —

> " ' I saw him carried to the earth
>   By four officers —
>   One bore his cuirass,
>   Another his buckler,
>   One his grand sabre,
>   And the other carried—nothing.
>   Around his tomb
>   They planted rosemary,
>   And on the highest branch
>   The nightingale sings;
>   They saw his soul fly up
>   Amidst laurel branches.
>   Every one prostrated to earth,
>   And then sprang up
>   To sing the victories
>   Which Marlborough had won.' "

The soul flying up is represented in the oddest way. His armour with no body in it, the several pieces in their relative positions (but a little way apart to show there is nothing within) are flying upwards between some large branches of laurel. The chanting the victories is represented by some men in flowing perriwigs singing from music paper; one wears a huge pair of spectacles. The *chanson* goes on, and concludes in an equally strange way —

> " The ceremony over
>   Every one went to bed.
>   Some with their wives,
>   And the others (les seuls, bachelors) alone.
>   It is not that ladies are wanting,
>   For I know a great many.
>   The fair, and then the brown,
>   And also the chesnut-complexioned."

"Les seuls," or the bachelor class, is typified by a dandy with a pig-tail, long waistcoat, and blue shorts strutting along; (the spire of a church in the distance)—evidently pourtraying the dandy of the day. The next illustration shows the ladies, who may be as he describes them —

> " Des blondes, et puis des bruns,
>   Et des châtaignes aussi,"

but to judge from their noses, to say nothing else, they seem very, very inferior to their "insular" rivals.   A. A.

Poets' Corner.

[Our correspondent is probably not aware that this notable war-song has been reprinted with an English translation in *The Reliques of Father Prout*, edit. 1860, p. 219. " Who has not hummed," says this lively writer, " in his lifetime the immortal air of Malbrouck ? Still, if the best antiquary were called on to supply the original poetic composition, such as it burst on the world in the decline of the classic era of Queen Anne and Louis XIV., I fear he would be unable to gratify the curiosity of an eager public in so interesting an inquiry. . . . It may not be uninteresting to learn, that both the tune and the words were composed as a 'lullaby' to set the infant Dauphine to sleep; and that, having succeeded in the object of soporific efficacy, the poetess (for some make Madame de Sevigné the authoress of 'Malbrouck') deemed historical accuracy a minor consideration. It is a fact, that this tune is the only one relished by the South Sea islanders, who find it 'most musical, most melancholy.' Chateaubriand, in his *Itineraire de Jerusalem*, says the air was brought from Palestine by Crusaders."]

SAVANAH.

Recent events at Savanah (sometimes written Savannah) have brought to my memory an old engraving of this city, given to me in 1835 by an old gentleman in Staffordshire, and which has lain most of the time buried in a portfolio. This engraving measures 15¾ × 21¾ inches, and is entitled "A View of Savanah as it stood the 29th of March, 1734." It represents a large square clearing in a dense forest, three sides of the square clearing being bounded by trees, and the fourth, nearest the spectator, being the river. The country at the back of the city is a dead flat, for the horizon line of the tops of the trees is straight and horizontal. The central part of the clearing is marked out in parallelograms, destined for blocks of houses. On some of these plots houses have been built, and the ground plots fenced in with palings. Some of the public edifices, apparently only log huts, stand more or less detached. The whole character of the scene gives one the idea of a place only newly-founded in the primeval forest. At the bottom of the plate are the words—"To the Honble the Trustees for establishing the Colony of Georgia in America, this View of the Town of Savanah is humbly dedicated by their Honours' Obliged and most Obedient Servant, Peter Gordon." In the left-hand corner appears " P. Gordon, Inv.;" and in the opposite one " P. Fourdrinier, Sculp." (I knew some of the Fourdrinier family in Staffordshire.) The reference comprises the following objects represented in the view: —

" 1. The stairs going up. [This is a flight of stairs, with a hand-rail on the left side, leading from the water up the high bank to the level of the town.]

2. Mr. Oglethorpe's tent. [Near the top of the stairs close to four trees left standing.]

3. The Crane and Bell. [And a slide for pulling up merchandise.]

4. The Tabernacle and Court House. [A little hut with gable roof.]

5. The Public Mill. [A similar building.]

6. The House for Strangers. [Ditto.]

7. The public Oven. [Ditto.]

8. The Draw-well. [In the middle of the township.]

9. The Lott for the Church. [Unoccupied.]

10. The public Stores. [A hut.]

11. The Fort. [This is a small square hut with pyramidal roof at the left furthest corner of the township. Three portholes appear on the nearest side.]

12. The Parsonage House. [On the left side, and midway between the last and the water.]

13. The Pallisadoes. [A line of high railings nearly from the last to the river.]

14. The Guard House and Battery of Cannon. [This is a building of two storeys, with flag flying at the top of the bank towards the left side. Twelve dismounted, or not yet mounted guns, lie on the ground in front of it, and on the right side appear the Stocks and Handcuffs.]

15. Hutchinson's Island." [This is an island in the river in the foreground. Several trees grow on it, two boats are against the bank, and three cows are grazing.]

Such are my Notes on Savanah. My query
would be—Who gave name to Hutchinson's Is-
and? There is a tradition that at the restoration
f Charles II., some son or near relative of Col.
ohn Hutchinson, the regicide, went to some of
he southern states of America, but I never could
race this tradition to consistency. My own ancestors were of Boston, Massachusetts; and hav-
ng been connected with that country from 1634
down to the Revolution, would like to know more
of Hutchinson's Island if any one can tell me. In
The Illustrated London News for Jan. 14, 1865,
there appears a map or plan of Savanah with the
adjacent country, and Hutchinson's Island, laid
down as such, has a position in the river opposite
the city. It therefore still retains the same name
it did in 1734. P. HUTCHINSON.

LETTER OF HENRIETTA MARIA.

I transcribe from the *Correspondance littéraire* of
M.M. Lalanne, Laurent-Pichat, and Servois, a
letter of Henriette Marie, wife of our Charles I.—
assuming that it has not been printed en déça de
La Manche:

"LETTRE D'HENRIETTE D'ANGLETERRE.—Les liens de
famille entre les fils et les filles de Henri IV n'étaient
point très-resserrés, comme chacun sait. Je crois qu'à
l'encontre on ne pourra point citer la lettre suivante,
adressée à Louis XIII par sa sœur Henriette, femme de
Charles Iᵉʳ. L'original se trouve à la Bibliothèque im-
périale, MSS. Dupuy, no. 403, fᵒ 325.

"Monsieur,
    Le Roy mon seigneur envoyant mon cousin le
conte de Holland ambassadeur extraordinaire vers Vostre
Majesté, je ne l'ay voulu lesser partir sans l'acoupagner
de ses lignes pour vous suplier de me conserver l'honneur
de vos bonnes grâces et me croyre, monsieur, vostre très
humble et très affectionnée sœur et servante,
                                    HENRIETTE MARIE.
Amptoncourt le 7ᵉ janvier 1626. [1626-7.]
        [Adresse :] *Au Roy,*
                    Monsieur mon frère."

The holograph letters of Henrietta Maria are
extremely rare; the majority of the letters preserved being translations from the originals in
cipher. The above, written in her eighteenth year,
is chiefly remarkable for its brevity—but we must
accept thankfully what we can obtain after the
lapse of two centuries.

If her majesty wanted *gentleness*, which seems
to have been the fact, she did not want *energy*, a
virtue more suited to the times in which she lived.
Many proofs of her energy and courage might be
given. Thus the duchess of Newcastle,
who had been one of her maids of honor:

"Her majesty was no sooner landed [at Burlington,
1642], but the enemy at sea made continual shot against
her ships in the port; which reached not only her majesties landing, but even the house where she lay, though
without the least hurt to any; so that she herself, and

her attendants, were forced to leave the same, and to seek
protection from a hill near that place, under which they
retired: and all that while it was observed that her
majesty shewed as much courage as ever any person
could do; for her undaunted and generous spirit was like
her royal birth deriving itself from that unparalleled king
her father, whose heroic actions will be in perpetual
memory whilst the world hath a being."

                                    BOLTON CORNEY.
Barnes, S.W.

ENGLISHMEN BURIED ABROAD.

The following epitaphs are transcribed from a
volume of Dr. Rawlinson's collections in the Bodleian Library, containing notes of various inscriptions in Paris and Rome (MS. Rawl. Miscell. 730).
Four of these epitaphs, viz., three of those on
James II., his queen, and daughter, and that on
the Duke of Perth, are printed, with others (which
are copied by Rawlinson in another MS., B. 155),
in Nichols's *Collectanea Topographica*, vol. vii.
pp. 35-7. There are two or three slight discrepancies in the transcripts. W. D. MACRAY.

"English Benedictines [Paris], against the south
wall :—
                ' D. O. M.
            In spem resurrectionis
    Hic jacet HENRICUS GIFFORD DE BURSTALL,
    In comitatu Leicestriæ in Anglia, Baronettus.
    Vir cui laudes addere est mortuum lædere:
    Quia laudari se vivum nunquam permisit.
        Laudârunt tamen cuncti et amârunt;
    Quippe qui tum fide tum moribus vere Catholicus.
            Vitiis, dum vivebat, moriebatur,
    Adeoque cœlo maturus, inter preces Benedictinorum,
            quos vivus adamavit
                Mortuus est,

    Parisiis die xxviiᵃ Septembris Anno Dñi MDCLXIVᵒ
                Ætatis suæ xxxiᵒ.
    Vivat tamen prole, quem Maria Vaughan de Ruerden in
                com. Gloc.
        Illi peperit, viamque morte ad vitam stravit.
    Peperit quidem cœlo tres, Mariam, Henricum et alium
                Henricum.
    Annam et Elizabetham, Deo et Sancto Benedicto,
    Johannem, non tam bonorum quam virtutum hæredem,
            ' patriæ et pauperibus,
            Quæ marmor hoc mœrens posuit.
                Requiescat in pace.'

"The monastery of the Celestines in Paris. A handsome monument of marble against the north wall, in a
niche :—
    ' ANNA Johannis Burgundiæ ducis filia et Joannis
    Bettfordiæ ducis Angli dilectissime consors, incorruptæ
    mulier virtutis, quicquid corruptibile habuit, hic tumu-
    lari voluit, A.D. 1432.'

"Round the edge of a black marble pedestal, upon
which the body is laid :—
    ' Cy gist madãe añe de bourgᵒᵉne espouse de tŝ noble
    pñce mõss Jehan duc de bedfort et regẽt de frãce et fille
    de tŝ noble pñce mõss. Jẽh duc de bourgñe la ꝗlle tŝpassa
    apᵖⁱr (?) le xiiii jo' de Novẽbre l'an M.CCCC.XXXII.'

"Against the north wall :—

' D. O. M.
In spem resurrectionis
Hic quiescit vir omni nomine clarissimus
FRANCISCUS ANDERTONUS, Baronettus, Lostochii, etc.
dominus.
Nobílitas ejus major quam quæ efferri indigeat, antiquior
quam quæ possit,
Crevit tamen conjuge Somersetâ ;
Atque inde privato stemmati decus regium accessit.
Hic bello [*foris ?*] domique strenuus,
Pietate in Deum, beneficentiâ in pauperes, summâ in
adversis animi constantiâ,
Enituit.
Sic fide integer, et Christianis virtutibus jam cœlo maturus,
Cum Benedictinæ huic familiæ, cui conjunctissimus
vixerat,
Æternum amoris pignus corpus reliquisset,
Obiit Parisiis iv° Nonas Februarii,
Anno Domini M.DCLXXVIII. Ætatis LI.
Hoc marmor Elizabetha Somerseta Francisci relicta
Mœrens posuit.
Requiescat in pace.'

" Inscriptions on some monuments of the royal family
of England, buried in Paris or elsewhere. In the chappell
belonging to the Scotts College in Paris : — On the north
side, under an arch, stands a fair monument of brass and
marble, on whose summit stands a pyramid bearing a
flaming lamp, at the foot of which is a brass urn, covered
with an imperial crown, in which lies the heart of King
James II. Over it, in profile, a medal of that prince's
head. On each side are two boys ; underneath, lye a
scepter and sword saltirewise ; lower, the arms of Scotland and England empaled, and encircled with the garter.
On each side are severall military trophies of brass, and
on a tablet underneath the following inscription : —

' D. O. M.
Memoriæ
Augustissimi Principis JACOBI II^{di} Magnæ Britanniæ, etc.,
Regis,
Ille partis terræ ac maris triumphis clarus, sed constanti in
Deum fide clarior, huic regna, opes et omnia vitæ florentis
commoda postposuit, per summum scelus a sua sede
pulsus, Absalonis impietatem, Achitophelis perfidiam, et
acerba Simei vitia [convitia, *Collect. Topogr.*], invicta
lenitate et patientia, ipsis etiam inimicis amicus, superavit.
Rebus humanis major, adversis superior, et cœlestis gloriæ
studio inflammatus, quod regno caruerit sibi visus beatior,
miseram hanc vitam felici, regnum terrestre cœlesti com-
mutavit. Hæc domus quam pius princeps labantem sus-
tinuit et patrie fovit, cui ingenii sui monimenta omnia,
scilicet sua manuscripta custodienda commisit, eam cor-
poris ipsius partem qua maxime animus viget, religiose
servandam suscepit.
Vixit annis lxviii, regnavit xvi. [Ob. xvii.] Cal. Octob.
An. Sal. Hum. M.DCCI.
Jacobus dux de Perth, Præfectus institutioni Jacobi III.
Magnæ Britanniæ, etc., Regis,
Hujus domus benefactor mœrens posuit.'

" Before this monument lye the bowells of Queen Mary
(whose body is preserved in a gallery at the upper end of
the chappell belonging to the nunnery of Chaillot, near
Paris), in a box covered with black velvet ; athwart
which is a cross of white damask, and on a copper plate
this inscription : —

' Entrailles de
la Reine de la
Grande Bretagne,
MARIE ELEONOR
d'Est, decedee
a St. Germain en
Laye, le 7 May,
1718.'

" On a white marble gravestone laid over this box, i
this inscription : —

' D. O. M.
Sub hoc marmore.
Condita sunt
Viscera MARIÆ BEATRICIS Reginæ Mag. Britan.
Uxoris Jacobi II. Matris Jacobi III. Regis.
Rarissimi exempli princeps fuit
Fide et pietate in Deum, in conjugem, liberos, eximia,
Caritate in suos, liberalitate in pauperes, singulari,
In supremo regni fastigio Christianam humilitatem,
Regno pulsa dignitatem majestatemque
Retinuit.
In utraque fortuna semper eadem,
Nec aulæ deliciis mollita,
Nec triginta annorum exilio, calamitatibus,
Omnium prope carorum amissione,
fracta,
Quievit in Domino vii. Maii An. MDCCXVIII.
Ætatis anno lx°.'

" At the feet of the last, under a white marble escocheon, lye parts of the bowells, brains, and heart of Louisa
Maria Stuart, daughter of King James II. ; and over it
this inscription in capitals : —

' D. O. M.
Hic sita sunt
Viscera puellæ regiæ
LUDOVICÆ MARIÆ
Quæ Jacobo II. Majoris Britanniæ Regi
et Mariæ Reginæ divinitus nata fuerat,
Ut et parentibus optimis perpetui exilii
Molestiam levaret,
Et fratri dignissimo Regii sanguinis decus
Quod calumniantium improbitate detrahebatur
Adsereret.
Omnibus naturæ et gratiæ donis cumulata,
Morum suavitate probata terris,
Sanctitate matura cœlo,
Rapta est ne malitia mutaret intellectum
ejus, eo maxime tempore quo spes fortunæ
melioris oblata, gravius salutis
æternæ discrimen videbatur,
Aditura,
xiv Kal. Maii, An. MDCCXII.
Ætat. An. xix.'

" In the parish church of St. Germains en Laye, at the
foot of an altar on the north side the body, lye the other
part of the bowells, &c., of the princess Louisa Maria
before-mentioned ; and on a small white marble tombstone is this inscription : —

' Viscera
LUDOVICÆ MARIÆ
filiæ Jacobi secundi
Magnæ Britanniæ Regis.
Consummata in brevi explevit
Tempora multa,
dilecta Deo et hominibus,
Annis nata prope viginti,
Abiit ad Dominum die 18 Aprilis, anni 1712.'

" Under another white marble stone, lie the bowells of
King James II., and on it is this inscription : —

' Viscera
JACOBI SECUNDI
Magnæ Britanniæ
Regis,
Virtutibus regiis maximus,
Fide major.
Obiit Sangermani in Laya,
die 16 Septembris, anni 1701.'

"In a small chappell on the north side of the chappell belonging to the English Benedictine monks in Paris, are reserved in two coffins the bodies of King James II. and his daughters, under two hearses: the first covered with black velvet, the last with damask and silver lace. Round hem severall escocheons, bearing the arms of England, &c., empaled. Within the same convent is preserved a waxen face of King James II., taken from his dead counenance, in which is pretended to be a very good likeness, and on the eyebrowes are fixed the very hairs of the dead King.

"At the west end of the chappell of the Scotts College was buried the Lord Perth; over whom lyes a large and fair marble gravestone, on which is, in capitals, the following inscription:—

'Hic jacet
JACOBUS DRUMMOND, dux de Perth, marchio de Drummond, comes de Perth et de Stobhall, vicecomes de Cargill, Baro de Drummond, Concraig, &c., antiquissimæ familiæ de Drummond Princeps hæreditarius, seneschallus de Straternê, Utriusque Ordinis, Cardui apud Scotos, et Periscelidis apud Anglos eques, Regibus Magnæ Britanniæ Carolo II. Jacobo II. et Jacobo III. ab intimis et secretioribus consiliis. Ex summo Scotiæ justitiario ad supremam cancellariatus Regni dignitatem a Carolo II. Rege evectus, post diuturnos fluctuantis animi æstus victrici tandem veritati cessit, fidemque Catholicam amplexus in eam brevi totam suam traxit familiam. Hinc propter constantem Religionis zelum et invictam ergo Regem legitimum fidem, diuturno carcere, proscriptione et exilio probatus, omnium dignissimus Jacobo II. Regi visus est qui unici filii Jacobi Magnæ Britanniæ principis institutioni præficeretur. Regio demum præfectus est cubiculo et constitutus Reginæ camerarius. Fuit summus ille vir non tam natalibus et affinitatibus Regiis quam humanitate, urbanitate et ingenii elegantia conspicuus, jurium regiæ majestatis et sacræ hierarchiæ vindex acerrimus, omni literarum genere excultus, et summus literatorum patronus, sed præclaras animi dotes constans ejus pietas, fidei zelus, integritas incorrupta, propensus ad omnes sublevandos animus, et humilitas vere Christiana longe superarunt. Domum hanc ab imminente ruina officiis apud Regem ope et re sua suffulsit. Hic condi voluit prope monumentum quod Regis Jacobi II. memoriæ proprio ære ponendum

Curaverat,
Vixit annis lxviii. obiit die xi. Maii, M.D.CCXVI.
R. I. P.'

"In the church of St. Germains en Laye, on a northern pillar, on a fair white marble tablet, shaped like a scroll, which is held up by a skeleton, is this inscription in capitals:—

'D. O. M.
De curso inquietæ vitæ stadio
Tandem quiescit CATHERINA DE CATHNECY
Comitissa de Arrol, comitis de Southasq filia, comitis de Arrol magni Scotiæ comes (sic) Tabuli vidua, natalibus et connubio clara, munere quo functa est clarior, virtutibus clarissima juidicio (sic in orig.), ingenio, moribus, et animi potissimum magnitudine, ultra sexum, par viris. Priscâ popularium in Reges fide Usurpatori (sic in orig.) Auriaci artibus graviter læsâ, suam servavit integritatem, aliorum confirmavit. Hinc carceri commissam, cum vel vinctam timeret tyrannos (sic in orig.) egit in exilium, sed exilium datum in pœnam cessit in præmium, nam Jacobus Mag. Brit. Rex, meritorum æquissimus judex, dignam censuit cui regimen infantiæ principis Walliæ demandaret. Hoc defunctam munere integro fere triennio mors rapuit die ii Octob. An. Dom. M.D.CXCII. Ætat. lvi.
Requiescat in pâce.

Ladt dame a faite une donâon a cette Eglise, et y'a fondée une messe basse anuelle le 2 Octbre, jour de son deceds (sic) par conet devant Guission de Fonteny, notre de ce lieu se (sic) 30 Xbre, 1694.'

"On a black marble gravestone in the body of the church is this mangled inscription, almost worn out by the people's feet:—

'D. O. M.
Quisquis peregrinus ades
Quiescentem hic spem beat, resurrectionis ad vitam vir pro sincera in Deum fide, pro inconcussa in Regem fidelitate, a patria . . . ædibus precibus oppos . . in . . . . .
Sub hoc etiam marmore jacet
HENRICUS DOMINUS DE WALDEGRAVE,
Baro de . . . Par Angliæ, ex antiqua nobilique Suffolciensi comitatu stirpe oriundus do . . . bis mortuum cum oneris vixerit par in (? sic) dicis id . . . ex eo conjicere quod Jacobus II. Magnæ Britanniæ Rex e tanto procerum regni numero . . . . . . carissimam Henrici . . . . . . collocaret, qui in honores cum . . . ab ipso regum . . . . Angliæ optimo D. Ludovici, M.XIV. Regum . . . maxim . . . An. 1688, Ablegatus arcanis . . . .'"

[Rawl. MS., B 155, fol. 10. "In the window at the west end of the Benedictines' chapell: Josephus Shirley, hujus monasterii prior, hanc ecclesiam, dormitorium, &c. ædificari curavit, A° Dm. 1676."]

(*To be continued.*)

THE CONFEDERATED COLONIES OF BRITISH NORTH AMERICA: WANTED, A NAME.—*Hesperia*, derived from "*hesper*, or *vesper*, the setting sun or evening," and used in the sense of "a western country," was a name applied by the Greeks to Italy, and by the Romans to Spain. Since the discovery of America, it belongs preeminently to the western hemisphere, as distinguished from the eastern.

In Webster's *Dictionary*, we find the following words and definitions:—

"HESPERIAN, *a.* (L. *hesperius*, western, from *hesperus*, *vesper*, the evening star, Venus, G. ἕσπερος), western, situated at the west."

"HESPERIAN, *n.* An inhabitant of a western country."

So that the above colonies are already "Hesperian," and the people "Hesperians," in relation to Europe; while they have an especial claim to the title from including also the westernmost shores of America, except the Russian territory.

Need we tax our inventive powers to supply a new name when we have one already at hand, which, though derived from antiquity, has not yet been specially appropriated by any other country, and is recommended by being at once brief, significant, and agreeable to the ear?   X.

INSCRIPTION AT HOLLAND HOUSE TO THE SECOND LORD CAMELFORD.—Among the Epitaphs and Inscriptions collected by Miss Frances Williams Wynn, and placed at the end of *Diaries of a Lady of Quality from 1797 to 1844*, edited by A. Hayward, Esq., Q.C. (second edition, 1864, p. 361,) is one—

"On a stone which marks the spot on which Lord Camelford fell in a duel..

" Placed by Lord Holland, written by Ugo Foscolo.

    " Hoc Diis Manibus
        voto
      deprecatione Iræ."*

Neither the inscription itself, nor its author, is here correctly stated. Ugo Foscolo came to England about the end of 1816. The duel between Lord Camelford and Mr. Best, in which the former was killed, was fought in 1804, and the monument on the fatal spot in the gardens of Holland House was erected by Lord Holland shortly after. An antique Roman altar was adopted for the purpose, raised on a square base for a pedestal, on the front of which was placed this inscription —

HOC

DIS MAN. VOTO

DISCORDIAM

DEPRECAMVR.

An engraving of the monument may be seen in Faulkner's *History of Kensington*, and in the *Gentleman's Magazine* for April, 1821, p. 325. It is not likely that the few words of the inscription were dictated by any other person but Lord Holland himself.   J. G. N.

MONEY POST OFFICE ORDERS were issued for the first time in the United States, on the 1st of November, 1864, and from the returns of 147 offices, which were all that had then been established, though the number hereafter will be greatly increased, I learn the amount transmitted during the month was $115,000, or a little more than 23,000*l.*, a very small sum, in comparison to what it will be when this important system of pecuniary remittances becomes better known by the people.

I notice in that interesting volume, *Her Majesty's Mails*, that money orders were first issued in England in 1839, and that " the annual amount transmitted has risen from 313,000*l.* to 16,494,000*l.*, it being fifty-two fold." Those persons who are living twenty-five years hence may see the same results in America.   W. W.

Malta.

TOLBOOTH: GROTESQUE: LACED MUTTON: WOLFGANG LAVIER.—1. The readers of Sir Walter Scott's captivating novels must be familiar with the "Tolbooth." I have noted the following use of this term in its original signification, viz. the covered place where custom or toll was paid, in Bishop Hall's *Contemplations on the New Testament*, Book III. Contempl. IV. " Matthew called " :

    " Those other disciples whom calling is recorded, were from the fisher-boat ; this from the *tolbooth*."

  2. *Grotesque* —

    " Morto da Feltro, an assiduous investigator of the decorative remains hidden and buried around Rome and Naples, in the numerous tombs, which, if we may use the expression, were preserved by their own ruins, had ex-

erted himself to revive the taste for what have been denominated *grottesche*, because the models were found in grottos."—*History of the Life and Works of Rafaello*, by Quatremère de Quincy (H. G. Bohn), p. 262.

  3. *Laced Mutton*, Shakspeare. See Vossius, *Etymolog.* p. 389 a, *s. v.* " Muto." Lactantius, *De Falsâ Relig.* p. 110; *British Magazine*, Feb. 1842, p. 162, *v. f.* (" Mutinus qui est apud Græcos Priapus.")

  4. A few months ago a coin, of which the following is a description, was dug up on the lands of Mr. John Southall, at Clare Hays, in the parish of Bobbington, Staffordshire, and is now in my possession. It is a thin brass token, unmilled, evidently of considerable antiquity, not only from the appearance of the entire coin, but also from the use of the *v* for *u* throughout. On the obverse, which is best preserved, I read the name of the person who caused the token to be struck : " WVLF. LAVIER . IN . NVRMBE." Beneath, in an inner circle are three crowns alternated with as many fleurs-de-lis. The reverse, which is much defaced, contains an inscription, which I read, " WER . GOT . VER . ER . GVT . HAT.," *i. e.* " Wer Gott verehrt er gut hat " : He who honours God is blest. In an inner circle is the orb surmounted by the cross. It is no doubt one of the numerous Nuremberg tokens; but who Wulfgang Lavier was I am not aware.   H. W. T.

PRICE OF A BIBLE IN 1660. — In a book intitled " *The Testimony of Truth Exalted*, by the Collected Labours of that Worthy Man, Good Scribe, and Faithful Minister of Jesus Christ, Samuel Fisher, M.DCLXXIX," are these words under the date of 1660, under the heading of " The Rustick's Alarm to the Rabbies " : —

    "And whereas a man may buy a whole Bible for *five shillings*, they [the Parsons] sell some one Verse of it, a little set out and flourisht and amplified with no other Trimming but their own fallible vain thoughts upon it, for Twenty shillings [that is, when they preach from a text] which Bible might serve a whole Town to read in ; one Chapter of which is worth twenty of their uncertain Sermons ; or if men be minded to have Sermons, these Nations are now so full of them, that for Groats a piece, one may buy Twenty Printed Sermons of men," &c. — P. 227.

               EDWIN ARMISTEAD.

Leeds.

AUSTRALIAN TOPOGRAPHICAL NOMENCLATURE. Mr. Isaac Taylor, in his *Words and Places*, mentions only two or three Australian names, and one of these he gives with a wrong spelling, in evident misapprehension of its derivation. He writes " Port Philip," as the original name of the colony of Victoria ; it should be " Port Phillip," for its discoverer was Governor Arthur Phillip, first Governor of New Holland.

It may be mentioned that Mr. Henry Kingsley, in his latest romance, *The Hillyars and the Burtons,*

names the capital of his imaginary colony "Palmerston," evidently in imitation of the origin of "Melbourne;" and Palmerston is the actual name selected by the South Australian Government for the capital of their new settlement on Adam Bay, at the mouth of the Adelaide River, on the northern coast of the continent.   D. Blair.
Melbourne.

A good Hint.—As your "N. & Q." fall, I have no doubt, into the hands of all classes, may I ask you to endeavour to put an end to a crying evil in the fine arts. I bought lately a collection of clever sketches of places in England and Wales, among which there are a hundred or more without any name of the place attached to them! Will you be so kind as to tell all artists and tourists that, unless they put the names of the places they sketch on the drawings themselves, they will be hereafter of no more value than a child's drawings at school. This will apply to lady artists as well as men; and I hope you will urge all who have any of their own sketches still in their possession, to sit down at once and write the names upon all of them. It will add greatly to the value of them when they are sold.

There is another crying evil, and a trying evil to old people with weak eyes, and young, too; namely, an extraordinary fancy for engraving the names of places in plates of views so faint that they cannot be read even with glasses. Pray do your best, Mr. Editor, to put a stop to such follies.   T. P.

Queries.

Apple-Pie.—What is the derivation and propriety of this in such phrases as "Apple-pie order"? I do not think that the origin is apparent on the face of the word.[*]
    Thos. Coward, M.A.
Cambridge.

Auvergne Poetry, etc.—Would you permit me to ask for the following information?—The titles of any books relating to the national poetry, fairy tales, legends, &c. of Auvergne, Limousin, and Poitiers. I have not been able to find any books as yet relating to these provinces of France and their legends, especially as regards Auvergne.
    A. W. Taylor.
3, Harwood Terrace, King's Road, Fulham.

Bible: Noad.—I have a Bible, printed in 1591 by Christopher Barker, and a Prayer Book without date; but King James being prayed for, it must have been published in his reign. Are these editions scarce, and of much value?[†]

[* For some conjectures respecting the origin of the phrase "Apple-pie order," see our 1st S. iii. 468, 485; vi. 109.]

[† Our correspondent has not stated the size of the Bible.—Ed.]

Would you also say if the family of Noad is of Saxon or Norman origin? I understand that it is a common name in some parts of Wiltshire, but have no means of ascertaining any particulars.
    Canada.
Quebec.

Bibliographical Queries.—

1. James McHenry, M.D. This gentlemen was author of The Antediluvians, a poem, London, 1839; The Pleasures of Friendship, and other Poems, 1825; and several novels and plays. Dr. Mc Henry was, I believe, a native of Ireland, but was for many years resident in the United States of America. Can any of your readers inform me whether he was an alumnus of Glasgow University? Is he still living?

2. John Douglas, author of Poems, Maryport, 1836. Can any of your Cumberland readers give me any account of this author, and his poetical works?

3. George Wilde, author of Poems and Songs, 1816, Plymouth. Can you give me any information regarding this Devonshire poet, and the titles of any of his other writings, poetic or dramatic?

4. There was published in 1822 a magazine, called The Constitutional Guardian, Bristol, J. M. Gutch. Can any reader of "N. & Q.," acquainted with Bristol literature, inform me who is author of the following papers in this periodical? I. Parody on Hamlet's soliloquy, p. 50. II. "Cleopatra's Needle," p. 203. III. Fragment from the History of Tom Thumb the Great, a tragi-comedy, p. 373.

5. Mrs. Crowther, author of Moral Tales and Poetical Essays, Huddersfield, 1802; with portrait. I only know this lady's book from seeing the title in a sale catalogue. Can any of your readers give me any account of the contents of this volume? Has the authoress written any other work, poetic or dramatic?

6. In the Biographia Dramatica there is a translation of Kotzebue's Pizarro (1799 ?) ascribed to Robert Heron, one of the biographers of Burns, and author of numerous miscellaneous works. This is a mistake. The author's name is Richard Heron. Can you tell me if Richard Heron has published anything else?

7. Junius. Another Guess at Junius, with a Dialogue in the Shades, &c., 1809. This pamphlet is, in Lowndes, ascribed to the Rev. Mr. Fitzgerald. Can you give me any information regarding the author?
    R. I.

S. Decharmes, London.—I have seen a very handsome repeating watch, which is still in good order, made by the above maker. Can any of your correspondents tell me when he flourished? I have a particular reason for wishing to know.
    G. G.

Dragon in Herefordshire.—There is a story of a dragon, that lived in a wood near Hereford, and was killed on its way to drink. What are the particulars of the story, and who is the hero of it?   T. C.

Sir Saunders Duncombe, etc.—Can any of your readers oblige me with any particulars of Sir Saunders Duncombe, of whom I have lately met with an original portrait bearing an inscription to the effect that he was distinguished for attainments in the mechanical sciences, and had a patent granted to him for the introduction of Sedan

·chairs into England. I have not, however, as yet met with anything further as to him.*

I have also met with another portrait, said to be painted by Benjamin West. It is that of a counsellor in wig and gown, holding a scroll, on which is written, as far as can be traced, an Act ———, Trade of ———, Rhode Island ———, Virginia ———, America. I shall be very glad if any clue can be afforded me to the identity of this portrait.   J. N.

"THE EUROPEAN."—I have five numbers of "The European, a Journal of the Progress of Society, Literature, the Arts and Sciences," published in November, 1839. Can you tell me who were its conductors, and how long it lived? It contains a review, with long extracts, of a poem called "The Re-advent of King Arthur or Ernest." Who was the author of this poem? If I remember right, a notice of it appeared in the *Quarterly Review* about the same time. Are copies to be had?   G. G.

FAMILIES OF GOODRICH, LINCOLNSHIRE.— The favour of information is desired, with descriptions of any monuments, &c., as to families of Goodrich or Goodrick, in Lincolnshire, anterior to 1700, including that of Thomas Goodrich, Bishop of Ely, who died 1554, Lord Chancellor to King Edward VI. and Queen Mary; and as to the emigration of persons of that name from Boston to Virginia, or elsewhere in America. Some information has been already obtained from East Kirkby and Bolingbroke.

Address, F. J. J., Box No. 62, Post Office, Derby.

GREEK CHURCH.—Can any of your readers tell me what is the precise relation in which the Greek Church stands, first, to the Roman Catholic Church, and second, to the English Church? or where can I get accurate information on the subject? Stanley does not seem to touch on it in his *Lectures.* Williams, in his *Holy City,* says, it is a "humiliating fact that while the Greek Church admits the orders of the Latins and Armenians, they do not recognise those of the Anglican Church, supposing them without the apostolic succession." Now how do these matters stand? I have heard it asserted that the Greek Church, as a Church, does not recognise the Roman Church; and I have also heard it asserted it does recognise the orders of the Anglican Church. I make the inquiry merely for information on a matter of fact, and not with the view of raising any controversy.   G. G.

HARD TACK.—

" In Dauphine, France, they make bread but once in six months, and bake it with the refuse of the fields. In

[* Sir Saunders Duncombe was a member of the Duncombe family of Battlesden, co. Bedford. See the pedigree in Harl. MS. 1531, fol. 152ᵇ.—ED.]

the winter it becomes so hard that they cut it with an axe, and soak it for twenty-four hours before they can eat it."

May I beg to ask if any of your correspondents can verify this statement, not from ersona, experience, but from having seen this "Hard tack" in France, or read of it, in other publications?
    W. W.

HERALDIC.—1. In Leland's *Collectanea* is a list of the names of those who came over to England with William the Conqueror. Amongst these we find "Percehay et Pereris." Query — Is the latter name a variation of that of "Henri de Ferrieres" mentioned in M. Leop. de Lisle's list?

2. A friend has copied for me the following extract from the Rev. W. K. R. Bedford's *Blazon of Episcopacy,* in reference to the celebrated Bishop of St. David's:—

" William Linwood, 1422 to 1446. Arms, a chevron. Coat of Arms at the beginning of his Register; communicated by Sir Frederick Madden."

" Note. Wm. Linwood (or Lindwood) was appointed to the See of St. David's Aug. 14th, 1442: ob. Oct. 21st, 1446."

Query. What authority is there for representing his arms as in the above extract—a chevron? (No tincture is assigned either to the field or to the ordinary so borne.)

All the heraldic authorities to which I have had access uniformly blazon the arms of Lyndwood (the ancient spelling) thus: *arg.* a fesse crenellée between 3 fleurs-de-lis, *sa.* Crest, a fleur-de-lis per pale *arg.* and *sa.*

In a copy of Bishop Linwood's great work, the *Provinciale, seu Constitutiones Angliæ,* London, 1505, there is a large coat of arms prefixed, with some complimentary hexameters, of which I subjoin a description: Quarterly, 1st and 4th arg. a fesse crenellée between 3 fleurs-de-lis sa.; 2nd and 3rd on a field semée of crosses crosslet a unicorn rampant. Crest, a fleur-de-lis per pale arg. and sa. Supporters; two unicorns coward. Query. To what family do the arms of the 2nd and 3rd quarters belong, and how did they come to be borne by the bishop? The supporters clearly belong to the same source.

3. I should be much obliged to any contributor to "N. & Q." who has access to works on Spanish and Portuguese heraldry, if he would furnish me with the armorial blazonry of the following foreign families:—Alvares; Carvalhal; Villarinho; Coelho; *De Haro; *De Castro; De Padilla; *Ponce de Leon; Mendes; De la Cerda; and Forjaz.

Those marked thus * may be found in Sandoval's " *Chronica del inclito Emperador de España Alonso VII.,* Madrid, 1600; but I have no means of consulting that work.

4. Gules, 2 bendlets vairé arg. and sa, on a canton or, a lion couchant of the second. Are these

the armorial bearings of some Staffordshire branch of the Stauntons? H. W. T.

"I GIVE YOU JOY!" — The following note on civic etiquette I copy from the *Gentleman's Magazine* for Nov. 1813: —

"The Aldermen, City Officers, and Members of the Livery Companies, then severally paid their respects to the new Lord Mayor, the Right Hon. [afterwards Sir] William Domville, agreeably to ancient custom, by *shaking hands* and *wishing joy*. (Note.) This custom of *shaking hands* and *wishing joy* is very ancient in the city of London. It is particularly practised in the Livery Companies when a young man takes up his freedom; and at the Chamberlain's Office the speeches made to the greatest personages uniformly begin with *I give you joy*."

In the *Gentleman's Magazine* for 1814, at p. 693 of part i., are printed at length the speeches made to Marshal Lord Beresford and Lord Hill, by the Chamberlain of London, on his presenting them with the Freedom of the City and a sword. Both these speeches commence with the formula, *I give you joy!*

If the last half-century has wrought any change in this good old custom, some other correspondent better acquainted than I am with the present manners of the City may kindly inform us. J. G. N.

RICHARD JAMES: ASSASSINATION OF THE DUKE OF BUCKINGHAM.—Sir James Balfour, in his *Annales of Scotland*, after narrating the execution of Felton for the murder of the Duke of Buckingham, makes the following statement: —

"At this same tyme, one Mr. James, ane attender one Sr Robert Cotton, a grate louer of his countrey, and a hatter of all suche as he supposed enimes to the same, was called in question for wretting some lynes, wich he named a statue to the memory of that vorthey patriot S. Johne Feltone."—Balfour's *Hist. Works*, ii. 174.

He then gives the lines (or rather what appears to be his Scottish version of them.) They commence thus: —

"Immortal man of glorie, whose braue hand
Hath once begune to disenchant the land
From magiq. thraldome!"

And thus conclude: —

".... To the neighbour flood
Then sincke olde fables of old Brute and Lud,
And giue thy statue place: in spight of charme
Of vitche or wizzard, thy more mightie arme,
With zeal and iustice arm'd, hath in treuth vonne
The prize of patriotts to a British sonne."

Mr. James here referred to was no doubt Richard James, a clergyman, the keeper of the Cottonian Library, who died in Dec. 1638. There is a memoir of this very learned man in Wood's *Athen. Oxon.* ed. Bliss, ii. 629. He is noticed in unfavourable terms in Sir Simonds D'Ewes's *Autobiogr.* ii. 39, and a letter from him to Viscount Dorchester, Secretary of State, is abstracted in Bruce's *Calend. Dom. State Papers*, chap. I. iv. 110. Where can I find other particulars of the proceedings against James for the panegyric upon Felton? S. Y. R.

P. V. MACHEREN.—I have in my possession a picture bearing the signature P. V. Macheren, 1645. I should state that there is some doubt whether the figure 4 in the above date is not a 2 or a 7, but I think it looks more like a 4 than either. The picture is about 4 feet square, the subject a violent storm at sea, in the foreground a galleon much after the Van de Velde type, driven hopelessly on the rocks, which rise precipitously on the right of the picture; while a little to the left, but still in the foreground, is another ship of the same character under heavy press of sail apparently on the point of wearing round, and so of avoiding the rocks. In the distance is another wreck with the masts gone. Near the first wreck, a boat full of men is being dashed on the rocks. A gleam of watery sunlight breaks from under a heavy drifting cloud. The execution of the immense lead-coloured waves breaking into spray upon the rocks appears to me wonderfully fine; and as I can find nothing in such books as I have consulted with regard to the painter, I shall feel greatly obliged to any of your readers who will either give me the requisite information, or put me in the way of obtaining it. I may add that the above signature, which appears on a spar drifting in the trough of the sea, is, as far as I can make out, what I have stated it, but as the colours are very dark, I may perhaps not be correct to a letter. AMATEUR.

"MUNGO."—In an article in a late number of *The Times* on "Old Clothes," the word "mungo" was used as meaning some material akin to shoddy. I have been told that in Leeds it is not uncommon to see handbills intimating sales of shoddy and "mungo." Can any of your readers tell me the origin and meaning of the term? Mungo is a somewhat common Scotch (Highland) name, and means, according to Miss Yonge, amiable or beloved. G. G.

PAINTING.—Wanted, the subject of the following painting: — An old man seated at table. On the right are two sprightly ladies: one of whom is holding up a flask, out of which she is inviting the old man to drink. Entering from the left is a very demure-looking young man, dressed in black. Lying down in front is a pug dog. The date, about the middle of the last century. Has it been engraved? J. C. J.

PONTIFICAL RINGS. — This subject has been illustrated in the most interesting and able manner by your valued contributor MR. OCTAVIUS MORGAN. Will he, however, permit me with all respect to ask him whether he has ever seen a very curious passage in Bishop Bale's *Image of both Churches*, no date, B. b. vii., vo. ? —

"Neyther regarde they to knele any more doune and to kysse their pontifical rynges, which are of the same metall" [*i. e.* fine gold].

Has this been the custom with regard to pontifical rings when borne by bishops, and has it any affinity with the custom of kissing the Pope's slipper? I am sure a reply would be gladly welcomed by all readers of "N. & Q."　　　A. A.

Poets' Corner.

RED LION.—In Lancashire, according to the last Directory of that county, there are eighty inns with the sign of the Red Lion. Where a lion is figured it is usually heraldically represented, and mostly rampant. In Yorkshire the sign is equally prevalent, and doubtless so in many parts of England. Whose arms are represented thereby? The Lacies, who received from the Conqueror large estates in Lancashire and Yorkshire, bore a lion rampant, but it was *purp.;* and the Percies, who also got many Yorkshire manors, bore, and still bear, a lion similarly represented, except it is *ar.* Whence, then, the Red Lion?　　　PRESTONIENSIS.

LEGEND OF ROSAMOND QUEEN OF THE LOMBARDS.—Where may authority be found for this legend, versified in *Once a-Week*, No. 27, November 30th, 1861, p. 631?　　　H. W. T.

ROYAL STANDARD. — When Charles II. landed in England to resume possession of his kingdom, what ensign did he hoist? I ask the question because I observe in one of the frescoes in the Palace at Westminster representing the event, that his majesty is depicted stepping from a barge with the *Union* hoisted at the stern. Now, I conceive in the first place, that the appropriate ensign, and probably that actually used, would be the royal arms; and, secondly, that if, under the circumstances of the time, that flag could not be readily supplied, but the Union was substituted, it must have been the Union Jack, consisting only of the colours of England and Scotland combined; whereas the artist in the fresco appears to have added the *saltire gules,* which formed no part of the national flag until the union with Ireland. I am fully aware that this sort of criticism may be regarded as idle, and as having nothing to do with the merits of the picture. I readily assent to that judgment. But when we consider the amount of observation, not only among ourselves but among foreign visitors, which our frescoes are likely to attract, it is surely desirable that they should be correct in points of detail.　　　R. S. Q.

"SECRET HISTORY OF THE CABINET OF BONAPARTE."—A work bearing this title was published in 1808 or 1809, and went through six editions. The author was Lewis Goldsmith. It contained many scandalous stories about the family of the Bonapartes, most of which are notoriously untrue. The work would be left to perish in obscurity by every honest historian. It is, however, referred to by Francis Lieber in his *Manuel of Political Ethics,* an English edition of which was published

by Moxon in 1839. On p. 360 of that edition he quotes in the text the following passage:—

"When Napoleon was at the summit of his power, the Archbishop of Paris wrote to his bishops in a pastoral letter: 'Servants of the altars; let us sanctify our words; let us hasten to surpass them by one word, in saying he (Napoleon) is the man of the right-hand of God.'"

Then Mr. Lieber adds in a note:—

"Goldsmith, *Histoire Secrète,* p. 130. Can the author have invented it? I only know it from that work. The Bishop of Amiens says in his *Mandement,* 'The Almighty having created Napoleon, rested from his labours.' Fabre de l'Aude, president of the tribunal, said to Napoleon's mother, 'The conception you have had, in carrying in your bosom the great Napoleon, was certainly nothing less than a divine inspiration.' It is well for us fearlessly to see how far man is ever ready to err as soon as opportunity offers. Shall we wonder that the Romans deified their emperors, and worshipped their images?"

Lieber leaves us somewhat in doubt whether he is indebted to the work of Goldsmith for the whole of these instance of glaring flattery and profanity. He uses them only as illustrations of the fulsome adulation which is often poured out on the shrine of absolute power, but it is a pity for a scientific writer to repeat such instances, unless he be satisfied of their authenticity. In the more recent histories of the Consulate and the Empire we do not find them recorded, and I have not access to the work of Goldsmith at present. As such stories have obtained currency, I quite agree with the concluding remarks of Lieber. He says:—

"I wish that some one would publish the most remarkable addresses made to Napoleon in and out of France; I wish it, that we may have them as a mirror of ourselves, for is it not our own time which committed these guilty follies?"

Can any of your readers give any authority, beyond that of Goldsmith, for the above?
　　　T. B.

A TOWN-CLERK'S SIGNATURE.—Why does a town-clerk sign his surname as a peer would, *i. e.,* without Christian name or initials?　　W. B.

LADY TEMPEST'S JURY.—I find in Woolrych's *Memoirs of Judge Jeffreys*—see note, p. 44—that Thwing and another were indicted for high treason at York, before Sir William Dolben; and in the course of his challenges Thwing said,—

"My Lord, I will willingly stand by the other jury.
Justice Dolben.—What Jury?
Thwing.—My Lady Tempest's Jury.
Justice Dolben.—Oh! your servant! You are either very foolish, or you take me to be so."

I wish to be informed, 1st. Who was Thwing? 2. Who was Lady Tempest? 3. To what circumstance allusion is here made?　　　C. H.

THE TIME OF DAY.—In Bunyan's *Holy War* (p. 9), Religious Tract Society's edition, one of the evil spirits uses this slangy phrase:—

" ' Besides,' said Legion (for he gave answer to this), ' a discovery of our intentions may make them send to their king for aid; and if that be done, I know quickly what time of day it will be with us.' "

I was surprised to meet this expression here. What is its exact meaning; of course, in its figurative application? I thought it modern, and could not expect to find it two hundred years' old. Is there any earlier instance of it? It might occur in the old English drama.   C. D.

TITHE BARNS. — Would some of your correspondents give me some information respecting the disputes between the clergy and the farmers in the old days of tithe barns, &c.? I know there was much hard hitting and discussion, which in one case, I believe, culminated in murder. But I am unable here to obtain exact information, or verified facts.   ARTHUR STUART.
Oldham.

YORK BUILDINGS FIRE ENGINE.—Can any of the readers of "N. & Q." tell me when the wooden tower of the York Waterworks Company, which formerly stood at the bottom of Buckingham Street, Adelphi, close to the York Water Gate, was taken down? There was an engine " for raising water by fire " (afterwards laid aside as too expensive), in the building. What kind of engine was this? It attracted the notice of the French traveller Mons. De la Mottraye. The York Waterworks Company were formed in the reign of Charles II.; and Canaletti, in his p c ure exhibited in the British Museum, has made the tower a prominent object.
WM. GEO. LARKINS.
23, Leamington-road Villas, Westbourne Park.

Queries with Answers.

BELL INSCRIPTION. — Can any bell-hunting reader of "N. & Q." interpret for me the following inscription, which occurs on a bell at Puncknowle, Dorsetshire, date 1629? —

" Hethatwilpvrchashonorsgaynemvstancientlathersstilmayntayne."

Is it an injunction against beard-growing?
L. B. C.

[The " honor's gayne," to be " pvrchas'd," as here set forth, by " mayntayneing ancient lathers," would seem to be the honour acquired by the ringers of a parish when they have rung a peal on the church bells, and rung it in good style. And what more worthy of honour than a well-executed " triple bob-major " ?

With respect to the word " lather," we may remark that lether, in provincial English, is, to make a noise. This comes from the A.-S. hleoðor, or hleoþor (hleothor), to sound; which, however, is particularly applied to the sound of a bell, as " Hleothor heora bellan "—the sound of their bell. " Hleothor " again, has been connected with the German

lauten, which, according to Wachter, meant (besides other significations), to utter a musical sound vocal or instrumental, to signify or notify by a sound—"signum dare sonitu ;" but which, at the time when Wachter wrote, was employed in this sense only with reference to the bell-ringer. " Hodie dicitur de ædituo tantum, qui campanæ pulsu cœtum ad sacra convocat." Compare also in Eber " Läuten, to ring a bell ;" " Zusammenläuten, to ring with all the bells ;" " Läuten, a ring of bells, the act of ringing the bells," &c. Läuten, lauten, hleother, lether, and here lather, seem all to be members of the same family.

" Ancient lathers," however, might possibly be read " Ancient fathers," meaning the Fathers of the Church ; or, by a slight mistake, it may have been substituted for " Ancient letters," which would come to much the same thing. But we have taken the word " lathers" as we find it; and prefer, on the whole, the explanation first given. If we may suppose either ringers or bell-founder to have had a voice in the inscription now under consideration, we may well imagine that such an opportunity of celebrating the praises of bell-ringing would not fail to be embraced.]

PRINCIPIO FABRICII, " DELLE ALLUSIONI." — Perhaps some of your readers can give me the name of the engraver of the following book of " Emblems," and also particulars of the author? I have not the means of referring to Mr. Stirling's Catalogue of books of this kind, and have consulted the almost never-failing Biographie Universelle, but in this instance was disappointed. Messrs. Willis and Sotheran, some time ago, catalogued a copy in calf, with a MS. note to the effect that no other copy is known, and that it was purchased at the Ercolani sale at Bologna. My copy is in limp vellum : —

" Delle Allusioni, Impresse et Emblemi, del Sig. Principio Fabricii, da Teramo, sopra la vita, opere et attioni di Gregorio XIII., pontifice massimo, libri vi." Small 4to. Roma, 1588.
A. H. BATES.
Edgbaston.

[Principio Fabricii, or Fabritii, was a secular priest of Teramo in the Ulterior Abruzzo (or, as more modern geographers would say, in Abruzzo Proper, or Abruzzo di Teramo, capital Teramo). His work Delle Allusioni, etc., consists of various ingenious fancies concerning the Life, &c., of Pope Gregory XIII. See Zedler under Fabritii, and Toppi (Biblioteca Neap.) under Principio. Zedler speaks of an edition in fol. 1588, but we suspect that this is a mistake for quarto.

If our correspondent will kindly put on his best glasses, and closely examine the title-page of the 4to edition of 1588, he will discover, supposing his copy to agree with that now before us, that the plates are by " Natal Bonifatio da Sib" (that is, of Sebenico near Venice). This artist published a " Descriptio " of the Ulterior Abruzzo, the country of Principio Fabricii. There are two copies of the Delle Allusioni in the British Museum, 4to, 1588.]

BOOKBINDING.—I am anxious to obtain information of any books on this subject. Below is a list of some half-dozen I have happened to have seen. Is there any Life or Memoir of Roger Payne to be had ?—

Arnett, J. A. "Bibliopegia, or the Art of Bookbinding." London, 1835. 12mo.

Arnett, J. A. "An Inquiry into the Nature and Form of the Books of the Ancients, with a History of the Art of Bookbinding." London, 1837. 12mo.

Cundall, J. "On Ornamental Art applied to Modern Bookbinding." London, 1848. 4to.

"Bookbinder's Manual of Leather and Vellum Bindings, with Directions for Gilding and Marbling the Edges." 12mo.

"Bookbinder's Complete Instructor in all Branches of Bookbinding, Marbling," &c. Peterhead, 1823. 12mo. n. d.

"The Handbook of Taste in Bookbinding." London. Churton. 8vo. n. d.

G. WESTON.

Croydon.

[Our correspondent's list contains the best works on the art of bookbinding. J. A. Arnett, whose name appears to the first two books, is a pseudonym for John Hannett. The fourth and best edition of *Bibliopegia*, with considerable additions, was published in 1848 with the author's real names. It also contains an interesting account of Roger Payne, with a rough engraving of him at work in his den. For additional particulars of this prince of English bookbinders, consult Dibdin's *Decameron*; *Gent.'s Mag.*, lxvii. 1070; lxxxiv. (i.) 440; Timperley's *History of Printing*; Chambers's *Book of Days*, ii. 596; and "N. & Q.," 3rd S. vi. 131.

A series of articles on "The History of Bookbinding" appeared in *The Bookbinders' Trade Circular*, vols. i. and ii., 1850–1859, containing some curious particulars of the art, as well as references to other works treating on this subject.]

BOARDS. — Mr. Fitzgerald, in speaking of the *Sermons* published by Sterne in 1767, says in a note, vol. ii. p. 327 : —

" 'Boards' and 'cloth' being as yet unknown, every book came out either in paper covers, like French books, or 'whole bound in calf.' "

When did boards first come into use ?

MELETES.

[The most ancient boards used for binding books were of wood. About the middle of the sixteenth century, leaves of paper were pasted together for this purpose, called pasteboards, until these were succeeded by millboards, which appear to have come into use in the seventeenth century. This change of material effected a great improvement in the art of bookbinding.—The originator of binding in cloth was Mr. R. E. Lawson, of Stanhope Street, Blackfriars, formerly in the employ of Mr. Charles Sully, and the first book bound in cloth was a manuscript volume of music, which was subsequently purchased by Mr. Alfred Herbert, the marine artist. On this volume being shown to the late Mr. Pickering, who was at that

time (1823) printing a diamond edition of "The Classics," he thought this material would be admirably adapted for the covers of the work. The cloth was purchased at the corner of Wilderness Row, St. John Street, and five hundred copies of the Diamond Classics were covered by Mr. Lawson with glue. Shakspeare's Plays were also issued in this form, and these works were the first books bound in cloth.]

THE WELSH TRIADS. — I find in two of the Triads, quoted in Jones's *History of Brecknockshire* (vol. i. p. 69), mention made of King Arthur as sovereign of three kingdoms, and of Cradoc as one of the officers of his court. What is the date at which the Triads are supposed to have been written, and how far are their historical statements to be relied on ?   T. C.

[The Cambro-British fragments called "The Triads," or metrical triplets, allude to circumstances connected with the first population and early history of our island, of which every other memorial has perished. Some are historical, whilst others are ethical, legal, and theological. Mr. Vaughan, the antiquary of Hengurt, refers them to the seventh century; and they have been noticed with respect by Camden. They were published in 1801, by the munificence of Mr. Owen Jones, and have since been edited by Mr. Probert, and their genuineness elaborately vindicated by Mr. Sharon Turner, and the Editors of the *Myvyrian Archaiology*. Consult *The Ecclesiastical Antiquities of the Cymry*, by the Rev. John Williams, 8vo, 1844; and especially the notice of that work in *The English Review*, vol. xv. pp. 1—24, which contains a brief examination of the evidence adduced in support of the authenticity of the Welsh Triads and other ancient records.]

WATERHOUSE OF KIRTON, — In Sylvanus Morgan's *Sphere of Gentry*, fol., London, 1661 (p. 84, recté 82), is an engraving of the "Effigies Gilberti Aquædomus, Ang. Waterhows, de Kirton Comitat. Lincoln, temp. H. III." I am anxious to know which Kirton is here meant. There are two places of that name in Lincolnshire : Kirton in Lindsey, and Kirton in Holland.   P.

[In the *Gentleman's Magazine*, vol. lxvi. pt. i. p. 460, Sir Gilbert Waterhouse is said to be of Kirton in *Low Lindsey*, co. Lincoln, which we take to be in the Holland division, divided into Upper and Lower.]

THE SUFFOLK PAPERS. — The amusing work, edited by John Wilson Croker in 1834, professes to give only a *selection* from the Countess of Suffolk's correspondence. Where are the rest of the papers ?   P.

[The original Correspondence and Papers of Henrietta Howard, Countess of Suffolk, 1712-1767, in five volumes large folio, are in the British Museum, Addit. MSS. 22,625—22,629.]

Replies.

UPCOTT'S REVISION OF 1808 FIRST FOLIO SHAKSPEARE.

(1st S. vii. 47.)

There is a notice of the reprint (1808) of the First Folio Shakspeare collated with the original by Mr. W. Upcott, who states that he found in the reprint no less than 368 typographical errors. That copy of Mr. Upcott's subsequently passed into the hands of J. W. Croker, Esq., and has recently come into my possession. On coming to examine it, I found on the first page a MS. note written by Mr. Croker. It is as follows: —

"Mr. Upcott collated this reprint most carefully with the original, and found, he says, 368 variances. I have noted all the variances in the margin of this copy from Mr. Upcott's notes. They are for the most part of little importance, and not quite so many as Mr. Upcott states; for in several places in which I myself collated this book and his notes with an original, I found he had marked variances where I found none. This copy may therefore be considered as perfect.
            "J. W. CROKER."

"3 Feb. 1842."

Now, as the reprint of 1808 is really a very handsome volume, and corresponds page for page and line for line with the Original Folio, it is a pity, I think, that its value should have been unduly depreciated by Mr. Upcott's account of it. For I have been at the pains to go through his notes carefully, comparing them in each instance with the actual text of the reprint. The following is the result of my examination, by which it will be seen how few errors there are, after all, of any serious importance. In the first place, then, he has marked 42 instances of variation in some very minute or trifling point, which are found, on closer scrutiny, to be either not such in the text of the reprint, or if so, to be no deviations from the original. 23 are corrections of obvious and manifest misprints in the Original, such as *all* for *nll*, *enter* for *entor*, *daughter* for *daughtet*, and the like. No less than 50 arise from the confusion of the long s and the f (f f), which, however, in only one instance (and I have verified them all), is likely to mislead the reader. 43 variances consist solely in the punctuation — a matter of no very great moment, considering the loose way in which the text is punctuated throughout in the original. 26 arise from the omission of the dot over the letter *i*. 21 from capital letters being substituted for small ones at the beginning of a word, or *vice versâ*. 15 from the letters *c* and *e* being interchanged; but this again, as in the case of f and f, is not likely to mislead the reader, the two letters being so nearly alike that he could seldom observe the difference unless it were pointed out. 10 trifling errors occur in the catchwords or headlines. 10 is the paging, 7 in the omission or need-

less addition of the mark of apostrophe ('), 7 in words partially disjointed or else improperly joined. 6 in letters accidentally reversed, 5 in the cross stroke of the A omitted (A), 2 in the hyphen mark omitted, 38 in arbitrary or archaic variations in the mode of spelling words, as *doe* for *do*, *oh* for *o*, *then* for *than*, *shortly* for *shortlie*, *return* for *returne*, and the like.

We have thus about 268 variances accounted for out of Mr. Upcott's 368. The remaining hundred do not admit of being easily classified, but they consist for the most part either in some glaring, though easily distinguished blunder, as *earrh* for *earth*, *supulcher* for *sepulcher*, or in an extra vowel, as *sweeetly* for *sweetly*, or the omission of a letter, as *squandred* for *squandered*, *dist* for *didst*, &c.

These being deducted, there remain about 40 material mistakes, quite sufficient indeed to convict the printers of gross carelessness in the execution of the reprint, but relieving it from the load of opprobrium which Mr. Upcott's account of it is naturally calculated to create.

Of these I now subjoin a list, for the benefit of all present and future possessors of this reprint, that they may, if they please, correct them in the margins of their copies, and thus render them, as books of reference, little inferior in value to the Original: —

Merry Wives of Windsor.

Page	Col.	Line	
49	1	24	pay *for* pray.

Merchant of Venice.

163	2	82	me *for* we.
177	1	53	about *for* above.
178	2	19	swayes to *for* swayes it to.

Love's Labour's Lost.

128	1	45	ligge *for* jigge.

All's Well that Ends Well.

242	1	44	Sir it *for* Sir it is.

Twelfth Night.

261	2	18	thou *for* you.
266	1	23	fee *for* see.

Winter's Tale.

279	2	25	you *for* your.
ib.	2	44	on *for* one.
287	2	41	torment *for* torments.
295	1	29	faith him *for* faith with him.

Richard II.

27	2	20	from bottom, y *for* y't.
32	1		last, come *for* comes.

Henry VI., Part I.

109	1	37	bad *for* hath.
118	2	6	gaced *for* graced.

Henry VI., Part II.

129	2	11	from bottom, and flye how *for* and flye thou how.
137	2	23	from bottom, supprized *for* surprized.
138	2	4	life *for* like.
145	2	30	are *for* art.

Henry VI., Part III.

Page. Col. Line.
147 2 7 Dare *for* Dares.
157 2 8 from bottom, rayle him *for* rayle at him.

Henry VIII.

206 1 33 give *for* gives.
220 1 49 should *for* shall.

Troylus and Cressida.

81 2 4 from bottom, whar *for* what.
89 2 11 from bottom, sweere *for* sweete.
93 1 26 cave *for* leave.

Coriolanus.

15 1 11 from bottom, their *for* there.

Romeo and Juliet.

60 1 3 then *for* they.

Timon of Athens.

89 2 3 dvet *for* dyet.
91 2 48 hast y more *for* hast yᵘ more.
93 2 10 are *for* art.

Macbeth.

147 1 11 from bottom, nor *for* not.

Hamlet.

258 2 8 from he *for* from the.
273 2 12 Now now *for* How now.
276 1 last, you *for* your.

King Lear.

296 2 7 from bottom, Ho *for* no.

Othello.

315 2 15 from bottom, conjuctive *for* conjunctive.
334 1 2 do *for* doth.

Antony and Cleopatra.

365 1 11 uine *for* ruines.

It will be seen, I think, that even of these forty misprints, which are the worst in the book, there are not very many which would seriously mislead the reader. There is one mistake in the Epistle dedicatory, viz. *nation* for *nations*, which I see I had overlooked. I have thus given you a faithful analysis of Mr. Upcott's list of variances, corrected by Mr. Croker, hoping it may be acceptable and useful to some of your readers.   C. H. G..
Henley-on-Thames.

THE PRIOR AND THE EXPECTED DELUGE.

(3rd S. vii. 57.)

Without it can be shown that the prior of St. Bartholomew's was a much more enlightened man than the foremost of his contemporaries, there appears no reason for treating as a joke the story of his journey to Harrow with boats and provisions in anticipation of a deluge. The astrologers of the time had predicted that a grand conjunction of the planets Saturn, Mars, and Jupiter, in the sign *Pisces*, almost identical in character with that which produced Noah's Flood, would occur in February, 1524, and be attended with most disastrous results. There can be no doubt that this prediction caused the greatest consternation,

and struck terror into high and low, learned and unlearned, throughout the whole of Europe. Bayle and Moreri furnish authorities for this statement in abundance.

John Stoefler (or Stofler), a famous mathematician and astrologer, who taught at Tubingen, first promulgated the prognostication in one of his *Ephemerides*, and it was supported by many of the best astronomers of the age. There were the incredulous, of course. Augustin Niphus, the amorous professor of divinity at Pisa, pooh-poohed it, and Paulus de Middeburgo, appealed to by the Duke of Urbino, "*ei liquido demonstrasset, inanem esse prorsus metum omnem, quem de futuro diluvio conceperat.*" (*Naudæus.*) On the other hand, the learned Cirvellus, Professor of Divinity at Alcala, admitted the value of precautions, though he denounced as "stupid" the sacrifice of property which the terrified people, living near the sea or rivers, were making in Spain. Peter Martyr, also, when consulted by the Chancellor of Charles V., thought the alarm exaggerated, but confessed his anticipation of fearful inundations. The Emperor's General at Florence employed a physician of Ravenna to write against the book of Niphus, lest the necessary precautions should be neglected, and suggested the selection of places of safety for men and beasts during the floods.

Nicolas Peranzonus followed suit with a book published at Ancona, and containing also accounts of twenty great inundations, as did Michaelis de Petra Sancta, Professor of Metaphysics in the College at Rome. There were many other publications on this subject *pro* and *con*: the writer would be glad to receive the full titles, &c., of any known to your correspondents.

Numbers of persons in France and other parts of the Continent provided themselves with ships, or fled to the mountains with provisions. The agitation must have been most intense and lamentable.

Stoefler's reputation was wrecked by the result. "The sun shone forth exceeding bright, and never was there a more pleasant spring."

Cardan and others make out that the prediction was a mistake, caused by Stoefler's want of skill; and that the particular conjunction of the planets from which he drew such dire forebodings indicated fine weather. The unlucky astrologer continued to shoot his arrows, and if we may credit the storytellers, his last shot was a "bull's eye." As Bayle quotes from Seth Calvisius, Stoefler foresaw that on a certain day he would be in great danger from something falling on his head. Feeling his own house secure, he invited some learned friends to bear him company in his study, and "while they were sitting over a moderate glass of wine, a small dispute arose, and Stoefler, to decide the controversy, took down a book from a high shelf; but the nail was loosened; the shelf fell on his head and gave the oor old man a grievous wound, of which he die̦at Tubingen, on the 16th February, 1531!"

AMOS CHALLSTETH.

1, Verulam Buildings.

TRADITIONS OF AN ANTECEDENT WORLD.

(3rd S. vii. 95.)

The inquirer will find much information on this curious subject in the *Præ-Adamitæ* of Isaac de la Peyrère, a French Calvinist, who published the work anonymously in 1655. See also the *Systema Theologicum ex Præ-Adamitarum Hypothesi* by the same author. The full title of Peyrère's work is —

"Præ-Adamitæ; sive exercitatio super versibus, 12, 13, et 14, capitis quinti Epistolæ Divi Pauli ad Romanos; quibus inducuntur primi homines ante Adamum conditi."

This work created a great sensation, and was translated into English the following year, under the title —

"Men before Adam; or a Discourse upon the Twelfth, Thirteenth, and Fourteenth Verses of the Fifth Chapter of the Epistle of the Apostle Paul to the Romans."

For writing this book Peyrère was forcibly carried off, and immured in the Inquisition; but being a follower and librarian of the Prince of Condé, he was soon afterwards released. Several scholars wrote vigorously against Peyrère's heretical ideas, and the smaller wits assailed them with ridicule. In the *Menagiana* there occurs a curious instance of a man reviewing a book without ever reading it, — not an uncommon practice, by-the-way, at the present day. The writer says, "that Peyrère would have been well pleased if he had known that a Rabbi had mentioned Adam's tutor." While the truth is, that Peyrère not only notices Adam's tutor, but actually says his name was Semboscer. Peyrère, founding his work on scriptural texts, expresses his disbelief of Rabbinical fables, though he acknowleges there are some traces of truth even in fables: —

"Quamvis parùm credam Rabbinorum fabulis, nihil tamen adeo fabulosum est quod non antiquam redoleat veritatem."

In relation to Peyrère's work, a laughable circumstance has lately occurred, affording considerable hilarity among literary circles during the dull days of winter. A few years past, a book was published, entitled *Genesis of the Earth and Man*, in which the author, though he travelled over the same ground, and even quoted the same texts, as Peyrère, never once mentioned his name. Later still, this last ear, another book was published of the same description, entitled *Adam and the Adamite*. Thereupon, the author of the first work challenged the author of the second for pla-

giarism; the gage was accepted, and the combat, a ve̦y lame affair, came off in *The Athenæum*. Though each doughty hero cuffed the other soundly, yet both, with true Spartan tenacity, held the secret intact; neither mentioned the well known name of Peyrère, but, like the cuttle-fish, purposely obscuring the water, each alluded to the French Calvinistic Protestant as an "Italian Monk." It would have been easy, even graceful, for the second author to say, in the words of a more distinguished writer, "the limits of fair appropriation are passed when the stream is purposely left sand-choked near the fountain-head;" and then the first author might have boldly and defiantly assumed the devout tone of St. Donatus, and exclaimed — "Pereant illi qui ante nos nostra dixerunt!" Or repeated the pleasanter epigram of the Chevalier d'Aceilly, thus —

"Dis-je quelque chose assez belle ?
L'Antiquité tout en cervelle
Pretend l'avoir dite avant moi.
C'est une plaisant donzelle !
Que ne venait elle après moi ?
J'aurais dit la chose avant elle."

The sect of the Pre-Adamites was founded soon after the issuing of Peyrère's work, but has long since disappeared. A few years ago I was attracted to stop a few minutes and listen to a street preacher in Brighton, through perceiving a Hebrew Bible in his hand—not knowing at the time that this is a common dodge used by the most illiterate of the street-preaching craft. The doctrine held forth seemed to me to be a mixture of Pre-Adamitism and Mormonism, and from the glibness of the speaker, and his peculiar selection of explanatory texts, I fancied he was well up in Peyrère; for the English translation, *Men before Adam*, though a rare, is not an uncommon work, and may frequently be picked up at an old book-stall. In the *Anthropological Review*, vol. ii. p. 109, there is an ably-written paper, entitled "Peyrerius and Theological Criticism," and well worthy of notice at the present time.   WILLIAM PINKERTON.

DUTCH EPITAPH: THE LEARNED PIG.

(3rd S. vi. 513.)

The subject of Major Clark's poor joke was Albert Pighe, a theologian of sufficient importance to have been fully noticed by Bayle, and to retain a place in the modern biographical dictionaries. To them I refer for his life, and shall omit what does not bear on the epitaph. He was born at Kempen in 1490, and died at Utrecht in 1542. He was a professor at Louvain and Paris, and a statesman at Rome. He wrote against the Protestants, and was groundlessly accused of Calvinistic "proclivities." Two epitaphs upon him are given by Casper Burman, but it is doubtful whether either was actually placed in the church of St. John at Utrecht, where he was buried : —

"Conditus vero dicitur in medio templi S. Johannis, et adsculpta ejus insignia cum signo sacri calicis, et super his mæandri sive gyri, et flexus hunc versiculum exhibentes :

'Pighius Albertus præpositus hic requiescit.'
Additque Valerius: 'Forte aliquando ibi lectum fuit hoc Epitaphium, Iconoclastarum rabie in Belgicis secessionibus deletum :

'Hic dormit ille Pighius mire sagax,
Mireque felix nactus ingenium, statim
Multis et amplis exercens se dotibus.
Lovanii primum, deinde Parisiis
Variis politus artibus, ac his optimis
Romæ Hadriani factus assiduus Papæ,
Comes est, amatus, nemo quantum amabitur,
In urbe Roma Pontifici ter maximo
Paulo supremo tunc Dei Vicario ;
Merito efferendus pluribus præconiis,
Quod pestilentes vindicavit hæreses,
Quibus Lutherus se, suosque perdidit,
Factos rebelles Principes Germaniæ ;
Quod et paratas negligens insidias,
Catholicorum sancta dogmata,
Ecclesiæque asseruit perstrenue.
Falsas Buceri dum parat calumnias,
Paucis, sed aptis, graviter convellere,
Vix absolutis operis primordiis,
Aqua gravatus, obrutusque intercute,
Scribendo summum finiit vitæ diem.'"

Hausse gives another epitaph, "hodie adhuc juxta chorum dictæ Ecclesiæ :

'Ne turba tumulum, Viator, istum,
Sed adsta reverenter, et saluta
Sacratum cinerem viri sacrati.
Ille est Pighius hoc loco sepultus,
Aures qui Batavas ita expolivit,
Ut dicas sapere Atticos lepores.
Quare tam bene dormiat, precare,
Quam docte nitideque et eleganter
Defendit Latiæ decus tiaræ,
Et morem statuit pium sacrorum,
Utro ut nomine debeant Latini
Plus illi addubitent ; utroque certe
Ingens promeritum viri fatentur."
          Caspari Burmani, *Trajectum Eruditum.*
          pp. 263-4. Traj. ad Rhen. 1738.

Burman says that he could not find the above in that church. Most likely it never was there, as he found an inscription in prose, put up sixty years after Pighe's death, and which, from the injury of time, was very difficult to read. It is too long to quote, and there is no reason to suppose that Major Clark had seen it. Perhaps he translated from a Dutch epitaph compounded of the two which I have quoted. The book in which his appears is dated 1724 ; Burman's is 1738. The line, "Yet Jove misliked his voice and face," was perhaps suggested by a quotation in Bayle :—

"Magnus hercle naturæ illudentis inverecundia, excellentem doctrinam cum illustri eloquentia conjunctam, si christiani scriptoris decus spectetur, multa infaceti oris truculentia operatum, in Alberto Pighio conspeximus. In disserendo vultus, Scythico more contusus et enormis,

et aspero gutture vox educta, et graviter resonantis nasi tumultus, totam fere sapientiæ gloriam deformabant." — Paulus Jovius, *Elogiis,* cap. cv. p. 245, ap. Bayle, Dic. art. *Pighius.*

The rendering of Jovius, by Jove, is in the same taste as Pighius, by "Pig."

I cannot refer to the passage in Ward. From the subject matter, I think it probable that not Ned, but Thomas Ward is intended. After the perusal of *England's Reformation,* I do not think Ned will seem dull.   H. B. C.
U. U. C.

Eɴɢʟɪsʜ Sᴏʟᴅɪᴇʀs ᴀᴛ ᴛʜᴇ Bᴀᴛᴛʟᴇ ᴏғ Lᴇɪᴘsɪᴄ (3ʳᵈ S. vii. 43.) — The following extracts from Carlisle's *Foreign Orders of Knighthood* (London, 1839), may perhaps interest Gᴀᴍᴍᴀ and others. The second class of the Imperial Order of S. Anne was conferred by the Emperor of Russia on Sir Wm. Congreve, Bart., "on account of the effect of the Congreve rockets at the battle of Leipsic in 1813." (P. 323.) Among the recipients of a gold medal from the King of Sweden was Lieutenant "Strangways of the Royal Artillery, who succeeded to the command of the Rocket Brigade, on the death of Captain Bogue in the neighbourhood of Leipzic, on the 19th of October, 1813." (P. 468.) The Marquis of Londonderry (then Sir Charles Wm. Stewart, K.B.) was decorated by the sovereigns of Russia, Sweden, and Prussia on account of (among other services) his gallantry "in the battles fought before Leipsic on the 18th and 19th days of October, 1813." (P. 312.) English officers and soldiers were also present at the siege of Dantzic in 1813. "Lieutenant and Adjutant Robert Gilbert, of the Royal Marine Artillery" received the fourth class of the Order of S. Vladimir, "in testimony of the approbation of his Imperial Majesty, the Emperor of all the Russias, of the signal intrepidity displayed by him in command of a corps of the Royal Marine Artillery (employed as a rocket corps), at the siege of Dantzic in the year 1813." (Pp. 317, 318.) Lieutenants George Macleod and Willoughby Montagu, both of the Royal Regiment of Artillery, Christopher Strachey, R.N., and Alexander Macdonald, R.H.A., were also similarly rewarded for their services on the same occasion.   Jᴏʜɴ Wᴏᴏᴅᴡᴀʀᴅ.
New Shoreham.

Cᴀʀᴇʏ (3ʳᵈ S. vi. 498) is from "cor cau," *a circle,* Celtic ; like eye, "isle," *the pupil of the eye,* Saxon. In fact both names have similar significations.   J. A. Dᴜɴᴋɪɴ.

Aʙʀᴀʜᴀᴍ Wᴏᴏᴅʜᴇᴀᴅ (3ʳᵈ S. vi. 475.) — Is it known whether there exists in any public or private collection, either in England or on the continent, a portrait of this distinguished writer ?
                                        Lʟᴀʟʟᴀᴡɢ.

"THE MIRROUR OF KNIGHTHOOD" (3rd S. vi. 310.)—I have an imperfect copy, in black-letter, of this old romance, containing the first part as far as page 179; wanting, however, the preceding pages (or rather leaves, for the right hand side only is numbered), viz., 137, 151, 152, 153, 157, 158, 159, and 176. The volume is otherwise in remarkably good condition; the title-page, dedication, and address to the reader, perfect; but it has been printed without date, the year 1595 being neatly inserted in writing by a former possessor. A long MS. note in a modern hand, is appended, from which I extract the following passage, notwithstanding its manifest inaccuracy, because it points to the whereabouts of a copy of this rare work, not mentioned in the Editor's reply to MR. WINNINGTON'S query, or in Bohn's edition of Lowndes. My copy has Thomas East, not Este, as the printer's name.

"*The First Part of the Mirrour of Princely Deeds and Knighthood*—so says the title, and adds, translated out of Spanish, but most likely is an original English composition. The date of the second part which was evidently published some time posterior to this, is 1596; the present part then we may justly suppose issued from the press of Thomas East, in 1595, and the age of the work may be, with pretty certainty, fixed at 200;[*] for this may be accounted an early edition, although most likely there never was other than one. All three parts are found in the library of Sir W. Dolben, Bart., at his seat at Finedon, Northamptonshire."

T. C. SMITH.

GENERAL HUGH MERCER (3rd S. vii. 40.)— Allow me to correct an error in M.'s reply as to the parentage of this general, &c. *Mercer's Chronicle* was *not* published by the "Spalding Club," but by that of the "Maitland Club, Glasgow." It is entitled *The Chronicle of Perth, a Register of remarkable Occurrences chiefly connected with that City from the Year* 1210 *to* 1668.. It was printed in 1831, and presented to the members by James Maidment, Esq., Advocate.   T. G. S.
Edinburgh.

JACK-STONES (3rd S. vii. 34.)—When I was at Eton some twenty years ago, as was befitting such a classic spot, ἀστράγαλοι, πεντέλιθοι, or *tali*, were much in vogue as a game in the long winter evenings, when "lock-up" was early. We called both the game and the implements used in it by the same name, "knucks," clearly a contraction of knuckles, as the knuckle or hucklebones of sheep were used for the purpose. The game required much quickness of eye and hand. I never heard the term jack-stones (or, no doubt more properly, jact-stones) used in England. BRUIN.

At a large school in Surrey, the knuckle bones from the legs of mutton, with which this game was there played, were called *dibs*.   M. S.

ANONYMOUS (3rd S. vii. 74.) — *Three discourses &c.* The author of this sensible volume was

[*] From this I infer the above note was written in 1796.

Thomas Sanden, M.D. of Chichester. See the *Biographical dictionary of living authors* by Watkins and Shoberl, 1816. The same information was given to me by Thomas Sutton, M.D. of Greenwich in 1822 or earlier.
BOLTON CORNEY.
Barnes, S.W.

METRICAL SERMON (3rd S. vii. 76.) — In the *Life of John Edwin*, the comedian, it is said when he was tramping through the south of Ireland, on a professional tour, with three others, they requested him, it being a Sunday morning, to favour them with a discourse suitable to the day. He began as follows: —

"In the fifth chapter of Job, seventh verse, you will find these words,—' Man is born unto trouble as the sparks fly upward.' I shall divide this discourse and consider it under the three following heads: 1. Man's ingress into the world; 2. Man's progress through the world; and 3. His egress out of the world.

"1. A man's ingress into the world is naked and bare,
 2. His progress through the world is trouble and care,
 3. And his egress out of the world is—nobody knows where!

"To conclude,—
 "If we do well *here*, we shall do well *there*;
 I can tell you no more if I preach a whole year."

I suspect the Derbyshire parson to whom W. D. refers was guilty of plagiarising the witty actor.
W.

THE INSCRIPTION ON THE CROSS (3rd S. vii. 75.) Though all the four Evangelists mention the inscription, none of them gives it in full. We collect it therefore from comparing all together. St. Luke gives the order of the three languages in which it was written, thus: Greek, Latin, and Hebrew. But St. John states it differently: Hebrew, Greek, and Latin. It is not certain that either intended to record the exact order in which the languages appeared, any more than the exact words of the inscription, of which they judged it sufficient to give the substance. It is most likely, however, that the Hebrew appeared at the top, or first in the title, as being the language of the Jews, and best understood; as in our own country we should write any inscription intended for general information, first in English, and next for the benefit of foreign visitors, in French, or German. But the remains of the original title are still to be seen at Rome, though much decayed, and with only the word *Nazarenus*, and the corresponding Greek word now legible. The Hebrew was at the top, but only a few faint traces of it are left. As the Hebrew was written from left to right, the Greek and Latin were written in the same way, as the Jews were accustomed so to read. The letters are in red. Now if the authenticity of this venerable relic be disputed, it must always be allowed to be of great antiquity; and the inference is just, that it was considered in the early times of the church that the Hebrew occupied the first or highest place on the title board. It may not be out of place to subjoin the comment of ·St. Augustin, on the adoption of the three languages : —

"Hæ quippe tres linguæ ibi præ cæteris eminebant. Hebræa propter Judæos in Dei lege gloriantes. Græca propter gentium sapientes. Latina propter Romanos, multis ac pene omnibus jam tunc gentibus imperantes." (*Tract.* cxvii. *in Joan.*)

F. C. H.

CHATEAUX IN FRANCE (3rd S. vi. 124, 190.)— No doubt there was in France as elsewhere a time when the castellated mansions of the feudal nobles were destroyed. Since that time country residences have sprung up in other parts of Europe. In England they abound. Those who have travelled abroad cannot have failed to observe that in France such residences are much more rare, and that of those that do exist many are in a dismantled and dilapidated state. How is this fact to be accounted for? I have frequently heard it attributed to the French revolution, and to the subdivision of property consequent on modern legislation. To this I reply, how then do you account for the same complaint being made by Laurence Sterne upwards of a century ago? I do not go so far as to suppose with MR. MACRAY, that Sterne may have recorded his own impressions; for I am not aware that when he wrote the first volume of *Tristram Shandy* he had ever been abroad. But however this may have been, I conceive it is no answer to say that Sterne's impressions were fantastical. His theories, social and political, may have been fantastical, if you please, and therefore I make no great account of the reason that he puts into the mouth of Mr. Shandy the elder. But in his perception of fact Sterne was remarkably acute, and though he may not have spoken from his own observation, I can have no doubt that his description was one of which the accuracy was so generally recognised, as to have warranted him in putting it forward as a thing about which there could be no question.

As regards the present state of things, it may be perfectly true that the Revolution, by breaking up extensive domains, may have had some effect in diminishing the number of the larger class of country residences. The great number of small proprietors must also be taken into the account; though I very much doubt whether the number of these small proprietors has been increased since the Revolution so much as is generally supposed. At all events the question still remains, whether the number of comfortable country houses is not remarkably small in proportion to the number of moderate sized estates. STAFFORD CAREY.

WORKS ON SATAN AND HIS DWELLING PLACE (3rd S. vi. 533.) — Amongst my Kentish Collections I have the following : —

"An Enquiry into the Nature and Place of Hell, showing—1. The Reasonableness of a Future State. 2. The Punishment of the next life. 3. The several Opinions concerning the Place of Hell. 4. That the Fire of Hell is not metaphorical but real. 5. The Improbability of *that* Fire's being *in* or *about* the Center of the Earth. 6. The Probability of the Sun's being the *Local* Hell, with Reasons for this Conjecture; and the Objections from Atheism, Philosophy, and the Holy Scriptures answered. By Tobias Swinden, M.A., late Rector of Cuxton in Kent. The second edition. With a Supplement wherein the Notions of Abp. Tillotson, Dr. Lupton, and others as to the Eternity of Hell Torments, are impartially represented. And the Rev. Mr. Wall's Sentiments of this learned Work."

I have given the title in full because I have never met with the book in a bookseller's Catalogue. My copy has a frontispiece, showing the face of the sun to be full of volcanoes belching forth flames and smoke. A. J. DUNKIN. Dartford.

LANCASHIRE: OLD TIMBER HALLS (3rd S. vii. 76.) —

"Clayton Hall, surrounded by a moat in the time of Charles I., was owned by the Byron family, now Lords Byron, Barons of Rochdale. It was afterwards sold to the Cheetham family, and at the death of the late Mr. Cheetham, was inherited by Mordecai Green, Esq. His son has since parted with it to several proprietors.

"Garrat Hall, in the time of Henry VII., belonged to George Trafford, Esq., and his wife Margaret, for whom the boys of the Free Grammar School in Manchester were bound to pray daily along with other benefactors."—Dr. Aiken's *History of the Country round Manchester*, London, 1795.

Ince Hall is near Wigan, and was formerly the property of the Gerard family, and is an interesting specimen of the half-timbered buildings once so common in Lancashire. H. FISHWICK.

WAKING TIME (3rd S. vi. 534; vii. 84.)—I believe I can now answer my own query, and, with your permission, will do so. This term had its origin amongst the weavers before the introduction of gas, when of course, during the winter, candles were used. By a figure of speech, candles were spoken of as "wicks," which in the Northern dialect becomes "wakes." Hence the time of year when it was necessary to use artificial light was called "Waking time." H. FISHWICK.

GAELIC GRAMMAR (3rd S. vii. 75.)—The ablest work on Gaelic Grammar, written by a native of North Britain, is unquestionably that by Alexander Stewart, late Minister of the Gospel at Moulin, the first edition of which was published in Edinburgh in 1801, and an improved edition in 1812. As the Highland Gaelic is essentially the same as the Irish, though it branched off as early as the sixth century, it may please HIGHLANDER to be informed that the best grammar of the Irish— the best preserved, most cultivated, and most polished dialect of the Gael—is " *A Grammar of the Irish Language*, published 1845, for the use of the Senior Classes in the College of St. Columba, by the late eminent scholar Dr. John O'Donovan." I fear they are both out of print, but each of them, I believe, may be obtained on application to Phelan, Bookseller, Lambeth Road, London.

J. Eugene O'Cavanagh.

Rev. John Brabant: Chronograms (3rd S. vii. 77.)—In the interesting editorial note upon the Rev. John Brabant, I observe these words:—

"It may be remarked, however, that P sometimes stood for 7, and that the age of John Brabant is *not given*, apparently, elsewhere in the inscription. P P, therefore, may have been meant to convey the information otherwise wanting, and to signify that he died aged 77. This method of indicating numbers, especially dates in letters larger than the rest of the text, is Jewish, and may be seen repeatedly in Jewish books."

This practice was not confined to the Jews. It occurs undoubtedly in Roman lapidary inscriptions. Here is one from Orellius (*Inscript. Latin.* N. 4852):—

" Dis Manibus, Claudia Ti. Augusti L. Toreumæ annor.
XVIIII.
" hæc ego bis denos nondum matura per annos
condor humo multIs nota toreVma jocIs.
exIguo VItæ spatIo felIcIter acto
effugI crImen longa senecta tuum."

With all modesty I am inclined to suggest that the Rev. Mr. Bedford's age may have been 55. I have no means of reference at hand, but I fancy that the majuscular P, in Greek at least, stands for five. H. C. C.

Latin Puzzle (3rd S. vii. 84, 85.)—The verses by Donne do not appear to come strictly within the class of Macaronics. They are a ludicrous jumble of English, Latin, French, Italian, and Spanish words, each of which stands distinct from every other. Macaronic verses are subject to the ordinary rules of scansion; but Donne's set all principles of prosody at defiance, as completely as most of the modern attempts at English hexameters. It does not, however, require any extraordinary effort to relieve CPL. from his real or pretended difficulty :

As many perfect linguists as these two distichs make,
So many prudent statesmen will this book of yours produce.

(Meaning obviously none at all.)
To me the honour is sufficient of being understood ; for I leave
To you the honour of being believed by no one.

This literally. The following attempt at a paraphrase may, I hope, be pardoned :—

Could these my couplets one sound linguist breed,
Then to true statesmanship your book might lead.
If I'm but understood, I aim no higher :
Be yours the honour to be deemed a liar !

But for a perfect appreciation of the author's sentiment, it is necessary to keep in view Coryat's introductory essay "On Travel in general," in which he urges the importance of visiting foreign countries towards the formation of a statesman's character. And it is not less essential to recollect the antecedent English lines of Donne, in which

the Odcombian traveller is treated with a degree of severity exceeding the ordinary bounds of banter. R. S. Q.

Bishop Thomas Sydserf (3rd S. vi. 356.)—I find that from my attention in this reply being directed solely to the spelling of the name, I have most unintentionally led some to suppose that the Diurnal writer was the bishop himself. It was his son, as indeed is expressly stated by Wodrow, i. 215. In a subsequent letter of Sharp's, 7th Feb. 1661, I find another notice of the Diurnalist : —

"They say they have discharged Thomas Sydserf. It is intolerable that a Papist shd bespatter the ministry of our church."

Sharp was then a moderate Presbyterian, but in fact attaching very little importance to the form of church government, except in so far as it might effect the tranquillity of the country in civil matters. In another letter dated the 2nd of March, after mentioning that it had been proposed in the Articles (a Committee of the Scotch Parliament by which all the business to be brought before the House was arranged) to repeal the Acts against Episcopacy, he observes :—

" If those Acts be rescindit, what confusion will be upon us. Bishop Sydserf may come and demand his place in Parliament."

George Vere Irving.

Miscellaneous.

NOTES ON BOOKS, ETC.

Practical Dietary for Families, Schools, and the Labouring Classes. By Edward Smith, M.D., LL.B., F.R.S. (Walton & Maberly).

This is an excellent and most opportunely published little work, on a subject, the great importance of which is only just becoming fully recognised. Dr. Smith was already known for his researches on subjects connected with diet, when he was entrusted by the medical department of the Privy Council with the task of inquiring into the dietary of the poorer classes throughout the kingdom, and the opportunities afforded by this extensive investigation have made him probably the first authority on the subject in this country. The design of the present work cannot be better explained than by stating, in the words of the Preface, that it is " intended to be a guide to heads of families and schools in their efforts to properly nourish themselves and those committed to their care, and also to clergymen and other philanthropists who take an interest in the welfare of our labouring population." The style is popular and little encumbered with technicalities, even in the more scientific parts, and the whole character of the book is essentially practical.

Libraries and Founders of Libraries. By Edward Edwards. (Trübner & Co.)

Mr. Edwards has been very fortunate in his choice of a subject ; for it would be difficult to find topics of greater literary interest than Libraries and Founders of Libraries. A small portion of the book, some thirty pages, had previously been published in the *Encyclopædia Britannica*, but with that exception, the contents of the present volume are now published for the first time, and have been based upon documents heretofore unused, and upon personal examination of the principal Collections which are here described. An outline of the contents of the volume will show the reader how much curious information he will find in it. After an introductory Sketch of the Ancient Libraries of Egypt, Judea, Greece, and Rome, Mr. Edwards gives us an account of the more remarkable Libraries, both abroad and at home. The Libraries of famous Authors next occupies his attention, and he furnishes curious notices of the Libraries of Plutarch, Boccaccio, Montaigne, De Thou, Grotius, Swift, Goethe, Scott, Southey, and De Quincey, The Royal Libraries of Isabel of Bavaria, Catherine de Medicis, Charles I., Frederick the Great, Napoleon, &c., are then reviewed, and the seventh chapter is devoted to the Old Royal Library of the Kings of England. The History of the State Papers and the Public Records of the Kingdom follows; and three chapters, devoted respectively to the Macclesfield Library at Shirburn Castle, the Sunderland Library at Blenheim, and the Spencer Library at Althorp, conclude the work.

A History of the Clanna-Rory or Rudicians, descendants of Roderick the Great, Monarch of Ireland. Compiled by Richard F. Cronelly, Constabulary Reserve Force. (Goodwin & Co., Dublin.)

A History of the Clan Eoghan, or Eoghanachts, descendants of Eugene the Great. By Richard F. Cronelly, Irish Constabulary Force. (Goodwin & Co. Dublin.)

We do not pretend to criticise or review these, the first two Parts of what promises to be a very curious Collection of Irish Family History. A glance shows the labour which its author — a member be it remarked of the Irish Constabulary Force — has bestowed upon it. All Celtic Antiquaries, especially all Irish Antiquaries, we had almost said all Irish men, would, we should think, be glad to aid by their subscriptions (the price of each Part is but 1s. 6d.) the patriotic labours of so intelligent a Constabulary Officer as Mr. Cronelly.

A Selection of Papers on Subjects of Archæology and History. By the Rev. John Kenrick, M.A. (Longman.)

In these seven Papers communicated to the Yorkshire Philosophical Society by their excellent Curator of Antiquities, which treat of the Knights Templars in Yorkshire; Historical Traditions of Pontefract Castle; The Relation of Coins to History; The Cause of the Destruction of Classical Literature; The Recovery of Classical Literature; The Reign of Trajan; Roman Waxed Tablets; and New Year's Day in Ancient Rome—Mr. Kenrick displays considerable learning, and tells what he has to say very pleasantly.

Books Received.—

The Irrationale of Speech. By a Minute Philosopher. (Longman.)

The reprint of an article from *Fraser*, which ought to be read by all Stammerers, and all who have to speak in public.

The Songs of Robert Burns. (Bell and Daldy.)

Tales of a Traveller. By Washington Irving. (Bell & Daldy.)

The time for criticising the Songs of Burns, or Washington Irving's *Tales of a Traveller*, has long since passed away. We can therefore only announce these handsome editions of them in Bell & Daldy's *English Elzevirs.*

Webster's Complete English Dictionary, thoroughly revised and improved. By C. A. Goodrich and Noah Porter. Part II. (Bell & Daldy.)

We are glad to see the Second Part of this cheap and excellent Dictionary.

We regret to announce the death, on Saturday last, of the Rev. Thomas Lathbury, Author of *The History of the Non-Jurors*; *The History of the Book of Common Prayer*, and other similar works. Mr. Lathbury, who was a frequent contributor to "N. & Q.," was in his sixty-sixth year, and was, we believe, the possessor of an extremely curious Library,

BOOKS AND ODD VOLUMES

WANTED TO PURCHASE.

Notices to Correspondents.

K. R. C. *Richardson's Dictionary*, 2 vols. 4to, contains quotations from our standard writers illustrating the various meaning of each word.

⁂ *The similarity referred to by our Correspondent has, we think, been frequently noticed.*

Whitmore of Whitmore. *Shem will send Mr. Whitmore a private answer to his query on this subject.*

E. J. Roberts. *The Register of Burials at Bunhill Fields, collected at immense labour and expense by Dr. Rippon and his son, are now in the College of Arms.*

H. Fishwick *will find in our* 1st S. vi. 358; viii. 242, *some interesting Notes on —*

" The conscious water saw its God and blushed."

Valentine's Day. *" One who wishes to know" should consult* " N. & Q." 1st S. v. 128; vii. 523; x. 5, &c.

A. F. Barton. *The beautiful proverb, " God tempers the wind to the shorn lamb," made so popular by Sterne, is fully illustrated in our* 1st S. i. 211, 236, 355, 557, 418; vii. 193.

J. Woodward. *Some account of the Emir Facardin will be found in the Biographie Universelle, ed. 1855, xiii. 339, and the Nouvelle Biographie Générale, ed. 1856, xvii. 27, art. " Fakhr-eddyn." Consult also Rees's Cyclopædia, art. " Druses." These notices of the Emir state that he visited the Court of the Medici at Florence.*

C. W. *King Henry VI. clearly intended his foundation at Eton to be collegiate from the first, which would of course include " the perpetual celebration of Divine service." The earliest act of the King respecting his projected College was his "Procuratory," dated Sept. 12, 1440, printed in Ackermann's History of the College, p. 13.—— Abp. Laud was buried under the altar of the church of Allhallows Barking; but on July 31, 1663, his body was removed to St. John's College, Oxford. See* "N. & Q." 3rd S. iii. 2.

Errata in our last number.—Page 120, col. 1. for " Thomas" Hailstone read " Edward."— Page 116, col. ii. line 12, *Farmer's Essay* first appeared in 1775, not 1755.

A Reading Case for holding the weekly Nos. of "N. & Q." is now ready, and may be had of all Booksellers and Newsmen, price 1s. 6d.; or, free by post, direct from the publisher, for 1s. 8d.

⁂ *Cases for binding the volumes of "* N. & Q.*" may be had of the Publisher, and of all Booksellers and Newsmen.*

"Notes and Queries" *is published at noon on Friday, and is also issued in Monthly Parts. The Subscription for Stamped Copies for Six Months forwarded direct from the Publisher (including the Half-yearly Index) is 11s. 4d., which may be paid by Post Office Order, payable at the Strand Post Office, in favour of* William G. Smith, 32, Wellington Street, Strand, W.C., *to whom all Communications for the* Editor *should be addressed.*

"Notes & Queries" is registered for transmission abroad.

LONDON, SATURDAY, FEBRUARY 25, 1865.

CONTENTS.—N° 165.

Notes.

EPIGRAMS.

In this month's *Quarterly Review* (No. 233), in a pleasant article on "Epigrams," it is remarked:—

"How many a drawer in a scholar's escritore contains, if we might rifle it, buried treasures of this kind, thrown off, perhaps, in lightness of mood, passed about to a friend or two, and then laid by and forgotten. . . . . It is a pity that these are not more carefully caught hp, as they drop, and communicated on the spur of the moment to *Notes and Queries*, where, at least, they would attain a longer and larger fame than their careless and indifferent progenitors have cared to secure for them."

I lately found in a book-shop a MS. volume by a Westminster scholar, H. H. dated 1840, containing a good many epigrams. Most of them are versifications of Irish bulls or well-known jokes; but some of them appear to be original. I transcribe a specimen of the different sorts. I have no clue to the author:—

"Per nemus omne notis inscripta tabella legendis,
 ' Hos,' monet, ' insidiæ mille tuentur agros.
Hic filo presso, illic ferro, fata lacesses
 Imprudens. Homines, vosque cavete, canes!'
Sic loca servantur, sic servatoribus ipsis
 Tutis per tutas vix licet ire vias."

" *Fronti nulla fides.*
"Nulla fides fronti. Ergo aversâ fronte sacerdos
Præcinit ante aram stans Pusyita fidem."

Inventis felix utitur.

" Angulo in obscuro parvus Johannulus Horner
 Artocreas, ut fert fama, sedebat edens;
Integrum et extrudens inserto pollice prunum,
 'Heus!' exclamat ovans, 'sum bonus hercle
 puer!'"

Μεταβολὴ πάντων γλυκύ.

" Quis ferat hos, inquit piscis, sartaginis æstus?
 Et saltu gratam quærit in igne vicem."

Οὐ πάντων μεταβολὴ γλυκύ.

" ' Bos meus, invitus fateor, laceravit in agro
 Communi taurum sævus, amice, tuum.'
' Ergo restituas.' 'Erravi: bos tuus est, qui
 Occidit nostrum.' ' Res meditanda magis.'"

Non tentanda via est.

" Cauta nimis mater puero: Noli, nisi postquam
 Noris nare, tuum credere corpus aquæ."

Crescit res.

" Ante reformatum radicali arte senatum
 Ad rem cernehdam nox erat una satis.
Nunc conscriptorum gravior sapientia patrum,
 Evolvit sese quinto operosa die."

Sane [Sawney] nollem hinc exitum.

" Sawney so fat in prison grows
 On wheaten bread and water,
That, dreading oatmeal, he avows
 His guilt in a manslaughter."

" The elm-trees in St. James's Park
 Were daily losing all their bark,
At which whoever look'd, or
From which whoever broke a piece,
He might the excavations trace
 Of *Scolytus destructor.*

" The ranger, knowing not what jaws
 The insect uses when he gnaws,
 Thought such tree-royal killing
By soldiers' bayonets must be done,
As if the guardsmen every one
 Had not enough of *drilling.*"

Ex fumo dare lucem.
(*On seeing some of my Scraps burned.*)

" Though dull my wit, my verses heavy stuff,
 That you make light of them is clear enough."
                                    JAMES HAMILTON.

GLEANINGS FROM AUSONIUS.—Having occasion to look over the Epigrams of this writer, who is not much read, I venture to think that a few specimens of his style may not be unacceptable to the readers of "N. & Q." The first epigram I shall select is very like the *Facetiæ* of Hierocles—that is in spirit, for its matter is quite original. The *rhetor* is just the *scholasticus* perpetuating a fresh absurdity:—

" Rufus vocatus rhetor ad nuptias,
 Celebri (fit ut) convivio,
Grammaticæ ut artis se peritum ostenderet,
 Hæc vota dixit nuptiis;
Et masculini et feminini gignite
 Generisque neutri filios."

" A pedant, when a wedding guest,
 The bride and bridegroom thus addressed:
' O may your union favoured be
 With children of the genders three!'"

The following epigram is an amplification of a maxim I have seen, whether older than Ausonius or not I cannot tell : *Bene cœpisse est dimidium facti.* The first word, which Ausonius has not, perhaps makes the maxim truer than the distich :

"Incipe : dimidium facti est, cœpisse. Supersit
Dimidium : rursum hoc incipe; et efficies."

" Only begin ; the half is done ;
Begin again : all will be won."

The next epigram also embodies a well-known and valuable maxim, *Bis dat qui dat cito,*—Who gives at once, gives more than once : —

" Si bene quid facias, facias cito : nam cito factum
Gratum erit : ingratum gratia tarda facit.'"

" Give quickly that your gift may please ;
A tardy gift will rather tease."

I give, but not in English verse, the following *recipe* for a drink of nine ingredients, which seems to have been famous. The distich is remarkable for its happy condensation : —

" *Dodralis Potio.*
"Dodra vocor. Quæ causa ? Novem species gero. Quæ sunt ?
Jus, aqua, mel, vinum, panis, piper, herba, oleum, sal."
LAURENCE MACKENZIE.

EPIGRAM AGAINST ARCHITECTS (3rd S. vii. 97, 119.) — If M. P. and A. A. will turn to the old-fashioned book, *Gay's Fables,* they will find in the second part (Fable 14) this couplet : —

" Make him (nor think his genius checkt)
A herald, or an architect."

Where the poet names Martial as his suggester, and where the allusion is evidently made to some occupation suitable for a dull boy. Having always had a strong turn for both heraldry and architecture, I remember in my young days thinking that there must be some error in the rendering, and fancying it to mean "an emblazoner or a bricklayer," or builder at the best. Z. Z.

Is your excellent correspondent A. A. quite serious in saying that "durus ad studia" means a hard student. To me—and if I am mistaken I shall be glad to be corrected—it seems to convey a very opposite idea. Certainly the passage referred to in Cicero, *Orat. pro Archiâ Poetâ,* will not support him in that assertion. I conceive the explanation in Facciolati is right (edit. Schneeb. 1831, fol.), which I will quote—"*Durus ad aliquid* est qui alicujus rei nullâ delectatione capitur," and he cites the very passage (Cic. *Arch.*) " Ipsi illi C. Mario, qui durior ad hoc studia videbatur, jucundus fuit." Nor can I agree with A. A. that "ingenium durum" is best explained by the term "hard-headed," which we use in the more favourable sense, implying intellectual solidity, compass,

and power. So to construe it would take away the whole point of Martial's epigram. The meaning of the epigrammatist surely is—"If your boy is a slow coach," a regular stupid (to use common expressions), "make him into an architect." And so the Delphin commentator (edit. Smid. Amst. 1701, 8vo), "Si puer videatur mentis stupidæ, efficias illum præconem aut architectum;" and in this explanation the other commentators on Martial whom I have met with seem to concur.
JAS. CROSSLEY.

AUTHOR OF EPIGRAM.—In an article on "Epigrams," in the current number of the *Quarterly Review,* the reviewer refers to a couplet of Sir Thomas More's—

" If evils come not, then our fears are vain ;
And if they do, fear but augments the pain,"—

as " an equivalent for only two lines of an epigram which in the Latin consists of four " : —

" Cur patimur stulti ? namque hæc vecordia nostra
Urat ut indomitus pectora nostra metus.
Seu mala non venient, jam nos metus urit inanis ;
Sin venient, aliud fit metus ipse malum."

Whose is this epigram ? Perhaps Milton had it in his mind when he wrote (*Comus*) : —

" Peace, brother, be not over exquisite
To cast the fashion of uncertain evils.
For grant they be so, while they rest unknown,
What need a man forestall his date of griefs,
And run to meet what he would most avoid ?
Or if they be but false alarms of fear,
How bitter is such self-delusion."
BRIGHTLING.

" THE MOTHER OF THE WESLEYS."

The foregoing is the title of an exceedingly pleasant volume by the Rev. John Kirk, Wesleyan Minister, much of the matter being of course derived from Dr. Clarke's charming account of *The Wesley Family.* My present object, however, is not to review either of these books, but merely to make a few remarks on the portrait of the excellent and remarkable woman above named. Several years ago, the late Mr. Tegg published an edition of *Wesley's Philosophy,* as revised . by the Rev. Samuel Dunn; and prefixed to this work was a portrait with the name of Susanna Wesley. Being a very pleasing face of a young woman, and bearing such a name, it was not only highly thought of by the Methodists generally, but by other persons who felt an interest in one of the most remarkable families of its class. I well recollect a framed impression of this print, which for years hung in the sitting-room of the poet James Montgomery, and often diverted his admiration from the fine engraving of Stothard's " Canterbury Pilgrims," which occupied an adjacent space. I had from the first, and for several reasons, grave doubts as to the genuineness of a picture which was so little like what one would expect of the daughter of good Dr. Annesley, the old Nonconformist minister; and still less, as I thought, either like, or likely to have been painted for the worthy rector of Epworth. Opportunity occurring, I mentioned these doubts to Mrs. Smith, one of the daughters of Dr. Clarke, and she asserted that the engraving was from a portrait with which she had long been familiar, of Miss Gwynne, a sister to Mrs. Charles Wesley. How it came to be used as I have stated; and why it continued to be so used after the mistake—if mistake there was — became manifest, I do not know. But now for the genuine portrait. Some time since, a painting of an elderly lady turned up in London, which the owner said had always been regarded and prized as the mother of the founder of Methodism : the look of the person represented, and history of the picture pointing towards its probable authenticity. The only *prima facie* feature of doubt being the occurrence of the towers of Westminster Abbey represented as seen through a window. After due inquiry, an old engraving of the picture was met with; and it turned out, on further evidence, that this was an undoubted, as it is a most pleasing original likeness of Mrs. Wesley, taken at a venerable age, for her son Samuel, when he was master of Westminster School : hence the characteristic accessories. This very interesting portrait, which, if I recollect rightly, is in the possession of Mr. Morley, of Leeds, has latterly been engraved in more than one size and style. It represents the good woman in a close-fitting full-bordered cap, suiting her sweet and saintly face: a white neckerchief; and long black silk mittens. I have been led to record these particulars in consequence of the interest I feel in the notices of and inquiries after original portraits of the Rev. John Wesley. Curiously enough, the " official portrait," now prefixed to most of the Wesleyan publications, is a compilation made by the late John Jackson, R.A., from all the accessible originals! A plan which, I must think—the *very flattering result* in this case, notwithstanding, and as I said to the artist—exactly adapted to *miss* the truth and discredit the trustworthiness of portraiture. D.

SIR JAMES OF ORMONDE.

There is a seal among those shown to visitors in the British Museum, which the authorities have labelled as belonging to "James Dormont, Knt., Captain of Gournay, 1441 ; " a designation which is, perhaps, correctly extracted from the accompanying document, but which will hardly enable a casual observer to identify the owner.

James Butler, son and heir to the fourth Earl

of Ormond, born in 1420, was knighted with King Henry VI. in 1426. Youthful as he was, his sovereign was even younger. In 1440, he is stated by Hall, who calls him Sir James of Ormond, to have accompanied the Duke of York to France, of which that prince had been made regent. Gournay, of which he was probably then appointed captain, was an important place ; and six years previously an English force under the Earl of Arundel had suffered a serious repulse there, the earl himself being wounded and made prisoner. In 1449, Holinshed names "the Lord Butler, sonne to the Earl of Ormond," as left in the hands of the French as an hostage. In the same year he was created, *vitâ patris*, Earl of Wiltshire; was advanced to the Lord High Treasurership of England in 1455 ; and was also elected a Knight of the Garter ; but, being made prisoner after Towtonfield, he was beheaded on May 1, 1461, and afterwards attainted.

The seal bears the arms of his ancient house differenced with a label, and he uses on it, like modern eldest sons of peers, the supporters belonging to the title to which he was heir apparent. When did the further use of the father's second title, and its distinguishing coronet, become general? Hotspur, who flourished at about this time, is not known as Lord Percy. Holinshed, as already noted, calls this Sir James "the Lord Butler," but I think incorrectly. The Earls (and Marquesses) of Ormond, whose second title of Viscount Thurles was conferred in 1537, do not use that of Butler, though they sat as magnates in the Irish Parliament before they were created earls.

Their sons, however, and those of the Earls of Desmond are frequently designated by the title instead of the patronymic of their family. In the case of the Desmonds, this custom continued until the destruction of that great house in the reign of Elizabeth. In the present instance we find it in use even after a distinct peerage had been conferred. Thus Hardyng, in cap. cxxxviii. of his metrical Chronicle, naming those who adhered to Henry VI. after the battle of St. Albans, includes "Sir James Ormond, Erle of Wiltshire"; and when the brother and eventual heir of this nobleman, Thomas, seventh Earl of Ormond, was summoned to the English House of Lords, the writ was addressed to "Thomas Ormond de Rochford." Whence did this custom arise? Unless as a mark of illegitimacy, I do not remember meeting any instance of it among English noble families, except that of Arundel. It was not practised by the Kildare Geraldines, the equals and rivals of the houses of Ormond and Desmond in Ireland, and is rather opposed to the Celtic ideas of a community which deemed it a higher distinction to be "The O'Brien" than to be Prince, or perhaps, King, of Thomond. S. P. V.

Six Hundred Years old.—A communication in "N. & Q." (3rd S. iii. 248) has brought me into trouble with the *Standard* of January 11th, which, in a leader on "Centenarianism," makes me relate that there is a man at Smyrna 600 years old, and that the governor-general knew it was true, "for he was present at his birth."

As neither Capt. Burton, nor any of the Mekkahites, has explained my note, I have now made inquiries, and am informed by Halikejee Hajji Ali Effendi, a very respectable and intelligent gentleman, that he met at Mekkah persons who had seen the aged Sheikh, that he lives in the Turkish province of Habesh in Abyssinia, about 40 hours (100 to 140 miles) from the sea; that notwithstanding his assumed age, he was in full possession of his faculties, and was very affable to strangers and foreigners. I have no doubt that my first hypothesis is right, and that this is a case of the succession of aged sheikhs like lamas. Ali Effendi says there are no cases of reputed extraordinary age at Mekkah, but that at Medinah there are many people of one hundred or thereabouts.   Hyde Clarke.

Smyrna, 27 Jan. 1865.

Curious Seal.—The impression in gutta percha of a curious mediæval seal was lately sent me for explanation. It is well-preserved, of oval form, and represents a female and a youth standing, each bearing a palm branch; and a nimbus surrounds the head of each. Underneath is the figure of a religious kneeling. The legend round the seal is as follows: s'ppositi . sci . qvirici . asten . ordis . hviliator'. I have given the inscription in Roman letters; but the characters on the seal are Lombardic. This seal is curious from having belonged to a religious congregation long since suppressed and abolished. It was that of the Humiliati, founded in 1017, confirmed by Pope Innocent III. in 1200, but abolished by Pope St. Pius V. in 1571, on account of the nefarious attempt of three of its members to assassinate St. Charles Borromeo. The superior of each House of this congregation was styled Provost; and this seal belonged to the convent of St. Quiricus, at Asti in Sardinia. Hence the inscription is in English: *The seal of the Provost of Saint Quiricus, at Asti, of the Order of the Humiliati.* The figures on the seal are St. Julitta and her young son St. Quiricus, or Cyr; and the religious kneeling below represents the Provost wearing the cap, or bonnet peculiar to that congregation.   F. C. H.

Incongruous Sayings. — These are no novelties. In the excellent edition of *Reynard the Fox*, published by the Percy Society, p. 54, the hero says:—

"Ye, my Lord, the Kynge, ye be also nyghe that as fro Rome to Maye."

The note quotes a French saying, "entre Maubeuge et la Pentecôte," and an English expression, "From the first of April to the foot of Westminster Bridge."

I have heard from some of the old four-in-hand whips, who prided themselves on their driving and their knowledge of town, that it used to be a sort of catch-question to a tyro in the art who might be talking of places and distances — "How far is it from the foot of Westminster Bridge to the 12th of August?"

The initiated would reply in a moment about two hundred yards. I have been told it was at this distance on the Surrey side that George IV. when Prince met Rodney in state when returning from sea after his victory over De Grasse. It is said the greeting of the former to the latter was, "Welcome, Rodney, to the Prince of Wales." Immediately after this a large public-house was built close to the spot, over the door of which were placed the portraits of the prince and the admiral, inscribed with the words of welcome stated above, and the *date of the meeting*. Very shortly after, the house was popularly known by the name of the date — "The 12th of August;" and thus to the habitués of London it was as much a locality as the foot of the bridge itself, and might be measured accordingly.   A. A.

Poets' Corner.

"No Man is a Hero to his Valet-de-Chambre."—The origin of this well-known phrase may be as old as Antigonus, who, on a poet flattering him with the title of the Son of God, answered — "My servant knows the contrary."

Francis Trench.

Islip.

Milton and his Illustrator.—In the volume of woodcuts illustrating Milton's noble poems, "L'Allegro" and "Il Penseroso," issued some years ago by the Council of the Art-Union of London to the subscribers, the designer of engraving V. seems quite to have misapprehended the allusion contained in two lines of the former poem; the two latter in the extract here given: —

> "While the ploughman, near at hand,
> Whistles o'er the furrow'd land;
> And the milkmaid singeth blithe,
> And the mower whets his scythe,
> *And every shepherd tells his tale
> Under the hawthorn in the dale.*"

The student of Milton needs not to be reminded that the expression, "tells his tale," as here employed by the poet, refers to the shepherd's practice of counting his flock. The artist, under the impression that a tale of love is implied, has represented the amorous swain engaged in breathing tender words into the ear of his fair one, whose waist he encircles with his arm.

I know not whether this misinterpretation of our great poet's meaning has been before pointed out. It certainly ought not to be permitted to pass unnoted.　　　　　　　　　　　　T. N.

Bacup.

CURIOUS ORIGIN OF A CHRISTIAN NAME. — I extract the following paragraph from a sister periodical published at New York, called the *Historical Magazine and Notes and Queries of America*, Feb. 1864, p. 71: —

"In Canada Delfma is a common and rather a pretty name for girls. Its origin would not easily be suspected. A clergyman from France had a child brought to him to baptize, and was requested to christen it by this name. 'This is not a fit name,' was his reply. 'You should give her the name of some saint.' 'But, M. le Curé, it is a saint's name.' 'No; there is no such saint in the calendar.' 'Why, M. le Curé, don't you know Ste Rose de Lima?' He certainly did, and found that people finding Rose de Lima too long, dropped Rose, and ran Delfma together.—A."

　　　　　　　　　　　　　　　　　　　P.

ENGLISH BEARDS. — The following note on this subject will not be considered ill-timed in the year 1865. The second half of our century having witnessed so remarkable a revolution of fashion from those days when the daily attendance of a barber with his razor was deemed indispensable. An able biographical work of contemporary biography was commenced in 1798 by Richard Phillips (afterwards Sheriff of London and Sir Richard), under the title of *British Public Characters*, and was continued for a considerable period in yearly volumes. In the first volume is a memoir of Matthew Robinson, then Lord Rokeby, to which is prefixed (pp. 494-496) *a Prefatory Dissertation on Beards*, concluding with the following passage: —

"These preliminary remarks will not appear totally misplaced, perhaps, to such as are acquainted with the person of the noble lord whose memoirs are here offered to the public, as *his beard forms one of the most conspicuous traits of his person*; and he is the only peer, and perhaps *the only gentleman of either Great Britain or Ireland* who is thus distinguished."

Is there any engraved portrait of this Lord Rokeby?*

At a much later date Mr. Muntz, the member for Birmingham, was long regarded as a singular example of a bearded Englishman: and I can well remember the time when a beard in the streets of London could only be supposed to be the property of some Turk or Oriental, or of the rabbis of the Jewish church.　　　　J. G. N.

CALVIN. — I have heard the name of the great Genevan Reformer quoted as if derived from *Calvus*, as though it meant Baldhead, or Baldy; but surely it represents rather *Calidum vinum*, from the French form *Chauvin*, i. e. *Chaud-vin*.

　　　　　　　　　　　　　　　　　　O. T. D.

[* Two engraved portraits of Lord Rokeby occur in Evans's *Catalogue of Portraits*, vol. i. p. 295.—ED.]

THE CAT. — I saw it stated recently, in the *Intellectual Observer*, that the modern name of this animal is Teutonic. Without denying this, allow me to say, that I some time since asked a Nestorian, a native of north-western Persia, what the cat was called by his people; and he answered, "Catto." This is the pronunciation; and, to prevent mistake, I asked him to write it down in Syriac characters. He did so, and with the same result.

　　　　　　　　　　　　　　　　　　B. H. C.

CONVENTUAL DISCIPLINE IN THE MIDDLE AGES. St. Bernard, who flourished in the twelfth century, and who occupies a high rank in the Romish calendar for his piety and austere sanctity, has left in his works a series of letters to a nun, *De modo bene vivendi*, giving her rules of conduct in all the duties of her monastic life.

In his chapter, "De Disciplinâ," he thus exhorts her: —

"Amabilis mihi Soror, melius est tibi manu Abbatissæ vel Priorissæ flagellis cædi quam in Inferno poenas pati; melius est tibi manu Abbatissæ vel Priorissæ flagellari in hac vitâ quam in Inferno cruciari in futuro; melius est tibi manu Abbatissæ flagellis verberari quam in Inferno torqueri; melius est tibi manu Abbatissæ temporaliter affligi virgulis quam cremari æternis incendiis."

Which may be briefly rendered—My amiable sister, it is much better for you to endure the wholesome smart of the rod from the hand of the abbess, than to suffer eternal torments hereafter.

None ever understood human nature better than the heads of the Catholic church, and they well knew that wherever strict discipline was required and the stubborn will brought into subjection, no means were so prompt and efficacious, with so little permanent injury to the sufferer, as moderate corporal punishment. There is not a matron in any of our gaols or houses of correction who does not deplore that the over-refinement of this age does not allow her to enforce order among the unruly and abandoned females she has to control, by the infliction of a whipping with a birch rod, which would effect more than days of solitary confinement in dark cells.　　　　　C. M.

SHAKESPEARE FAMILY. — Perhaps the following extract from Aubrey's *Natural History of Wiltshire* (written about the year 1680) may interest your readers: —

"Jo. Shakespeare's wife, of Worplesdowne, in Surrey, a North Wiltshire woman, and an excellent huswife, does assure me that she makes as good cheese there as ever she did at Wraxhall or Bitteston, and that it is meerly for want of art that her neighbours doe not make as good."

　　　　　　　　　　　　　　　　　　C. J. R.

FIRST AMERICAN STEAMBOAT. — I trust the following authentic notice of the first ship navigated by steam in American waters may claim a remembrance in "N. & Q.": —

" Fulton's Steamboat.—In a speech in New Orleans recently, Jacob Barker mentioned incidentally that when Robt. Fulton's machinery for the first steamboat came from the manufactory in England to New York, it was consigned to him, and that it actually remained in the commission warehouse six months before the money could be raised to pay the charges of importation."

W. W.

Malta.

The Venality of Chatterton.—Chatterton's sister, a Mrs. Newton, in a letter first published in the pamphlet entitled *Love and Madness*, thus vindicates her brother's morality :—

" My brother would frequently walk the College Green (Bristol) with the young girls that statedly paraded there to'show their finery ; but I really believe he was no debauchee, though some have reported it ; the dear unhappy boy had faults enough : I saw with concern he was proud, and exceedingly imperious : but that of *Venality* he could not be justly charged with."

This is a curious use of a common word : the good lady evidently derived it from *Venus*.

X. Y. Z.

Elma, a Female Christian Name.—The following passage occurs in *The Historical Magazine and Notes and Queries* of America, September, 1864, p. 312. It ought to be reproduced in " N. & Q." :—

" In London *Notes and Queries* (3rd S. v. p. 97) an enquiry is made as to the origin of Elma, the Christian name of a daughter of the Earl of Elgin. The quærist supposes it formed from the initial syllables of her mother *Elizabeth Mary*. In this country the name exists, but is an abbreviation of Gulielma. The victim of the Manhatten Well murder in New York, many years since, was Elma Sands, whose real name was Gulielma."

P.

Adverbs improperly used. — Bartlett, in his amusing *Dictionary of Americanisms* (p. 28 of the Introduction), protests against the use of adverbs where idiomatic usage requires an adjective, as " I feel very *badly*," " you look *charmingly*," &c. " So that," he continues, " we may expect soon to hear ' She seems *ignorantly* ;' ' he became quite *crazily*, &c. ; and to be unable any longer to make the distinction between ' He feels *warmly*,' and ' he feels *warm*.' "

He should have added that this usage is common in Shakspeare. Thus, in *As You Like It*, we have —

" You look merrily."—Act II. Sc. 8.
" Looks he as freshly."—Act III. Sc. 2.

And in *Julius Cæsar* —

" Look fresh and merrily."—Act II. Sc. I.

S. W. P.

New York.

Queries.

CIVIL WAR SERMONS, MS.

Two MS. sermons preached before Charles I. and his court, at Oxford, in the civil wars, are now *penes me*. They are in the handwriting of the time, and so copiously blurred with corrections and interlineations as to be evidently, in the opinion of clerical experts, the actual pulpit copies. No name is given, but I have some reason for conjecturing that the name of one of the preachers was Benet. Query, Do any records exist of the Oxford transactions of that time which would give the court preachers? They are of octavo size, bound together in a dark calf, and written on paper so coarse as almost to suggest a scarcity of stationery in that beleagured city. The first states that it was

"preached before yᵉ King, yᵉ Prince, yᵉ Duke, and yᵉ Lords at Oxford, on Christmas Day, being Munday,1643, in yᵉ time of yᵉ great Rebellion."

The text is from

" 1 Jo. iii. 8 : ' For this purpose yᵉ Sonn of God was manifested, that hee might destroy yᵉ workes of the Deuill.' "

There are, of course, occasional references, in describing the works of the Devil, to agencies then close at hand ; thus,—

" That if we finde in the world a generation of men compacted as it were of pride, and crueltie, and calumnie, and hypocrisie, and lying, we may sadly conclude they shake hands with the Devill, and have entred a covenant with hell, and death, and damnation, without Repentance. . And then, I beseech you, consider awhile what is Luciferian Pride if this be not, to offer at the Croᵂne, to endanger the Royall throne, to say in effect, Sʳ, lay by your Scepter, deliver us your sword, if not we will take it by violence. What is barbarous Crueltie and hellish barbaritie if this be not ? to send out bloodie edicts (executed accordingly) for killing, and slaying, and destroying all their fellow subjects and servants that shall dare to resist their rebellious insurrection ? . . . . If these be not τὰ ἔργα τοῦ διαβόλου, the workes of his masterpeeces, certainly there is either no difference betwixt Virtue and Vice, or we must graunt of necessitie a parietie of transgressions, and so blott out τὰ ἔργα in the text."

The second sermon has marks of a still darker time, its date being but a month before the king delivered himself up at Newark, " *mæstissimo tempore*," as the preacher notes at the end. The text is,—

" 1 Cor. xv. 57 : ' But thanks be to God who giveth us the victorie through oʳ Ld. Jes. Xt.' A sad time to preach of victories, in such a low condition, when yᵉ enemie presseth on so fast, and lookes so bigg, not only insulting and flying upon us *gladio oris*, with the base and barbarous sword of their mouth—for swords are in their lipps (Ps. lix.), *et ore gladii*—and with the mouth of their bloody sword ; but, what is more, openly confessing they intend no longer to deale with us by way of retayle, but to take us off totally at a blow, as by whole sale, and so to make havock of us altogether. For any one then to treate of victories at such a time as this, may it not be thought an . . . . argum^t . . . . It were to be wished that too, too many, had not too much cause to be troubled with the same contemplation at this day; when they behold (as they doe) in this deluge of miseries the best of men in the worst condition; being forced to forsake howses, and brethren, and fathers, and wife, and lands, and possessions; hunted and proscribed from citie to citie; many of them tortured and tormented from top to toe; undergoing the trial of cruel mockings and scourgings," &c.

Mem. at end of sermon: —

"Deo gratias, before ye King, ye Duke of York, and P. Rupt., &c., March 29, A^o 1646, moestissimo tempore."

The remainder is on the inside the cover: seem hints or fragménts: —

"That these words may be treated on to . . . . .
"More especially let us pray for the churches under . . . . [Seems incomplete, like the preceding line and others below.]
"And let us pray for ye King's Majestie, that God would look upon his pson with the watchfull eye of his gratious consideration—that he would comfort him in all his troubles, that he would deliver him out of all his dangers, and that he would crown his pious endeavours with happie successe, to the glorie of his great name, the preservation of his poore church, and ye peace and safetie of his kingdoms.
"Let us pray also for his royall Consort . . . . that they may in their severall places serve faith . . . ."
                                        BIBLIOPOLA.

JOHN ANDERSON, FOUNDER OF FERMOY: SIR JAMES CALEB ANDERSON.—In Mr. D. Owen-Madden's *Revelations of Ireland*, is an interesting account of John Anderson; an enterprising character, founder of the town of Fermoy in Ireland, who appears to have been living in 1816. Mr. Madden's account forms the basis of an article in Mr. William Anderson's *Scottish Nation* (a very excellent work, which ought to be better known south of Tweed); and some details respecting John Anderson may be found in Burke's *Peerage and Baronetage* for 1861, pp. 23, 24. None of these authors give the date of John Anderson's death. I hope it may be supplied.

John Anderson's son, Sir James Caleb Anderson, Bart., died, aged sixty-eight, April 4, 1861; when, leaving no male issue, the baronetcy became extinct. He was at one period celebrated for his efforts to improve steam locomotion. His death is duly recorded in the *Gentleman's Magazine* and the *Annual Register*, but without any allusion to the circumstances which once made him famous.
                                        S. Y. R.

CALAMY'S "ABRIDGMENT," CHAP. IX.—I should be very much obliged to any of your correspondents who could assist me with information on the two following points? —

1. The names of those in the list who simply gave up their livings in 1660 to the rightful owners. I have already, by a careful search

through Walker's *List of the Suffering Clergy*, discovered 218 who did so.

2. The names of any in the list who were ejected for refusing to take the engagement. Calamy himself says that many of the Lancashire ministers were ejected for refusing, and writing against the engagement. He, however, distinguishes them in no way, and puts them all down as sufferers in 1662.

I shall also be glad to know from what sources I can best verify Calamy's List?
                                        JOHNSON BAILY.
Bishop Middleham, Ferry Hill Station, Durham.

CHURCH DESECRATION.—These lines were written on seeing the vaults under a church used as wine cellars: —

"A spirit above, and a spirit below,
A spirit of weal, and a spirit of woe.
The spirit above is the spirit divine,
The spirit below is the spirit of wine."

Who was the author?   J. B. G.

"GOD US AYDE."—At the sale of Antiquities from Bramhope Manor, Yorkshire, which took place at Messrs. Christie, Manson, and Wood's rooms on February 6, there occurred a ring thus described in the Catalogue: —

"25. A curious old ring, chased with the Nortons' motto, *God us ayde*."

As the metal in which the ring is wrought is not named, it is, I suppose, of gold. I am anxious to know whether the above motto has been used by any family except the Yorkshire Nortons, and also whether it is known to occur as a posy on wedding rings. Everything that relates to the sufferers in the Rising in the North is interesting to many of us.   EDWARD PEACOCK.
Bottesford Manor, Brigg.

EDMUND HOYLE. — Can any of your correspondents help me to any facts relating to Edmund Hoyle (the celebrated writer on cards) as to his parentage, life, descendants (if any), or family? Has any memoir of him ever been written? He was born in 1672; and died in Wellbank (qy. Welbeck) Street, Cavendish Square, in August 1769. Any further particulars respecting him would be most acceptable. If any of his family are living, I should feel greatly obliged to them to put themselves in communication with me.
                                        CAVENDISH.

"IN THE TIMES."—I shall be obliged if some of your poetical readers will furnish me with a copy of a touching little poem entitled "In the Times," or refer me to any publication in which it has appeared. The first verse runs thus: —

"Married! married! and not to me!
Is it a dream, or can it be
That the final vow is plighted?

Is there no chance of error here
In the cruel lines traced fair and clear,
By which my hope is blighted ? "
                   WILLIAM GASPEY.
Keswick.

INFANTRY IN LINE.—I should like to know if
it is true, that the Duke of Wellington was the
first general in the British army who introduced
the formation of infantry in line, in preference to
column, when attacking an enemy; and if he
carried out that formation in all his battles in the
Peninsula, and also at the battle of Waterloo ?
Has any continental nation ever employed
the formation of infantry in line in any of their
great battles, as an attacking force ?   FUSILIER.

"JEAN-FRANÇOIS, LES BAS BLEUS."—The *Athenæum* for 1833 (p. 792), contains a review of *Les
Cent-et-Une Nouvelles nouvelles des Cent-et-Un*,
Vol. I.; Paris, Ladvocat; London, Dulau & Co.:
a work, as it seems, contributed to by several
writers, among them, M. Charles Nodier. He
wrote a tale therein called "Jean François les Bas
Bleus," of which an abridged translation is given.
I am very anxious to know whether this story is
told as a work of fiction, or whether it is a narrative of facts. There is perhaps nothing impossible in it; but it is altogether so contrary to the
experience of most persons, that if the circumstances related really occurred, one would like to
have proof that they did so. I should not have
thought of asking if a story in such a collection
was true, were it not for the fact that some passages in it, *as translated*, seem to claim credence.
                          P.

YOUNG JOHNSON.—Can any of your readers
give me a copy of the once celebrated lyric, recording the sad fate of a young man named Johnson from the neighbourhood of Malton, who was
executed for forgery, which contains the injunction—

    " O beware of pen and paper,
       For 'tis called forgeree " ?
                 C. J. D. INGLEDEW.
Tyddyn-y-Sais, Carnarvon.

LONGEVITY: MISS MARY BILLINGE UPWARDS
OF 112.—In *The Times* of January 26th, Mr. John
Newton of 13, West Derby Street, Liverpool,
communicated the following remarkable instance
of longevity of an old lady, whom he had attended
in her last illness. The account was written by
Mr. Newton at the time of her death, and was
published in *The Times*, the *Gent. Mag.* and other
periodicals : —

"Dec. 20th, 1863, at her residence, Edge Lane, Liverpool, aged 112 years and six months, died Mary Billinge.
She was born at Eccleston, near Prescot, on the 24th May,
1751. She retained her faculties in a very remarkable
degree to the last, and was never known to have been
confined to her bed for a single day until the week preceding her decease."

On the 27th, a correspondent who avowed "that
he shared Sir George Lewis's doubts as to the
majority of statements of longevity, and his wish
to ascertain the precise facts in all alleged cases,"
invited Mr. Newton to furnish some particulars
of the evidence which satisfied him that the lady,
Miss Mary Billinge, who died on Dec. 20, 1863,
was the same person who was baptized on May 24,
1751.
I, who am also a doubter in these cases, have
looked with some anxiety for Mr. Newton's reply.
That gentleman has as yet made no sign. Parliament is now sitting; *The Times* will have little
space for such matters, and I hope therefore
"N. & Q." will admit an old correspondent,
through its columns, to call the attention both of
Mr. Newton and its Liverpool subscribers to this
curious instance.
The subject of longevity has long attracted the
attention of men of science, actuaries, and others;
but I believe that since the present century no
case at all approaching to that of Miss Mary Billinge has been found to bear the test of examination.   A DOUBTER.

LORD MACAULAY'S ANCESTRY.—His grandfather
was the Rev. John Macaulay, minister of Inverary; whose brother was the Rev. Kenneth Macaulay, minister of Calder, Nairnshire, author of
the *History of St. Kilda*. Who were these two
the sons of, and who did they marry? They are
both frequently mentioned in Boswell's *Johnson*.
Were the Rev. Robert Macaulay, minister of
Inchinnan, Renfrewshire, in 1703, and the Rev.
Robert Macaulay, minister of Stirling about the
same date, relations of the above? or were the
two latter one and the same?   F. M. S.
229, Clarendon Villas, Plumstead.

LADY MARJORY MURRAY.—I have before me
the following books : —

1. "*Essai d'Imitation Libre de l'Episode D'Ines de
Castro dans le Poème des Luziadas de Camoens*. Par
Mlle M. M. 1772 . . . . 8vo."
2. "*Essai d'un Éloge Historique de Maria-Thérèse,
Archiduchesse d'Autriche, &c. &c.* Par M. M * * * * *.
Brussells, 4to, 1781."

In a hand of the period, a former owner has
filled up the asterisks in the title of the latter
work with the name Murray, and has written
Murray on the title of the first-named book.
I surmise that the person meant was Lady
Marjory Murray, who died at Twickenham 19th
May, 1799. She was the second daughter of
David Murray, sixth Viscount Stormont, by Anne,
only daughter and heiress of John Stewart of
Innerbye, and was called *Miss Marjory Murray*
until 30th April, 1793, when she and her eldest
sister Anne obtained the royal warrant to enjoy
the same place and precedence as the daughters of

an earl of Great Britain. Thenceforward she appears to have been designated *Lady* Marjory Murray. In Mary Granville's (Mrs. Delany's) *Autobiography* she is called Miss *May* Murray at a period before 1793. Perhaps some correspondent can confirm or rebut my supposition that these works are by Lady Marjory Murray.   S. Y. R.

THE NETHERLANDS.—At the time of the separation of the seven united provinces (1579) was Dreuthe part of either Friesland or Gröningen? Which three of the other ten provinces were ceded to France in 1748? A card, containing the arms of the Netherlands (1677), gives the seventeen shields; but leaves out Liege and West Flanders, and puts in Malines and Aras (Arras).
                                JOHN DAVIDSON.

" OH, OH, RAY, OH AMBORAH."—

  " No pow'r on earth can e'er divide
    The knot that sacred love hath tied;
    When parents draw against our mind,
    The true love's knot they faster bind.
    Oh, oh, ray, oh Amborah.
    Oh, oh," &c.

Polly sings the above air in the *Beggar's Opera*, Act II. Sc. 2. The burden seems a strange unusual sort of one. Had it any meaning at the time the *Opera* was written?   W. B.

PURITAN PEW. — It would be interesting to ascertain how many of these curious enclosed seats still remain untouched in our churches. W. T. T. D. (3rd S. vii. 116) mentions one in Long Melford church, "entirely covered in." There is another pew of the kind in the church of Langley V. Mary (commonly called Langley Marsh), in West Drayton. It is on the north side, separated from the nave by a wooden lattice work. The pew communicates with a small library of books on divinity, to which the occupant of the pew might retire without being noticed from the body of the church. The domestic chapel attached to Littlecote Hall, near Hungerford, still retains the distinctive arrangements peculiar to the Puritan age, in the position of the communion table, seats, &c. Can any of your readers supply other instances of this kind?
                            BENJ. FERREY, F.S.A.

QUOTATIONS. —

  " . . . . a gleam,
    A light that never fell on sea or land;
    The artist's fancy, and the poet's dream!"

  " . . . . in a season of calm weather,
    Though inland far we be,
    Our souls have sight of that immortal sea
    Which brought us hither,
    Can in a moment travel thither,
    And see the children sport upon the shore,
    And hear the mighty waters rolling evermore."
                                        A.

PEWTERERS' COMPANY. — The *Athenæum* of Feb. 4, 1865, contains a review of Dr. Hook's

Lives of the Archbishops of Canterbury (vols. iii. and iv.), which concludes with the following words: —

" When these volumes close, the Statute was in force which legalized the burning of heretics; and the Pewterers' Company were then, or soon after, in possession of the estates which they held under the pleasant service of furnishing all the faggots required for the fires in which the heretics of London were to expiate their offences against Rome."

Will you kindly allow me to propose the following queries: — Where can the authority be found for this assertion with respect to the Pewterers' Company? When, and by whom, were estates granted to them on the condition mentioned? What were the estates? Does any evidence exist of the service having been rendered? Did the Company lose the estates when the service was no longer required?

An answer to any of these inquiries will be highly acceptable to   A LONDON ANTIQUARY.

PRACTICES OF THE ROMAN CHURCH. — In an article entitled " The Reformation," in *The Saturday Review*, of Jan. 28, 1865, the writer says: —

" Vernacular services, communion in both kinds, and the marriage of the clergy, are all freely allowed to large national communities in strict communion with Rome."

I wish to ask, to what communities does he here refer?   W. T. T. D.

SAM SHARPSET. — Will some clever kindly disposed reader inform me who is the worthy alluded to in the following comparison, which appeared in the 10th of December number of *The Reader?* —

" A momentary enthusiasm might perhaps greet a tragedy by Sophocles, a decade of Livy, or the now missing portions of the *Annals* or *History of Tacitus*" . . . . . " A few scholars would cherish the resuscitated worthies, but nine-tenths of the literary world would receive them as coolly as Sam Sharpset received his brother Matthew at Barbadoes."

                          ALFRED JOHN DUNKIN.

SKETCH BY LESLIE. — Can any correspondent suggest for what subject the late Mr. Leslie intended a sketch, which is now in my possession? It is a single figure, apparently of a Welshman. He has his head tied up in a napkin; one hand he holds to his breast, with the other he very sorrowfully holds out a piece of money as if particularly objecting to part with it. It is very spirited, and finely touched. He evidently intended to introduce it into some large picture, by the pains he took to finish the flesh parts.
                                        J. C. J.

R. SMITH, author of *A Wonder of Wonders, or a Metamorphosis of Fair Faces into Foul Visages; an invective against black-spotted Faces, temp.*

James I.* Any particulars of his life will oblige me. ST. T.

"STILL WATERS RUN DEEP."—I have been accustomed to hear this phrase used for the last fifty years. Where does it first occur in print?
G. H. OF S.

STORMSTEAD.—Will any of your readers kindly give me information as to the orthography of the word "stormstead"? Is it "stead," "sted," or "staid"? H. B.

"VITULUS AUREUS."—Who, under the name of Philander, wrote this work?
JOHN DAVIDSON.

SIR WALTER SCOTT.—Did Sir Walter Scott ever visit Melrose Abbey by moonlight, or is the well-known description in the Lay of the Last Minstrel wholly the result of imagination?
J. B. G.

Queries with Answers.

"COLLECTION OF POLITICAL TRACTS."—Chance threw in my way a book bearing this title:—"A Collection of Political Tracts. Dublin: Printed by George Faulkner, in Essex Street. M.DCC.XLVIII." In the Preface are these words:—"Some of them were ushered into the world from a printing-press under the sanction of a late noble Duke." Who was the "noble Duke"? The tracts are signed as if by different writers, but the style of all is so alike as to lead one to the conclusion that they are all by the same hand. By whom were they written? I give some of the names found at the end of the various papers: "The Occasional Writer;" "From my Garret"; "John Trot"; "Phil-Athenus." The following names appear in one of the articles thus entitled: "An Answer to the London Journal of Saturday, December 21, 1728:"—"Benjamin, Lord Bishop of ******;" "Ben"; "Robin"; "Numb Fish"; "Raleigh;" "Publicola"; "A Person." For whom did these names stand? PAUL À JACOBSON.
West Derby.

[The Tracts contained in the volume purchased by our correspondent are from the pen of Lord Bolingbroke, and some of them are reprinted in Mallet's edition of his Lordship's Works. The Rev. William Mason, in a letter to Mr. Bryant, dated Nov. 13, 1747, informs him that "Lord Bolingbroke has advertised a Collection of Political Tracts, but I suppose they will be only such as have before made their appearance in the weekly papers." (Nichols's Literary Anecdotes, ii. 711.) This volume was reprinted verbatim in Cadell's edition of Bolingbroke's Works, ed. 1788, 8vo, with the following title: "A Collection of Political Tracts, by the Author of the Disser-

[* Temp. Charles II. "Lond. 1662, 4to." A copy was in Heber's library, Pt. iv. 3037.—ED.]

tation upon Parties." Warburton said that his "Occasional Writer" (printed in this Collection) is one of the best things Bolingbroke ever wrote." By "Robin of notable memory" is probably meant Robert Harley, Earl of Oxford; and "Benjamin, Lord Bishop of ******," is clearly Benjamin Hoadly, Bishop of Bangor.]

LATIN NAMES OF TOWNS.—Is there any dictionary or work that gives a list of the Latin names of the principal European towns? Without some list of that sort, one is apt to make mistakes in reading small coins where the words are much contracted. I had a small silver coin of Louis XIV., with MO. NO. ARGEN. (or some contraction like it) on the reverse, and I considered it to mean new silver money; however, I came across a demiecu of the same most Christian king, on which the legend was given in full—"MONETA . NOVA . ARGENTINESIS." New money of Strasburg struck 1710, a few years after that beautiful city gave given itself up to France as the comet-thaler of 1681 says:—

"Strasburg die schœne statt;
An Frankreich sich ergeben hat."

MON . NO . TUGI . was to me a great puzzle till I found it to mean of Zug (Tugigensis). If any correspondent of "N. & Q." can inform me where I can find such a list I shall be much obliged.
JOHN DAVIDSON.

[The following works may be consulted for the Latin names of towns: 1. Lexicon Geographicum in quo universi orbis urbes, provinciæ, regna, maria, et flumina recensentur. Illud primum in lucem edidit Philippus Ferrarius Alexandrinus, in Ticinensi Academia Mathematices Professor. Nunc vero Michael Antonius Baudrand, hanc editionem emendavit, illustravit, et dimidia parte auctiorem facit. Paris. 1670, 1677, fol.—2. J. B. Riccioli's Geographiæ et Hydrographiæ reformatæ libri duodecim. Bonon. 1661, fol. et Venet. 1672, fol.—3. Dictionnaire interprète manuel des noms Latins de la Géographie ancienne et moderne [par Espr.-Jos. Chaudon]. Paris, 1777, 8vo. Vide "N. & Q." 1st S. i. 474; v. 235, 305.]

CROMWELL: PALINURUS.—In the Miscellaneous Writings of Lord Macaulay, the following passage occurs:—

"A few days more, and his head is fixed to rot on the pinnacles of that very hall where he sat on a throne in his life, and lay in state after his death."—Conversation between Mr. Cowley and Mr. Milton.

He is here speaking of the Protector. Is it a fact that such occurred to him?

To whom does Pope allude in the following line—

"Even Palinurus nodded at the helm"?
The Dunciad, canto iv. line 614.
E. L.

[Pepys shall reply to our correspondent's first question. "Washing-day. My wife and I by water to Westminster. She to her mother's, and I to Westminster

Hall, where I saw the heads of Cromwell, Bradshaw, and Ireton, set up at the further end of the Hall." (*Diary*, Feb. 5, 1660-1.) *Vide* also " N. & Q." 2nd S. xii. 193.

Palinurus, noticed in the *Dunciad*, may probably be intended for Sir Robert Walpole, and Pope may have been thinking of the following passage in his friend Bolingbroke's first letter to that minister in *The Occasional Writer*, No: I. : — " Should any of those flatterers, who often betray their patrons into a fatal security speak to you much in the same manner as Sleep addresses himself to Palinurus in the *Æneid*, book v. : —

' Palinure, ferunt ipsa æquora classem,
Æquatæ spirant auræ, datur hora quieti :
Pone caput, fessosque oculos furare labori.'

You would answer, as I am persuaded, as this pilot did —

' Mene salis placidi voltum fluctusque quietos
Ignorare jubes ? mene huic confidere monstro ? '

But Palinurus slept, and you know the consequence."]

DISSENTERS' COLLEGES OR PUBLIC SCHOOLS.— Can any reader inform me what pu c places of education (if any) there existed fob Dissenters about the years 1700-20, and more especially belonging to Wales ?   E. J. ROBERTS.

[Bogue and Bennett, in their *History of Dissenters*, ed. 1833, vol. i. pp. 297—342, have given a long "Account of the different Seminaries and Tutors among the Dissenters." The only one in Wales noticed by them was at Llangynwyd in Glamorganshire, of which Samuel Jones, Fellow of Jesus College, Oxford, was the tutor. They also speak of "Mr. Stephen Hughes of Carmarthen ; Mr. Samuel Jones of Brynllywarch ; Hugh Owen of Montgomeryshire ; Marmaduke Matthews of Swansea ; Peregrine Philips of Haverfordwest, and a few others, who, though not regular tutors, occasionally assisted in preparing young men for the service of the sanctuary.]

"NOT PROVEN."—Could you, or one of your correspondents inform me, whether, if a person be tried in a Scotch Criminal Court, and the jury return a verdict of "Not proven," he can be tried again in Scotland for the same offence ?
            CHIRURGUS.
Lucknow.

[Paterson, in his *Compendium of English and Scotch Law, stating their differences*, states that, besides our English Verdicts of Guilty and Not Guilty, there is in the Scotch Law, " an intermediate verdict of ' not proven,' which is substantially a verdict of ' Not Guilty,' and is *res adjudicata*, barring another trial." See also Hume's *Commentaries on the Criminal Law of Scotland*, ii. 439.]

REV. GEORGE SECKER.—I have a beautiful copy of Samuel Clark's Bible, printed 1690, with a portrait of George I. engraved by Vertue from a picture by Sir Godfrey Kneller, bearing this inscription : —" Martha Bankes, widow of Richard Bankes, bequeathed this Bible as a testimony of her respect to the Revd Mr George Secker, 1758." Can any of your readers tell me who Mr. George

Secker was ? what preferments he held ? and whether he were related to the Archbishop of Canterbury, Dr. Thomas Secker ?   E. W.

[Most probably the Rev. George Secker, D.D., Canon residentiary of St. Paul's Cathedral, and nephew of the Archbishop of Canterbury. He died in March, 1768, and his library was sold in the same year.]

PARAMATTA.—Whence does this stuff derive its name ? Surely not from Paramatta, in New South Wales.   A. B.

[The soft woollen fabric called Paramatta is named from the town of New South Wales, which has obtained a high character for its manufactures of cloth, not only in the colony, but also in the mother country.]

Replies.

THE DERIVATION OF THE WORD MISTLETOE.
(3rd S. vii. 76.)

The history of this word is curious, showing on the part of our remote ancestors a greater amount of observation on matters of natural history than is commonly ascribed to them. The original form of the word in A. S. was *mistil-tan;* in Old Norse, *mistil-tein*, meaning literally dung-plant. The Latin name for the plant, *viscum*, is from a root of similar signification. Pliny, lib. xvi. cap. ult., says,—

" Viscum satum nullo modo nascitur, nisi per alvum avium redditum, maxime palumbis et turdi. Hæc est natura, ut nisi maturatum in ventre avium, non proveniat."

Wachter (*Gloss. Ger., sub voc.*) adds, — "Ergo *mistel* est a *mist* stercus, quod ex stercore avium pronascatur, nec aliter pronasci possit." The *missel*-thrush is so called from the idea that it is one of the chief means of this method of propagating the plant, and as bird-lime was formerly made of the glutinous berries, the proverb arose, "*turdus malum sibi cacat*, quia ex baccis visci fit gluten quo turdi capiuntur." By Junius (*Etymol. Angl.*) the word is spelled *missel-den*. Cotgrave has it *missell*, *misseltoe*, *misseldine*. Wachter has mistaken the A. S. corruption, *mistel-ta*, to mean the bird-lime instead of the plant, and thus explains the last syllable, "altera digitum pedis significat, eam scilicet partem, qua avis tenetur a visco." This absurd etymology has been reproduced by Dr. Richardson, for which there is no excuse, as Johnson had pointed out long ago the true derivation to be from *tan*, a twig or branch. Johnson, however, is mistaken in his explanation of *mistel* as originally meaning bird-lime, and thence transferred to the plant. The converse is really the case, the ultimate radical to which the word can be traced being the Sanskrit root मिह्, *mih*, which means, according to Bopp, " Effundere, præsertim mingere," and derivatively " stercus egerere." From this root a large number of words are derived both in the classical and Teutonic families. Johnson does not seem to be aware of the mode of propagation of the plant alluded to above; but his description (too long for quotation here) is well worth reading.

The Latin name of the plant, though bearing the same meaning, is derived from a different root, विष्, *vish*, disjungere, separare, from which *vishtá*, stercus. Virgil (*Æneid*, lib. vi. ver. 205) appears to allude to the mode of dissemination: —

" Quale solet silvis brumali frigore viscum
Fronde virere nova, quod *non sua seminat arbos*,
Et croceo fetu teretes circumdare truncos."

I am not able to say why Shakspeare should attach the epithet *baleful* to the plant, except in connection with the cruel superstitions of the Druids, from whose festivities at the winter solstice the modern associations of the plant may be derived. J. A. P.

Liverpool.

It would take up more room than I think the Editor would like to allow to answer the inquiries of A. A. fully. It is a very curious subject, and one little known. By far the best account of mistletoe, of its growth, its properties, and the superstitions connected with it, that I know, was read at Hereford last spring, before the Woolhope Naturalists' Field Club, and has since been printed, with some additions, in the *Transactions* of that society. It is shown there to have been regarded as a "mirth-provoking plant" only of late years, since the knowledge of it has extended from the counties where it grows into London and the large towns. In Herefordshire it is associated not with Christmas but with the new year. Shakspeare's discernment did not fail him when he called mistletoe a *baleful* plant. It is always most abundant on the oldest and most unhealthy trees in an orchard, and in the oldest orchards; its presence is probably the consequence and not the cause of their unhealthiness; but the coincidence is strongly marked. It is a popular but erroneous belief that the berries are poisonous; and this may be what Shakspeare referred to. Its medicinal properties are, in reality, very slight, and rather beneficial than otherwise.

T. C.

Hay, Hereford.

IS IT A FOSSIL?
(3rd S. vii. 75.)

No! it is simply the head of a real crocodile. But the head of a dragon said to have been strangled by St. Martha's garter, and preserved

with great veneration at Aix, is undoubtedly the fossilised head of an extinct Saurian reptile. The best authenticated dragon story is that of the one said to have been killed by Dieudonné of Gozon, Knight of Rhodes, and afterwards Grand Master of the Order, who died in 1353. Gilles de Chin died in 1137, yet the traditions of Hainault attribute to him the most striking traits of the exploit, said to have been performed two centuries later by Dieudonné. The difficulty of obtaining permission to fight the dragon, the care with which a figure resembling it was previously made to accustom the horse to such a terrific sight, the training and employment of fierce dogs, the precaution of being followed by devoted servants to near the place of combat, — all these circumstances are common to both combats. The head of Dieudonné's dragon was carefully preserved as a trophy at Rhodes till the knights were driven out of the island.

The Turks in turn preserved the head with equal care, so it was actually seen by Thévenot, the traveller, as late as the middle of the seventeenth century; and from his description it appears to have been the head of a hippopotamus. And I believe it really was that animal, which, before the invention of fire-arms, would prove no contemptible antagonist to a knight on horseback confined in heavy armour, and armed only with sword and lance. But how did it get to Rhodes? Dr. A. Smith, in his *Illustrations of the Zoology of South Africa*, gives a remarkable account of the migrations of this animal; and Sir C. Lyell, without any reference to this subject, says: —

"The geologist, therefore, may freely speculate on the time when herds of hippopotami issued from North African rivers, such as the Nile, and swam northwards in summer along the shores of the Mediterranean, or even occasionally visited islands near the shore. Here and there they may have landed to graze or browse, tarrying awhile, and afterwards continuing their course northwards." — *Geological Evidences of the Antiquity of Man*, p. 180.

In that interesting and valuable miscellany, *The Book of Days*, edited by Mr. R. Chambers (vol. i. p. 541), will be found many curious dragon legends both British and foreign; also notices of several continental churches where parts of crocodiles are preserved, and shown as dragons killed by saints. See also *Recherches Historiques sur Gilles Seigneur de Chin et la Dragon*, Mons, 1825; Thevenot, *Relation d'un Voyage fait au Levant*; *Dictionnaire de Moreri*, art. "Gozon" (Dieudonné); Bottin, *Traditions des Dragons Volans*; and an excellent paper by Lenoir, "Du Dragon de Metz," published in the second volume of *Mémoires de l'Académie Celtique*.

St. Romanus, about 720, is said to have delivered the town of Rouen from a monstrous dragon. This deliverance seems to have been raising banks to restrain the floods of the Seine, as quoted in the following strophe from the hymn of Santeuil: —

"Tangit exundans aqua civitatem ;
Voce Romanus jubet efficaci ;
Audiunt fluctus, docilisque cedit
Unda jubenti."

Servin, in his *History of Rouen*, says it is more probable that the fable of the destruction of the dragon is founded on the fact of St. Romanus having destroyed the remnants of idolatry, and levelled with the ground temples of Venus, Jupiter, Apollo, and Mercury which existed in his diocese. Butler, in his *Lives*, says: —

"No traces of this story are found in any life of this saint, nor in any writings before the end of the fourteenth century. The figure of a serpent called Gargouille seems here, as in some other towns, originally to have been meant to represent symbolically the devil overcome by Christ."—Oct. 22.

The Emperor Sigismond founded the Order of "The Vanquished Dragon" in celebration of the anathema denounced by the Council of Constance against the doctrines of John Huss and Jerome of Prague. Louis XIV. had himself painted, wig and all, in the character of St. Michael, spearing the infernal dragon, to commemorate his Revocation of the Edict of Nantes.

A curious instance of the foundation of a dragon story may be told in a few words. Augustus Cæsar, wishing to immortalise his conquest of Egypt, gave as a type for the medals of a colony which he had founded in Gaul, the device of a crocodile tied to a palm tree. The town, in which the colony settled, had for several centuries previous recognised one Nemausus, whose name it bore as its local divinity, and this name could not fail to be on its medals. Notwithstanding that the palm tree and crocodile were not natives of Gaul, the legend arose, the animal was a devastator that poisoned the fountains and Nemausus was the saint who killed it, and thus gained and transmitted his name to the town,* having performed what others had never dared to attempt—*Nemo ausus.*   WILLIAM PINKERTON.

A late learned antiquary and naturalist, Colonel Hamilton Smith, was of opinion that many of the local traditions of encounters between knights and dragons may have had their origin in fact, and that in all cases the so-called dragon was a crocodile. In support of his opinion he showed a drawing made from a mural painting in a church in the island of Rhodes, representing a combat between a knight of St. John and an unmistakeable crocodile; and, as well as I can remember, he asserted that a record of the fact was preserved in the annals of the order, in which, however, the

* The modern Nismes.

monster was styled a dragon. Crocodiles are said to attain to a very great age, and Col. Hamilton Smith believed it possible that some of the many imported into Europe by the Roman emperors, may have escaped and survived to later times.

E. M'C.

SYMBOLIZATION OF COLOURS IN HERALDRY.

(3rd S. vii. 64.)

MR. WEALE'S reply to my note appears to me a satisfactory answer to his claim for De la Colombiere. It explains why, for more than two hundred years, men of letters interested in heraldic pursuits have treated De la Colombiere's pretensions with neglect, and have unanimously attributed to Silvester Petrasancta the merit of having fixed the present method of employing dots and lines.

I do not undertake to explain De la Colombiere's statements, nor to suggest any motives beyond what I suggested in 2nd S. ix. 509. But I must remark that MR. WEALE's suggestion, that Cardinal Barberini may have communicated the invention to Fr. S. Petrasancta, is corroborated by no proof of any kind; and, which is most noticeable, is not alleged by De la Colombiere himself. The *Tesseræ Gentilitiæ*, published in 1638, the year before De la Colombiere's *first* work, contains an immense number of plates. I have it on the table before me now; and, as it is a book of extreme rarity, I may venture to say a few words about it. It is a folio of middle size, and has 678 pages, besides the title-page, and a page covered by the Barberini arms, the Letter of Dedication, Letter to the Reader, Approbations, Index Capitum, Index of Names, Errata, Regestum, and Vocabulary of Terms in Latin and Italian. My copy has a fine print of "Thadæus Barberinus Almæ Urbis Præfectus," &c.; but I am not sure whether it is or is not an insertion. The greater part of the 678 pages shew, each, five shields on separate plates. Some pages shew six, some four, some two, some three. When he comes to treat of helmets and exterior ornaments, he is equally profuse in his illustrations. Some few pages have no engravings. Such a work as this must also have occupied a long time in preparation; and will, therefore, carry back the arrangement of the invention to a date a good deal before 1638. I have no doubt that the work was put in hand immediately after the issue of Fr. S. Petrasancta's first work, the *De Symbolis Heroicis* in 1634. And this work raises the final, and I think insuperable difficulty, to which MR. WEALE has made no reference. De la Colombiere talks, as quoted by MR. WEALE, of the *Tesseræ Gentilitiæ* published in 1638. This is sufficiently astonishing. But why did he omit to mention the *De Symbolis Heroicis*, published in 1634, on pages

313, 314 of which the invention is detailed; and on p. 314, illustrated by a plate of the tinctures, all except *purpure*—which purpure was added in the *Tesseræ* in 1638. De la Colombiere had to shew, not only that a work published in 1638 imitated a work published in 1639—an enterprise of sufficient difficulty—but he had to show that a work published in 1634 was guilty of the same imitation. His entire silence as to the *De Symbolis Heroicis* of 1634 appears to me, as I suppose it has appeared to most other persons conversant with the facts since his time, to remove all ground for further inquiry. No edition of the *Tesseræ Gentilitiæ* appeared after 1638. Fr. S. Petrasancta had no proper opportunity, therefore, of contradicting De la Colombiere. Probably he and his friends thought, as I think now, that no special occasion was to be made for the purpose of contradicting an assertion which would be sure to refute itself.   D. P.

Stuarts Lodge, Malvern Wells.

WINTHROP FAMILY.
(3rd S. vii. 96.)

"The family of the Winthrops came antiently from Northumberland, they afterwards settled in a village not far from Newark, which was called Winthorpe; from thence they came up to London, and owned Marribone [Marylebone] Park; from thence they went to Groton, in Suffolk, where they lived many years; and when the great persecution of good men was in England they came to America." *

John Winthrop, Governor of Massachusetts Bay, 1630, Lord of the Manor of Groton, Suffolk, England; born Jan. 12, 1577-8; died in Boston, U. S., March 26, 1649.

John Winthrop (his eldest son), born Feb. 12, 1605-6; elected Governor of New Haven Colony in 1657, and on the union of Connecticut and New Haven Colonies in 1665, was the first governor under the charter; died April 5, 1676, in Boston, U. S.

Fitz-John Winthrop (his eldest son), Governor of Connecticut; born March 14, 1638-9; died Nov. 27, 1707.

Wait Still (second son), Major-General and Chief Justice of Massachusetts; born Feb. 27, 1641-2; died Sept. 7, 1717.

John Winthrop (his only son), born Aug. 26, 1681; married Ann, daughter of Governor Jos. Dudley, and died Aug. 1, 1747, at Sydenham in England; buried at Beckenham, in same county.

John Still Winthrop (his son) born Jan. 15, 1720; married Jane Borland of Boston, U. S.; and secondly, Elizabeth Shirreff of Annapolis, Nova Scotia, widow of Captain John Hay, of the 40th

* Extract from a paper in Wait Still Winthrop's handwriting, in the possession of the late William H. Winthrop, Esq., of New London, Connecticut, U. S.

regiment; died June 6, 1776, leaving the following sons : —.

Francis Bayard Winthrop, of New York, who died in 1817.

William Winthrop, of New London, Connecticut; died 1827.

Joseph Winthrop of Charleston, South Carolina; died 1828.

Thomas Sindall Winthrop, Lieut.-Governor of Massachusetts; died 1841.

Benjamin Winthrop of New York.

Robert Winthrop, Admiral in the British Navy; died 1832.

There are numerous descendants of the above now living in Boston, New York, and other parts of the United States.

Of the issue of John Winthrop and Ann Dudley, Mary married Joseph Wanton, Governor of Rhode Island; Rebeckah married Gurdon, son of Governor Gurdon, Saltonstall, of Connecticut.

Thomas Sindall Winthrop (son of John Still Winthrop) married Elizabeth Bowdoin, eldest daughter of Sir John Temple, Bart., by which marriage this branch of the Winthrops are of course connected with the families of the Duke of Buckingham and Viscount Palmerston.

Hon. Robert C. Winthrop, *now living* in Boston, U. S., is the representative of this branch. Some years since he was United States senator, and at another time Speaker of the House of Representatives. Admiral Yates, of the British navy, is a first cousin.

H. O'D. will find a complete pedigree of the Winthrops, after their intermarriage with the Dudleys, in the *Sutton-Dudleys of England, and the Dudleys of Massachusetts in New England*, 8vo, 1862.*   Geo. Adlard.

Barnsbury.

THE CHURCH OF ENGLAND AND IRELAND.
(3rd S. vii. 122.)

The Right Hon. Joseph Napier delivered a lecture before the Young Men's Christian Association in Dublin on the evening of the 8th of February, the subject being "The Irish Difficulty." In the course of his address, the learned gentleman partially answered a question of mine in "N. & Q." on the application of the term used in our title. His words, as reported, were to this effect : —

"The Protestants of Ireland had been assured that they would occupy under the Union an improved position. The State, the Church, and the Legislature of Ireland were to be united with those of England. It was an international treaty in its very nature permanent, because on each side there was the giving up of the separate and independent existence of a State, a Legislature, and a

* One volume, 8vo, J. Russell Smith, Soho Square.

national Church. The weaker party could only be effectually secured by the peculiar wording of the treaty. It professed to be based upon the union of the two national Churches as the fundamental article of the treaty. They had long before been one in doctrine, discipline, and ceremony, with the same relation to the mixed monarchy and settled Constitution of England. In the State documents for centuries before they had been described occasionally as 'The Church of England and Ireland.' In the Injunctions of Edward VI., in the English Articles of 1552, and in the Injunctions of Queen Elizabeth, the collective title is used. The first of the Irish Canons of 1634—said to have been drawn up under the supervision of Strafford—is entitled:—' Of the agreement of the Church of England and Ireland, in the profession of the same Christian religion;' also in the 31st Canon. The two Churches constituted one episcopal Church, but at the time of the Union they were distinct national Churches. The effect of the Act of Union was to incorporate them into one undivided United Church of England and Ireland."

Before the Union at the beginning of the nineteenth century, it is interesting to know that the Churches of England and Ireland were commonly designated as one. Allow me now to ask, were the reformed Churches so designated under Henry VIII.? And was the same title in use at any period since the Conquest of Ireland in application to the Roman Catholic Church of Ireland, or the Church of the pale? It is requested that the answer be as specific as possible.

The Rev. R. Staveley, private Chaplain to the Bishop of Meath, has obligingly communicated the following note in illustration of the identity of the Churches of England and Ireland in earlier days than the Act of Union:—

" In Bishop Mant's *History of the Irish Church*, vol. ii. p. 338, there is an interesting letter (1719) of Archbishop King's to the Archbishop of Canterbury on the contract of conformity between the Churches of England and Ireland.

" I believe also that Irish Bishops (perhaps expelled by the Celtic savages) were frequently employed as suffragans in English dioceses in pre-Reformation days."

O. T. D.

The following notes may serve to reply to the query of O. T. D., "The Church of England and Ireland," namely, "Where is that name first found in print, and when was it first used by authority?"

In the Acts of Parliament, as far back as Edward IV. (which is the first collection I have seen), the preamble reads: "Edward, by the Grace of God, King of England and of France, and Lord of Ireland." Richard III. (1483) the same. First Parliament and the last of Henry VII. (1485), the same. Henry VIII. (1509), the same; but in 1531, the title reads: "King of England and of France, Defender of the Faith, and Lord of Ireland." In the statutes made at Westminster, 1540, the king is styled: "Defender of the Faith, Lord of Ireland; and in Earth, under Christ, supreme Head of the Church of England," but in 1541, the heading is: "Henry the Eighth, by the Grace

of God, King of England, France, and Ireland, Defender of the Faith, and of the Church of England, and also of Ireland, in earth supreme head."[*] The Irish Act of 33 Henry (1542): "Henrici Octavi, Dei gratiâ Angliæ, Franciæ, et Hiberniæ Regis, fidei defensoris, ac in terrâ ecclesiæ Anglicaū et Hiberū supremi capitis." Edward VI., same title, 1547; Mary the same, 1553; but in 1554, the title reads, "Lord and Lady Philip and Mary, by the Grace of God King and Queen of England, France, Naples, Jerusalem, and Ireland; Defenders of the Faith; Princes of Spain and Sicilie, Archduke of Austria, &c., Dukes of Milaine, &c., Counties of Hapsburg, &c." Elizabeth, 1558, the title simply is, " by the Grace of God of England, France, and Ireland, Queen, Defender of the Faith, &c." This is continued (except in the time of Cromwell) to William and Mary.[†] There may be some slight alteration in the spelling or wording, but it is not of any consequence. I have seen in print, in the course of compiling a *Bibliotheca Hibernica*, some works, published about the beginning of the seventeenth century, the term "Church of England and Ireland." If O. T. D. wishes, I will make a note of it when next I meet it, and let him know the title of the work and where it is to be found.

JOHN POWER.

3, Grove Terrace, St. John's Wood, N.W.

JACOBITE SONG.

(3rd S. vii. 54, 121.)

The following version of "The Tartan Plaidie" has been kindly sent to me by a correspondent in Edinburgh, who says it is the only one known or sung in that part of Scotland, and is copied word for word as usually sung:—

CHARLIE STUART.

" When Charlie first came frae the North,
   The manly looks o' our Hieland laddie,
Made every true Scottish heart to warm,
   When they view'd the looks of the Hieland laddie.
     Chorus. Love farewell, friends farewell,
         To guard my King, I'll bid all farewell.

" When King George he heard o' this
   (He had gone north to heir his daddy),
He sent Sir John Cope
   To catch the lad wi' the Tartan Plaidie.

" When they came to Inverleith,
   The English fleet was lying ready :
Five hundred Pounds it's I will gie
   If you catch the lad wi' his Tartan Plaidie.

* See *Irish Statutes* (vol. i. p. 175, folio). Note, the Preamble to the Acts of 25 Hen. VIII. (D. p. 63) only says, "Henrici Octavi vices. quinto," etc.
† The Preamble to the Acts of William and Mary (an. 1694) states, "England, Scotland, France, and Ireland;" but at the time of the Union in 1800, it was changed to "The United Kingdom of Great Britain and Ireland."

" Sir Johnny Cope addressed his men,
  Saying, If that you'll be stern and steady,
Five hundred pounds again I'll gie,
  If you catch me the lad wi' his Tartan Plaidie.

" Our noble prince addressed his men,
  Saying, If you'll be stern and steady,
I'll set you down in a kingdom free,
  If you fight with me to keep my Plaidie.

" The Duke o' Perth stood on his right,
  Brave Montrose and brave Glengarry,
From the Isle of Sky the brave Lochiel,
  M'Larens bold, and brave M'Cready.

" Painted rooms, an' feather beds,
  Could hardly please a German lairdie ;
But a better prince than ever he was,
  Lay among the heather in his Tartan Plaidie."
                        JAMES GIBSON.

23, Spring Gardens, Bradford.

BARLEY.

(3rd S. v. 358; vi. 481; vii. 84.)

This query reminds me of a mystic jingle used by Lincolnshire boys when claiming any treasure-trove, whether a bird's nest or otherwise : —

  "All my awn (own) !
  Barley-corn !
  Bar ha'avs (halves) and quarters ! "

The second line is exquisitely obscure, still there seems a family likeness to the Lancashire instance given by T. T. W. in your January part (p. 84), so far as the right to a " find " is concerned. Whether the other sense of " barley ;" viz. a prohibitive or cautionary one, may be connected with the verb " bar," I merely throw out as a hint. I think that monosyllable is still in use in boys' games to stop any irregularity, as " bar that ! " " bar striking ! " &c. Among Lincolnshire phrases one may hear, " It's a bargains on it ! " or " Oh, a bargains on (or of) him ! " when one would depreciate a man or a thing.

In a little threepenny tract, *Notes on Lincoln-shire Words*, in form of a glossary (Lincoln, Brookes), " bargains " in this phrase is explained by the old negative " bar ; " viz. *no gains*, no profit, no good of him or it. The late Rev. Jas. Adcock, Mr. Halli-well's chief Lincolnshire correspondent, once gave this to the writer. '(N.B. I have just seen — not without a certain indignation — *bar* and *barring*, in the sense of *excepting* [a perfectly legitimate sense] inserted in the *Slang Dictionary*.)

Apropos of Lincolnshire words, which have re-ceived very little attention generally, a *local* classi-fication of the several dialects is very desirable, by which some estimate of the local immigrations at the era of the sea kings might perhaps be approached. A walk of a few hours introduces a new dialect. Rambling on the wolds, not far from Horncastle, I asked a shepherd boy the way to a certain farm-house which I was bound for. In showing me its

direction, he added—" It's a pla'as uncommon hard to *fin*." Now, nearer to Lincoln, *foind*, with a splendidly full and broad enunciation, would have been the word. The Danes (per Mr. Worsaae) claim our country as their own. On the coast near Wainfleet is the popular bathing village, *Skegness* ; the *Notes* just mentioned connect it with some Baltic prototype, *Skaegnaes* ; but query if Danish, as I have been assured that the *k* is soft in Denmark, and that it would have come down to us as *Shagness*. The word would imply a ragged shore, a rough cape, which scarcely applies to the flat Lincolnshire beaches.

I am glad to see on p. 31 of your January part a " Lincolnshire Dialogue " by C. P. T., but in a county some eighty miles from north to south, the locality should have been given. *Sthrange*, as the pronunciation of strange, is, I confess, quite strange to me ; *taving* (restless) is probably south Lin-colnshire. It is given in Thompson's *Boston*, and Skinner (*temp.* Chas. II.) has " to tave, *furere*," as a Lincolnshire word. He was a Lincoln physi-cian. *Wetchard* must be the common corruption of *wet-shod*, and only applicable to *wet feet*. C. P. T. mentions in a note (as if it were the *bona fide* name) " *Marquery*, a vegetable peculiar to Lincolnshire, resembling spinnach." I presume the same as the mercury of the gardeners. I hope the writer will pursue the subject, but not omit to tell the district he illustrates.

There are some curious instances in the above-quoted *Notes* of words lost since Skinner's time from our local vocabulary. A tom-cat was then a *karl-cat*, meaning no scandal on the joyous Stuart on the throne, but simply thus (according to Skinner) — " Lincoln. usitatissima pro feli mare, ab A.-S. karl, *i. e.* masculus." *Scathe*, to hurt ; *snithe-wind*, a cutting wind ; *beesen*, blind, with many more, which have perhaps only retreated northward since those days, have likewise disappeared from among us. In the fourteenth century old parish docu-ments show that *gar*, *speer*, and other Scotticisms, as they are now considered, were current in the district.   LINDENSIS.

INVOICE OF CARGO, 1803: A BUSINESS COM-MUNICATION (3rd S. vii. 72.)—The document of which you insert a copy is very interesting, as illustrating the mode in which a former gene-ration of merchants conducted the slave trade. It is, however, *not* an invoice, but a bill of lading. An invoice is a document stating the description and quality in detail of certain goods or live stock which may be sold by one party to another, specifying the price and charges of transmission, if any. A bill of lading is a receipt given by the master or purser of a vessel for certain goods or live stock shipped on board such vessel, contracting to convey the same from one port to another in consideration of certain freight money: and the document above referred to is of the latter class. If your correspondent could furnish you with a copy of the invoice, it would be a curiosity, as showing the price then paid for human beings in Africa, and the charges incurred in shipping them abroad. The fact that the payment was probably made in beads, hatchets, guns, ammunition, and other goods, instead of in money, would add to the interest.　　　　　　　　　　ARTHUR SHUTE.

1, Romford Place, Liverpool.

TITHE BARNS (3rd S. vii. 137.)—If MR. STUART wants anecdotes about the old state of things before the Tithe Commutation Act, I doubt whether many will be forthcoming. But the general condition that then prevailed is well known, and was a main ground for the alteration of the law. The clergy, from time immemorial, were entitled literally to one-tenth of *certain* produce; as Sydney Smith said of the Archdeacon of Newfoundland, that he "sat bobbing for cod, and pocketing every tenth fish." Many things were in the way of the view of those who maintained the absolute divine right of the church to the full and exact tithe; as the exemption from various causes, both of certain lands and of certain other properties, from tithe. A common subject of litigation was the definition of the latter kind; but the squabbles which MR. STUART refers to, I imagine, were as to the actual amount of corn, &c. (brought into this "Tithe Barn") from year to year. The clergy's right was to the thing itself as it stood on the ground. Such a state of things was more fitted for times of primitive simplicity than for those of cash and commerce; and in many cases the clergy, who otherwise had simply to get the tithe as they could for themselves, had voluntarily agreed with the parish for a fixed money commutation: a sure sign that the times were ripe for a change in the law. The present law, which fixes the tithe on a settled principle, and determines the amount by an easily-ascertained rule, has done away with the old grounds of quarrel, and very little, if at all, diminished the real incomes of the clergy. The rent charge is often paid by the owner, not by the occupier, of the land.　　　　　　　LYTTELTON.

Hagley, Stourbridge.

W[ILLIAM] ALEXANDER (3rd S. vi. 434), born in Philadelphia, Dec. 5, 1808, was living in 1859, and I believe is so still. He entered the Sophomore Class of the University of Pennsylvania, 1828; B.A. 1831. He is, or was, a schoolmaster. The title of his book inquired for, is —.

"The Poetical Works of William Alexander, including his Christiad, Dramas [*not* Christian Dramas], and Minor Poems; with Dissertations on Poetry, and a Sketch of his Life." Philadelphia, 1847. 8vo.

A most stupid book. It contains a portrait of the author.　　　　　　　　　　　　　　ST. T.

MUM (3rd S. vi. 434, 503; vii. 41, 101.) — It may be worth recording that the word *mum* is at least as old as the beginning of the sixteenth century. In the treatise, *De Generibus Ebriosorum et Ebrietate Vitanda*, written A.D. 1515, occurs a chapter on the various kinds of beer then in use in Germany. Among a host of other names occurs that of "*Mommom, sive Mommum Brunsvigen*." The catalogue which follows shows that even the names of fancy drinks are not new under the sun; and that the "Eye-openers" and "Cocktails" of the Yankee bars had their prototypes in the mediæval tap-rooms. I select a few of the most presentable: Cow's-tail, Calves-neck, Buffalo, Slip-slop, Stamp-in-the-ashes, Knock'em-down, Crowing-cock, Wild-oats, Red-head, Raise-head, Swell-nose, and Gnat's-mustard. These and other designations were so delectable in the ears of the beer-bibbers that, whenever they were mentioned, the Sirens seemed to be singing and thirst reigned around.　　　　　　　　JOHN ELIOT HODGKIN.

HEREFORDSHIRE QUERIES: TUMP AND TOFT (3rd S. vii. 101.)—Agreeing with your correspondent as to τύμβος, *tumulus, twmp*, &c., "descending from the same ancestor," I will add that I have frequently met with the name *tump* in Gloucestershire, and there on my own estate, in places where a tumulus or round mound exists, which *cannot* by possibility *have had a building on it*.

But not so with respect to *toft*. There is a manor of that name adjacent to Knutsford, in Cheshire, with a noble mansion of the Leycesters (of Toft) upon it.

Sir P. Leycester (of Tabley) in noticing this place in his *Historical Antiquities* (edit. 1673, p. 375) makes this remark: —

"The word *toft* signifies a parcel of land *wherein a house hath stood* (Camden's *Remains*, p. 120), and in that sense it was taken by the judges and expounded (2 & 3 Philip and Mary), Plowden's *Commentaries*, Hill *versus* Graunge, p. 170."

LANCASTRIENSIS.

THE QUAKER'S DISEASE (2nd S. x. 305; xi. 196.) Seed cast into the kindly soil of "N. & Q." may be long buried without showing any signs of vitality, but it seldom fails in the end to reward the sower with some measure of increase. The perusal of Mr. John Hill Burton's interesting work, *The Book-hunter*, enables me to furnish your correspondent, THE AUTHOR OF "TWENTY YEARS IN THE CHURCH," with a quotation, which, although entirely at odds with the one he gives from the *Life of Lord Jeffrey*, is nevertheless, and perhaps I may say on that account, not unworthy of his attention. In a note, p. 8, our author remarks:—

"It has often been observed that it is among the Society of Friends, who keep so tight a rein on the passions and propensities, that these make the most terrible work when they break loose. De Quincey, in one of his essays on his contemporaries, giving a sketch of a man of great genius and high scholarship, whose life was early clouded by insanity, gives some curious statements about the effects of the system of rigid restraint exercised by the Society of Friends, which I am not prepared either to support or contradict. After describing the system of restraint itself, he says: 'This is known, but it is not equally known, that this unnatural restraint falling into collision with two forces at once—the force of passion and of youth—not unfrequently records its own injurious tendencies, and publishes the rebellious movements of nature by distinct and anomalous diseases. And further, I have been assured upon most excellent authority, that these diseases—strange and elaborate affections of the nervous system—are found *exclusively* among the young men and women of the Quaker Society; that they are known and understood exclusively amongst physicians who have practised in great towns having a large Quaker population, such as Birmingham; that they assume a new type and a more inveterate character in the second or third generation, to whom this fatal inheritance is often transmitted; and, finally, that if this class of nervous derangements does not increase so much as to attract public attention, it is simply because the community itself—the Quaker body—does not increase, but on the contrary is rather on the wane.' "

In 1860 I called the attention of a medical man, residing in one of the strongholds of Quakerism, to the assertion of Lord Jeffrey, but he would not allow that those born in the drab were more liable to "die of a sort of atrophy" before the age of fifty than were any of their more lively fellow-creatures. I have not yet had the advantage of his opinion concerning the neurotic affection. Perhaps DR. CAPPER of Liverpool may be induced to favour us with another communication.

ST. SWITHIN.

MAGNA CHARTA (3rd S. vi. 533.)—Finding that no one has yet sent a reply to this query, which somewhat surprises me, I give the authority, and fuller quotations. On May 17, 1628, during the debate on the Petition of Right, Sir Edward Coke said:—

"Sovereign Power is no parliamentary word. In my opinion it weakens *Magna Charta* and all our Statutes: for they are absolute, without any saving of sovereign power; and, shall we now add it, we shall weaken the foundation of Law, and then the building must needs fall. Take we heed what we yield unto. *Magna Charta* is such a fellow that he will have no sovereign. If we grant this, by implication we give a sovereign power above all these laws. We must not admit of it; and to qualify it is impossible. Let us hold our privileges according to the law."—See I. Rushworth, 568.

The whole speech is to the same effect. Sir Edward Coke had been Lord Chief Justice of England, Speaker of the House of Commons, &c.

TOULMIN SMITH.

ARMS OF A CONQUERED KNIGHT (3rd S. vii. 46.) MR. DYMOND appears to have committed an inadvertence (3rd S. vi. 540) in identifying MR. RYE with the passage that he extracted from Burke's *Extinct Peerage* (3rd S. vi. 483). It must, however, be observed that the passage so extracted by

MR. RYE has not added materially to our knowledge. For the Robert Carey mentioned by Burke is no other than *Robert Cary*, respecting whom the question originally arose. And if MR. RYE wishes for some authority for the supposition that the statement contained in the extract is erroneous, he will find it in the passage quoted from CURIOSUS in a former communication of mine (3rd S. vi. 313). This communication MR. DYMOND perhaps thought it unnecessary to cite, as it had already been referred to by MR. RYE (3rd S. vi. 483).

R. J. F. has given an instance of the arms of a knight, taken prisoner in war, being conferred on his captor (3rd S. vi. 401). I am not sure that this is quite a case in point. Still it appears to have some bearing upon it; and I therefore beg to add another case of the same kind that I have lighted upon in Clark's *Introduction to Heraldry* (1818) p. 58:—

"No. 33. Argent, on a bend gules, between three pellets, as many swans proper—rewarded with a canton sinister azure, thereupon a demi-ram mounting argent, armed or, between two fleurs-de-lis of the last; over all, a baton dexterwise, as the second in the canton. This is the arms of *Sir John Clarke*.

"*Note.* The canton was the arms of the *Duke of Longueville*, and was given as a reward to *Sir John Clarke* for his taking in lawful war *Lewis de Orleans, Duke of Longueville, and Marquis of Rotueline* (Rothelin), *prisoner* at the battle of Bomy, near Terovane, August 16, anno Hen. VIII. 5."

The Duke of Longueville, mentioned in the foregoing extract, was the first husband of Mary of Lorrain, who was afterwards married to James V., King of Scotland. The battle at which he was taken prisoner is sometimes called the battle of Guinegate, but more commonly the battle of Spurs. In his enumeration of the prisoners taken on that occasion, Dr. Lingard speaks of the Duke of Longueville and the Marquis of Rotelin, as two separate and distinct persons. MELETES.

Morgan le Yonge, of the family of the Yonges of Bryn Yorcin, co. Flint, had lands granted him in the reign of Richard II., for having taken prisoner a Spanish grandee of great note, and was permitted to bear his arms, "Gules, a toison, or," in a canton on his own shield. (*Archæologia Cambrensis,* i. 44.) MORRIS C. JONES. Liverpool.

MY (3rd S. vi. 435.)—Is MR. KEIGHTLEY correct in stating broadly that, in common conversation, *my* is pronounced so as to rhyme with *lie, fly?* It undoubtedly is so pronounced where it is emphatic, as in—"That is *my* hat, don't you run away with it." It is also pronounced somewhat in the same manner, though not so strongly, when it begins a sentence, as in—"My hat wants brushing." But when it comes in the middle of a sentence, and is not emphatic, the sound of the *y*, though not entirely lost, is much less clearly marked. Thus, in—"He knocked me down, and smashed my hat:" here the *y* in *my* appears to me to have, as nearly as possible, the same sound as it has in the last syllable of *gladly*.

The fault that I have heard attributed to the school of the Kembles was, that, in such a sentence as the last, they would pronounce the *my* in "smashed my hat" exactly in the same manner as they did the *me* in "knocked me down;" and that they even went so far as to adopt the same pronunciation where the *my* stood at the beginning of a sentence.   MELETES.

CUDDY: MAN, BIRD, AND BEAST (3rd S. vii. 53.) It appears that in different parts of England the abbreviation of the commonest Christian name has been applied to the ass by way of endearment or familiarity. Thus your correspondent, CUTHBERT BEDE (though certainly no one would be inclined in any other respect to write down that gentleman an ass), claims the useful animal as a namesake under the style of "Cuddy," an abbreviation of Cuthbert; and no doubt many a southern reader of *Old Mortality* misses the latent wit in the name Cuddie Headrigg. MR. BEDE also speaks of asses being called "Edward," or "Neddy," in the midland and southern counties. I have always heard that in the eastern counties they were called "Dickies," and if it be so, they certainly bear this abbreviation, as well as that of Cuthbert, in common with men and *Dicky*-birds. Whether Richard is a commoner name in the eastern than in other counties in England (and if so, why?), I must leave it to those learned in name-systems to determine. The abbreviation Jack (in jack-ass) is, I fancy, common throughout England, and is not a term of endearment but of distinction of sex, as in jack-hare, jack-snipe, and the proverb that tells us "Every Jack has his Jill."

I would ask with MR. CUTHBERT BEDE, what is there so distasteful in the word "ass" (applied to an animal) as to make so many euphemisms necessary, as Donkey, Moke, Jerusalem pony, Cuddy, Neddy, and Dicky, and I dare say many others?   C. A. L.

"THE IRISH TUTOR" AND TYRONE POWER (3rd S. vii. 99.)—In 1821 Mr. Power was playing heavy melo-dramatic business at the Olympic, in such characters, for instance, as Baron D'Herstal, in the *Solitaire*, or the *Recluse of the Alps*. I think he came to the Olympic from Astley's. At the former theatre he played, in 1822, Timothy in *Life in London*, but he subsequently played *Jerry*. In 1824, I remember, when a boy, seeing at the Variétés, in Paris, *Les Deux Precepteurs, ou Asinus Asinum fricat*. I soon after saw the *Irish Tutor* at Covent Garden, and recognised it as a translation of the French vaudeville. Both in London and Paris the translator was well known—Lord

Glengall. MR. HUSK is not quite correct in stating that *Dr. O'Toole* fixes clever O'Connor as a player of Irish parts. Long before that character fell to him I had seen him play Irish parts, with great effect. His Irish haymaker in *Rosina* was a rich and masterly "bit," that used to rejoice the audiences of the old "Little Theatre in the Haymarket."   J. DORAN.

LORD WILLOUGHBY (3rd S. vii. 96.)—The date assigned to the marriage of Lord Willoughby by the authority referred to is a mere misprint. Mary, heiress of Gwydyr, was born at Gwydyr on the Feast of All Saints, Nov. 2, and baptized in the church of Llanrwst, Nov. 7, 1661. She was the only child of Sir Richard Wynn, fourth Bart. of Gwydyr, who was buried at Llanrwst, Nov. 4, 1674, by Sarah his wife, who died June 16, and was buried at Llanrwst June 23, 1671, dau. of Sir Thomas Middleton, Bart., of Chirk Castle. The heiress of Gwydyr married, July 30, 1678, Robert Bertie, thirteenth Lord Willoughby de Eresby, who succeeded on the death of his father, May 8, 1701, as fourth Earl of Lindsey, was created Marquess of Lindsey 1706, and Duke of Ancaster and Kesteven, 1715. The Duke died July 26, 1723. The extract cited from Mr. Dineley's work describes the Lord Willoughby who married the heiress of Gwydyr as Lord Willoughby of *Parham*. This is obviously an error attributable to inadvertent substitution of one designation for another. The Lords Willoughby of Parham were a junior branch of the Lords Willoughby de Eresby, derived from Sir William Willoughby, created Lord Willoughby of Parham by letters patent, dated Feb. 16, 1547, son of Sir Christopher Willoughby, Knight, younger brother of William, ninth Baron Willoughby de Eresby.

PHILIPPA SWINNERTON HUGHES.

Mr. Dineley is incorrect in giving Lord Willoughby of Parham as the husband of Mary Wynn of Gwydyr: "perhaps the two baronies of Willoughby may have confused the Duke of Beaufort's chronicler," as SIR THOMAS WINNINGTON suggests. Sir Bernard Burke is also incorrect with regard to the date of her marriage. Her husband was Robert (Bertie) eldest son of Robert, third Earl of Lindsey. He was called up by writ to the House of Peers as Lord Willoughby of Eresby, during his father's lifetime, April 27, 1690. He succeeded as fourth Earl of Lindsey, 1701; was created Marquess of Lindsey Dec. 24, 1706, and Duke of Ancaster and Kesteven July 20, 1715. His marriage with Mary, dau. of Sir Richard Wynn, of Gwydyr, co. Carnarvon, took place July 30, 1678, which lady left two sons and three daughters, and died Sept. 20, 1689. (See Collins's *Peerage*.)   CROWDOWN.

FLEMISH STAINED GLASS IN ENGLAND (3rd S. vi. 472, 541.)—I believe the glass in Rugby

School chapel was brought from Flanders; but the character of several of the windows has been entirely changed (I might say destroyed) during the recent alterations. A very poor woodcut of the east window forms the frontispiece to the *Book of Rugby School.*   A ẟ.

THE QUEEN'S MARIES (3rd S. vii. 69.)—W. H. C. has in the foot-note confounded two incidents connected with the history of Mary, Queen of Scots, which are quite distinct from each other; and between the occurrence of which there was a long interval.

When the queen at a very early age was sent to France, she was accompanied by four little ladies (all about her own time of life), daughters of noblemen, and all having the Christian name of "Mary." I have seen given the whole four sir-names (where I cannot remember), but one of them I am certain was Fleming; and very likely Livingstone was that of another.

The second incident took place when the queen lived at Holyrood Palace, during her marriage with Darnley. She had then *four* female attend-ants, all named Mary. One of whom was a French girl, who was executed in Edinburgh for child-murder; and it is to this the lines of the old ballad (quoted, in part, by your correspondent) apply—not to the little Maries of the queen's childhood. This appears clearly, from the only three verses of the ballad which are preserved; and which, as they have a kind of wild pathos, and may probably be new to many of your readers, I use the freedom to give in full :—

" When she came to the Netherbow Port,
    She laughed loud laughters three ;
But when she came to the gallows' foot,
    The tear stood in her e'e.

" O ye mariners, mariners,
    That sail upon the sea,
Let not my father or mother to wit,
    The death that I'm to dee.

" Last nicht the Queen had four Maries,
    The nicht shall hae but three ;
There was Mary Seaton and Mary Beaton,
    And Mary Carmichael and me."
                                        G.
Edinburgh.

ROMNEY'S PORTRAITS OF WESLEY AND MRS. TIGHE (3rd S. vii. 103.) — MR. BURTON gives an interesting note on Romney's portrait of Wesley. It will cause one of your correspondents, at all events, to make some endeavour to see it when next in Ireland. Every portrait by that prince of English portrait painters is precious indeed, and Wesley was a fine subject for an artist.

MR. BURTON ends his note with a reference to Mrs. Tighe, adding, that "all we know of the *personnel* of the lady of that name—the authoress of *Psyche,* first published, I think, in 1805—comes to us from the picture for which she sat also to Romney."

Looking to my quarto edition of *Psyche* (Lon-don, 1811), I find an exquisitely beautiful portrait of its "authoress," as I suppose here referred to. The readers of "N. & Q." are encouraged to look at it, if they can. It is in small medallion form, with costume of the utmost simplicity—scarcely more than that which would be worn by a peasant girl. It is quite in the Romney style; but the inscription is as follows, wanting farther explana-tion to those unacquainted with the history of the portrait : " Comerford, after Romney, *pinxit; Caroline Watson, Engraver to her Majesty, sculpsit.*"   FRANCIS TRENCH.
Islip Rectory.

Romney's portrait of Wesley became the pro-perty of the late Mr. Butterworth, M.P., some thirty years ago; and it may be presumed, is in the possession of the family.

About 1817 it was copied, with the permission of the excellent lady for whom Romney painted the portrait—the late Mrs. Tighe of Rossana—for the Rev. Mr. Roberts of Bristol; and the copy was done by the late Mrs. John Taylor, the ta-lented daughter of Mr. Spilsbury, who, about 1789, engraved the mezzotinto alluded to.

As names have been introduced—although, as MR. BURTON observes, parenthetically—I think it right to correct a little mistake : — The authoress of *Psyche* was not Mrs. Tighe of Rossana, but her daughter-in-law Mrs. Henry Tighe. All are now dead. *Psyche,* alas ! died young —

    " Ere yet her form had lost its vernal bloom "—

and before she could know the wide-spread fame her poem attained.   A. W. DAVIS, M.D.
Toppington Vicarage, Shrewsbury.

HORKEY.—In "N. & Q.," 1st S. i. 263, the de-rivation of this word was asked by LORD BRAY-BROOKE; and in 1st S. i. 457 various solutions, all in my opinion very unsatisfactory, were offered. I beg to suggest one that has my preference, and which, I think, is calculated to command more general assent. I mean the Greek word ὄργια (Latin, *orgia*), " orgies "; which, though originally applied to the feasts of Bacchus, was afterwards used to denote any revel or feast.
                                        THOS. COWARD, M.A.
Cambridge.

KNIGHTS BACHELORS (3rd S. vii. 76.)—Sir Daniel Williams is unquestionably dead. The precise date of his decease I do not recollect, but it must be forty or fifty years ago. It can, no doubt, be ascertained by application to the clerk of the peace for Middlesex.

It is a mistake to call Sir Daniel chief of the *Lambeth* Court. That court had no existence in his day, not having been established in fact until the reconstruction of the police districts, about twenty-five years ago. The court over which he presided was that of Lambeth Street, White-chapel. Since Sir Daniel, the following magis-trates have occupied that bench :

Matthew Wyatt, deceased.
John Hardwick, retired.
Thomas Walker, deceased.
Hon. G. C. Norton, now at Lambeth.
Thomas Henry, now at Bow Street.

The court of Lambeth Street was abolished at the time referred to, and the business divided be-tween Worship Street and the Thames.

R. S. Q.

In answer to some of the inquiries of L. H., I am able to state that —

Sir Daniel Williams died at Stamford Hill on the 16th August, 1831, aged seventy-nine, *Gentle-man's Magazine* of that month, p. 187.

Sir Alexander Wilson, M.D., of Bath and of Stroat, near Gloucester, died May 10, 1813, as is stated in the *Gentleman's Magazine* for Feb. 1848, p. 219; when his widow was recently de-ceased at Cheltenham. J. G. N.

Lᴏᴘᴇ ᴅᴇ Vᴇɢᴀ (3ʳᵈ S. vii. 114.)—E. F. will find Lope de Vega's *Jerusalem Conquistada* and *La Dragonetta* in Mr. Grenville's library. Y. S.

Mʀ. Gᴏᴏᴅᴡʏɴ, ᴛʜᴇ Mᴀᴛʜᴇᴍᴀᴛɪᴄɪᴀɴ (3ʳᵈ S. vii. 114.)—Mr. Goodwyn, the mathematician, was the head of the firm of Goodwyn & Co., the great brewers, whose brewery was near the Tower. The firm is now changed, if the brewery still exists. I think the mathematician's Christian name was Henry. I believe, but am not certain, that papers by him will be found in the *Philosophical Trans-actions*. He died very early in the present century. And now I will treat you with a reminiscence of mine. I was at Burney's school at Greenwich ; and well I remember, quite at the end of last cen-tury or the beginning of this, the above-named Mr. Goodwyn coming with his son into the play-ground at Greenwich to see his three grandsons : Henry, Thomas Wyldman, and Charles Goodwyn, and his great-grandson Sam. Enderby. And for fun, the old gentleman would play a game at marbles. In my mind's eye, I now see the four generations playing together, and the old gentle-man's cocked hat "lives in my memory still." Sam. Enderby was older than his uncle Charles Goodwyn. Some forty years ago, the Burney Club partook of a "stoke-hole" dinner at the brewery as guests of Thomas Wyldman Goodwyn. I think Mr. Goodwyn lived on Maize Hill, Greenwich, near Blackheath.* H. F.

Aʀᴜɴᴅᴇʟʟ ᴏғ Lᴀɴʜᴇʀɴᴇ (3ʳᵈ S. vi. 248, 523.) A short time since I constructed a genealogy of

[* Henry Goodwyn, Esq., resided at Bastile-house, Maize-hill, which was built by Sir John Vanbrugh. Mr. Good-wyn died on Sept. 27, 1824, aged seventy-nine, and his eldest son, H. R. Goodwyn on Jan. 2, 1815, aged thirty-one.—Eᴅ.]

the Arundell family from Burke, Lysons, Hals, Tonkin, and other authorities, from which I find that Sir Thomas, who married Catherine, dau. of Sir John Dynham, was succeeded by his son, Sir John (brother of Humphrey, beheaded 1549), who married, 1st, Lady Eleanor Grey, dau. of Thomas Marquis of Dorset ; and, 2nd, Jane, dau. of Sir Thomas Granville. He was succeeded by his son, Sir John, who, *temp.* Mary (1553-8), m. Anne, dau. of Sir Henry Gerningham. Sir John was sheriff of Cornwall, 1555. His son, or grandson, John, m., says Hals, Chydiock, which I think is a mistake, as Burke says the father of the above Sir Thomas, m. the heiress of Chydiocke. The son of John, Sir John, m. 1st, Elizabeth Roper, dau. of Lord Teynham ; 2nd, Ann, daughter of John Arundell, of Trerice, and died at an advanced age in 1701, having settled his estates on Richard Billing, his grandson, on condition that he took the name of Arundell. Now the great break in the genealogy is between Sir John, who m. the dau. of Sir H. Gerningham in the reign of Mary, and the Sir John who m. the dau. of Lord Teynham, and died in 1701. Where is the Sir John who m. Anne, widow of Lord Stourton, to be placed ?

Tʀᴇᴛᴀɴᴇ.

Tʀᴜғғʟᴇs (3ʳᵈ S. vi. 209.) — Truffles are found in several parts of the South Downs. The only ones I have eaten in Sussex were grown at Lord Gage's, at Firle Place. His lordship informed me that he had never found them except under the shade of beech trees in his park. They are also found in Stanmer Park, and in the beech woods of West Sussex. They are usually hunted by dogs, which so much affect this delicacy that they can only be bribed into giving it up to the hunter by a bit of raw meat. In Cartwright's *History of the Rape of Bramber*, 1830, p. 73, is the following statement : —

"The beech-woods in this parish (Patching) are very productive of the truffle (*Lycoperdon tuber*). About forty years ago (circ. 1790) Wm. Leach came from the West Indies with some dogs accustomed to hunt for truffles, and proceeding along the coast from the Land's End to the mouth of the Thames, determined to fix on the spot where he found them most abundant. He took four years to try the experiment, and at length settled in this parish, where he carried on the business of truffle-hunter till his death."

Pigs are occasionally used for truffle-hunting.

Mᴀʀᴋ Aɴᴛᴏɴʏ Lᴏᴡᴇʀ.

Lewes.

Yᴇᴡ Tʀᴇᴇs ᴄᴀʟʟᴇᴅ Pᴀʟᴍs (3ʳᵈ S. vii. 96.) — In Ireland the branches of the yew are blessed and given to the people in the Roman Catholic churches on Palm Sunday. On that day the male peasants may be seen returning from mass with sprigs of yew in their hats or buttonholes, which are generally worn till replaced by the shamrock on Patrick's Day, March 17 ; the women carry home the blessed branches also, and on entering a peasant's cottage a tuft of yew may be seen at the bed-head, or round the crucifix which hangs on on the wall. Hence yew trees are almost universally called palms in Ireland, even by persons who know the proper name for them.   CYWRM.

Porth yr Aur, Carnarvon.

REGIMENTAL BADGES: THE PASCHAL LAMB.— In the interesting article on "Regimental Badges" (3rd S. vii. 5), it is said that the Queen's Royal Regiment derives its—

"Badge, 'The Paschal Lamb,' from the Royal arms of Portugal; the regiment being raised for service in Tangiers, part of the dower of Catherina, Queen of King Charles the Second, and who was, previous to her marriage, Infanta of Portugal."

But at p. 49 it is stated this badge was "granted for having been a guard of honour to the queen of Charles II. on her progress to London."

May I ask JUVERNA if both these statements are correct? I should be glad also if he, or any other of your correspondents, would kindly inform me how the "Paschal Lamb" is connected with the arms of Portugal. It does not appear in them at present; and after diligent search, I have failed to find that it has ever done so, or been associated with them as a crest or supporter.

JOHN WOODWARD.

New-Shoreham.

PASSAGE IN "DON QUIJOTE" (3rd S. vii. 25.)— When translating Don Quijote, I was much puzzled by the expression "mil velos"; and my master, who was a Spaniard well acquainted with English, told me that "mil velos" meant a very large or long veil, and that it gave the idea of reaching down to the feet. Of course, velos is in the plural, because preceded by mil. Its number, therefore, is no proof that more than one veil is meant.   A. DE R.

FIRST DUKE OF MARLBOROUGH (3rd S. vi. 376.)— Perhaps MR. HUTCHINSON is not aware that the Duke's mother was Elizabeth Drake, daughter of Sir John Drake, Knt., of Mount Drake and Ashe, by Helen, daughter and co-heir of Sir John Butler, Bart., of Hatfield Woodhouse, Herts. I should be much obliged if MR. HUTCHINSON can tell me to whom the property of Ashe now belongs?

W. T. T. D.

THOMAS BUDD (3rd S. vi. 418.)—With Governor Jenings he was, in 1684, chosen a commissioner "to negotiate in England" the "matter relating to" the People of West New Jersey's "demand and vindication of their right to the Government, against Edward Billing's pretence to the same." Other persons were elected in the same year to fill the public offices in New Jersey held by Budd, which makes it probable that he went to England. Can anything be learned of his sojourn there, and its results? His book on Pennsylvania, &c., was published in 1685—the following year: possibly in England, and under his own supervision. I find that he copies, literally, passages from Yarrenton's work (to which you kindly referred me) without any marks of quotation. He was a member of the Society of Friends, was involved in the Keith controversy, and, I have heard, became a member of the Church of England. On this latter point I would be glad of information.

ST. T.

"HARD CASH:" "JUPITER AID US" (3rd S. vii. 94.)—The symbol which is usually prefixed to a medical prescription undoubtedly now stands for the word Recipe, just as the French physicians use P, or the word Prenez, at the beginning of their formulæ. But there is as little doubt that this letter has replaced the somewhat similar symbol of the planet Jupiter, used by the physicians of heathen times, as an invocation to the deity whose aid and blessing they sought in their professional labours, just as the Mahometan writers invoke Allah, poets propitiate the Muse, and, in days of more simple and earnest faith, the merchant headed his invoice with the words "Laus Deo," or some similar address to the Deity who alone giveth the increase. I cannot say when the change in the symbol took place; but should infer from the following explanation that the astrological character was in use a century and a half ago:—

"R. Take, which also represents Jupiter's Arms, as if Physicians would first of all invoke the Deity. 'Tis marked thus ♃ at the beginning of a prescription."—Physical Dictionary, by Stephen Blancard, 8vo, London, 1715.

It now, however, much more nearly resembles the letter R, and, as Dr. Paris remarks:—

"It is at present so disguised by the addition of the down-stroke, which converts it into the R, that, were it not for its cloven foot, we might be led to question the fact of its superstitious origin."—Pharmacologia.

Mr. Reade thinks the doctors fair game, and perhaps he wishes, too, to insinuate that a less reliance on their own skill would be as well, at least for their patients; seeing, moreover, that, according to the old epigram, the former have such a powerful auxiliary on their own side:—

"Death and the Doctor to destroy
   All mankind have agreed;
But why should both their power employ,
   When one can do the deed?"

WILLIAM BATES.

Birmingham.

"It is generally supposed that ℞ is short for recipe." This is true, but how came the word recipe, or its initial letter, to be placed at the beginning of medicinal formulæ? It is not the most appropriate Latin word for the meaning it there assumes. A reason is given by a late president of the London College of Physicians, Dr

Paris, in his *Pharmacologia* (8th ed. p. 13). He says: —

" The salutary virtues which many herbs possess were, in times of superstitious delusion, attributed rather to the planet under whose ascendency they were collected or prepared, than to any natural and intrinsic properties in the plants themselves; indeed, such was the supposed importance of planetary influence, that it was usual to prefix to receipts a symbol of the planet under whose reign the ingredients were to be collected ; and it is not perhaps generally known, that the character which we at this day place at the head of our prescriptions, and which is understood and supposed to mean *Recipe*, is a relic of the astrological symbol of Jupiter, as may be seen in many of the older works on pharmacy, although it is at present so disguised by the addition of the down stroke, which converts it into the letter B, that were it not for its *cloven* foot we might be led to question the fact of its superstitious origin."

Dr. Paris then shows in a drawing how easily the symbol of Jupiter (♃) could be turned, by the addition of a back, or first stroke, into the modern ℞. His inference from this is plausible, and probably true, but it would have been more satisfactory if he had given a reference to some old work on pharmacy, in which the symbol of Jupiter, without the modern addition, is placed at the beginning of a medicinal formula. Will any correspondent of " N. & Q." supply the omission?
D.

"Bailler aux Corneilles " (3rd S. vi. 94.)— The excellent Phraseological Dictionary of Tarver gives "bayer aux corneilles," to look about idly, vacantly. The old meaning of *bayer* seems to be to gape or stare about; but *bailler* seems to be a different word, and to signify in old French, to give, or rather more closely rendered, to "hand over," as we should say in vernacular English. The whole expression seems so closely to resemble the often-used phrase of Aristophanes, βάλλ' ἐς κόρακας (see Nubes, 134), that we should believe one is derived in some way from the other. Perhaps the learned Examiner at Woolwich himself would oblige us by his own impressions on the point.
A. A.

Poets' Corner.

Bell cracked, 1594: Old Churchwardens' Accounts (3rd S. vii. 89.) — All thanks to Mr. Tyssen for publishing to the wide world in " N. & 'Q." "the slothfulness of a sexton" in 1594, whereby a noble bell at Reading was cracked, as many hundreds have been, by pulling the clapper to the side for tolling. Thanks, too, for such interesting extracts from old churchwardens' accounts.

I beg to suggest that much information of bygone proceedings in our parishes would be elicited if the several Archæological Societies throughout the kingdom would set some simple machinery at work, by which the contents of all the old parish coffers within their districts might be examined.

And, with regard to bells being cracked by lazy sextons—as it is a well-known fact they are—will any scientific reader of " N. & Q." explain the reason why ? And here I would ask whether any person ever heard of a bell being cracked by tying a string round it, and then sounding it, as I heard a village blacksmith boast some sixty years ago that he could do ? To the same point I annex a quotation from *Neckam de Naturis Rerum*, a volume lately issued under the sanction of the Master of the Rolls, p. 63, "De Campana: " —

"Campana maxima si pulsetur, filo circumdata etiam tenui, findetur."
H. T. Ellacombe, M.A.

Numismatic Query (3rd S. vii. 76). — It is of course extremely difficult to pronounce on a coin without having seen it, but the probability is that it is one of Philip IV. of France (Philippe le Bel); that the crosses are simply the abbreviation of the name of Christ; and that the legend is the same as that given on the reverse of the coin figured in Bordier and Charton's *Histoire de France*, Paris, 1689, vol. i. p. 426; namely, "Christus imperat, Christus vincit, Christus regnat." The coin is supposed to have been struck about 1290. The reverse has a cross flory in a quartrefoil, and the legend goes round it. We must all congratulate its possessor on its extreme curiosity and value.
A. A.

Poets' Corner.

The legend on the gold coin mentioned appears to run thus: "XPC imperat, XPC regnat, XPC vincit." I believe the three Greek letters are not the date of the coin, as Geo. Moore supposes. They are simply the common abbreviated form of the word XPICTOC, " Christ rules, Christ reigns, Christ conquers."
J. A. Wick.

Mollitious (3rd S. vi. 524.) — I see no reason to regret having made the suggestion contained in my former communication (3rd S. vi. 337); for though it may have failed to set your correspondent upon analysing what was passing in the mind of the poet, it appears to have led him to answer his own question in a manner satisfactory to himself.
Meletes.

Countess of Suffolk (3rd S. vii. 94.)—Zuccaro came to England in 1574. At that time no lady bore the title of the Countess of Suffolk; and as Frances, Duchess of Suffolk, mother of Lady Jane Grey died in 1563, the portrait referred to (if authentic) must be that of her stepmother, Katherine, Baroness Willoughby de Eresby and Duchess of Suffolk, who died in 1580. Much curious information about her will be found in Lady Georgina Bertie's *Five Generations of a Loyal House.*
S. P. V.

Barapicklet (3rd S. vii. 113.)—Is equivalent to the Cymric *bara-planc*, or griddle-bread—*i. e.*

small flat cakes baked on a portable iron plate, which is suspended a few inches above the fire-place. *Bara*, baked after this primitive fashion, constitutes the ordinary diet of the Welsh pea-santry at this day; and, when properly made, surpasses all other kinds of bread. The story of King Alfred and the cottier's wife will recur to the minds of your readers. Whence comes *picklet*, unless from the French, I know not. The term is still applied to those pancake-looking delicacies vended by dealers in muffins and crumpets, and made it would seem of similar materials. I have usually heard the term pronounced as if it were spelled *pike-let*. But this, no doubt, is an Angli-cism.   W.

An oval cake about the size of one's hand, slightly sweetened, and not thicker than half a muffin, to be eaten toasted, is called a *picklet;* sometimes also, in contempt, "buttered flannel."
                                        Cywrm.
Porth yr Aur, Carnarvon.

Barapicklet, Welsh. (Bailey's *Dict.*) *Beatille pies*, giblet pies.   E. Marshall.
Sandford.

Bailey gives this apparently as a compound word of Welsh origin: "*Bara-picklet*, cakes made of fine flower kneaded with yeast."
                                        F. Phillott.

In the midland districts of England, I first made the acquaintance of a table-delicacy called a "pyflet"—a round, flabby, spongy cake, baked I believe in a metal ring; but on this point I do not presume to speak as an authority. I have heard it spoken of, by native tongues, as a "pike-let." And does not this sound like an abbrevia-tion of *barapicklet?*   J. C.
Newcastle.

Surgeon executed for Murder (3rd S. vii. 112.)—In a useful old volume, entitled *A Chro-nology of some Memorable Accidents, from the Crea-tion of the World to the Year* 1742, Dublin, 1743 (p. 107), the following entry appears:—
"1728, June 5. Mr. Audouin was executed at [St.] Stephen's Green [Dublin], for cutting his Maid's Throat."

This supplies your correspondent with the name of the criminal. I have certainly read, within the last few years (and there is probably in my possession), a full account of the trial and execu-tion; but I cannot remember in what publication.
                                        Abhba.

Cary Family (3rd S. vii. 117.) — Your corre-spondent is in error when he states that, "in 1588 there was a Cary, or Carey, Bishop of Killaloe," no one of the name having been at any time in charge of that diocese. He probably refers to Mordecai Cary, D.D., who was "a native of Eng-land, educated at Trinity College, Cambridge;" and who, having been rector of St. Catherine's, in

Coleman Street, London, and chaplain to the Duke of Dorset, Lord-Lieutenant of Ireland, was promoted to the bishopric of Clonfert in the year 1731, and translated to Killala (not Killaloe), and Achonry, 1735-6. See Harris's *Works of Sir James Ware*, vol. i. pp. 646, 657; and Archdeacon Cotton's *Fasti Ecclesiæ Hibernicæ*, vol. iv. pp. 75, 170. Bishop Cary died at Killala, October 2, 1751; and was buried in his cathedral, where his monumental stone may be seen. There has not been a second Irish prelate of the name; but in Archdeacon Cotton's very valuable work, mention is made of several of the Cary family amongst the inferior clergy. The Bishop's son, Henry Cary, was Archdeacon of Killala.   Abhba.

Gladys (3rd S. vi. 334, 538.)—I am greatly obliged to Mr. Carmichael for so satisfactorily answering my query as to the origin and pronun-ciation of the name "Gladys." The previous answer of Schin failed of its kind intention to satisfy my curiosity. I already knew that *Gladiss* was a Silesian surname; but that did not help me towards understanding the origin of *Gladys*, the Christian name. "There is a river in Macedon, and there is also moreover a river in Monmouth." Mr. Carmichael states that Gladys is more correctly written *Gwladys*, and he goes on to say that it is considered to be the equivalent of Claudia.

Now the latter is a genuine Latin word, and of course could not have been derived from Gladys. Does Mr. Carmichael mean that early British writers adopted Gladys as the equivalent of Clau-dia, on account of the mere similarity of sound? The writer of the article "Claudia," in Smith's *Dictionary of the Bible*, supposes that the Claudia mentioned in the Second Epistle to Timothy, iv. 21, was a British maiden, whose father took the name of his imperial patron, Tiberius Claudius.

I know next to nothing of the Welsh language, and can only cling to my Dictionary, where I find *Gwlad* translated "country," and *Gwlad ac Eglwys* cited as meaning "Church and State." Does *Gwlad*, then, mean "country" in the sense of *patrie*, or in that of *pays? Patria* or *terra?* J.

Token: Thomas Johnson (3rd S. vii. 78.) — I extract the following from Bromley's *Catalogue of Engraved British Portraits*:—
"Thomas Johnson, Pugilist, wh. len. prefixed to *Boxing Revised*, 1790, 8vo. Basset.
" ———— fighting Isaac Perrins, an etching. Metz. J. Grozer. 1789.
"Isaac Perrins, Pugilist, in the print with Tho. John-son, above."

I happen to possess the coin described by E. M'C., as well as another of similar character, but having a different bust and the name "Isaac Perrins." The reverse has the same date and in-scription in the middle; but the legend round is,

"Strength and Magnanimity." Both pieces are of very good workmanship. I have also a sort of "Brummagem" halfpenny: *obv.* a bust, "Johnson, Pugalist;" *rev.* a harp, "Music Charms."

The following extract is from the *Gentleman's Magazine* for October, 1789, p. 947:—

"On Thursday the 22nd inst. a great boxing match took place at Banbury, in Oxfordshire, between two bruisers, Perrins and Johnson: for which a turf stage had been erected 5 feet 6 inches high, and about 40 feet square. The combatants *set-to* at one in the afternoon; and, after sixty-two rounds of *fair and hard-fighting*, victory was declared in favour of Johnson, exactly at fifteen minutes after two. The number of persons of family and fortune, who interested themselves in this brutal conquest, is astonishing: many of whom, it is proper to add, paid dearly for their diversion."

J. C. WITTON.

Bath.

"WHEN OLD ADAM FIRST WAS CREATED" (3rd S. vi. 308) is part of an old song I was accustomed to hear above sixty years ago. I do not know who is the author of it. The first verse is—

"When old Adam first was created,
And lord of the universe crown'd,
His happiness was not completed
Until a companion he'd found."

J. H.

SIR ANDREW RAMSAY (3rd S. vii. 123.)—HIBERNICUS and N. H. R. seem to come, on insufficient grounds, to the conclusion that the letter referred to shows that, before its date, the Provost of Edinburgh was not called "*Lord* Provost," for it is obvious that the letter may bear two interpretations, viz., that of constituting the title for the first time, or that of debarring other Provosts from using it. That the latter is no strained construction, but on the contrary the true one, appears from the former article in "N. & Q.," alluded to by HIBERNICUS, and to be found in vol. iii. 404. On looking at that article, it will be seen that the writer of it cites an entry in the City Council Records of the Scottish capital, in which, seventy years before the date of the letter, viz. in November, 1597, the Provost is denominated *Lord* Provost; and it is not improbable that were these Records more minutely examined, they would show instances of the same thing at a still earlier date.

As to the "place and precedency" which the latter declares that the Lord Provost should have within the precincts of the city, there is no inconsistency in it with the view I have above suggested. It is not to be supposed that, as Chief Magistrate, he had not already such place and precedency, so that the declaration was not enactive, but confirmatory and expletive.   G.

Edinburgh.

PEPYS'S MEMOIRS (3rd S. vii. 93.) — MR. EVANS's suggestion, that a new edition of these most interesting Memoirs should be published,

including *all* that Pepys wrote, with the exception of the indecent passages, will, I am sure, meet with a cordial response from many readers of "N. & Q." The subject brings to my remembrance a question I have often thought of asking with regard to a peculiarity in Pepys's phraseology. Instead of "he tells me," "he thinks" this or that, we find "he do tell me," "he do think."

Now this was not the ordinary mode of expression in Pepys's day. We know that his Diary was kept in short-hand, and that it was from an expanded transcript of the MS. that Lord Braybrooke compiled his edition. I would ask whether the peculiar phraseology I have alluded to was really adopted by Pepys, or whether it originated in some mistake of the transcriber who wrote out the fair copy? Now that we possess the key to the original, it would, I presume, be easy for a careful examiner of the MS. to answer the query I have proposed.   JAYDEE.

Miscellaneous.

NOTES ON BOOKS, ETC.

Itinerarium Peregrinorum et Gesta Regis Ricardi; auctore ut videtur Ricardo, Canonico Sanctæ Trinitatis Londinensis. Edited from a MS. in the Library of Corpus Christi College, Cambridge. By William Stubbs, M.A., &c. (Longman.)

Recueil des Croniques et Anciennes Istories de la Grant Bretaigne, à present Nommé Engleterre, par Jehan de Waurin, Seigneur de Forestel. Edited by William Hardy, F.S.A., &c. *From Albina to A.D. 688.* (Longman.)

A Collection of Chronicles and Ancient Histories of Great Britain, now called England, by John de Waurin. Translated by William Hardy, F.S.A., &c. (Longman.)

Leechdoms, Wortcunning, and Starcraft of Early England, being a Collection of Documents for the most part never before printed, illustrating the History of Science in this Country before the Norman Conquest. Vol. II. Collected and Edited by the Rev. T. Oswald Cockayne, M.A., &c. (Longman.)

The good work, which was originally suggested by Sir John Romilly, and which that sound scholar and enlightened statesman, the late Sir George C. Lewis, enabled the Master of the Rolls to carry out, is progressing so quickly, although as satisfactorily as quickly, that, with the limited space We can devote to the notice of new publications, We find some difficulty in keeping that progress before our readers. The books whose titles head this notice are the latest of these valuable contributions to English History. The first, the *Itinerarium* of Richard Cœur de Lion, the authorship of which seems pretty clearly brought home to Richard, the Canon of the Holy Trinity in Aldgate, who having been formerly in the service of the Templars, was afterwards Prior of the House, has been most carefully edited by the present librarian of Lambeth, whose sketch of the character of the impetuous monarch and view of the times, as narrated in his able introduction to the Chronicle of Richard the Canon will be read with considerable interest. The interesting French Chronicle, the editing and translating of which has been entrusted to Mr. William Hardy, peculiarly well fitted for the task, embraces a period from the first fabled settlement in Britain to the author's own time,' namely, to the expedition undertaken by King Edward IV. against the Bastard of Falconbridge, after the defeat of Queen Margaret and death of the Prince of Wales, at Tewkesbury, in the year 1471. The text of the present volume is printed from a MS. of the fifteenth century, preserved in the Imperial Library at Paris, believed to be the only complete and nearly contemporary copy of Waurin's entire work now in existence. The portion now published concludes with the cessation of rule of the Britons and their final expulsion into Wales by the Saxons after the death of Cadwallader in 688. The whole of the MS. has been transcribed, and is now ready to be prepared for press. With regard to Mr. Cockayne's second volume of *Saxon Leechdoms*, we have only space left to reiterate the praises which we gave to his first volume. It is a book replete with information as to the state of science among the Saxons, and will interest the Antiquaries of Germany to the full, as much as it will their brethren in this country. The Glossary is very full and valuable.

Diary of Mary, Countess Cowper, Lady of the Bedchamber to the Princess of Wales. 1714—1720. *Edited by the Hon. Spencer Cowper. Second Edition.* (Murray.)

We are glad to see the favourable opinion we expressed of the value of the *Diary* of this amiable and accomplished woman recognised by the reading public, and that the second edition of the work, which that recognition of its merits has called forth, was not issued until there was time to include in it the interesting Letter from the lady which we published in "N. & Q." a few weeks since.

Debrett's Illustrated Peerage of the United Kingdom of Great Britain and Ireland. Under the immediate Revision and Correction of the Peers. Published annually. 1865. (Bosworth.)

Debrett's Illustrated Baronetage and Knightage of the United Kingdom of Great Britain and Ireland, &c. (Bosworth.)

These revivals of a Peerage and Baronetage, which were first published upwards of a century since, seem to have been carefully superintended; and as the Editor states that they have had moreover the benefit of the revision and correction of the noble and eminent persons whose names and arms figure in them, they bid fair to deserve and thereby to secure the favour with which *Debrett* was always regarded in the old times "when George the Third was King." Some of the arrangements by which the Peers who are ordinarily known by higher titles than those by which they sit in the House of Lords, and those bearing courtesy titles may be readily recognised, give a peculiar and useful character to the present *Peerage*.

The High Commission. Notices of the Court and its Proceedings. By John Southerden Burn. (J. Russell Smith.)

The High Commission was something like the Star Chamber, only while the latter dealt with Civil, the former busied itself with Ecclesiastical matters. This is, we believe, the first attempt that has been made to collect the materials for its history; and it is somewhat remarkable that the researches of so diligent an inquirer as Mr. Burn into a Court "which drew many more cases within its clutches, and was less merciful in its proceedings" than the justly dreaded Star Chamber, should not furnish material for more than a hundred pages. The book, though small, is a valuable contribution to English History, for which Mr. Burn deserves the thanks of all historical students.

Notices to Correspondents.

In consequence of the great number of Replies waiting for insertion, We have enlarged the present Number to thirty-two pages.

A. E. L. (Oxford.) *Colnaghi's, Graves', or Hogarth's. The prices depend altogether upon the condition.*

Arthur G. *Salep or Saloup is a decoction of the dried roots of the Orchis mascula.*

A. Teacher. *Cowper's allusion in the line*—
      " So sit two kings of Brentford on one throne,"
is to the Duke of Buckingham's celebrated farce, The Rehearsal, *where the two kings figure " hand in hand," &c.*

H. F. *will find the line*—
      " Too fair to worship, too divine to love,"
in Milman's Prize Poem on the Apollo Belvidere.

Grace Macaulay. *We have a letter for* T. G., *whose communication on this subject appeared ante p. 49.*

F. F. Sulbent. *What was the subject of your communication ?*

E. S. C. *"The Yorkshire Volunteers' Farewell to the Good Folks of Stockton," is printed in Ritson's Bishopric Garland, p. 35, edit. 1810, and in C. J. D. Ingledew's Ballads and Songs of Yo: kshire, p. 221, edit. 1860.*

Sigma. *The extract from Stow's Annals on Bombs has appeared in our 2nd S. xi. 178. See also pp. 29, 74, of the same volume.*

A Reading Case for holding the weekly Nos. of "N. & Q." is now ready, and may be had of all Booksellers and Newsmen, price 1s. 6d.; or, free by post, direct from the publisher, for 1s. 3d.

⁂⁂ Cases for binding the volumes of "N. & Q." may be had of the Publisher, and of all Booksellers and Newsmen.

⁂⁂⁂ "Notes and Queries" is published at noon on Friday, and is also issued in Monthly Parts. The Subscription for Stamped Copies for Six Months forwarded direct from the Publisher (including the Half-yearly Index) is 11s. 4d., which may be paid by Post Office Order, payable at the Strand Post Office, in favour of William G. Smith, 32, Wellington Street, Strand, W.C., to whom all Communications for the Editor should be addressed.

"Notes & Queries" is registered for transmission abroad.

LONDON, SATURDAY, MARCH 4, 1865.

CONTENTS.—N° 166.

Notes.

CHORISTER ACTORS.

The employment of the Children of the King's
Chapel and other choirs as actors, was of frequent
occurrence during the reigns of our Tudor sovereigns. The Household Books of Henry VIII.
contain entries of the payment of sums of 6l. 13s. 4d.
each to "Maister Crane," master of the children
of the Chapel-royal, "for playing before the King
with the Children of the Chapell, in rewarde," on
the New-year's days of 1529, 1530, and 1531 ; and
the Household Books of Edward VI. show that
similar payments were made to Richard Bower,
the then "Mr of the Children of the Kinge's
Chappell, for playinge before the Kinge's Majestie
with the saied Children" in 1548 and 1549. In
the reign of Elizabeth, the children of the chapel,
under Richard Edwards, and the children of St.
Paul's Cathedral, became famous as actors, and
all Lyly's plays and many of those of Ben Jonson
appear to have been acted by them.

Jonson's well-known poetical epitaph on Sala-
thiel Pavy, a boy actor who was famed as the
representative of old men, and who died about the
year 1601, at the age of thirteen, will doubtless
recur to the recollection of most readers. This
boy was probably a chorister as well as actor.
The choir boys continued to act on the stage
until the early part, at least, of the reign of

James I., but a change of feeling afterwards
arose, for we find that a warrant, granted in 1626
to Dr. Nathaniel Giles to take up singing boys for
the service of the chapel-royal, contained a pro-
viso that the children so to be taken should not
be employed as comedians or stage-players, or
act in stage plays, interludes, comedies, or tragedies, "for that it is not fitt or decent that such
as sing the praises of God Almighty should be
trained or imployed on such lascivious and pro-
phane exercises." The very spirit of Puritanism
breathes in these words, which might almost be
taken for a production of the same hand that, a
few years later, penned the *Histrio-Mastix*.

It is not quite clear that the chorister boys resumed their occupation as stage performers after
the restoration of the monarchy in 1660, but it is
certain that the gentlemen of the Chapel-royal
were so engaged, and continued to be until Queen
Anne forbade the practice for reasons similar to
those expressed in the warrant of 1626 before
mentioned.

We learn, however, from Dr. Burney, that on
Wednesday, February 23, 1731, Handel's oratorio
of *Esther*, was represented, *in action*, by the children of his Majesty's chapel, at the house of Mr.
Bernard Gates, their master, in James Street,
Buckingham Gate ; the chorus being "placed,
after the manner of the ancients, between the
stage and orchestra." Amongst the boys who
performed on this occasion were John Beard,
afterwards the famous tenor singer ; John Ran-
dall, afterwards Doctor in Music and Professor at
Cambridge ; and Thomas Barrow, afterwards Gentleman and Music copyist in the chapel-royal.
The oratorio was afterwards publicly performed
by the same singers at the Crown and Anchor
Tavern, but does not appear to have been then
given in action or on a stage.

Exactly twenty-four years after the performance in James Street, viz. on 23rd February, 1755,
Horace Walpole wrote to Richard Bentley as follows :—

"Garrick has produced a detestable English opera,
which is crowded by all true lovers of their country. To
mark the opposition to Italian operas, it is sung by some
cast singers, two Italians and a French girl, and the
Chapel boys ; and to regale us with sense, it is Shakspeare's
Midsummer Night's Dream, which is forty times more
nonsensical than the worst translation of any Italian
opera books."

The opera here spoken of was produced at
Drury Lane Theatre on February 3rd, 1755, under
the title of *The Fairies*. The piece was concocted
by Garrick out of Shakspeare's play, by excising
the comic characters, "sweet bully Bottom" and
his fellows, and adding songs from others of
Shakspeare's pieces and elsewhere. He also wrote,
and himself spoke, a prologue to the opera. The
music was composed by John Christopher Smith,
the friend and amanuensis of Handel. The two

Italian singers mentioned by Walpole were Signor Guadagni,* who played the part of Lysander, which Garrick is said to have (with great pains) taught him to act; and Signora Passerini, who performed Hermia. The "French girl" was Miss Poitier, who during the run of the opera married Joseph Vernon, the tenor singer, and who played Helena. The boys who took part in the piece as principal performers were Master Reinhold, who personated Oberon; Master Moore, who played Puck; and Master Evans, who represented the first Fairy. The remaining chapel boys probably appeared as Fairies in the chorus. The other singers employed were Beard as Theseus, Champness as Egeus, and Miss Young as Titania. The chapel boys were at that time still under the mastership of Bernard Gates.

I should be glad to know whether this was the last occasion on which choristers appeared on the stage as actors; and if so, whether their further appearance was prohibited by any and what authority? As also what, if any, other instances are known of the employment of the boys of the Chapel-royal or other choirs as actors?

W. H. Husk.

HOMER AND HIS TRANSLATORS.

"Though I am willing to make all the allowances possible to an author who raises our admiration too often not to have a right to the utmost candour wherever he fails, yet I can find no excuse for an unaccountable absurdity he has fallen into, in translating a passage of the tenth book. Diomed and Ulysses, taking advantage of the night, set out in order to view the Trojan camp. In their way they meet with Dolon, who is going from thence to the Grecian, upon an errand of the same kind. After having seized this unfortunate adventurer, and examined him concerning the situation and designs of the enemy, Diomed draws his sword, and strikes off Dolon's head, in the very instant that he is supplicating for mercy:—

Φθεγγομένου δ' ἄρα τοῦγε κάρη κονίῃσιν ἐμίχθη.
Book x. ver. 457.

"Mr. Pope has turned this into a most extraordinary miracle by assuring us, that the head spoke after it had quitted the body:—

'The head yet speaking mutter'd as it fell.'

"This puts me in mind of a wonder of the same kind in the *Faery Queen*, where Corflambo is represented as blaspheming after his head had been struck off by Prince Arthur:—

'He smote at him with all his might and main
So furiously, that e're he wist he found
His head before him tumbling on the ground,
The whiles his babbling tongue did yet blaspheme,
And curse his God, that did him so confound.'
Book iv. canto viii. 45.

"But Corflambo was the son of a giantess, and could conquer whole kingdoms by only looking at them. We may perhaps, therefore, allow him to talk when every

---

* Tate Wilkinson, in his *Memoirs*, calls him Giordani, and Genest, in his *Account of the Stage*, gives the name as Curioni. Both are wrong.

---

other man must be silent: whereas there is nothing in the history of poor Dolon that can give him the least pretence to this singular privilege. The truth is, Mr. Pope seems to have been misled into this blunder by Scaliger, who has given the same sense to the verse; and then, with great wisdom and gravity, observes: 'falsum est a pulmone caput avulsum loqui posse.'"—Fitzosborne's (Melmoth's) *Letters on Several Subjects*, vol. ii. p. 146.

In Clarke's *Homer* is the following note:—

"Ver. 457. Φθεγγομένου δ' ἄρα τοῦγε κάρη κονίῃσιν ἐμίχθη.] Vide nimiam celeritatem, salvo pondere, ad quam non potuit conatus Maronis accedere:

'Tum caput orantis nequicquam, et multa parantis
Dicere, deturbat terræ.'—*Æn.* x. 554.

In quibus mihi visus est (Virgilius) gracilior auctore. *Macrob.*, lib. v. cap. xiii. Scaliger e contrario locum hunc Homeri vituperans, 'Falsum est, inquit, a pulmone caput avulsum loqui posse.'—*Poëtic.*, lib. v. cap. 3. [p. 563]. Quod plane est nodum in scirpo quærere. Hoc enim ait Poëta, caput jam *inter loquendum* fuisse abscissum: 'Εἰς γῆν ἔπεσεν ἡ κεφάλη ἐκείνου, ἀρξαμένου μὲν φωνὴν ἀφιέναι, μήπω δὲ διασαφήσαντος τὸ λεγόμενον.'—*Eustath.* 'Γράφεται μὲν, "φθεγγομένη δ' ἄρα τοῦγε κάρη." Οὐχ Ὁμηρικὴ δὲ ἔστιν ἡ φράσις, οὐ γὰρ ἔστι Δηλυκῶς ἡ κάρη παρ' Ὁμήρῳ.—*Idem.* Meminit et Aristoteles, *De partibus Animalium*, lib. iii. cap. 10; qui hic legerent, φθεγγομένη, non φθεγγομένου."

But Pope is not singular in this supposed perversion. Chapman translates it thus:—

"And suddenly his head, deceiv'd, fell speaking to the ground."

Cowper thus:

". . . . with a stroke so swift, that ere
His tongue had ceased his head was in the dust."

Unfortunate indeed would have been this greatest of "the interpreters of the gods," had he been misinterpreted by all his translators. His meaning is faithfully given by Hobbes:

"That from his shoulders fell his head away
As he was speaking, and lay in the dust."

By Morrice:

"But the swift sword descending cut in twain
The nerves whilst yet he spake; his sever'd head
And lifeless corpse lay mingled with the dust."

By the Earl of Derby:

"Ev'n while he spoke, his head was roll'd in dust."

Here is the "nimia celeritas" which, as Macrobius observes, Virgil could not attain to. "Ev'n while he spoke"—dicto citius—"his head was roll'd in dust." But Scaliger's motto must have been "Ne quid nimis," for he adds, "et durum est, Caput mistum pulvere, non enim miscetur, quod apparet et extat." Perhaps Melmoth also was hypercritical.

. Bibliothecar. Chetham.

Shakspeariana.

Mr. Keightley's "Shakespeare Expositor."
The readers of "N. & Q." will, I am sure, not grudge me a little space on my own account. In the Preface to my edition of Shakespeare, I wrote as follows: —

"The corrections I have made will be explained, and the principles by which I have been guided shown, in a volume named *The Shakespeare Expositor*, on which I have been engaged some years."

In the Preface to the one-volume edition, last December, I added: "and which will shortly appear."

It is true I had made no regular agreement on the subject; but I regarded it as a clearly understood matter that, when I gave in the text the corrections, the result of several years' study, the comment explaining and justifying them should follow as a matter of course. The publishers however, taking a Trade-view of the matter, declined printing that moderate-sized volume, on the grounds that such works did not pay; that readers in general, when they got the results, cared little for the reasons, &c., &c.

This may be, and probably is, all very true; but if I had known it, I should either have declined the editing altogether, or I should only have given the simplest and least disputable corrections: for now I stand exposed, without the power of reply, to the sneers and taunts of any one who chooses to assail me.

This, however, I care not very much about. I never expected to make anything by the work, and fame is what I have never thought of. It has given me agreeable occupation for thousands of hours, that I might not otherwise have known how to employ. I will go on improving it: for it must, I am convinced, be published some day or other, though probably not in my time; and it will probably be all the better for the delay. I may here add, that it is adapted to any edition of Shakespeare, and has no peculiar connexion with my own.

It only remains for me to request of the readers of "N. & Q." to believe that I can give, if not convincing, at least very probable reasons, for even the boldest corrections I have made; and to judge of me as a critic by my perfect Milton, rather than by my imperfect Shakespeare.

Belvidere, Kent.

THOS. KEIGHTLEY.

Shakespear Family (2nd S. x. 188, 402.)—
E. A. T., S. W. Rix, T. C. N., and W. S., are informed that John Shackspeer (Shakespear), of Rope Walk, Upper Shadwell, was born in 1612; that on July 14, 1654, he married Martha Seeley, aged nineteen, by whom he had four sons and four daughters; and dying in September, 1689, at the age of seventy-seven, he was succeeded in the business of rope-making by his youngest child Jonathan, who was born Feb. 6, 1670.

This Jonathan married, April 26, 1689, Elizabeth Shallott, and by her had thirteen children; and dying April, 1735, aged sixty-four, left his business to be carried on by his eldest son Arthur, who was born Nov. 3, 1699.

This Arthur died May 9, 1749; leaving his property and the rope-making to be carried on by his younger brother John, on condition that he John "brings up his heir to carry on the trade of rope-making."

This John was the twelfth child of Jonathan, and was born March 16, 1718. He married, 1745, Elizabeth Currie; and by her had eleven children. He died May 19, 1775, an alderman of Aldgate Ward.

In regard to this family being connected with him, "who was not of an age, but for all time," there is neither proof, that it is or that it is not. But there are circumstances which lead me to believe that it is.

The dramatic poet lived in St. Helen's Place, Bishopsgate, within two miles of the parish of St. Dunstan's, Stepney; in which parish, and close to where John of Rope Walk lived, are Ben Jonson's Fields. Clearly our poet was often on the scene of the Rope Walk.

About 1580, the poet's father and mother were in London, and would probably be in the same locality. It also appears that several Shakespears came to London about this time.

It seems also strange, that Jonathan Shakespear, in the rope-making trade, should have been of the Guild of Broiderers; unless, indeed, he had been influenced by Quincy, a connexion of the poet's youngest daughter, who was a citizen and Broiderer at that time.

There can be no doubt that there was a relation of the poet's alive in London, about 1660, at a very advanced age. May not this Shakespear, very old in 1660, have been the father of John, born in 1612, and who now has a great-great-great-great-grandson?

My great grandfather has left a document, saying "that their family is from the poet's grandfather, Richard Shakespear."

ARTHUR SHAKESPEAR.

Richmond.

"**Cling.**" — This word occurs but twice in Shakspeare, namely, in *Macbeth*, Act I. Sc. 2:— "That do cling together";—Act V. Sc. 5: "Hang alive till famine cling thee." As it seems to me strangely ungrammatical to use the verb in an active sense, I think it probable that the word in the second quotation is a misprint. About Leeds, *clam* is used in the sense of "to pinch"; as, for instance, "I'se clammed wi' hunger." About

Newcastle-on-Tyne it is written and pronounced " clem." The word "clams" is also the technical name given to nippers or pinchers of various kinds used in several trades. I therefore suggest that the quotation should be read :—"Hang alive till famine clam thee." Clam, I think, is derived from the Saxon clæmian, German klemmen, to pinch. G. H. OF S.

PASSAGE FROM "MACBETH" (3rd S. vii. 51.)— If, in the wide variety of Shakspeare's Drama, an incongruous word occurs, his editors will proffer their own conjectural substitution; a process, however, which mere homeliness — the habit (not the vice) of his age — can hardly justify. Certainly MR. JESSOP's blankest is the nearest typographical approach to the eminently domestic word which our poet, without incurring any emendation, has more than once seriously used, and which sufficiently accords with his simplicity and directness. Neither Coleridge nor Mr. Collier have, in my poor judgment, mended the matter. If the stage substitutes, as I believe it does, the more elegant word curtain, let the printed text of his Macbeth abide intact by the variable and fantastic notion of gilding his gold, which is all the more pure and precious as it first came from his alchemic hand. I fully assent to J. DIXON's suggested restoration of faint (p. 52); it relieves a world of idle conjecture. E. L. S.

PASSAGE IN "MUCH ADO ABOUT NOTHING" (3rd S. vi. 324.) — In "N. & Q." the well-known passage —

" And sorrow wag, cry hem, when he should groan,"—

in Much Ado about Nothing, is briefly commented on. Will you please put a comma after "And," and alter "sorrow" to "sorry," and present it thus to your numerous readers? It will then read : —

" If such a one will smile, and stroke his beard,
And, sorry wag, cry hem when he should groan,
Patch grief with proverbs," &c., &c.

I know not if this reading has been given before, but have long thought it the true one.
                                                    H. J. L.
Cambridge Terrace, S.

THE ORIGIN OF INFIRMARIES IN ENGLAND.

In a thick octavo volume of tracts, the dates extending from 1710 to 1715, I have one with the following title : —

" The Charitable Society : or, a PROPOSAL for the more Easy and Effectual Relief of the SICK and NEEDY. I was sick, and in Prison, and ye visited me. London : Printed by G. James, for JONAH BOWYER, at the Rose in Ludgate Street, 1715." Pp. 27.

After a Preface of four pages, the body of the pamphlet opens with a declaration of the necessity and usefulness of such societies; and urges their establishment, as a duty towards God and man. The consideration of the subject is comprised under three general heads : — 1st. The Scheme of such a Society. 2nd. By what Means it may easily subsist. 3rd. The great Benefits and Advantages.

It would occupy too much of the space of "N. & Q." to give even an outline of the scheme, which is set forth in detail in thirteen propositions. Suffice it to say, that the constitution includes all the features of the modern "Infirmary," though the word itself had not then come into use.

Women, under the denomination of "Visiting Sisters," were rightly expected to take a prominent part; both in the internal management, and in obtaining funds. Besides a monthly meeting of all the members, it was considered desirable that the President, Steward, and Sisters, should have a meeting once a week. There is a naive simplicity in the following recommendation : —

" XII. If the Meeting be in some convenient Room of some of the Members' Houses, let there never be any Treat given ; and, as far as is possible, let all Discourse be avoided which is foreign to the Business in hand."

Among the means proposed for supporting the Society, in addition to the canvassing for subscriptions —

" It is to be hoped and expected that many will, of their own accord, send in their charity ; particularly those who are in conscience bound, as they value their Salvation, to make Restitution of their unjust Gains ; and know not the persons whom they have wronged, and to whom they are obliged to make Restitution."

In setting forth the benefits and advantages, the writer refers to a French author, who shows that such Societies have been already established in Paris ; and that —

" the Princesses, Duchesses, and those who are of the highest quality, and nearest to the Crown, do with chearfulness enter into this Charitable Society for the Relief of the Sick and Needy ; and take pleasure in visiting them, and in ministering to them with their own Hands."

After speaking of the benefit and advantage of such Societies, not only to the bodies and souls of those relieved and comforted, but also to those employed in so good a work, the writer adds:

" And now let it not be objected, that this Work of Charity is a troublesome and unpleasant Work. It is true indeed, that a poor Cottage where the Wind blows in on every Side ; a hard Bed stuffed with Straw, on which the poor sick Wretch lies ; a few Tattered Rags, which served to be a Covering to his weak and naked Body ; but above all, that noisome Smell which ordinarily attends him languishing upon the Bed of Sickness in such a mean and streight Place, is no very agreeable and inviting Sight. But if we consider the poor Wretch as a

Representative of *Jesus Christ*, and with the Eye of Faith behold Him, as it were, lying upon the Bed of Sickness. If we consider farther the great Benefit and Advantage which we by this *Labour of Love* shall bring to others, and to our own Souls; we shall acknowledge it to be the most delightful and profitable Sight we can behold; the best and most useful Visit we can make; and the most pleasant and advantageous Work we can be employed in."

My brief account of this tract will have shown that it is, in itself, interesting; but I have a more special object in bringing it before the readers of "N. & Q."

Behind the title-page of my copy is written a curious autograph note, which I copy verbatim:—

"Mem^d. The Revd Mr Bowyer having communicated to me a Scheme he had met with in a French Sermon concerning of Infirmaries in France, we agreed to have ye Substance translated and published in ye manner it is in this Pamphlet, w^h first produced, by God's great Blessing, the Infirmary in St Marg^ts Westm^r, and afterw^ds the Hospital at Hide Park Corner, at Winchester, Bath, and one in Dublin."

Was the "Rev. Mr. Bowyer" connected with *Jonah Bowyer*, the publisher of the pamphlet; and what further is known of him? Who was his worthy coadjutor—the anonymous writer of the above note?   W. LEE.

BLACKFRIARS BROKEN-BRIDGE.

When I was a little boy I used very often, on winter evenings, to stop and enjoy the Galantee Show, then to be met with in the streets of my native town, as also in the streets of the adjacent neighbourhood: where, occasionally, Galantee Shows are still to be observed. I remember being particularly delighted with the broken bridge of cardboard; on which the cardboard man, while vigorously working away with his cardboard pickaxe, used to sing:

"The bridge is broke, and it must be mended,
    Right fol, de diddy dol de day."

It is not long since that I stopped, in broad daylight, to look down upon and meditate over the fate of another kind of broken bridge: for such, indeed, Blackfriars Bridge has been for many years past.

One afternoon, last summer, I tarried in Amwell churchyard to transcribe the monumental inscription of Robert Mylne, the architect of the broken bridge; which, after much labour, and spending of "coined money," was found to be past all possible mending. The inscription just alluded to, although in a country churchyard, is particular to tell that Robert Mylne was not only buried in the vaults of St. Paul's Cathedral, but that "his remains were interred near to those of Sir Christopher Wren." And further, to arrest the Weeverish visitor on his pedestrian way, the inscription records the fact that Robert Mylne "designed and

constructed the magnificent bridge of Blackfriars, London."

When I stood the other morning upon the high-up-in-the-air temporary wooden foot-bridge — looking down on the half demolished and stone-by-stone pulled asunder "magnificent bridge of Blackfriars, London"—I could not help thinking of the cardboard broken bridge, as exhibited in the Galantee Shows of my boyhood time, and of the above quoted words, which I had so recently copied in a country churchyard—far, far away "from the busy hum of men."

And anon, when I take up *The Westminster Magazine* for 1773, Time's Galantee Show reveals to me another picture, very interesting at this time; when we are compelled to see that Master Father Thames is more constant in his ablutions, so as to appear every day, and indeed all the year round, with a healthy and odoriferous "shining morning face."

"Thursday, June 24, 1778. At noon, the tollmen at Blackfriars bridge were all removed to the Surrey end, all the commissioners being present; so that any person from the city may take an airing on the bridge without taxation."

So says *The Westminster Magazine*. And such trivial facts and scraps as these, when they meet together, seem almost to resemble the sweet revival of a dying echo. Doubtless the time will arrive again, when we shall be able to take an airing on the Blackfriars Bridge of the *future*, free at least from taxation to our olfactory sensibilities: especially when we remember, that old John Norden, writing towards the end of the reign of that great Queen Elizabeth — "the most comfortable nursing mother of the Israel of God in the British Isles," as he terms her—was able to record, speaking of Somerset House, that its principal front towards the south, that "the sweete river Thamise offereth manie pleasinge delightes."

EDWIN ROFFE.

Somers Town.

SHERMAN'S "WHITE SALT." — My copy of *White Salt, or, a Sober Correction of a Mad World, in some Wel-wishes to Goodness*, by John Sherman, B.D., London, 1654 (pp. viii.—242), is bound in old morocco, from which silver (?) clasps, corners, and centre-pieces have been removed; and has the following curious inscription on the fly-leaf, in a contemporary hand, possibly that of the author:—

"*Salsâ molâ litabat cui defuerint Thura.*

"Who wanted Ox, or Lamb, or Dove,
    With Salt did his Devotion prove.
If heaven, I hope then you'l dispense
And make my Salt your Frankincense.
When Sodom in her Flames was Burn'd,
Lott's wife in Salt a pillar turn'd:

> But you a liveing pillar stand
> Of salt, to season this Fresh land.
> Each pious teare from your faire eyes
> Is salt, and also sacrifice.
> The tomb I wish for is, to be
> Well pickled in your memory."
>
> EDWARD RIGGALL.

Bayswater.

THE SEA SERPENT.—This irrepressible monster has been seen again, *teste* the following cutting :—

" 'THE SEA SERPENT AGAIN.'—We are in a position definitely to set at rest the much vexed question—discussed so earnestly a few years ago—as to the reality and *bona fide* existence of the Sea Serpent. A credible correspondent assures us that he has himself seen the creature, and found her (as he calls the Sea Serpent) to be quite a comely object. She made her appearance in these seas a few days ago, and is at the present moment in the waters of our harbour. The Sea Serpent was seen not long since off Tauranga, and had been previously observed among the Chatham Islands. The length of the creature is, we should say, not less than 70 feet ; and as she moves along the water, which is occasionally done with considerable rapidity, the body appears a good many feet above the surface. The Sea Serpent presents exactly the appearance of a tight and well-rigged schooner, or perhaps we might say a brigantine, and is under the care of a highly respectable mariner."—*New Zealander*, Aug. 20, 1864. B. H. C.

REMARKABLE CASE OF REANIMATION AND CONFESSION.—In one of his sermons, preached before King Edward, Bishop Latimer relates an extraordinary instance of reanimation and confession. During his stay in Oxford, he says, he "heard of an execution done on one who suffered for treason." The man was tried, found guilty, and sentenced to be hung, drawn, and quartered. Though the rope was about his neck, he continued to protest his innocence to the last ; after some delay, he was hung and cut down ; but life not being quite extinct, the wretched man was brought before a fire, and revived—and in that state of recovered consciousness, he confessed his guilt. "It may well be said," exclaims Latimer, "*Pravum cor hominis, et inscrutabile*, a crabbed piece of work and unsearchable." F. PHILLOTT.

CURIOUS BAPTISMAL NAMES.—I may add to the list of curious baptismal names, the following: "Artules" and "Arculus," from gravestones in Clutton churchyard, Somerset, both evidently a corruption of Hercules ; which seems to have been a fashionable name here. Also "Iearenery," from a stone in the churchyard at Geldeston, Norfolk. The last is a corruption of Irene. C.

ANCIENT SPECIFICS AGAINST HUNGER. — In Xiphiline's epitome of Dion Cassius, inserted among the fragments of the latter by Reimar, (book lxxvi. sec. 12-16, Hamburg, folio, 1752, p. 1281), is a statement .that the ancient Britons could endure all sorts of hardships ; that they could remain plunged in the marshes many days, their heads alone being out of water ; that in the woods they subsisted on bark and roots ; that on all occasions or emergencies (περὶ πάντα) they prepared a sort of food of which, *eating the size of a bean*, they neither hungered nor thirsted (τι βρῶμα ἐφ' οὗ κυάμου τι μέγεθος ἐμφαγόντες, οὔτε πεινῶσιν οὔτε διψῶσι). Sir Robert Sibbald supposed this to be the root of a sort of liquorice, which he says the mountain Scotch call *karemyle*, and used for the purpose of warding off hunger in his time. Pliny is cited (*Nat. Hist.*, xi. 119 ; xxii. 11), as attributing such properties to the liquorice (*glychyrrhiza*). *Caramel* is the French word for a preparation of sugar, a sort of inspissation, and may have been adopted into the Scottish vernacular in the time of Mary Queen of Scots, when so many French words and customs were in vogue.

Now however useful and pleasant the liquorice may be, and however correctly Pliny may state (*loc. cit.*) what a valuable a remedy it is for coughs, injury to the fauces, and for the thorax and liver, yet we know that if we take the best preparation of liquorice (Savory and Moore's Pontefract cakes), the size of a bean of this delectable concoction would be a poor substitute for ever so slight a lunch. It is probable our author exaggerates a little, as he may do when he talks of the Britons being whole days in marsh-water up to the chin ; but still there is every probability they had some prophylactic, or palliative against hunger, or it would not have been so prominently stated. Concentrated meat, or *pemmican*, requires concoction in hot water before it is eatable, though a little goes a great way ; and much has been talked in late years of the specific virtues of the Arabian *haksheesh*. Is it possible the Britons may have used some of our native sedative plants for the purpose of deadening hunger? The subject is very curious, and worthy of illustration by our naturalists. A. A.

UNCONSCIOUS IMITATION.—The Court of Queen's Bench was amused some days ago by a case of Breach of Promise of Marriage, in which the gallant captain, who was defendant, had written to the plaintiff a letter referring to a fishing excursion, and wishing that he had been able to use the photograph of the plaintiff as a bait. Probably he was not aware that the idea had been previously used by Dr. Donne, as quoted in Isaac Walton's *Complete Angler :* —

> "Thou thyself art thine own bait,
> The fish that is not catched thereby
> Is wiser sure, alas ! than I."
>
> JOB J. B. WORKARD.

ONE BECCARIA.—

"The English society for abolishing punishment by death has found little favour of late in British eyes, and it has therefore expended its sympathy at the considerable distance of Milan, by subscribing a round sum for the completion of a monument in that city to one Beccaria, *who is said to be a warm partisan* of the benevolent theory of letting off with his life the enemy of life."

The above is "going the rounds." Perhaps it may be worth preserving in "N. & Q." as a specimen of what distinguished writers may come to.

AN INNER TEMPLAR.

Queries.

SEALS OF GEORGE ABBOT, ARCHBISHOP OF CANTERBURY, 1611 TO 1633.—Can any of your readers refer me to impressions of the archiepiscopal and personal seals of Archbishop Abbot? There are no impressions of these seals in the British Museum.   J. J. HOWARD.

Ashburnham Terrace, Greenwich.

BIBLIOGRAPHICAL QUERIES.—Can you give me any information regarding Wm. Meeston, M.A., author of a translation of St. Pierre's *Harmonies of Nature*, 3 vols. 1815? I think he published a work on education about 1822.

Who is author of the English translation of Madame De Stael's *Germany*, 1813?

Wanted, any information regarding the Rev. J. Thomson, author of *Poems, Moral, Elegiac, Descriptive*, 1807, 12mo.

Can any of your readers inform me who was editor of *The Lapsus Linguæ, or College Tatler*, an Edinburgh University periodical, 1824–5; published by Sutherland, Edinburgh? It contains original essays, sketches of the professors, dramatic sketches, poetry, &c. The initials of some of the contributors are, "J. S. M.," "A. F. S.," "R. W.," "S. G.," &c.

Can any of your American readers give me any information regarding J. W. Simmons, author of a volume of poetry published at Philadelphia in 1821? He published one or two other volumes, and was author likewise of *Valdemar*, a tragedy. Is Mr. Simmons still living?   R. I.

SIEGE OF MALTA: "CAVALIER."—In the accounts of the siege of Malta frequent mention is made of the "Cavalier," which was evidently a work of different character to that which we call by the same name in modern fortification. What was it? Was it a retrenched bastion? There is, I think, a description of similar works in *L'Architecture Militaire du Moyen Age*, par M. Viollet-le-Duc; but that book is inaccessible to me at present.   J. WOODWARD.

"FALL" FOR "AUTUMN."—It is usual to consider this peculiarly American, and it has probably now become so. How early an instance can be cited of its use in England? I have an impression that it is much older than the following passage from the *Journal* of one Samuel Bownas, an Englishman, about 1696: "Towards the fall I bought a horse" (p. 10, London edition of 1795). Is not the next use of the word, in a public Act, somewhat curious?—

"There shall be four Days in a Year for Training or Mustering, two in the Spring, and two in the Fall of the Leaf."—Chap. v. of *Laws passed at Perth Amboy in New Jersey*, in 1693.

Dr. Latham, in his notes on the *Germania* of Tacitus (p. 76), calls it American, and a "recent term." It may be recent, in his sense; and yet much older than the English language in America, or the "American language" as some are pleased to style it.   ST. T.

HOWELL'S "LETTERS," EDIT. 1754. —

Grunnius Sophista (p. 337).—Who was this testator, who, "having nothing else to dispose of but his body," devised it in the quaint manner there related? Was he a *Grynæus*? If so, which? And where can I find more of him and his will?

"The *Extended Woman* meaning the blessed Virgin" (p. 440).—Why, how, when, or where *extended*?

Corinth now *Ragusa* (p. 53).—"We passed by Corinth, now Ragusa, but I was not so happy as to touch there; for, you know, 'Non cuivis homini contingit adire Corinthum.'" What is the meaning of *now Ragusa*?

Captain Mahun (p. 282).—"And Captain Mahun was pitifully massacred by his own men lately." (Date of letter May 2, 1640.) Where can I find the story of Captain Mahun?

Ragged-staff of the Spaniard (p. 115).—"Therefore, rather than they [the Protestants] should be utterly suppressed, I believe the Spaniard himself would reach them his *ragged-staff* to defend them." What is the allusion here?

"The *Lady Southwell's* news from Utopia, that he who sweareth when he playeth at dice may challenge his damnation by way of purchase" (p. 208). — Wanted, information about this lady and her book. The biographical dictionaries and Lowndes afford none.   H. L. T.

"HYMNS ANCIENT AND MODERN."—Hymn 20, entitled "Sunday," commencing—

"Morn of morns, and day of days!
Beauteous were thy new-born rays."

The first and third lines are sung to music identical with that of the beginning of the beautiful song, "Oh! Nanny, wilt thou gang with me?" Which is the more ancient, the hymn or the song? By whom was each composed?*   SENESCENS.

[* The air of "Oh! Nanny, wilt thou gang with me?" has been generally considered the composition of Thomas Carter, a native of Ireland, and brought up in the choir of Christ Church Cathedral, Dublin. He died on October 12, 1804. But in the *Gentleman's Magazine* for May, 1847, it is attributed to Joseph Blaidon, of Great Queen Street, Lincoln's Inn Fields, who died on May 7, 1774. It is there stated by Blaidon's grandson that Carter was a purchaser at the sale of his grandfather's library, and among other things of the air of "Oh! Nanny," then in manuscript. Carter, it appears, subsequently published it as his own composition.—ED.]

HYMNOLOGY.—Can any of your readers tell me the authors of the three hymns which are numbered 61, 137, and 165, in the " Ancient and Modern " Collection? The first lines are : —

61. " The people that in darkness sat,
A glorious Light have seen."

137. " Three in One, and One in Three,
Ruler of the earth and sea,
Hear us, while we lift to Thee
Holy chant and psalm." *

165. " Take up thy Cross, the Saviour said."

The second of these hymns is, I understand, taken " from the German "; but I should like to know where the original is to be found.　D. Y.

LLANDAFF CATHEDRAL. — A Welsh lady has lately written to me as follows : —

" He took me over Llandaff Cathedral, now being restored under the superintendence of Mr. John Pritchard, the diocesan architect. The restorations are carried out, in what I consider excellent taste, with one or two slight exceptions ; one of them being that the verse selected for the emblazonment of the otherwise beautiful organ bears the following astonishing ejaculation : ' O all ye Beasts and Cattle, bless ye the Lord ! ' Considering the congregation, this is certainly not complimentary."

Your readers, most probably, will agree with my fair correspondent ; but can any of them inform me what special lesson is intended to be conveyed by this odd-sounding text?　W.

LONGEVITY.—In the churchyard of Hampton, co. Middlesex (or perhaps in that of Hampton Wick), is a monumental inscription to a Mrs. Hannah Brown, who is stated to have died in 1785 at the age of 103. She was, I believe, the widow of Mr. Lancelot Brown of Hampton Court, who was, I think, a gardener of some repute; and their grandchild was another Lancelot Brown, some time M.P. for Hunts, and resident at Fenstanton, in that county, in 1788.

Though sceptical of most instances that have been publicly alleged, I have some reason to think the above is worthy of credit, and desire to know more about this supra-centenarian.　C. Ross.

HENRY MARTYN was a contributor to the Spectator in 1711. Paper No. 200 is among his contributions. He is believed to have been a Wiltshire man, and to have married an heiress of a family of the name of Bendall. His son, Bendall Martyn, was Secretary to the Board of Excise. I should be greatly obliged if any of your correspondents could give the arms of these two families, and any further particulars concerning their pedigrees, and especially the name of the wife of Bendall Martyn.　MARTYNET.

PHONETIC HEADSTONES. — In a little kirkyard, near Elgin, I noticed a gravestone with an inscription beginning " Hêr liz θe bodi," and written

[* Attributed to Mr. Marriott.—ED.]

throughout in phonetic characters. Can any of your readers inform me if this is common? I should like to hear of another.　T. W. HORSLEY.
Pembroke College, Oxon.

RAGUSA.—Who was Governor (Rector) of Ragusa in 1773 ? Where can I find a tolerably full account of the republic, and a list of its Governors or Doges ? What metal is the shield—Or, or Argent, with four bars gules ?　JOHN DAVIDSON.

SPANISH JEWS.—It may be worthy of observation, whether the Spanish language of the Jews in Constantinople, Salonika, and Smyrna, is not giving way to the Italian ? Such is certainly my view. Formerly the Spanish standard was maintained by the occasional arrival of emigrants, or exiles, from Spain, of whom I have seen in the Jewish burial grounds old tombs, with coats of arms and Spanish inscriptions; but now there is nothing to keep up the purity of Spanish, and its extinction seems imminent in the rivalry of Italian.　HYDE CLARKE.
Smyrna, Turkey.

SWEEPING THE HEARTH, OR THE THRESHOLD.— A friend informs me that, in Hertfordshire and the adjacent counties, this custom prevails among the cottagers. If a visitor comes in who is welcome, they immediately sweep the hearth. But if it be one with whom there is some secret feud, or who they consider de trop, the earliest decent opportunity is taken of sweeping the threshold of the door. This is a matter quickly understood, and the intruder walks off in a great huff. Does the custom prevail elsewhere in England ?
　　A. A.
Poets' Corner.

FAMILY OF DE VAUDIN, OR VAULDIN. — Can any of your readers direct me where to find the history of the ancient Breton family of De Vaudin, or Vauldin ? Branches of it appear to have settled in Normandy and other northern provinces of France at a very early date.
　　J. BERTRAND PAYNE.
Brompton.

HENRY WALKER, MINSTREL. —I shall be much obliged by your insertion of the following matter, and queries arising out of it : —

Henry Walker, musician, of London, by his will, dated April 17, 1612, gave to the master wardens and assistants of the Company of Musicians in London 120l., for the benefit of the poor of Kington, Herefordshire.

John Walker, his brother, and the surviving executor of his will, by deed dated May 6, 1626, conveyed lands in the parish of Kington to trustees, with a view to give effect to his brother's will.

The Company of Musicians is supposed to have been incorporated by King James I. Arms were granted to this Company in 1614. (Stow's *London*, by Strype, 2nd App., p. 16).

In the account of the sale of the articles, which formed part of the Sainsbury Museum, recently sold, occurs : —

" Indenture of bargain and sale between Henry Walker, citizen and minstrel of London, and William Shakespeare of Stratford-upon-Avon, in the county of Warwick, gentleman, William Johnson, citizen and vintner of London, John Jackson, and John Hemyng, gentleman, for 140*l.*, of a house or tenement, with the appurtenances situate within the precincts of the late Black Fryers, London, March 12th, 1612, 55*l.*"—Mr. Halliwell. (See *Times.*)

Does any list of the Company of Musicians exist ?

Can Mr. Halliwell, or any of your readers, say whether Henry Walker, the testator, was the same person as Henry Walker mentioned in the bargain and sale ? And whether Henry Walker, minstrel, was associated with William Shakespeare ?
JAMES DAVIES.

Moor Court, Kington, Herefordshire.

"DRAGON OF WANTLEY": JOHN, THIRD EARL OF BUTE.—If any of your correspondents would kindly oblige me with the following, I will most willingly enclose you postage stamps to cover any expenses : —

1. The music of the *Dragon of Wantley.*
2. The burial place of John, third Earl of Bute, and his epitaph.

JAMES DAVIDSON, Head Master.
Grammar School, Bowness, Windermere.

THE WELCHES IN ENGLAND. — Extracting the following from Thafarzik's *Slowanski Starozitnosti* (Slavonic Antiquities), — a valuable work of ancient history and ethnology,—I solicit the attention of the friends of these sciences to this subject; and beg them, for the sake of English and Slavonic ancient history, to devote themselves to the investigation thereof.

After having substantiated his proofs of the nationality of the Welches, one of the Slavonic tribes now extinct, the above historian proceeds to speak of their settlements in Batavia and Britain on the 800th page as follows : —

" Still more dark and uncertain are the accounts of the sojourn of the Welches in England, especially in that part of the country which was termed, after the arrival of the Anglo-Saxons, Wiltseater, or Wilts, the present county of Wiltshire. There are mentioned early enough the town of Wiltun (now Wilton), and the inhabitants, Wiltuns and Wiltunisc.

" It is probable that in the great migration of the North Western Nation which ensued in the fourth and fifth centuries, there arrived there some of the troops of the warlike Welches, and, having liked that already considerably fertilised country, settled there. That may account for the great amount of original Slavonic terms in the modern English language. But as I am at present unable to follow this very important subject to its entirety, I postpone the investigation thereof to a better time."

The author mentions on the same page that, according to "Cron. de Trajecto," the Welches and Slavonians came to Friesland from England, and also that the historian Mone declares, without hesitation, the Wilts in England to be the Welches.
CORCONTIUS.

Queries with Answers.

BISHOP PERCY OF DROMORE (3rd S. vi. 261, 338.)—Your correspondent H. S. G., at p. 338 of the last vol. of "N. & Q.," doubts very strongly the connection of the good bishop with the house of Northumberland. He is on this point by no means singular, for several eminent antiquaries are quite as sceptical. It would, however, seem as if Percy persuaded himself fully into the belief of the connection, and was justly proud of it. One thing is very clear that he was received on the most intimate footing by the duke and duchess of Northumberland of that day, though I cannot of course say whether they allowed the claim of relationship.

I transcribe the following passages from Leigh Hunt's amusing book *The Town* (edition 1859, pp. 187, 188) : —

" Northumberland House was discovered to be on fire March 18, 1780, at five o'clock in the morning, which raged from that hour till eight, when the whole front next the Strand was completely destroyed. Dr. Percy's apartments were consumed ; but great part of his library escaped the general ruin."

This is a quotation recorded from Malcolm, vol. ix. p. 308. Here follow Mr. Leigh Hunt's comments upon it :—

" Mr. Malcolm has spoken of the apartments of Dr Percy. This was Dr. Percy, Bishop of Dromore, who gave an impulse to the spirit of the modern muse by his *Reliques of Ancient English Poetry.* He was *a kinsman* of the Northumberland family."

Percy was at this time Dean of Carlisle, which preferment he had obtained in 1778. In 1782 he became Bishop of Dromore, and there died Sept. 30, 1811. He was, I presume, buried in the cathedral there, far from the little country church of Easton-Maudit in Northamptonshire, in which he had so long ministered, and the sepulchre of three of his children.

I should be glad to be informed whether there is any memorial of him in Dromore cathedral; and if so, whether alliance is thereon claimed for him with the ducal house ? Such a record, if existing, might be worthy of a niche in the pages of "N. & Q.," and would be valuable evidence.
OXONIENSIS.

[The inscription to the memory of Bishop Percy on a marble tablet in the north transept of Dromore cathedral does not allude either to his parentage or family. It is printed in Cotton's *Fasti Ecclesiæ Hibernicæ*, iii. 287. The Bishop's connection with the house of Northumberland has not been satisfactorily proved; but on this subject consult Nichols's *Leicestershire*, iv. 708; Nash's *Worcestershire*, ii. p. iv.; Green's *Worcester*; *Gent. Mag.* lxxx. (i.) 502; lxxxii. (i.) 225; and "N. & Q." 2nd S. vi. 410; vii. 34.]

CÆSAR AND THE DELPHIC ORACLE.—It is stated that Augustus Cæsar having sent an embassy to Delphos to inquire concerning his successor about the time of Christ's birth, the oracle gave the following reply: —

"Me puer Hebreus superum Rex linquere tecta
Hæc jubet, et Ditis cæcas remeare sub umbras;
Ergo silens aris tu nunc abscedito nostris."

Can any of your readers inform me in what Latin author the above account is to be found?

QUERIST.

[We believe that these oft-quoted lines can be traced no higher than the era of Suidas, to whom they are referred by Anthony Van Dale in his *De Oraculis*, 4to, Amstd. 1700, p. 444. Sir Thomas Browne of Norwich, in his *Pseudodoxia Epidemica* (s. v. Cessation of Oracles), gives both a Latin and an English translation of Suidas's Greek triplet; which, in all probability, were made by the eccentric knight himself, who offers, however, no authority for them — a very unusual thing with him. Sir Thomas being a firm believer in the supernatural and satanical character of oracles will account in some measure for this omission. Gibbon, the historian, is silent on this subject; and, we may add, every other trustworthy biographer of Augustus.

The supposed oracle is thus given in Greek by Suidas (Lexicon, Oxford ed., fol. 1834,) under Αὔγουστος :—

Παῖς Ἑβραῖος κέλεταί με, Θεοῖς μακάρεσσιν ἀνάσσων,
Τόνδε δόμον προλιπεῖν, καὶ ἄϊδην αὖθις ἱκέσθαι.
Λοιπὸν ἄπιθι σιγῶν ἐκ βωμῶν ἡμετέρων.

Suidas adds that Augustus on returning to Rome set up an altar with the inscription Ὁ βωμὸς οὗτός ἐστι τοῦ πρωτογόνου Θεοῦ (Hæc est ara primogeniti Dei).

Among the middle-age writers who have cited the "oracle" in question, it is remarkable that Cedrenus alleges no less an authority for it than Eusebius: —

Ὁ δὲ αὐτὸς φησὶν Εὐσέβιος ὅτι οὗτος ὁ Αὔγουστος ἀπελθὼν εἰς Δελφοὺς κ.τ.λ. (See the *Corpus Scrip. Hist. Byzantinæ*, Bonn, 1838, vol. i. p. 320.) This would bring us back to the fourth century. Van Dale, however, as cited above, states that he has failed in discovering the place in Eusebius, and so have we.]

FANNY RUSSELL AND FREDERICK PRINCE OF WALES.—Walpole, in his Letter to the Countess of Ossory, dated 26 August, 1784, speaks of "Fanny Russell's reply to the late Prince of Wales, on the 30th of January, as an anecdote especially worthy of being remembered." Who was Fanny Russell, and where can I find the anecdote?

F. R.

[In the suite of the Princess Amelia, daughter of George II., was a lady of the name of Fanny Russell, the great granddaughter of Oliver Cromwell. One day, it

happened to be the 30th of January, the anniversary of the martyrdom of Charles I., she was in waiting, and occupied in adjusting some part of the Princess's dress, when Frederick, Prince of Wales, came into the room, and sportively said, "For shame, Miss Russell! why have you not been at church, humbling yourself for the sins on this day committed by your ancestor?" "Sir," replied Miss Russell, "for a descendant of the great Oliver Cromwell, it is humiliation sufficient to be employed as I am in pinning up the tail of your sister." Miss Fanny Russell married John Rivett, Esq., formerly of the Guards; he died in 1763, and his wife in 1775.]

WELLESLEY. — On October 10, 1797, Richard, second Earl of Mornington, afterwards Marquis Wellesley in Ireland, was elevated to the British peerage by the title of Lord Wellesley, of Wellesley, in the county of Somerset. Where is Wellesley?

P. S. C.

[The manor of Wells Leigh, which gave name to the eminent family of Wellesley, is in the ancient parish of St. Cuthbert, nearly two miles south of the city of Wells. (*Vide* Collinson's *Somersetshire*, iii. 405, and "N. & Q." 1st S. vi. 585; viii. 255; 2nd S. vii. 164.) Playfair in his *British Family History*, iv. 62, ed. 1810, informs us, that "the ancient family of Wellesley is of Saxon origin, but derives its name from the manor of Wellesley (originally Welles-leigh), in the county of Somerset, which it held under the Bishop of Bath and Wells, and to which it removed soon after the Conquest, having been previously seated in Sussex. Avenant de Wellesleghe, in the fourth year of Henry I., obtained from that prince a grant of the grand serjeantry of all the country east of the river Perret as far as Bristol Bridge; in the centre of which district lay his manor of Wellesleigh, in the hundred of Wells, and near the city of that name."]

OBADIAH WALKER'S PRIVATE PRINTING PRESS.—Where will I see a list of the books *printed* at the private printing press set up at his lodgings by Obadiah Walker, Master of University College.

AIKEN IRVINE, Clk.

Kilbride, Bray.

[In the reign of James II. Obadiah Walker "set up cases of letters and a press in the back part of his lodgings, belonging to him as Master of University College, where he printed the works of Abraham Woodhead, his quondam tutor, and would have printed many more (all, or most, against the Church of England), had King James II. continued longer on the throne." (Wood's *Athenæ* (Bliss), iv. 440.) Walker had a license granted to him by the king, dated May, 1686, for the exclusive sale of certain books for twenty-one years. The license as well as a list of the books to be printed will be found in Gutch's *Miscellanea Curiosa*, i. 287—289.]

LADY ELIZABETH TREVOR.—Sir Richard Steele's daughter married Lord Trevor, and had a daughter Diana. Did this daughter ever marry? If so, who did she marry, and had she any issue, and has she at the present day any descendants?

R. W. E. L.

U. U. Club.

[John, third Lord Trevor, married Elizabeth, daughter of Sir Richard Steele, on May 31, 1731. His lordship died at Bath on Sept. 27, 1764, at which place their only child, Diana-Maria, died on Jan. 29, 1778. She was remarkably beautiful, though unfortunately an idiot. Lady Elizabeth Trevor died on Jan. 1, 1782, and was privately interred in the parish church of Walcott, near Bath.]

URICONIUM, OR WROXETER. — Where can I find a good account of this place, and more especially of the explorations of the ruins? Are these still going on?

ÆSICA.

[For particulars of the excavations at Wroxeter, the ancient Uriconium, consult the *Journal of the Archaeological Association*, xv. 205—224, 311—317, 350, 352, 358; xvi. 342, 349; xvii. 100—110, 218, 329; xviii. 75—78, 398; xix. 106—111. *The Times* newspaper of July 25, Aug. 16, Sept. 3 and 26, Oct. 19, 1859; June 23, July 19, Aug. 13, 1860; Oct. 5, 1861; and Jan. 11, 1862; also an article by Mr. C. Roach Smith in the *Gentleman's Magazine* for Nov. 1862, pp. 598—601.]

BACHELOR OR WIDOWER. — By which of the above is a man to be designated when divorced? A lady, I believe, regains her maiden name.

K. R. C.

[In Macqueen's *Practical Treatise on Marriage, Divorce, and Legitimacy*, the author, speaking of how divorced persons will appear before a clergyman for matrimony, says distinctly (p. 110), "The man will present himself as a bachelor; the woman will come, not as a married person or as a widow, but as a spinster. In a word, the sentence of divorce will effectually restore the parties to their original state."]

Replies.

RED LION.

(3rd S. vii. 136.)

The communication of PRESTONIENSIS respecting the numerous signs of the Red Lion to be found in Lancashire, brought to my recollection a story about that popular animal, which Canning introduced into one of his speeches delivered in Liverpool; and which is so good, that it deserves to be embalmed in your columns. The speech, in which the passage I refer to occurred, was spoken at the Canning Club on the 23rd of August, 1822; when the illustrious orator, alluding to those who put forward "parliamentary reform as the panacea for every evil," proceeded to say: —

"I read a few days ago (I cannot immediately recollect where) a story of an artist who had attained great eminence in painting, but who had directed his art chiefly to one favourite object. That object happened to be a red lion. His first employment was at a publichouse, where the landlord allowed him to follow his fancy. Of course, the artist recommended a Red Lion. A gentleman in the neighbourhood, having a new dining-room to ornament, applied to the artist for his assistance; and, in order that he might have full scope for his talents, left to him the choice of a subject for the principal compartment of the room. The painter took due time to deliberate, and then, with the utmost gravity and earnestness: 'Don't you think,' said he to his employer, 'that a handsome red lion would have a fine effect in this situation?' The gentleman was not entirely convinced, perhaps; however, he let the painter have his way in this instance, determined, nevertheless, that in his library, to which he next conducted the artist, he would have something of more exquisite device and ornament. 'He showed him a small panel over his chimney-piece. 'Here,' says he 'I must have something striking. The space, you see, is but small: the workmanship must be proportionably delicate.' 'What think you,' says the painter, after appearing to dive deep into his imagination for the suggestion, 'what think you of a small red lion?' Just so it is with parliamentary reform. Whatever may be the evil, the remedy is a parliamentary reform; and the utmost variety you can extort from those who call themselves 'moderate reformers,' is, that they will be contented with a *small* red lion."

C. ROSS.

SOBRIQUETS OF REGIMENTS.

(3rd S. vii. 70, 120.)

I wonder that I never heard of the sobriquet of the 33rd Regiment, "Havercake Lads;" as one of my most valued friends, who is yet living, served in that corps in every rank, from ensign to lieut.-colonel inclusive. He gave me the following anecdote of a recruiting-sergeant belonging to the regiment, who addressed his wondering Yorkshire listeners as follows: — "Come, my lads, don't lose your time listening to what them footsogers says about their ridgements. List in my ridgement, and ye'll be all right. *Their* ridgements are obliged to march on foot, but my ridgement is the gallant Thirty-third—the First Yorkshire West Riding ridgement; and when you join head quarters ye'll all be mounted on horseback." My friend Colonel —— assured me that the *ruse* was nearly always successful.

After the death of the late Duke of Wellington, this corps received its present title, "The Duke of Wellington's Regiment," which superseded its former title. During the lifetime of the Duke, he was requested to apply to Her Gracious Majesty for permission to have the 33rd Regiment named after himself; but he firmly declined to do so, stating that such an application must be postponed until after his decease. He died in September, 1852, and the change of the regimental title was gazetted about July, 1853.

Thus far in reply to MR. HAILSTONE.

Your correspondent SCHIN is right as to the 53rd Regiment being called "The Five-and-Threepennies;" and I can assure him that the 76th

Regiment is spoken of by its officers as "The Old Seven-and-Sixpennies"—five-and-threepence being the daily pay of an ensign in our army, and seven-and-sixpence being the daily pay of a lieutenant, whose commission as *lieutenant* is dated seven years since.

The history of how the 76th Regiment obtained red facings is curious. In the year 1718, a regiment was raised and formed from invalids. On the 1st of July, 1751, it was numbered "The Forty-first Regiment;" and was disembodied in 1787, when another regiment was raised and received the same regimental number as the invalid corps which had been disembodied—the colonel of which was appointed colonel of the newly-raised regiment. The new regiment had red facings, and was quartered at Windsor soon after it was raised. In the autumn of that year, it became necessary to raise several regiments for service in India — the present 74th, 75th, 76th, and 77th; and the adjutant proceeded to Windsor, in order to receive His Majesty's commands relative to the equipments and facings of the newly-raised regiments. After deciding on the facings of the 74th and 75th, the King seemed uncertain, and at last remarked: "Seventy-sixth, eh? Seventy-sixth! Why the Forty-first were here lately, and looked very well in their red facings. Let the Seventy-sixth have the same."

In April, 1822, the facings of the 41st Regiment were changed from red to white; and on the 19th of March, same year, the Head Quarter division, under Colonel Godwin, embarked at Gravesend for India. Indeed, I hardly remember any distinction being conferred on a regiment without its being soon followed by an order from the Horse Guards to proceed for a lengthened service on a bad foreign station. Thus, the 13th Regiment was made "Light Infantry" when the corps was on board transports conveying it to India; and, as soon as I saw that the Queen's Bays had had their buff facings restored, April 7, 1855 (after having been for seventy-one years in mourning, *i. e.* wearing black facings), I knew that the Queen's Bays would certainly proceed to India on their next tour of foreign service; and, accordingly, the regiment went to India July 24, 1857, and is still quartered there. The facings were changed from buff to black, in 1784, at the request of the colonel of the regiment, George, fourth Viscount Townshend, and Baron of Lynne; who became Earl of Leicester May 18, 1784. On what grounds did he apply to have the "Bays" put into mourning? Was the previous Earl of Leicester his relative? He was created Marquis Townshend, October 27, 1787; and died September 14, 1807, exactly thirty years after the death of his first wife, Lady Charlotte Compton, only surviving child of the then Earl of Northampton.

With respect to the regiment stated by SCHIN

to have borne an uncomplimentary *sobriquet*, I beg to observe, that I have heard offensive sobriquets applied to regiments; and that such titles shall never be imparted to the readers of " N. & Q." by

, JUVERNA.

A correspondent begs to ask JUVERNA if the 68th Light Infantry, or "The Faithful Durhams," has not been accidentally omitted in his amusing list of Regimental Sobriquets? L.
Brussels.

DUNCANSON FAMILY, OF CANTIRE.

(3rd S. vii. 96.)

All the information I possess about the Duncansons is at the service of F. M. S. From the Army Lists in my possession, 1756-1807, and others which I have consulted from the latter year to 1856, I have gleaned, in chief, the following particulars: —

1. A Robert Duncanson was in the army in 1747, at which time he held rank as second lieutenant in the twelve independent companies formed for service in the East Indies under Admiral Boscawen. With that expedition Duncanson was present in 1748, in the action at Ariacoupan, and the unsuccessful siege of Pondicherry. On the return of the force to England, the independent companies were disbanded on December 25, 1750, and Duncanson placed on half-pay still as a second lieutenant. In 1786 most probably he died, as in 1787 his name disappears from the lists.

2. Duncan Duncanson was a lieutenant in the 100th foot on half-pay in 1772. His regiment was disbanded about 1763. I cannot trace when he first received his commission. In 1773 he disappears altogether from the Army List.

3. Robert Duncanson (written Robertson Duncanson in Army Lists in error, see Stewart's *Highlanders*, ii. 113; 3rd edition, 1825), joined 2nd battalion 71st foot on its formation, and was commissioned as lieutenant Dec. 1, 1775. Next year he was serving in the American war. On Nov. 12, 1778, he was promoted to be captain in the same regiment, and was still in America. When his regiment was disbanded in 1783, he was placed on half-pay; but returned to the service on full-pay as captain of the 77th foot, Nov. 6, 1788. In the Army List, 1791, under the head of "Alterations while Printing," p. 440, Robert Duncanson appears as captain in the 23rd foot, not, however, in the roll of the regiment; and, as his name is altogether dropped in the Army List, 1792, most likely he quitted the service by sale of his commission.

4. William Duncanson was ensign in 82nd foot, Jan. 3, 1778, and served in the American war, obtaining his lieutenancy, Sept. 18, 1780. About

1784 his regiment was broken up, and he placed on half-pay. In 1785 he occurs on the half-pay of the 25th foot, as one of the additional lieutenants; and in 1820 his name disappeared from the roll.

5. James Duncanson was assistant-surgeon of the 81st foot, April 25, 1811; but his connexion with it was soon at an end, as his name is dropped in the List for 1813. He turns up again in an inferior capacity on May 26, 1815, as Hospital-Assistant, with the degree of M.D. added to his name three years later. In 1817 he was on half-pay as Hospital-Assistant, from which he was removed Oct. 27, 1825, as Assistant-Surgeon to the 49th foot, to return again to the half-pay June 25, 1828. In time he assumed his place on the full-pay as Assistant-Surgeon on the staff of the Medical Department. On June 1, 1838, he joined the 1st West India regiment as surgeon, and died at Barbadoes while surgeon of the 46th foot, April 17, 1843. (*Unit. Ser. Jour.* 2, 1843, p. 639.)

F. M. S. speaks of a Captain John Duncanson, who was killed in a duel at Malta. No officer of that name was in the army during the last hundred years.

Some of the earliest Army Lists have no indexes, and the half-pay for many years after was published without this useful means of reference. I have however gone through every page of these unindexed volumes, and the above details may be accepted as the entire information they contain relative to the Duncansons.

A few of the names may be new to F. M. S. Of their connexion one with another I can offer no clue; but, as they all possess a strong family likeness, I thought it well to adduce all I could collect about them for the use of F. M. S., and any of your readers interested in the family.

M. S. R.

Brompton Barracks.

RICHARD JAMES: ASSASSINATION OF THE DUKE OF BUCKINGHAM.

(3rd S. vii. 135.)

Your correspondent, S. Y. R., will find the lines quoted in Sir James Balfour's *Historical Works*, ii. 174, more correctly printed, but without proper punctuation, in Mr. Fairholt's *Poems and Songs relating to George Villiers Duke of Buckingham, and his Assassination by Felton*, Percy Society, 1850, p. 69. No author's name is there subjoined, but there is no doubt that the lines are, as mentioned in Balfour, by Richard James, whose poetical style is a peculiar one, and can scarcely be mistaken. There is, indeed, the copy of a letter without any address or date, amongst his MSS. (Preface to *Iter Lancastrense*, pp. 56-58), containing his "Reasons concerning the Attempts on the Lives of great Personages," in which he concludes that "personages of state, though they deserve ill, may not be violated mortally out of any man's religion and pietie." But this may have been written as a blind, and if even his opinions were contrary to this conclusion, it is very unlikely that he would have deliberately avowed them when called upon to advise or pronounce dogmatically in a written document which might afterwards have been traced back to him. The most elaborate account of this learned man, and which is not noticed by your correspondent, is that prefixed to James's *Iter Lancastrense*, edited by the Rev. Thomas Corser for the Chetham Society in 1845, in which are inserted several specimens of his poetry. Great interest attaches to his occasional verses, as Mr. Hunter has attributed to him, and is followed by Mr. Singer, Mr. W. W. Lloyd, and others, the admirable lines first prefixed to the second folio edition of Shakspeare, signed J. M. S.; and there is sufficient similarity in style and general character between those lines and others to which he has appended his name, to make the question one which may be considered still *sub judice*.

Of the proceedings against James for the panegyric upon Felton, I am not aware of any other mention than that made by Balfour. No such proceedings appear to be noticed in Mr. Bruce's *Calendar of State Papers for* 1628-9. His other troubles arising from his intimacy with Sir Robert Cotton, and the manuscript entitled *A Project*, &c., are well known.

Mr. Forster, in his excellent *Life of Sir John Eliot*, edit. 1864, vol. ii., gives the substance of an interesting letter from James to him on literary subjects, not before published, and some notes on Eliot's *Monarchy of Man*, which are very curious.

Jas. Crossley.

DOCKING HORSES (1st S. vi. 43.) I beg to forward you a more correct version of the Epigram attributed to Voltaire by your correspondent F. B—w:—

" Vous fiers Anglois,
    Barbares que vous êtes,
    Coupez la tête aux Rois
    Et la queue à vos bêtes ;
    Mais les François,
    Polis et droits,
    Aiment les lois,
    Laissent la queue aux bêtes
    Et la tête à leurs Rois."

Omega.

Jersey.

Passage in Eusebius: Dr. Cureton and the "Quarterly Review" (3rd S. vii. 110.)—Lælius is no doubt correct in his conjecture, that Dr. Cureton did not fall into the mistake ascribed to him by the reviewer. I have referred to Heiniken, and only find what exactly accords with Dr. Cureton's notes, but in a shorter form. The Syriac of the *Martyrs of Palestine* gives us the name of Valentina's companion three times: first in the title to the section, and afterwards in a passage which Dr. Cureton thus rendered: —

" He caused both the young women, Hatha and Valentina, to be bound together, and gave sentence against them of death by fire. The name of the first was Hatha, and her father's house was in the land of Gaza; and the other was from Cæsarea, our own city; and she was well known to many, and her name was Valentina."—P. 30.

I need scarcely say, that this justly represents the Syriac text. With regard to the passage in the Greek, where the word ἀδελφὰ occurs, it differs from the Syriac; in which no such idea is conveyed, at least not in similar diction. I need not repeat the Greek which your correspondent has quoted, but I copy Dr. Cureton's rendering of the Syriac which answers to it: —

" Then, at that time of terror, the noble maiden showed the courage of her mind and gave the altar a kick with her foot, and it was overturned; and the fire that had been kindled upon it was scattered about," &c.—P. 29.

I venture to append as literal a translation as I can make of this sentence: —

" Then the noble maiden, in that time of fear, the courage of her mind displayed; and kicked the altar with her foot, and it was overturned, and the fire that upon it was burning she scattered."

The late—alas, that it must be said!—*the late* learned Canon has stumbled at the last word; but he has not made the mistake ascribed to him by the reviewer, who cannot have carefully read the passage.   B. H. C.

Street Melody: "Young Lambs to sell" (3rd S. vii. 118.)—I well remember this cry in Birmingham full sixty years ago; and the seller must have been the old sailor described by Hone in his *Table Book*, p. 397, or rather by some correspondent, as the article bears the signature of an asterisk. But I also recollect seeing the old soldier, William Liston, who followed up the trade of the old sailor. This was in Northampton, about forty years ago; and I distinctly recollect his peculiar appearance with his wooden leg, iron hook for a right hand, and his remarkable way of crying his "Young lambs to sell." He first gave a prelude of a few bars without words, of which I could not convey an idea without musical notation; and this served to collect boys and girls about him, and excite attention. Then came his cry,—

"Lambs to sell,
Young lambs to sell;
If I'd as much money as I could tell,
I never would cry: 'Young lambs to sell,
Young lambs to sell.'"

This was his cry, as I remember it. I quite agree with Mr. Roffe that the "Young lambs"

we purchased in our childhood were far superior to those of modern manufacture.   F. C. H.

Readers (3rd S. vii. 109.)—The office is described at large, with the declaration which Readers have to sign since the Reformation, in Burn's *Eccles. Law, sub tit.*, and in Hook's *Church Dictionary*.   E. Marshall.
Sandford.

Weever, in his *Funeral Monuments*, p. 127, ed. 1631, says,—

" Readers, quos Pastores (à pasco) nominatos putat Ambrosius, matutino tempore Prophetarum Apostolorumque scripta legebant, ac populum divinis lectionibus quasi pascebant. Which Saint Ambrose supposeth to be called Pastours by the Apostle Paul: did rede the writings of the Prophets and Apostles, at the time of morning prayer, and did feede, as it were, the people with such divine lessons."
                                                                J. H. S.

"For a Year and a Day" (3rd S. vii. 116.)—S. inquires the origin of the above phrase. In English it is as old as the thirteenth century, at least, for it occurs in Magna Charta; by which it is declared that—

" The King do not hold the lands of them that he convicted of felony longer than a year and a day (' Nisi per unum annum et unum diem '), after which they shall be restored to the lord of the fee."

But the use of the phrase is probably antecedent to this: for as Magna Charta was not a new legislative creation of the reign of King John—but consists, at least in part, of re-enactments from earlier laws, Norman, Saxon, or British—this article may probably be traced to a prior date. From feudal associations, one would conjecture that it was Norman; but Barrington, in his *Observations on the more Ancient Statutes*, points out that an equivalent French law omits the "one day," and gives the king possession only for the year—" pour la première année;" whilst he quotes from the Danish law an instance, in which the term of the "year and the day" occurs: " Si agricola domum reliquerit, vicini *per annum et diem*, quo minus destruatur, custodiant" (p. 15).

The precise period of a year and a day is fixed for other purposes in the statute of Gloucester in the reign of Edward I., and in many laws later than Magna Charta. Barrington suggests that the "addition of the day to the year may have been made with a view to prevent all disputes about inclusive and exclusive" (*ib.*). Was it for a similar reason that a youth's majority has been fixed at twenty-one? so as to be absolutely certain that he had attained twenty.

Amongst the natives in some parts of India, the number of blows legally inflicted for certain offences, is thirty-nine: being the "forty stripes save one," which St. Paul complains that he had so frequently received from the Jews. Has this precise figure been fixed on to ensure that the punishment shall not be excessive, by keeping the number of lashes *under* forty?

There is an oriental air about the addition of the unit, especially when the numbers are large, that reminds one of *The Thousand* AND ONE *Nights* of the King Shahriyar, and recalls the dreamy stories of the Princess Shahrazade.

J. EMERSON TENNENT.

QUOTATION WANTED: "OH! WHY WER'N'T YE CUNNING," ETC. (3rd S. vii. 56.)—These lines form a portion of a song called "The Widow M'Gra." I have never seen it in print, but it runs thus:—

"If ye'll listen to me now, without any fun,
Sure I'll tell ye how the war begun:
But of all the wars, both great and wild,
There was that betune widow M'Gra and her child!
Musha tooral loo, &c.

"Now if Teddy would list, the serjeant said,
That soon a captain he'd be made;
With a fine long soord, and a big cocked hat,
'Arrah! Teddy, my child, wouldn't you like that?'
Musha tooral loo, &c.

"Then Teddy he fought his way through Spain,
And to the Indies back again—
And the hundreds and thousands that he kilt,
Sure a mortial volume might be filt!
Musha tooral loo, &c.

"Then Widow M'Gra waited on the shore,
For the space of seven long years and more—
'Till she saw two ships sailing over the say,
Crying, 'Phililu, hubbaboo, whack, clear the way!'
Musha tooral loo, &c.

"Then Teddy he lighted on the strand,
And Widow M'Gra seized him by the hand;
But after she had given him a kiss or two,
Sez she, 'Teddy, my child, this can't be you!'
Musha tooral loo, &c.

"'Arrah! my son Teddy was straight and trim,
And had just one leg to every limb;
Arrah! my son Teddy was straight and tall,
But the divil reçave the leg have ye got at all!'
Musha tooral loo, &c.

"'Oh! why weren't ye cunning, and why weren't ye cute?
And why didn't ye run away from the Frenchman's shoot?
To think that I my child should call
A man, who couldn't stop the force of a French cannon ball!'
Musha tooral loo, &c.

"'But a thundering war I will proclaim
Against the King of the Frinch, and the snuffy ould Queen of Spain;
And I'll make them sorely to rue the time,
That ever they shot off the legs of a child of mine!'
Musha tooral loo, &c."

The first two lines of each verse are sung twice over. I have heard the song sung more than twenty years ago by poor Johnstone, the scene-painter of the Adelphi, and never by any one else. JOHN PAVIN PHILLIPS.
Haverfordwest.

VENERABLE BEDE (3rd S. vi. 358, 401, 480.)—In the edition published in 1848 of Wheatly's

Rational Illustration of the Book of Common Prayer of the Church of England, the following passage occurs at p. 64, and refers to the Venerable Bede:—

"His learning and piety gained him the surname of *Venerable*. Though the common story which goes about that title's being given him, is this: his scholars having a mind to fix a rhyming title upon his tombstone, as was the custom in those times, the poet wrote,

HAC SUNT IN FOSSA,
BEDÆ   OSSA.

Placing the word OSSA at the latter end of the verse for the rhyme, but not being able to think of any proper epithet that would stand before it. The monk being tired in this perplexity to no purpose fell asleep; but when he awaked, he found his verse filled up by an angelic hand, standing thus in fair letters upon the tomb;

HAC SUNT IN FOSSA,
BEDÆ VENERABILIS OSSA."

I look on this passage as a literary curiosity, the style and punctuation of which are alike worthy of each other. I should hardly have liked to send up such an exercise

"At Merchant Taylors' School, what time
Old Bishop held the rod."

I remember at a Divinity Examination at Oxford more than twenty years since being furnished by the Examiner with the following paper: "State what ou know of the History of the Venerable Bede." My answer was that, "His learning and piety had rendered him conspicuous, and the epithet of 'Venerable' was probably conferred upon him for *that* reason, but certainly not on account of his advanced age, as he died in his sixty-second year." My venerable Examiner, being then but forty-five years old, may have taken my answer as a sly compliment to himself, as I was ordained very high up in the list of candidates for Priest's Orders in a few days after my examination.

One question remains to be asked—If the monk were asleep when the epithet "venerabilis" was added to the inscription, how could he be certain that the verse was "filled up by an angelic hand?" EIN FRAGER, M.A. OXON.

"JOANNES AD OPPOSITUM": TRANSLATION OF ENGLISH PROVERB (3rd S. vii. 114.)—

"To be Jack on both sides; 'Coser a dos cabos,' Span. 'Αλλοπρόβαλλος, a turncoat, a weathercock."—Ray's *Proverbs*.

E. MARSHALL.
Sandford.

SUPERSTITION OR SYMPATHY, WHICH? (3rd S. vi. 496; vii. 45.)—That gifted and admirable man, the late Dr. George Wilson of Edinburgh, thus describes his own sensations subsequent to the amputation of his foot:—

"I have no feeling of the want of a foot, and seem still to feel toes, great and small. John Cairns [*] thinks this

* The Rev. Dr. Cairns of Berwick.

must arise from a pre-ordained harmony between the soul and body!!! Well done, John!"—*Memoir by his Sister*, p. 301.

A recent American writer, in a very curious and objectionable book, says:—

"Within the corporeal frame there is another body, constituted of more ethereal elements, and an imperishable organisation. It is a curious fact, that persons who have lost a limb always have an internal consciousness that the body is still complete. Although an arm or a leg may have been amputated years before, and its decomposed elements scattered to the winds and waves, the individual still feels that the lost member is with him, and sustaining its proper relations; and his sensation extends to the very extremity, almost as perfectly as when the limb was there. This may seem incredible, but the fact is confirmed by the uniform experience of all who have suffered the loss of one or more of their members. The sphere of their conscious existence is never circumscribed by this partial destruction of the body. From this significant fact we can only infer that the individuality of man does not belong to his body, but, on the contrary, that it inheres in a super-mortal and indestructible constitution."—Dr. S. B. Brittan, *Man and his Relations*, pp. 574, 575.

Dr. Kerner tells us that Madame Hauffé, the "Seeress of Prevorst," when she saw people who had lost a limb, saw the limb still attached to the body; that is, she saw the nerve-projected form of the limb.

"From this interesting phenomenon," he adds, "we may, perhaps, explain the sensations of persons who still have feeling of a limb that has been amputated: the invisible nerve-projected form of the limb is still in connexion with the visible body."

Fancy or fact, which? *one* at least of your readers is disposed to ask.
W. MAUDE.
Birkenhead.

DIGHTON'S CARICATURES (3rd S. iv. 410; vii. 119.)—Bos PIGER has furnished you with several racy anecdotes of the medical practitioners at Oxford in the early part of this century. May I be allowed to fill up his line,

"Optat ephippia bos piger, optat arare caballus."

As a scholar at Alma Mater in their day; I was well acquainted (happily not as a patient) with these doctors, and remember their professional phizzes, dress, &c. Grosvenor sported a venerable powdered pate, and wore a blue coat with brass buttons, the correct thing in that day for an elderly surgeon. Dr. Bourne, on the contrary, clad himself in a sober suit of brown, with a neat brown wig to match, and carried a gold-headed cane in his hand. Dr. Wall, another eminent medical, was attired pretty nearly after the same fashion of the time. *Ex uno disce omnes.* In the Vista, when the two doctors chanced to walk in High Street; they heard the description of family likeness, often quoted from Ovid;

"Qualis decet esse sororum,
Non eadem facies omnibus, una tamen."

Of the skill in these learned practitioners we

undergraduates did not pretend to judge, but like the Dons in Common Room, sometimes perpetuated wretched puns upon their names, over our wine and walnuts; *e. g.*, The weakest go to the Wall; the Bourne from whence no traveller returns—were the *post prandial* jokes of unfledged scholars with gooseberry beards. The Fellows, old grey-beards, confined themselves to Attic wit from the Greek and Latin classics. Bos PIGER has omitted to mention a contemporary professor with Bourne and Wall; the late Sir Christopher Pegge, who had the good fortune to be dubbed, at the same time with Sir Edward Hitchins, a knight of the thimble, in the presentation of a loyal address from the city of Oxford. On their return from London, Sir Edward was proud of the royal honour conferred upon the mayor; not so Sir Christopher. His new title did not settle comfortably on the stomach of the professor. His appetite began to fail; his clothes (made by Hitchins) hung loosely about him; he could get no sound sleep when he went to his bed; his medical brethren, Wall and Bourne, were called in, and consulted long and thoughtfully on the seat of the disease. It was beyond doubt their patient was a *peg* too low from some nervous affection. From whence did it arise? They determined to call in Grosvenor to help them in council. When the "Rubber" obeyed the call, post haste, of his medical brothers, both of them anxiously exclaimed, "What *is* your opinion?" The Rubber, with a look not to be mistaken, whispered in a slow and solemn tone—"*night-mare.*"
QUEEN'S GARDENS.

LUNATIC LITERATURE (3rd S. vii. 120.)—In justice to our American friends I would refer your readers to Mr. Sala's "Echoes of the Week," in the *Illustrated London News* of Feb. 11, in which he entirely refutes the statement that one of the principal New York papers was edited by a lunatic.
EDWARD C. DAVIES.
Cavendish Club.

XIMENES, ETC. (3rd S. vii. 102.)—The arms of Cardinal Ximenes were chequy or and gu. In Goussencourt, *Martyrologe des Chevaliers de Malthe*, Paris,1643, tome ii. p. 257, the arms of this family are blazoned correctly; but the engraving would make the tinctures *arg.* and gu. Very few indeed of the engravings, either in this work or in Favyn's *Théâtre d'Honneur et de Chévalerie* (Paris, 1620), have the *hachures* in accordance with the blazon: and that Favyn knew nothing of the system at present in use is proved by his speaking with praise of the German method of indicating the tinctures by small initial letters, as in Siebmacher's *Wäppenbuch*, &c. He says (tome ii. p. 1797):—

"Il y pouvoit demonstrer les Couleurs, et Metaulx du moins, ce qui luy estoit assez aisé de faire, s'il cognoissoit et sçavoit la façon admirable et gentille dont les Alemans (Doctes et Curieux en Armes s'il y en eut jamais) se servent.

"Façon que nos Graveurs devroient imiter, et ensuivre. Les Alemans (dis-je) representât l'arme d'une gentilhomme, ont des Lettres qui leur servent de Marques et de Notes, pour representer les Metaux et Blasons de l'Escu, les Cimiers, Lambrequins et Supports," &c. &c.

J. WOODWARD.

New Shoreham.

In answer to LÆLIUS, as to the coat of the Cardinal, I am afraid I shall only increase his difficulty instead of helping him; as he will find a third coat assigned, differing from either of the two he mentions. In the frontispiece of the *Missa Gothica seu Mozarabica*, published at "Angelopoli, MDCCLXX.," the arms are given, with the tinctures marked as chequy or and azure; and a dissertation upon them in Latin and Greek, with a translation into Spanish.   W. A. F. A.

SOLICITOR AT GOLDSMITHS' HALL (3rd S. vii. 42.)—Commissioners for compounding the estates of the cavaliers sat at Goldsmiths' Hall as well as at the Haberdashers'. A list of those from whom fines were forced will be found reprinted in Morgan's *Phœnix Britannicus*. Dr. Grey, in his *Notes to Hudibras* (pt. I. c. iii. l. 878), quotes a cavalier song which declares —

"Our money shall never indite us,
Nor drag us to Goldsmiths' Hall:
No pirates nor wrecks can affright us.
We that have no estates,
Fear no plunder nor rates,
We can sleep with open gates;
He that lies on the ground cannot fall."

It is probable that the passage in Cowley alluded to the solicitors who practised before the commission?   P. W. TREPOLPEN.

CHEVISAUNCE (3rd S. vii. 114.) — Spenser elsewhere uses this word in the sense of an achievement, performance, or acquisition. It is derived from the French verb *chevir*, which means to master, or overcome. Hence I think it most probable that the name of *chevisaunce* was given to the herb *masterwort*, which, though now fallen into disuse, was formerly cultivated in gardens, and is extolled for its virtues in old herbals. The German apothecaries call it *Ostericium* or *Astrencium*: Dioscorides (bk. iii. ch. 17) describes it under the name of *Smyrnon*; but the usual botanical names are *Imperatoria*, *Astrantia*, or *Magistrantia*. Our English name *Masterwort* is evidently borrowed from the German *Meisterwurz*.

F. C. H.

"THE VICAR AND MOSES" (2nd S. iii. 112; 3rd S. vii. 125.)—MR. ALLBUTT's communication is interesting and curious, and would be valuable were it less vague. Are we to understand that the great grandfather of his own name had the *Christian name* of T. Clifford? There is perhaps some reason for suppressing the name of the parish in which was

situate his "small country house in Herefordshire;" but I should like a reference to the particular volumes of the *Gentleman's Magazine* which contain "several satirical poems and like pieces by his hand." The date of his death should also I think be furnished. I don't press for the name of "the squire of the parish" to whom allusion is made, inasmuch, as by giving it, a clue might be afforded to the identification of its drunken vicar. Will MR. ALLBUTT pardon my observing that, unless he is more specific and precise, the claim of his great grandfather to the authorship of "The Vicar and Moses" will hardly be considered as well made out?   S. Y. R.

I heartily thank MR. T. CLIFFORD ALLBUTT for his interesting information of the author of the favourite old song, "The Vicar and Moses." Referring to my former communication on the different versions of it (2nd S. iii. 178), I find I have there mentioned a new song on the same subject of my own composition. I fear it would not be admissible into "N. & Q." on account of its length, as it contains twenty-two verses; but any intimation from the editor in the "Notices to Correspondents" to the contrary would at once induce me to send a copy, though it has never yet travelled out of the author's possession.   F. C. H.

BATTLE OF LEIPSIC: ROCKETS (2nd S. viii. 537; 3rd S. vii. 43.)—How is it this weapon appears to have fallen out of use? It seems to have done the greatest service at Leipsic and at Waterloo, and yet we hear nothing of it in the struggle in the Crimea, nor in that now going on in America. It would be very interesting if some military engineer would enlighten us on the point. From all accounts, the rocket seems to have been peculiarly terrible to cavalry.   A. A.

Poets' Corner.

DAVISON'S CASE (3rd S. vii. 80.) — In the case related in the *Story Teller*, the murder was committed by "prussic acid," and the prisoner was tried on the Northern Circuit by Lord Mansfield. The existence of prussic acid is recorded to have been discovered in 1709, and it was first obtained in a separate state about 1782 six years before the retirement of Lord Mansfield from the bench. I do not find that his lordship ever took the Northern Circuit but once, and that was in 1758; and I would ask some of your correspondents, familiar with the matter, whether murder by prussic acid was known "in the last century." I have been under the impression that no such case was ever tried in this country till the present century had been more than a quarter gone.

J. C.

THE INSCRIPTION ON THE CROSS (3rd S. vii. 75, 143.)—The oldest post-biblical copy of this inscription which I remember, is in the book of Antoninus Martyr, *De Locis Sanctis*, about A.D.

570. This writer says he saw the title, which was placed above the head of Jesus; and upon it was written: "Jesus Nazarenus Rex Judæorum." He says he held it in his hand and kissed it, in the church of Constantine at Jerusalem (sec. 20). He is silent in reference to the Greek and Hebrew. The most recent article upon the subject is in the *Sunday at Home* for 1864, p. 804. I may remark that, in one MS. of Antoninus, the reading is "Hic est Rex Judæorum;" and that there is considerable diversity in Greek MSS. of the Gospels as to the words employed by Pilate. The actual order of the languages cannot be determined, and the question is rather curious than important. For a description of the title, as shown at Rome, see Severano, *Memorie Sacre delle Sette Chiese di Roma* (Rome, 1630), p. 626. This title was found in 1492, and is mentioned by writers soon after.
                                                            B. H. C.

"Mungo" (3rd S. vii. 135.)—Was not the term "mungo" given to a low class of woollen goods in consequence of the manufacturer, when the bad quality of them was pointed out to him, saying: "Well—well—there they are, and they mun go;" "mun go" being a provincialism for "must go": meaning thereby, that they *must be sold* at any sacrifice, rather than *not be sold at all?*
Hence low rubbishy woollens have taken the name of "mungos."   J. B. C.

I cannot help G. G. to the origin of the term "mungo," as applied to shoddy, or devil's dust; but I can inform him that the name "mungo" is applied, in the north of Ireland—and, for aught I know, in Scotland also—to an alkaline liquid used for cleansing linen yarns. What the mungo is composed of I have no notion; but I can answer for it that it is useful for cleansing other things besides yarn: since when, boy like, I had my hands covered with thick dirt, I have often made them perfectly clean and white by simply washing them in a vat of mungo in a friend's mill.
                                                            C. W.

Greek Church (3rd S. vii. 134.)—I will keep clear of all controversy in a brief reply to the inquiries of G. G. As to the precise relation of the Greek Church to the Roman Catholic: it is the relation of a schismatical and heretical church, entirely separated from her communion. It is so in consequence of its denying the Procession of the Holy Ghost from the Father and the Son, and maintaining that the Holy Ghost proceeds from the Father *only;* and also, from its denial of the Pope's supremacy. In every other article of faith, the Greek Church agrees with the Roman Catholic, believing in the same seven sacraments, the mass, purgatory, &c.
As to the precise relation in which the Greek Church stands to the Church of England, it agrees with it in one only point—the denial of the Pope's

supremacy. The Greek Church does not acknowledge the validity of the Anglican Orders. Copious information on the Greek Church may be had by consulting the great and learned work, *La Perpetuité de la Foi;* which gives professions of faith, definitions of synods, liturgies, and ecclesiastical records, in abundance. Much information may be derived also from Bergier's *Dict. de Théologie,* and Bell's *Wanderings of the Human Intellect.*
                                                            F. C. H.

The best and fullest account of the Greek Church in our language, I believe, is the Rev. J. Mason Neale's *History of the Holy Eastern Church* (Masters or Rivington, I think). G. G. will probably find there what he wants.   Lyttelton.
Hagley, Stourbridge.

An article, entitled "The Greeks of the Greek Church in London," by William Gilbert, appears in the number of *Good Words* for the present month. I think it will prove interesting to G. G., and afford him the information he requires.
                                                            C. K.

Limehouse (3rd S. vii. 35, 121.) — May I quote the following from *An Account of Millwall,* published in 1853 ? —

"In behalf of the common derivation of this name, we may quote Mr. Pepys. In his *Diary* under date, October 9, 1661, we find the following : — 'By coach to Captain Marshe's at Limehouse, to a place that hath been their ancestors' for this 250 years, close by the *lime-house* which gives the name to the place.' The lime-house is there to this day, and also a house, which, if I mistake not, is either the same, or occupies the same site, as the one mentioned by Mr. Pepys. John Stow, a man possessing far more of the spirit of an antiquary, and who made such things his particular study, adopts the view that Limehouse is a corrupt spelling for Lime-host, or Lime-hurst ; the latter of which denotes a plantation or a place of lime-trees. John Norden, in 1592, rather earlier than Stow, gives the more usual explanation, and, as we have seen, refers to the lime-kilns. These lime-kilns are very ancient, and must have existed for 450 years."

The reference to Limehouse by Norden mentioned previously seems to be the insertion of the name in his map. (See the *Account of Millwall, &c.,* pp. 12, 108.) There is a good plan of Limehouse in Gascoyne's *Survey of Stepney,* 1703 — a large map of the old parish of Stebonheath. The plate comprising the Limehouse section was a few years since at the Town Hall of the parish, and I have an impression (modern of course) taken from it. This is what I was told on the spot.   B. H. C.

S. Decharmes, London (3rd S. vii. 133.) — Mr. Simon De Charmes, the eminent watchmaker, flourished about the beginning of the last century. He built a house at Hammersmith, which is now called Grove Hall (at present unoccupied). The estate contained about twenty-five acres. About 1730 his son, David De Charmes, resided here, and was buried in the churchyard, in which is now a gravestone to the memory of Mr. David De Charmes (probably the son of the last named), who died March 15, 1783, aged fifty-six years. John De Charmes, Esq., died July 15, 1801, aged forty-seven years. Mrs. Ann De Charmes, relict of the above, died Nov. 20, 1812, aged eighty years. Also Mrs. Mary Ann De Sailly, daughter of David and Ann De Charmes, who died March 24, 1822. The estate referred to has passed through several possessors during the present century, but Mrs. Mary Ann De Charmes, wife of David De Charmes, enjoyed an annuity of 200*l.*, payable out of the property, to her death, which occurred in the month of July, 1856. It is said (Faulkner's *Hist. of Hammersmith*) that the ancestor of this family came to England at the time of the Revocation of the Edict of Nantes, but I do not find the name in the Lists of Foreign Protestants and Aliens settled in England between 1618 and 1688, edited by Wm. Durrant Cooper, Esq., F.S.A., for the Camden Society, in 1862. Isaac *des Camps* obtained letters of denization in 1684.   JOHN MACLEAN.

Hammersmith.

COLOURS IN HERALDRY (3rd S. vi. 394, 480; vii. 102.) — I have seen some woodcuts in an old German work, *The Council of Constance*, published early in the sixteenth century, in which the distinction between *metal* and *tincture* was given by *white* for the first, and *black* for the second. It would be interesting to trace the commencement of this mode of distinction. It would probably date from the invention of block printing.   Z. Z.

HAYS OF ERROL (3rd S. vii. 84.) — If H. will carefully read over my article on the Hays of Errol, he will find it perfectly correct. Sir David de Haya de Erroll, who commenced the existing *Tabill* about 1346, says that many names of his ancestors were wanting from the time of the battle of Luncarty, DCCCCLXXX., to his commencement of the *Tabill* in 1346.   JAMES DAVIDSON.

Bowness.

CRINOLINE (3rd S. vi. 512.) — I have impressions of two engravings, in large folio, of the street cries of some Italian city. They are on copper, apparently by different artists, and seem to be from the sixteenth century, or the first half of the seventeenth. In both the figures of the cries are arranged in five long lines, eight or nine figures in each line. The one unsigned has forty-three criers, each with a descriptive cry, a couplet in Italian below. The other has the engraver's monogram at the lower corner on the right, but it is very faint, apparently MB, which I cannot identify. It has forty-one such cries and criers, with similar couplets in Italian at the foot of each. The third in the third line is a man selling crinolines, exactly as we see them in our shop windows. He has three of these hateful objects slung on his back, which he holds by a string in his right hand, while he holds one such in his left hand. The lines below are,—

"Correte o donne che hauete i puscini
A comprar questi belli nostri crini."

Am I right in translating this —

"Who will my fine new crinnies try !
Come, girls with child, make haste to buy !"

If so, and if they were properly designed to hide pregnancy, and supposing that these abominations must still be used, might they not be brought back to their original moderate size, and confined to their original mock-modest object?
GEORGE STEPHENS.

Cheapinghaven, Denmark.

TOWN CLERK'S SIGNATURE (3rd S. vii. 136.) — The clerks of assize of the various circuits, and several officers of the courts of justice, sign by their surnames only the various writs which they issue.   G.

YORKSHIRE POET (3rd S. vi. 389.) — Why a *Yorkshire* poet? Has the author ever been identified? My copy is in 8vo, and has the following title: —

"Pecuniæ obediunt Omnia. Money masters all things: or, Satyrical Poems, shewing the Power and Influence of Money over all Men, of what Profession or Trade soever they be. To which are added, A Lenten Litany, by Mr. C——d, a Satyr on Mr. Dryden, and several other modern Translators; also, a Satyr on Women in general; together with Mr. Oldham's Character of a certain Ugly Old P——.

" ' Tho' Jews, Turks, Christians, different tenets hold,
Yet all agree in idolizing gold.'

"Printed and sold by the Booksellers of London and Westminster, 1698."

The poem has no merit as such, but it contains many valuable illustrations of the social and domestic manners of the seventeenth century, particularly among the lower and trading orders. This edition has first two pages of poetry, "To the Reader." The following recommendatory verses are signed not in full but with initials only. Those by R. J. are "To his Honoured Kinsman," not "Uncle," as in MR. HAILSTONE's copy. Section LXXXV., "On Booksellers," p. 58, in my copy, commences thus: —

"The Bookseller for ready cash will sell
For as small profit as other traders will;
But then you must take special care, and look
You no new title have to an old book;
For they new title pages often paste
Unto a book which purposely is plac'd,
Setting it forth to be th' second edition,
Or third, or fourth, with 'mendments and addition;
But when you come for to peruse and look,
You will not find one word in all the book
Put either in or out, no, nor amended,
For that's a thing that never was intended
By the author; but when a book begins to fail,
This is their trick to quicken up the sale.

And if a new edition comes indeed,
From all th' old books they have, they then with speed
The title-pages oft pluck out and tear,
And new ones in their places fixed are;
Then have the confidence to put to sale
Such books for new they know are old and stale;
And th' buyer thus, if he does not descry,
Will have a cheat put on him purposely."

All the rest of this severe but true description is well worth reading. Many curious words occur throughout the book. The last section, No. CLXXVI., "The Epilogue," is only of two lines: —

"My Muse is tir'd, so has no more to say,
But that *Pecuniæ obediunt omnia.*"

GEORGE STEPHENS.
Cheapinghaven, Denmark.

Miscellaneous.

NOTES ON BOOKS, ETC.

Haunted London. By Walter Thornbury. *Illustrated by F. W. Fairholt.* (Hurst & Blackett.)

Horace Walpole praised St. Foix's *Rues de Paris,* and proposed to write a book on London of the same character. What Walpole proposed Mr. Thornbury, who claims to be the Old Mortality of bygone London, has accomplished for the western part of it; and starting from Temple Bar, and walking westward until he turns up St. Martin's Lane, he returns by Long Acre and Drury Lane to Lincoln's Inn Fields; and as he leads us with him, points out "the legendary houses, the great men's birthplaces, the haunts of poets, the scenes of martyrdoms, and the battle-fields of old factions." He tells us how "the tombs of great men, in the chinks of which nettles have grown undisturbed ever since the Great Fire, are now being uprooted;" and "how busily Time, the destroyer and improver, is working—erasing tombstones, blotting out names on street-doors, battering down narrow streets, and effacing one by one the memories of the good, the bad, the illustrious, and the infamous." The book overflows with anecdotical gossip; and as Mr. Thornbury is scrupulous in quoting his authorities, and indexing his facts, he has produced a volume which will make all who read it look anxiously for its successors. One word more in justice to Mr. Fairholt, whose drawings on wood from the old prints of London add alike to the value and interest of the book.

A Famous Forgery; being the Story of the Unfortunate Dr. Dodd. By Percy Fitzgerald, M.A. (Chapman & Hall.)

The story of Dr. Dodd—his strange career, his wretched crime, his melancholy death, the great moralist's interference in his behalf, the apparent indisposition of Lord Chesterfield to save his unfortunate tutor from the penalty of his misdeeds—furnish Mr. Fitzgerald with materials for a very readable little volume; in which the principal incidents of Dr. Dodd's career are so illustrated by contemporary gossip, as to bring them very vividly before the reader. We wish Mr. Fitzgerald had been able to cast some light upon the terrible insinuation thrown out by Walpole.

Bibliotheca Americana: a Catalogue of Books, Pamphlets, Manuscripts, Maps, Engravings, and Engraved Portraits, illustrative of the History and Geography of North and South America, &c., on Sale. By J. Russell Smith.

Though it is not our practice to call attention to Bookseller's Catalogues generally, the present, containing as it

does nearly seven thousand articles relating to America, certainly claims recognition as a valuable contribution to American Bibliography.

We are glad to see that Messrs. Longman announce a new edition of Brande's *Dictionary of Science, Literature, and Art,* reconstructed and greatly extended, to adapt it to the present state of knowledge.

BOOKS AND ODD VOLUMES

WANTED TO PURCHASE.

Particulars of Price, &c., of the following Books to be sent direct to the gentlemen by whom they are required, and whose names and addresses are given for that purpose:—

⁎ The bookseller, who intimated a copy of TINDAL'S RAPIN for sale—*vide* "N. & Q." February 11th, is requested to send his *full* address, as money and letters have been returned by Post Office, to *Mr. J. W. Fleming, F.R.C.S.,* Surgeon, 37th Regiment, Dover.

FIGURES DU VIEUX ET NOUVEAU TESTAMENT, par G. C. T. 'A Lyon: Pour Estienne Michel M.DLXXXII.
  Wanted by Rev. *J. C. Jackson,* 5, Chatham Place East, Hackney, N.E.

THE ATHENÆUM from the First Number to the end of the year 1831. ANTHROPOLOGICAL REVIEW. Nos. 1, 2, and 3. (1s. each will be given.) ARCHÆOLOGIA. Vol. XXXVI. Part II. JOURNAL OF THE ARCHÆOLOGICAL ASSOCIATION. Nos. 2—12. (1s. each will be given.)
  Wanted by *Edward Peacock, Esq.,* Bottesford Manor, Brigg.

GRABE'S SEPTUAGINT. Last Volume.
  Wanted by Rev. *E. Knowles,* Abbey Hill, Kenilworth.

Notices to Correspondents.

F. W. C. *Wm. Prynne's Brief Survey and Censure of Mr. Cozen's cozening Devotions,* 1628, 4to, *is a coarse tirade against the Collection of Private Devotions by that excellent prelate, John Cosin, the learned Bishop of Durham. See Kippis's* Biog. Britannica, iv. 285.

J. S. *The writers in the* LYRA APOSTOLICA *were a., Bowden; β., Froude; γ., Keble; δ., Newman; ε., Wilberforce; ζ., Williams. Vide "N. & Q."* 1st S. ix. 407.

F. J. SPARLER. *Either of the following works may be consulted for a description of the manners, customs, &c. of the English: Craik and Macfarlane's Pictorial History of England,* 8 vols. imp. 8vo, 1849; *or Charles Knight's Popular History of England,* 8 vols. 8vo. 8vo. 13s. 6d.

INQUIRER. *We believe the best collection for a history of the Audley family (the Touchets) has been compiled by Mr. John Tuckett, of 66, Great Russell Street, Bloomsbury.*

GEORGE J. COOPER. *Dr. Hawtrey, late Provost of Eton died on Jan. 27, 1862.—A short notice of Forshall and Madden's edition of Wickliffe's translation of the Bible appeared in "N. & Q."* 1st S. ii. 501.

J. L. (Dublin.) *We cannot discover any remarks on Rev. xviii. 13, in "N. & Q."*

C. W. H. *The arms of Barton Holyday, as recorded by Wood, were—Sable three helmets close argent, in the centre point a fleur-de-lys or, within a border engrailed of the second.*

WORKHOUSE CHAPLAINS.—URIEN REGRED *will find a list of these officials in the* Poor Law Union Almanack, *published by C. Knight of Fleet Street.*

Replies to other Correspondents *in our next number.*

ERRATUM.—In our last number, p. 154, col. 1. line 10, *for* "Dreuthe" *read* "Drenthe."

A Reading Case for holding the weekly Nos. of "N. & Q." is now ready, and may be had of all Booksellers and Newsmen, price 1s. 6d.; or, free by post, direct from the publisher, for 1s. 8d.

⁎ Cases for binding the volumes of "N. & Q." may be had of the Publisher, and of all Booksellers and Newsmen.

"NOTES AND QUERIES" is published at noon on Friday, and is also issued in MONTHLY PARTS. The Subscription for STAMPED COPIES for Six Months forwarded direct from the Publisher (including the Half-yearly INDEX) is 11s. 4d., which may be paid by Post Office Order, payable at the Strand Post Office, in favour of WILLIAM G. SMITH, 32, WELLINGTON STREET, STRAND, W.C., where also all COMMUNICATIONS FOR THE EDITOR should be addressed.

"NOTES & QUERIES" is registered for transmission abroad.

MORE CURES OF COLDS, ASTHMAS, AND COUGHS BY DR. LOCOCK'S PULMONIC WAFERS.—From Mr. H. Armstrong, Chemist, Church Street, Preston. — "Of elderly people, numbers have obtained the greatest benefit from them; many with the first or second box. To the greatest invalid I can recommend them with confidence, having seen the most magical effects produced by them on coughs, hoarseness, and difficulty of breathing." They have a pleasant taste. Price 1s. 1½d., 2s. 9d., and 4s. 6d per box. Sold by all druggists.

LONDON, SATURDAY, MARCH 11, 1865.

CONTENTS.—N° 167.

Notes on Books, &c.

Notes.

THE VISITS OF PRINCE CHARLES EDWARD TO LONDON.[*]

NO. I.

The long letter to the Editor of *The Times*, signed J., which closed the communications to that journal upon this subject, was a *résumé* of all the stories respecting it. The first visit is said to have occurred in 1748, upon the authority of Forsyth's *Remarks on Italy*. This visit Lord Stanhope rejects; and rightly, as I think I can show quite satisfactorily. The Stuart Papers, as I stated in my first letter, are made up of *two* collections. I have no doubt that one consisted of the papers of the Chevalier de St. George, and the other of those of his son, the Prince Charles Edward. They contain the whole correspondence between the father and son, and the drafts or copies of their letters, which were kept on each side, for the year 1748, so that we have the entire series being missing. From Jan. 1, 1748, to Dec. 9, there are letters from the Prince to his father weekly. In general they are not very interesting;—the weather is very cold, or very hot; he hopes it will change; he is in perfect health; and, as

[*] *Vide antè, 1—3.*

the custom was, he always "lays himself at his Majesty's feet." Those in reply to "Dearest Carluccio" most frequently state that the French post has not arrived, and that he has nothing to say, but (the letters being principally in Edgar's handwriting, he adds with his own hand, what does not appear in the copies, that) "he embraces him, &c." The Prince's letters during the negociations of the Treaty of Aix-la-Chapelle, and the events immediately preceding it, contain matter of more interest. He was fully alive to the effects of that treaty upon their cause, which his father appears to have perceived in a very somnolent manner. And he prepared, without consulting his father, the Protest which, it is known, was delivered in their behalf, though necessarily in vain, against it. On the other side, the correspondence is enlivened by complaints that the Prince does not confide in his father, and has other counsellors, &c. The letter warning the Prince against the danger of attempting to resist the King of France is perhaps the wisest of the whole. Great affection is expressed, under courtly forms, on both sides.

Besides these letters, there are drafts of letters, dated in full, to all the Prince's real confidants and counsellors, which disclose what he so carefully concealed from his father.

The dates of these letters never show an interval greater than seven days. Frequently they follow at much smaller intervals. This is conclusive evidence against Forsyth's statement, which makes the Prince remain *a week* in London: for, on his hasty return from London to Paris, in 1750—according to the memoranda, printed in my first letter—the journey consumed two days. So that four days, at least, out of any one of these intervals must have been taken up in travelling. Besides, not one of all these letters, or drafts, speaks of such an expedition. Two expeditions are spoken of: but one is that to Madrid, in the preceding year; and the other is that made by an agent of his, whose letters are signed "Jo. Smith," to Frankfort, in the vain hope of procuring the hand of the Princess of Hesse Darmstadt for his master. [This expedition, it may be well to say, is usually placed a year later.] Still further:—The Chevalier, writing from Albano on June 25, 1748, says: "I look upon it to be very sure that you will be out of France when this letter arrives at Paris." And on July 15, the Prince replies from Paris: "Your Majesty has been misinformed as to my leaving this cuntry."

His Majesty it appears had a correspondent, who signed "Watson" simply; and who was, during part of this time, certainly in Paris, and communicated to him what he could learn or observe about the Prince. His letters are very much of the same quality as those of some of "Our own Correspondents" in the present day. For instance, he tells Edgar in one, of the Prince's addiction to the *demi-monde.* But every soul in Paris knew of this. In another, dated March 9, 1748, he says, with characteristic irony : —

" We have now given up all thought of business, even our favourite project 75, 1024, 1305, 1630 [*decyp.* " of declaring Protestant"] is no more spoke of, nor that of 75, 407, 1330 [" of a Protestant"] marriage. We have no thought or mention of anything but money, our whole time is swallowed up in a round of pleasure ; and could we be recovered out of this lethargick disease, we are assured that no discreet man 108, 46, 433, 100, 99, 579, 109, 101 [" will have anything to do with us "]."

Yet, in a draft of a letter addressed to some one in " Edingburg," dated the day before this communication, the Prince specially speaks of such a marriage as " necessary and proper for him." And after this it was, that the Hesse Darmstadt attempt was made, and the protest against the Treaty of Aix-la-Chapelle. The mention of " declaring Protestant," at this date, shows that the unhappy Prince had learned something from the fatal '45.

This, I think, fully supports Lord Stanhope in rejecting Forsyth's story of a visit to London in 1748. Hearsay evidence, considerably after date, cannot stand against the negative and positive evidence which these letters present. In my next note I will trace the Prince's movements, from his arrest in Paris in Dec. 1748, to his visit to London in Sept. 1750.   B. B. Woodward.

Royal Library, Windsor Castle.

BLOW'S BELFAST BIBLE.

I may be excused for introducing a subject of local, though certainly of considerable bibliographical interest to " N. & Q." In Mr. Berwick's *Historical Collections relating to the Town of Belfast* (Belfast, 1817), there is the following passage under the date 1696 : —

" The art of printing was introduced into Belfast this year by James Blow and his brother-in-law Patrick Neill, who came over from Glasgow by invitation from Mr. Crawford, then Sovereign of Belfast, who entered into partnership with them. After the death of Neill, the business was continued by Blow, who, about the year 1704, printed the first edition of the Bible in Ireland, and many succeeding editions."

Mr. Berwick gives the *Belfast Newsletter* as his authority, without reference to date or number; and I may observe that Mr. Crawford was not Sovereign in 1696, though he held that office in 1693 and 1694.

Again, in a *History of the Rise and Progress of Belfast*, by J. A. Pilson (Belfast, 1846,) will be found under the date 1704, as follows : —

" The first Bible ever printed in Ireland was published this year by Messrs. Blow & Neill at Belfast."

Again, in *Belfast and its Environs*, by J. H. Smith, A.M., M.R.I.A., is the following notice at p. 54 : —

" In 1716 there was printed in this town (Belfast), by James Blow, the first edition of the Holy Bible produced in Ireland."

In the *Ulster Journal of Archæology* (No. 9, p. 76,) there is a communication from Mr. John Hodgson—whose mere name alone, on a question of this kind, is a great authority—corroborating Mr. Smith. There is also a notice of Blow's Bible in Bohn's *Hudibras;* and later still we find in Bohn's *Lowndes' Bibliographer's Manual* the following entry : —

" The Bible, Belfast, James Blood, 1716, 8vo. First Edition of the Scriptures printed in Ireland. An error occurs in a verse of Isaiah. *Sin no more* is printed *Sin on more.* The error was not discovered until the entire impression (8000 copies) were bound and partly distributed."

This is circumstantial enough—the size of the book, the number of copies, even the very error—but it is nevertheless apocryphal. There is no such verse or passage in Isaiah as " Sin no more," at least I cannot find it, and Blood is evidently a typographical error for Blow,* not requiring further notice. But what is really worthy of attention is, that there are several distinct authorities asserting that the first Bible printed in Ireland, was printed at Belfast in 1716, while, in the British Museum, there is an excellent folio edition of the Authorised Version of the Scriptures that once belonged to the celebrated Archbishop Synge, bearing on its title-page the following imprint : —

" Dublin : Printed by A. Rhames, for William Binauld at the *Bible*, in Eustace Street, and Eliphal Dobson, at the *Stationers' Arms* in Castle Street. MDCCXIV."

Here, then, is conclusive testimony that the alleged Blow's Bible of 1716 was not the first printed in Ireland. I use the word alleged advisedly, for the bibliographers, who have made the various editions of the Bible their particular study, do not mention it. The writer, after many years' search, under rather favourable circumstances, has never been able to see it or even to meet with any one who had seen it ; and, consequently, is now led to believe that it never had an existence. The well-known Irish antiquaries, the Messrs. Benn of Glenravel, have assiduously hunted among the old Presbyterian families in the north of Ireland, but in vain ; Jas. Blow's descendants, still alive in Belfast, know nothing of it. Mr. G. Benn, in his very valuable *History of the Town of Belfast* (Belfast, 1823,) with his usual good judgment, omits all reference to the alleged Blow's Bible. Nor in the *History of the Presbyterian*

---

* The same error occurs in Bohn's *Hudibras*, but the text is correctly mentioned, viz. John viii. 11.

Church in Ireland (London, &c., 1853,) probably the most accurate ecclesiastical history ever compiled, written by that most conscientious and liberal-minded gentleman, the late Dr. Reid, is this Bible noticed. No man was better acquainted with the early typography of Belfast than Dr. Reid; he expressly mentions Blow and Neill, and would certainly have been most gratified to observe that they had printed a Bible in Belfast — the first printed in Ireland! — if he could have found sufficient authority for doing so.

But, *audi alteram partem.* In the Rev. H. Cotton's *Typographical Gazetteer* (Oxford, 1831,) I read under the heading of Belfast at p. 29, as follows: —

"In 1714 James Blow printed the works of Sir David Lindsay, a Bible, Prayer-Book, Psalms in Metre, and 20 or 30 other books."

A copy of this very curious edition of Lindsay's *Works* is now before me, and I may be excused for quoting the title in full: —

"'The | Works | of the | Famous and Worthy Knight, Sir | 𝕯𝕒𝕧𝕚𝕯 𝕷𝕚𝕟𝕯𝕤𝕒𝕪 of the *Mount,* | alias, Lyon, King of Arms. | Newly corrected and vindicated from the | former Errors wherewith they were cor | rupted: And augmented with sundry Works, &c. | Job vii. | *Militia est vita hominis supra terram.* | Vivit etiam post funera virtus. | BELFAST. | Printed by *James Blow,* and are to | be sold at his shop. 1714."

The book ends at p. 268, in the old style, thus— "*Quod* LINDSAY at *Command of King James the Fifth.*"

Then follow three unpaged pages of contents, and then two unpaged pages, headed "*Books Printed and Sold* by James Blow *in* Belfast." Among which I find —

"The Holy Bible" in several volumes.
"The New Testament of our Lord and Saviour Jesus Christ."
"The Psalmes of David in Meeter."
"The Bible the best New Year's Gift; containing the Contents of the Old and New Testament in Verse."

This last-mentioned work is also found in a list of books "printed and sold by Patrick Neill and Company at *his* shop, Belfast," at the end of "*The Psalms of David in Meeter.* Belfast: Printed by Patrick Neill and Company, and Sold at his Shop. 1700." This very remarkable volume is inscribed *David Smith's Gift to Belfast Meeting-house,* 1705, and is carefully preserved among the archives of the First Presbyterian Congregation, Belfast, of which D. Smith's descendants are still members.

Besides the above, there are twenty-eight other well-known trade books—such as Bunyan's *Pilgrim's Progress, Academy of Compliments,*[*] &c. Only two books that are actually known to have been printed by Blow are in the list; one is "The Warks (*sic*) of Sir David Lindsay;" the other is the

---

[*] Still printed and sold as a Chap-Book in Ireland.

well-known work, the title of which is so long that it is generally quoted as *Presbyterian Loyalty,* written by Dr. James Kirkpatrick, the first minister of the Second Presbyterian Congregation of Belfast. Blow's name is not attached to this last work, for high churchism was then rampant, and Queen Anne's funeral sermon had not been preached in a hundred dissenting congregations to the text, "Go, see now this cursed woman, and bury her; for she is a king's daughter," 2 Kings ix. 34.

The signatures to this copy of Lindsay's works are irregular, but it may be said to be 24mo; and I have been the more particular in describing it, as it seems to differ from a copy printed at Belfast in 1714, described by Mr. George Chalmers, as being in the possession of the Rev. J. Brand, Secretary to the Society of Antiquaries. I think, however, it is more likely that Mr. Brand's copy may have been misdescribed, than that Blow should publish two editions in one year.

Two of the works, we know, were *printed* by Blow, and if the others had merely been *sold* by him, the words at the head of the list would still be correct. If Blow did not print a Bible, the error must have arisen in this manner. Probably Mr. Cotton, now the venerable Archdeacon of Cashel, founded the extract I have given from his *Typographical Gazetteer* upon this very copy of David Lindsay's *Works.* At any rate he considered it untrustworthy, for in his *Editions of the Bible and Parts thereof in English, from the Year MD. to MDCCCL. Second Edition, Corrected and Enlarged* (Oxford, 1851,) this most skilful of bibliographers does not notice Blow's Belfast Bible.

I may add that there was no Patent required to print a Bible in Ireland, so that Blow might have printed as many as he thought proper. But I consider that the want of education, and limited number of Bible readers then in Ireland, would render the speculation of printing a Bible an exceedingly unremunerative one. Excellent English Bibles were then printed in Holland, and Belfast may have been supplied from thence. For Bible printing being then in Scotland a strict monopoly, it followed, as a matter of course, that the Bibles were most wretchedly printed. And even so late as 1824, when Principal Lee of Edinburgh University opposed this monopoly, showing how badly the Scottish Bibles were printed, in some instances the word Judas being indecently substituted for Jesus, his *Memoir* in favour of the Edinburgh Bible Society and against the monopolists, was suppressed and interdicted by order of the Court of Session.

No one need be surprised at Lindsay's works having been published in Belfast. Their antipapistical tendencies, which helped to bring about the Reformation in Scotland, would render them very welcome to the Scoto-Irish of Ulster. In fact, from their notices of Old Testament history, they were considered next best to the Bible. In the description of Ralpho's library in Colvil's *Scotch Hudibras* we may read : —

> " And there lyes books, and here lyes ballads,
> As Davie Lyndsay, and Gray Steel,
> Squire Meldrum, Bevis, and Adam Bell."

From Kelly's *Scottish Proverbs* we learn they were used as a school-book. A man, perfect in every art and science, was said to have read from Wallace to Lindsay, an allusion to Blind Harry's *Life of Sir W. Wallace.* A doubtful statement was gently contradicted by saying—"It's no atween the brods o' David Lindsay." *Anglice*, it is not within the covers of Lindsay's works. Such was the repute and confidence in which the works of the Lyon King of Arms were held. The Scoto-Irish of Ulster ever delighted in Scottish poetry, and did not write it badly themselves. It may not be generally known that the fourth edition of Burns's *Poems*, the first printed out of Scotland, was printed and published in 1787 by James Magee, at the sign of the *Bible and Crown*, Bridge Street, Belfast.

I think I have stated the question as fairly as I can; I might say a great deal more on this, to me at least, very interesting subject; but, like the imp of the old enchanters, my pen is circumscribed by a magic circle, which must not be overpasse . I ask, then, can any one give me any direct information of a Bible printed at Belfast early in the eighteenth century ? I have heard so much hearsay and traditional evidence regarding this Bible, that I respectfully decline to receive any more. Nothing, in fact, will satisfy me but the statement of a person who has seen the Bible in question, with the imprint of Belfast upon it. I would be happy also to receive any information respecting the early typography of Belfast—say previous to the year 1740. I may be communicated with either through " N. & Q.," or my address as underneath.

WILLIAM PINKERTON, F.S.A.

Hounslow, W.

CARABOO.

The following paragraph is transcribed from *The Times* of Jan. 13, 1865 : —

" Such of our readers as are interested in the history of impostors will remember that many years since a person who styled herself the 'Princess Caraboo,' created a sensation in the literary and fashionable circles of Bath and other places, which lasted till it was discovered that the whole affair was a romance, cleverly sustained and acted out by a young and prepossessing girl. On being deposed from the honours which had been accorded to her, the 'Princess' accepted the situation, retired into comparatively humble life, and married. There was a kind of grim humour in the occupation which she subsequently followed,—that of importer of leeches ; but she conducted her operations with much judgment and ability, and carried on her trade with credit to herself, and satisfaction to her customers. The quondam ' Princess' died recently at Bristol leaving a daughter, who, like her mother, is said to be possessed of considerable personal attractions."

A full account of the singular imposition practised by the subject of the foregoing lines was published by Mr. Gutch, and is entitled : —

"CARABOO. A Narrative of a Singular Imposition practised upon the benevolence of a Lady residing in the Vicinity of the City of Bristol, by a Young Woman of the name of Mary Willcocks, *alias* Baker, *alias* Bakerstendht, *alias* Caraboo, Princess of Javasu." Illustrated with two Portraits, engraved from drawings by E. Bird, Esq., R.A., and Mr. Branwhite, &c., royal 8vo. Bristol, 1817, price 5s., pp. 68.

This curious volume has become very scarce ; but it is needless to occupy space with details from it, as a summary of the case, with copies of the portraits, will be found in Hone's *Every Day-Book*, vol. ii. p. 1631. From this latter source I glean the further information that in the year 1824, Caraboo, on her return from America, made a public exhibition of herself in New Bond Street, at a charge of one shilling each person; but that she did not attract any great attention. See also *Sketches of Imposture, Deception, and Credulity*, p. 159.

The reader cannot fail to be here reminded of the equally extraordinary, and still more notorious imposture, practised half a century before by George Psalmanazar, "a reputed native of Formosa." He, like Caraboo, sought to sustain his imposition by the invention of hieroglyphics and characters to represent his native language; but went further than his successor by the publication (1704, 2nd ed. 1705), of a thick 8vo, containing a description and history of Formosa, the island of his alleged nativity. Of this fabulous narrative, a translation into French, as of a veridical production, is before me : —

" Description de l'Ile Formosa en Asie, avec une ample, et exacte relation de ses voyages, traduit de l'Anglais de George Psalmanazaar par le Sieur N. F. D. B. R.," 8vo, Amsterdam, 1705.

Psalmanazar repented in after life of the deception he had practised, and the other irregularities of his " hot youth." He wrote his life, a valuable and interesting, but neglected piece of biography : —

" Memoirs of . . . . commonly known by the name of George Psalmanazar; a reputed Native of Formosa, written by himself, in order to be published after his Death, containing an Account of his Education, Travels, Adventures, and Connections, Literary productions, and pretended Conversion from Heathenism to Christianity ; which last proved the Occasion of his being brought over into this Kingdom, and passing for a Proselyte, and a Member of the Church of England." Second edition, London, 8vo, 1765.

And he became in his latter days so exemplary a member of society, that Dr. Johnson, upon being asked by Boswell "who was the *best* man he had ever known?" to the surprise of his interrogator, answered "Psalmanazar." For an account of Psalmanazar, see the article on "Literary Forgeries" in Disraeli's *Curiosities of Literature;* and an essay on his life and character will be found in *Malvern Hill, with Minor Poems and Essays,* by Joseph Cottle, 8vo, London, 1829, vol. ii. p. 433.

In comparing the imposture of Caraboo with that of Psalmanazar, it must not be forgotten that the former was an illiterate servant girl, and the latter a man of good education and uncommon mental abilities.

But though I have associated Caraboo, the Princess of Javasu, with the notorious Formosan, I must not forget to inform the reader that a contemporary parallel may be found for her in the annals of imposture. In the same year in which her narrative appeared, was published —

"Companion for Caraboo : a Narrative of the Conduct and Adventures of Henry Frederick Moon, &c. &c., a native of Brighthelmstone, Sussex, and now under sentence of imprisonment in Connecticut, in North America ; containing an Account of his unparalleled Artifices, Impostures, Mechanical Ingenuity," &c. By Walter Bates, Esq. High Sheriff of King's County, in New Brunswick, &c., 8vo, 1817.

By way of rounding off the foregoing notes, I transcribe a passage from an old record, from which it will be seen that Caraboo had a predecessor in the same walk of imposture, as far back as the reign of King Stephen : —

"In this king's time also there appeared two children, a boy and a girl, clad in green, in a stuffe unknown, of a strange language, and of strange diet ; whereof the boy being baptized, dyed shortly after, but the girl lived to be very old ; and being asked from whence they were : she answered, they were of the land of St. Martyn, where there are Christian Churches erected : but that no Sun did ever rise unto them ; but where that land is, and how she came hither, she herself knew not. This I the rather write, that we may know there are other parts of the World, than those which to us are known ; and this story I should not have believed, if it were not testified by so many and so credible witnesses, as it is." — Baker's *Chronicle*, folio, 1660, p. 56.

WILLIAM BATES.

Birmingham.

DAVID HUME : JAMES BOSWELL.

I enclose two extracts from the Edinburgh Baptismal Register, which may be interesting to your readers. The first relates to David Hume, and the other to James Boswell.

The historian's family name was Home, but he fancifully spelt it Hume. This change was a subject of amicable controversy between the historian and the author of *Douglas*, who stood out for Home as being more correct. The respective merits of Port, the favourite beverage of the Philosopher, and Claret, which the Dramatist preferred, was also a subject of dispute between the two, and is alluded to in Mr. David Hume's will thus : —

"I leave to my friend John Home, of Kilduff, ten dozen of my old Claret, at his choice, and one single bottle of that other liquor called Port.

"I also leave to him six dozen of Port, provided he attests under his hand, signed John Hume, that he has himself alone, at two sittings, finished that bottle.

"By this concession he will at once terminate the only two differences that ever arose between us concerning temporal matters."

The will is dated 17th Aug. 1776, eighteen days prior to his death. Ninewells is near Dunse, in Berwickshire.

"Edinburgh, 26 April, 1711.

"Mr. Joseph Home of Ninewalls, advocate, and Katherine ffalconar, his lady, a Son named David. Witnesses, George, Master of Polwarth, Sir John Home of Blacadder, Sir Andrew Home, advocate, and Mr. Alexander ffalconar, advocate. Child born this day."

"Saturday, 18 October, 1740.

"To Mr. Alexander Boswell, younger, of Auchinleck, and Mrs Euphanie Erskine, his spouse, a son named James. Witnesses, Walter M'Farlane, of that Ilk, Allan Whitefoord, Receiver-General for North Brittain, and Dr. John Pringle, Physician, in Ednr. Born the same day in the morning, and baptised by the Revd Mr Robert Wallace, one of the ministers of the City."

James Boswell died in London, 19 June, 1795. His eldest son Alexander was created a baronet in 1821, and was killed in a duel on the 26th March, 1822. His son Sir James died in 1857 ; not having heirs male, he was desirous of breaking the entail of his property, and succeeded in this in 1851. The entail, which had been an object of great anxiety to his father and grandfather, was set aside in consequence of the letters "irred" of the word "irredeemably" having been written over an erasure. What dire effects from trifling causes spring !   SEARCH No. 2.

"THE FOURTH OF MARCH."—The following extract from last week's *Owl* may be interesting to the readers of "N. & Q. : " —

"FOURTH OF MARCH. — It is not perhaps generally known to our readers that the reason which the founders of the American Republic had for selecting the 4th of March for the inauguration of their president, was to avoid the occurrence of a 'dies non' by the incidence of that date on a Sunday. By calculation it was ascertained that for many hundreds of years the quadrennial recurrence of that day in the year of election invariably falls on a week day."

A. L. M.

[We fear that in this, as in some other American speculations, events have not justified the previous calculations. If there is any reliance to be placed on PROFESSOR DE MORGAN'S *Book of Almanacks*, in the year 1821, the 4th of March fell on Quinquagesima Sunday, and in 1849 on the Second Sunday in Lent.]

NELSON'S ATTACK ON THE BOULOGNE FLOTILLA IN 1801.—I have just accidentally met with the following passage in the *Biographie Nouvelle des Contemporains*, tome i. p. lix.: " An 9 (1801), 26 therm. . Combat naval entre l'amiral Nelson et la flotille de Boulogne: *les Français sont victorieux*." Now as it happened that I was in some degree an eye-witness of what was passing on the French coast, I beg leave to offer a few remarks on the above statement.

It is well known that in the summer of 1801, Buonaparte had mustered a large army upon the heights of Boulogne for the alleged purpose of invading England, while the harbour and the surrounding parts of the coast were occupied by an armed flotilla to assist in carrying out his projected attack. There was not any supineness or want of diligence on the part of our country. Lord Nelson was stationed in the British Channel to watch the movements of the enemy, and to act upon any emergency he might judge necessary to defeat this hostile attempt. At break of day on Tuesday, Aug. 4, 1801, Lord Nelson commenced his attack on Boulogne and on the armed flotilla in the harbour. The booming of the guns and the cannonading were distinctly heard and seen from the heights of Dover Castle. On this side of the Channel nothing was known of the proceedings until the following morning. It was by some conjectured that the French had quitted the harbour either with an aggressive design upon the English coast, or that a conflict in some way or other had arisen between the rival powers. Nelson's attack unfortunately turned out to be a *coup manqué*, as the French vessels, being guarded by strong wire-netted gratings and iron bars, became irresistible. (Vide the *Annual Register*, xliii. 266.)

In conclusion, permit me to state how I became acquainted with the circumstances above narrated. In 1801, I was surgeon and ensign of a militia regiment then stationed at Dover Castle. It may be necessary to state that, in the militia, as was the custom in the Fencible Cavalry, &c., the surgeon's stipend when held alone being 4s. per day, was considered unremunerative, unless a subaltern's commission and pay were allowed in addition. It was in this two-fold capacity that I was placed on the outlying piquet on the night of Monday, Aug. 3, to patrol the beach from sunset until the following morning, when on returning to my quarters in the Castle, I could observe from the heights what was then passing off Boulogne. In the *London Gazette* of August 8, 1801 (No. 15,394) is a letter from Lord Nelson respecting his bombardment of Boulogne on August 4, from which it appears that Capt. Lieutenant Peter Fyers of the Royal Artillery was wounded on that occasion.   Φ.

BAPTISM OF A BLACKAMOOR. — The following entry appears in the Record of Baptisms for the Parish of Canongate (Edinburgh), and seems to merit insertion in " N. & Q." from its quaint and singular character : —

" 30 September, 1686. The same day y[r] was baptized a Blackmore Servant to My L. Duke of Queensberry, named John ; who, being about 10 years of age, made publick profession of the Christian Faith, and solemnly engaged to live according to it. Witnesses y[e] whole Session of the Abbey Church."

On the margin is written: "Blackmore John Drumlanrig."

Drumlanrig is the seat of the Queensberry family, in Dumfriesshire, and their town residence in Edinburgh still remains under the name of " Queensberry House " in the Canongate ; but was disposed of by them many years ago, and is now a house of refuge.   G.

Edinburgh.

"STRAWBERRY" PREACHERS.—Latimer, preaching in the shrouds at St. Paul's, makes the following quaint allusion to the *non-resident* clergy of his day : —

" Great is their business, and therefore great should be their hire. They have great labours, and therefore they ought to have good livings, that they may commodiously feed their flock : for the preaching of the word of God unto the people is called meat. Scripture calleth it meat ; not strawberries, that come but once a year, and tarry not long but are soon gone, but it is meat, it is no dainties . . . Many make a strawberry of it, ministering it but once a year ; but such do not the office of good prelates."

["A Bachelor of Divinity, named Oxenbridge, in a sermon preached at St. Paul's Cross, Jan. 13, 1566, says, ' I will shew you the state and condition of this my mother Oxford : for a piteous case it is, that now in all Oxford there is not past five or six preachers. I except Strawberry Preachers.'"]—*Foot-note* by the Editor.

Your readers will, no doubt, accept the testimony of *Oxenbridge* as that of the *arch*-denouncer of Oxen-ford.   F. PHILLOTT.

MYLNE OF BALFARG. — The following very remarkable genealogy of a family of builders is deduced from the master-mason of King James III. of Scotland (a monarch whose architectural taste did not suit his rude nobility, and who was murdered in Sauchie), is extracted from an old transcript of the Lyon record, made by Robert Milne, a Scotish collector of the last and preceding century.

Whether *old* Robert—for he died at the age of 103—was of the same family, does not appear : —

" Mylne, Robert, of Balfarg, his Maiesties' Master Masson, nevoy and representer of the deceased John Mylne, late Master Masson to his Majesty, which John was lawful son to the deceased John Mylne, also his Majestie's Master Masson, and which John was lawful son to the deceased John Mylne, lykewise his Majestie's Master Masson, and which John was lawfull son to the deceased Thomas Mylne, in lyke manner his Maiestie's

Master Masson, which Thomas was son to the deceased Alexander, lykewise his Maiestie's Master Masson, and which Alexander wes son of the deceased John Mylne, also his Maiestie's Master Masson, by vertue of ane gift granted to him thereof be King James the 3d of ever blessed memory, of the date the　　day of yeares, BEARS Or a cross moline azure quarterly perced of the field, betwixt 3 mullets of the 2d. Crest, Apelles' head couplé at the shoulders proper, vested about the neck, vert, on the head a helmet azure, bever turned up, and a plumaish Gules. Motto, Tam arte quam Marte."

J. M.

EPITAPH BY J. HOOKHAM FRERE.—I have had the following lines in my possession for nearly twenty years. They were copied from an inscription on a tombstone; and were written, as it was supposed, by the Right Hon. John Hookham Frere, and I have no doubt that you will think them worthy of insertion in "N. & Q."

I have taken the liberty with the original inscription of inserting "Britain" instead of "England," in the first line, as including the country indicated by my signature; but if you quote Mr. Frere as the author, I shall leave it to yourself to decide as to the change which I have made:—

Lines copied from a Tombstone intended to be erected in England.

" Heroic Britain, prodigal of life,
　Sends forth to distant enterprise and strife
　Her daring offspring : we must not repine
　If, from the frozen circle to the line,
　Our graves are scatter'd : and the sole relief,
　For kindred sorrows and parental grief,
　Is to record upon an empty tomb,
　Merit and worth, and their untimely doom."

The subject of the above lines died in India.

SCOTUS.

HERALDRY AS AN ACCESSORY TO HISTORY.—In the *Illustrated London News* (March 12, 1859, p. 266), is an engraving of an ancient marble bas-relief of the "Madonna and Child," which was purchased at Naples, and attributed to Giotto:—

" The work itself (observes the writer who communicates the fact to the above journal), though undoubtedly of the Giottesque school, bears internal evidence of being of a later period than that of the great founder of that school. . . . In addition to this, there is the fact of the arms of Aragon, somewhat effaced and not very clearly defined, being on the border of the lowest part of the frame. The house of Aragon did not come into possession of the Neapolitan dominions until a century after the death of Giotto ; and some such date would in all respects better tally with the character of the work than a much earlier one."

H. W. T.

Queries.

ANONYMOUS. — By whom were the following publications?—

1. "Six Dramas, illustrative of German Life, from the Original of the Princess Amalie of Saxony."
2. "English Life, Social and Domestic, in the Middle of the Nineteenth Century."

3. "Reverses ; or, Memoirs of the Fairfax Family. By the Author of 'English Life.'"
4. "Second Part of the History of Rasselas, Prince of Abyssinia."

ABHBA.

Who is the author of the following?—

"Meditations of a Divine Soul ; or, the Christian's Guide. . . . . . also Arguments to prove there is no Material Fire in Hell. . . . . . to which is added 'An Essay of a retired Solitary Life, with an after-thought on King William III.' London, printed for *John Kersey*. . . . . . and sold by *Ralph Simpson* . . . 1703."

It is not mentioned by Lowndes. I have curtailed the running title of the book as much as possible.

GEORGE LLOYD.

Thurstonland.

MOUNT ATHOS. — Professor Carlyle, who with Dr. Hunt visited the monasteries on Mount Athos in 1801, states, in a letter to the Bishop of Durham, published in Walpole's *Turkey* (vol. i. pp. 194—197), that he made "a very detailed catalogue of the whole of the contents of these celebrated repositories" (referring to the libraries). Dr. Hunt also (same volume, p. 220) states : "We had now taken catalogues of all the MSS., each of which we had ourselves individually examined." Are these catalogues in existence now, and where? *

F. M. S.

229, Clarendon Villas, Plumstead.

COURTENAY QUARTERINGS. — On a picture of Henry Courtenay, Marquis of Exeter, is the following coat of arms:—Quarterly of six : 1. Plantagenet. 2. Courtenay. 3. Redvers. 4. Vert, two bars argent. 5. Chequey or and azure, two bars argent (Brionis?). 6. Fitz Osborne. Can any of your readers inform me to what persons, or families, the fourth and fifth quarterings belonged?

E. M. B.

ERIN. — In *Postulates and Data* (vol. i. p. 347) there are fourteen Greek lines with the heading : "Nundinis Donnybrycæis nomen vernaculum 'Erin' luculenter exponitur." I am anxious, for a particular purpose, to know their author's name, and perhaps you may be able to assist me.

ABHBA.

OLD HOUSE AT HASTINGS.—In the *Sussex Archæological Collections* (vol. xiv. p. 107) we find these words:—

" We give an engraving of the largest of the old houses, which was situate in *High Street*, and was standing in 1815 ; when a sketch was taken by Mr. Prout, for the use of which the Society is indebted to the kindness of John Pitman Shorter, Esq."

[* Some interesting notices of the libraries in the monasteries of Mount Athos will be found in Curzon's *Visits to Monasteries of the Levant*, 1849, 8vo. In the library of Lincoln College, Oxford, is a MS. of the sixteenth century, entitled "Catalogus monasteriorum in monte Atho." See Coxe's *Catalogus Oxon.*, i. Lincoln. p. 7.—ED.]

Facing what page is this engraving? Fronting p. 106 we have an engraving of an old house "formerly at [the] eastern entrance of the town." At p. 107 we have Pelham House, still standing, in High Street, and Mrs. Shovell's house in All Saints' Street. On p. 108, Salmon's House; and, fronting p. 108, two old houses in All Saints' Street; and on p. 110, an old house, date 1657, known as Mrs. Boadle's, in George, i. e. Suburb Street; but where is the old house that was standing in 1815? Can MR. DURRANT COOPER—can MR. Ross—inform me through "N. & Q."?

                       W. J. B.

HERALDIC QUERY. — Do any English counties, towns, or families, bear St. George's cross (Argent, a cross gules,) as their arms, or any part of their arms? Can any correspondent of "N. & Q." add to the following list of foreign counties, &c., bearing it?—

1. Barony (Herrschaft) of Padua.
2. Island of Cephalonia.
3. Republic of Genoa.
4. Bishopric of Treves.
5. County of Pyrmont.
6. Imp. free town Memmingen (sinister part per pale).
7. Principality of Ratzeburg (sometimes a cross calvary, pendant).

I ask the same questions with reference to: Gules, a cross argent (foreign):—

1. Duchy of Savoy.
2. Barony of Vicenza.
3. Town of Vienna.
4. Bishopric of Constance.
5. Principality of Kammin, or Camin.
6. Family of Von Rotthal (Austrian, 1620).
7. Town of Elbing (borne in a chief).
8. The Order of St. John, Malta. (On coins the cross is not eight pointed).

Are these crosses, more especially in the second list, all exactly the same shape when properly represented?   JOHN DAVIDSON.

HOLY-WATER-SPRINKLE.—Can any of your military correspondents explain the nature of this ancient weapon or fire-arm, which has been described as having one of its ends armed with a gun—the particular use of which seems to have puzzled Grose? Are there any weapons of this description now in the Tower? I presume they were possessed of some explosive power. The name seems to imply as much.   F. PHILLOTT.

JEWS AS ARTISANS. — Are there any Jews who, answering to what we call "artisans," work as such in any of our large manufacturing towns, or in any of our cotton mills? I know there are Jews who keep shops; but are there any who work, as do our carpenters and labourers? Are there, in fact, any "class of Jews" answering to

our class of artisans? I should feel much obliged by this information.   W. J. CHARLTON.
Lansdown Terrace, Cheltenham.

PICTURE BY MR. LE JEUNE.—There was a picture painted, some years ago, by Mr. Le Jeune for H. R. H. Prince Albert, whose subject was the "Release of the Captives from Exodus." Can any contributor tell me in what number of the Art Journal it was engraved?   J. C. J.

HUGH MORRELL. — Looking over the Burnet Papers at the Bodleian Library, I met with a letter of Hugh Morrell, dated Paris, April 10, 1651, relating to some transactions with the French government. Can any of your readers inform me to what family and county he belonged, and what arms he bore? Also, the position he held in the government of the Commonwealth? W. H. T.

REGIMENTAL PECULIARITIES.—When and why was the Light Company of the 46th Regiment permitted to wear red tufts in their shakos, instead of green tufts? The regiments of the Coldstream Guards and 42nd Highlanders now wear red feathers; but I think that I remember the time when green feathers were worn by the Light Companies, both in the Coldstreams and "The Black Watch." I know how, and when, the latter corps obtained permission to wear red feathers. Why do the 5th Fusiliers wear white plumes tipped with red? All other Fusilier (Line) regiments wear white plumes. The Fusilier Guards do not, I think, wear any plumes in their bearskin caps.   JUVERNA.

STICK. — "Our Author, to shew how angry and froward he resolues to be, . . . makes his first Paragraph a Compleat Stick of Railing;" and a marginal note, "J. B. a compleat Railer." (Works of Robert Barclay, London, 1692, p. 854.) Is stick used in the sense of a stab, or has it some other meaning now obsolete?   ST. T.

SUN-DIALS.—Is there any work from which, with but slight mathematical knowledge on my part, I could learn "to carve out dials quaintly, point by point?" Where can I find designs for sun-dials copied from existing specimens?   S. W. P.

TRANSMUTATION OF METALS. — The following note deserves a place in the pages of "N. & Q.":—

"The extraordinary price attained by this metal (bismuth) was due to a circumstance which would scarcely be suspected in the present day. A Company was formed in London, under the direction of a foreigner, for the purpose of making gold. Very large premises were taken, and much apparatus placed in position, to carry out the most recent attempt at transmutation. Bismuth was to have entered largely into the process, and all that could be obtained was purchased regardless of price. Of course no gold has been made, and to save out of the wreck as much as possible, the deluded shareholders are cautiously selling their stock of bismuth, so as to obtain as high a price as possible." — *Quarterly Journal of Science*, vol. i. p. 693, Oct. 1864.

Will some readers of "N. & Q." kindly give a brief note respecting the Company here alluded to? adding, if possible, some quotations showing the variation of price at which bismuth has been sold since its formation. The existence of a Company formed in the present day for such a purpose, presents something more than a mere ephemeral interest.   AIKEN IRVINE, Clk.

Kilbride, Bray.

WILLIAM, SON OF KING STEPHEN. — William, Earl of Bologne, son of King Stephen and his Queen Matilda, was killed at the siege of Toulouse in October, 1159, *s. p.*

William, *a* son of King Stephen, married Isabel, Countess of Warrenne and Surrey in her own right, and died *s. p.*

Can any one kindly help me to ascertain the correct solution of the following queries? —

1. Are the above-mentioned Williams different, or identical?

2. Had King Stephen a natural son of this name?

3. If they are not identical, which of them married the Countess Isabel?

Matthew of Westminster (ed. Bohn, ii. 55), speaks of William, Earl of Moreton *and Warrenne*, as "the bastard son of King Stephen." Anderson (*Royal Genealogies*, p. 741) mentions "William, a natural son, *mistaken* for William, Earl of Surrey." The *Annals and Antiquities of Lacock Abbey* state that "the heiress of the Warrens . . . was bestowed first on an *illegitimate* son of King Stephen" (p. 104). Burke (*Extinct Peerage*, p. 557) evidently supposes the two identical: for he says that Isabel married "William de Blois, Earl of Moreton, *natural* son of King Stephen, killed at the siege of Toulouse in 1163, *s. p.*" While Vincent (*Discoverie of Errours*, p. 519,) boldly asserts that the husband of Isabel was "William de Bloys, Earl of Mortaigne and *Bologne*, Lord of the Egle," adding : "It is not so necessary here as elsewhere to show whether this William were a bastard or not—*a thing earnestly denied by good writers*." The Registry of Lewes (Cott. MS. Vesp. F. xv.), which I hoped would have cleared up the doubt, leaves it undecided by simply calling the Countess's husband "Willm͞s de Bloys, Steph͞n de Bloys Regis Anglie fili⁹ et Comes Surreyis . . . Dominus de Aquila . . . jacetque Tolosane" (fol. 106).

It is of considerable importance to me to ascertain beyond doubt whether the husband of Isabel de Warrenne was the legitimate or legitimate son of Stephen. And I entertain strong hopes that some of your correspondents, many of whom have so kindly assisted me before, may be able to help me out of this difficulty also, which will increase the obligations which I already owe to "N. & Q."   HERMENTRUDE.

Queries with Answers.

"THE VAMPYRE." — Can you tell me in what magazine, published in 1819, appeared the tale or fragment of *The Vampyre*, ascribed to, but repudiated by Lord Byron, and by him referred to Polidori?   A. BLANE NEWBERY.

[*The Vampyre* was published in *The New Monthly Magazine* for April 1, 1819 ; but it appears to have been previously printed as a separate pamphlet, entitled " *The Vampyre*, a Tale by the Right Hon. Lord Byron. Lond. : Printed for Sherwood & Co., Paternoster Row, 1819, 8vo. Entered at Stationers' Hall, March 27, 1819." It is probable that the pamphlet was not issued until after the publication of the Tale in *The New Monthly Magazine*. The "Extract of a Letter to the Editor" prefixed to it has been attributed to J. Mitford. *The Vampyre* was repudiated by Lord Byron in a letter to the editor of *Galignani's Messenger*, an English daily paper published in Paris, and reprinted in *The Gentleman's Magazine*, lxxxix(i.) 633. Lord Byron, in his characteristic letter, justly remarks : "If the book is clever, it would be base to deprive the real writer, whoever he may be, of his honours ; and if stupid, I desire the responsibility of nobody's dullness but my own." Besides publishing this letter in his paper, Galignani appended a lithographed copy to his 8vo edition of Byron's *Poems*. Consult also the *Letters and Journals of Lord Byron*, by Thomas Moore, edit. 1833, ii. 462, 466. In the May number of *The New Monthly Magazine* appeared the following letter from the real author of the Tale : —

" MR. EDITOR.—As the person referred to in the Letter from Geneva, prefixed to the Tale of the Vampyre, in your last number, I beg leave to state, that your correspondent has been mistaken in attributing that tale, *in its present form*, to Lord Byron. The fact is, that though *the groundwork* is certainly Lord Byron's, its development is mine, produced at the request of, a lady, who denied the possibility of any thing being drawn from the materials which Lord Byron had said he intended to have employed in the formation of his Ghost story. I am, &c. JOHN W. POLIDORI."]

RIDDELL OF GLENRIDDELL. — Can any of your correspondents inform me if there exists any considerable collection of the books and MSS. of Robert Riddell of Glenriddell, the friend of Captain Grose, whose death in 1794 was the subject of an elegy by Burns? In a library to which I have access I have met with several books profusely annotated by him, and five or six odd volumes of a MS. series, entitled "A Collection of Scottish Antiquities," one or two of which contain journals of tours made in company with Captain Grose, from Mr. Riddell's house at Friars' Carse, near Dumfries, to various objects of archæological interest in Scotland, and are illustrated with several excellent water-colour drawings by the Captain. There are also MS. collections of Scottish ballads, glossaries, and historical notices of families and peerages. I should like to discover where the remainder of this interesting series is deposited. J. E. O.

[There can be little doubt that the books and MSS. were sold as well as Friars Carse, the residence of Mr. Riddell, near Dumfries, where the contest for the Whistle, so well known by Burns's poem, took place. From a communication by our correspondent, MR. CARMICHAEL, which appeared in the last number of *The British Archæological Journal*, p. 358, we find that some interesting relics of Mr. Riddell's antiquarian researches are still preserved at Friars Carse in the shape of carved and engraved stones.]

PATRICK ANDERSON, son of James Anderson, the celebrated editor of the *Diplomata Scotiæ*, is stated in 2nd S. viii. 476 (note), to have been afterwards the "celebrated President of the Court of Session;" and yet no such name appears in the Chronological List of the Lords President. How is the contradiction to be reconciled? I suspect the asterisk referring to the note has been misplaced, but there is no other name in the page to which it can refer. F. M. S.

229, Clarendon Villas, Plumstead.

[Patrick Anderson was Comptroller of Stamps at Edinburgh. The meaning of the note appears to be that he obtained this office through the influence of one who was afterwards "the celebrated President of the Court of Session;" no doubt Duncan Forbes of Culloden, at least he best answers the dates. It is curious enough, that though Anderson is a common name in Scotland, and more than one advocate bearing it have held good positions at the bar, none have ever been raised to the judicial bench.]

CLERK OF THE CLOSET. — What are the duties attaching to the office of Clerk of the Closet to the sovereign, which is usually held by one of the bishops? E. H. A.

[Chamberlayne, in his *Present State of England*, 1673, p. 165, states, that "the King hath a Clerk of the Closet, or Confessor to his Majesty, who is commonly some reverend discreet Divine, extraordinarily esteemed by His Majesty, whose office is to attend at the King's right hand during Divine service, to resolve all doubts concerning spiritual matters, and to wait on His Majesty in his private oratory or closet."]

COOKERY: "AU BLEU." — Will one of the correspondents of "N. & Q." contribute to it, for the information of an untravelled Englishman, the signification in French culinary science of the process designated *au bleu*? Has it any connection with the *Cordon Bleu*, the badge or decoration popularly assigned to *chefs de la cuisine*? CLERICUS.

[To cook a carp or any other fish *au bleu* is to boil it awhile in a sort of *court-bouillon*, which imparts a blueish tinge. This kind of court-bouillon is a sauce chiefly consisting of wine. We question whether, thus prepared, any

fish that swims would beat our own stewed carp, though we never saw it look blue.]

KING OF JERUSALEM. — I shall be glad to know what kings have been designated by this title, and what present potentates call themselves by it, or claim right over the Holy Land? E.

[A tabular list of the successive Christian Kings of Jerusalem, from Godfrey of Bouillon, A.D. 1099, to Emperor Frederick II., A.D. 1250, is printed in Anderson's *Royal Genealogies*, ed. 1782, Table 159; and in Betham's *Genealogical Tables*, ed. 1795, Table 171.]

Replies.

GREEK CHURCH.

(3rd S. vii. 134, 190.)

On so grave a subject as that which F.C.H. treats, it would surely be right rather to refer to authoritative statements than to make strong assertions. The Greek Church is not separated from the other part of Christendom because of its "denying the procession of the Holy Ghost from the Father and the Son," but because of its protest against the insertion of these words into the Nicene Creed without the sanction of a General Council. That this is so is clear, from a conversation lately held between the Patriarch of Constantinople and an American clergyman. Pointing to the first suffrages in the Litany of the English Church, the Patriarch said: "That is your Litany; I see nothing here to hinder Communion, though you assert the double procession; but I protest against any part of the church altering a creed which is the common property of the Church Universal." Whatever differences then may exist as to doctrine, and these are, as they seem to me, differences of words rather than of facts, or rather differences in the stating of the same fact, the protest of the Greek Church has been against the foisting of words without authority into the common creed of the Church; and not, or at least not primarily, against the doctrine itself.

But your correspondent goes on to say, that the Greek Church agrees with the English Church "in one only point—the denial of the Pope's supremacy." Surely, not to mention other points, F. C. H. has forgotten that the Greek Church, in common with the English Church, maintains the Communion in the Liturgy under both kinds, and gives the cup in accordance with Christ's own command, and with primitive usage, to all. But F. C. H. adds, that "the Greek Church does not acknowledge the validity of the Anglican Orders." Where does this appear? What act of the Greek Church will bear out this assertion? Does the Greek Church re-ordain priests who have received "Anglican Orders"? Will F. C. H. point out any instances of this? In my intercourse with the authorities of the Orthodox Church, I have always found that my orders were unquestioned by them. In a short tour made a few years since in Servia, the Metropolitan of that country—a man whose ecclesiastical knowledge is above the average of western bishops—fully and frankly recognised my orders. He took me within the *Iconostasis*, or sanctuary, of his own chapel, not permitting an English layman who accompanied me the same privilege; gave me the benediction appropriate to a priest on leaving him, and in writing to me afterwards addresses me as a priest. Other Orthodox bishops have done the same. But I am able to refer to something more official, which will, I hope, convince F. C. H. that he is misinformed on this point. Recently an English clergyman, who a few years ago withdrew from the English Church, applied for baptism to the Holy Synod of Russia, saying that he did so because he doubted the validity of his baptism. This request was considered; and the answer was returned, that the Russian bishops had no doubt about the validity of his baptism, and could not re-baptize. Upon this he intimated to the Archbishop of Moscow his intention to apply for Orders in the Russian Church. "To which," said the Archbishop to a friend of mine, "he will receive the same answer. We have no doubt about the validity of English Orders. We cannot, therefore, confer what he already has." But indeed, if F. C. H. will reflect a moment, he must need own this to be antecedently the only course open to the Orthodox, or Eastern Church. By no authoritative document, no brief, bull, nor any other official instrument, has the Roman Church questioned *the fact* of the English succession; the best canonists and ecclesiastics of that Church only question the validity of the English Orders because of circumstances arising out of the denial of the Pope's supremacy. But since this "supremacy" is equally denied by the Greek and the English Churches, it would be impossible for the Greek Church to question the English Orders on any such ground.

W. Denton.

The *odium theologicum* with which the members of the Greek and the Roman Church persecute each other is well described by Sir J. Emerson Tennent in his very interesting *Letters from the Ægean*, 1829, vol. i. pp. 101-2:—

"It is not the Turk alone who is honoured with the hatred of the Greek; to him his aversion bears only political invetaracy; but it is the members of the Church of Rome who feel the full bitterness of his soul's aversion. With them, as with every other sect, it is the most trifling discrepancy of faith which makes the widest breach of friendship; and as the Latin dissents only in a few points of church government, he is treated with a double portion of religious hatred. The Turk differs too widely in his faith to produce any collision; but the texture of Catholicism and the Greek Church come so closely in contact

as to produce incessant eruptions, attended with all the fulmination and flames of polemic combustion. In the Islands, at one time, no intercourse was held with the apostates, and at the present moment Christian burial is denied them, unless performed by their own sect; and absolution in his dying moments has been refused to an orthodox Greek because in the service of a heretic Romanist.

"The hatred, however, is not confined to one side the house; it is returned with ardent fervour by their Vatican brethren. Father Jerome Dandini, the Pope's envoy to the Maronites of Mount Libanus towards the end of the seventeenth century, thus characterises the Greek Christians of Crete, amongst many others, to whom he pays like compliments," &c.

Dandini's *Voyage to Mount Libanus*, translated from the Italian, Lond. 1698, 8vo, was reprinted in the *Oxford Collection of Voyages and Travels*, vol. i., and also in the tenth volume of Pinkerton's collection.

The endeavours which have mutually been made by the Eastern Church and the Anglican to form one communion as members of the primitive Catholic Church are exhibited in the *British Magazine*, vol. xv. pp. 495-504, 616-630, and vol. xvi. p. 16-26; and in Lathbury's *History of the Nonjurors*, pp. 309-360. Bibliothecar. Chetham.

CARY FAMILY.

(3rd S. v. 398; vi. 173, 217, &c.; vii. 117.)

The statement that a Cary was Bishop of Killaloe in 1588 is altogether without foundation. The occupant of that see from 1570 to 1612 was Maurice or Martough O'Brien-arra.

Mordecai Cary, sometime Fellow of Trinity College, Cambridge, was appointed Bishop of Clonfert 1731, and translated to the see of *Killala* in 1735. He died 2 Oct. 1751.

On the south side of the hall of New College, Oxford, are the arms of *John* Cary, M.A., Fellow, viz., Argent, on a bend sable three roses of the field, a crescent for difference. (Wood's *Colleges and Halls*, ed. Gutch, Append. 259.) We suppose him to have been the person of that name who went out, B.A. 12 June, 1718, and M.A. 4 April, 1722. He was probably a benefactor to his college, but when or to what extent we know not.

Walter Cary was a Fellow of New College, being elected from Winchester, in 1704. He was B.A. 25 Nov. 1708, and was created M.A. 15 Sept. 1730. He was M.P., Clerk of the Privy Council, and of the Board of Green Cloth, and Secretary to the Lord Lieutenant of Ireland. (Walcott's *William of Wykeham and his Colleges*, 425.) He died 27 April, 1757. (*Gent. Mag.* xxvii. 189.)

The following coat is in a window of the Middle Temple Hall:—Quarterly, 1. Argent on a bend sable, three roses of the field, a martlet for difference; 2. Or three piles, Azure; 3. Gules, a fess between three crescents argent; 4. Argent, on a fess sable, three pears, or.

This is ascribed to *George* Cary (Dugdale's *Orig. Jurid.* 229.) The quarterings may assist to determine the individual. One George Cary, Recorder of Londonderry in 1618, obtained a grant of Red Castle, in the barony of Innishowen, co. Donegal, and died 22 April, 1640. A Sir George Cary was author of *Reports of Cases in Chancery*, out of the labours of Mr. William Lambert. These were printed 1650, and reprinted 1665 and 1820.

We have no information when Sir George Cary, the reporter flourished; but from the mention of Lambert [Lambarde] on the title-page of his book, he was probably dead long before its first publication. He may have been identical with George *Carye*, Esquire, who on 19 June, 1568, gave commandment from the queen to the Lord Keeper not to dismiss a certain suit, and brought unto his lordship from her highness a ring for that purpose. (Monro's *Actæ Cancellariæ*, 372.) We incline to think that the reporter may have been Sir George *Carew*, LL.D., Master in Chancery, who died at an advanced age in Nov. 1612.

The Dr. Carey who was brought to the Bar of the House of Lords in 1677 (1 March, 1676-7), and who was imprisoned and fined 1000*l.*, was named *Nicholas.*|

The book for which he was called in question, was entitled, *The Grand Question concerning the Prorogation of this Parliament for a Yeare and three Months stated and discussed.* The author was not the Earl of Shaftesbury, but Lord Holles. (See *Lords' Journals*, xiii. 54, 55; Cooke's *Life of the Earl of Shaftesbury*, ii. 163.)

It is to be observed that before Dr. Carey was punished by the Lords, he had two interviews with Charles II. at Whitehall on the subject of the authorship of the above work.

More information about him will, it is hoped, be given. Peculiar interest attaches to the names of those who have courageously withstood efforts to repress free discussion.

The arms of Dr. William Carey, successively Bishop of Exeter and St. Asaph, were, Argent on a bend sable, three roses of the field, on a chief, gules, *three* crosses patee or. (Bedford's *Blazon of Episcopacy*, p. 11 and pl. 6.)

Walter Cary, M.A. and Student in Physic, was author of *A Book of the Properties of Herbes called an Herbal.* Lond. (Kyngston), n. d.; *The Hammer for the Stone*, Lond. 1581; and *A briefe Treatise called Caries Farewell to Physicke*, Lond. 1583, 1597, 1598, 1611, 1625.

To T. Carey is ascribed a version of Psalm xci., apparently written at the close of the reign of Elizabeth. (Farr's *Select Poetry, chiefly devotional, of the reign of Queen Elizabeth*, pp. xxx, 338.)

Henry Cary was author of *The Fruit of Pleading in Sir Edward Coke's Reports*, 1601, and *The Law of England; or a true Guide for all Persons concerned in the Ecclesiastical Courts*, n. d. Dugdale (*Orig. Jurid.* 61) calls him Richard, and this mistake has misled Watt, who ascribes the *Fruit of Pleading* to both Henry and Richard Cary.

Two letters of Sir George Cary of Cockington, Lord Deputy of Ireland (who died 1615) are given in Monro's *Acta Cancellariæ*, 20, 127.

Walter Carey (apparently a different person from the medical writer of that name) was author of *The Present State of England, expressed in this Paradox, Our Fathers were very rich with little, and We Poor with much.* Lond. 4to, 1626, 1627. It is reprinted in *Harl. Miscell.* ed. Park, iii. 206; ed. Malham, iii. 552. The author was seventy-six years of age when the work was written.

Grace Cary, an extraordinary enthusiast, was widow of Walter Cary of Bristol, and resided at one period at Usk, in Monmouthshire. There is an account of her in Seyer's *Bristol*, ii. 338 *seq.*; *England's Forewarninge; or, A Relation of true, strange, and wonderful Visions and propheticall Relations concerning these Tragicall Tymes, shewed four or five years since to Mrs. Grace Cary of Bristoll* (dated June, 1644), forms MS. Egerton, 1044.

Under the name of Walter Cary appeared — *England's Wants; or, several Proposals probably beneficial to England; offered to the Consideration of all good Patriots in both Houses of Parliament.* Lond. 8vo, 1685. We can find no particulars of this author's history.

Robert Cary, LL.D., rector of East Portlemouth, and sometime Archdeacon of Exeter, published, *Palælogia Chronica a chronological Account of ancient Time*, in three parts. 1. Didactical; 2. Apodeictical; 3. Canonical. Lond. fo. 1677. This is said to be a work of considerable merit. The author was born at Cockington, Devon, and was buried at East Portlemouth, 19th Sept. 1688.

John Cary, merchant of Bristol, who died soon after 1704, was a voluminous writer on commerce. (See *Autobiography of Edmund Bohun*, 131 *seq.*; "N. & Q." 1st S. xi. 1; Watt's *Bibl. Brit.*; and M'Culloch's *Lit. of Pol. Econ.* 46.)

Thomas Cary, M.A., of Oxford, and who was incorporated in that degree at Cambridge, became a Canon of Bristol, 1693, and died in 1711. Two of his sermons are in print.

C. H. & Thompson Cooper.

Cambridge.

A more careful and extended search among original authorities has led me to modify and correct some of the conclusions which I had previously adopted upon this subject. I feel less confidence than heretofore in assuming that the descendants of the first Lord Hunsdon are to be looked for *only* in the issue of his third surviving son, Sir Edmund Cary.

I will explain my reasons as briefly as possible. 1st. I have good authority (Segar's *MS. Baronagium penes Coll. Arm.*) for stating that William, fourth son of the first Lord Hunsdon married Martha, daughter of Thomas Turner of Wratting, co. Suffolk; and there can be little doubt that he is identical with "William Cary of Barwick," to whose effects his relict, Martha, administered, 18 May, 1593. (See *Durham Wills*, ii. 231, published by the Surtees' Society.) Whether there was any issue by this marriage is not recorded; and, as the widow was twice married afterwards, there is some difficulty in ascertaining the date of her death. The possibility, however, still exists that there might be descendants from this younger son.

2nd. Again; John, third Lord Hunsdon, had a second son Charles Carey, who married Elizabeth, daughter of Sir John Whitbroke, Knt. In the funeral certificate of his mother (penes Coll. Arm.) it is stated that, at her death, he had one child, Mary, aged three in 1627. It is by no means improbable that other children might have been subsequently born, and I should certainly be very glad to ascertain the fact, one way or the other. When and where did Charles Carey die?

3rd. Sir Pelham Carey, Knt., a younger son of Henry, fourth Lord Hunsdon, married Mary, daughter and heir of Sir John Jackson *, of Berwick, Knt.; but whether he left issue, I know not. I can only ascertain that he was eight years old in 1621, and was knighted in Scotland 16 July, 1633.

4th. I now come to Thomas, the third son of Sir Edmund Cary. As his elder brother Robert was baptized in 1582-3, we may conclude that he was born *circa* 1590. He was alive in 1620 (*Visitation of Devon*), and in 1707, when the last Lord Hunsdon claimed the title, is spoken of as having had issue, believed at that date to be dead. (See Sessions Papers, 1707.) As, however, their existence would not interfere with the petitioner's claim, the question was not entertained. Whether this son was identical with Sir Thomas Cary mentioned in Bramston's *Autobiography*, I know not, but I thank MELETES for the suggestion. I am aware that many families in Ireland, bearing the name of Cary, claim descent from the Hunsdon branch, and perhaps the records at Dublin might furnish information on this point.

Let me take this opportunity to state that further investigation does not confirm my idea that Rowland Cary was a brother of Col. Ernestus Cary. He is not mentioned in the pedigree signed by the latter at the Heralds' College, and his

* Probably the "Mr. John Jackson," who, with Sir Robert Jackson, of Berwick, Knt., is mentioned as a ——— in the will of Bishop Valentine Carey. (See "N. & Q." 3rd S, vi. 174.)

administration (dated 16 Jan. 1651-2) only furnishes the name of his son, Edward Cary. The Registers of Everton commence in the seventeenth century, and notice the descendants of Rowland, viz. Edward Cary, buried 1657, and Walter Cary, buried 1679, and others, but nothing more.

With regard to Bishop Valentine Carey, it should be observed that there was in the North of England another member of the Cary family contemporary with the first Lord Hunsdon. In 1542 "Thomas Carye, Esq.," was constable of Prudhoe.

In reply to your correspondent, I must add that Alitha Cary was a daughter of Sir Ferdinando Cary (not of Sir Edmund), and certainly married Sir William Quirinson, of Middleburgh, in Zealand. Sir Edmund's two daughters were Anne and Catharine; the former wife to Sir William Uvedale, of Wickham, co. Hants, and the latter to Sir Francis Rogers.

I do not know of any Irish bishop of the name except Bishop Mordecai Cary. He was of Trin. Coll. Camb.; Master of Morpeth Grammar School in 1718; Bishop of Clonfert in 1732, and translated to Killaloe in 1735, of which see he died bishop in 1751. (Hodgson's *Northumberland*.)

The collections which I have made upon the subject of this note are too extensive for admission into the pages of "N. & Q." I purpose publishing them in a complete form in forthcoming numbers of the *Herald and Genealogist*, a publication which is no rival, but a valuable adjunct to that in which this discussion has taken place. In thanking MELETES and other correspondents for their aid, let me invite them to continue it, and in case their communications should be unsuitable for a popular periodical, to address them directly to me, by whom they will be gladly received.　　CHARLES J. ROBINSON, M.A.

Harewood Parsonage, Ross.

P.S. Since writing the above, I have discovered one or two additional facts which should not be overlooked.

William Cary, son of Henry, first Lord Hunsdon, died *without issue*, and his brother Robert, afterwards Earl of Monmouth, thus became heir to Colombine Hall, co. Suffolk. (See Lord Monmouth's *Autobiography*.)

Valentine Cary owed his elevation to the Bishopric of Exeter wholly to the personal influence of Lord Hunsdon with James I. (See *Court and Times of James the First*, ii. 275.)

The Sir Thomas Cary whom your correspondent mentions was evidently Sir Thomas Carew, a younger son of Sir Richard Carew of Anthony. I have been frequently puzzled by this common practice among old writers of writing Carey for Carew. A notable instance may be found in Smyth's *Obituary*, where the public execution of Sir Alexander *Carey* is recorded, though there can be no doubt that the sufferer was Sir Alex. Carew (half-brother of Sir Thomas) who was beheaded on Tower Hill, Dec. 23, 1644.

The only instance I have found of Cary arms differenced with a mullet occurs in a volume of Painters' Work in the College of Arms, viz.—

"1687. July 1. Arms of Forster impaling Cary with a mullet charged with a crescent for difference."

Perhaps your correspondent may be able to make something of this entry, which of course refers to a funeral. C. J. R.

The Rev. W. Bedford in the *Blazon of Episcopacy*, p. 11, gives the arms of William Carey, Bishop of St. Asaph, and afterwards of Exeter, as follows: arg. on a bend sa. three roses of the first, on a chief gu. *three* crosses patée or, on the authority of the Bishop's seal. J. Woodward.

New Shoreham.

"IL FORTUNATO INFORTUNATO."

(2nd S. ix. 282.)

The play is "*El Dichoso Desdichado, Poncio Pilato,* de Don Juan de Espinosa Malagon y Valenzuela," 4to, p. 24. There is no date, but at the end is: "En Sevilla, en la Imprenta de Joseph Padrino, Mercader de Libros, en Calle de Genova."

Pontius Pilate is represented as depressed in spirits by excess of good fortune: everything which he undertakes is successful, and his blunders are as fortunate as his designs. He is weary of this, and wants a change. He says:—

> "Si no conoce el pesar
> Un hombre, lo que es placer ?
> Siempre el plácer viene á dár
> Enfado, que es necio el gusto.
> Que se gusta sin azar,
> Porque el placer sin disgusto
> No es placer sino pesar."—P. 3.

As a contrast to Pilate, Brodio, one of his officers, is always unlucky, but cheerful. Pilate desires Brodio's company to death; Brodio suggests to dinner, *á comer*. Pilate afterwards relates his life, and bemoans his prosperity, concluding—

> "Y assi, la muerte has de darme,
> Pilato soi yo soi Poncio,
> Porque si tu no me matas
> He de matarme yo proprio.
> *Brodio.* Yo, gran señor, vivir quiero
> Que soi desdichado en todo."—P. 8.

Saint Veronica, Tiberius, and various other persons are introduced, and the events are jumbled in the usual manner of Spanish plays. Tiberius has heard of Jesus as a curer of diseases, and, being very ill, sends for him to Rome. Hearing that he has been put to death by Pontius Pilate, he summons Pilate, and gives orders for his execution. Pilate reappears in the coat of Jesus, and is loaded

with compliments and promotion. When out of sight, Tiberius again decrees his death, but again changes on Pilate reappearing in the coat. At last he throws it off, Tiberius puts it on, and orders Pilate to be put to death without delay. Pilate enters, half naked—*medio desnudo*—with a dagger in his hand. A crucifix appears to him; he soliloquizes at some length, and with some affectation of argument, ending—

> "Oy, Christo vos me matais,
> Y en el Tribunal os veo
> En la Cruz, y como à reo
> Maldito me sentenciais,
> A la justicia me dáis,
> Que me hiera, y no me amague,
> Que me confunda y estrague
> Por perverso, y por mal quisto:
> Si esta justicia hace Christo
> Quien tal hace, que tal pague.
> *Dase de puñaladas y cae muerto*."—P. 24.

Perhaps I have trespassed too much on your space by these extracts, the interest of which I may have measured more by the time and the great number of volumes which I turned over before finding the play than by their real value. I have looked without success for some account of the author. I am not sufficiently familiar with Spanish typography to guess the date from print or paper; both are bad. I find other plays by the same publisher, better printed, but without date. Should any reader of "N. & Q." know a book, with the date, published by Joseph Padrino of Seville, I shall be glad of it, as a help to discover who Malagon was. H. B. C.

U. U. Club.

EVIDENCES OF DISTANT LIGHT AND SMOKE.

(3rd S. v. 329.)

Sir Thomas E. Winnington mentions a brilliant illumination of the sky as being distinctly visible at night in the direction of Dudley, but at a distance of twenty miles; and that he had found the larch plantations, near the summit of Brown Clee Hill, in Shropshire, fourteen miles distant, covered with a smoky deposit, similar to the trees in the London parks. He asks—"Has such a phenomenon of distant smoke been observed elsewhere?"

Brown Clee Hill is, I think, not many points from due *west* of Dudley; and it is a fact that the prevalent winds there are *westerly*. I believe it would be found that the wind blows from the *east* only a small portion of the year; and your correspondent may possibly be mistaken as to the substance upon the trees being brought from Dudley. I suggest a careful detachment of a sufficient quantity (without removing any of the cortex of the tree) for chemical examination. If the substance should be found almost, or quite, pure carbon, Sir T. E. Winnington will have established a very interesting and valuable fact.

The vitiated air of large towns is undoubtedly prejudicial to both animal and vegetable life, and it is important to know how far that influence may, in extreme cases, extend.

Some years since I was staying with the vicar of Dudley, who complained of injury to the health of his large family, from residing at the vicarage, nearly in the centre of the town. On this account he had taken a house and grounds two or three miles distant *eastward*. There I saw that the fruit, when ripe, was coated with soot, and was informed that currants could not be eaten because they were so bitter.

Sheffield has long been called the "City of Soot;" and since the epidemic of "rifled cannon" and "armour plates" set in, I think it may fairly vie, in obscure atmosphere, with any town in the "Black Country." Yet the hills *west* of the town, within three miles, are dotted with pleasant residences, where smoke and soot are almost unknown. At Rotherham, five miles *northeast*, vegetation is slightly affected by Sheffield smoke. The distances, therefore, to which these disagreeable and deleterious influences extend, from any great centre, must depend upon the directions of the prevalent winds.

I have no doubt Sir T. E. Winnington has seen the illumination of the sky at a distance of twenty miles from Dudley. It might be seen at a greater distance,—even from the Wrekin, and at Malvern. Dudley is situated on the watershed of the country, and the highest points of the parish are nearly 1000 feet above the sea. The rain falling on one side of High Street flows into the valley of the Tame, and thence by the Trent into the German Ocean; while that falling on the other side of the same street flows into the river Stour, and thence by the Severn into St. George's Channel.

In constructing the framework of the Ordnance Survey, (after measuring the base lines,) some of the operations of the first triangulation were executed during dark nights; and the surveyors, with their theodolites upon one eminence, were able to measure angles, whose sides extended from 50 to 70 miles in length, by beacon lamps placed upon other distant mountain tops.

Since writing the above, I am informed by a friend, who has recently visited the hydropathic establishment of Ben Rhydding, in Yorkshire, that the proprietor entertains no doubt the trees there are affected by the smoke from Bradford, fourteen miles distant. W. LEE.

LONGEVITY: MISS MARY BILLINGE (3rd S. vii. 154.)—Your correspondent, A DOUBTER, has asked **me to furnish** some particulars of the evidence **which satisfied** me that Miss Mary Billinge, of

Edge Lane, near Liverpool, who died on December 20th, 1863, was the same person who was baptized on May 24th, 1751. In answer, I may say that it was only by a mere accident we were able to obtain even the scanty particulars furnished. The old lady had outlived all her early friends. She had long been looked on as a sort of fossil relic of a byegone age. Her old servant, who had faithfully served her for nearly fifty years, died two years before herself. She was the only depository of the secret as to the great age of her mistress; and, though often questioned, she never communicated it to any one. But to her sister, who succeeded to her place beside Miss Billinge, she told that years ago, it had been necessary, in connection with a will, to obtain needful certificates of relationship or identity, and that Miss Billinge had then sent her to Eccleston, near Prescot, assuring her that that was the place of her birth. We had traditional and other evidence to the same effect. She had, it is known, a brother and sister, and she was the senior of both. The brother died in 1817, aged forty-seven years. The Health Committee in this town employed an officer to make inquiries as to the matter, who, I understood, after some research, rested quite satisfied with the truth of the certificate. Miss Billinge would never speak of the past, and always resented any reference to her great age. She had long been bent almost double with years, her skin hung extremely loose, and was most curiously wrinkled. An old lady, herself upwards of eighty years, who wished to see her in my presence, looked quite fresh and youthful in comparison. Should any further particulars as to dates come to hand, I will communicate them. JOHN NEWTON.

13, West Derby Street, Liverpool.

KEIGHTLEY'S "SHAKESPEARE EXPOSITOR" (3rd S. vii. 175.)—In reference to MR. KEIGHTLEY'S article on this subject in "N. & Q.," No. 166, will you allow us to deny having ever made any engagement, *either expressed or understood*, to print that work. MR. KEIGHTLEY undertook to make the First Folio Edition of Shakespeare the basis of the reprint we have recently issued, and to clear it as far as he could of printers' errors. We agreed to his inserting a few conjectural emendations, on condition that attention was specially called to them, and the old reading given at the end of each play; but he never asked us to undertake the *Shakespeare Expositor*, nor even showed it to us, till after half of the Shakespeare itself was printed; and had he in any way given us to understand that his preparing the text would involve the publishing of his Comments, we should have been obliged to decline his assistance. BELL & DALDY.

THE SLAVONIANS IN ENGLAND (3rd S. vii. 181.) Permit me to correct the following errata in my

Query on p. 181: for Welches there should be Weletes; for Thafarzik, Shafarzik; for nation, nations.

I have to add, that as a further proof of the Slavonic origin of the Weletes, the former inhabitants of Wiltshire, there seem to serve efficiently the fact that Old Sarum was called by the Britons *Sorbiodunum*: that is, the town of the *Sorbes*. Now *Sorbi, Serbi, Sierbi, Sirbi, Srbi, Sarbi* was the native name of the ancient Slavonians; and even until now more than 7,000,000 of Slavonians under Austrian and Turkish rule call themselves Srbi; and signifies, according to Shafarzi, a countryman, a native, and is related to the Indish term *serim* (natio.)

A similar term have the Germans in Thiutisk, Diutisk, Deutsche, Teuton, from Gothic *thuida* (natio, gens.)   CORCONTIUS.

GLEANINGS FROM AUSONIUS (3rd S. vii. 148.)—
Will MR. L. MACKENZIE accept the following translation of the Latin distich, on the *Dodralis Potio?*—

" I am called *Dodra*: do you ask me why ?
Because my compound nine good things supply.
Broth, water, honey, wine, and bread combine
With pepper, herbs, oil, salt to make the nine."
                                        F. C. H.

MATFELON (3rd S. v. 223.)—It will be remembered that B. H. C. supposes that *Matfelon*, as the name of a plant, is a compound of the old verb *mater*, to macerate, and *felon*, a boil. This derivation—somewhat different from any that I have seen elsewhere—receives confirmation from two articles that I have lighted on in M. Métivier's Glossary to his *Rimes Guernesiaises*, published some years ago, but without a date, by Simpkin, Marshall, & Co. :—

" FLON, *s. m.* Clou, froncle; mal St. Antoine.
" FLON, Herbe au, *s. f.* Herbe qui guérit le mal St. Antoine. Ang. *Matfelon, Knapweed."*

It is clear that the *Flon* of Guernsey—probably known by the same name on the neighbouring coast of Normandy — is no other than the *felon* of B. H. C., or, as it is spelled in the *Promptorium Parvulorum, felone.* And as this is clearly at the root of the name—*Herbe au flon*—it seems almost beyond a doubt that the English name *Mat-felon*, given to the same plant, must have a similar origin.

Whether the parish of St. Mary Matfelon owes its name to the abundance of this medicinal herb once growing on its open commons, or, as B. H. C. suggests, to some medical virtues of its patron saint, is still a question open for discussion.

The French word *froncle* evidently comes from *furunculus.* But how came a boil to be called *furunculus* (a thief) in Latin, and *felon* in English? Might we not go a step further? and, as there is a striking similarity of sound between *whitlow* and *outlaw*, might we not be led to suspect that originally these two words had something to do with one another?   P. S. C.

ROYAL STANDARD AND UNION FLAG (3rd S. vii. 136.)—At Hampton Court are two very interesting pictures, which severally represent the embarcation of Charles II. from Holland, in 1660, and that of William III. in 1688, both monarchs being on their way to the shores of England. The Royal Standard in both pictures is a large red flag, upon the centre of which King Charles charges his Stuart shield-of-arms, while King William, in the same manner, displays his royal shield, with its accessories of supporters, crest, motto, &c. This usage is still prevalent in the blazonry of the sovereigns of continental states, but the sovereign of our own country now blazons the charges of the royal arms over the *entire field* of the Royal Standard or Banner. I think we may assume that both King Charles and King William, when landing, displayed the same standards that were hoisted by them on the occasion of their embarcation; and, accordingly, I believe, R. S. Q. may confidently consider the Royal Standard of Charles II. when he landed " to resume possession of his kingdom," to have been a large *plain red flag*, charged with the *Royal Shield* of the Stuart sovereigns of Great Britain.

As a matter of course, whenever the *Union flag* was displayed by Charles II. it was the *first* of the two Union brethren which had been adopted by James I. in 1606, and which symbolized the union of England and Scotland in the union of the Crosses of St. George and St. Andrew; the incorporation of the red saltier of St. Patrick into the Union Flag marks the political union of the three kingdoms of England, Scotland, and Ireland, in the commencement of this present century.

The *ensign* in use in the time of Charles II. appears to have been a red flag cantoning the St. George; this ensign, with a plain red flag, and another red flag containing the *first* Union in place of the St. George, appear in the Hampton Court picture of the embarcation of William III., and I know no earlier example of such an appearance of the Union in an ensign.

The criticism of R. S. Q., as he very justly admits, has " nothing to do with the merits " of the fresco in the Palace of Westminster, to which he alludes; still I cannot admit that his is " idle " criticism, since he would seek by it to secure for our national works of art of the highest order consistent historical accuracy. Bad heraldry may not necessarily imply bad art; but surely noble art has a right to expect good heraldry; at any rate, it must be a grave imperfection in an historical painting, which professes to deal historically with an important incident in history, should such a picture unequivocally record the return of Charles II. to England, to " enjoy his own again," to have taken place in the nineteenth century. Such at this moment is the record of the fresco in question.   CHARLES BOUTELL.

LATIN PUZZLE (3ʳᵈ S. vii. 85.)—The four maccaronic verses by Donne, prefixed to Coryat's *Crudities*, respecting which your correspondent CPL. inquires, are written in a mixture of five languages — Latin, - Spanish, English, Italian, and French. They may be literally though clumsily translated thus; but they are not very intelligible : —

" As many as two perfect linguists shall make these couplets,
So many prudent statesmen this thy book shall make.
Enough to me is the honour to be here understood ; for I leave
The honour of being believed by nobody to thee."

The *Latin* words are—Quot, hæc, disticha, tot, hic, tuus, hic, sat, tibi.
Spanish—Dos, cuerdos, l'honra.
Italian—Perfetti, fara, a mi, inteso, creduto.
French—Fairont, livre, l'honneur, estre, car, de personne, n'estre.   P.

METRICAL SERMON (3ʳᵈ S. vii. 76, 143.)—Allow me to mention, as an illustration of this subject, a parallel passage from a once well-known and generally read book—*The Tour of Doctor Syntax in search of the Picturesque*. Singular to say the sermon preached by Doctor Syntax, is precisely on the same text as that recorded by your correspondents, W. D. and W. : —

"Then in loud tones, though somewhat hoarse,
He gave the following discourse.
' The subject I shall now rehearse
Is Job the *fifth*, and *seventh* verse :
*As sparks rise upward to the sky,
So man is born to misery.'* "

The whole sermon is admirable, and the progress of man from the cradle to the grave most effectively painted. It is, as I think, one of the best passages in *Doctor Syntax*.   OXONIENSIS.

APPLE-PIE ORDER (3ʳᵈ S. vii. 133.) — I have referred to your 1ˢᵗ S. iii. 468, 485; vi. 109, for the different conjectures that have been given respecting the origin of this phrase. As I do not think that they are at all satisfactory, I venture to suggest that "apple-pie" is a corruption for "alpha-beta," and that the phrase means nothing more than *alphabetical*, or *regular*, *order*.

THOS. COWARD.

Cambridge.

FAMILIES OF GOODRICH (3ʳᵈ S. vii. 134.) — I address this to "N. & Q." because what I have to say concerns not a mere private family, but a known character in history. Thomas Goodrich, or Goodrich, was made Bishop of Ely in the reign of Henry VIII., and consecrated April 19, 1534. He was Lord Chancellor of England in the time of Edward VI., but *not in the reign of Queen Mary ;*

for on her accession to the throne, she appointed Stephen Gardiner, who was Bishop of Winchester, to be Lord Chancellor. Goodrick was not likely to find favour with Queen Mary, seeing that he was one of those bishops and noblemen who signed the letter to her denying her right to the crown, and defending the claim of Lady Jane Gray. Bishop Goodrick died May 10, 1554, at Somersham, where he lies buried, with an inscription on his tomb. There is a fine brass to his memory in Ely cathedral, on which he is represented in full pontificals, with the name spelt "Goodryke;" but by a strange mistake of the artist, the ends of the stole are seen pendant between the dalmatic and tunicella. (See Dodd's *Church Hist. of England*, vol. i., and Lingard's *History*, "Qu. Mary.")   F. C. H.

QUOTATIONS (3ʳᵈ S. vii. 155.)—It is the second time within a few weeks that one of your correspondents, and I presume yourself also, have been at fault about a passage from Wordsworth's finest production. The passage beginning "In a season," is from his "Ode on the Intimations of Immortality from the Recollections of Early Childhood."   LYTTELTON.

Hagley, Stourbridge.

MILTON AND HIS ILLUSTRATOR (3ʳᵈ S. vii. 150.) I do not mean to question the correctness of the interpretation here given; but I may observe that it seems to have been a new one at the time that Professor Warton published Milton's Minor Poems. In his note on the passage he says it was suggested to him "by the late ingenious Mr. Headley." (2nd edit., 1791.) Mr. Warton seems to speak of the previous interpretation as being merely "shepherds telling stories," love having nothing to do with them : stupid enough. He argues in favour of Mr. Headley's view, and well adduces Shakspeare, *Third Part of Henry VI.*, Act II. Sc. V.,

" Gives not the hawthorn bush a sweeter shade
To shepherds *looking on their silly sheep*."

If Milton had this in his mind, it much confirms this rendering. Mr. Hayman has lately well translated it —

" sub arbuta vallis
Quisque gregem pastor confert et ovile recenset."
LYTTELTON.

Hagley, Stourbridge.

As a rider to the note on this subject, permit me to add that a *Times'* reviewer a few years ago actually took an artist to task for *not having taken* the same view of the "shepherd's tale" as the designer of No. V. in the volume issued by the Art Union of London, mentioned by your correspondent. This has ever appeared to me the most ludicrous of blunders. I give *ipsissima verba* from an article on "Illustrated Books" published in *The Times* of December 24, 1858 : —

"Mr. Creswick's 'Dappled Dawn' rises naturally enough, but if 'every shepherd tells his tale under the hawthorn in the dale,' the shepherd of Mr. Redgrave is a notable exception; for, so far from telling any tale of his own, he is not even inclined to listen to the tale of his fair companion, being entirely preoccupied in opening the hurdles for his sheep"!!

A. CHALLSTETH.

1, Verulam Buildings, Gray's Inn.

T. N. is rather too dogmatic on this subject. In my note on this place of the *Allegro* in my edition of Milton's *Poems* I have shown that "the almost invariable meaning [of 'tell a tale'] is, to narrate something."   THOS. KEIGHTLEY.

Several writers give the same explanation as T. N. of the shepherd's telling —

" his tale
Under the hawthorn in the dale."

Mr. and Miss Edgeworth, for example, in their *Readings on Poetry*, 2nd ed. 1816, p. 213, say,—

" The word *tale* here means the *tally*, or the account of the flock which each shepherd *numbers* or *tells* in the morning, and not a love tale."

But I doubt the correctness of this explanation. The hawthorn is in flower in May, and in many parts of England is commonly known by the name of that month; but May is especially the month of love.

" Hail! bounteous May, that dost inspire
Mirth and youth, and *warm desire.*"

In this the physiologist agrees with the poet. Hence the propriety of making the shepherd tell his tale of love under the hawthorn; but what propriety is there in making a shepherd count his sheep under a hawthorn rather than under any other tree? It may be added that a *dale* is a comparatively secluded place, in which sheep are much less frequently kept than in upland pastures, but which is all the more suitable for the lovesick swain.   D.

Your correspondent T. N. in your number for Feb. 25 has certainly enlightened me as to the proper meaning of the "tale" which Milton's shepherd is supposed to "tell." In confirmation of his correctness, allow me to say, that when geologising a few years ago in Devonshire near Span Head, Isle of Barnstaple, I found on the Ordnance Map a place called "Telling House," and the people about spoke of "The telling house." On inquiring the meaning of the term, I found it was the place to which the sheep were brought down from the hill to be counted, or, in other words, to have their *tale told*.   BETA.

PONTIFICAL RINGS (3rd S. vii. 136.)—In answer to the enquiries of A. A., I have to state that it has been long customary in this country for Catholics to kneel for a blessing from their bishops; but the custom of kissing the bishop's ring, when kneeling before him for a blessing, is not so

common in England as on the Continent. Canons do not kneel, except to the Pope: to all other bishops they only bow when they receive the blessing, or kiss the pontifical ring. As to the affinity between kissing a bishop's ring, and kissing the Pope's slipper, both are marks of respect and veneration: the latter being more profound, as the dignity of the supreme Pontiff is so much greater.   F. C. H.

TRADITIONS OF AN ANTECEDENT WORLD (3rd S. vii. 95, 141.) It may be useful to note, in addition to the valuable information by MR. PINKERTON, that the absurd book of Isaac de la Perreyre was pretty effectually stifled at its birth by the refutation published by a Professor of Theology at Gröningen, named Desmarais, though La Perreyre wrote a reply to it. He was condemned by the Inquisition in Flanders, but appealed from the sentence to Pope Alexander VII., who received him with kindness. While at Rome he printed a retractation of his book, and retired to the Convent of our Lady of Virtues; where he died, having been converted from Calvinism to the Catholic faith. (See Bergier, *Dict. de la Théologie*, art. "Preadamites.")   F. C. H.

BAZUBEND (3rd S. vii. 113.) — Your correspondent is right in supposing that *bazu-bend* is an article of dress. It is used in Persia, and, I may add, in India. The word is good Persian, adopted also in Hindustani, from *bāzū*, the arm; and *band*, a band or fastening, and signifies an armlet worn above the elbow.   EDMUND BELL.

DRAGON IN HEREFORDSHIRE (3rd S. vii. 133.)— Mordiford is a small village near the junction of the rivers Lugg and Wye, four miles and a half south-east of Hereford. It is celebrated in a traditional history as the scene of a furious combat between a winged serpent and a condemned malefactor, who was promised pardon on condition of his destroying this monster, who had spread terror and destruction all around. The contest was of some continuance. At length, however, the serpent was killed, but his poisonous breath proved fatal to his destroyer. In memory of this event, a large green dragon, with expanded wings and web-footed, is (1808) painted on the west end of the church. (*Hereford Guide*, Wright, 1808.)

But the Rev. John Duncumb gives a more probable version of the legend: —

"Soon after this period (A.D. 448) Uther, surnamed Pendragon, was chief of the Silures; the cognomen was probably acquired by some signal exertion of valour under the insignia of the dragon, which was common to the banners of all the British chiefs, and was a sacred symbol amongst them, and many other nations of antiquity. The dragon is not only often mentioned in various records, but respect has been shown towards it in several places by particular customs, some of which exist even at this day (1804). Thus the supposed form of a dragon has been described and renewed on the west end of the church of Mordiford from time immemorial."—*History and Antiquities of the County of Hereford*, vol. i. pp. 31-2.

In addition to these authorities, the legend was amplified in a pamphlet written by a shoemaker, Mr. Dacres Devlin, about the year 1841, and formed the groundwork of a romantic tale.

C. N.

T. C. will find an account of this dragon in *Helps to Hereford History, Civil and Legendary, &c. The Mordiford Dragon, &c.*, by J. Dacres Devlin, a curious little book, which may be obtained of J. R. Smith, Soho Square. SAMUEL SHAW.
Andover.

VOLTAIRE (3ʳᵈ S. vi. 533.)—The passages quoted as from Newton and Voltaire, and well described by MR. ROOPER as "most astonishing, striking, and interesting," have not yet been found in the works of either. I have more than once in "N. & Q." asked for references to the writings of Voltaire for words ascribed to him. I now ask if there is any evidence of the following account of his death?—

"Fury and despair succeeded each other. He had near the appearance of a demon than a man. To his physician he said, 'Doctor, I will give you half of what I am worth if you will give me six months of life.' To which his physician replied, 'Sir, you will not live six weeks.' 'Then,' said Voltaire, 'I shall go to hell, and you shall go with me,' and soon after he expired."—*A Sermon preached at the Baptist Chapel, St. Albans*, April 28, 1862, by Danzy Sheen, p. 18.

FITZHOPKINS.
Garrick Club.

SAM SHARPSET (3ʳᵈ S. vii. 155.)—Sam Sharpset did not receive his brother Matthew coolly at Barbadoes, but Matthew received Sam coolly at Surinam.

Matthew is surrounded by creditors, whom Sam and Fogrum suppose to be paying court to a great man. They approach:—

"*Sharpset.* Strangers and countrymen,—a double claim to my protection.

"*Sam Sharpset.* We are both strangers, noble Sir; but not both countrymen, because he's a Londoner, and—Lud a mercy! may I just ask your noble name?

"*Sharpset.* Matthew Sharpset, Esquire.

"*Sam Sharpset.* 'Tis him—huzza! (*Snaps his fingers.*) 'Tis brother Matty! Yorkshire for ever! Why Matty, hast thou forgotten little Sammy?

"*Sharpset.* The devil! Ah! little Sammy, is it you? How do you do?"—*The Slave*, Act I. Sc. 2.

FITZHOPKINS.
Garrick Club.

FOUR-AND-TWENTY SWORN MEN OF GOOS-NARGH (3ʳᵈ S. vii. 75.)—A gentleman who has access to the vestry books of Goosnargh has forwarded to me the subjoined extract, which I think may be interesting to many of the readers of "N. & Q." It is taken from a page bearing the date of 1678:—

"Here ensueth the form of the Oath wᶜʰ of antient time hath beene used to be ministered unto every person elected into the number, Company, or Societye of the Four-and-Twenty sworne men of the chappellrye of Goosnargh in the countye of Lancʳ at the time of his election into that Societye, viz.—You shall well and truly observe and keepe all antient lawfull and laudable Customes as heretofore in this place have been observed and kept, so far as they shall agree with the laws of this Realme and the good and benefit of this Chappell and Chappellrye according to your power and best understanding and your own Counsell and your fellowes you shall keepe. So helpe you God."

H. FISHWICK.

SIR WALTER SCOTT (3ʳᵈ S. vii. 156.)—It is certain from his own acknowledgment, that Sir Walter Scott never did visit Melrose Abbey by moonlight. In *Views a Foot* by J. B. Taylor, it is stated that Bernard Barton once wrote to Sir Walter on behalf of a young lady who wished to have his description of Melrose Abbey in his own hand-writing. Scott sent it with the following addition:—

"Then go and muse with deepest awe
On what the writer never saw;
Who would not wander 'neath the moon
To see what he could see at noon."

F. C. H.

YEW TREES CALLED PALMS (3ʳᵈ S. vii. 167.)—It is customary in many parts of England still, as well as in Ireland among Catholics, to bless sprigs of the *yew*, and distribute them from the altar on Palm Sunday. Our ancestors made use of it for the same purpose; and hence it was common to plant yew trees in the churchyards, and particularly one or more near to the church porch, for the convenience of providing small branches for blessed palms. An aged yew tree is still to be seen near some of our church porches, and there is one standing within a few miles of the place from which I write. In other parts of England sprigs of different trees are blessed, and distributed in Catholic churches and chapels on Palm Sunday—as of box, broom, laurel, and sallow. The last has been used so much in many places, that the tree itself is commonly called palm, especially by the children. In every house of Catholics, the palm, of whatever tree it may be, is to be found hung up in some conspicuous place, usually at the bedhead, during the whole year. The ashes of a few of the blessed palms burnt are used for the expressive ceremonial of marking the foreheads of the faithful, in the form of a cross, on Ash Wednesday; and all the other palms are burnt on the morning of Palm Sunday, previous to receiving the newly-blessed palm. The same customs prevail in all Catholic countries as well as in Ireland; but real palm branches are of course used where they can be had. F. C. H.

SIR THOMAS FORTESCUE (3ʳᵈ S. vii. 94.)—Anne Lady Parry, widow of Sir Adrian Fortescue, bequeathed the manor of Charlton, Kent, to Thomas Fortescue, who was probably the person after whom C. J. R. makes his inquiry. I shall be glad to know more of these Fortescues.　C. P.

Donkey (3rd S. vii. 165.)—There is one appellative of this interesting quadruped not noticed by C. A. L. In Nottinghamshire an ass is called "Bunkus;" witness the following speech from a stable-boy, who saw a lad beating a donkey in the yard : " What's thee arter, bensilling Bunkus a' that how ? "　　　　　　　　　　　　A. T.

Miscellaneous.

NOTES ON BOOKS, ETC.

Historical Studies. By Herman Merivale. (Longman.)

When a sound scholar, who thinks for himself like Mr. Herman Merivale, puts forth in a collected form his published and unpublished Essays in the wide fields of History and Literature, he is sure not only to add to our stores of pleasant reading, but to do good service to the great cause of historical truth. The interesting *Historical Studies* contained in the present volume are devoted—first, to the illustration of " Some of the Precursors of the French Revolution," in biographical sketches of Joseph the Second, Catherine the Second of Russia, Pascal Paoli, Voltaire, Rousseau, and Goethe, &c. Next, to " Studies from the History of the Seventeenth Century," which are devoted to the Streets of Paris at that period, and to visits to Lutzen and Marston Moor. Lastly, some pleasant papers on " The Scenery and Antiquities of Cornwall," " The Landscape of Ancient Italy, as delineated in the Pompeian Paintings," and a " Visit to Malta in 1857," complete a volume of very varied interest and character, the contents of which the author modestly describes as " the attempts of a learner to assist fellow-learners with himself."

A Catalogue of the Collection of Tracts for and against Popery (published in and about the Reign of James II.) in the Manchester Library, founded by Humphrey Chetham, in which is Incorporated, with large Additions and Bibliographical Notes, the whole of Peck's List of the Tracts in that Controversy, with his References. To which are added a Tabular Index to the Tracts in both Editions of Gibson's Preservative, and a Reprint of Dodd's Certamen Utriusque Ecclesia. Edited by Thomas Jones, B.A. Part II. (Printed for the Chetham Society.)

This ample title-page will show what a valuable contribution both to the history and bibliography of the times of James the Second, the learned Librarian of the Chetham Library, has here given to the world. An inspection of the book itself can alone show how much information Mr. Jones has thrown into the notes and extracts, with which he has diversified the monotony of a long enumeration of Tracts, and the pains which he has taken, lest, through any inadvertence on his part, anything should creep in calculated to give reasonable cause of offence to any reader, whatever his faith may be.

The Souldier's Pocket Bible. Printed at London by G. B. and R. W. for G. C. 1643. Reproduced in Facsimile, with an Introduction by Francis Fry, F.S.A. (Willis & Sotheran.)

The Christian Soldier's Penny Bible. London, Printed by R. Smith for Samuel Wade, 1693. Reproduced in Facsimile, with an Introductory Note by Francis Fry, F.S.A. (Willis & Sotheran.)

Two more of Mr. Fry's admirable facsimiles of rare and early tracts. The first is a facsimile of the Pocket Bible

with which the soldiers of Cromwell's army were supplied ; and of which only two copies are known to be now in existence. The second is a somewhat altered and enlarged work having a different title, and the extracts being taken from the Authorised instead of the Genevan Version. We hope Mr. Fry will be encouraged to continue his most useful labours.

Charles Dickens's Works.—A new and cheap edition of Mr. Dickens's matchless pictures of English life is announced by Messrs. Chapman & Hall. It will appear in Monthly Volumes, the first two of which will contain his earliest and almost his best story, *Pickwick.*

BOOKS AND ODD VOLUMES

WANTED TO PURCHASE.

Particulars of Price, &c., of the following Books to be sent direct to the gentlemen by whom they are required, and whose names and addresses are given for that purpose:—

A Ballad in Macaronic Latin, entitled Rustica Descriptio Visitationis Fanaticæ. By John Allibond, D.D. The Oxford edition of 1634 required.

Wanted by *Mr. James Yeowell*, 4, Minerva Terrace, Barnsbury, N.

Gudge on the Epistle to the Hebrews.
The Way of Life. By Charles Hodge, D.D.

Wanted by *Rev. C. S. Ward*, Brenchley, Staplehurst, Kent.

Notices to Correspondents.

Canon Dalton *will find, on reference to the Indexes to our First and Second Series, that his communication on the MSS. used for the Complutensian Polyglott has been anticipated.*

J. D. Campbell. *Oliver Cromwell's dying prayer is printed by Carlyle, iii. 373.*

S. Tucker. *The Register of Burials at Bunhill Fields is at the College of Arms. See our Notices to Correspondents on Feb. 18th.*

R. W. E. L. *He was thrown when hunting. Full details of the accident will be found in the Gents. Mag. for Feb. 1815, p. 189.*

T. G. C. (Newcastle-on-Tyne.) *The Rolls of Parliament are printed in six vols. folio, and extend from 6 Edw. I. to 19 Hen. VII. There is a very copious index, which forms an additional volume.*

L. B.'s *Queries being purely scientific should be addressed to one of the scientific journals.*

Oxoniensis *is referred to our 2nd S. iii. 206, 238, 257, 355, 471, for information respecting the First Actress.*

Acha. Irby, of Boston—Argent, a fretty sable, on a canton gules, a chaplet or. *The Epitaph on Dean Bill is printed in Dart's Westminster, vol. i. 100.*

A Wykehamist *will find Swift's Epitaph on Schomberg in our 1st. S. vii. 341.*

G. E. N. *The legend on which Roger's Ginevra is founded is very widely spread.*

W. R. G. E. " *Vive Henri Quatre.*"

A Reader of " N. & Q." (Kettering.) *It is impossible from the description given to ascertain the artist by whom the pictures were painted, or whom they are intended to represent.*

T. F. *The print is certainly not by Hogarth. If left at the Office of* " N. & Q." *for a few days, we might be able to give our Correspondent information respecting it.*

T. G. Stevenson *will accept our best thanks for the list of the contributors to* The Lounger: *but we find it has already been printed in Alex. Chalmers's* British Essayists, vol. xxx.

E. E. *The passage on the Burial Service is from a Latin antiphon. See* " N. & Q." 3rd S. v. 177.

A Reading Case *for holding the weekly Nos. of* " N. & Q." *is now ready, and may be had of all Booksellers and Newsmen, price 1s. 6d. ; or, free by post, direct from the publisher, for 1s. 8d.*

*** *Cases for binding the volumes of* " N. & Q." *may be had of the Publisher, and of all Booksellers and Newsmen.*

"Notes and Queries" *is published at noon on Friday, and is also issued in* Monthly Parts. *The Subscription for* Stamped Copies *for Six Months forwarded direct from the Publisher (including the Halfyearly* Index*) is 11s. 4d., which may be paid by Post Office Order, payable at the Strand Post Office, in favour of* William G. Smith, 32, Wellington Street, Strand, W.C., *where also all* Communications for the Editor *should be addressed.*

"Notes & Queries" *is registered for transmission abroad.*

LONDON, SATURDAY, MARCH 18, 1865.

Notes.

LEGITIMATION PER SUBSEQUENS MATRIMONIUM.

Most persons interested in Scotish history are aware of the discussions on the subject of the legitimacy of King Robert III., whose lawful descent became the subject of great and angry controversy. All doubt on the point has been excluded by recovery from the Papal Records of a copy of a dispensation, which, after disclosing the nature of the antecedent connexion—the objection to it—the cohabitation—and distinctly recording the fact that the parties had begotten " prolis utriusque sexus multitudinem "—permits the marriage, and removes all impediments which might prevent the celebration of a marriage *in facie ecclesiæ*. This document is dated in the sixth year of Clement VI., and therefore must have been issued in the year 1347.*

The case of Robert III. becomes a direct precedent of the antecedent existence of the law of legitimation " per subsequens matrimonium," and demonstrates that, prior to 1342, the doctrine of Glanville, as imported into the Regiam Majestatem, had met with no countenance in Scotland. A more direct proof of the recognition and application of the civil and canon law on this point in this country can hardly be figured. Not only is there

* The Dispensation printed in the Appendix to Andrew Stuart's *History of the Family of Stewart.*

cotemporary historical evidence that the future monarch and a " multitude" of children were in existence before the celebration of the nuptials *in facie ecclesiæ* took place, but the papal dispensation discloses the fact at its date, that a mid-impediment existed to their legitimacy which could only be removed *benignitate apostolica*. Whether the Pope could wipe out the ordinary effect of incestuous intercourse, is, we suspect, the point which gave rise to the question as to Robert's legitimacy. That his holiness intended to do so is palpable; but his powers to do so have been questioned by many learned persons, including the learned Scotch lawyer John Riddell, Esq.

Be this as it may, nothing is more certain than that, to a very considerable extent, the general law of Scotland is based on the civil law; and, as legitimation *per subsequens matrimonium* was legalised by Justinian without any qualification, it is not surprising that it became part and parcel of our law; the more especially as the canon law was equally explicit and pointed. One quotation from the Decretals of Pope Gregory IX. may be given:—

" Naturalis, ex soluto genitus et soluta, legitimatur per subsequens parentum conjugium, etiam quoad hæreditatem." . . . " Conquestus est nobis Herbertus quod cum quandam mulierem in uxorem acceperit, R., ipsam exhæredare conatur, eo, quod ante dispensationem matris suæ nata fuerit ; licet postea pater mulieris præfatæ matrem ipsius acceperit in uxorem."

Although the rule is clear that the subsequent marriage of the parent legitimates the children that previously had come into existence, this admits of some qualification, and may not always follow. Thus, if a man should be father of children by an unmarried female during the lifetime of his own wife, his subsequent marriage with this person would not make such children legitimate. At one time there was a general belief that legitimation arose out of the legal fiction that the parties who subsequently had become man and wife, originally cohabited with a view to marriage, and thus the marriage must be presumed to draw back to a period antecedent to the birth of the child. This supposition has now been overturned by the decision in the case of Kerr v. Martin.* The facts were these: In 1780, Mary Bone, an unmarried woman, was delivered of a daughter, named Agnes, whose reputed father was John Kerr, an unmarried man. In 1781, John Taylor married Mary Bone. Several children were born of this marriage, which was dissolved by the death of Taylor in 1793. In 1794, his widow, Mrs. Mary Bone, or Taylor, was regularly married to John Kerr, the father of her child Agnes. John Kerr had a younger brother James, who on his death left a lawful

* March 6th, 1840. Dunlop, vol. ii.

daughter Isabella. She possessed certain burgage subjects, besides property held under a long lease, which had belonged to her uncle John, and also some moveables, derived from her father James, all of which she conveyed, in February, 1821, to her husband Alexander Martin, residing in Laigh Craighmore. She died in May 1821, leaving no issue.

Agnes Kerr, the admitted daughter of John Kerr by Mary Bone previous to her marriage with Taylor, asserted that by reason of her father's subsequent marriage with her mother, she was legitimate in the eye of law, and entitled to the estate real and personal that belonged to her deceased father. Proceedings had been adopted by her and her husband, M'Robert, against Martin the husband and disponee of Agnes' cousin Isabella. He in his turn brought a reduction of a cognition of certain burgage subjects which Agnes had procured from the magistrates of Stranraer. In this proceeding he was successful, and the cognition and sasine following upon it were set aside. There was a cessation of litigation for some time, and the interlocutor of the Lord Ordinary was allowed to become final; but in 1834 Agnes was induced, with consent of her husband, to institute new proceedings, which came to depend before Lord Cunninghame, and in which the only question substantially agitated was that of the lady's legitimation, which her opponent contended was barred by her mother's intermediate marriage with John Taylor. The case was deliberately considered, and the opinion of the whole judges of the Court of Session taken. The authorities for the presumed fiction were carefully examined and sifted, and although a minority of the Judges clung with great tenacity to it, the majority thought otherwise, and were of opinion that, as both by the civil and canon law there was no qualification adjected to the imperial edict which had been incorporated into the canon law, legitimation must be taken unconditionally, and must be held in all cases absolute unless some *fatal* mid-impediment intervened.

This decision at the time startled many eminent lawyers, who having been accustomed to receive the fiction as conclusive, could not at first be reconciled to a judgment decidedly adverse to preconceived notions. Time and consideration led ultimately to the proper result, and we believe that the judgment is considered as in every way sound. Indeed, if the edict of Justinian and corresponding authority of the canon law, rule the point, as to which we presume there can be now little question, our only surprise is, that the fiction which owed its origin to fanciful theorists, could so long have held its place as an unassailable legal axiom.

A difficulty has been suggested, which merits attention. It is this: what place is the person so

legitimated to assume in the succession of his parents? Is he to take according to seniority of birth, or from the period when he was first legitimated? We venture to think that it must be from the period of his legitimation. Neither the edict nor the canon law fix this; but if the fiction we have noticed be only a fiction and not a reality; then as the child was not made legitimate until the marriage of his parents, he had no title, either in law or equity to take a higher position than from its date. The subsequent marriage of his father and mother was an accident; but the antecedent marriage was a reality, and the birth of children, resulting from *bona fide* espousals, ought not, and we believe could not be injured by any such subsequent occurrence.

The object of these remarks has been to ascertain whether in any Christian country excepting England and its dependencies, the doctrine of legitimation *per subsequens matrimonium* has been repudiated. It would be also desirable to know what is the rule in foreign countries as to mid-impediments? for instance, if cohabitation between persons within the forbidden degrees can, by a papal ordinance, be legalized to the effect of removing the stain of incest; and if an intervening marriage excludes the legitimation of previous offspring by individuals subsequently becoming husband and wife?

It is but right to mention that the legal victory achieved over the prejudices of Scotch jurists was effected by the historiographer of her Majesty for Scotland, George Brodie, Esq., the learned editor and continuator of Stair, and Robert Robertson, Esq., now Sheriff-substitute of Stirling.

J. M.

THE "ÉCOLE DES CHARTES" AND THE SCIENCE OF PALÆOGRAPHY.

It has often struck me, and I speak from experience, that the correspondents who supply "N. & Q." with extracts from old literary muniments must very often be stopped in their researches by the difficulty of making out a crabbed piece of handwriting, and the still greater one of determining whether the piece in question is authentic or not. You alight upon a curious letter, a scrap containing the key to some interesting historical problem — a bull, an edict, a decree; you purchase it at a very high price, and while you are rejoicing at the idea of possessing a treasure, you discover, to your utter dismay, that the document is a forgery, and therefore utterly worthless. Perhaps you may have seen in some collection what appears to be an autograph of Luther, or of Corneille, or of Leo X. You get it printed; and, the next day a critic tells you that a word which you had overlooked, the crossing of a' t, the colour of the ink, the subscription — in fact, a mere trifle, as you deem it, decides against the authenticity of the MS., and consigns it to the waste-paper basket.

' It is, therefore, absolutely indispensable that all those who have anything to do with the middle ages and with mediæval lore should secure a guide, both trustworthy and clear-headed, to accompany them in their researches; moreover, considering the extraordinary development given during the last twenty years to historical studies, it seems almost unaccountable that no *English* work should have appeared on the subject of palæography; at least such is the impression I have derived from the perusal of a small *brochure* lately composed by M. Léon Gautier,* and one of the purposes of the present article is to ascertain whether this deficiency is or is not a fact.

M. Léon Gautier, like a true enthusiast, describes first the rise and progress of the Paris *E'cole des Chartes*, to which he belongs, and the design of which is to prepare duly qualified librarians, archæologists, keepers of record-offices, and critics. Napoleon I., who amongst other useful ideas, had that of organising what he called a community of *lay Benedictines*, could not, unfortunately, carry his plan into execution; and it was only in 1821, that a royal decree called into existence the *E'cole des Chartes*. The first results of this new institution were not very happy; in 1829, a fresh attempt was made by the government to revive it, and in 1846, under the ministry of M. De Salvandy, a second and thorough reform took place. Since that epoch the school has gone on prospering; and it now occupies a proud position on the list of useful foundations belonging to the University of France.

Without going through all the suggestive details given by M. Léon Gautier, I shall just say that the curriculum of studies followed at the *E'cole des Chartes* extends over three years, and that it embraces ten different courses of lectures. As for the fruits produced, French *savants* can point with very legitimate satisfaction to the periodical issued by the members of the institution,† and to the numerous works for which both masters and pupils are equally responsible. Two yearly examinations test the proficiency of the students, and a *thesis* or disquisition crowning the whole, entitles the candidate to a diploma showing his proficiency, and qualifying him to hold an appointment as librarian or record-keeper. A list of some of the subjects for the terminal essays issued in 1860 will interest the reader: — " The War of Flanders (1299—1304); Historical Researches in the Reign of Charles the Bald; Sketch

of the Royal Administration in Touraine, from the Reign of Philip Augustus to that of Philip the Fair; on the Merits of Gregorius Turonensis as Annalist; Enquiries into the Language spoken in Gaul from the fifth to the ninth centuries, &c.

M. Léon Gautier's purpose is to prove the importance of the study of palæography, and the portion of his work I have just analysed is merely a preface or introduction to the end. He illustrates by a variety of examples the use of his favourite science; he then enumerates the principal rules which young tyros should follow if they aim at being thoroughly proficient, and after having drawn the programme of a course of lectures both on palæography and on diplomatics, he concludes by a *catalogue raisonné* of the chief works accessible to modern successors of the Benedictines.

It is amusing to see the real zest with which our author discusses every branch, every feature in the science of deciphering MSS. How rapturously he talks of Papebroch, Mabillon, Baronius, and the Bollandists! Yet such enthusiasm should not be sneered at, because if it were not for men fired with the zeal which animates M. Léon Gautier, what would become of literature? In the meanwhile, I hope some reader of "N. & Q." may be induced to treat more fully the question of an English *E'cole des Chartes*, and the subsidiary one of publishing for the use of English students some work similar in style to M. Natalis de Wailly's *E'léments de Paléographie*, or better still, to the excellent hand-books of M. Alphonse Chassant.*

Harrow-on-the-Hill.   GUSTAVE MASSON.

LOCALITY OF ZION IN EARLY WRITERS.

Mr. Fergusson says (Smith's *Dictionary of the Bible*, i. 1026),—

" It cannot be disputed that from the time of Constantine downwards to the present day, this name (Zion) has been applied to the western hill [rather, south-western hill] on which the city of Jerusalem now stands, and in fact always stood."

As Mr. Fergusson, who makes this statement, earnestly maintains that Zion was the eastern hill, it is natural that others, including those who advocate the same opinion, should assume, from his not having stated it, that there is no evidence later than the time of Constantine for supposing Zion to be the Temple Hill; hence the point has not, it seems, been properly investigated. It will hardly be thought any want of respect to Mr. Fergusson if it be supposed that he has not the same acquaintance with early patristic writers that he has

---

* *Quelques Mots sur l'E'tude de la Paléographie et de la Diplomatique.* Par Léon Gautier. 8vo. Paris: Aubry.

† *Bibliothèque de l'E'cole des Chartes.* 23 volumes published.

* *Paléographie des Chartes et Manuscrits du XIe au XVIIe Siècle*, 8vo; *Dictionnaire des Abréviations Latines et Françaises usitées dans les Inscriptions.* 8vo. Both these works are published by M. Aubry.

with architecture. That it has been generally applied to the south-western hill (on which part of the city stands) is certain, but in and from the time of Constantine this has not been universal.

Eusebius, in his *Life of Constantine*, seems to make Zion the south-western hill; but he appears to do this by mystically applying the name to the side of the valley opposite to the Temple Mount. I rely on him as a witness that the hill on which the Temple had stood was then known as identical with Zion. Eusebius says (*In Esaiam* xxii.), — Σιὼν μὲν γὰρ ὅρος ἐστὶν ὑψηλόν, ἐφ' οὗ ὁ νεὼς τοῦ θεοῦ ᾠκοδόμητο. (Montfaucon, *Collectio nova Patrum*, ii. 442ᵇ.)

Epiphanius, in the latter part of the fourth century, thus identifies Zion with the eastern hill on which the fortress (ἄκρα) had stood (north of the Temple, on the same ridge, be it remembered). In speaking of Golgotha he says, — ἄντικρυς γάρ ἐστι τὸ τοῦ Ἐλαιῶνος ὅρος ὑψηλότερον, καὶ ἀπὸ σημείων ὀκτὼ ἡ Γαβαὼν ὑψηλοτάτη· ἀλλὰ καὶ ἡ ἄκρα ἡ ποτὲ ἐν Σιὼν νῦν δὲ τμηθεῖσα, καὶ αὐτὴ ὑψηλοτέρα ὑπῆρχε τοῦ τόπου. (Epiph., *Panarium*, ed. Petavii, i. 394ᵃ, ed. Dindorf, ii. 415.) Probably for σημείων ὀκτὼ we should read σημείων πίντε (ὲ instead of ἡ); for this would be about the distance to Neby Semwil, the only place it seems that could be intended. It may be worth mentioning that Origen in the third century identified Zion with the Temple mountain. He says (*In Johan.*, tom. xiii. 12), οἱ δὲ Ἰουδαῖοι τὸ Σιὼν θεῶν τι νενομικότες . . . . καὶ διὰ τοῦτο ἐν αὐτῷ ᾠκοδομῆσθαι τὸν ναὸν ὑπὸ τοῦ Σολομῶντος λέγουσι. (Ed. De la Rue, iv. 222ᵈ.)

As every locality connected with Jerusalem is so earnestly discussed, every contribution in the way of *evidence* has its value. I believe that the passage from Eusebius and that from Epiphanius have never been brought forward before on this subject; at least I do not remember to have seen them, and I noted them in the course of my own patristic studies.

Many who do not at all agree with Mr. Fergusson in his strange theory as to the site of the Holy Sepulchre being where the Mosque of Omar now stands, fully hold that the Zion of Scripture was the eastern hill, the fortress ("City of David"), occupying the northern part; amongst these I may mention the Rev. J. F. Thrupp, in his *Antient Jerusalem*, 1855, and Mr. Lewin, in his *Sketch of Jerusalem*, 1861. Has Mr. Lewin published any more recent work on the topography of the Holy City?   S. P. Tregelles.
Plymouth.

[Mr. Lewin has since published, "*The Siege of Jerusalem by Titus*, with the Journal of a Recent Visit to the Holy City, and a general Sketch of the Topography of Jerusalem from the earliest times down to the Siege." With a Map. Lond. 8vo, 1863.—Ed.]

JACOBITE BANK NOTES.

At a recent meeting of the Scottish Society of Antiquaries in Edinburgh, there was exhibited an engraved copper plate, found near the west end of Loch Laggan, which was one of those engraved by Sir Robert Strange for Prince Charles Edward shortly before the battle of Culloden. It is engraved for notes of " one penny," " two pence," " three pence," and " six pence." Each note has a background of a trophy of arms, with the letters " P. C." in the centre, surmounted by a crown and three feathers; and, although slightly engraved, is marked by the graceful manner of the engraver. This interesting relic seems to have been lost in the retreat from Culloden, and was found near the west end of Loch Laggan. In the brief paper of Memorabilia of Sir Robert Strange, dated 1797 (and in the possession of Sir Patrick Murray Thripland, Bart., of Fingask, whose grandfather, Sir Stuart, was his comrade in arms, and friend in their consequent exile), these notes are mentioned as follows:—

" During this period that the army were stationed in and about Inverness, the first battalion of the Life Guards, commanded by Lord Elcho were billeted upon Culloden House. One evening, after I had retired to rest, an express arrived from Inverness between eleven and twelve, acquainting me that the Prince was desirous of seeing me as soon as possible. I that instant got up, and my horse being saddled, I made the best of my way to town. Upon my being announced at the head quarters, I was desired to be shown into the Prince's bed-chamber. There was this evening a ball. After having waited but a short time, the Prince, accompanied by Sir Thomas Sheridan and Mr. Murray, the secretary, came into the room. Sir Thomas Sheridan took the lead, and, addressing himself to me more particularly, told me that His Royal Highness was desirous of taking my opinion, relating to a circulation of one species of money or another, which it had been thought expedient to issue for the service of the army in general, but more particularly amongst the soldiers, and that they were desirous of knowing what plan I could recommend as the most eligible. I answered Sir Thomas that the subject was entirely new to me; 'that, so far as regarded my own profession, I thought everything of the kind exceedingly practicable, but that it was a question with me whether or not the town of Inverness could afford me what assistance would be necessary in executing a work of this kind, particularly a rolling-press, which would be indispensable on the occasion; but, if they would indulge me with a few hours the next day, I should then have put my thoughts together upon the subject, have considered it in every point of view, and give my opinion of course. It was agreed upon that I should return the next evening between eight and nine. I attended soon after eight, and was again shown into the same apartment as I had been the night before. Soon after the Prince appeared, accompanied as the preceding evening, with the addition of a third gentleman. Sir Thomas Sheridan again accosted me, and asked me what I had done. I answered, that it was just as I had apprehended, for that there was no such thing in the town of Inverness as a rolling press; but, that I had had recommended me a very intelligent man of a carpenter, and an excellent mechanic, who had entered into my ideas, and perfectly comprehended the construction of what was required, and was even ready to begin such, were it necessary. I then proceeded towards explaining what I had in view, and with that intention pulled out of my pocket a small device I had put together, the better to communicate my ideas. It consisted, I said, of nothing but the slightest compartments, from behind which a rose issued on one side, and a thistle on the other, as merely ornamental ; the interior part I meant should be filled up by clerks, with the specific sums which were intended, &c. ; and I proposed etching or engraving, in the slightest manner for expedition, a considerable repetition of this ornament on two plates, for the facility of printing ; that such should be done on the strongest paper, [so] that, when cut separate, they should resist, in some measure, the wear they must sustain in the common use of circulation. The Prince had at this time taken the compartment out of my hand, 'and was showing [it] to Mr. Murray, and seemed much pleased with the idea of the rose and the thistle. In short, everything was approved of, and the utmost expedition recommended me. We now talked of a circulation of larger sums, which would likewise be required. I gave it as my opinion, that I thought they could not do better than issue notes in imitation of the Bank of England, or the Royal Bank of Scotland, in the execution of which there was very little labour: that it would be necessary, if possible, to see such notes, in order to concert a form how they were to be drawn up, by whom paid, or at what period ; if at a given time, that of the Restoration, I imagined, would be the properest. This produced a general smile. Mr. Murray at this instant left the room ; and soon after, returning on his steps, brought with him two notes of the Bank of England, one for one hundred pounds, and the other for two, and which, though different in appearance, yet both were payable on demand. On examining those notes, I observed the impossibility of having a proper paper made for the occasion, but that I did imagine the finest post-paper would be sufficiently adequate for the purpose ; that it had strength enough, as the notes would be less subject to friction in the wear than the smaller paper, which would be in circulation amongst the soldiers. All this was agreed upon ; and Mr. Murray said, as I would have occasion for the notes to regulate me in the engraving, I might then put them in my pocket, and that, in the course of a few days, I should hear from them, when they had considered of a proper form for drawing up what was intended. The Prince, on my leaving the room, recommended me all diligence. Next day, being Sunday, my carpenter was early employed in cutting out the wood, in order to begin on Monday. It was not so with a copper-smith, whose assistance I more immediately required. He was a good Presbyterian, and thought he would be breaking the Lord's day. But necessity has no law ; he turned out even better than his promise, overcame his prejudice, went to work, and furnished me with a copper plate on Monday about noon. I had passed that morning in making a composition of etching-varnish, but had not perfectly proportioned the materials, for I well recollect the aqua-fortis playing the devil with it, but which was repaired with some little trouble. In short, it mattered not much, provided the purpose was answered ; and, indifferent as things might be, I would at this moment purchase a series of them even at a considerable expense, to decorate as it were this volume with the more juvenile works of its author. Such would be a curiosity of its kind. The reader may naturally conclude that, on this occasion, I lost not a single hour. Solicitous in the service in which I was employed, my activity was, if possible, redoubled ; I laboured till late at night, and saw with regret the approach of day with impatience. Not a fortnight had elapsed when I was ready to begin printing, and had even forwarded the notes for a larger circulation.

Such was the position of my undertaking when, all of a sudden, news was brought to the Duke of Cumberland, with his army, had passed the Spey on the 13th of April. The town was in a general alarm, and even confusion. Nothing was heard but the noise of bagpipes, the beating of drums, and the clash of arms. The field of Culloden was the following day to be the general rendezvous, and every individual betook himself to his corps. The next morning I went betimes to the secretary's office, and delivered over the whole of my charge, together with the notes I had been entrusted with. I told the treasurer that an account would be presented by a carpenter who had been very active in serving me ; that there would be added to it a few articles he had disbursed, and requested the whole might be paid ; which was accordingly done. I now returned to Culloden House. My companions were, in general, glad to see me, and, joking, asked me when they were to have any of my money. I replied that, if they gave me a good account of the Duke, I hoped his treasury-chest would supply us."

W. H. C.

CASE OF CIRCUMSTANTIAL EVIDENCE.

This subject derives importance from the inquiry which is now being made by the Royal Commission as to capital punishment ; and authentic cases, where such evidence has led to the condemnation of the innocent, will be of much value to those who, like myself, are interested in the conclusions to which that Commission may come. One of the most remarkable cases within my own knowledge is that related in *Household Words* (No. 31, October 26, 1859), in an article on "Duties of Witnesses and Jurymen." Unfortunately, the author of the article has omitted to give any of the particulars by which the authenticity of his facts can be shown. He does not give the name of the judge, nor date of the trial ; neither are we supplied with the names of the persons placed for trial. The facts are, however, well known to have transpired : as I have conversed with persons in Nottingham who knew all the circumstances, and related many particulars of a conspiracy which had been entered into at that eventful time ; but I am not able to supply the date of the trial.

In this case it was not an innocent man who was condemned, but a guilty one who escaped. A concerted plan defeated the prosecution ; and I have heard it stated that, so desperate were the men engaged in the conspiracy, that persons were in court with loaded pistols, intending to shoot the judge if the prisoners were condemned ; and to follow that by an attempt at rescue. Few persons have any adequate idea of the feelings which prevailed at that period among the labouring classes, and which threatened the peace and security of the manufacturing districts ; but such incidents as the following will afford evidence of the existence of a state of things which almost exceeds belief, in these more prosperous times. I will give the history in the author's own words:—

"In one of the trials arising out of the outrages committed by the Luddites, who broke into manufactories and destroyed all lace frames of a construction which they thought oppressive to working men, an *alibi*," he said, "had been concocted; which was successful in saving the life of a man notoriously guilty, and which had therefore added to the disrepute of this species of defence. The hypothesis was, that the prisoner, at the time when the crime was committed, at Loughborough, sixteen miles from Nottingham, was engaged at a supper party at the latter place; and the prisoner having the sympathy of a large class in his favour, whose battle he had been fighting, no difficulty was experienced by his friends in finding witnesses willing to support this hypothesis on their oath; but it would have been a rash measure to have called them into the box unprepared. And when it is considered how readily a preconcerted story might have been destroyed by cross-examination, the task of preparing the witnesses so as to elude this test was one requiring no ordinary care and skill. The danger would arise thus:— Every witness would be kept out of court, except the one in the box. He would be asked where he sat at the supper? Where the prisoner sat, and each of the other guests? What were the dishes, what was the course of conversation?—and so forth. The questions being capable of multiplication, *ad infinitum:* so that, however well tutored, the witnesses would inevitably contradict each other upon some matters on which the tutor had not foreseen that the witness would be cross-examined, or to which he had forgotten the answer prescribed. The difficulty was, however, surmounted.

"After the prisoner's apprehension, the selected witnesses were invited to a mackerel supper, which took place at an hour corresponding to that at which the crime was committed; and so careful was the ingenious agent who devised this conspiracy against the truth, that, guided by a sure instinct, he fixed upon the same day of the week as that on which the crime had been committed; though without knowing how fortunate it would be for the prisoner that he took this precaution. When, on cross-examination, it was found that the witnesses agreed as to the order in which the guests were seated, the contents of the dishes, the conversation which had taken place, and so forth, the counsel for the crown suspected the plot; but not imagining that it had been so perfectly elaborated, they inquired of their attorneys as to whether there was any occurrence peculiar to the day of the week in question; and were told that, upon the evening of such day, a public bell was rung, which must have been heard at the supper if it had taken place at the time pretended. The witnesses were separately called back, and questioned as to the bell. They had all heard it; and thus, not only were the cross-examiners utterly baffled, but the cross-examination gave tenfold support to the examination in chief: that is, to the evidence as given by the witnesses in answer to the questions put by the prisoner's counsel on his behalf.

"The triumph of falsehood was complete. The prisoner was acquitted."

T. B.

THE CLEMENCY OF THEODOSIUS.—Many weekly newspapers give a column of interesting scraps, in which the newest *facetiæ* of *Punch* are mixed with jokes and anecdotes which have been used for similar purposes from the times of Hierocles and Plutarch till now, with no change but in the

names. George Selwyn and Wilkes being succeeded by the Prince of Wales and Charles Fox, and they by Sydney Smith and Theodore Hook. Sometimes real history is so changed that it cannot be identified. Here is an example; which, on first reading, I cut out as a piece of pure fiction with an ill-chosen hero; as Theodosius was not very merciful to the traitorous or seditious.

"A WISE MONARCH. — The Emperor Theodosius ridiculed the idea of *laws for treason and sedition*, and passed a decree to this effect:—'If any person commits an offence against us, let him escape punishment. If he does it from levity of disposition, he deserves our contempt; if from madness, our compassion; if from malice, we pardon him, as having done the greater injury to himself."—*Reynolds' Newspaper*, January 1, 1865.

Yet this is founded on a rescript, cited with approbation, and translated by Montesquieu, *Esprit des Loix*, liv. xii. c. 12. The original is:

"Si quis modestiæ nescius, et pudoris ignarus, improbo petulantique maledicto nomina nostra crediderit lacessanda, ac temulentiâ turbulentus obtrectator temporum nostrorum fuerit, cum pœna nolumus subjugari, neque durum aliquid nec asperum volumus sustinere: quoniam si id ex levitate processerit, contemnendum est; si ex insania miseratione dignissimum; si ab injuria remittendum, unde integris omnibus, hoc ad nostram scientiam referatur, ut ex personis hominum dicta pensemus, et utrum prætermitti an exquiri debeant censeamus."—Cod. ix. t. 7.

On this Gibbon says:

"Montesquieu praises one of the laws of Theodosius addressed to the prefect Rufinus, to discourage the prosecution of treasonable or seditious words. A tyrannical statute always proves the existence of tyranny; but a laudable edict may only contain the specious professions, or ineffectual wishes, of the prince or his ministers. This I am afraid is a just though mortifying canon of criticism."—*Decline and Fall*, c. xxix. note f.

I never heard of a monarch or state which went so far as to repeal the laws against treason and sedition.   FITZHOPKINS.

Garrick Club.

HOURS OF SUNDAY SERVICES IN LONDON, A.D. 1714.—Paterson, in the introduction to his *Pietas Londinensis, or the Present Ecclesiastical State of London*, which was published in the year 1714, says:—

"In all Parish Churches especially, and Chapels, within my Compass, Morning Prayers and Sermon begin every Sunday at ten, and between two and three in the Afternoon. . . . And, moreover, on all Sacrament Days the Morning Service begins commonly a quarter of an Hour sooner, and in the Evening [*i. e.* the afternoon] as much later than the usual Time."

This is the reason in all probability, why, at St. Paul's Cathedral, where there is every Sunday a weekly mid-day celebration of the Holy Communion, the morning service commences at 9·45 A.M.; whereas at Westminster Abbey, which has not I believe a weekly mid-day celebration, the morning service begins at 10 A.M.

About the time of Queen Anne, our forefathers

seem to have been one hour earlier risers than the present generation.

I think I have seen it stated somewhere, that the present hours of the Sunday services at St. Paul's Cathedral were fixed with the sanction, and during the episcopate of Compton, Bishop of London. They enable such of the minor canons, as are also incumbents in the City, to take part afterwards in the morning services of their respective parish churches. LONDINENSIS.

FAMILY OF CONINGSBY. — Those contributors to "N. & Q." who are interested in the family of Coningsby, may like to be informed that I possess an old well-executed oak panel, on which are carved in relief the following arms: Quarterly, 1st and 4th, gu. three bars gemelles or; on a canton sa. a crescent of the second : 2nd and 3rd or, a boar passant sa. in chief, a crescent of the last. Impaling gu. three conies sejant arg.

Beneath the shield is this inscription in raised letters, divided into two semicircular compartments, and gilded : —

" Oliver Brigges Armiger et Anna Vxor ejvs, filia Hvmfridi Coningesby Armigeri de " (cætera desunt).

The above-named Oliver Brigges belonged to the family of Sir Hugh Briggs, of Haughton, co. Salop, Bart.; whose second sister Elizabeth married Leigh Brooke, Esq., of Blacklands, in the parish of Bobbington, co. Stafford. The oak carving in question was removed, many years ago, from a mansion (now pulled down) in the said parish; and came into the possession of the last owner, who presented it to me. H. W. T.

OLD SAYING. — You used to have some curious specimens of folk lore and quaint expressions, suggested by correspondents. An expression, apparently proverbial, was used the other day by a gentleman in conversation with me, which I never heard before ; and which is, I think, curious.

Speaking of a person who had been brought down terribly in the world, and from a state which in his own estimation at least had been rather an important one, the gentleman said: "His noble has come down to ninepence." If this expression show a lingering tradition of the coin " so called, from the purity and excellency of the gold of which it was coined," it is very singular; and owes its preservation, probably, to the idea of undue self-estimation which seems to be included in the word "noble"—for the coin of that name was struck in the reign of Edward III., five hundred years ago.

Is this expression familiar to any of your numerous readers and correspondents ?

E. S. S. W.

LETTER OF GENERAL LEE.—The following extract from a letter of advice addressed by the great Confederate General to his son in 1852, on his leaving home for New Mexico, seems to deserve a corner in the pages of " N. & Q." : —

" In regard to duty, let me, in conclusion of this hasty letter, inform you, that nearly a hundred years ago there was a day of remarkable gloom and darkness, still known as the dark day, a day when the light of the sun was slowly extinguished, as if by an eclipse. The legislature of Connecticut was in session, and as its members saw the unexpected and unaccountable darkness coming on, they shared in the general awe and terror. It was supposed by many that the last day, the day of judgment, had come. Some one, in the consternation of the hour, had moved an adjournment. Then there arose an old Puritan legislator, Davenport of Stamford, and said, that if the last day had come, he desired to be found at his place doing his duty, and therefore that candles be brought in, so that the house could proceed with its duty. There was quietness in that man's mind, the quietness of heavenly wisdom and inflexible willingness to obey present duty. Duty, then, is the sublimest word in our language. Do your duty in all things, like the old Puritan. You cannot do more, you should never wish to do less. Never let me or your mother wear one grey hair for any lack of duty on your part."—Guardian, Feb. 15, 1865, p. 142.

E. H. A.

THE REVOLUTIONARY VETERANS. — Extracted from the New York World newspaper of Feb. 3, 1865, reporting the proceedings of the United States Senate of that day in Washington: —

" The House to-day unanimously passed a bill giving a gratuity of $300 a-year to each of the five surviving revolutionary pensioners, in addition to the pension of $100, which they now receive. In January, 1864, there were only twelve remaining, seven of whom have since died. The names of the only survivors are as follows : Lemuel Cook, enlisted in Hatfield, Mass., 98 years of age, now residing at Clarendon, Orleans county, N.Y. ; Samuel Downey, enlisted in Carroll county, N.H., 98 years of age, now living at Edinburg, Saratoga county, N.Y. ; William Hutchins, enlisted in Newcastle, Me., 100 years of age, residing at Penobscot, Me. ; Alexander Maroney, enlisted at Lake George, N. Y., as a drummer boy, 94 years of age, residing at Yates, Orleans county, N. Y. ; James Beartham, a substitute for a drafted man in Southampton county, Va., living in Missouri, in his 101st year.

T. P.

Queries.

BELL INSCRIPTION. — Can any learned reader of "N. & Q." explain the word IᴄɴɪᴏꞘᴍᴀʀᴘ (Lemosmary) repeated nine times on a bell at Abbotsham, North Devon ? All the letters are in small church text, and each word about four inches apart. The bell is long-waisted, 40 inch. diam,, G♯, and good tone, by tradition a foreigner. There is no incipient cross to mark the beginning. The words are stamped in upside down.

H. T. ELLACOMBE, M.A.

Clyst St. George.

BIBLIOGRAPHICAL QUERIES. — The Rev. C. Malan published Le Veritable Ami des Enfans, 1838, London. Does this volume bear any resemblance to Berquin's work, L'Ami des Enfans?

Does Mr. Malan's volume contain any juvenile dramas, dialogues, &c.

1. F. P. Wilmsen, of Berlin, died 1831, author of *The Children's Friend*. 2. C. T. Thieme, author of *Gutman's Children's Friend in Saxony*, 4 vols. 1794. Can any of your readers inform me whether these collections contain any dramas for children?

Who is the author of a French translation of the Latin tragedy of *Freewill*, by Franc. Negri Basantinus, of which there is an English translation by H. Cheke, son of Sir John Cheke? The French translation was published about 1558. Is the translator named by Barbier?

In Brunet's *Bibliogr. Manual* there is the title of a French drama on the subject of the Triumph of the League, 1607, Leyden. (Anon.?) The author said to be R. J. Nerce. Wanted, some account of this writer. Was he a French Protestant?

There is a Latin translation of Beza's tragedy of *Abraham*, by Joannes Jacomotus Barenses, Geneva, 1598. Can you tell me anything regarding the history of the translator?

Can you give me the dates of the German translations of Racine's *Esther* and *Athalia*, and the names of the translators, as given in Ersch's *Lexicon of German Bibliography*?

Wanted, biographical particulars regarding—1. Sixtus or Sextus Betterlejus, or Birch, Principal of the College at Augsburg, who died about 1554. He was author of Latin Dramas. Was he of the Romish or Protestant party? 2. Vincent Boltz, author of the *Mirror of the World*, a Play, acted at Basle in 1550, and one or two other dramas.

Has F. Gerstaecker, a living German novelist, and well-known author of Travels, &c., written any dramatic works?   R. I.

ALVOISE CONTARINI.—When was he doge of Venice? I have a ducat having the legend " S. M. V. Aloysius Cont. D."

Only five Contarini were doges, and their names were Francesco, Nicolo, Carlo, Dominico, and Luigi. The only doge having the Christian name of Alvoise (since 1413) is Alvizzo Moncenigo, 1763.

I suppose the list I have is not correct. Where shall I find a better one? I have taken mine from "Sketches of Venetian History," *The Family Library*, vols. xx. and xxx. 11.*

JOHN DAVIDSON.

EXECUTIONER OF CHARLES I.—In 2nd S. ix. 41, I read: —

" The burial register of St. Mary Matfelon has the

[* On referring to Antonio Nani's *Serie dei Dogi di Venezia* (2 vols. 4to, Ven. 1840), we failed to discover any doge of the Contarini family bearing the Christian name of Alvoise. Has our correspondent correctly read the legend on his coin?—ED.]

entry on the 21st [June, 1649]: 'Buried in the church-yard, Richard Brandon, a *ragman* in Rosemary Lane;' to which has been added : 'This R. Brandon is supposed to have cut off the head of Charles I.'"

In Ellis's *Letters* (2nd Series, vol. iii. p. 343 n.), the entry on the register is given, on the authority of the Rev. D. Mathias, the rector of Whitechapel, as follows : —

" 1649. Buriall, June 21st. Rich. Brandon, a *man* out of Rosemary Lane."

The marginal addition is stated by Mr. Mathias in the words you quote. Which is correct—the " man," or the "ragman"?   J. B.

GRINLING GIBBONS.—Lysons, in his *Environs of London*, iv. 87, mentions that at Valentines in Barking, Essex, " a large mansion built by James Chadwick, son-in-law of Archbishop Tillotson," there " was some fine carving by Gibbons." And in the Supplement (p. 342) that Valentines was purchased in 1808 by Charles Welstead, Esq., and that " the carving by Gibbons had been removed." Where is this carving? And what is known about it?   M. C. J.

THE IGELER SÄULE.—Has any illustrated account ever been published of the sculptures on the " Heidenthurm" or Igeler Säule in Rhenish Prussia?   J. WOODWARD.

KELLAWAY, CO. DORSET. — In Harl. MS. 1165, fol. 75, Visitation of Wilts, A.D. 1623, it is recorded that Thomas Weston, son and heir of John Weston, of Canings (Bishops Cannings), co. Wilts, and then living, married Anne, daughter of Thomas Weston of Kellaway, co. Dorset.

Was this Kellaway a tenement, an estate, or a hamlet, and where was it situated? Neither the *Index Villaris* nor Potts's *Gazetteer* makes mention of it, nor have local inquiries resulted in aught satisfactory.   G. W.

WORKS ON SATAN, HIS OFFICE AND ABODE.—Thomson's *Vindication of Eternal Punishment in Hell*.

Bailey on *The Extent of the Kingdom of Hell*. I found these titles in sale catalogues, but have failed in the attempt to identify the writers. Can any correspondent assist me?

The date of the *second edition* of Tobias Swinden's *Enquiry*, of which the full title is given by MR. DUNKIN (3rd S. vii. 144), is 1727. It was published after the author's death, and I wish to learn the name of the editor, who made considerable additions to it, and also of the writer of a letter appended to the volume signed "Philalethes."

" A gentleman of Wadham College, Oxford " (a MS. note in Museum copy says " Swinton ") published in 1738 a letter on a kindred subject entitled *A Critical Dissertation concerning the*

Words ΔΑΙ′ΜΩΝ *and* ΔΑΙΜΟ′ΝΙΟΝ. It is signed
" Philalethes." Who was he?

*An Enquiry into the Scripture Meaning of the
Word Satan, &c.* London : J. Wheble, 1772, in
8vo.

In the Museum copy a MS. note assigns the
authorship on hearsay " to one Barker, a curate of
Dr. Hershaw's at Leeds." Is this correct? Note
that one Thomas Barker wrote on *The Nature.
. . . . . of the Demoniacks in the Gospels, &c.*
London : B. White, 1783, in 8vo.
                                    A. Cʜᴀʟʟsᴛᴇᴛʜ.
1, Verulam Buildings.

Sᴛᴀʟᴇ Mᴀᴛᴇ.—Can any of the chess-players
who read " N. & Q." inform me the French technical term for what we call in English a *stale
mate?* in German it is *schach-patt,* in opposition
to *schach-matt,* our check-mate. The French
consider a game so concluded a drawn one (*re-
mis*). The Germans allow no defeat: in England
alone do we punish the generally superior power
of the antagonist whose inattention drives his
adversary into an immoveable position. The
technicals for the same condition in any other
language are also requested.
                            Wɪʟʟɪᴀᴍ Bᴇʟʟ, Phil. Dr.
6, Crescent Place, Burton Crescent.

Aʙʙᴇʏ ᴏғ Sᴛʀᴀᴛᴀ Mᴀʀᴄᴇʟʟᴀ.—Why was this
abbey so named? Are any views or drawings of
it or its ruins extant? In Dugdale's *Monasticon,*
it is said to have been a timbered structure. In
some of the neighbouring churches some relics of
it are preserved. In Buttington church there are
some fragments of stained glass and a font, and
in the chancel of Guilsfield church a carved oak
roof.   M. C. J.

Sᴜɴᴅʀʏ Qᴜᴇʀɪᴇs.—1. In the *British Critic,*
vol. xix. p. 252, occurs a striking passage, cited by
Coleridge from some Anti-Romanist publication of
Spanzotti. What are the titles of the known works
of this author? and are there copies of them in
the British Museum or Bodleian Catalogues?

2. Desiderius, the last King of the Lombards,
had a son Adalgisius. Is anything known of his
descendants? and what is the title of the Drama
written by Manzoni, of which Adalgisius is the
subject?

3. In a small *History of England,* much used
in schools some forty years ago, I remember a
note, in which were quoted the first lines, in Latin
and English, of some singular verses, to which (if
I recollect rightly) some popular tumult had given
rise. The commencement of each of these lines
will perhaps enable some of your readers to revive
facts, and to furnish the pages of " N. & Q."
an authentic copy of the whole. I regret
cannot recall more than one line of each
. . . :—

" Watte vocat, cui Thoma venit," &c.
" Watt cries, Tom flies, while Tib stands grinning by.

4. In M. Bouchot's *Histoire du Portugal* (Paris,
L. Hachette, 1854) p. 62, the celebrated hero
Dom Nuno Alvarez Pereira — whom our own
Southey had signalised as " a perfect example of
patriotism, heroism, and every noble and lovely
quality above all others of any age or country"—
is said to have resembled his patron, King John,
in the character of his birth. He is described as
" Bâtard comme don Juan." In a beautifully
printed folio life of D. N. A. Pereira, by Frey
Domingos Teixeyra, published in Portuguese at
Lisbon, he is represented as one of the very large
progeny of sons born to Dom Alvaro Gonçalves
Pereira, Prior of Crato, whose wife was a person
of distinction, Eyria Gonçalves de Carvalhal,
principal Lady of the Bedchamber to the then
queen, Dona Brites. I do not remember, throughout the entire work, that there is any reference to
the illegitimacy of Nuno Alvarez Pereira's birth.
I should be glad to known on what authority M.
Bouchot's statement rests.

5. Can any correspondent supply information
respecting the pedigree and armorial bearings of
the late Dr. Jonathan Pereira, F.R.S.?

6. Required, the arms of Fretwell, of Hellaby,
co. York.

7. In Gilbert White's *Natural History of Selborne,* notes, it is stated that Hugh Tybbe was
rector of Selborne ᴀ.ᴅ. 1411. Can any reader of
" N. & Q." oblige me with information respecting
this clergyman's family and armorial bearings?
                                             H. W. T.

Pᴏʀᴛʀᴀɪᴛ ᴏғ Tᴀʏʟᴏʀ, ᴛʜᴇ Pʟᴀᴛᴏɴɪsᴛ. — Mr.
W. Meredith, the person who furnished Thomas
Taylor the Platonist, with money to pay for print-
ing several of his translations, had a portrait of
Taylor by Sir Thomas Lawrence. I am anxious
to know where this picture is now.
                                    Eᴅᴡᴀʀᴅ Pᴇᴀᴄᴏᴄᴋ.
Bottesford Manor, Brigg.

Tʜᴇ Oʀɪɢɪɴ ᴏғ Vᴀʟᴇɴᴛɪɴᴇs. — In Bailey's
Dictionary we have this word under two head-
ings :—
" Vᴀʟᴇɴᴛɪɴᴇs (in *England*). About this Time of the
Year, the Birds choose their Mates, and probably thence
came the Custom of the young Men and Maidens chusing
Valentines, or special loving Friends on that day.
" Vᴀʟᴇɴᴛɪɴᴇs (in the church of *Rome*). Saints chosen
on *St. Valentine's* day as Patrons for the Year ensuing."

In that curious Dictionary (*sine not. aut ann.*) I
have referred to before, we get this explanation :
" Vᴀʟᴇɴᴛɪɴᴇs, saints chosen for special patrons, for
that year, or (among us) men and women chosen for
special loving friends."

I have heard of the custom of selecting a special
patron saint every year in Roman Catholic countries. In fact, I remember being told by a lady at

Naples, that a friend, who had just taken leave of her, had stated she thought this year she should change from Santa Lucia to Santa Catarina, the reasons for which I do not remember; but I never heard such a thing took place *de rigueur* on St. Valentine's Day. If this really were the case, it might readily be understood how one custom slipt into another. The probable way to unravel this mystery, which has puzzled antiquaries for many years, would be, if the correspondents of "N. & Q." would give what information they can, first, as to the custom of choosing patron saints *annually*; second, Whether such choice be, or be not, on the 14th of February; and third, how early we have notice that the choice is recorded as that of " special loving friends."

A. A.

Poets' Corner.

Abp. Whately's Family.—Thomas Whately, of Norwich Park, the Archbishop's grandfather, married Mary, daughter and heiress of Joseph Thompson, Esq., a cousin of Lord Haversham.

I should be greatly obliged to any of your correspondents who will favour me with a clue to the name of the father of Thomas Whately, and his relationship to the " painful preacher of Banbury," who died in 1639, and who is believed to have been a member of the same family ; and also for any clue to the relationship of Joseph Thompson to the Haversham Thompsons.

Investigator.

St. Catharine's Wheel.—In the table of authors at the commencement of the first volume of *Le Martyrologe des Chevaliers de Malthe* (Paris, 1643), par Mathieu de Goussancourt, is a passage which has puzzled me. It is (*verbatim et literatim*) as follows : —

" Cahorsi Vice-Chancellier de Malte, en ses commentaires du siege de Rhodes l'an 1480. Il portoit d'argent à une roüe de saincte Catherine de gueulles, de six rayons, *qui est celle des hommes; celles des Dieux est de huict, celles des demons est de quatre.*"

Can any of your correspondents inform me what is the meaning of the passage in italics ?

T. Woodward.

New Shoreham.

Queries with Answers.

Thomas Earl of Effingham, 1775.—In Mason's *Correspondence with Walpole*, vol. i. p. 194, Mason says : —

" You are always telling me of your additional noble authors, and do not mention one worth all the rest of the Bunch : I mean my neighbour here, Lord Effingham. Was there ever anything, ancient or modern, better either in sentiment or language, than his late speech ? "

Thomas, Lord Effingham, was also the author of a " celebrated Whig Song," to which I have seen frequent references.

Can any reader of "N. & Q." say where I can see, at length, the above speech and song, or refer me to any other production of Lord Effingham ?

T. S. B. E.

[Mason's allusion is probably to the speech of the Earl of Effingham on the debate in the Lords on the Memorial of the General Assembly of New York, May 18, 1775, printed in *The Parliamentary History*, xviii. 686—688. The Earl was bred to arms, and held a captain's commission in the twenty-second regiment of foot. As a peer in parliament, he uniformly opposed the whole system of measures pursued against the Americans, and finding at length that his regiment was intended for the American service, he thought it inconsistent with his character, and unbecoming of his dignity, to enforce measures with his sword which he had so utterly condemned in his legislative capacity. He accordingly forwarded a letter of resignation to the Secretary at War, for which he received the thanks of the cities of London and Dublin. The Earl also published anonymously *An Essay on the Nature of a Loan, being an Introduction to the Knowledge of the Public Accounts.* York, 1782, 8vo.]

" Rustica Descriptio."—I have now before me in MS. in rhyming Latin, a squib on the Reformation at Oxford, of which I can decipher only a very little beyond its title, as follows : — *Rustica Academiæ Oxoniensis nuper Reformatæ Descriptio, &c.* An. Dom. 1648. What is it ? At the end is the signature, J. Alibourn. Querist.

[The author of this satirical work was John Allibone, D.D., Vicar of Bradwell, in Gloucestershire—" a witty man of Magdalene College," says Antony Wood. John Allibone, with other wits of the University, found some solace for their woes, or some vent for their indignation under the persecution of the triumphant Puritans in 1648, by exhibiting the *dulmanity* of their persecutors in literary attainments, and their ruthless *immanity* in matters of right, property, and personal liberty. On the visitation to Oxford by the parliamentary visitors, he put forth his " Seasonable Sketch of an Oxford Reformation," a poem of considerable humour.

" When rakes reforming tracts compose,
And sober blockheads read 'em,
Oxford, beware of godly foes,
And doubly guard thy freedom !

" Lest pious knaves and canting fools
Should crow o'er men of letters,
And once more turn thy public schools
To sanctuaries for traitors."

The *Rustica Descriptio* was so popular, that, in spite of the visitors' orders against printing and publishing abusive pamphlets, it was printed on a single sheet twice in the year 1648. It was reprinted at London in 4to, without date (about 1700), and in 8vo, with an English version in 1717. The best edition is the one printed at Oxford, 8vo, 1834, with a " Preface and Notes, the verses being done into Doggrel in usum Parliamenti Indoctorum ejusdem nominis secundi."]

"TENTAMEN MEDICINALE."—I possess a small volume, entitled—

· "*A Short Answer to a late Book entitled Tentamen Medicinale.* With which are reprinted several papers formerly published, touching the Rise, Growth, and Usefulness of the DISPENSARIES erected by the College of Physicians for the benefit of the Sick Poor in and near London. London: Printed for A. Roper at the Black Boy against St. Dunstan's Church in Fleet Street, 1705."

Can any of your readers give me any information as to the *Tentamen Medicinale?*   T. B.

· [The work is entitled "*Tentamen Medicinale;* or, an Enquiry into the Differences between the Dispensarians and Apothecarys: wherein the latter are prov'd capable of a Skilful Composition of Medicines, and a Rational Practice of Physick. To which are added, Some Proposals to prevent their Future Increase. By an Apothecary. London, Printed and sold by John Nutt, near Stationers' Hall. 1704, 12mo." In the Preface, the author states, that "The principal reasons that put me upon this undertaking were to vindicate the Apothecarys from those unjust reproaches which of late have been cast upon them by such whose private interest has induc'd to be their enemies, I mean the *Dispensarians,* and to remove those infamous obloquies which the profession lies under by the admission of several into it almost altogether unqualified."]

THE IRON CROWN. — Have we any certain authority for believing that Napoleon crowned himself with the iron crown at Milan in 1805?
     QUERIST.

[It was in March, 1805, that a deputation of the consulta or senate of Italy proceeded to Paris, to request Napoleon to accept the ancient iron crown, the crown of Italy, with the condition that the two crowns of France and Italy should remain united only on Napoleon's head. On the 26th of May, 1805, the ceremony of the coronation was performed in the Cathedral of Milan, by the archbishop of that city. Napoleon seized the iron crown of the old Longobard kings, and placed it on his brow, saying, "God has given to me; woe to him who shall attempt to lay hands on it." After his coronation at Milan, Bonaparte instituted a new order of knighthood for Italy, entitled "The Iron Crown," on the same principles as that of "The Legion of Honour" for France. An account of his coronation will be found in the *Gentleman's Magazine,* lxxv. (i.), 569—572; and an engraving of the iron crown in Chambers's *Book of Days,* i. 673.]

THE REV. JAMES SCOTT was one of the ministers of Perth from 1762 to 1806, when he resigned from age and infirmity. He was author of *History of the Lives of the Protestant Reformers in Scotland,* 1810; *History of John, Earl of Gowrie.* Edinb. 8vo, 1818. The latter work was posthumous. He was the founder of the Antiquarian Society at Perth, and made considerable MS. collections relative to the history of "the fair city." These, after his death, were purchased by the Faculty of Advocates, Edinburgh.

I presume Mr. Scott's death took place between 1811 and 1818. Can any of your correspondents supply the correct date?   S. Y. R.

[The Rev. James Scott, late senior minister of Perth, died at the advanced age of eighty-five on April 27, 1818. Mr. Scott was ordained minister of Kinfauns in 1759; admitted minister of Perth 1762; and resigned his charge, in consequence of the infirmities of age, in 1807.—*Scots Magazine,* New Series, ii. 597.]

"CONFESSIONS OF A METHODIST."—By whom were *The Confessions of a Methodist* written? They were published in 1810, and originally appeared in *The Satirist.* I am also desirous of knowing when this Magazine was commenced, and at what time was it discontinued. Also by whom edited?   C. K.

[A copy of *The Confessions of a Methodist* in the British Museum contains the following MS. note: "This work was bought up by the followers of Huntington, and the publication stayed. Not more than three hundred were printed, the greater portion of which were destroyed."—*The Satirist, or Monthly Meteor,* commenced on Oct. 1, 1807, and we believe was discontinued with the number dated Dec. 1, 1813, making 13 vols. The last three volumes were called a "New Series."]

"CALAMY'S ABRIDGMENT," CHAP. IX.—Walker, in his *Sufferings of the Clergy,* Part II., p. 240, in his account of Fullham —, D.D., says:—"The Right Reverend Bishop of Worcester, in some short Manuscript Notes of his on Mr. Calamy's *Abridgment,* saith, &c." Have these manuscript notes ever been published? If not, is it known whether they are still in existence?
     JOHNSON BAILY.

[There is a copy of Calamy's *Abridgment,* 8vo, 1702, with manuscript notes, in the Bodleian Library. Bishop Kennett, in a letter to the Rev. Thomas Baker, dated June 13, 1728, says, "I have delivered to our good friend Dr. Knight, your second volume of Dr. Calamy's *Abridgment,* with your exact notes upon it; and thank you for the use of that and many like favours." (Nichols's *Lit. Anecdotes,* i. 383.) Consult also Masters's *Memoirs of the Rev. Thomas Baker,* 1784, 8vo, pp. 75—77.]

SIR ROBERT DOUGLAS, of Glenbervie, Bart., well known as the author of the *Peerage of Scotland* (published before his succession to the baronetcy) was dead in 1798, when his *Baronage* was published, but appears to have been alive when the 18th page of that work passed through the press. The exact date of his decease would oblige.

His only son, Sir Alexander Douglas, M.D., died 28 Nov. 1812, although his name continued on the list of the London College of Physicians till 1822.   S. Y. R.

[Sir Robert Douglas, Bart., died at Edinburgh on April 24, 1770, in the seventy-seventh year of his age. See *Scots Magazine,* xxxii. 230.]

Replies.

LADY TEMPEST'S JURY.

(3rd S. vii. 136.)

A correspondent under the initials C. H. has three queries: 1. Who was Thwing? 2. Who was Lady Tempest? 3. To what circumstance allusion is made in the extract he gives from Woolrych's *Memoirs of Judge Jeffreys?*—To the first,—Thwing was the Rev. Thomas Thwing, a Catholic priest, who was executed at York, October 23, 1680. Mr. Salmon, in his *Examination of Burnet's History of the Reformation*, p. 880, observes that the encouragement given to Titus Oates and Bedloe occasioned others to profess to discover plots in various parts of the kingdom. One of these was laid in Yorkshire, and Mr. Thwing was accused by two discharged servants of Sir Thomas Gascoyn, of having conspired with Sir Thomas, who was his uncle, and with Sir Miles Stapylton, Lady Tempest, and others, to kill the king. The others were acquitted; but Mr. Thwing, being a priest, did not meet with equal justice, but was condemned upon the testimony of the same two miscreants, whose evidence had not been admitted when the others were tried upon the same indictment. He was sentenced to death on the 2nd of August, but reprieved till the 23rd of October, and then hanged, drawn, and quartered, having solemnly protested his innocence in a noble speech at the gallows. The following inscription was placed over him when interred by his friends:

" R. D. Thomas Thwing de Heworth, Coll. Anglo-Duaceni Sacerdos, post Annos 15 in Missione Anglicana transactos, Eboraci condemnatus et Martyrio affectus est Octob. 23, 1680.

" A duobus falsis testibus, ob crimen conspirationis tunc temporis Catholicis malitiose impositum."

To the second,—Who was Lady Tempest? I can give no more direct answer than that she was a Catholic lady well known in Yorkshire, and most probably of the Tempest family of Broughton.

To the third,—by " Lady Tempest's Jury," Mr. Thwing evidently meant the jury on her trial. He petitioned the Court that he might be tried by the same jury which had been impanelled at the trial of Lady Tempest, who had been tried on the same evidence, and acquitted; but this request Judge Dolben refused, in the words quoted by C. H. (See Dodd's *Church Hist. of England*, vol. iii., and Challoner's *Memoirs of Missionary Priests*, vol. ii.)

A piece of the rope with which Mr. Thwing was hanged is preserved in one of the Catholic colleges in England, and has been often seen by

F. C. H.

Thomas Thwing was tried at York for high treason, 24th July, 1680. A jury had acquitted

Lady Tempest the day before. " Mr. Justice Dolben, taking notice of a gentleman near the prisoners, demanded, 'What is that gentleman? We are all beset; he was one of the jury yesterday.'"

He afterwards says to the prisoner: " Really methinks you that are priests should be more dextrous. My Lady Tempest managed her business much better, and had her witnesses in more readiness." (*State Trials.*)

Thwing was convicted and executed. His trial is one of the most monstrous of the time. Sir Thomas Gascoigne, my Lady Tempest, and others agree to kill the king, and in hopes it will take effect, they will erect a nunnery at Dole Bank, of which Thwing shall be chaplain!   E. G.

The passage quoted by Woolrych is from the trial of Thomas Thwing and Mary Pressicks for high treason at York in 1680. (See *State Trials*, vol. vii. p. 1163.) " Lady Tempest," it says in a note, " was probably the daughter of Sir Thomas Gascoigne. No report of her trial has been found." Sir Thomas had been previously tried in the King's Bench for high treason (p. 959), in which she perhaps was in some measure implicated. He was acquitted, and no doubt her trial and acquittal immediately preceded that of Thwing, who naturally, therefore, wished to be tried by the same jury, and the judge as naturally refused the request. Poor Thwing was convicted and hanged.

EDWARD FOSS.

SIR WILLIAM WESTON,
LORD PRIOR OF THE ORDER OF ST. JOHN OF JERUSALEM, *temp.* HENRY VIII.

(2nd S. vii. 317, 405, 496.)

The late MR. PISHEY THOMPSON in his reply to P. S. C. regarding the knight above named, refers to Cromwell's *History of Clerkenwell* for a representation and description of the very fine and curious monument to the memory of the last Lord Prior of the Knights Hospitallers in England, which adorned the old church of St. James's at Clerkenwell prior to its demolition in 1788, when, as recorded by MR. PINKS (2nd S. vii. 496), to the eternal disgrace of the parties concerned, *it was sold* to the Rev. Sir George Booth, and conveyed to Burghley, co. Lincoln [?]. Cromwell speculates at some length (pp. 189-191) on the signification of the extraordinary motto ANY BORO on the scroll beneath the sculptured arms of Sir William Weston; and premising that it had given rise to some antiquarian discussion, supposes it to be a corruption arising perhaps from the ignorance of the sculptor of SANS BARO, " Truly a Baron!" or " A Baron indeed!" and infers that it was the motto borne officially by the Grand

Prior of the Order of St. John, as Premier of the Baronage of England.

I question the correctness of this assumption for the following reason:—In the Heralds' College is preserved "A Description of the Standards borne in the Field by Peers and Knights in the Reign of Henry VIII.," compiled between 1510 and 1525; and in it is delineated the standard OR and VERT of Sir Richard Weston, brother of the Lord Prior, on which in transverse, diagonal, counptercharged bars, the motto ANI BORO twice occurs.

Sir Richard Weston was not a Knight of St. John; but even had he belonged to the Order, his brother, whose banner figures in the same MS., was at the time Grand Prior and bearing a like motto. Sir Richard, then, must have borne, and the heralds must have recorded, the motto of his family.

Major Whitworth Porter, in his notice of Sir William Weston (*History of the Knights of Malta*, vol. ii. p. 323), states that the Grand Prior of England ranked as premier baron, and describes the distinctive dress worn by him and barons generally; but he makes no mention of any distinguishing motto, which he undoubtedly would have done had he been satisfied that such was borne *ex officio* by that officer.

Can any of your readers adduce evidence in support of the view taken by Cromwell? Can any suggest a more probable meaning to ANI BORO than that assumed by him, or can any of them bring forward proof of another motto having been borne by Sir William and Sir Richard Weston and their family in the time of Henry VIII.? W.

ADVERBS IMPROPERLY USED.

(3rd S. vii. 152.)

I apprehend Mr. Bartlett is wrong, at least as to the use of many of the adverbs he appears to refer to; and that it can be shown without relying on Shakspeare's authority. In answer to the common question, "How do you do?" it is quite correct to answer, "I do well, or ill;" as in the Bible, "He shall do well." Now "well" and "ill" are adverbs, and correspond to "how." But the other common phrase shows the double usage most clearly when one says, "I *am* well," in answer to "How are you?" I say the double usage, for, of course, it is equally correct to say, "I am healthy," or "sick," using the adjectives. No doubt in colloquial usage "well" as much as "ill" is almost regarded as an adjective, as is shown by the derivative "unwellness," though "well" is never used as an adjective, while "ill," "of course, is: "it is an ill wind," &c. As is continually the case in English, it may not be easy to draw the dividing line, or to define the *rationale*. But I

apprehend for practice the rule might be found from what I have indicated. Wherever in a question the adverb can be used, another adverb can be used in the answer, and that, whether the question is asked or not. No one would say, "How do you become?" for "What do you become?" it would mean something quite different. Nor, I think, would one say, "How does it seem?" for "what does it seem to be?" except by a very loose colloquialism. But we should say, "How do they look?" or "How do they feel?" "He feels warmly" is different from "He feels warm," because the verb is used as a transitive, and elliptically. It means "he has or entertains (*certain feelings*) in a warm manner," or "to a great degree of warmth."

The quotation from *Julius Cæsar* shows the double usage, unless "fresh" is used adverbially.

LYTTELTON.

Hagley, Stourbridge.

Your correspondent, S. W. P., quotes from Shakspeare the phrases—

> "You look merrily,"
> "Looks he as freshly,"
> "Look fresh and merrily,"

in order to defend such expressions as "I feel very badly," "You look charmingly," against the censures of Mr. Bartlett. Now he must allow me to point out a distinction where a real difference exists. Our word "to look" may be equivalent either to δοκεῖν, or to βλέπειν; and as it is wrong to say φαιδρῶς δοκεῖς· ἱλαρῶς δοκεῖς, so is it wrong to say "You look merrily," if we mean "You appear merry." The expression "You look charmingly," evidently means "You have a charming appearance," and is therefore *incorrect*. But as it is right to say, φαιδρῶς βλέπεις, ἱλαρῶς βλέπεις (Cf. Mel. in *Anth.* xii. 159, ἱλαρὸν βλέπειν, and Xen. *Memor.* iii. 10, 4, ἆρ᾽ οὖν, ἔφη, γίγνεται ἐν ἀνθρώπῳ τό τε φιλοφρόνως καὶ τὸ ἐχθρῶς βλέπειν πρός τινας;) so is it right to say, "You look merrily," if we mean "When you look at me you do so merrily." Βλέπειν, "to look," in this sense has an active signification, and the action is properly qualified by an adverb. This active force of βλέπειν is still more strongly seen in an idiom common in Aristophanes, and familiar to ourselves. Compare Aristoph., *Vesp.* 455,—

> . . . . ἀνδρῶν τρόπος
> ὀξυθύμων καὶ δικαίων, καὶ βλεπόντων κάρδαμα,

with our expression, "He looked daggers at me." Cf. also Soph., *Œd. Col.* 319,—

> . . . . φαιδρὰ γοῦν ἀπ᾽ ὀμμάτων
> σαίνει με προστείχουσα.

"She cheers me with the glad radiance of her eye," where we are usually told that φαιδρά is used adverbially. Here, however, as often elsewhere, the neuter adjective is far more expressive than the simple adverb. The idiom σαίνει με φαιδρὰ ἀπ' ὀμμάτων is very nearly akin to κάρδαμα βλέπειν.

The distinction which I have attempted to point out above, holds with regard to the word "to feel," and Mr. Bartlett is aware of the distinction. "He feels warm" means "he experiences a sensation of warmth"—"he knows by his sensations that he is warm," and we accordingly use an adjective, and we condemn as incorrect the phrase "He feels badly," because an adverb is employed to convey a precisely similar notion. For as "he feels warmly" means "he is one who when he experiences sensations, does so in a warm manner;" so "he feels badly" should strictly mean, "His sensitive faculties are impaired;" a signification which we never intended the words to bear.

FABIUS OXONIENSIS.

MISTLETOE.

(3rd S. vii. 76, 157.)

That J. A. P. should have followed Wächter in his very erroneous deduction of this word, and thence too followed up the argument to ascribe to the Druids its origin from so despicable a word as *mist*, dung, shows that he has not consulted Pliny in the original. The passage he cites from Pliny after Wächter is from lib. xvi. cap. 93, in which three sorts of viscus are given: *Stelin, Hyphear* (called also *Dryos Hyphear, copiosissimum in quercu*) and *Viscus*; and then follows the quoted passage, which is more in relation to the mode of its propagation than to the derivation of its name. Had either J. A. P. or Wächter gone on to the next chapter but one, xcv., their error as to the derivation would have been very plain; and it would show a wonderful proof of the enduring powers of language, and of Pliny's knowledge of German and British, that his translation of our indigenous term should be still perfectly recognisable. This Teutonic lore of Pliny had already been recognised by Sir Francis Palgrave, in his translation of *Bodenlos* by *fundo carens*. But I will give you the principal portion of this chapter, in which, as Britons regardful of our ancestry, we have even a domestic interest: —

"Non est omittenda in ea re (nempe Visco) et Galliarum admiratio. Nihil habent Druides (ita suos appellant Magos) visco, et arbore in qua gignatur, si modo sit robur, sacratius. Jam per se roborum eligunt lucos nec ulla sacra sine ea fronde conficiunt, ut inde appellati quoque, interpretatione Græca, possint Druides videri. Enimvero quicquid adnascatur illis e cœlo missum putant, signumque esse electæ ab ipso Deo arboris.—*Omnia sanantem appellantes suo vocabulo*, sacrificiis epulisque rite sub arbore preparatis duos admovent candidi coloris tauros, quorum cornua tunc primum vinciantur. Sacerdos candida veste cultus arborem scandit; falce aurea demetit; candido id excipitur sago."

Omnia sanantem as translation of the indigenous term is still best retained in the German

mistel, contracted merely from *meist heil(sam)*, and not very dissimilar from our English equivalent, *most heal(ing)*. Even *mist*, German for dung, philosophically considered as nature's balmy restorer, may not be inaptly deduced from the same considerations as producing fecundity, which Pliny, in continuation, makes one of the attributes given to the *omnia sanantem* herb: —

"Fecunditatem eo poto dari cuique animalium sterili arbitrantur; contra venena omnia esse remedio." ·· (

It may be doubtful whether superstition has taken or given one of its traits from the mode of the mistletoe's growth, and gathering into the white robe of the principal Druid, to prevent its ever coming in contact with the earth, so that in Shakspeare's days contact with the soil would weaken a charm or invalidate witchcraft. Hecate in *Macbeth*, says,—

"Upon the corner of the moon
There hangs a vaporous drop profound,
I'll catch ere it come to ground,
And that, distilled by magic slights,
Shall raise such artificial sprites
As by the strength of their illusion
Shall draw him on to his confusion.
He shall spurn fate, scorn death, and bear
His hopes 'bove wisdom, grace, and fear;
And you all know security
Is mortals' chiefest enemy."

The peculiarity of growth, coupled with the sanctity attached to the plant, will also give an answer to a question asked in "N. & Q." which I have not seen answered, — "Whence originates the custom of kissing under the mistletoe?". In our merry Christmas time the practice would lose all efficacy was it not *under* the mistletoe, and we therefore very correctly hang it from our ceilings; for in this position it aptly represents the native growth and place of potent vantage. We may fancy that three thousand years ago, if not more, our ancestral tribes in their youthful days of tryst and courtship, danced under the gnarled oaks of our primæval forests wherever the outstretched bough bore the sacred emblem, exchanging vows of troth and *oscula dulcia*, and may they continue to do so still for an equal space of time.

WILLIAM BELL, Phil. Dr.

6, Crescent Place, Burton Crescent.

Mr. Prior, in his very excellent little book *On the Popular Names of British Plants*, derives *mistletoe* from the Anglo-Saxon *misteltan*, from *mistl*, different, and *tan*, twig, being so unlike the tree it grows on.

W. J. T.

T. C. is of opinion that the presence of mistletoe is "probably the consequence and not the cause of the unhealthiness" of the trees on which it is found. If he will consider how the mystic plant is propagated, I think he will be ready to change his note. One of the most exhaustive articles on the mistletoe which I can now call to mind, appeared in *Once a Week* for December 31, 1864. In it the writer, Mr. Walford, makes the following quotation from a paper read by Dr. Harley before the Linnæan Society in March, 1863. After the seed of the parasite has been deposited and has begun to germinate — .

" the branch still struggles vigorously with its enemy, but as fast as one generation of roots are dying off, a later and more numerous progeny attack it in another place. The affected branch moreover assumes various contortions, in the hope of escaping, being twisted sometimes in one direction and sometimes in another, and frequently being bent at right angles to itself; but it wrestles in vain as with a veritable hydra, which having killed its centre, spoiled and occupied its bark, and invaded anew the living wood that remains, now gradually completes the work of destruction."

Thus far Dr. Harley; Mr. Walford continues —

"It is to this power of the mistletoe to seize on one branch of a tree after another, and to reduce them to a desolate woe-begone appearance, that Shakespeare is thought to allude when he says of the limes in Datchet Mead,—

" 'The trees, though summer, yet forlorn and lean,
O'ercome with moss and baleful mistletoe.' "
Tit. Andr., Act II. Sc. 3.
St. Swithin.

A curious practice illustrating the properties of this strange plant was communicated to me, now many years ago, and is, I think, note-worthy, although it may not throw any light on the peculiar epithet used by Shakspeare. In the palmy days of " Cranborne Chase," the season for killing "dry" does began at Martinstide (Nov. 11) and ended at Candlemas (Feb. 2). Now it was customary with the keepers to produce the effect of natural sterility by inducing abortion in the female deer, and this they did by laying branches of mistletoe in their feeding grounds some two or three months before the season commenced. The plan succeeded, but it was said that the venison in such cases was deficient in flavour. I was likewise informed that mistletoe would produce the same effects in the canine race. This property of the plant is not, I believe, generally known; for the practice founded on it was a piece of woodcraft probably confined by traditional usage to the district I have named. The fact is singular and suggestive. W. W. S.

Longevity: Miss Mary Billinge (3rd S. vii. 154, 207.)—I am obliged to Mr. Newton for his courteous reply; but he will, I trust, excuse my saying that I am not yet satisfied as to the great age of Miss Mary Billinge. Her brother, who died in 1817, aged forty-seven, must have been born in 1770, nineteen years after Miss Mary Billinge, a fact which adds to my doubts rather than removes them. Would Mr. Newton, as he is a resident on the spot, kindly apply to the Officer of Health for Liverpool, who made the researches, and was satisfied with the result, and request that gentleman to give your readers the benefit of those researches? The question is not an idle one: it involves much of social and physiological interest, and I hope for Mr. Newton's assistance in settling it. A Doubter.

Barley (3rd S. v. 358; vi. 481; vii. 84.) — Among the many conjectures that have been offered as to this expression, may I be permitted to intrude my own humble opinion: that the interpretation furnished by Halliwell in his *Dictionary*, after all, approaches nearest to the truth, viz. that it signifies "to bespeak or claim." This has been well illustrated by T. T. W. in the instance of children searching in company for an object, when the first fortunate discoverer of it calls out in haste, "Barley," or, as the version of P. P. has it, "Barley me,"—thus asserting a right to it as his own. I would therefore suggest, that Barley is nothing more nor less than a contraction of the phrase, "By your leave;" as may be perceived by pronouncing it glibly over the tongue, without dwelling upon the labial *ve* at the close. The addition of "me" only serves as a confirmation of the original claim; and is as much as to say, elliptically and hastily, without any unnecessary circumlocution, "It is for me," or "It is mine."

Then more particularly as to "me:" if I may be allowed without affectation of pedantry to employ a classical allusion, I would add, that this little *me* is Nature's most appropriate language of highly wrought hurried excitement, rising at once to the lip on the spur of the moment, and beautifully exemplified by Virgil in his episode of Nisus and Euryalus: —

" Me, me, adsum qui feci."—*Æneid*, l. ix. v. 42.

But, to descend from heroics:—At the hazard of being thought fanciful, I venture to put forward the above interpretation till a better is found; and, if it be admitted, shall assert my right among my fellow-inquirers to the privilege attendant upon the discovery by adopting the expression "Barley me" — "By your leave, it is mine."
U. U.

Edmund Hoyle (3rd S. vii. 153.)—Your correspondent Cavendish will find a short account of Edmund Hoyle, in Chambers's *Book of Days* (vol. ii. p. 282). It is as follows: —

" Of this celebrated writer of treatises on games of chance, including, among others, whist, piquet, quadrille, and backgammon, and whose name has become so familiar, as to be immortalised in the well-known proverb, 'According to Hoyle,' little more is known than that he appears to have been born in 1672 ; and died in Cavendish Square, London, 29th August, 1769, at the advanced age of ninety-seven. In the *Gentleman's Magazine* of December, 1742, we find among the list of promotions:

'Edmund Hoyle, Esq., made by the Primate of Ireland register of the Prerogative Court there, worth 600l. per annum.' From another source we learn, that he was a barrister by profession. His treatise on whist, for which he received from the publisher the sum of 1000l., was first published in 1743 ; and attained such a popularity that it ran through five editions in a year, besides being extensively printed. He has even been called the inventor of the game of whist ; but this is certainly a mistake, though there can be no doubt that it was indebted to him for being first-treated of, and introduced to the public in a scientific manner. It first began to be popular in England about 1730 ; when it was particularly studied by a party of gentlemen, who used to assemble in the Crown Coffee House, in Bedford Row. Hoyle is said to have given instructions in the game, for which his charge was a guinea a lesson."

THOMAS T. DYER.

PHILIPPINES: "VIEL LIEBCHEN" (3rd S. vi. 458, 501 ; vii. 24, 104.) — In explanation of the term Philippines, as referring to the double kernel of a nut, it was suggested in " N. & Q." (Queries with Answers, vi. 458), that the name of Philippines may have been connected with the two Philippinæ, daughters of St. Philip, who were interred in one burial-place.

A correspondent, however (vi. 501), offers what he thinks is a more satisfactory explanation of the name than that contained in your " editorial suggestion." In many parts of Germany, he says :

" The fixed salutation is 'Guten morgen, viel liebchen,'— 'Good morrow, well-beloved ;' and the similarity of pronunciation between 'viel liebchen' and 'philippines,' the English substitute, is quite marked enough to account for the name."

Your "editorial suggestion" is thus set aside. The term Philippines, as employed in reference to two kernels in one shell, is not traceable to the two Philippinæ laid in one burial-place; but is an "English substitute" for the German "viel liebchen."

But let us look a little further. Granting that "viel liebchen" is the phrase now commonly used in German, does it follow that Philippines is merely an English substitute? Far from it. On the contrary, your learned correspondent HERMENTRUDE informs us (vii. 104) that Philippe, or Philippine (as the case may be), was the term connected with the twin kernels which she heard employed in French by a native of Austria. It would appear then that Philippine, so used, is no merely English term. And it may be remarked in support of this conclusion, that Philippine, though not a common, is a well-known German Christian name, as in the case of Philippine Welser.

On the whole, then, I would offer this suggestion. Philippine and "viel liebchen" have undeniably so much "similarity of pronunciation," that, in their common application to the case of twin kernels, one of them is in all probability the other's "substitute." But which? Is Philippine the mere English substitute for "viel liebchen"? We have already seen reason for concluding that this view is untenable. May we not rather, then, suppose the reverse? — Namely, that "viel liebchen" is after all a German substitute for Philippine?

Give but precedence to the sainted Philippinæ who were laid in one burial-place, your original explanation will then stand good, and we shall at once perceive the connexion with the two kernels in one shell.   INVESTIGATOR.

ADULATION OF BUONAPARTE (3rd S. vii. 136.)— The profane adulation of Buonaparte ("the Almighty having created Napoleon rested from his labours ") cited in the Manual of Political Ethics of Lieber, as attributed to the mandement of the Bishop of Amiens, has also been ascribed to the Prefect La Chaise, who is stated to have inscribed under a portrait of the emperor, "Dieu créa Napoléon et reposa," which elicited two contemptuous French lines allusive to his name, marked by wit and point, but unsuited for general perusal. Did one of these plagiarise the impious parody from the other, or was it one of those inspirations in which " les beaux esprits se rencontrent ? " That there is nothing intrinsically improbable in the servile incense stated to have been in this, as in other instances, offered to the first emperor, will be admitted by the contemporaries of the advent to presidential and imperial power of the third. Authentic instances of this abject prostration of self-respect in reference to both, would supply a singular and instructive chapter to "N. & Q." As antidote to the bane, curious notices might also be contributed of the satires, both pictorial and literary, of which the first emperor, now within the domain of historical criticism, was the object. Of these pictorial satires, I cite from a German work the following notice of a political caricature in reference to the murder of the Duc d'Enghien : —

"Nach des Herzogs von Enghien schändlichem Mord erschien eine Karikatur. Napoleon, den Kopf des Gemordeten in der Hand, besprengte Joseph, Ludwig und Murat mit dem Blute: ' Je vous fais princes du sang.' Bruder Hieronymus konnte die Bluttaufe noch nicht empfangen, und Lucian verschmähte sie, doch sagte er dem Königmacher bei weiterem Andringen: ' Nun ja ! so will ich König von England sein.' "

Is there any proof of the publication of this caricature ?   JOHN HUGHES.

INFANTRY IN LINE (3rd S. vii. 154.) — I can give your correspondent, FUSILIER, some information on the subject of his inquiry, having been instructed from the lips of Colonel M'Murdo, C.B., the late Inspector-General of Volunteers, and now Honorary Colonel of the Inns of Court ("Devil's Own"). Colonel M'Murdo told us (the "Devil's Own" aforesaid) that the Duke of Wellington, in the Peninsular war, noticed how the French advanced under fire in column; and then deployed into line, and his (the Duke's) plan invariably was to bring guns to bear upon the enemy's heads of columns in process of formation, so as to break them and throw them into confusion. He added that Sir Charles Napier, in the Indian campaign, introduced the system of advancing under fire in column; and, whilst deploying into line, the files, as they came to the front, commenced firing, thereby doing execution at once, and at the same time, by the smoke of their musketry, preventing the artillery of the enemy from playing upon them with such effect during the deployment, as would otherwise have been the case. I know nothing of the manœuvres of foreign troops.   A Volunteer.

"Hard Cash:" "Jupiter aid us" (3rd S. vii. 94, 168): Scabious. — If the astrological symbol of Jupiter, ♃, was partially in use in 1715, it seems to have been entirely superseded by the ℞ very shortly after. The *New English Dispensatory* of Dr. James Alleyne appeared in 1733; and throughout that work the ℞ is not only used exclusively at the head of every prescription, but in the English translations of the prescriptions it is always rendered by the word *Take*. Nor is there in any part of the book any intimation of the former use of the ♃, or of the substitution of the ℞ for it. My copy of Bailey's *Dictionary* is the seventh edition, published in 1735, and I find there that the "℞ in a physician's bill stands for *Recipe*, L. Take."

In old works of astrology, the symbol ℞ meant *Retrograde*: as, for example, "We find ♃ (*Jupiter*) located in the 10th house, and there afflicted by a ▢ (*Quadril*) of ♄ (*Saturn*) ℞ (*Retrograde*) in the 6th house."

Though in no way connected with the above, the following amusing eulogy of the Scabious, attributed to Pope Urban, may be worth embalming in "N. & Q." with a German translation appended to it in a curious old German Herbal, printed at Strasbourg in 1589 :—

" *Versus de Scabiosa.*

Urbanus per se-nescit pretium scabiosæ,
Nam purgat pectus,—quod comprimit ægra senectus :
Purgat pulmonem,—lateris simul regionem :
Rumpit apostema,—et lenit virtute probata,
Emplastrumque foris—necat anthracem tribus horis.

" *Zu Teutsch.*

Bapst Urban saget für sich,
Er wisse nicht wie wunderbarlich
Das er möcht Scabiosen preisen,
Ja ihr Lob und Tugend beweisen.
Die Brust macht sie weit und rein,
Reiniget die Lungen und Seittenfein,
Bricht die Apostema innerlich gemein.
Pflasters weiss auff den Anthrax gelacht,
Inn dreyen Stunden den auffmacht."

F. C. H.

(3rd S. vii. 102.)—It is thought by Lin- that this word *bar* is in use in boys' games

to stop any irregularity, as "bar that!" "bar striking!" &c. In the school in which I was educated, many years ago, the word was in constant use, but in a very different sense. It signified with us to call or claim a thing, as "bar that place," "bar first go;" also to claim exemption from any disagreeable job, as "bar not to fetch coals." When a boy had first *barred* anything, his right to possession or exemption, as the case might be, was indisputably established.

F. C. H.

D'Abrichcourt (3rd S. v. 320.) —

"In the church (1360), Elizabeth, daughter of the Marquis of Juliers, and widow of John Plantagenet, was married to Sir Eustace Dabrieschescourt. The lady had taken the veil at Waverley, and for this breach of her vows was condemned daily to repeat the seven penitential psalms and the fifteen graduals, once every year to visit the shrine of St. Thomas at Canterbury, and once every week to wear no 'camisia,' and to eat nothing but bread and a mess of pottage. This penance she endured fifty-one years."—Murray's *Handbook for Kent*, article "Wingham Route," x.: p. 209.

R. J. F.

Martial's Epigram (3rd S. vii. 97.) — In this epigram, which has recently been criticised by several of your correspondents, two points require consideration, "duri puer ingeni," and "architectum." I entirely agree with your correspondent, Mr. Jas. Crossley (3rd S. vii. 148) that the former description is depreciatory, seeing that it is applied to "præconem," and no one can suppose brilliant abilities or even hard study to be necessary in an auctioneer. *Durum ingenium* is an imputation only a degree better than *pingue caput*, a thick head. But I think that the whole puzzle of the epigram lies in the meaning, or rather the shade of meaning, ascribed to *architectum*, on which term I venture to make a simple suggestion, not essentially verbal, but rather referring to fact and observation. How can architecture be regarded as the resource of a heavy youth, mainly anxious to make money, who, in the words of the epigram,—

" Artes discere vult pecuniosas"?

How can an auctioneer and an architect be fitly conjoined, as in the last line,—

" Præconem facias, vel architectum " ?

I answer that translators and commentators have assigned too high a meaning to "architectum." We ought to understand it as at most builder, or as master-mason. Seeing the word, we are apt to think of architecture as one of the fine arts, and to take it for granted that a person is meant ranking, not with tradesmen or mechanics, but with sculptors, painters, composers, and poets. But every architect is not a Vitruvius or a Palladio. Architecture is not like the other four fine arts, refined originally and unchangeably, but is also a useful and necessary art. It is not like the others, addressed solely to the other sentiments and emotions, but provides us with habitations, and with other structures required by the common affairs of life. There must have been in Martial's days, as there are in ours, many builders, successful, wealthy, respectable, who yet, as their works sufficiently testify, have the slenderest pretensions to taste or genius, and to whom it is no disparagement to be classified with auctioneers, skilled in the value of goods and the credit of persons, and finding their calling most lucrative. I see nothing then incongruous in the ideas of the epigram, which may be thus paraphrased: — "Whatever you do with your son, do not let him pursue poetry or eloquence, which are unprofitable. If he wishes to make much money, let him become a great musician, if he can. If he is incapable of any such pursuit, he may still get rich if you make him an auctioneer or a builder."   K.

FIGHTS WITH DRAGONS (3rd S. vii. 159.) — A correspondent of "N. & Q." alludes to the authority of the "late naturalist and antiquary, Colonel Hamilton Smith, who was of opinion that many of the local traditions of encounters between knights and dragons may have had their origin in fact, and that in all cases the so-called dragon was a crocodile." However this conjecture may be applicable to the mythic chivalry of Egypt and the East, it can hardly reach the difficulty of explaining such traditions in Great Britain, where the crocodile was not indigenous.

A more probable solution may possibly be found in the encounters between the native chieftains of these islands, and the Norsemen and Vikings, who gave to their war ships the name of "Dragons." This term occurs constantly in the Sagas. In the Frithiof Saga, Thorstein, when setting out to recover the golden armlet, which Soté the pirate had carried off to Britain—

"Mounted his *dragon-bark*, and steered to the place o'er
    the ocean."

Again, amongst the heirlooms of Thorstein which descended to Frithiof —

"Ellida, the war ship, belonged to the family treasures;
    Fair was the ship to behold, for the open planks of its
        structure
    Grew into one of themselves, and had never been bolted
        together :
    It was framed like a huge sea-snake o'er the stem,
        which loftily tow'ring,
    Lifted its grisly crest, and breathed gilt flames from
        its nostrils.
    Rose o'er the stern its glittering tail, all scaly with
        silver.
    Filled with warriors in arms, 'twas as though some
        kingly castle
    Or fortress embattled, were sailing abroad on the ocean ;
    Black were its wings, with a border of red, and when
        they were extended,
    It rivalled the tempest in speed, and distanced the
        following eagle."
        Muckleston's *Translation*, p. 35.

Again, when Frithiof asks Ingeborg in marriage —

"Then Frithiof his *dragon-bark* unmoor'd,
    And the breeze blew fresh, and the billows roar'd,
    As northward she flew
    Toward Bele's Cairn o'er the waters blue."
        Ib. 1. 43.

Is it not probable that a combat and conquest of one of these formidable craft, with its ominous name, may have conferred on the vanquished the distinction of having slain the dragon?
        J. EMERSON TENNENT.

SPANISH AND PORTUGUESE FAMILIES (3rd S. vii. 134.) — I am happy in being able to supply H. W. T. with some of the heraldic information which he desires : —

Alvarez. — Huit points d'azur équipollés à sept d'arg. (Chequy of 15 panes, az. and arg.)

Carvajal or *Caravaial* (= *Carvalhal?*). — D'or à la bande de sa. ; au chef cousu du champ, chargé d'un tourteau de sin., surchargé d'un croix d'or. (Or. a bend sa., on a chief of the field a pomeis charged with a cross or.)

De Haro. — D'arg., à l'arbre de sin. accosté de deux loups pass. de sa. (et portants la proye), à la bordure de gu. chargée de huit flanchis d'or. (Arg., a tree vert accosted by two wolves passant sa. on a bordure gu. eight saltires or.)

De Castro. — D'arg. à six tourteaux d'azur. (Arg. six hurts 2, 2, 2.)

Padilla. — D'azur à trois poêles à frire, rangées et mises en pals, adextrées chacune d'un croissant contourné, surmontée chacune d'un croissant versé, et soutenues chacune d'un croissant montant, le tout d'arg.

Ponce de Leon. — Parti de Leon et d'Arragon, à la bordure de Bidaure. (Party per pale—1st, arg. a lion ramp. gu. ; 2nd, or, four pallets gu. All within a bordure az., charged with eight escutcheons, or, a fess azure.)

Mendez. — D'arg. au lion de gu., chargé de trois bandes d'or. (Arg. a lion ramp. gu. charged with three bendlets or.)

De la Cerda. — Ecartelé aux 1 and 4, parti de Castille et Leon ; aux 2 and 3, de France. (Quarterly, 1 and 4, per pale, gu. a castle or. (for Castile), and arg. a lion ramp. gu. crowned or. (for Leon) ; 2 and 3, az. three fleurs-de-lis or, for France.)

I have not been able as yet to find the arms of Villarinho, Coelho, or Forjaz.   J. WOODWARD.
New Shoreham.

SIR WALTER SCOTT (3rd S. vii. 156, 211.) — When Mrs. Beecher Stowe was in Scotland, she and her party felt themselves in duty bound to visit Melrose by "pale moonlight," and she says (*Sunny Memories*, p. 79) : —

"In the course of the evening came in Mr. ——, who had volunteered his services as guide and attendant during the interesting operation. 'When does the moon rise?' said one. 'Oh a little after eleven o'clock, I believe,' said Mr. ——. Some of the party gasped portentously. 'You know,' said I, 'Scott says we must see it by moonlight; it is one of the proprieties of the place, as I understand.' 'How exquisite that description is of the effect of moonlight!' says another. 'I think it probable,' says Mr. —— drily, 'that Scott never saw it by moonlight himself. He was a man of very regular habits, and seldom went out evenings' (*sic*). The blank amazement with which this communication was received set S—— into an inextinguishable fit of laughter. 'But do you really think he never saw it?' said I, rather crest-fallen. 'Well,' said the gentleman, '*I have heard him charged with never having seen it, and he never denied it.*' Knowing that Scott really was as practical a man as Dr. Franklin, and as little disposed to poetic extravagances, and an exceedingly sensible family kind of person, I thought very probably this might be true, unless he had seen it some time in his early youth. Most likely good Mrs. Scott would never have let him commit the impropriety that we were about to (*sic*), and run the risk of catching the rheumatism by going out to see how an old abbey looked at twelve o'clock at night . . . . In the day time we had criticised Walter Scott's moonlight description in the lines which say —

'The distant Tweed is heard to rave,
And the owlet hoot o'er the dead man's grave.'

'We hear nothing of the Tweed at any rate,' said we, 'that must be a poetic licence.' But now at midnight, as we walked silently through the mouldering aisles, the brawl of the Tweed was so distinctly heard that it seemed as if it were close by the old lonely pile, nor can any term describe the sound more exactly than the word 'rave' which the poet has chosen. It was the precise accuracy of this little item of description which made me feel as if Scott must have been here in the night."

ST. SWITHIN.

BIBLIOGRAPHICAL QUERIES (3rd S. vii. 133.) — I am able to give your correspondent R. I. the information he asks about Mrs. Crowther of Huddersfield. The full title of the book runs thus —

"Moral Tales and Poetic Essays. By Mrs. Crowther. *Elle n'a aucun autre objet que celui de plaire.* Huddersfield : Printed by Brook and Lancashire, for the Subscribers, 1802."

There is a short introduction written by Mrs. Crowther, but the editor of the book says that she did not live to publish, as was evidently her intention when she penned it. He further adds : —

"It is to be lamented that the author was deprived of those advantages of education which her birth seemed to require, and which her singular genius would have done honour to. She certainly possessed many requisites for a good writer: a strong and fertile imagination, a sportive and elegant fancy, and a species of delicate wit, peculiar to elegant and superior minds."

The *Moral Tales* consist of "Zulima and Fatima," an eastern tale, and "Cephisa." They are both in prose, and occupy pages 1 to 54. The *Poetic Essays* consist of nineteen poems, generally short, and occupy the pages 55 to 136 of a foolscap octavo book. The work was only printed for circulation amongst subscribers and friends. Should R. I. desire it, I will send him the full list of the titles to the poems.   ABRAHAM HOLROYD.
Bradford.

AUVERGNE POETRY, ETC. (3rd S. vii. 133.) — There will be found some specimens of the *patois* of Auvergne in M. Bouillet's *Album Auvergnat*, which contains Noels, &c. There is a "Chanson Hugenote, en patois d'Auvergne," quoted by M. Doniol, in his *Ancienne Auvergne*, tom. iii. p. 52. There is also a poem in the same *patois*, with the title of " L'Homme Content, par Joseph Pasturel ; " and another poem, " Sur les Vendanges, par M. Laborieux," which will be found at p. 158 of the *Album.*

In the library at Clermont it is said that there are MSS. in the *patois* of Auvergne ; and among them a "Thesaurus Linguæ Limanicæ, par J.-B. Tailhandier."   J. MACRAY.

Miscellaneous.

NOTES ON BOOKS, ETC.

The Great Governing Families of England. By John Langton Sandford *and* Meredith Townsend. *Two Vols.* (Blackwood.)

" England," says Mr. Meredith Townsend, " is governed in times of excitement by its people, in quiet times by its property." This property is, in a great measure, represented by the thirty-one families whose histories (originally printed in *The Spectator* newspaper, where they excited great attention by their ability,) form the subject of the present volume. The object of the writers is clearly avowed. It is to elucidate the half-forgotten but cardinal fact of British constitutional history, the existence in the empire of a few great families, who have exercised from age to age an unbroken influence upon its policy, who have occasionally been powerful enough to govern the country as if it were their property ; and who even now, when opinion has become an executive force, when ultimate power has been legally transferred to the whole middle class, are stronger than any other single interest. But it will be a comfort to those who may be frightened at this picture, to find that, though the power of this aristocracy is still the most direct and constant of the five influences — the landlords, commerce, the priesthood, the press, and the population — still this influence would appear always to have been exercised for the benefit of the realm, from the time when it wrested from the people the spoils of the monasteries till when Stuart Anne died childless, these great governing families summoned the German House, under whose reign they and we alike have flourished beyond human precedent. The historical and biographical matter, contained in these histories of the Percies, Stanleys, Talbots, Russells, &c., is at once instructive and amusing.

Memorials of Angus and the Mearns ; being an Account, Historical, Antiquarian, and Traditional, of the Castle, and Towns visited by Edward I., and of the Barons, Clergy, and others who swore Fealty to England in 1291-6 ; also of the Abbey of Cupar and the Priory of Rostinoths &c. By Andrew Jervise. (A. & C. Black.)

A work of considerable learning and research, and valuable not only as a contribution to local history, but for the light it throws upon the recognition of the supremacy of England by many of the most eminent Scottish

Barons and Churchmen during Edward the First's subjugating tour through Scotland in 1296.

Of the Orthographie and Congruitie of the Britan Tongue. A Treates, noe shorter than necessarie, for the Schools. By Alexander Hume. *Edited from the original MS. in the British Museum* by Henry B. Wheatley. (Early English Text Society.)

This early treatise on English Orthography, written by Alexander Hume, who was at one time Head Master of the High School, Edinburgh, is printed from the MS. copy which the author dedicated to James I. It is a very fitting Essay to have been printed by the Early English Text Society.

A Biographical Memoir of Samuel Hartlib, Milton's familiar Friend; with Bibliographical Notices of Works published by him, and a Reprint of his Pamphlet entitled " An Invention of Engines of Motion." By H. Dircks, Esq. (J. Russell Smith.)

By this little book Mr. Dircks has done good service both to literary history and to the history of mechanical progress in this country.

BOOKS AND ODD VOLUMES
WANTED TO PURCHASE.

Particulars of Price, &c., of the following Books to be sent direct to the gentlemen by whom they are required, and whose names and addresses are given for that purpose:—

Cole's (Elisha) Dictionary, English-Latin and Latin-English, 4to. London, 1677. Two guineas offered for a good copy.
Wanted by *Mr. J. O. Halliwell*, 6, St. Mary's Place, West Brompton, near London.

Garmann, L. C. F., de Miraculis Mortuorum libri tres. Dresden 1709. Five shillings will be given.
Wanted by *Mr. Edward Peacock*, Bottesford Manor, Brigg.

Account of Ejected Ministers, by Calamy.
Wanted by *Mr. Johnson Baily*, Bishop Middleham, Ferry Hill Station, Durham.

Notices to Correspondents.

Among other articles of interest which are in type, and will be inserted in an early number, are —
Death caused by drinking Cold Water; Breakneck Steps; Assumption of Arms; On a Passage in Pericles, by *Dr. Bell;* Daniel Defoe, the News-Writer, &c.

E. S. Lascelles *will find articles on the "Nicæan Barks" in "*N. & Q.*" 3rd S. iii. 287, and v. 268.*

The Greek Church. *We are compelled for obvious reasons to discontinue the discussion of this question.*

H. P. G. *will find the "Union Jack" treated of in "*N. & Q.*" 2nd S. iii. 17, 70, and in a very recent number.*

Z. *The motto "Min, Sucker, Reap," is Irish, and means " Gentle, Prudent, Ready."*

W. W. *The following works on writing in Cipher may be consulted:* La Cryptographie Dévoilée, *par Ch. Fr. Vesin (Bruxelles, 8vo, 1848);* Martens's Guide Diplomatique, *p. 570, et seq., and the Works of Dr. John Wallis, iii. 659. It is probable that the cipher occasionally seen in newspapers may be a regular code arranged between the corresponding parties. Vide "*N. & Q.*" 1st S. xii. 112, 305, 413.*

A Reading Case for holding the weekly Nos. of "N. & Q." is now ready, and may be had of all Booksellers and Newsmen, price 1s. 6d.; or, free by post, direct from the publisher, for 1s. 8d.

*⁂ Cases for binding the volumes of "*N. & Q.*" may be had of the Publisher, and of all Booksellers and Newsmen.*

"Notes and Queries" *is published at noon on Friday, and is also issued in Monthly Parts. The Subscription for Stamped Copies for Six Months forwarded direct from the Publisher (including the Half-yearly Index) is 11s. 4d., which may be paid by Post Office Order, payable at the Strand Post Office, in favour of* William G. Smith, 32, Wellington Street, Strand, W.C., *where also all Communications for the Editor should be addressed.*

"Notes & Queries" is registered for transmission abroad.

LONDON, SATURDAY, MARCH 25, 1865.

Notes.

BREAKNECK STEPS IN A LITERARY "LONDON FOG."

The London, Chatham, and Dover Railway, a work which will be of wonderful use when completed, has nevertheless caused a great gap in the City: a "breach in nature" as it were. Pistol-like, the London, Chatham, and Dover Railway is having "incision" in the Civic bosom, and in this cut-and-thrust performance, I am afraid the London, Chatham, and Dover Railway has not merely *thrust* on one side, but has entirely *cut* away, the Breakneck Steps of Goldsmithian reputation. Upon this interesting point, and upon sundry other points thereabout, some citizen, whose words are of credit, though at present his name may not be one of renown, might very well employ himself in re-surveying whatever is left undisturbed by the interesting line of railway, three times named in full already.

I lately tried to discover Breakneck Steps, but every lane or alley I went down, and every street I went up, I came upon the London, Chatham, and Dover Railway works, so that in many cases former thoroughfares were transformed into "No-thoroughfares," with Turn-*back*-again Lanes in all directions. I found hoardings "awest my pwogress" such a number of times, that I felt compelled, as the saying is, "to fly away," and in despair give up my search for this famous flight of Steps.

A certain reference in *London and its Environs Described*, published by R. and J. Dodsley, 1761, in six volumes, was the cause of my attempt to survey this Breackneck locality, now so completely cut through by this almost-everywhere-to-be-handily-met-with railway. Of this locality, however, thank heaven! master John Strype, of laborious memory, has, in his edition of old Stow, 1720 (Book III. p. 280, vol. i.), laid down the following map-like description:—

"On the North side is *Seacoal lane*. This Lane is very ordinary, both as to Houses and Inhabitants. Out of this Lane is a passage to *Snow Hill*, another into *Green Arbour*, and a third into *Bishop's Court*; the two last ascended up by a great many Steps, or a pair of Stairs, made through *London Wall*; but having their chief Entrance out of the *Little Old Baily*, shall be here taken Notice of. On the West side of this Lane are these Allies, which fall into the *Ditch side; viz. George Alley*, or *Yard*, an open Place, and unbuilt, except the *George* Brewhouse, and the end next this Lane, and that is but ordinary. *Bear Alley*, an indifferent open Place, and reasonably built and inhabited. On the South side of this Alley, is another small one, called *Little Bear Alley*, very ordinary. *Goose Alley*, indifferent good, but narrow. And against this Alley is a small Place called *Ford's Rents*."

In *London and its Environs Described*, 1761, we are directed to "BREAKNECK *alley*, in the Minories," and also to "BREAKNECK *court*, Blackhorse alley, Fleet Street." Both alley and court are followed by this note mark ‖, and all places so marked, we are informed, derive their names "from ridicule." The Breakneck Court, which, in 1761, was to be found by those who dived into Blackhorse Alley, may possibly have been the narrow passage to be observed in 1865, leading from the aforesaid alley into Farringdon Street. From the end of this little passage, in days of yore, there existed great facilities, no doubt, for tumbling into the Fleet Ditch, when that once smiling rivulet was open to the public view, from the silvery Thames, through the Holborn Hill valley, right away to the vicinity of old St. Pancras Church, and elsewhere.

Of these probable Fleet Ditch dangers we have a peep or two in *A Survey of the Cities of London and Westminster, Borough of Southwark, and the Parts Adjacent*, 1734-5, by one Robert Seymour, concerning whom, and his book, the following note from Henry G. Bohn's enlarged edition of Lowndes' *Bibliographer's Manual*, is worth being "made note of" in these pages:—

"The real author of this work was John Motley. Some copies are dated 1736, others 1754. A collation, with some curious particulars respecting the work, will be found in Upcott's *Bibliographical Account of the principal Works relating to English Topography*, p. 620, and in *Chronicles of London Bridge*, p. 393."

Robert Seymour, at page 795 of his first volume, speaking of "Black-horse-alley," calls it "ordinary," and further adds:—"Out of this Alley is a Passage to Fleet-ditch," which passage might, with great propriety, have been called, once upon a time, and for the sake of " ridicule "—" BREAK-NECK Court." Strype, who seems to have poked his antiquarian nose into every hole and corner with great earnestness, remarks, " *Black-horse-Alley*, ordinary, and nastily kept. Out of this Alley is a passage to *Fleet Ditch*." Robert Seymour further tells us of " *Eagle-and-child-alley*, narrow, hath a Passage into *Fleet-ditch*, down Steps." Brewer's-yard, George-alley, Currier's-alley, and Harp-alley, are all mentioned as making their way to Fleet-ditch, but without any notice of doing so " down Steps." Stone-cutter-street is a way " good and open." He records, however, " *Queen's-arms-alley*, but narrow, with a Free-stone Pavement, which leads to the Ditch-side, down Steps." Originally, perhaps Break-neck Court had a few steps down to, as it was called, the " Ditch-side "; though we are not called upon to suppose that at any time, Oliver Goldsmith, Bishop Percy, or anybody else, had to " climb from the brink of Fleet Ditch,'—which, by-the-bye, was covered in to a point beyond the south corners of Ludgate Hill and Fleet Street, and occupied by the old Fleet Market, as early as 1737, full twenty years before Goldsmith went to reside above the Breakneck Steps of our own times. When there were ways to the Ditch-side, " down Steps," the chance of danger to those ascending or descending seems to have been confined to the immediate possibility of a tumble and a broken neck, without the cruel addition—supposing a tumble and *no* broken neck — of a roll over the " brink of Fleet Ditch," with a watery-grave ; or, in this case, to use Queen Gertrude's apter words, a " muddy death." This view of the matter may be prettily observed by another extract from the book of Robert Seymour, otherwise John Motley:

" The *Ditch-side*, called *Fleet-ditch*, is a spacious Place, with good Buildings on both Sides of the Canal, so made since the Fire of LONDON, and has on both Sides a broad Passage for Carts to the Wharfs next the *Thames* ; this Canal is railed in, for fear of Danger of People's falling into it."

Messrs. R. and J. Dodsley having kindly directed the STOW-ically inclined antiquary to Breakneck Alley, and Breakneck Court, while Lord Macaulay, according to the extract sent by J. E. J. ("N. & Q." 2nd S. ix. 280), chose poetically to exclaim — " Goldsmith took a garret in a miserable court, to which he had to climb from the brink of Fleet Ditch by a dizzy ladder of flagstones called Breakneck Steps. The court and the ascent have long disappeared ; but old Londoners well remember both,"—I was led to dive into divers old " Londons" for references to *Breakneck Steps*, but could find no mention of them by that name.

Strype, in 1720, as we have seen, speaks of Bishop's Court, and Green Arbour Court, as being

reached " by a great many Steps, or a pair of Stairs, made through *London Wall*." Robert Seymour, in 1734, observes, " *Green-arbour-court*, at the upper End is a very good Square with tolerable good Houses, and Inhabitants answerable. Out of this Court is also a Passage down Steps into *Seacoal-lane*."

In *The History and Survey of London*, 2 vols. 1756, " By William Maitland, F.R.S. and Others," —the title-pages of which further affirm that it was published " By the KING's Authority,"—the " Others," I fancy, assisted William Maitland by thieving pretty freely—" *convey* the wise it call " —from Robert Seymour, otherwise John Motley. Not only do the "Others " give Seymour's words about Green Arbour Court, even to " Out of this Court is also a Passage down Steps into *Seacoal-lane*," but the " Others " at page 963, of their *History and Survey of London*, quaintly observe :—

" The *Ditch-side*, called *Fleet-ditch*, is a spacious Place, with good Buildings on both Sides of the Canal, so made since the Fire of *London*, and has on both Sides a broad Passage for Carts to the Wharfs next the *Thames* ; this Canal is railed in for fear of Danger of People's falling into it."

And thus it is our merry-minded surveyors of Stow's London go on ringing the changes against each other, without remorse, for these words used by the " Others " in 1756, when (for nineteen years) the Fleet Ditch had been filled up and made of *market*-able value, are the very words spoken by Robert Seymour in 1734, at which time Fleet Ditch was a *real* ditch, as we learn from Maitland's *original* edition of his *History of London*, published in 1739. At page 352 thereof he observes :—

" But this new and spacious Canal' filling with Mud and Dirt as formerly, the Charge of Cleansing it above *Fleet Bridge* amounted to more than its annual Produce ; wherefore 'twas again neglected, and the Rails on each Side being decay'd, many Persons perish'd, by falling therein by Night, and Beasts by Day ; so that it was become a very great and dangerous Nuisance : which occasion'd the City to apply to Parliament for a Power to arch over and level that Part of it above *Fleet Bridge*, which being readily granted, the Work was begun about the Beginning of *March, Anno* 1734."

This filling up, or ditch-arching-over " consummation devoutly to be wished," was finally effected in 1737, in which year, according to Maitland, " *Fleet-Market* was open'd on the Thirtieth of *September*." But all these varied says—first of Strype, then of Seymour, next of Maitland, and those " Others" who helped him, are necessary to be studied for the slight purpose of endeavouring to ascertain *when* Breakneck Steps were first called " Breakneck Steps" *in print*. Also whether it was likely that Oliver Goldsmith, when he repaired to his " Smoky, miserable one-pair-of-stairs room in Green Arbour Court, near the Old Bailey"—as a writer expresses it in *The*

Westminster Magazine for April, 1774—was under the dangerous necessity of having to " climb from the brink of Fleet Ditch "—a very poetical idea, but not exactly correct.

In such " Londons" as I have been able to consult, I get no glimmer of Breakneck Steps, by that name, until David Hughson, in 1806, published a work entitled *London ; being an accurate History and Description of the British Metropolis.* This work extends to six goodly octavo volumes, and in the third of them, speaking of Green Arbour Court, David Hughson (otherwise E. Pugh) remarks : —

" In the latter court, at the top of BREAK-NECK STEPS, stands a house in which Goldsmith dwelt when he composed the Vicar of Wakefield, the Traveller, &c."

And so—in this neighbourhood—with the exception of the Dodsley " Breakneck court" in 1761, it is not until 1806 that I find (as yet) a mention of anything Breakneckish in name. However, from all these " Londons" there is something to be gained, notwithstanding the wholesale re-churning up of each other to be observed in them all. As for instance — of the " something to be gained " — during the summer of 1864 I was baffled many times in attempting to copy the crumbled inscription to Amey Constable on the monument erected to that lady's memory in old St. Pancras churchyard : but in Robert Seymour's *Survey of the Cities of London and Westminster, Borough of Southwark, and the Parts Adjacent,* 1734-5, I find Amey Constable's monumental inscription accurately and completely given. I come to the conclusion of its completeness from the stray parts I myself recovered with so much trouble. From this circumstance I entertain some respect for Seymour's title-page announcement, which in part reads as follows :—

" The Whole being an Improvement of Mr. STOW's and other SURVEYS, by adding whatever Alterations have happened in the said CITIES, &c., to the present Year ; and by retrenching many Superfluities, and correcting many ERRORS in the former WRITERS."

However it may have been with the " former writers" and their doings, I know not, but Amey Constable died in 1731, and Seymour printed her tomb-inscription by 1734-5, whereas Master William Maitland in 1739, and the " Others "in 1756, cut poor old St. Pancras off, as it were, with a literary shilling, for they do not condescend to notice *one* inscription at that, then, out-of-town churchyard. Consequently, as Robert Seymour is the first and only one of these Londoners I can find who gave Amey Constable's inscription to the printing press, I think we may venture to attach some sort of value to that " *Motley* performance," as Upcott good-humouredly calls John Motley's pseudonymic Survey. As John Motley, *alias* Robert Seymour (who nineteen years afterwards was to be met with as a " Gentleman of

the Inner Temple "), has been so often mentioned, the following note, taken from page 620 of Upcott's *Bibliographical Account of the principal Works relating to English Topography,* may here be deemed interesting : —

" The real author of this book was *John Motley,* the more celebrated compiler of *Joe Miller's Jests.* He also wrote a Life of Peter the Great, as well as some pieces for the stage ; and was the son of Colonel Motley, who fell at the Battle of Turin, 1705, in the service of Louis the Fourteenth."

To deprive antiquity of its dry, high-top baldness, is a very desirable consummation ; while to infuse the spirit of poetry with *inch-measured truth,* is to produce that juiciness of being, so observable in the more renowned of our worthies.

Old Weever, when recording of rebels, exclaims about the " distorted visage of Plebeian fury," while the venerable Stow, when his heart was troubled over demolished monuments, cried out against the " bad and greedy men of spoil." But to talk as Lord Macaulay talked—according to the extract given by J. E. J. — of Oliver Goldsmith clambering from the brink of the Fleet Ditch by a dizzy ladder of flagstone steps, when that ladder of steps was a good quarter of a mile from the spot where the brink of the Fleet Ditch *had* been, is a process of poetry destructive to truth. Poetical expression is the life of antiquarian discourse, dry words the way to its " dusty death ; " but in the midst of the most poetical of antiquarian discourse, inches must be measured by inches, feet measured by feet, or truth, " white-robed truth"—to use the words of the immortal Milton — becomes at once as dirty as Ditch-water.

EDWIN ROFFE.

Somers Town.

LETTER TO R. B. SHERIDAN.

Perhaps the following unpublished letter, containing a strange jingle of words, addressed to the late Mr. R. B. Sheridan, may amuse the readers of " N. & Q." It is signed " W. R. Spencer," a son of Lord Charles Spencer. He was the author of *Leonora ;* a translation from the German. *Urania, or the Illuminé ;* a comedy. *The Year of Sorrow,* and other poems, 1796-1811 : —

" I only write you a few words by way of apology for not having sent, and for not sending now, those foolish things you were so good to desire. You shall have them all as soon as I have them myself, and you cannot desire them sooner. I hope you scolded Pitt confoundedly, and your friends still more than him, if they made themselves fools, which they were very likely to do. Dr. Parr begs you will cut Pitt's throat without loss of time, and destroy all the worshipers of Baal without distinction. Pray drive the dog and all his whelps to the D——l, and purge the House of C's of its filth, for it is an Augean stable of muck and nastiness . . . . . Do send us some account of what you are doing or not doing, saying or not saying, &c. &c., and whether Pitt trembles on the treasury bench. We drank your health yesterday, and various other orthodox toasts, and will drink it again to-day and every day, please God, *dum spiritus hos regit artus.* So good bye, God bless you and yours, and do punish me for puzzling you with these hieroglyphics by sending me some of your own to decipher.

            " Yours sincerely,
Without dissimulation,
With the greatest admiration
Of your rank and station,
Which, without ostentation,
In my estimation
Is the first in the nation ;
So with due consideration
And perfect adoration
Of your Foxite situation,
And the truest execration ·
Of the damn'd simulation
And curst peculation,
Of which long observation,
And keen penetration,
And investigation,
And deep speculation
On the scheme and formation
Of Pitt's administration
Have giv'n me confirmation,—
With argumentation
And ratiocination,
Severe accusation
And quick refutation,
Which this generation,
From infatuation,
To my consternation
And heartfelt vexation,
Have giv'n his Broggation
And vociferation,—
So to Pitt here's damnation,
To Fox exaltation,
To you recreation
Beyond all numeration
Or multiplication,
With which supplication
Here ends my Rhymation.
           " Yours, &c. &c.
              " W. R. Spencer."
                 B. S.

DEATH CAUSED BY DRINKING COLD WATER.

A fact which, although apparently well known in the East and in some parts of Europe, appears to have escaped the notice, or at least not to have occupied the attention, of writers on physiological subjects, seems worth making a note of in the " N. & Q."

To the believer in the Christian faith, the subject derives additional interest from the connexion it has with the most awful mystery of our religion, the Crucifixion. The commentators on those parts of the Gospels which relate our Lord's sufferings on the Cross do not mention the fact, probably unknown to them, that drinking cold water whilst suffering very severe pain, produced by torture, causes immediate death.

As has been noticed, most commentators on the New Testament pay but little regard to the incident of our Lord drinking on the Cross; but in a very rare and little known work (*Nov. Test. Cathol. expositio ecclesiastica, auctore* A. Marlorato, 1559), the commentator on Matth. c. xxvii. remarks that the writer of the Gospel —

" Loquitur tanquam de re usitatâ : ac probabile est genus potionis fuisse confectum ad mortem accelerandum quum miseri homines satis diu torti essent."

General Kleber fell by the hand of a fanatic at Cairo, June 14th, 1800. The assassin was soon secured, and sentenced by the French to be impaled alive. This horrible sentence was carried out, and borne by the criminal with that fortitude and stoicism which is so often witnessed among the barbarous or semi-barbarous nations of the East or the extreme West.

     " Fine tamen laudandus erit ; qui morte decorâ
     Hoc solum fecit nobile, quod periit."

In the French account of this execution it is stated that, after the assassin had been impaled alive, he asked for drink. A French soldier who was about to give the wretch some water, was prevented by the chief of the Mamelukes, who said, " Gardez-vous en bien; vous feriez mourir à l'instant ce criminel." The unhappy man remained alive upon the stake for four hours ; at the end of which time, the executioners having departed, a French soldier, moved by a sentiment of humanity, gave a cup of water to the tortured wretch, who immediately expired. Moore had probably some such history as this in his remembrance when, in the " Veiled Prophet of Khorassan," he wrote the following lines : —

     " Such treacherous life, as the cool draught supplies
     To him upon the stake, who drinks and dies."

Cotterell, in his *Recollections of Siberia,* states that prisoners who are allowed to satisfy their thirst after suffering the severe punishment of the knout immediately die.   J. V.

PASSAGE IN "PERICLES,"

In the following beautiful death oration of Pericles over the corpse of his Queen Thaysa, who had just died in child-birth, and whose body the superstition of the sailors insisted on being thrown from the ship in which they were sailing into the ocean, I find an additional proof to the many I have already published, in my *Shakspeare's Puck,* of our great poet's intimate knowledge and consequent residence in Germany. For it is only explainable from a very popular but peculiar fallacy in natural history of our neighbours of Fatherland, still fully prevalent among them. The following is the passage (Act III. Sc. 1) : —

     " *Per.* A terrible child-bed hast thou had, my dear :
No light, no fire : the unfriendly *elements*
Forgot thee utterly ; nor have I time
To give thee hallow'd to thy grave, but straight ·

Must cast thee, scarcely coffin'd, in the oozes ;
Where, for a monument upon thy bones,
The *air-remaining lamps,* the belching whale,
And *humming* water, must o'erwhelm thy corpse
Lying with *simple shells.*"

Elements in the plural, where only fire is referred to, is certainly wrong. We may retrench
the final *s*.

" The air-remaining lamps, the belching whale,"—
has given rise to much unnecessary comment ;
and Mr. Malone's *aye-remaining* has been indorsed
by all the commentators with much commendation, instead of Steevens's *air-remaining,* which is
more to the purpose. Though Steevens fortifies
his alteration with much learning for a very ridiculous paraphrase. It is : —

" Instead of a monument erected above thy bones, and
perpetual lamps to burn near them, the spouting whale
shall oppress thee with his weight ; and the mass of the
water shall roll, with low heavy murmur, over thy head."

The error of all these gentlemen lies in mis-
understanding the word *lamps,* which has here
nothing to do with *burning lights,* whether perpetual or otherwise. It is here put for one of the
lowest, and of the most loathed species of fish—
the *lamprey.* This animal, as is well known, has
seven spiracula or air-holes on its side. These
with the Germans, according to a wide-spread and
popular belief, are taken for seven eyes ; which,
with the two real ones the animal has, make up the
Teutonic tale of nine, to give it the only name
by which it is known of *Neunaugen,* or nine eyes.
But consequently, from this view, no orifices remain for respiration ; and it follows that, not being
able to emit the air, it must retain it : so that by
the change of a single letter in the line, a *t* for an
m, we have a perfectly consistent epithet, and a
perfect solution, viz. : —

" The *air-retaining* lamps, the belching whale."

And what a most beautiful and comprehensive
idea does not this reading offer,—the whole range
of ichthyology, from the lowest species, the inver-
tebrate lamprey, to the blatant belching whale, in
a single line ! The contrast, too, is so forcible :
betwixt the lamprey emitting no air, and the whale
spouting it so furiously, and in such columns.
These still serve his persecutors, the whalers of the
Arctic Seas, to follow him as a signal

" Which lure *them* on to his destruction."

There is also another point of contact between
these two denizens of the deep, which possibly
may have been the first germ of their position in
this place. The Lamprey, like the Sturgeon, is a
regal fish. Pennant tells us, " That it has been
an old custom for the city of Gloucester annually
to present the sovereign of the realm with a Lamprey pie, covered with a large raised crust ; " and
it may have been one of these luscious presents
which so tickled the palate of our first Henry

that, by excess of eating it, he died of the surfeit.
The Whale, too, is also claimed for the second
person in the realm. Our Queens Consort have,
according to Blackstone, the right to all the
Whales stranded on the British coast, to provide
whalebone for the stomachers of her Majesty and
her ladies.

Our name of Lamprey is merely a false translation of the French Lamproie, to which we also
unnecessarily add Mud and Sand-lamprey ; for I
take the French to mean by it a Sand-borer.
Those arid tracks of sand betwixt Bourdeaux and
Bayonne are emphatically designated *Les Landes,*
and *proue,* our *prow,* stands here for borer, or to
penetrate, as it is the custom of these fishes to bury
themselves in the mud like the eels, or in running
water to affix themselves by their sucker-like
mouths to stones or rocks, whence their generic
name of *Petromyzon.*

Humming water is certainly not in character
with the tossing, tumbling waves of an angry
ocean, which cannot be said to murmur softly over
the queen's coffin : the single interchange of a
letter would give a better reading, as *hemming
waters, i. e.* surrounding the body on all sides.

Lying with *simple* shells. The addition of the
epithet simple induces me to believe that the
sentence alludes to a very ancient practice, in
which shells were connected with the dead : from
the Roman times their leaden coffins were largely
ornamented with scallop-shells affixed as their
principal ornament. Such a one was lately dug up
near the Roman wall in the Minories in London,
and was fully described by Mr. C. Roach Smith,
in the *Collectanea Antiqua :* others have also been
dug up with similar shells. Pilgrims' shells, first
taken only by those whose pilgrimage had St.
Iago de Compostella for its object, originated also
from the coffin of this saint, which, though of
heavy weight, was, according to the legend,
floated from the place of his martyrdom in Palestine, to the north-western coast of Spain with
the body, about 800 A.D. ; and these ornaments
would be gladly received by those whose piety
and zeal induced them to the long journey into
Gallicia, as proofs of their enterprise. The practice became subsequently extended to all pilgrims,
irrespective of the shrine they sought. The name
Compostella for the locality is another feature
of the legend, which declares that a bright star
settled over the spot to which the coffin and its
sainted freight was driven ; and it is possible that
a comet may have been in the heavens over this
portion of northern Spain at the time when a
Roman coffin, thus decorated, had been thrown
up by the waves, or from which the superincumbent earth had been washed away. The contained body, from this very circumstance, may
have been considered that of a saint ; but why
St. James was fixed on more than any of the

other eleven Apostles, I cannot conjecture, unless the Hagiology had already given these other eleven their final resting places. For this view of the shells connected with the coffins of the dead, I surmise that the epithet *simple* is here cited, to distinguish between one which would have the orthodox ornament and that in which the queen lay, with only the natural shells of the ocean around it.　　　　　　　WILLIAM BELL, Phil. Dr.

ß, Crescent Place, Burton Crescent.

LETTER OF OUR LORD TO ABGAR.

Among the very ancient and interesting documents in the recently-published posthumous work of the late Canon Cureton,[*] the letter said to have been written by King Abgar to our Lord, and that of our Lord to Abgar in reply, are now I believe for the first time printed in the original Syriac. It is well known that the learned Canon entertained a strong conviction of the genuineness of these letters; but the grounds on which he mainly rested this belief, so contrary to the opinion generally maintained at the present day, can unfortunately never be made known. The discussion of this, and of many other highly interesting matters, having been reserved for a preface, which his untimely death prevented him from adding to the volume; which although, with the exception of the last sheet, it was printed under his own super-intendence, he did not live to publish. In the notes which accompany the English translation of these letters, we find a curious bit of "folk lore," which may be worth recording in "N. & Q." After alluding to the fact (mentioned by Procopius) that the people of Edessa, firmly persuaded of the genuineness of this letter of our Lord, had a copy of it affixed to the gates of their city, which was supposed to act as a sort of phylactery, Dr. Cureton adds:

"Nor did the belief in the protecting power of this letter of our Lord prevail in the East only ; for we find, at a very early period also, that it obtained even in our own British Isles."

This statement he confirms by a reference to an MS. service book of the Anglo-Saxon times, now in the British Museum; and afterwards quotes Jeremiah Jones (*New and Full Method, &c.*, Oxford, 1798, vol. ii. p. 6), as stating that—

"The common people in England have had it (*i. e.* the letter) in their houses in many places in a frame, with a picture before it, and they generally with much honesty

* "Ancient Syriac Documents relative to the Earliest Establishment of Christianity in Edessa and the Neighbouring Countries, from the Year after our Lord's Ascension to the Beginning of the Fourth Century ; discovered, edited, translated, and annotated by the late W. Cureton, D.D., &c., with a Preface by W. Wright, Ph.D., LL.D." 4to.　London, 1864.

and devotion regard it as the word of God, and the genuine Epistle of Christ."

Dr. Cureton adds, finally : "I have a recollection of having seen the same thing in cottages in Shropshire."　　　　　　　　　　　　　Q.

CURIOUS PAMPHLETS.—In lately turning over a pile of old books which have been bequeathed to me, I have met with three which seem to be rare. One is—

"The Secret History of the Most Renowned Queen Elizabeth and the Earl of Essex. By a Person of Quality. Cologne : Printed for Will-with-the-Wisp, at the Sign of the Moon in the Ecliptick. 1695." Pp. 115.

It has an engraved frontispiece of a rather indelicate character; but there is nothing in the contents to correspond with the insinuation conveyed in the engraving. Is it of any value.[*]

Next I have a small pamphlet, pp. 39 —

"White Ladies ; or, His Sacred Majestie's most miraculous Preservation after the Battle at Worcester, September 3, 1651. Faithfully imparted for the Satisfaction of the Nation by Eye-witnesses. *By Special Command.* London : Printed for the Author, and are to be sold at the *Royall Exchange*, and at *Westminster*. 1660."

It has an engraved portrait of Charles II., arrayed in crown, ermine mantle, and collar of the Garter. The publisher promises that this "first part only of his Majestie's Preservation" will, "if it find a favourable acceptance," be followed by the "narration of the residue of his dangers." Is anything known of this pamphlet ? And did the "residue" ever appear ?

The third is—

"Honesty the best Policy" (no date). Dedicated by Is. Pinckney, " to His Grace John, Duke of Marlborough, Captain-General of His Majesty's Forces."

It is a ranting defence of the Duke against—

"The high Ingratitude, and most unparallel'd Inhumanity of the monstrous, savage, and brutish wild Boars of our British forest ; Who have thrown their most horrid Indignities, and vile Aspersions, on this great Hero (you know)."

It is abundantly larded with texts of Scripture and Latin phrases; and, as well as the other two, may be of interest to some of your readers—to any of whom I shall be glad to lend them for a time.　　　　　　　　　　　　　　　C. W.

43, Union Grove, Clapham, S.

LOUIS XIV., AUTHOR OF A "VIE DE CÉSAR."—The rumour of the existence of a *Vie de César* by Louis XIV., according to the *Independance Belge*, has some truth in it. It would seem likely that only a portion of the work was printed, if printed at all, as another rumour states, that five chapters of a *Vie de César* by this monarch have been found in a bundle of autograph letters of Madame

[* Frequently reprinted.—ED.]

de Maintenon, endorsed "Letres aux Prives." Another report says that the work, of which only two copies were printed, is a translation of Suetonius' *Vies des XII Césars* and not a *Vie de Jules César*.

Can any of the correspondents of "N. & Q." give further information?　W. H. C.

"HE'LL NEVER SET THE TEMSE ON FIRE." — Many years ago, before machinery was introduced into flour mills for the purpose of sifting the flour, it was the custom for the miller to send it home *unsifted*. The process of sifting was done thus, but principally in Yorkshire. The *temse* or sieve which was provided with a rim which projected from the bottom of it, was worked over the mouth of the barrel into which the flour or meal was sifted. An active fellow, who worked hard, not unfrequently set the rim of the temse on fire by force of friction against the rim of the flour-barrel; so that in fact this department of domestic employment became a standard by which to test a man's will or capacity to work hard: and thus of a lazy fellow, or one deficient in strength, it was said, "*He* will never set the temse on fire." The long misuse of the word *temse* for *sieve*, as well as the superseding of hand labour by machinery in this particular species of work, may possibly have tended to the substitution of sound for sense, in such phrases as "He will never set the *Thames* on fire," the Mersey on fire, or any other river.

I do not recollect having seen any notice of this phrase in "N. & Q.," and should be glad to know whether it is familiar to many persons.

P.

Burslem, Staffordshire.

GLIBBY.—I heard this word in use in Huntingdonshire during the late frost. Its meaning was "slippery," or (as it was locally explained to me) "sleathery."　CUTHBERT BEDE.

"AS GIPSIES DO STOLEN CHILDREN."—It is rather amusing to find wits abusing the plagiarists, and yet condescending to act the same part themselves. Fox traced the thought given above from Sheridan, through Churchill, to Wycherley—and might have gone still farther. Davenant had long before used the same idea; in his Preface to *Gondibert* (p. 772, Anderson), he says:—

"Because they commonly make such use of treasure found in books, as of other treasure belonging to the dead and hidden underground : for they dispose of both with great secrecy, defacing the shape and image of the one as much as of the other, through fear of having the original of their stealth or abundance discover'd."

P. W. TREPOLPEN.

MOORE'S "POEMS."—Written, after reading a collection of Moore's *Poems*, by the late Rev. John **Parsons**, sometime Fellow of Oriel College, **Oxon**:—

" Yes, thou hast fancy, taste, and feeling,
　Grace to trifle, skill to move,
O'er the lonely bosom stealing
　Many a ray of pensive love.

" But ne'er let youth where peace reposes,
　O'er virgin's lips thy light strain breathe ;
For vice still lurks beneath the roses,
　And pleasure twines her serpent wreath.

" Oh ! had thy syren lyre been given,
　An offering pure on Virtue's shrine,
An angel might have lean'd from heaven,
　To list to strains so sweet as thine."

The above, I believe, have never appeared in print, and may be worthy of a niche in "N. & Q."
R. W. F.

NEOLOGISM : "HOLD-FORTH."—
"The Non-conformists took up the word *hold-forth* in the year 1642, which was never known before."—Hearne's *Diary*, Feb. 3, 1705-6.

P. W. TREPOLPEN.

THE LION ON NORTHUMBERLAND HOUSE.—The following cutting is from the *Court Journal* of March 4; and, as I have some doubts about the correctness of the moving of the lion, I would feel obliged if any of your readers would inform me whether the statement is correct or not ?—

"A former Duke of Northumberland, holding high office in the State, had become somehow obnoxious to the City folks and Corporation of London, and had received some insult from that quarter, in the discharge of what he deemed his duty to the country at large. What was his revenge ? He simply persevered in putting British interests before those east of Temple Bar ; but the Percy lion, which formerly looked in that direction, had his head forthwith turned towards Westminster Abbey, and his tail to this day indicates from what point the Duke had received unmerited contumely."

I may add, that the position of the lion's tail is made the subject of many wagers in India.
EDWARD C. DAVIES.
Cavendish Club.

Queries.

APPARITIONS OF RECULVER AND ROCHESTER.—Can any of the readers of "N. & Q." inform me what they were ? They are mentioned in Fox's *History of Pontefract*. As the connection appears to be with the Roman epoch, I have looked through Charles Roach Smith's Index to his *Antiquities of Richborough, Reculver, and Lymne*, and can find no allusion whatever to any "story of a local ghost, which the common people do still believe haunt cities, towns, and family seats famous for their antiquity and decay" (p. 5). I have also in vain referred to various books of reference, which I considered probably might contain accounts of Kentish legends.　ALFRED JOHN DUNKIN.
Dartford.

THOMAS BILBIE. — Can any of the readers of "N. & Q." inform me when a bellfounder of this name flourished in Bristol, and where he resided? In 1746 he set up a foundry at Collumpton. Any other particulars will oblige. H. S. W.

BIOGRAPHICAL QUERIES.—Can you help me to any information about the following? —

1. Thomas Windsor, son of Sir Thomas Windsor, who married, *ante* 1630, Anne Carey.

2. Dudley Weld or Wild, of co. Kent, who married about the same time Mary Carey. She subsequently became the wife of Sir Alexander Fraser, Bart. (query, ob. 1681?); and by him had a daughter Carey, who married Charles Mordaunt, the great Earl of Peterborough.

3. Henry Picks, of Crayford, co. Kent, who married Dorothy Carey. (A Sir *Edward* Picks, of the city of Westminster, Knt., died in 1681, leaving his widow Dorothy sole executrix. He had property in Kent, Sussex, and Hants.)

4. Bevil Skelton, Groom of the Chamber to Charles II., and husband of Simona Carey.

5. Who was Catherine, wife of Sir Francis Rogers, of Cannington, co. Somerset, living (a widow) in 1629? C. J. R.

MARCHIONESS OF CORNWALLIS. — In the Ninth Report of the Deputy-Keeper of the Public Records, p. 195, Augmentation Office Grants, the Marchioness of Cornwallis is set down as a grantee of monastic property. There is no date, but the reference to the late monastery of Dartford makes it probable that the time was that of Henry VIII. Who was the Marchioness of Cornwallis? Or if a clerical error, will some of the record officers oblige us with its correction? C.

CINNAMON.—Whence comes the phrase —
"Cur moriatur homo, qui sumit de cinamomo?" *
J. G. T.

THE REV. SAMUEL ELSDALE, sometimes Fellow of Lincoln College, Oxford (B.A. 1803, M.A. 1809), published —

"Death, Judgment, Heaven, and Hell: a Poem, with Hymns and other Poems," 8vo, 1812, 3rd edit. 1813.

In 1814 he was elected Master of the Free Grammar School at Moulton, Lincolnshire. He was alive in 1818. When did he die?
S. Y. R.

MEANING OF "FOWERMEN."—The first entry in the church book of the parish of Plympton-Maurice, in Devon, dated "Anno Dni. 1650," records the election of "a churchwarden for the year following by the old warden." Then follow the

[* This phrase is thus noticed in Thomas Cogan's *Haven of Health*, 4to, 1596, p. 109 : — "I have read in an old author of Phisicke this meeter following,—
'Cur moriatur homo, qui sumit de cinamomo?'"
See "N. & Q." 1st S. x. 454.—ED.]

names of "sydemen" (two), "ffowermen" (four), "seattsetters" (two), and "waywardens" (two). Can any reader of "N. & Q." inform me what was the office of the "ffowermen"? I can find nothing about them in any of the glossaries that I have had opportunity of searching. The title (in later entries written "fourmen") continues until 1700. After that date it does not appear, but in 1702 for the first time, and in following years, there are chosen four "rators." Was their office the same as that of the "fourmen"?

It has occurred to me that the title of the latter may have been derived from the word "fowe," to clean ("to fowen out an old diche," *Beves of Hamtoun*, quoted by Halliwell), and that their duty was to superintend the cleaning of the streets. Scavengers were elected annually in Plympton to a recent time, but I believe that they were elected at the "mayor-choosing," and that their office was municipal, not parochial. It is possible that the name may refer only to the number of the officers — four men.

As regards the "seattsetters," I may mention a note made in 1764, that the sum of two shillings and sixpence had been paid by the ancient custom of the parish by the inhabitants for their sittings. At the beginning of the eighteenth century and afterwards the title is written "seat *sitters*," the true meaning of the word (*set*, to let, still used in leases) being probably at that time forgotten.
J. SHELLY.

OLD INNS OF HOLBORN, ALDGATE, AND BISHOPS-GATE. — May I ask if any thing has been done to illustrate the old inns in Holborn, Aldgate, and Bishopsgate? They are, I think, some of the most interesting relics left us of Old London; and as they are fast disappearing, I should be glad to know if there are any descriptions and illustrations in the way of engravings, water-colour drawings, or photographs, of the following old inns, viz.: The Old Bell; Black Bull; Blue Boar, afterwards called the George and Blue Boar Inns, in Holborn—this latter inn was pulled down in 1863; The Bull and the Three Nuns, in Aldgate High Street; and the Bull, Green Dragon, Four Swans, and Vine Inns, in Bishopsgate Street. The Bull Inn has just been sold to the City Offices Company, and is now being demolished. The following extract from the *Herts Guardian* of Saturday, March 11, relative to the demolition of the Bull Inn, Bishopsgate, may at this time be interesting to some of your readers. It states that—

"Under the yew-tree, against the steeple of All Saints' Church, Hertford, is a small ordinary looking gravestone, having the following quaint inscription : 'Here lyeth Black Tom of the Bull Inn, in *Bishopgate*, 1696.' The Bull Inn was one of the oldest of the many hostelries for which London was noted. It had a special license granted for the performance of theatricals. Here some of our earliest actors played, and Black Tom was probably one of them. The stage was erected across the Inn yard, at the side of which there is a room still called the Shake-speare Coffee-room."

· If there are no drawings in existence of the above old inns, I think that photographs should be taken of those remaining before they are demolished. I may state that the Vine Inn, Bishopsgate Street, was pulled down last year; and we are, I am informed, shortly to lose the Old Spread Eagle Inn, in Gracechurch Street.   W. D.

INSCRIPTION ON A TOMBSTONE. — Will any of your readers say what author the following line, which I found on a gravestone in a Highland churchyard, is taken from, if it is not original? —

" Homo fugit rapide lethumq: invadit inermes."

It is intended for an hexameter, but as it stands there is neither "rhyme nor reason" in it, though if we read "Hora" for "Homo," the scansion and the sense will be made out.   STRLE.

THOMAS OUGHTON, a proctor in the Court of Arches published —

"Ordo Judiciorum ; or, Method of Proceedings in the Ecclesiastical Courts of England and Ireland, relating to the Canon and Civil Law, with large Notes and Observations." Lond. 2 vols. 4to, 1728, 1738.

· Where can any account be found of the author of this learned and valuable work?   S. Y. R.

POLITICAL SATIRES : "NEW TORY AND WHIG GUIDE." — In the year 1819 there appeared two exceedingly clever works of a satirical description, the *New Tory* and the *New Whig Guide*. The former is perhaps the best of the two, although the latter is exceedingly good. In a leading article in a number of the *Standard* published last year, it is asserted that the admirable squib denominated "The Trial of Henry Brougham for Mutiny," in which the future chancellor is charged with calling the Right Honourable George Ponsonby, the leader of the opposition, "an old woman," was written by Lord Palmerston. Is this the case? I know from positive testimony that the *English Melodies* were written by the late Sir Alexander Boswell, Bart.

From an entry in the sixth volume of Moore's *Journal*, we learn, p. 178, that Paul Methuen, Esq., afterwards Lord Methuen, was the "author of almost all those [in the *Tory Guide*] about the Rat Club, which are certainly some of the best." It would be very desirable to ascertain the respective authors of the other articles in these very amusing volumes, which merit a place in the library of those who collect facetiæ.*   J. M.

WESTON, EARL OF PORTLAND.—Where can I find any detailed account of the descendant of Richard Weston, first Earl of Portland, and particularly of Thomas, the fourth and last Earl,

[* In the Catalogue of the British Museum it is stated that the articles in the *New Whig Guide* were written by H. J. Temple, Viscount Palmerston, and others.—ED.]

who died A.D. 1688 ; whereupon, as Banks states in his *Extinct and Dormant Peerages*, the title became extinct for want of heirs male of the first Earl surviving?   HISTORICUS MINOR.

"PRIMITIVE HISTORY FROM THE CREATION TO CADMUS."—Some years ago I purchased at an obscure book-stall a portion of this work in sheets, comprising the first 200 pages, the margins of which are literally covered with additions and corrections in the hand of the writer, evidently with a view to its future republication. Subsequent to this I obtained the remainder of the work also in sheets but without any writing on it, and had the whole carefully bound so as to preserve the notes. It was published at Chichester in 1789, and dedicated by the writer, "W. Williams, Esq., formerly of St. John's College, Cambridge," to the Prince of Wales; but this dedication has been crossed over, and on the blank side of the leaf another appears in MS. addressed, "To the Members of the University of Cambridge in General; To the Members of St. John's College in Particular." As the work contains an immense amount of research and much recondite learning, I would be glad to obtain some information respecting the writer, for whose name I have searched several biographical dictionaries in vain.   T. C. SMITH.

QUOTATION WANTED.—Christopher Love being brought to trial on a charge of High Treason in 1651, made a long defence, in the course of which he said—

" It is a maxim in the Law (I have read it in Divinity-Books), *Ampliandi sunt favores, et in pœnis benignior interpretatio facienda.*"—See *State Trials*, folio, 1742, vol. ii. p. 138.

Where is the foregoing maxim to be found?   MELETES.

READING POINTER. — Some years ago a person was convicted of stealing a *reading-pointer*, an instrument in the form of a hand and finger extended, used by the readers of the Hebrew Scriptures. Can any reader of "N. & Q." give a reference to the trial?   E.

SHELVES IN WILTSHIRE. — Mr. Cobbett, in his *Rural Rides* through the down counties, refers to "the thousands and thousands of acres of ploughed lands in *shelves*, in Wilts alone." "The side of a steep hill," he tells his readers, "is made into the shape of stairs; only the rising *parts* more sloping than those of a stairs, and deeper in proportion" (p. 437). On these *shelves* Mr. Cobbett founds his hypothesis of population, which he contends was as great in the early days of England as in the present; and he adds :

" The fact is, I dare say, that the country has never varied much in the gross amount of its population ; but formerly the people were evenly spread over the country, instead of being, as the greater part of them now are, collected together in great masses ; where, for the greater part, the idlers live on the labour of the industrious."

I will not trouble you with a refutation of Mr. Cobbett's hypothesis of population in England; but shall, on the present occasion, confine myself to an inquiry of the origin of the *shelves* in Wiltshire. I have not access to the local histories of that country, save *The Beauties of England and Wales*. The author does not mention the *shelves;* nor, so far as I remember, are they referred to in any article in the *Quarterly*, or any other reviews, on the history of counties in which downs prevail. May I ask the favour of any of your readers conversant in the history of the down counties to give me, through the medium of your journal, the origin of these *shelves*, and any information which he may think will be useful to be made known of them?

·I cannot conclude without expressing my desire to see a *new edition* of Cobbett's *Rural Rides* published; but stripped of all the abusive epithets of men, and of political and religious questions, which disfigure the *Rides*. I am persuaded it would become a very popular book in this day.

                         Fra. Mewburn.

Larchfield, Darlington.

.Supersedeas. — Will any of your readers oblige me by explaining this word? A reviewer in *The Athenæum*, Feb. 18, p. 226, writes: —

·· "We suspect that college terms are sometimes irrecoverably lost. It appears in Newton's private account-book, that while at Cambridge he bought, for a few shillings, a *supersedeas*. But all our inquiries, both in and out of Trinity College, have failed to discover what this was."

                         F. Phillott.

Queries with Answers.

When was Cannon first Made? — I have cut the following from the Miscellaneous paragraph column of a newspaper, but, as is too often the case, it gives no date, nor does it quote the authority on which the statement is made. It originates an inquiry of some importance—What is the actual date of the first cannon made, and which was the first battle in which they were employed? —

"A small brass cannon has been found at the bottom of a deep well of the Castle de Cluey, in France, with the date 1258 upon it. The date of the invention of cannon has historically been assigned to the year 1324, 66 years later."

                         T. B.

[Artillery was in use much earlier among the Eastern than the Western nations. Chased, the Hindú bard, says, "Oh! Chief of Gajné, buckle on your armour, and prepare your fire-machines," and he adds (stanza 257), that the culivers and cannons made a loud report when they were fired off. As this took place about A.D. 1200, during the Ghorian dynasty, the fact of cannon balls having been propelled by means of gunpowder in India,

at that early period, appears to be established. With the exception of certain weapons, called by John Barbour, Archdeacon of Aberdeen, "crakys of war," which Edward III. had during his campaign against the Scots in 1327, the use of artillery in Europe appears to have been confined to Spain till about the year 1339, when ten cannons were prepared for the siege of Cambray by the noble Chevalier Cardaillac. It has been stated that Edward III. owed his great victory at Cressy in 1346 to the effect produced by some pieces of artillery placed in front of the army. This important circumstance appears to rest chiefly on the authority of Villani (see " N. & Q." 1st S. x. 534). For some interesting historical notices of the early use of cannon, consult Col. Chesney's *Observations on the Past and Present State of Fire-Arms*, 8vo, 1852.]

"Ivanhoe." — This novel has been dramatised in England and France. Can any one tell me where I shall find the English adaptation? Also, is there any trace of Sir Walter Scott ever having passed any time in or near Rotherham, Wentworth, Doncaster, or other spot in or near the Valley of the Don, in which the action of Ivanhoe principally takes place?   T. S. B. E.

[The English adaptation is entitled " *Ivanhoe; or the Knight Templar*; adapted from the novel of that name. First performed on March 2, 1820, at Covent Garden. The music selected by Dr. Kitchener: the Stage management and the whole piece produced under the direction of Mr. Farley. Lond. 8vo, 1820." A copy is in the British Museum. *Ivanhoe* was dramatised by Mr. Daniel Terry, the actor, to whom Sir Walter Scott wrote from Abbotsford on Nov. 10, 1819: "I go to town on Monday, and will forward under Mr. Freeling's cover as much of *Ivanhoe* as is finished in print. It is completed, but in the hands of a very slow transcriber. When I can collect it, I will send you the manuscript, which you will please to keep secret from every eye. I think this will give a start, if it be worth taking, of about a month, for the work will be out on the 20th of December. It is certainly possible to adapt it to the stage; but the expense of scenery and decorations would be great, this being a tale of chivalry, not of character."

Of the French adaptation of *Ivanhoe*, Sir Walter subsequently remarked, " It is an opera, and of course the story sadly mangled, and the dialogue, in great part, nonsense."

Scott certainly paid a short visit to Sheffield, and the district referred to in September, 1815, but the dates show it must have been a hurried one. It is, however, probable that he had been there previously, although there is no positive record of the fact.]

Matthew Hopkins, the Witch-finder. — "Who after proved himself a witch," &c.

" These verses (says Dr. Hutchinson, *Historical Essay*, p. 65) relates to that which I have often heard, that Hopkins went on searching and swimming the poor creatures till some gentlemen, out of indignation at the barbarity, took him and tied his own thumbs and toes, as he used to tie others; and when he was put into the water, he himself swam as they did. *This cleared the country of him*, and it was a deal of pity that they did not think of the experiment sooner." — *Hudibras*, Grey's edition, note to part II. c. iii. v. 153.

How did it clear the country? Did Hopkins run away, or was he tried and executed? Is any more known about him?   J. M. K.

Malvern.

[In the account of Matthew Hopkins printed in the *Anthologia Hibernica*, i. 427, it is stated, that "the experiment of swimming was at length tried upon Hopkins himself, in his own way, and he was upon the event condemned, and, as it seems, executed as a wizard." The writer, however, gives no authority for his conjecture. Mr. G. BLENCOWE in our 1st S. x. 285, discovered the following entry in the register of the parish of Mistley-cum-Manningtree in Essex : "Matthew Hopkins, son of Mr. James Hopkins, Minister of Wenham, was buried at Mistley, August 12, 1647." This is supposed to refer to the noted witch-finder general of the associated counties. It is not known that any writer has made any mention of Hopkins after 1647. In whose library is the manuscript account of this notorious impostor formerly in the possession of the late Mr. W. S. Fitch of Ipswich ?]

QUOTATIONS. — The following lines are taken from the mottos of Sir Walter Scott's works. Who is the author, and what is the name of the book ? —

"Away ! our journey lies through dell and dingle,
    Where the blithe fawn trips by its timid mother ;
    Where the broad oak, with intercepting boughs,
    Chequers the sunbeam in the greensward alley.
    Up and away ! for lovely paths are these
    To tread, when the glad sun is on his throne,
    Less pleasant and less safe, when Cynthia's lamp
    With doubtful glimmer lights the dreary forest."

Underneath is written "Ettrick Forest." Having but a treacherous memory, though knowing the following lines full well, yet I cannot remember the name of the poet : —

"The warbling woodland, the resounding shore,
    The pomp of groves—the garniture of fields,
    And all the dread magnificence of Heaven."

I have looked over Milton, Pope, Cowper, and Thomson in vain, or perchance I may have overlooked those lines in my hurry to find them.
                                     DROGO DE M.

[The lines from Scott are prefixed to the nineteenth chapter of *Ivanhoe*. They were written by Sir Walter himself: see Scott's *Poetical Works*, edited by Lockhart, edit. 1848, p. 677. The words "Ettrick Forest" are only one of Sir Walter's mystifications. "Whenever memory failed to suggest an appropriate epigraph," says Lockhart, "Scott had recourse to the inexhaustible mines of 'Old Play' or 'Old Ballad,' to which we owe some of the most exquisite verses that ever flowed from his pen." The second quotation is from Beattie's *Minstrel*, book i. stanza 9.]

"AS DRUNK AS DAVY'S SOW!"—What is the origin and meaning of this phrase? Is it only a corruption the idea of the sow returning "to her wallowing in the mire ?"   R. C. L.

[Capt. Francis Grose, in his *Classical Dictionary of the Vulgar Tongue*, informs us that this saying took its rise from the following circumstance :—" One David Lloyd, a Welshman, who kept an ale-house at Hereford, had a living sow with six legs, which was greatly resorted to by the curious ; he had also a wife much addicted to drunkenness, for which he used sometimes to give her due correction. One day, David's wife having taken a cup too much, and being fearful of the consequences, turned out the sow, and lay down to sleep herself sober in the stye. A company coming in to see the sow, David ushered them to the stye, exclaiming ' There is a sow for you ! did any of you ever see such another ? ' all the while supposing the sow had really been there. One of the company, seeing the state the woman was in, replied, ' It was the drunkenest sow he had ever beheld.' Whence the woman was ever after called David's sow."]

PAGAN CARICATURE. — I am quite certain that I have met somewhere with the information that at an early period of the Christian era a famous caricature of our Lord represented him as a man with an ass's ears, and one foot hoofed, holding in his hand a book inscribed "Deus Christianorum, ὀνοχήλον." My impression is that the note I have of this was taken from some cyclopædia ; but I have recently searched right and left in vain for its corroboration. Can you or some correspondent tell me where the assertion is to be found, and whether it is to be relied on ?   R. C. L.

[The Pagan caricature referred to by our correspondent is doubtless that discovered at Rome in the Palace of the Cæsars in Dec. 1856, and noticed by Garrucci in his *Graffiti de Pompei*. It is described very fully in the *Edinburgh Review*, vol. cx. pp. 436-7, and it is this article, we presume, which our correspondent has seen. The caricature is engraved in Mr. Wright's lately published *History of Caricature and Grotesque in Literature and Art*, p. 39, where also some remarks upon the subject will be found.]

MEN OF GENIUS IN BERNERS STREET. — Can you tell me who De Quincey alludes to in his *Essay on Murder* as the men of genius in Berners Street ? —

"To begin with S. T. C. One night many years ago I was drinking tea with him in Berners Street (which, by-the-way, for a short street, has been uncommonly fruitful in men of genius.")
                                     G. B.

[Cunningham, in his *Handbook of London*, tells us this street was chiefly inhabited by artists, and points out the houses respectively occupied by Sir W. Chambers, Fuseli, Opie, and Bone the enameller.]

MARY DE VALENCE, COUNTESS OF PEMBROKE.— Can you tell me where I can find any historical account of Mary de Valence, Countess of Pembroke, daughter of Guy de Chatillon, Count de St. Paul in France? She married Audamarie de Valence, second Earl of Pembroke, who was slain at a tournament on the day of his nuptials. She was the foundress of Pembroke Hall, Cambridge.

DROGO DE M.

[Some biographical particulars of Mary de St. Paul, Countess of Pembroke, who, says Fuller, was "maid, wife, and widow, all in a day," will be found in Dyer's *History of the University and Colleges of Cambridge*, ii. 94, ed. 1814; Carter's *History of the University of Cambridge*, p. 62, 8vo, ed. 1753; and *A History of the University of Cambridge* (Ackermann), vol. i. p. 51, ed. 1815.]

Replies.

DANIEL DEFOE, THE NEWS WRITER.
(3rd S. vi. 527; vii. 58.)

In a former article I epitomised the "history" contained in the recently-discovered "Letters of Daniel Defoe," and made some remarks on the criticism of the *London Reviewer*. I reserved for consideration what Defoe did under his engagement, therein mentioned, with the government;—and, the morality, or otherwise, of his conduct.

To form an accurate judgment as to the actions and conduct of men, we must place ourselves, as far as possible, in the midst of the circumstances by which they were surrounded. In 1718, when the Letters in question were written, all authors, of any considerable reputation and standing, had themselves been subjected to a rigid official censorship of the press. It cannot be doubted that the abolition of such censorship tended greatly to consolidate the principles of the revolution, and to establish the freedom we now enjoy; but another century required to elapse before Governors would be able to bear free public discussion of their policy. The Lord Treasurer for the time being was the head of the Government, and exercised some general superior authority; but there was then no Cabinet, as we now know it. The administration often consisted of discordant members, acting in their respective departments as judgment or caprice might dictate. The struggle of the preceding reign, for and against High Church principles, had scarcely ceased; and recently had given place to a fiercer conflict between the adherents of the newly acceded House of Hanover, and the friends and followers of the Pretender. The gaols still contained numerous Jacobite rebels; and more were at large, who did not always conceal their disaffection to the existing Government.

We can scarcely wonder that State authorities of the Home Department should, in such circumstances, evince great jealousy and over-sensitiveness as to public criticism; or should, under feelings of official isolation and insecurity, use what they considered effectual means to ward off, or punish, all attacks on their administration. Newspapers and other periodical publications were therefore all examined, and frequently, for offensive comments or opinions (that would not, in our day, excite more than a good-natured smile on the face of a minister), "messengers" were dispatched to search and ransack the premises of the printer and publisher; and to take into custody, not only him, but all persons found there. The zeal of the myrmidons was sometimes excessive to a ludicrous extent: not only compositors and pressmen, with their copy and sheets, but the "devil," and the old housekeeper, and any unfortunate lodger who happened to be under the same roof,—all were seized, and carried before the proper members of the administration. After examination, the innocent were released, the mere instruments discharged with suitable admonition, and the actual delinquent dealt with according to the degree of his political turpitude. For a minor offence, detention for a time in the private dwelling-house of the messenger sufficed, with a subsequent release upon recognizances, which the culprit was compelled from time to time to renew. Graver faults ensured committal and trial, with the punishment of pillories, whipping, fines, and imprisonment. For printing a pamphlet stating that James was the rightful king, a young man named Matthews was, in the following year, (1719) sentenced to be hanged, drawn, and quartered.

This will show that the conduct of a public journal was attended with much and continual danger to its proprietor; especially if it ostensibly took the side opposed to the Government.

Defoe knew, by sad experience, what it was for "an unhappy author" to suffer the displeasure of Government; and, on entering into the engagement we have now to consider, urged that the setting up a Weekly Paper to answer scandalous attacks on the Government, would be inadequate either to prevent such attacks, or, to avert the punishment of the offenders. He therefore too readily agreed to lay that aside, and accept the proposal of Lord Townshend, that he might be more serviceable by writing as if "under the displeasure of the Government, and separated from the Whigs." His great talent as a writer made him an acquisition to any journal, and his connection with its management would enable him, on the one hand, to serve the Government, by suppressing the treasonable or seditious papers of contributors, and on the other, to save the owner of the paper from fines, imprisonment, and, the common result, absolute ruin.

The details of the arrangement were left to the direction of a subordinate officer, Mr. Buckley. The journals in which Defoe was to write were

" to seem to be on the same side as before, *to rally the Flying Post*, the Whig writers, and even the word ' Whig,' &c., and to admit foolish and trifling things in favour of the Tories."

The "recently discovered Letters" show that he insisted on these conditions with the owner of one of the papers in which he was to write. When Mr. Mist did not faithfully adhere to the compact, Defoe threatened not to "serve him any farther, or be concerned any more."

That I might be qualified to state what Defoe did under this engagement with the Government, and, to form a judgment on the morality or otherwise of his conduct, it became necessary to examine the publications referred to in his Letters—namely, *Mercurius Politicus, Dormer's News-Letter,* and *Mist's Journal.* I intended at first only to make such an investigation as would enable the readers of "N. & Q." to say, *Guilty,* or, *Not Guilty,* on the indictment against Defoe in the *London Review.* My manuscript of his hitherto unknown writings has, however, now grown to the capacity of an ordinary octavo volume; and I must, therefore, after a few brief illustrations of what he *did,* incur the risk of pronouncing a somewhat dogmatic judgment on his moral and political conduct; promising, that if all be well, the whole shall be laid before the public for final decision.

I. Mr. Buckley had directed — "Seeming to be on the same side as before."

With respect to the condemned rebels, especially in Scotland, he says, in *Mercurius Politicus* May, 1716 : —

" It has been a mightily disputed case amongst the Parties here, whether Justice, so it is call'd as respects the Publick ; or Revenge, so it is call'd as respects Parties, should be extended against the Rebels in general ; or whether Mercy should interpose to the saving them from the Hand of the Executioner ?

" It is not the business of these Collections to enter into the debate, neither does it consist with the Impartiality professe'd in the Introduction, and to which we resolve steadily to adhere," &c.

In the same number, however, he finds nearly eight pages octavo, to print in full an able memorial by Sir David Dalrymple, Lord Advocate of Scotland, pleading for mercy towards the Scotch rebels. In *Mist's Journal,* Oct. 4, 1718, he says:—

" Our Scout employed in the districts of Long Acre, Covent Garden, and Drury Hundreds, writes us an account that a Parrot in Henrietta Street, having spoken very Seditious and Scandalous Words, a neighbouring Justice of *De Peace* had consulted several of his Brethren, in what manner they should proceed against the Parrot, or his Master."

In the same Number is the following characteristic anecdote : —

" They write from Edinburgh, that by a Commission of Oyer and Terminer at Perth, several Bills of Indictment were drawn up, and presented to the Grand Jury there, against several that were supposed to have been in the

late Rebellion, and came home from France, and the Bills were all returned Ignoramus ; upon which the Prisoners were discharged, and the Cryer, thereat standing up, proclaim'd it in Court ; at the end of which, as usual, he spoke, with a loud Voice, — God *save the King and the Judges.* At which a Gentleman standing by added, *and this Jury :* The Cryer hearing it, and thinking it was a Direction to him, he likewise bawl'd out, and this Jury."

II. The papers under Defoe's management were to " rally the *Flying Post*, the Whig writers," &c. In *Mist's Journal,* July 19, 1718, is a communication as to the general incredulity of some persons, and especially of a Whig whom he had recently met. He says —

" I quoted the *Flying Post,* and ask'd him if he believ'd that ? He told me, with a sneer, I had clench'd it now, by asking him if he believ'd a Paper that no Body believ'd."

In the *Journal* of April 18, 1719, was inserted the following paragraph of false news : —

" On Monday last died Mr. Cibber, an Actor at the Theatre in Drury Lane ; he was notorious for his late comedy called the *Nonjuror,* which was calculated to triumph over the misfortunes of those unhappy Gentlemen, who lately fell under the Displeasure of the Government for their attempt in favour of the Chevalier, and by which he lost himself much of the Reputation he acquired by his former Performances."

In the *Journal* of May 2, Defoe corrects the error as follows : —

" It seems, by an Advertisement published last Thursday se'nnight, that *Mr. Flying Post* is very angry that *Mr. Cibber,* who was reported to be dead, is alive ; and appears to Act upon the Stage again, and a great Triumph he makes over *Mr. Mist* for having been wrong inform'd, to which *Mr. Mist* answers—

" 1. As to Mr. C——, he says, as the famous Tatler said of old Partridge, the Almanack maker, that if he was not dead, he should ha' been dead, for any good he was like to do while he was alive.

" 2. If *Mr. Mist* has gained *Immortal Honour* by believing a Lie of another Man's making, how many Immortalities of Praise are due to *Mr. Ridpath,* that has made so many for other People to believe ?

" All this is upon a Supposition that Mr. C—— is alive ; he does not indeed know but he may be so, and should have been inclin'd to ha' believ'd it, had'n't it been publish'd in the *Flying Post.*"

On the same day that he wrote the third of the letters to Mr. De 'la Faye, " recently discovered " in the Record Office, namely, May 10, 1718, he " rallied the Whigs," in *Mist's Journal,* thus : —

" One *Mr. Oliver Testy* has sent us a very good-natured peevish Letter, wherein he threatens Mr. Mist to write a Satyr on him shall make him go hang himself ; and all this for taxing the Whigs with being the Chief Favourites of *Curlicism,* or Bawdy Books ; but, by the way, does not deny the Thing to be true, so we need say no more of that."

III. As to his manner of dealing with the High Church and Jacobites, and the suppression of sedition and treason.

The *Journal* of the date just quoted contains an instance : —

i" We heartily fall in with the opinion of the Reverend *Mr. Jonathan Cassock* relating to the Government of the Church ; but, it being too tender a point for us to meddle with, we desire to be excus'd."

This must have been merely a questionable communication. The following reply, in *Mist's Journal* of March 29, 1718, probably relates to the subject of his Letter to Mr. De la Faye, dated April 12, 1718 : —

" Among other Letters, we have lately received two from *Mr. Paul Fogg,* we should say, two Treasonable Papers ; we hope, if he expects we should publish them, he will first come and set his Name to them, which, if he thinks fit to do, in the cause of Murther and Assassination of Kings, he may hear farther ; but we cannot but wonder to what purpose any Man should send Letters to be put into a Publick Paper, when he must needs think, whoever should Print them could expect nothing but to be try'd for *High Treason,* and sent to the Gallows. However, we are bound to thank our Cozen Fogg for his good will, and take our leave of him in the terms of an Old Parliament Satyr, which may serve to answer him and those of our loving Friends who desire we should hang for them, viz. —

'Mist, at this time, having no need,
Thanks you as much as if he did.'"

IV. His impartiality in writing the foreign and other news.

In *Mist's Journal* of July 5, 1718, after deprecating the exaggerations, untruthfulness, and contradictions of the Foreign Affairs in other newspapers, he says : —

"In this Madness we shall endeavour, as we have hitherto always done, to relate the events of this approaching War, which we believe will be very obstinate and bloody, with the utmost Exactness, and with a perfect Impartiality. We are utterly ignorant of the Necessity there is to lessen Things on one Side, or double them on the other, to please one side or other. We do not see that it is of such a mighty consequence to us which Popish Prince prevails over the other, that we should be afraid to give a full and true Account of any Action, let it fall how it will. The giving true Intelligence is the business before us, and we resolve to favour neither one side nor the other."

The above are fair examples, from the mass of manuscript now in my possession, of what Defoe *did* under his engagements with the Whig Government and with the Tory newspapers, respectively mentioned in his Letters " recently discovered." In other papers, Whig and Tory, of the same period, I have observed much pandering to the prurient passions of readers ; but not in any of the papers with which Defoe was connected. The continual tendency of them was to promote religion and virtue. With respect to politics, he constantly aimed at impartiality ; and I have not found that he actually wrote, in any Tory journal, anything contrary to the liberal principles he had all his life professed. He was undoubtedly restrained by his position from writing in such journals directly in favour of his own political views ; but it is right to add, I have discovered that those principles were freely expressed and advocated in another journal, established in September, 1718, under the management of Defoe, and published thrice a week ; and also, in a daily paper established the following year.

In connection with Tory journals Defoe had to meet continually persons very uncongenial to him, and to suppress, or remodel, Tory advices, essays, and letters, often of most objectionable character. He had further to contend against the prejudice, bigotry, and *quasi* loyalty of his printers and publishers ; and to bear, in silence, the most virulent personal odium from two of the contemporary Whig journals. His motives and his conduct in so trying circumstances appear to have been upright, and the consciousness of this sustained him ; but he had certainly placed himself in an irksome and a questionable position, and I cannot doubt he felt it most bitterly, when he wrote the words — " Thus I bow in the house of Rimmon."

The proper name of Mist's paper was, *The Weekly Journal, or Saturday's Post ;* and as far as *it* was concerned I am able to add, in further proof of Defoe's strict integrity—that he firmly adhered to his determination of suppressing all offensive articles, or ceasing to be connected with the journal. In October, 1718, when a letter to which he objected was inserted, he added a long note replying, and disavowing its principles in the name of Mr. Mist, and at once severed himself entirely from the management of the paper.

Mr. Mist discovered his mistake by finding himself and his servants shortly in the custody of government officials ; and after his liberation, on security given for future good behaviour, he very soon further discovered, by a rapidly declining circulation, that the good genius of his journal had departed. Self-interest compelled him to seek, and put himself again into the hands of, Defoe, who resumed its management at the end of January, 1719, on his own absolute terms ; and it so continued for several years, exhibiting nothing of Toryism in its character beyond the mere pretension of adherence to its past reputation.

My judgment, after more than two months' careful investigation is, that in his connection with the Government, and the several Tory journals mentioned in his "recently discovered Letters," Daniel Defoe unwisely consented to place himself in a very questionable position ; but that, in such position, he did nothing to disparage, positively, his moral character as a man, a patriot, and a Christian.   W. Lee.

LOPE DE VEGA.

(3rd S. vii. 114, 167.)

Sismondi says of Lope : —

"'A temps perdu il ait encore écrit vingt-un volumes in 4to de poésies, parmi lesquelles cinque poëmes épiques. Ces derniers ouvrages ne meritent point une analyse ; il suffira de les indiquer. Il y a une *Jerusalem Conquistada,* en octaves et en vingt chants; une continuation de Roland Furieux sous le nom de *La Hermosura de Angelica*, aussi en vingt chants, en sorte que pour lutter avec le Tasse et l'Arioste, il traita, en deux poèmes épiques, *presque le même sujet que l'un et que l'autre.* — *Littérature du Midi de l'Europe*, t. iv. p. 46, Paris, 1813.

From the above I think it probable that Sismondi had not read the *Jerusalem Conquistada*, which bears little resemblance to the *Gerusalemme Liberata.* The American critic is bolder, and especially wrong. Rinaldo and Armida do not talk like Marini's Venus and Adonis, for they do not appear in the poem, which is an epic of the third crusade, with Richard Cœur de Lion as one hero, and Alfonso XI. of Castile, who never was in Palestine, as another. Ticknor (t. ii. p. 281, Spanish version) gives a good account of *Jerusalem Conquistada*, but hardly says enough on its great occasional beauties.

I think I have found the passage which E. F. desires. It does not exactly correspond with the extract, but the writer is nearer to the text here than in his description of the characters. At a feast, Saladin talks of the crusaders who have landed, and his brother Sirasudolo tells him that, not only France, Germany, and England have arrived, but also the divine Alfonso of Castile. He proceeds: —

> "Es una fiera gente la de España
> Que, quando á pechos una empresa toma,
> Los tiembla el mar, la muerte los estraña
> *Diga Numancia, que le cuesta a Roma.*
> Ni se le da marchando en la campaña
> Aunque vaya desnuda y hierbas coma,
> De la fiera canicula, ni teme ·
> Que el Capricornio frigido la queme.
>
> "Pregunta tú quien son los Castellanos
> Al gran Carthagines, que en sangre tinto
> Passó el Tajo, y venció los Carpentanos,
> Castigo de un exercito distinto:
> Los firmes Saguntinos por sus manos
> Muertos en mas confuso labyrintho
> Te digan su valor, que su arrogancia
> Saben hasta los niños en Numancia."
>
> Lib. vi. st. 11, 13.

Allow me to quote one more stanza to show that Lope, who was in most things quite up to the intolerance of his age and nation, appreciated the greatness of Saladin, whose death he describes very beautifully, and thus apostrophizes him: —

> "O capitan gallardo en experiencia
> Ingenio, industria, y fuerza el mas dichoso
> De tu edad, en que hiciste competencia
> A tanto Rey y Principe famoso!
> Si añadieras, o Persa, a la excelencia
> De tu valor heroyco y generoso
> El ser Christiano, ahora merecieras
> Que de los de tu edad el mejor fueras."
>
> Lib. xx. st. 35.

Perhaps Saladin ought to be treated as the hero of the poem. He conquers Jerusalem at the beginning, holds it till he dies, and it is not retaken at the end.

Jerusalem Conquistada is in volumes xiv. and xv., and *La Dragontea* in vol. iii. of Lope's *Obras Sueltas*, 4to, Madrid, 1776.   H. B. C.
U. U. Club.

GREEK CHURCH (3rd S. vii. 134, 190, 202.)—I cannot complain of the Editor's putting a stop to discussion on this subject; but it should in fairness have been stopped earlier. A correspondent asked some questions respecting it, which I answered briefly, and with scrupulous avoidance of any approach to controversy. But I was regularly called to account by another correspondent for my statements; and he also made some new assertions, which I could not admit. I wrote a very temperate reply in vindication of my statements, and a very short refutation of my opponent's assertions: and now I am refused admission; and these things will be allowed to go forth in "N. & Q." far and wide, without any contradiction. This is not fair. Either the communication of REV. MR. DENTON should have been declined, or a temperate answer to it should have been allowed, before the discussion was editorially closed.   F. C. H.

[We are sorry to have appeared guilty of injustice to our valued Correspondent; but We are satisfied that, even at the cost of that *apparent* injustice, We adopted the right course in stopping a controversy unsuited to the columns of "N. & Q."]

ROCKETS IN WARFARE (3rd S. vii. 189.)—Will A. A. allow me to say that he is a little mistaken in supposing that rockets "have fallen out of use," and that they were not used in the Russian war? The 6- and 12-pounders are still used for field service, and the 24-pounder for siege purposes. They were certainly employed both by the English and French armies in the Crimea, though at the battle of the Alma the rocket practice was unsatisfactory. I do not recollect having seen any mention of them in the accounts of the recent battles in America, but I should be surprised to find that so formidable a weapon had been unemployed by either of the belligerents.   J. WOODWARD.

New Shoreham. ·

BELFAST PRINTING (3rd S. vii. 194.) — I have nothing to say about the *Blow Bible*, but should MR. PINKERTON not be aware of it, he may like to hear that James Blow continued to gratify the Scoto-Irish love for Scottish poetry by publishing—

"The Life and Acts of the most famous and valiant Champion, Sir W. Wallace, Knight of Ellerslie, Maintainer of the Liberty of Scotland," &c. Belfast, printed by James Blow, and are to be sold at his Shop. 1728.

a beautiful copy of which I possess. How long he continued printing I know not; but in 1741 Saml. Wilson and Jas. Magee were ministering in like manner to the prevailing tastes, as I have

The Whigg's Supplication, by Sam. Colvill, a neat 24mo, published by them in that year. At the end of this is a list of "Books lately printed by and for them," in which is one in the same line of literature, *The History of Sir Eger, Sir Grahame, and Sir Gray Steel,* a copy of which I should like to hear of. Your correspondent is no doubt right about the improbability of two *Davie Lindsays* having issued from the Belfast press in 1714. The copy in the British Museum corresponds exactly with the one he describes.   J. O.

S. DECHARMES (3rd S. vii. 133.) — I do not find the date of Simon Decharmes' arrival in England, but in 1696 a Simon Decharmes was married at the Chapel of Le Quarré to Elene Dieu. In 1725 a Judith Decharmes was married at the French Chapel in Hungerford Market to Jean La Sage. The name is very uncommon, and must not be confused with the numerous *Deschamps*. Should G. G. desire Simon's parentage or place of business he had better look at the Register of Le Quarré, at Somerset House.   JOHN S. BURN.
The Grove, Henley.

MUNGO AS A CHRISTIAN NAME (3rd S. vii. 135.) I think that some of the Glasgow readers of "N. & Q." must be rather surprised at seeing this name mentioned as if especially belonging to the Highlands. The name Mungo is formed from the epithet by which St. Kentigern, the patron saint of Glasgow and founder of that bishoprick, is often known. This Kentigern is, according to the British or Welsh spelling of his name, Cyndëyrn; he was the son of Owain the son of Urien Rheged. The designation which he received because of his amiable disposition was Mwyngu (gently dear), which has been converted into Mungo.

"When he grew up he founded the bishoprick of Glasgow, or as the Welsh writers term the place, Penryn Rhionydd; but after a time the dissensions of his countrymen forced him to retire to Wales, where he was kindly received by St. David. While he remained in Wales he founded another bishoprick at Llanelwy (St. Asaph) in Flintshire, about A.D. 550." — Professor Rees's *Welsh Saints,* 261-2.

Cyndëyrn was afterwards recalled to Glasgow, which see he resumed after resigning Llanelwy to one of his companions called Asaph, whose name remains as the permanent English (and Latin) designation of the see, which the Welsh still know as Llanelwy. In the sixth century the language of the south of Scotland was certainly Cymric, a dialect cognate with the Welsh, if not identical. Thus there can be no surprise that Cyndëyrn Mwyngu should be equally at home as to language in Wales as in his own native Scotland. Of the Welsh authors of the sixth century Aneurin and Merddin Wyllt belonged to what is now Scotland, and Llywarch Hên was a Cumbrián. It is in connection with the north that Cyndëyrn is mentioned in the Triads. May I venture

to correct an expression used by the Editor of "N. & Q." (p. 136) who calls the Triads "metrical"?—they are plain prose, and many embody historical facts of great value. Besides the Triads, in the remains of early Cymric literature, there are several collections of *metrical triplets*, but these things are wholly distinct from each other.
                                                    LAELIUS.

LANCASHIRE: OLD TIMBER HALLS (3rd S. vii. 76, 144.)—Your correspondent, H. FISHWICK, has incorrectly stated the succession to the property of Clayton Hall. It passed to Mordecai Greene in right of his wife, Miss Chetham, and was inherited by their only child James Greene, at whose death the lands at Clayton Hall and elsewhere were divided amongst his daughters; and Clayton Hall fell to the lot of Arabella (the second daughter), wife of Peter Richard Hoare, of Kelsey Park, Kent, in whose possession it still remains.
                                         GEO. E. FRERE.
Roydon Hall, Diss.

LORD WILLOUGHBY (3rd S. vii. 96.) — Collins, in speaking of Robert Bertie, who, in 1715, was created Duke of Ancaster, expresses himself as follows: —

"His Grace married to his first wife, July 30th, 1678, Mary, daughter to Sir Richard Wynn, of Gwedier, in the county of Caernarvon, Bart., who dying September 20th, 1689, left issue two sons and two daughters." — *Peerage* (1812), vol. ii. p. 21.

This Robert, afterwards Duke of Ancaster, was the eldest son of Robert Bertie, third Earl of Lindsey, and at the time of his marriage with the daughter of Sir Richard Wynn, he bore his father's second title, that of *Lord Willoughby of Eresby*.

The foregoing statement will, I think, enable SIR THOMAS WINNINGTON to extricate himself from the manifold inaccuracies with which he has been perplexed.

I avail myself of the opportunity of drawing the attention of your readers to a singular circumstance in the descent of the title of Lord Willoughby of Parham. Charles, the second baron, who died in 1603, had six sons. The title descended in the line of the eldest son till the death of Charles, the tenth baron, in 1679. The line of the eldest son of the second baron having then become extinct, Thomas Willoughby, who traced his descent from the *fifth* son, was allowed the barony on the supposition—which turned out to be erroneous—that the issue male of all the elder brothers was extinct. The title, however, descended in the line of the *fifth* son, till that line became extinct on the death of Hugh, fifteenth baron, in 1765.

On his death, Henry Willoughby, who traced his descent from the *third* son of the second baron, claimed the dignity, which was ultimately adjudged to him, and he took his seat in the House of Peers, April 25, 1767.

It thus appears that the issue of the *third* son had been kept out of their right for nearly a century. ' What was there to prevent their making their claim during that time?

STAFFORD CAREY.

ARUNDEL OF LANHERNE (3rd S. vi. 248, 523; vii. 167.)—TRETANE, in his note last referred to, mentions Humphry Arundell, the leader of the Cornish Insurgents of 1549, as the brother of Sir John Arundel of Lanherne, and the son of Sir Thomas, by Catherine daughter of Sir John Dinham. This is unquestionably a mistake. He was the son of Roger Arundell, of Helland, near Bodmin, by Johanna, daughter and heiress of Humphry Culwoodleigh of East Stodleigh, and of Culwoodleigh in Devon, son and heir of Thomas C. by the daughter and heir of Otho Colyn of Helland. Humphry Culwoodleigh died 15th Nov. 12 Hen. VIII., when Johanna, the wife of Roger Arundell, was declared to be his heir (her brother, William C. having died previously). (*Inq. post mortem,* 12 & 13 Henry VIII.) Roger Arundell died 12 June, 28 H. VIII., when Humphry Arundell was declared to be his heir, and to be of the full age of twenty-three years and more. (*Inq. p .m.* 27 & 28 H. VIII.) Johanna, widow of Roger Arundell, died Sept. 29 H. VIII., when her son Humphry Arundell was declared to be her heir, and to be of the age of twenty-four years and more. (*Inq. p. m.* 30 H. VIII.) The Manor of Culwoodleigh, in Devon and Hellands, and other manors and estates in Cornwall held by Humphry Arundell were, of course, forfeited upon his attainder, and were granted to Sir Gawen Carew for his zeal in suppressing the rebellion. (*Pat. Rolls,* 4 Edw. VI. p. 6.) Hals says that Humphry Arundell was of the Lanherne family. I should be very glad if TRETANE can connect Roger A., Humphry's father, with that family; and I shall be pleased to hear from him privately, if he will do me the favour to write direct.

JOHN MACLEAN.

Hammersmith.

CONFIRMATIONS OF ARMS (3rd S. vii. 65.)—I must apologise to MIDDLE TEMPLAR for not complying sooner with his request. In the first case, the party wants his arms confirmed and his crest altered. Dalton, Norroy, recites the arms and crest hitherto used, and changes the crest. In the second case, the applicant wants his arms confirmed and a crest granted, he not having one. Dalton confirms the arms and grants a crest without any make believe that he is only confirming that appendage. Both documents are dated 1560, and *both families* are registered as bearing arms in *the Visitation of* 1583.

Heralds required positive proof, when this could be given. If the first grant had been lost, a confirmation would be the next best thing. And as the original grant, if existing, would be with the head of the family, confirmations would be of great importance to the younger' branches, as saving them from the trouble of going over all their proofs again whenever the Herald went his rounds. Hence the number of these documents.

P. P.

DUKE OF BUCKINGHAM (3rd S. vii. 94.)—In the Gallery at Hampton Court Palace, your correspondent X. will find two portraits of the Duke of Buckingham, described by the late Mrs. Jameson in her *Guide to the Public Galleries,* 1845, as No. 197:—

" The family of George Villiers, 1st Duke of Buckingham, by Honthorst. The Duke is seated; on his right is his Dutchess (Lady Katherine Manners), and another lady in a rich dress (probably his sister Lady Denbigh), on the left his mother (Mary Beaumont, widow of Sir Geo. Villiers, created 1618 Countess of Buckingham for life). Two men in black are standing by. There are three children, the youngest of whom is his son, afterwards the witty Duke of Buckingham, the favorite of Charles II., who was born 1627, consequently this picture must have been painted just before the Duke was assassinated by Felton, 1628.

" It was in King James's Collection, and is engraved in Jesse's *Memoirs of the Stuarts.*"

The other picture is described as " No. 652 by C. Jansen; Villiers, 1st Duke of Buckingham, half-length in the robes of the Garter."

ALBERT BUTTERY.

TITHE BARNS (3rd S. vii. 137, 163.)—

" The Devil's Barns in Hell are filled as full of the *damned* souls of those that have defrauded God's ministers of their maintenance as the Tythe-Robber's Barns, Houses, and Purses have bin and are filled with unjust gain."—Richard Culmer, in his *Lawles Tythe-Robbers Discovered: who make Tythe-Revenue a mock Tythe-mayntenance.*" London, 1655, 4to (pp. 39, and one leaf.)

Culmer appears to have been a hot-headed and eccentric man, and he wore blue in opposition to black, and was hence dubbed " Blue Dick of Thanet," and MR. STUART will find the parson's side of the case urged in the above tract with some vigour and more asperity. The "generation and spawn of unconscionable men!" as he terms the farmers, had no doubt something to say on the other side, but for this your correspondent must look elsewhere.

A. CHALLSTETH.

1, Verulam Buildings.

CHURCH OF ENGLAND AND IRELAND (3rd S. vii. 160.)—O. T. D. asks whether the reformed Churches were so designated under Henry VIII.? In Part III. of the valuable *State Papers* of that reign, p. 564, he will find " The Church of Inglande and Ierlande" treated as the official designation of that church, of which the King was " Supreme Hedde in yerthe immediate under Godd."

S. P. V.

This matter has been ventilated with the most satisfactory results. It only remains to embrace

Mr. Power's offer of further references, that shall show how far back the identity of the English and Irish Churches has been assumed.

A reference to the *Bullarium Magnum*, or kindred publications inaccessible here, might possibly prove that in the time of Henry II., or at any period intervening between his date and that of the Reformation, the Popes recognised the Church of the Pale, at least, as one with the Roman Catholic established Church of England.

O. T. D.

CLASSICAL WASHERWOMAN (3rd S. vii. 34.)—My son reminds me that this is a translation of the chorus beginning 'Ωκεανοῦ τις ὕδωρ in the *Hippolytus* of Euripides, line 121.

E. H. A.

COLOURS IN HERALDRY (3rd S. vii. 191, &c.)—A Nurenberg Wappenbuch (1605) in my possession marks the sable only, and that with lines in any direction; in fact shades the sable, giving no other distinction between the metals or tinctures. When the field is sable the lines are always horizontal, and in one or two cases crossed with a few perpendicular scratches; when an ordinary is sable it is marked by lines which vary according to its size or shape, generally with slanting lines drawn from its dexter to its sinister side.

JOHN DAVIDSON.

HYMNOLOGY (3rd S. vii. 180.)—I have not seen the hymn-book mentioned by D. Y., but from what he quotes of No. 61 there is, I think, reason to suppose that it is taken from No. 19 of the "*Translations and Paraphrases in Verse of several Passages of Sacred Scripture*, made under authority of the Church of Scotland, and used in it and the other Presbyterian Churches in that country." That to which I have referred begins as follows, and is a paraphrase of Isaiah, chap. ix. 2nd to 8th verses:—

> "The race that long in darkness pined
> Have seen a glorious light,
> The people dwell in day, who dwelt
> In death's surrounding night;
> To hail thy rise thou better sun,
> The gath'ring nations come
> Joyous as when the reapers bear
> The harvest treasures home."

These beautiful translations of the Scotch Church are transferred to various hymn-books used in English Established and Dissenting Churches, sometimes entire, often injured by attempts to improve them, but in no case which I have seen is any acknowledgement made of the source from which they are taken—a want of candour not to have been expected.

G.

Edinburgh.

"HYMNS ANCIENT AND MODERN" (3rd S. vii. 179.)—Hymn 20 is from the Parisian breviary, and is of course many centuries old. The English words are by the Rev. Isaac Williams, but are somewhat altered from his translation. The tune in the *Ancient and Modern* collection is "Innocents."

D. Y.

JACKSTONES (3rd S. vii. 34, 143.)—In reply to the last query of SIR J. EMERSON TENNENT, the term *jackey*-stones is quite common in Cumberland and Westmoreland. In Yorkshire the pebbles are called jacks and five-stones. The game is played in Durham and Northumberland under the name of chucks, and as to chuck anything in those counties means to throw or toss it, the suggestion in the second query is probably correct. There is, however, a curious application of the word jackey, both in the north of England and in Scotland to a pocket knife, such a knife being called a jackeylegs knife. Do any of your numerous readers know the origin of the expression?

J. WETHERELL.

"WHAT'S IN A NAME?" (3rd S. vii. 115.)—How would our Literary Artillerymen like to call themselves the *Pennyroyals*, or to band themselves together for the defence of their country under the title of the *Press*-Gang, their motto being "All right," or "write," as they might choose to spell it?

ST. SWITHIN.

"MORS MORTIS MORTI," ETC. (2nd S. ix. 445, 513.) The distich annexed, whose author was inquired for in vain some years ago, is inscribed on the tomb of the Twemlow family in Witton churchyard, Northwich, co. Chester; and is said to have been the composition of the late incumbent, the Rev. —— Littler. (See Grocott's *Familiar Quotations*.)

There is an immaterial difference between the lines given by W. B. and the subjoined. W. B.'s version reading *dedisset* for *dedisses*:—

> "Mors mortis morti nisi morte dedisses,
> Æternæ vitæ janua clausa foret."

JOHN WOODWARD.

New Shoreham.

SEA SERPENT (3rd S. vii. 178.)—A friend going some short time ago on a trip in a yacht in the north of Scotland, saw what he thought was the undoubted sea serpent. There was a long succession of undulations of a black substance swimming in the sea, and extending several hundred yards. The motion was exactly like the up and down contortions of a snake or eel, certain portions alternately appearing above, and sinking beneath the waves. His friends smiled, and steered towards the object, which gradually developed itself as a number of porpoises following (as often is their custom) closely in the wake of each other, and swimming in a straight line much as wild ducks fly. Their alternate pitching, head and tail, gave so exactly the appearance of the wriggling motion of a huge snake that my friend says it was a considerable time before he could possibly believe that it was not one long animal. He is firmly of opinion that

similar appearances have given rise to the story of the Great Sea Serpent.   A. A.
Poets' Corner.

HERALDIC (3ʳᵈ S. vii. 95.) — There is no doubt a misprint as to the first coat. It should probably be "bordé componé de mesme." The blason would then be quarterly gu. and or, a fess quarterly counter-changed within a bordure gobonated of the same.

It should be remembered in delineation that the bordure should pass round the ends of the fess as well as the sides.

The second coat may be tricked thus—Draw a line across the shield as per fess. Below this, at the width of a fess, draw another line potentée. The blazon will be—A fess abased potentée of Champagne towards the point. The peculiar potent of Champagne may be seen in Bouton, Nouveau Traité de Blason, p. 199 (Paris, 1863.) See also Berry, art. "Potentée," and vol. iii. pl. xv. fig. 27.   A. A.
Poets' Corner.

SOBRIQUETS OF REGIMENTS (3ʳᵈ S. vii. 5, 168.) Perhaps some one of your numerous readers may be able to afford me information, not of the sobriquet, but the proper patronymic of the 25th regiment of foot. This regiment is said to have been originally raised in Edinburgh, and to have at first borne the name of that city; but, according at least to what I have often heard, the authorities there having prohibited it beating for recruits within their bounds, Lord George Lennox, who was its colonel for about forty years, felt so displeased that he got permission to change the name. I observe from almanacs in my possession, that it was named "Sussex," at least from 1781 till 1807, when it appears as the "King's Own," which name it retained till 1818, when it is styled "The King's Own Borderers," by which it is still designated; but in 1833 it got permission to wear on its colours the arms of Edinburgh with their motto, "Nisi Dominus frustra," and continues to do so.

This shows the pro a it of its having at first borne the name of the city; and possibly some of your correspondents may have access to Army Lists previous to 1781 (beyond which the almanacs I have do not go back) which may bear on the point, and may be able too to confirm the explanation I have heard, and stated above, as to the reason of the change of name.   G.
Edinburgh.

If MR. WOODWARD will refer more carefully to page 5 of this volume, he will find that the statements there made originated with a General Officer in Her Majesty's service, and not with JUVERNA, who only quoted the General's letter written fourteen years since. The statement relative to the Queen's Royal Regiment, inserted at page 49,

originated with the Naval and Military Gazette newspaper, and MR. WOODWARD will find it at p. 652 of the number of that journal which was published on October 8, 1853. According to Mr. Cannon's Historical Record of the 2nd or Queen's Royal Regiment, page 2, this regiment "was designated 'the Queen's;' and the Paschal Lamb, the distinguishing badge of Portugal, was placed on its colours, and has ever since continued to be borne by the regiment." I have seen a statement in print that this badge was granted to the regiment in consequence of its having been a Guard of Honour to Queen Catherine, Infanta of Portugal, wife of King Charles the Second, on her progress to London on the occasion of her marriage.
JUVERNA.

THE PASCHAL LAMB IN THE ARMS OF PORTUGAL (3ʳᵈ S. vii. 5, 168.)—When the arms of Portugal are represented in full, with crest and dragon supporters, the chain of the Order of Christ hangs round the shield, from behind which the points of a cross are seen. This is the cross of the Order of Christ, and in all probability has the Paschal Lamb on it; but as I have never seen more than its points, I am unable to say for certain whether it is so or not. The earliest account I can find of this order is (in the words of my book) "Heinrich der Seefahrer Grossmeister des Christ-ordens, 1415," son of John I. of Portugal.
JOHN DAVIDSON.

YEW TREES CALLED PALMS (3ʳᵈ S. vii. 96, 167.) Is there not some little error in CYWRM's communication? Palm Sunday has only preceded the 17th March four times during the last eighty years—viz. in 1788, 1845, and 1856, when it was on the 16th March, and in 1818 when it was on the 15th March.   THOMAS LEWIS.
Dover.

"GOD US AYDE" (3ʳᵈ S. vii. 153.)—This motto, with the cipher "I. N.," is on one of the bells of Rylstone church. See Canto VII. of Wordsworth's White Doe of Rylstone.   CUTHBERT BEDE.

THE QUEEN'S MARIES (3ʳᵈ S. vii. 60, 166.)— In the latter notice (p. 166) G. gives three verses as the only three verses which are preserved. This seems a mistake. I refer to Robert Chambers's Scottish Ballads, printed by William Tait, 78, Princes Street, Edinburgh, 12mo, p. 120, "Marie Hamilton." Where many more verses are given, and much information respecting them, and many references to authorities.   J. Ss.

SCARLETT FAMILY OF SUSSEX (2ⁿᵈ S. x. 196; xi. 192; 3ʳᵈ S. i. 231, 299.) — The first notice of this name is also to be found in the same list of Pevensey freemen, in 1342, as John "Schakelot." They remained at Pevensey till the time of Elizabeth, if not later.   WM. DURRANT COOPER.

St. Mary Rouncival (3rd S. vi. 329.) — Sundry lands that belonged to the Guild of our Lady of Rouncival were granted by Edw. VI. on Nov. 16, in the sixth year of his reign, to Edward, Lord Clinton, and Lord Saye. In my *History of Deptford* (p. 148), I have given reference to Augmentation Off. Box G. 34.

Dartford.   Alfred John Dunkin.

Miscellaneous.

NOTES ON BOOKS, ETC.

History of the Reformation of the Church of England. By Gilbert Burnet, D.D., Bishop of Salisbury. *A New Edition carefully revised, and the Records collated with the Originals. By* Nicholas Pocock, M.A., late Michel Fellow of Queen's College. *7 Volumes.* (Oxford: Clarendon Press.)

When Burnet published the first part of this book in 1680, the thanks of both Houses of Parliament were voted to him. Nay, the Commons did more: they desired him "to proceed with, and complete, that good work begun, in writing and publishing 'The History of the Reformation of the Church of England.'" Though it may perhaps be doubted whether a similar vote would now receive the sanction of either Lords or Commons, the work has assumed such a position among Standard Historical Books, as to justify all the pains which a judicious editor could bestow upon it. The Delegates of the Clarendon Press have therefore shown good judgment in issuing a new and carefully-revised edition of it. Seven years have been devoted by Mr. Pocock to a task which he had originally supposed he might have accomplished in two ; while every page furnishes evidence of his industry, the list of corrigenda and addenda which appears in the seventh volume shows that, like a true scholar, Mr. Pocock has been more anxious to make the book as complete as possible than "to spare," to use his own words, "his own reputation as an editor." Another point for which Mr. Pocock deserves high commendation, is the facilities which, by means of precise references, he has afforded to the critics to discover whether he has committed any errors either of copying or of any other description. How numerous were the errors in former editions one short fact will show: — In the *Catalogue of Resignations* from the Augmentation Office, the errors averaged one in every line.

The seventh volume of the present edition contains an elaborate preface by the editor occupying nearly 250 pages, in which he exhibits a view of the literary history of the book, its origin, its gradual progress, the various collections of MSS. which Burnet made use of, the assistance which he received, and the criticisms which he provoked — all which points the editor has investigated with much care and patience. This is followed by the *Corrigenda* and *Addenda*, to which we have already referred. We have then a *Chronological Index of the Documents* used by Burnet, an Index drawn up at the suggestion of one who well knows the value of such aids to students, the Rev. J. S. Brewer ; and thus by a *General Index* to the whole book (adapted from the good index compiled for the edition of 1829) which occupies no less than 329 pages.

Such is the new edition of Burnet's work, which, though it can never be considered an adequate account of the Reformation in this country, must, with its Records

and Strype's Ecclesiastical Memorials, which are a supplement to it, be used as the groundwork by any one who may hereafter undertake to write the Church History of the period, and be consulted by all who are at all interested in the history of those eventful times. It is scarcely necessary for us to add, that Burnet can only hereafter be safely consulted in the edition for which we are indebted to the learning and industry of Mr. Pocock, — an edition which must at once take its place in every library which claims to be considered as approaching completeness in the department of English History.

The Autograph Souvenir. A Collection of Autograph Letters, interesting Documents, &c., executed in Facsimile by F. G. Netherclift. *With Letter-press Transcriptions, and occasional Translations, &c. By* Richard Sims. *Part XII.* (Netherclift.)

This twelfth part of *The Autograph Souvenir* contains autographs of the Cardinal de Lorraine ; St. Vincent de Paul ; Katherine, Duchess of Buckingham ; George Villiers, Duke of Buckingham ; Henry, Prince of Wales ; Louis XIV., and General Delambre. This completes the first volume of this very interesting and ably executed collection. The title-page, index, and dedication to the Prince of Wales, are issued with the present part.

Artemus Ward, his Book. With Notes and a Preface, by the Editor of the "Biglow Papers." (Hotten.)

A series of short papers replete with humour, but disfigured by that intermixture of sacred allusions which characterises the writings of too many modern humorists, especially among our American brethren. Mr. Hotten, who has edited the volume, ingeniously attempts to derive this peculiarity from the old Puritans.

Notices to Correspondents.

Mr. Keightley's "Shakespeare Expositor." — *We have received another Letter from Mr. Keightley reiterating his assertion, that the publication of this work was a part of the scheme connected with his edition of Shakespeare. But if We insert Mr. K.'s letter, Messrs. Bell and Daldy will claim to be heard in reply ; and We cannot afford space in "* N. & Q." *for such a controversy.*

T. D. Dyer. *Similar stories of persons being "kept above ground" are current everywhere.*

W. T. *should consult vols. vii. viii. and ix. of our First Series respecting the line —* "Could we with ink the ocean fill."

W. R. Tate. *The coins are of no value.*

P. S. C. *will find references to Demosthenes' praise of Action in our* 2nd S. vi. 114, 115.

T. C. H. F. *"What will Mrs. Grundy say ?" is a phrase which occurs repeatedly in Morton's comedy, Speed the Plough.*

D. *will find some notices of artificial teeth among the Romans in "* N. & Q." 2nd S. xii. 417, 481.

R. C. L. *The book was written in sober earnestness. The author, a man of learning, was convinced of the truth of his theory.*

Mr. Wilkins *will find specimens of early Naval terms in a Military and Sea Dictionary of which the 4th edition was published in 1711.*

Errata. — 3rd S. vii. p. 230, col. 1. line 1, *for* "other sentiments" *read* "higher sentiments;" p. 222 col. 1. line 20, *for* "Norwich" *read* "Nonsuch."

A Reading Case for holding the weekly Nos. of " N. & Q." *is now ready, and may be had of all Booksellers and Newsmen, price 1s. 6d.; or, free by post, direct from the publisher, for 1s. 8d.*

*** *Cases for binding the volumes of "* N. & Q." *may be had of the Publisher, and of all Booksellers and Newsmen.*

"Notes and Queries" *is published at noon on Friday, and is also issued in* Monthly Parts. *The Subscription for* Stamped Copies *for Six Months forwarded direct from the Publisher (including the Half-yearly* Index) *is 11s. 4d., which may be paid by Post Office Order, payable at the Strand Post Office, in favour of* William G. Smith, 32, Wellington Street, Strand, W.C., *where also all* Communications for the Editor *should be addressed.*

"Notes & Queries" *is registered for transmission abroad.*

LONDON, SATURDAY, APRIL 1, 1865.

CONTENTS.—N° 170.

Notes.

REMARKS ON THE ORIGIN OF "COLD HARBOUR."

In different parts of England, Ireland, and America we still meet with the name of *Cold Harbour*
given to places, farms, lanes, &c. Persons not acquainted with the etymology of this expression,
and who only think of *harbour* in its more restricted signification of a *port* for shipping, are
generally at a loss to understand how "Cold Harbour" can be found in the middle of a wood or on
the top of a mountain. This apparent anomaly
is, however, easily explained if we trace the word
back to its origin and original application.

In old English writers we frequently meet with
a place called "Cold Harbour," often corrupted
into Coal or Cole Harbour, and which, according
to Nares, was an ancient mansion situated in Dowgate or Down-gate Ward, London. This place
was the residence of Tunstall, Bishop of Durham,
in the reign of Henry VIII., when probably it
obtained the privileges of a sanctuary,* and was
pulled down by Earl Gilbert about the year 1600.
At an earlier period, in a grant of Henry IV., it is
called "quoddam hospicium, sive placeam, voca-
tum le Cold Herbergh." Now *herbergh* is an old
Germanic word, introduced into the English language from the Anglo-Saxon.

* The tenaments being afterwards built on the spot,
which thus well, being a protection to persons in debt.

In Ettmüller's *Lexicon Anglosaxonicum* we find,
"*Hereberge*, statio militaris, hospitium." In Graff's
Althochdeutscher Sprachschatz (Old High German
dictionary), we have—"*heriberga*, from *heri*, an
army, and *bergan*, to cover, to shelter—hospitium,
statio, castra." In the present German, *herberge*
signifies an inn, &c.; with which compare mediæval Latin, *herebergum*; Span. *albergue*; Ital. *al-
bergo*; Fr. *auberge*.

Our English word *harbour*, therefore, meant
originally a military station, a shelter, a retreat;
and *Cold Harbour*—cold, from Anglo-Saxon *ceald*,
cald—now signifies nothing more than a cold
abode, a cold retreat, the primitive signification
of the word *harbour* being still kept up in the
present English, as is easily seen by opening
Walker, where we find—"*Harbour*, a lodging, a
place of entertainment, a port or haven for shipping, an asylum, a shelter."

The transition form of our word from *herbergh*,
as found in the grant of Henry IV., to our present
harbour, was *herborow* or *herborw*. The Germanic
gutterals *g*, *k*, preceded by *z*, softened down under
the influence of the Norman-French to *ow* (e. g.
Germ. *Mark*, *Sorge*; Eng. *marrow*, *sorrow*); and
the form *herborw* is to be met with in Tyrwhitt's
note to v. 342 of the Prologue to Chaucer's *Canterbury Tales*, where T. says:—

"St. Julian was eminent for providing his votaries with
good lodgings and accommodation of all sorts. In the
title of his Legende, MS. Bod. 1596, fol. 4, he is called
'St. Julian, the gode herberjour.' It ends thus:—

"'Therefore, yet to this day thei that ever lond wende,
Thei biddeth Seint Julian anon that gode *herborw* he
hem sende,'" &c.

The proper name Cold Harbour was no doubt
brought over to England by our Saxon ancestors,
for Germany has also its Cold Harbours up to the
present day. About four German miles south of
Aix-la-Chapelle there is a village called Kaltherher-
berg, which is proverbially known in those parts as
one of the coldest, most dreary, and dismal places
any one can possibly imagine, being situated in the
middle of the forest of the Eifel, where snow lies
during the whole of the winter.

In the southern part of the Grand Duchy of
Baden, in a mountainous country, there is a large
farm called Kalteherberg situated about 1750 feet
above the level of the sea, also a small village,
Kaltenherberg, near Lörrach, on an elevated spot.
Having lived chiefly abroad I am not acquainted
with the different Cold Harbours in England; but
from a passage in Hall, quoted by Nares, the London Mansion Cold Harbour was a cold place; and
a friend of mine tells me there is a Cold Harbour
farm near Exeter, situated on the brow of a hill,
and much exposed to wind and weather.* The
German Cold Harbours in the Eifel and Baden,

* On the road to Holcomb Burnell from Ide.

are all very cold places, so that I very much suspect that wherever we may meet with other Cold Harbours, whether in England or Germany, we shall find them all in refreshing situations. I mention this particularly to show that *cold* is the Anglo-Saxon *ceald, cald;* Germ. *kalt = frigidus,* and by no means an old Celtic word, with an unknown signification, as some persons have been led to believe.

An interesting paper might be written on this proper name, and I much regret only being able to offer the above few remarks, not having the necessary works of reference at my command to enter into a fuller investigation of the subject.

J. C. HAHN, Ph. D.

Heidelberg.

P.S. There is a Cold Harbour Lane at present at Brixton. Dowgate was granted for ever, so Mr. Lodge says, to the College of Heralds by King Richard III., who had lately granted them their charter; and Henry VII., willing to annul every public act of his predecessor, gave it to the then Earl of Shrewsbury.

In Ben Jonson (*Silent Woman*, Act I. Sc. 3) we find —

"Or its knighthood shall do worse, take sanctuary in Cole Harbour sanctuary and fast."

"Here is that ancient modell of Cole Harbour, bearing the name of the 'Prodigall's Promontorie,' and being as a sanctuary for banquerupt detters."—Healy's *Discovery of a New World*, p. 182.

HERCULES IN DANTE'S "DIVINE COMEDY."

To those who know the diligence with which Dante studied the classical mythology (especially as illustrated in Virgil's sixth Æneid), and the subtlety with which he expounded it, it will not be uninteresting to consider whether he has visibly introduced the majestic shade of Hercules, to whose exploits, in connexion with the Centaurs, Cacus, Antæus, and the rocks at the entrance of the Mediterranean, he has so many striking references. I think he has introduced him; and I should be obliged to any of your correspondents who can inform me whether this opinion has yet been propounded and discussed.

When Virgil and Dante have traversed half the infernal circles (see cantos viii. and ix.), they reach the city of Dis; corresponding historically to the defences of Tartarus in the Æneid (mœnia Ditis), and morally to the barrier between sins of infirmity (*incontinentia*) and sins of perversity (*bestialitas, malitia*). Here a troop of fiends shut the gates in their faces, and Virgil remains outside awaiting help from a higher power. The Furies appear on a tower, threatening to call up the Medusa; which makes it likely that Dante was acquainted with the 11th Odyssey, where Ulysses, amid his communings with the spirits of heroes, stops short

in fear that Proserpine will make the dreadful Gorgonian head appear to him. Then a mighty form, whom Virgil has been awaiting, comes to the rescue. The choleric spirits plunged in Styx flee before him. The Demons and the Furies are seen no more. He reaches the gate, "appearing full of disdain;" opens it by a touch of a wand, and retires without noticing the two poets—after he has rebuked the powers of Hell for their vain resistance to the will of Omnipotence, and has, in conclusion, recalled to them the example of what Cerberus suffered through their obduracy : —

" Your Cerberus, if ye recollect it well,
Keeps yet therefrom his chin and throttle peeled."
(*Rossetti's Translation.*).

Now this deliverer ("sent from heaven," as we read,) has been considered as an angel; but Dante is less accustomed to feign angelic interpositions than those of human spirits; besides which, an angel need not have appeared disdainful or discourteous even in Hell, nor have —

" .   .   .   .   .   semblance made
Of a man whom other care constrains and bites,
Than that of him who is before his face."

Hence the late Professor Rossetti judged that we had here a spirit from Limbo, or a virtuous Pagan, who allegorically represented an important personage in Dante's own time. As a general view, I have no doubt that this opinion is perfectly correct; but I question the propriety of the added intimation that this spirit is specially, according to the letter, Julius Cæsar; because the conjuncture demands a man of physical strength, and not a general or an emperor. In brief, I think that he who here bursts the gate of Hell, is the same hero who long before performed a like exploit, according to the ancient poets; and the reference to Cerberus, which in the mouth of any other would be abrupt and uncouth, comes naturally from Hercules; who, with his own hands, chained the hell-hound after dragging it from under the throne of Pluto, as Virgil writes —

" Tartareum ille manu custodem in vincla petivit,
Ipsius a solio regis traxitque trementem."
Æn. vi. 395.

Dante may have seen more full and particular accounts of the transaction in Seneca's *Hercules Furens.*

It may seem strange that Hercules should not be expressly named in the canto; but we hear that Virgil gave Dante some explanations, which the latter's troubled feelings prevented him from bearing in remembrance.   C. B. C.

WORDS IN DALYELL'S "SCOTTISH POEMS."

At the end of the Glossary to this book, Dalyell gives a list of "Words imperfectly Understood." Many of these I fancy I can understand, but there are others of which I can make nothing : —

Hag matines.

".Their haly *hag matines* fast they [the priests] patter."
P. 189.

Can this have anything to do with "Hogmanay?"

Foster.

" The sisters gray before this day,
Did crune within their closter:
They feeit ane frier their keyis to beir,
The feind ressave the *foster* ;
Syne in the mirk he weill culd werk,
And kittil them wantonly."—P. 192.

Query, One who is over pampered, or one who is a guardian, or a rogue ? See Florio, s. v. "*Bricco*, a rogue, a *foist*, a nip."

Tinsell. (Kittie=wench, a name of contempt.)
" . . . . filthy speich and counsell
That she did heir of sum curst kittie *tinsell*."—P. 244.

Pluckup fair.—The *Sege of the Castel of Edinburgh*, by R. Sempill. "Lanuoy to the Ambassade," p. 299.

Half mark steikis.

" Vpone that spuilzie I will spend na tyme,

Sum gripit gold, and gat the thing he seikis ;

Sa gat thair handfull of thir *half mark steikis*,
Will have na mair within ane ẟeir nor we."
Ibid., p. 294.

Foundit (is an old word for *fed*, and a common word for *clothed*, but neither makes sense).
" [Prelattis] Makand thair godis of warldie gudis and geir,
The flock new *foundit*, and thay in furringis happit."
The Legend of the B. of Sanctandrois Lyfe, p. 303.

Tottis, adj. ; *Kelt*, sub.

" Of *tottis* russet his ryding breikis ;
Ane hamelie hat, a cott of *kelt*,
Weill beltit in ane lethrone belt."—*Ibid.*, p. 327.

Cashmaries. (Query, *Cadge-mary*, possibly a name for a female pedler ?)
" Na mulettis thair his cofferis caries
Bot lyke a court of auld *cashmaries*,
Or cadyers ctiig to ane fair."—*Ibid.*, p. 328.

Bryde. (Query, *Brood*, family ?)

" Bot ay the mair this smatcher gettis
The closer garris he keip the yettis ;
Feiding his bellie, and his *bryde*
Begging and borrowing ay besyde."—*Ibid.*, p. 340.

Dysertis Duschet : Dussie. Ibid., pp. 312, 317
("Dussie"), 315.

Bedene. (Query, Offer, promise, *i. e.* of thy love to sinners ?)
" My lippes, Lord, then louse thou sall,
Whilke closed lang haue beene
From thy louing, sair bound in thrall,
Brekand thy sweit *bedene*."—*Ibid.*, p. 119.

I am quite sure of *all* the rest, but my notes are quite at the service of anyone who finds a difficulty with the interpretations.   J. D. CAMPBELL.

LETTERS OF THE STADTHOLDER JOHN DE WITT.

A very interesting and important work has recently been published, in Holland, by way of supplement to M. Groen van Prinsterer's *Archives, ou Correspondance inédite de la Maison d' Orange-Nassau.* It consists of an analysis of the letters in the Royal Library at the Hague, written in reference to the Act of Seclusion and its repeal; and of a very valuable essay, by M. J. W. Van Sypesteyn, on the state of Dutch-English politics from 1552 to 1688. Among the letters given in the Appendix are two, written confidentially, by the Stadtholder John de Witt (which have never before been published) to the Dutch Ambassador in London.

Whatever may be said — and much may with justice be said — of De Witt's complete statesmanship, these letters can scarcely fail to bear condemnatory witness to his time-serving state craft. I append copies of those letters for such of your readers as may feel any interest in a matter which even the researches and industry of Macaulay have not exhausted.

John de Witt to Louis of Nassau, Lord of Beverweerde, Ambassador in England : —

" Monsieur,
" Je m'assure que le Roi de la Grande Bretagne aura eu occasion de pénétrer au fonds de tout ce qui s'est passé à l'égard de l'acte de séclusion de Monsieur le Prince d'Orange en l'année 1654 ; et qu'il aura trouvé que non seulement l'on n'a donné aucune occasion de ce côté-ci pour disposer le feu protecteur à demander la dite séclusion, mais qu'au contraire les ministres de cet état, tant ceux qui étoient sur le lieu, que ceux qui participoient au maniement des affaires ici, ont fait toute la diligence et touts les devoirs possibles pour détourner cet esprit capricieux d'une si fâcheuse demande, et quoiqu'en ce regard il ne leur peut rester en leur particulier aucune inquiétude ni scrupule, et que Messeigneurs les E'tats d'Hollande et West-Frise, par une résolution publique se soient expliqués nettement sur la direction de cette affaire et en ayant déchargé absolument les dits ministres ; neanmoins, considérant qu'il y a encore des esprits qui par malice ou parceque le soupçon leur est naturel, tâchent de se persuader eux-mêmes, et de faire croix aux autres le contraire, et que l'on a fomenté cette affaire d'ici, ce me seroit une satisfaction particulière comme aussi à tous ceux qui participent au maniement des affaires, et que l'on peut tirer sans le même soupçon s'il plut à sa Majesté, renvoyant l'instrument de séclusion à Messeigneurs les E'tats d'Hollande, de donner ce témoinage de verité dans sa lettre de laquelle il accompagneroit le dit instrument. Et si vous trouvez moyen d'obtenir ce témoinage, vous aurez acquis une nouvelle obligation sur celui qui est et demeurera toujours," etc.

Copy of the letter (accompanying the foregoing) which De Witt requested the King of England to send, with the original Act of Exclusion, to the States of Holland. The request was not complied with by his majesty : —

" Hauts et puissants Seigneurs,
" Le Sieur de Beverweerde m'a donné part de votre résolution solennelle par laquelle il vous a plu déclarer

que l'acte de séclusion, touchant l'emploi du Prince d'Orange, mon nevew, dont je vous renvoie ici l'original, selon vos desirs, est et demeurera, à l'avenir mortifié et de nulle valeur, et comme ce m'a été une nouvelle preuve de la bienveillance et de l'affection que vous avez témoigné pour lui en plusieurs autres occasions, aussi ne m'a ce pas donné une moindre satisfaction d'avoir rencontré ici des occasions pour pénétrer au fonds du tout ce qui s'est passé à l'égard de la dite séclusion en l'année 1654; et surtout d'avoir eu cet éclaircissement, que non seulement de votre côté l'on n'a donné aucune occasion pour disposer ceux qui n'étant pas contents d'esperer ici leur domination, la tâchoient aussi d'étendre sur vous, à demander la dite séclusion; mais qu'au contraire vos ministres, tant ceux qui étoient ici sur le lieu, que ceux qui participoient au maniement des affaires chez vous, ont fait toute la diligence et touts les devoirs possibles pour détourner ces esprits capricieux d'ici d'une si fâcheuse demande.

" 1 Octobre, 1660."

C. H. Gunn.

Municipal Collegiate Institution,
　Amsterdam, March, 1865.

Original Portraits of John Wesley.—In 1790, the year before he died, John Wesley paid his last visit to Sunderland, in the county of Durham, and was the guest of Mr. Lipton, who resided in Green Street, Bishop Wearmouth. During his sojourn, he was prevailed upon by his host to sit for his portrait to Mr. Thomas Horsley, a local artist of considerable eminence (who studied under Romney), and from whose surviving son, Mr. Thomas John Horsley, also a Sunderland portrait-painter, I derive this information. Mr. Horsley, senior, then produced a *replica*, somewhat varied in detail, which now hangs in the large vestry of Sans Street Chapel. The first of these pictures remained in the family for which it was painted till a recent period, when it was presented to the Methodist Institution at Richmond, in Surrey. My father, who knew Mr. Wesley well, used frequently to tell me that the best likenesses of him were Romney's portrait, taken Monday, Jan. 5, 1789, and a bust of black porcelain, I believe by Wedgwood. The portrait made up by John Jackson, R.A., for the Methodist Conference from a series of likenesses of various dates, my father said conveyed no idea of the man. The Conference picture makes him look full-faced, portly, and rather tall; whereas Wesley, was meagre in feature, slender, and short of stature. The two Horsley portraits seem to have been the last taken from the life; and the late Mr. George Harrison, shipowner, of Sunderland, who stood at the Great Methodist's side, Sunderland Street, opposite the Pann Field, Bishop Wearmouth, when he preached to several thousands of people on Sunday evening, June 13th, 1790, frequently told me that Mr. Horsley's pictures were striking likenesses. Why not engrave one or both?

G. H. of S.

Dr. Bisset, Bishop of Raphoe.—In Mr. Fitzpatrick's *Memoirs of Archbishop Whately*, there is a statement at p. 169, vol i., which gives pain to the surviving relatives of Dr. Bisset, the Bishop of Raphoe, in 1831. Having referred to a report that the archbishoprick of Dublin had been declined by Dr. Bisset, Mr. Fitzpatrick says,—

" No offer of the see had been made to Dr. Bisset at all; but a translation to Derry, which fell vacant at the same time, was tendered to him, but which, owing to advanced age, he declined."

A friend of mine, who was nearly related to the bishop, and who passed some years of her life under his roof, has written to me to say, that there is not the shadow of a doubt but that the archbishoprick of Dublin was distinctly offered to Dr. Bisset; and, as indisputable evidence of that fact, the lady has in her possession an autograph letter of the bishop to herself, dated Sept. 24, 1831, mentioning the official letter which he had received tendering to him the see of Dublin, and his feelings that the arduous and important post could be better filled by a younger man, and that he had consequently declined it. The lady has also preserved a newspaper called *Stewart's Despatch*, which thus refers to the death of Bishop Bisset. After deploring the loss sustained by the diocese of Raphoe, the writer adds,—

" When the see of Dublin became vacant by the death of Archbishop Magee, the government offered to Dr. Bisset the vacant archiepiscopal dignity; but his lordship declined it, assigning as his reason the increasing and multiplying infirmities of age, and his anxious desire to spend his days among the clergy whom he knew and loved."

Additional evidence could be produced, but what has been placed is probably enough to show that Mr. Fitzpatrick was mistaken when he wrote the paragraph to which I have taken exception; and if you will allow this correction to appear in your columns, you will afford satisfaction to the feelings of my friend, and be doing justice to the memory of a prelate, to the appreciation of whose character such an offer as that of the archbishoprick of Dublin, affords a most distinguished testimony.

E. S. S. W.

Manual of Palæography.—Permit me to attach my signature to Prof. Masson's plea for a Palæographical Manual for English students. I know Wright's *Court Hand Restored*, which is a useful book; and I also know the two valuable manuals of M. Chassant, the *Paléographie*, and the *Dictionnaire des Abbréviations* mentioned by your correspondent. There is also a third work by the same author on the reading of " seals," &c. But we want more than we have—a comprehensive manual, which shall serve as a key to the writing of successive centuries in our own country; and which shall furnish an introduction to French, Italian, Spanish, and other documents not of modern date. The difficulty of decipherment leads to the neglect and destruction of many important records. I believe, therefore, that the compiler of such a work as M. Masson recommends would be a public benefactor; and if undertaken I shall give my name as a subscriber. B. H. C.

Coshering. — The Times, in its issue of March 11, says of this word—"Its derivation is more than doubtful." This may be true of London, but elsewhere its derivation is not doubted. The English verb "to cosher" is formed from cios, rent, and the offence under the statute was the levy of rent in kind or otherwise by those who had been, or who pretended to have been, dispossessed.
H. C. C.

Ship v. Sheep.—The agricultural pronunciation of the word sheep, which is sounded as ship, is common, I believe, to most English counties. I had imagined that the proverb about "spoiling a ship for a ha'porth of tar," referred to the sailing vessel; but a farmer, the other day, used it in my hearing, as applying to one of his sheep, and the tarring upon its back of his initials or private mark. "Losing a hog for a ha'porth of tar," is another variation of the proverb, given by Ray, and used in Northamptonshire and Yorkshire— the hog being the yearling sheep.
Cuthbert Bede.

Postage Stamps.—In a notice of the late William Humphrys, the engraver, in the Athenæum of Jan. 28 of this year, it is stated that—

" The well-known portraits of Queen Victoria, on the postage stamps, are all produced by mechanical multiplication from the one steel plate originally engraved by Humphrys."

I know not on what authority this statement is made, but it is erroneous. The plate in question was engraved by Frederick Heath, son of the celebrated engraver Charles Heath. Q.

St. Anne's Chapel on Caversham Bridge.— Tanner, p. 427, ed. 1744, mentions a patent of the 50th of Edw. III., by which was granted to the Canons of Nottely, in Buckinghamshire, the Chapel of St. Anne on Caversham Bridge, in which, says Dr. Loudon, one of the visitors in Henry VIII.'s time was a famous relict, being "An angel with one wing, which brought to Caversham the spear-head that pierced our Saviour on the cross."

The foundation of this chapel is still to be seen under the houses upon Caversham Bridge, and one of the arches is likewise remaining. The Canons of Nottely had probably a cell at Caversham, and the church itself was part of the endowment, as appears in the Monasticon, tom. ii. p. 154.

The ancient house close to the church now occupied by Mrs. Monck was built by Cardinal Wolsey, and still has great remains of antiquity.

One wing was taken down some years ago; the long gallery was converted into bed-rooms. The chapel I went to see some years ago under the centre arch of the bridge; the boatman kept his oars there, which prevented me going to the east end or ascertaining the length of it.
Julia R. Bockett.
Bradney, near Burghfield Bridge.

Cæsar a Grammarian.—The following paragraph, quoted by The Times, March 23, 1865, may interest some of your readers : —

" We are surprised to find no mention of his [Cæsar's] fondness for grammatical studies. On a point so illustrative of his inquisitiveness and versatility, we are glad to quote the words of Professor Max Müller : —

" ' We learn from a fragment of Cæsar's work, De Analogia, that he was the inventor of the term Ablative in Latin. The word never occurs before, and of course could not be borrowed, like the names of the other cases, from Greek grammarians, as they admitted no ablative in Greek. To think of Cæsar fighting the barbarians of Gaul and Germany, and watching from a distance the political complications at Rome, ready to grasp the sceptre of the world, and at the same time carrying on his philological and grammatical studies, together with his secretary, the Greek Didymus, gives us a new idea both of that extraordinary man and of the times in which he lived.' "
F. Phillott.

Queries.

WYVIL OF CONSTABLE BURTON.

The following queries respecting the ancient Norman family of Wyvil of Constable Burton, in the North Riding of Yorkshire, are asked, from no mere spirit of idle curiosity, or desire to pry into matters that do not concern me, but only to clear up some papers in my hands. I need not say I shall be greatly obliged to any one who can assist me.

Before putting the queries, it will be necessary to prefix some genealogical details.

Sir William Wyvil, fourth baronet of Constable Burton (born 1645), left two sons: Sir Marmaduke, fifth baronet, and D'Arcy. The line of Sir Marmaduke the fifth, failed in his grandson the seventh Sir Marmaduke; who died s. p. m. in 1774, when the succession reverted to the descendants of D'Arcy, second son of the fourth baronet as above.

D'Arcy Wyvil had two sons: 1st, William, who settled in America and left as Marmaduke, de jure, eighth baronet, on the death of Sir Marmaduke, seventh baronet above, in 1774; and 2nd, Edward, general supervisor of Excise at Edinburgh in 1737, who married Christian Catherine Clifton, daughter of William Clifton, Esq., Commissioner of Excise there, and left a son, the Rev. Christopher Wyvil, who succeeded to the estates in 1774, on the death of Sir Marmaduke the seventh baronet.

My queries are : —

1. Did the eighth Sir Marmaduke ever assume the title; did he marry; and are any of his descendants still in existence? Perhaps some of your Transatlantic correspondents (and they are numerous) can furnish information on this point.

2. If there are any descendants still in America, are they not (being naturalised Americans) debarred from succession to the title; and should it not, therefore, come to the descendants of the Rev. Christopher Wyvil?

3. Of what family was William Clifton descended, whose daughter Christian Catherine was the mother of the successor to the estates in 1774, and from whom the present family is descended? That he was an Englishman I know; and it seems probable that he was a member of the neighbouring family of Clifton and Lytham in Lancashire. I am very anxious to know more of his descent, and where he was settled before going to Edinburgh. He had one son William (?), Vicar of Embleton, in Northumberland; and David Clifton, Clerk of Excise in Edinburgh, 1745, was probably another.

Possibly there may be some monument in the churches at Fingall, Spennithorne, or Masham, which may throw light on the last query. Any notice of such, communicated to me privately, or through "N. & Q.," will confer a great favour.

As the Wyvils were connected with Edinburgh, may not Sir Walter Scott have taken the idea of Waverley-Honour, or Osbaldistone Hall, from Constable Burton?

Finally, Has the novel, *Marmaduke Wyvil*, by H. W. Herbert, published in 1843, any reference to the family? F. M. S.

229, Clarendon Villas, Plumstead.

AGUDEZA.—If any of the readers of "N. & Q." could offer me an explanation of the "point" of the following *agudeza*, I should be much obliged; as, although I have asked many Spaniards, and among them several Andalucians, to explain it, not one has been able to do so : —

"Acababan de nombrar alcalde de un pueblo muy desmoralizado á un vecino que se propuso por cuantos medios estuviesen á su alcance moralizarlo. Con este fin suplicó al cura que le indicase las mujeres que daban escándalo y que convenia amonestar. Acordaron ponerse juntos en la plaza y que cuando fuesen entrando las susodichas, diria el cura :—Haba. Pero fué el caso que á cuantas entraban decia el cura :—Haba. Señor, reponia el alcalde, si es la mujer de mi compadre. . . . . Haba ! recalcaba el cura. Llegó en esto la mujer del alcalde. Haba ! dijo el cura. Señor, si es mi mujer y dice Vd. haba ! ! Y Tarragona, repuso el cura."—*Fernan Caballero, Cuentos y Poesias Andaluces.*

The joke evidently lies in the "haba—y Tarragona." ff.

ANNE, COUNTESS OF ARGYLE.—Anne, daughter of Sir William Cornwallis, the second wife of Archibald Campbell, seventh Earl of Argyle, was living in 1633. The date of her death is required. Her husband died in 1638. S. Y. R.

FRANCIS DICKENS.—What were the arms and crest of Francis Dickens, Esq., M.P. for Northampton for the fifth time, 1802. Whom did he marry? And had he other issue besides Maria-Isabella, wife to the last Earl Cornwallis; and Mary, married to Samuel Ravenscroft, attorney-at-law? SAMUEL TUCKER.

20, Doughty Street, Mecklenburgh Square.

DE QUEIROS FAMILY. — Your correspondent SCOTUS (1st S. ii. 478) appears to have access to an ordinary of Portuguese heraldry. I should be much obliged to him, or to any correspondent of "N. & Q.," for the arms of the Portuguese family De Queiros. H. W. T.

GENERAL RICHARD FORTESCUE. — Who was General Richard Fortescue, a Parliamentarian officer, who died about 1656 while Commander-in-Chief in Jamaica, as appointed by Cromwell? His will shows that he had a house and land at Bray, houses in Reading, and an estate at Halskott bought from the trustees of the Marquis of Winchester. To what branch of the Fortescues did he belong? KAPPA.

HAWKE AND BLADEN FAMILIES.—Who was the grandfather of the first Lord Hawke, and where did the family spring from? The father was Edward Hawke, a barrister of Lincoln's Inn, and it is supposed that the family originally came from Cornwall.

Also, What is the origin of the Bladens, and where did they hold property? Col. Martin Bladen, uncle of the first Lord Hawke, at one time held the property of Barmoor Castle, in the parish of Lowick, in Northumberland; and also some property at Alborough Hatch, in Essex; but how these properties were inherited, or parted with, is not known. This Col. Martin Bladen was a Lord of Trade. There was a Col. Thomas Bladen, Governor of Maryland, after whom Bladen county, in North Carolina, was named; as the town of Bladensburg, in Virginia, was named after another member of the family. The Governor of Maryland is thought to have married a daughter of a Sir Theodore Janssen, Bart., said to be a grandson of the Baron du Hèze, who was Governor of Brussels in Alva's time. Another daughter married Calvert, Lord Baltimore, and hence the Governorship of Maryland came. A William Bladen is supposed to have been a Lord Mayor of Dublin a long time ago. The Governor of Maryland is supposed to have been a brother of Col. Martin Bladen. E. W.

Hampstead.

HÆVER, OR ÆVER, OR EAVER.—I do not know the exact orthography of the above word, and hence have made as near an approach to the pronunciation as I could. It is a common Lancashire word, denoting the *direction of the wind*. "What *haver* is the wind in this morning?" is a frequent inquiry; and the answer may be from any point of the compass, as the case may be. What is the etymology of the word?   T. T. W.

"IRELAND IN PAST TIMES."—Two octavo volumes, entitled *Ireland in Past Times; an Historical Retrospect, Ecclesiastical and Civil*, appeared anonymously in London, 1826. By whom written?   ABHBA.

'LOBECK'S "AGLAOPHAMUS."—There is no copy of this work, to my knowledge, in Australia. I have noted references to it in De Quincey's essay on "Secret Societies," and in Mr. W. C. Kent's article on the "Eleusinian Mysteries" in *Blackwood's Magazine* some years ago, which article has since been included in that gentleman's collection of miscellanies, entitled *Footprints on the Road* (Chapman & Hall, 1864).

Will any of your correspondents who have recently been referring to the *Aglaophamus* in your columns be kind enough to inform me where a review, or analytical account, of the work may be found in any accessible book, English, French, or German?   D. BLAIR.
Melbourne.

NUMISMATIC QUERY.—I shall be obliged to any correspondent of "N. & Q." who will explain to me the mint marks upon the present French coinage. Taking the copper series for an example, I find on the obverse, on each side of the date, a mint mark: before 1856, it is (almost) invariably a greyhound's head on the right side; but after 1855, an anchor takes its place. The left side is occupied by a bee, an antique lamp, crossed hammer, and pick, &c., apparently without regularity. Has this mark, on the left of the date, anything to do with the number struck on the reverse? Again occurs another mint mark, showing the place where struck: A—Paris; B—Bordeaux; BB—Lille (?); W—Lyons (?); D—(?).

Will some correspondent of "N. & Q." correct and complete this list? M. Huhlmann, who was the Mint Master of Lille (the mint there is now converted into a school, the last coins struck there being some silver *jettons* celebrating the visit of their majesties to the bourse, 1853; and the monument erected in the bourse to Napoleon I., 1864), gave me a list of the mint and their marks, but I have lost it.

I should also like to know how many five or ten *centime* pieces there are differing in their mint-marks.   JOHN DAVIDSON.

PAYLER AND CARY.—Can you afford me any information respecting the persons mentioned in the following note, taken from the Administration Acts at the General Registry, York?—

"Admon., 3 Dec. 1680, of Dame Mary Cary *alias* Payler, late of Nun Monkton, to James Porter, principal creditor."

She also administered the same day to her husband George Payler of Nun-Monkton, Esq., and to Nathaniel Payler his son—all of whom died intestate.

I can find nothing in Dugdale's *Visitation of Yorkshire*, 1666; or in the brief pedigree of Payler, given in Sir B. Burke's *Extinct Baronetage*.   C. J. R.

MARY PRICE, Spinster, born about 1700, married, in or near London, to one Mr. Reynolds; and died, prior to 1789, leaving a daughter if not more issue. Can any reader oblige by giving any further particulars to William Price, Glannantyllan, Llanffwyst, Abergavenny?   GLWYSIG.

WARD.—Rev. Nathaniel Ward, who was educated at Emmanuel College, Cambridge, taking the degree of A.M. in 1603, is said to have died in 1653, at Shenfield, in Essex, of which parish he was the minister. Cotton Mather, in his *Magnalia* (ed. 1702, part iii. p. 167), informs us that he was "born at Haverhill, in Essex, about 1670." Subsequent writers have copied this date from Mather; but there is reason for believing it to be too early.

Will some reader of "N. & Q.," residing at Shenfield, ascertain if there is a tablet to his memory in that church giving the exact date of his death and his age? And, if so, copy them for me?

I would like also to obtain the date of death and age of his father, Rev. John Ward of Haverhill, whose quaint Latin epitaph is quoted by Fuller in his *Worthies of England*, edit. 1840, vol. iii. p. 186.   MASSACHUSETTS.
Boston, U. S.

Queries with Answers.

"OH! NANNY WILT THOU GANG WITH ME?" (3rd S. vii. 179.)—SENESCENS, alluding to a hymn which is sung to music identical with that of the beginning of the beautiful song, "Oh! Nanny, wilt thou gang with me?" inquires by whom each was composed. It is not very clear whether he asks about the words or the tunes; but the editor assumes the latter, and acquaints him with the names of two persons, to each of whom the music has been attributed. Is there any doubt as to the authorship of the words, which in the north of Ireland have always been ascribed to Dr. Percy, the Bishop of Dromore, and author of the *Reliques of English Poetry*? They are believed to have been addressed to his wife, who rests in the same grave with him in the transept of the cathedral. In Ulster the first line is always written "gang wi'" me, thus rendering it consistent with the Scottish idiom which prevails in the county of Down.

J. K.

[Bishop Percy's ballad " O, Nannie wilt thou gang wi' me?" may have been suggested by " The Young Laird and Edinburgh Katy," by Allan Ramsay (*Tea-Table Miscellany*, 1724). We quote as a specimen the second verse from the edition of 1733, vol. i. p. 67 : —

> " O Katy, wiltu gang wi' me,
> And leave the dinsome town a while ?
> The blossom's sprouting frae the tree,
> And a' the summer's gawn to smile :
> The mavis, nightingale and lark,
> The bleating lambs and whistling hynd,
> In ilka dale, green, shaw, and park,
> Will nourish health and glad ye'r mind."

The occasion of Bishop Percy's writing this exquisite ballad is thus related by Miss Lætitia Matilda Hawkins, in her *Memoirs, Anecdotes, Facts, and Opinions*, ed. 1824, i. 271 : " It is well known that Bishop Percy was the author of the elegant popular song, ' O Nanny, wilt thou gang wi' me ? ' " And in a note she adds, " Recollections of the tenderest kind are called up by the mention of this exquisite ballad, which I have been told was Dr. Percy's invitation to his charming wife, on her release from her twelvemonths' confinement in the royal nursery, in attendance on her charge, Prince Edward, the late Duke of Kent. His Royal Highness's temper as a private gentleman did not discredit his nurse, for his humanity was conspicuous."]

SIR THOMAS BURGH, OR BOROUGH, heir-general of Lord Cobham of Sterbury, created Baron Burgh by Hen. VIII. [VII. ?], had a son Edward. I am very anxious to know whom this Edward married. He had also another son William, Lord Burgh; who married Catherine, daughter of the Earl of Lincoln, by whom he had Thomas, Lord Burgh, K.G. I wish also to know to whom this Thomas was married ? Whoever she was, she was " famous for charity," and died in Westminster about 1638—1640. The name is now commonly written "Burgh."

C. P.

[Edward Burgh, the second Baron, married Anne, daughter and heiress of Sir Thomas Cobham of Sterborough. William Burgh (son of Thomas, the fourth Baron), who married Catherine, daughter of Edward Clinton, Earl of Lincoln, was the fifth Baron, and was succeeded by his son Thomas, K.G., who died Lord-Lieutenant of Ireland in 1597. We cannot discover the family name of his wife Frances, who, says Fuller, " was famous for her charity, and skill in chirurgery." She died in 1647.]

MANOAH SIBLY. — This man was a short-hand writer and bookseller in London, and the author of several works, which he published between the years 1777 and 1795. Can any of your readers

refer me to any particulars of his life, and when and where he died, &c. ?

G. P. O.

[Mr. Manoah Sibly is better known as the Pastor of the New Jerusalem Society assembling at a meeting-house in Friars Street, Blackfriars, where he officiated from the year 1792 until his death on Dec. 16, 1840. The following inscription has been placed on his tombstone in Bunhill Fields burial-ground : " Sacred to the memory of the Rev. Manoah Sibly, who for fifty-two years faithfully, ably, and zealously preached the doctrines and truths of the New Church, signified by the New Jerusalem in the Revelations, from her commencement in the year 1788, and rejoined his beloved conjugal partner in a glorious and blessed state of Immortality, on the 16th of December, 1840, in the eighty-fourth year of his age." For biographical particulars of Mr. Sibly consult *The Intellectual Repository, and New Jerusalem Magazine*, for 1841, being vol. ii. of the New Series, pp. 40, 132—139, and 288. Mrs. Sibly died on Oct. 31, 1829, and some account of her is given in the same periodical for 1831, vol. i. p. 45.]

PAINTED WINDOW AT ST. MARGARET'S, WESTMINSTER.—Can any of your correspondents inform me if the fine painted glass at St. Margaret's, Westminster, is of Flemish origin? I have heard it was once in Westminster Abbey.

THOMAS E. WINNINGTON.

[It was presented by the magistrates of Dort to Henry VII., and intended for his chapel at Westminster, but never put up there. It was at Waltham Abbey, and removed by the last prior to a private chapel at New Hall. This estate passed through many hands—Ratcliff, Earl of Sussex, Villiers, Duke of Buckingham, Oliver Cromwell, General Monk; and the window having eventually become the property of Mr. Conyers, of Copt Hall, Essex, was sold by him in 1758 to the parish of St. Margaret's, Westminster, for four hundred guineas.]

ADDISON FAMILY. — Can any one tell me whether the family of which Joseph Addison was a member is extinct, and whether he had brothers or sisters who left issue? Also his mother's maiden name?

R. W. E. L.

U. U. C.

[Joseph Addison's mother was Jane, daughter of Nathaniel Gulston, Esq., and sister to Dr. William Gulston, Bishop of Bristol. Addison's only child, born just before his death, survived her father seventy-eight years, and died unmarried at Bilton Hall in March, 1797. He had two brothers and three sisters : 1. Jane died in her infancy. 2. Gulston died Governor of Fort St. George in the East Indies. 3. Dorothy, who married first Dr. Sartre, formerly minister at Montpellier, afterwards prebendary of Westminster. Her second husband was Daniel Combes, Esq. 4. Anne, who died in early life. 5. Launcelot, Fellow of Magdalen College, Oxford.]

"BIOGRAPHICAL ANECDOTES OF THE FOUNDERS OF THE FRENCH REPUBLIC." — This work was published in the year 1797 in two volumes, and I should feel much obliged if you could give me information concerning the author of it. At the beginning of vol. i. there is a plate, with the following inscription : " Address of Louis XVI. at the Bar of the Convention, on the 26th of Dec. 1792 ; " and at vol. ii. "Attack of the Thuilleries, on the 10th of Aug. 1792, sketched by an eye-witness."   T. T. DYER.

[This work is the first literary production of the late John Adolphus, the celebrated common-law barrister. He also assisted the historian Coxe in preparing for the press *The Memoirs of Sir Robert Walpole*, 3 vols, 4to, 1798. Mr. Adolphus died on July 16, 1845, aged eighty.]

BRADSHAW'S "RAILWAY COMPANION, OR GUIDE."—What is the exact title, size, and date, or other distinguishing mark of the first edition ?   KAPPA.

[The work was originally entitled Bradshaw's *Monthly Railway Guide*, Manchester, 1842, 16mo, and continued as Bradshaw's *Monthly General Railway and Steam Navigation Guide for Great Britain and Ireland*, Manchester, 16mo. We have only met with one number of Bradshaw's *Railway Time Tables* for Sept. 1842, Manchester, Sm. sh. fol.]

DR. FERNE AND LORD CAPEL.—In the *Catholic Miscellany*, 1825, it is stated that Dr. Ferne, who, after the Restoration, was made Bishop of Chester, was previously chaplain in Lord Capel's family. To this Anthony Wood makes no allusion, neither is it noticed in Ormerod's *History of Cheshire*. I wish to ask, therefore, what documentary, or other satisfactory evidence, is there to substantiate the above statement ?   LLALLAWG.

[The statement has probably been made from the fact, that Dr. Ferne accompanied Lord Capel and the other commissioners from King Charles I. to treat with the Parliamentarians at Uxbridge in matters relating to the Church. *Vide* Clarendon's *History of the Rebellion*, ed. 1849, iii. 498.]

"WIRE-IN."—Mr. Hotten, who, in his amusing and interesting *Slang Dictionary*, solves so many difficulties of our London vernacular, has himself met with a poser, as he intimates at p. 271 :—

" WIRE-IN, a London street phrase in general use at the present time, the meaning of which I have not been able to discover."

Can any one clear up this difficulty ?   SPECTACLES.

[Wire-in and wire-up are Dorsetshire phrases. A friend who in 1863 passed his summer holidays at Weymouth in that county formed the acquaintance of a resident, who occasionally employed one expression or the other, wire-in or wire-up—both, apparently, in the same sense. They seemed to be familiar and conventional terms of invitation, exhortation, and encouragement. Thus, in summoning him to dinner : "Now then, *wire-in*."]

HISTORICAL VALUE OF POPULAR BALLADS: MALBROUGH.

(3rd S. vii. 127.)

There is in the Library of the Sacred Harmonic Society a volume of French *chansons* published at Paris about the year 1842. It is of a large octavo size, has no general title, nor any signatures or paginal or other numbers to indicate the order of succession of its contents, which are printed in sections of eight pages, each complete in itself, and containing one long or two short chansons, and terminating with the printer's name (F. Locquin, 16 Rue N. D. des Victoires), showing the work to have been issued in numbers. Each chanson is preceded by an historical notice, and followed by the music to which it is sung, and each page of the words of the chanson itself is surmounted and bordered by ably-designed and well-executed etchings, many of them of a remarkably humorous kind, illustrating the song.

The first song in the volume is the same which your correspondent A. A. has described. It is here given under the title of *Mort et Convoi de l'Invincible Malbrough*. The introductory notice is so curious and interesting, that I think it better, notwithstanding its length, to transcribe it *in extenso* than to give a condensed account of it. It is as follows :—

" NOTICE.

" La célèbre chanson de *Malbrough* fut certainement composée après la bataille de Malplaquet, en 1709, et non après la mort de Jean Churchill, duc de Marlborough, en 1722, comme l'ont pensé quelques graves commentateurs de cette facétie historique.

" Aucune des circonstances de ce petit poème populaire ne peut se rapporter à la mort véritable du duc de Marlborough. Lorsque cet illustre général mourut, dans sa terre de Windsor-Lodge, le 17 Juin 1722, des suites d'une attaque d'apoplexie, il n'avait point paru à la tête des armées depuis plus de six ans ; depuis plus de dix, il ne jouait qu'un rôle obscur et secondaire dans la politique de l'Europe, et les Français, plus légers encore à cette époque qu'ils ne le sont aujourd'hui, avaient en tout le temps nécessaire pour l'oublier. George I, en arrivant au trône, rappela le duc de Marlborough à la cour, dont la reine Anne l'avait éloigné ainsi que sa femme ; mais il ne lui demanda plus des conseils qu'il ne suivait pas toujours. Le duc vivait donc fort tristement dans ses domaines, où l'argent lui manquait pour l'achèvement du magnifique château de Blenheim, que la reine Anne et le parlement d'Angleterre avaient voulu faire bâtir, à leurs frais, en mémoire de l'éclatante victoire d'Hochstett : il tomba presque en enfance, et s'éteignit enfin sous les yeux de Lady Marlborough, qui se chargea elle-même de lui faire des obsèques triomphales.

" La chanson est donc antérieure à cette mort, qui n'eut guère d'écho au delà de l'Angleterre, et, à défaut d'autres preuves, nous pourrions citer l'ancienne légende en prose qui accompagne la chanson, et dans laquelle il est dit que Malbrough fut TUÉ à la bataille de Malplaquet, qui se donna entre Mons et Bavay, le 11 Septembre, 1709. Dans cette bataille si glorieuse pour les

Français, de l'aveu même des historiens Anglais, le maréchal de Villars fut blessé au genou, lorsqu'il allait envelopper le duc de Marlborough et l'écraser entre les deux ailes de l'armée Française ; en ce moment décisif, Marlborough courut les plus grands dangers et faillit partager le sort de cinq de ses lieutenants-généraux, qui furent tués dans la mêlée.

" Le bruit de sa mort se répandit sans doute, et quelque chansonnier badin lui fit cette oraison funèbre, au bivouac du Quesnoy, le soir de la bataille, pour se consoler de n'avoir pas de chemise et de manquer de pain depuis trois jours : ainsi va l'esprit Français. Le duc de Marlborough, grand capitaine et négociateur habile, avait fait bien du mal à la royauté de Louis XIV : pendant trente ans, il l'avait poursuivie, attaquée et affaiblie sur tous les champs de bataille et dans tous les cabinets de l'Europe ; il s'était montré digne élève de Condé et de Turenne à Hochstett, à Oudenarde et à Ramillies : son nom faisait la terreur et l'admiration du soldat. Faute de pouvoir le vaincre, on essaya de le chansonner, et chacune de ses victoires fut marquée par une nouvelle chanson satyrique. La chanson était encore en France, comme au bon temps du Cardinal de Mazarin, l'expression la plus ordinaire des vengeances et de représailles du peuple.

" Et cependant la chanson de Malbrough ne survécut pas au héros de Malplaquet ; elle se conserva seulement par tradition dans quelques provinces, où l'avaient rapportée probablement des soldats de Villars et de Boufflers ; elle ne fut pas même recueillie dans les immenses collections des chansons anecdotiques qui faisaient partie des archives de la noblesse Française. Mais en 1781, elle retentit tout à coup d'un bout à l'autre du royaume.

" Marie-Antoinette mit au monde un dauphin qui devint le nourrisson d'une paysanne, nommée Madame Poitrine, qu'on avait choisie, entre toutes, à son apparence de santé et de bonne humeur. Madame Poitrine chantait en berçant le royal enfant, qui ouvrit les yeux au grand nom de Marlborough. Ce nom, les paroles naives de la chanson, la bizarrerie de son refrain, et la touchante simplicité de l'air, frappèrent la reine, qui retint cet air et cette chanson. Tout le monde les redit après elle, et la roi lui-même ne dédaigna pas de fredonner à l'unisson Malbrough s'en va-t-en guerre. On chantait Malbrough des petits appartements de Versailles aux cuisines et aux écuries ; la chanson faisant fureur à la cour, quand elle fut adoptée par la bourgeoisie de Paris, et elle passe successivement de ville en ville, de pays en pays ; elle retourna d'abord en Angleterre, où elle fut bientôt aussi populaire qu'en France.

" A Paris, Beaumarchais, dans son Marriage de Figaro, fit chanter a Chérubin l'air de Malbrough, en remplaçant l'antique refrain Mironton ton ton, mirontaine, par ce vers langoureux, Que mon cœur, que mon cœur a de peine !

" A Londres, un gentilhomme Français, voulant se faire conduire par son cocher à Marlborough Street, et ne se rappelant pas le nom de cette rue, chanta l'air de Malbrough, et le cocher comprit aussitôt l'adresse qui lui indiquait la chanson.

" Goethe, qui voyageait en France dans ce temps-là, fut assourdi par un concert universel de mirontons, et prit en haine Marlborough qui était la cause innocente de cette épidémie chantante. Malbrough dansa son nom aux modes, aux étoffes, aux coiffures, aux carrosses, aux ragouts, &c., Malbrough revenait sans cesse à propos de tout et à propos de rien. Le sujet de la chanson était peint sur les paravents, sur les éventails, sur les écrans, brodé sur les tapisseries et sur les meubles, gravé sur les jétons, sur les bijoux, reproduit sous toutes les formes et de toutes les manières. Cette rage de Malbrough dura plusieurs années, et il ne fallut rien moins que la chute de la Bastille pour étouffer le bruit d'une chanson.

" A present que nous sommes loin de la chanson et de Marlborough, qui sont à jamais acquis à la France, nous avons récherchés quelle devait être l'origine de cet air guerrier et melancholique à la fois, que Napoléon entonnait a haute voix, malgré son antipathie pour la musique, chaque fois qu'il montait à cheval pour entrer en campagne, et nous ne répugnons pas à croire, avec M. de Chateaubriand, que ce pourrait bien être le même air que les Croisés de Godefroid de Bouillon chantaient sur les murs de Jérusalem, pour s'encourager à délivrer la ville sainte et le tombeau du Christ. Les Arabes le chantent encore, et l'on prétend que leurs ancêtres l'avaient appris à la bataille de Massoure, où les frères d'armes du sire de Joinville le répétaient en choquant leur boucliers et en poussant le cri national, Montjoie Saint Denis !

" P. L. Jacob, Bibliophile."

This "Notice" occupies two pages, the next four are devoted to the words of the chanson, the engravings round which represent, 1. The hero in ancient armour on horseback, preceded by trumpeters and drummers, and attended by a numerous train, emerging from the gates of a fortified town ; 2. The duchess on the top of her tower, with two ladies ; the black-habited page on a terrace beneath, bowing ; 3. The funeral procession, the body preceded by the four officers carrying the arms of the deceased ; and 4. The ascent of the soul (a very substantial figure crowned with a nimbus, rising from a tomb), the prostration of the soldiers, and their departure, gaping, to their homes. The music fills two pages more.

There are upwards of thirty other chansons in the volume, amongst which are Le Juif Errant, Le Roi d'Yvetôt, La Machine Infernale [de la Rue Nicaise], Le Comte Orry (from which the plot of Rossini's opera is taken), Fanfan la Tulipe, Paris à cinq heures du Matin (which possibly suggested the well-known " London at Five in the Morning," sung by the late Charles Mathews), L'Enfant prodigue and Le Roi Dagobert et Saint Eloi.

W. H. Husk.

Five generals had fallen on the field of Malplaquet, and Churchill's completion of the half dozen was too desirable not to be—telegrammed, I was near saying—to Paris without waiting its verification. So the chanson was extemporised in the guard-room, and—

"Malbrough s'en va-t-en guerre,"

sung and whistled over Louis le Grand's dominions, while its living subject—præsenti largimur honores — was knocking his majesty's maréchaux about right and left. So tells us P. L. Jacob, Bibliophile (La Croix).

Like other celebrities "Malbrough" had its day, and was heard only in the provinces till "Madame Poitrine" (the nom de lait, I suppose, of a βαθύκολπος paysanne) brought it back to the Tuileries ; Louis Seize sang it in the royal nursery, whence it was caught up the courtiers, echoed by the bourgeoisie, and reverberated over France. Silenced by the cannon of 1789, its refrain found a patron in the elder Buonaparte, who, little as he loved music, sang it at the *ouverture* of his several campaigns. I wonder, did his biographical nephew hum it at Balaclava?

What, however, are these reminiscences to the Orientalism ascribed to this popular tune by Chateaubriand, as having been picked up by Godfrey of Bouillon's Crusaders in the Holy Land? Of a truth, the duke in his chain-mail, the duchess on the top of her tower, and Buttons at the barbican in his black dittoes, as they appear in A. A.'s illuminated broadsheet, have a very troubadourish aspect.

When, why, and from whom will be heard the next revival of " Malbrough"?   E. L. S.

Your correspondent A. A. does not seem to be aware that this ballad is a permanent memorial of a false and transient rumour. Neither, indeed, could the writer, who bears the literary name of *Father Proud*, have been aware of its origin when he wrote the remarks which you extract, though I doubt not that he has long ago learned it. After one of Marlborough's battles a report was spread that he, already renowned and dreaded, had been slain. The news ran like wildfire, and for a few days was believed, amongst others by one who vented his feelings in an air and words, which the dissipation of the delusion could not deprive of immortality. The whole subject was treated in an exhaustive article in *Chambers's Journal* of Jan. 20, 1844, in which were given full particulars of the date and occasion of the false report, the authorship of the ballad, and its speedy and continued popularity.   K.

The following anecdote respecting the popular ballad of " Malbrough" is related in the Biographical Memoir of the Hon. Wm. R. Spencer, prefixed to his *Poems*, ed. 1835, p. 13:—

" Whilst at Harrow Mr. Spencer frequently visited his uncle at Blenheim, of whom he was a great favourite, as well as of the Duchess of Marlborough. During one of his visits to them, the Duchess received from the unfortunate Queen of France, Marie Antoinette, a present of a very beautiful fan with the well-known song of ' Malbroug' written upon it, and a letter by which it appeared that she supposed it to have been written on the great Duke of Marlborough, according to the general belief. In the discussion that took place as to whether her mistake should be set right, or be left unnoticed, when the Duchess wrote a letter of thanks to her, Mr. Spencer learned that this popular and hacknied song was in fact written on the Duke's father, Charles, second Duke of Marlborough, when he set off from a village in Germany, to take the command of the British forces serving on the Lower Rhine, and that the village barber was the author of it. The author of the music is still unknown."

J. Y.

SIR WILLIAM WESTON,

LORD PRIOR OF THE ORDER OF ST. JOHN OF JERUSALEM,

(2nd S. vii. 317, 405, 496 : 3rd S. vii. 224.)

As I ventured in the last number of "N. & Q." to question the accuracy of the interpretation, and assignment by Cromwell (*History of Clerkenwell*, pp. 187-191), of the motto sculptured beneath the arms of Sir William Weston on the once splendid monument of that knight, it may not be uninteresting to consider the correctness or otherwise of the description, and of the engraving given of the armorial bearings themselves. The following remarks, however, chiefly apply to the engraving. After describing the injuries from which the monument had suffered from the ravages of time, the wanton mischief and the thefts of the sacrilegious, and the *beautifying* it received in 1780, Cromwell continues:—

" The other indentations appear to have been made by plates of arms, one of which had evidently been Sir William Weston's coat, as represented among the decorations at top : bearing ermine in chief 6 bezants ; quartering 3 camels passants ; crest, a Saracen's head on what appears to be intended for a Prior's cap ; motto, ANY BORO."

Aubrey, in his description of Sutton Race, Surrey, the residence of Sir Richard Weston, says:—

" In the hall is the crest of Weston, viz. a Saracen's head with a black beard, and a wreath of white linen. This does not exactly tally with our crest : but the difference may have arisen from the sculptor's ignorance."— P. 189.

The Westons bore five not six bezants, but the causes above adverted to doubtless led to the inaccuracy. In the " Description of the Standards borne in the Field by Peers and Knights in the reign of Henry VIII." in the College of Arms, Sir William Weston's banner bears—1st and 4th Erm. on a chief Az. five bezants ; 2nd and 3rd Ar., three camels statant Sa. The cross of the Order of Knights Hospitallers is borne in chief, and the banner is supported by a camel Sa. crined, hoofed, and garnished Or. His crest is not given, but in the same MS. where the standard and arms of his brother Sir Richard Weston are emblazoned, occurs the Saracen's head, not full, but three-quarter faced, bearded, and with protruding tongue, collared, bound with a fillet Ar. and Az! and resting on a wreath Ar. and Sa. The head has all the characteristics of the best type of Arab, with high features, massive brow, flowing hair, full beard and moustache, and rich brown complexion ; and the face, in spite of its distortion and fierceness, is not ill-favoured. In the crest on the monument the sculptor fell into the modern and conventional rendering of the heraldic Saracen, the thick-lipped, beardless, black, bloated, woolly-haired negro.

The fillet round the head was converted either by the sculptor, draughtsman, or engraver into the jewelled or embroidered band of a kind of skull-cap, and in the arms the bezants have, in the first and fourth quarters, been sown broadcast on the field.

In the first quarter they have fallen in two equal and parallel rows, whilst in the fourth they have distributed themselves more artistically in three rows, numbering three, two, and one respectively. The engraver, moreover, has allowed his fancy to run wild in the adornment of the chief in the above bearing, which is far beyond any attempt at heraldic description.

I should be glad if some of your correspondents would reply to Mr. Pinks' query (2nd S. vii. 496) regarding the Lord Prior's monument. Is it still at Burghley, and in whose memory has it been erected?   W.

EPIGRAMS.
(3rd S. vii. 97, 117, 147.)

Plus its Laconism, the "Epigram upon an Epigram," recorded by M. N. S., is better conceived and more neatly pointed than Warton's — which of the brothers, Tom or Joe, I forget. Unless it be too familiar for repetition, here it is : —

" One day in Christchurch meadows walking,
   Of poetry and such things talking,
      Cries Ralph—a merry wag :
   ' An Epigram, if right and good,
   In all its circumstances should
      Be like a *Jelly-bag*.'

" ' Your simile, I own, is new ;
   But how dost make it out ? ' says Hugh.
   · Quoth Ralph ' I'll tell thee, friend :
   Make it a-top both wide and fit
   To hold a budget-full of wit,
      And point it at the end.' "

Ausonius's "Dodra" — which he relished well enough to give its receipt in two Latin epigrams (*epigraphs* rather), and one Greek — had tempted me to a translation. May I, notwithstanding Mr. Hamilton's note, venture to append it ? —

" Men call me *Niner :* bread, broth, water, wine,
   Salt, pepper, oil, herbs, honey, make my Nine,"—

a mixture, fit only to wash down the classical dinner of Smollet's Antiquarian !

As also one of Martial's, which is eminently terse and poignant : —

" Cum sitis similes, paresque vitâ,
   Uxor pessima, pessimus maritus,
   Miror, non bene convenire vobis."
                          Lib. viii. Ep. xxxv.
" So like your tempers and your lives,
   The worst of husbands, worst of wives,
   'Tis odd, how ill your union thrives."

Before I had seen Mr. Mackenzie's note of the Ausonian "Dodra," I was thinking of its mono-linear version. To compress nine ingredients (three of them being impracticable dissyllables)

within an English heroic line, were about as easy as packing Falstaff into a pepperbox : so I tried it with an Alexandrine's *twelve*, which, I need not say, is shorter by *five* than the original Latin ; and will be accounted, I hope, at least as condensate as Ausonius's seventeen. No easy task it was ; but easier than it would have been to swallow its practical brewage : —

" Men call me *Niner*. Why ? Thrice three is nine :
   Bread, broth, salt, honey, herbs, oil, pepper, water, wine.":

Martial's "duri ingeni puer" is simply a *block-head :* fit only to be a town-crier, a costermonger, an auctioneer's or tumbler's touter, or such other brazen-lunged *præco ;* or else a bricklayer or hodman. Heraldry and architecture are beyond his blockheadism. The trivial class of these *præcones* was oddly played upon by our grave lexicographer—paronymously, he would term it : —

" If the man who turnips cries,
   Cry not when his father dies ;
   'Tis a proof that he had rather
   Have a turnip than his father."

The point of this epigram is, I believe, contemporaneous with Jack Bannister's story.

Dryden uses the term "hardhead" as a *street-mêlée* word ; wherein the "roughs" butt each óther in the Taurine fashion—a brutal sort of head-work : yet preferable to the Italian knife. In some old play (I forget its title) there is a parish-constable—a cross between Dogberry and Bumble—by name, Authority *Hardhead*.

Turning, too abruptly perhaps, to a very different view of our subject, long ago I "made a note of " a distichon, which we may not term an epigram. What other than φαντασία, animo concepta, an illustration applicable only by something lower than itself of "The Mystery of Mysteries," I know not how to term it : —

" Nix, Glacies, et Aqua ; tria Nomina, Res tamen una :
   Sic in personis trinus Deus, et tamen unus."

Having common-placed it, in the days when "N. & Q." was not, I unfortunately neglected to set down its authorship ; but among the learned contributors to our weekly *necesse est*, it will hardly fail of a reference. I venture this inadequate rendering : —

" Snow, Ice, and Water ; one, yet three in name —
   Father, Son, Spirit ; three, yet each the same."
                                          E. L. S.

I do not think the following are generally known. They are given as original in *The Green Book* (Dublin, J. Duffy, 1845) : —

" When I meet Tom, the purse-proud and impudent blockhead,
   In his person the poets' three ages I trace :
   For the *gold* and the *silver* unite in his pocket,
   And the *brazen* is easily seen in his face."
Feb. 16, 1830.

On Two Pretty Girls.

" 'How happy could I be with either,' was said
    By Macheath to his wives in the play ;
But were two such charmers as you in their stead,
    He could not wish either away.

" Oh ! no, until death with such angels he'd grapple ;
    Then both are so temptingly fair,
That, as Adam lost Heaven by eating an apple,
    I'd forfeit *my* chance for a pair."

On Miss ——

" Thrice happy the man who gets thee for a wife !
    Thrice happy, indeed, since he's sure of salvation !
For if Heaven's to be gained, we are told that this life
    Must be spent in Repentance and Mortification."

Jan. 20, 1830.

The author of the volume, which is a curious Irish nationalist production, was " John Cornelius O'Callaghan, Esq., a " literary agitator."   C. W.

43, Union Grove, Clapham, S.

The maxim " Cœpisse," &c., is certainly older than Ausonius. See Horace, 1 *Epis.* ii. 40 —

" Dimidium facti qui cœpit habet : sapère aude :
Incipe."

Where does the other maxim referred to in the same note come from, " Bis dat qui cito dat " ?

O. P. Q.

APPLE-PIE ORDER (3rd S. vii. 133, 209.)—A lady has very kindly informed me that she remembers being told by an ancestress, the custom many years ago was to take off the top crust of an apple-pie, to mash up the fruit with sugar and cream, and then to cut the crust into triangular pieces like sippets, and stick them ends downwards into the fruit in various patterns, as circles, crowns, stars, &c. This seems to be a more probable origin for the phrase than any yet offered.   A. A.

AN OLD RAPIER (3rd S. vi. 308, 521.) — By a strange oversight I had not observed, until three months after its appearance, MR. W. J. BERNHARD SMITH's obliging reply to my query. I would add that the blade is not flat, but rounded on both sides. What is the meaning of the four perforations in the blade immediately below the hilt? Were they to make the thrust more deadly if it reached as far ? Being unskilled in such matters, I will not venture to describe the hilt, but I send an accurate drawing of it, with this further query, and hope it may reach my correspondent's hands.

ALFRED GATTY, D.D.

TRUFFLES (3rd S. vii. 167.)—Truffles are plentiful occasionally in Hampshire. In the village of Cheriton, about three miles south of Alresford, when I was a boy, there were two families whose principal means of support depended upon the success of their truffle-hunting ; and, remarkable enough, their name—like that of the man said by MR. M. A. LOWER to come from the West Indies—

was Leach. At present there are three brothers in the village who follow the occupation of their sire. These men do not, as your correspondent says, bribe the dogs by giving them meat to prevent their eating the luxury, but they give them a piece of bread now and then as a reward for their discoveries. Nor do the dogs, as might be inferred from the communication, get possession of the truffles. They find them, and their master digs them up with a pike he carries on purpose. The dogs used by these men are white ones, very similar to the French poodle. The hunting is not limited to any particular places ; but in all the hedgerows round, and fir plantations are the truffles found.   J. W. BATCHELOR.

MY (3rd S. vii. 164.)—I am very glad to find from MELETES' reply, that the use of the egotistical *my* is not universal ; but that it is very prevalent I know by fatal experience ; and surely Thackeray's ridicule of the Irish for their adherence to Walker, as I may term it, was proof sufficient of my statement. Let not, however, the neophonists lose courage ; they are sure to carry the day ; for novelty, however erroneous, always beats old-fashion, however logical and correct. Has not *kerb-stone* nearly driven *curb-stone* out of use ? While we write *epigram*, *diagram*, &c., have we not *programme*, *à la Française* ? Do we not meet, even in books of some pretence, *to clearly see*, *to truly narrate*, and such like atrocities ? I could, of course, find many other instances of the triumph of ignorance over knowledge, but where would be the use ?

THOS. KEIGHTLEY.

RAGUSA (3rd S. vii. 180.) — Triers, in his *Einleitung zu der Wapen-Kunst* (p. 785), gives the arms of Ragusa thus : —

" In silbernem Felde drey blaue rechte Schräg-Balcken mit dem Worte LIBERTAS, welches mit gülden Buchstaben quer durch geschrieben ist." (Arg. three bendlets az. ; over all, the word " Libertas" in fess or.)

He adds : " Es ist nicht ausgemacht zu welcher Zeit diese Republice entstanden."

J. WOODWARD.

HOLY-WATER-SPRINKLE (3rd S. vii. 200.) — This was a weapon of the mace kind, and was another name for the " Morning-star," the head being furnished with a number of radiating spikes. In the Tower Survey of 1547, *penes Soc. Ant.*, is the following entry : —

" Great holly water sprincles, 118 ; Holly water sprincles with gonnes in th' ende, 7 : Little holly water sprincles, 392 : Holly water sprincle with three gonnes in the topp, 1."

This is no doubt the MS. cited by Grose (ii. 286), and the last item, in all probability, the arm called King Henry VIII.'s Walking Staff, still preserved in the Tower. See Hewitt's *Anc. Arm.* iii. 604.   S. D. S. '

This weapon is properly a long club of wood; its head armed with iron spikes, standing out in all directions at right angles from its axis. It was a rude implement, mostly used in the defence of breaches and trenches, and sometimes called a "morning star." The name was derived from the resemblance to the "Aspergillum" for holy water, which is much in the form of a bottle-brush. A modification of the weapon was, and perhaps is still used, by the watchmen in Denmark and Sweden. It may be remembered that the late Marquis of Waterford was nearly killed by a Scandinavian watchman, armed with a "morning star." That instrument was, however, described at the time as a long staff with a spiked shoe, and leaden ball at its top. The spiked head was probably thought too formidable to be entrusted to a guardian of the peace. There are examples in the Tower, and elsewhere, of match-lock guns combined with the weapon; but they formed no part of the "morning star" proper, which was simply a thick staff, or club, studded with iron points.   W. J. BERNHARD SMITH.

Temple.

BURIAL IN COFFINS (3rd S. vii. 113.)—It would seem from the apparently studious avoidance of any mention of coffins in the Burial Service of the Church of England, that at the period of compilation of that service, uncoffined interments were common. "Corpse" or "body" alone is spoken of. Sir Henry Spelman says in his Works, interments without coffins were common amongst the humbler classes even so late, as the year 1650. Some decent involucra, or coverings, were deemed to be necessary, but this was all.
          GEO. VICKERS.

Shimpling, Bury St. Edmunds.

KING OF JERUSALEM (3rd S. vii. 202.) — My query, what present or more recent potentates call themselves by the above title, awaits an answer. In proclamations, or coins, I see that the King of Sardinia, King of Naples, Queen of Spain, and Grand Duke of Tuscany, all claim the title. Have the rulers of Austria, Germany, Turkey, France, or any other kingdom, since Frederick II. in 1229–39, in public deeds or coins, been so styled?
          E.

The only reigning sovereigns of Europe who use this title, and habitually quarter the arms of Jerusalem with their own, are, I believe, the Emperor of Austria and the King of Italy. The other potentates who have, or have had, pretensions to the sovereignty are, the Pope, the King of Spain, the King of France, the King of the Two Sicilies, the Duke of Lorraine, and the Duke of Mantua. The Republic of Venice, on the involuntary abdication of the throne of Cyprus by Catarina Cornaro, the last queen, annexed her dominion to the Republic; and at her decease,

whatever rights she possessed over the throne of Jerusalem, escheated to the state of which she was an adopted daughter, and the arms of Jerusalem, with those of the kingdom of Cyprus, were incorporated with those of the Venetian Republic.
          JOHN WOODWARD.

New Shoreham.

In answer to the latter half of E.'s question, I think that at the present time no potentate bear the title of King of Jerusalem. The title was born by the kings of Sardinia, and on their coins generally ran as follows (legend of a Doppia in full 1773) — "Victor Amadeus Dei Gratia Rex Sardiniæ Cypriæ et Ierosolymæ."
The arms of Jerusalem are in the first quarter of the full Sardinian shield quartered with Cyprus, Armenia, and Luxemburg—rather a funny combination.
A year or so ago the King of Sardinia changed his title to Re d' Italia, and then I should imagine dropt the inferior titles.   JOHN DAVIDSON.

SEALS OF GEORGE ABBOT, ARCHBISHOP OF CANTERBURY (3rd S. vii. 179.)—MR. HOWARD wishes to be referred to an impression of the archiepiscopal and personal seals of Archbishop Abbot. Among the muniments of Lord Willoughby de Broke at Compton Verney in this county, I found some years ago the appointment of his ancestor, Sir Robert Heath, to be one of the Governors of the Charter House, signed and sealed by this Archbishop, January 25, 1 Charles I. (1625); in others, his personal seal, of course, is used, and I enclose a very rough sketch of it; it is a plain shield, bearing a chevron between three pears.   E. H. SHIRLEY.

PASSAGE FROM "MACBETH" (3rd S. vii. 51.) In old English Dictionaries, probably in Bailey's, the word blonket, which means a thunder-cloud, is given. It may be that this is the original reading of the passage.   B. T.

WORKS ON SATAN AND HIS DWELLING-PLACE (3rd S. vi. 533; vii. 144.)—I have now before me two editions of the work of Dr. Swindon, one being the second ed. 1727, described by your Kentish correspondent, and the other an anonymous edition of 1724; full title, An Enquiry into the Nature and Place of Hell. London: Printed by W. Bowyer, for W. Taylor at the Ship in Paternoster Row, and H. Clements at the Halfmoon in St. Paul's Churchyard, 1714. Frontispiece of the sun taken from Kircherus and Scheinerus. Are these works scarce? The edition of 1727 only is mentioned in Bohn's Lowndes, and not as a second edition.   A. B. MIDDLETON.

The Close, Salisbury.

HERALDRY (3rd S. vii. 184.)—I am very much obliged to your correspondent H. W. T. for having called attention to an error in my Blazon of

Episcopacy. · The coat of Bishop Lyndewode ought there to have been given as a chevron between three leavés, the latter clause having slipped out in the transcription of my memoranda for the press. The coat will thus be found to be the same as that upon the brass for John de Lynde-woode (of 1421), at Linwood, co. Lincoln. I have examined the edition of the *Provinciale* referred to by H. W. T., and I cannot believe that the coat there engraved is intended for the arms of the bishop; as in addition to the supporters, a most unlikely adjunct to episcopal arms, they are surmounted by a close helmet. I hope to be able to discover to whom they really appertain; but if intended even for the bishop's, I should prefer the contemporary evidence of his own Register to the coat attributed more than half a century after his decease.

Had your correspondent's friend who made the extract from my book looked back to the name before Linwood's, Thomas Rodburn, 1433 to 1442, he might have saved himself the trouble of correcting the obvious misprint of 1422 for 1442.

W. K. RILAND BEDFORD.

PEW (3rd S. vii. 155.)—A pew, somewhat similar to the one described by MR. FERREY, is extant in the small church of Shellesley Walsh, in the valley of the Teme, Worcestershire. It is enclosed with richly carved woodwork, to the height of the rood screen to which it is adjacent, on the south side of the small nave; and, I presume, was the seat in ancient times of the lord of the manor.

THOMAS E. WINNINGTON.

DR. MOISEY (3rd S. i. 290.)—Perceiving that the query of MR. R. INGLIS concerning this gentleman has never been replied to, I mentioned the fact to a friend; who, I conceived, might possess a "note" upon the subject. We at once dived into his MS. collection:—

"MS. S—20. *Othello.* and *Il Bondocani,* see Bill. The 'Othello' of this evening is said to have been a Mr. Moisey, of the medical profession—he failed decidedly." [Saturday, December 20, 1800.]

This immediately caused a search to be made high and low—"up stairs and down stairs," in the literal sense of the word; and amongst almost endless histrionic archives, stowed away in huge cupboards, the following extracts formed the total result of our searchings:—

"19. [20]. — *Othello.* A gentleman of the name of Moisey, whom we had only an opportunity of seeing in one scene, made his *debut* in this arduous character. We understand that he spoke with 'good emphasis and discretion;' but having other prospects in life, and his success not being such as to promise a very lucrative engagement, he has prudently resigned all thoughts of the stage as a profession."—*The Monthly Mirror,* 1801, vol. ix. p. 55.

"20. [December, 1800]. A Gentleman of the Faculty (of the name of Moisey) made his *debut* at Covent Garden in the part of *Othello.* Of the expression of his countenance, the disguise did not permit us to judge: his person

appeared to be genteel, and above the middle size. His action was rather free than graceful, though he trod the stage not without dignity; but whatever merits he may possess, they were all insufficient to compensate for a voice without volume or compass, having neither modulation for scenes of pathos, nor strength for declamation. The impression it made on us was similar to what we should have received from a person enacting Othello in a small parlour, and restraining his voice lest he should be heard by the people overhead. We need only add that, though he was not loudly censured, his reception was such as we think would not encourage him to renew the attempt, at least in the higher walks of Tragedy."—*The European Magazine,* 1801, vol. xxxix. p. 40.

EDWIN ROFFE.
Somers Town.

PHYSICIANS' FEES (2nd S. v. 495.)—Sir Alexander Croke, in his edition of the *Regimen Sanitatis Salernitanum* gives quotations from some works written in imitation of the subjoined celebrated compound of poetry and physic, which is thus prefaced: —

"The following prudential advice, given by Otho of Cremona to medical practitioners, enters too deeply into the mysteries of the profession to have been designed for the use of the profane: —

"*De prudentiâ Medici sumentis pro labore.*

"Non didici gratis, nec sagax musa Hippocratis
Ægris in stratis serviet absque datis.
Sumpta solet care multum medicina juvare,
Si quæ datur gratis — nil habet utilitatis.
Res dare pro rebus, pro verbis verba solemus.
Pro vanis verbis montanis utimur herbis,
Pro caris rebus, pigmentis et speciebus.
Est medicinalis Medicis data regula talis,
Vt dicatur ' da, da,' dum profert languidus 'ha, ha.'
Da medicis primo medium, medio, nihil imo;
Dum dolet infirmus, Medicus sit pignore firmus;
Instanter quære nummos, ut pignus, habere, ,
Fœdus et antiquum conservat pignus amicum,
Nam si post quæris, quærens semper eris."

JUVERNA.

H. H. PRINCE FRANCIS RHODOCANAKIS (3rd S. iv. 453.) — Besides the *History of the Ancient Dukes and other Sovereigns of the* (Greek) *Archipelago, &c.,* mentioned in "N. & Q.," he wrote many other literary and philosophical works; among which may be noticed the following biographical one, as its perusal will greatly assist your correspondent DE RHODES in his researches regarding the state of the Byzantine nobility after the conquest of Constantinople by the Turks: —

"Les Hômmes Nobles et Illustres de l'Isle de Chio; escrit par Son Altesse Monseigneur le Prince François D. Rhodocanakis,* Duc de la Tour Rhodocanaki, Seigneur de la dite Isle, etc.; et adressé à S. A. le trés-illustre Prince Gaston, Duc d'Anjou, etc. [afterwards Duc d'Orleans, younger brother of H. M. King Louis XIII. of France]; à Paris, Sam. Thiboust, 1620, in 4º."

* He assumed the family name of his wife after his own, two years after his marriage; and he dropped it a few years afterwards, having ascertained that her only brother, and consequently the inheritor of the titles and name of Justiniani, had not being killed in the battle, as reported. (See p. 5 of the above-mentioned biographical work.)

It contains the biographies, not only of all the members of the author's family who flourished before him, but of many others of the nobility of the island of Chios, who distinguished themselves by their talents. C. R.

NOTE FOR SPANISH SCHOLARS (3rd S. vii. 73.)—I beg to submit the following, as a more correct translation of Cervantes' sentence than that given by MR. PLATT:—

"And observe, Sancho, that those works of charity which are done reluctantly and lazily, possess no merit, and are of no value." ·

H. W. T.

FAG: A REMNANT (3rd S. vii. 110.)—This word is now of common use; but the original term for an end, strip, or remnant, was the Saxon *dag*. In the *History of Henley* (p. 256), is an account of the goods of John Knight, in 1438, which were forfeited by the killing of his wife: "In primis j daggon de Walssh clothe, verid color." And in Chaucer's *Sompner's Tale*, the mendicant friar begs:—

"Or yeve us of your brawne, if ye have any,
A *dagon* of your *blanket*, leve dame
Or suster dere."

· JOHN S. BURN.

The Grove, Henley.

WATERHOUSE OF KIRTON (3rd S. vii. 138.)—The county of Lincoln is divided into three "parts," namely, Lindsey, Kesteven, and Holland; but, until the answer to P.'s query, I had never heard of either the "parts of Lindsey, or Holland," being again subdivided, so that there should be a· district known as *Low* Lindsey.* P. may possibly feel interested in learning that there is, in the church of Kirton in Lindsey, the recumbent figure of a knight in chain armour, which may probably be that of Sir Gilbert Waterhouse. It was discovered, some four years ago, deeply embedded ·under the floor of the church at the eastern end of the south aisle; and, after narrowly escaping a "restoration," found a resting-place upon the top of the old stone altar of Catholic times.

I may add, that the name of "Waterhouse" may frequently still be met with in villages adjoining the River Trent, which is only a few miles distant from the town of Kirton, in Lindsey.

WM. E. HOWLETT.

Kirton in Lindsey.

PHILIP VAN MACHEREN (3rd S. vii. 135.)—

"A marine painter, who lived at Middelbourg towards the end of the seventeenth century. In 1672 he entered .one of the vessels of war of the republic, for the express purpose of seeing a ˛naval combat—a subject which he ˛delighted to represent. He also made several voyages in

[* "Holland is divided into two parts, the *Upper* and the *Lower*; the Upper contains the two wapentakes of Skirbeck and Kirton; and the Lower only the wapentake of Ellow."—*Magna Britannia*, 1720, ii. 1406.—ED.]

Danish and Swedish vessels for the same purpose. His works are rarely seen with his name; nor are there any further particulars recorded of him, except that Balkema says he died at Amsterdam, and Immerzeel at Rotterdam."—Bryan's *Dictionary of Painters*, London, 1849.

'Ἁλιεύς.

Dublin.

ENGLISHMEN BURIED ABROAD (3rd S. vii. 129.)—Some years ago, visiting a school-girl relative, in the English convent at Bruges, I was admitted to its beautiful chapel, where I copied the following:—

.   I.
" D. O. M.
Hic
manet depositum
COR
Generosæ Dominæ
MARIÆ ANNÆ GIFFORD,
filiæ Joannis Gifford equitis
aurati et illustrissimæ
Dominæ Catharinæ Middleton.
Ætatis suæ 53 obiit
Die 23 Aprilis, An.
Dom. 1759.
R. I. P."

II.
" Deo optimo maximo.
Hic prope jacet
Prænobilis Puella
CAROLINA MARIA TALBOT,
Filia nobilissimi Domini Caroli Talbot
ex antiquâ et nobilissimâ familiâ de
Shrewsbury,
et illustris Dominæ Mariæ
Mostyn.
Annos nata 16
obiit ad hunc conventum,
Die 10 Januarii, 1782.
Hoc marmor in testimonium sui amoris afflicta mater
poni jussit.
R. I. P."

I noted at the same time two other epitaphs in this chapel: the one on "Lucia Theresia Herbert de Powis," professed 1693, deceased 1744; and the other over "Maria Augustina More," a descendant of the great Sir Thomas More, ending: "Sacræ huic Domui annos præfuit 41. R. I. P."

JOHN W. BONE.

· 41, Bedford Square, W.C.

QUEEN OF QUERUMANIA (3rd S. vi. 287.)—On the death of Chrononhotonthologos̓, Aldiberontiphoscophornio and Rigdum Funnidos are about to fight for the hand of the Queen Fadlodinida, who stops them with—

" Well, gentlemen, to make the matter easy,
· I'll have you both, and that I hope will please ye." .

She afterwards changes her mind, and settles the matter more in accordance with the court-morals of those days than of the present.

· In the early editions of *Tom Thumb*, the passages imitated are given in the notes. No such assistance is given in any copy of *Chrononhoton-thologos* which I have seen. ··Some parts look very like parodies. Are they such, or only general imitations of the grand style ? 　　　　W. D.

THOMAS SANDEN, M.D, (3rd S. vii. 74, 143.)—He was an eminent physician at Chichester, and the author of the —

" Three Discourses : 1. On the Use of Books. 2. On the Result and Effects of Study. 3. On the Elements of Literary Taste," &c.

He also published Strictures on Dr. Dawson's Treatment of Acute Rheumatism, 12mo, 1781 ; and contributed articles to Duncan's Annals of Medicine. His name will be found in the Biographical Dictionary of Living Authors, 8vo, 1816.
　　　　　　　　　　　　　　　　F. B.
Caton.

" IN THE TIMES " (3rd S. vii. 153.)—The poem thus entitled will be found in London Society for November, 1862, p. 449. The poem is anonymous, and is illustrated by J. D. Watson.
　　　　　　　　　　　　　　CUTHBERT BEDE.

The verses so entitled appeared in London Society, vol. ii. 449. MR. GASPEY probably has access to this publication ; but if not, I shall be happy to furnish him with a copy of the lines.
　　　　　　　　　　　　　　ST. SWITHIN.

CARABOO (3rd S. vii. 196.) — The utility of MR. BATES's interesting communication would be enhanced if Caraboo's maiden name were given. Cannot your correspondent MR. PRYCE supply it, as also the exact date of her death? 　　S. Y. R.

I well recollect the imposture of " The Princess Caraboo " in Bristol. My father was mainly instrumental in her detection. As a linguist, he had been invited to pay her a visit, with a view to ascertaining what language she spoke. When he entered the room some gentlemen had just placed before her an Oriental MS., making signs to her to read it. She at once began to read it with great apparent facility, and aloud. My father observed quietly to a gentleman near him, but loud enough to be heard by " Caraboo," that the language of that MS. was read, like Hebrew, from right to left. In a few minutes she had changed her mode of pretending to read, and now traced the words from right to left. This opened the eyes of those in the room to her imposition, and she was soon forced to own it. She afterwards said that when she saw my father enter the room she dreaded him. He was persuaded from the beginning that she was an impostor, and probably his countenance and manner indicated such persuasion. I remember that, among other tricks, she used to go upon the roof of the house every day to worship the sun. 　　　　　　　　F. C. H.

WINTHROP FAMILY (3rd S. vii. 160.)—Corrections of Typographical Errors : Second column, which line, for " Sindell" read Lindall, and the version twenty-first line. On line twenty, omit

the comma between Gurdon and Saltonstall : the former being the Christian name, as we term it, but as the Americans (I think more properly) term it, the given name.

A late writer, in speaking of the Winthrop family, has assumed that John Winthrop (only son of Wait Still Winthrop) had returned to England. I presume in consequence of his death occurring at Sydenham, in Kent. Such, however, was not the case ; he was merely on a visit to England (leaving his wife and daughters in New England), attending to a law-suit that he had against Samuel Sparrow and others, arising from a contract with these parties to work a blacklead mine on his estate on Long Island, near New York city. He was accompanied by his son, John Still Winthrop ; and they were for some time, between 1737 and 1743, residing with Mrs. Henrietta Hyde, " in the parish of St. Mary-le-bone," widow of Nathaniel Hyde of Harriott, in Hampshire, and second cousin of John Still Winthrop. The son returned to New London ; and the cousin (Mrs. Hyde) went to New London, probably in company with him, and there resided till her death. She was the daughter of Robert Woodward, D.D., Dean of Salisbury. Her grandmother's sister was the wife of Wait Still Winthrop, and mother of John Winthrop, the father of John Still. It is presumed that Nathaniel Hyde was related to the Hydes, Earls of Clarendon : Sir Lawrence Hyde, uncle of the first Earl of Clarendon, residing at the Close in Salisbury.

I shall be glad if any of the readers of "N. & Q." can inform me whether a Nathaniel Hyde was a grandson of Sir Lawrence. Robert, second son of Sir Lawrence, was Chief Justice of the Common Pleas, and died in 1665 ; and Alexander, the fifth son, was Bishop of Salisbury, and died in 1667.

Mrs. Hyde had three children, who all died in infancy, or very young. An interesting portrait of her and her children is in the possession of Thomas C. Winthrop, Esq., of New York city.
　　　　　　　　　　　　　　GEO. ADLARD.
Barnsbury.

COUNTESS OF SUFFOLK (3rd S. vii. 94, 169.) — I doubt very much whether S. P. V. has hit upon the right person. I think it much more likely that the Countess of Suffolk, to whom a portrait by Zuccaro has been assigned, should be Catherine, the second wife of Thomas Howard, first Earl of Suffolk of that name. But if X. will kindly furnish a description of the portrait to which his inquiry relates, the problem might easily be solved.

In the collection at Gorhambury there was, and probably there still is, a full-length portrait of the Countess of Suffolk above adverted to. She there appears as a lady of well-developed embonpoint, and altogether an easily recognisable personage. Who was the painter ?

In the collection at Castle Howard there was,

and probably there still is, a portrait of the Earl of Suffolk himself (represented as not a very young man), attributed to Zuccaro. What is the size of the picture? When was it painted?

MELETES.

EDMUND HOYLE (3rd S. vii. 153.)—He is said to have been born near Halifax, in Yorkshire. The family of which he was a member came from Flanders or Brabant, and settled and acquired estates in the neighbourhood of Halifax, temp. Edw. III. Branches of the family lived at Swift Place, Hoyle House, Light Hazels, and Hollings, in the same locality. They continued to rank as gentry there, till the end of the eighteenth century. One representative of the family is Fretwell W. Hoyle, of Ferham House, near Rotherham, who bears for arms, ermine, a mullet sable; crest, an eagle's head erased proper; and another is Richard Hoyle, of Denton Hall, near Newcastle, who bears ermine a mullet or; crest, a griffin's head erased. I am not aware that any memoir of Edmund Hoyle has ever been written.

RANGIORA.

ANONYMOUS (3rd S. vii. 199.)—The Meditations of a Divine Soul, 1703, inquired about by MR. LLOYD, is a work of Charles Povey's, and was published again in 1705. The dreamy author was mighty proud of this curious compound; in his Torments after Death, seventh edition, 1742, he says,—

"My work entitled Meditations of a Divine Soul (ten thousand copies of which have been sold at four shillings each) contains several tenets of atheism," &c.

Povey's books are numerous. I have before brought some of them to notice in "N. & Q.", and hope, as his name is again on the tapis, that some of your curious contributors will ventilate through the same channel any notes they may have about the life or works of this remarkable man, who died in 1742 or '43, at the great age of ninety.

J. O.

The Dramas (five not six) of the Princess Amalie of Saxony, were introduced to the English public by the late Mrs. Anna Jameson, under the title of Social Life in Germany, 2 vols. 1840, Saunders and Ottley. My copy is one of a second issue published by G. Routledge in 1846, and has Mrs. Jameson's name on the title-page. ABHBA will find the translation attributed to her in Men of the Time, p. 838, ed. 1857, Kent and Co. (late Bogue).

ARCHIMEDES.

HUGH MORRELL (3rd S. vii. 200) was a merchant at Exeter; and afterwards, for several years, agent at Paris for the English government. It seems that he was residing at Dover in November, 1662; and we find him mentioned in a letter from the Earl of Dorset to Secretary Bennet, March 7, 1662-3. It is probable that he was then advanced in life.

Particulars respecting him may be collected from Green's Calend. Dom. State Papers, James I., iv. 515; Bruce's Calend. Dom. State Papers, Chas. I., iv. 424; v. 197, 200, 202, 223, 250; vi. 230, 240, 292, 377; MS. Tanner, liv. 31, 33; lxvi. 252; Cary's Civil War, ii. 264; Thurloe's State Papers, ii. 61; iii. 444; iv. 524, 669, 692; Green's Calend. Dom. State Papers, Chas. II., i. 383, 421; ii. 554; iii. 71.

C. H. & THOMPSON COOPER.
Cambridge.

OLD HOUSE AT HASTINGS (3rd S. vii. 199.)— The woodcut facing p. 106, in the 15th volume of the Sussex Arch. Collections, is one of the old house of which Mr. Prout made the sketch in 1815. The woodcut has his monogram, and the date. In my day, the house (which stood at the extreme eastern entrance of the town, not precisely in High Street, but eastward of the space where All Saints Street and High Street diverge,) was used as a place for storing wool.

WM. DURRANT COOPER.

"STILL WATERS RUN DEEP" (3rd S. vii. 156.) Is not the following line from Shakspeare's Second Part of Henry VI., Act III. Scene I. the original of this phrase?—

"Smooth runs the water where the brook is deep."

E. R.

"Vada sonant, alta quiescunt."
By whom written?

R. W. F.

FORGED ASSIGNATS (3rd S. vi. 217.)—The late MR. GEORGE OFFOR gave me for my Dartford collections an assignat, the paper for which was supposed to have been made at Dartford. It purports to be an

"ASSIGNAT
de cent francs
Série
621
No. "Ogé." *
287.

The border of the assignat has classic emblems. On the top of the assignat is printed, in lower-case type, about the size of that known in England as bourgeois (but the printing was certainly done in France, and with type cast from French matrixes): "Hypothéqué sur les domaines nationaux;" and at the foot, "Créé le 18 nivose l'an 3e de la République française." On the sides, in small capitals, upright:

"LA LOI PUNIT DE MORT LE CONTRE-FAC-TEUR." d
"LA NATION RÉCOM-PENSE LE DÉNON-CIA-TEUR." f

The hyphens show where the words have been divided in upright columns. MR. OFFOR, in the note he sent to me with the assignat, said:

---

* The signature "Ogé" is printed in script character, in the centre, from a small wood block. At the end of the accented é is a flourish, which might have been intended for either a Q or L.

"The one enclosed is the kind said to be the forgery. It was pasted tight down on a sheet of paper. Soaking it to get it off has injured the stamp [this damage it has now partially recovered]; otherwise it is in fine condition, with the water-marks very perfect. The cap of liberty [these are on the opposite top corners] was a good emblem." "I have two large sheets, showing every form of assignat, with emblems," &c.

Mr. Finch, who made the paper for the forged assignats at the Dartford paper mills, has repeatedly told me that he entered into a contract with a stationer in St. Paul's churchyard to make the paper. The moulds were sold by Mr. Hubbard, the auctioneer, in 1832, after the failure of Mr. Towgood, who, till then, occupied the mills. For further particulars, *vide* my father's *History of Dartford*, p. 233*, 310.

ALFRED JOHN DUNKIN.

Dartford.

REV. JOHN LAWSON (3rd S. vi. 311, 439.) — A memoir of this distinguished geometer, by T. T. Wilkinson, Esq., F.R.A.S., &c., will be found in Alfred John Dunkin's *Archæological Mine*, vol. i. p. 109.   Δ.

BELL CRACKED (3rd S. vii. 169.) — I am happy to be able to give MR. ELLACOMBE a little information on this subject. Several years ago I paid a visit to the church at Hanbury, near Burton-on-Trent, and ascended the tower, in which a new set of bells had recently been hung. I was then informed that, on the completion of the restoration of the church, the workmen employed obtained permission to sound the bells in honour of the architect. One of them, by way of a practical joke, thinking to deaden the sound, suddenly clasped his legs around one of the bells at the moment when his comrade struck it. He succeeded beyond his wishes; for the bell cracked on receiving the blow, and had to be recast. On some surprise being expressed at this accident, the founder observed, that a piece of packthread tied tightly round a bell would have produced the same result. The story made an impression on my mind at the time, and I am now glad that I remember it.   W. J. BERNHARD SMITH.

Temple.

PEPYS'S MEMOIRS (3rd S. vii. 93, 171.) — I have little doubt that the peculiar expressions, occurring in the printed version of Pepys's *Diary*, are due to want of care in deciphering the shorthand characters in which the original is written. The stenographic system used by Pepys was that known as "Rich's;" and one peculiarity of it is, that the letter *s*, when terminating a word, is denoted by a small dot placed under the preceding consonant. Very probably experienced writers of the system often omitted this dot, trusting to the general context to render the meaning sufficiently precise; and I think it extremely likely, that a minute examination of the MS. would show that

this has led to most of the peculiarities of phraseology alluded to by your correspondent JAYDEE. I would venture to suggest that, in case a new edition of the *Diary* should be contemplated, the present printed text ought to be diligently compared with and corrected by the original shorthand MS.

In offering the above remarks, I have no desire to disparage the labours of the Rev. John Smith, the original decypherer of the *Diary*. He appears, on the whole, to have performed a very tedious and difficult task in an extremely satisfactory manner. Indeed to him belongs the chief merit of giving the inimitable *Diary* to the public: for, though the late Lord Braybrooke has gained all the credit for doing so, his sole share in the work consisted in making omissions from Mr. Smith's transcript, and adding the foot-notes.

GAMALIEL EVANS.

"SEDES STERCORARIA" (3rd S. vii: 102.) — See the preface to Peter Langtoft's *Chronicle*, p. xli., where Hearne quotes an ancient MS., entitled "The Ceremonies of the Holy Church of Rome," giving a curious account of what takes place on the occasion of the newly-elected Pope's visit to the Lateran.   E. H. A.

WHITBREAD FAMILY (3rd S. vii. 35.) — There were two distinct families in Sussex, *temp.* Edward III. The one inquired for by your correspondent, as being of the German family "Weitbrecht," was probably of Pevensey, where Stephen "Wittberd" was a resident freeman in 1342. They were distinct from the Witbreds who were freemen of Seaford.   WM. DURRANT COOPER.

Miscellaneous.

NOTES ON BOOKS, ETC.

Polychronicon Ranulphi Higden Monachi Cestrensis; together with the English Translations of John Trevisa, and of an Unknown Writer of the Fifteenth Century. Edited by Churchill Babington, B.D., &c. (Vol. I.) *Published under the Authority of the Master of the Rolls.* (Longman.)

This edition of the *Polychronicon* of the worthy monk of Chester, to whom we owe not only this curious and interesting work, but the equally curious and interesting Series of *Chester Miracle Plays*, promises to be one of the most valuable of the Series of Chronicles now in the course of publication under the authority of the Master of the Rolls. In the first place it will furnish English students with a genuine text of Ranulph Higden; to this is added the translation by Trevisa, a work of great interest to English philologists; and, lastly, a more recent English translation, now printed for the first time from a MS. in the British Museum, No. 2261, in the Harleian Collection. The edition was originally entrusted to Archdeacon Hardwick; but in consequence of his lamented death, has been transferred to Mr. Churchill Babington, who is obviously well qualified to do full justice to Higden and his translators.

Historical Narrative of certain Events that took place in the Kingdom of Great Britain in the Month of July, in the Year of Our Lord 1553. *Written by* P. V. *Now first reprinted from the Latin.* (Bell & Daldy.)

A reprint and translation of an interesting cotemporary tract, written it is supposed, by Peter Vermilly, *alias* Peter Martyr, for the purpose of showing that the death of Edward VI. was not the result of natural causes, but accelerated by unfair means.

Atalanta in Calydon: a Tragedy. By Algernon Charles Swinburne. (Moxon & Co.)

Moulded on the form of the ancient tragedy, and introduced by a long tribute, in Greek verse, to the memory of Walter Savage Landor, this very able and powerfully written drama does not present temptations to general readers. But the time will come when its merits will be widely recognised.

A Dream of Idleness and other Poems. By W. Cosmo Monkhouse. (Moxon & Co.)

A little volume, which shows that the writer is one who thinks deeply, and finds utterance for his thoughts in graceful and flowing verse.

The Herald and Genealogist. Edited by J. Gough Nichols, F.S.A. *Part XIII.* (Nichols & Son.)

The new number of this periodical, which stands in such high favour with genealogists, opens with the first of a series of interesting papers on the Origin and Development of Coat Armour by the editor, which will be found novel and instructive. The number contains also some good papers on the Bibliography of Heraldry, Historical and Heraldic Cards, the Cary Family, &c.

The London Diocese Book for 1865, *containing a Variety of Information for Clergy and Laity. By* John Hassard, Private Secretary to the Bishop. (Rivingtons.)

A little volume, carefully compiled, containing much more information respecting the ecclesiastical arrangements of the diocese of London, both for the Clergy and Laity, than was contained in its predecessor, the *London Diocesan Calendar.*

Stammering and Stuttering: their Nature and Treatment. By James Hunt. (*Sixth Edition.*) (Longman.)

The sixth edition of a work, which all ought to consult who have friends afflicted with impediments of speech.

Notes on the South Lancashire Dialect. By J. A. Picton, F.S.A.

This curious and interesting pamphlet has just come to hand. On the title-page are the warning words, "printed for private circulation," which is as much as to say to the critics "procul estote." Our present impression is, if the author will venture to make the brochure public, we should certainly spare a good word for the little work. If he chooses to maintain his privacy, it is not for us to invade it,

BOOKS AND ODD VOLUMES
WANTED TO PURCHASE.

Particulars of Price, &c., of the following Books to be sent direct to the gentlemen by whom they are required, and whose names and addresses are given for that purpose:—

Newman's Apologia. Part VI.
Cookesley's Pindar. Part III. Nemean and Isthmian Odes.
Willmot's Sacred Poets. 2nd Series.
Sir A. Grant's Aristotle. Vol. I.
Journal of Classical and Sacred Philology.
E. Greswell's Translation of Comus.
The Cloister and the Crowd. Wix, 1834.
　　　Wanted by *R. S. D.*, Union Society, Cambridge.

Tappan's Treatise on the Will. (? Boston, Mas.)
　　　Wanted by *the Rev. J. Maskell*, Tower Hill, London, E.C,

The Life of Robert Raikes, the Founder of Sunday Schools.
　　Wanted by *Mr. John Handcock*, 26 & 27, Commercial Street, Leeds. ·

Choir Books (early), especially any containing Music by Dr. Fairfax and other early English Composers.
Book of Common Prayer, 4to. Barker, 1639.
　　　——————, small 12mo, 1660.
　　　——————, Edinburgh, 1637. Any of them perfect or imperfect.
Missale Augustense. Meyre, 1555.
Canon Missæ. Folio on Vellum. Any edition by Radbalt.
　　　Wanted by *Rev. J. C. Jackson*, 5, Chatham Place East, Hackney, N.E.

Notices to Correspondents.

J. C. (Cambridge.) *Consult Trusler, or some of the other commentators on Hogarth.*

Our Shakesperian Correspondents *will, we hope, not be offended at our postponing their communications until Saturday, April 22.*

T. Davidson. *Heraldic Anomalies was written by the Rev. Edward Nares, D.D., the biographer of Lord Burleigh.*

J. B. Rowlands, *whose query respecting the "Delalaunde" family appears in "*N. & Q.*" 3rd S. V. 377, is requested to say where a letter will reach him.*

Scotus. *The best edition of Alexander Ross's* Helenore *; or the Fortunate Shepherdess, was published by his grandson, the Rev. Alexander Thompson (Dundee, 12mo, 1812), to which is prefixed a Life of the Author. There is also an excellent account of Alex. Ross in Chambers's Biog. Dict. of Eminent Scotsmen, i.v. 198.*

P. (Oxford.) The New Monthly Magazine *commenced January, 1814. It was a separate series that commenced in January, 1821.*

A Reading Case for holding the weekly Nos. of "N. & Q." is now ready, and may be had of all Booksellers and Newsmen, price 1s. 6d.; or, free by post, direct from the publisher, for 1s. 8d.

*⁂ Cases for binding the volumes of "*N. & Q.*" may be had of the Publisher, and of all Booksellers and Newsmen.*

"Notes and Queries" *is published at noon on Friday, and is also issued in* Monthly Parts. *The Subscription for* Stamped Copies *for Six Months forwarded direct from the Publisher (including the Half-yearly* Index*) is 11s. 4d., which may be paid by Post Office Order, payable at the Strand Post Office, in favour of* William G. Smith, 32, Wellington Street, Strand, W.C., *where also all* Communications for the Editor *should be addressed.*

"Notes & Queries" *is registered for transmission abroad.*

LONDON, SATURDAY, APRIL 8, 1865.

CONTENTS.—N° 171.

Notes.

PRECEDENCY OF BISHOPS' WIVES.

The exclusion of the Wives of Bishops from any defined precedence in the social order of Society, has been at various periods subject to remarks and complaints, which in some respects have been considered not altogether unfounded.

The accompanying letter, written many years since, though not publicly avowed, was said to be from the pen of a very eminent Prelate, and as showing his views and arguments upon the subject, may be worthy of preservation in a page of " N. & Q.," as affording all the arguments which could be offered in favour of the exercise of the Grace of the Crown which the writer was anxious to obtain; and which went so far as to suggest the form of an Order, by which he might accomplish the object under royal authority.

In suggesting the *rank* of daughters of Barons for their Wives, it is singular that the *style* and *title* proposed was that of Earls' daughters.　　　　　　　　　　X. Y. Z.

It is said (*vide* Blackstone, bk. I. c. ii. ed.14), that "the Bishops are not *in strictness* held to be Peers of the Realm, but only Lords of Parliament," and (*vide* Brydson's *View of Heraldry,* that " the maxims of the municipal Law in contradistinction to that of Chivalry, ascribes Nobility of *Blood* to none but the Peerage (or Temporal Lords) only," and that, " *hence* it results that the Spiritual Lords are not Barons by tenure or otherwise, in the same sense wherein the Peers or Secular Lords are, else their Wives and families would

certainly share in their honors, though they be not transmissible by inheritance." But this statement is by no means an *explanation* of the *ground* for the *custom* which has hitherto prevailed respecting Bishop's Wives, but merely an ingenious supposition to account for it. It cannot, when compared with the *principles,* or *fact,* upon which the *Temporal Rights* of the Spiritual Lords are *founded,* be made to apply to the case in point; and the *real origin* of the custom is to be found *in a combination of circumstances* which History very fully displays.

It is certain (*vide* Blackstone, bk. I. c. ii. p. 156, ed. 14) —

" The Archbishops and Bishops hold or are supposed to hold, *certain antient Baronies under the King,* for William the Conqueror thought proper to *change* the *Spiritual tenure* of *frank-almoigne* or *free-alms,* under which the Bishops held their lands under the Saxon government, into the *Feudal* or *Norman tenure by Barony,* which subjected their estates to all civil charges and assessments from which they were before exempt, and *in right of Succession to those Baronies* which were *unalienable* from their respective dignities, the Bishops and Abbots were allowed their Seat in the House of Lords."

" Baronies (*vide* Brydson) were formerly *territorial,* but have long become merely *personal.*" Thus it appears that the Bishops sit in the House of Peers *not* in right of their *Bishoprics* or *Spiritualities* (which give their place in Convocation), but in right of the *Temporal Baronies* annexed to the *Bishoprics,* whence is derived their title of *Spiritual Lords*—and this is further proved, by all the *Writs of Summons* — by their title of Baron, Viscount, or Earl, according to the title attached to each See—by the Ceremonies of Investiture of Temporalities— and by the title of Lordship being given *constantly* to the Bishops, and *not only* when in the House of Parliament. It is therefore evident that their Dignity is *personal* and not merely *Official,* like that of the Judges in the Courts of Law. " Bishops are comprehended under the denomination of *Nobility,* and *enjoy the privileges common to all Peers.*" (*Vide* Porney, Blackstone, Clarendon, Hume, &c.) And although it be allowed that the Spiritual Lords hold their dignities by a " Tenure *in some sense different*" from the Temporal Lords, .it *cannot* be proved that this difference affects the point of right in question. The Temporal Lords receive the *Right of Succession* upon their creation, which *ennobles their blood,* and transmits their honors to their posterity, because theirs are *only personal;* but the Spiritual Lords *cannot* receive this Right of *Succession* because their temporal dignity is unalienably attached to the Bishopric, and *therefore their blood* is *not* ennobled. And it is for *this* reason they are not " *in strictness* Peers (*Pares*) of the Realm," viz. because they do not possess *this* right *in common* with all other Peers; but in all other respects it is certain " *they enjoy the privileges common to all Peers.*" It may be further observed, in answer to the supposition that Bishops sit in the House of Lords *as Lords of Parliament in their Ecclesiastical character,* that this is true *only in so far* as their *Ecclesiastical office* enables them to hold *the Barony annexed* to the Bishopric (in token of which Bishops *vote* in their *Episcopal robes,* not in their *Baronial robes*); but it is clearly the Barony *only* which gives them their *Temporal rank.*

"When the Parliament (*vide* Burnet's *Hist. of the Reformation,* Part ii. Book 1. p. 47) was divided into two Houses, then the Clergy made likewise a Body of their own, and sate in Convocation, which was the third Estate. But the *Bishops,* having *a double capacity,* the one of *Ecclesiastical Prelature,* the other of being the *King's Barons,* they had a Right to sit with the Lords *as a part of their Estate,* as well as in Convocation."

Bishops are indeed *Barons* in a twofold manner, viz., *Feudal,* in regard of lands as Baronies annexed to their Bishoprics; and *by Writ,* as being summoned by Writ to Parliament. That *the Barony alone* gives Bishops their *Temporal rank* is clear, because Temporal rank *cannot be derived from Ecclesiastical Office.* It *cannot be a part of it*—it must be *distinct from it,* though *connected with it* by the *authority of the Sovereign.* In its *Origin,* and *traced from its origin,* it will be found to be in nothing different from the Baronies of the Secular Lords, *except* the right of descent, from the cause above mentioned — (even the *now* commonly supposed mark of inferiority of Bishops not sitting in Judgment as Peers in all cases, *originated in a claim of Privilege.*) This Barony therefore must, and *in fact does,* give *Personal Rank.*

The point of *Personal Rank* being ascertained, it follows consequently, that *the Wives of Bishops* have a right to share in their dignity *as Barons,* since it is *a maxim* in Law and in *Heraldry* that " all Wives participate in the Rank of the Husband, either *Personal* or *Hereditary.*"

"By Marriage (*vide* Blackstone, bk. i. c. xv.), the Husband and Wife are one person in Law . . . . . upon this principle depend almost all the legal rights, duties, and disabilities that either of them acquire by Marriage . . . . . married women and widows are *entitled* to the same rank among each other, as their husbands would respectively have borne among themselves, *except* such rank is *merely professional* or *official.*"

And to make the case yet stronger, it may be observed, that the Wives of Judges and of *Privy Counsellors* (an *Office* held only during Pleasure), take place of the Wives of Baronets. "The Wives of Privy Counsellors, Judges, &c. are to take the same place their husbands do" (*Vide* Porney's *Elements of Heraldry*), which rule *must* include the Wives of Bishops, even if Bishops were *only Lords of Parliament,* since there is *no-where any exception in their disfavor.* The rank of Privy Counsellors' Wives has indeed been recently ac-

knowledged in a very remarkable manner. At the Marriage of the Prince of Wales, the Wives of Privy Counsellors were admitted to the Royal Presence, while Bishops' Wives, though the Wives of Peers of the Realm, were excluded—a circumstance very generally considered as a striking indignity to the Bishops themselves, as well as a glaring proof of the impropriety of the present situation of their Wives.* *It was expected* that this opportunity would be taken to raise the Wives of Bishops to their proper station in society; and *it has been said* that the difficulty of fixing the place of *Archbishop's Wives* prevented it. But this supposed difficulty will be entirely removed by recurring to the *foundation* of the claim of Archbishops and Bishops to Temporal rank, and to the causes which have hitherto operated against the acknowledgment of the Right of their Wives to share that rank. *Thence* it will appear evident that in strictness the Wives of Archbishops can only rank as the Wives of *Barons.* The right to personal rank as Barons, Bishops and Archbishops *equally* possess, in virtue of original grant and by the laws of the realm; but *precedence* among the Peers (originally *Lords alike*) is determined *solely* by the King's pleasure. When, therefore, King Henry VIII. assigned to the Archbishops their high place in the Table of Precedence, it must be considered as a mark of respect due to their *Ecclesiastical character* — upon which principle the *Spiritual Lords* are named before the *Secular Lords* in all acts of state—*but the marriage of Bishops not being allowed* when the order of precedence was determined, and the claim of Bishops' Wives to rank being derived from the antient Baronies *annexed* to the Bishoprics by William I., it seems very clear that the Wives of the Archbishops are *not* entitled to the same elevation with their husbands in the precedence granted to their *Archiepiscopal,* and therefore *official* character; which is a matter quite distinct from their right to rank as the Wives of Barons — a right which they also possess by the *laws of the realm,* the *maxims of heraldry,* and *the courtesy of England,* although it has hitherto lain dormant from a combination of circumstances, which shall be briefly mentioned in order to account for a *custom* as singular as it is mortifying to the persons concerned, both in its origin and its consequences. At the time of the Reformation the Bishops were not all agreed concerning the important point of marriage; and those Bishops who did marry, married very privately, and kept their wives concealed, and in a sort of obscurity, in order to avoid giving offence to those who, from Popish prejudices in favour of celibacy, questioned the lawfulness of their marrying. Queen Elizabeth's avowed aversion to the

* From this it would appear that the letter was written soon after April, 1795.

marriage of the clergy is well known. She even chose to consider their wives as *concubines*, and yet on *one* occasion she contessed the strange impropriety of their situation, though she could not bring herself to allow them any rank. (*Vide* Strype's *Life of Archbishop Parker*, *Hume*, &c.) In the succeeding reigns the prevailing spirit of Puritanism on one side, and the continual *attempts* to effect a reconciliation of parties on the other, contributed alike in their turn to lower the rank and importance of Bishops themselves; and it could not therefore be possible for their wives to acquire any new privilege declaratory of rank which it seemed the common object to deny. In *a late reign*, however, rank *was actually promised* to the Wives of Bishops; but a circumstance of a peculiar and personal nature *postponed* the performance of this promise, and *a change of Court* taking place before that impediment was removed, this promise was left unfulfilled. In the present times, various causes concur to make the acknowledgment of this right politically desirable, and it will be peculiarly hard if, when titles and honors have been so profusely distributed among all descriptions of people, the class of persons *who possess a right to them* should be suffered to remain in their present humiliating condition, which is now most universally confessed to be more strikingly improper than ever. The condition of Prelates' Wives is, indeed, truly termed *humiliating*, not only because, according to the wish and design of Queen Elizabeth to throw an odium upon all married Bishops, it does, in fact, *resemble* the state of "*concubinage*" rather than that of *marriage*, since the common privilege *enjoyed by all other wives* of sharing the *personal dignity* of their husbands is withheld from them— but because *no place* being appropriated to them in that society in which they are necessarily led to live, they are thus singularly subjected, by the elevation of their husbands, to the awkward and distressing situation of persons suddenly brought forward into a circle, without being directed to their place, and involuntarily exposed, often without the protection of birth or connexions, to the coldness of disdain, and the impertinence of envy, while they are expected to support the *indefinable dignity*, of which they cannot but be conscious, of their *undefined station*—and farther, because the wives of physicians, surgeons, painters, drawingmasters, bankers, merchants, grocers, &c. &c., are continually invested with titles and rank, denied to them, though the Wives of Peers of the Realm; and all the daughters of all Baronets have precedence, however circumstanced, though it sometimes happens (as in an existing case [*]), that the

At Norwich the Bishop's Chaplain's Wife constantly takes her place as the daughter of a baronet above the Bishop's Lady, though the Bishop himself is of a noble family.

Wife of the Bishop's Domestic Chaplain thus takes place of the *Wife of the Bishop.*[*]

(*To be concluded in our next.*)

FOLK LORE.

CAKES ON PALM SUNDAY.—It has been the custom from time immemorial to mark the return of Palm Sunday at Hentland church, Herefordshire, in a peculiar manner. The minister and congregation receive from the churchwardens a cake or bun, and, in former times, a cup of beer also. This is consumed within the church, and is supposed to imply a desire on the part of those who partake of it to forgive and forget all past animosities, and thus prepare themselves for the festival of Easter.

I should be glad to know whether these peaceofferings are a relic of a more general custom, and whether it prevails in any other part of England. Hentland is memorable as the site of Dubritius's College, from whence issued the opponents of Pelagianism.   C. J. R,

HOW TO PREVENT A WOUND FROM LEAVING A SCAR.—One of my children being badly cut on his forehead, a Huntingdonshire woman told his nurse that if she wished the wound not to leave a scar, she must wet it every morning with her spittle before she had eaten or drunk. The force of the charm lay in the latter part of the injunction; and the woman said that she had always known it to be effectual when strictly carried out.
   CUTHBERT BEDE.

TURKISH FOLK LORE.—The Anatolian Turks will not eat the red-legged partridge, because they say its legs are bloody, which arises from this circumstance:—A prophet had taken refuge in a poplar tree (*kavak* in Turkish); and when his pursuers came up, the partridge pointed him out by calling *Ka-kavak kavak ka ka kavak.* Of course, the version varies.

It will be observed that this legend is, from its nature, peculiar to a Turkish population. It depends for its basis on the cry of the bird and the name of a tree. It is most likely very old, and brought in from Turkestan. It cannot exist among the allied Madyars, as the word for poplar is different in that language.   HYDE CLARKE.
Smyrna; Jan. 14, 1865.

WAITS AT YORK.—I am not aware if a custom which exists in York, in connection with the

[*] This lady was Sarah, daughter of Sir John Hinde Cotton, of Landwade, Bart., wife of the Rev. John Oldershaw, Archdeacon of Norfolk, 1797, and Chaplain to the Right Rev. Charles Manners Sutton, Bishop of Norwich, 1792 to 1805, when he was translated to the see of Canterbury.

waits, has yet appeared in your pages. For the five successive Mondays preceding Christmas, a band of waits perambulate the principal streets; and after serenading the inhabitants with an air, proceed to salute the heads, and sometimes the individual members of each house, by name. Not long ago I was *en pension* at St. Mary's convent, better known as "The Bar," from its vicinity to Micklegate Bar—one of the many grand old gates of the city. Being a light sleeper, and having a quick ear, I was always deputed on these exciting occasions to be the rouser of the seven other girls, who formed the complement of our jealously guarded dormitory. Arrived beneath the convent windows, the one air common to the nocturnal entertainment was performed. This over, a stentorian voice roared out:—

"Good morning to the Lady Abbess!—Good morning to the nuns!—Good morning to the young ladies!—Three o'clock in the morning: a fine [or otherwise] morning!—Good morning to the chaplain! [his house immediately adjoined the convent].—Good morning to all!—Good morning!—Good morning!"

Immediately after Christmas, the waits called at all the houses thus honoured; and a tradition existed among the girls, that half-a-crown was presented on the occasion to these speculative philanthropists by the Reverend Mother.

BRUSSELLS.

JEWISH FOLK LORE.—A Polish Jew once gravely informed me that it was his own firm belief, and that of his co-religionists, that the sun was to shine on some part of every Wednesday; because the sun was "created" on the fourth day of the week.   H. W. T.

"TAKE A HAIR OF THE DOG THAT BIT YOU."— This homœopathic cure of the effects of excessive joviality is, at least was, very well known; but I have never met with any account of its origin. This may no doubt be owing to the limited extent of my reading; but I will venture to give the following passage from *La Gitanilla*, one of Cervantes' *Novelas*:—

"A young man, on approaching a gipsy-camp by night, was attacked and bitten by the dogs. An old gipsy woman undertook to cure his wounds, and her procedure was, 'she took some *hairs of the dogs*, and fried them in oil, and having first washed with wine two bites he had in the left leg, put the hairs and oil upon them, with a little chewed green rosemary over them; she then bound the wounds up with clean cloths, and made the sign of the cross over them,'" &c.

The wine and oil may remind us of the parable of the good Samaritan.   THOS. KEIGHTLEY.

DRAGON IN HEREFORDSHIRE (3rd S. vii. 133, 210.)—In addition to other answers it may be

stated, that the tradition of the "Dragon" still lives in this neighbourhood of Mordiford in *the name* given to a deep ravine and pathway leading from the main road overhanging the Wye, far away and up into the hilly tableland and forest district of the "Woolhope Valley of Elevation." *Serpent's Lane* is well known to all here, and even to geologists and fern-hunters from a distance. The whole of this region has a special interest geologically and archæologically. Not only are fossils of the Devonian and Silurian periods to be found, and traces of British and Roman camps and battle-fields still survive in *the names* of many places; *e. g.* Cradock = *Caractacur;* Caplar Wood = (a camp) Ostorius *Scapula;* Oyster Hill (latterly called Din-dor Hill = Dun-Dwr, the fort by the water), which commands the Wye near Hereford, and traces its pedigree from the same commander, *Ostorius;* Colwall = *Collis Vallum;* and many others. In later days Offa's Dyke, which joins the Wye near Byford, west of Hereford, formed the limit of the Mercian kingdom. Welsh names consequently prevail on the south and west of this boundary line, Saxon on the north; but Roman traces appear on both sides. It should be added that the *Dragon* was the heraldic bearing of Wales, and it is possible that the Mordiford legend may represent some defeat near that place in Saxon times of a local Cymric chieftain, who may have still held out, like his greater chief in earlier days, Uther Pen Dragon, in the rough and inaccessible district forming the "Silurian upheaval" of Sir Roderick Murchison, and of which Woolhope is the centre.   T. W. W.

Hampton Bishop, Hereford.

OLD AGRARIAN WORDS. *Too late*

In a Wiltshire Rent Roll of *temp.* Elizabeth, I have met with the following words and phrases, some of which are now obsolete, others not quite so. To students of words they may be interesting, as there are some that I do not see in our Archaic and Provincial Glossaries.

Relating to land.

"One messuage and other housing, containing in all six *romes* or *feilds*, and one *acreman of land*, and two *cotes* containing three closes of pasture."

"A messuage, &c., containing one *stych* and one *acreman.*" [Stitch means ridge.]

"One messuage, and one *place*, and one *acreman of land*, which contain three closes and xxv acres of land."

"Every of the *place-holders* shall fynde a maker to make the hey: lykewyse shall the viij *acreman-holders.*"

"Every *place-holder*, whereon any house is standing," &c.

"A *rowlease tenement*, and half yarde lands with common for two *ruther beasts.*"

"Any tenant being a *place-holder* of a *row-lease tenement* without a house belonging therto," &c. [I have elsewhere seen "a ruinose or rollesse tenement."]

"Four *cotes*, which contain one smyth's forge, one close

of pasture called ' The four cotage,' and sundry other small parcels of ground."

" One rod and one *shermegold* of mead." " Two *plecke* of void ground. " A little *pocke* of meade." " One *parrock* of pasture." " A *corsettell* of land." " A *farundell* " [sometimes ' A *fardingale* '] of land." " Half an acre and two *hornes* of land containing three rodds: of lotts in Westmead acre."

" The Lord to enter to the *steanmead and vallo* [fallow] at Lammas."

Relating to Timber.

" Except to the Lord all timber trees and *trees of warrant.*"

" Towards the reparacyon of their houses, the tenants to be allowed wyndfalls and *starvelings* that leave noe green leaves."

" The tenant to take and have *fryth* bryars and thornes."

Relating to Commons.

" None but their feild, wherein they *stynte* themselves with sheep as they thinke most meete."

" Pasture for cc sheep, four oxen, and two *hallyers.*"

" For vij *ruther beasts*, one *horse beast* and *one colt called a hallyer.*"

" Heyne."

" Eckmead to be *heyned* at th' annuncyacion of Our Lady, and to be cutt before Midsummer." [" To heyne a field " is still a phrase in constant use, meaning to close it up for the grass to grow.]

To " Showle-cast."

" To carry out once in the yere all the donge that shall happen to be made in the shepe-house, and also to *showlecast* togeather one third part of the soyle upon the grange barton." [To " showle cast " is of course to heap together with a shovel always called a " showle " by Wiltshire labourers.]

" Mow."

[To mow, according to modern usage, always means to cut with a scythe ; but in the next extract it clearly meant, *temp.* Eliz., some variety of stacking, as " a barley-mow," *i. e.* barley stacked under cover."] " To hold for xxi yeres, paying yerely of rent the thirdes and tythes of the corne growing upon the errable land : the tenant to sow and dress 60 acres with wheat and 60 with barley : to cut down, sheafe, *pooke*, and rake the said thirdes and tenths, and when ready to be carryed, to carry for the Lord into hys barne or *rekehey*, there to be *mowed* or *reaked* at the choice of the Lorde."

Farm-house Words.

" The south-end of the oxe-house belonging to the grange, containing two *feilde*, the old kytchen," &c.

" A *dwelling house containing fyve feilds*, whereof two are newly builded."

" One parlour, a buttery, a *whyte-house* [dairy], one house for *fearne*."

Livery.

Tenants to wear livery. On the back of a lease an agreement was written — " That the said John shall during his life serve the said Sir Walter and wear his lyvery, if the said Sir Walter will bestow his cloth upon hym : and also ride with the said Sir Walter upon reasonable warnyng, and to make hys lyving hymself at his own charges."

Another tenant " Shall and wyll make and weare the lorde's lyvery when yt shall please hym to geve the same to make the same, and also shall not at any tyme weare the lyvery of any other person without the Lorde's good wyll therto fyrst had."

A Mortuary Fee for Pigs.

" Every tenant shall pay to the Lord for pannage of piggs, for every pigge that every of them shall kill at slaughter time, 1ᵈ."

" Imphayes."

This is the name of a field. In a second parish it is called " Nymph-hay." In a modern rate-book of that parish it has been degraded into " Empty field."

" Far-leve."

" The best piece of plate, bedde, or other chattell, in the name of an heryott, or *far-leve*."

" Hipple."

" Two acres at the *hipple* of stones in Hide-field."

J. E. J.

LEEDS DIALECT.

I have cut the following from a Leeds newspaper, and send it to you, as you may think it worth preservation in " N. & Q." It gives with much correctness the peculiar pronunciation of the district, and the sentiment is unobjectionable. The phraseology is also characteristic of the class, amongst whom the speaker might be expected to be found. In my early days I have heard sermons, by local preachers, in the same style as to language and utterance. And I much question whether pure English, as spoken by the educated classes, would have been understood by many of those to whom such sermons were addressed.

" T'OWD COLLIER'S LAST WORDS.

(*Founded on a true incident.*)

" Cum in and see me agean lad,
　Sed t'Collier tul his mate ;
　Am gettin varry owd,
　An sadly aght a date.

" Sumhah I feel sa wake nah,
　But wunce wor strong enuf ;
　Wi' dewin t'least it world
　Am clean knock'd aght a puff.

" We've hed a lot a barns—true,
　But then I luv 'em, mun ;
　An I sud find it hard
　Ta pairt wi' even wun.

" They may hav kept uz poor,
　But still I'll trust an pray
　At God al bless em all
　Wen I am tane away.

" An then there's t'wife—poor lass —
　It trubbles me, indeed,
　Ta think wen I am goan
　At shoo may ivver need.

" But then I pray agean,
　An sooin I think I hear
　A anser thro' aboon,
　At bids me nivver fear.

" It seems ta giv ma hoap
　At t'barns al nut neglect
　Ta lewk ta all her wants,
　An show her due respect.

" An then my thowts go back
  Tut bygone, happy day,
  When t'parson made us wull
  On that bright morn e May.

" We've trudged on hond e hand,
  Till ower t'top ut hill ;
  But I mun leave her nah,
  I feel it's Natur's will.

" Then cum an see ma agean lad,
  It glads my heart ta see
  Owd mates I've knawn sa long,
  Nah, wen am bahn ta dee."

T. B.

WORDS USED IN DIFFERENT SENSES. — It has been remarked, I think by Archbishop Trench, and is well known, that several words in the English language, which were formerly used in different senses, have gradually become restricted to one, and that the worse signification. *Resentment* and *censure*, the former of which was once used to express gratitude as well as revenge, and the latter an opinion generally either good or bad, are instances that occur to me. *Officious* is a word generally, I think, now used in the bad sense of fussy and meddlesome ; yet it could not have been always so, or an old parishioner of mine on her deathbed would not have told me that her relatives had been very officious, evidently meaning that they had been kind and attentive ; in short, mindful of their duty towards her. In a letter from John Johnson, Esq., to Henry Liddell, Esq., dated Newcastle, Oct. 9, 1715, and printed in the Appendix to Lady Cowper's *Diary*, is proof of another word—viz. *insinuation* having once been capable of a good as well as a bad meaning : —

" Sir Charles Hotham's regiment is expected here upon their route for Berwick, but I hope, through the insinuation [*i. e.* the friendly interposition] of Lord Scarborough to keep them here till further orders from Government."

E. H. A.

COPY OF ST. MATTHEW WRITTEN BY BARNABAS. The following curious passage, in an obscure chronicle, will no doubt interest some of your readers : —

" A.D. 477. Hoc tempore corpus Barnabæ Apostoli, et Evangelium Matthæi stylo ejus scriptum ipso revelante reperitur."—*Hermann. Contract. Chron.* ed. 1579. p. 205.

A copy of St. Matthew written by Barnabas would be of inestimable value. I believe a recent publication professes to contain a facsimile of part of the first gospel from a MS. of the apostolic period. Of course all such professions are more than suspicious.   B. H. C.

ART IN AUSTRALIA.—In these days when there is scarcely the person who has not a relation or friend at the antipodes, it becomes very interesting to watch the efforts of our Australian colony to advance itself in the polite arts. By English artists in particular, I think the following extract will be read with exceeding gratification. I take it from the *South Australian Government Gazette*, No. 23, Adelaide, Thursday, June 2, 1864, and "Published by Authority." This number contains pp. 443 to 476, 4to : —

" TO ARTISTS.

"Notice is hereby given that the Government of Victoria has determined to offer the sum of 200*l.* for the purchase of a painting or paintings, by an artist or artists resident in Australia, provided such painting or paintings possess sufficient merit to qualify it or them to compare favourably with the works of eminent living artists in Europe. Such painting or paintings to be placed in the Public Gallery of Art of Victoria.

" Every picture submitted must be painted and finished in oil on canvas, panel, or other suitable material, or in water colours.

" The subject of the picture is left to the judgement and taste of the artist."—[&c.]

EDWIN ROFFE.

Somers Town.

BISHOP HEBER. — Amongst the recollections of Bishop Heber's early life, in the first volume of Mrs. Heber's biography of her deceased husband, there are at p. 346 some humorous lines sent to a fellow collegian (Lord Ebrington), from Birmingham, where, on his way to Oxford, he had been kept awake throughout the night by the noisy revelry of a public ball held at the Hen and Chickens. The fifteen Greek lines are a supposed Homeric fragment, with a bald translation into Latin, and copious notes in the old editorial style, and describe his then present situation. The whole *jeu d'esprit* is well worth turning to ; but the object of this communication is to "make a note" elucidating, on the authority of personal recollection, the supposed commentator's explanation of the first line : —

˝Ω πόποι· ἢ μέγα πένθος ὁδοιπόρῳ ἔσσεται ἀνδρί.

V. 510. ὁδοιπόρῳ ἀνδρί. Quis foret ille peregrinus non adhuc satis constat. Herculem scholiastes, Thesea alii intelligunt. Non animadvertêre scilicet boni *interpretes* de seipso poetam hic loqui, quem Poetam Jaspida fuisse Anglo-Phœnicem ipse suprà demonstravi : Excurs. i. ver. 17 hujus libri. Et tamen cl. Turnebo Moses his versibus annui videtur ; quàm verè judicent alii.

The few surviving contemporaries of the good bishop may remember, 1st the fact, though perhaps none ever knew the wherefore, of his having always gone amongst his familiars in college by the name of *Jasper ;* and, 2nd, that he was a most popular member of the *Phœnix*, the membership of which club was then, and probably is still, sought after as a social distinction by the undergraduates of Brasenose. It may help, for the instruction of posterity, to whom it must otherwise be lost, to note this meaning of the bishop's own description of himself, as "Jaspida Anglo-Phœnicem."   SEPTUAGENARIUS.

HAZLITT'S EDITION OF TUCKER'S "LIGHT OF NATURE."—In a very able criticism of Tucker's well-known book, in the *Saturday Review* for

Nov. 12, 1864, the reviewer speaks of the desirableness of publishing a condensed edition of that work, and states his conviction that such a volume would be both valuable and popular. He appears not to be aware that there is in existence an abridgement of Tucker by William Hazlitt, with a preliminary essay written with all Hazlitt's accustomed acuteness and power of abstract thought. The copy I possess is of the first edition (John Johnson, London, 1807). I am inclined to think no second edition was ever published. But I am convinced, with the *Saturday Reviewer*, that a réprint of an abridgement of Tucker would pay well, and there can be none better than Hazlitt's.

D. BLAIR.

Melbourne.

GREAT SEAL OF SOUTH CAROLINA. — Without affecting, avowing, or disavowing proclivities, as they are called, I may fairly at the present moment extract the following from the *Universal Magazine* for February, 1778 (p. 107), for the readers of "N. & Q.": —

"February 10.

"The device for the Great Seal of South Carolina : — A palmetto tree, supported by twelve spears, which, with the tree, are bound together in one hand [qu. band], on which is written, 'Quis separabit?' On the tree are two shields, the one inscribed March 26, the other July 4 ; and at the foot of the palmetto an English oak fallen, its root above the ground and its branches lopt.

"In the Exergue,
'MELIOREM LAPSA LOCAVIT,'
1776.

."Legend : 'South Carolina' immediately over the palmetto, and on the opposite part of the circle, 'Animis ad fata paratis.'

"*Reverse :* —

"Hope advancing over a rock, which is rugged and steep behind her, but smooth and of gentle ascent before. The way is strewed with the arms of an enemy. She holds a laurel-flower in her right hand, and has a view of the sun rising in full splendour.

"In the Exergue,
'SPES.'
"Legend : 'Dum spiro spero.'"

W. J. B.

Queries.

THE AMERICAN REGIMENT. —Where can I find a list of the officers in Colonel Gooch's regiment (the Americans) in 1741? When the regiment was disbanded in October, 1742, what became of the Colonel?

P. S. C.

VISCOUNT CHAWORTH. — Can any one furnish me with the date of the death of the last Viscount Chaworth, which took place between the years 1673—1700?

F. P. L.

DELVED, DOLYE, OR DALF? — The *Athenæum* of March 18, points out some printer's errors in a very useful book of quotations, compiled by Mr. J. Hain Friswell, and just published under the title of *Familiar Words.* In this work are given the lines : —

"When Adam dolve, and Eve span,
Who was then the gentleman ? "

According to the *Athenæum* there are two mistakes here, and the lines ought to run,—

"When Adam delved, and Eve span,
Where was then the gentleman ? "

Thinking *delved* (a "weak" form) much less likely to be the past tense of *to delve*, in Richard II.'s reign, than *dolve* (a "strong" form), I turned to the only histories I had at hand, and found the lines differently given in each. Keightley gives —

"When Adam dalf, and Eve span,
Who was then the gentleman ? "

Hamilton reads —

"When Adam delved, and Eve span,
Who was then the gentleman ?" *

Will some of your readers settle which of the four versions is correct? It seems odd that there should be so many different versions of the lines, and it seems to me unfair to condemn Mr. Friswell in two mistakes because his version does not agree with the *Athenæum's.* Mr. Keightley's seems to me the best, and the *Athenæum's* the worst: for Richardson shows that Chaucer makes the past tense *dalfe*, and the perfect participle *dolven.* Any reader of Chaucer would require the citation of some authority before believing that the past tense of *delve* was *delved* in Richard II.'s time. As to *where* versus *who*, I should vote for the latter, on the score of probability.　N. N.

DISCIPLE. —Where did the word *discipulus* get its letter *p*, which appears also in *disciplina?* But for its presence in the latter word, I should have suggested *puellus* as its possible parent, i. e. *discens puellus.* But etymologists only give *disco* as the root ; whereas, it is clear to me, that somewhere there must exist another root which supplied the *p ;* unless, indeed, it is simply euphonious.

ALPHA BETA.

POWER OF FRANKING. —I have in my collection of franks one of the late Duke of Gloucester's. It is not signed, as would be expected, with the name of H. R. H.'s peerage, as is the case with all the other royal franks I have ; but with his Christian name, "William Frederick," being the usual way in which royalty signs except in the cases of franks. This leads me to ask, whether the royal family had the power of franking independently of the peerages they held? I shall be glad of information on the subject, either in "N. & Q." or privately from any one who could tell me. With whom I should be glad to exchange franks, or autographs, if they liked.　H. F.

Union Club, Oxford.

[* This is the reading adopted by Southey in his *Wat Tyler.* —ED.]

FUSTIAN IN NAPLES.—The following occurs in an inventory of the time of King Henry VIII. What does it mean?—

"Itm̄, a new cushion of *fustian in naples* wᵗʰ knoppes of black silke."

A. O. V. P.

THE O'CONNORS OF KERRY.—I am desirous of knowing whether there has been any late publication in regard to the history of this Sept. David O'Connor, of this race, founded the "Siol-t-Da," a sept of Kerry. Where can I find a full account of him? What are the sources (at present available) for information? X. Y. X.

"MAHOGANY," A CORNISH BEVERAGE. — In Croker's *Boswell's Life of Samuel Johnson* (edit. 1835, vol. viii. p. 53), we read:

"Mr. Eliot mentioned a curious liquor peculiar to his country, which the Cornish fishermen drink. They call it 'Mahogany'; and it is made of two parts of gin and one part treacle, well beaten together. I (Jas. Boswell) begged to have some of it made, which was done with proper skill by Mr. Eliot. I thought it very good liquor; and said it was a counterpart of what is called Athol porridge in the Highlands of Scotland, which is a mixture of whisky and honey. Johnson said, 'That must be a better liquor than the Cornish, for both its component parts are better.' He also observed: 'Mahogany must be a modern name: for it is not long since the wood called Mahogany was known in this country.'"

1. Who was Mr. Eliot?*
2. Does any one know of Cornish fishermen having a drink called "Mahogany"?
3. If so, can the name "Mahogany," applied to this drink, be explained?

GEORGE C. BOASE.

Penzance.

ST. MAGNUS, ORKNEY.—Is it true that Sir Henry Dryden, of Canons Ashby, co. Northampton, Bart., went several successive summers to Orkney for the purpose of taking drawings, and architectural plans, with other details, of the cathedral of St. Magnus? Is it true that he entered most perseveringly into the whole scope, plan, and particulars of this ancient and interesting building, and compiled an elaborate record of its present state? Is it true that, in his zeal for minuteness, he had scaffolds erected under the vaulting of the roof, and thereon lay upon his back, close under the bosses of the ceiling, in order that he might copy them the more correctly? If these things are true, as alleged, and that only one copy of these drawings and memoranda exist, it is highly desirable that others be made therefrom. Surely this point is worthy the consideration of Scotland, if Sir Henry would permit his handy work to be multiplied. P. HUTCHINSON.

[* Edward Eliot, created Baron Eliot of St. Germains, co. Cornwall, Jan. 30, 1784; ob. 1804. He is frequently mentioned in Lord Chesterfield's *Letters to his Son.*—ED.]

POWLETT MSS.: MARY, QUEEN OF SCOTS. — I have heard it asserted that there was formerly in the possession of the Powlett family a collection of MSS., contained in several volumes, bound in old red morocco, small folio size; consisting principally of copies of letters to and from Sir Amyas Paulet, during the time that he was Governor of Fotheringay Castle and gaoler of Mary, Queen of Scots; and that, about twenty-six years ago, these papers passed into the hands of a Mr. Blackett, a surgeon in Green Street, Grosvenor Square.

Mr. Blackett has been dead some time. Is it known what has become of these MSS., or in whose keeping they are at present? They may possibly be known to some of the many writers who have made the history of this unfortunate Princess their peculiar study; and there can be no doubt that they must contain information of the highest interest in connection with the last years of her life. E. M'C.

QUOTATIONS WANTED.—

"The sun slept on his clouds, forgetful of the voice of the morning."

"Immortal till his work is done."

"The storm that wrecks the winter sky,
No more disturbs their soft repose,
Than summer evening's latest sigh
That shuts the rose."

[The second stanza of a poem entitled "The Grave," by James Montgomery. See "N. & Q.," 1st S. x. 353.]

F. R. S.

Can any of your correspondents tell me where I shall find these lines:—

"Sometimes the young forgot the lesson they had learn'd,
And loved where they should hate (——) like thee."

Is not this the original of the saying attributed to Napoleon I. about the sublime and the ridiculous?—

"L'on ne sauroit mieux faire voir que le magnifique et le ridicule sont si voisins qu'ils se touchent."—Fontenelle, *Dialogues des Morts, Sénèque et Scarron.*

X. H.

"Retribution in a *human* hand is Havock, and not Justice."

J. H.

Youghal.

THOMAS RUDDIMAN AND JOHN DRUMMOND, M.D. — Some time ago I purchased a copy of a book published in Edinburgh, 1720, called—

"The Letters and Negotiations of Sir Ralph Sadler, Ambassador to King Henry 8th of England to Scotland; containing the Transactions of two memorable Embassies."

On the fly-leaf, written in Ruddiman's fine bold manly style, was the following interesting memorial of friendship for a man of whom we should like to know something more; and an important literary acknowledgment not mentioned in Lowndes:—

"Viro longe optimo ac eruditissimo Joanni Drummond, M.D., hunc Librum, sua precipue cura in lucem editum, lubens meritoque dono mittit, studii sui in eum, existimationis, et grati animi qualecunque monumentum futurum.
                                                "Tho. Ruddiman.

"22 Junii, 1720."

Can any of your readers give information about Dr. Drummond?   J. G.

Roman Tesseræ.—Some years ago I purchased about a peck of tesseræ which had been taken from the floors of a Roman villa, some portions of which had been discovered in a field about two miles from Lyme, in Dorsetshire. (The discovery is mentioned in *Arch. Journal*, March 1854, p. 49.) These tesseræ are made of chalk, white lias, blue lias, and red brick. About one-third part of them have been reset, and placed in the centre of the floor of a small antique building belonging to me. They were reset, not on the earth, but in a shallow hollow, or dish, about an inch deep, cut out of a slab of stone. The cement used was Portland cement: the water was from a well in the valley of Sidmouth, away from the sea—good, pure, drinking water. Not long after the slab of stone, with the tessellated pavement set in it, all in one solid mass, had been placed in the floor resting on the solid earth, I observed that a white efflorescence formed on the surface of the pavement; as if some salt were issuing from the work, and crystallising. This crystallisation proceeded, and proceeds most rapidly in dry weather. After an absence of a month, I once found that the undisturbed action had produced an effect nearly an inch thick: so that the tessellated pavement looked as if it were covered with a quantity of white cotton wool. This, however, is only one instance out of many. On brushing it off, and putting my tongue to it, it tasted like saltpetre; and it produced combustion, like that salt, when thrown into the fire. I am anxious to stop the formation of this salt, be it nitrate of potash or anything else: for not only does its appearance spoil or hide the colours of the tesseræ, but they themselves are thereby receiving injury, as in some places their top surfaces have broken up and flaked off. Some have suggested painting over the work with oil, but I fear this would darken the colours of the tesseræ. I have several times applied washes of Bartlett's silicate of potash, but altogether without any good effect. Could any correspondent of "N. & Q.," learned in chemistry, point out to me any remedy?
                                                P. Hutchinson.

Song.—"When he thinks of the days that are gone." Some fifty years or more since, I met with a short piece the burden or refrain being the above line. As an old man, I would be thankful to any one who would help me to it again.
                                                Sexagenarius.

Spinning-Jenny.—What is the origin of the name "Spinning Jenny"? Guest, in his Com-

pendious *History of the Cotton Manufacture*, says, at p. 13, that Highs "produced the ingenious machine known by the name of the Spinning Jenny, and which he so called after his daughter, her Christian name being Jane."

Most, if not all, other writers on the subject state, that Hargreaves (for whom the invention is also claimed) named it after his daughter Jane; but he never had a daughter.*   B. W.

Stained Glass in Cologne Cathedral.—In the north aisle of Cologne Cathedral, near the western entrance, are four or five of the finest old stained glass windows I have ever seen. They are, I think, immediately opposite to the beautiful modern windows in the south aisle, presented by Ludwig, King of Bavaria, and contrast curiously with them. I should be glad to know the date, artist, and donor of them—the latter especially. The only shield of arms that I remember is that of the Counts of Leiningen (ancestors of Her Majesty the Queen), which is several times repeated.   John Woodward.
New Shoreham.

Joseph Vien, Artist.—In the *Athenæum* of the 25th of March, there is the following paragraph relative to the chestnut tree which is popularly believed to burst into leaf about the 20th March. I should be glad if authorities can be given by any one for the tradition with regard to Vien, and if any record of the trial can be found.

"The celebrated chestnut-tree of the Tuileries that bursts into leaf before its neighbours, and generally enters an appearance by the 1st of March, is a laggard this year. Crowds stare up at its bald crown in disappointment. The tradition which has given the people faith in the precocity of this tree dates, neither from the birth of the King of Rome, nor from Napoleon's return from Elba. The date is the 20th of March, 1746. A celebrated painter was accused of having assassinated his rival at the Royal Academy on that day. The painter's name was Joseph Vien. He proved before the tribunal of the Châtelet that at the moment of the murder he was standing, gossiping with the Duchess de Roncevaux, under a chestnut-tree. He said he could identify the tree, for it was the only one in leaf. 'This *alibi*,' we are told, saved Vien's head; and from that time the people have watched the precocious tree. It has seldom failed; but the cold of the present year has been too much for it."
                                                Percy B. St. John.

Williams Family.—Roger Williams died 1691, aged sixty-eight; David Williams died 1726, aged seventy; John Williams died 1741, aged seventy-

[* In Pulleyn's *Etymological Compendium*, edit. 1853, p. 64, it is stated that "the term Jenny was derived from Hargreave's *wife*, whose name was Jane, but whom he used to address by the familiar name of Jenny; thinking, no doubt, as the latter had been very prolific (which was the case), that his new invention would be equally so, under a similar appellation. The result justified such a conclusion." On turning, however, to Baines's *History of the Cotton Manufacture*, pp. 177, 178, we find that *Elizabeth* was the name of Hargreave's wife.—Ed.]

seven. Three inscriptions on the same gravestone, inside Lantarnam church, co. Monmouth; presumed to have been a father and two sons. Can any reader of "N. & Q." give any clew to the ancestry of either of those? He will oblige by giving such through "N. & Q.," or to Mr. Wm. Price, Glannant-y-llan, Llanfoist, near Abergavenny. GLWYSIG.

RICHARD WISEMAN, SERJEANT-SURGEON TO CHARLES II. — When and where was he born? In what year did he die? And where was he buried?* JAYDEE.

Queries with Answers.

MOTTO OF THE ARMS OF NOVA SCOTIA. — I enclose a woodcut taken from a Halifax newspaper representing the arms of Her Majesty's old and flourishing province of Nova Scotia, and shall be glad if any of your readers can explain the meaning of the motto, which is a standing puzzle to the learned on that side of the Atlantic. The arms are thus described in the patents granted to the baronets of Nova Scotia by Charles I. previous to 1629: —

"Ar. a cross of St. Andrew azure charged with an inescocheon of the royal arms of Scotland, supported on the dexter by the royal unicorn, and on the sinister by a savage or wild man ppr.; and for the crest a branch of laurel, and a thistle issuing from two hands conjoined, the one being armed, and the other naked, with this motto—'Munit hæc et altera vincit.'" — Berry's Encyc. Heraldica.

The usual local rendering is "One defends and the other conquers." Or it might be "He defends these, and conquers the others." Either way how does it apply? X.

[The true import and bearing of an old motto is often a hard nut to crack; but we think the specimen before us admits at any rate of a fair conjecture. From one hand issues a thistle; from the other a sprig of laurel: the one protects, the other vanquishes. The protective or defensive character of the thistle, indicated by its prickles, is clearly referred to in the motto of "The Knights of the Thistle," "Nemo me impune lacessit " (No one provokes or attacks me with impunity). The laurel is now so generally recognised as the emblem of victory, that not a word need be said on the subject.

It is remarkable that as the old motto of the Baronets of Nova Scotia now figures as the motto of the colony, so the motto of the Knights of the Thistle is the motto of Scotland.

Some of our readers may be old enough to recollect that in former days the national motto, "Nemo me impune lacessit," was malevolently transferred from the Scotch thistle to a certain cutaneous malady disagreeably affecting the interstices of the fingers. No one, it was pretended, could safely shake hands with his dearest friend

* [* See a note respecting this eminent surgeon in our 1st S. x. 424.—ED.]

if he came from North Britain : the motto of his own land indicated the danger—"Nemo me," &c. But with reference to this vulgar prejudice we beg leave to place on record a little anecdote. A venerable friend, a physician still living in Canada West, was ere the present century had entered its teens, surgeon to a Scotch regiment, the Musselburgh militia. Talking over the various forms of disease which he had to treat, while serving in the regiment, an acquaintance remarked, "I suppose you had plenty of this," scratching with one hand between the fingers of the other. "No," said the doctor, "during the whole time I was in the regiment, we had not a single case.—Oh, yes, I forget. On one occasion our men went into barracks that had previously been occupied by an English regiment, and a few days after several of them had the itch."]

REFORMADES. — In the Holy War of Bunyan, which is the second best religious allegory in the language, and, in Lord Macaulay's opinion, narrowly escaped being the first, the author being his own successful rival in his Pilgrim's Progress, occurs the following stirring picture : —

"But when they set out for their march, oh, how the trumpets sounded, their armour glittered, and how the colours waved in the wind ! The Prince's armour was all of gold, and it shone like the sun in the firmament : the Captains' armour was of proof, and was in appearance like the glittering stars. There were also some from the court that rode reformades for the love they had to the King Shaddai, and for the happy deliverance of the town of Mansoul."—P. 88, Tract Soc. Ed.

Reformades—what and why, and instances of equally early use ? The word occurs again on p. 106 : "Those that rode reformades, they went about to encourage the captains."

By-the-way, is there any commentary on Bunyan's Holy War ? Pilgrim's Progress has been annotated in profusion. LECTOR.

[Bunyan's Holy War has been illustrated with notes by William Mason (8vo, 1782), by the Rev. George Burder (8vo, 1803); as well as by Mr. George Offor in the collected edition of Bunyan's Works (3 vols. roy. 8vo, 1862). Mr. Burder has the following note on the above passage : "Reformades, an old word signifying volunteers. The angels are intended, because 'ministering spirits,' who delight to explore the wonders of redemption, and to serve the heirs of salvation." Mr. Offor adds, " Reformades, angel volunteer officers, not attached to any troop or company." Phillips, in his New World of Words, fol. 1706, explains "Reformado, or Reformed Officer, as an officer whose company or troop is disbanded, and yet he continued in whole or half-pay; still being in the way of preferment, and keeping his right of seniority. Also, a gentleman who serves as a volunteer in a man-of-war in order to learn experience, and succeed the principal officers."]

SALT SPILLING: ALLUDED TO BY CLASSIC WRITERS. — Is there any allusion, in Latin or Greek classical authors, to the superstition about spilling salt? Any kind friend who will supply a reference, or references, will much oblige

IGNORAMUS.

[There are very many allusions to the sacred character of salt, not only in the Holy Scriptures, but also in the classic writers. Salt was used in all sacrifices (St. Mark, ix. 49), and was especially offered to the Penates (Horace, Ode iii. 23 ; Livy, xxvi. 36) ; but we remember no classic allusion to the superstition attached to spilling it. Our correspondent will find a very interesting investigation of the subject in Sir Henry Ellis's excellent edition of Brand's *Popular Antiquities*, London, 1842, vol. iii. p. 82. The earliest notice given there is from Bishop Hall (characters of Virtues and Vices, 1608—The Superstitious Man); but here the idea of the ill-luck is the salt *falling towards* a person, not merely the spilling it. In Leonardo da Vinci's wonderful picture of the Cenacolo (" Last Supper "), at Milan, Judas Iscariot is represented as overturning the salt-cellar as he stretches out his hand to receive the sop. Some persons have supposed this action alludes to the superstition, and some in fact say it was its origin ; but in Italy very little is thought of upsetting salt—the dread there is to spill *oil*. This is thought to be an omen of severe sickness or death. Spilling *wine*, on the contrary, is thought lucky, and everybody cries out "allegria." We should be glad to receive from our readers the earliest notice they may come across of this superstition.]

" JERUSALEM THE GOLDEN." — I shall be much obliged to you if you will inform me where I can find the Latin original of the hymn commonly known by the name of "Jerusalem the Golden."

E. F. S. S.

[The Latin original of this beautiful hymn, by Bernard, a monk of Clugny, is printed in Abp. Trench's *Sacred Latin Poetry*, second edition, 1864, p. 307, to which is appended the following note : "In these lines the reader will recognise the original of that lovely hymn, which within the last few years has been added to those already possessed by the church. A new hymn which has won such a place in the affections of Christian people as has ' Jerusalem the Golden,' is so priceless an acquisition that I must needs rejoice to have been the first to recall from oblivion the poem which yielded it. Dr. Neale, as is known, no doubt, to many of my readers, in his *Rhythm of Bernard de Morlaix on the Heavenly Country*, London, 1859, has translated a large portion of the poem."]

HERALDIC.—I should feel much indebted to any of your readers who would be obliging enough to tell me to what families the subjoined arms belong :—

(*a*) Bendy of six gu. and arg. within a bordure (erm. ?), charged with seven bezants.

(*b*) Paly of six az. and ar., a fesse chequy az. and or.

W.

: [The coat which most resembles (*a*) is that of Valetort; bendy of six arg. and gules on a bordure sable, bezants. See Papworth's *Ordinary*, p. 345.

(*b*) Is probably not quite correctly blazoned, and might be paly with a fess, *counter-company*, Courtoys, or Curtis. We are glad to learn that Mr. Papworth is fast recovering from his late severe illness, and that his excellent and useful work is likely to proceed as heretofore.]

Replies.

WILLIAM, SON OF KING STEPHEN.

(3rd S. vii. 201.)

The *Art de Vérifier les Dates* makes this William the second legitimate son of King Stephen, by Maude, heiress of the Counts of Boulogne. When Stephen seized the English crown, he transferred the county of Boulogne to his eldest son, Eustace, who died without issue 11 Aug. 1153, when this William (with Stephen's consent) inherited Boulogne and Moreton. In 1159 he joined the expedition to Toulouse, and died, either there (Vaissette), or on his return (Ralph de Diceto), leaving no issue by Isabel de Warren, his wife. Thereupon his sister Mary, Abbess of Ramsey, in England, becoming his heir, was induced to abandon her nunnery, by Matthew, brother of the Earl of Flanders, and to marry him, who thereupon seized the county of Boulogne, and maintained himself in its possession in spite of the pope's efforts to have it given up to Constance, widow of Count Eustace, who claimed it in dower; Matthew's marriage with a nun being deemed of no validity. Nevertheless Ida, daughter of this marriage, being legitimated by the pope, inherited the county of Boulogne (*Art*, &c. iii. 2nd part, p. 298.)

S. P. Y.

I beg to send the following answers to HERMENTRUDE's queries (3rd S. vii. 201):—

1. The Williams she mentions are identical. See Watson's *History of the Earls of Warren and Surrey*.

2. King Stephen had a natural son named William. His mother was named Dameta. See Rapin's *History*.

3. The legitimate son married the Countess Isabel.

The fact that the husband of the Countess was confessedly Earl of Boulogne and Lord of the Eagle appears to me in favour of his legitimacy : for these were hereditary honours in the house of Blois, and it will be remembered that this William, if legitimate, was his father's only surviving son and male representative, as the two eldest sons, Baldwin and Eustace, died *vitâ patris*.

CHARLES F. S. WARREN.

VOLTAIRE.
(3rd S. vii. 211.)

Though I cannot produce evidence of the dreadful dialogue between Voltaire and his physician, it will not appear improbable, when the following authentic account is considered. In the work entitled, "*Voltaire, particularités curieuses de sa vie et de sa mort*, par M. Elie-Harel," occurs an exact copy of the Memoir of the Abbé Gaultier, presented by him to the Archbishop of Paris, detailing all that passed at the death of Voltaire. This contains the notes that passed between the Abbé Gaultier and Voltaire, his visits to Voltaire, and the retractation which Voltaire wrote himself and signed. This, however, was not sufficiently ample to satisfy the Archbishop, and M. Gaultier prepared a fuller form of retractation, which he read to Voltaire's nephew, the Abbé Mignot, when he came at six o'clock in the evening of the 30th of May, 1778, to fetch the Abbé Gaultier to hear his uncle's confession. " *Votre dernière lettre*," said he " *lui a fait une grand impression : il veut se confesser, et ne se confesser qu'à vous.*"

The Abbé Gaultier handed the form of retractation to the nephew, who quite approved of it, and promised him that Voltaire should sign it. They went to call the curé of the parish, St. Sulpice, and they all three entered together the room where Voltaire lay. They found him wandering so much in his mind that the abbé could not say anything to him, either about confession or retractation : he could only request that he might be sent for again when Voltaire should be more composed ; and this was promised. After these priests had left him, his physician, M. Tronchin, came and found him dreadfully agitated, and crying out in despair : " *Je suis abandonné de Dieu et des hommes ; et portant les mains dans son vase de nuit, et saississant ce qui y était, il le mangea.*"

This Dr. Tronchin related to several respectable persons, and added : "I wish that all those who have been seduced by Voltaire's books had been witnesses of his death ; no one could have borne such a spectacle." Voltaire died at about eleven o'clock on the same night. I think it, therefore, very likely that the dialogue referred to did occur between Voltaire and Dr. Tronchin.   F. C. H.

I cannot trace any reliable evidence as to Voltaire's death-bed. The *Penny Cyclopædia* (vol. xxvi. p. 438, art. " Voltaire," states " the details of his death are contradictory : he seems to have been exhausted, and only to have wished to die quietly."   W. POLLARD.
" Herts Guardian," Hertford.

The *Biographie Universelle*, generally considered to be a very trustworthy authority, says on this point that —

" A cloud of obscurity and contradiction surrounds the last moments of Voltaire. . . . It has been constantly asserted that, when summoned by the *curé* of St. Sulpice to say whether he acknowledged the divinity of Jesus Christ, he turned round and said : ' Laissez-moi mourir en paix.' According to other authorities he said : ' Au nom de Dieu ne me parlez plus de cet homme-là.' This sacrilegious antithesis is not very probable, considering his extreme weakness both of body and mind at that time. However this may be, the *curé*, turning to the Abbé Gauthier, said with prudent moderation : ' Vous voyez bien qu'il n'a plus sa tête.' "

RICHARD B. PROSSER.
25, Southampton Buildings, W.C.

SIR ROBERT DOUGLAS OF GLENBERVIE.
(3rd S. vii. 223.)

The following inscription, copied from the tombstone of Sir Alexander Douglas, Bart., in the Howff burial ground, Dundee, may interest your correspondent S. Y. R. : —

" Sacred to the Memory of SIR ALEXANDER DOUGLAS, Bart., of Glenbervie, physician in Dundee, and of Dame Barbara Carnegy of Finhaven, his spouse ; also of Robert Douglas, Esq., their only son — who all lie interred here. Sir Alexander, born 1738, died 1812 ; Lady Douglas, born 1741, died 1815 ; Robert, born 1776, died 1780. By the heirs of Lady Douglas.

Sir Alexander was physician to the forces in North Britain. His name appears upon the Staff down to 1802, and for several years previously.

I may add, that I have in my possession a copy of Sir Robert's *Baronage of Scotland*, printed upon large and fine stout paper, beginning at p. 1 and ending at p. 562 (properly p. 560, for that folio, as well as the three preceding, are misprinted) ; being (as stated in foot-note to p. 563 of the complete book) the portion of the work as far as carried on by Douglas. This copy of the *Baronage* bears the book-plate of George, Lord Macartney ; and contains a MS. index to the families, with corrections and additions throughout the volume, written in a small neat hand. To the first marginal note on the left of p. 13 (Innes of Innes), are added the words : —

This Charter is lost, but there is a Transcript of it in the possession of the family under the subscription of Gavin Dunbar, Lord Register in the reign of King James the 5th."

" This Charter is in the possession of the Family," is added to the first note on the right of same page.

At p. 47 (Moncrieff of that ilk), the following curious note is written, opposite to the paragraph beginning, " XI. THOMAS " : —

" This Person was a servant of John, 14th Earl of Crawford, Lord Treasurer. He made much money by the purchase of Prizes in the time of the 1st Dutch War in K. Chas the 2ds Reign. 'Tis said that his name was not Moncreiff, but that he assumed that Name upon his purchase of the Estate of Moncreiff."

Can any reader of "N. & Q." throw light upon the origin or truth of this statement, and the original surname of the person referred to? Or give any idea of who wrote these notes? The writer seems to have been well acquainted with the history of Scotch families, particularly those in the North. The following, inserted after the word "deduced," line 11 from foot, col. 2, p. 335 (Cuming of Altyr), may afford an additional clew to the writer:—

" . . . He bought several Debts against the Family Estates, which his brother James had much encumbered; had it adjudged and brought to sale, and became the Purchaser. He died unmarried, leaving his fortune to his grand Nephew Alexander [the undoubted head or chief of that illustrious family], who married —— daughter of Sir Ludovick Grant, of Grant, Baronet, and has issue."

The Alexander above referred to married in 1773; was created a baronet in 1804, died in 1806, and was grandfather of the present Sir A. Gordon-Cuming, Bart.　　　　　　　　　　　A. J.

WATTE VOCAT (3rd S. vii. 221.) — The verses referred to by your correspondent H. W. T. are to be found in a note to p. 119 of Pinnock's Goldsmith's England, where they are attributed to Gower the poet, and are said to have been written on Wat Tyler's insurrection. I subjoin a copy of the verses as given, with Andrews's translation.

" Watte vocat, cui Thoma venit, neque Symme retardat,
　Bat que, Gibbe simul, Hykke venire jubent.
Colle furit, quem Bobbe juvat, nocumenta parantes,
　Cum quibus ad damnum Wille coire volat.
Grigge rapit, dum Davie strepit, comes est quibus Hobbe,
　Larkin et in medio non minor esse putat.
Hudde ferit, quem Judde terit, dum Tibbe juvatur,
　Jacke domosque viros vellit, et ense necat."

The translation by Andrews is as follows:—

" Wat cries, Tom flies, nor Symkin stays aside;
　And Bat, and Gibb, and Hyke, they summon loud,
Colin and Bob combustibles provide,
　While Will the mischief forwards in the crowd;
Greg hawls, Hob bawls, and Davy joins the cry,
　With Lary, not the least among the throng;
Hodge drubs, Jude scrubs, while Tib stands grinning by,
　And Jack with sword and firebrand madly strides
　　along."
　　　　　　　　　　　　　　　　　　P. M.

KELLAWAY, CO. DORSET (3rd S. vii. 220.)—The hamlet or tything of Weston, or Stalbridge Weston, co. Dorset, the early residence of the Weston family in that county, and more anciently in deeds and monuments called Calewe Weston (from its proximity to the river Cale), is doubtless the place indicated by your correspondent. Thomas, son of Sir Wm. Weston, Knight, Lord Chief Justice of Ireland (most probably referred to by G. W.) is buried on the north side of the chancel of Stalbridge church. (Vide Hutchins's Dorset, under "Stalbridge," where a description of the monuments is given.) Some notices of the Weston

family will be found in "N. & Q.," 2nd S. x. 266, 395, 500. Although Hutchins, in the earlier editions of his work, states that no pedigree of the family occurs in the Visitation Books, there is a descent of four generations of Westons of Callew Weston, deduced from the Lord Chief Justice, given in Her. Visit. co. Dorset, 1677 (penes Coll. Arms, Lond.)　　　　　HENRY W. S. TAYLOR.
Halifax.

There can be but little doubt that Thos. Weston of Kellaway, co. Dorset, must be Thos. Weston of Callow-Weston, a manor in the parish of Stalbridge, belonging to the Abbots of Sherborne, and long held by the family of Weston. In a monument in Stalbridge church, of about a hundred years since, the word is spelt Calewe, as also in a much older one; and in the registers of Sherborne, the name, now more commonly written Kellaway, appears under the various forms of Calway, Callway, Keylway, and Keyleway.
　　　　　　　　　　　　　　C. W. BINGHAM.

STALE MATE (3rd S. vii. 221.) — Check-mate (German, schach-matt) is in French échec-et-mat, while schach-patt (stale-mate), has its equivalent in the French pat, the final t being pronounced in the French as in the German words. Landais derives pat "(suivant Ménage) de l'Italien patto ou patta, qui signifie la même chose, et dont l'origine est très-incertaine." In Spanish stale-mate is mate ahogado, literally "smothered mate," a term known in our own game in a different sense.
　　　　　　　　　　　　JOHN W. BONE, B.A.
41, Bedford Square, W. C.

I think DR. BELL will find pat to be the French term for stale mate; and faire pat to be the phrase for giving stale mate.　　　　　P. M.

BARLEY (3rd S. v. 358; vi. 481; vii. 84, 162.) The remarks on "barley" and the Lincolnshire dialect, by LINDENSIS, remind me of a boyish play in which I was once very fond of indulging. We used to form ourselves into a line, and then select one of our company to stand out a few yards to the front. As soon as he had taken his position he called out at the top of his voice,—

　" Black-thorn, Black-thorn;
　Blue milk and barley-corn.
　How many geese have you to-day?"

Our reply was,—

　" More than you can catch and carry away."

A race then took place to certain points, and the one he caught not only took his place at the mark in front, but was obliged to carry him on his back to the line. We called this "playing at blackthorn." I may add, that from long and careful observation, I have come to the conclusion that East Lancashire is quite as Danish as Lincolnshire. The Ordnance Maps supply us with numerous farmsteads, &c., whose names are very little changed, either in orthography or pronunciation, from their Danish originals. Our local dialect, too, abounds in terms from the same source. "I can't *fin* o' my hart," is to be heard any day amongst us; and to be "*witsherd*" this snowy and wet weather is no uncommon occurrence. "Eearn yo felly ah du*rnd* kno, but yo ma gooa raand't cornur and then *sper*," was a reply given to me by a female not long ago, of whom I asked the road to a street in the town of Preston. I afterwards found that she came "fra Blegburn" (Blackburn), and was no longer surprised at her answer. Mr. Arnold, in his recent *History of the Cotton Famine in Lancashire*, has noticed the Anglo-Saxon element in our local dialects, but he seems to have been unaware of the extensive admixture of Danish and Scandinavian terms. A stranger, such as Worsaae, would also find the intermixture of races quite as remarkable as the dialect. The inhabitants of this portion of Old Northumbria have not yet lost all traces of their descent from the Danes and Northmen who at different times colonised the county.　T. T. W.

Burnley, Lancashire.

The Mace of Kinsale (3rd S. vi. 159.)—The old mace of this corporation did not long remain in the possession of the Rev. Dr. Neligan after its sale. I found it in the hands of Mr. Cooper of Holborn, and purchased it from him at the request of my friend, Sir George Bowyer, who wished to present it to the mayor and corporation of Margate. A notice of this presentation has appeared in the present volume of "N. & Q." and in several papers. It is engraved in the *Illustrated News*. When I obtained it the cross was lost from the mound: this has been restored.

　　　　　　　　　　W. J. Bernhard Smith.

Temple.

Goodrich Family, Lincolnshire (3rd S. vii. 134.)—There is now living at Hagg, near Spilsby, a Mr. Thomas Goodrich, aged eighty-one, whose progenitors were allied to the East Kirkby Goodriches, and no doubt that of the old Bishop of Ely.　　　　　　　　　　Wm. Bailey.

The Dodralis Potio (3rd S. vii. 208.)—I am very well pleased with the four lines of your correspondent, F. C. H., but I think it necessary to translate a distich by a distich. This was my difficulty, which I now try to meet:—

" *The Nonal Drink.*

" I'm Nine, for I bread, water, honey, wine,
　With broth, salt, pepper, herbs, and oil combine."

　　　　　　　　　　　　　　　　　　K.

Inscription at Chillingham Castle (3rd S. vi. 384.)—See in *Archæologica Æliana*, new series, vol. iii. p. 1, a learned paper, explanatory of the above, by the Right Hon. Lord Ravensworth, President of the Society of Antiquaries of New-

castle-upon-Tyne; and another paper in the same volume, p. 279, by the late lamented Dr. Raine, respecting the authorship of it.　　E. H. A.

American Depreciation of Currency (3rd S. vii. 6.)—This note reminds me of an "historic doubt" which I would much thank you to solve for me in relation to the American continental money, hundreds of dollars of which, fallen to me from my ancestors, I have from time to time given away to curious collectors. Is it true that the British government, or its officers with its knowledge, helped the depreciation by the issue of counterfeit bills? The last four of the following lines, from the fourth canto of John Trumbull's *Mc Fingal*, printed at Hartford, in America, in 1782, point to the popular belief:—

" When lo! an awful spectre rose
　With languid paleness on his brows;

His breast-plate grav'd with various dates,
' The faith of all th' United States.'

I started, and aghast I cried—
' What means this spectre at their side ? '

' Alas!' great Malcolm cried, ' experience
Might teach you not to trust appearance:
Here stands, as drest by fierce Bellona,
The ghost of Continental Money.'

In vain great Howe shall play his part,
To ape and counterfeit his art;
In vain shall Clinton, more belated,
A conq'rer turn to imitate it."

In a late reprint of this "epic poem" (New York, 1864,) the editor does not hesitate to assert that such counterfeits were distributed "by cartloads," and adds—"Such was one of the dishonourable modes of warfare employed by the British commanders here."　　　　　St. Th.

Massachusetts Stone (3rd S. v. 298.)—If I have properly consulted the indexes of "N. & Q." the query under the above reference has never been answered. In Mr. Laing's *Trans. of Snorro Sturleson's Heimskringla*, Lond. 1844, or rather in the Preliminary Dissertation thereupon (vol. i. p. 172), will be found some extended remarks upon the well-known stone on the river Taunton, in Massachusetts, covered with what have been called Runic characters, and known as the Deighton Writing Rock. The commentator's estimate of the historical value of the inscription is not high. On p. 175 is a drawing of the rock, and at p. 176 a larger copy of the writing as given by Dr. Baylie and Mr. Goodwin in 1790, and by the American antiquaries in 1830. The author refers to *Antiquitates Americanæ* (Hafniae, 1837), and to a communication of the Rhode Island Hist. Soc. to the Soc. of Northern Antiquaries at Copenhagen, 1830, and observes that other rocks similarly marked are found in various parts of the interior of America, far from the coast — as on the Alleghany and Connecticut Rivers, about Lake Erie, on Cumberland River, about Rockcastle Creek. I have an impression that there is also an account of the Deighton Rock in one of Prof. Edward Hitchcock's *Reports* and in Silliman's *Journal*.

St. Th.

Dr. Percy (3rd S. vii. 181.)—

"Dr. Percy knowing himself to be the heir male of the ancient Percies,* and having the warmest and most dutiful attachment to the noble house of Northumberland, could not sit quietly and hear a man praised who had spoken disrespectfully of Alnwick Castle, and the Duke's pleasure grounds, especially as he thought meanly of his (Pennant's) travels."—Boswell's *Life of Johnson*, 9th edit. vol. iii. p. 273.

E. H. A.

Lady Tempest's Jury (3rd S. vii. 136, 224.) — The Lady Tempest, who was tried for high treason, was Anne, wife of Sir Stephen Tempest, of Broughton, the eldest daughter of Sir Thomas Gascoigne, of Barnbow, the second baronet, who at the time of his trial must have been about eighty-four years of age. See Dugdale's *Visitation of Yorkshire* (edit. Davies), 289, 361.

The following extracts from Luttrell's *Diary* may further elucidate the matter to which your other correspondents refer: —

"1679-80, March. The Lady Tempest, daughter to Sir Thomas Gascoign, by order of councill was the 3d committed to the Gatehouse, in order to her tryall at next assizes at York, whither she is to goe.

"The 17th, at the assizes at York, the Lady Tempest, Thomas Thwing, and Mary Pressick were arraigned on an indictment of high treason for conspiring the death of the King, &c.; but they excepting against so many of the jury, their triall could not be proceeded with, but is putt off till next assizes.

"1680, July. At the assizes at York, the 24th, Thomas Thwing and Mary Pressicks came to their tryall on an indictment of high treason on account of the Popish Plott; and on consideration of the evidence, the jury found Thomas Thwing guilty, and Mary Pressicks not guilty.

"At the same assizes Sir Miles Stapleton came to his

---

* See this accurately stated, and the descent of his family from the Earls of Northumberland clearly deduced, in the Rev. Dr. Nash's excellent *History of Worcestershire*, vol. ii. 318. The Doctor has subjoined a note, in which he says: 'The editor hath seen and carefully examined the proofs of all the particulars above mentioned now in the possession of the Reverend Dr. Thomas Percy.' The same proofs I have also myself carefully examined, and have seen some additional proofs which have occurred since the Doctor's book was published; and both as a lawyer accustomed to the consideration of evidence, and as a genealogist versed in the study of pedigree, *I am fully satisfied*. I cannot help observing, as a circumstance of no small moment, that in tracing the Bishop of Dromore's genealogy essential aid was given by the late Elizabeth, Duchess of Northumberland, heiress of that illustrious house; a lady not only of high dignity of spirit well as became her noble blood, but of excellent understanding and of lively talents. With a fair pride I can boast of the honour of her grace's correspondence, specimens of which adorn my archives."

---

tryall; but he challenged so many of the jury, that he could not be tryed this assizes, but was to stay till next.

"The same assizes, the Lady Tempest (daughter to Sir Thomas Gascoign) and Mr. Charles Inglesby came to their triall for high treason on account of the plott, and were by the juries acquitted."

It is satisfactory to add, that Sir Miles Stapleton (who was a nephew of Sir Thomas Gascoigne) was acquitted in July, 1681.

The right name of the priest, who is called Thwing, was Thwenge. He was also a nephew of Sir Thomas Gascoigne. (See Howell's *State Trials*, vii. 1181.)

From Dugdale's pedigree of Gascoigne we ascertain that this Thomas Thwenge was a son of George Thwenge, of Kilton Castle, in Cleveland, by Anne, fourth daughter of Sir John Gascoigne, the first baronet.

A Mrs. Ravenscroft, Sir Thomas Gascoigne's granddaughter, appeared at his arraignment and trial. Can the Yorkshire genealogists assign her place in the pedigree?

C. H. & Thompson Cooper.

Cambridge.

The Crosses of St. George and St. John (3rd S. vii. 200.)—The cross of St. George is borne by the following families, &c., as well as by those in Mr. Davidson's list: —

St. Georges, Marquis de Verac.
St. Georges de Kerroualt. (Brittany.)
Giorgi (Italy) in chief.
Cibo, Prince of Massa, in chief as an augmentation from Genoa.
Sedeigno, arg. a cross gu., within a bord. az. (otherwise az., an escutcheon of St. George.)
Grégoire, the cross slightly patée throughout. This is also the case with the cross in the dexter half of the arms of the Abbey of Creutzling.

The city of Lincoln bears the cross of St. George charged with a fleur-de-lis or. Arg. the cross of St. George, in the dexter canton a sword erect gu., are the well known arms of the city of London.

The cross of St. George is also the armorial bearing of the most noble Order of the Garter. With a different chief in each case it forms the arms of the four Kings-at-Arms, Garter, Norroy, Clarencieux, and Ulster. It also appears in the arms of the College of Arms, of the Trinity House, and of the East India Company. With other charges it forms the arms of the kingdom of Sardinia (not the duchy of Savoy, which bears the cross of St. John), and of the Florentine family of Machiavelli.

The cross of St. John is also borne by the following: —

Bishopric of Vienna (with an escutcheon of the arms of Austria).
Bishopric of Costnitz.
Family of Aspremont.
Family of Bécherel.

Family of Kinzich (Prussia).
Family of Roquette.
Counts de Rottal, Bohemia.
Family of Rougé (usually patée throughout).
Family of Bulgarini (Tuscany) surmounted by a chev., reversed *az.* moving from the chief. As given by Siebmacher, the cross in the arms of the Bishopric of Constance is slightly patée.

The cross of the Order of St. John is never eight-pointed in the arms of the order or of its knights. It was only the *decoration* which was so formed.　　　　　　　　JOHN WOODWARD.
New Shoreham.

DE BEAUVOIR FAMILY (3rd S. vi. 147.)—Allow me to refer JUXTA TURRIM to Smyth's *Life and Services of Captain Philip Beaver, R.N.* (London, 1829); and to inform him that in the early part of the last century, a gentleman named Peter Beaver, whose daughter, Martha, was married in 1739 to Latham Blacker, Esq. of Rathescar, in the county of Louth, resided in the old and fashionable town of Drogheda. I have their portraits, which are large-sized and in good preservation.
ABHBA.

SLOW TUNES AND QUICK TUNES (3rd S. vi. 27.)—I have heard the anecdote attributed to Rowland Hill; who, being annoyed at his footboy singing profane songs whilst cleaning the knives and the forks, ordered him, under the penalty of dismissal, to sing hymns. But as the work proceeded only to the tune of the solemn yet slow measure, Rowland Hill was compelled to tell the boy to return to his old style of profane music, otherwise his knives and forks would not have been ready for dinner.
ALFRED JOHN DUNKIN.
Dartford.

FIENNES FAMILY: SAYE AND SELE (3rd S. vi. 455.) — Amongst my father's MSS., I find in a MS. pedigree that—

"Sir Wm Fienys, Kt, made Viscount Say and Sele by Pat. 7 Jul., 22 Jac. I., ob. at Broughton, 1662. He married Elizabeth, daughter of John Temple of Stow, co. Bucks."
ALFRED JOHN DUNKIN.
Dartford.

RAMPERS (3rd S. vi. 45.)—The root of this word is *ripa,* a bank. Whence the shoal off Dungeness is termed *Rip-rapps.* In my *Cæsar's Cantian Campaigns,* I have given the present French name for this shoal, which is Celtic.
ALFRED JOHN DUNKIN.
Dartford.

MOROCCO (3rd S. vii. 73.) — I tasted this drink when at Levens. It is, as C. C. P.'s friend states, "almost dark, pours like oil, and tastes mild as milk in its treachery." The Morocco is always brought in an immense and curiously wrought glass to every one who dines at Levens for the first time; and the visitor is expected on no account to refuse the glass, but to taste it and say—"To the health of the Lady of Levens!" there being a current story of a curse on the house, viz. that, since the alienation of certain property from the Grahams, there should never be a male heir to Levens. I believe the recipe for making Morocco, is kept strictly secret.

Your correspondent has made two mistakes in his query. Levens Hall is in Westmoreland, not Cumberland, as stated by C. C. P.; and it belongs to a branch of the Suffolk, not the Carlisle family.
W. I. S. HORTON.
Rugely.

MEDIÆVAL CHURCHES IN ROMAN CAMPS (3rd S. vi. 37.)—The churches of Caistor, Lincolnshire, and Porchester, Hants, are built in Roman enclosures.　　　　　ALFRED JOHN DUNKIN.
Dartford.

"PISCIS FLOTANS" (3rd S. vii. 55, 124.)—In acknowledging my obligations to MR. BINGHAM, I must at the same time express my regret that in my former communication I did not give some further intimation of the context: for, with that before him, I am persuaded that he would not have suggested the possibility of a duty having been laid specially on the exportation of dabs, or flounders. In the days of King John and Henry III., the fishery of Guernsey consisted mainly of congers — at that time a considerable article of trade. In summer they were dried. In winter they were pickled. In either case, there was a duty paid on them. Besides which, if *Piscis flotans* was exported to Normandy, a duty was imposed upon the boat. This *Piscis flotans* I suppose to have been the fish that was neither dried nor pickled; but sent off, as it was caught, fresh and flabby. I should, however, be glad to have some authority to support this conjecture of mine.
P. S. C.

THE COLLIER'S CONFESSION OF FAITH (1st S. v. 523, 571.)—I have just met with an earlier mention of the above than any yet referred to. It is quoted by Erasmus in his excellent treatise, *De Præparatione ad Mortem :* —

"Narrant quiddam non quidem è sacris voluminibus, sed tamen ad id quod nunc agimus satis accommodatum, de duobus quos imminente morte de Fide tentavit Diabolus: alter philosophiæ peritus erat, alter nihil aliud quàm Christianus, rudis et anormis. Priori suggessit quid crederet, an Christum Deum et hominem, an natum de Virgine, an Resurrectionem mortuorum. Cœpitque Philosophiæ rationibus demonstrare, non posse conjungi in unum ea inter quæ nulla esset affinitas, velut inter finitum et infinitum, creatum et increatum. . . . . Quid multis? Vacillavit homo, et præcipitatus est; hostis victor abiit. Alter ille rudis percontanti quid de hoc et illo crederet respondit compendio, *Quod credit Ecclesia.* Rursum objicienti quid crederet Ecclesia, *Quod ego,* inquit. Quid tu? *Quod credit Ecclesia.* Quid Ecclesia? *Quod ego.* Ab hoc imparato ad disputandum, sed simplici fide stabili, Tentator victus discessit. Hoc responsum satis est ad abigendum insidiosum hostem. Maxime tamen valet in obscuris ac dubiis."—Editio princeps, *Basil*, 1534, 4to, pp. 69—70.

EIRIONNACH.

THE ANSTRUTHER LIBRARY (3rd S. vi. 326.) — Will J. M., who speaks with such gusto of "the glorious Anstruther Library," or some other learned Scot, kindly give me some information respecting the same? This collection was dispersed, I believe in 1832, but I have never seen the sale catalogue. I possess a volume of pamphlets which belonged to this library, having the autograph of "W. Anstruther," written in a fine bold hand, apparently at the close of the seventeenth century; also having a book-plate, with the arms of "Sir John Anstruther of that ilk, Baronet." The name Anstruther is now commonly shortened into Anster. EIRIONNACH.

MR. GOODWYN, THE MATHEMATICIAN (3rd S. vii. 114, 167.) — I do not think there are any papers by Mr. Goodwyn in the *Philosophical Transactions.* In 1823, he published a work in two volumes royal 8vo, of which the following is the title : —

"A Table of the Circles arising from the Division of a Unit, or any other Whole Number, by all the Integers from 1 to 1024; and a Tabular Series of Decimal Quotients for all the proper Vulgar Fractions."

The late Dr. Olinthus Gregory, of Woolwich, proposed Question 1418, or the Prize Question for the *Ladies' Diary*, 1824, as an example of the use which could be made of Mr. Goodwyn's series. He terms them "Curious Tables of Circulating Periods." The work appears to have been sold by "Richardson, Cornhill." T. T. W.

DOCKING HORSES (1st S. vi. 13 ; 3rd S. vii. 185.) — OMEGA does not give any authority to show that his version of the epigram is a more correct one than that of F. B. I send you my version and my authority.

In my youth, more than sixty years ago, an uncle of mine had in his garden a summer parlour, the walls of which were adorned with caricatures—some of them French. One, and one only, has fixed itself in my memory. It was this : —

The drawing represented a macaroni in a phaeton, driving a pair of long-tailed ponies, and his footmen standing behind the carriage. The ponies had their tails buckled up in large bunches, to keep them out of the mud. The master, and each of his footmen, had large heads of hair, also tied in a large knot behind. And beneath the picture was this inscription : —

" Les Anglais barbares, du même couteau,
Coupent aux rois leur têtes et les queues aux chevaux ;
Les Français plus polis laissent aux rois leur têtes,
Et aussi, comme vous voyez, les queues à leur bêtes."

Mine probably is only an adaptation of the
to the picture. I however give some authority for my version. J. Ss.

"CONFESSIONS OF A METHODIST" (3rd S. vii. 223.)—The first number of the *Confessions of a Methodist* appeared in *The Satirist* of January 1, 1809, and was continued in subsequent numbers. No. 1 of *The Satirist* is dated October 1, 1807. The 23rd, and last number of the New Series, was dated June 1, 1814. It then changed hands; and, July 1, appeared under the title of *The Tripod, or New Satirist.* Of the last work I have the first two numbers, and I doubt whether any more were published. The caricatures of these numbers have the titles : — " Satirist, July 1st, 1814. Doctor Blucher." " Satirist, August 1, 1814. The Modern Don Quixote, or the Fire King." I do not know who was the editor. E. H.

THE MICKLETON HOOTER (3rd S. vi. 464.)—Can any of your correspondents say whether our illused little English bear (the badger) haunts Mickleton Wood? Years ago, in Rockingham Forest, I heard his cry. It is *eerie* enough. C. W. BARKLEY.

7, Paulton's Square, Chelsea.

SANCROFT (3rd S. v. 290.) — All the sources of information so kindly suggested by your correspondent were, I find, tested some years ago, without result. Your correspondent says that, about the year 1661, Archbishop Sancroft's sister Catherine lived with him; but in the same communication states that the Archbishop had six sisters—Deborah, Elizabeth, Alice, Frances, Mary, and Margaret—which agrees with my own information. Was Catherine a seventh sister, or is the name a second name of one of those in the list? Who were the two nephews to whom the Archbishop made a deed of gift shortly before his death? ST. TH.

COOKERY: "AU BLEU" (3rd S. vii. 202.) — The editorial note appended to the query of CLERICUS explains the process of cooking *au bleu*, and the blue tinge imparted by it to fish. The change of colour thus effected is associated with an anecdote of the Court of Louis XV. of France.

When the Marquise de Pompadour, daughter of Poisson, a butcher to the Invalides, but apocryphally elevated by the flattery of her *quondam* friend Voltaire to the status of a farmer of Ferté-sous-Jouarre, and wife of the Sous-Fermier, Le Normand d'Étoile, solicited the French monarch to invest her brother, Abel François Poisson, with the Order of the "Saint Esprit," the riband of which is blue, Louis declined, observing, or his court circle for him, that the brother of the favourite, " était trop petit poisson pour être mis au bleu." The monarch, however, relented; and yielding to the fascinations and influence of "sa Pompadour," later in the same year, an office connected with the coveted Order was granted to Poisson, which authorised him to bear a decoration rivalling in lustre those of the Garter and the Golden Fleece. Marmontel waited on the *parvenu* to offer his compliments on the distinguished honour thus achieved, when the new *Cordon Bleu*, more consonantly with truth and fact than elegance and self-esteem, exclaimed to Marmontel's astonishment, " *Le Roi me decrasse.*"

The territorial designations of Abel François Poisson were changed three times. When created Marquis *de Vandières*, the wits of the court happily termed him "Marquis *d'Avanthièr*"; and, in reference to this play of words, when the name of *Marigny* was assumed by him (why does not appear), he remarked, " *On m'appelle Marquis d'Avanthièr; on m'appellera encore Marquis de Marinée, sachant que je suis né Poisson.*" Succeeding under the will of his sister to the estate of Menars, he finally adopted that name.

The title of Pompadour, become unenviably historic as associated with the scandal and disgrace of a corrupt court, was that of an honourable family which had but recently become extinct before the assumption of its designation and arms by the daughter of M. Poisson.

The editorial note does not reply to the concluding inquiry of CLERICUS; nor can I contribute to supplying the omission unless by the suggestion that, as we speak of "the Derby" being, in allusion to the riband of the Garter, the "Blue Riband of the Turf," so the *Cordon Bleu* of the Order of the Saint Esprit is figuratively assigned to expert *artistes de la cuisine* by the French.

JOHN HUGHES.

STICK (3rd S. vii. 200.) — Does not "stick" in the sentence quoted suggest in sound, as also in signification, the adoption of a German word which may have been in use in this country in 1692? " *Stück*, a piece, is constantly used in German in an analogous manner : *ein Stück Eitelkeit*, a piece of vanity ; *ein Stück Frechheit*, a piece of arrogance ; *ein Stück Spott*, a piece of railing. Thus,—

" Our author, to shew how angry and froward he resolves to be . . . makes his first paragraph a compleat Stick [*Stück*, piece] of Railing."

PHILIPPA SWINNERTON HUGHES.

"THE WHOLE DUTY OF MAN" (3rd S. vii. 124.) Allow me to correct an error in the reference made by JUXTA TURRIM to the *Journal of Sacred Literature.* The articles he alludes to are in N. S. vol. v.* (pp. 185, 433), and not vol. xiv. I am the more anxious to point out this error, as I happen to know of one person, at least, who on the faith of " N. & Q." has been ·disappointed on purchasing the wrong volume.   Q.

BELL INSCRIPTION (3rd S. vii. 219.) — It often happens .that in inscriptions in what is here called

* *I. e.* Nos. 9 and 10 (April and July, 1864).

"church text," a letter *i* and an *n* in close proximity appear so like an *m* as to be read for it. I believe this has been the case in reading the word on the bell at Abbotsham. I have no doubt that the word is intended for *elemosinary*, the initial *e* being either omitted, or indicated only by a small ('); and that the word was adopted to signify that the bell was presented as an *elemosinary*, or deed of pious alms to the church.   F. C. H.

THE ORIGIN OF VALENTINES (3rd S. vii. 221.)— The custom of choosing a patron saint for the year prevails among Catholics; but choosing a monthly patron is perhaps more common. The choice of a patron for the year is not observed on St. Valentine's Day among seculars; but in religious communities, it is quite customary on St. Valentine, not to choose, but to draw a billet for the ensuing year, which is headed by the name of some saint, followed by the virtues for which he was most remarkable. Here is a copy of one of these billets lying now before me : —" St. Mechtildes V. Abbess. Compunction, zeal for the observance of regular discipline, and abhorrence of all worldly discourse." This was drawn in a Dominican nunnery, several years ago. The person who draws the billet, proposes to invoke the intercession of the saint, and to endeavour to imitate his virtues, particularly during the ensuing year. As to the profane custom of choosing on St. Valentine " special loving friends," I think there can be no doubt that it is a remnant of the Pagan practice in honour of Juno Februata, on which I enlarged in a former article on St. Valentine in " N. & Q." vol. iii. of the present series, p. 169.   F. C. H.

"THE FOURTH OF MARCH" (3rd S. vii. 197.) — In " N. & Q." of March 11, 1865, there is a reference to this day as not often occurring on a Sunday. My friend, Mr. Robert Robson (a man far too modest for his attainments), has given me the following retrospective and prospective Sundays falling on the fourth of March; and of course they might be extended : —

" *Fourth of March on Sunday.*

" 1804, 1810, 1821, 1827, 1832, 1838, 1849, 1855, 1860, 1866, 1877, 1883, 1888, 1894, 1900, 1906, 1917, 1923, 1928, 1934, 1945, 1951, 1956, 1962, 1973, 1979, 1984, 2001, 2007, 2012, 2018, 2029, 2035, 2040, 2046, 1057, 2063, 2068, 2074, 2085, 2091, 2096, and so on."

JNO. KITTS, Librarian, Sunderland.

MOUNT ATHOS (3rd S. vii. 199.)—The catalogues referred to by F. M. S. are in the possession of Professor Carlyle's daughter, Mrs. Maclean, of Lazonby Hall, in the county of Cumberland.
E. F. BURTON.

Carlisle.

OLD SAYING (3rd S. vii. 219.) —I believe the saying is in general use, though I can speak from my own experience only of Oxon and Bucks, where it is applied to persons supposed to be living beyond their means:—

" To bring a noble to ninepence, and ninepence to nothing.

" *Il fait de son teston de six sols.* To bring an abbey to a grange. *Fare di trenta tre undici.* The Italians also say, *Far d'un lancia un fuso.* To cut a cloak to a button."
(Bohn's *Hand-Book of Proverbs*, p. 172.)
                                                        H. B. C.

U. U. Club.

SUN-DIALS (3rd S. vii. 200.) — Very simple directions for making sun-dials will be found in Procter's *Dictionary of Arts and Sciences.* For an account of the various kinds of sun-dials consult Brewster's *Furguson's Lectures.*   H. FISHWICK.

TRADITIONS OF AN ANCIENT WORLD (3rd S. vii. 95, 141, 210.)—There is a very interesting article on the speculations of Isaac de la Peyrère, in the fifth number of the *Anthropological Review*, May, 1864. There is also, I believe, some mention of him in Bayle's *Dictionary*, and M. M. Hagg's *La France Protestante.*   EDWARD PEACOCK.

FLEMISH STAINED GLASS IN ENGLAND (3rd S. vi. 472.)—In Gessert's *Geschichte der Glasmalerei in Deutschland und den Niederlanden, Frankreich, England, &c.* (8vo, Stuttgart, 1839), an attempt is made to give a list of the stained glass windows in the principal countries of Europe, and of the artists by whom they were executed. The celebrated windows of Fairford are particularly mentioned as having come from the Netherlands, owing to the capture, about the year 1492, of a Spanish ship, which Dallaway supposes was bound for South America; but whose destination was more probably Spain itself, as at that time there were no churches in South America; and Columbus only returned from his first voyage, after an absence of seven months and twelve days, in March, 1493.

Martin Guerards, of Bruges, is mentioned by Herr Gessert as one of the innumerable Flemings who emigrated to England about the year 1590; and who is more celebrated as a designer of outline sketches for stained windows, than as a painter of them. I cannot find any other particulars at all relevant to MR. WEALE'S inquiry, in this German compilation.   J. MACRAY.

Oxford.

THE BIDDING PRAYER (3rd S. vii. 152.) — BIBLIOPOLA closes his extracts from the Oxford MS. Sermons with portions from the Bidding Prayer. Could you find room for the whole prayer, as it would prove an interesting addition to your bill of fare? I heard Dr. Hook, at Leeds, use the Bidding Prayer before sermon; entering into much detail of title and function of the nobility and gentry of Yorkshire, with good effect.   A. B. C.

[The Bidding Prayer varies according to circumstances.—ED.]

Miscellaneous.

NOTES ON BOOKS, ETC.

Life and Times of Sir Joshua Reynolds, with Notices of some of his Cotemporaries : *commenced by* Charles Robert Leslie, R.A. *Continued and concluded by* Tom Taylor. *In Two Volumes. With Portraits and Illustrations.* (Murray.)

A biography of the great English painter, whose immortalising pencil has preserved to us " in their habits as they lived," so many hundred likenesses of his contemporaries eminent for wit, beauty, or eloquence, with such a fidelity that we feel we know them all;—a biography of the painter friend of Johnson, Burke, and Goldsmith ; a biography of Reynolds, which should be at once worthy of the man and of the artist, has long been wanted. To produce such a work was a labour of love which the late worthy successor of Sir Joshua, Leslie, the Royal Academician, had imposed upon himself, and it occupied him until the last moment of his life. On his death, the task of completing and concluding what he had left unfinished, was entrusted to Mr. Tom Taylor, who clearly has entered heart and soul into the work. He has felt that to write the Life and Times of Reynolds was to record, not only the history of the painter's works, but to tell, it may be briefly but still distinctly, who were his sitters, and not to give us a bare list of their names, but to recall them to our memory by characteristic illustration. To do this he shows us Sir Joshua at all seasons, and in all company ; and the result is, that while the life of Sir Joshua forms the prominent object of his picture, the background is a rich mixture of anecdote and gossip, called forth by the mention of all the chief men and women of his time for beauty, genius, rank, power, wit, goodness, or even fashion and folly, who were either his friends or the subject of his pencil. A very full Index gives completeness to the book, which is to be followed by a *Catalogue Raisonné of the Works of Sir Joshua Reynolds, with Notices of their present Owners and Localities,* by Mr. Tom Taylor and Mr. Charles W. Franks, who invite information on the subject.

A Dictionary of Science, Literature, and Art ; *comprising the Definitions and Derivations of the Scientific Terms in General Use, with the History and Descriptions of the Scientific Principles of nearly every Branch of Human Knowledge. Edited by* W. T. Brande, D.C.I., &c., *and the* Rev. George W. Cox, M.A. *Assisted by Gentlemen of Eminent Scientific and Literary Acquirements. Part I.* (Longman.)

Such of our readers as have, like ourselves, been in the constant habit of referring to Brande's *Dictionary of Science, Literature, and Art,* will be well pleased to know that a new and enlarged edition of this useful compendium of useful knowledge is in course of publication. How much it is enlarged we may show by a very simple statement. The number of articles has been so greatly increased that, judging from the examination we have made of this first part, they are half as many again in the present edition as in the edition of 1852 ; so that it is clear the book is keeping pace with the advancement of knowledge. One other claim to public favour which the new issue puts forth deserves especial notice—namely, it is even more clearly and distinctly printed than the last—a great virtue in a book of reference. So there can be little doubt that whatever may have been the popularity of the book in its original shape, that popularity will increase in the ratio of the increased utility and fulness of the present enlarged and reconstructed issue.

The Lineage and Pedigree of the Family of Millais; recording its History from 1331 to 1865, being an Extract from the "Armorial of Jersey," by J. Bertrand Payne. With Illustrations from Designs by the Author. Privately printed.

The words "privately printed" forbid criticism; but the work is so beautifully printed, got up, and illustrated, that it cannot fail to be eagerly sought after by all admirers and collectors of handsome books on genealogy. The "Millais" are traceable in Jersey as early as A.D. 1331; and, from the names of those well-known localities *Les Monts Millais* and the *Cueillette de Millais*, are supposed to have been, in yet earlier times, among the opulent and powerful "dwellers within the isle."

BOOKS RECEIVED.—

An enlarged and illustrated Edition of Dr. Webster's Complete Dictionary of the English Language. Thoroughly revised and improved. By C. A. Goodrich, D.D., and Noah Porter, D.D. Parts III. and IV. (Bell and Daldy.)

Every fresh part of this work which we receive serves to justify the high terms in which we spoke of it on its first appearance. When completed it will be a most valuable dictionary.

Lives of the Queens of England, from the Norman Conquest. By Agnes Strickland. Vols. V. & VI. (Bell and Daldy.)

Though grave critics may deny the claim of this work to be considered of historical authority, there can be no doubt of its great popularity; and by reproducing it in its present form—it now occupies only six volumes—Miss Strickland will assuredly largely increase the number of her readers.

The Autographic Mirror (L'Autographe Cosmopolite), *Nos. 26, 27, 28.*

This marvellously cheap collection of photo-lithographic facsimiles of the autographs of illustrious and distinguished persons of past and present times is continued with great spirit. Every number contains articles of considerable interest.

BOOKS AND ODD VOLUMES
WANTED TO PURCHASE.

Particulars of Price, &c., of the following Books to be sent direct to the gentlemen by whom they are required, and whose names and addresses are given for that purpose:—

FLETCHER'S FAMILY DEVOTION. Second-hand copy.
　Wanted by *Mr. Joseph Simpson*, Bookseller, High Street, Edgware, London, N.W.

TOUR OF DR. SYNTAX IN SEARCH OF THE PICTURESQUE.
　Wanted by *Dr. Fisher*, 5, Appian Way, Upper Leeson Street, Dublin.

PSALTERIUM S. BONAVENTURÆ. Manuscript or printed.
Old English Manuscripts.
Good Specimens of Binding.
　Wanted by *Rev. J. C. Jackson*, 5, Chatham Place East, Hackney, N.E.

Notices to Correspondents.

G. S. MITCHELL. "*A Hawick Gill*" is half an English pint, and a "*Tappit Hen*," a tin measure containing a quart.

J. R. FOWLER. *So much depends on state, date, &c., it is impossible to answer your inquiries. A fair price will no doubt be procured for them from Mr. Taylor, or any other respectable dealer in coins.*

S. & R. *Steamboats which date from 1815; railways from 1825.*

SYDENHAM PERRAGE. *Charles Poulett Thomson was created Baron Sydenham, Aug. 19, 1840, and died Sept. 19, 1841, never having taken his seat.*

HERALDIC ANOMALIES. *I beg to correct the statement in your Notices to Correspondents (p. 272) that this book was written by the Rev. Edward Nares, D.D., the biographer of Lord Burghley. It was a work of the Ven. Robert Nares, M.A., Archdeacon of Stafford, author of the valuable Glossary of Old Words and Phrases, and for some time editor of The British Critic.—N.*

[*Our authority was the New Edition of Lowndes.*—ED. "N. & Q."]

E. W. *We cannot find that the three Bibles of 1652, 1657, and 1661, are of any special value. Lea Wilson states that the edition of 1657 is very incorrect, but the typography good. That of 1661 has the mistranslation in Acts vi. 3, "Whom ye may appoint."*

ERRATA.—3rd S. vii. p. 259, col. i. line 18 from bottom, *for* "struck on the reverse? Again," *read* "struck? On the reverse again"; line 15 from bottom, *for* "Huhlmann" *read* "Kuhlman."

A Reading Case for holding the weekly Nos. of "N. & Q." is now ready, and may be had of all Booksellers and Newsmen, price 1s. 6d.; or, free by post, direct from the publisher, for 1s. 8d.

‡‡‡ *Cases for binding the volumes of* "N. & Q." *may be had of the Publisher, and of all Booksellers and Newsmen.*

"NOTES AND QUERIES" *is published at noon on Friday, and is also issued in* MONTHLY PARTS. *The Subscription for* STAMPED COPIES *for Six Months forwarded direct from the Publisher (including the Half-yearly* INDEX*) is 11s. 4d., which may be paid by Post Office Order, payable at the Strand Post Office, in favour of* WILLIAM G. SMITH, 32, WELLINGTON STREET, STRAND, W.C., *where also all* COMMUNICATIONS FOR THE EDITOR *should be addressed.*

"NOTES & QUERIES" *is registered for transmission abroad.*

LONDON, SATURDAY, APRIL 15, 1865.

CONTENTS.—N° 172.

Notes.

SITE OF GOLGOTHA.

Those who deny that the Church of the Holy Sepulchre does or *can* occupy the real locality, and that the true Golgotha and the true sepulchre *must* have been elsewhere, have been accustomed boldly to assert that before the investigation of Constantine there is no trace whatever in Christian writers of any acquaintance with the locality; this argument *e silentio* was strongly pressed by the late Dr. Robinson, and his remarks have been so re-echoed by others, that this assertion has been allowed to pass as a fact. Thus, those who show that the Church of the Holy Sepulchre was not included within the wall of Jerusalem in our Lord's time, have admitted too readily that no notice is to be found that before the time of Constantine the Christians knew the spot. It has been continually said that this is admitted on both sides.

But what if there is evidence that the Christians did know the place? What if Robinson imagined, from his want of acquaintance with early Christian writers, that nothing was to be found in them which would not suit his theories? and what if his opponents, in this case at least, gave him credit for completeness and accuracy of information to which he was not entitled?

Now in the answer of the martyr Lucian, before he suffered, there is a passage which bears closely on this subject. After speaking of the sufferings and resurrection of our Lord, he thus continues:—

"Quæ autem dico, non sunt in obscuro gesta loco, nec testibus indigent. Pars pene mundi jam major huic veritati adstipulatur; urbes integræ: aut si in his aliquid suspectum videtur, contestatur de his etiam agrestis manus ignara figmenti. Si minus adhuc creditur, *adhibebo vobis etiam* LOCI IPSIUS, *in quo res gesta est, testimonium.* Adstipulatur his ipse in Hierosolymis locus, et *Golgothana rupes sub patibuli onere disrupta; antrum quoque illud, quod avulsis inferni januis corpus denuo reddidit animatum; quo purius inde ferretur ad cælum.*"— Routh, *Rel. Sac.* iv. 6, 7 ; e Ruffini *Hist. Ecc.* ix. 6.

The cogency of this passage must depend on its genuineness; as to which, however, there seems to be no reasonable ground for distrust. For though it may be said that this may be an embellishment brought in by Ruffinus, yet, on the other hand, it is important to notice that it contradicts Ruffinus's own opinions relative to the *discovery* of the places. It could scarcely therefore be an invention of Ruffinus. The whole tone of the reply of Lucian savours of the beginning and not the close of the fourth century; if it be Lucian's own, it shows that before the reign of Constantine the localities of the suffering and burial of our Lord were *well* known; but even if it be argued that the statement proceeds from some one subsequent to Lucian, though prior to Ruffinus, even then it would show that it was the opinion of Christians that the localities were known before any investigation on the part of Constantine.

I have no doubt that this quotation from Lucian the martyr will be to many a piece of perfectly new evidence; for although I brought it forward nine years ago (in the *Journal of Classical and Sacred Philology*, March, 1856), I am not aware that it received the smallest attention. I was thus like George Primrose, whose "Paradoxes" were thus treated by the world, as he had to inform his father, the Vicar of Wakefield. I showed the passage in Lucian to a foreign writer on the Holy Land, who has declaimed earnestly against the *fraud* of those who defend the received localities of Jerusalem; but to my astonishment he asserted that it *could* not really mean what the words say; I then found to my surprise that this writer, although in his books he most fluently quotes ancient authors, is wholly ignorant of all ancient languages. I quite expect that publication in "N. & Q." will be enough to call attention to this piece of evidence, so that it will not in future be passed by in silence by those who discuss the localities of Jerusalem.

But perhaps Lucian is not a mere solitary witness; perhaps there is some evidence, direct or indirect, that the place was known between his time and the apostolic age. Origen *seems* to know something of the place:—

Περὶ τοῦ κρανίου τόπου ἦλθεν εἰς ἡμᾶς ὅτι Ἑβραῖοι παραδιδόασιν ὅτι τὸ σῶμα τοῦ Ἀδὰμ ἐκεῖ τέθαπται· ἵνα ἔπει ἐν τῷ Ἀδὰμ πάντες ἀποθνήσκουσι, πάλιν ἐν τῷ Χριστῷ πάντες ζωοποιηθῶσι (iii. 920, ed. De la Rue).

If a tradition be attached to a place, it assumes (without proof being needed) that the place is known. However groundless be the story that Adam was buried at Golgotha, yet this was the Jewish tradition in the former part of the third century, and whether Origen personally knew the place or not, he knew that the Jews attached that story to the place—a known and definite locality. The same traditions are mentioned by Epiphanius, a native of Palestine, and a Jew by nation, after the time of Constantine.

Ὡς ἐν βίβλοις ηὑρήκαμεν τὸν κύριον ἡμῶν Ἰησοῦν Χριστὸν ἐν τῷ Γολγοθᾷ ἐσταυρῶσθαι, οὐκ ἄλλη που ἀλλ' ἢ ἔνθα ἔκειτο τὸ τοῦ Ἀδὰμ σῶμα . . . . ἐκεῖσε ἐτάφη ἐν τῷ τόπῳ τῷ Γολγοθᾷ· ὅθεν εἰκότως τὸ ἐπώνυμον ὁ τόπος ἔσχε. (Panarium, i. 394, ed. Petavii; ii. 415, ed. Dindorf.)

We may be very sure that Epiphanius did not use Origen as an authority, but it is evident that they both of them mention the same Jewish tradition; both of them thus appear to refer to the same place. Epiphanius, of course, means that on which Constantine had built a church, the locality of which has never from that day been forgotten; and Origen, by speaking of the tradition, identifies the spot as that which was known in his day.

Why did Constantine search on that spot? The only reasonable answer is, because the Christians knew it to be Golgotha. The idol temple marked it; and even if hid, yet the words of Lucian show that they knew the cleft rock and the empty sepulchral cave to be there. Recently some have chosen to mix up the narrative of Eusebius with later accounts about "the invention of the cross," and dreams and miracles of which he says not a word; and after ridiculing these tales they say,—"These are the grounds on which the identity of the Holy Sepulchre rests." But this is an entire misrepresentation: they might as well affirm that the real existence of the Khalif Haroun-al-Rashid, and of the city of Bagdad, depended on the authenticity of the *Arabian Nights*. We know of the existence of that Khalif and of that city, *although* they are introduced into amusing fictions.   S. P. TREGELLES.

Plymouth.

PRECEDENCY OF BISHOPS' WIVES.*

With respect to the political expediency of publicly acknowledging this right, the advantage to be derived from giving weight and consequence to a class of persons who seem absolutely obliged

[* Continued from p. 275.]

by their situation to observe a peculiarly exemplary course of conduct, and to form some barrier against the sweeping torrents of irreligion and licentiousness, cannot be deemed a trifling consideration: and it should be observed that this acknowledgment would furnish a complete answer to the various Sectarists, who in the old style of Puritanism, and in the new style of Socinianism, profess themselves scandalized at this *semblance* of Popish error respecting *ecclesiastical rank and title*, and inveigh against the rank of *Bishop* being now so opposite to their situations and pretensions in the primitive ages of Christianity, in a matter which excites doubts of its propriety even among zealous Episcopalians. It being in vain to urge that it is the *Barony* annexed to the Bishopric which gives them *temporal rank*, while rank is withheld from their Wives. For it is artfully maintained, in order to *degrade* the Bishops, and to stigmatize the Church in the eyes of the people, that this singular distinction *proves* not only that they sit in the House of Peers in their *Ecclesiastical character*, but that they have no other—"no temporal rank as Peers"—and that "having no rank in right of their *Temporalities*, or *Baronies*, *as they are called*, they can have no *right to the title of Lords*, (except *when sitting in the House officially* as Lords of Parliament or Counsellors of State) which it is highly improper to give them *as Bishops*, &c. &c." —an opinion growing more and more prevalent in this age of *research* into the *foundation* of rights, titles, claims, and privileges, and of invidious attack upon all. The declaration and protection of a right considered to be, or pretended to be considered to be, of a doubtful nature, cannot be esteemed any *innovation*, or *alteration* of a long established *system* in the estate of the Bishops. This right to *personal* rank and dignity the Bishops have, in fact, possessed ever since the Conquest, and their Wives have *consequently* a right to share that rank and dignity. Were they to assert this right of place as Barons' Wives, it could not be denied them with the shadow of justice. But many circumstances connected with the spirit of the times, and the peculiar situation of the Wives of *Bishops*, render it far more desirable that this right, which has been suffered to lie dormant so long, should be called forth by a *special command* from the throne, rather than be *claimed* by the parties themselves. And as the suppression of a privilege without just cause is an acknowledged grievance, from which every subject may properly demand relief, it is surely advisable in every case to redress a grievance (especially one not likely to be silently endured much longer) as a mark of favor, before a just complaint of neglect from persons who really deserve attention, precludes the idea of gratitude, and yet secures its object. With a view to such a measure, the following Form of an Order for the public acknowledgment of the right in question is subjoined to this private representation of this literally singular case.

It is presumed that this Order may easily be made applicable to the Bishops on the Irish Bench by *special grant*, if they cannot plead *a claim;* and that it will be found to preserve the distinction of *blood* so highly valued by the hereditary nobility. Bishops precede Barons upon the same principle which placed Archbishops before Dukes; but the Wives of Barons must precede the wives of Archbishops and Bishops, because "*Hereditary* dignities have place before *Temporary* dignities, except when otherwise ordered, as some of the Officers of State, &c." (*vide* Porney, Blackstone, &c.), though the Baronies annexed to the Bishoprics are, with few exceptions, the most *antient.* And the *antient Baronial fillet,* which the Bishop's mitre now surmounts in like manner as the Archbishop's mitre surmounts the ducal coronet, instead of the *coronet* given to the Secular Barons by King Charles II., will further distinguish the Wives of Bishops from the Wives of Barons; and their title, according to the signature of their husbands, will distinguish them from the Wives of the younger sons of Dukes and Marquises who take the name of their family. Bishops have a right to the style of "Right Honble" as Barons. They were addressed by titles of equivalent temporal rank, as well as by others of ecclesiastical dignity, before titles and precedence became fixed and appropriate; and the custom of sinking the "Right Honble" in the *superior* title of "Right Reverend" or "Most Reverend," upon the principle already mentioned, and of adding the *inferior* title of "Honble" *as a mark of distinction,* which has lately prevailed, has contributed something towards the error respecting their real dignity *as peers* which it is the object of the following order to correct.

PROPOSED FORM FOR THE ORDER.

The King having taken into his Royal Consideration that the Wives of the Archbishops and Bishops have a just Claim to Rank and Precedence as the Wives of Barons from the Antient Baronies annexed to each of the Bishoprics (by virtue of which Baronies, or Temporal and Personal Dignities, the Bishops and Archbishops take their Seats in the House of Lords, and possess the Privileges common to all Peers), and this Right having been suffered, hitherto, to lie dormant, His Majesty is graciously pleased to Command that from henceforth the Wives of Archbishops and Bishops shall take their Rank as Wives of Barons, for Life, and shall take their Style and Title according to the Signature of their respective Husbands, their Family distinctions, and the accustomed Precedence in the manner following:—

The Right Honble Lady John Canterbury.
The Right Honble Lady William York.
The Right Honble Lady Bielby London.
The Right Honble Lady Shute Durham.
The Right Honble Lady Brownlow Winchester.
The Right Honble Lady James Ely.
The Right Honble Lady Richard Worcester.
The Right Honble Lady John Hereford.

The Right Honble Lady James Litchfield and Coventry.
The Right Honble Lady Richard Llandaff.
The Right Honble Lady George Lincoln.
The Right Honble Lady John Salisbury.
The Right Honble Lady William Bangor.
The Right Honble Lady Samuel St. Asaph.
The Right Honble Lady Richard Bath and Wells.
The Right Honble The Lady Anne Edward V. Carlisle.
The Right Honble Lady Charles M. Norwich.
The Right Honble Lady Spencer Peterborough.
The Right Honble Lady Henry R. Exeter.
The Right Honble Lady Foliot H. W. Bristol.
The Right Honble Lady John Chichester.
The Right Honble Lady John Oxford.
The Right Honble Lady Henry W. Chester.
The Right Honble Lady George Murray St. Davids.
The Right Honble Lady George F. Gloucester.
The Right Honble Lady Thomas Rochester.

The King is pleased to Command that the Wives of Archbishops and Bishops, or Spiritual Barons, shall rank after the Wives of the Temporal Barons; and that the Widows of Archbishops and Bishops shall give Place to the Wives of Archbishops and Bishops.

HOG FEAST.

I am called upon to-day to write a letter for a poor neighbour, in reply to an invitation from his granddaughter, that he would come and visit her "for hog-feast." I am not aware if this Huntingdonshire expression and custom obtains elsewhere; and, as it has not yet been mentioned in the pages of "N. & Q.," I here make a note of it. The Huntingdonshire "hog-feast" is the domestic rejoicing that follows upon that important event in a cottager's family—the killing of the pig. The relatives and friends of the pig's proprietor are summoned by him to partake of a feast, the chief dishes of which are composed of those portions of the pig's interior economy which are unsuited for the purposes of salting. A part of the spare-rib, or one of the choicer joints, is usually cooked; but the brunt of the hog-feast is borne by those other porcine parts which may not be cured into bacon. In return for their dinner, the guests assist the good wife in the salting of her pig. The old man for whom I wrote the letter waxed loquacious as his memory recalled the various hog-feasts in which he had taken an active part. Said he:—"I mind the time when hog-feast cost a mort' o' money. That was before George the Fourth took the tax off salt. When you killed a pig, before George the Fourth's day, you was obligated to part with the bald-ribs and spare-ribs, and all the best joints, to buy salt with, afore you could salt the flitches and hams. And now, look at the salt that you can get for fourpence! Oh yes! we are greatly obligated to George the Fourth; and when I lived as ostler at the Inn on Alconbury-hill, George the Fourth he came and slept the night there. Our boys went out to meet him beyond Buckden; and he came with two fours and a pair. There was a many gentlemen with him, but no ladies. It was the time when he and Caroline didn't keep company. We all hurrahed, and Old Tom, that's now dead and gone, blessed him for cheapening hog-feast; but I don't suppose as George the Fourth would know the meaning of hog-feast. He went away the next morning for Wansford; and then turned off somewhere Wisbeach way, and back home by way of Cambridge: so he did not come again by our Great North Road. When he started off I was close to him, putting in the near wheeler; and George the Fourth was smoking a long pipe that came as low as the bottom of his waistcoat. It wasn't a clay, you understand; but had a large bowl to it, and a great gold stopper on it. He made hisself very free and pleasant; but what we thought most of was, his taking the tax off salt and cheapening hog-feast."

There is a story current of a clodpole who had been at a dinner, and was asked as to the bill of fare. His reply being: "There was all sorts o'meat, Sir; there was roast pork, biled pork, pig's face, and bacon, Sir." Which repast, doubtless, was a superior kind of hog-feast.

CUTHBERT BEDE.

JUNIUS.—In the *Intermédiare* (a professed and very deserving French imitation of "N. & Q.") there appeared in the No. for June 15, 1864, a communication signed "E. Pieraggi" (Suresnes) to the following effect, on the subject of the *Letters of Junius* : —

" Among some old papers that belonged to my mother, an Englishwoman, and daughter of Walsh Porter, of Alfarthing, who was a frequent visitor at the Court of the Regent, afterwards George IV., I found a card, enclosed in a slip of paper, on which was written : '*A Secret.*' On the card was written, in two different hands, one of them very tremulous, no doubt designedly : ' *The author of Junius, Charles Lloyd.* LOYD. *He was private Secretary to the present Lord Grenville ; father and teller of the Exchequer.*' The words *Charles Lloyd* are underlined once, and Loyd twice. But this is not all. The words, ' *Honor bright, until the poor son be provided for,*' are written inside of the envelope. There is no date or signature ; and even the handwriting is unknown to those of my mother's relations whom I have interrogated on the subject. However, what may give some value to this little document is the fact of its evidently having passed through the hands of my grandfather, who lived in a circle where this secret was no mystery : perhaps in his childhood he had even known Junius. In short, Charles Lloyd figures among the number of supposed authors, as well as Lord Grenville. The objection derived from the style of Junius, which is so remarkable, and betrays, it is said, the composition of Sir Philip Francis ; and from the cessation of the letters the day after his departure for America, is this objection as insurmountable as it seems to be ? Have we not here a three-fold coadjutorship, an *inspiration*—to make use of a term employed by writers for the newspapers ? Has not Sir Philip revised, annotated, and corrected this work, inspired by Lord Grenville, and edited by Loyd ?

" Here, it seems to me, is an interesting occasion for having recourse to comparative bibliography ; and for inquiring whether there are not circumstances, either in the style or in the lives of these three individuals, which correspond with certain expressions or allusions contained in the *Letters*. Lloyd's situation in the Exchequer, and his intimacy with Lord Grenville, and consequently in the ministerial world of that time, would singularly facilitate that merciless knowledge of secret affairs of which the author gives proofs. E. PIERAGGI."

J. MACRAY.

Oxford.

IGNITION OF WOOD BY FRICTION.—In an early number of "N. & Q.," I inquired whether there was any known instance in this country of success in the experiment of producing fire by rubbing one piece of wood against another, as constantly practised among the South Sea islanders and elsewhere. I believe the answer was in the negative. But in the last number (p. 239) we are told that it is possible — not to say was once common in Yorkshire—to "set the temse on fire," by merely rubbing the rim of a riddle on the top of a flour barrel ! I say nothing about the actual meaning of the familiar phrase alluded to, and I hope P. is not joking ; but surely a more unfounded notion than that of the *possibility* of setting *a* "temse on fire " by the domestic operation described — and which, when a boy, I often witnessed—would only be the likelihood of setting *the* "Thames on fire " by some of the steamers plying thereon !

J. H.

NAMES OF RIVERS.—In a recent number of "N. & Q." there were some remarks on the origin of the names of rivers. May I suggest that the name of *Esk*, in the Lowlands of Scotland, is probably not derived, as stated, from a word signifying water, but from the old Scotch word for an *asp*.

In the ballad of the "Young Tamlane," the youth was transformed while in the arms of his mistress into an *esk* (asp). The idea of likening the course of a stream to a snake is common enough. *Serpentine* in modern times is well known.

Apropos, the *Goomtee* on which Lucknow stands is synonymous with our adopted meaning of the word *meander*. S.

HUNTERIAN SOCIETY.—I know no receptacle but " N. & Q." in which to lodge the following amusing blunder. In a publication entitled *The Royal Album*, designed partly for tradesmen's advertisements, but edited, it seems, by French and German editors for the guidance and information of their countrymen in London, and printed in English, French, and German, appears in a list of public societies, "The Hunterian Society," translated "Société des Chasseurs," and "Jagd-Gesellschaft."

Foreigners, and particularly Frenchmen, when they know a little of English have unbounded confidence in that little; and I once myself received at Hâvre a tradesman's card in the following terms:—

"So-and-so, Merchant, and Fabricant of Umbrellas and Parapluies. Make and repair all things who concern his state, at juste price. The persons whom ar far can write him he shall go directly."

F. J. J.

THE THIRD PLAGUE OF EGYPT.—When Aaron was commanded to smite the dust of the land with his rod, he did so, and the dust "became *lice* in man and in beast," according to the rendering of the Authorised Version (Exodus, viii. 16). Dr. Kalisch, however, in his *Historical and Critical Commentary on the Old Testament* (Exodus, chap. viii. p. 137, ed. London, 1855) endeavours to prove, and I think successfully, that the Hebrew word כִּנִּים = Kin-nim, ought to be translated by the term *gnats*. His reasons for this rendering are given at length in a long and learned note (pp. 136-137). The Septuagint, which is of great authority in all points relating to the natural history of insects in Egypt, translates the Hebrew word by σκνῖφες, mosquito gnats. Niebuhr mentions (*Description de l'Arabie*, Pref. p. 39), that when he was in the East he once inquired into this very subject, and asked the Greek Patriarch, and also the Metropolitan at Cairo, what they supposed was the species of insect mentioned in Exodus, chap. viii.? Their answer was, that they believed the *gnat* was the insect. (Kitto's *Cyclop. of Biblical Literature*, vol. ii. p. 249, ed. Edinburgh, 1847.) Kalisch observes, that though Josephus, Jonathan, Onkelos, Hesychius, Taylor, Buxtorf, Le Clerc, and Bochart, adopt and maintain, as the most correct translation, the word *lice*, yet their arguments are not supported with sufficient proofs. As, however, there are great names on both sides of the question, it is now probably impossible to ascertain for certain whether the little animals were lice or gnats. Either must have been very tormenting, especially the *gnats*, which, according to Philo and Herodotus, have always been numerous in Egypt.

J. DALTON.

Norwich.

ABRAHAM LINCOLN A POET.—I have not seen any allusion to the curious instance of involuntary rhyme afforded in the President's recently delivered inaugural address, yet it seems worth making a note of. The President said—

"Fondly do we hope,
Fervently do we pray,
That this mighty scourge of war
May speedily pass away :
Yet if it be God's will
That it continue until —"

but here the strain abruptly ceases, and the President relapses into prose.

W. S.

THE BELL OF ST. CENEU, OR ST. KEYNA.—Perhaps the following may be worthy of preservation in "N. & Q.," copied from Mr. Kerslake's *Bristol Catalogue*, 1859, pasted in my copy of Jones's *History of Brecknockshire*. Where now its place of deposit?

"ANCIENT-BRITISH CHURCH BELL: THE BELL OF ST. CENEU or ST. KEYNA, daughter of Brychan, Prince of the province called from him Brecknock, found on the site of her oratory at Llangeney, Brecknockshire.

"This most venerable relique of the ancient British Christianity is of an oblong plan, and conical figure. It consists of a single plate of iron, gathered up into its present form, and rivetted down through the middle of each of the narrow sides. At the top is a bow or loop for the handle, and it was evidently intended to be rung by swinging in the hand. The strip of metal which forms the handle is continued through to the inside where it formed a smaller loop, from which the clapper was suspended but is now wanting. After the iron substructure was finished, the whole appears to have been coated with bell-metal, or other brass-like compound; and this was evidently applied by dipping or washing the finished iron utensil in fluid metal, as all the joints, and the rivets themselves are covered, and the seams and interstices filled with it. Being corroded through in some places, the amalgamated contact of the metals is apparent. The result is similar to that of electrotype. Iron was perhaps in ancient times, as now, very commonly washed with tin and its compounds; but was brass usually applied in this manner?

"In Jones's *History of Brecknockshire*, published 1809 (ii. 469), there is a long account of this bell and of its discovery; but there appears to be some mistake in his description of the dimensions. The actual height is 10 inches, without the handle; size at top, 5½ by 3 inches; at the mouth, 7¼ by 6 inches; weight rather more than 6 lb. 15 oz.

"The town of Keynsham, near Bristol, arose out of an oratory founded there by this St. Keyna. See her legend in Cressy's *Church History of Britain*, A.D. 490, b. x. ch. xiv.

"Two views of the bell of St. Mura, attributed to the seventh century, may be seen in the *Ulster Journal of Archæology*, No. 4, Oct. 1853. This has a general resemblance to that of St. Ceneu; but was decorated, and not so large.

"Although the sonorous quality of the bell is, no doubt, diminished by the holes which are fretted through it, the voice which called our countrymen to church, perhaps even before St. Augustine came from Rome for the same purpose, can still be most distinctly elicited."

GLWYSIG.

Queries.

BIBLIOGRAPHICAL. — Perhaps a reader of "N. & Q." who has a marked copy of "*Bibliotheca Reediana*, the Catalogue of the Library of Mr. Isaac Reed sold 1807," would kindly inform me who was the purchaser of "Lot 8536," viz. "Shaksperiana,—a large assembly of Tracts by various Authors relative to Shakspeare, neatly bound in 9 vols. 8vo." I am desirous also to learn if it is known in whose possession these volumes are now. Were any copies of Douce's *Illustrations of Shak-*

speare, 2 vols. 1807, taken off on large or thick paper? *
E. N.

BRETON MUSIC. — The air called "An Aliké, or the Shepherd's Call," in Tom Taylor's *Songs of Brittany*, is that called "Ballinderry," in Bunting's *Collection of the Ancient Music of Ireland*. In Jephson's *Walking Tour in Brittany* occurs a tune which is identical with that in the *Irish Melodies*, to which Moore has written the words "Silent, O Moyle, be the roar of thy water!" What was the original home of these tunes? Ireland or Celtic France?
O. T. D.

CURIOUS COINCIDENCE OF NAMES. — In the third volume of the *Sussex Archæological Collections* (for 1850), p. 117, there is a paper communicated by Mr. R. Willis Blencowe, containing extracts from the journal and account-books (1683-1714) of Timothy *Burrell*, of *Ockenden House*, Cuckfield; which house, then (1850) in the occupation of Mr. J. P. Fearon, belonged to the late *Sir C. Merrik Burrell*, of Knepp. In the *Universal Magazine* for November, 1747, p. 245, it is stated that the present [members for Great Marlow, Bucks,] are William *Ockenden*, Esq., of Temple Mills, and *Merrick Burrell*, Esq.

Query, was there any original connection, local, personal, or family, to account for this coincidence?
W. J. B.

DIOGENES' LANTERN. — Can any one tell me the authority on which the repartee about "the lantern" and the "honest man" is ascribed to Diogenes? And why does Æsop, to whom Phædrus gives the credit of the saying, never come in for the benefit of it?
MEDIO SOLE.

INFORMATION WANTED FOR A SCOTCH MONASTICON AND EPISCOPAL CHRONICLE, ETC. — As I am presently preparing a Chronicle of all the Bishops in Scotland, down to the present day, with minute details of their lives and jurisdiction, from correspondence, &c., based on Keith's *Catalogue*, but much amplified; as also a Scotch Monasticon, containing notices of abbeys, abbots, religious houses, &c., will you be so kind as allow any information thereanent, or corrections and defects in Keith, to come through your columns, if this intimation should be replied to, which it is certain to be? Any correspondence, if too lengthy for "N. & Q." can be posted direct to myself.
J. F. S. GORDON, D.D.,
Incumbent of St. Andrew's Church, Glasgow.
247, Atholl Terrace, Bath Street, Glasgow.

KATHERINE HARMAN. — In 1692 Dame Katherine Harman, widow of Admiral Sir John Harman, was living. Her daughter (heiress of Sir John and of her brother, James Harman) was

[* Twelve copies were printed on large paper of Douce's *Dance of Death*; but we have never met with a large paper copy of his *Illustrations to Shakspeare*.—ED.]

wife of Dauntesey Brouncker, of East Stoke, Wilts. He was the last heir male of the Brounckers of East Stoke, and died, 1693, leaving two daughters married, who died without issue. I am anxious to ascertain whose daughter Lady Harman was, and also any particulars of Admiral Harman's birth and parentage which may be matter of record. The arms on his picture are those of Harman of Suffolk. I am aware of the notices of him in Pepys's *Diary*.
E. W.

LAVINGTON BURNT. — In an old almanac by Gabriel Frend, 1598, I find the following memorandum in the handwriting of that period : —
"August 20. Lavington burnte by mishape."

Can any readers of "N. & Q." inform me to which of the Wiltshire Lavingtons this refers, or where I can probably meet with some particulars of a brief issued, or the like, and thus fix the place either as Lavington Forum or Lavington West?
E. W.

"OCULUM SACERDOTIS."—Is anything known of a mediæval treatise called *Oculum Sacerdotis*, by an Englishman, somewhat similar to *Pupilla Oculi*?
J. C. J.

PLANTS IN ROOMS.—Will *any* plants grow in rooms in which gas is burned; or does the gas poison *all* plants? Is there any way of preserving plants from its poisonous effects? Will covering them with a bell glass at night do?
P.

QUOTATIONS WANTED.—In the *Simple Cobbler* (p. 25) will be found this passage : —
"I can hardly forbeare to commend to the world a saying of a lady living sometime with the Queen of *Bohemia*. I know not where she found it, but it is pity it should be lost : —
  'The world is full of care, much like unto a bubble ;
  Women and care, and care and women, and women and
  care and trouble.'"

This couplet sounds familiar. Does any reader of "N. & Q." know its origin?
On p. 34, the following occurs : —
"Some ten or twelve years before these Wars, there came to my view these two Predictions :
1. 'When God shall purge this Land with soap and nitre,
  Woe be to the Crowne, woe be to the Mitre.'
2. 'There is a set of Bishops coming next behind,
  Will ride the divell off his legs and break his wind.'"

Can these predictions be found in print or manuscript before that time?
MASSACHUSETTS.
Boston, U. S.

"THE SENTIMENTAL AND MASONIC MAGAZINE." May I ask you to be so kind as to tell me how many volumes of the above-named periodical were published? I have a copy of six half-yearly volumes (from July, 1792, to June, 1795), and I have never met with any others, though I have searched the library of Trinity College, Dublin ;

but I am informed by a friend, that, to the best of his belief, five more subsequently appeared. To judge from what I have seen, it was a really good Dublin publication of the last century. Who was the editor? * ABHBA.

SHAW OF SAUGHIE AND GREENOCK. — Where can I see a pedigree of this family? F. M. S.
229, Clarendon Villas, Plumstead.

THE "SIMPLE COBBLER'S" REFERENCES. — In the *Simple Cobbler of Aggawam*—a book written in New England in 1645 or 6, and published at London in 1647, four editions being issued that year, there are some references that I should like explained, viz.: —

1. The Cobbler says :—

" If Truth be but One, methinkes all the Opinionists in England should not be all in that One Truth, some of them I doubt not are out. He that can extract an unity out of such a disparity, or contract such a disparity into an unity, had need be a better Artist then ever was *Drebell*."—P. 10.

Is Cornelius Drebell, the Dutch alchymist, who died at London in 1634, meant?

2. In another place he says : —

" Brethren, have an extraordinary care also of the late Theosophers, that teach men to climb to heaven upon a ladder of lying figments. Rather then the devill will lose his game, he will out-shoot Christ in his own bow. He will outlaw the Law, quite out of the word and world ; over-Gospell the Gospell, and quidanye Christ with Sugar and Ratsbane. He was Professour not long since at Schlestat in *Alsatia*, where he learned that no poyson is so deadly as the poyson of Grace."—P. 17.

What Professor is referred to?

3. Addressing King Charles I., the Cobbler says :—

" Is your father's Sonne grown more Orthodox then his most Orthodox father, when he told his Sonue that a King was for a kingdome, and not a kingdome for a King?"—P. 54.

Did James I. so tell his son?

4. The Cobbler tell us that the Irish —

" Have a Tradition among them, That when the Devill shewed our Saviour all the kingdomes of the Earth and their glory, that he would not shew him Ireland."—P. 72.

Is this a fact?

5. Again, he says : —

" Not long since I met with a book, the best to mee I ever saw, but the Bible : yet under favour, it was somewhat underclad, especially by him who can both excogitate and expresse what hee undertakes, as well as any man I know —

The world is growne so fine in words and wit,
That pens must now *Sir Edward Nich'las* it.
He that much matter speaks, speaks ne'er a whit,
If 's tongue doth not career 't above his wit."

" Sir Edward Nicholas," I take it, means Secretary Nicholas. But what book is referred to?
MASSACHUSETTS.
Boston, U. S.

[* Our correspondent is the fortunate possessor of a periodical not to be found in the British Museum.—ED.]

WOODWARD FAMILY. —

" In 1552 King Edward VI. by Letters Patent, 8 March, granted, *inter alia*, a field called Le Humme, with its appurtenances in the Lordship of Ditton, to George Woodward for twenty-one years @ 106s. 8d. rent ; and on its surrender in 1563, Queen Elizabeth regranted the same premises to John Woodward for a farther term of twenty-one years on the payment of a fine of £21 6s. 8d. In 1584 (26 Eliz.) the Queen demised the same premises to George Woodward, gent., and Edward and George his sons, at the same rent, for their lives and the life of the survivor, with a heriot of 26s. 8d."

These Woodwards were of Upton, co. Bucks; the first George and Richard his second son were " Clerks of the honor and Castle of Windsor." (*Visitation of Hampshire* in 1576 and 1602.)

Can any one of the readers of " N. & Q." inform me whether Robert Woodward, D.D., who was Dean of Salisbury from 1691 to 1701, was of this family ; and if so, was he descended from Edward or from George, the last named in the above grant?

Lipscombe, in his *History of Buckinghamshire*, states that there is a monument of white marble at Hillesden church, co. Bucks, to George Woodward " Envoy Extraordinary from the King of Great Britain to the King and Republic of Poland," that he was the grandson of George Woodward, of Stratton Audley, co. Oxford, and that he died at Warsaw, March 10, 1735, in the thirty-eighth year of his age, and was buried at Hillesden.

Query, Were these descendants of the Upton family? GEO. ADLARD.

Queries with Answers.

" LONDRES," 1770. — Being at Paris in 1862, I fell in with a book, in four duodecimo volumes, entitled *Londres*, and containing an account of a Frenchman's travels in England in 1766-7. It is anonymous. My copy is a new edition, " corrigée et considérablement augmentée," printed at Lausanne in 1774. The preface tells me that the first edition was printed in 1770, and that mine is the second. It also contains a notice that, in 1773, an English translation of *Londres*, by Dr. Nugent, was published " avec le plus grand soin, par l'Imprimeur de la Société Royale ;" and complaints are made of pirated. editions being printed in Flanders and elsewhere : and of the author of the *Voyageur François*, who, in his work, " a fait entrer le *Londres* à large dose, c'est-à-dire par paquets de 4, de 7, de 18 pages continues." It is also mentioned, that the book had been reviewed in the *Journal Encyclopédique* of Oct. 1773, by M. de la Condamine, who had since honoured the author with his friendship, and to whom several corrections in this new edition were owing. The writer of the preface (who seems not to be the author) indulges in a bit of sarcasm against one set of his critics : —

" Pour ne rien omettre de ce qui peut présenter avantageusement un ouvrage que j'ai l'intérêt de faire valoir, j'ajouterai qu'il a complètement déplu aux auteurs de l'*Année Littéraire*."

I have not been able to discover any traces of the name or quality of the author. He evidently was a learned man, and had access to the best society. I shall be glad if any of your correspondents can give me information respecting the authorship.

I may mention, that my attention was drawn to the book from the circumstance of four exceedingly well-bound volumes being offered for sale at a bookstall on the Quais at 60 *cents* the volume. I was again in Paris the other day, and saw copies for sale at 40 *cents* the volume.   H. A.

Deanery, Canterbury.

[The author of this work was Peter John Grosley, a French antiquary, born at Troyes, Nov. 18, 1718, and educated in the profession of the law ; but a decided turn for literary pursuits induced him to travel, in search of knowledge, twice into Italy, twice into England, and once into Holland, besides passing a considerable part of every year at Paris, where he was received into the best company. He died at Troyes on Nov. 4, 1785, being then an Associate of the Academy of Inscriptions and Belles-Lettres, and a member of the Royal Society of London. Although in his *Tour to London* the author appears as a philosopher and a man of taste as well as learning, nevertheless his remarks on England and its inhabitants are very imperfect, and frequently erroneous. At the particular request of Mons. Grosley, Dr. Nugent in his translation corrected some of those obvious inaccuracies animadverted upon by the writer in the *Journal Encyclopédique*. For some biographical notices of Grosley, and a list of his numerous productions, consult the new *Biographie Universelle*, 1857, xvii. 604, and the *Nouvelle Biographie Générale*, 1858, xxii. 179.]

DEATH OF ADMIRAL BYNG.—I find it stated that Sir George Rooke refused to sign the death-warrant of Admiral Byng, saying : " It might be presumptuous in an individual to differ from so great an authority as the opinion of the twelve judges ; but when the shedding of blood was concerned, a man must act on his *own* conscience and not the opinions of *other* men." As Sir George Rooke had been dead many years, who was the member of the Board of Admiralty who refused to add his signature to the death warrant ? It is undoubted that Sir George Rooke observed to a friend, just before his death, that his property was such, " it had never cost a sailor a tear or the nation a farthing." These two speeches seem to have been strangely jumbled together.

H. W. D.

[It was Admiral John Forbes, then one the Lords Commissioners of the Admiralty, who refused to sign the war-

rant for carrying out the sentence of death on Admiral Byng, and prepared a paper in which he assigned his reasons for his refusal. Admiral Forbes's " Reasons for not signing Admiral Byng's Dead Warrant," were printed in 1757 as a hand-bill in small folio, and we possess a cutting of the document from some periodical of the time. The original, we believe, is still in the Admiralty Office at Whitehall. Who were the members of the court-martial, and other circumstances connected with the trial, may be found in Schomberg's *Naval Chronology*, i. 281 ; *The London Magazine* for Feb. and March, 1757 ; and *The Gentleman's Magazine* for Feb. and March, 1757.]

MONUMENTAL INSCRIPTION. — Does the following very remarkable inscription, quoted by Bishop Jeremy Taylor in his *Rule and Exercises of Holy Dying*, chap. iii. sect. ix. § 6, still exist in the parish church of Faversham, Kent ? —

" Whoso him bethoft
    Inwardly and oft
    How hard it were to flitt
    From bed unto the pit,
    From pit unto pain
    That nere shall cease again,
    He would not do one sin
    All the world to win."

H. W. T.

[This epitaph on Richard Colwell, Mayor of Faversham, ob. 1535, is printed in Weever's *Funeral Monuments*, p. 276, and in Pettigrew's *Chronicles of the Tombs*, p. 432. It would seem that the brass was still at Faversham in 1804, from the following notice of it in *The Beauties of England and Wales*, viii. 740 : " In the south aisle are various memorials for different civil officers of Faversham, one of whom, Richard Colwell, Mayor in 1555 [1535 ?], is represented by a brass figure standing between his two wives, with groups of children beneath, and at the corners a well, with the letters C. O. L. forming the rebus of his name."]

THE CHURCH OF NOTRE DAME, CALAIS. — Can you furnish information as to whether the church at Calais called " St. Mary's," or " of Our Lady," in the time of the English occupation of the town, was built or only enlarged by the English ?

M. E.

[It is stated in most topographical dictionaries that St. Mary's at Calais was built during the English occupation of the town. Mr. T. Mot, F.S.M., minutely inspected this large church in April, 1816, and communicated an interesting account of it to the *Gentleman's Magazine* in Sept. 1816, p. 220. He says, " The church, from its structure and appearance, I have no doubt, was erected whilst Calais was in the possession of the English, *i. e.* in the fourteenth century, as was the castle of St. Risban, Basseville church, and many other of the public buildings, not excepting some of the present houses, and most of the defences of the town." An engraving of St. Mary's church by Mr. Topping is given in the *Gent. Mag.* for May, 1814, p. 433.]

, EPISCOPUS HAMENSIS.—Amongst the illustrious persons who were buried in the Carmelite convent at Norwich, occurs the following record : "Frater Gilbertus de Norvico, Episcopus Hamensis (alias Hamerensis), obiit A.D. 1287, 9 Die Octobris.[*] Query, What is the modern name corresponding with Hamensis or Hamerensis? J. DALTON.

[This suffragan bishop is noticed in Stubbs's *Registrum Saorum Anglicanum;* p. 143 : "Gilbert Hammensis; buried at the Carmelites, Norwich, Oct. 9, 1287. Granted forty days' indulgence to all who should attend the preaching of the Carmelites, 1273, 1274, and 1276. He was probably the Bishop Hamerensis in Norway, consecrated 1263." Hammer, the modern name, is a town in the province of Aggerhuus in Norway, which was formerly the see of a bishop, until removed to Christiana, from which it is distant 100 miles to the N. E.]

EARL SPENSER'S "BOCCACIO," 1471. — I have seen this celebrated edition at Althorpe, but have never read, except in Dibdin, a really accurate account of the purchase of it, and of the *exact* price given for it by his lordship. Is there any other account extant besides that given by Dibdin, which I understand is exaggerated?
 J. DALTON.

[We have consulted the priced Catalogue of the Roxburghe Library, and find that the enormous sum given for this single volume, as stated by Dr. Dibdin, is perfectly correct. " *Il Decamerone di Boccaccio,* fol. first edition, printed at Venice by Valdarfer, 1471." To which is added the following note : " Of the extreme scarcity of this celebrated edition of the *Decameron,* it will perhaps be sufficient to say, that no other perfect copy is yet known to exist, after all the fruitless researches of more than three hundred years." It was knocked down to the Marquis of Blandford for 2260*l.* ! when it was said Lord Spenser took off his hat, and, bowing to the Marquis, thanked him for saving him four hundred a year.]

SAINT NIERSIS. — When did St. Niersis live, and where can I find an account of him? I have a work in twenty-four languages printed at Venice, 1823, entitled *Preces St. Niersis Clajensis Armeniorum Patriarchæ Viginti quatrici Linguis coitæ.*
 JOHN DAVIDSON.

[Nersès IV., surnamed Shnorhali (*i. e.* the graceful), patriarch of Armenia, was born shortly before the close of the eleventh century, and died in 1173. During the last twenty-six years of his life, he resided at Hromkla, commonly called Rumkala, a fortified place on the Euphrates. He is considered as the inventor, or principal cultivator, of rhymed poetry. With the exception of a brief *History of Armenia,* his works are mostly theological. A long account of him is given in the new edition of the *Biographie Universelle,* xxx. 325.]

[*] Bale, *Cent. Script.* iv. 31. See also Kirkpatrick's *History of the Religious Orders and Communities of Norwich,* p. 172, 1845.

HIGH CHURCH AND LOW CHURCH. — Is there any small work which states clearly the differences both as to points of *doctrine,* and as to *forms* and *practices,* between the parties of the Church of England, known popularly as the "High" and "Low" Church? P.

[Our correspondent will probably find as much as he desires to know on this subject in the concise Essay, entitled "Church Parties," by the late W. J. Conybeare, M.A., which originally appeared in *The Edinburgh Review* for October, 1853. The Essay has been frequently reprinted, and the fifth edition of it will be found in Mr. Conybeare's *Essays Ecclesiastical and Social,* pp. 57-164, Lond. 8vo, 1855. Consult also "N. & Q." 1st S. viii. 117; x. 260, 278.]

"THE POLITICAL MAGAZINE."—Can you inform me how long *The Political Magazine and Parliamentary, Naval, Military, and Literary Journal* was issued, printed for J. Bew, Paternoster Row? It was commenced in 1780. I have the volumes for 1780, 1781, and 1782, and am desirous of obtaining any further volumes which may have been published. W. TUCK.
 15, Milsom Street, Bath.

[A copy of *The Political Magazine* in the British Museum consists of twenty-one volumes, 8vo, 1780-1791.]

Replies.

SHELVES IN WILTSHIRE.

(3rd S. vii. 241.)

MR. MEWBURN's note refers to a most interesting subject, and one to which the attention of those archæologists who have applied themselves to the study of pre-historic earthworks has long been directed. The reason why some definite theory as to those shelves, or rather terraces, has not been submitted to the public is the fact that they are to be found all over the kingdom — from the lowlands of Scotland to the Downs of Wiltshire ; that they are not like a camp, a thing to be surveyed in an hour, but extending as they do for miles and miles, and varying in breadth from a few feet to many yards, many of them would be the work of weeks. Therefore, until the details of a sufficient number collected by local antiquaries can be obtained, it would be utterly futile to make any attempt at a general theory. Every fact regarding them is however of importance, and I am certain if MR. MEWBURN will be so good as to draw up a detailed statement of the length, elevation and breadth of any such terraces in his neighbourhood, it will not be the least interesting paper that will be read at Durham during the next congress of the British Archæological Association.

In the meantime I may inform him that there is a capital description of one of those groups of terraces (Peebleshire) in the *Proceedings of the Society of Antiquaries of Scotland,* 1861, 2, or 3, and that the well known Scotch antiquary, Mr. Sim of Culter, pointed out to me a most remarkable instance occurring on his property in Lanarkshire, which I hope to have an opportunity of surveying next month.

The most striking Scotch instance, however, occurs in Galloway, where an insulated hill overlooks the mouth of the River Orr (pronounced Urr). The terraced outline of this hill strikes every one that approaches it. It is known as the *Moat* of Urr, and there is a tradition that it was the place of a Witagemot.

It might be interesting to ascertain how far the valloys which these terraces overhang were not swamps in olden times.   GEORGE VERE IRVING.

What Cobbett termed "Shelves in Wiltshire" are common in Scotland, Ireland, and all hilly and grazing countries. And Cobbett's notice of them is an instructive fact, showing how readily an otherwise shrewd man may commit a gross absurdity, for the sake of finding a convenient peg to hang a theory upon. Similar "shelves" in Ireland have frequently been pointed out to me as positive proofs of the very great population, and the superior knowledge of agriculture possessed by those in Ireland in ancient times. But the real truth is, that those so-called "shelves" are not ancient plough-marks: they are simply formed by sheep and black cattle when grazing on the hill-sides, as any person who chooses to use his eyes may almost any day observe; for these ancient tracks, though formed by the constant treading of centuries, are still used by sheep and black cattle when grazing on steep hill-sides.

WILLIAM PINKERTON.

THE STORM OF 1703.

(3rd S. iii. 168, 197, 273, 319; v. 504.)

Admit the following correction of the last article above quoted. I know not whether the error is the printer's or mine. The work referred to in the eighth line, is "The City Remembrancer," &c. &c.

When writing my last note on the subject, I had not time to look over my collection of pamphlets. I have now pleasure in sending you the following: —

"An Elegy on the Author of the True-born Englishman. With an Essay on the late Storm. By the Author of the *Hymn to the Pillory.* London: Printed in the Year 1704."

The tract is in verse, and the essay on the Storm occupies eighteen pages *quarto.* In the list of Defoe's works, contained in the new edition of *Lowndes,* it is stated to be in 8vo: —

"The Lay-man's Sermon upon the late Storm; Held forth at an Honest Coffee-House Conventicle. *Not so much a*

Jest as 'tis thought to be. Printed in the Year 1704." [4to pp. 24, and Title.]

This is also attributed to Defoe; making, with the 8vo volume referred to by J. H. G., three distinct works on the subject, by the same author, during one year.

"Mr. Collier's Dissuasive from the Play-House; in a Letter to a person of Quality, Occasion'd by the late Calamity of the Tempest. London, 1703," 8vo, pp. 15.

On the last page, the writer says: —

"What Impression this late calamity has made upon the *Play-House,* we may guess by their acting *Macbeth* with all its Thunder and Tempest the same Day: where at the mention of the *chimnies being blown down* (*Macbeth,* p. 20,) the Audience were pleas'd to *clap* at an unusual Length of Pleasure and Approbation," &c. &c.

The last work I shall notice, at present, is entituled —

"An exact Relation of the Late *Dreadful* TEMPEST: or, a Faithful Account of the most *Remarkable Disasters* which happened on that Occasion. The Places where, and the Persons' Names who suffer'd by the same, in City and Countrey; the Number of Ships, Men, and Guns that were lost, the Miraculous Escapes of several Persons from the Dangers of that *Calamity,* both by Sea and Land. Faithfully collected by an Ingenious Hand, to preserve the Memory of so Terrible a Judgment. *Nos fatis agimur Variis: contenditur fatis.* London: Printed and Sold by *A. Baldwin* at the *Oxford Arms* in *Warwick Lane,* 1704," 4to, pp. 24.

W. LEE.

"COLD HARBOUR."

(3rd S. vii. 253.)

Taking up my last number of "N. & Q." I was surprised to find, at the reference indicated, a note professing to contain "Remarks on the Origin of Cold Harbour." The author, DR. J. C. HAHN, certainly has the good sense to conclude by saying, "an interesting paper might be written on this proper name, and I much regret only being able to offer the above few remarks," &c. &c.

Permit me to state for the information of DR. HAHN, and your readers interested in such inquiries generally, that a series of learned, and I may add exhaustive, papers on this and its kindred nomenclature, written by your frequent correspondent, DR. HYDE CLARKE, appeared in the *Freemason's Magazine* (vol. v. July to December, 1858), under the title of "Anglo-Saxon History, as illustrated by Topographical Nomenclature." These papers will be found at pages 99-102, 162-8, 213-7, 251-4, 350-6, 399-403, 448-53, 492-6, 546-50, 630-5, 678-82, 733-7, 871-6, 967-9, and 1117-19. The portions that more particularly relate to the Cold Harbours are those at pp. 213 and 350, they enumerate the positions of the various Cold Harbours, and the forms of "kill," "cool," "harbour," "bower," and "wind."

We are all prone to give the Germans credit for searching and multifarious reading on almost every subject they write upon, but the article in "N. & Q." is so superficial when placed in juxtaposition with that of our English Mezzofanti that, in justice to him, and believing the Magazine one not much known to your readers, I have taken the earliest opportunity to indicate where a series of papers on Cold Harbours may be found.

MATTHEW COOKE.

The Rev. Mr. Hartshorne, an eminent antiquary, whose recent death we lament, once told me that he believed this name was a corruption of *Coluber*. He said it was to be found in some twenty places in England, and always near to a *snake-like curve* in an old Roman road.

LYTTELTON.

In reference to the word "herbergh" I would observe that the Charter of Foundation of the Abbey of Holyrood, by King David I. of Scotland, a copy of which is in Maitland's *History of Edinburgh*, pp. 144-5, contains the following grant to the Canons, — "Concedo etiam eis *herbergare* quoddam burgum inter eandem ecclesiam et meum burgum." Maitland makes the mistake of supposing that "herbergare" was an old name of the Canongate of Edinburgh, or of a town which formerly stood on that site; but Arnot, the more recent historian of the city, shows (foot note, p. 4) that it is the infinitive of a barbarous Latin word, signifying *to build*, in which sense of it the grant can obviously be read. He refers as his authority to Dalrymple's *Annals*, p. 97, and he is confirmed by the *Cartulary* of Coldingham, a copy of which is in the Advocates' Library, in p. 15 of which it will be found that it is used in the same signification. The similarity of the word to those noticed by your correspondent is somewhat curious.   G.

Edinburgh.

THE ORDER OF CHRIST: THE PASCHAL LAMB.

(3rd S. vii. 5, 168, 251.)

In directing JUVERNA's attention to the discrepancy which appeared to me to exist between the account on p. 5, and that on p. 49, I did not at all mean to imply that he was responsible for the accuracy of the statements contained in the "General Officer's" very interesting letter; but I was and am anxious to know how, and when, the Paschal Lamb was connected with the Portuguese royal arms. This connection up to the present time I have failed to discover.

I have to thank MR. DAVIDSON for his ingenious suggestion, but fear it is untenable for the following reasons. First, the cross *behind* the shield of Portugal is *not* that of the Order of Christ. Secondly, the cross of the Order of Christ is not, and I venture to say never has been, charged with the figure of the Paschal Lamb.

The badge of the Order of Christ, which is suspended from the triple gold chain around the arms, is—"A cross patée, red, charged with a cross white." While the floriated green cross, placed *behind* the shield, is the badge of the *Order of Avis*.

Out of abundant proofs of the correctness of these assertions I may cite the following:—

"Um den Schild hänget der Orden Jesu Christi, und hinter demselben ragen die Spitzen des Avischen Ordens-Creutzes hervor."—Triers, *Einleitung zu der Wapen-Kunst* (Leipzig, 1744), p. 286, Wapen des Königs in Portugall.

Again, Spener, the great German herald, in his *Insignium Theoria*, or *Opus Heraldicum* (Frankfort-on-the-Main, 1680), pars specialis, lib. i. cap. lxxii. p. 283, says:—

"*Ordo* militaris est, quem *Jesu Christi* vocant, cum cruce inde dependente; additur etiam post scutum crux viridis in liliorum flores terminata, pro ordine *Avisio*."

In Siebmacher's *Wappenbuch* (Nürnberg, 1734), vol. vi., the arms, &c., are correctly engraved.

The *Order of Christ*, which arose out of the ruins of the Order of the Knights Templars, was founded by King Dionysius about the year 1320. The *Order of Avis* arose about the middle of the twelfth century. MR. DAVIDSON will find full information about both Orders in Favyn's *Théâtre d'Honneur et de Chevalerie* (Paris, 1620), pp. 1265—1272; Carlisle's *Account of the Foreign Orders of Knighthood* (London, 1839), pp. 231—234, 238; Marquez, *Tesoro Militar di Cavalleria*, Madrid, 1642; Sansovino, *Della Origine dei Cavalieri*, Venetia, 1570; and in the books of Clarke, Ashmole, Robson, Burke, &c.

JOHN WOODWARD.

New Shoreham.

Your correspondent, MR. JOHN DAVIDSON, says:—

"When the arms of Portugal are represented in full, with crest and dragon supporters, the chain of the Order of Christ hangs round the shield, from behind which the points of a cross are seen. This is the Cross of the Order of Christ, and in all probability has the Paschal Lamb on it."

On referring to Elias Ashmole's *Order of the Garter*, I find this not to be the case. He has given an engraving of the Cross of "Jesus Christ in Portugal" on which no Paschal Lamb appears. At p. 83 he describes the dress of this religious order of knighthood:—

"They were clothed black, wearing upon their breasts a cross patée of red silk, and upon that another of white. This Order (as that d' Avis) became at length annexed to the Crown of Portugal; whose kings have ever since taken upon them the title of perpetual administrators of both."

Elias Ashmole gives the following interesting account of the origin of "The Order of Knights of Christ in Portugal:"—

"As the Knights of Montesa sprung from the ruine of the Knights Templars in Valentia, so did this Order of Christ (or of the Warfare of Christ) succeed them in the Kingdom of Portugal. For the Knights Templars having been very serviceable to the Kings of Portugal, in their wars against the Moors, the Kings gave unto them divers lands and revenues, which, when their Order came to be dissolved and their estates confiscate, King Dom Denys, surnamed Perioca, sent to Pope John the 22nd (then at Avignion) to desire that the Knights Templars' lands might not be disposed of out of his kingdom; which, though he did not readily grant, yet he gave way for the King, to render him the reasons of his request. Hereupon King Denys sent his embassadors to the Pope, in the year 1316, not only to back his desire, but withal to declare to his Holiness the great vexations and evils the neighbouring Moors in Algarves did to his kingdom. And forasmuch as the town of Castra Marin was a frontier of the enemy, and the site thereof very commodious for the building of a fort to resist them, he farther moved the Pope for licence that an Order of Knights might be instituted in that town, and withal offered to him the rents and jurisdiction thereof, and all dominions over it. This request being thought just, and the remedy so necessary, the Pope did afterwards (namely in the year of Our Lord 1315) give foundation to this new Order, dedicating it to the honor of God, and the exaltation of the Catholick Faith, under the title of the Military Order of our Lord Jesus Christ, because of the miraculous apparition which this King had seen of Christ crucified when he went to fight against the Moors."

It appears also from the same author that "The Order of Knights d'Avis in Portugal" have for badge a green cross flory, for he says —

"The badge of this Order is a green cross flory, such as the Knights of Alcantara wear, and said to be given them by Don Pedro, but before they used the like cross with those of the Order of Calatrava, two birds being added at the foot thereof, in allusion to the later name given to this Order, as appears from the ancient seal."

In neither of these Orders does the Paschal Lamb appear. Did the Kings of Portugal use badges like the Kings of France, and was the Paschal Lamb a badge of one of them?

W. H. C.

The Knights of this Order, founded by Dom Diniz King of Portugal, A.D. 1318, were clothed in black, and wore upon the breast "a cross pattée of red silk, and another full cross over the red." (Favyn, ii. 188); *i. e.* a cross pattée gules, surmounted of a plain cross arg.

There is nothing in Favyn's description to indicate that the Paschal Lamb, or any other emblem, formed any part of the original badge. Nor is there any addition to the above description of the cross of the order in the shield of Dom Henriqué (second son of King John of Portugal by Philippa of Lancaster), which is sculptured on his monument in the church of Batalha, and figured in Mr. Murphey's beautiful work on that edifice.

An exact representation of this double cross may be seen in a portrait of Charles III., Prince of Monaco, published some years ago in the *Illustrated London News.* H. W. T.

WELSH PARALLELS FOR CORNISH PROVERBS.
(3rd S. v. 208, 275.)

In reading the two chapters on Cornish Proverbs contributed by your correspondent Trepolpen, it occurred to me that I had often heard similar sayings among the folk of this locality; and on making search I was able to find very literal parallels to some of those adduced by him, which I herewith transmit you. If you deem them worthy of insertion in "N. & Q." they are at your service; and with your approbation, I shall on another occasion send some more : —

I. Cornish.
"He that hurts robin or wren
Will never prosper boy nor man."

Welsh.
"Ysawl â dorro nŷth y druw;
Ni chaiff iechyd tra fo byw;
Ysawl a dorro nŷth ywennol
Ni chaiff iechyd yn drag'wyddol;
Ysawl a dorro nŷth y robin
Agaiff waed ô fewn e'i goffin,"

which I have thus Anglicised into doggerel rhyme : —

"Whoso the wren robs of its nest
Health loses in a day ;
The spoiler of the swallow's house
Will ail and pine for aye ;
And he who with his ruthless hands
Shall tear the robin's cot,
In his coffin shall have a guilty mark—
A deep-red gory spot."

The wren was, and still is, a general favourite in this neighbourhood. Not long ago an old custom was prevalent of carrying about a wren secured in a cage, decorated with ribbons and artificial flowers in the most fantastic manner, on the Twelfth Night. The owners of the concern used to visit the principal houses in the neighbourhood. On their arrival they formed themselves into a crescent, and sang encomiums to their little "king," as they termed their little prisoner; for this they were rewarded by the good folks of the house with some money, and a free libation of "cwrw da."

The swallow is also an object of veneration, as it is the happy harbinger of the pleasant summertide. But *the* favourite is the wee red-breasted robin, whose solitary note breaks the monotony of a dull winter's day; and any one guilty of cruelty to her is doomed to a violent death (for such, I presume, is the signification of "gaiff waed yn e'i goffin").

We shall now proceed to the magpies: —

II. Cornish.
"One for sorrow, two for mirth,
Three for a wedding, four for a birth."

Welsh.
"Piogen â chroesdra."—A magpie and disappointment.

This unfortunate bird in this part of the country is no more the bane of gamekeepers than it is the

dreaded enemy of all superstitionists. If a person
is on a journey, and one of the species cross his
path, it will turn out unlucky. If one is in search
of something and see a magpie, he will not find
what he seeks. It is always an evil omen, and
invariably "one for sorrow" in this locality; and
it is customary with the superstitious whenever
they see one, to draw the figure of a cross with
their right foot on the ground, and then to spit on
it,—a charm powerful enough to resist the impending doom even of magpyism. A person
affirmed to me the other day that whenever he
hears magpies chattering near his house, it is a
certain forerunner of a word-battle between him
and his better half. Little regard have magpies
for domestic felicity !　　　　　J. R. PHILLIPS.
Cardigan.

DANTE: HERCULES.

(3rd S. vii. 254.)

The conjecture of C. B. C., that it was Hercules
who opened the gate of the city of Dis for Virgil
and Dante (*Inferno*, ix.), is hardly to be sustained.
It is indeed less probable than that of the old
commentator Benvenuto da Imola, who would
have it to be Mercury; whose function in heathen
mythology as the messenger of Jove, and duties
(as described by Virgil) in the infernal regions
would render him much more fit for such a
task than Hercules, whose attribute of physical
strength is not appropriate on an occasion of overcoming the resistance of evil spirits. But in truth
both are very wide of the mark. The event to
which reference must be made, in considering this
passage, is the descent of Christ into hell, which
took place on the day of the year to which the
action of Dante's *Inferno* in this place must be
referred; and nothing *less* than an angel sent from
the immediate presence of God would satisfy the
requirements of the poem—the allusion being to
a similar resistance, supposed to have been made
to Christ's entrance into hell.

All the associations of the passage point to a
biblical, and not a pagan origin. In the service of
the Roman Catholic Church for the Saturday in
Holy Week (the time in question), there occur
the words: "Hodie portas mortis et seras pariter
Salvator noster disrupit." It is difficult also to
believe that the magnificent line—

"Dinanzi polveroso va superbo,"—

was not suggested by Psalm xxxv. ver. 1 to 5:—

" Plead thou my cause, O Lord, with them that strive
with me : and fight thou against them that fight against
me. Lay hand upon the shield and buckler : and stand
up to help me. . . . . Let them be confounded and
put to shame, that seek after my soul : let them be turned
back, and brought to confusion, that imagine mischief for
me. Let them be as the dust before the wind : and the
angel of the Lord scattering them."

Comparison may also be made with a sentence
from Augustine (*De Resurrectione*) : —

" *Portam Inferni et vectes ferreos confregit*, et omnes
justos qui originali peccato adstricti tenebantur, ab-
solvit."

Much illustration, too, of the passage may be
obtained, by reading the account of the Descent
into Hell in the *Vision of Piers Ploughman* (probably composed in 1362) : —

" What lord artow ? quod Lucifer.
　　Quis est iste?
　' *Rex Gloria*,'
　The light soon seide,
　'And lord of myght and of man,
　And alle mannere vertues.
　Dominus virtutum.
　Dukes of this dymme place,
　Anoon undo thise yates,
　That Crist may come in,
　The kynges sone of hevene ! '
　And with that breeth helle brak,
　With Belialles barres,
　For any wye or warde,
　Wide opned the yates."
　　V. 12,710, &c. (London, Pickering, 1842).
　　　　　　　　W. F. P.

LOBECK's "AGLAOPHAMUS" (3rd S. vii. 259.)—
MR. D. BLAIR, of Melbourne, will find an analytical account of Lobeck's *Aglaophamus* and the controversy it provoked in Renan's *Essais d'Histoire
religieuse*, article headed " Les Religions de l'Antiquité."　　　　　　　　A. R.

ANGUS M'DIARMID (3rd S. vi. 507 ; vii. 43.) —
I happened, within two or three years after the
publication of Angus M'Diarmid's pamphlet, to be
with some of my family and relations on a shooting party on the Breadalbane property at Loch-
earnhead. The house of Edinample is within a
mile or two of it. We had several gillies in hired
attendance upon us in our several shooting parties.
In mine, I was very soon made acquainted with
the talented Mr. Angus M'Diarmid, who was one
of them; and in consequence, we became purchasers of his work, and got him to read it to us—
to the great amusement of his fellow gillies as
well as ourselves. They constantly called him the
poet.

Angus's native tongue, of course, was Gaelic;
and in it his work was originally composed. We
were informed that, in translating it into English,
he was much indebted to a dictionary; and his
knowledge of English not being extensive, whenever he was in want of a word he looked into his
dictionary, and adopted generally the most im-
posing-looking word connected with the one he
was looking for, whether it might be noun, verb,
adverb, or otherwise. Thus he used more than
once the words "asperity aspect," to express the
wild appearance of mountains.

Our information was that a Colonel O'Reilly, who had been shooting there two or three years before, had, for his own amusement and for the benefit of Angus, edited his work; and had got an edition printed, which he gave to Angus to sell for his own benefit. I still possess a copy of it at home.

The poet did not seem to be much the richer for the sale; as, though ground officer to the Earl, he was, I remember, the worst dressed of all the gillies: not in the highland fashion, as the others were, but with a black coat and a hat; and, as I remember his comrades observed, a pair of white cotton stockings not very sound at the heel.

J. Ss.

"Oh, oh, ray, oh Amborah" (3rd S. vii. 155.) This burden of one of Polly's songs in the *Beggar's Opera*, is an Anglicised version of "The Irish Howl," to the tune of which the words were sung in the Opera. Your correspondent refers us to Act II. *Scene* 2, but in the original edition (8vo, 1728) the words occur in the fourteenth scene of Act II. The air is printed at the end of the book as No. 21 of the second act.   Wm. Chappell.

Red Lion (3rd S. vii. 136.) — In Yorkshire the sign of the Lion is very common, and as many have changed since the last *Directory* (1857), the following numbers are given: Red Lion, 90; Old Red Lion, 13; Little Red Lion, 2; Golden Lion, 44; Old Golden Lion, 3; Blue Lion, 2; Black Lion, 16; Lion, 4; Lion and Lamb, 3; Lion and Key, 1; Rampant Lion, 1.

C. J. D. Ingledew.

Locality of Zion in early Writers (3rd S. vii. 215.) — Will Dr. Tregelles excuse me for saying that I am unable to see how the passage from Epiphanius shows that he supposed Zion to be the *eastern* hill? There were more *akras* than the one "north of the temple, on the same ridge." In truth, Josephus uses the word (1) in reference to the *hill*, or "lower *agora*;" (2) in reference to the fort upon that hill; (3) in reference to the fort on the higher hill, or "upper agora," which, however, he generally calls φρουρίον; (4) in reference to Antonia, which however he generally calls *Baris*. The use of *akra* in the passage cited affords no clue to the site of the hill. Even in Josephus it is only from the context that you can know frequently which of the *akras* he is speaking of.

Let me suggest the following remark to Dr. T. Zion was predicted to be "ploughed as a field." This has been fulfilled *only of the southern hill*; the eastern hill has always been built upon, not cultivated, and has always been within the city walls. If the eastern hill be Zion, how is this prophecy accomplished?

Zion is very frequently spoken of in connection with *Judah*. It was Judah's hill, David's hill.

If it was the eastern or north-eastern, it was not Judah's, but Benjamin's. Dr. T. knows that the oldest Hebrew tradition draws the line between Judah and Benjamin right across *Moriah*, leaving all the southern part of Jerusalem and its hills in Judah. Taking this in connection with the fact that Zion was specially Judah's hill, we have immemorial Jewish tradition (as well as Christian) in favour of the southern hill.

It is likely that *Gabaon* is Nebi-Semwil; but there is no need to change the *eight* into *five*,—as Nebi-Semwil is, by the *nearest* road, seven miles from Jerusalem; by the farthest, nine. But, rather than alter the reading without MS. authority, I should have said Epiphanius meant the Herodium or Frank hill, which is quite as conspicuous an object from the city. Josephus, however, frequently mentions *Gabaon* (meaning *Gibeon* apparently), which lies down in the western valley below Nebi-Semwil; and Gabaon, if I remember right, was a crusading name for Nebi-Semwil.

Horatius Bonar.

Nolo Episcopari (3rd S. vii. 42, &c.) — Is the following statement, by a popular lecturer, a joke, or has it any true historic foundation? —

"A curious example of *Nolo Episcopari* was afforded by the Rev. Dr. John Bull, Canon of Christchurch, who refused the see of Oxford for the reason that he would not give up the venerable signature of John Bull for that of John Oxon — a species of pluralism at which his conscience rebelled."

Durotrix.

Jackey-legs Knife (3rd S. vii. 250.)—To *shake* is pronounced in Yorkshire (at least in north-east Yorkshire) to *shak*; and a knife, of which the blades have become so loose in the handle as to shake about, is called, not a *jacky*, but a *shaky-legs* knife.   D.

A corruption of the old Scottish word *jocteleg*, used for a knife, and itself a corruption of *Jacques de Liege*, whose name was stamped on large pocket knives used *temp.* Jac. VI. See Sir Walter Scott's *Life, Letters, and Works, passim.*   Crwym.

Porth yr Aur, Carnarvon.

Temse (3rd S. vii. 239.) — The word *temse* is in common use in Lincolnshire, to signify the sieve used by brewers to remove the hops from the beer.   K. P. D. E.

Yew Trees called Palms (3rd S. vii. 251.) — Mr. Lewis is quite right; I wrote hurriedly; I merely meant that the sprig of yew was worn in the hat by the peasants in Ireland for a considerable time, probably till about Whitsunday, or so.   Crywm.

Porth yr Aur, Carnarvon.

I was not aware that yew trees were ever called palms until the quotation from Hunter's edition of Evelyn's *Sylva* appeared in "N. & Q.," but it had long been the custom in this part of England, though recently discontinued, to decorate the churches with yew boughs at the season of Easter. Their first appearance on Good Friday led me to suppose it was a funereal emblem appropriate to that solemn fast day. I venture now to suggest that possibly this yew decoration may have continued until its origin was forgotten, and that the greater celebration of Good Friday and Easter Day caused the village authorities to appropriate to these days the emblem originally intended for the preceding Sunday.

THOMAS E. WINNINGTON.
Stanford Court, Worcester.

LETTER OF OUR LORD TO ABGAR (3rd S. vii. 238.)—On this curious subject the following passage, from the Hon. Robert Curzon's *Armenia*, is worth reproducing:—

"Some years ago I was informed, while in Alexandria, that a papyrus had been discovered in upper Egypt in an ancient tomb. It was enclosed in a coarse earthenware vase, and it contained the letter from Abgarus to our Saviour, written either in Coptic or uncial Greek characters. The answer of St. Thomas was said not to be with it. I was told that the manuscript afterwards came into the possession of the King of Holland; but I have no means at present of ascertaining the truth of the story, or the antiquity of the papyrus of which it forms the subject."

K. P. D. E.

I can confirm the late Dr. Cureton's testimony respecting the popularity of this letter amongst the poor. I have seen it in many cottages both in Nottinghamshire and in Warwickshire. The copy now in my possession was given to me by a poor woman in the latter county as a kind of farewell memento.

H. W. T.

CHURCH DESECRATION (3rd S. vii. 153.)—The lines referred to by J. B. G. were written on a window in a spirit vault in Rothesay. The building was originally a church. In course of time the congregation had to erect a larger building, and the old property was then altered by flooring across the gallery. The upper portion of the building was used as a place of worship by another body of Christians, and the lower portion let as spirit and beer vaults. The lines as I have heard them repeated on the spot, were written thus:—

"There's a spirit above, and a spirit below,
A spirit of love, and a spirit of woe;
The spirit above is the Spirit divine,
But the spirit below is the spirit of wine."

The last time I visited the place, the old church was occupied by an auctioneer on the top story, and the same jolly old fellow who deals in the spirits and wine, as its first occupant, on the ground floor. I do not know the author.

WM. M°K.
Glasgow.

A knowledge of the locality which called forth the epigram—

"There's a spirit above and a spirit below,"

may lead to the discovery of the author's name. The Independent Chapel in Bridge Street, Bristol, is the upper story of a wine and spirit vaults, and I have heard that the lines were written by the late Rev. Robert Hall.

U. O. N.
Westminster Club.

DEATH CAUSED BY DRINKING COLD WATER (3rd S. vii. 236.)—How this subject can derive additional interest to a Christian from its connexion with the crucifixion of our Blessed Saviour, is to me inconceivable; for it has no connexion with it at all. Commentators may well omit to mention, "that drinking cold water whilst suffering very severe pain, produced by torture, causes immediate death," since the case never came before them. Our Saviour drank no *water;* he merely tasted a little *vinegar.* His death, therefore, in a mere natural sense, could not have been caused or accelerated by drinking cold water.

But can any Christian seriously suppose that our Saviour would have done anything to hasten his own death? or ought we, like modern infidels, to reason on the awful and mysterious death of the Son of God, as we might upon the death of any criminal? Does not the Gospel disclose the real motive, and describe the actual event, too clearly for the interference of any comment or calculation? Undoubtedly it does. St. John says that our Lord cried out, "I thirst" (xix. 28), in order "that the Scripture might be fulfilled." What was this Scripture? Evidently the prophecy of the Psalmist (Ps. lxviii., *Hebr.* lxix. 22): "In my thirst they gave me vinegar to drink." St. John says, "He knew that all things were now accomplished." There had remained only this prophecy; to fulfil it, it was necessary to make known his thirst; and therefore our Lord said, "I thirst." The sacred text informs us, that "there was a vessel set there full of vinegar." They dipped a sponge into it, placed the sponge in a bunch of hyssop, to be able to convey it safely, and having tied this to the end of a reed, lifted it to our Saviour's lips. He tasted the vinegar, and thus the last prophecy relating to his passion was fulfilled. If he died immediately, it was not from drinking cold water, for he drank none; nor from drinking vinegar, of which most probably he only tasted; but because then, as he declared, "all was consummated," and it only remained for him to die.

F. C. H.

MARRIAGE RINGS (3rd S. vii. 12.)—I am grateful for your reply to my query, so far as it goes; but I am still anxious to know if there are any recorded instances in which a plain gold ring has been determined to be indispensable for the marriage service; or in which a priest has refused to solemnise it with a ring of any other sort. One of my reasons for pressing for this information is, that I heard recently of a clergyman in India stopping the ceremony because the would-be bridegroom proffered a diamond ring instead of one of the fashion prescribed by "traditionary practice," the only law, you say, on the subject. Your quotations from " N. & Q." (2nd S. x. 290), seem to confirm my belief that a couple might be lawfully married, even in England (as we all know is a frequent custom abroad), without any ring at all, in which case the rubric is of no legal force. But if the rubric is of legal force, is it true that "a ring" no longer satisfies its demands if an odd gem or two adorn it? And if so, I beg you will allow me again to ask—how, when, where, and why, did this innovation arise?

The truth is, I believe it is very doubtful whether the rubric is part of the ἄγραπτα νόμιμα, our common law, at all. A year or two ago this interesting question was raised in a curious case, which came before the Court of Queen's Bench, but was somehow shelved, and consequently never decided. A clergyman (not far from Windsor) refused to proceed with the marriage service, unless the man at its appointed stage laid the ring "*with the accustomed duty*," upon the book. Query, does the law give the priest a right to sue for this, because the rubric gives him a right to demand it?

R. C. L.

SUPERSEDEAS (3rd S. vii. 242.) — It often happens that a grave inquiry is made after some very common and obvious matter; and I strongly suspect that the present is only another instance. Might not the *supersedeas* entered by Newton in his private account book, as bought for a few shillings, have been merely a comfortable arm-chair, or some less honourable seat, which he preferred to enter in his accounts under this name?

F. C. H.

SATIRICAL ENGRAVING (3rd S. vi. 456; vii. 124.) I have looked through Machiavelli's few poems without finding the lines, which I think are translated from Æschylus: —

Μὴ νῦν βροτοὺς μὲν ὠφέλει καιροῦ πέρα,
Σαυτοῦ δ'ἀκήδει δυστυχοῦντος · ὡς ἐγὼ
Εὔελπίς εἰμι τῶνδέ σ' ἐκ δεσμῶν ἔτι
Λυθέντα, μηδὲν μεῖον ἰσχύσειν Διός.
Prom. Vinct. vv. 507-10.

The chief figure and the harpy, seem to be adaptations of Prometheus and the eagle. I am ignorant of their modern application. H. B. C.
U. U. Club.

GÆLIC GRAMMAR (3rd S. vii. 75, 144.) — As J. E. O'CAVANAGH says, in answer to HIGHLANDER'S query, Stewart's *Gælic Grammar* is the best, and the 1812 edition preferable to that of 1801. He might perhaps also consult with profit Shaw's *Analysis of the Gælic Language*, published in 1778, and the later works of Armstrong and Munroe. HIGHLANDER is throwing his time away if he

studies the Gælic of Scotland except through the parent Irish, which once mastered, opens the door to all the cognate Celtic tongues. I divide the Irish grammars under the following heads: — 1. Early grammars: Kearney's *Alphabeticum Hibernicum*, 1571; O'Molloy's *Grammatica Latino-Hibernica*, 1677; Lhuyd's *English-Irish Do.*, 1707; McCurtin's *Elements*, 1728 and 1732; and Donlevy's *Irish Language*, 1742. 2. More modern grammars: Vallancey's *Irish Grammar*, best edition, 1782; Neilson's and Lynch's *Introduction to Irish*, 1808; McElligot's *Observations on Irish*, 1808; O'Brien's *Practical Grammar*, 1809; Halliday's, or E. O. C.'s *Grammar*, 1803; Lynch's *Introduction to Irish*, 1815; O'Reilly's *Compendious Irish Grammar*, 1817 and 1821; and S. O'M.'s *Grammar*, 1841. 3. Recent grammars: O'Donovan's *Grammar of the Irish Language*, 1845; Wright's *Grammar of Modern Irish*, 1855; O'Daly's *Self Instruction*, 1853; Bourke's *Self Instruction*, 1864. The last four are all that are needed however to master the Irish tongue. O'Daly's little book (McGlashan, Dublin, 1853) will enable one to master the pronunciation; Bourke's *Easy Lessons* (Mullany, Dublin, 1864) which are given *à l'Ollendorf*, will teach the colloquial Irish; and O'Donovan's *Masterpiece* (Hodges and Smith, Dublin, 1845) will exhaust all the student's other needs. The above information may be useful to some of your readers, and save them much trouble.

In conclusion I beg to add, that neither Irishman, Welshman, or Scotchman, should be without O'Reilly's *Irish-English Dictionary*, with O'Donovan's great Supplement, just finished, publishing in thirty-three sixpenny parts, by J. Duffy of Dublin. W. EASSIE.

SINGULAR CHRISTIAN NAMES (3rd S. vii. 152.) I have noted in my parish register that the name "Marchina" was given in 1805 to the daughter of a temporary "sojourner" in the village. As the child was baptized, and probably born, in *March*, this singular name may be of the same class as "May," which is, I know, sometimes bestowed upon a child born in the month so designated. H. W. T.

SLEATHERY (3rd S. vii. 239.)—Rather, perhaps, *slithery* (th as in *wither*), A.-S. sliðor, *slippery*, either physically or morally; and *slither*, sub., a slippery place on ice, made by and for sliding; also, a small stream that gently flows or slides out of a bottle. A woman unintentionally poisoned her child with laudanum. She said she had given it only three drops and a *slither*. D.

It may interest your correspondent CUTHBERT BEDE to know, that the word *glib* is in constant use in Lincolnshire for *slippery*; and the verb *to slither*, for "to slide." A LINCOLNSHIRE MAN.

METRICAL SERMON (3rd S. vii. 76, 143.) — In 1837, John Bromley (the author of *Bromley*

Chapel, &c.,) preached a sermon twice in vérse in Bromley chapel, co. Kent. The second occasion was at "the particular desire" of his congregation. Portions of this production the author read to my father and myself, and we both advised him to print the sermon. I am inclined to think that it was printed, and the profits arising therefrom given to some charitable institution connected with the chapel; which was a pet child of Mr. Bromley's, as he wished to be known (as he phrased it) as "Mr. Bromley of Bromley Chapel, Bromley, Kent." Mr. Bromley in early life was an auctioneer. After retiring from business, he was the chief promoter of the construction of Bromley Chapel, where he preached for many years. Mr. Bromley was the cause of the public obtaining free admission into St. Mary's Chapel, in Moor Fields. Previously to his taking legal proceedings, entrance into that sacred fane could only be had by a cash payment. A notice of two of Mr. Bromley's publications will be found in J. Russell Smith's *Bibliotheca Cantiana*. The latter one contains the history of the differences between the pastor and his flock (p. 105).

ALFRED JOHN DUNKIN.

Dartford.

"NO MAN IS A HERO TO HIS VALET-DE-CHAMBRE" (3rd S. vii. 150.)—In Smith's *Classical Dictionary* I find fourteen Antigoni. May I ask to which of them, and on what authority, the clever saying is ascribed?   J. M. K.

"PLAIN SERMONS BY CONTRIBUTORS TO TRACTS FOR THE TIMES" (3rd S.vii. 57, 124.)—The following list of the seven contributors to this excellent series of sermons may be acceptable to GAMMA:—

A. 139. (vols. i. ii. iv. vi. vii. viii.)	Rev. John Keble.	
B. 78. („ ii. iv. vii. ix. x.)	„ Isaac Williams.	
C. 20. (vol. iii.)	„ Dr. Pusey.	
D. 86. („ v.)	„ J. H. Newman.	
E. 55. (vols. i. ii. iv. x.)	„ Thomas Keble.	
F. 12. } (vol. vii.)	}	„ Sir Geo. Prevost, and Rev. W. J. Copeland, but not known which is which.
G. 7. } („ vii.)	}	
347		GRIFFIN.

ARMS OF LYNDWOOD (3rd S. vii. 134.)—The arms assumed by John Lyndewood, the father and John the brother of the bishop, are a chevron between three linden leaves (tinctures not expressed), as may be seen on their brasses in Linwood church, near Market Rasen, Lincolnshire.

F. P. L.

DONKEY (3rd S. vi. 432.)—Is not this word merely a corruption of Fr. *donc*, from the common ejaculation addressed to animals by their drivers, "Marche donc," misinterpreted for joke, as "Get up, Donk"? There is a vehicle in Canada, which, from the same expression, is called a *marche-donc*.

P.

ALVOISE CONTARINI (3rd S. vii. 220.)—I am much obliged to the editor for the reference in his note to my query. I find that my list, as far as it goes, is correct; and I have been told that *Alvoise* is no more than a form of Luigi. Ludovicus, Ludwig, Louis, Lewis, Luigi, *Aluisi*, Aloise, Alvoise, Aloysius.

Is *Aluisi* (or any name of the sort to take its place in the above string) known as a Christian name? *Alvizzo*, which I thought was *Alvoise*, is, I fancy, a family name.   JOHN DAVIDSON.

SIR JOHN FENWICK (3rd S. vi. 478.)—Sir John Fenwick's library exists at Castle Howard, and the papers relating to his trial, and a portrait of Lady Mary (*née* Howard) his wife, holding a miniature of his portrait in her hand.   W. H. C.

PICTURE BY MR. LE JEUNE (3rd S. vii. 200.)— "Release of the Captives from Exodus" appeared in the number of the *Art Journal* for February, 1860. The number can still be had.   R. W.

BAPTISMAL NAMES (3rd S. vii. 178.)—Bishop Aylmer's sixth son was—

"*Tobel* (i. e. God is good), of Writtle in Essex. Archbishop Whitgift was his godfather, and the reason for his singular appellation was his mother's being overturned in a coach without injury while she was pregnant."—Cooper's *Ath. Cant.* ii. 172.

"At Dr. Whitaker's death his wife is described as being 'partui vicina,' and a week afterwards her child was christened by the name of Jabez, doubtless for the scriptural reason, 'Because,' she said, 'I bare him with sorrow.'"—*Ib.* 197.

I was not long ago called upon to christen a girl by the name of Nicholas, and on my hesitating and expressing surprise, was told that the child's grandmother bore the name, the use of which, as a female appellation, was not at all uncommon in Scotland.   E. H. A.

DUDLEY FAMILY (3rd S. ii. *passim.*)—Your correspondent H. S. G. and others also may be interested in the following extract from the Marriage Register of Newington Butts:—

"157⅞, Jan. 27. Thomas Dudley and Helen Winnington."

C. J. R.

BERNARDINO (3rd S. vii. 9.)—By reference to biographical and literary sketches of Italian authors, I find record of one who, I think, is most likely the man in question. Let me premise, what all Italian and other scholars well know, that it is usual to find men of note in Italy called by their *first* name as if it were the family name: for instance, *Dante*, whose second name is Alighieri; *Galileo*, whose added name is Galilei, and many others.

The one with which I have met is *Bernardino Baldi*, of whom it is recorded that he held lineage from a noble family, A.D. 1553. Having completed in his native land the course of elementary studies, he seemed to feel a special inclination for medical science. So his father sent him to the University of Padua, where he applied himself to everything else than medicine. He is said to have traced an encyclopædia of subjects of study, always excepting those of Hippocrates. He busied his mind with logic, mathematics, jurisprudence, and languages, of which latter he is said to have mastered fourteen. After this, clerical and pastoral engagements engrossed his fervent care. He produced various noble works in prose and verse, orations, idyls, &c. To cut short a biography of no small interest and moral worth, I offer the sequel and close in Tuscan tongue, from Costantini's *Scelta di Poesie Italiane:* —

"Nella sua patria di Urbino, il 10 Octobre del 1617, chiuse il Baldi con morte assai pia una vita integerrima. Il genio enciclopedico di Monsignor Bernardino (Baldi) divagò intorno ad una soverchia varietà di fiori, così che ebbe in parte difetto di squisitezza il *mele* ch' ei distillò. Potrebbe egli figurar nobilmente come poeta, se lo stile non di rado raffinato e concettoso non gli scemasse una parte di merito. Egli in poesia fu assai fecondo, e scrisse prosopopeje di eroi romani, epistole, madrigali, epitaffi, concetti morali, etc.—oltre alcuni poemi in versi sciolti."

S. C. FREEMAN.

Adelaide House,
148, Highbury New Park, N.

HÆVER, AEVER, OR EAVER (3rd S. vii. 258.) — May not this be merely a peculiar pronunciation of *ever*, so that the inquiry would be in plain English, "*Whatever* is the wind in this morning?" that is, whatever point of the compass, or in whatever direction?

F. C. H.

" BIS DAT QUI CITO DAT? " (3rd S. vii. 265.) — This maxim comes from the famous poet, *Publius Syrus*, who flourished at Rome in the reign of Julius Cæsar, and supplanted Laberius in his favour. He has another proverb somewhat similar:
" Bis est gratum, quod opus est, ultro si offeras."

F. C. H.

CARABOO (3rd S. vii. 269.) — I have no doubt the real name of this impostor was Mary Baker. We are told that after her exposure she went to America, where she remained about seven years, when she returned to England, and exhibited in New Bond Street, London, from whence she made her way westward. The last I heard of her was that she married, and once more took up her residence in this city, where her latter days were spent very creditably as an importer of leeches, and in applying them when requested by her customers. She appears to have died about the close of the year 1864, leaving an only daughter. I believe the exact date of her decease is unknown, as well as her age and place of interment.

GEORGE PRYCE.

City Library, Bristol.

CAREY FAMILY (3rd S. vii. 203, &c.) — I have heard it alleged that the names *Carey* and *Carew*

were originally the same, and that the two families are both descended from the same stock. The assertion ran to the effect, that the name of the remote ancestor was written *Careu*, which, in Welsh, was pronounced pretty much as the modern word Cary or Carey; hence the name Carey, by those who followed sound only. On the other hand, others articulated the Welsh word more after an Anglicised bias, sounding the last letter *u* as an English *w*, thereby making it *Caroo*. A name pronounced *Caroo* would naturally be written *Carew*, differing only in its last letter from its infantine construction. I should like to know whether there is any philological or historical truth in all this.

P. HUTCHINSON.

JOHNSONIANA : CONTINUITY (3rd S. vii. 6, 42, 123.)—

". . . . . Leibnitz di Lipsia sino dal 1693 avesse fatto presentire nel mondo materiale e morale la grande legge di *continuità* nell' infinito del tempo o dello spazio." *Idea fondamentale e bisogno d'una Storia delle Storie.* See article in "Il Politecnico," Gennaio, 1865.

The Abbé Draghesti, in his *Dissertazioni Psicologiche*, asserts that the celebrated scholar, Pontanus (1426-1503), was the first who called attention to the law of continuity; and was also the first among the moderns who revived the opinion of Democritus on the subject of the milky way, which he maintained to be composed of an infinite number of small stars.

J. MACRAY.

Oxford.

RAGUSA (3rd S. vii. 180, 265.)—The arms given on the silver ducat and a half that I have of Ragusa, differ from those mentioned by MR. WOODWARD, being Barry of eight, argent and gules; perhaps they are the arms of the governor (1773), whose bust is on the obverse. Was Ragusa ever independent of Venice?

As MR. WOODWARD has been so kind as to answer my query and as he has given me an extract from a German work on heraldry, may I ask him what heraldic word have we for that triangular quartering one finds not uncommonly in foreign shields: a pointed quartering *pushed up*, as it seems to be considered; I mean "Die Spitze" "Der untere *eingeschobene* spitzige Theil," seen in the Georges German shield, containing the arms of the city of Granada in the Spanish shield, &c. &c. Is it a pile issuing from the base?

JOHN DAVIDSON.

TITHE BARNS (3rd S. vii. 137, 249.) — LORD LYTTELTON states accurately the clergy's right to the produce itself as it stood on the ground, previous to the Tithe Commutation Act. When at a school near Shrewsbury, where the master was also rector of the parish, I can remember the schoolboys' assistance in the harvest collection, which was effected by placing a stick on every tenth sheaf in the cornfield, to be afterwards conveyed by the clergyman's team to his tithe barn.

THOMAS E. WINNINGTON.

THOMAS BILBIE (3ʳᵈ S. vii. 240.)—In the List of Bell Founders, printed in the first volume of the *Wilts Magazine*, Mr. Lukes has given "Thomas Bilbie" as a bell-founder, 1746, at Kew- or Chewstoke, near Bristol. Bells of his casting are often met with in the western counties.   E. W.

Miscellaneous.

NOTES ON BOOKS, ETC.

The New Testament of Our Lord and Saviour Jesus Christ. Illustrated in a plain explanatory Comment, and by Authentic Views of Places mentioned in the Text, from Sketches and Photographs taken on the Spot. Edited by Edward Churton, M.A., *and* William Basil Jones, M.A. *In Two Volumes.* (Murray.)

This beautiful edition has been produced for the purpose of furnishing such a plain explanatory comment, that any portion selected for daily reading might be found so far historically, critically, or doctrinally interpreted, as to leave the words of the sacred lesson itself first and last in the reader's mind. Its illustrations are, for the most part, true and accurate views of the places which they represent as they exist at the present day, taken from sketches or photographs made on the spot; and they are introduced from the conviction, that "it surely lends vividness to the impression with which we read the New Testament, to find the fisherman still casting his net into the Sea of Galilee—the women of Palestine still grinding at the mill, or lighting the oven with grass from the field." In the panoramic illustrations—so beautiful in themselves, and so appropriately introduced—the journeys of Our Lord around the shores of the Sea of Tiberias, from Galilee and Nazareth to Jerusalem, and from Bethany to Jerusalem, may partly at least be traced. Mr. Murray modestly describes this beautiful *New Testament Illustrated* as a Book for Easter — it is more, it is a Book for all Time.

Historical Notes to the Lyra Germanica: containing Brief Memoirs of the Authors of the Hymns therein translated, and Notices of Remarkable Occasions on which some of them or any of their Verses have been used. With Notices of other German Hymn Writers represented in other English Collections. Compiled and translated from authentic German Sources. By Theodore Kübler. (Longman.)

It was a saying of Coleridge, "That Luther had done as much for the Reformation by his hymns as by his translation of the Bible;" and there can be little doubt as to the good service rendered to the cause of religion and piety by the hymn writers, both of Germany and of this country. In the preface to the present work the author tells us, that the earliest attempts at introducing the German hymns to the religious world of England were made by the brothers John and Charles Wesley; who were for a time intimately connected with the Moravians, when Count Zinzendorf and A. G. Spangenberg first came over to this country. And many will be surprised to hear that some of the most effective and popular of Wesley's hymns, are translations from the German. In more recent times, F. E. Cox, the Rev. A. T. Russell, Mr. Massie, and more especially Miss Winkworth, have opened the treasures of the German hymnologists to English religionists. The popularity of Miss Winkworth's *Lyra Germanica* has called forth the present volume, which abounds in biographical notices of the principal German hymn writers, and notices of remarkable occasions on which the hymns have at times been used. Independently therefore of its own merits, the work has scarcely secondary value as an illustration of Miss Winkworth's deservedly popular book.

Israel in the Wilderness; or Gleanings from the Scenes of the Wanderings. With an Essay on the true Date of Korah's Rebellion. By the Rev. Charles Forster, B.D., Rector of Stisted, Essex. (Bentleys, 1865.)

This is a work which will be read with much interest by all who hang fondly over every detail of Holy Scripture, and delight to identify every spot, and verify every circumstance connected with the Exodus of the Israelites. Mr. Forster stoutly insists, that the mysterious inscriptions of the Peninsula of Sinai are the Jews' own record of their sojourn there. The sculptured ostrich of Djebel Maghara is the emblem of the wanderers in the wilderness ; the corpses of those that died in the plague of Kibroth-Hattaavah were interred in the cemetery of Sarbut-el Khadem ; the "quails," after which the people lusted, are figured on the tombstones there ; and whereas it is said that Eldad and Medad "were of them that were written" (Num. xi. 26), the true meaning is, that they were engaged on the inscriptions. We cannot say that Mr. Forster's arguments are as convincing as his subject is interesting. And he surely strains a point when he appeals to the poetic strains of Moses' song, and of the later Psalms, as literal descriptions of the passage of the Red Sea and the "smiting of the rock."

The Books of the Vaudois. The Waldensian Manuscripts preserved in the Library of Trinity College, Dublin. With an Appendix containing a Correspondence (reprinted from the British Magazine) on the Poems of the Poor of Lyons, the Antiquity and Genuineness of the Waldensian Literature, and the supposed loss of the Morland MSS. at Cambridge; with Mr. Bradshaw's Paper on his recent discovery of them. By James Henthorn Todd, D.D., &c. (Macmillan & Co.)

All who have studied the history of the Waldenses know how much depends upon the age of the tract called *Qual Cosa sia l'Antichrist*, and of the vain endeavours which have been made to discover the MS. of it which Morland deposited in the Public Library of Cambridge. They will also remember the interesting correspondence connected with this subject between Dr. Todd, Dr. Gilly, Dr. Maitland, and the Hon. Algernon Herbert in the *British Magazine*. Of these correspondents, Dr. Todd says truly, " Never were men more honestly in search of truth, or more ready to embrace what they discovered of it, in defiance of all consequences." But the learned Doctor tells us, that while all this correspondence was going on, the supposed missing volumes were lying unknown and buried in their dust untouched for upwards of 200 years on the very shelf where Morland placed them. Mr. Bradshaw's account of their discovery and description of the tiny MS. volumes of which they consist is not the least of the many interesting papers which the present volume contains.

BOOKS AND ODD VOLUMES

WANTED TO PURCHASE.

Particulars of Price, &c., of the following Book to be sent direct to the gentleman by whom it is required, and whose name and address are given for that purpose:—

THE HISTORICAL EDUCATOR. Vol. II. London: John Cassell, La Belle Sauvage Yard, Ludgate Hill. 4to, 1854.

Wanted by *Varlo Hellyer, Esq.*, Coleshill Street, Eaton Square.

Notices to Correspondents.

Shakespeariana. "N. & Q." of Saturday next will contain several articles uPon Shakespeare.

Charles Povey. Our next number will also contain an article of this extraordinary projector, the originator of the Sun Fire Office, &c.; together with a copy of his will.

E. U. (Croydon) will probably find what he requires in Collins' Peerage. Of course we mean the edition published by Sir E. Brydges.

T. The picture representing Edward VI. granting the Royal Charter to Bridewell is at Bridewell.

May Marriages. "One who wishes to know" will find this subject very fully treated in our First Series.

Omega. The date of Wace's death is not known. He is supposed to have died soon after the completion of his Roman de Rou in 1171.

A Reading Case for holding the weekly Nos. of "N. & Q." is now ready, and may be had of all Booksellers and Newsmen, price 1s. 6d.; or, free by post, direct from the publisher, for 1s. 8d.

*** Cases for binding the volumes of "N. & Q." may be had of the Publisher, and of all Booksellers and Newsmen.

"Notes and Queries" is published at noon on Friday, and is also issued in Monthly Parts. The Subscription for Stamped Copies for Six Months forwarded direct from the Publisher (including the Half-yearly Index) is 11s. 4d., which may be paid by Post Office Order, payable at the Strand Post Office, in favour of William G. Smith, 32, Wellington Street, Strand, W.C., where also all Communications for the Editor should be addressed.

"Notes & Queries" is registered for transmission abroad.

LONDON, SATURDAY, APRIL 22, 1865.

CONTENTS.—Nº 173.

Notes.

CHARLES POVEY.

On paying a visit to the Probate Office lately, I had the curiosity to look up the last will and testament of this "extremely foresighted, thoughtful, but eccentric man," as he is styled in the new edition of Lowndes, and carried away in my memory as much of the curious contents as it would carry; particularly the fact, that the testator directed its publication in the daily papers twice within a month after his decease, which appears to have occurred on April 2, 1743.[*] At the Museum to-day I sought and discovered the document in the *London Daily Post* of the 1st and 8th July of that year; but on perusal, found it denuded of much of its *Povian* peculiarities. However, I made a jotting, and now send the same for your inspection. If deemed of sufficient interest, it may obtain a place in the columns of "N. & Q.": for it serves to identify a few extraordinary books that sometimes fall into the hands of the collector of oddities, and lead to queries about their author,—Povey's works being privately, or irregularly published, and many of them anonymous. In the earlier part of his life, Povey was in a constant state of warfare with authorities of all kinds. The government deprived ... of the advantage of his *Halfpenny Carriage* ... Charles Povey died on May 4, 1743, aged ninety.

scheme; the Excise stripped his brewery at Hampstead of its utensils for their duty; his partners in his own *invention* of the Sun Fire Office, wheedled him out of the concern, by which he lost a fortune; the magistrates imprisoned him, with his servants, for writing his two large octavos—the *Meditations* and *Holy Thoughts*—rambling treatises eulogistic of King William and the Revolution, and abuse of the Highflyers: these, and many more of his grievances, are set forth at large in his *English Inquisition*, 1718, and his *English Memorial*, 1737. The first an appeal to the nation, and the last a representation to Parliament, unsuccessfully claiming indemnification for the sacrifices he had made for the public benefit. With his literary contemporaries he was in no better odour. John Dunton says, "Povey not only steals my projects, but reprints those very questions and answers I formerly published in *The Athenian Oracle*," in his *General Remark upon Trade*: which last publication was in rivalry, I think, of Defoe. He envied the popularity of Addison and Steele, and clumsily imitated the *Spectator* and *Tatler* in his *Visions of Sir Heister Ryley*; in his *Virgin in Eden*, he attacks *Pamela*; and, indeed, managed to render himself so unpopular that another of his complaints is, that the *false wits* were down upon every move he made, "taking the liberty to brand me with the odd characters of Maggot, Projector, Madman, or worse titles." Povey was, nevertheless, a man before his age in some respects, and crude though some of them may be, suggested many social improvements; professing a large philanthropy, and very latitudinarian views upon religious matters. Our subject was, moreover, an outrageous egotist; his works being filled with the most amusingly self-complacent examples of what he had done "to promote virtue, loyalty, wit, honour, truth, and moderation; and to extinguish vice, rebellion, bribery, pride, and ambition:" to say nothing of his magnified labours to ameliorate the condition of the poor, both physically and mentally. All of which can only, however, be effectively maintained by a cordial reception, and a large demand by the public for his works![*] The

[* Charles Povey must have been a most voluminous writer, as he tells us that "the large 4to and 8vo volumes, with other small treatises and pieces I have writ, exceed six hundred in number!" (*English Inquisition*, 1718, 8vo, p. 8.) Alas! how few of them are known to the present generation of bibliographers. A recent glance over the Registers at Stationers' Hall enables us to spot two works by this prolific writer which appear unknown:—1. *A Memorial of the Proceedings of the late Ministry and Lower House of Parliament*, entered Dec. 15, 1714. 2. *The English Parliament represented in a Vision*; this work was entered on March 7, 1714-5, at the same time as *An Inquiry into the Miscarriage of the Four last Years' Reign*, noticed in our 2nd S. i. 322. Some interesting particulars of Povey will be found in Park's *Hampstead*, 4to, 1814, p. 156.—ED.]

suppressions in this printed will illustrate some of these points in the testator's character. His comments upon the *dole* to the widows, for example, inform us that he has been labouring all his life to reconcile religious sects; as far at least as to secure the Christian virtue of cordial co-operation in works of mercy and charity, of which he furnishes a practical proof. It is to be feared, however, that the literary gift which accompanied the pecuniary one must have been distasteful to both Church and Meeting-house—the orthodoxy of their widows being endangered thereby: for Povey, like some moderns, roundly rejects the belief of material fire in his Tophet:— with him, the torments after death are the immaterial stings of a guilty conscience. Again, the persecutions which Povey met with from unjust judges, false witnesses, &c., &c., all come afresh into the poor old man's mind when settling his worldly affairs, at the age of threescore years and ten; and his early cantankerous spirit returns to the charge, with an appeal to his Maker that he is innocent of the *crimes* they attempted to fix upon him: accompanied by a special denouncement against one Ladd, a judge or magistrate— one of the most virulent of his enemies.

The affair of the Sun Fire Office, too, comes again under review; and an intimation that, if his annuity from that flourishing concern is not continued after his death, the proprietors will forfeit their claim to be men of honour.

The widows and children, as well as the *perjured and vile incendiaries* who had embittered his existence, had intimation during his lifetime: a paragraph in his *Torments* announcing, that his benevolence to the first, and his *remembrance* of the last would be found in his *Last Will and Testament*; which he there says he had directed to be printed, not out of vanity, but to set his character in its true light; but we have seen that this rod in pickle for his enemies was suppressed in the copy for the public eye.

Except naming a brother, I nowhere observe that Povey mentions his family. Was he a son, or otherwise related, to Thomas Povey, who held a public office in the time of Charles II.?—whose house, and style of living "did surpass all that ever I did see of one man in all my life," says the envious Pepys.

The Copy of Mr. Povey's will, published according to his own desire.

" In the name of God, Amen. I, Charles Povey, of the parish of St. Mary Whitechapel, in the county of Middlesex, Gent., being aged and infirm in body, but of sound and perfect mind, memory, and understanding (praise be given to Almighty God for the same), and considering the certainty of my death, and the uncertainty (of the time) thereof, do therefore, for the avoiding controversies after my decease, make, publish, and declare this to be my last will and testament, in manner and form following (that is to say): first, and principally, I recommend my soul to the mercies

of God, believing I shall certainly rise again to life eternal through the merits and mediation of Jesus Christ my Saviour and Redeemer; my body I commend to the earth, to be decently buried by my executors hereinafter named, in the parish church of St. Mary, Newington Butts, in the county of Surrey, in the same grave wherein my late wife Ann Povey now lieth interred: and as for and concerning the disposal of all such worldly estates and effects, which it has pleased God of his great goodness to bestow upon me, I give, devise, and bequeath, the same as followeth: and first, I will and order that only four or five mourning coaches and one hearse, shall be employed at my funeral, and that my pall shall be supported by six gentlemen whom my said executors shall think fit to appoint. Item, I give and bequeath unto Mr. Obadiah Jones of the parish of St. Andrew, Holborn, London, all my land lying and being at Cheagle, near Boos in Staffordshire. I also give and bequeath to him, the said Obadiah Jones, all that which will descend of right belonging to me, after the decease of Dorothy Povey, widow of my late brother Josiah Povey, deceased; who was minister of Rodom and Kescom, near Lewes, in Sussex. Item, I give and bequeath to and for the use of the parish of St. Mary, Newington, aforesaid, my great organ, being 5 feet in depth, 6 feet in front, and 9½ feet in height: containing three sets of keys; Mr. Aaron Davis, an organ maker, having contracted and agreed with me to make, or cause the said organ to play six several Psalm tunes, and four voluntaries, and to perform the same from time to time at pleasure, without any person playing upon the keys thereof; as also the bellows of the said organ, to move and perform the same by clockwork. Item, I give and bequeath fifteen guineas for, or towards, the erecting and setting up the said organ in the said parish church, and for other uses which shall and may be necessary to or for the ornament thereof. Item, I give and bequeath to and for the use of the Charity School of the said parish, fifty guineas. Item, I will and direct that my said executors shall, on every Saturday during the space of six months next after my decease, give to the poor of the parish of Whitechapel aforesaid 100 penny loaves. Item, I give and devise to 100 poor tradesmen's widows, who shall be arrived at the full age of forty-five years, each one guinea a-piece. Item, I give and bequeath to 100 poor ministers' widows, of the like ages, five guineas a-piece; and I give and bequeath to each of the said 200 widows, one book of my treatise, intitled *The Virgin in Eden, or, the State of Innocence*; and one book each of my other treatise, intitled *Torments after Death, upon Atheism and Charity*. And I do direct and appoint that the said 200 widows shall be chosen in manner following (that is to say): the morning preachers who reside in and about London, and consecrate bread and wine of the parish churches of St. Mary Whitechapel, St. Botolph-without, Aldgate, St. Thomas's, St. George's, and St. Mary's, Newington, aforesaid; each of the said divines to nominate ten ministers' poor widows of the Church of England, and ten tradesmens' widows of the same Communion; and each of the said is to produce a certificate under the hand of one of the aforesaid clergymen, whereby it shall be sufficiently certified that they know and believe such widows to be reduced, and to be of sober conversation, and to have no settled income whatsoever: and the other 100 poor widows shall be chosen by the ministers of the Meeting-houses under named (that is to say): that of Dr. Watts, in Duke's Place; Mr. Denkam (?), in Old Gravel Lane, Houndsditch; Mr. Wilson, in Prescot Street, Goodman's Fields; Mr. Read, near Guy's Hospital; and Mr. Oldfield's, near Deadman's Place, Southwark: each of the said ministers to nominate ten Dissenting ministers' widows and ten tradesmen's widows, of the same persuasion; each and every of which said widows to produce a certificate signed by one of the said ministers, in the same form as those of the Church of England above-named; and I order and appoint all and every the said legacies to be paid within the space of four months next after my decease. Item, I give and bequeath unto J—— S——, of the parish of Aldgate aforesaid, Gent., twenty guineas, to be paid him on delivering up to my said executors a bond and assignment from me, unjustly detained by —— and ——, clear of all charge except law expenses. Item, I give and bequeath unto A—— H——, of the parish of St. Giles's-in-the-Field, widow, the like sum of twenty guineas, to be paid to her on the delivery of the said bond and assignment, upon the forms and conditions aforesaid. Item, I order and appoint Thos. James, now or late of the parish of St. Clement Danes, to be sole proprietor of all my copies of the several treatises here under-mentioned (being my works, that is to say): *The Meditations of a Divine Soul*, price 4s.; *Holy Thoughts on God made Man*, price 4s.; *The Visions of Sir Heister Ryley*, price 2s. 6d.; *The Treatise of Trade and Employing the Poor*, price 1s. 6d.; the treatise entitled *The Virgin in Eden, or State of Innocency*, price 1s.; and the treatise entitled *Torments after Death upon Atheism and Charity*, price 6d.; with all and every other copies whatsoever heretofore wrote and published by me; the testator, upon this condition, that he the said Thos. James, his executors, administrators, and assigns, do and shall well and truly pay, or cause to be paid, 1s. 6d. out of every pound or 20s., which he or they shall receive and take by sale of all and every, or any, of the said copies: 9d. out of every pound to be paid to the rector (for the time being) of St. Mary's, Newington Butts, aforesaid; and the other 9d. to be paid to Dr. Guyse, the elder Dissenting minister at the Meeting-house in Broad Street, London, or any other minister (for the time being) of the same congregation; the said monies to be by them (according to their discretion) distributed in and amongst poor ministers' widows of their own persuasion, who shall not have received any benefit by or under this my will. And the said Thos. James is to pay to my said executors a certain price, to be agreed upon between him and me, at or before the time of my executing this my will, for all the printed copies which are now in my possession of two of the said treatises entitled, *The Virgin in Eden* and *Torments after Death*; and shall sell and dispose of all reprinted copies thereof, before he shall be entitled to demand or receive the said several copies hereinabove devised to him; and all the rest and residue of estate, real and personal, of what nature or kind soever, after my debts and funeral expences, and the above legacies are fully paid and satisfied, I will appoint the same to be fairly divided into three equal parts. Two-third parts, or shares whereof, I give, devise, and bequeath to my niece Eliz. Smith, widow, now living with me; and the other third part, or share thereof, I give and bequeath unto Margaret Stringer of St. Martin's-le-Grand, widow. And I do hereby make, order, constitute, and appoint my said niece Eliz. Smith, and the said Margaret Smith, joint executrixes of this my last will and testament. And lastly, I do hereby revoke and make void all former wills by me at any time heretofore made; and do declare this present writing, contained in three sheets of paper, to be my last will and testament. And I do order and direct my said executors, within one month after my decease, to cause the same to be printed twice in one of the daily papers. In witness whereof I, Charles Povey, the testator, have, to the bottom of the first and second sheets of this my will, set and subscribed my name; and the third, and last sheet, have subscribed and set my hand and seal this 13th January, [...] year of our Lord, 1742, and in the 16th year of the [...] of our Sovereign Lord George the Second, by the

Grace of God of Great Britain, France, and Ireland, King, Defender of the Faith, &c.

"CHARLES POVEY.

" Signed, sealed, published, and declared by the said Charles Povey, the testator, as and for his last will and testament, in the presence of us; who, in his presence, have set and subscribed our names as witnesses thereto, the day and year last above written:

(Signed)　" JOHN DODD,
　　　　　　　REBECCA NEWTON,
　　　　　　　SUSANNAH LOWE."

London Daily Post, Friday, 1st and 8th July, 1743.
　　　　　　　　　　　　　　　　A. G.

Shaksperiana.

NEW SHAKSPERE EMENDATION.

In Mr. J. A. Heraud's new work, *Shakspere, His Inner Life*, he has ventured with some confidence to submit a suggested reading of a passage in *Julius Cæsar*, Act II. Sc. 1, which has long been regarded as corrupt. Coleridge, he tells us, had noticed the line—

" For if thou *path*, thy native semblance on,"

and had set it down as a misprint or a miscript; asking the pertinent question, "in what place does Shakspere (where does any other writer of the same age?) use *path* as a verb for *walk*?" His own reading was *put* for *path*, ingenious, but, as we shall see, involving one objection. But Mr. Heraud, who is entitled to respectful hearing if only on the ground of having been Coleridge's friend and disciple, goes further than the master. He says, "To me it is clear that the line contains *two* errors. It should have run—

" For if thou *pall* thy native semblance o'er,"

and supports it by an allusion to the context, "their faces *buried* in their cloaks."

"It is to this statement," he says, "that Brutus refers in the line in question, which simply means that if the conspirators come with 'their faces buried in their cloaks' their conspiracy will be naturally suspected;—that the true mode of concealment is to let their naked faces (their ' native semblance') be seen, and only to 'hide' the ' monstrous visage' of conspiracy in 'smiles and affability.' With this interpretation the passage reads intelligibly enough, and the line as amended falls naturally into its proper place."

Now, is this so ? I think not.

Let us examine the passage. Let us reduce it to simple prose, and see the result. Speaking in the language of every-day life, Brutus would have said, "O conspiracy! Do you fear to show your brow by night? Where then by day will you find a cavern dark enough to hide its monstrosity? Best seek none. ' Hide it in smiles and affability:' for if you appear in your native semblance, not hell itself is black enough to hide you."

Now, in this view of the passage, the text of Shakspere as it stands, per ect　accords if we grant the use of *path* in the sense of *walk*.

With this also Coleridge's emendation is consistent, having only this objection, that conspiracy can hardly be required in strict sense to "put on" what is "native" or natural to it.

But how does it fare with my friend Heraud's reading?

Passing over his substitution of the conspirators for the abstract conspiracy (wholly indefensible as it seems to me), how does the passage read as he would amend it? —

"O, then by day
Where wilt thou find a cavern dark enough
To hide thy monstrous visage?   Seek none, conspiracy.
             [Not "conspirators."]
Hide it in smiles and affability."

Why? ' '

"For if thou pall thy native semblance o'er."

That is, as Mr. Heraud tells us, "if thou 'hide' thy 'monstrous visage' in 'smiles and affability,'" what will happen? —

"Not Erebus itself were dim enough
To hide thee."

No! Shakspere could not have meant to say that. If thou hide thyself Erebus is not dim enough to hide thee? Impossible! Adopt Mr. Heraud's reading, and the sequence should have been:—

"Not even Heaven itself has light enough
To reveal thee."

The fact is, Mr. Heraud has stumbled through confounding the "native semblance" of conspiracy with the naked faces of the conspirators, and the lection which this has induced him to offer is in consequence, in my judgment, wholly inadmissible.

One word more. I do not with Halliwell and Knight defend path. I think the solitary use of the word as an active verb in this passage lays it open to suspicion; but walk (with a comma after it) clearly gives sense, and any one who will write the two words in the style of the sixteenth century writing, beginning the w with a tail, and omitting to cross the t, will see that they are sufficiently alike to have deceived the eye of scribe or printer.   W. Sawyer.

54, Crowndale Road, Oakley Square, N. W.

Passage in "Pericles" (3rd S. vii. 236.) — In the name of common sense what can your correspondent, William Bell, mean by saying that the passage from Pericles which he quotes —

"The air-remaining lamps, the belching whale"— ,

is an additional proof "of our great poet's intimate knowledge and consequent residence in Germany"? Will Mr. Bell forgive me for saying, that as he has not produced one tittle of evidence to show that "lamps" means "lampreys," I do not accept that interpretation? But not content with assuming that "lamps" is put for lampreys, Mr. Bell proceeds to point out that, as "a peculiar

fallacy in natural history" still "prevalent among our neighbours of Fatherland," they call the lamprey Neunaugen; and this is a wonderful proof that Shakspeare was in Germany. One might almost be pardoned for exclaiming with Mr. Burchell, "Fudge!" Let Mr. Bell refer to Halliwell's Glossary, and he will find that calling the lamprey "Nine eyes" is as much a "peculiar fallacy" in England as in Germany; and forgive me, Mr. Editor, if I add, that but for your well-known "proclivities" to the theory of Shakspeare's visit to Germany, I suspect we should have been spared. Mr. Bell's far-fetched and illogical attempt to improve a passage in Shakspeare rendered sufficiently intelligible by Malone's simple emendation "aye" for "air"—"the aye-remaining lamps."   R. A.

"A Dish of Carraways" (Hen. IV., Part II. Act V. Sc. 3.) — This passage has given rise to some amusing comments. Warburton was justly ridiculed for a note, which simply stated that in the sixteenth century the French were very fond of lozenges. Whereupon Goldsmith, with an air of authority, observed, that "the dish of carraways here mentioned was a dish of apples of that name." Steevens, after giving four quotations to show that carraways were not apples, but some kind of comfit, added: "There is a pear, however, called a carraway." In a later note he cites a passage from Cogan's Haven of Health (1595), which, as he truly states, "settles the question." The old physician, with droll plainness of speech, says: —

"Howbeit, we are wont to eate carawaies or biskets, or some other kind of comfits or seeds, together with apples, thereby to breake winde ingendred by them; and surely it is a very good way for students."

Is it worth while to add another quotation, to corroborate this from Cogan? William Vaughan, in his Directions for Health, &c. (4to, London, 1626, 6th edition), says: —

"Apples, suffered to grow to their maturity and perfection, surpass all other fruits whatsoever, if they be eaten in winter with carraways or comfits."

           Jaydee.

Passage from "Macbeth." — A correspondent, B. T., in your number of April 1, under the above heading writes, that "in old English dictionaries, probably in Bailey's, the word blonket, which means a thunder-cloud, is given;" and he suggests that this may be the original reading of the passage in Lady Macbeth's soliloquy (so long disgraced by the unquestionable corruption of blanket). I should be obliged to B. T. to inform me in what dictionaries the word blonket, with the interpretation he gives to it, is to be found. It is not in Bailey's; and the only one in my possession which contains it is that of Ashe, who calls it, "an incorrect spelling of blanket."

-Is it a provincialism, or has it been employed by any known author of any date, or is there any reasonable probability that Shakspeare could be cognizant of it?

I ask these questions because, if it can be shown that it is a word which an audience in the reign of King James I. would have understood in the sense of "thunder-cloud," it appears to me to solve the long vexed question; and, by the change of a single letter, supply an image at once correct and dignified,—qualities in which the word *blanket* is so offensively deficient.   G. K.

"TWELFTH NIGHT," ACT II. SC. 3 (*sub fin.*).—

"Call me cut."

I do not know whether any of your readers are acquainted with the boyish game still in vogue in Cumberland, and with which I have been for many years familiar. It will throw, I think, some light upon the phrase above quoted. The game, or whatever it may be called, is conducted thus. Two boys of equal years and strength are pitted against each other; lots are drawn by means of two unequal straws or slips of paper, and the boy who draws the longest piece, if he wish to fight his schoolfellow calls him "cut;" the other, if in the same mind, retorts "Jack-hazel,"—then the *mêlée* commences.

I cannot doubt that Sir Andrew's "instinct" would have brought him well out of the difficulty, though he had called Sir Toby "cut," and left him "to take it how he would;" in fact to return or not "Jack-hazel." In calling "cut" it sometimes happens that a lad who wishes to stand well with his schoolfellows, but does not care to fight, spells the word deliberately "c-u-t" (which is not a challenge until every letter is pronounced to a "t"), in order that he may have time to calculate whether his antagonist will fight or not. Does this throw any light upon the mysterious letters in the fifth scene of this act? "Her C's, her U's, and her T's: why that?"

           J. WETHERELL.

Middlesbro'.

CUE.—The word *cue* occurs twelve times in the plays of Shakspere, and once in the plural number. In the voluminous edition of 1803 we have six notes in illustration of its meaning, two of which I must transcribe:

"*Had you not come upon your cue.*] This expression is borrowed from the theatre. The *cue, queue, or tail* of a speech, consists of the last words, which are the token for *entrance or answer. To come on the cue,* therefore, is to come at the proper time."—JOHNSON [1765. v. 297.]

"*__ and all.*] A *cue,* in stage cant, is the last words of the preceding speech, and serves as a hint to him who is to speak next."—G. STEEVENS [1790, ii. 484.]

Johnson and Steevens report correctly the *stage cant* of their times, which is also that of our time, but how was the word *cue* understood when Shakspere flourished? On that point we have no information, unless we rely on *Quince the carpenter* and *Bottom the weaver*—entertaining fellows, no doubt, but quite inadmissible as authorities on philological matters. I shall therefore produce the sober decision of a learned grammarian of the year 1634:

"Q. A note of entrance for actors, (because it is the first letter of *quando,* when,) showing when to enter and speak." Charles BUTLER, M.A.

In confirmation of the statement of Butler, I add examples from the best authorities now at hand; the first, from the quarto edition in photo-lithography, and the others from the excellent reprint of the folio of 1623, published by Mr. Lionel Booth:

"*Beatrice.* Speake Counte, tis your Qu."
           Much adoe, 1600.

"*Ford.* . . . The clocke giues me my Qu, and my assurance bids me search."— *M. W. W.*

"*Mi. Ford.* . . . Mistris *Page,* remember you your Qu."
           M. W. W.

"*Mountjoy.* . . . Now wee speake vpon our Q."
           Henry V.

"*Buck.* Had you not come vpon your Q my Lord."
           Richard III. "
           BOLTON CORNEY.

Barnes.

BIBLIOGRAPHIC (3rd S. vii. 297.)—The *Shakspeariana* of Mr. Isaac Reed, in 9 volumes. This lot was purchased by lord Spenser at 23*l.* The copy of the *Bibliotheca Reediana* whence I derive this information has been just thirty years in my possession, and was priced by Mr. Alexander Chalmers. The prices are thus authenticated: "*Twelve copies of this catalogue were printed on a large paper, and given by the auctioneers to the particular friends of Mr. Reed. The prices here are copied from one of these. A.C. March 1809.*"

           BOLTON CORNEY.

ASSUMPTION OF ARMS.

I want to provoke a little discussion on a fresh branch of a subject often already treated of in the columns of "N. & Q."

I set out with two propositions:—

1. All cognizances, devices, or armorial bearings were, I apprehend, originally adopted at the fancy of their bearers; *i. e.* arms existed long before their multiplication gave birth to Heralds (in the Doctors' Commons sense of the word), and were, in all such cases, "arms of assumption," of which

the college became, at some latter epoch, the registrar.

2. Whatever may have been the practical value of armorial bearings in actual middle-age warfare, —or whatever may be, now and hereafter, their importance as auxiliaries to historical, antiquarian, or genealogical inquiry (an importance which I am far from underrating), — they are not *used now* by those who bear them with the slightest view or reference to any such ends. Their principal and only present practical value is for purposes of harmless and elegant display, and ornamentation: to make a gay flag over a stall or in a pageant; to crown a stately entrance arch, or relieve a carriage panel; to mark a tankard or a dinner-plate; to make a fanciful heading-stamp for a sheet of note-paper, or an imposing device for a family seal on its envelope; to deck a leather chair back, or, more usefully, to enliven a "dull cold marble," or enrich a gorgeous memorial window. In a word, to set on a multitude of chattels an elegant and distinctive mark of ownership. There may be plenty of enthusiasts (with whom I shall decline to dispute) to tell me that this is a disgustingly low view of the matter. I know that it is true in the main.

Now I who write this, by name Neumann Weissenschild, am by education, by membership of a learned profession, by all social habit and circumstance, and I hope, by higher and better intrinsic claims, a gentleman; and eke, by the courtesy of the nineteenth century, an Esquire: though I cannot, with strict veracity, Latinize the latter title into "Armiger," because, though I can trace back my honest and worthy ancestors for a couple of centuries, I have no record or evidence of their having borne "arms." Garter, Clarencieux, and Norroy have "in the great heap of their learning" no grain of information on that subject.

Being what I have above attempted to describe, and intending, from my union with a daughter of the ancient house of Eberswursten, to beget and leave behind me a numerous and flourishing family, I have—without the slightest yearning by any awful device to strike terror into the souls of modern Paynims, or to rally my faithful vassals round my banner in the approaching war with the North American States—I have, I say, a harmless enough desire to invent and adopt some badge, which shall serve henceforth to distinguish and adorn the carriages, books, plate, seals, &c. &c., of the Weissenschilds, a family of much future consideration, and make them recognisable thereby to the observant eyes of the twentieth and all subsequent centuries. And I mean this badge to take the shape of what is called a "coat of arms."

What *moral* objection is there to my so doing? I know, of course, that I *can* do it without inter-ference, save from the taxgatherer, so long as I don't assume the cognizance of any existing armi geri, or perhaps even if I do.

I also know that Norroy and the rest will, for "certain considerations," be too happy to "grant" or "confirm" to me such bearings as I choose to assume, provided my tinctures are all "selon les règles," and that I don't put metal upon metal, or commit some similar heraldic "gaucherie." But I don't happen to care a farthing for the sanction of these worthies, and I certainly don't mean to pay the very serious "certain considerations" which they would extort for its accordance. As for the tax-gatherer, I have no notion of cheating the queen, and *he* is, or shall be, welcome to his annual receipt of her royal impost.

Well, then, I am about, without troubling the Heralds, to assume a "coat" — say on a field *vert*, within a bordure *or*, semée with cocoa-nuts, three monkeys gambadant, langued *gules* and queued *azure* (a bearing, I believe, which will not infringe upon the rights of any existing armigerous gens); with, for crest, on a branch proper, a female ape *sejant* and *scalpent*, with an appropriate motto from Juvenal. I may possibly make some alteration in the design before final adoption; but that is immaterial. Homo sum, and the coat is Darwinian and ingenious.

Now, what I want to know is—why am I, as I am told in all treatises of sound heraldry, a "snob" for so doing? My badge will not set up any claim of descent from Courtenay, Montmorency, or Plantagenet. If it did I should be the first to admit the justice of the appellation. But I make no effort to hang myself upon the Past, and only look forward to the Future. Why may I not mark my books (for instance), the weapons of the noblest warfare waged in our time, as old Raoul de Fitz-Battleaxe marked his shield and surcoat in darker days? Why may I not "assume" as he did before Rouge-Croix was born or thought of?

It may be that I *am* a "parvenu," *i. e.* I have made my way in the world to a higher status than that of my fathers, and by my brains instead of my fists: a fact which, after all, is not much to my discredit. But what then? Is the register of families closed "Libro d'oro?" and are no new ones to be founded, or rather no hitherto-undistinguished ones to become distinguished, hereafter? If I am capable of achieving and transmitting social position and consideration among gentlemen, why am I a "vulgar pretender" and a "snob" for adopting, albeit without the sanction of Messieurs the Heralds, a badge for myself and my posterity, any more than for setting up my brougham, butler, library, pianoforte, or any other article of luxury or fancy ordinarily used among the class to which I have ascended? Or is the whole thing only a wretched matter of £. s. d.

and am I a "snob" only because Norroy and the rest don't get their "considerations"?

. I know I can assume a *name*, and make my way with it as best I can without any leave either of her most gracious Majesty or Messieurs her Heralds; for being, as will have been observed, of Teutonic extraction, and whilome called "Schweinsfleisch" (and thereby the subject of much unseemly jocularity), I some years ago altered my patronymic to the more euphonious but unpretending " Weissenschild,"—a change for which the descendants I propose to leave will, or I mistake, be eternally grateful. Was I a "snob" for that too? I am afraid some folks will call me so, for I know I paid no fees for it.

Will somebody convince me that I am a "snob" (and, if so, an ass into the bargain)? or can and will some "novus homo" take up the anti-Heralds' College side of the question more ably than   Neumann Weissenschild?

ROBERT BRUCE.

In support of his claim to the crown of Scotland in 1291, Bruce urged (among other arguments) that he had been formally recognised as rightful heir in the reign of Alexander II.

This argument is set out in several documents:—

1. In the appeal of the seven Earls of Scotland. See *Documents and Records illustrating the History of Scotland*, edited by Sir Francis Palgrave, p. 20.

2. In a Petition in the French Language presented by Bruce to Edward I. (*Id.* p. 26.)

3. In the Petition presented by Bruce to the Arbitrators at Norham. (*Id. Illustrations*, p. xv.; and *Fœdera*, n. e. vol. i. p. 777.

I here subjoin the statement contained in the French petition, as reduced into modern spelling by Sir Francis Palgrave:—

"Pour ce, que le Roi Alexandre, père du Roi Alexandre que derein [dernièrement] mourut, quand il alla en guerre sur les îles, graunta et ordonna (comme celui qui mieux fut avisé de son sang) par commun assent des Evêques, Contes, et de son Baronage que si Dieu voulût, qu'il mourût sans heirs de son corps, Sir Robert de Brus, comme plus prochain de son sang, fût tenu son hoir au Royaume d'Ecosse avoir. Et de ce fut fait un écrit, scellé du scel du Roi et des evêques et autres grands Seigneurs, lequel écrit demeura en la Trésorie du Roi."—*Documents and Records, &c.*, Introduction, p. xxiv.

At what time is this recognition supposed to have taken place?

The warlike expedition to the Isles that Bruce speaks of would enable us to fix the date if it were itself known to history; but I have hitherto searched for it in vain.

In his petition to the arbitrators at Norham, Bruce furnishes us with another clue. Alexander II. is there spoken of as "desperans de hærede de corpore suo." The seven Earls of Scotland in

their appeal enlarge upon this point. I quote from the translation given by Sir Francis Palgrave:—

"Alexander II. having advanced almost to the verge of senile age, and there being no expectation of his having an heir of his body, he assembled all the Nobles and Magnates of Scotland, the Bishops, and other Clergy and Laity, as many as could be brought together at a certain time and place, in order to prevent the dissensions which would arise in the event of his death without issue."—*Introduction*, p. xvi.

Poor old king! When did this despair come upon him? At the time of his death in 1249 he was only in his fifty-first year, and he left a son of seven years old and upwards. If ever he recognised Bruce as heir to the throne, it clearly must have been before the birth of this son in 1241. Sir Francis Palgrave carries the time somewhat further back:—

"The declaration," he says, "must have been of course made before there could be any probability of that event, and the period to which it must be assigned, must be found between the 4th March, 1238, when Queen Joan died, and the 15th May, 1239, when Alexander II. married his second wife, Mary de Coucy."— *Introduction*, p. xxviii.

We are thus required to believe that King Alexander, despairing of any issue of his own, must have looked out for a collateral heir before he had completed the forty-first year of his age, somewhere in the interval of fourteen months that elapsed between the death of his first wife, and his marriage with the second. Surely this has a very suspicious aspect.

But let us proceed with the statement of the seven earls :—

"Unto this Parliament or Convention he declared the state of his age, and that he had no issue of his body; but that his Uncle David had three daughters, the first of whom had a daughter, and the second a son; and he enjoined them all, as they were bound to him by their allegiance, fealty, and homage, that they would decide and adjudicate between the parties, which and whether of them should inherit the crown—the daughter of the eldest sister, or the son of the second sister. And the Great Council being assembled together, they decreed and adjudged by all their own laws, and by the imperial and other laws, that the son born of the second sister should inherit in preference to the daughter born of the eldest sister; and all present, clergy as well as laity, unanimously declared the same as a true judgment to the King. Such judgment being given by the Great Council, and accepted by the Sovereign, he, King Alexander, took Robert Bruce, Lord of Annandale who now is, by the hand, and presented him to all the Nobles and Magnates, Clerks and Laymen then and there present, as his true and legitimate heir to the Kingdom of Scotland; and all such Magnates by the King's command, and in his presence took the oath of fealty to the Lord Robert Bruce upon the Holy Gospels."—*Introduction*, p. xvii.

It is material to observe that Alexander's object is represented to have been, not to select a successor, but to obtain the recognition of the rightful heir; and it is stated to have been the *judgment* of the council that Bruce, as the son of the younger sister was, in law, to be preferred before the daughter of the elder sister.

The question to which I would wish to invite attention is, whether any such judgment could really have been given? and upon this point I beg to offer the following observations:—

1. When the judgment was appealed to, no record of it was produced, nor has any trace of it been since discovered.

2. It is remarkable that in that part of the document where the issue of *David*, Earl of Huntingdon is spoken of, no mention should be made of his son *John le Scot*, Earl of Chester and Huntingdon, who, after surviving his father somewhere about eighteen years, died no longer before the date of the supposed judgment than the year 1237.

Here let me pause to remark by the way, that Dugdale erroneously assigns the death of John le Scot to the year 1244 (*Baronage*, vol. i. p. 45); and in this he is followed by Nicolas in his *Synopsis*, under the title of "Chester" (edit. 1825). Whether the error has been created in the new edition I do not know. At all events, under the title "Huntingdon," Nicolas gives the true date 1237.

But to proceed with my observations:—

3. At the time when the judgment is supposed to have been given, Robert Bruce's mother, Isabella, was alive; and no right, derived through her, could have vested in her son.

4. It must be borne in mind that Alexander II. had three legitimate sisters; and I may here take the opportunity of observing that, according to the allegations of Balliol (id. *Illustrations*, p. xxv.), Margaret was the eldest, Marjory the second, and Isabella the youngest. Margaret, the eldest, was married to Hubert de Burgh, Earl of Kent; and, from Balliol's allegations, it would appear that she had a daughter and heir also named Margaret, who died *s. p.* But without pursuing at present the inquiry respecting the issue of the Countess of Kent, it is sufficient to remark that at the time when the recognition is supposed to have been made, Margaret, the Countess, Alexander's eldest sister, was herself alive.

It may be proper to add, that the force of the last two observations does not in the slightest degree depend upon any critical inquiry into the precise date of the recognition.

Alexander II., by whom the recognition is stated to have been made, died on July 8, 1249.

Robert Bruce had livery of the lands of his mother's inheritance in 36 Hen. III. (1252). See Collins's *Peerage* (1812), vol. v. p. 112. She must therefore have survived Alexander II. by at least two years.

John de Burgh, on the death of Margaret, Countess of Kent, was found to be his next heir in 44 Hen. III. (1260.) See Dugdale's *Baronage*, vol. i.

p. 700. The Countess must therefore have survived Alexander II. somewhere about ten years.

It will thus be seen that at no time during the life of Alexander II. could Robert Bruce have been recognised as the rightful heir to the throne without his mother Isabella being passed over; at no time during his life could Alexander II. have searched for an heir among the descendants of his uncle David without setting aside the undoubted right of his own sister. MELETES.

NON-CON NOTES.

The antiquities of the Conventicle are scarcely, it will be said, a vein worth the working; but I merely propose to jot down a few recollections and traditions that occur to me. Dissent, like everything else in this nineteenth century, is putting on new phases, and the old ones are being fast forgotten—rather a pity, methinks. In my boyhood the old folks would still talk of "going to meeting," though "chapel" had become naturalised; in our day the Quakers have the term to themselves. How did the change originate? Was it from the Wesleyans? "Chapel," an old minister once assured me, began in a Popish relic—*St. Martin's Hat*, or "chapelle," which used to accompany the French Kings in their wars; the tent, or other receptacle for the hat (with its masses, ceremonies, &c.,) in course of time taking its name. Let philologists settle that point.

Although a Presbyterian of three or four generations back, I could not but enjoy a grim jest upon my own "denomination," heard the other day for the first time. A friend, visiting the south, was inspecting an ironmonger's stock-inventory, in which he found, to his surprise, "Two Presbyterians," meaning, he was told, two of the cowls or hoods which are attached to certain chimnies, and shift with the wind. Herein lay the sting. "Turned by every wind of doctrine" was doubtless the sentence of some severe Independent or Baptist on his heterodox brother, whose primitive Calvinism of the Commonwealth has been insensibly "toning down" during the eighteenth century into a quiet contemplative Arianism, ending at length in Unitarianism.

Among the usages of the sect was the standing in prayer, and being seated at the singing. They partake of the Lord's Supper round a table, and a "Table-pew" may generally be noticed in front of the pulpit. Baillie, in his *Report to Scotland on the Westminster Assembly of Divines* (Hanbury, ii. 430), describes the Presbyterians as sitting round a table, but the Independents as keeping in their pews. The broad centre aisle in the late Edward Irving's gothic structure in London was; I believe, so arranged to allow of a long communion table or tables.

. *Nicodemus's Seat.* —When a boy I remember a certain pew in the chapel I attended, which was so named of course from the disciple who came to Jesus by night. The pew was darkened by an overhanging staircase, and being close to the door seemed a tempting shelter for any timid listener, though scarcely contrived on purpose. A desponding prophecy used to be heard in dissenting communities, that when a family set up a carriage in the third generation, it would go back to the church. Priestley's remark was in the same spirit when signing a petition against the Test and Corporation Acts—viz. that he was petitioning for the break-up of his own flock. But I have trespassed long enough perhaps. Non-Con.

THE COUNTESS OF TYRCONNEL.

The following paragraph has once more been sent flying through the rounds of the papers by a late publication : —

"The White Widow.—The Strand Exchange, in the time of William and Mary, was the scene of the pretty story of 'The White Widow.' For several days a sempstress appeared at one of the stalls, clothed in white and wearing a white mask. She excited great curiosity, and all the fashionable world thronged her stalls. This mysterious milliner was at last discovered to be no less a person than the Duchess of Tyrconnel, widow of Talbot, the detested Lord Deputy of Ireland under James II. Unable to obtain a secret access to her family, and almost starving, she had been compelled to turn shopwoman. Her relatives provided for her directly the story became known. This duchess was the Frances Jennings mentioned by Grammont, and sister to the Duchess of Marlborough."—Thornbury's *Haunted London.*

This dateless story is wretchedly vague, and scarcely deserves a notice in these columns. It is almost beyond probability that the sister of Sarah Duchess of Marlborough, related to some of the first families of the kingdom, and an exceedingly clever woman besides, should have adopted such a course. When the dastard James, the first to fly, carried the news of his own defeat at the Boyne into Dublin, he ironically complimented Lady Tyrconnel on the quickness of her husband's countrymen's heels, to which she readily rejoined, "His majesty in that respect had the advantage of them."

There is a doubt, however, respecting where the Countess of Tyrconnel died and was buried. I say Countess for, as her husband did not receive the title of Duke till after King James had abdicated, the epithet Duchess is improper. According to Prior's *Life of Goldsmith*, we find that she ░░ed in Dublin, where she died at her lodgings ░Ormond Quay, on Sunday, March 7, 1730-1. I ░░░ seen an elegy by White, the Westmeath ░░░░ her death, among the eighty lines of ░░░ it is constructed there are the following : —

"Tyrconnel, once the boast of British isles,
Who gained the hearts of heroes by her smiles ;
Whose wit and charms throughout all Europe rang,
From whom so many noble peers have sprang ;
Whose virtue, carriage, parts, and graceful mien,
Made her a fit companion for a queen."

Notwithstanding we have the preceding testimony of her death at Dublin, there is still to be seen among the Jacobite sepulchral monuments in the chapel of the old Scots College, in the Rue des Fosses St. Victor, at Paris, a plain tablet bearing the following inscription : —

D. O. M.
Æternæ Memoriæ
Illustrissimæ et Nobilissimæ Dominæ
Franciscæ Jennings,
Ducissæ de Tyrconnell,
Reginæ Mag. Brit. Matronæ Honorariæ,
Hujus Collegii benefactricis,
Quæ Missam quotidianam in hoc sacrario
Fundavit perpetuo celebrandam
Pro animâ suâ et animâ ejus Dom Georgii
Hamilton de Abercornæ, Equitis aurati,
Conjugis sui primi, et Dom Ricardi Talbot,
Ducis de Tyrconnell, Proregis Hyberniæ,
Secundi sui conjugis.
Obiit die xii Martii, An. Domini
MDCCXXXI.
Requiescat in Pace.

Tyrconnell was undoubtedly a brave man, and *la belle* Jennings a fair and witty woman. Among hundreds of traitors, he alone was faithful to his king ; that the latter was obstinate, pig-headed, and probably cowardly, was not Dick Talbot's fault. The greatest temptations were held out to Tyrconnell by William, but in vain. Rank, fame, fortune, all might have been retained by playing a double part, but Tyrconnell was faithful to the last ; and so it is that, even at the present day, in the absurd stories of venial Whig journalists are raked up in modern books of gossip, and the faithful nobleman is styled "the detested Lord-Deputy of Ireland." *Risum teneatis amici?*

I must add, that being away from my books at present, I am indebted for one notice of Tyrconnell expressed above to an able article on that nobleman, written by H. F. Hore, Esq., and published in vol. v. of the *Ulster Journal of Archæology.* William Pinkerton.

THE EASTERN ORTHODOX CHURCH. —

Whilst suggesting a reprint in "N. & Q." of the following paragraph, which appeared in the *London Guardian,* I cannot be supposed to be actuated by a desire to resuscitate the controversy on the churches, since the extract furnishes a very striking incident irrespective of their comparative orthodoxy, and the more memorable because it is *toto cœlo* irreconcilable with the subjoined declaration of Dr. Constantine Simonides.

"An event which has recently taken place in America in connection with the movement of the renewal of friendly

relations and intercommunion between the eastern orthodox and Anglican churches, deserves something more than
a passing notice. If, as is possible, this step should lead
to other and more important results, and if the courtesies
interchanged between individual churchmen should extend to the clergy generally, the service celebrated on the
2nd of March, 1865, in Trinity Chapel, New York, will be
referred to as an historical incident; for on that day, for
the first time in a thousand years, the Liturgy (or Eucha-
ristic Service) was celebrated in a western church by a
priest of the Holy Orthodox Communion, and the creed of
Christendom was chanted in English without that *Filioque*
clause which caused the great schism of East and West."
The Guardian, March 29, 1865.

'Απάντησις Σιμωνίδου σύντομος πρὸς τοὺς ἐρωτήσαντας
αὐτὸν "Αγγλους περὶ τῶν ἐξῆς ζητημάτων.

'Η Ἐκκλησία τῶν ὀρθοδόξων ἡμῶν Ἑλλήνων, καθολικὴ
καὶ ἀποστολικὴ οὖσα, καὶ κεφάλην ἔχουσα τὸν Κύριον
ἡμῶν Ἰησοῦν Χριστὸν, οὐδεμίαν οὐδαμῶς ἀναγνωρίζει ἐπὶ
τῆς γῆς ἑτέραν ἐκκλησίαν· οὔτε τὴν τῶν Ἀγγλων ἑκατον-
κέφαλον "Ὕδραν ὁηλονότι, οὔτε τὴν Παποκέφαλον τῶν
καινοτόμων Ῥωμαίων, ὡς οὐδ' ἀλλήν τινα. Καλεῖ δὲ πάσας
ταύτας συναγωγὰς ἀνθρώπων αἱρετικῶν· 'Αναγνωρίζει δὲ
οὐδὲ τὴν ἱερωσύνην αὐτῶν: ὅτι οὐκ ἔχουσιν ἱερωσύνην.
'Ορθοδόξων Ἑλλήνων Θεολόγικαι Γράφαι Τέσσαρες.
Ἐν Λονδίνω, 1865, ad calc.
BIBLIOTHECAR. CHETHAM.

PRICE OF SALMON. — In an inquiry now being
held at Limerick, before the Fishery Commissioners, Mr. Andrew J. Watson, who had managed
the salmon weir there from 1827 to 1834, "in
reply to Mr. Brewster, said, that in 1882 they
caught an immense quantity of fish. The fish
was so numerous, that he could see their fins over
the water; and as there was then no demand for
them, he opened the weir and let them all escape."
He "recollected when he used to see salmon
boiling at the head of cellars, and a cut of it could
be had for one penny; and the price in the shops
was twopence per pound." S. P. V.

DROITWICH REGISTER. — In the Register of St.
Peter's Church, Droitwich, several Latin verses on
the uncertainty of life, &c., are interpolated among
the usual entries, and the following advice to his
successors, by a rector in the olden time: —

" All you, my successors, that my benefice shall take, .
Keep well this Register for my sake ;
And as I have left yt faire and pure,
So I would have yt for ever to endure."
THOMAS E. WINNINGTON.

MARRIAGES OF KNIGHTS. — The following, from
the Registers of Newington Butts, are worth a
note: —
" 160⅘, Feb. 10. Sir Anthonie Forester and Judith
Riche. Lic.
" 1638. May 27. Sir Thomas Bludder, Knt. and Mrs.
Jane Lucas. Lic." .
C. J. R.

SIGNIFICANT NAMES. — Have you a department
in your Notes for curious names? Some firms

present a curious conjunction. I add localities to
prevent forgeries. Stone and Flint, London
Bridge; Flint and Steel, Oxford Street; Heath
and Waterfall, Sheffield ; Salmon and Rice, Dub-
lin; Blood, Phayre, and Furey (called commonly
Blood, Fire, and Fury), Dublin.
Of single names I remember Tredaway, Shoe-
maker, Hammersmith ; Last, Shoemaker, Exeter ;
Trulock, Gunsmith, Dublin. Ireland also has a
Mr. Beauchamp Urquhart Colclough, pronounced
Beecham Urcurt Cokely, a rather odd trio of
names to be borne by a single person.
Will you kindly admit additions to a list that
ought to form an amusing department of " N. & Q."
OWEN TUDOR.

JULIUS CÆSAR AND BRITAIN : LINE IN LUCAN.
" Territa quæsitis ostendit terga Britannis."
(ii. 572.)
Would not these words, so descriptive of the
connection of Julius Cæsar with our island, be
suitable as a motto for any English life of that
famous Roman ? LÆLIUS.

EPIGRAM: on a very tall Barrister of the name
of *Long*, by the late T. Dunbar, Esq.: —
" Longe longorum longissime, Longe, virorum,
Dic mihi, te quæso, num BREVE quidquid habes ?"
W.

LATIN EPIGRAM. — The following couplet was
addressed to a clergyman, who used to preach
Hare's Sermons: —
" Ne vendes lepores alienos, prome leporem
Nativum : melior syllaba longa brevi."
J. C. J.

Queries.

" THE TRAGEDIE OF ALCESTE AND ELIZA, 1638.
By Fr. Br."—Any correspondent of " N. & Q.,"
who happens to have access to the Registers of
the Stationers' Company, would greatly oblige
me by endeavouring to ascertain if there is any
clew upon the face of the entry of the work above-
named there to the name of the translator. The
tragedy of *Alceste and Eliza* is a free paraphrase of
portions of the *Croce Raccquistata* of Fr. Br., i.e.,
as my correspondent the Rev. Thomas Corser,
M.A., and myself agree in thinking, Francesco
Bracciolini, the original writer. On the title-page
of the English book, these initials occur as if " Fr.
Br." was the translator; but that circumstance
probably arose from a misplacement of the lines.
It would present a very remarkable coincidence
indeed, if the initials of the author and his translator were identical. Besides, I am not acquainted
with any English writer of the time to whom
such initials could appertain.
At Lloyd's sale, in 1819, the volume in question produced a large figure. I believe that Mr.

Lloyd's copy was afterwards in the hands of Mr. Rice and Sir F. Freeling; at whose auction, in 1836, it passed into the possession of the Rev. T. Corser. The only other copy which seems to have occurred for sale, is one I found bound up at the end of an imperfect copy of May's *Henry the Second*, 1633. It is an 8vo of thirty-nine leaves: the last being blank, but necessary to complete sig. E. W. CAREW HAZLITT.

BREMEN.—1. What was the political condition of Bremen from 1731, when it was taken possession of by Denmark, to 1757, when it was taken by the French?

2. What means the letter *s* in the following inscription upon a Bremen coin of 1750 — FRANCISC. I. D. G. ROM. IMP. S. A.? E.

EARLY BRITONS. — Pearson, in *Early and Mediæval Ages of England*, p. 6, in speaking of our British ancestors from " the few skulls and other bones," says : —

" Modern theory would view with suspicion the prehensile thumb, equalling in length the forefinger of the hand, as if something of a lower nature had not yet been worked out in the growth of the race."

If but few bones have been found, how has it been possible to decide on the " prehensile thumb " in Britain ? Has it been found in any other country ? F. C. B.

CLINT HILLS.—

" The most celebrated spots of Druid worship are Stonehenge and the Clint Hills in England, Karnak in Brittany."—*Travels by Umbra*, p. 83.

How are the Druids connected with Clint hills, which are probably Danish ? Our Clint hills have no features in common with Stonehenge or Karnak. F. C. B.

THE CRUSADERS.—A friend writing from Naples mentions a recent visit to the convent of Trinità la Cava, and says : —

." There is a magnificent collection of MSS. and illuminated books (missals) of the seventh, eighth, ninth, and tenth centuries. Amongst others, a sort of map or chart of the time of the Crusades, on which are introduced the banners and coats of arms of the Crusaders, including our Richard Cœur de Lion," &c.

Is there any detailed account of this chart ? If so, where is it to be found ? R. W. F.

Bath.

EPIGRAMS ADDRESSED TO THE DUCHESS OF MARLBOROUGH. — G. Steinman Steinman will feel greatly obliged by being referred to the printed volume in which the three epigrams addressed to the celebrated Duchess of Marlborough by H. G., and entitled severally " The Royal Sapling Oak," " The Reasonable Caution," and " The Murmurs of the Oak," are to be found. (*Vide* Miss Strickland's *Queens of England*, 1848, xii. p. 206.)

Sundridge, near Sevenoaks.

JOHN FITZGIBBON, FIRST EARL OF CLARE. — This eminent individual was born in the year 1749; but where did the event take place ? Having a particular object in view, I have examined different biographical works, and made sundry inquiries, but as yet without success. In 1763 Lord Clare's father had a house at Donnybrook, near Dublin. ABHBA.

"THE GOBLINS OF NEAPOLIS."—Who wrote a small 12mo volume, entitled *The Goblins of Neapolis*, Dublin, 1836 ? ABHBA.

HISTORIOGRAPHER ROYAL. — Query, Has any one held the office since Richard Stonehewer, Esq., who held it in 1782 ?

The office was created soon after the Restoration, and was conferred upon, if not created for, James Howell (*Biog. Dict.*, art. " Howell "). In France such an office was of earlier date : for Mons. De la Terre, who wrote the account of the " Entrée de la Reyne Mère *temp*. Chas. I.," 1639, was Historiographer Royal.

It would seem, however, that some persons held a similar appointment much earlier, viz. Matthew Paris was historiographer to King Henry III. (Drake's *Parl. Hist.*, vol. i.) Dryden was made historiographer to King James II. (Johnson's *Life of Dryden*, p. 96.) J. R.

LETTERS OF ALEXANDER KNOX AND HANNAH MORE. — A few years ago three unedited letters to the Rev. Geo. Miller, D.D., of Armagh, relative to his *Philosophy of Modern History*—one from Alexander Knox, and two from Hannah More—appeared in an English periodical. Dr. Miller died in October, 1848, and the letters in question were published not long after his death. Will you, or some one of your correspondents, kindly refer me to the periodicals. ABHBA.

"MAJESTAS INTEMERATA, or, the Immortality of the King : Printed in the year 1649," 12mo.— Hearne, in his Diary, Aug. 23, 1715 (*Rel. Hearnianæ*, 341), observes : —

" To enquire particularly who was the author of *Majestas Intemerata, or, the Immortality of the King*, which was printed in the year 1649, in 12mo."

In a note to which passage, Dr. Bliss says : —

" It is the general report that Jno. Cleveland, the poet, was the author. So Hearne, in a subsequent note . . . . But neither does that author [Nichols] nor Wood appear to have seen the tract in question. . . ."

In a copy of *Majestas Intemerata* now before me, however, a contemporary hand has made a large number of MS. annotations and corrections; and in the title-page has written, " By Francis Whyte, of Greye's Inne." Lowndes assigns to a gentleman of this name a legal treatise, printed in 1652. The only ground that exists, so far as I am aware, for attributing the piece to Cleveland, is, that there is the same extract from Lydgate to be found here which occurs before Cleveland's *Idol of the Clownes*, 1654.

The character of the emendations in my copy, and their correspondence with the coeval hand-writing on the title, together with the legal complexion of the whole volume, leads one in the absence of any direct evidence of Cleveland's authorship to incline to Whyte's claim to the book. Can any reader of "N. & Q." speak more authoritatively on this point?

W. CAREW HAZLITT.

"ODE TO SPRING."—Can any one tell me where the remaining verses of the subjoined ode to spring are to be found? —

An Ode to Spring.

"Spring, the sweet spring is the year's pleasant king :
Then lovers meet, old wives a sunning sit ;
And through the fields, those sounds our ears do greet,
Coo coo, ju ju, pee wee, too wit-a-woo."

H. B. JOHNSTON.
Dublin.

PROCURATORS. — In the Ecclesiastical Courts prior to the Reformation, what were the qualifications required for admission as a Procurator, and how was he admitted? Could a layman be admitted as a Procurator? Could a Procurator, admitted by one official, practise before another official?

D. M.

SPUR MONEY IN BELFRIES. — One of the rules for the guidance of the ringers of Burnley Church (Lancashire) is "Any person attempting to ring with spurs on, to forfeit 6*d*." I believe I have seen this rule in other churches. What can have been its origin? To descend a staircase, such as usually leads to a church belfry, with spurs on one's heels, would be sufficiently unpleasant without the additional *spur* of the 6*d*. forfeit.

H. FISHWICK.

"WILLIE IS GONE," ETC. — Will one of your musical correspondents oblige me with information where the melody and the rest of the words of the old Scotch song are to be obtained, beginning—

"Willie is gone to Melville Castle
To bid the ladies there farewell ;
The first he met was Lady Bet

(and ending)

"And I'll come back and wed ye all?"

M. A. BROWNE.

Queries with Answers.

OSBORNE'S CATALOGUES OF BOOKS. — I have copies of two Catalogues of Books, which were issued by Thomas Osborne, the well-known London bookseller of the last century, for the years 1764 and 1765. Can you tell me whether he issued any more? And if so, how many, and for what years?

ABHBA.

[Osborne is best known as the publisher of the *Catalogus Bibliothecæ Harleianæ*, or a Catalogue of the printed books of the Harleian Library, in five vols. 8vo, 1743—1745. This Catalogue was edited by Dr. Johnson and William Oldys. Osborne also published a series of trade Catalogues between the years 1729 and 1768, which are now become extremely scarce. These are literary curiosities in their way, not only for the information they afford of the prices of books in his day, but for the quaint notes, and still more for the queer prefaces contained in them. They are also valuable as consisting of the purchased libraries of the most eminent men of that time, and as containing many thousand volumes of the greatest rarity and interest in English literature. Here will be found the contents of the libraries of Charles Hulton, Henry Smith, Rev. Mr. Ilive, Philip Duke of Wharton, Dr. Robert South, Tom. Hearne, the antiquary, William Stuart, part of the collection of Robert Harley, Earl of Oxford, Dr. Edward Halley, Nathanael Boothe, Rev. Mr. Comarque, Rev. Mr. Johnson, Thomas Coxeter, Anthony Kecke, Governor Winthrop, W. Kynaston, Rev. Dr. Baker, Dr. Tyson, Counsellor Webbe, Lady Mary Worsley, Dr. Abraham Hall, Dr. T. Stack, Rev. John Gaudy, Bishop Chandler, Dr. Butler, Bishop of Durham, Dr. Horsman, Sir Thomas Burnet, Dr. Cromwell Mortimer, Edmund Pargiter, Dr. James Foster, Counsellor Hamilton, Henry Viscount Colerane, Hon. Baron Clarke, Dr. Samuel Dunster, Dr. Thomas Gale, Roger Gale, Henry Wotton, Bishop Conybeare, Gilbert Walmsley, Chancellor of Lichfield, Rev. John Creyke, Heneage Earl of Winchilsea, Sir Luke Schaub, Edmund Sawyer, Dr. G. Hepburn, Dr. E. Hody, Dr. Philip Bearcroft, John Twisleton, Dr. T. Morton, and other eminent antiquaries. In 1851 Thomas Thorpe, the bookseller, possessed the most complete collection of Osborne's Catalogues, bound in forty-three volumes 8vo, 1729 to 1768, which he priced at 6*l*. 16*s*. 6*d*. Only five odd volumes of the series are to be found in our national library, namely, 1736, 1753, 1754 (2 vols.), and 1761. It is evident that Osborne must have carried on a successful trade as a book-broker, for at his death on August 27, 1767, he left behind him the comfortable assets of 40,000*l*.]

GAVELKIND. — What makes the difference between a "woman of Kent" and a "Kentish woman"? The women of Kent are, or were, entitled to certain privileges under the law of gavelkind. In what part or district of Kent must one reside to be a "woman of Kent"? Had it not something to do with one side or the other of Rochester bridge?

JOHN DAVIDSON.

[The provincial distinction of "men of Kent" and "Kentish men" no doubt equally applies to the fair sex of that county. The West Kent men, according to the tradition, are styled "Kentish men ;" whilst those of East Kent are more emphatically denominated "men of Kent." When St. Augustine, with the assistance of King Ethelbert, founded another episcopal see at Rochester, he thus divided the Kentish kingdom into two dioceses—the eastern Canterbury, the western Rochester; the men of the former retaining their ancient name of " men of Kent;" whilst those of the latter adopted that of " Kentish men." The Gavelkind tenure and free Kentish customs gave rise to the well-known old provincial song of " The Man of Kent," its burden being—

" Of Briton's race if one surpass,
' A man of Kent' is he."

Consult Sandys's *Consuetudines Kanciæ*, and an article on this local distinction from the same gentleman in "N. & Q." 1st S. v. 615.]

HUNTINGDON STURGEON. — What is the allusion to, in the following passage in Pepys's *Diary*?

" 1667, May 22nd. This day, coming from Westminster with W. Batten, we met at Whitehall Stairs a fisher boat with a sturgeon that he had newly catched in this river; which I saw, but it was but a little one; but big enough to prevent my mistake of that for a colt, if ever I become Mayor of Huntingdon."

F. A. E.

[In the later editions of Pepys's *Diary* Lord Braybrooke has added the following note to this passage: " During a very high flood in the meadows between Huntingdon and Godmanchester, something was seen floating, which the Godmanchester people thought was a black *pig*, and the Huntingdon folk declared was a *sturgeon*; when rescued from the waters, it proved to be *a young donkey*. This mistake led to the one party being styled ' Godmanchester black pigs,' and the other ' Huntingdon sturgeons,' terms not altogether forgotten at this day. Pepys's *colt* must be taken to be the *colt of an ass*."]

ATLAS OF HISTORY. — I think I have seen an *Atlas* containing maps on which under, or instead of the names of the places, historical events that took place, or the names of celebrated persons who were born or resided at them, were printed.

What is the title of the book, and who was the author? . E. N.

[Probably the following is the work required: " A Concise Historical, Biographical, and Genealogical Atlas of the principal events in the Histories of England, France, Spain, Portugal, Germany, and Italy. Also the celebrated European Treaties, Painters, &c. Designed and Compiled by Heneage Lowth, with the addition of the valuable Historical Summary and Observations of Lesage." Londfol. 1851.]

Replies.

EVIDENCES OF DISTANT LIGHT AND SMOKE.
(3rd S. v. 329; vii. 206.)

I have frequently noticed the trunks and stems of larch trees to be covered with a black deposit, and have always attributed it to blight. I should suppose to account for the " smoky deposit " which SIR THOS. WINNINGTON found on the larch plantations on Brown Clee Hill in the same man-

ner. The " larch blight " is due to the attacks of an insect known as the *coccus* or *eriosoma laricis*, and the eggs—

" may be detected even by the naked eye, thickly crowded together around the base of the buds, and in the small depressions and crevices of the bark of the last year's wood, in the form of *small black grains*. . . . . The trees become clammy and *black* with the honey-dew or excrementitious discharge of the insects, which live upon the resinous sap of the tree." (Selby, *History of British Forest Trees*, p. 516, Lond. 1842.)

Another form of larch disease is noticed in the *Quart. Journ. of Agriculture*, vol. v. p. 536, by Mr. Webster, who says,—

" When the trees infected shed their foliage they appear in winter all covered with *blackish strands* [*stains?*] both on the trunk and branches, and especially on the south side, as the rains are more severe from that quarter than any other."

The italics in these quotations are mine. If SIR THOMAS WINNINGTON's theory be correct, it must necessarily happen that the smoky deposit is more abundant on the *east* side, Dudley being about due east of Brown Clee Hill. There would be no difficulty whatever in ascertaining this. If I may express my opinion, I am decidedly against the theory that the sooty deposit is carried from the Dudley iron works.

The instances brought forward by MR. LEE as to the distance at which the light of a lamp is sometimes visible, are scarcely to the point. The light from the furnaces in the " Black Country," as from large fires in general, is not seen directly, but by reflection from the clouds. On cloudless nights the light is not so intense as when the sky is slightly overcast. The beacon lights used in the Ordnance Survey were seen by direct vision. MR. LEE gives 70 miles as the distance at which they were visible; but some of the lines were much longer than this. The mean length of the sides of the principal triangles was 35·4 miles; 37 were between 80 and 90 miles; 18 between 90 and 100 miles; and 11 exceeded 100 miles in length: the longest was 111 miles. In many cases the light used was that of the sun, reflected to the distant station by means of a mirror adjusted at the proper angle. The first idea of this is, I believe, due to Professor Gauss, who, in 1820, was engaged at Lüneburg in trigonometrical observations, to combine the Hanoverian and Danish triangles. He perceived that when he directed his telescope towards the steeple of St. Michael's church at Hamburgh, a window in the upper part reflected the sun's image towards him, and thus impeded his operations. This gave him the idea of using the sun's light for signals, by catching it with a mirror and reflecting it to the place where the signal was to be given. (Newton's *London Journal*, 1820, iv. 198.)

RICHARD B. PROSSER.

25, Southampton Buildings, W.C.

BLADEN FAMILY OF ALDBOROUGH HATCH.

(3ʳᵈ S. vii. 258.)

I can give E. W. a few particulars of this branch of the Bladen family, although unfortunately the Bladen pedigree is one of the most unsatisfactory in my Essex collections. I shall be very glad if your correspondent's query elicits further information.

Martin Bladen, of Aldborough Hatch, Lieut.-colonel under the Duke of Marlborough, Comptroller of the Mint in 1714, Commissioner of Trade and Plantations, and M.P. in five successive Parliaments, was son of Nathaniel Bladen of Hemsworth, co. York, and of Lincoln's Inn, by Isabella, daughter of Sir William Fairfax. Nathaniel Bladen was son of the Rev. Dr. Bladen and Sarah his wife, daughter of Henry, second Lord Blayney. He had at least three children besides Martin : William, father of Colonel Thomas Bladen, M.P. for Old Sarum, ob. 1780, aged eighty-two ; Frances, wife of William Hammond ; and Elizabeth, first married to Col. Ruthven, and secondly to Edward Hawke, of Lincoln's Inn, by whom she became the mother of the great Lord Hawke.

Of the early life of Martin Bladen, I know little or nothing. He is stated to have first married Mary, daughter of a Col. Gibbs, and to have had two daughters : one of whom, Isabella, became the wife of George Blount, Esq., of Pembridge. However this may be, in 1728 (the marriage settlement is dated March 29) he married Frances, niece and heir of Joseph Jorye, Esq., of Bethnal Green, widow of John Foche, Esq., of Aldborough Hatch. She had inherited the mansion and estate of Aldborough Hatch from her uncle. Col. Bladen pulled down the old house—which had been the seat of two eminent Puritan families, the Kightleys and the Neales ; and in which, before their day, Dr. Donne was seized with his last illness*—and built, at the expense of 14,000l., a stately mansion of red brick, in which he lived for many years. He was a man of literary habits, and published a translation of Cæsar's *Commentaries*, which I believe is now very scarce. I have never even seen a copy. Col. Bladen died in February, 1746, aged sixty-six, and was buried in Stepney church. A monument was raised there to his memory, which I am sorry to hear is no longer in existence. The inscription is preserved in Lysons. His widow died in 1747. She devised the Aldborough Hatch property to her kinswoman Ann, daughter of Sir Francis Hodges,† wife of John Lambert Middleton, of Freeman's

Court, Cornhill, afterwards of Belsay Castle, and fourth baronet of that name.

Aldborough Hatch was sold by the Middletons, in 1828, to the Crown. The mansion has long since been pulled down, and a public footpath now passes over its site. The chapel, which was evidently much older than the house—and where it may not improbably be imagined that Donne may have worshipped—was endowed with 20l. per annum under the will of Mrs. Bladen ; and is, therefore, still standing, with a portion of the old Kightley mansion. A particular of sale of Aldborough Hatch, sixty-three years ago, in my possession, gives a very full description of the house. I have also two spirited drawings of the mansion and chapel, taken for the late Dr. Wellesley about 1792.

Only one Bladen entry appears in the Register of Barking : the burial, Sept. 30, 1737, of John Sepio Bladen. The burials of two daughters of Capt. Edward Hawke are recorded at Barking ; Frances Isabella, Sept. 13, 1739, and Isabella, April 3, 1740. These entries illustrate the connection between the families of Hawke and Bladen. There are several entries of Foche and Jory. In those days Aldborough Hatch was included in the parish of Barking : now in the parish of Great Ilford.

I may conclude with a query : Is there an engraved, or other portrait known, of Col. Martin Bladen?   Eᴅᴡᴀʀᴅ J. Sᴀɢᴇ.

Stoke Newington.

* So it is commonly stated ; but there is reason to believe that Samuel Harvey, Donne's son-in-law, lived in a house situated a little to the south of the great house at Aldborough Hatch.
† Query, Sir Nathaniel Hodges ?

MISTLETOE.

(3ʳᵈ S. vii. 76, 157, 226.)

Will you kindly allow me a small space for a little explanation of my former communication, and in reply to Dʀ. Bᴇʟʟ's article of March 18.

It is important in all philological inquiries that we should adhere to the true principles of etymological analysis, and not be led away by mere guesses, however plausible. In searching for the origin of a word, the natural course seems to be that of tracing it through its various permutations of form and meaning as far back as our literature will allow ; of comparing its equivalents in other languages, both cognate and alien ; of ascertaining the primitive idea involved in it, and thus arriving at length at the primary root. This I endeavour to do by showing that in all the Teutonic languages the name *mistel* or *mist-il* is closely connected with the word *mist*, mist ; that the Latin name for the plant, *viscum*, can be traced to a similar connexion ; that the mode of its propagation has always been supposed to be from the dung of birds, and that this idea running through the whole can be traced to two Sanskrit roots having a similar meaning. I wish to give a few further illustrations in confirmation of what has been thus advanced.

Dr. Bell must have greatly misunderstood me in supposing that I ascribed the origin of the name either to Pliny or to the Druids. The former I merely cited to prove the mode of propagation of the plant. The information we have of the latter is far too apocryphal to found any serious argument upon. Dr. Bell assumes that I had not consulted Pliny in the original. I gave Pliny's exact words so far as related to the subject, and they are surely no less original because they had been previously quoted by Wachter (not Wächter, as Dr. Bell writes it). The fact is, the quotation was taken from the Leyden edition of Pliny, 1668-9, in which the chapters are differently arranged from the Delphin editions, but I have since verified it by collation with other copies. I have also examined *all* the passages in Pliny's *Natural History* which relate to the *viscum*. They are very numerous, occurring in books 13, 16, 17, 20, 22, 23, 24, 27, 28, 32. His observations throw considerable light on the views of the ancient world concerning the plant. Whatever the opinion of the Druids may have been, Pliny considers it for the most part baleful both to the tree on which it grows, and to those who eat of its berries. It must be said, however, that he attaches the name, *viscum*, to several different plants—to the ξία of Theophrastus and Dioscorides, to the στελίς and ὑφεαρ of the former, as well as to the *viscum* proper. I dare not indulge in quotations illustrating this, but the passages are numerous.

A word or two as to Dr. Bell's derivation of *mistletoe*. He quotes from Pliny, book xvi. chap. 95, an account of the doings of the Druids, "In which," he says, "as Britons, *regardful of our ancestry*, we have even a domestic interest." Surely this is very loose talk when applied to the Saxon inhabitants of England. But the Druids, according to Pliny, called the mistletoe "*suo vocabulo—omnia sanantem.*" "This translation of the indigenous term," says Dr. Bell, "is still best retained in the German mistel, contracted merely from *meist heil*(*sam*), and not very dissimilar from our English equivalent *most heal*(ing)." Dr. Bell does not give the "indigenous term," of which *omnia sanantem* was the equivalent. I will supply the omission. It was "*uchel-wydd*, virgulam eximiæ virtutis." The equivalent, in Old German, is *gut-hyl*. The meaning of *omnia sanantem* is rather *all-heil* than *meist-heil*. Now *all-heil* does exist in German, but it has no reference to the mistletoe. It means, as in English, a sovereign remedy. We have *all-heal* in English applied to a plant (the herb *basil*), but its equivalent in German is *kraft-wurzel*.

To sum up: there is not the slightest evidence in any Teutonic language that the mistletoe was ever called *meist-heil*. The word *mistil* or *mistel* is found in Swedish, Danish, Anglo-Saxon, High and Low German, Dutch, and Flemish, constantly in juxtaposition with *mist*, stercus. It is traced in this form by Graff (*Althochdeutscher Sprachschatz*, vol. ii. p. 890), back to MSS. of the ninth century. I have also found it in the same form in an Anglo-Saxon vocabulary of the eleventh century. Every German philologer who mentions the word comes to the same conclusion, which can hardly be set aside by a mere conjecture, entirely unsupported by a single fact.　　J. A. P.

THE WORD DISCIPULUS.

(3rd S. vii. 279.)

In reply to the question, "Where did the word *discipulus* get its letter *p*?" I would suggest that the word is a substitute for *disc-iculus*, the presence of the two consecutive gutturals being offensive to the ear. That the Romans (and Greeks too) were influenced by such a feeling in the formation of words seems to be proved by examples such as the following:—The Latin *furca* meant properly "a prong," hence a plural *furcæ* or *furculæ* was at first required to denote "a fork" to which two or more prongs are essential. This meaning of *furca* is further proved by the compounds *bifurcus*, "two-pronged;" *trifurcus*, "three-pronged;" and by its derivation from *for* or *fod*, as seen in *fora-re* and *fod-ere*. Now from the simple *furca* instead of forming a diminutive *furc-ex*, the Romans produced three varieties: *forceps*, or rather *forcipes*, *forfex* or *forfices*, and *forpex*.

So again from a base *ak*, denoting sharpness, as in ἀκμή, *acidus*, *acetum*, *acus* "a needle," *acu-ere*, was deduced a diminutive *apex*, rather than *acex*, "a point."

But a more instructive example occurs in a word selected by Prof. Max Müller, in his first series of lectures for special consideration, which he calls the root *pac*, "look" of the Sanskrit. This Sanskrit verb is by all etymologists identified with the *spec* of the Latin *species spectare*, and ἰσκεπ of the Greek σκέπτομαι. But with submission to the Oxford Professor, I would ask whether the base of the verb be not a syllable *sec*, corresponding to *seh* of the German *sehen*, and our own *see*, so that *pac* would be no root at all? A derivative *sec-ec* being intolerable alike to Greek and Roman ears, the difficulty was avoided in different ways, the one language giving a preference to a form σκεπ (for σεκ-επ), the other to *spec* (for *sep-ec*). Exactly in the same way our own language, which possesses the same suffix of diminution in the form *ock* (*bull-ock*, *hill-ock*) from a simple *scale* = *shell*, has a secondary *scall-op*.

I have omitted to notice the somewhat familiar fact that the Latin abounds in secondary, or per-

haps tertiary, diminutives, corresponding to the supposed *disc-ic-ul-us*, as in *homun-c-ul-us, nav-ic-ul-a, opus-c-ul-um*.   T. HEWITT KEY.
Univ. Coll., London.

QUOTATION (3rd S. vii. 241.) — Christopher Love's quotation was probably from memory, and inaccurate. He seems to refer to two maxims in the *Digest*:—"Favorabiliores rei potius quam actores habentur" (50, 17, 125), and "In pœnalibus causis benignius interpretandum est" (F. 50, 17, 155, § 1).   R. C. L.

The maxim inquired for is thus expressed in Canon Law:—

"Leges favorabiles ampliori interpretatione sunt intelligendæ; seu in materia favorabili verba Legis accipi debent secundum amplam suam significationem." (See Ferraris, *Prompta Bibliotheca Canonica, Juridica*, &c., ad verb. *Lex*, art. v. 38.)

F. C. H.

LEGITIMATION PER SUBSEQUENS MATRIMONIUM (3rd S. vii. 213.) — The student of history and heraldry combined will not fail to notice, under this head, both the fact that an act was passed in 1397 for the legitimation of the De Beauforts, the sons of John of Gaunt and Catherine Swynford, and the alteration consequent upon this, in the coat armour of the children of those personages; the effects of which are still to be traced in the heraldic insignia of some of our highest nobility at the present day.   H. W. T.

"SECRET HISTORY OF THE CABINET OF BONAPARTE" (3rd S. vii. 136.)—A correspondent (T. B.) quoting a note from Lieber's *Manual*, which contains the following sentence—

"The Bishop of Amiens says in his *mandement*, 'The Almighty having created Napoleon, rested from his labours,'"‡

asks whether any authority, beyond that of Goldsmith can be given for these instances of glaring flattery and profanity.

I do not know whether the above quoted expression is to be found in the bishop's pastoral, but if I am not very much mistaken, this identical phrase will be found in a speech addressed to Napoleon I., and reported in the *Moniteur*. In 1808, on the occasion of the great reviews and military manœuvres executed in the neighbourhood of Arras, Napoleon visited that city. A M. La Chèze was at that time prefect, and concluded his complimentary speech to the Emperor by saying, "Dieu créa Bonaparte, puis il se reposa." The zeal of the prefect was rewarded with the following quatrain, which was widely circulated at the time:—

"Il n'en resta pas là;
Il fit encore La Chèze;
Puis il se reposa
Beaucoup mieux à son aise."

The same phrase has appeared during the present empire, on a transparency, I think at Lille, under the auspices of M. de Calvimont.   J. V.

WHO WAS PHILALETHES? (3rd S. vii. 220.) — The Rev. Thomas Stackhouse, author of the *History of the Bible*, and many other valuable works, used the signature "Philalethes" to most of his smaller works.   JAS. COLEMAN.

JOHN BARCROFT (3rd S. v. 11.)—

"In the year 1723, being the sixtieth of his age, and about the twenty-seventh of his ministry, died John Barcroft of Arkill, near Edenderry. He was the son of William and Margaret Barcroft, born at Shralegh, near Rosenallis, in the Queen's County, in the year 1664. He was the first friend who came to settle near Edenderry after the Wars."—*Hist. of the Quakers in Ireland*, by Thomas Wight, Dublin, 1751, p. 295. See also Gough's *Hist. of the Quakers*, vol. iv. p. 261.

"In 1708, a meeting settled, and a Meeting-house built, at Ballytore, in the county of Kildare."—*Hist. of Quakers in Ireland*, p. 347.

I was under the impression that the subject of the foregoing notice was the originator of the colony of Balitore, which was founded by John Barcroft and another, as we learn from the Leadbeater Papers, in the latter part of the seventeenth century. But the statement of URSAGELLUS, that the colonist had been, before his conversion to Quakerism, one of Cromwell's officers, is quite inconsistent with my previous belief. There is but one John Barcroft mentioned in the two books cited above, and had there been another of a character and career so interesting as to have distinguished him in the humble annals of Quakerism, the omission of his name from these carefully compiled works would be singular. My John Barcroft would have been old enough in the latter part of the seventeenth century to have undertaken the enterprise; and my second quotation offers some slight presumption that the colony may have been founded very near the end of the century, as the earnest reformers would probably set up a "Meeting" as soon as possible. Will URSAGELLUS favour me with the source of his information? I wish to identify the founder of Balitore.   ST. TH.

RICHARD ALLESTREE (3rd S. vii. 124.) — In the *Journal of Sacred Literature* for July, 1864 (vol. v. n. s. p. 435), Mr. Barham includes among other works supposed to have been written by Dr. Allestree, *The Government of the Thoughts*, and *The Duty of Christian Resolution*. As Mr. Barham has investigated the question touching the authorship of these and the other works attributed to Dr. Allestree he will probably be able to furnish a reply to the following inquiries:—

1. Has Bishop Fell stated that the MS. of *The Government of the Thoughts* was found among Dr. Allestree's papers after his decease?

2. In what year and by whom was *The Government of the Thoughts* published?

3. What is the date of the first edition of *The Duty of Christian Resolution?* Who was the editor of it?   LLALLAWG.

"IVANHOE" (3rd S. vii. 242.)—An adaptation of this novel to the stage, more popular than that of Terry, was made by Thomas Dibdin; and produced at the Surrey Theatre, when under his management, on January 20, 1820. It bears the title of *Ivanhoe, or, the Jew's Daughter,* and is printed in *Cumberland's Minor Theatre.* Some ten years later, an adaptation of an operatic character was brought out at Covent Garden Theatre under the name of *The Maid of Judah,* but I believe the songs only were printed.
W. H. HUSK.

JACOBITES AND JACOBINS (3rd S. i. 425; ii. 282.)
"The most difficult, and at the same time amusing examples of Amphibology, are those which commonly go by the name of Jesuitical verses,— verses which receive directly opposite meanings, if read in different order. Thus the following lines, if read as they stand, must be admired for their staunch loyalty; but let them be perused according to the order of the figures prefixed to them, and nothing can more strongly savour of rank Jacobinism:—

1. I love my country—but the King
3. Above all men his praise I sing,
2. Destruction to his odious reign
4. That plague of Princes, Thomas Paine;
5. The royal banners are display'd
7. And may success the standard aid
6. Defeat and ruin seize the cause
8. Of France, her liberty, and laws.

"The above, I am sorry to say, was not sported off as a mere *jeu-d'esprit*, but was actually composed to lend its artful aid to the cause of anarchy. I have it from a friend, who himself picked it up with many other similar publications, as they were circulated, previous to the rebellion in 1798, amongst the United Irishmen! I do not doubt but the following translation of another such poem into monkish Latin was applied to the very same laudable purpose!:—

1. Pro fide teneo sana
3. Quæ docet Anglicana
2. Affirmat quæ Romana
5. Videntur mihi vana
4. Supremus quando rex est
7. Tum plebs est fortunata
6. Seductus ille grex est
8. Cui Papa imperator.
9. Altare cum ornatur
11. Communio fit inanis
10. Populus tum beatur
12. Cum mensa, vinum, panis
13. Asini nomen meruit
15. Hunc morem qui non capit
14. Missam qui deseruit
16. Catholicus est et sapit.

"I have here ventured to supply myself a couplet that was wanting, but I will not so affront my reader's penetration, as to point out to him which couplet that is." — Addison's *Indian Reminiscences*, pp. 209, 210, Lond.

CRUX (2.)

BOOKBINDING (3rd S. vii. 138.)—Will your correspondent add to his list a modest 12mo of 310 pages, entitled —
"A Manual of the Art of Bookbinding: containing full Instructions in the Different Branches of Forwarding, Gilding, and Finishing; also the Art of Marbling Book Edges and Paper," Philadelphia, 1856,

by James B. Nicholson, a worthy Englishman settled in Philadelphia?   ST. TH.

"BRADSHAW'S RAILWAY COMPANION" (3rd S. vii. 261.)—I have before me a copy two years older than the one you cite as the original edition, with the following title:—
"Bradshaw's Railway Companion, containing the Times of Departure, Fares, &c., of the Railways in England; and also Hackney Coach Fares from the principal Railway Stations, illustrated with Maps of the Country through which the Railways pass, and Plans of London, Birmingham, Leeds, Liverpool, and Manchester." Manchester, 1840, 16mo.

Is not this the original edition?   KAPPA.

WILLIAM WILLIAMS (3rd S. vii. 241.)—In 1810 he resided in Ivy Tower, in the parish of St. Florence, near Tenby, Pembrokeshire, where his death occurred on Nov. 16, 1813. Five letters written by him in 1810 were addressed to Theophilus Jones, the historian of Breconshire. They have been published in the *Archæologia Cambrensis* for 1858 and '59 (iv. 376-82, and v. 13-20). For further account of Mr. Williams and his works see *Gent. Mag.* for 1813, lxxxiii. 624-5.
LLALLAWG.

FREEMASON (2nd S. xii. 219.)—The passage I quoted from Cawdray's *Similies* ("As the freemason heweth the hard stones," &c.), I find is taken from a work of Werdmuller's, translated by Bishop Coverdale, and published in 1550, under the title of *A Spiritual and most precious Perle*, &c. It occurs at the close of chapter vi. It is a pity that Cawdray does not give any references. He borrows largely from Werdmuller, whose writings abound in similies.   EIRIONNACH.

PAGAN CARICATURE: QUOTATION WANTED (3rd S. iii. 89, 456; vii. 243.)—In *Nova Variorum Scriptorum Collectio*, t. iii. 8vo, Halæ, Magdeb. 1717, the frontispiece to t. ii. is a restoration of the picture described by Tertullian, and the print mentioned at iii. 89 is probably a copy cut down by the binder, the upper part having a scroll, on which is "Ononychotus." The fifth dissertation is,—
"Idoli, quod apud Tertullianum Christianis affingitur, verum nomen esse *Ononychotus*, demonstratur." The author is J. P. Heinius. It is short, occupying only twenty-two pages, but learned and well-written. The various readings are discussed, and the result is given at p. 85:—
"Emensi pene sumus viam, et tredecim eruditorum virorum conjecturas a scopo abludentes perlustravimus; nostram nunc proferamus sententiam, et exploremus,

albone clarius, quam ceteræ absit. Substituimus pro 'Ononychite' 'Ονούχωτος, vocabulum conflatum ex ὄνος, asinus, ὄνυξ, ungula, οὖς, auris. In ignominiosa tabula conspiciebatur monstrum auribus asininis, et ungulato pede. Asini ergo pars inerat, inerat etiam ungula.''

See also Farrar, *Bampton Lectures*, 1862, p. 573.
　　　　　　　　　　　　　　　　H. B. C.

U. U. Club.

· R. C. L. will find the quotation *Deus Christianorum ὀνοκοίτης* (not *ὀνόχηλον*, as he writes it) in one of the early chapters of Tertullian's *Apology*. I regret that I have not the work at hand to refer to.　　　　　　　　　　　E. WALFORD, M.A.

· Balliol College.

LYNCHETS, OR SHELVES IN WILTSHIRE (3rd S. vii: 241, 302.)—Having been brought up on Salisbury Plain, where those shelves are common enough to form a characteristic feature of the scenery, and to have the local name of *lynchets*, I can assure the querist that Cobbett's expression, "thousands and thousands of acres of [formerly] ploughed land on shelves, in Wilts alone," is perfectly correct; but their description in the latter part of the quotation seems absurd. The "rising parts" of stairs do not slope at all. Those of terraces formed in chalk must of course slope as much as chalk railway banks, or about forty-five degrees. · Their commonest height is from ten to twenty feet. They are perfectly similar to the "terraces of Zion" in Seddon's picture, but confined always to the steep middle part of the slope's height, because all chalk hills are left by the diluvial scour imperceptibly rounded off both above and below. Throughout the interior of the Plain, where its utmost undulations are nearly confined to 200 feet, I remember no hillsides marked with more than four "lynchets," but the higher downs toward its outer escarpments, rising to 400 and 600 feet, may have many series of seven or eight, such as I have seen near Calne, and near Cranbourne. It is quite exceptional to see any of these terraces cultivated, and they always, since I was old enough to know they were artificial, impressed me, without having read Cobbett, with an idea of the dense population that must once have dwelt on those now lonely pastoral wilds; though perhaps a greater share in conveying this impression is due to the immense military works, the ever-present entrenched camps or cities, mostly larger than Old Sarum, and almost as deeply fortified, the twenty-mile rampart of Wansdyke (Woden's dike), and others hardly inferior, and the great sepulchral barrows, dotted *by hundreds* within sight of Stonehenge, and in smaller numbers about Avebury temple, and the barrow of Silbury, itself *exceeding in cubical contents the third Pyramid.*

　　　　　　　　　　　　　　E. L. GARBETT. ·

. MR. PINKERTON is perfectly right in his definition of these so-called archæological remains. The

"shelves" are the work of cattle, as can be easily seen if the hilly feeding grounds be visited when stocked with cattle. In Devonshire the shelves are very common; in the immediate vicinity of Exeter you can walk to a set of hilly fields, and verify MR. PINKERTON's statement in a few minutes. The cattle begin feeding from the bottom of the hill, and gradually work their way to the top; in so doing they tread down these terraces or shelves. In wet weather the cattle soon make these tracks, and with constant use for some time the shelves become widened and hardened with the weather. When once formed, and the pastures shut up for some time, the shelves get overgrown with grass, and any one passing by and not knowing how they were made, would be sorely puzzled to account for so singular a sight on the steep hill side.　　　EDWARD PURFITT.

Devon and Exeter Institution.

In Gloucestershire these shelves are called *linchets*. (In Kent the word is used for a bank or boundary.) They are supposed to be formed by sheep and cattle grazing on hill sides for many centuries. Any observer may notice *little ones*, only a few inches wide, on the sloping sides of sheep-walks. These small beginnings getting wider and wider by constant treadings, would no doubt be further widened if the land was turned into arable, and then being levelled to a certain extent would be more easily cultivated by spade or plough, and eventually have the appearance of *shelves* or *steps*.　　　H. T. ELLACOMBE.

ALVOISE CONTARINI (3rd S. vii. 220.) — The name *Alvoise* is miswritten or misprinted for Aloysius, which follows. But Aloysius is the same name as *Luigi*, the last Contarini Doge mentioned by MR. DAVIDSON. This appears to be the favourite mode of the Italians for Latinizing Lewis. Thus, St. Luigi Gonzaga (the one specimen of chastity in that most licentious race), is often called St. Aloysius Gonzaga; and on the coins of the Empress Maria Louisa as Duchess of Parma, she is called Maria Aloisa. Is not Heloise another form of this feminine?　　　　　　　LAELIUS.

WORDS USED IN DIFFERENT SENSES (3rd S. vii. 278.)—Your correspondent E. H. A. should hardly have omitted *garbled*. This, Sir E. Coke, in his fourth Institute, tells us was a grocer's word; and "*garbled* spices," expressed the best spices, carefully selected and picked out. "*Garbled* extracts," in the present day, expresses just the reverse, *i. e.* extracts dishonestly and unfairly chosen.　　W.

SONG (3rd S. vii. 281.)—I send you some lines which may be those after which your correspondent SEXAGENARIUS inquires. They are printed in Kelly's *Reminiscences* (vol. ii. p. 289), and entitled "Ballad by Sheridan." And unless they are more known than I imagine, their tenderness and delicacy may perhaps induce you to insert them in your pages : —

"No more shall the spring my lost pleasure restore,
  Uncheer'd I still wander alone ;
And, sunk in dejection, for ever deplore
  The sweets of the days that are gone.

"While the sun as it rises, to others shines bright,
  I think how it formerly shone ;
While others cull blossoms I find but a blight,
  And sigh for the days that are gone.

"I stray where the dew falls, through moon-lighted groves,
  And list to the nightingale's song ;
His plaints still remind me of long banished joys,
  And the sweets of the days that are gone.

"Each dew-drop that steals from the dark eye of night,
  Is a tear for the bliss that is flown ;
While others cull blossoms I find but a blight,
  And sigh for the days that are gone."
                     X.

Can SEXAGENARIUS be seeking for the words of a song which Miss Edgeworth's sister sang to Sir Walter Scott? It was a fragment, and related the woes of an Irish girl with a *petticoat of red.* The chorus was —

  "Shool, shool! Ochone, ochone !
Thinking on the days that are long enough agone."

I copy the words of two verses, which Sir Walter Scott said he had recovered by accident : —

  "I went to the mill, but the miller was gone—
  I sat me down, and cried ochone,
  To think on the days that are past and gone,
  Of Dickie Macphalion that's slain.
    Shool, shool, &c.

  "I sold my rock, I sold my reel,
  And sae hae I my spinning-wheel,
  And all to buy a cap of steel,
  For Dickie Macphalion that's slain.
    Shool, shool," &c.

These particulars I have gathered from Lockhart's *Life of Scott*, 7th volume, pp. 198, 199, second edition. I should be glad to see the whole of the song, and to get the music if possible.

               C. W. BARKLEY.

DELVE, DOLVE, DALF (3rd S. vii. 279)—It may not be very easy to find full or fair proof. I have examined at least five probable sources of information.

The word *dalf* is, I believe, not often heard of; I do not find *dolve* in two very likely places; nor even *delve* where it might be expected to appear.

I am inclined to think that, though *dolve* may have its advocates, *delve* is perhaps as legitimate as any, if not more so—e. g. "delve of coals." For the word *delve*, however, the reference in one authority is to *delf*—with the quotation, "The delfs would be overflown."—*Ray*. The heraldic *delf-ten*, indicative of abatement, and expressive of cowardice, may here perhaps be noted.

As to the couplet—whether the Gothic, Belgic, or Saxen, is taken into consideration—the absolute correctness may be somewhat questionable accord-

ing to the estimate of *Dolf* (G.), *Delfan* (S.), or *Delven* (B.).

Query. Since there are such various readings, may there not be something in the *channel* through which they flow? It is not impossible that persons, times, and circumstances, may account for much.

Literary usage, as well as criticism, may have some variations from age to age. We may indeed have met with names, altered by the lapse of time; and it may be difficult to trace to their original exactness in some instances.   B.

BISHOP LINWOOD (3rd S. vii. 134, 266.) — MR. BEDFORD will do good service to the cause of historical and heraldic accuracy if he will pursue the task now set before him, and thoroughly sift the authorities on this subject. In the meantime I beg to make a query, and to add a note or two on this head : —

1. Are the tinctures which belong to the shield described by MR. BEDFORD known? Is there any authority for this bearing (a chevron between three leaves) except the Register; and on what ground is it considered that the addition of these arms is contemporaneous, and not added by a later hand?

2. Will MR. BEDFORD oblige me by a reference to any trustworthy *illustration* of the brass for John de Linwood? Gough, *Sep. Mon.*, ii. 53, mentions John, a brother of the bishop, who died 1420. Is this the person indicated by MR. BEDFORD as "John de Lyndewoode" of 1421?

3. Can your correspondent refer me to any armorial in which the arms he claims for the bishop are assigned to *any* form of the name Linwood? Gwillim and others to whom I have had access, uniformly blazon Lyndwood, arg. a fesse crenellée between 3 fleurs-de-lis sa.

4. As Bishop Linwood was a Fellow of Pembroke Hall, Cambridge, perhaps your very able correspondents, MESSRS. C. H. & THOMPSON COOPER, may be able to bring their extensive and ready learning to bear upon our inquiries.

5. It was not my friend, to whom I am indebted for the extract from the *Blazon of Episcopacy*, who made the note of correction, although by a printer's error the text of "N. & Q." was made to represent the case in that light. Not having the book before me I was, of course, not aware of what preceded the extract, and simply made a "note" correcting the error in the date.
               H. W. T.

MEAT AND MALT (3rd S. vii. 73.) — Many years ago we were advised to suspend a raw beef steak in a tub of home-made elder wine. I think we did so, but after the lapse of forty-five years I am more certain of the excellence of the wine than of the contribution of the beef. If it improved wine it is worth trying in ale.   F. C. B.

ROMAN TESSERÆ (3rd S. vii. 281.) — If MR.
HUTCHINSON had washed off the inflorescence every
morning with pure water, he would not now have
to lament over his incrusted pavement. The evil
of which he complains is well known to all who
have had anything to do with flooring tiles. The
remedy for it is a very simple one, and like that for
many ailments of the body; daily washing with
pure water will effectually remove the malady.
                                        A TILER.

COPY OF ST. MATTHEW WRITTEN BY BARNABAS
(3rd S. vii. 278.) — The legend that the original MS.
of St. Matthew's gospel was discovered in the
tomb of St. Barnabas, the apostle, was very widely
spread and firmly believed in during the middle
ages. The story is in a high degree improbable.
A modern critic would naturally ask how the
relics of St. Barnabas were identified four centuries after his death? How the manuscript was
proved to be of the age attributed to it? And
how, granting the authenticity of the relics and
the age of the book, it was proved to be in the
handwriting of the evangelist? To none of these
questions do the writers who mention this discovery furnish any rational answers. See *Martyr-
olog. Rom. 2 Sep.; Surius de probatis Sanctorum
Historiis, 11 Junii; Capgrave, Chron. p. 87; Elo-
gium Historiarum*, pp. 201, 344; *Beyerlinck, Mag.
Theat. Vitæ Humanæ*, t. i. 953, C.; t. ii. 1000, E.;
t. iii. 398, H.; t. vi. 937, C.
                                  EDWARD PEACOCK.
Bottesford Manor, Brigg.

Miscellaneous.

NOTES ON BOOKS, ETC.

*The Court of Final Appeal; or the Appellate Jurisdiction
of the Crown in Ecclesiastical Cases.* By the Rev. M.
J. Fuller, M.A. (Parkers: Oxford and London.)

The author's attention was first directed toward his
subject by the Gorham Case about fifteen years ago,
since which time he has been accumulating materials on
the subject. His little volume contains, among other
matters, a History of the Court from the earliest times to
the present, an Analysis of the Debate on Bp. Blomfield's Bill in 1850, and the Opinions of the Judges upon
the Authority of Convocation in 1711; and the result at
which he arrives is, that "the present Appeal Court is
opposed to all scriptural, apostolic, and primitive prece-
dents, and most unsatisfactory in every respect." The
work is carefully executed, and will be a convenient
manual for those who desire to see a synopsis of a large
subject in a little space.

The Secrets of Angling. By A. S. Moffat, Author of
"Reminiscences of Otter Hunting." (A. & C. Black.)

Of a surety, the mind of an angler is a psychological
study. Professing to imitate the great master of their
art, and make it a rule of life to be "quiet and go a-
angling," he no sooner takes rod in hand than he becomes
a very enthusiast. Mr. Moffat is no exception to this

rule: his preface is an outburst in praise of the delights
of a country life, with its piscatorial pleasures, as con-
trasted with that of life in cities, "the squalid haunts of
vice, pestilence, and immorality." But when he comes to
treat on "the gentle art," Mr. Moffat is a quiet, sober,
practical teacher. He seems to have practised successfully fishing in all its branches. His instructions are
clear and intelligible; and as he not only tells how to
fish, but where to fish, and how to cook salmon and trout,
his *Secrets of Angling* is a book which every Waltonian
will be pleased to add to his library.

Shakspeare's Editors and Commentators. By the Rev. W.
R. Arrowsmith. (J. R. Smith.)

Such of our readers as remember Mr. Arrowsmith's
occasional Shakesperian papers in "N. & Q.," will not
require to be told how thoroughly that gentleman has
studied the writings of the great dramatist. They will
remember too that his criticisms did not err on the side of
mercy, and will readily anticipate the slashing style in
which he here "exhibits the degeneracy of the existing
breed of expositors."

*Shakspeariana from 1564 to 1864. An Account of the
Shakspearian Literature of England, Germany, and
France during three Centuries, with Bibliographical In-
troductions.* By Franz Thimm. (Thimm.)

This useful little manual of Shakspeariana will give
English readers a good insight into the progress which
France and Germany have made in the study of Shak-
speare.

BOOKS AND ODD VOLUMES
WANTED TO PURCHASE.

Particulars of Price, &c. of the following Books to be sent direct to
the gentlemen by whom they are required, and whose names and addresses are given for that purpose: —

WHITE'S (HENRY GOSTLING) SERMONS. 2 Vols. 8vo(?), 1817.
  Wanted by *X. Y. Z.* care of the Librarian, City of London College,
    Leadenhall Street, London, E.C.

CATALOGUE OF THE EXHIBITION OF WORKS OF ART, &c. on Loan at
the South Kensington Museum. June, 1862. 8vo. Part IV. and following parts, if any, or a complete copy.
MASON'S SURVEY OF IRELAND. Vol. III. (Preferred in boards.)
  Wanted by *Mr. Andrew Jervise*, Brechin, N. B.

THE PROCEEDINGS OF THE CHURCH CONGRESS AT OXFORD in 1862.
PAPERS ISSUED BY THE CAMBRIDGE CHURCH DEFENCE ASSOCIATION. (A
set.)
  Wanted by *Rev. Aiken Irvine*, Kilbride, Bray.

Notices to Correspondents.

Answers to Correspondents in our next.

A Reading Case for holding the weekly Nos. of "N. & Q." is now
ready, and may be had of all Booksellers and Newsmen, price 1s. 6d.;
or, free by post, direct from the publisher, for 1s. 8d.

⁂ *Cases for binding the volumes of* "N. & Q." *may be had of the
Publisher, and of all Booksellers and Newsmen.*

"NOTES AND QUERIES" *is published at noon on Friday, and is also
issued in* MONTHLY PARTS. *The Subscription for* STAMPED COPIES *for
Six Months forwarded direct from the Publisher (including the Half-
yearly* INDEX) *is* 11s. 4d., *which may be paid by Post Office Order,
payable at the Strand Post Office, in favour of* WILLIAM G. SMITH, 32,
WELLINGTON STREET, STRAND, W.C., *where also all* COMMUNICATIONS
FOR THE EDITOR *should be addressed.*

"NOTES & QUERIES" is registered for transmission abroad.

CURE OF ASTHMATIC COUGH AT THE AGE OF EIGHTY-FIVE, BY DR.
LOCOCK'S PULMONIC WAFERS. — "Wm. Taylor, The Cape, Heathwick,
aged eighty-five, says he for many years suffered from a heavy asthma-
tical cough. To get rest at night was almost out of the question,
although he tried many things; but for the last four years, since he
commenced taking the Wafers, he can insure a good night's rest, &c.
— Witness, R. Brown, Chemist 55, Spring Hills, Birmingham." Price
1s. 1½d., 2s. 9d., and 4s. 6d. per box, of all Druggists.

LONDON, SATURDAY, APRIL 29, 1865.

CONTENTS.—N° 174.

Notes.

"THE LADY OF THE HAYSTACK."

"Louisa: a Narrative of Facts, supposed to throw light on the Mysterious History of 'The Lady of the Haystack.' Translated from a French Work, published in the Imperial Dominions, A.D. 1785, by the Rev. G. H. Glasse, A.M., Rector of Hanwell, Middlesex. The Second Edition. London, 1801. Fcap. 8vo, pp. [xxxii.] 111. Printed by P. Norbury, New Brentford."

In the year 1776, a poor unfortunate female was found beneath a haystack at Bourton, near Bristol. She appears to have wandered about the neighbourhood during the day, subsisting on the charity of the country people, and returning regularly to the same shelter at night. After about four years of this life, during which time no word of her former history could be extracted from her, as evident symptoms of insanity appeared, she was taken to the lunatic ward of St. Peter's Hospital, at Bristol; whence she once escaped, and returned to her former shelter—a distance of six miles. Moved by the helpless state of this unfortunate, the benevolent Hannah More removed her to Bitton, in the county of Gloucester, and provided a person to attend her.

The little volume quoted has the above story, for the title of a "Tale of Real Woe," written by Hannah More, by way of introduction. It was first published in the *St. James's Chronicle* in 1785. The translation is from an anonymous

work, *L'Inconnue, Histoire Veritable;* being some particulars of the life of an adventuress, La Freülen, who, under pretence of being a daughter of Francis I. of Austria, victimised many persons in Bourdeaux, Hamburg, and Stockholm, about the year 1768. In 1769, in consequence of a letter, apparently written by Joseph II., then on his travels in Italy, to the King of Spain, and by him forwarded to the Empress of Austria, La Freülen was, on the requisition of the Austrian Court, arrested and sent under a strong guard to Brussels, where she was to be examined by M. de Cobenzel and the first President M. de Nancy. She was conducted to Fort Monterel under the guard of Major Camerlang, who, as she could neither read nor write, taught her to sign her name. The examination, after twenty-four sittings, being entirely finished—

"Messrs. De Cobenzel and De Nancy being desired to give their opinion, the Court agreed that the most prudent measure would be to place the poor girl in some distant convent, and there to keep her, till time should throw some light on this mysterious affair."

The elder De Nancy, Secretary to the Empress, thus wrote:—

"Though it appears to me that the prisoner is not the daughter of the Emperor, there are, however, circumstances in her story which throw a mysterious perplexity over her birth."

The day before the death of M. de Cobenzel, which occurred shortly afterwards (speaking of a letter he had received from M. de Kaunitz), he said: "I have just received despatches from Vienna, charging me to acquaint the Court with the prisoner's whole history, by no means to dismiss her, and to take no step without further order."

"Four days after his death, the stranger was taken out of prison—a sub-lieutenant of the Maréchaussée of Brabant conducted her to Quiévraing, a small town between Mons and Valenciennes—fifty louis-d'ors were put into her hands—and she was abandoned to her wretched destiny."

If La Freülen (or Mademoiselle de Schonau, as she is sometimes styled) is to be believed, she was visited at Bourdeaux by the Duke of York, who presented her with 700 *louis-d'ors*, and promised to furnish her with money sufficient to pay her debts. The Duke does appear to have written to her from Monaco an unfinished letter, referring to the Princess d'Aversberg; and after his death, which shortly followed, La Freülen sent to the persons appointed to examine his papers, by whom her own portrait and another picture were returned to her.

In the appendix (p. 77) a letter by the translator of the narrative, which was published in the *Gent. Mag.* (1785, vol. lv. p. 791), points to many circumstances tending to prove the identity of La Freülen and Louisa. Five letters by Hannah

More (unsigned), with various particulars follow. One passage tells the sequel: —

" Finding the recovery of her limbs as hopeless as that of her understanding, and fearing that she might eventually be left in a situation wholly unprotected, I obtained for her an asylum in the Hospital; allowing a certain sum annually to clothe her, and to furnish her with such comforts as she had been accustomed to enjoy. I visited her more than once in this her last retreat, till she had so far lost all sensibility or knowledge of me as to make it no longer necessary."

Every effort appears to have been made to trace the history of this poor woman without success, and she died at Guy's Hospital Lunatic House on the 19th December, 1800. A certificate to that effect, dated Feb. 18, 1801, signed by Thomas Callaway, Steward, Alfred Wm. Roberts, Chaplain, is printed at p. xxxi. The date of her removal from Bitton to Guy's Hospital is not recorded.

It is possible that the sympathy excited by this mysterious lunatic may have had some share in originating the marvellous imposition of the Princess Caraboo (" N. & Q.," 3rd S. vii. 196).

The little volume is a literary curiosity.

　　　　　　　　　　　　　　　　　HUGH OWEN.

Westminster Club.

UNIVERSAL CATALOGUE OF ENGLISH BOOKS.

No one, I think, would deny that a complete Catalogue of all books, printed in the English language since the invention of printing, would be a work of the highest utility and interest. At the same time too many, I fear, are disposed to think with Mr. Bohn (Preface to his edition of Lowndes, vol. i. part II.), that "such a consummation is rather to be sighed for than expected," and with this feeling make no effort to remedy the deficiency. My object in writing this letter is to draw attention to the subject, with the hope that the discussion of it in the pages of " N. & Q." may educe some practical suggestions on the matter.

I would now add a few remarks on one or two points: —

1. *As to contents.* The catalogue I propose would comprise all books ever printed in English, specifying the various editions, with their date, size, and place of publication; and, in the case of very rare books, noting in what libraries they exist. It might also, unless it were found to swell the size of the work to too great an extent, contain brief bibliographical notes on the more important books; or, at all events, references to notices, reviews, &c., in other works.

2. *As to arrangement.* All who have considered the point will I believe agree with me, that the catalogue should be arranged in alphabetical order according to the names of authors, or the titles of the books. A classified catalogue might possibly be afterwards prepared; but the first thing to be done is, to form a simple alphabetical register of every book.

3. *As to the means by which the work might be effected.* It has occurred to me that a Society, somewhat similar in its constitution to the Philological Society, might undertake the compilation of the catalogue; the work being divided amongst a certain number of its members, and the necessary expenses before publication being defrayed by an annual subscription.

Some may perhaps doubt whether a catalogue, such as that I now propose, would obtain a sale sufficient to repay the expenses of its publication; but I believe that, if the work is well executed, it may safely be assumed that the volumes would be purchased by all the larger public and collegiate libraries in the United Kingdom, by many American and continental ones, besides by a certain number of private individuals.

I am aware that on almost every point it is easy to suggest difficulties and objections. One stock objection to such a work as that I propose, is, that it must soon get out of date; but this is almost equally an objection to all bibliographical catalogues. They can only, any of them, be complete up to the date of their publication. Other catalogues, or supplementary volumes, must be consulted for books published at a subsequent date; but this surely should not be a bar to so desirable a work as a complete Catalogue of the whole of English Literature. 　　　G. W. J.

" LANG-NEBBED THINGS."

The prayer for protection against " witches and warlocks, and lang-nebbed things," is familiar amongst the peasantry of Scotland, by whom it has also been implanted in the folk-lore of Ulster. Sir Walter Scott introduces it in the second chapter of the *Black Dwarf :* —

" Well, Hobbie," said the Laird, " for one who believes so deeply as you do in supernatural appearances, I must own you take heaven in your own hand rather audaciously, considering where we are walking."— " What need I care for the Mucklestane Moor, ony mair than ye do yourself, Earnscliff," said Hobbie, somewhat offended; " to be sure, they do say *there is a sort of worricows and lang-nebbit things* about the land, but what care I for them I "

This superstition has obviously some reference to birds; and so far as regards Scotland and Ireland, one circumstance is curious, that the word *whaap*, which is the popular name of the Curlew (*Numenius arquata* of Linn.), a bird notorious for the length of its bill — is also the term used to signify a " hobgoblin "; which, as Jamieson says in his *Scottish Dictionary*, is believed to have a *long beak*, and to haunt the eaves of houses after nightfall.

Thompson, in his *Natural History of Ireland*, vol. ii. p. 194, says the word *whaap* is a near approach in sound to the alarm-cry of the curlew when disturbed; and if this has anything to do with the popular belief, the instance is not without a parallel, inasmuch as the night-scream of the owl has given rise to a similar superstition, which has had an unusually extended prevalence. Ovid and Tibullus commemorate it, and Statius alludes to the same circumstance : —

" Nocturnæque gemunt striges; et feralia bubo
Damna canens," &c. (*Thebaid.* lib. iii. 1. 511.)

In India, the unearthly yell of one variety of the owl—the *Sirnium indranee* of Sykes—has obtained for it the mysterious dread of the people, and associated its voice with unutterable horrors.

But in the case of the owl, the length of the *beak* has nothing to do with the dread inspired by its cry; and the epithet " lang-nebbed " certainly cannot apply to it. Why, then, in the instance of the curlew has the accident of the prolonged *bill* inspired a kindred dread, there being nothing in the tone of its voice to give rise to terror? Jamieson, in allusion to the feeling in Scotland, speaks only of the bill, and makes no mention of any cry in connexion with the goblin *whaap*.

Nor is there wanting at least secondary evidence to imply that in Italy and elsewhere in Europe, there is some association of the long beak with the imagery of witchcraft, vampyrism and diablerie. Salvator Rosa, in his well-known picture of the " Persecution of St. Anthony," invests his principal tormentor, a creature something between a reptile and a human skeleton, which bestrides the saint as he lies prostrate, with an enormously prolonged beak, whose dimensions approach those of a crane rather than a curlew. And Mr. Wright, in his charming *History of Caricature and Grotesque*, has given numerous examples from the sixteenth to the eighteenth century, in which the artists have always combined a prolonged beak with the other attributes of demons and incubi. Breughel in Flanders, and Callot in Lorraine, were each prolific in these " long-nebbed " monsters—thus demonstrating the prevalence of the superstition extensively in Europe. Callot, as an artist, belongs to Italy rather than to France. Is there any theory or conjecture to elucidate this legendary belief, or to account for the connexion of the *long bill* of the grallatorial birds with this midnight superstition?

J. Emerson Tennent.

ENGLISH ACTORS IN FRANCE, *temp.* HENRY IV.

In the *Intermédiaire*, a valuable French imitation of " N. & Q." there is a notice in the number for June 1, 1864, of some English actors who performed before the king and the court at Fontaine-

bleau. The whole notice had best be quoted in the writer's own words : —

"Dans le Journal Manuscrit du Médecin Héroard, qui se trouvait autrefois dans le Cabinet de M. de Genas (N° 21,448 de la Bibl. Hist. du P. Lelong) il est dit que le samedi 18 Septembre, 1604, le Roi et la cour étant à Fontainebleau, le Dauphin (Louis XIII, qui entrait alors dans sa quatrième année) est mené dans la grand salle neuve, ouïr une tragédie représentée par des Anglais. Il les écoute avec froideur, gravité et patience 'jusques à ce qu'il fallut couper la tête à un des personnages.' Le mardi 28, le Dauphin se fait habiller en masque et imite 'les Comédiens Anglois qui étoient à la Cour et qu'il avoit vus jouer.' Enfin, le Dimanche 3 Octobre de la même année, l'enfant se fait encore habiller en comédien, et, marchant à grands pas, imite les Comédiens Anglais, en disant, *Tiph! toph! milord!* Voilà donc, à l'époque de Shakespeare, des Comédiens Anglais jouant à Paris en 1598, et à la Cour de Fontainebleau, devant Henri IV en 1604. Serait-il possible de connaître le personnel de ces troupes et les pièces de leur répertoire ? "

The passage relating to the actors of 1598 is as follows : —

"Dans l'inventaire des titres et papiers de l'Hôtel de Bourgogne se trouvent mentionnés : 1° un bail de la grande salle et théâtre du dit Hôtel, passé le 25 mai 1598, devant Huart et Claude Nourel, Notaires à Paris, par Jehan Sehais, Comédien Anglais; 2° une Sentence du Châtelet, rendue le 4 juin 1598, à l'encontre desdits Comédiens Anglais, tant pour raison du susdit bail que pour le droit d'un écu par jour, jouant par lesdits Anglais ailleurs qu'au dit Hôtel."

In answer to the query respecting the names of the actors, and the pieces performed, a reply was inserted in the No. for Fevrier 25, with the signature "Henry Ch. Coote" (Londres) chiefly to the following effect. Mr. Coote is inclined to think that the English words, incorrectly quoted by the Dauphin, are from Shakespeare, and are as follows: "Tap for tap, my Lord," which words occur in *Henry IV*. Act II. Sc. 2, and are part of an apostrophe addressed by Sir John Falstaff to the Lord Chief Justice of England in the following language: —

" This is the right fencing grace, my lord, tap for tap, and so part fair."

Mr. Coote leaves it to his readers to judge as to the correctness of his conjecture respecting one of the plays acted before the court of the gallant monarch. If they think he is in the right, then he says the fact is proved, that English actors—of whose names he is ignorant—performed some of Shakespeare's plays in France in 1604, or perhaps earlier; for if they acted one play, Mr. Coote is of opinion that more than one were performed; but this at present seems to be matter of conjecture. J. Macray.

Oxford.

LE DERNIER VOLUME DES ŒUVRES DE VOLTAIRE.—Un livre est tombé sous ma main, il est intitulé *Le dernier Volume des Œuvres de Voltaire* (Paris, 1862, Henri Plon, éditeur). Je tiens à redresser cette erreur; le dernier volume de Voltaire reste à publier; ce sera, je crois, bien le dernier et le plus intéressant des deux.

Le Sottisier, suivant le titre écrit par Voltaire lui-même, est tout entier de sa main, qui a rempli les 133 feuillets dont il se compose.

Vers et prose citations, réflexions, notes, bonsmots, toute espèce de fragments recueillis à droite et à gauche, tout s'y trouve rassemblé de la manière la plus bizarre, sans suite aucune et sans choix; espèce de poche où cet esprit prodigieux jetait pêle mêle tout ce que la fantaisie du moment, le caprice, le besoin d'annoter et de se rappeler, lui faisait trouver à mesure que sa fiévreuse activité s'exerçait autour de lui.

Il y a enregistré jusqu'aux injures lancées contre lui (celles de Dom Calmet par exemple).

'A côté de "Apulée rapporte," etc., il y a "Louis XIV se levait à 8 heures et quart." De petites rubriques — "Bons Mots," "Absurdités," "Jugements Salomoniques" (d'après lui, Voltaire), "Contradictions," etc.—sont entrelacés de "Confucius et ses sentences," "Les Anglais c'est une grande baleine: et latum sub pectore possidet æquor," "Réflexions sur la Liberté" (pour la nier), "Notes sur Descartes," "Le Roi de Prusse a écrit," etc., "Mémoires de Sully," "Anecdotes de Berlin," "Anecdotes sur la Comédie," "Chiffres statistiques," etc.

Ce repertoire, formé des éléments les plus disparates, est comme une espèce de mosaïque littéraire semée de pointes quelquefois plus que lestes, toujours aiguës, que l'on est étonné de trouver au milieu des pensées les plus sérieuses.

Après tout c'est un certain miroir offrant ou réflétant les mille facettes de cet esprit universel.

Ce volume unique dans son genre a été peut-être pendant un demi-siècle sous la main de Voltaire, et il se trouve maintenant avec la bibliothèque du grand philosophe à St. Pétersbourg à l'Ermitage impérial de Cathérine II, où je l'ai vu il y a trois ans.   STÉFAN POLÈS.

[No one interested in the literary history of Voltaire would desire to see this communication *traduced* into English. We trust, therefore, that our correspondent will excuse our inserting it in his own language.—ED.]

KAR, KER, COR. — In *The Dolomite Mountains*, by Gilbert and Churchill (p. 84), occurs this remark: "It is singular how frequently the element *Kar* appears in the nomenclature of this valley" (the Eisach Thal). And after giving some instances, the author asks: "Is *Kar* a German element; and if so, what becomes of the asserted Celtic or Etruscan origin of Kardaun, the ancient Cardunum?" A note to this refers the *Car*, in *Carinthia*, to a Slovenic source; and says that *Gora-tan*, "mountain land," became in time *Carinthia*. Also, that the *Carni* would mean "the mountaineers." But *Cor* has also a particular meaning, relating to sheep and shepherds, and

hence applicable to a mountainous district; and we find tribes, whose names include *Cor* or *Car*, stretching from the banks of the Volga across Europe even to our own island. The Coraxi, adjoining the Colchi on the eastern coast of the Euxine, were famed for the production and manufacture of wool. Of this tribe, Mr. Yates, in his *Textrina Antiquorum* (p. 31), gives some information partly quoted from Klaproth. Of course we do not forget that *Corydon* was the classical name for a shepherd. Tracing this syllable westward, we find it bearing, in Brittany, rather a different meaning—a *point, end, height;* and strange to say, the Breton fairies, called *Korigans*, are dwarfs. Dr. Latham says *k—r* means, a boundary: hence we can well account for its entering into so many Breton appellations; and our own Cornwall probably received its name from the same source as the Breton *Cornouaile*. Was this Celtic? I think not; though we find *Kar, Cor*, side by side with *Cen, Hen, Ven*,—the former passed north of the Euxine, the latter south of it. I do not suppose either was the earliest race in Western Europe.
                                                F. C. B.

NAVAL VICTORY OF JUNE, 1665. — This newsletter may be read with interest, and confirm the narrative in Pepys's *Diary* in connexion with the first report of the victory of that date June, 1665 : —

"Mr White,
"By Mr Whittingham's desire, in his Lettre from London now before me, I write you the news (viz.), That ye Duke of Yorke is expected in London to-morrow wth Joy and triumph, for it's credibly reported yt all the Dutch Admiralls (except *Everts*.) [Evertsen?] are suncke and burnt, and 17 shipps taken, 34 escaped at most, and ye rest [perished?]. Wee lost ye Lord ffitzharding, Lord Portland, Lord Musgrove [Muskerry?], and Mr Boyle, 2d sonne to ye Earle of Corke, soe neare his Highnesse that theire Blood flew on his Robes. And yr Earle of Marlborough was slayne in ye old James. The Duke of Munmouth, Earle of Sandwitch, Sir John Pawson, and 1150 Soldiers wounded; we lost 500 Soldiers, and noe more. And there were 20 of ye old Captains did intend to revolt. The Duke of Yorke, when he drew his sword in engaging, threw his scabard in ye Sea. Brave Holmes suncke vapri'g Trumpe. Wee lost one shipp cald ye Charity, and noe more. Vera copia. ffrom, Sr,
                    "Yr assured friend to
                              "serve you,
"10 Junii, '65·   WM. HEWER."

Mr. Hewer was an apprentice to White's brother, a London cloth dealer. Certainly not the Wm. Hewer of that date, officially connected with Pepys.   E. W.

BARDOLPH'S COUNTENANCE.—I have lately come across an amusing literary blunder in the *Life* of Alexander Wilson, the ornithologist, by his American biographer Mr. Jared Sparks. He says (*Library of American Biography*, ii. 122) : —

"While at New York, Wilson had the curiosity to call on Paine, the author of the *Rights of Man*. . . . Wilson seems to have been struck with the *brilliancy of his countenance—which answered to his imagination of Bardolph*—even more than with the glow of his conversation. Paine examined his book with great attention," &c.

This I find, on reference, is simply a paraphrase of a passage in one of Wilson's letters as follows : —

" While in New York, I had the curiosity to call on the celebrated author of the *Rights of Man.* . . . Paine's face would have excellently suited the character of Bardolph ; but the penetration and intelligence of his eye bespeak the man of genius and the world. . . . He examined my book, leaf by leaf, with great attention," &c."

It is evident that Mr. Sparks is not a Shaksperian reader ; and that he has made his first acquaintance with Bardolph, and his immortal face, in this passage, which he so innocently construes into a compliment to the countenance of the author of *The Rights of Man.*

W. MOY THOMAS.

THEODOLITE. — Has not an accident discovered the true derivation of this word ? I have before me a copy of *Exegeses Physico-Mathematicæ, de momentis gravium, de vecte, &c.,* dedicated to D. Carolum Theodolum, Marchionem S. Viti. Romæ, 1685.

He is described as belonging to a family renowned for their interest in mathematical studies. Is it not very probable that the instrument was named after him or one of his ancestors ? I have less doubt in offering this suggestion, as all others hitherto given seem so manifestly impossible.

J. C. J.

THREE PARALLEL PROVERBS. — The Paris Correspondent of *The Times,* April 15, quotes an old French proverb of caution against too early adopting a summer dress : —

" Au mois d' Avril,
Ne quitte pas fil."

I have learned from an Italian gentleman, that there is a similar though amplified proverb in the Piedmontese dialect : —

" Avril, pó un fil,
Maggio, addagio,
Guing, slarga l'pugn."

That is to say : In April don't put off a thread ; in May gently begin ; in June slack your fist, or change freely.

There is also a Scotch proverb (I know not if it is used in England to the same effect), but I think it the best of all, being both comprehensive and laconic : —

" Ne'er cast a clout,
Till May be out."

K.

PARALLEL PASSAGES IN SHAKSPEARE AND OTHERS. — Vegetating at the Antipodes, I know not whether the following parallelism has been

noticed. There appears to me to be more than a mere coincidence of thought and expression : —

" Nay, mother,
. . . . you were used
To say extremity was the *trier* of spirits ;
That common chances common men could bear ;
That when the sea was calm, all boats alike
Showed mastership in floating. Fortune's blows
When most struck home [. . . . .
. . . . . .] being gentle wounded craves
A [No] noble *cunning.*"

Coriolanus, Act IV. Sc. 1.

" It is not but the tempest that doth show
The seaman's *cunning ;*—but the field that *tries*
The captain's courage ;—and we come to know
Best what men are in their worst jeopardies."

Daniel to H. F. Wriothesley, E. of Southampton.

It may be worth adding, that the unexpressed continuance of the negative in this last passage illustrates a similar form in *Cymbeline ;* but the naturalness so to speak, and propriety of the omission, is with Shakspeare. " Mine eyes," says the King, meditating on what he has heard : —

" . . . . Mine eyes
Were not in fault, for she was beautiful ;—
Mine ears that heard her flattery ; nor my heart
That thought her like her seeming."

So where, according to the editions to which I have access, Marina says : —

" I never did her hurt in all my life ;
I never spake bad word nor did ill turn
To any living creature : believe me, la,
I never killed a mouse nor hurt a fly ;—
I trod upon a worm against my will,
But I wept for it."—*Pericles,* Act IV. Sc. 1.

" I trod " should be " Aye trod."

B. NICHOLSON.

Queries.

ARCHDEACON, AN IRISH ARTIST. — Can you or any of your Irish correspondents, furnish me with a few particulars of this artist, who, if I mistake not, resided for some years in or near Dublin ? When did he die, and what is known of his drawings ? I have two very neatly done ; one of old Monkstown church, co. Dublin (taken about the year 1795), and one of Delgany church, co. Wicklow.

ABHBA.

BERKELEY ARMS. — Can any correspondent of " N. & Q." oblige me with instances in which the Berkeley arms appear as gu. a chev. arg., without the crosses patées (as at present borne) or any other charge ? I am aware of the instance supplied by the Roll of Henry III. Over the door which leads from the south aisle into the vestibule of the Berkeley Chapel (now the minor canons' vestry), in Bristol cathedral, are four shields, two charged with the chevron and crosses patées, two charged with a chevron only. And in one of the windows on the south side of the chancel is the

figure of a knight bearing a shield, gu. a chev. *or.* Mr. T. W. King, York Herald, once suggested to me, that this shield was originally gu. a chev. arg., but that the tincture had been changed at its restoration. J. WOODWARD.
New Shoreham.

CUSHA: CUISHEAG.—In the *Transactions of the Kilkenny Archæological Society*, vol. i. 375, *first* series, I find it stated that the Hindùs of the present day regard the *cusha* grass as sacred, and use it in their lustrations; and that an Irish native grass called *cuisheag* was once used for similar purposes. What are the botanical names of the plants referred to. AIKEN IRVINE.
Kilbride, Bray.

DALLAS, ETC. — In the Decrees of a Provincial Synod, held at Ardpatrick, near Louth, in 1678, I find the following entry : —

" 7. Decernimus, ut nullus Sacerdos adoptet, aut acceptet alumnos, vulgo *Dallas*, directe vel indirecte, per se vel per alium, et qui hoc decretum transgressus fuerit, careat beneficio et officio ad arbitrium ordinarii."

In a letter of Dr. O. Plunket to the Internunzio at Brussels, which followed the transmission of the Decrees of this Synod, the word *Dallas* is thus explained : —

" Some wicked priests becoming *nutritors* [fosterers], took to their care the children of Protestants, that thus they themselves might be defended against their ecclesiastical superiors; these children were called *Dallas*." *—
Moran's *Life of Plunket*, p. 136.

Where can I get any further information respecting these pupils. What is the origin of the word ?

Before closing this query, may I express my thanks to EIRIONNACH for calling attention to a former query of mine as to the words *Arrha*, *Vrrhusc*, and *Esane*, which still remain a puzzle to me; as none of the solutions, either forwarded me directly or through " N. & Q.," are satisfactory. (See 3rd S. vi. 205, 275, 482.)
AIKEN IRVINE.
Kilbride, Bray.

"A DESCRIPTION OF LOVE," ETC. — Can any of your correspondents favour me with the dates of the first, third, fourth, and seventh editions of this once popular and interesting little volume ? The second edition was printed in 1620. A very fine copy of the sixth, unnoticed by Lowndes, is in my possession : " Printed by M[iles] F[lesher] Francis Coules, at the vpper end of the Old Baily, neere Newgate, 1619," 8vo, thirty leaves, unnumbered, not including title. It came into my hands accidentally, bound up with two works of no value. The ninth edition, presumed to be the latest, appeared in 1638, and sold at Heber's sale for 3*l*. 1*s*. W. CAREW HAZLITT.

[* May not *Dallas* be a misprint for *Daltas?* According to O'Reilly (*Irish-English Dictionary*) a " Dalta is a foster child, a pet, a disciple, a ward."—ED.]

SIR FRANCIS DRAKE.—A year or two ago, either in a modern book of biographies or in a recent review, I saw a statement that Admiral Sir Francis Drake, though at the time of the Armada a resident in the west country, was of a Yorkshire family, who had migrated thence to take part in the cloth manufactures, of which the western counties had then a monopoly.

Can any reader of " N. &. Q." refer me to this biography or review. T. S. B. E.

"DU PLESSIS'S MEMOIRS," ETC.—Who was the author of two small volumes, entitled *Du Plessis's Memoirs; or, Variety of Adventures, &c.*, Dublin, 1757? The preface begins with these words : —

" The following Memoirs were originally wrote at the Request, and for the private amusement of a Gentleman of the Kingdom of Ireland, an intimate Friend of the Author's, but never intended for Publication."
ABHBA.

" FINE ROMAN HAND." — What is the origin and precise meaning of this phrase ? It is thus used in a review of certain *cause célèbre* in *The Saturday Review*, vol. xviii. p. 765 :—

" But whether the idea of the . . . . episode was a real inspiration of ——'s, or an *ex post facto* thought due to *the fine Roman hand* of —— ——, can never be clearly decided till —— determines on explaining to the public what as yet he has chosen to leave unexplained."
Y. X.

FLEUR-DE-LYS. — The old arms of France were, Azure sémé de lys, and were changed by Charles VI. (what year?) to azure, three fleur-de-lys, or, two and one.

Edward III. first quartered the French arms with the English, giving the precedence to the former.

I want to know if the first and fourth quarter of the English shield was changed at the same time, and if not, when ? JOHN DAVIDSON.

FOXES OR SHEAVES ?—Who first suggested the substitution of *sheaves* for *foxes* in Judges xv. 4 ? Mr. Dawson, in his *Illustrations of some remarkable Events recorded in the Old Testament*, p. 210, London, 1861, 8vo, refers to a scarce treatise, intituled, *Dissertation sur l'Anesse de Balaam, les Renards de Samson*, &c., and states that

" if we admit that instead of *shuâlim* we ought to read *sheâlim*—שעלים, instead of שועלים, the ו in the latter word having been inserted through the inadvertency of the transcriber — the narrative becomes perfectly natural and credible."

He evidently considers that the omission of the ו converts the Hebrew equivalent for *foxes* into that for *sheaves* (p. 209). Our translators have not made that distinction. If there be an error of the kind supposed in the original text, it would, I presume, be in the insertion of שעלים or שועלים,

for some form of the root אלם. Has any such form been proposed, and if so on what authority?

JOSEPH RIX, M.D.

St. Neot's.

"FROM OXFORD TO ROME." — Can any of your correspondents inform me who is the author of a work, whose third edition appeared in '47, entitled *From Oxford to Rome?* [*] Also who were the originals of the characters, particularly (1) Eustace A.; (2) His Friend, the distinguished Fellow;" (3) Dr. L. and Mr. Mac N.; (4) Mr. F.?

F. W.

HERALDIC QUERY. — On some of the thalers of Rudolph II. of Germany, the third quarter of the shield contains three leopards' heads caboshed, two and one. Are these the arms of Dalmatia? The coin bears the date 1578, and the legend says "Archduke of Austria, Duke of Burgundy, Margrave of Moravia." Dalmatia, quartered with Croatia, Rascieu, and Albania, makes the fourth inescutcheon in the arms of Venice.

JOHN DAVIDSON.

HERALDRY ACCESSORY TO EMINENCE.—In Taylor's *Modern British Plutarch*, the following extraordinary incident is related of John Scott, afterwards Lord Eldon: —

"While a barrister on the Northern Circuit, I was counsel in a cause, the fate of which depended on our being able to make out who was the founder of an ancient chapel in the neighbourhood. I went to view it. There was nothing to be observed which gave any indication of its date or history; however, I observed that the Ten Commandments were written on some old plaster, which, from its position, I conjectured might cover an arch. Acting on this, I bribed the clerk with five shillings to allow me to chip away a part of the plaster, and after two or three attempts I found the keystone of an arch, on which were engraved the arms of an ancestor of one of the parties in the law case. This evidence decided the cause, and I ever afterwards had reason to remember with some satisfaction my having on that occasion broken the Ten Commandments."

It would be interesting to know the chapel in question and the family concerned.

GEORGE VICKERS.

Shimpling, Bury St. Edmunds.

THE IMMORTALITY OF THE BRUTE CREATION.— To what extent has this opinion been held amongst naturalists and really scientific men? A few not very distinguished *divines* of the last century asserted that animals had souls, and were immortal.

JOSEPHUS.

NOSSELLS. — In looking over some churchwardens' accounts for the eighteenth century, I made note of the following entries: —

"1736. To mending *nossells* for Hirst, 6d.
"1738. To 2 *nostles* for Hearst, 6d."

[* By Miss Harris of Windsor. In the *Gent.'s Mag.* for August, 1852, p. 213, it is stated that she died on June 2⁴, 1852.—E⁵.]

Can any one inform me what part of a hearse is meant by the term *nossells* or *nostles?*

H. FISHWICK.

REV. GEORGE RYE'S SERMON.—

"The snake, unless soothed by soft words, shall deceive the leathern eagle.

"The sea god's dog shall tear the lion, who, burnt alive with unkindled fire, shall revive, losing nothing but his mane.

"If there be rain enough, and not too many weeds; not so much frost or hail as to hurt the young ears; and the birds of the air and the beasts of the field do thee no hurt, thou wilt have nothing to fear but the locusts."—*A Sermon preached at St. Martin's Church, Oxford*, by George Rye, B.D., Fellow of Oriel College, on the 8th day of January, 17¹³/₁₄.

The sermon is on prophecy. The first two are given as examples of what heathen priests did to puzzle the learned; the third to show how they imposed upon the simple.

Can any reader of "N. & Q." tell me whence they are taken. The third looks as if invented for the occasion, as even a farmer of the last century would hardly have been imposed upon by it, unless put into ornate language.   E. F.

SHORT SERMONS. — Can you decide a question as to the paternity of this anecdote: —

"Mr. Canning was once asked by an English clergyman how he liked the sermon he had preached before him. 'Why, it was a short sermon,' quoth Canning. 'Oh, yes,' said the preacher; 'you know I avoid being tedious.' 'Ah! but,' replied Canning, 'you *were* tedious.'

It has been attributed to Mr. Hookham Frere, the friend of Mr. Canning; but claimed for Coleridge and Rogers.   ALIQUIS.

TOAD IN STONE.—I have cut the enclosed paragraph from the *Leeds Mercury* of April 8. Statements of this kind are common enough; they seldom, however, are made in such a circumstantial manner. Will not some north-country correspondent of "N. & Q." investigate the matter, and send you the results of his inquiries for publication: —

"AN EXTRAORDINARY TOAD.—During the excavations which are being carried out under the superintendence of Mr. James Yeal, of Dyke House Quay, in connection with the Hartlepool Water Works, the workmen yesterday morning found a toad, embedded in a block of magnesian limestone, at a depth of twenty-five feet from the surface of the earth, and eight feet from any spring-water vein. The block of stone had been cut by a wedge, and was being reduced by workmen, when a pick split open the cavity in which the toad had been incarcerated. The cavity was no larger than its body, and presented the appearance of being a cast of it. The toad's eyes shone with unusual brilliancy, and it was full of vivacity on its liberation. It appeared when first discovered desirous to perform the process of respiration, but evidently experienced some difficulty; and the only sign of success consisted of a 'barking' noise, which it continues invariably to make and present on being touched. The toad is in the possession of Mr. S. Horner, the President of the Natural History Society, and continues in as lively a state as when found. On a minute examination, its mouth is found to be completely closed, and the barking noise it makes proceeds from its nostrils. The claws of its fore feet are turned inwards, and its hind ones are of extraordinary length, and unlike the present English toad. The Rev. R. Taylor, incumbent of St. Hilda's Church, Hartlepool, who is an eminent local geologist, gives it as his opinion that the animal must be at least 6,000 years old. The wonderful toad is to be placed in its primary habitation, and will be added to the collection in the Hartlepool Museum. The toad when first released was of a pale colour, and not readily distinguished from the stone; but shortly after its colour grew darker, until it became a fine olive brown."—*Correspondent.*

K. P. D. E.

"ULRICH MOLITOR DE CONSTANTIA." — Should any of your readers possess early copies of the *De Lamiis et Pythonicis Mulieribus Dialogus*, they would confer a great favour on the writer either by affording him an opportunity of examining them, or by forwarding minute descriptions of them to the care of the editor of " N. & Q."

A. C.

DEATH OF WACE.—It is generally believed that Wace, the Anglo-Norman poet, of the twelfth century, born in the Isle of Jersey, died in England in the year 1184. Could any of your numerous readers give me positive information on the fact? It would be rendering a service to history, and to his admirers. The time of his birth is not positively known. Information on that point would be considered a favour.

OMEGA.

Queries with Answers.

VALENTINE BROWNE. — Where can I obtain any information respecting Sir Valentine Browne, of Croft in Lincolnshire, of whom mention is made in Collins's *Peerage* (1812, vol. vii. p. 232) as having married Elizabeth, the eldest daughter of Sir John Monson, who died in 1593?

What relation was this Sir Valentine to Master Valuntyne Browne, who, as we read in Machyn's *Diary*, p. 280, married a niece of Lord Keeper Bacon's in 1562?

Had this Master Valuntyne Browne ever been married before?

Who was the Valentine Brown, Esq., that is spoken of in Collins (vol. iv. p. 394) as being one the Commissioners for the Management of the Crown Lands in Ireland in the year 1554?

MELETES.

[Valentine Browne, Esq., noticed in Collins (iv. 394) as one of Queen Mary's commissioners in Ireland died on Feb. 8, 1567. He was the father of "Master Valuntyne Browne" alluded to in Machyn's *Diary*, p. 280, who was a privy counsellor to Queen Elizabeth. The latter married first Alice, daughter of Robert Alexander of London; and secondly, Thomasine, daughter of —— Bacon of Northall, co. Middlesex (Harl. MS. 1550, 131b.) By his

first wife he had Valentine Browne, who married Elizabeth, daughter of Sir John Monson of Carlton, co Lincoln. (Cf. Harl. MS. 1550, 131b, and the inscription on his monument in Croft church in Saunders's *History of Lincolnshire*, ii. 141.) The best account of the Browne family of Croft will be found in Lodge's *Peerage* by Archdall, edit. 1789, vii. 51-58; but the writer does not appear to have consulted the short pedigree of the family in the Harl. MSS.

The following Order of Council, describing the costume of a page to Sir Valentine Browne, the privy counsellor to Queen Elizabeth, may probably amuse many of our readers. It is said to have been copied from a manuscript in the library of Thomas Astle, Esq. :—

"THESE are to praye and requier you to make psent serch within your ward & charges p'sently to macke hew & cry for a yong stripling of the age of xxii yeres, the coler of his aparell as foloweth : One doblet of yelow million fustion th'one half therof buttoned with peche color buttons, & th'other halfe laced downwards one payer of peche color hose laced with smale tawnye lace a graye hat with a copper edge rounde abonte it with a bande pcell of the same hatt a payer of watched [blue] stockings. Likewise he hath twoe clokes th'one of vessey collor garded with twoe gards of black clothe & twisted lace of carnation colour & lyned with crymson bayes & th'other is a red shipp russet colour striped about the cape & downe the fore face twisted with two rows of twisted lace russet & gold buttons afore and uppon the sholdier being of the clothe itselfe set with the said twisted lace & the buttons of russet silke & gold. This youthes name is Gilbert Edwodd & page to Sir Valentine Browne Knight who is run awaye this fowerthe day of January with theis parcells following, viz. A chaine of wyer worke golde with a button of the same & a smalle ringe of golde at it two flagging chaines of golde th'one being marked with theis letters v. & b. uppon the locke, & th'other with a little broken jewell at it, one carkanet of pearle and jasynitts thereto hangeing, a jewell like a marimade of gold enameled the tayle therof being set with diamonds the bellye of the made with a ruby & the shilde a diamond the cheine of golde whereon it hangeth is set with smale diamonds & rubyes & certeyne money in golde and white money.

	To all Constable, Bayliffs, &
	Hedboroughs, & to all other
Burghlye, Warwick,	the Quene's Officers whatsoever
Hunsdone, Howard.	to whome the same belongeth
	& apperteyneth.
	Valentine Browne."]

BISHOP HALL'S "BALM OF GILEAD," AND "THE ART OF PATIENCE." — On comparing a modern copy of Bishop Hall's *Balm of Gilead* with an old volume in my possession, entitled *The Art of Patience*, I find that they are substantially one and the same treatise under different titles. The volume appears from its typography to be of King Charles II.'s time; but as the title-page is wanting, the precise date and professed author cannot be ascertained. In one of its sections—that on "Public Calamities"—reference is made to the Great Plague and Fire of London, events which I believe did not occur before the death of Bishop Hall.

Can any of your readers, who are conversant with the old divines, inform me whether the good bishop gave his consolatory treatise to the world as the *Balm of Gilead*, or as *The Art of Patience?*

G.

[*The Art of Patience* is a reproduction of Bishop Hall's *Balm of Gilead*, with additions and alterations. The title-page of the former reads as follows : " The Art of Patience and the Balm of Gilead under all Afflictions : an Appendix to the Art of Contentment, by the Author of the *Whole Duty of Man.* London, 8vo, 1693 ; second edition, 1694." In the Preface the editor informs the reader, that " the original part of this Discourse was extracted from a foundation laid by a learned and reverend prelate [Bishop Hall's *Balm of Gilead*] upon whose basis this superstructure is erected. He, like a wise master-builder, laid the corner-stone, as a pattern for others to imitate ; and they which attain to his height of perfection shall enjoy what Christ said to his disciples : ' In their patience they shall possess their own souls.'"]

THE SOCIETY OF ANCIENT SCOTS.—Is the above society still in existence ? It was stated to have been established time out of mind, and about the year 1820 published, in half-a-crown parts, several volumes of most excellent biographies of eminent Scotchmen. SCOTUS.

[*The Lives of the Scottish Poets*, published by T. Buys of Ludgate Hill in 1821-22, and said to be " by the Society of Ancient Scots re-established A.D. 1770," made Six Parts, or three volumes. The Society was probably located in the city of London.]

CHARLES THEYER'S MSS. — What is the present place of deposit of the MSS. which belonged in the latter end of the seventeenth century to Charles Theyer, gent., of the county of Gloucester ? They are described in *Catalogi Librorum Manuscriptorum Anglice et Hibernicae*, Oxoniae, 1697, tom. ii. pt. I. pp. 198-203. A. O. V. P.

[Charles Theyer's manuscripts are now in the King's Library in the British Museum. See David Casley's *Catalogue* of this Library, 1734, 4to.]

MR. GEORGE ROGERS AND MR. WILLIAM CHIVERS.—Mr. Rogers I believe was a commissioner of the navy, and living in 1798. I shall be glad to know the date of his death. His widow married Mr. Chivers. This gentleman, I am told, having a quarrel with a labourer in his employ, struck him, upon which the man, in a fit of passion, knocked him down with his spade, and killed him, and was in consequence tried for murder and executed. I shall feel much obliged to any of your correspondents who will inform me of the date of this trial, and where I can find an account of it. CPL.

[William Chivers, Esq., of Battersea Rise, was murdered by William Duncan his gardener, on Jan. 24, 1807. The prisoner was tried at Kingston on March 20, 1807, and found guilty of murder, but we do not find

that he was executed. Consult the *Gent. Mag.* for 1807, pt. I. pp. 185, 270, *Annual Register*, xlix. 410. A monument in memory of William Chivers, Esq., was put up in the churchyard of Lee.]

Replies.

GENERAL RICHARD FORTESCUE.

(3rd S. vii. 258.)

General Richard Fortescue, was undoubtedly Col. Fortescue ; for whose prowess in the West of England, in 1646, consult Joshua Sprigge's *Anglia Rediviva* (*England's Recovery*, 4to, 1647). He was distinguished as a great Parliamentary officer ; took Pendennis Castle in Falmouth Bay, in Cornwall ; which was the last fortress which held out for the king in the west after the capture of Exeter, and the defeat of Lord Hopton at Torrington ; named also in Clarendon. His regiment is probably enumerated in the list at the end of Sprigge's work — which gives an elaborate summary of the forces of the Roundheads, subsequent to the capitulation of Truro and the fall of Oxford.

Sprigge was an Independent preacher: appears to have been attached to Sir T. Fairfax's army. His book is dedicated to Lenthal, the Speaker of the House of Commons, and is now rare. It gives all the operations of the Parliamentarians, subsequent to the Self-denying Ordinance ; Naseby fight (with plate) ; and all the events of note (after the capture of Basing-house), which took place in Devon and Cornwall. He was a native of Banbury, Oxon. A portrait of Fairfax on horseback sometimes adorns the work.

Gen. Fortescue, who was probably an ancestor of a branch of the Devon family, now seated at Castle Hill, near South Molton, must have been the first Governor of Jamaica, as that island fell into Cromwell's hands in 1656: after the check experienced by Penn and Venables at Hispaniola (for which *vide* Ludlow's *Memoirs*), where Major-Gen. Haines, his forlorn hope, and a great portion of his forces perished. The well-known motto of the family—" Forte scutum, salus ducum "—is very appropriate to the lofty name.

The estate at Halskott must have been purchased from the trustees of that unfortunate papist lord and royalist of the first water, the Marquis of Winchester, when, after the storm of Basing-house and its dismantlement, the estates were forfeited ; and, like the Marquis of Worcester at Ragland Castle, the family reduced to indigence.*

The Devon Fortescues seem to have sided with

---

* He was the fifth Marquis. The house was leaguered, and then stormed and burnt, by Cromwell and that " godly and pious man," the butcher Harrison, a Major at the time.

the Parliament. At Edghill, 1642, a Sir Faithful Fortescue went over to the king, with all his troopers, after discharging their pistols into the ground—so says Clarendon, however.

In that rare work, *Politicus sine Exemplo*, translated into German and published at Nuremberg in 1663 (12mo), there occurs the following notice of Pendennis Castle, p. 32 : —

"Nichts war mehr übrig in den Westen als das Castell *Bendennis*, welches vom Col. Fortescue belägert, sich bald ergeben."

This publication, which was a memoir of the Protector—with a bust, supporters to it, and his armorials above—contains a great number of interesting particulars of the time; with a list of his Privy Council, the members of his House of Lords, Justices of the Peace, and other officials of rank ; also the general officers who were appointed to the various districts into which the kingdom was divided. It is entitled : —

"Kurtzer Begriff der Kriegs und Staats-Handlungen seiner Hoheit Olivier Cromwels, Lord Protectors in Engel- Schott- und Ireland."

In the *Englischer Geschichts Calender* (p. 24, ed. 1698, Leipsig, J. L. Gleditsch), Aug. 16, 1646, occurs : —

"Gleng Pendennys, des Königs lezte festung in Cornwallia, verlohren."[*]

It was held by a *Killigrew* (one of the Cornish lineages, whose name implies the "Valley of Eagles") for the king, and whose pistol burst and harmed him.

Pendennis was, till of late years, a sinecure retreat or appanage for retired military officers of rank. The last was Lieut.-Col. Fenwick of my old regiment (the 34th, Cumberland), who lost a leg at the battle of Albuera, in Spain, I believe, or on the Pyrenees ; and enjoyed the pleasures of retirement, and a comfortable pension, as Governor of the Castle. Major Hovenden, who was then lieutenant in the Light Infantry Company, I well recollect as stating that he assisted to bind up his wounds.

Major Hovenden afterwards perished in the wilds of Australia, years later. After being swindled out of his property by a scoundrel attorney, he died of starvation, and was devoured by the wild dogs of the desert !   BREVIS.

THE "SIMPLE COBBLER'S" REFERENCES.
(3rd S. vii. 299.)

MASSACHUSETS asks if it be a fact, that the Irish, according to the Cobbler—

"Have a Tradition among them, That when the Devill shewed our Saviour all the kingdomes of the Earth and their glory, that he would not shew him Ireland."

[*] Possibly also recorded in the German "*Judas Maccabæus*, or, Eulogium of Sir T. Fairfax," 12mo.

I reply, No! The Cobbler is mistaken, the Irish have no such tradition. The story arose in this wise : — In 1602, after the battle of Kinsale, when Don John de Aguila had surrendered to the Lord Deputy, the Spaniard in a conference with Sir William Godolphin said that the Irish were—

"Not only weake and barbarous, but perfidious friends. Presuming," he continued, "in their promise that they would join me, I in vaine sustained the brunt of the Viceroy's Armes. I then saw these Counts (the rebels O'Donnell and O'Neill) take their stand within two miles of Kinsale, reinforced with some Companies of Spaniards, and every hour repeating their promise to join us in forcing the world—O'Donnell into Spaine, O'Neill to the furthest part of the North ; so that now I find no such Counts *in rerum natura*."

Subsequently, in allusion to the barbarous state of the country, the want of roads, the scarcity of provisions, the perpetual moisture, and the then great unhealthiness of the climate, Aguila said : —

"Surely, when Satan tried to tempt our Saviour by displaying before Him all the Kingdoms of the Earth, the wily Enemy of Mankind did not exhibit this wretched and most untempting country of Ireland."

This is the sense; though, as I quote from memory, probably not the exact words used by Aguila. They will, however, be found in the Record Office among the Irish Papers : so ably arranged, and partly calendared, by Hans Hamilton, Esq. The profanity of the saying might almost be palliated, if we take into consideration how truly fatal Ireland had been to the Spaniards. On their previous invasion at Smerwick, the garrison, after their surrender at discretion, were according to the usage of the period cruelly butchered in cold blood. Of the Invincible Armada, intended to sweep the English heretics off the earth, and burst the bonds of the Irish Roman Catholics, no less than seventeen tempest-tost ships were cast away on the coast of Ireland. All their crews, upwards of 5,000 men, were either drowned or slaughtered by the barbarous Irish. One Gallagher, more merciless than the ocean waves, killed sixty Spaniards with his axe, as the unfortunate wretches gained the shore by swimming. The rich dresses and gold buttons of the Spaniards proved irresistible temptations to the wild Irish; only a very few officers were preserved for ransom. Bacon tells the story of De Aguila in a slightly different manner, in his treatise *Of a War with Spain*, thus : —

"Aguila said, in open treaty, 'That when the Devil upon the Mount did show Christ all the Kingdoms of the Earth and the glory of them, he did not doubt that the Devil left out Ireland, and kept it for himself.'"

The discomfited Spaniard may almost be excused for saying so; but at a later period, when William III. saw the fair fields of Ulster, as he rode onwards to try the *ultima ratio regum* at the Boyne, he exclaimed: "This, truly, is a country well worth fighting for!"

WILLIAM PINKERTON.

DANIEL DEFOE THE NEWS-WRITER.

(3rd S. vii. 58, 244.)

Pursuing my investigations as to the hitherto unknown writings of Defoe, I have disinterred the following. It may be taken as supplemental to what has already appeared in "N. & Q." under his name. I must however premise a few words.

Defoe was left in the management of *Mist's Journal*, but Mr. Mist had so great a tendency to gravitate towards Jacobitism, that, about the middle of the year 1720, a separation again took place (except as to the articles on "Foreign Affairs"), and Defoe connected himself with *Applebee's Original Weekly Journal*.

As on a previous occasion, poor Mist was no sooner left to himself than he fell into trouble, but this time it ended in ruin. Omitting, for brevity, all that intervened, I quote the following from *The Post Boy* of February 14th to 16th, 1721: —

"Last Monday Mr. Mist appeared on his Recognizance at the King's Bench Bar, Westminster, to receive Judgment for some Reflections on his Majesty's Interposition on behalf of the Protestants in the Palatinate, of which he had been convicted the last Term; and the Court pronounced Judgment, as follows, viz. That he stand in the Pillory, at Charing Cross and the Royal Exchange; pay a Fine of 50*l.*; suffer three months' Imprisonment in the King's Bench, and give Security for his good Behaviour for seven years."

Editorial leading articles in the public journals of the early part of last century appeared in the humble forms of Letters Introductory, with continual changes of the subscribed initials, or fictitious signatures. On February 18th appeared the following Introductory Letter by Defoe in *Applebee's Original Weekly Journal:* —

"Sir,—It is a Rule in our Accidence, and which in Latin begins with *Felix quem faciunt*, that they are happy who take warning by other Men's Disasters: I think this is a Time of Day when this Rule stands in Need of much Application; and there are many Occasions which tell us *who*, and *who*, and *who* ought to take Notice of it.

"You publish, it seems, *Dying Speeches*, and from thence 'tis natural to preach to the Gentlemen of the PAD, that they BEWARE, or else that they provide their last Speech and Confession, and send them to your House to be ready for the Press.

"The *South Sea* Company have chosen new Directors; and the Conduct of their Predecessors, or rather the Consequences of that Conduct, stands as so many Warning Pieces, or Mementos, to bid them beware how they go on; and, as a Beacon upon a Sand, to bid them stand off, and live,—draw near, and dye; to call to them to take Care, lest they run a Ground, and are stranded, as others did before them.

"A Brother Journal Man has fallen into the Pit lately;

Humanity directs you not to insult him in his Disaster, but the contrary to an extream; but Prudence gives a Hint; *Guardez Vous, Monsieur*, take care of yourself, lest unwarily you fall into the like Snare.

"Another bold Journal Scribe writes strongly for *Freedom of Speech*, by which may be understood, he would have a Freedom for the Press to speak what it would; the Truth is, by the Liberty he takes, one would hardly think there was any Freedom deny'd, or which he could not venture upon: But I counsel you, wonderful Sir, to remember that the Press and the Pit are alike open, and stand very near together: the Press is open, that is true; and the Prison is open, that is as true; *Guardez Vous*, Mr. App; write warily, write cautiously.

"But you will say, What must a poor Printer do? Must he turn his Tale as the Weather-cock of State turns? And when the Wind blows a Whig Gale from Court, turn Whig; when it blows a High Church Gale, face about to the High Church; and in Times of the unsteady Gales, trim and look every Way,. and no Way, all at once? What must he do?

"No, no, Mr. App, be honest and be wise; be steady to yourself; but knock your Head against no Stone Walls, lest the few Brains you may have go to wreck in the Storm, and the little Money you have follow after them.

"It is the Wisdom of a Publick Writer to give no Offence to the Powers to which his Allegiance is due, or such whose Authority he is subject to; and yet no Man seems to be under the Necessity, either of Flattery or Falsehood, in any Reign, or under any Times whatever. If we look back upon all the Prosecutions and Tryals which have been against Printers, or Authors, in our Age, not in this Reign only, but also in the Reigns precedent, they have not been for the plainness of their Writing so much as the Passions, *that is to say*, the Follies of the Writers.

"*Plainness* is a Virtue in Writing, and no Author that is honest ought to go from it : But Passion, in the very same Cause, may be the height of Folly ; even a Satyr may be so couch'd in its Terms, as to give no legal Offence, and yet no Part of the Edge, or Point, be abated.

"Let him that writes Satyr, then, take care to have it sharp, but not sour ; mettled, but not raging ; *full*, but not *foul:* How many a gallant Prince has borne the Edge of the Satyr, for the Wit of it ? But remember, that all the Wit of a Satyr perishes when the Manners decay.

"But, after all, what have you Men of Scribble to do with the Times ? Or why must you dip into the Passions and Parties which agitate the People ? Leave off the Comment, and keep to the Text (*Facts*) ; when a Wretch, in contempt of God and Government, hangs himself, and robs the King of a Subject, however worthless and useless, it is a Crime no doubt ; But what have you to do with that ? Your Business is to tell us the Story, and leave the World to its relish of it their own Way ; *and the like*, of all other cases : Suppose 'tis of Rebellion, Treason, South Sea Thievery, or of any other sort of R——y, be the Story your Province; leave the Reflection to the Readers ; lay your Finger on your Mouth, and when you talk of State Affairs, *ware Pillory, ware Printer;* be wise and be wary ; you may have room enough to please your Friends, without displeasing those who have Power to resent and to punish.

"What Business have Printers to espouse Parties at their own Expense ? Make the Passions of private Men speak in Publick, and take a Liberty of Speech not supportable in itself, and which Men in Power, let them be of which Side they will, cannot bear ?

"If you are prepar'd for Martyrdom indeed, 'tis another Case ; then you may come with Vox Populi, and Vox Dei, and Vox any Body ; you know the Way that has been trod before you : But, if you will act the prudent

Part, cut no Throats but with a Feather,—shoot no poison'd Arrows: Let Wit and Waryness joyn in your Work;
and so I end my Advice to you where I began it: *Felix
quem faciunt aliena Pericula cautum.*

"Your Friend,
"SOLOMON WARYMAN."

Vox Populi Vox Dei was the title of a treasonable publication, for r n n which a young man
named Matthews had been hanged at Tyburn during the preceding year.   W. LEE.

THE IGELE SÄULE.

(3rd S. vii. 220.)

In vol. ii. part II. of Pococke's *Travels* (1745) a
fine plate of the sepulchral monument at Igel is
given at page 221. He says: —

"I could see no entrance to this monument, but the
people say there is one, which, I suppose is underground,
and that it is lined with copper adorned with figures."

In a note, he gives the following description of
the sculptures: —

"It is raised on a pedestal or basement, which is on
two plinths; the corner one being two feet deep, and the
upper three, both setting in six inches: the die of the
pedestal consists of two tier of stone and is about five
feet deep; it was adorned with reliefs, those to the east
and north are defaced; on the west side there is a loaded
car drawn by two horses with a man on the further side
of each horse; they seem to have a thyrsus in their
hands. To the north a person sits with a book in his
hand, there being another behind him; and on one side
of him, two sit at a table, and two stand to the east of it;
this also is much defaced. In the die of the pedestal to
the east and west, the reliefs are almost entirely defaced,
and much ruined to the south; but I could discern a
person sitting, with one standing on each side, that to the
east holding the person who sits by the hand. In the
frieze to the west are eight persons in procession; to the
east is a person sitting and a boy standing at a round
table, another likewise at a table, and two persons standing. The frieze to the south is divided into two parts by
three pilasters; in the middle compartment one sits at a
table, and two at each end; to the west there is a table
and other utensils, and two persons standing; to the east
one as at a stove and two as walking off towards the
middle. To the east a woman sits near a bed, on which
there is a man, a person standing at the feet of the bed;
to the west there is a man in a car drawn by beasts,
which seem to have horns; to the south are two persons,
and there was a third in the middle probably sitting. In
the pediments the reliefs are all defaced, except to the
south, in which there are three figures; the middle one,
which is naked, seemed to resemble Hercules."

JOHN DAVIDSON.

Mr. WOODWARD will find in *Ersch und Grüber's
Allgemeine Encyclopädie der Wissenschaften und
Künste*, art. "Igel," a long list of works containing
accounts, in some cases accompanied by plates, of
The Igeler Säule. The most accessible is perhaps
the *Mém. de l'Inst. Nat. des Sciences et Arts; Litt.
et Beaux Arts*, vol. ii. p. 549. (Paris, Fructidor

An. vii.) Besides this I would refer him to Neu-
rohr's *Abbild. des röm. Monuments zu Igel* (Trier,
1826), and also to Osterwald's *Das röm. Denkmal
in Igel und seine Bilderwerke* (Coblenz, 1829.)
RICHARD B. PROSSER.
25, Southampton Buildings, W.C.

COLD HARBOUR, ORIGIN OF THE NAME.

(1st and 2nd S. *passim*; 3rd S. vii. 253, 302. Various in England, 2nd S. vii. 143, 200, 317, 357.)

The bibliography of this *quæstio vexata* is as
follows: —

"Hartshorne's *Salopia Antiqua*; or, An Enquiry from
Personal Survey into the Druidical, Military, and other
early Remains in Shropshire and the North Welsh Borders; with Observations upon the names of Places, and
a Glossary of Words used in the County of Salop, 1841.
pp. 253—258.—*Archæologia*, vol. xxxiii. on the Designation of "Cold Harbour." By Capt. W. H. Smyth, R.N.,
F.R.S.

I shall quote a paragraph from the *Archæologia*,
in illustration of the derivation referred to in
"N. & Q." (3rd S. vii. 303) by LORD LYTTELTON:

"Now it is not a little remarkable that, though these
places are found recurring along the line of the Chilterns,
the Cotswolds, and other ridges, yet they predominate on
or near the old Roman roads; sometimes where there is a
rise in the ground, and often in the very angle where a
turn in the direction becomes necessary, not only in the
occasional deviations from the main *viaria*, but also in
those which were made for forming *diverticulæ*, or cross
communications. May not these ascents and winding
turns therefore have been named after the significant tor-
tuosities of the *coluber?*" &c., p. 126.

An enumeration of Cold Harbours on or near
Roman roads is given in *Salopia Antiqua*, pp. 255-
258.   BIBLIOTHECAR. CHETHAM.

In 1860, in communicating to "N. & Q." (2nd
S. ix. 139, 441) a proposed derivation of this word,
I noticed the greater frequency of its occurrence in
the south-eastern counties of England, where the
iron manufacture was formerly carried on to a
very large extent, in which charcoal was the fuel
employed.

Other names of places there also have reference
to the same industry, such as "Hammer Posts"
and "Hammer Ponds." "Collier Farm" is of
frequent occurrence. There is a "Charcoal Lane"
and "Colmonger Farm," all evidently connected
with the same manufacture.

Cold Harbour, or as sometimes written, Cold
Harborough, is a corruption from Coaled-arberye,
that is, charcoal.

"Arbery" is an old English word for wood-
fuel, which is preserved in the following passage
from Maundeville's *Travels*, cited by Mr. Halliwell
in his *Dictionary of Archaic Words:*

"In that contree is but lytille *arbery*, ne trees that
beren fruite, ne othere. Thei ly3n in tents, and thei
brennen the dong of bestes for defaute of wood."

The word therefore means wood-fuel turned
into coal; in modern phrase, charcoal. It was
applied to places where charcoal was made, or
where it was sold, or to the road leading thereto.

Formerly the word coal or cole simply meant
charred wood, and not the mineral now known by
that name.

Thus Chaucer, in the Prologue of the "Channon Yeman's Tale," when he speaks of —

　　"Dyvers fuyres maad of woode and cole,"

meant charcoal, as is evident from a few lines
further down, where he says the Channon —

　　"Out of his bosom took a *bechen* cole."

And again —

　　"And whan that the channones *bechen cole*
　　Was brent."

This derivation satisfactorily explains how
"Coldharbour" can be found in the middle of a
wood," and "Kalterherberg," near Aix-la-Chapelle is "situated in the middle of the forest of
the Eifel."

In England, the places so named lie chiefly in
a warm situation.

The Coldharbour mentioned in Upper Thames
Street, in Dowgate Ward, was probably built
upon the site of a charcoal maker's yard, and the
satirical allusions to it probably arose from the
warmth of the charcoal fires attracting those
houseless vagrants who had no settled lodgings.

　　　　　　　　　　　　　　　　　C. T.

GAELIC GRAMMAR.

(3rd S. vii. 75, 144, 308.)

W: Eassie's information on Gælic Grammars
(p. 308) is instructive, and must be interesting to
students and proficients in the Celtic language.
Some of his statements, however, challenge comment, and though his list of printed Grammars is
cop ous, it is not exhaustive, and therefore I am
led i to hope that space may be afforded to the
explanatory and the supplementary matter which
I now supply.

In reply to Highlander's queries (p. 75), I
confined myself to giving the information he had
sought, mentioning (p. 144) that "the ablest
work in Gaelic Grammar, written by a native of
North Britain, is unquestionably that by Alexander Stewart," and I added—

"As the Highland Gaelic is essentially the same as the
Irish, though it branched off as early as the sixth century, it may please Highlander to be informed that
the best grammar of the Irish—the best preserved, most
cultivated and most polished dialect of the Gael—is *A
Grammar of the Irish Language* by the late eminent Irish
scholar, Dr. John O'Donovan."

W. Eassie suggests, that Highlander might
perhaps also consult with profit Shaw's *Analysis
of the Gaelic Language*. Of this work, thus recommended, Stewart entertained no favourable
opinion. In his introduction to the second edition of his *Grammar* (1811, p. xiii), he refers to
it in these not complimentary terms: "I know
but one publication professedly of Gaelic Grammar
written by a Scotsman (Shaw). I have consulted
it also, but in this quarter I have no obligations
to acknowledge." And of it O'Donovan, in the
introduction to his *Grammar* (p. lvii.), says, "This
Grammar is confined to the Erse or Gaelic of
Scotland, and its merits are very questionable."
Irrespective of my own convictions, these authorities are my justification for not recommending
Shaw's work. It is evident that some of the
books classified by W. Eassie as grammars have
not been examined by him. He names as the
first grammar Kearney's *Alphabeticum Hibernicum*,
1571. This work is not a grammar. It is a small
volume of 54 pages, all Irish, containing as the
title-page announces, an Irish Alphabet and
Catechism : —

"I. An Exposition of the Christian Doctrine, and Articles of Faith, &c., translated by John O'Kearnaigh,
printed in Irish in Dublin, at the expense of Mr. John
Uiser (Usher), Alderman, at the head of the bridge on
the 20 June, 1571."

The Irish Alphabet and remarks on the powers
and modifications of the letters occupy five pages.
Dr. O'Donovan, or rather the author from whom
without acknowledgment he borrowed the title,
is responsible for the erroneous description. In
his *Grammar* (p. lv.), O'Donovan says, "The only
known copy of this rare book is preserved in the
Bodleian Library, Oxford." This is also a mistake ;
there is a second copy in excellent preservation, in
the British Museum, press mark C. 33, A. 1. I
know of no grammar called Donlevy's *Irish Language*, 1742, but am aware of Donlevey's *Irish-
English Catechism* published at Paris in that year,
to which is appended brief instructions for reading
the Irish Language, entitled "The Elements of
the Irish Language." This treats of Orthography
only, as O'Donovan correctly remarks (p. lvii.)
M'Eligott, though he compiled an Irish Grammar,
still extant in manuscript, never had it published.
And his *Observations on the Gaelic Language* is
merely a contribution to the Transactions of the
Gaelic Society of Dublin in 1808. O'Daly's
valuable little tract has no pretensions to be
classed as a grammar. The following grammars
and instructions for reading Irish, if known to
Mr. Eassie, have been unaccountably omitted :
Theobald Stapleton's *Catechism*, to which is subjoined in Irish and Latin, *Modus perutilis legendi
linguam Hibernicam*, 4to, Louvain, 1639. There
is a copy in the Library of Trinity College, Dublin, and in the British Museum, of Godfrey Daniel's

Church Catechism with the Elements of the Irish Language, 1680. John O'Connell's *True Wisdom*, by Paul Segnary, to which is prefixed *Short Instructions for reading Irish*, Cork, 1813. James Scurry's *Introduction to the Irish Language*, Waterford, 1820; Barron's *Irish Primer*, 1833; H. J. M. Mason's *Irish Grammar*, 1834, and a second edition has since appeared; Owen Connellan's *Irish Grammar*, 1842. The Rev. Mr. Nangle, of Achill, has brought out a second edition of Neilson's *Irish Grammar*, with some judicious additions and corrections. Bourke's *College Irish Grammar* has also reached a second edition; and I may worthily close the list with the *Irish Grammar* of the very learned linguist and accomplished Irish Scholar, Martin A. O'Brennan, LL.D. To none, however, of these native writers is the language and literature of the Gael more deeply indebted than to J. C. Zeuss, whose *Grammatica Celtica* is a profound, unique, and invaluable scholastic tribute to the structure and old extant treasures of the Celtic. His materials he has drawn from the ancient records of the Irish, dating from the seventh century, still preserved in Continental libraries and of the dialects of Britain, Wales, Cornwall, Armorica, and the literary remains of Ancient Gaul. His *Celtic Grammar*, written in Latin, was printed in two large octavo volumes, comprising 1229 pages, Lipsiæ, 1853.

Though my notes of Irish printed books are the accumulations of the gleanings of many years, I think some, if not many, elementary treatises on the Irish language may have escaped my notice, but — and I hope I am not out of Court in saying so — I am glad to know that there is a gentleman in the field, Mr. John Power, whose zeal, intelligence, and persevering research promise a *Bibliotheca Hibernica* which, supplementing Harrison and Nicholson, will index those literary treasures which Irishmen have produced, or their country or their deeds have suggested, at home and abroad, "from the introduction of printing to 1860."

JOHN EUGENE O'CAVANAGH.

GOODRICH FAMILY (3rd S. vii. 134, 203.)—With reference to a paragraph taken from the *Stamford Mercury* of February 24th, asking for information respecting the family of Goodrich, of Lincolnshire, anterior to 1700, including that of Thomas Goodrich, Bishop of Ely, who died in 1574, and who was a native of East Kirkby, near Spilsby, a parishioner of mine, Francis Goodrich, has asked me to write to you.

His family have been resident at Wrangle since the early part of the sixteenth century, where they still have a small property, though this unfortunately (for tracing descent) only came into their possession about thirty years ago. They were tenant farmers for a very long period on a different estate in that parish.

None of them now reside at Kirkby, but several of the name live in the neighbouring places; our Francis Goodrich is considered apparently the head of the family. He is seventy-eight years old, and has always heard it as a tradition that the Bishop of Ely, at the time of the Reformation, belonged to it.

He has asked me to find out anything I could about his ancestor at various times. I have no doubt that a careful examination of the tombstones of Wrangle churchyard, and the parish register, would materially assist any one desirous of searching into the family records.

W. S. THOMASON.

An account of an American family of this name will be found in Goodwin's *Genealogical Notes, or Contributions to the Family History of some of the First Settlers of Connecticut and Massachusetts*, Hartford, 1856. See also the eighteen volumes of the *New England Historical and Genealogical Register*, published in Boston, Mass. S. W. P.

UNACKNOWLEDGED REPUBLICATION (3rd S. vi. 284.)—My attention having just been called to a paragraph in the page above-named, headed "Unacknowledged Republication," I find that the writer, after mentioning a work of mine published more than twenty years ago, under the title of *Aphorisms and Reflections, &c.*, says, in reference to the one entitled *Sunshine and Shadows, or Sketches of Thought, Philosophic and Religious*:—

"I had scarcely opened this volume, when I discovered that it was nothing more than a republication of the *Aphorisms and Reflections*, slightly re-arranged and very much abridged."

On which I have thus much to say:—That a very considerable proportion of the work so impeached, including the pieces which I consider the most elaborate, is entirely new; that the portions of the *Aphorisms* incorporated into it are either more or less modified, or introduced in connexions that give them a new significance; and lastly, that the work was intended to be but a companion volume to another, since published, entitled *Essays of a Recluse; or Traces of Thought, Literature, and Fancy;* in which, if your correspondent should ever honour it with an inspection, he will find a prefatory note, informing him that "both together include all that the author cares to retain of whatever he has hitherto published."

I leave you and your readers to judge whether the "laws of literary," or other "ethics," have been most infringed; by me or by a person who could pronounce, so categorically, on the contents of a book which he had scarcely opened.

W. B. CLULOW.

OLD SAYING ABOUT A PERSON WASTING HIS SUBSTANCE (3rd S. vii. 219, 290.)—I have heard another saying with a similar import to that named by your correspondent. A person going back in the world is said to "Make his pack into fardel, and the fardel into nout" [nothing]. Fardel, it scarcely need be added, is a small pack.

                                   WM. DOBSON.

Preston.

THE DODRALIS POTIO (3rd S. vii. 148, 208, 286.) I was not aware that the Latin distich was required to be translated by a distich in English. The lines of K. have the defect of changing the order of the ingredients: it is preserved in the following attempt:—

    " Dodra I'm called, of nine things made, without a fault, Broth, water, honey, wine, bread, pepper, herbs, oil, salt."

                                   F. C. H.

WESTON (3rd S. vii. 224.) — Sir John Rogers of Bryanstone, in the county of Dorset, who died in 1565, married Katrine the daughter of Sir Richard Weston. (See Symonds's *Diary*, published by the Camden Society, p. 125.)

Who was this Sir Richard Weston? His arms, as given by Symonds, were ermine, on a chief [vert] five bezants. These arms are altogether different from those of Sir Richard Weston, brother of the Lord Prior, as described by W. I presume, therefore, that he did not belong to the same family.   P. S. C.

REMARKABLE AS TO BISHOPS' WIDOWS (3rd S. vii. 273.)—The Canon Law calls a bishop "Maritus Ecclesiæ;" and we read elsewhere "as if they were knit in nuptial bands of love and care for their diocess." Yet it is of note, that a bishop's widow "has a right to exhibit the arms of the see;" and that "she has a right to emblazon all that will honour her deceased husband." Hence, the bishop appears (*quasi*) alienated from his wife for church purposes; and it seems as if, during life, in this case, the "one flesh" was regarded as superseded, and that, contra, after death of the bishop, there was a reflex honour upon his widow, and a right of exhibiting and emblazoning. Some explanation may perhaps be considered to lie in the episcopal and baronial properties being peculiar to a bishop as such.

It is said, as a principle, "fulget radiis mariti," but this (as to bishops) must be a particular exception if an apparently appropriate place according to position is not assigned. Importance being attached in consequence of marriage, precedence would be otherwise imagined as consecutive.

We are informed that bishops, "by virtue of baronies annexed to their bishopricks, always had place in the Lords' House of Parliament, as Barons by succession." (Segar, *On Honour*, lib. iv. cap. 13.)

The baron, "imprimis," has been deemed "quasi robur belli." Of the episcopal one we read " ex

solâ liberalitate Regum," and "a Regibus in feudum tenetur."

A possibility of being "aliened or entailed," and of honour passing is, I believe, held in point of baronial circumstance; which may not apply to the "tenure of barons by succession."   B.

PRECEDENCE OF BISHOPS' WIVES (3rd S. vii. 294.) — There is a considerable similarity to the position of Bishop's wives in that of the wives of the judges in the Scottish Court of Session. I extract the following paragraph from Sir Walter Scott's note to chap. ii. of *Redgauntlet*:—

    "The Scottish judges are distinguished by the title of 'lord' prefixed to their own temporal designation. As the ladies of these official dignitaries do not bear any share in their husbands' honours, they are distinguished only by their lords' family name. They were not always contented with this species of Salique law, which certainly is somewhat inconsistent; but their pretensions to title are said to have been long since repelled by James V., the sovereign who founded the College of Justice. 'I,' said he, 'made the carles lords, but who the devil made the carlins ladies?'"

The title of "lord" thus assumed is sometimes taken from the name of the judge's property, and sometimes is prefixed to his ordinary surname. Of the present thirteen judges *nine* are designated from properties, and the rest from surnames. As the ladies in all cases retain the surname of their husbands, some inconvenience, it is understood, has occasionally been felt when their lordships travel with their wives on the continent, and the husband has found it prudent to drop the titular appellation *pro tempore*, the announcement of "Lord A. and Mrs. B." giving occasion to uncomplimentary conjectures. It was at one time proposed that the title of "lord" should be dropt and "judge," or "Mr. Justice," adopted in lieu of it; but, independently of the objection to the change of a national distinction, the proposal was made at the period of the French Revolution, and was of course characterised in the stereotyped cant of the day as part of a conspiracy against social order.   J. R. B.

THE CONTINUANCE OF VALENTINES (3rd S. vii. 290.) — The drawing of names from a box would seem to savour more of heathenism than Christianity. If we are to associate the name of Valentine with Feb. 14, it should be for *some recognition of a saint and martyr* (cir. 270 A.D.) in the reign of Claudius — "He was eminently distinguished for his love and charity." It appears that "the pastors of the early Christian Church" were anxious to substitute saints for women in order to commemoration.

As "the earliest known poetical Valentines were written by Charles, Duke of Orleans, taken prisoner at the battle of Agincourt, October 25, 1415," which are "in the library of the British Museum," we have a trace of 450 years.

In our own day, the style and character have been rather altered; clearly there has been a great amount of abuse, likewise a change of fashion —

> " Some Valentines should alter'd be
> Or change their names to flippancy."
>
> B.

DUKE OF MARLBOROUGH: MALPLAQUET (3rd S. vii. 261.) — It is not generally known, that John Churchill, the great Duke of Marlborough, and husband of the celebrated Sarah Jennings, paid a visit to Heidelberg, April 20, 1705, after visiting the Landgrave of Hesse at Schlangenbad the day before. He only passed the afternoon there, going next day to visit the Prince Lewis of Baden, his ally, at Rastadt. Tradition says he put up at the old Hôtel Ritta, built in 1572 by a French Huguenot, and named after the old Pretender, Chevalier St. George: others think at the Hirsch, in the Markt-Platz (north-east corner, now Schützendorf, the Tapezierer), while at Heidelberg. After a conference with the Prince of Baden, about reinforcements and other military matters, on the 22nd, after visiting the lines of Biehl and Stolhoffen, he went to Mannheim; and thence to Triers, where the English and Dutch forces were encamped near Igel, on the Moselle—where the famous Roman obelisk is still to be seen.

With respect to Malplaquet battle (Aug. 13, 1709), and the frivolous *chanson* or *réfrain* about his grace's imaginary death there, I will only remark, that the French endeavoured to conceal their check, and affected not to have been beaten; although, in spite of P. Daniel's garbled statement, their loss in officers alone was about 540 killed, 1068 wounded, and 310 made prisoners; and yet they made out their casualties of private soldiers, very modestly, as not exceeding 1500!

The victorious Duke of Marlborough had, nevertheless, two horses killed under him, but escaped unhurt. Prince Eugene was slightly touched on the head, and the Duke of Argyle had shots through his clothes and periwig. How was it that no *chansonnier badin*, among the allies did not substitute an *oraison funèbre* for Villars, with his shot in the knee, and his ten general officers and three brigadiers, who perished at the wood of Taisnières that bloody day ?—or, as the Malplaquet medal, " Gallis ad Taisnière devictis," has it.

> BREVIS.

PRINCE FRANCIS RHODOCANAKIS (3rd S. vii. 267.)—Qu. Who was Constantine Rhodocanacides, who collected the "Breves Sententiæ Græcæ, Latinè explicatæ," in which all the Greek primitives are in a particular manner comprehended under twenty heads or chapters; and which was published at the end of Schrevelius's *Greek Lexicon*, and also at the end of the *Clavis Græcæ Linguæ* of Eilardus Lubinus, published at Leyden by F. Heger, with Elzevir type, in 1644? Was he also of the " Isle de Chio"?

> BREVIS.

QUOTATIONS WANTED (3rd S. vii. 280.) —

> " The sun slept on his clouds, forgetful of the voice of the morning."

This is an incorrect quotation from Ossian's address to the sun, which occurs in the poem of Carthon. The exact words in Macpherson's *Ossian* are these : —

> " Thou shalt sleep in thy clouds, careless of the voice of the morning."

I possess an imperfect copy of an old work in small 4to size, printed by Geo. Smart at Wolverhampton in 1769, entitled *Poems on several Occasions.*" They are published anonymously, but the author was the Rev. Thomas Moss. The opening poem is the " Beggar," so well known afterwards as the "Beggar's Petition." In this work occurs the " Address of Ossian to the Sun," attempted in blank verse, and, as I have always considered, very happily accomplished. I extract that portion which includes the above quotation : —

> " But thou perchance like me art for a season,
> And time shall put a period to thy years :
> *Thou in thy clouds perhaps shalt one day sleep*
> *Careless for ever of the morn's sweet voice;*
> Exult then, O thou sun ! in youthful strength.
> Age is unlovely, desolate and dark ;
> 'Tis like the feeble splendour of the moon
> That shines through broken clouds, when rising mist
> Enwraps the hills, and blots them from the sight,
> When the North blast is howling on the plain,
> When in his journey shrinks the traveller,
> Weary and half-way distant from his home."

And being upon Ossian, I may append a note relative to his poems. The late Dr. Macdonald, Bishop of Kingston in Upper Canada, told a friend of mine, that Mrs. Fraser of Culbokie possessed MS. copies of several of Ossian's poems long before Macpherson's work appeared. Moreover, that this lady lent the MSS. to Macpherson, but never had them returned.

> F. C. H.

> " Sometimes
> The young forgot the lessons they had learnt,
> And loved where they should hate—like thee, Imelda ! "
>
> From *Italy*, a poem by Samuel Rogers.

The story of Imelda is beautifully told by Mrs. Hemans in her *Records of Woman.* Also *vide* Sismondi's *Histoire des Republiques Italiennes*, vol. iii. p. 443.

> JOHN PAVIN PHILLIPS.

Haverfordwest.

JUDAS OVERTURNING THE SALT-CELLAR (3rd S. vii. 283.)—In the celebrated picture of the Last Supper by Leonardo da Vinci, Judas is represented as overturning the salt-cellar; but not " as he stretches out his hand to receive the sop." The time chosen for the scene represented is when our Blessed Saviour startled his Apostles with the

alarming declaration that one of them would betray him. Surprise, grief, and consternation are marvellously depicted on the countenances, and in the attitudes of the Apostles. Judas wishing to appear as innocent as the rest, lifts up his left hand as in astonishment; while, as he clutches the money-bag with his right, he upsets the salt, which falls away from him. At the same moment he is supposed to be saying what St. Matthew records (xxvi. 25),—" Is it I, Rabbi ? " To which our Saviour answers: " Thou hast said it." The incident of our Lord reaching to him the bread dipped (St. John xiii. 26), occurred just after, in answer to the enquiry which St. John made at the suggestion of St. Peter: " Lord, who is it ? " (v. 25.) But in the picture before us, our Blessed Saviour is neither dipping the morsel, nor giving it to Judas; but has both his hands upon the table, and his face cast down, expressive of acute sorrow.
　　　　　　　　　　　　　　F. C. H.

SNAIL-EATING (3rd S. vi. 268, 296.) — A correspondent has been pleased to demolish the story of the poor widow of the Irish gravel-digger at Blackheath, who fed her stout and ruddy brood on a diet of which snails formed the only animal portion, by asserting that snails would melt away on the application of salt " like ice before a fire." Now fearing, Mr. Editor, lest this very confident assertion should deter any of your readers, who were so minded, from endeavouring to procure a wholesome and probably palatable article of food, a matter of prime importance in these days when butchers' meat is so dear, and South American beef so *stinking*, I have made a little experiment; the result you have now before you in the shape of a *salted snail*, prepared according to the widow's recipe, which has lost but little of its bulk and less of its weight. You are at perfect liberty, Sir, to munch this "dainty bit," * an it so please you. To encourage you in the venture I may add that the daintiest dish of which I have ever had the good fortune to partake, was a *caterpillar stew*,† which followed a boiled monkey, or baked porcupine (on this point my memory fails me), on the banks of a certain tropical river, where of old Sir Walter hunted for his El Dorado.　　A. CHALLSTETH.
Gray's Inn.

SPINNING-JENNY (3rd S. vii. 281.)—It is stoutly maintained by many that Thomas Highs, a reedmaker of Leigh, co. Lancaster, was the real inventor of " the Jenny," and that he called it after his favourite daughter, Jane; and that it was for an improvement of this machine that Hargreaves obtained a patent, but which was afterwards an-

----

　[* Remembering how a certain illustrious personage was laughed at by Theodore Hook for " munching " the last golden pippin, we respectfully beg leave to decline.— ED.]
　† Gru-gru worms, the larval state of a beetle.

----

nulled. I believe it is certain that neither wife nor daughter of Hargreaves bore the name of Jane.
　　　　　　　　　　　　　　H. FISHWICK.

VISCOUNT CHAWORTH (3rd S. vii. 279.) — All ordinary accounts agree in assigning 1640 as the year in which this title became extinct by the death of the last viscount, *s. p. m.* His only daughter and heiress, Juliana, m. Chambre (Brabazon) fifth earl of Meath, by which alliance the baptismal name, and more recently the title, of Chaworth has been introduced into that family. On Feb. 7, 1831, an English barony was conferred on the tenth Earl of Meath, who was created Lord Chaworth of the U. K., under which title the present earl sits as a member of the Upper House. Guillim states that Patrick Chaworth, Esq., created " Viscount Chaworth of Ardmagh, in the kingdom of Ireland," was of the old baronial family of Chaworth, or de Cadurcis, and bore the same arms, viz., Azure, two chevronels, or. Sir George Chaworth, Knight (an ancestor of the Viscounts Chaworth), m. Alice, dau. and sole heiress of John Annesley (who d. 15 Henry VI.), and with her the manor and estate of Annesley passed to the family of Chaworth, represented in 1833 by John Chaworth-Musters, Esq., of Colwick Hall, Notts. (*Vide* Burke's *Commoners.*)
　　　　　　　　　　　　HENRY W. S. TAYLOR.
Halifax.

URICONIUM, OR WROXETER (3rd S. vii. 183.) — Will you permit me, through your columns, to refer your correspondent for the information that he desires to a paper written by me, which appeared in Cassell's *Family Paper* of Oct. 31, 1863, I believe under the signature of " Decanus."
　　　　　　　EDWARD N. HOARE, Dean of Waterford.

" Cole's *Tourist's Guide Book, a Visit to the Wonderful City of Uriconium,* &c. By W. F. Peacock. Manchester, Coles; London, Simpkin & Co., 4th or 5th edition. 6d."
　　　　　　　　　　　　　　GLWYSIG.

TONED PAPER v. WHITE PAPER (3rd S. vi. 454; vii. 64.)—I sincerely hope that we may never see *toned* paper in general use; I must raise my voice against such a proposition. Short-sighted men like me must have clear print, white paper, and good light, or else lay by their books. I never, if I can avoid it, read a book, the paper of which is coloured; it is painful and distressing to my eyes, and strains my sight when I am obliged to do so. It may suit EIRIONNACH and J. F. S., but I trust that "N. & Q." will continue to retain its clear print and white paper, to the great comfort and ease of one who, short-sighted as he is, has contrived to read through glasses for more than half his life.　　　　　　　　　　　　F. S. M.

COUNTESS OF SUFFOLK (3rd S. vii. 94, 169, 269.) In reply to the kind answer of MELETES, the lady represented in the portrait referred to has a rather small face, broad forehead, eyes so placed as to remind one of the Chinese type, *nez retroussé*, thin clever mouth, the whole countenance possessing great intelligence and piquancy. The hair is combed tightly back from the face, and surmounted by a lace cap or coif, a fearfully starched ruff environs her neck, and her gown is fronted by a strip of broidered work as stiff and gorgeous as the door of an old India cabinet. From her ladyship's hair a jewel in true *cinque-cento* taste, hangs on her forehead, little pearls are in her ears, strings of seed-pearls are round her neck, and altogether she looks as fresh and sprightly a lady of some eight and thirty years as one could expect to have seen about the year of grace fifteen hundred and eighty, at which time, as I take it, she was put on panel.   X.

MARRIAGE RINGS (3rd S. vii. 12, 307.) — In the remarks upon this subject made by R. C. L. in your last number, he says a clergyman (not far from Windsor) refused to proceed with the marriage service, unless the man, at its appointed stage, laid the ring, with the accustomed duty, "upon the book." This reminds me of what happened to a clerical friend of mine, a bishop's son, and a very strict ritualist. The late Archbishop Howley, hearing that he was about to be married, kindly offered to perform the marriage ceremony at Lambeth; accordingly on the appointed day the bride and bridegroom, with their friends, attended at the private chapel at Lambeth. The service having proceeded to the point where the ring with the accustomed duty should be laid on the book, the bridegroom, in compliance with the rubric, placed the ring, with a little paper envelope containing a twenty-pound note, upon the service book. The archbishop, thinking that the little packet was only the folded paper which had contained the ring, proceeded to the end of the service, when he quietly shut the book and placed it on the communion table. Nobody seems to have remarked the circumstance, and it was not till some weeks afterwards that the archbishop's chaplain accidentally discovered the envelope, folded within the leaves of the book, which held the bank note, with a memorandum inside the cover that it might be given to the fund of the Society for the Propagation of the Gospel. Of course my friend could not offer the archbishop a fee, and therefore in acknowledgment of the compliment, made this offering of twenty pounds to the society of which the archbishop was the president. Let "would-be bridegrooms," therefore, take a hint, and whether the ring be jewelled or plain, let there be no mistake about "the accustomed duty" being in the hard coin of the realm.

BENJN. FERREY.

GENERAL HUGH MERCER (3rd S. vi. 537; vii. 40.) — General Mercer was not a member of the family of Mercer of Knockbally Style, co. Carlow.

No such Christian name as "Hugh" occurs in their pedigree. Capt. Thomas Vigors m. 2ndly in 1737, Elizabeth, eldest dau. of Edward Mercer, Esq., of Knockbally Style (who d. Feb. 3, 1762). Mr. Mercer was second son of Richard Mercer of Dublin, who died in 1694, leaving three sons, Richard, Edward, and William. I have examined an extensive pedigree of Mercer of the co. Down, but likewise failed to find a "Hugh" in it. The co. Carlow family bore for their arms "Or, a fess gu. charged with 3 bezants in chief 3 crosses patée of the 2nd and in base a mullet azure." Crest, a stork's head couped, holding in its bill a snake embowed. Motto, "The Grit Doul."

H. LOFTUS TOTTENHAM.

POWER OF FRANKING (3rd S. vii. 27.) — The late Duke of Kent sometimes franked as "Edward;" at other times as "Kent and Strathearn."

JOSEPH RIX, M.D.

Miscellaneous.

BOOKS AND ODD VOLUMES
WANTED TO PURCHASE.

Particulars of Price, &c., of the following Books to be sent direct to the gentleman by whom they are required, and whose name and address are given for that purpose:—

COMMON PRAYER, 1660. Black-letter, 4to.
VIRGILII OPERA. 4 Vols. Frontispiece engraved by Pitteri.

Wanted by Rev. J. C. Jackson, 5, Chatham Place East, Hackney, N.E.

Notices to Correspondents.

We are compelled to omit our usual Notes on Books.

PASSAGE IN "PERICLES."— *We have received from Dr. Bell a long letter in reply to R. A. Had the letter contained the evidence which R. A. called for, that the name lamps was ever used for lamprey, or disproved R. A.'s assertion that Nine eyes, is a common name for lampreys in this country, we should of course have at once given it insertion. But beyond some strong language directed against R. A., and a challenge to him to produce from any English dictionary ancient or modern (with the exception of Halliwell, the mention of Nine eyes at all, and an assertion that on the continent "the animal is known by no other name," Dr. Bell's letter does not touch upon the real points at issue between him and R. A. We must, therefore, decline to insert the communication in question.*

THOMAS T. DYER. *The lines—*

"Only the actions of the just
  Smell sweet and blossom in the dust,"

are from Shirley's Contention of Ajax and Ulysses.

P. (New York) *is thanked for his hints, which shall not be lost sight of. The term has been used here in the same way that John Bull is applied to all Englishmen.*

COLD HARBOUR. *We are so overwhelmed with communications on this subject, which was very fully discussed in our former series, that We must crave the forbearance of many of our contributors. An esteemed lady correspondent will, We think, admit on reconsideration that her communication breaks the very rule which she herself would lay down.*

LOVILL. *Prospectuses of the Early English Text Society may be obtained from the Hon. Sec., Henry B. Wheatley, Esq., 53, Berners Street, London, W.*

HYPOKEIMENOI (Cape Town.) "X. Y. Z. Junr., Esq.

SAMUEL SHAW. The Tablette Booke of Ladye Mary Keys, London, 1861, is a fictitious historical production. Vide The Athenæum of July 23, 1861, p. 50.

P. P. *We have received a letter for this correspondent; where shall it be forwarded?*

A Reading Case for holding the weekly Nos. of "N. & Q." is now ready, and may be had of all Booksellers and Newsmen, price 1s. 6d.; or, free by post, direct from the publisher, for 1s. 8d.

*** Cases for binding the volumes of "N. & Q." may be had of the Publisher, and of all Booksellers and Newsmen.

"NOTES AND QUERIES" is published at noon on Friday, and is also issued in MONTHLY PARTS. The Subscription for STAMPED COPIES for Six Months forwarded direct from the Publisher (including the Half-yearly INDEX) is 11s. 4d., which may be paid by Post Office Order, payable at the Strand Post Office, in favour of WILLIAM G. SMITH, 32, WELLINGTON STREET, STRAND, W.C., where also all COMMUNICATIONS FOR THE EDITOR should be addressed.

"NOTES & QUERIES" is registered for transmission abroad.

LONDON, SATURDAY, MAY 6, 1865.

CONTENTS.—N° 175.

Notes.

CAPITAL PUNISHMENTS IN RUSSIA.

Mr. Basil Montagu, in his valuable work, *Opinions of Different Authors on the Punishment of Death*, published in 1813 (in vol. iii. p. 195), gives an extract from the Code of Laws adopted by the great Catherine; by which it appears that, following the example of her predecessor Elizabeth, she abolished the punishment of death for all crimes but those grave offences against the state which have always been marked out for great severity by despotic rulers. I need not give the passage at length, as it has been so often quoted both by writers and speakers on the subject of capital punishment. It is said that during the whole reign of Elizabeth—that is, for twenty years—the punishment of death was never once inflicted. And Schnitzler, in his *Secret History of the Court and Government of Russia* (vol. ii. p. 339) says (writing in relation to the execution of Pestel and his confederates for their leadership in the revolt of 1825, and which execution took place in the first year of the reign of the autocrat Nicholas, 1826,) that "For the last eighty years St. Petersburgh had not witnessed a capital punishment."

Having had occasion of late to make many inquiries as to the operation of the criminal law in the several European states, I have found the greatest difference of statement in relation to

capital punishment in Russia; and great difficulty in procuring accurate information, as the same facilities are not afforded through official sources as in other states in Europe. By some persons who have had opportunities of observation by residence in Russia, it is asserted that the capital penalty is often inflicted; while others assert that it is substituted by a punishment of greater severity, inasmuch as many criminals die under the knout, or almost immediately after it; and that others perish on the way to Siberia, or shortly after their arrival there. I find nothing more satisfactory than the general statement I have given. The abolition of the punishment of death is therefore nothing, if it is succeeded by a system of torture which brings only a more lingering and more horrible death. Schnitzler says (vol. ii. p. 317): —

> "Though the law does not mention death, it is nevertheless frequently given by the knout: we must, therefore, not laud too highly the pretended sensibility of Elizabeth Pétrovna, who, in abolishing capital punishments in ordinary criminal cases, allowed this other punishment, which is much more barbarous and often followed by the same effect, to subsist. In what relates to political crimes, the pain of death is expressly maintained. People may still be torn in quarters in Russia, even as they may be impaled at Constantinople and broken alive on the wheel in Prussia—an enlightened country, where the most solid civilisation has penetrated into every class. . . . . It is for none but the most obscure criminals that the atrocious punishments of the old Muscovite legislation are reserved: for instance, that of *running the gauntlet*; where honest soldiers are transformed into ignoble executioners, and blood runs no less plentifully than beneath the iron thongs of the knout."[*]

I am very desirous of obtaining further information, if any of your readers can help me to it. I cannot procure any statistical information as to the number of criminals condemned to the punishment of the knout, nor of those sent to Siberia. I believe that such returns are not obtainable.

While consulting the work of Shnitzler, I find the account of a horrible circumstance connected with the particular execution to which I have referred; and which strikes the mind with greater force, after the recent accident to the wretched man Atkinson at Durham. In the case under notice, Pestel, and four of his comrades, were doomed to death by the hangman. The remainder must be told by Schnitzler himself, who it appears was a spectator of what he describes: —

> "They ascended the platform and the benches placed in front of the gibbet one by one, in the order allotted to them by their sentence. Pestel first occupying the right side, and Kakhofski the left. The fatal noose was then passed round their necks; and no sooner had the executioner stood aside, than the platform fell from under their feet. Pestel and Kakhofski were strangled immediately; but death refused, as it were, to reach the three others

---

[*] The sufferer has to walk five or ten times through the open ranks of a thousand soldiers.

placed between them. The spectators then beheld a terrible scene. The rope being badly adjusted, slid over the heads of these unfortunate men, who fell altogether into the hole under the scaffold pell mell with the trap-door and the benches. Horrible contusions must have been the consequence; but as this lamentable accident caused no alteration in their fate, for the Emperor was absent at Tsarsko-Sélo, and nobody ventured to grant a respite, they had to suffer the agony of death a second time. As soon as the platform was replaced, they were again brought under the gibbet. Although stunned at first by his fall, Ryleïeff walked with a firm step, but could not help uttering this painful exclamation: 'Must it be said that nothing succeeds with me—not even death!' According to some witnesses he exclaimed also: 'Accursed country, where they know neither how to plot, to judge, nor to hang!' But others attribute these words to Sergius Mouravieff-Apostol, who, like Ryleïeff, courageously ascended the scaffold. Bestoujeff Rumine, doubtless more injured than the others, had not strength enough to support himself. It was necessary to carry him under the gibbet. A second time the fatal noose was placed round their necks, and this time without slipping."

I quote this account without being able to give any opinion as to its accuracy. It differs from the contemporaneous accounts of the execution in all matters but the fact of the three criminals being precipitated to the earth from the slipping of the noose.   T. B.

ADAM SMITH AND MANDEVILLE.

None of your readers, who are acquainted with Dr. Adam Smith's *Wealth of Nations*, can fail to recollect the description in his first chapter of what is required for the accommodation of a common artificer. The passage is too long to be copied, and is so well known as not to require it. I refer to it at present because, in reading "A Search into the Nature of Society," by Mandeville, annexed to his *Fable of the Bees*, I have been struck with the following passage, which, in point of general character and expression, so much resembles Dr. Smith's description that I cannot help supposing that it must have suggested the passage in his work; if, indeed, the latter has not been in a great measure borrowed from it, and afterwards altered and extended. The passage is as follows:—

"What a bustle is there to be made in several parts of the world before a fine scarlet or crimson cloth can be produced! What multiplicity of trades and artificers must be employed! Not only such as are obvious—as woolcombers, spinners, the weaver, the clothworker, the scowrer, the dyer, the setter, the drawer, and the packer—but others that are more remote and might seem foreign to it—as the millwright, the pewterer, and the chymist: which yet are all necessary, as well as a great number of other handicrafts, to have the tools, utensils, and other implements, belonging to the trades already named. But all these things are done at home, and may be performed without extraordinary fatigue or danger. The most frightful prospect is left behind, when we reflect on the toil and hazard that are to be undergone abroad, the vast seas we are to go over, the different climates we are to endure, and the several nations we must be obliged to for their assistance. Spain alone, it is true, might furnish us with wool to make the finest cloth; but what skill and pains, what experience and ingenuity are required, to dye it of those beautiful colours! How widely are the drugs and other ingredients dispersed thro' the universe that are to meet in one kettle. Allom, indeed, we have of our own; argol we might have from the Rhine, and vitriol from Hungary—all this in Europe; but then for saltpetre, in quantity, we are forced to go as far as the East Indies. Cochenille, unknown to the ancients, is not much nearer to us, tho' in a quite different part of the earth. We buy it, 'tis true, from the Spaniards; but not being their product, they are forced to fetch it for us from the remotest corner of the New World in the East Indies. Whilst so many sailors are broiling in the sun, and sweltered with heat in the East and West of us, another set of them are freezing in the North to fetch potashes from Russia."
                                        J. R. B.
Edinburgh.

THOMAS FULLER'S UNPUBLISHED EPIGRAMS.

In a copy of Crashaw's *Steps to the Temple, with the Delights of the Muses*, second edition, 1648, 8vo, which fell in my way about three years ago, I discovered, written upon the blank leaves, as a portion of the copy was printed on one side only, a large quantity of curious manuscript matter, consisting partly of *excerpta* from printed works, but partly of original and inedited compositions. Among these are upwards of fifty epigrams, chiefly upon religious subjects, by "Mr. Thomas Fuller," and I forward herewith some account of the collection, which, as I have little or no doubt that "Mr Thomas Fuller" is identical with the church historian, cannot fail to be of interest to some of your readers:—

"EPIGRAMS BY Mr THO: FFULLER.

1. On Adam.
2. On Noah, a Ridle.
3. On Leah.
4. On Joseph and his Mrs.
5. On Ziporah circum. her sons.
6. On Moses Strikinge ye Rocke.
7. On the Batle with Amelecke.
8. On Joshauah [sic].
9. On an Altar Ed. [?]
10. Sampson's Jawe Bone.
11. On Elijah taken vp into Heaven.
12. On Zacheus.
13. On ye Powder Plot.
14. On vaine Excuses.
15. On Gallants' Cloakes.
16. On Popish Interpretation of Scripture.
17. On Sin.
18. Whether Scripture or Tradition ye Mother of Faith.
19. On Pope Innocent.
20. On Corn hoorders.
21. On Joseph's Mrs. [Different from No. 4.]
22. On Jacob.
23. On Paul's Journey to Damascus.
24. On ye Philistines.
25. On Bugbears.
26. On Sampson.
27. On Jacob.
28. On Noah's Doue.
29. A Prayer.

30. On Pride in Cloaths.
31. On Musculus.
32. On the Men of Sodom.
33. On Ehud.
34. On Naboth accused.
35. On Jacob.
36. A Prayer.
37. On yᵉ Israelites in yᵉ Wildernes.
38. On Sampson's Weapons.
39. On Jepthaes Daughter.
40. On Ely yᵉ Priest.
41. On Sampson and John Baptist.
42. On Christ lookinge on Peter. [With about a dozen more.]

In a different hand from the above are other epigrams, among which are several of an amatory cast. At the close of the volume occurs, with considerable appearance of having been written by the same person, who has composed or transcribed other pieces, the autograph of Dudley Lovelace, who has written his name a second time with an eye to a little *jeu de mots*, thus: Dudley Lovelasse, and this gentleman has apparently (for they are in the same hand, or a very similar one) copied out portions of his brother's *Lucasta* upon some of the spare leaves, with here and there a variation from the printed edition. On the recto of p. 96 there are four verses from *Lucasta* with the signature of *Richarde Lovelace*.

The true history of the little book before me might be curious and interesting, if it could be ascertained. There is surely ground for presuming that it has once been possessed by Dudley Posthumus Lovelace, the younger brother of the ill-fatal Cavalier Poet, Richard Lovelace, if not by the latter himself. I referred to the curiosity of the present copy of Crashaw in a note at p. 42 of my edition of the *Poems of Richard Lovelace*, 1864.   W. CAREW HAZLITT.

RECIPES IN OLD MSS.

An old parchment oak-bound MS. copy of the Statutes, from Magna Charta to the *Articuli Exon*, has descended in my family, containing some singular and characteristic entries that may interest your readers.

It appears originally to have belonged —

" Reūs Utring, a brother of the Order of Eremite Friars of St. Augustin, in the Convent of Waryngton, near Westchester (?)."

In process of time it descended to "Thomas Ernele," probably an ancestor of my own, whose name appears, in a blank page in the middle of the book, in rather ominous connexion with that of "Susan Calley"; suggesting a contemplated union, at least, between those members of two very well-known old Wiltshire families.

In the blank pages at the end are the following curious recipes, written in a very good hand. Of some of the ingredients, however, in the first I am not quite sure : —

" Colycompotus   .   .   .   .   .   .   iid.
  Venykreki   .   .   .   .   .   .   ii½d.
  Long pep   .   .   .   .   .   .   id.
  Gr. Aynys   .   .   .   .   .   .   id.
  Z. Bayes .   .   .   .   ii½d.
  Lycorys .   .   .   .   iid.
  Agnēs sede (?)   .   .   .   .   .   .   iid.
  Z. Butt .   .   .   .   id.
  A gallon and a halffe off good Ale
" A drench ffor horsys ; thys wul suffice iiii horsys well."

Then follows : —

" Thom's Rollys off Kynswode."
" An erbe callyd ffymytory put yn a bundell, and sodyn wᵗ a coney or chekyns, and use hytt ; and hyt ys good to Avoyde a consumpcion."

" A drenche ffor a horsse that hathe the glandres, or the Coffe.

" ffirst take Mystyldew that growythe on a Appull tree, ffor that is best ;.and take ii handffulls theroff, off the branche and levys to gether ; ii handffulls of garleke clovys, and brose them yn a vessell ovyr the ffyer yn a pottell off stale ale, and sethe hyt to a quarte. And then take and strayne hyt, and putt there in ii sponeffulls off powder off brymstone, ii sponeffulls off powder off lycoryse, and one sponeffull off powder off comyn, and then geve hyt yower horse to drynke warme. And aftur he hathe drynkyd, lett hym be softely laboryd li over or iii myles, and then sett hym uppe yn a warme stabull, and don hym wᵗ a good warme clothe, and sett a pan off colys as nere hym as ye can, to cast hym yn a swete. And then take good ale, oyle, and venygar, and meddyll them to gyther, and rubbe hym well there wᵗ all ovyr a gaynst the heyre, that yt may soke in to the skyn ; and thus serve hym, and geve hym thys drynke iii tymes, one a day, and so therbe a whole daye and a nyght betweene evry drynkyng tyme. And then he schal voyde moche ffleme at hys moth and nose by great quantyte ; wyche ffleme ys cause off hys desease, and thys schall heyle hym off hys Wynde."

" Memᵈ, hyt nede not to anoynte hym wᵗ oyle and vynegre, onles hys skyn stycke ffast to hys fflesh, and that wryll lose hytt.

" Memᵈ, also, to geve yower horse aftur hys drynke sooden barley ffor hys pvendur."

The only other name I can find among a few more scribblings, is that of "Dorothe Smyth."

                                        C. W. BINGHAM.

LORD DERBY, GOETHE, AND MANZONI.

Reverting to a subject touched upon in your pages some years ago (1855), viz. Lord Derby's and Goethe's translation of Manzoni's *Ode on Napoleon Bonaparte* (" Cinque Maggio "), I wish to call the attention of Italian scholars to the rendering, in both cases, of two lines in the seventh stanza : —

" E ripensò le mobili
  Tende, e i percossi valli."

I have not Lord Derby's since printed (though not published) volume of translations to refer to; but I have seen it, and observed in it the same interpretation of the passage in question as your correspondent B. (1.) (" N. & Q." 1ˢᵗ S. ix. 109.) quoted from memory—

" He saw the quick struck tents again,
  The hot assault—the battle plain," &c.

Goethe has —

" Da schaut er die beweglichen
  Zelten, durchwimmelte Thäler," &c.

About this last interpretation there can be no doubt whatever. Goethe has taken *valli* for the plural of *valle*, a valley or plain; and what I submit is, is he not wrong? Poetical licenses are scattered rather freely in Italian poetry, but I do not see the loophole by which *percosso* could make its plural feminine in *i*. And if not, the word *valli* is from *vallo*, a rampart, instead of *valle*, a vale; a solution which makes the expression *percossi* intelligible as well as grammatical.

I approach Lord Derby's translation with more hesitation, for he has given two descriptions to Manzoni's one. He has both a " hot assault" and a " battle-plain"; and perhaps no one but himself can say which of the two he intended to represent *percossi valli*, and which to fill up space or afford a rhyme. Some idea of something assaulted seems to have passed through his mind; at the same time that the *battle-plain* stands there most suspiciously, as the equivalent for *valli*.

If two such great men have really by some accident misinterpreted the *valli* in this case, it is a curious coincidence, and worth noticing.

As to commendation of Lord Derby's noble version of the Ode, it would be absurd to express it to any one who has had the good fortune of judging for themselves. Perhaps, however, only those who have made the same experiment and failed, in consequence of what seemed the almost insuperable difficulties surrounding the task, can fully estimate the beautiful as well as masterly touches which abound in this wonderfully successful effort. Among the unsuccessful labourers, I once ranked myself; but the labour was not lost which brought almost every word of the Ode under careful consideration. Of this, however, I shall be more satisfied if I find I am right in insisting on *valli* as the plural of *vallo*, and *percossi valli* as better translated by " stormed ramparts" than " durchwimmelte Thäler."

MARGARET GATTY.

Ecclesfield.

PALESTINE EXPLORATION FUND.

The gratifying intelligence that such a fund is about to be raised suggests an inquiry, which does not appear to have hitherto received the attention of travellers in Palestine. We read, in 2 Kings xx. 20, that Hezekiah "made a pool and a conduit, and brought water into the city." Now, on a due consideration of the localities, it seems difficult to understand how that water could be brought into the city, unless it were by an aqueduct or by a pipe: the pipe first descending and then ascending, on the principle that water will rise to its own level. There seems no reason for concluding that Hezekiah erected an aqueduct. Was it then known to him, or was it known to those whom he employed to carry out his design, that the water, if conveyed in a channel properly secured, would rise to the elevation of the site from which it came, and so *come up* to where it was wanted? This idea is in a measure countenanced by the fact that the " conduit," by which Hezekiah is said to have brought the water into the city, is in Hebrew—תעלה, from עלה, " to go up;" and it would be curious if it should appear on investigation, that the " conduit" was in fact a pipe, or channel, through which the water, first descending, ultimately *ascended* to the level at which it was required for use or distribution. This idea will not be found, on examination, to clash with 2 Chron. xxxii. 30.

It has been supposed that the Romans built aqueducts through ignorance of the hydrostatic principle—that a fluid will rise to a level at the opposite ends of properly adjusted pipes. Some, however, have imagined that the Romans were well acquainted with this principle, but were unable to give effect to it because unable to fabricate pipes of adequate strength and magnitude. It would appear that Hezekiah surmounted this difficulty by excavating the rock.   SCHIN.

THE CAISTOR WHIP. — The following note, which is worth preserving, occurs in a Catalogue of Books now on sale by Puttick & Simpson. The Whip will be sold on Monday the 8th: —

"1416 THE CAISTOR GAD (or Whip).—An estate at Broughton, near Brigg (co. Lincoln?) is held by the following old and singular custom. On the morning of Palm Sunday, the gamekeeper, or some servant on the estate, brings with him a large gad, or whip, with a long thong; the stock is made of the mountain ash, or wicken tree, and tied to the end of it is a leather purse, containing thirty pence (said to have in it formerly thirty pieces of silver); while the clergyman is reading the first Lesson (Exodus ix.), the man having the whip cracks it three times in the church porch; and then wraps the thong round the stock, and brings it on his shoulder through the church, to a seat in the chancel, where he continues till the second Lesson is read (Matthew xxvi.); he then brings the gad, and kneeling upon a mat before the pulpit, he waves it three times over the clergyman's head (the thong is fastened as before observed), and continues to hold it till the whole of the Lesson is read, when he again returns to his seat, and remains till the Service is over. He then delivers the gad to the occupier of a farm called Hundon, half a mile from Caistor."

Perhaps you or some of your correspondents could throw light on the origin of this curious custom.   SPENCER HALL.

GABRIEL HARVEY AND SPENSER.—I forward to you, just as it was obligingly communicated to me:

by a literary friend, the accompanying memorandum of a MS. note by Gabriel Harvey discovered in the Bodleian. It came too late to find a place in the notes to *Old English Jest Books.* Gabriel Harvey says, that "Mr. Spensar gave him Howleglas, Skoggin, Skelton, and . . . ., on 20 Dec., 1578, on condition he should read them over by a stated time." These are not the words of the note, but are its *substance,* and all that can be made out, as the writing is partly illegible.

W. CAREW HAZLITT.

GABRIEL HARVEY'S "COMMONPLACE-BOOK."— I have before me what I judge to be the only remaining fragment of the commonplace-book of Gabriel Harvey. It consists, in its present state, of ten pages only. There are quotations from various authors, in English, &c.; but what renders it of peculiar value is that it preserves to us, by a lucky accident, the whole of an unknown and curious English poem, copied by Harvey in 1584 from an original, which must be presumed to have perished. The production in question is entitled—

"A View or Spectacle of Vanity: A Sober and Serious Moral Lesson, composed in an Hundred excellent Verses, aswell for matter as stile very notable."

At the close, Harvey has written: "Incerti Auctoris, anno 1584." I conceive that it is one among the objects of "N. & Q." to place on record short notices of any inedited and uncatalogued English MSS.   W. CAREW HAZLITT.

ALLAN RAMSAY.—On the fly-leaf of a copy of Allan Ramsay's *Poems* (2 vols., Edinburgh, 1721, 8vo), there is the following inscription : —

" To Dr. Robinson, when at Edinburgh, July 30th, 1734.

"Now troth, dear Doctor, it is kind,
And shaws a cowthie crefauld mind
In you, who live sae far away,
On Brittain's sunny side of the Brae,
To dawt and clap a northren pow,
Owning his roundels easy row.
I own I like the scawpy height,
Where men maist sib to God's delight,
Yet pay my debts, and school my weans
By canny conduct of my gains :
And fowk think that ane unko ferly,
'Cause poets play that part sae rarely !
Thanks to Queensberry and the rest,
Wha gave what biggit up my nest ;
When Quarto volume chanc'd to get in ·
Five hundreds frae the best in Brittain,
For which I'll chant, and shaw I'm gratefull,
Till canker'd Eild make singing hatefull."

In the original there is no pointing. *Queensberry* was Gay's Duke. By "Quarto volume," he signifies the subscription edition of his *Poems,* in 1721.   W. CAREW HAZLITT.

EARL SPENCER'S "BOCCACCIO."—This book, so remarkable for the price given for it, was once shown to me by Mr. Payne, of Pall Mall. An anecdote regarding the sale is given in "N. & Q.," 3rd S. vii. 301. I have heard that the call of "Hats off!" was uttered when the book was brought forward, out of respect to the volume ; and that, on Lord Blandford's apologising to Lord Spencer for his successful competition against him the latter observed, that it was quite unnecessary, as it had saved him from doing a very foolish thing.   FRANCIS TRENCH.
Islip Rectory.

CHAINED LIBRARIES IN PARISH VESTRIES.— How many church vestries are there in this kingdom known to be in possession, by bequest or otherwise, of libraries chained or fastened to the shelves? By the inclosed extract you will perceive that we have one such collection in our city : —

"THE CHAINED LIBRARY OF ALL SAINTS.—Many of our citizens are not aware that the vestry of the church of All Saints possesses an almost unique evidence of 'the, . dark ages,' when books were chained to the shelves, and a money pledge given before the sacred volume could be obtained for perusal. We refer to Dr. Brewster's Library, given to the parish in the last century. The books have been only once removed from their holding. This method of diffusing knowledge was only short-lived, it occurring in the time of a thrifty and generous churchwarden, who sold the books to a London bibliopolist at what was deemed a long figure, and the profit was intended to be carried to the year's receipt. The *Hereford Journal,* however, took up the matter in correspondence, and the books were saved from the impending confiscation. They have since remained on the shelves of the vestry. There are some interesting works in the collection, and a catalogue of them was published in the *Journal* at the time of their sudden removal to London. Luther's "Common-place Book " is one, as we heard the vicar remark, affording· an interesting memento of the eminent man, who took so large a share in the bringing about of the Reformation. A very fine specimen of early printing (1541) in rubric and black-letter, came under our observation on Thursday ; but the books are too thickly bedizened with dust to invite any but a book-worm to dive into their mysteries. The collection would form an excellent nucleus to a Free Library."

C. N.

Hereford.

BISHOPS' OATHS OF OFFICE.—Oath taken by the Bishop of Exeter in the early part of Queen Elizabeth's reign : —

" I, Wylliam Alley, Busshop of Exeter, do most humbly acknowledge and confesse your most excellent majestie to be my most true and undoubted Soveraigne Lady, and I utterlie renownce and refuse all obedience for anye thinge I possesse or enjoy, or hereafter shall possesse within anie your majesties realmes and domynions, to any foreyn power or potentate ; and humbly confesse your majestie to be the supreme governor in all thinges as well ecclesiasticall as temporall within this realme, and with all obedience do make my homage for the temporalities and possessions of the Busshopricke of Exeter which I hold and enjoy ; and I protest, by this my presente Othe, that I shall remayne your true, faythfull, and obedyent subjecte during my naturall lief, as God shall helpe me and the contentes of the booke touched by me. At Richemonde, the seconde day of August, 1560, and the seconde yere of your majesties most prosperous reigne.

" WILLIAM EXON."

The original of the above is on parchment, and is preserved among the Lansdowne MSS. in the British Museum. G. A.

Barnsbury.

Queries.

MR. JOHN BOTRIE. — In Manning and Bray's *Surrey*, vol. iii. p. 681, is a list of those appointed "Triers" of the conduct of the clergy of the co. of Surrey, Feb. 16, 1647, one of whom was Captain Buttery of Dorking. Was he identical with John Botrie of Lincoln's Inn, and Marston St. Lawrence, co. Northampton ? His will was proved April 14, 1654, by Eliz. Bootrye, his widow; and letters of administration were granted to John Buttrey of Lincoln's Inn, armiger of the estate of his brother Aug. 3, 1639. Eliz. Buttery, spin., by her will dated Dec. 8, 1642, leaves a legacy to her brother John Buttery of Lincoln's Inn ; also—

" Unto the godly and religious ministers that have heretofore been plundered and pillaged by the cavilleers 20l., and unto such souldiers as shall be maymed and wounded for and on the right and behalf of the parliament, 20l. ; to be paid unto my brother-in-law, John Sedgwick the elder, B.D., and minister of St. Alphage, Cripplegate, for their use."

Can I ascertain if John Botrie was called to the bar at Lincoln's Inn. ALBERT BUTTERY.

178, Piccadilly.

"CHRISTIAN BREADBASKET."—After the paper duty ceased to exist some years since, did a religious periodical, whose title remind us of the puritan æra, ever appear under the designation of *The Christian Breadbasket?* which reminds us of those of Cromwell's time, such as *A Shove for Heavy "Sterned" Christians ;* or *Hooks and Eyes for Believers' Breeches*, as appears in D'Israeli.

BREVIS.

THE COURT, 1730. — I am at present engaged in investigating a case of propinquity, which turns on the evidence of the birth of a child in London, 1728-30. The birth of this child does not appear to have been registered in London, though the mother was a lady moving in the court circles. Our only chance left of finding a clue seems to be that the birth *may* be noticed in some of the memoirs, letters, &c., in print or MS., which particularly refer to the gossip, tattle, and scandal in and about the court at that date.

I have tried a great many such in vain, but am unwilling to throw up the cards yet. Walpole and Lord Hervey are a little too late ; the same applies to Bubb Dodington. Lady M.

Wortley Montague's letters are unfortunately deficient at the date in question. Are there any unpublished MSS. of hers anywhere ? The Suffolk papers, both the printed and the MS. in the British Museum, have been ransacked to no purpose. Can the editor or any of his correspondents kindly suggest a source of information, such as I have indicated, either in print or MS. ? P.

BENJAMIN FRANKLIN. — According to Parton's *Life of Benjamin Franklin*, the latter, while residing (1724-1726) in London as journeyman printer, lodged "in the street called Little Britain," and afterwards in Duke Street. Are the houses still standing, and where ? S. W. P.

"GOD IS THE SEA OF LOVE."—

" God is the sea of love,
Where all my pleasures roll ;
The circles where my passions move,
And centre of my soul."

This verse is found in Watts's *Hymns* in the hymn commencing "My God, my life, my love." It is attributed to Sir Thomas Browne, who lived before Watts. Can any reader inform me which of the two is the author ? If my memory serves me, the verse is found in *Religio Medici*, but I am not sure. J. F.

GERVASE HOLLES.—I wish to be informed whether any part of this gentleman's collections for Lincolnshire and Notts has ever been printed. Of his MSS., forming several volumes, now among the Lansdowne MSS. in the British Museum, I am aware. But I am constantly meeting with quotations from Gervase Holles without its being stated whether it is the original MS. or some publication from which the quotations are made. More particularly I desire to know whether any of your readers can refer me to any full and finished printed account (taken from Gervase's manuscripts) of the families of Holles Earl of Clare, Densel, Musard, Clifton of Clifton, Freschville, and Kingston. J. E. J.

LAYSTONE ABBEY.—Did Turner, or any artist, at the beginning of this century, execute a drawing of Laystone Abbey, Suffolk ? If so, has it been engraved ? J. C. J.

PRINCIPAL LEE'S MSS. — At the sale of the MSS. of Principal Lee of Edinburgh University a few years ago, the following MS. was sold for a small sum —

"325. Scroll index to the Particular Register of Sasines, Inverness, Cromarty, and Sutherland, 1627—1690."

The purchaser will confer a great favour by communicating with me. F. M. S.

229, Clarendon Villas, Plumstead.

MANETHO.—This writer is generally believed to have lived about 280 B.C. in the reigns of Ptolemy Lagi and Philadelphus. It is also said that he

was a priest of Heliopolis. Many of your readers are, however, probably aware that Hengstenberg, in his work entitled *Die Bücher Moses' und Aegypten* (pp. 237-245, &c.), maintains, with great learning and good arguments, that Manetho never resided in Egypt; and also that he did not live earlier than about the commencement of the vulgar era. Can any one throw any additional light on his history? And what authority is due to those extracts from his writings which are given by Eusebius, Josephus, Plutarch, Julius Africanus, &c.?   J. DALTON.
Norwich.

¹ THE NEW VERSION OF THE PSALMS was introduced into general use in consequence of the Order in Council of William III., December 3, 1696. At the end of the New Version there are several hymns, but the selection is not the same in all copies. By what authority have the changes in these hymns been made, and when did the hymns "My God, and is thy table spread," by Philip Doddridge, and "Hark! the herald angels sing," by Charles Wesley, first appear at the end of the New Version?   W. L. D.

EARLY METRICAL VERSION OF THE PSALMS.—Can you, or any of your readers, tell me whether the sixteenth century metrical version of the Psalms in the Inner Temple Library has ever been printed, or whether anything is known of its author? I enclose a transcript of the first psalm, on the chance of some of your readers recognising it:—

"Argumentum.

This psalme in sence } of men both good and bad:
Shew'th difference }
Yt shew'th their frutis } thir endis both glad and sad.
Their hartis pursutis }

Psal. I. Beatus vir.

"1. Man blest is he: whose lyffe doth fle
     To walke men's wyked featys:
     And stondeth no daye [tyme]: in synners' waye
     Nor syttith in skorners' seatys.
"2. But lovyth in wyl: in hart and skyll
     The lordis good lawe and lore,
     Yea daye and nyght: his lawe wil right
     Revolve to kepe the store.
"3. And lyke is he: the plantyd tre
     Nye ryvers set forsoth,
     Who frutith in tyde: whose leavys abide,
     Al prosper what he doth.
"4. Not so, not so: the wicked do [be]
     Thei be lyke dust in wynd:
     Both voyde and vayne: as chaffe is playn
     From earth cast forth by wynde.
"5. Therfor these men: so wiked then
     In Jugement shal not stond,
     Nor synners be [rest]: in companye
     With rightwise men of hond.
"6. For God doth knowe [see]: and wyl avowe
     The waye of men vpright
     Wher shal deraye: the croked waye [ways]
     Of wiked men ful quyte.

"Oratio.

"O blissed father: make vs to be as fruteful trees before thi presence: so watryd bi the dewe of thi grace, that we maye glorifie the bi the plentuousnes of swete frute in our dayly conversation, through Christ."
     F. J. FURNIVALL.

ODE TO SHAKESPEARE.—In an old magazine, I read, when a boy, an ode to Shakespeare. It was a somewhat lengthy production, and full of the heroes of the mythology; indeed some one of them took Shakespeare to heaven, where every heathen deity made him some gift. The first two lines, if I remember rightly, were—
"When Nature to Athens and Rome bid adieu,
 To Britain the goddess with ecstasy flew;"
and the last line of all was—
"One Shakespeare on earth, and one Jove in the sky."
Wanted, for a particular purpose, a reference where the entire ode may be found by   M. C.

SHOOTER'S HILL.—Is there any good reason for supposing that Shooter's Hill, near Woolwich, is so called from its having once been much used for archery? In an act of Richard II. it is called Shetere's Held; and in Henry VIII.'s reign it is called Shutter's Hill? See Richardson's *Greenwich.*   F. A. E.

THE STYRING FAMILY.—Could you or any of your correspondents kindly give me any information as to the origin or history of this family? Misson, or Misterton, in Notts, *seems to be* their first settlement.   C. W. SINGLETON.
Leeds.

SULTANA.—Webster and Worcester agree in saying that this word means the *wife* of a sultan. But Hope in *Anastasius* (i. 116) states that it is used to designate only the sultan's *sisters* and *daughters*, whom of course he cannot marry. Which definition shall we accept?   S. W. P.
New York.

TORCHLIGHT FUNERAL AT WESTMINSTER ABBEY.—There is said to have been a funeral by torchlight at Westminster some forty years since. Who was so buried, and is that the last instance of a funeral by night at Westminster Abbey?   T. L.

OLD WALL PAINTING.—The figure, of which I enclose a sketch, was found over the door of the south wall of a church now in course of restoration. It consists of a large circle with two diameters, each about five feet crossed at right angles, and in the upper right hand quarter a small circle filled by a star of eight points, each about three inches long. The whole is coloured red except the star, which is black. I shall feel greatly obliged to any of your readers who will suggest an explanation.   CPL.

WART STONE.—At Whitechurch, near Dublin, there is a large flat stone of irregular outline, in which a small (evidently artificial) excavation retains rainwater. The stone is known as the "wart stone," and it is locally believed that by immersing a wart-troubled finger in the water, the growth will be removed. Can any of your readers give me information about this superstition, or mention other localities in which a like belief obtains? ACHENDE. Dublin.

Queries with Answers.

FENIAN. — What is the origin of the name Fenian, applied to a section of the revolutionary party in Ireland? ACHENDE. Dublin.

[For the following explanation of this word we are indebted to our valued correspondent J. E. O'CAVANAGH, Esq.:—

This question was asked in the columns of the *Times*, October 20, 1863. It provoked three replies, from Hibernicus, Monkbarns, and George Ballentine. The note which Hibernicus then quoted from Moore's *Irish Melodies*, and which is affixed to the song commencing —

" The wine-cup is circling in Almhin's hall,"

gives the correct derivation, in my opinion, of the name by which those Irishmen, both in America, Ireland, and elsewhere are called, who aim at the overthrow of English dominion in Ireland, namely —

" The Finians, or Fenii, were the celebrated National Militia of Ireland, and derived their name from Fin, the son of Cumhal—pronounced Cooal."

Some of the readers of " N. & Q." may desire further information of this force and its leader. This celebrated warrior was of the royal line of Heremon, and son-in-law of King Cormac, A.D. 213—253, and hereditary general of the standing army of that monarch. Pinkerton, in his *Inquiry into the History of Scotland*, ii. 77, thus speaks of him:—

" He seems to have been a man of great talents for the age, and of celebrity in arms."

" It has been the fate of this popular hero," says Moore, in his *History of Ireland*, " after a long course of traditional renown in his country, where his name still lives, not only in legends and songs, but yet in the most indelible of scenery connected with his memory, to have been all at once transferred, *by adoption*, to another country (Scotland), and start under a new but false shape, in a fresh career of fame." The army, or rather the military order, of which Finn was the chieftain, was called the " Fiann of Erin." The word is used by Irish writers, as well as the peasantry, in a collective sense, and understood as *the order of men called the* " Fiann." Its plural, " Fianna," means *bands or bodies of the Fiann*. An individual member was styled " Feinnidhe." Should our modern Finians take the field, and remain true to the injunctions imposed on their ancient prototypes, though formidable to their male adversaries, the fair sex will

have little to apprehend. There were four injunctions, Keating tells us, laid upon every person admitted into the order of the Fiann : the first, never to receive a portion with a wife, but to choose her for her good manners and virtues ; the second was, never to offer violence to any woman ; the third was, never to give a refusal to any mortal for anything of which one was possessed ; the fourth was, that no single warrior of them should ever flee before nine champions. Though my own convictions have been thus submitted, it may be well to add that some archæologists think the word Fiann comes from " Phenician." " It possibly may," says O'Mahony, who adds, " It is, however, just as likely to come from the same origin with Feadhach (pronounced Feeagh), *i. e. a hunt*, and to mean an order of hunters. Thus the name of a member of that modern German light cavalry corps, ' Jäger,' means hunter. The 'Fianna' seem to have done nothing but hunt and fight." From some of the Finian tales and poems now in course of publication—to the elucidation and vindication of ancient Irish history— one would imagine that they monopolised all the game, as well as all the fighting, of Ireland in their day. A Finian warrior may thus be synonymous with the Latin " Venator " or the German " Jäger," and have no relationship at all with the word Phenician. The bands of Kerns and Galloglasses, supported by the Irish chieftains of later times, it is conjectured, have been affiliations of these more primitive Fianns, who are still, after the lapse of many centuries, so vividly and popularly remembered ; while, singularly enough, the Kearns and Galloglasses of comparatively recent existence, have secured no perpetuity of fame in the poetry, prose, romances, or traditions of their country; and by the uneducated peasantry are now nearly forgotten.]

ANSAREYS. — Can any of your readers give me any information respecting the " Ansareys" and " Gindarics" mentioned in the third volume of *Tancred*, by B. D'Israeli, M.P.? I wish to know whether such a sect really exists, or did exist up to a short time; or are they only a creation of the novelist's brain? W. A. M.

[The Ansareys, also called Ansarians, Ensarians (properly Nassaris and Ansayri), are a people of Syria. The territory occupied by them is that chain of mountains which extends from Antakia to the rivulet called Nahrel-Kabir, or the Great River. The history of the origin of this people, though little known, is instructive. The following account is given in the words of a writer (Assemani, *Biblioth. Orientale*), who has drawn his materials from the best authorities. " In the year of the Greeks, 1202 (A.D. 891), there lived, at the village of Nasar, in the environs of Koufa, an old man, who, from his fastings, his continual prayers, and his poverty, passed for a saint : several of the common people declaring themselves his partisans, he selected from among them twelve disciples to propagate his doctrine. But the magistrate of the place, alarmed at his proceedings, seized the old man and confined him in prison. In this reverse of fortune his situation excited the pity of a girl who was slave, the gaoler, and she determined to give him his liberty. An opportunity soon offered to effect her design. One day, when the gaoler was gone to bed .intoxicated, and in a profound sleep, she gently took the keys from under his pillow, and after opening the door to the old man, returned them to their place unperceived by her master. The next day, when the gaoler went to visit his prisoner, he was extremely astonished at finding he had made his escape; and the more so since he could perceive no marks of violence. He therefore judiciously concluded he had been delivered by an angel, and eagerly spread the report, to avoid the reprehension he merited. The old man, on the other hand, asserted the same thing to his disciples, and preached his doctrines with more earnestness than ever." — Volney's *Travels through Syria and Egypt*, ii. 1—8, ed. 1787.

The Ansarians are divided into several tribes or sects, among which are distinguished the Shamsia, or adorers of the sun; the Kelbia, or worshippers of the dog; and the Kadmousia, who are said to pay a particular homage to that part in women which corresponds to the priapus; and who hold nocturnal assemblies, in which, it is said, after certain discourses, they extinguished the light, and indulge promiscuous lust. For other particulars of these people consult Burckhardt's *Travels in Syria and the Holy Land*, 155—158, 4to, 1822; Chesney's *Survey of the Rivers Euphrates and Tigris*, i. 542, ed. 1850; *The Modern Syrians*, ed. 1844, pp. 276—282, and "N. & Q." 1st S. ix. 169.]

CARLO BOTTA. — Where shall I find the best biography of this author? He was, I believe, a surgeon in Buonaparte's army of Italy, and was an Italian by birth. He was distinguished by several works of great merit in his native language, but of all, his *Storia della Guerra dell' Independenza degli Stati Uniti d'America*, 4 vols. 8vo, Milano, 1819, stands pre-eminent, and in this the conflict with the "Serapis" and the pirate Paul Jones's two ships, equal in size with the English frigate, on 23rd September, 1779, is described as graphically as any such combat we have on record. Sir Richard Pearson, who commanded our "Serapis," was afterwards promoted to be Lieut.-Governor of Greenwich Hospital.

INQUIRER.

[Carlo Giuseppe Botta was born at San Giorgio in Piedmont in 1766, studied medicine in the University of Turin, and took a doctor's degree in 1786. In 1796, after the first success of Bonaparte, he followed the French through their campaigns in Lombardy, and in the following year was present at Venice at the fall of that ancient republic. In June 1800 he was appointed member of the Consulta, or council of administration for Piedmont. When Napoleon resolved, in 1803, to unite, definitively, Piedmont to France, Botta was one of the deputation sent to Paris on the occasion. In 1804 he was elected deputy to the French legislative body. After the fall of Napoleon, he availed himself of his ample leisure in preparing for the press his *History of the North*

American Revolution and War of Independence. In 1815, Napoleon's restored government appointed him Rector of the University of Nancy. He resigned his rectorship at the second Bourbon restoration, and was appointed Rector of the University of Rouen, an office he did not retain long, for in 1816 he was living at Paris without employment or pension. He now applied himself to write his great work, a contemporary History of Italy, during the French occupation, which he published at Paris in 1824, entitled *Storia d'Italia dal 1789 al 1814*, 4 vols. 8vo. Botta died in reduced circumstances at Paris in August, 1837. The longest biographical notice of this celebrated writer, with a list of his works, will be found in the *Biographie Universelle*, Nouvelle édition, v. 149, Paris, 1843.]

GARRICK'S BOOK-PLATE.—I was lately induced to buy a copy of *Shakspeare*, 10 vols. Tonson, 1728, by the book-plate. On a scroll is "David Garrick," above it an esquire's helmet; and for crest a panther's head holding a caduceus in its jaws. The whole is embedded in foliage, flowers, and shells. In the righthand corner is "S. W. inv. et sc."

Is this the book-plate of the great actor? What were his arms?　　F. R. C.

Rue Angoulème.

[The arms of David Garrick given in Burke's *Armory*, are "Per pale, or and az. on the dexter compartment a tower gu., and on the sinister, on a mount vert, a sea-horse ar. mane, fins, and tail, of the first; on a chief, gold, three mullets of the second. *Crest*—a mullet or." The following notice of his book-plate appeared in our 1st S. vii. 221: "The name, David Garrick, in capital letters, is surrounded by some fancy scroll-work, above which is a small bust of Shakspeare; below, and on the sides a mask, and various musical instruments; and beneath the whole, the following sentence from Menage: 'La première chose qu'on doit faire quand on a emprunté un livre, c'est de la lire, afin de pouvoir le rendre plutôt.'— *Menagiana*, vol. iv."]

ROAN. — What is the etymology of *roan*, the leather used in binding in imitation of morocco, and prepared from sheep-skin?

A FAITHFUL READER.

[In common parlance, when a book is spoken of as being bound in roan, we think the reference is primarily to the *colour*, just as when we say "a roan horse." In this latter sense the French have the word *rouan*, formerly *roan*, which seems to be the immediate source of our English *roan*."]

TRÈS, THE FRENCH COMPARATIVE. — Does this literally mean *three times*, as, for instance, *très bon*, thrice good — that is, excellent, superlatively good? *Très hardi*, very bold, exceedingly audacious.

GALLUS.

[This is a question which French scholars do not appear to have yet settled among themselves. Some of them seem to be quite satisfied that *très*, used to express the superlative, does literally signify *thrice*, so as to be the

true equivalent of *ter*, or τρίς. In support of this view they cite such Greek words as τρισόλβιος, τρισευδαίμων, and τρισμέγιστος. Others, however, maintain that the true root of *très* is *trans*, citing the example of *transpassare*, which in Fr. becomes *trépasser*; in Old Fr. *trespasser*.]

Replies.

NEW SHAKSPERE EMENDATION.

(3ʳᵈ S. vii. 315.)

It is fortunate, in regard to the question which Mr. Sawyer has raised to my emendation of the line in Brutus's soliloquy (*Julius Cæsar*, Act II. Sc. 1.), that there is no doubt as to the meaning of the speech itself. The question merely relates to the single line, and the removal of an evident corruption. Of that line we have now (including my own and Mr. Sawyer's) four readings, namely,

" For if thou *path*, thy native semblance on."—Folio.

" For if thou *put* thy native semblance on."
Coleridge.

" For if thou *pall* thy native semblance o'er,"
Heraud.

" For if thou *walk*, thy native semblance on,"
Sawyer.

Mr. Sawyer has himself disposed of Mr. Coleridge's reading; but his own is equally untenable. " Walk " by itself is certainly an incomplete phrase; the sense requires "walk forth," or " walk abroad." He likewise mistakes my meaning. I have nowhere said, " If thou hide thy monstrous visage in smiles and affability," that " not Erebus itself were dim enough to hide thee;" but precisely the contrary. My words are, " That the true mode of concealment is to let their naked faces (their 'native semblance') be seen, and only to *hide* ' the monstrous visage ' of conspiracy in smiles and affability."

Mr. Sawyer mistakes the meaning of the phrase " native semblance." I have explained that it simply means " naked faces," as the context proves. Lucius enters to Brutus, announcing the arrival of Cassius and his companions: —

" *Bru.* Do you know them ?
Luc. No, sir; their hats are plucked about their ears,
And half their faces buried in their cloaks,
That by no means I may discover them
By any mark of favour."

Whereupon Brutus exclaims: —

." They are the faction. O Conspiracy !
Shamest thou to shew thy dangerous brow by night,
When evils are most free ? O! then, by day
Where wilt thou find a cavern dark enough
To mask thy monstrous visage ? "

Now here the term " monstrous visage " means the naked faces which they had " buried in their cloaks," the " dangerous brow " which they were ashamed to show. But thus to cover the face is

to excite suspicion. Brutus rules that it is better to wear an open brow, a smiling and affable countenance. To attempt to hide their purpose in any other way is worse than vain, it is full of peril. No cavern—not even Erebus would avail to ensure the success of the attempt, should they persist in mantling up their naked features,—in other words, " pall *their* native semblance o'er." It is true that what belongs to the concrete conspirators is in the text transferred to the abstract personification, *thou* and *thy* being used for *they* and *their*; but it is a license frequently employed by Shakspere, the prosopopeia being simply in such cases indicated as a slight elevation of the style, and not intended for a perfect figure.

The number of synonyms for the countenance in this speech and that of Lucius is remarkable. Take them in order: "faces "—"favour "—"dangerous brow " — " monstrous visage " — " native semblance." In like manner, we have " a cavern dark enough " — leading ultimately to " Erebus dim enough." This is the wonted genetic process of Shakspere's style, by reason of which, as Coleridge has shown, each speech or even sentence in the dramatist's works frequently becomes " a living organism,"—that is, a product naturally generated and not mechanically constructed. It is quite probable, therefore, when Brutus recurs to Lucius' statement of the conspirators coming with " their faces buried in their cloaks," that he should so far idealise it as to express the same fact, by the line —

" For if thou pall thy native semblance o'er."

We thus see how the line was generated. I may mention that it was not by guess, but by intuition, that the line as amended occurred to me.

Coleridge evidently mistook the meaning of " native semblance." He had in his mind *the likeness with which Conspiracy was born*, and associated this with a *mantled countenance*, as if, like Minerva from the head of Jove, this malign deity had sprung to birth already equipped in appropriate costume. And, truly, a sculptor might well represent Conspiracy as a goddess with a muffled face; but Shakspere had no such idea, for there is nothing in the context to generate it. An artificial poet might, indeed, have dragged in such an image by the head and shoulders, but this is not Shakspere's " creative way," whose works in whole and in part are " living organisms," not mechanical structures. John A. Heraud.

ORIGIN OF THE WORD SUPERSTITION.

(2ⁿᵈ S. v. 125, 242; vi. 301; 3ʳᵈ S. i. 243, 335, 391, 475; ii. 17, 234, 516.)

Although the impression is very prevalent that *superstitio* means *quid nimis*, that is, that *super* is the principal element, something excessive or above the standard of right (cf. Riddle's *Bampton Lectures*, p. 434, *sq.*), and its being used as the equivalent of δεισιδαιμονία appears favourable to this view, I cannot agree with your excellent correspondent EIRIONNACH, when he writes : —

" " It might be said that when the doctrine of the Soul's immortality was first introduced amongst the ancient Romans, they who first embraced it and believed that they should *survive* death were called Superstites and Superstitiosi, or Survivors; this is far more probable than most of the derivations assigned for Superstitio, and yet it has not an historical leg to stand on." (2nd S. vi. 301.)

So far from the definition of Superstition being groundless and wanting in historical foundation, I believe that in his reflections on the consecration of the image of his lamented daughter, Tullia, Cicero did himself acknowledge this *cultus* to be both nominally and really *vana superstitio*.

" M. Tullius," remarks Lactantius, " who not only was a perfect orator, but philosopher, and indeed the sole imitator of Plato, in that book in which he sought consolation for himself after the death of his daughter, hesitated not to declare that the deities who received public worship had been men. . . . Within a few lines he has imparted to us two facts. For whilst he professed he would consecrate the image of his daughter in the same way their statues and images were of old consecrated, he both inculcated that they were deceased men, and exhibited the origin of this vain superstition." — *De Falsa Religione*, cap. xv. p. 67, edit. Paris, 1748.

Again, the Christian Cicero observes : —

" Wherefore Cicero admitted it was without limitation evident, that we may infer the same thing respecting Jupiter and the senior gods ; that if our forefathers consecrated their memory, for the same reason he designed to consecrate his daughter's image and name; the mourners should be pardoned, but the believers (in this *superstition*) can not. For who so senseless as to think that through the consentient *placitum* of innumerable dotards the heaven can be opened to the dead ? or that any one can confer on another what he does not himself possess ? "—*Ibid.* p. 69.

The piety of Æneas he shows to have been superstition only : —

" An potest aliquis dubitare quomodo religiones [sive superstitiones] deorum sint institutæ, cum apud Maronem legat Æneas verba sociis imperantis : —

'Nunc pateras libate Jovi, precibusque vocate
Anchisem genitorem'?

" Cui non tantum immortalitatem, verum etiam ventorum tribuit potestatem," p. 66.

It is satisfactory to find my etymological suggestion (2nd S. v. 242) confirmed by Bp. J. Taylor in his Sermon *On Godly Fear*, quoted by EIRIONNACH (3rd S. i. 391), though the latter supposes the term refers to the survivors and their intense feeling for the departed as shown in the old ἀποθέωσις, or deification, in prayers for the dead, and the oriental honour performed to spirits of their ancestors. " Hence came the etymology of Superstition: it was a worshipping or fearing the Spirits of their dead heroes, quos Superstites credebant," &c.—Bp. Taylor, *ut suprà*. Cf. Cicero, *Pro Murenâ*,—

" Utrisque Superstitibus præsentibus. Id est, sanis et incolumibus, ideoque præsentibus. Qua in re id verbum a veteribus usurpatum fuisse Nonius Marcellus scribit. Superstitibus igitur est sanis et incolumibus, ideoque præsentibus." Sylv. edit. Amstelodami, 1696, p. 41.

That the words *superstitio* and *superstitiosus* were employed as terms of ridicule by materialists is, I think, supported by the authorities above cited, Cicero and Lactantius. I beg further to remark that, from the peroration of Cicero's magnificent Oration for Archias, he appears to have substantiated what he apprehends to be the Utopia of immortality by the ambitious expectation of posthumous fame.

" He cared not for his life resumed in heaven,
He'd lived to ev'ry end for which 'twas given."

Even granting that Cato and Cicero were convinced of the important doctrine of the soul's separate existence in a future state, we are not justified in attributing the same belief to the generality of his contemporaries. In the celebrated words of Tacitus : " If in another world there is a pious mansion for the blessed; if as the wisest men have thought, the soul is not extinguished with the body," we may observe he says, *ut sapientibus placet*, not *plerisque*.

A Christian only could confidently maintain—

" Nec dissolvetur anima dissoluto corpore, nec eo pereunte peritura est. Sed vitam sibi propriam possidens, manet *superstes* et immortalis, futuræ capax miseriæ aut fœlicitatis."—Burnetius, *De Statu Mortuorum et Resurgentium*, p. 41, 1733.

" The ancient Hindus believed in immortality and in personal immortality, and we find them in the Veda praying to their gods that they might see their fathers and mothers again in the bright world to come. *We can hardly imagine such a prayer from the lips of a Greek or a Roman;* though it would not surprise us in the sacred groves of ancient Germany. What a deeply interesting work might be written on this one subject—on the different forms which a belief in immortality has assumed among the different races of mankind ! "—" On Manners and Customs," a review of *Researches into the Early History of Mankind, and the Development of Civilization*, by Edw. Burnet Tylor, in *The Times* of April 21, 1865.

It will perhaps be objected that Lactantius used the word referred to in its common acceptation as opposed to *impietas*; but it must be acknowledged that he probably designed to include this original or etymological signification here proposed; inasmuch as the lesson which he says ought to be derived from the bereaved father's *cultus* was this —; not that the worshippers were δεισιδαίμονες, but that the honours paid to these consecrated individuals implied an affectation of belief that the *mortui* were *superstites, incolumes, præsentes*.　　BIBLIOTHECAR. CHETHAM.

HERCULES: DANTE.
(3rd S. vii. 254, 305.)

I have read with attention the reply of W. F. P. to my query on this subject; on which he will believe, I hope, that I did not write without due consideration of Christ's descent into Hell, to which Dante refers so pointedly at the end of canto viii. But the invader of Hell, in canto ix. asks the fiends —

"Perchè ricalcitrate a quella voglia
A cui non puote il fin mai esser mozzo,
E che più volte vi ha cresciuto doglia?"

substantially meaning, "Why do you infernal powers resist that will whose consummation can never be imperfect, and which has *more than once* increased your punishment?" This implies, I venture to believe, that there had been, under divine sanction, several invasions of Hell (besides our Lord's), which the fiends had vainly opposed in such a way that they had suffered for their temerity. In fact Virgil himself had been to the lowest circle (ver. 25 to 31 of the canto discussed, the 9th), and had encountered some resistance from the demons in Malebolge (c. xxi. v. 63). Hence we need not imagine (on Dante's authority) that the omnipotent Visitor of Hell added to His work the (for Him) paltry exploit of chaining Cerberus, on which performance we may more becomingly leave Hercules alone to plume himself. Furthermore, the object of our Lord's Descent was to lead away the spirits of Adam, Abel, and the others who had fulfilled the conditions of salvation under the dispensations previous to the Christian: hence it does not appear that He went further into Hell than the First Circle, or that He was resisted anywhere else than at the Upper Gate, described in canto iii., and subsequently mentioned in canto viii., *sub finem.* We can hardly be called on to imagine that the conflict was carried into the third circle (to which Cerberus was attached), or that Cerberus was allowed to quit his bounds and ascend to the scene of action. I do not know what notions the author of *Piers Ploughman* may have entertained respecting the history or mystery to which I have had to refer; but I never heard that Dante, or any of Dante's commentators, had consulted him.

I have been told that the words "del Ciel Messo," in v. 85, refer distinctly to an *angel.* But the "Messo di Dio" of Purgatory, c. xxxiii. v. 44, is always understood to be a man acting under the Divine sanction.

Will you now permit me a digression? In a recent review of Mr. W. Rossetti's *Dante's Comedy,* it is remarked *obiter* that the phrase, c. i., v. 20 —

"Che nel lago del cuor m'era durata,

becomes *nonsense* in Cayley's rendering,—

"Which in the lake, even my heart, had stay'd,"

while Mr. Rossetti's —

"The which within my heart's lake had endured,"

preserves the substance, though not the spirit, of the original. I have vainly endeavoured to imagine, or to get the irresponsible reviewer to explain to me what substantial difference there can be between "my heart's lake," and "the lake, even my heart." Will any of your correspondents on the Italian poet, or on the English language, help me to solve this difficulty?

C. B. C.

LYNCHETS, OR SHELVES, IN WILTSHIRE.
(3rd S. vii. 241, 301, 330.)

I had yesterday the pleasure of inspecting the most curious artificial terraces in this vicinity, and also comparing them with the almost exhausting notices of such earthworks in Chambers's *History of Peebleshire,* p. 39, *et seq.,* wherein reference is made to a remarkable instance recorded by Gordon in his *Itinerarium Septentrionale,* p. 114.

To those who are accustomed, like myself, to traverse the hills of the Lowland Highlands of Scotland, the idea that shelves like these were formed by the passages of sheep or cattle only excites a smile. We have thousands, I might almost say millions, of the tracks made by those animals, the ovines being quite distinct in character from the bovines, and both from the shelves and terraces in question, of the artificial nature of which Chambers gives us the uncontradictable proof, that in the instance of one on Arthur's Seat, near Edinburgh, it is like those on the Rhine, *faced with rude masonry.*

Every hill in this district, however, gives us evidence of the extension of cultivation to a height we would not dream of attempting now. And why? Labour was cheap in those days, and artificial manures unknown. The manure that they had was applied to some small patch of ground round the homestead; while year after year virgin soil, whenever it could be conveniently found on the holding, was broken up, and then again let run to grass. Where then the inclination was such that the plough could be used that implement was employed. Where, however, the slope was too steep, and the soil at the same time rich, the exposure being also favourable, terraces were gradually formed by the spade, very much in the way that what are called "lazy beds" in this district are to the present hour.

GEORGE VERE IRVING.
Culter Mains, April 26, 1865.

It is evident that these terms are applied to two very different features of the land, and that the "shelves" of Devon and Gloucestershire are not of the same character as those of Wilts, to which Cobbett alludes. Lynchets are paths along the hill sides, trodden by sheep and cattle in the way to their pasture grounds; shelves are broad terraces following the contour of the hills of the chalk formation, and which are occasionally, where the ground permits, brought under cultivation, but from their inaccessible situation remain more frequently uncultivated. They are well-known features of the landscape to such as, like Mr. Garrett and myself, are familiar with the scenery of Wilts and Dorset, and no doubt we have speculated at times in common on the causes of their formation, and with various conclusions; but as for myself I do not hold with the opinion that the lynchets have an archæological significance. In some localities they certainly assume very much the appearance of artificial ramparts, and may possibly have been used in primitive ages for purposes of defence, but closer observation leads me to conclude that the idea of artificial construction must be abandoned, and that they are, in fact, the work of nature, not of man. The most plausible explanation of their origin that occurs to me is, that they may be of the nature of raised beaches, indicating successive stages of that great geological process which effected the gradual elevation of the chalk above the then surrounding ocean This hypothesis, however, requires confirmation. W. W. S.

MISTLETOE (3rd S. vii. 76, 157, 226, 326.)—A rejoinder to J. A. P. will, I trust, be allowed me, as my last on the subject, as other more important occupations preclude their further interruption.

The discussion arose upon the query of A. A. as to the meaning and derivation of the word *misletoe*, and J. A. P., entirely ignoring Pliny's account of its meaning at his time in Gaul, gave only that writer's account of its propagation from a previous chapter, thus travelling out of the record; to which I endeavoured to call his attention.

In his rejoinder, however, Pliny's knowledge is seemingly disavowed, contrary to what I think has been the invariable opinion, not only of contemporaries (he refused for his MSS. *cccc millibus summum*, equal to 3242l.); and I need not repeat the encomiums of posterity, down to the opinion I have given of the late Sir Francis Palgrave, who first taught me his knowledge of German. It cannot therefore be denied that Pliny did not know the form and meaning of the indigenous word. Whatever Pliny's private opinion of the injurious effect of the parasite might be is here nothing to the purpose. In the passage I cited, the Druids are said to have held a directly different view—to have considered it of the most potent efficacy, which J. A. P.'s exposition of his own favourite word *virgulam eximiæ virtutis* exactly expresses, and which great repute, if we

could not gather from our own Christmas festive observance, may be found in one of the most celebrated recitals of the Edda, where the Misletoe is the only herb potent enough for the arm of Loke to slay the best-beloved son of Odin, the mild Baldur. As for the indigenous form of the word, it is, I believe, an etymological axiom that when the consonants—the bones and sinews of a word, disregarding the vowels, which are merely the filling in and covering of the frame—have a significance in a tradition, those consonants are the true root. *Omnia sanantem* would certainly be more literally expressed in German by *all-heil*, but, as J. A. P. admits, there is no significance in these words to the plant in question; there is this requisite, however, in *mistel*, which, as a contracted form of *meist-heil(sam)*, is a true exponent of Pliny's version, and consequently the indigenous term. WILLIAM BELL, Phil. Dr.
6, Crescent Place, W.C.

ADVERBS IMPROPERLY USED (3rd S. vii. 152, 225.)—"Oh, she is very poorly;" "Thank you, she is very nicely."

What are we to say of these two expressions, one of which has been admitted into use, the other is knocking at the door? P. S. C.

SOBRIQUETS OF REGIMENTS (3rd S. vii. 4, 251.)—With reference to G.'s question, I have referred to the official Army Lists from 1754, the earliest date from which they exist, and find no trace of the 25th Regiment having ever borne the name of "Edinburgh." Until the year 1782 it had no other designation than its number. In that year I find "The Sussex" interlined in MS., and in the following years printed. It continued to be called by this name until 1805, when Lord George Lennox, the colonel, died. The Hon. Charles Fitzroy was appointed colonel, and the designation of "The Sussex" was transferred to the 35th Regiment in lieu of "The Dorsetshire," which that regiment had borne for twenty-five years. On 14th May, 1805, a letter was addressed to the colonel, acquainting him, "That His Majesty has been pleased to order that the Regiment of Infantry under your command shall in future be styled *the 25th Regiment, or the King's Own Borderers.*"

I have not been able to find the authority for the designation "The Sussex" as applied to the 25th Regiment. JOHN MACLEAN.
Hammersmith.

The 97th, "the Celestials," from the light blue facings.

2nd Dragoon Guards, "Queen's Bays."

"The Enniskillins" and the "Carbineers" seem to be omitted from the list. The 33rd are certainly "The Havercake Lads." Are not the 2nd Life Guards the "Nulli Secundus?"

ANON.

THE O'CONNORS OF KERRY (3rd S. vii. 280.)—
X. Y. X. will find a genealogy of the O'Connors
of Kerry in the first part of Mr. R. F. Cronnelly's
Irish Family History, now in course of publication by Messrs. Goodwin, Son, and Nethercott,
Dublin. A work valuable to Irish historical students, lately noticed in " N. & Q."

                          JOHN MACLEAN.
Hammersmith.

THOMAS MAY, DRAMATIST AND HISTORIAN (3rd
S. vi. 286.)—The arms borne by him were, Gu. a
fesse betw. 8 billets or. The crest was out of a
ducal coronet or., a lion's head gu. The family
first came into Sussex from Kennington, Kent, on
the marriage of John May with Alice Shoyswell
of Etchingham.   W. D. C.

HOG FEAST (3rd S. vii. 295.)—This custom,
now nearly obsolete, prevailed in parts of the
West Riding of York under the name of Bedlam
Feast. It may have had its origin from the same
cause as the hog feast, but at one I was invited to,
the host dispensed with our assistance in salting
the flitches and hams. Our servant (a native of
Barnsley) tells me that her mother has a " spit "
called a " Bedlam-spit," consisting of a number
of hooks, one above the other, tied to a rod of
iron, with wire, upon which the " offal" parts
were hung to roast. What may be the derivation of the word " Bedlam" in connection with
this feast I do not know.   A. GOLDTHORP.
Wakefield.

A very pretty illustration on this subject will
be found in the fourth part (Herbst) of Ludwig
Richter's *Für's Haus*, published at Leipzig in
1861 or 1862.   JOHN DAVIDSON.

DISSOLUTION OF RELIGIOUS HOUSES (3rd S. vii.
94.)—Dugdale in his *Mon. Angl.*, vol. vi. of Cayley and Ellis's edition, gives a full account of the
possessions of the Knights of St. John of Jerusalem. The outlying societies of the Hospitallers
were called Commanderies, those of the Templars
being distinguished as Preceptories.   CPL.

"NO MAN IS A HERO TO HIS VALET DE CHAM-
BRE " (3rd S. vii. 150, 309.) — J. M. K. inquires
about the Antigonus, whose saying I forwarded to
"N. & Q." I found it in the following passage of
William Penn's *No Cross, No Crown* (p. 305, ed.
1806), which I copy out in full : —

" Antigonus being taken sick, he said, ' It was a warning
from God to instruct him of his mortality.' A poet flattering him with the title of the Son of God, he answered,
' *My servant knows the contrary.*' Another sycophant
telling him, that the will of kings is the rule of justice.
'No,' saith he, 'rather justice is the rule of the will of
kings;' and being pressed by his minions to put a garrison into Athens to hold the Greeks in subjection, he
answered, he had not a stronger garrison than the affections of his people."

I believe that this special Antigonus was the
King of Macedonia, who was the cotemporary and
correspondent of Zeno; and if we may judge from
a letter preserved by Stobæus, and also to be
found in the work above quoted, the sayings here
given seem very much to suit his character.

                         FRANCIS TRENCH.
Islip Rectory.

YEW TREES CALLED PALMS (3rd S. vii. 306.)—
Looking over the accounts of the churchwardens
of Woodbury, I find the following : —

" Memorandum, 1775.—That a Yew or Palm Tree was
planted in the church yard, ye south side of the church,
in the same place where one was blown down by the
wind a few days ago, this 25th of November."

Signed by the churchwardens and eight parishioners.   H. T. E.

DALYELL'S " SCOTTISH POEMS " (3rd S. vii. 254.)
Haly hag matins.—" *Halyoch* (gutt.)," according
to Jamieson, is "a term used to express that strange
gabbling noise people make who are talking in a
language we do not understand.—*Gall.*" The Celtic word *Goilemach* signifies prating, tattling.

Foster.—Celtic *Foisteachair*, a hireling. I think,
but cannot be sure, that I have heard the word
foster applied to a steward or overseer of workers
in the south of Scotland, where *wood-*foster was a
common term for a forester—one who had the
charge of woods. In this case *foster* may be merely
a corruption of forester; but why *wood-*foster ?

Half mark steikis.—May not this be the same
as *hamart steiks*, home-made clothes ? See Jamieson, *Hamart* and *Steiks.*

Tottis russet.—Tots or taits, that is, locks of
wool or hair; russit or rushit, from *rush*—diar-
rhœa. These rushit, or rushid, locks are cleared
away from the clean parts of a sheep's fleece; and
are, or rather were, often scoured and manufactured into cloth, blankets, or stockings for home
use.

A cott of kelt.—Sibbald (*Chronicles of Scottish
Poetry*) explains the word *kelt* to mean " cloth
with a frieze, commonly made of native black
wool."

Cashmaries, according to Jamieson, " fish car-
riers, or people who drive fish from the sea through
the villages."

Bryde.—*Bred, brod:* a board, a shelf (?).

Bedene.—Unless this is bidding, command, I
know not what it means.

Duschet, Dussie (Dulset?).—A musical instrument. See Jamieson, *Scot. Dict.* : —

" He toned his dussie for a spring."—P. 315.
" Vpon his duschet vpe he played."—P. 317.

                             ANON.

THOMAS BILBIE (3rd S. vii. 240.)—The Bilbies
were a firm of bellfounders at Chewstoke, Somerset, and at Collumpton, Devon, in which counties,
as also in Dorset, Gloucester, and Wilts, their
bells are found. Their names were Thomas, 1734-

1766; Abraham, 1769; William, 1780-1783; and Thomas, 1791-1805. The earliest date occurs in an inscription on a bell at St. Peter's, Dorchester:—

"Mr Renaldo Knapton saw me cast the 21st Septr 1734. Mr Daniel Arden, Mr. Joseph Gigger, Chwardens. Tho. Bilbie cast all these six bells. Ring to the praise of God."

A curious inscription occurs at Kenton, Devon:—

"T. Bilbie cast all we, 1747."

See the Rev. W. C. Lukis's *Account of Church Bells.* Parkers, 1857. A most interesting work on the subject.   CPL.

CLINT HILLS (3rd S. vii. 323.)—This should be spelt Clent. I am not sure if Umbra (Mr. Charles Clifford) and F. C. B. mean the same place. Umbra, no doubt, refers to Clent Hill in this neighbourhood, on the top of which are four stones of immemorial anti uity, placed in a slight artificial cavity. It is,qI believe, generally supposed that they are Druidical, and of the same character as those on Stonehenge; but there is no record about them, and only a foolish legend, probably not very ancient, calling them Ossian's tomb.

Hagley.   LYTTELTON.

THE THIRD PLAGUE OF EGYPT (3rd S. vii. 297.) Your respected correspondent, J. DALTON, in an interesting note on this subject, seems inclined to adopt the theory of Dr. Kalisch and others, who have argued that *gnats* and not *lice* were the "little animals" that visited the Egyptians in the third plague. It will be borne in mind, however, that the plagues of Egypt were of a remarkably *distinctive* character, directed with a punitive virulence and force against local peculiarities and superstitions, and to shock local faith. The *flies* of the fourth plague we know were especially calculated to wound the idolatrous sensibilities of the people: if such an effectual instrument in fulfilling this special purpose, is it probable that a torment would have been prepared so similar in character to its immediate predecessor? Moreover, the expression is remarkable; it is said that "the dust of the land became lice *in* man and *in* beast;" *gnats*, it is true, especially those of the mosquito kind, would be a terrible scourge, but *lice* would be a still sorer visitation, afflicting the flesh, and at the same time holding up to the Egyptians a shocking and loathsome picture of their *uncleanness.*   F. PHILLOTT.

To the authority of Dr. Kalisch may be added that of Dr. Davidson (*Introduction to the Old Testament*, vol. i. (1862) p. 220), who takes the word commonly rendered *lice* as meaning *marsh gnats.* The same writer is of opinion that the fourth plague consisted of swarms of the beetle, *i. e. Blatta orientalis*, adding, however, that "many authorities are in favour of the *dog-fly.*"   Q.

PHILLIPS FAMILY (3rd S. iv. 230.)—The subject of your correspondent's query was the son of Christopher Phillips. See Savage's, *Genealogical Dictionary of the First Settlers of New England,* iii. 410. It is to be regretted that nothing more is known of one whose descendants are so respectable and numerous in America.   S. W. P.
New York.

BOOKBINDING (3rd S. vii. 138.)—Some valuable remarks on this subject are contained in the preface to the *Catalogue of the Choicer Portion of the Magnificent Library formed by M. Guglielmo Libri,* London, 1859. See also the splendid work, *Monuments Inédits ou peu connus, faisant Partie du Cabinet de Guillaume Libri,* London, 1862.   S. W. P.
New York.

BARLEY (3rd S. v. 358; vi. 481; vii. 84, 162, 285.) — Considerable information as to this word will be found in Jamieson's *Scotch Dictionary, sub voc.* "Barla-breikis, Barla-fummil, and Barley." Barla-fumill, in his secondary sense of a fall, occurs in a letter from Sir Robert Moray to the Earl of Lauderdale, in August 1663. Brit. Mus., Add. MS. 23,118, f. 52.   GEORGE VERE IRVING.

May not this be a corruption of By'rlady or Barlady as it used to be written? *e. g.* By'rlady, I claim this! By'rlady, I shall have half! By'rlady, I do this! or as a small boy ought to say, Barley me this! Barley ha'avs! Barley! (suiting the action to the word).   J. WETHERELL.

THE BELL OF ST. CENEU, OR ST. KEYNA (3rd S. vii. 297.)—Some years ago I bought a bell of this description from a shepherd on the borders of Salisbury Plain. It had been used as a sheep bell. It is not so large as the indicated size of that of St. Keyna. I have, however, seen one as large in the private museum of a friend in Northamptonshire, which had been used as a cattle bell. I forget whether he got it in Northamptonshire or Scotland. My bell is made of sheet iron, hammered into the rude form described, and rivetted, with clapper, and a loop for the handle. It is also imperfectly coated with brass. Such bells, though fashioned after the most ancient type, have still been made in modern times. I understand they were coated with brass in the following manner:— When the iron part was completed, the workman bound the bell round and round in various directions with thin brass wire. This done, he submitted it to the heat of the furnace, when the brass melted, and ran over the surface of the iron. Such bells, though getting scarce, are met with in the great sheep grazing districts. They are being superseded by the common house bells. As a concluding paragraph, I would ask, whether the bell of St. Keyna has been preserved, and if so, where?   P. HUTCHINSON.

"ONE STEP' FROM THE SUBLIME TO THE RIDICULOUS" (3rd S. vii. 280.)—This saying, generally attributed to Napoleon I., occurs in the writings of a too-noted Englishman, Thomas Paine: of a date prior to any supposable appropriation of it by the great emperor. Paine says: —

"The sublime and the ridiculous are often so nearly related, that it is difficult to class them separately. One step above the sublime makes the ridiculous; and one step above the ridiculous makes the sublime again."

Possibly this is but a re-echo of the idea of Fontenelle. β.

LETTERS OF ALEXANDER KNOX AND HANNAH MORE (3rd S. vii. 323.)—ABHBA will find the three letters to the late Dr. Miller in the Church of England Magazine (1849), vol. xxvi. pp. 206, 266. B. E. S.

CURIOUS NOMENCLATURE (3rd S. vii. 322.)— Should you be disposed to adopt the suggestion of your correspondent OWEN TUDOR of a list of curious names, I beg to inform you that a few years ago this town could boast of four surgeons in active practice, who bore the appropriate names of Sharp, Keen, Steel, and Hardy. The first and two last are still living, but the second fell a victim to his efforts in the relief of the poor during an irruption of Asiatic cholera. M. D. Warrington.

SPUR MONEY IN BELFRIES (3rd S. vii. 324.)— Quoting from the two General Indexes of "N & Q," MR. FISHWICK will easily find an answer to his Query if he will refer to 1st S. i. 373-374, 462, 494; 2nd. S. xi. 508; xii. 37, 97, 140, 176, 229, 259, 276, and to other vols. of 3rd S.

Will MR. FISHWICK favour me with a copy per post of the rules he saw in Burnley Belfry? He will much oblige H. T. ELLACOMBE. Rectory, Clyst St. George, Devon.

VOLTAIRE (3rd S. vii. 211, 284.)—The considerations urged by F. C. H. will undoubtedly claim our utmost attention whenever we have before us the authority on which Mr. Danzy Sheen founded his statement. In the meanwhile I feel assured that F. C. H. will agree with me that such considerations are not of themselves sufficient to establish an historical fact. MELETES.

LOCAL GHOSTS (3rd S. vi. 268.)—When "making up" your last volume for the binder, a fortnight ago, I noticed two queries, on p. 268, on which I may be permitted a word or two.

ANON asks, "What was the black dog of Winchester?" The same probably, I would answer, as the black dog of Colchester; and what he was is declared, without doubt or misgiving, by Mr. Thomas Woodcock in a letter to Richard Baxter, printed in The Certainty of the Worlds of Spirits, London, 1691, 8vo: —

"I remember," writes Mr. Woodcock, "a story of one at Colchester, who, in a bravado and defiance of the Devil,

would walk in the night to the churchyard, where it was reported he appeared and walked; and he met him in the shape of a Black Dog with terrible eyes, which brought him by terrors into such a mind, that he was never quiet in his mind till he got into good Society" [!].

It must be added, however, that a black dog often serves to mask a supernatural visitor; and Mrs. Crowe, in her Night Side of Nature, mentions two families (one located in Cornwall) who are warned of approaching deaths by apparitions in this shape.

The "Barguard of York" refers, no doubt, to the "Barguest" of the northern counties: a spirit which is sometimes seen "sitting on a rail" of a gate or style at high noon, in this respect resembling the classical "Empusa" (of his legs we have no report), and in disposition showing his kinship with the "Bogle," "Hobgoblin," and "Robin Goodfellow."

The only apparition connected with Rochester that I can recall, is that of a dying mother to her children there (vide Beaumont, and others), and this does not fall into the category of "local ghosts." A. CHALLSTETH.
1, Verulam Buildings, Gray's Inn.

"WATTE VOCAT," ETC. (3rd S. vii. 285.)—It may possibly interest your correspondent H. W. T. to know that, in addition to the version by Andrews of Gower's lines, "Watte vocat," &c., there is a characteristically quaint and amusing translation "bestowed" by Fuller in his Church History, 1655, book iv. p. 139. The original verses (which, it may be added, are from the first book of the Vox Clamantis), differ, as quoted by Fuller, in one or two trifling particulars from the copy given in a recent number of "N. & Q." (vide suprà), e. g. Betteque for Batteque; Lorkin for Larkin; Tebbe for Tibbe; vovet for volat; quos for quem; and, in the third line, Gibbe (a misprint?) for Bobbe.

The translation runs (? limps) as follows: —

"Tom comes thereat, when call'd by Wat, and Simm as forwarde we finde;
Bett calls as quick, to Gibb and to Hykk, that neither would tarry behinde.
Bobb [Gibb?], a good whelp of that litter, doth help mad Coll more mischief to do;
And Will he doth vow, the time is come now, he'l joyn with their company too.
Davie complains, while Grigg gets the gaines, and Hobb with them doth partake;
Lorkin aloud, in the midst of the crowd, conceiveth as deep is his stake.
Hudde doth spoil, whom Judde doth foile, and Tebb lends his helping hand;
But Jack, the mad patch, men and houses doth snatch, and kills all at his command."

"Oh, the methodical description of a confusion!" continues our author. "How doth Wat lead the front, and Jack bring up the rere! . . . . All men without sir-names (Tiler was but the addition of his trade, and Straw a mock-name, assumed by himself; though Jack Straw would have been John of Gold had this treason took effect), so obscure they were and inconsiderable. And, as they had no sir-names, they deserved no Christian names for their heathenish cruelties."

JOHN B. SHAW, M.A.

Old Trafford, Manchester.

WORDS USED IN DIFFERENT SENSES (3rd S. vii. 278.) — In addition to the instances quoted by E. H. A. from Archbishop Trench, let me add the following use of the word *prostitute*. It occurs in —

"The Original of Idolatries; or the Birth of Heresies. First faithfully gathered out of Sundry Greeke and Latine Authors, &c., by that famous and learned Isaac Casaubon, and by him published in French for the Good of God's Church; and now translated into English for the Benefit of this Monarchy. By Abraham Darcie. London, 1624."

In the Epistle Dedicatory to Prince Charles, Darcie subscribes himself —

"Your Highnes most
Humble and devoted prostitute,
AB. DARCIE."

The word is evidently used in the sense of "your humble servant." The word as now used is so thoroughly different, that it would be interesting to trace the change of it.   G. W. N.

Other than phonetically, it cannot be taken as the same word; but the oddity of its application may render it worth "making a note of." When an Irish peasant has a point to gain, or a grievance to complain of, he sets off to his landlord, or to some other gentleman at a reasonable distance, with: "Your honour's so good, I'd always sooner trouble your honour nor any jontleman in the county; so, if you plaze, I'll *insense* ye wid' the whole matter." Not meaning to incense his auditor, but to put sense into him of Paddy's particular purpose: after his own fashion, of course.

E. L. S.

SPILLING SALT (3rd S. vii. 282.) — In Dacier's *Life of Pythagoras* there is the following passage, alluding to this subject (I quote from the English translation, p. 60): —

"He said that 'Salt was the emblem of justice: for as salt preserves all things and prevents corruption, so justice preserves whatever it animates, and, without it, all is corrupted.' He therefore ordered that a saltcellar should always be served on the table, to put men in mind of this virtue. And doubtless this was the reason the heathens sanctified the table by the saltcellar, which custom was perhaps taken from the law that God gave to his people: 'You shall offer salt in all your offerings' (Lev. iii. 13). And who knows but the superstition that was so ancient, and that reigns to this day, concerning the spilling of salt, came from the opinion of the Pythagoreans, who regarded it as a presage of some injustice?"

G. E.

"OCULUM SACERDOTIS" (3rd S. vii. 298.) — This treatise is generally considered to have been the work of William de Pagula, who was Vicar of Winkfield, in Berkshire; and died about 1350. It does not appear to have been ever printed.

Several copies of it are to be found in MS. The Cambridge University Library possesses two copies: one in folio, and one in octavo, both written in hands of the fifteenth century. Trinity College, Oxford, has a copy, which in Mr. Coxe's *Catalogue* has this title: —

"Liber qui dicitur Oculus Sacerdotis, in tres partes distinctus, auctore forsitan Gulielmo de Pagulo [sive Gualtero Parker, sive cujuscumque sit]."

There is also a copy in the library of Balliol College, in which the title runs: —

"Johannis de Burgo, sive cujuscumque sit, Oculus Sacerdotis," etc.—Coxe's *Cat. Cod. MSS.*

Joh. de Burgo was the author of *Pupilla Oculi*. In the same library is a continuation of the work, with the title *Cilium Oculi Sacerdotis*.

A copy of the *Oculus Sacerdotis* is also in the Lambeth Library, but is there said to be in *two* parts; so probably the third part is wanting. See Todd's *Catalogue*.

The Cambridge octavo copy consists of nearly 400 closely written pages, and is entitled *Oculi Sacerdotum*. The first part is called "Pars prima Oculi Sacerdotum;" the second, "Dextera pars Oculi Sacerdotum;" and the third, "Sinistra pars Oculi Sacerdotum."

Some notice of the work will be found in Tanner's *Bibliotheca*, p. 570.   E. V.

Cambridge.

SUNDIALS (3rd S. vii. 200, 291.) — A great deal of useful and valuable information on the construction of sundials may be found in Emerson's *Dialling, or the Art of Drawing Dials, on all sorts of Planes whatsoever*, London, J. Nourse, 1770. Very little mathematical knowledge is required in order to understand this excellent treatise, and be able to construct many useful kinds of dials.

T. T. W.

Heather, *On the Use of Mathematical Instruments*, Weale, London, will give S. W. P. some information on this head.   WILLIAM BLOOD.

"CLEANLINESS IS NEXT TO GODLINESS" (3rd S. vi. 259, 337.)—Amongst the instances in which this proverb was quoted some time ago in "N. & Q.," I did not see the sense in which my old nurse employed it many years ago. In my childhood, she urged it as a reason why the Saturday night's tub-washing should precede the Sunday morning's appearance at church.   M. D.

WASHINGTON ARMS (3rd S. vii. 11.) — Seeing in "N. & Q.," an article headed "Washington Arms," and implying a curiosity respecting the relatives of Washington in England, I note that in the churchyard of Sedberg, in Yorkshire, there are, or were in the year 1800, several tombstones of families of that name in the neighbourhood, and there was a local tradition that the American leader, or his progenitors in America, were relations of these. The tombstones were of the upright kind, four or five feet high, with more than one name on each, such as are common among substantial yeomen.   T.

RAGUSA (3rd S. vii. 180, 265, 310.) — I have no doubt that Ragusa was at one time independent of Venice. The blazon of its arms, which I gave from Triers at p. 265, occurs among the "Wapen der kleinen *Frey-Staaten*," the others so given being those of Lucca, Geneva, and San-Marino. I have never seen a shield of the arms of Venice in which the arms of Ragusa appeared among the quarterings.

I think it possible that at one time or other Ragusa may have borne for arms Barry of eight arg. and gu., as MR. DAVIDSON says, that a shield so charged appears upon the coinage of the state. For, on referring to Rietstap, *L'Armorial Général* (Gonda, 1861), I find that Marshal Viesse de Marmont, who was created Duke of Ragusa by the Emperor Napoleon I., bore those arms in the first and fourth quarters of his shield.

But, again, in *L'Armorial Général de l'Empire Français* (folio, Paris, 1812), published by Henry Simon, "Graveur du Cabinet de sa Majesté l'Empereur et Roi, et du Conseil du Sceau des Titres," a work, therefore, in which we may expect accuracy; both the engraving (tome i. planche 13) and the description make the first and fourth quarters of the arms of the Duke of Ragusa to be arg. three bendlets *gu.*

After all, I suppose the best authority we can have is "L'Ecu Complet" of the Emperor of Austria, the present possessor of Ragusa, in which it appears as I blazoned it at p. 265 (arg. three bendlets az.), but with the significant omission of the golden word—LIBERTAS.   JOHN WOODWARD.
New Shoreham.

THE SCOTCH WORD "ESK" (3rd S. vii. 296.) — Permit me to correct your correspondent S., who says that this word means an *asp*. It means, and is still commonly used for, an *eft* or *newt*. S. spells it *esk*, but that he and I mean the same word is plain from his reference to the ballad of "Young Tamlane," who was transformed certainly not into a poisonous asp, but into a harmless, though not lovable, newt. That this word cannot have given its name to the river Esk is also certain, since the *ask* or *newt* does not frequent rivers but pools or ditches. Even if it had meant *asp*, the derivation could not be supposed, since the asp has never existed in the British islands, whose sole noxious reptile is the viper or adder.
      K.

DIOGENES' LANTERN (3rd S. vii. 298.) — The "*honest* man" is as old as Charles Dibdin, probably older: —

" Diogenes, who was a wag in his way,
 Took a lantern and candle one sunshiny day,
 For a man that was honest to search all about,
 But before he could find one the candle went out."

Diogenes Laertius says : — Λύχνον μεθ' ἡμέραν ἄψας, "Ανθρωπον φησὶ ζητῶ (*De Vitis Philos.*, l. vi. c. 41), which looks as if he had prepared the answer, and lighted the candle to be asked. Phædrus avoids this, and gives the air of an impromptu by saying that Æsop's master sent him for a light.

" Tum circumeunti fuerat quod iter longius
 Effecit brevius : namque recte per forum
 Cœpit redire, et quidam e turba garrulus,
 ' Æsope, medio sole quid cum lumine ? '
 ' Hominem,' inquit, ' quæro,' et abiit festinans domum."

What word would Diogenes have used for *honest?* Καλοκάγαθος? χρηστός?

Another saying (c. 40) illustrates the use of ἄνθρωπος alone. 'Εκ τοῦ βαλανείου ἐξιών, τῷ μὲν πυθομένῳ εἰ πολλοὶ ἄνθρωποι λοῦνται, ἠρνήσατο· τῷ δὲ, εἰ πολὺς ὄχλος, ὡμολόγησε. The small wit of this answer is scarcely conveyed in Mr. Yonge's translation : —

" Once, when he was leaving the bath, and a man asked him whether many men were bathing, he said, 'No ;' but when a number of people came out, he confessed that there were a great many."—P. 231.

Some questions have been asked about kindling fire by rubbing two pieces of wood together. The difficulties of the ancients must have been great, when Phædrus, who always regards probability, represents the master of a house, with such a slave as Æsop, obliged to send beyond the market-place for a light.   H. B. C.
U. U. Club.

FAG, A REMNANT (3rd S. vii. 110, 268.) — The term *fag*, in the sense here applied, is in common use in many parts of Scotland. Not long ago I saw the death of a child certified by a skilful, though a somewhat waggish, medical practitioner, as having been caused by " the *fag-end* of nirls," *i. e. sequelæ* of measles. And, but very recently, I happened to be in a draper's shop in the city of Aberdeen, when a person from the country came in, and, on presenting a piece of cloth to the merchant, and asking if he had any of the web on hand from which the piece had been previously cut off, the latter replied, " I ha'e only the *fag* o't left ;" at the same time he exhibited the remnant, or fragment of the web to the enquirer. The words *fag* and *lag* are often applied synonymously to the person who is the last to enter appearance at an assembly or meeting. Both words are also used in the different senses given in Jamieson's *Dictionary of the Scottish Language, q. v.* "He's a *fag* o' a chiel," (Angl. fellow), is often applied to idle or indolent workmen in the north-east of Scotland ; and the opprobrium of " lazy *faggot*" to women of the like stamp.   A. J.

VISCOUNT CHAWORTH (3rd S. vii. 279.) — Burke's *Extinct Peerage*, edit. 1850, states the last Viscount died Feb. 15, 1699.   D. D. H.

"FROM OXFORD TO ROME" (3rd S. vii. 339.) — The writer of this work was a Miss Harris. Its opening advertisement is dated "Windsor, Christmas Day, 1846." The authoress subsequently became a Catholic; and in a letter in the *Tablet* she thus wrote: —

"I am anxious to express my deep regret for having given publicity to unauthorised statements, or false impressions, concerning the Church of Rome and its members, in this and in other instances. I lament the publication of my work; I would gladly recal it, if it were under my controul."

As to the characters introduced in the book, I never heard that they referred to any individuals. I believe them to have been purely imaginary.
F. C. H.

The "distinguished Fellow" was Dr. Newman.
LYTTELTON.
Hagley, Stourbridge.

THREE PARALLEL PROVERBS (3rd S. vii. 337.) — The contributor of the note, under the above heading, expresses a doubt whether the one which he thinks the best of all —

"Ne'er cast a clout
Till May be out,"—

is used in England, as well as in Scotland. I can inform him that it is well known in Norfolk. It was quoted to me very lately; but with an apology for its being vulgar, which I think it as fully deserves to be called as to be styled "comprehensive and laconic." It was cited in consequence of my having just repeated the French proverb; but as the person to whom I spoke did not understand French, I extemporised it in English thus for the occasion : —

"In April dread,
To throw off a thread."

F. C. H.

NOSSELS (3rd S. vii. 339.) — This word I take to be identical with *Nosles;* and as applicable to a hearse, to mean the projections on the top on which the plumes were fitted; or wooden pegs, more or less ornamental, in default of plumes.
F. C. H.

WOODWARD OF UPTON (3rd S. vii. 209.) — I hoped to have been able to supply MR. ADLARD with some of the information he requires, but find I have not here the papers which might enable me to do so. In the course of a few weeks I shall be able to make a search for them elsewhere. At present I have only a pedigree from John Woodward of Upton (father of the George Woodward first mentioned as being Clerk of the Castle of Windsor), for six generations down to the year 1644. It appears to be extracted from Harl. MSS. 1198, 1391, 1533, &c. These references may help

MR. ADLARD, if the reading room at the British Museum is accessible to him.
JOHN WOODWARD.

DOCKING HORSES (3rd S. vii. 185.) — I have heard or read, I cannot say where, a translation of the French lines, which, perhaps, is worth preserving : —

"Capricious, proud, the self-same axe avails
To chop off monarchs' heads and horses' tails.
O, barbarous English ! decency you shock;
Tails you curtail, and sentence block to block.".
FITZHOPKINS.
Garrick Club.

PATRICK ANDERSON (3rd S. vii. 202.) — In your note on the query of F. M. S. regarding Patrick Anderson, you observe, "that although Anderson is a common name in Scotland, and more than one advocate bearing it have held good positions at the bar, none have ever been raised to the judicial bench." There is, however, one instance to the contrary, and that at no distant period, in Adam Anderson, a son of the late Samuel Anderson, Esq., of Moredun, who was raised to the bench in 1852 (after having previously held the office of Lord Advocate) by the title of Lord Anderson. But he did not long enjoy the dignity, having died in London on September 28, 1853, aged fifty-six.   W. E.

"DIE SPITZE" IN GERMAN BLAZON (3rd S. vii. 310.) — There is, I think, no exact equivalent in English heraldry for the German "Spitze." I should make use of the French equivalent "enté en point," or "la pointe entée."

Thus I should blazon the royal arms of Spain — "Quarterly, 1 and 4, Castille; 2 and 3, Leon.; enté en point de Grenada," &c.

The English word *grafted* might perhaps be used, but I doubt its being generally intelligible.
J. WOODWARD.
New Shoreham.

Miscellaneous.

NOTES ON BOOKS, ETC.

Ten Years in Sweden; being a Description of the Landscape, Climate, Domestic Life, Forests, Mines, Agriculture, Field Sports, and Fauna of Scandinavia. By An Old Bushman. (Groombridge & Son.)

The "Old Bushman" has here undertaken a task for which he has shown himself fully qualified by previous publications. He has lived among the Swedes till he has learned to appreciate their good qualities, while he does not hesitate to point out in a kindly spirit some of their defects. His views of the social and material condition of the country deserve attention, because they are based upon a ten years' residence in it; and what he has, during those ten years, observed carefully, he tells us very pleasantly. His notices of the Swedish *fauna* will interest students of natural history.

Biographies of Eminent Soldiers of the last Four Centuries.
By Major-General John Mitchell. *Edited, with a Me-*
moir of the Author, by Leonhard Schmitz, LL.D.
(Blackwood.)

The reputation of the author of *The Life of Wallen-*
stein and *The Fall of Napoleon*, as a military critic and
biographer, is too firmly established and too widely recognised to render further allusion to it necessary; and we
shall most fitly commend the present series of sketches to
the notice of our readers by pointing out of what they
consist. The eminent soldiers, whose lives are here described by General Mitchell, are Zisca, the Hussite, Scan-
derbeg, the Chevalier Bayard, the Constable of Bourbon,
the Duke of Alba, Field Marshal Suwaroff; Marshal
Massena, Field Marshal Schulenburg, Max Emanuel,
and Charles XII., Prince Eugene, the Duke of Marlborough, Marshall Saxe, and Frederick II. Two Essays
"On the French Army," and "The British Army in the
World of 1850," complete a volume which is sure to find
a place in every military library.

El Consultor Universal (Notes and Queries Español), &c.
Nos. I. to IV. (Barcelona, London, Molini.)|
Bradshaw's Illustrated Hand Book to Spain and Portugal.
By Dr. Charnock, F.S.A. (Adams.)

We doubt if any better proof could be given of the
rapid strides which Spain is making to regain her place
among the nations of Europe, than is evinced by the publication of the two works whose titles we have just transcribed. A Spanish *Bradshaw* says much for her advance;
but to our thinking, a Spanish *Notes and Queries* says far
more. We heartily welcome our fellow labourer, who has
adopted for his model our French cousin, *L'Intermediare*;
and Spanish scholars in England will, we are sure, join
us in such welcome.

E'pis et Bluets. Par Le Chevalier de Chatelain. (Rolandi.)
Fleurs des Bords du Rhin. Par Le Chevalier de Chatelain. (Rolandi.)

The first of these handsomely printed little volumes
contains a number of original poems by the Chevalier de
Chatelain, among which our Shakspearian friends will
find some dozen graceful sonnets on Shakspeare. The
second, on the contrary, contains a series of translations
from the poets of Germany, executed with that facility
for which the author has now established a peculiar
reputation.

Brande's Dictionary of Science, Literature, and Art.
Part II. (Longman.)

The new Part of this useful encyclopædia-in-little,
which extends from "Baptistery" to "Cofferdam," fully
justifies the favourable opinion which the first Part called
forth from us.

THE SHILLING MAGAZINE.—This new monthly candidate for public favour is under the management of Mr.
Samuel Lucas, who will be assisted by a large circle of
literary friends. The first number exhibits plenty of
variety; Fiction, Science, Archæology, Poetry, by some
of the ablest writers of the day, make up an excellent
opening number.

CAMDEN SOCIETY.—At the General Meeting of the Camden Society on Tuesday last, the Council, in announcing
the early completion of the *Promptorium*, added that, with
the view to the requirements of English philologists, they
had made arrangements for the sale of a limited number
of copies of the complete work. It was announced, too,
that the Camden Society, in concurring with the Society
of Antiquaries in an application to the Chief Judge of the
Probate Court for facilities for taking photographs of
wills of distinguished persons, had recalled Sir James

Wilde's attention to their former joint application on the
subject of the extension of the privileges now enjoyed by
literary men at Doctors' Commons, to the Registries of all
Local Courts where early wills are deposited.

THE HANDEL FESTIVAL.—The proposed Handel Festival, at the Crystal Palace, progresses in the most satisfactory manner. The alterations made in the corner
galleries were completed and tested on Good Friday with
great success. Many hundreds of excellent additional
seats have by this means been provided on the floor of
the Centre Transept. It has been decided by the Directors that the Shakspeare House shall be removed, and it
is intended to raise the seats near the garden front of the
Great Transept, which will doubtless command for them
a ready sale. The tickets for the Great Rehearsal have
also been issued, and they are being sold very rapidly.

BOOKS AND ODD VOLUMES

WANTED TO PURCHASE.

Particulars of Price, &c., of the following Books to be sent direct to
the gentlemen by whom they are required, and whose names and addresses are given for that purpose:—

ETCHINGS BY RADEMAKER about 1620.

Wanted by *Rev. J. C. Jackson*, 5, Chatham Place East,
Hackney, N.E.

LITERARY GAZETTE for July 6, 1861.
BANCROFT'S SERMON AT PAUL'S CROSS FEB. 9, 1588 : A brief Discoverie
of the Untruthes and Slanders against the true Government of the
Church of Christ.
A CHRISTIAN LETTER OF CERTAINE ENGLISH PROTESTANTS, unfained
Favourers of the present state of Religion authorized and professed in
England: unto that Reverend and learned Man, Mr. R. Hooker, re-
quiring resolution in certain matters of Doctrine, &c. &c., expresslie
contained in his Five Books of Ecclesiastical Policie. Small quarto,
1599.

Wanted by *G. W. Napier, Esq.*, Alderley Edge, near Manchester.

VOLTAIRE'S WORKS IN ENGLISH. Vol. I.
FOX'S LECTURES TO WORKING MEN. Vol. I.
GIBBON'S ROME. Vol. I. 8vo edition, in 12 vols.
RAPHAEL'S ASTROLOGY. Or any Works on Astrology.
DE CANDOLLE'S CACTI.

Wanted by *Mr. Thomas Millard*, 38, Ludgate Hill, City.

BOOK OF BRITISH BALLADS. Edited by S. C. Hall. 12th (and last) Number. 1842.

Wanted by *H. E. Dobbin, Esq.*, 2, Lower Belgrave Place, S.W.

Notices to Correspondents.

F. C. *will doubtless find the Greek Epigram on Chantrey's Woodcocks,
and many others on the same subject, in the Collection of the Verses written on the occasion, and published by Murray in* 1847, *under the title of*
Winged Words on Chantrey's Woodcocks.

CYRIL. *For the authorship of* Captain Carleton's Memoirs, *see*
"N. & Q." 2nd S. vi. 329; vii. 11, 74, 93, 150; 3rd S. vi. 375, 443; *and for
that of* Robinson Crusoe, 1st S. x. 345, 448. *The query on a pretended
resuscitation appeared in our last volume, p.* 183.

CHARLES WYLIE. *The* Twelve Golden Rules *attributed to Charles I,
are printed in* "N. & Q." 3rd S. iii. 167, 215. *After all, we are inclined
to think that these Rules were agreed to by Ben Jonson and his fellow
poets, and called by them* "Table Observations."

ERRATA.—3rd S. vii. p. 290, col. i. line 23, *for* "created" *read* "corrected;" last line but one, *for* "his next heir" *read* "her next heir;"
p. 338, col. i. 9th line from bottom, *for* "1619" *read* "1629;" p. 346, col.
i. line 38, *for* "Harrison" *read* "Harris;" and in the following line,
for "Nicholson" *read* "Nicolson."

A Reading Case for holding the weekly Nos. of "N. & Q." is now
ready, and may be had of all Booksellers and Newsmen, price 1s. 6d.;
or, free by post, direct from the publisher, for 1s. 8d.

*** *Cases for binding the volumes of* "N. & Q." *may be had of the
Publisher, and of all Booksellers and Newsmen.*

"NOTES AND QUERIES" *is published at noon on Friday, and is also
issued in* MONTHLY PARTS. *The Subscription for* STAMPED COPIES *for
Six Months forwarded direct from the Publisher (including the Half-
yearly* INDEX) *is* 11s. 4d., *which may be paid by Post Office Order,
payable at the Strand Post Office, in favour of* WILLIAM G. SMITH, 43,
WELLINGTON STREET, STRAND, W.C., *where also all* COMMUNICATIONS
FOR THE EDITOR *should be addressed.*

"NOTES & QUERIES" *is registered for transmission abroad.*

LONDON, SATURDAY, MAY 13, 1865.

CONTENTS.—N° 176.

Notes.

GOLDSMITH'S PAMPHLET ON THE COCK-LANE GHOST.

Describing Smithfield and its locality, old Stow says, " Over against the said Pie-corner lieth Cock-lane, which runneth down to Oldborne-conduit." This narrow lane was the scene, in the months of January and February, 1762, of that celebrated imposition, the Cock Lane ghost.

Almost every one of us, young and old, have heard how cunning "Fanny," with her mysterious knockings, contrived to hoax the wonder-loving Londoners, until at length the cheat was discovered and its chief contriver brought to condign punishment. Dr. Johnson, at the head of a band of savans, solemnly investigated the affair; and Goldsmith wrote a pamphlet on the subject, for which Newbery paid him three guineas. Mr. Forster, in his *Life of Oliver Goldsmith* (1848, p. 240), says : —

" But whether with Johnson, he thought the impudent imposture worth grave enquiry ; or with Hogarth, turned it to wise purposes of satire ; or only laughed at it as Churchill did ; the pamphlet has not survived to inform us."

Mr. Forster was mistaken here : the pamphlet survived, and an account of its existence was communicated to the public in an early volume of " N. & Q." (1st S. v. 77).

In the fourth edition of his entertaining biography of the poet (1863, p. 160), Mr. Forster modifies his former statement by saying : —

" It is not quite certain that the pamphlet has survived to inform us. But if, as appears probable, a tract on the *Mystery Reveal'd*, published by Newbery's neighbour Bristow, be Goldsmith's three-guinea contribution, the last is the most correct surmise. It is, however, a poor production."

This tract now lies before me. I was fortunate enough to pick it up the other day for a few shillings, from a dealer in " odds and ends," who exposes his wares to the curious at most "reasonable rates." I was going to mention his locale ; but, upon second thoughts, may not be unacceptable to the readers of " N. & Q."

To begin. It is an octavo of thirty-four pages, exclusive of title-page and bastard-title. The latter informs us that it was published at "one shilling." The former reads as follows : —

" THE MYSTERY REVEALED ; containing a SERIES of TRANSACTIONS and AUTHENTIC TESTIMONIALS, respecting the supposed COCK-LANE GHOST ; which have hitherto been concealed from the PUBLIC.

' Since none the Living [sic] dare implead,
Arraign him in the Person of the Dead.
Dryden.

London : Printed for W. Bristow, in St. Paul's Churchyard ; and C. Ethrington, York. MDCCXLII." [The date is a mistake for MDCCLXII.]

The writer commences by saying : — :

" It is somewhat remarkable that the Reformation, which in other countries banished superstition, in England seemed to increase the credulity of the vulgar. At a time when Bacon was employed in restoring true philosophy, King James was endeavouring to strengthen our prejudices, both by his authority and writings. Scot, Glanville, and Coleman, wrote and preac ed with the same design ; and our judges, particularly Sir Matthew Hale, gave some horrid proofs of their credulity."

After remarking that, "since that time, arguments of this kind have been pretty much rejected by all but the lowest class," he goes on to relate, at a considerable length, the cause of the manifestations of the Cock Lane ghost. The summary of this is, that the whole was a plot devised by one Parsons, the parish clerk of St. Sepulchre's, and carried out by his daughter, a girl of twelve years ; the object being to malign a gentleman of Norfolk, who had sued him for a debt. This gentleman was a widower, who had taken his wife's sister as his mistress (the marriage being forbidden by law), and had brought her to lodge with Parsons ; from whom he had removed her to other lodgings, where she had died suddenly of small- ox. Parsons' object was to obtain the ghost's declaration that she had been poisoned by his (Parsons') creditor.

" When, therefore (says the writer), the spirit taught the assistants, or rather the assistants had taught the spirit (for that could not speak), that Mr. K—— was the murderer, the road lay then open; and every night the farce was carried on, to the amusement of several who attended with all the good humour which the spending one night with novelty inspires. They jested with the ghost, soothed it, flattered it, while none was truly unhappy but him whose character was thus repeatedly rendered odious, and trifled with, merely to amuse idle curiosity.

" To have a proper idea of this scene, as it is now carried on, the reader is to conceive a very small room with a bed in the middle; the girl at the usual hour of going to bed, is undressed and put in with proper solemnity; the spectators are next introduced, who sit looking at each other, suppressing laughter, and wait in silent expectation for the opening of the scene. As the ghost is a good deal offended at incredulity, the persons present are to conceal theirs, if they have any; as by this concealment, they can only hope to gratify their curiosity. For, if they show either before, or when the knocking is begun, a too prying, inquisitive, or ludicrous turn of thinking, the ghost continues usually silent; or, to use the expression of the house, Miss Fanny is angry. The spectators, therefore, have nothing for it but to sit quiet and credulous; otherwise they must hear no ghost, which is no small disappointment to persons who have come for no other purpose.

" The girl who knows by some secret, when the ghost is to appear, sometimes apprizes the assistants of its intended visitation. It first begins to scratch, and then to answer questions, giving two knocks for a negative, and one for an affirmative. By this means it tells whether a watch, when held up, be white, blue, yellow, or black; how many clergymen are in the room, though in this sometimes mistaken; it evidently distinguishes white men from negroes, with several other marks of sagacity; however, it is sometimes mistaken in questions of a private nature, when it deigns to answer them: for instance, the ghost was ignorant where she dined upon Mr. K——'s marriage; how many of her relations were at church upon the same occasion; but particularly she called her father John instead of Thomas, a mistake indeed a little extraordinary in a ghost; but perhaps she was willing to verify the old proverb, that *it is a wise child that knows its own father*. However, though sometimes right, and sometimes wrong, she pretty invariably persists in one story, namely that she was poisoned, in a cup of purl, by red arsenic, a poison unheard of before, by Mr. K—— in her last illness, and that she heartily wishes him hanged."

The ghost, it appears, was a particular enemy to the light of a candle, and "always silent before those from whose position and understanding she could most reasonably expect redress." A memorable meeting, by the ghost's desire, " of gentlemen of eminence for their rank, learning, and good sense," took place in the vault of St. John's church, Clerkenwell, upon the night of Feb. 1, 1762; and Dr. Johnson, who was present, printed at the time an account of what they saw and heard. After quoting the whole of Dr. Johnson's statement, which is distinguished by inverted commas, the writer adds:—

" Such an account will convince those who are under the influence of reason; but nothing can gain over some, who from their infancy have been taught to believe, but not to think. To convince such it were to be wished that the Committee had continued their scrutiny a night, or two longer, by which means the impostor would in all

probability be caught in the fact, or at least most thoroughly detected. For if the ghost persisted in such company to continue silent, it would then be obvious that it was afraid of the discovery it pretended to aim at; or if it continued to knock or scratch, the noises, by explaining themselves, could not long frustrate a judicious enquiry.

" But as it is, the ghost still continues to practise as before, and in some measure remains undetected; and it is probable that she will thus continue for a much longer time, to exhibit among friends who desire no detection, or among the curious, whose pleasure is in proportion to the deception."

After a number of interesting details connected with the story, the writer says:—

" I have now as briefly, and indeed as tenderly as I could, stated the whole of this most surprising transaction, and the reader by this time sees how far Mr. K—— is culpable. He sees him living affectionately with a woman as his wife, whom the laws of nature allowed him to love, but the strictness of the canon law forbade him to marry. He sees every possible method to preserve this woman's reputation and life, and the most reputable persons produced as witnesses of her end. He sees men of the highest rank, both for birth, character, and learning joined to acknowledge the whole [story] of the pretended ghost as an imposition upon the public; and, lastly, he sees those who pretend to bear witness to the accusation, persons of a mixed reputation, of gross ignorance, great cruelty, and what is more armed with resentment against him. I would not wish, however, to turn the popular resentment upon any particular person, but I think it my duty to divert it somewhere from the guiltless."

We have then the story of the "famous impostor" Richard Hathaway, and a remarkable one of Zachary of Poland, who was personated, after death, by a false spirit, who took his likeness and wooed the object of his love. The writer concludes with these sensible words:—

" One would think that a story of this nature could hardly gain credit, and yet it deceived a whole nation for five years successively: what is still more surprising, it deceived a Protestant divine, otherwise of sense and of learning. I cannot avoid thinking that there are several similar circumstances between this Polish ghost and the ghost of Cock-lane. The ghost at Cock-lane answered questions, so did Zachary; the Cock-lane ghost is visited by the nobility, so was Zachary; the Cock-lane ghost plays tricks, so did Zachary; the Cock-lane ghost follows a girl, so did Zachary. There is one circumstance, however, in which the parallel will not hold good; Zachary was believed to be a real ghost by a Protestant divine; but I fancy no Protestant divine can be found among us, so much the old woman, as to lend even a moment's assent to the ghost in Cock-lane."

The fear of the contrivers, and their consequent inability to carry on the imposition before the committee of gentlemen who had undertaken to investigate the matter, coupled with Dr. Johnson's printed statement, gave the death-blow to the Cock Lane ghost. Parsons stood three several times in the pillory, and was imprisoned for one year in the King's Bench Prison.

" London mobs," remarks Peter Cunningham, "are curiously composed; instead of pelting Parsons in the pillory, they collected a subscription for him."

Edward F. Rimbault.

A GENERAL LITERARY INDEX: INDEX OF
AUTHORS.*

EUTHYMIUS ZIGABENUS AND THE MANICHÆANS.

"Though Euthymius Zigabenus is a writer well known to scholars, his *Panoplia Dogmatica*, in many respects the most valuable of his works is, I believe, an exceedingly rare book. The only printed edition of the original text appeared at Tergovist, in Wallachia, in the year 1710 . . . . . . and very few copies seem to have found their way to the west of Europe. The copy which was used by Fabricius (*Bibl. Græca*, vol. vii. p. 461) had been given to his friend Mich. Eneman in the East by the Patriarch of Jerusalem. It is not in the Bodleian, nor in the British Museum; and the only copy I ever saw was in the King's Library at Paris, till a few months ago I purchased one from a bookseller in London. . . . . . . The fly-leaf of the book in question exhibits the following inscription written by the same hand in Greek and Latin . . . . . . A present of books from the Patriarchs to the 'Catholics' of Britain indicates the existence of a kind of intercourse with which I was not at all acquainted. It is the Roman Catholics who are plainly intended."—*British Magazine*, vol. xiv. p. 286.

Euthymius Zigabenus (or Zygadenus), a Greek monk of the Order of St. Basil, flourished in the beginning of the twelfth century under the Emperor Alexis Comnenus, by whom he was highly esteemed, and by whose command he compiled the *Panoplia*. (See Anna Comnena's *Alexias*, p. 490.) "The Greek text of this work," says Du Pin, "never as yet came to our hands, only a Latin version made by [Petrus Franciscus] Zinus, printed at Lyons, A.D. 1536, at Paris in 1566, at Venice in 1575, and in the *Bibliotheca Patrum*" [Lugdun. 1677, vol. xix. in which are all his published works in Latin.] MS. copies of the *Panoplia* are described by Lambecius in the *Bibliotheca Vindobonensis* [or *Viennensis*], lib. v. pp. 51, 52; MSS. are also in the Vatican, see Possevinus, *Appar. Sacr.* pp. 74, 79, 89; in the *Bibliotheca Regia Gallica*, Codd. 1990, 2399, 2939, &c.; in the Bodleian, see Oudin, vol. ii. 979; in Trinity College, Dublin, see *MSS. Librorum Angliæ et Hiberniæ Catalogus*, Oxonii, 1697, vol. ii. One of the MSS. in the *Bibliotheca Vindobonensis* contains nine large excerpts from the *Panoplia*, a description of which is given by Oudin as well as Lambecius, with an enumeration of the Fathers, from whose writings it is compiled.

They here follow in succession, as I find them in the Latin Version: Gregorius Theologus, *i. e.* Nazianzenus, Gregorius Nyssenus, Jo. Damascenus, Dionysius Areopagita, Athanasius, Basilius Magnus, St. Maximus, Leontius Cypri pontifex, St. Chrysostomus, St. Cyrillus, Leontius Byzantinus, Anastasius Sinaita, Germanus Patriarcha, Nicephorus Patriarcha Constantinopolis, Theodorus, Photius.

The heretics refuted by this "Malleus Hæreticorum" are enumerated in the third book of

---

* Continued from 3rd S. iv. 458.

Lambecius, p. 168. In the edition of 1714, the Patriarch Chrysanthus omitted the chapter against the Saracens and what relates to the Trinity, being apprehensive of the same cruelty from the Turks which they had exercised against Cyril Lucaris. Cf. T. Smith's *Account of the Greek Church, &c.* 1680; Mosheim's *Inst.*, Cent. xvi. sect. 3, ch. 2; and Cent. xvii. sect. 2, ch. 2. Neither is the Latin Version by Zinus complete; *e. g.* the extract from *Photius* concerning the procession of the Holy Spirit is omitted; viz. tit. xiii. in the Greek MSS. On this subject there is a separate treatise by him, but according to Simon (*Critique de la Bibliothèque des Auteurs Ecclésiastiques, &c.*, par M. Elies Du Pin, p. 318) it differs but little from this portion of the *Panoplia*. For authorities on this celebrated controversy, see Mosheim's *Instit.*, Cent. viii. pt. II. ch. 3, and Cent. ix. ch. 3; Gieseler, Third Period, Div. 1. ch. 3.

With reference to Du Pin's account of Euthymius's works, Simon remarks, *quot verba, tot errata.* The rarity of the Greek edition will account for the misstatement in Smith's *Dictionary*, that the Greek original of the *Panoplia* has not yet been published except the last title, which is contained in Sylburg's *Saracenica*. Adam Clarke makes the same error, although he contradicts himself; and the continuator of his *Succession of Sacred Literature*, vol. ii. p. 666, states that "only part of the original has been published, but the whole is extant in the Ambrosian Library at Milan."

BIBLIOTHECAR. CHETHAM.

(*To be continued.*)

A MAY-DAY SONG.

In the issue of this journal for July 29, 1854, (1st S. x. 91), I described the May-day customs as then existing in Huntingdonshire; and, in the *Illustrated London News* for May 2, 1857, I gave a sketch of "The May Queen and her Garland, at Glatton, Huntingdonshire." The May-day customs at Glatton and the adjacent village have been observed up to the present year; but, as they present no novelties, it is needless for me to encumber your space by a repetition of what I wrote eleven years ago. The description under the above reference in your first series would stand for an account of the May-day customs in 1865, at Glatton, Stilton, Denton, Caldecote, Folkesworth, and other Huntingdonshire villages. The immediate object of my note is to record in " N. & Q." the words of a May-day song, sung by "the Mayers" on May-day, 1865, in the village of Denton and Caldecote, when they went round with their "garland." The song, I may observe, was taught to the children by the mother of one of the singers; and the woman had learnt it as a child from her mother, who had been taught it, in turn, by *her* mother. Like the songs of the Christmas Mummers, it would appear to have been compiled by an uneducated person from odds and ends of verse. I give it precisely as it was sung : —

" Here comes us poor Mayers all,
   And thus we do begin
To lead our lives in righteousness,
   For fear we should die in sin.

" To die in sin is a dreadful thing,
   To die in sin for nought ;
It would have been better for our poor souls
   If we had never been born.

" Good morning, lords and ladies,
   It is the first of May ;
I hope you'll view the garland,
   For it looks so very gay.

" The cuckoo sings in April,
   The cuckoo sings in May,
The cuckoo sings in June,
   In July she flies away.

" Now take a Bible in your hand,
   And read a chapter through ;
And when the day of Judgment comes,
   The Lord will think of you."

The sudden variations of this song between theology and ornithology, and its very slight relation to May-day, certainly invest its composition with a daring originality. It was sung to a tune that was "most melancholy," but not "most musical."   CUTHBERT BEDE.

ORIGIN OF NAMES.

The amusing example given by H. T. E. (3rd S. v. 71) of the mode in which names are coined in Kaffirland, reminds me of the following parallel instance.

When stationed on the Burmese frontier, my brother officers and myself were known to the natives with whom we were brought in contact by nick-names indicative of some marked peculiarity, and which soon completely superseded with them our own proper appellatives.

Our Colonel was too mighty and exalted a being to be known save by his dignity, as " The Great Chief," but irreverent subalterns had long rendered any additional sobriquets superfluous ; smaller stars, however, were recognised each by his light. The varied colour of the hair of the European is very striking to the Oriental, and it is not surprising, therefore, that individual peculiarities in this respect determined the names of many. A red-hirsute Highlander was y'cleped *Shue-Mong,* " The Golden-haired." A fair Saxon-blooded ensign was known as *Sani,* " The White-haired" ; whilst *San-Crou,* " The tangled thicket," was very properly given to a bushy-haired brave little fellow, who has since done the state some service. At first they called me *Bo-gleai,* or " The young Chief," but when subsequently I went into mourning, new acquaintances, from the

crape on my arm, distinguished me as *Meam-Meam-Keala,* " The one wearing a black band." A fat, flabby, round-faced youngster was much exasperated at being styled *La-Bye,* " The full moon," whilst a lieutenant of elongated visage, saintly port, and unspotted morality, deemed, as we asserted, the name of *Phoonghee,* or " The Priest," a mild heathen tribute to his superior sanctity.

I remember but one other, *Bobrong,* " The Creator of Disturbances"; richly deserved by a turbulent, roistering, rack-loving Irishman, one of the most noisy and most kind-hearted of mortals, but now, alas ! no more.   W.

NOTE ON TWO MISTAKEN ETYMOLOGIES.

1. *Tattoo.* — The derivation, *tapotez vous,* was certainly never invented by a Frenchman ; nor is the term *tattoo* known in French, nor in any other Latin tongue, but is peculiar to the Germanic dialects. Sir James Turner, in his *Pallas Armata* (a treatise on military affairs, *circa* 1627), gives it as *taptoo,* and explains it as the signal for closing the sutlers' canteens. The original appears to have been the Dutch *taptoë,* tap signifying as with us either a spigot or public; and *taptoë* being equivalent to the spigot or tap closing. In accordance with this, there is no verb to *taptoo, taptoen, &c.,* as might have been expected had the word *aught* to do with the tap or beat of the drum ; but the phrase in Dutch, English, or Swedish, is, to beat the tattoo — *die taptoë slaan, &c.* The true origin is further proved by the German form *zapfenstreich* (verb, *zapfenstreichen*), the striking of the *zapfen* or spigot into the cask.

2. *To run the Gantlope.* — The derivation of this, from *Gand,* is an example of the manufacture of historical facts for etymological purposes; and that of *gant,* all (for *ganz,* I presume), is on the *lucus a non lucendo* principle, since all except the delinquent stand still. Sir James Turner uses the form *gatlope,* and rightly derives it from the Dutch or Low German *loopen,* to run; and *gat* (our *gate*), a passage or strait — as for example, in *keel-gat,* the throat : a term metaphorically applied by Dutch sailors to a dangerous and rapid narrow near New York, and transformed by the English sailor into " Hell-gate." The present Dutch phrase for *gatlope* is different; but, as above, the derivation is proved by the German form *gassen-laufen,* to run through the street or lane of men : *gasse* being the German military term for the interval between tents, ranks, regiments, brigades, and the like.

Since writing the above, I find that Webster adopts a similar derivation. He says, probably from *gang,* a passage ; but as *ganglope* and *gang-loopen* are as yet conjectural, I am still inclined to think the *n* a euphonic addition. Possibly, however, *gangloopen* may have been the form used in some one of the German dialects with which our Low Country soldiers became familiar.

B. NICHOLSON.

THE CHARTERS OF HOLYROOD.

"HERBERGH," "HERBERGARE," "HARBARGARIE."

Upon an examination of the *Liber Cartarum Sancti Crucis: Munimenta Ecclesie Sancti Crucis de Edwinesburg*, published by the Bannatyne Club in 1840, I find it mentioned that the convent was placed at first within the fortress of Edinburgh Castle; but that the canons must have soon found the castle, however desirable as a place of security, a narrow and inconvenient residence. The foundation charter is of no earlier date than between 1143 and 1147, although there is no reason to doubt that the year 1128 was the date of the building of the Abbey of Holyrood on its present site. Whether the convent had been moved to its final situation in the year now assigned or not, it would appear that it must have been settled there previous to the great charter of the founder; which, in permitting the canons *to found a burgh* between their church and the King's Burgh, points distinctly to what was afterwards, in consequence of that permission, united to the city of Edinburgh by "the Abbots Burgh of regality of Canongait": "Concedo etiam eis herbergare quoddam burgum inter eandem ecclesiam et meum burgum." These words have been the fruitful source of much curious blundering; which, taking its origin in the mistake of some monkish lawyer, has been perpetuated by scholars and lawyers down to the present day. It might be permitted to the abbot of the sixteenth century to allege, that—

"we culd not find in Latine sic ane word as harbargary to be ane verb, and thairfor apperandlie the saidis boundis now callit the Cannegait wes a befoir callit Harbargary."

In the Appendix to the Preface of the *Charters of Holyrood*, there is given a series of Law or Session Papers (curious specimens of old Scotch pleadings) regarding the privileges of the burgh of Regality of Canongait, and illustrating the curious interpretations put upon the word "herbergare." The grammatical disputations—

"quhidder Harbargary be ane verb or ane nowne substantive, quhilk we reckin to be ane nowne substantive and sumtyme to be ane propir name in auld dayes of the boundis now callit the Cannogait," concludes, "and thairfoir quhidder Harbargary be ane propir name of burgh than ane verb *signifiand power to big ane burgh*, yet insafar as the samyn wes to be biggit within the boundis libellat now callit the Cannogait, and erectioun of the said burgh maid within the boundis libellat, the titill producit is sufficient."

T. G. S.
Edinburgh.

KIRBY HOOKS. — The lovers of the sport of angling will not forget Izaak Walton's praise of the Kirby hook; whether it has since gone out of fashion, or been succeeded by some more approved hook, I know not; but the anglers who read "N. & Q." will not be displeased to read the following advertisement, published in the *London Journal* of March 24, 1721: —

> "*To all Gentlemen and others.*
>
> "I, Charles Kirby, son of Timothy Kirby, grandson to old Charles Kirby, have left off dealing with William Browne, of Black Horse Alley, near Fleet Bridge, for two years past, and now have contracted and agreed with Mr. Robert Hopkins, of Bell Yard, near Temple Bar, at the sign of the Salmon, and with him only: and whereas the said William Browne has pretended to sell fish-hooks under the name of Kirby, these are to advertise that they are not *my* hook, but an imposition upon the world."

H. E.

EPIGRAM.—I find, in one of my note-books (but unluckily without a reference), an epitaph, which we may venture to call an epigram, on some not very creditable person whose English name was Nunn; and, in humble imitation of Ulysses' *paronomasia*, was latinized into *Nullus:*—

> "Hic situs est Nullus: nunc Nullo Nullior iste;
> Et quia Nullus erat, de Nullo Nil tibi, Christe!"

E. L. S.

A HINT TO ATLAS PUBLISHERS. — Why do not our atlas publishers adopt some system of *marginal reference*, such as is used in ledgers? It is exceedingly inconvenient to be obliged to hunt through a bulky volume of maps before finding the one we are in search of. I speak as one who has experienced much vexatious delay from the want of some such contrivance. S. W. P.

IRISH PARLIAMENTARY REPRESENTATION.—The following is a copy of a curious document which was lately lent to me: —

> "I shall bring Mr. Flood into Parliament for the Borough of Baltinglass next General Election for Eighteen hundred pounds, with re-election in case of the King's death; and Mr. Flood will, as I have really refused two thousand down for a seat, endeavour to let me have eight hundred [now or] as soon as he can.
> "May 21st, 1789.   ALDBOROUGH."
> "Henry Flood, Esq., is the person to be brought in."

The words "now or" are erased in the original. The Earl of Aldborough, it is almost needless to say, was "patron" of the borough of Baltinglass; and his family received compensation for the loss of its members at the Union with Great Britain.

H. LOFTUS TOTTENHAM.

TAYLOR THE WATER-POET. — On a spare leaf before a copy of Taylor's *Works*, 1630, folio, I find this written: —

> "Geven me by my well-wishinge frende, John Taylor, 1633: 'Valeant qui me volunt.'
>
> "Had I dipt my pen in the . . . . of Parnasus, like

other of your frends, my raptures had not prooved so barren, but yet take this : —

" ffull many things within this Vniuerse,
This spetiall booke doth wittely rehearse,
In thunderinge prose and able verse.
· Who censures not so, I will . . . . . non,
He is like to that which Balaam rid on.
"W. C."

On the title-page, in a different and very clear hand, is the autograph of "Robert Cranmer." Was this person of the archbishop's family ? Izaak Walton was connected by marriage with the Cranmers, having married Rachel Cranmer. The two words indicated by dots are, to me, illegible.

W. CAREW HAZLITT.

TABOUROT AND LE SIEUR GAULARD. — The *Bigarrures et Touches du Seigneur des Accords, avec les Apothegmes du Sieur Gaulard et les Escraignes Dijonnoises*, form a volume, which enjoyed at one time considerable popularity. The book is a tissue of silliness and indecency. In the department of silliness, there are stories resembling some narrated of English royal Dukes in bygone days. In its original shape, it has passed through numerous editions, as may be supposed from the character of the contents; but I have before me an unnoticed English version of M. Gaulard's Apothegms and the Escraigns, of which it is my object to forward you a brief account. The volume is a small 8vo, of thirty-five leaves, and is thus entitled : —

" Bigarrures ; or the Pleasant, and Witlesse, and Simple Speeches of the Lord Gaulard of Burgundy. Translated by J. B. of Charterhouse."

The work is written in a very minute, but clear and legible hand, of the period of the Restoration, and is evidently the MS. prepared by the author for the press. There are signatures throughout. Here is one of the *Bigarrures* : —

' " Being advertised by one with him, that the Deane of Besançon was dead, he said to him, ' Beleeue it not, for if it were so, he would write to me ; for he writes to me of all things.' "

The " Escraignes" are not indicated on the title ; but they occur in the present volume on the nineteenth leaf, and run to the end. I have had the misfortune to peruse many books of equivocal morality—*The Decameron*, the *Cent Nouvelles Nouvelles*, many of our jest-books, and so on; but it has never been my lot to meet with a volume so abounding in gross sentiments and expressions, or rather so full of nothing else, as this. It is worse than Durfey's Pills ! W. CAREW HAZLITT.

EPISCOPAL BLAZON. — It is a generally received rule in heraldry that bishops do not either assume or retain a crest upon their elevation to the bench. Examples to the contrary are I believe rare, but I have one before me now. It is the seal of the Right Rev. Stephen C. Sandes, D.D., successively Bishop of Cashel and Killaloe. In this example the episcopal mitre surmounts his family crest, viz. a griffin segreant. W. H. T.

BRIGGLE. — In describing the quick, pert, and half impudent gait of a little bird which frequently hops close to the open doorway of a cottage, the mistress of the house a few days ago employed the unusual word to "briggle," apparently in the sense of bridling up in a bold and rather intrusive manner. I had never heard this word before, but its meaning was obvious enough.
H. W. T.

MILTON, SHAKSPEARE, RALEIGH, ETC.—
" 'The 20th day of December, 1608, was baptized John, the sonne of John Mylton, scrivener.' Twelve days old ! Thus little Johnny Milton ' played ' about the parish of Richard Stock — ran past the 'Mermaid' all unconscious of one Shakespeare, one Ben Jonson, one Sir Walter Raleigh, and other immortals, within."

These words are from the preface of Mr. Grosart's edition of Stock and Torshell *On Malachi*. The said preface contains a memoir of Richard Stock, the clergyman from whose hands John Milton received baptism. The register of this event, with the observation following it, I give above. Is not this observation more than unfounded ? Do the histories of Shakspeare and Raleigh allow us to regard Mr. Grosart's supposition as even a possibility, so far as they are concerned ? Milton was not seven years and a half old when Shakespeare died. B. H. C.

Queries.

CHANGE OF SURNAME. — Since the celebrated Jones Herbert case, the change of surname by mere publication of an intention to do so, seems common. Can any of your readers inform me whether this act does or does not *legally* change the name of children *living at the time* when their father indulged his innocent fancy by giving himself a new name ? It strikes me they retain the one to which they were born. CAMBRIAN.

CHARTULARY OF WHALLEY ABBEY. — In the *Coucher Book, or Chartulary of Whalley Abbey*, vol. i. p. 95 (Chetham Society) occurs the following clause in a charter : —

" Preterea ad supradicta uberius vallanda renunciavi pro me et posteris meis omni juris auxilio canonici et civilis privilegiis clericatus et fori et statuto, actionibus de dolo et *in factum* et omnibus aliis exceptionibus personalibus et realibus que possint *obiti* contra instrumentum vel factum."

Can any of your readers who are versed in the terms of canon and civil law tell me what is the proper reading instead of in *factum*, which is a misreading on the part of the editor ? I have seen several charters in which a similar clause occurs, but in none of them has this word been extended. It is plainly a noun in the dative case, such as *infirmationi* or *infractioni*, but I cannot hit upon the right word.

In passing, I may remark that this Chartulary is full of editor's blunders; in the same clause the word *obiti* is put for what is clearly *obici* (objici); and on page 186 a sheet of facsimile enables one to test the editorship of this chartulary still further. In the first line of the print is " carta, duplex, Edwardi." Now the fac-simile gives not the slightest authority for the introduction of such a word as *duplex*, which is a matter of imagination entirely, and the next line gives *post conquestu*, which the fac-simile (and also the simple rules of grammar) show to be utterly incorrect.

Again, on the same page, *viris religionis* should be *viris religiosis*—a phrase familiar and well-known to all readers of monastic charters.

On p. 27, l. 10, *preservet* should be *perseverct*, and this mistake occurs throughout the book. An active verb like *preservo* makes simple nonsense.

However, without going further into this part of the subject, I will return to the first point, and beg leave to ask for an elucidation of the doubtful word represented by *in factum*.　MONASTICUS.

ROBERT DUDLEY'S MARRIAGE.—Has any one a clue to the Papal Dispensation for Robert Dudley's marriage with Elizabeth Southwell, sometime between 1605 and 1607 ? or the *Ceremoniale di Roma* of the year 1630, wherein is inserted the Pope's patent to Robert Dudley, making him a Roman Patrizio, &c., and giving him power to create nobles ? or to the reports or decisions in the Papal courts (la Rota ?) in favour of R. Dudley's claims for compensation from the crown of England (the date of such decisions may be about 1618 or 1628 or 1638)?　　M. P.

WAS EUGENE A DEIST ?—The following was the passage which led me to think so —

" Reflecting that Marlborough was a heretic, and Eugene a Deist."—Brougham's *Lives of Men of Letters*, vol. i. p. 15; ed. 1845.

　　　　　　　　　　　　　　　CYRIL.

FLYING BUTTRESSES. — Are there many cases known of flying-buttresses being hollow and containing a flight of steps, such as in those at the end of the north transept of Westminster Abbey ? Where do others occur ? 　JOHN DAVIDSON.

HOOL-CHEESE.—

" She scarce knew the meaning of the orders she received. She set the kettle on the table, and placed the tea-board on the fire ... and said, ' Yaw may think . as haw ai've yeaten *hool-cheese* but it y'an't soa, I'se think I'm bewitched.'"—*Sir Launcelot Greaves*, ii. ch. 3.

What is hool-cheese ?　　CYRIL.

LAWRENCE. — Henry Lawrence, President of Cromwell's Council, died in the year 1664. In 1690 was recorded in Jamaica the will of John Lawrence.

The late James Lawrence (Knight of Malta) published an account of the various families of Lawrence in the *Gentleman's Magazine* (1815-29), and asserted that John Lawrence, who died in 1690, was a younger son of the President of Cromwell's council, and that he emigrated first to Barbados and then to Jamaica, with James Bradshaw, a *nephew* of the regicide Judge.

This assertion has been generally adopted and repeated. It was reiterated with some singular anachronisms in the obituary notice of Sir William Stephenson, late Governor of Mauritius, in a popular paper.* It is to be found in Burke's *Peerage and Baronetage, voce "* Abinger," &c.

It would be desirable to know on what foundation so general a belief rests. Facts indisputable in one generation are supposed to be so patent as not to require any great attention to the preservation of *proofs*. In the next generation, however, the fact is questioned, and it is then perhaps extremely difficult to produce the legal proof requisite to substantiate the descent. I am now desirous of eliciting any information that may exist on the present subject, based upon positive documentary evidence, for the will of John Lawrence, proved in 1690, contains no allusion whatever to his relations in England or elsewhere; and Henry Lawrence, President of Cromwell's Council, left no will. Is this John Lawrence of 1690, then mentioned in the will of Sir —— Lawrence, Bart., of St. Ives, and his brother, or in the wills of the Dowager Lady Lawrence or Lady Baltimore ?　　　　　　　　SPAL.

N.B. In seeking for the *proof* of this link in the pedigree of Lawrences, I by no means deny its truth. It is only the *legal* proof that I question.

LE POER QUERIES. — I am anxious to know —
1. What were the arms, crest, and motto of Robert le Poer, who was marshal to Henry II. in 1172, when he went over to Ireland, and who afterwards settled in co. Waterford ?
2. Did the Le Poers (or Powers) bear the same about 1600 ? if, not, what were their arms, crest, and motto at that time ? and does the Marquis of Waterford quarter the same now as the representative of the family ?

It is said that a branch of the Power family settled in England about the year 1600, and about 1680 assumed other arms, which they have retained ever since. A friend of mine who is descended from the above branch, has in his possession some ancient relics, with armorial bearings upon them, and if any of your correspondents can answer the above questions so as to supply the missing links, it is believed that he will be able to prove some curious facts respecting the family.

　　　　　　　　　　　　　E. WALFORD.
Hampstead, N.W.

* *Illustrated London News.*

COOTE MOLESWORTH, M.D., a younger son of the first Viscount Molesworth, is stated in the modern Peerages to have died in 1782, æt. 85, *unmarried.* Surely this is an error. In the contemporary accounts of the great fire which occurred at Lady Molesworth's house in London in May, 1763, where several members of the family perished, it is stated that Dr. Coote Molesworth, with his wife and two children, were on a visit to Lady Molesworth at the time, and describes the manner of their escape; and a pedigree now before me mentions that " Margaret," only child and heir of Jervas Wright, M.D. of Sheffield, married " Bourchier Molesworth," son of Coote Molesworth, a younger son of Lord Molesworth. Mrs. B. Molesworth married, secondly, Rev. —— Sealey, and, thirdly, —— Holmes, and died in Ireland in 1811 or 1812, without issue. Any information as to the marriage and issue of the foregoing Coote Molesworth would be esteemed.   G. B.

A PAIR OF IRON ORGANS.—I shall feel obliged if some one of your many ecclesiastical correspondents would explain the following extract from Hutchins' *Notice of the Church of Buckland Abbas, Dorset :* —

" In 1550 here were a pair of *iron* organs, weighing about 200 l., which were probably then taken down and sold."

Both the rectory and vicarage of this parish formerly belonged to the abbots of Glastonbury, and hence the ecclesiastical adjunct to the Buckland, a name given to several other parishes in the Vale of White Hart, down to King Stag Inn, in the Royal Forest, where the beautiful white hart of King Henry III. was killed by Thomas de la Lind, a great hunter of the time, for which a fine was laid on all the lands of himself and of the other squires in at the death; and this *amerciament* is still annually paid into the Exchequer as " White Hart Silver."   QUEEN'S GARDENS.

PHILIPS, EARLS OF PEMBROKE. — Where did the two Philips, Earls of Pembroke in the seventeenth century, die, and where were they buried?   M. P.

DESCENDANT OF SARSFIELD.—I am acquainted with a gentleman, who claims to be the only living representative of the celebrated General, through a female line. To my mind he establishes his claim; but I wish to know if there is any other claimant, or if it is known whether the general left any one to transmit his line. Some correspondent, versed in such matters, will no doubt enlighten me on this point.   S. REDMOND.
Liverpool.

TAVERN SIGN.—Dr. Adam Clarke says, on the first clause of Prov. xii. 10, " A righteous *man* regardeth the life of his beast," that, " Once in

my travels I met with the *Hebrew* of this clause on the *signboard* of a public inn." The doctor does not mention where it was, but perhaps some of the readers of " N. & Q." can tell, and if it is still extant.   GEORGE LLOYD.
Thurstonland.

ROBERT WALLACE OF KELLY.—It is well known that this gentleman, late M.P. for Greenock, was the pioneer of those measures which resulted in the Post Office reforms effected by the uniform Penny Postage of Sir Rowland Hill's bill. It is stated in the *Gentleman's Magazine* for Oct. 1855, p. 397 (in a paragraph copied from the *Caledonian Mercury*), that Mr. Wallace had bequeathed his papers relating to the Post Office, &c., to the Watt Institution at Greenock. In an obliging letter received from the Secretary of that Institution, now before me, he states that " no manuscripts belonging to the late Mr. Wallace are in the Greenock Library, nor can any information be given where such are to be found." Can any one kindly inform me where Mr. Wallace's manuscripts are now reposited?   J. YEOWELL.
4, Minerva Terrace, Barnsbury, N.

" WODROW'S PRIVATE LETTERS," edited by Mr. Maidment in 1829, were reviewed in *Fraser's Magazine*, where, I understand, the whole work is treated as a fabrication. I shall be obliged by a reference to the year and month of the review.
                                   F. M. S.
229, Clarendon Villas, Plumstead.

Queries with Answers.

BP. TAYLOR'S SECOND MARRIAGE. — In Bishop Heber's Life of Jeremy Taylor (Taylor's *Works*, 10 vols., London, 1854, vol. i. p. xxxv.), there is the following passage : —

" This second wife was a Mrs. Joanna Bridges, who was possessed of a competent estate at Mandinam, in the parish of Llanguedor and county of Carmarthen. Her mother's family is unknown ; but she was generally believed to be a natural daughter of Charles the First, when Prince of Wales, and under the guidance of the dissipated and licentious Buckingham. That the martyr's habits of life at that time were extremely different from those which enabled him, after a twenty years' marriage, to exult while approaching the scaffold that, during all that time, he had never even in thought swerved from the fidelity which he owed to his beloved Henrietta Maria, there is abundant reason to believe ; nor are the facts by any means incompatible. The former indeed rests chiefly on the authority of Mr. Jones's papers."

And in Wilmott's *Jeremy Taylor* (edit. 1847, p. 118), in speaking of Bishop Jeremy Taylor's second wife, and her supposed parentage, Mr. Wilmott says : "This relationship is claimed on the single authority of the Jones MSS."
Can any more light be thrown on this subject? I suppose "the Jones MSS." are the same as "Mr.

Jones's papers." What and where are Mr. Jones's papers? I should be much obliged if you could find space for this.   X. Y. Z.

[William Todd Jones, of Homra, co. Down, was Bishop Taylor's lineal descendant in the fifth degree, and was employed at one period of his life in collecting and arranging materials for the biography of his distinguished ancestor. Mr. Jones possessed, among many other interesting documents, a series of autograph letters to and from the Bishop; and a family-book also in his own handwriting, giving an account of his parentage and the principal events of his life. At his death, in the year 1818, the greater part of his family papers had been deposited at Montalto, under the care of the late John, Earl of Moira. Their subsequent fate has unfortunately not been ascertained. At Donnington, whither all the papers found at Montalto are said to have been transferred, no traces of them remain; and there appears but too much reason to apprehend that they were consumed, together with some other packages belonging to the Marquess of Hastings, in the fire which destroyed the London Custom-house. All which the family yet retain consists of some extracts made by Mr. Jones from these documents with a view to his intended work, and which were liberally communicated to Bishop Heber. Consult his Life of Bishop Taylor, as reprinted by the Rev. C. P. Eden in Taylor's *Works*, edit. 1854, vol. i. pp. x., cxxii. and ccci.]

" Sermons upon the Quadragesimall Gospells." — Can any of your readers acquaint me with the title of a book, containing forty-two sermons on the Quadragesimal Gospels? evidently published toward the end of the sixteenth or in the beginning of the seventeenth century. My copy has, I conjecture, been royal property. On the binding are embossed the letters " C. R.," surmounted by a crown; which I cannot otherwise interpret, than by " Carolus Rex." These marks I only recently discovered, but there are six on each side. The title is gone, but the dedication runs: —

" To the two noble knights, Sir John Strangwayes and Sir Lewis Dive; and their vertuous ladies, the Lady Grace Strangwayes and Lady Howard Dive, in acknowledgement of his own true love and respect, Don Diego Puede-Ser dedicateth these his indeavours."

    J. H. H.

Louth.

[The title-page is an engraving of scriptural subjects in nine compartments. The work is entitled " Devout Contemplations expressed in Two-and-Fortie Sermons upon all the Quadragesimall Gospells, written in Spanish by Fr. Ch. de Fonseca. Englished by I. M. of Magdalen Colledge in Oxford. London, Printed by Adam Islip, Anno Domini 1629." Don Diego Puede-Ser is the pseudonym for James Mabbe, of whom an excellent account was furnished to "N. & Q." (2nd S. xi. 3) by Mr. Bolton Corney. Consult also Wood's *Athenæ* (Bliss), iii. 53. There is an unpublished work of James Mabbe in Harl. MS. 5077, entitled " Observations touching some of the more Solemne Tymes and Festivall Dayes of the Yeare." The Advertisement is addressed " To my worthy Friend, Mr. Jhon Browne," and is signed " James Mab, from my Chamber at St. Mary Magdalen Colege, December 27, 1626." In this Advertisement Mabbe mentions another of his works published during the preceding year, and which we have not been able to trace. He says, " This is but an Appendix, or little piece of building annexed to that great work wherewith I presented you the last year. The other was the mansion-house; this the out-offices, without which latter, the former could not conveniently consist. This Part had been finished with the other, had not sickness (an inevitable stop) been an hindrance to that business. Now to those *Practicks of Meditations* I have added certain Observations upon your more solemn Festival Days. You were pleased to take the first in good part; and I am so confident of your love, that I rest most assured you will afford this other the like kind of entertainment."]

Thomas à Kempis. — In what work of Thomas à Kempis does any equivalent for the following distich occur, and what are the original words?—

" I never find, whichever way I look,
True joy, but in some corner with a book."

(Quoted in *The Catholic Choralist*, by W. Young, Dublin, 1842, p. 166.)

    H. W. T.

[" I have sought for rest every where,"Thomas à Kempis often said towards the close of life, " but I found it no where, except in a little corner with a little book." (Charles Butler's *Life of Thomas à Kempis*, prefixed to *The Following of Christ*, ed. 1852, p. xix.) Dr. Dibdin says that " Mr. Butler notices this memorable aphorism as occurring in the 21st chapter of *The Imitation*, where I find it not." Dibdin has also the following note on this passage: " Dr. Hickes says, that Thomas of Kempis was much delighted with this motto: ' *In Hoeckens und Boeckens:*' that is, ' In Little Corners and Little Books;' meaning, that his only sure rest was found in such situations and with such companions; or, adds the biographer [C. Butler] it was sometimes ' *In een Hoecken met een Boecken;*' that is, ' In one little Corner, with one little Book.' There was, accordingly, continues he, ' a rough portrait or picture of this venerable man, done either by himself or by one of his contemporaries, with the foregoing inscription; which an hundred years after his decease was still kept in the same house where he had lived, though very much then defaced; and which I find (*Tolans Vit. Kemp.*) was shewed as a devout curiosity to such as visited the place.' From such an anecdote, to have represented our author *without* a Book, would have been scarcely a venial heresy."]

Great Tom of Oxford. — Can any one inform me why the principal gate and quadrangle of Christ Church, Oxford, is called by the extraordinary name of " Tom"? I am not certain whether the bell takes its name from the quadrangle, or the quadrangle from the bell. I am aware that Wolsey's name was Thomas; but I am afraid this common solution of the difficulty cannot be received, as Anthony Wood mentions the bell as having been taken away from the cathedral, and after having been recast, as having been put in the tower, since called. "Tom Tower;" and this in Cardinal Wolsey's time, and mentions it as being already called "Tom." Not having the book by me, I cannot quote the exact passage, but it will be found in his description of Christ Church.   H. W. Z.

[The great bell Tom in the campanile of the tower of Christ Church belonged formerly to the right tower of Osney Abbey, and was recast in 1680, when Dr. Fell, Bishop of Oxford, was Dean. The old inscription on this bell was, " In Thomæ laude resono Bim Bom sine fraude." The present inscription is, "Magnus . Thomas . Clusius . Oxoniensis . renatus . Aprilis . viii . Anno . MDCLXXX . Regnante . Caroli . II . Decano . Joanne . Oxon . Episcopo . Subdecano . Gul . Jane . ss . TH . P . et arte Christ: Hodson." It has been conjectured with some probability that Great Tom was named after Thomas à Becket. The great gate, commonly known as Tom Gate, is so named from the cupola containing the great bell.]

CHAP.—Is there any instance of the use of this favourite slang word so early as the following? —

"The purchaser will look upon himself as a provident chap that has secured . . . heaven by that wise bargain."
          Capt. Carleton, p. 275, ed. 1743.
          CYRIL.

[Webster quotes an earlier use of this word from one of Steele's works: " If you want to sell, here is your chap."]

Replies.

WAITS AT YORK.
(3rd S. vii. 275.)

Of the custom described I had never before heard. But in the collection of Proclamations, Broadsides, and Ballads, presented by Mr. J. O. Halliwell to Chetham's Library, Manchester, and bound in thirty-two folio volumes, No 1524, is an old song engraved with music, entitled "York Waits,"—too long and too "free" to print entire; from which I extract the lines exhibiting the "Waits" themselves. It begins: —

"In a winter's morning
Long before the dawning,
Ere the cock did crow,
Or stars their light withdraw,
Waked by a hornpipe pretty,
Play'd along York city,—

In a winter's night
By moon or lanthorn light,
Through hail, rain, frost, or snow,
Their rounds the Music go,
And each in frize or blanket
(For either Heaven be thanked)
Lined with wine a quart,
Or ale a double tankard,

Burglars send away,
And bar-guests dare not stay.

Candles, four in the pound,
Lead up the jolly round;
Whilst Cornet shrill i'th' middle,
Marches, and merry Fiddle;
Curtel (?) with deep hum, hum,
Cries ' We come, we come, we come; '
And Theorbe loudly answers
Thrum, thrum, thrum, thrum.
But, their fingers frost-nipt,
So many notes are o'er-slipt,
As that you'd take sometimes
The Waits for the Minster chimes.
Then, Sirs, to hear their music
Would make him sick, or you sick;
And much more to hear a ropy fiddler call
With voice like her that cries,
' Who shrimps or cockles buys? '
' Past three ! fair, frosty morn ;
Good morrow, my masters all ! ' "*

These lines show that the York Waits were the musical watchmen of the old city. Their instruments seem to have been the cornet, the fiddle, the curtel (? citole), and the theorbo, which may indicate the period depicted. " We come," &c., is probably a line from Henry Purcell's chorus, "Come if you dare." The " bar-guests " classed with burglars, may mean late topers at public-house bars, or the old Yorkshire hobgoblin bargheists (i. e. gate-ghosts) or boggarts.   CRUX.

ASSUMPTION OF ARMS.
(3rd S. vii. 317.)

There may be no law on the statute-book which shall forbid a man from wearing coat armour. Neither is there any law which shall forbid him to walk about out of doors with his coat covered over with gold lace or turned inside out, or with one red leg and one blue leg to his trowsers, or with a cap and bells on his head. But if he thinks that the wearing of the gold-lace coat or any of the other things named will confer an honour, or raise him in the estimation of his neighbours, he is mistaken. The honour must come first; the badge by which it is revealed should follow. In past times heraldic bearings have always been understood as a distinction conferred by the king, as a mark of favour for some good service done. A man, therefore, who displayed a device on his shield, was known to have done something to have earned it, and hence he was honourable in the eyes of his fellow men. This is evidenced in history, where a young esquire would appear in the lists bearing a white shield, a virgin shield, or vierge escue, showing that he had not performed any feat of arms, or other deed, which he could record before the eyes of the world: hence the

[* These lines on the York Waits, with a few variations, appeared in our last volume, p. 510.—ED.]

term, an heraldic achievement. It is a mistake to suppose that any man could assume what he liked according to his mere whim, or that such a whim would be acknowledged by his fellow men.

The devices in heraldry were not fanciful; or if they were fanciful, they were not arbitrary. Throughout the best ages of this practice they were typical and significant, like hieroglyphics on an Egyptian monument. They had their meanings, though many of those meanings have been lost in the lapse of time. The cross was a favourite device with the Crusaders, who loved to display it in their conflicts with the Infidels, to distinguish them from their opponents, and to show for what they were fighting. Scallop shells were adopted by those who went on pilgrimage, especially to Compostella; spears, swords, and other weapons of war are sufficiently significant amongst those who lived in a rude age, and whose business was arms; the chevron, representing the roof beams, or principals in the roof of a house, is said to have been generally given to the younger son, to show that he must be the architect of his own house or fortunes, as he did not inherit the family patrimony. The same pr nc p e in modern times guided the granting of a new coat, or augmentations on a former one. Witness the ship and other things on the shield of Nelson, typical of his great naval fame. One of Nelson's admirals had two or three typical augmentations granted by the hereditary Earl Marshal, on the part of the king, for services performed: a chief azure wavy to represent the sea, on which was placed a naval crown or. An anchor was also added. The crest had previously been a stag standing on the ground. It is now a stag standing on a naval crown, azure. Grants were made for single acts of bravery or incidents in life. Thus the Hamiltons have the oak tree for a crest half cut through with the saw, according to the legend, too long to give here. The Dalzells bear a dead man in pale, the founder of that family having received large grants of land and this bearing from the king, for having rescued the dead body of a friend from the enemy by whom he had been taken and hanged. Some devices are plays upon the bearer's names. Thus, Whitlock bears three padlocks; Cotton, three hanks of cotton; Ducke, three ducks, and so on. All this shows, and scores of other examples might be adduced, that the devices in heraldry were not meaningless.

People may try and twist their arguments as they choose, but no sophistry can explain away the general impression of society, that heraldic bearings are the badges of a gentleman—of some one elevated above the common herd. It was so in ancient time, and the impression has naturally descended to our own day. No successful tradesman thinks his gentility complete until he sports his emblazoned shield. To sport his carriage is not enough. This, of course, is a weakness. It is one way in which the vanity of human nature betrays itself. People who do this flatter themselves that no one will ask questions, and that no one will know anything about it; or they console themselves by thinking that people will conclude that they and their ancestors always had a coat of arms, but that they had never displayed it until now.

No one who invents a coat of arms and has it put either upon his plate or his carriage, would like to confess to the proceeding, because he knows that he would meet with derision instead of respect. Those, therefore, who do the thing surreptitiously try to keep the secret, and hope no one will find it out. They fail, however, to give to their coat of arms the very value which would alone make it really worth having; namely, the having got it in the regular way. To speak of a brougham or any other carriage, or a butler, as luxuries, and a coat of arms as a luxury to a rich man, is a mistake. A coat of arms, if honourably obtained, is not so much a luxury as an honour. Besides, in a well-appointed establishment, a carriage cannot be looked upon as a luxury; it is necessary. Its owner makes use of it for himself where a poorer man would call a cab, or hail a 'bus; and it is moreover available for the use of his friends or visitors. In a wealthy house, where there is much dinner company, a butler is a necessary also.

No man can shed honour on himself. He may perform some good or great deed worthy of honour, and when the world has seen it, he will be honoured in consequence. The monarch, as supreme head of the nation, has been designated "the Fountain of Honour," because all honourable distinctions emanate from the crown. The person who assumes armorial bearings surreptitiously does it in the very way to render them of no value even in his own eyes, to say nothing of the eyes of his neighbours. But, as I said before, he will hope that nobody will know anything about it. He will bear them as if he had a right to them, and he will hope that people will suppose he really has the right, and that they will not ask questions. Every sensible man would think that honours borne in this way were not worth having. Some successful tradesmen put their initials in cypher on the panels of their carriages. No one can find fault with this. It is amusing to observe that, whilst the weak vanity of some people urges them to covet honours, which would turn out to be no honours unless regularly obtained, they seem to be fully aware that they will not escaping fixing upon themselves, the dreaded term "snob." Myself, I should like to have a good definition of that word. However, such a term is never applied to those who obtain their honours honourably. This ought to be quite enough to satisfy every sensible man.   P. Hutchinson.

NEUMANN WEISSENSCHILD seems to me to be right in both his positions; but he loses sight of the fact that hereditary arms have become identified with families as honorary social distinctions, and have in many instances for generations been used as such on public monuments and in other ways. Armorial bearings have thus been rendered indirect evidences of the consanguinity and long established respectability and dignity of certain families. They have therefore served a purpose not recognised in NEUMANN WEISSENSCHILD's letter, and one which deserves due consideration and respect; and on this ground the claims of the Heralds' College to authority may be consistently advocated. But it is quite a fair question, I think, to propose that that venerable body should adapt its regulations and requirements to the altered times in which we live. At present many people send up "name and county" to some unauthorised herald in the metropolis, who furnishes a coat to order (like a tailor) for a sum that is moderate in comparison with the demand of the functionaries of the college. Now, if they were to be content with say 10l. for a grant, and 5l. for a confirmation, and be empowered to require a guinea a-year regularly for their authority to the grantee to use the coats conceded or confirmed— the Chancellor of the Exchequer to go shares with the Heralds by the levying of a stamp on the grants and confirmations, and of fifty per cent. on the yearly permits, the duty on armorial bearings being abolished, the kings-at-arms, pursuivants, and so forth, would increase their labours largely and profitably, and the unauthorised pretenders to arms might be rendered amenable to fines and penalties, which would scarcely be risked under the circumstances, as they would be enforced by government in the usual manner.

It is probable that by regulations framed on the principle above imperfectly explained, the unauthorised use of arms would be prevented; for no one would be entitled to "sport" armorial bearings unless he had a college grant or confirmation to show in justification of his so doing. If any person exhibited arms publicly, as on a carriage or a house, or privately by sealing letters with an armorial signet, and causing such insignia to be engraved on silver spoons, and so forth, he would be liable to be called on to produce his grant or certificate by the excise officers. If he could not do so, his evasion of the government stamp would be detected, and his further pretensions to armorial bearings without authority would be stopped. The punishment for such attempted evasion, on proof before a county court judge, might be a fine equal in amount to the charge for a grant. It might be advisable to call even on all authorised bearers of armorial insignia, without exception, to pay a fee of 5l. for a confirmation or registration grant; so that the Heralds' College would thus be provided

with a complete register of all the families in the country using arms.

If the readers of "N. & Q.," interested in this question, would discuss it, perhaps an improvement might be effected in the present system.

MEDIUS.

"Let it be granted that armorial bearings existed long before Heralds as now technically understood, and that in the first ages of their use, they were *assumed*, in most if not all cases, according to taste or fancy. In any case they were assumed for distinction's sake. To preserve this distinctiveness and avoid confusion should more than one person or family claim the same arms, registration be came necessary, and this led to the appointment of Heralds. The possession of this, an authorised registry by the Heralds, placed them in the position of referees, and the Earl Marshal, whose officers they were, became the final arbiter and judge in all disputed points. To those persons or families, who having assumed certain coats, had used them without dispute, these same arms were confirmed by being entered in the registry; while to those who, not having previously borne arms, were by their position entitled to that distinction, coats of arms were assigned by the College of Heralds. In either case these arms were acknowledged and legitimate bearings; they told their own story, were capable of being verified, they were borne by right, and their title ascertainable."

In early times arms were assumed because there was no authority to grant arms; but, with the establishment of the Court of Heralds, assumption ceased. The intervention of that body, as agents of the crown, henceforth became imperative. To grant the power of assuming arms to whosoever chooses is to confuse and render useless the most exact and scientific as well as the most picturesque of historic records. "Assumed" arms are fictitious arms; to say that they are the coat of arms of him who assumes them, is to speak an untruth.

That every man has the power of making this assumption is beyond denial. A man may assume a title and call himself a duke, no one can prevent him; but he is no duke for all that. The ambitious citizen of Baltimore, who insisted on having the arms of the English ambassador painted on his carriage, acquired no coat by his vulgar impertinence.

In these days, when changes in social position are so frequent, there are many who desire to find themselves "at home" in the rank to which their exertions have raised them. Many, no doubt of high descent, are rising from the obscurity into which they had fallen; and if these can prove their descent, arms are theirs by inheritance. But to assume them without proof, simply from similarity of name, is to proclaim as a truth that which is only conjecture or a hope. There are others like your correspondent, NEUMANN WEISSENSCHILD, whose forefathers have confessedly never borne arms, and who can therefore have no right to arms. To both these the Heralds' College is the only legitimate resource. By that body a coat can still be granted, and the true state of the case will be registered for reference by future generations—that at such a time, to such a person, for such a reason, such a coat was granted, to be borne by him and his descendants, and by none else. The coat becomes distinctive and his own. Whereas to the assumed coat everyone has an equal right; it belongs to no one in particular.

It is a common weakness of the day—a weakness of the fastidious *parvenu*—to feel ashamed to acknowledge or to have it registered, that he cannot *prove* his descent from a certain ancient namesake, or that his ancestors have never borne "arms." If it be true why should a man be ashamed of it? It is no disgrace, but an honour to have raised oneself. Let it only be borne in mind that there can be no gentility apart from *truth*. The infraction of this principle is involved in the unauthorised " assumption " of arms, or of another man's name, and is the essence of what your correspondent calls " snobbism " or " snobbishness."

What is a " snob ? " Not a man of humble birth or mean extraction, or low social position or rustic manners. The " snob " is the man who assumes to be what in truth he is not, and tries to conceal what he really is.

" Quod non est simulat, dissimulatque quod est "— are applicable descriptions of a snob. He sails in society under false colours, he affects to be other than he is; all such affectation is vulgarity or " snobbism."

Your correspondent deludes himself in supposing that his coat of arms will be *only* an elegant badge to adorn his carriage. This it may be, but its effect, whatever its intention, will be to deceive those who do not know better—all not in the secret. It will be a palming himself off in the crowd of non-heraldic admirers as a gentleman—a Weissenschild too ! entitled to bear arms without having any such right. If this be not " snobbish," because false, it is difficult to apprehend where the peculiar idiosyncrasy begins.

But my knowledge of human nature tells me that the real stumbling-block is the money to be paid for a grant; the struggle is between vanity on one side, and parsimony on the other. If a coat of arms could be had for a guinea, no more would be said, the money would be paid. Well, no doubt, in fees and stamps the outlay is considerable for a poor man; let such a one wait till he is richer, and has made good his position; but for a man who has already raised himself "by his brains," who is "by education and membership of a learned profession," and by other claims, a gentleman—nay, an esquire!—who has "set up his brougham, butler, library, pianoforte, and other articles of luxury," surely the sum asked is after all a very great thing. It would only purchase a moderate picture. As there is no necessity to spend money on such an *objet de luxe* as a coat of

arms, I do not see that any one can of right complain. The legislature considers that they who aspire to these distinctive emblems of gentility should pay for them as for other needless luxuries, and there should be no objection to pay. Why should the whole thing be looked on as a " wretched matter of £. *s. d.*" more than paying the legal fees on being made a peer, or a knight, or bishop, or a serjeant-at-law? The charge is but for fees to those who have the trouble, and for stamps to the government; and the assuming without payment, and by a side wind, *proprio motu*, that for which the law provides an authorised channel in order to save one's purse, appears to my view to partake no little of the nature of fraud,—as much so as evading a stamp or legal fee in any business transaction.

A Nemesis has pursued your correspondent in the selection of the coat he so elaborately blazons. " To ape " is a function of " to assume," and one of the peculiarities of the genus snob; and the whole bearing of Weissenschild late Schweinsfleisch will be complete by adhering strictly to the Darwinian theory, and assuming as a motto "Simius sum." The space I have occupied forbids my entering on the subject " Change of Name."

Crowdown of that Ilk.

"THE VICAR AND MOSES."

(3rd S. vii. 125, 189.)

Constant engagement must be my excuse for the delay of the present letter, and for the carelessness of my former one. In reply to your correspondents allow me to say, that by the hasty expression " of my own name," I meant surname only. My great-grandfather's name was, I believe, John Allbutt. The date of his death I really do not know, without inquiries as yet unmade. I have, however, often heard my father speak of his grandfather as a very fine old man, whom he just can remember as remarkable for a blue coat, powdered wig, large shoe-buckles, and most imposing-headed cáne. I should suppose, therefore, that my great-grandfather, who wrote " The Vicar and Moses," died somewhere about 1808, at an advanced age. His character and doings have often been talked of among us, as he seems to have been a man of considerable originality, and of no mean attainments. In his earlier years he was a good deal attracted by the teaching of the Encyclopædic Schools in France, and hence the readiness of his satire upon the local parson. Like the Roman magistrates, however, he considered forms of religion very useful for the " commoner sort," and on the appearance of the Methodist revival he ordered down a preacher for the " squire's " servants and his own. This ended in the conversion of some members of his own family, much to his annoyance. We have an excellent portrait of him as a young man, and the face is one showing much character and humour. I am sorry that I cannot refer your correspondent to the pieces in the first numbers of the *Gentleman's Magazine*, which were written by my progenitor; it is quite possible that some records of them exist, but being as I am far from my relations I cannot make any search. When at my father's house in Suffolk, a short time ago, I put the question to him, and he replied that he really had never thought of making any minutes of the matter, and had no records at hand, but that the *Gentleman's Magazine* always laid, number after number, upon his grandfather's table, and that he used to correct proofs for it, and would occasionally refer to his effusions. It seems, indeed to have been so well known as to excite no question or inquiry. All I can add is, that if your correspondent will turn, as I have lately done, to the first few numbers of the *Gentleman's Magazine*, he will light upon several pieces bearing a great resemblance to "The Vicar and Moses." Finally, let me say that 1 make no claim on behalf of my ancestor for the authorship of a piece which has no great literary merit, as it appears to me, but seems to have hit the public fancy. The authorship of it has always been looked upon in our family as a matter of certain knowledge, and my letter was only drawn forth by the interest taken in the question by a leading antiquary, my personal friend.   T. CLIFFORD ALLBUTT.

LOCALITY OF ZION IN EARLY WRITERS.
(3rd S. vii. 215, 306.)

The words of Epiphanius, on which I rest as showing what hill he regarded as Zion, are νῦν δὲ τιμηθεῖσα; this he affirms of ἡ ἄκρα ἡ ποτὲ ὑπάρχουσα ἐν Σιών; so that although, as DR. BONAR states, another *akra* is mentioned in Josephus (and I may add in the Maccabees), and though the word may be used of any fortress, yet here we have distinctly *the akra that was formerly in Zion, but which is now cut down*. This identifies it with the *akra* on the same hill as the temple to the north, marking the eastern hill as Zion. That the temp e hill was ploughed we know as an historical fact : —

; "The Jewish writers relate, and their account is adopted by Jerome, who has unfortunately confounded the events of the times of Titus and Hadrian, *that the plough was drawn over the site of the temple*, as a mark of perpetual interdiction . . . . . There is in this instance the less reason to doubt the substantial truth of the statement, since the Jews specify the name of the Roman, Turranius Rufus, by whom the ceremony was performed."—*Antient Jerusalem*, by the Rev. J. F. Thrupp, p. 201.

I ought perhaps to have mentioned that the passage from Epiphanius has been used by Mr. Fergusson for another purpose; he, like DR. BONAR, seems not to have noticed the identification shown

by the mention of the *akra* in Zion, *now cut down*.

Apart from *evidence* I cannot believe that there is any Jewish identification of Zion with the south-western hill. We know that the name of Zion for that mount gradually grew up amongst Christians; but it could not have been a settled point when Eusebius in the fourth century, and before him Origen, in the third, knew well that Zion was the temple hill. I do not believe that any one, from scripture alone, and except on the ground of comparatively modern traditions, has ever thought, or could think, that Zion was other than the temple hill : —

"For the Lord hath chosen Zion : He hath desired it for His habitation : this is *my rest for ever*. Here will I dwell, for I have desired it."—*Psalm* cxxxii. 13, 14; (see too Psalm lxxiv. 2, 3.)

I am perfectly willing to receive DR. BONAR's correction as to the distance of Neby-Semwil from Jerusalem, although in Van de Velde's *Survey* the road marked is not quite five miles. There is no temerity, however, in conjecturing a wrong numeral in Epiphanius; such mistakes of copyists are *habitual*, and in the case of Epiphanius, MS. authority is not very abundant. Prof. W. Dindorf, in his late edition of Epiphanius, has done much for the criticism of the text; and to his clear statements I must refer those who wish to know what MSS. exist of that writer, and how far they have been available for the emendation of the text: a thing which Dindorf has well performed.

Any reference to what might be the *Gabaon* of Epiphanius is wholly irrespective of the subject of the present inquiry, as to which I maintain that the evidence of Epiphanius, Eusebius, and Origen is free from a shadow of ambiguity.

S. P. TREGELLES.

Plymouth.

"PISCIS FLOTANS" (3rd S. vii. 55, 124, 288.) — I know not whether it may be worth while to add that the *fletta, flet*, might probably be, not the dab, or flounder, as P. S. C. seems to conclude, but the holibut, which is called by Lacépède *Pleuronecte fletan*, and *Hippoglossus* by most of our best modern naturalists. See Couch's *Fishes*, art. "Holibut," vol. iii. p. 149.   C. W. BINGHAM.

THE FLEURS-DE-LYS OF FRANCE (3rd S. vii. 338.)—The change in the royal arms of France was made by Charles V. about the year 1365. On the Great Seal of Henry IV. of England the banners appear charged with France Modern. (See Boutell's *Heraldry, Historical and Popular*, 1865, pp. 296-7.)   J. WOODWARD.

KINGDOM OF DALMATIA (3rd S. vii. 339.)—The leopards' heads on the thalers of Rudolph II. would be the arms of the kingdom of Dalmatia, viz.: az. three leopards' heads caboshed, crowned or. It was united to Hungary about the year 1087, at the death of King Zolomerus.

J. WOODWARD.

New Shoreham.

SONG (3rd S. vii. 281, 330.) — Will the following prove an illuminator in reference to the song sought after? It is not as full as I could wish, but it is all I possess on the subject. Any one who may remember, and who had the *entrée* to certain literary society in Dublin from 1835 to about 1842, must have clear recollection of the following. There was a lady who had a remarkable voice—indeed I have often heard judges pronounce her to have been superior to Jenny Lind—who, however, had not appeared at the time.* The lady was the guest of all parties, particularly literary. She used to sing a song which was translated from the Irish, but I regret I have not a copy of the translation; but, from some passages which I quote from memory, I am of opinion it must be the song sought after. The fate of the gifted creature, who charmed and almost entranced thousands by her magic voice, was a sad one indeed; but I am precluded from alluding to it further here. The only portion of the song that clings to my memory are these —

> "I'll sell my rock, I'll sell my reel,
> When my flax is gone I'll sell my wheel
> To buy my love a sword and shield.
> Ma Veeth a Vourneen slawn.
>
> "Shool, Shool, Shool arhoo,
> There's none but he can ease my woe
> Since the lad of my heart from me did go.
> Ma Veeth a Vourneen slawn."

I only give the last line as it struck on the ear. I know it is Irish, but regret I cannot translate it. If it be true that this is a translation from an Irish original, and that it is identical with that sung by Miss Edgeworth's sister for Sir Walter Scott, either the learned baronet or Mr. Lockhart must have taken strange liberties with it. The air I know is peculiarly Irish, and, to a judge, of a deliciously plaintive character. The song was no doubt of Jacobite origin.　S. REDMOND.

SHORT SERMONS (3rd S. vii. 339.)—The speech attributed to Canning is such as Lord Brougham once described as "an epigram with the knob on." Canning is said to have made the speech thus: — On coming from a church in Dorsetshire, the clergyman who had preached said unwisely, "I knew you would like a short sermon." "But it seemed long," was the ready rebuke of Mr. Canning.　T. F.

It was Mr. Canning who made a young clergyman aware that in accuracy of language his ser-

* I have heard Jenny Lind, Catherine Hayes, Piccolomini, and all the celebrated singers since 1840, and I think the lady alluded to was superior to any of them, but she could not be induced to appear publicly.

mons might be tedious, though they were not long. They were walking from church after one of the clergyman's first sermons, when this dialogue took place : —"Well, Legge, you were not long." "I was afraid of being tedious." "Oh! you were tedious." Mr. Legge became a bishop. He was then walking home from his church at Lewisham.

S. D.

THE IMMORTALITY OF THE BRUTE CREATION (3rd S. vii. 339.)—JOSEPHUS probably knows that the opinion of the immortality of animals is advanced by the Rev. S. R. Maitland, in *Eruvin*.

CHARLES F. S. WARREN.

HUBERT DE BURGH (3rd S. vi. 415.)—It is not easy to trace the proceedings taken against Hubert de Burgh, Earl of Kent. In the *Additamenta* to Matthew Paris, HERMENTRUDE will find the earl's defence, drawn up by Master Laurence of St. Alban's, in answer to the articles pressed against him in 1239. In this defence the articles are set out at length, and I presume set out correctly. I suppose these articles to be, if not in form, at least in substance, identical with the charges brought against the Earl by Henry III. in 1231. Such, at all events, the Earl represents them to be, when he says, in his defence : —

"All the foregoing charges were let pass, and legally remitted to him, when he made peace again with the King."

One of the articles contains some very strange allegations with respect to the Earl's marriage with the daughter of the King of Scots. But before entering upon this field of inquiry, it would be satisfactory to be assured of the precise form in which the charge was made in 1231.　MELETES.

POWER OF FRANKING (3rd S. vii. 279, 350.)— The evidence on which I relied will not, I find, sustain my statement that the duke was accustomed to frank as "Edward." I beg leave to apologise for my error.　JOSEPH RIX, M.D.

St. Neot's.

JUDAS OVERTURNING THE SALT (3rd S. vii. 282, 348.)—Amongst every class in Ireland, it is accounted what is designated "unlucky" to upset a salt-stand at a dinner table; and hundreds of times I have been told that the reason was, Judas upset the salt before he betrayed our blessed Redeemer. May I ask, why in Leonardo da Vinci's celebrated picture of the "Last Supper" Judas is painted very nearly black—black, at least, when compared to the faces of the other Apostles. I speak of a fine copy of the picture, not having seen the original.　S. REDMOND.

Liverpool.

MODERN BELIEF IN THE BROWNIE (3rd S. vi. 511; vii. 46.)—Sir Walter Scott stated that the last place in the *south* of Scotland supposed to have been honoured or benefited by the residence of a Brownie was Bodsbeck in Moffatshire. In *The White Wife*, I showed that belief in the Brownie existed in the Western Highlands in 1863; and, in these pages, at the above references, it was shown by F. A. M. and myself that the Carskey Brownie (*Beag-bheul,* or "Little-mouth") was supposed to exist so late as the Christmas of 1864. A correspondent of the *Argyllshire Herald* carries us down to a date still more recent; for, in the issue of that paper for April 22, 1865, the writer, in describing the island of Cara (one of the south Hebridæan group, to the west of Cantire) speaks of the rock called "the Brownie's Chair," and of the Brownie who was supposed to have his habitation there. He then says,—

"Many are still alive who are able accurately to rehearse the doings and misdoings of this mysterious personage, and it is unquestionably true that some are to be met with who do not hesitate to declare their belief in his existence still, and who would much prefer his favour to his frown."

CUTHBERT BEDE.

CARABOO (3rd S. vii. 196, 269, 310.)—Reference on this subject may be made to a brief article entitled "Notice of the pretended Princess Caraboo," by Archbishop Whately," published in *The Rose, the Shamrock, and the Thistle Magazine* for April, 1863. The Archbishop gives her name as Mary Baker—thus confirming the statement of your correspondent, MR. GEORGE PRYCE; and he further tells, how he exhibited specimens of her writing "to my friend Hawkins (now Provost of Oriel College), to Dr. Copleston, who was then Provost, and to Dr. Macbride, the Principal of Magdalen Hall; all of whom concurred in my judgment that the scrawls were specimens of the Humbug language." On this circumstance, however, becoming known to a certain person, he stated in the *Times*, that a specimen of Caraboo's handwriting "had been sent to the University of Oxford, which had pronounced it to be the writing of no known language!" The Archbishop considered Caraboo "a professed and notorious liar;" and, in speaking of the credence given to her later statements, says,—"Some persons appear to consider mendacity as a disease analogous to the measles, from which a person who has once *had* it is thenceforth secure." CUTHBERT BEDE.

VALENTINE BROWN (3rd S. vii. 340.)—The following extract has been recently forwarded to me from the British Museum, but I do not know from what source. It is very possible it may be of service to your correspondent:—

"Sir Robert Browne (?) married —— Dabeney, and quartered his wife's arms, which are those of the D'Albeneys of Wymondham, Earls of Arundel."

Different branches of this lady's family were settled in the fifteenth century at Melton Parva, and in the sixteenth century at Barnham Broom,

Costessy, and Colton, all in the vicinity of Wymondham, and an elder branch at Snetterton near Thetford. H. DAVENEY.
Blofield.

FLEURS-DE-LYS (3rd S. vii. 338.)—MR. DAVIDSON will find an answer to his query in Sandford's *Genealogical History*, pp. 270, 239. He says:—

"This Henry (V.), being Prince of Wales, as appeareth by his seal annexed to two several indentures, the one dated the 6th day of March, An. 6th, and the other on the 7th of May, An. the 8th of Henry the 4th, his father . . . . . did bear azure, 3 flowers de lys or, for the kingdom of France (reducing them from semée to the number 3, as did Charles VI. the present French King, quartered with 3 lyons of England: which makes me of opinion that King Henry IV., this prince's father (although he made use of no other seal than that in which the flowers-de-lys are semée) was the first king of England that, in imitation of his said contemporary Charles VI., reduced that number to 3 flowers-de-luce; for I find them so in his escocheon, impaling the arms of Joanne of of Navarre his second wife, at the head of his tomb at Canterbury.

"By this seal of Prince Henry it most certainly appears that he, so early as the 6th year of Henry IV. his said father, bare in his achievement only 3 flowers-de-lys." (Cf. Willement's *Regal Heraldry*, pp. 32, 33.)

LEWIS EVANS.

ARMS OF FRETWELL (3rd S. vii. 221.)—In No. 1067 of the Harl. MSS., at fol. 46, there is a pedigree of the family of Spencer, of Bramley Grange, co. York, in the handwriting of Geo. Owen, York Herald; and in it is sketched the coat, "Argent, three fleurs-de-lis gules" as belonging to Ralph Fretwell of Hellaby. W. D. HOYLE.

PEREIRA FAMILY (3rd S. vii. 221.)—Perhaps the following notes may be of service to H. W. T.:—

From *The Universal Pocket Companion*, 1741:—
"David Lopez Pereira, merchant, St. Mary Axe.
Francis Pereira, *ibid.*
Isaac Alvarez Pereira, merchant, Bury Street.
Pereira and Lima, Jeffery's Square."

From Boyle's *City Companion*, 1798:—
"B. M: Pereira, Esq., 5, Finsbury Square. [In another place, Finsbury Terrace.]
Mrs. Pereira, 6, Church Row, Fenchurch Street.
Isaac Lopez Pereira Esq., Artillery Street."

R. I. F.

WRITERS ON GAME COCKS (2nd S. xii. 210.)—Εἰς μὲν γὰρ μάχην ὁρμωμένῳ καλῶς ἔχει κρόμνον ὑποτρώγειν, ὥσπερ ἔνιοι τοὺς ἀλεκτρυόνας σκόροδα σιτίσωντες συμβάλλουσιν.—Xenophontis *Convivium*, c. 4, § 7, p. 17, ed. Bornemann, Lipsiæ, 1824.

Chor. Ἔχε νῦν, ἐπέγκαψον λαβὼν ταδέ. Bot. τί δαί;
Chor. Ἵν᾽ ἄμεινον ᾦ᾽ τὰν ἐσκοροδισμένος μάχῃ.
Equites, v. 491.

The scholiast says: Μετήνεγκεν ἀπὸ τῶν ἀλεκτρυόνων, ὅταν γὰρ εἰς μάχην συμβάλλωσιν αὐτοὺς, σκόροδα διδόασιν αὐτοῖς ἵνα δριμύτεροι ὦσιν ἐν τῇ μάχῃ.—Sch. ad locum. FITZHOPKINS.
Garrick Club.

BISHOPS' BARONIES, ETC. (3rd S. vii. 273.)—In the interesting article on the Precedency of Bishops' Wives, it is said that bishops sit in the House of Lords in right of the temporal baronies attached to their bishoprics, and that this is proved "by their title of baron, viscount, or earl, according to the title attached to each see." I suppose the bishopric of Durham to be that to which the title of earl is, or was, attached, in right of the county palatine of Durham and the earldom of Sedburgh, but to which bishopric was the title of *viscount* attached? Was it to any?

New Shoreham.　　　　　　　　　　　　J. WOODWARD.

MARRIAGE RINGS (3rd S. vii. 12, 307, 350.)—I know there is a general impression amongst the peasantry in Ireland, that a marriage without a gold ring is not legal either by canon or civil law; and at one time I knew a parish town in the south-east of Ireland, where a person kept a few gold wedding-rings for *hire*. When the parties being married were too poor to purchase a ring of the precious metal, the person alluded to lent a ring, for which he received a small fee, the ring being returned after the performance of the ceremony.　　　　　　　　S. REDMOND.

Liverpool.

The shrewd remark of Swinburne, "the oracle of canon law," that—

"it skilleth not at this day, what metal the ring be of; the form of it being round, and without end, doth import that their love may circulate and flow continually,"

ought perhaps to have been satisfactory and decisive to R. C. L. and all impatient bachelors. The example, however, of the ancient Hebrew is in this respect worthy of imitation:—

"They acknowledged also the planet Jupiter (which they called מזל טוב, *Mazal Tob*) to be a very favourable star. For which reason it was that the new married man was wont to give his bride a ring, whereon was engraved the forenamed words, מזל טוב; that is to say, in the natural signification of the words, a good star, or good fortune, desiring by this ceremony that she might be delivered of all her children, under this favourable starre; as it hath been observed, both by Munster, Aben-Ezra, and Chomer."—*Unheard of Curiosities*, by James Gaffarel, chap. xi.

　　　　　　　　　　　　　　J. WETHERELL.

BURGH (3rd S. vii. 260.)—"We cannot discover the family name of *Frances* the wife of Thomas Lord Burgh, who died 1597." Since the above appeared in "N. &. Q." I have seen the will of Mrs. Blanche Parry, dated 1589 [1590], in which she gives "to the Right Honourable the Lady Frances Burghe, *my niece*, one hundred pounds." This niece was the daughter of her (Mrs. Blanche's) sister, Elizabeth Parry, and wife of Thomas, Lord Burgh, who died in Ireland, 1597. Mrs. Blanche Parry also gives in her will "to Mrs. Frances Burgh, *my god-daughter*, 20l., and to

Mrs. Elizabeth Burghe 20l." These two last-named girls were daughters of Thomas Lord Burghe, who married *Frances*, the niece of Mrs. Blanche Parry.　　　　　　　　　F. C.

[We shall feel obliged by the copy of the will so kindly offered by our correspondent.]

GENERAL RICHARD FORTESCUE: LIEUT.-COL. FENWICK: FORTESCUES OF FALLAPIT (3rd S. vii. 341.)—As in future ages "N. & Q." may be quoted as an authority for any statement found in it remaining uncorrected, I may inform BREVIS that Lieut.-Col. Fenwick did not lose his leg "at Albuera, in Spain, or on the Pyrenees," but at Busaco. I knew Lieut.-Col. Fenwick forty years ago; I last saw him at the landing at Falmouth, in Sept. 1828, of Queen Maria da Gloria of Portugal; he was then grandly decorated with Portuguese orders. I have always been interested in Pendennis Castle; an ancestor of mine is (traditionally) known as one of its defenders. Not all " the Devon Fortescues sided with the Parliament;" witness Sir Edmund Fortescue, of Fallapit, the loyal defender of Fort Charles in 1646. For the siege of Fort Charles, list of the garrison, &c., see *Kingsbridge and Salcombe, with the intermediate Estuary described*, [by Abraham Hawkins, of Alston, Esq.], 1819, pp. 87-93. A photograph of the ruins of Fort Charles is given in *Kingsbridge Estuary*, compiled by S. P. Fox, 1864. There is also one of Fallapit, the abode of its brave defender.　　　　　　　　　　　　LÆLIUS.

PEWS (3rd S. vii. 267.)—For the information of SIR THOMAS E. WINNINGTON, and other of your readers interested in the matter, I beg to state that two pews, formerly the seats of the Earls of Oxford (De Vere), and the family of the Springs, are still standing in the interesting church of Lavenham, Suffolk. They are highly finished specimens of the style of Henry VII.'s Chapel at Westminster, most elaborately wrought; if possible that of the latter family more so than that of the former. They are both however somewhat decayed, and the Oxford bearings have in every instance been removed from the shields in the decorations. This may probably be accounted for by the fact that in the former case they were affixed to the shields, while in the latter they were carved upon them.

　　　　　　　　　　　　　GEORGE VICKERS.

Shimpling, Bury St. Edmunds.

WORDS USED IN DIFFERENT SENSES (3rd S. vii. 278.)—The word *nervous* is either used to imply energy or feebleness. It is an old joke against magistrates that they administer *indifferent* justice. The riddle tells us the soul is *immaterial*. We use the verb to *incense* in the north of England not as meaning to make one angry, but to make one understand; but as this is a provincialism it may be that *insense* is the properer way to spell it.

　　　　　　　　　　　　　　　　　P. P.

TOAD IN STONE (3rd S. vii. 339.)—I inclose extracts of a letter recently addressed to me by the Rev. Robert Taylor, the eminent local geologist mentioned by your correspondent:—

"The toad continues in good health, is still an object of great interest, and daily has many visitors. I have little more to add than what I have before stated to you, except that I have carefully examined the rock from which the block was hewn. I have also carefully examined the man who found the toad, and those whom he immediately called to witness the discovery of the stranger. I may add that the quarry, or that part of it where the toad was found, was a few years ago abandoned on account of water; but since then, in an adjoining old-worked quarry the water-works which supply the Hartlepools have lowered the surface of the water in this quarry about five feet, and in there the toad was found. The rock might be damp, but I am perfectly convinced there was neither vein nor chink, and am still ready to maintain that the animal must have been alive in a dormant state since the deposition of the material of the rock; and, according to my theory of geology, this, the magnesian limestone, was formed before the foundations of the Yorkshire hills were laid; so that it may be affirmed that it is older than these hills, and that it is fully six thousand times six thousand years old. Of course the uninitiated will think this wild kind of language; but I am ready to maintain my opinion."

J. WETHERELL.

THE CAISTOR WHIP (3rd S. vii. 354.)—MR. SPENCER HALL, and all who feel interest in the Caistor Whip, will find in The Archæological Journal, vol. vi. p. 239, an admirable article on "The Gad Whip Service," by Mr. W. S. Walford, F.S.A.

THOS. PURNELL.

BERKELEY ARMS (3rd S. vii. 337.)—In an old pamphlet which I have (bound with some more Guides), The Gloucester Guide, among the arms said to have been in the east window of that cathedral, are these: Gules, a chevron, ermine, between ten crosses, patée, argent, for Berkeley.

R. H. RUEGG.

H. M. Customs, W. I. Docks.

BREMEN COIN (3rd S. vii. 323.)—The letter s stands for semper. The full inscription is—FRANCISCUS I. DEI GRATIA ROMANORUM IMPERATOR SEMPER AUGUSTUS.

T. W. W.

COUNTESS OF SUFFOLK (3rd S. vii. 94, 169, 269, 349.)—From the description given by X., I think there can be little doubt as to the identification of the portrait. The second wife of Thomas Howard was clearly the only Countess of Suffolk that it could represent. But I conceive that it could not have been painted till many years later than the date that X. would assign to it. I do not know the date of the lady's birth; but Thomas Howard, her husband, was born in 1561, and it is hardly to be supposed that when he was not more than nineteen his wife should be verging upon fat, fair, and forty. I think it more probable that this likeness of the countess should have been taken at the same time as that of her husband

(also attributed to Zuccaro), an engraving from which is to be found in Lodge's Portraits. He is there represented with the collar and badge of the Garter; and, as his installation did not take place till May, 1597, the picture could not have been painted till after that date.

I may here mention that there are several portraits attributed to Zuccaro that could not have been painted by him till long after his visit to England in 1574. Without going beyond Lodge's Collection, I may particularise the portraits of Edward Somerset, Earl of Worcester; George Carew, Earl of Totnes; Robert Cecil, Earl of Salisbury; and Henry Howard, Earl of Northampton.

MELETES.

D'ABRICHCOURT AND WINGHAM CHURCH (3rd S. vii. 229.)—The most curious part of the penance upon this nun for breaking her vows and remarrying will be found (p. 269) in Dunkin's Report of the Proceedings at the Congress of the British Archæological Association, held in Canterbury, 1844. It will not well bear admission into the columns of "N. & Q." Not having access to a copy of Murray's Kent Hand-Book, I am unable to say whether the penance is given there in full.

Mr. Dunkin thus writes:—

[After the death of John, a brief time after his marriage,] "his disconsolate widow, shortly after—in the bloom of youth and beauty—vowed chastity, and was, solemnly veiled a nun by the Bishop of Winchester, at the convent of Waverley; but afterwards repenting of having so precipitantly quitted the world, she secretly withdrew from the monastery, and about eight years after, 'before the sun rising upon Michaelmas day, A.D. 1320, was clandestinely married to Sir Eustace Dabrieschescourt in a chapel of the mansion house of Robert de Brome, a canon of the College of Wingham, by Sir John Ireland, a priest. Such a striking violation of ecclesiastical discipline necessarily called forth condign punishment upon the culprits. The Archbishop of Canterbury summoned them both before him at the mansion-house, Maghfield, upon the seventh ides of April, and had not their high rank and riches intervened, would have instantly pronounced the marriage null and void. As it was, he enjoined for their penance," * &c. For which, see p. 269.

Αλφρεδ.

VOLTAIRE (3rd S. vi. 533; vii. 211, 284.)—Le Roi Voltaire is the eccentric title of an 8vo volume by M. Arsène Houssaye (Paris, 1858), which seems, from a short account of it by Edward de Barthélemy in his Essais Critiques, to be not so much a biography of Voltaire as a disjointed and somewhat paradoxical éloge, full of humour, verve, and esprit. A very brief and imperfect account of Voltaire's last hours is contained in the following extract from M. Barthélemy's Essais:—

"M. Houssaye retrace sa mort, couverte d'un nuage, mais qui eût été peut-être Chrétienne sans un empressement maladroit, par lequel échouèrent les sages dispositions d'un ecclesiastique qui, bien qu'éssentiellement,

* In despite of the indelicacy of this astonishing penance, the lady endured it fifty one years.

dévoué à la foi, plaisait à Voltaire et s'était déjà fait en-
tendre."
                                          J. MACRAY.

, FOXES OR SHEAVES (3ʳᵈ S. vii. 338.) — In reply
to the question, who first suggested the substitution of *sheaves* for *foxes* in Judges xv. 4, I may
state that this subject is discussed in Harris's
Natural History of the Bible, from which it appears that the notion of sheaves is first found in
the *Republ. des Lettres*, Oct. 1707; and Dr. Ken-
nicott refers to the *Memoirs of Literature*, 1712,
p. 15, for a like translation. Sewall, Hollis Professor of Hebrew in Harvard College, Cambridge,
U. S., replied. Some think the jackal and not
the fox is intended, but Gesenius has shown that
the proper Hebrew name for jackal is אׇ ee (= a
howler), whilst שׁוּעָל, *shual*, is by the best modern
scholars rendered *fox*, as in our version.
                                          T. J. BUCKTON.

MANETHO (3ʳᵈ S. vii. 356.) — To counteract the
attempt to disparage the authority of Manetho by
Hengstenberg, who has probably confounded some
other of that name, it may be useful to state that
in Heeren's *Manual of Ancient History* (pp. 51-54,
Oxf. 1833), the Greek authority for the first period of Egyptian history, after Herodotus and
Diodorus, is Manetho, described as the

" high priest at Heliopolis, who flourished under the reign
of Ptolemy Philadelphus, about B.C. 260. He wrote the
Ægyptiaca, of which, besides several fragments in Josephus,
the enumeration of the kings has been preserved in the
Chronicles of Eusebius and Syncellus. The authenticity
of Manetho is now completely established, since the names
of the Pharaohs mentioned by him have been deciphered
on the Egyptian monuments. It is worthy of observation,
that in Herodotus we have the documents of the priests of
Memphis; in Diodorus those of the priests of Thebes; in
Manetho those of the priests of Heliopolis — the three
principal seats of sacerdotal learning: perfect consistency
cannot, therefore, be expected in the accounts of those historians."

Bunsen, Lepsius, and Osburn concur in this
eulogy of Manetho.   T. J. BUCKTON.
Lichfield.

CLINT OR CLENT: OSSIAN'S GRAVE (3ʳᵈ S. vii.
323, 365.) — LORD LYTTELTON'S note, at the last-
quoted page, puts me in mind of a curious monu-
ment(?) situate on the apex of a wild and desolate
mountain pass, not far from the small town of
Borris, county of Carlow, on the road leading
from Kilteally to Borris. There are nine stones
set up in a peculiar perpendicular manner, and the
place is called the "Nine Stones." The stones
are about from four to six feet above the ground,
and set very irregular as to form. There is a
world of local tradition and mystery about these
——, which are of rough granite, and appear in a
—— natural form; the stone is plentiful in the
locality. One of the traditions, credited by the
people in the neighbourhood, is, that these stones

mark the grave of Ossian.* A quantity of fairy
and folk lore (enough to fill a volume) is in exist-
ance about these "Nine Stones." This may elicit
something more about them.   S. REDMOND.
Liverpool.

HENRY MARTEN (3ʳᵈ S. vii. 114.) — Your correspondent P. wishes to know the arms of Marten
the Regicide. I do not know if it is worth mentioning, but in the chancel of Ewelme church,
Oxon, is a monument to Colonel Francis Martyn,
who is believed to have been a relation of Henry
Marten. The arms are uncoloured: A chevron,
between three lions passant gardant, impaled with
a fess ermine between three anchors. As though
the monument is mentioned in Skelton's *History
of Oxfordshire*, the inscription is not given, I copy
it from my father's notes, as possibly interesting
to the readers of "N. & Q.": —

" Hic juxta situs est FRANCISCUS MARTYN de Ewelme,
in Comitatu Oxon. Armiger, qui obiit nono die Junii
Anno Domi 1682, Ætatis 74. Hoc monumentum Johis
Martyn unus Executorum posuit."

Francis Martyn built a large house in Ewelme,
which was pulled down between forty and fifty
years ago. He was an officer in Cromwell's army,
and it is supposed his influence was used for the
preservation of the monuments in Ewelme church
during those troublous times.   L. C. R.

"CHRISTIAN BREADBASKET" (3ʳᵈ S. vii. 356.)
A periodical under this title was issued some
three or four years ago, price 2d., monthly, published by Houlstone & Wright, but it lived, I
think, only seven months. Each number was
brought out, near the end, with *The Basket of
Crumbs*, being short pieces, under such titles as
the following: "How to make a Fast a Feast,"
"He is a Babe," "Temptation," &c. I trust
this will give BREVIS all he requires on this head.
                                          W. WILLEY.
Birmingham.

GERVASE HOLLES (3ʳᵈ S. vii. 356.) — Gervase
Holles' "Church Notes" have never been printed
in a complete form. The quotations occasionally
seen in small topographical works relating to
Lincolnshire have been obtained by the compilers
from the MSS. in the British Museum. Edward
Peacock, Esq., F.S.A., of Bottesford Manor, near
Brigg, has had in contemplation of publishing
these remarkably interesting records with notes.
The late Lord Monson incurred the expense of
obtaining a copy of Colonel Holles' Notes, and
this, we believe, is the only complete one in the
county to which they chiefly relate. The Dean
and Chapter of Lincoln's Library does not possess
a copy!   STAMFORDIENSIS.

* Ossian is said to have been the son of the great giant,
warrior, Finn M'Cool (?).   ΤΑ ΤΙ

Sobriquets of Regiments (3rd S. vii. *passim*.)
I have just met with the inclosed, and have copied
it, not knowing, however, whether it has been
already inserted among your articles on the sobriquets of regiments or no.

46th. *The Lacedemonians.*—Enoch Markham, a
younger brother of the Archbishop of York, was
Lieut.-Colonel of the 46th Regiment, which was
employed in America during the War of Independence. The following anecdote is related of
him:—

"Having halted his men under a heavy fire, whilst he
was for a few moments considering the best mode of attack, he heard talking in the ranks, upon which he coolly
turned round, and, commanding silence, harangued the
men upon the discipline of the Lacedemonians, and their
mode of marching to an attack in perfect silence. This
circumstance gained the regiment the sobriquet of *The
Lacedemonians.*"—*History of the Markham Family,* 8vo,
1854, p. 57.

J. G. Nichols.

White Ladies at Worcester (3rd S. vii. 238.)
In the *Report of the Congress of the British Archæological Association,* held in 1847 in Worcester, by
Alfred John Dunkin (p. 298), is an account of the
excavations made with the consent of the proprie-
tress of the White Ladies, in search of a subterranean passage said to exist between that nunnery
and Hindlip House. There is also an engraving
of the ruins of the chapel as it existed in 1847.

Αλφρεδ.

Anne Lady Parry and the Manor of Charlton (3rd S. vii. 211.)—I find in Hasted's *Kent*
(folio edit. i. 35), that Queen Elizabeth in her
fifth year granted the manor to Lady Anne Parre.
I find, however, no mention therein that she was
the widow of Sir Adrian Fortescue; nor do I find
that she bequeathed the manor to Thomas Fortescue, but that King James I. granted the manor
to Sir Adam Newton, knight and baronet.

Alfred John Dunkin.

Dartford.

Miscellaneous.

NOTES ON BOOKS, ETC.

*The Holy Sepulchre and the Temple at Jerusalem. Being
the Substance of Two Lectures delivered in the Royal
Institution, Albemarle Street, on the 21st February, 1862,
and the 3rd March, 1865. By James Ferguson, F.R.S.,
&c. (Murray.)*

These two lectures contain a *resumé* of all the main
points of the argument, with a sufficient amount of illustration and references to make it intelligible, by which
Mr. Ferguson believes he establishes the fact that the
building popularly known as the Mosque of Omar is, in
reality, the sepulchral building which Constantine erected
over what he believed to be the tomb of Christ. The
subject is one of great interest; and the volume is, for
many reasons, well timed. The appendix contains some
interesting extracts from a small volume entitled *Theo-
doricus de Locis Sanctis,* lately published by Dr. Titus
Tobler, of St. Gall.

*The Wedgwoods : being a Life of Josiah Wedgwood, with
Notices of his Works and their Productions, Memoirs of
the Wedgwood and other Families, and a History of the
Early Potteries of Staffordshire. By Llewellyn Jewitt,
F.S.A. With a Portrait, and other Illustrations.*
(Virtue Brothers.)

The complaint made by Mr. Gladstone in his admirable
eulogium on Wedgwood, that it was strange that the life
of such a man should, in this nation of shopkeepers, yet
at this time remain unwritten, is no longer called for.
The groundwork of the present volume, which has been
one of serious labour to the editor, is to be found in the
chapters of Wedgwood and Etruria which form a part of the
series of histories of the porcelain and earthenware manufactories of this kingdom, which Mr. Jewitt is giving in
the pages of the *Art Journal.* These have been remodelled and re-written, and the additional matter has swelled
the narrative to more than double its original size. It
now contains a very interesting history of the "great
Josiah and his family," and his works: and the latter
being profusely illustrated (the book contains 145 woodcuts), the editor is justified in regarding it as a pleasing
and lasting Wedgwood memorial.

*The Annual Register ; a Review of Public Events at Home
and Abroad, for the Year 1864. New Series.* (Rivingtons.)

There is obviously a new and long career of usefulness
opening to the New Series of this valuable Compendium
of Home and Foreign History. Our newspapers get too
large for private individuals to file, but the more prominent features of them are here condensed and indexed
ready for immediate reference.

*The Romance of the Scarlet Leaf, and other Poems, with
Adaptations from the Provençal Troubadours. By
Hamilton Aidé.* (Moxon & Co.)

The opening poems of this little volume remind us
strongly of Rogers's *Italy*; not so much as being imita-
tions of it, as being the emanations from a kindred mind.
Is Mr. Aidé right in supposing he is the first to give in
English any poetical adaptations from the Provençal
Troubadours ?

*The Early English Organ Builders and their Works from
the Fifteenth Century to the Period of the Great Rebellion. An unwritten Chapter in the History of the Organ.
By Edward F. Rimbault, LL.D.* (A. Whittingham.)

All admirers of the King of Instruments will receive
with thanks from Dr. Rimbault this interesting contribution to the early history of Organ-building in England.
Dr. Rimbault's industry in research, and judgment in
selection, give ample security for the value of his information.

Notices to Correspondents.

*We have lately received so many Queries accompanied by requests for
private letters in reply, that We think it right to announce that We
cannot undertake to furnish private Replies to any inquirers.*

*Our Correspondent, who writes to us on the subject of a recently pub-
lished tract on " Genealogies," will, on consideration, see that his remarks are of too personal a character.*

Errata.—3rd S. vii. p. 364, col. ii. line 21, *for* " Gollemach " *read*
" Golleamach;" line 34, *for* " rushid " *read* "rashed."

A Reading Case for holding the weekly Nos. of " N. & Q." is now
ready, and may be had of all Booksellers and Newsmen, price 1s. 6d.;
or, free by post, direct from the publisher, for 1s. 8d.

*** Cases for binding the volumes of " N. & Q." may be had of the
Publisher, and of all Booksellers and Newsmen.

"Notes and Queries" is published at noon on Friday, and is also
issued in Monthly Parts. The Subscription for Stamped Copies for
Six Months forwarded direct from the Publisher (including the Half-
yearly Index) is 11s. 4d., which may be paid by Post Office Order,
payable at the Strand Post Office, in favour of William G. Smith, 32,
Wellington Street, Strand, W.C., where also all Communications
for the Editor should be addressed.

"Notes & Queries" is registered for transmission abroad.

LONDON, SATURDAY, MAY 20, 1865.

CONTENTS.—N° 177.

Notes.

WHAT IS A COSHERER?

Public attention was excited to some extent by the singularity of the presentment case, which in March last was brought before Mr. Baron Hughes, at the Kilkenny Assizes, when Patrick Doyle was impeached, under the statutes of Queen Anne and Geo. III., *inter alia*, for "coshering" from house to house; and the jury found that "he was an Irish gentleman, and would not work," and he was sentenced to find two securities in 10*l.* each for his good behaviour for seven years, or to be imprisoned during that period.

The objects of this contribution are to correct what appear to me to be errors of the several scribes, who have attempted to define what a "cosherer" was, and whence the word is derived.

The Times, in an editorial article, March 11 last, says, "the derivation of the term 'cosherer' is more than doubtful;" and conjectures that "he is one who pretends to be an Irish gentleman, and will not work." And again adds: —

"A cosherer is described by some etymologists as a man who goes about from house to house claiming food and lodging, sometimes as a feudal superior, sometimes as a kinsman; cousining himself upon the inmates, and cozening them out of their substance."

On the 13th of the same month a correspondent, "Pacilla," writes, "cosherer is obviously derived from the French word *coucher* (to lie down,

to sleep)," and thinks there is no doubt about the derivation.

In the columns of the *Daily Telegraph* of the 24th March, an oriental etymological origin is sought for the word; and on the 27th following, "Philologist," in an erudite and interesting contribution to it, exhibiting an acquaintance both with the oriental languages and the Irish or Keltic, says very truly: —

"Their correspondence of form proves their unity of origin. But for the etymological meaning of 'cosher,' or 'cosherer,' an oriental origin need not be sought. Its import in Hiberno-Celtic excludes the possibility of doubt. Cosher is another name for the class called in Hiberno-Celtic 'Tories,' or 'plunderers,' 'searchers,' 'seekers,' &c. But the same parties were also called 'cosherers,' which literally means footmen—etymology: *coss*, a foot; and *ear*, a man."

One of our own respected correspondents, H. C. C., acutely, though equally at fault with the others, suggests *cios*, rent.

Learning and ingenious philological conjecture have been thus expended on the roots and meaning of the word "cosherer;" and now I respectfully, though confidently, submit my conviction that all these conjectures and disquisitions are at variance with the derivation, accurate definition, and the historical and legal significance of the word.

In a *Treatise of Ireland*, by John Dymmok, supposed to be in attendance upon Essex when he was Lord-Lieutenant of Ireland, written about 1600, published by the Irish Archæological Society, we are told that —

"Irish taxes or services are of two sortes, either made unto the queene by the gentlemen towards their defence and mayntenance of her forces in the countrye, as Rysingout, Bonaght, and Soren, or els by the Lord upon his tennant, as Coynye, Livery, Cashery," &c.

The writer proceeds then to explain the meaning of these terms, and the word "cashery" (coshery), he thus defines: —

"Cashery is certeine feastes which the Lord useth to take of his tennants after Easter, Chrismas, Whitsontyde, Michaelmas, and all other tymes at his pleasure; he goeth to their howses with all his trayne and idlemen of his cuntrye, &c., and holdeth on this course till he have visited all his tenants one after another."—Pp. 8, 9.

Sir James Ware's *Antiquitates Hibernicæ* confirms the statement of Dymmok: —

"Coshery exactio erat Dynastæ Hibernici, quando ab incolis sub ejus potestate, et clientela, victum et hospitium capiebat pro seipso suaque clientela."—Sec. 12.

"Coshering" was a custom not peculiarly Irish; it was an ordinary custom, though not so named, also of feudal rule.

"The Lords," says Sir Henry Spelman, "might take not only of their tenants, but of all the country thereabout, victuals and all other necessaries for furnishing their castles, &c. And by *signorial authority* as to lye and feast themselves and followers (called 'coshering') at their tenants' houses; and when any matter of extraordinary charge fell upon them, then to extort the same amongst the tenants, which the Irish about forty years since (*circiter* 1550) of my own knowledge, still continued, calling it *cuttings*, according to our word *tallagium*. But amongst us it was taken away by the *Magna Charta* of King John."—Spelman, *Of Parliament*, London, 1723.

Abolished as the custom had been by Magna Charta, it was not taken away, as Spelman asserts; for we find that during the " visitations " or " progresses " of Queen Elizabeth, she obtruded her royal presence, " eating the landlord out of house and home."

In that patriarchal phasis of society which Ireland shared with other nations, where all members of a sept were " of the one blood," and had the same social status, those primitive and inartificial customs, which prevailed, worked well and harmoniously, and were seldom or never impeded or disturbed by those irregularities, which the Anglo-Norman officials so conveniently for themselves detected, and so indignantly denounced in later years. On the contrary, we have it upon the best authorities, that the colonists adopted them, and exposed themselves to the odium subsequently involving them. Sir John Davies says :—

" But when the English had learned it (coshering), they used it with more insolence, and made it more intolerable, for this oppression was not temporary or limited either to place or time, &c., and this crying sin did drawe downe greater plagues uppon Ireland than the oppression of the Israëlites did drawe uppon the land of Egypt. For the plagues of Egypt, though they were grievous, were but of short duration ; but the plagues of Ireland lasted four hundred years together, that is, from the invasion of the English."—*Discoverie of the True Causes why Ireland was never entirely subdued, &c.* London, 1612, p. 174.

The author of the *Faerye Queene*, the poet Spenser, in his *View of the State of Ireland*, 1596, a few years before Dymmok wrote, describing " coshery " and " kindred " customs, gives the following apologetic explanation, and singularly, though I am convinced inaccurately, attributes its introduction into Ireland to the English colonists:

" The which is a common use amongst the landlords of the Irish, to have a common spending amongst their tennants at will, they use to take of what victuals they will, for of victuals they were wont to make small reckoning ; *neither in this was the tennant wronged, for it was an ordinary and knowne custome*, and HIS LORD USE TO SO COVENANT WITH HIM, which if at any time the tennant disliked, he might freely depart at his pleasure, &c., *the which* (I thinke) *were customs at first brought in by the English upon the Irish*."

By the Irish custom of *Tanistry*, the chieftain of every country and the head of every clan had only a life interest in their "chieferies." Sir John Davies, Attorney-General for Ireland in the reign of James I., states that their cuttings and " cosheries," &c. constituted their revenues. When the chieftain died, their sons and next of kin did not succeed to him. The " Tanist " succeeded, and had been elected during the lifetime of his pre-

decessor. Personal qualifications and consanguinity were the only requisite recommendations. Every hale male of the sept was eligible. On the death of a clan's man, his portion was not divided amongst his sons, but the chief made a partition of all the lands belonging to his sept, and gave every one his part according to his "antiquity;" and however small their allotments, or indigent their circumstances, " yet did the military men scorn to descend to husbandry or merchandise." They were the ruling class. With the sword they won the " Green Isle; " with the sword they were always ready to stand up for their inheritance; their claims for support on their territory, "never receiving other pay," was equal if not superior to those of the cultivators of the soil and other producers of wealth. To a free maintenance the warrior and the chief had at least as strong a hereditary claim as had or has a feudal lord to his inheritance.

In the ceaseless strifes with alternating advantages, between the English settlers and the natives, for centuries, the men who bore arms were the most troublesome, most dreaded, most detested, most abused by their adversaries ; thus the harshest measures, the most virulent abuse, the most opprobrious epithets were applied to the. Kearns, Galloglasses, and Dalteens, and found a resting-place even in the statutes.

The total destruction of the "Men of Warres," the retainers of the chieftains of the " Irish enemies," and of the "English rebel Lords," became at an early period the chief aim of the English Government; and to ensure this politic resolve, recourse was had, not only to arms, but to legislation, and many Acts of Parliament were made in consequence.

William Burke, Earl of Ulster, and Lord of Connaught, was slain in Ulster by his English attendants. He left an only daughter to inherit his vast possessions. She was afterwards married to. Lionel, Duke of Clarence, second son of Edward III., but that prince never came into possession, for the next male heirs of the deceased earl seized upon his extensive territories, according to the Brehon laws, and afterwards retained them in despite of the English government. Duke Lionel came twice to Ireland, in the capacity of Lord Lieutenant, to gain possession, but in vain. By this prince was summoned at Kilkenny, A.D. 1367, the most famous parliament that till then had been held in Ireland, in which the statute of Kilkenny was passed. By its provisions, the most stringent measures were applied for the extinction of Coyne and Livery, &c., Idlemen, &c., and the reformation of the colonists, who had adopted the laws, language, and manners of the " Irish enemies," and had conciliated the natives by intermarriages and other alliances. "If any did submit himself to the Brehon law, he should be adjudged a traitor." De Lolme thus speaks of this enactment : —

"The fact is, that it was no more than a peevish and revengeful expression of the resentment Duke Lionel felt from the opposition he had met with, and the loss of those lands he had come over to claim."—*Strictures on the State of Ireland*, 4to, p. 31.

In the Irish State Papers, vol. xv. there is an interesting document bearing date December 2, 1565, No. 55, p. 281, &c., thus described : —

"From a book to be exhibited unto the Rt. Hon. the Lᵈ Lieut. (Sir Henry Sydney) agayst Coyn and Livery wᶜʰ thearle of Kildare taketh by exforce of thenhabitants of the Countie Kildare wᵗʰ other the sayd earles enormities and abuses."

Amongst several items it contains the following : —

"And it was enacted in the time of King Ric. the Second, at his personall being here in this realme of Ireland, that Coyn and Livery should be abolished the Englishe pale as Methe (Meath), the countie of Dublin, the countie of Kildare, and the countie of Catherlaghe, wᶜʰ acte was newly confirmed by Kynge Edward IIIIᵗʰ, as doth appear by record, &c.

"Item, in the rayne of Kinges Henry VIIᵗʰ, there paste an acte within this realme of Ireland Wᶜʰ is called thacte of Marches and Maghery, that such as take coyn in the Maghery or Englishe pale should be estemed felons.

"Item, Sir Anthony Fitz Harbard Knighte, and other commissioners, sent hither by the late prince of famous memory, Kinge Henry VIIIᵗʰ, took order that thactes aforesayd should stand in pour.

"Item, in the tyme of Sir William Sheryngton, beinge deputie of this realme, ther paste an acte for the extinguishment of the sayd coyn and livery as playnly may appere by the same acte in print, conferminge likewise thactes aforesayd," &c.

In the same volume of this Series of State Papers, Eliz., an. 14 (1565), October 5, are "Instructions to Sir Henry Sydney, Lord Deputie and Council." In which it is stated that her "Matie is informed," &c., that —

"there are sufficient provisions already made against the greatest abuses found in that Realme as against coinyng Livery and 'Coshery,' against wearing of Irish apparel, against succouring of felons, against Ryots and unlawful assemblees, against Retayners, against taking of Tributes, against marrying or fostering wᵗʰ Irishmen : And special lawes also, according to the Statute of Winchester," &c.

Her Majesty then concludes by charging and commanding her Lieutenant —

"to cause searche to be made as well for the said Lawes, as for any other lyke to the same, and therof to make advertissment what shall be thought meete, with the publishing of the same."

On the termination of Tyrone's war with James I., the spirits of the people were broken; and Sir John Davies, in the work already quoted, says that —

"Sir George Cary did, in the first year of his Majesty's reyne (1603), make the first sheriffes that ever were made in Tyrone and Tirconnell; and shortly after, sent Sir Edmund Pelham, Chief Baron, and myselfe, thither—the first Justices that ever sat in those countries. The com-

mon people were taught, &c., that the Cuttings, Cosheries, Sessings, and other extortions of their Lords, were unlawful; and that they should not any more submit thereunto. Thereupon the power of those Irish Lords over the people sodainly fell and vanished."—Pp. 264—268.

The fact is by what, in legal phrase, is called the forfeitures to the crown, the septs were deprived of their lands, till then their common property, reduced to a state of indigence and helpless dependence; subjected as tenants to fixed rents, and other obligations, arbitrarily imposed and rigidly exacted, outraging their sense of justice. This is the fount and source of many of the evils which afflict Ireland.

To the acts of Anne and George, which suggested and sustained the presentment against Patrick Doyle, it is needless to refer. There now remains merely to explain the derivation of the word *Cosherer*.

Cosherer, a free feast-er, a free guest; compounded of *cosair*, a feast, a banquet; and *fear*, a man. The initial being aspirated, fear is pronounced *ar* or *er*, and is the agglutinated affix in "Cosherer." This affix, I would suggest, is to be found elsewhere than in the Irish, and probably in those nouns in the English language ending in *er*, and in their signification including an agent. *Coshair*, a feast, a banquet—in the Irish *co-sair*, for the Irish *s* is invariably *sh*—is also a compound word, the components being primitives; thus abnegating the oriental descent in its integrate form. *Cot*, meat, victuals—the final *t* being aspirated, *cot* is pronounced *co*; and *saor*, free, voluntary. See Reilly's, Begley's, O'Connell's, and O'Brien's *Irish Dictionaries*, and Shaw's and Armstrong's *Gaelic Dictionaries*, under these words.

"Cosherer" is found in our *Law Dictionaries*—Blount, Jacob, Cowell, and Tomlins; but it is acknowledged that they obtained it from Spelman, who recognises it as used by the Irish.

JOHN EUGENE O'CAVANAGH.

Lime Cottage, Walworth Common, London.

BALLAD : BATTLE OF HARLAW.
ORIGINAL VERSION.

In order that the original words of this old ballad may not be lost, they are sent to "N. & Q." in the hope that they may find a place there.

I.

"As I cam in by Dunidier, and down by Wetherha', There was fifty thousan' Hielan' men a' marchin' to Harlaw,
(*Chorus*)　　In a dree, dree, drady drumtie dree.

II.

"As I cam on, and farther on, and doun an' by Balquhain,
Oh, there I met Sir James the Rose, wi' him Sir John the Gryme.

III.

"'Oh, cam ye frae the Hielans, man, and cam ye a' the wye,
Saw ye MacDonell an' his men come marchin frae the Skye?'

IV.

"'Yes, she cam frae the Hielans, man, and she cam a' the wye,
And she saw M'Donell an' his men, come marchin' frae the Skye.'

V.

"'Oh, were ye near an' near eneuch, did ye their nummers see?
Come, tell to me, John Hielanman, what micht their nummers be?'

VI.

"'Yes, she was near, an' near eneuch, an' she their nummers saw,
There was fifty thousan' Hielan men, a' marchin' for Harlaw.'

VII.

"'Gin that be true,' quo' James the Rose, 'we'll no come muckle speed;
So we'd best cry in our merry men, and turn our horses' heeds.'

VIII.

"'Oh no! Oh no!' quo' John the Gryme, 'that thing maun never be,
The "Gallant Grymes" were never beat, we'll try what we can dee.'
[N.B.—The battle has now commenced and is raging.]

IX.

"As I cam on, an' farther on, and doun an' by Harlaw,
They fell fu' close on ilka side, sic fun ye never saw.

X.

"They fell fu' close on ilka side, sic fun ye never saw,
For Hielan swords gaed clash for clash, at the battle o' Harlaw.

XI.

"The Hielan men, wi' their lang swords, they laid on us fu' sair,
And they drav back our merry men, three acres breadth or mair.

XII.

"Brave Forbes did to his brither say, 'Now, brither, dinna ye see,
They beat us back on ilka side, and we'll be forced to flee.'

XIII.

"'Oh no! Oh no! my brither dear, that thing maun never be,
Tak ye your guid sword, ie yr han', and come your wyes wi' me.'

XIV.

"'Oh no! Oh no! my brither dear, the clans they are ower strong,
An' they drive back our merry men wi' swords baith sharp and lang.'

XV.

"Brave Forbes to his men did say, 'Noo tak your rest awhile,
Until I to Drumminnor send, to fetch my coat of mail.'

XVI.

"Brave Forbes' {hinchman} {servant} then did ride, and his horse it did na' fail,
For in twa hours an' a quarter, he brocht the coat o' mail.

XVII.

"Then back to back the brithers twa gaed in amang the thrang,
And they hewed doun the Hielan men wi' swords baith sharp and lang.

XVIII.

"M'Donell he was young an' stout, had on his coat o' mail,
And he has gane oot through them a', to try his han' himsel'.

XIX.

"The first ae stroke that Forbes struck, made the great M'Donell reel,
The second stroke that Forbes struck, the great M'Donell fell.

XX.

"An siccan a 'pilleurichie' the like ye never saw
As there was amang the Hielanmen, when they saw M'Donell fa'.

XXI.

"An when they saw that he was dead, they turned an' ran awa,
An they buried him in 'Seggatt's lan'* some twa three miles awa.

XXII.

"They rode, they ran, and some did gang, but they were of sma' record,
For Forbes and his merry men slew maist a' by the road [sword?].

XXIII.

"On Munonday at morning the battle it began,
On Saturday at glo'min', ye'd scarce tell wha had wan.

XXIV.

"An sic a weary burying, the like ye never saw,
As there was the Sunday after that on the muirs down by Harlaw.

XXV.

"An gin Hielan lasses speer at yu, for them that gaed awa
Ye may tell them plain an' plain eneuch they're sleepin' at Harlaw."

N.B. This, the *original version* of this ballad, one of the oldest in Scotland, has, it is believed, *never been printed;* various editions have, but never this. It is sung to a quaint lively air, and years ago might have been heard not unfrequently in the farmhouses in Aberdeenshire. The words must be pronounced in the broadest Aberdeenshire dialect. M'Donald is here spelled throughout M'Donell, simply for the sake of dropping the "d." It might have been better to have written "M'Donal'," but it is given *literatim* from the manuscript. A. FERGUSON.

* Qy. Where is "Seggatt's lan'?" It can scarcely be Seggat in Auchterless. The manuscript is indistinct, and it would read equally well "Leggalt's lan'." Where, again, is that, or is there such a place? Seggat, in Auchterless, would be some fifteen or sixteen English miles from Harlaw? Can any of your correspondents answer?

ANTONY AND CLEOPATRA.

" *Cleopatra.* . . . . It is great
　To do that thing that ends all other deeds;
　Which shackles accident, and bolts up change;
　Which sleeps and *never palates more the dung,*
　The beggar's nurse and Cæsar's."—Act V. Sc. 2.

Before examining the italicised phrase let me
say a word or two on the interpretation of the
verbs in this fourth line. In the third and fifth,
Death, the "thing" of the second line, is personified, and the words "never more" forbid us to
take sleeps and palates as attributives of such a
being. Neither as a second supposition can it be
believed that Shakspeare clumsily or sleepily forgot that he had thus personified death and so
spoke of it in the intermediate line as a state into
which the living being falls. It is more natural
to consider the personification of death as one acting on us, to be carried on throughout, and to interpret sleeps and palates as casual verbs. Death
which shackles, which bolts up, which causes
sleep, which never causes or allows of palating, the
nurse of Cæsar and the beggar. Linger and fall are
familiar examples of this causal usage.

Now if the reader adopt the first or second of
the above interpretations, then he must at once
reject Warburton's change of "never palates more
the dug," for this makes Shakspeare represent death
first as an infant, and then as a nurse. On the
other hand, if he reads the verbs as causals, though
this objection does not hold, yet the phrase, on
close examination, will be seen to be neither suggested by any word used by Cleopatra, nor by any
thought which can be supposed to have entered
her mind. Life to her was the time since she had
become a woman and a queen. That life she
thoroughly enjoyed; but her infantile life and its
pleasures would be the last thing she would think
of, and that life was to her as great a blank as
death itself. In fact Warburton formed his thought
on Cleopatra's after-thought, and this gives it its
apparent suitableness.

The original reading again —"to palate the
dung," gives, I conceive, somewhat of the sense
intended; but the word is objectionable on three
grounds. Shakspeare was a great chooser of words,
and generally very happy in his choice, but though
the produce of the earth may, in any one's estimation, be as dung, it can in no other way be or be
likened to dung, and therefore I do not think it
would be used in this sense, when it is no way
pre-shadowed or led up to, without some defining
word, such as — of the earth, or vile, &c. Secondly, the luxurious Cleopatra did not so estimate the good things of this world. Her "better
life," that she speaks of, is clearly nothing more
than the doing, after the old Roman fashion, of
something more noble than the consenting to live
as a captive. Her pride and all the habits of her
life revolted against being shown in triumph, and

being then banished into desolation. It is the
sense of this change that makes her think of death,
"which shackles accident and bolts up change."
It is because she can no longer live the only life
she cares for, and because of Antony's death, that
she thinks the world not worth leave taking. But
her last commands are —"Give me my robe, put
on my crown;" and among her last thoughts are—
　　　　"Now no more
　The juice of Egypt's grape shall moist this lip."

Thirdly, Cleopatra was a thorough woman in
her mobility, and power of identifying herself with
the spirit of the hour. When enraged with her
messenger, she might have called him dung of
the earth (though even then Shakspeare avoids
putting into her mouth worse epithets than horrible villain, or cuckold), but it is certain that
when moralising, her delicacy or unconscious raising herself to the height of that great argument;
or if you will, her sense of fitness would revolt
against the utterance of so gross a word.

But when we sleep two acts are unperformed,
one essential to life itself, the other essential to
social life, and both of the very essence of life to
Cleopatra. We neither taste food nor talk; and,
as exemplified in the words taste, talk, *dicere*,
gouster, λαλεῖν, "gluck," and others; the palating
the tongue, or touching the tongue with the palate,
is essential to, and will therefore express, both
these acts. As to taste, if the reader will place
any savoury scentless matter on his tongue, he can
test the truth of this for himself. I would therefore read—" And never palates more the tongue,"
or as it was often spelled, "tong."

　　　　　　　　　　　　　B. NICHOLSON.

SCOTCH PEERS, 1713–14.

The following notanda, from the collections of
a Scotch genealogical writer, are worthy of preservation. The notes are by the writer: —

23rd January, 1713, N. S. The Earl of Melfort died at
Paris.—*Political State of Great Britain*, p. 78.

24th January, 1713. The Earl of Selkirk set out by
Dover and Calais for France, to renew his solicitations
about his pretensions to the Dutchy of Chastel Herault.—
Ibid. p. 77.

14 June, 1713. The Earle of Blantyre, one of the sixteen Scotch Peers, died in Westminster of a fever, much
lamented. He is succeeded in his honours and estate by
his brother, then a Captain in Port Mahon.—*Ibid.* p. 459.
[The Earldom is in the creation of the author. His Lordship was only a Scotch baron.]

4th January, 1714. The Earl of Crawfurd, a North
British Peer, Colonel of the second troop of her Majesty's
Horse Grenadier Guards, died of a phthisick. — *Ibid.*
p. 71. [This nobleman was the Lord Whigridden of
Pitcairn's witty comedy of *The Assembly.*]

18th May, 1714. Lord Irwin dies of small-pox. —
Ibid. p. 449. [He was the fourth Viscount, and died at
the early age of twenty-eight, unmarried. The founder
of the family was an Alderman of London: he died in
1612.]

. On Friday, 17th of August, 1714. The Earl of Cromarty died in the North of Scotland, in the eighty-fourth year of his age. He was made a Baronet by King Charles. He was a person of universal learning, the oldest officer perhaps in the world. In his time a very able statesman, and a great honour to his native county.—*Ibid.* p. 246. [A tolerably correct enumeration of his Lordship's works will be found in Wood's edition of Douglas's *Scotish Peerage.*]

18th November, 1714. The Earl of Dunbar, a Scotch Roman Catholic Peer, dyed in London, and was succeeded in his honours and estate by his brother, William Constable, Esq. [This nobleman was only a Viscount. His only daughter Anne became eventually heiress of line. She married Simon Scrope of Danby. The patent, being to heirs male bearing the name and arms of Constable, has been in abeyance since the death of William Constable, who did not long survive his brother.]

24th November. The Lord Aston, another Roman Catholic, who was succeeded by his son [Walter].—*Ibid.* p. 469. [This Peerage was created by Charles I., Nov. 28, 1627, with a remainder to heirs male for ever. In consequence of this, after the failure of heirs male of the body, the title went to a cook and a watchmaker—for to this humble position the male representatives of this noble family had been reduced. The last Lord was the 9th Baron. He was in holy orders ; though married, he had no issue, and, since his death, no claimant to the honours has appeared.]

J. M.

THE ROMAN HYPOCAUST AT SLACK. — When this hypocaust was discovered about forty years ago, a sketch of it was made by the late Mr. Tayler, of Halifax, architect. This sketch was subsequently deposited in the Museum of the Leeds Philosophical Society, but now—*non est inventus.*

Mr. Tayler had also a rough outline of the hypocaust in one of his sketch books, but it was sold with some other of his plans and drawings some few years ago.

Let me now say through " N. & Q.," in the hope that it will reach the possessors of either of these sketches, that a copy, or the loan of either of them, will greatly oblige the Council of the Huddersfield Archæological Association. Address, Rev. George Lloyd, Hon. Sec., Thurstonland, Huddersfield. GEO. LLOYD.

THE METROPOLITAN ROADS IN 1692.—There is a curious entry in the *Lords' Journals* for March 1, 1692, which shows the difficulties of travelling even in the neighbourhood of London at that time. The House had assembled at one o'clock to meet the Commons at a Conference ; but the Speaker, Sir Robert Atkyns, the Chief Baron of the Exchequer, not having arrived, the Duke of Somerset was chosen Speaker *pro tempore.* The cause of his absence is shown by an entry in the latter part of the day's proceedings : —

" A message was sent to the House of Commons by Sir Miles Cook and Sir Adam Ottley :
" To let the Commons know, that the Speaker of the House of Lords, living two miles out of town, and the badness of the roads at this present, was the only occasion of their Lordships not coming to the Conference at the time appointed."

Sir Robert Atkyns, it is understood, was then living at Kensington. M. N. S.

DE GUSTIBUS, ETC. — I enclose you for publication a letter from Mr. Maywood, the American actor, to my grandfather, introducing Mr. Greenhow. The postscript is very curious.

" Dear Sir,
" I trust time has not intirely erased my name from the tablets of your memory, and that you will pardon a moment's intrusion.
" Mr. Greenhow, the gentleman who will present this, is a warm admirer of your talents ; and finding occasion to brave the world of waters which lie between this vast continent and the emporium of learning and genius, wished an opportunity of seeing you. I have, therefore, taken the liberty of introducing him, in the hope of double gratification. He is a gentleman of good mind, extensive reading, and well acquainted with the history and all particulars relative to his country. He is, too, a profound lover of the drama. He will be happy to inform you of its state in this country ; which, with other matters, may while (*sic*) away an hour, and perchance amuse you. Your society and converse will on his part be highly valued. I learn that poor ' Ogilvie ' has passed that ' bourne whence no traveller returns :' his troubled spirit now finds rest. In the confidence that you do not think me presuming, and that your literary labours may ever be crowned [*crowed* in MS.] by a golden harvest, I remain yours, with great respect,
" New York, R. C. MAYWOOD. -
April 29th, 1821.
" William Hazlitt, Esq.

" P.S. I feel assured that any parts of so great a being as George Cooke, will be esteemed a curiosity, and richly valued. The bearer of this will offer a morsel of the liver of this wonderous man. R—— [*sic*]."
W. CAREW HAZLITT.

FLY-LEAVES. — A spare page, before a copy of the *Works of William Gouge,* 1627, folio (which belonged to the Earl of Harborough), exhibits the following interesting particulars : —

" Yorke, 10th 18o Ano Dni., 1626. .
For Mrs Mary Cholmeley. HEY FAIRFAX.

MARY CHOLMELEY.
Anagrams.
Hail, comely Mrs. S. *super est.*
Mal, y'are comely. H. *non est . . .*[*]

' Though tricksy to see, too be gallant to driue,
Yet comely and wise is ye huswife to thriue.'
Tusser.

MARY CHOLMELEY.
Anagram.—' Oh I'me all mercy.
M. My hand, my heart, my selfe, and what doth make it,
C. Claime to bee mine, *Oh I'me all mercy,* take it.
HEY FAIRFAX.

Fly, restless thoughts ! But, heark ye, stay ;
I need not question where you goe.
The haste you make doth that betray ;
Salute my Loue, and let him know

* A word here is illegible. -

My weak estate, when you did part;
You left mee neither Thought nor Heart.

If he reply and say, that I .   .   .
  Possest his heart, when mine I gaue,
Beleeu[e] it not ; its fals, for why
  I haue none, but one would gladly haue.
If carelessly hee say, Take either,
Answer, I will haue his or neither.

If falsly hee asure them doth,´
  And fly, still follow : finde him out.
Say I'le exclude him : yet I'me loath,
  For why, I haue no heart to doo't.
You leau[e] me neither Heart nor Thought,
And I'le conclude I'me good for nought.
  M. C. of ever happy memory.

M. High dying Thoughts and Heart of thine,
Ff. Finde rest in Heaveⁿ. These wee resigne."

Upon the title-page of the book, is "Fare fac |
M. F." ; and throughout the earlier portion of the
volumes (two in one, original binding), are copious MS. annotations by Henry Fairfax : conclusive as to the careful perusal by him of the copy
of the work, which he presented to Mary Cholmeley, afterwards Mary Fairfax.

W. Carew Hazlitt.

Toasts. — It appears to me that " N. & Q."
might be made the means of rescuing from oblivion many of the toasts of former days, valuable
on account of their wit, quaintness, or historical
bearing. Hitherto, I think, no attempt of any
magnitude has been made. I give my quota to
the undertaking : —

" May the last king be strangled in the bowels of the
last priest."—(Given at the meetings of the revolutionary
Societies of the close of the last century.)

" Here's a health to those that we love, here's a health
to those that love us ; here's a health to those that love
them that love those that love those that love them that
love us."

" Here's a health to you and yours who have done
such things for us and ours ; and when we and ours have
it in our powers to do for you and yours what you and
yours have done for us and ours, then we and ours *will* do
for you and yours what you and yours have done for us
and ours."

These two were given me .some years ago by
an old gentleman who remembered them as favor-
ites in the last century. One of them was composed by Dr. Enfield.

" May the trade of Kidderminster be trampled under
foot by all the world."

Said to have been given by Pitt at a dinner in
that town.

" Sink your pits, blast your mines, dam your rivers."
—(By Henry Erskine.)

" May all our labours be in vein."—(Mining toast in
Yorkshire.)

Cyril.

Batler. — In *The Reader* of April 27, is a notice of the finding in an old house in Yorkshire
of a batler, or batlet, such as the enamoured

Touchstone kissed (*As You Like It*, Act II. Sc. 4.)
These *batlers* or *battledores*, as they are now generally called, are still in use in Yorkshire. They
are the prototype of the " patent mangle," and
consist merely of a flat rectangular piece of wood,
some two feet long, and six inches broad, with a
thin short handle. The linen to be mangled is
coiled round a roller, which is placed on a table,
and then the batler is placed on the top, and
pushed forwards and backwards on the roll under
pressure of the hands.

.They were not used in Yorkshire only. I procured a very handsome specimen in Suffolk some
years ago, the upper surface of which is rather
elaborately carved with a Gothic design. The
initials of the owner are burnt in in Gothic letters,
and the article cannot have been made more
lately than the beginning of the sixteenth century.
J. Eliot Hodgkin.

The Epistle to the Laodiceans. — Many
have supposed from an expression in Col. iv. 16,
that St. Paul wrote an Epistle to the Church of
Laodicea. The following cutting now going the
round of the newspapers bears upon this subject,
and seems to call for a remark : —

" At a recent sale by auction at Mingdon, a magnificent
illuminated Latin manuscript of the Bible, written in the
twelfth century, and containing, in addition to the Apo-
crypha, the Epistle of Paul to the Laodiceans (long received as a canonical book), was knocked down to Mr.
Thomas Hughes, of Chester, for thirty-two guineas. It
is said that this precious manuscript will be deposited in
the Chapter Library, Chester."

It is well known that no ancient Greek text of
this forgery is extant, and that we have no proof
that the Latin text is identical with the Epistle to
the Laodiceans mentioned, and rejected by Jerome,
Theodoret, Gregory the Great, and Timotheus the
Presbyter. The statement that it was " long received as a canonical book " is utterly untrue, and
I hope will not be adopted by the authorities at
Chester. (See Herzog's *Real-encyklopädie*, xii.
335). The text has been many times printed, and
even appended to some editions of the Latin Vulgate.   B. H. C.

" That's the Cheese."—Popular slang phrases,
however absurd in themselves, are usually corruptions of expressions in our own or other languages. Such would appear to be the case with
" That's the cheese." A friend of mine, who has
just returned from India, has suggested that it is
derived from a word very common in Bengalee
as spoken in Calcutta. The word *chiz* is used
in the sense of " thing ; " *e. g.* " That's the *chiz*
for me," or " That's the *chiz.*" It is easy to see
how, in its transit to this country by means of
the P. and O. company, *chiz* becomes " cheese ; "
and hence our slang phrase. Such varieties of it
as " That's the Stilton," " That's the Cheshire,"

&c., are mere offshoots of the parent stem, due to the fancy of the ingenious.   .   W. S.

Crowndale Road.

COUPLETS.—I do not know whether the following couplet has ever appeared in " N. & Q.," or, indeed, whether it is current. At all events it deserves so to be, from the noble sentiment conveyed : —

> " Chi vuol Catone amico,
>   Facilmente l'avra : sia fido a Roma."

I copy it as found in a letter addressed to Mr. (afterwards Sir William) Jones in 1782, by the Duchess of Devonshire. The same letter contained another couplet of a very different character, being nothing less than a Greek epigram, which may specially amuse all who bear the same honourable name : —

> Αἱ Χαρίτες, τέμενός τι λαβεῖν ὅπερ οὐκὶ πεσεἴη
>   Ζητοῦσαι, ψυχὴν εὕρον 'Ιωνίανου.

In sending it, the Duchess adds this graceful compliment,—

" I will attempt to copy it : and after the various characters I have, in days of yore, seen you decipher, I will not despair of your making out Greek, though written by me."—*Life and Writings of Sir W. Jones*, by Lord Teignmouth, vol. i. 398, ed. 1807.

                  FRANCIS TRENCH.

Islip Rectory.

Queries.

"NAN HARTLIB" AND "CLODIUS."

In Pepys' *Diary* are the following entries, mentioning two persons about whom I am anxious to get some information : —

" Home and called my wife, and took her to Clodius's,* to a great wedding of Nan Hartlib to Mynheer Roder, which was kept at Goring House, with great state, cost, and noble company."—July 10, 1660.

" While I was at dinner, in came Samuel Hartlib and his brother-in-law, now knighted by the King, to request my romise of a ship for them to Holland."—August 7, 166þ

The question is, Who was Nan Hartlib ? I believe that she was the sister of Samuel Hartlib, the particular friend of Milton. But, on the contrary, Mr. Keightley, in his *Account of John Milton* (p. 107), after quoting the above passages, says: "Nan Hartlib was then evidently the *niece*, not the daughter, of the elder Hartlib."

If this statement is correct, then the Samuel Hartlib mentioned by Pepys must have been the nephew of him to whom Milton dedicated his *Tractate of Education*. That he had a nephew is shown by his Letter to Lord Herbert (Nov. 22, 1660), where he says: " I have nothing left to keep me alive, with two relations more, a daughter and a nephew, who are attending my sick condition." It was the younger Samuel Hartlib who annoyed Pepys at Bartholomew Fair : —

[* The name is spelled " Clodins " by Pepys.—ED.]

" . . . and so we ended, and took a link, the women resolving to be dirty, and walked up and down to get a coach ; and my wife, being a little before me, had like to be taken up by one, whom we saw to be Sam Hartlib. My wife had her vizard on : yet we cannot say that he meant any hurt ; for it was just as she was by a coach-side, which he had, or had a mind to take up ; and he asked her, ' Madam, do you go in this coach ? ' but, as soon as he saw a man come to her, I know not whether he knows me, he departed away apace. By-and-by did get a coach, and so away home."—Sept. 6, 1667.

The question then is, To which of the Hartlib's does Pepys allude in the entry of August 7, 1660 ? Lord Braybrooke thought clearly to the elder ; and so does Mr. Dircks, in his recently published *Memoir of Samuel Hartlib*.

The next query is, Who was Clodius, who was concerned in the marriage of Nan Hartlib ? Lord Braybrooke gives no note to the passage, but if I may be allowed to conjecture, he was the person of whom William Wotton, writing to John Evelyn (Aug. 13, 1703), asks, " Do you know anything of one Clodius a chemist ? Was he (or who was) Mr. Boyle's first master in that art ? ". Evelyn, in his answer, says : —

" Claudius, whom you inquire after, was his [Hartlib's] son-in-law, a professed adeptus, who by the same *methodus mendicandi* and pretence of extraordinary arcana, insinuated himself into acquaintance of his father-in-law : but when or where either of them died (though I think poor Hartlib's was of the stone), or what became of them, I cannot tell."

From this it is clear that " Claudius " the chemist is the person alluded to by Pepys. Query, did he marry an older daughter of Hartlib's, or was it the one who attended him in his sickness in 1660 ? The points I have mooted concerning Hartlib's relatives are important ones, and it is a pity that Mr. Dircks did not investigate the matter more fully when engaged upon the subject. A good biography of this old worthy is still a desideratum. The voluminous correspondence and state papers of the period would surely yield ample material if carefully examined.

                  EDWARD F. RIMBAULT.

BISHOP BEDELL.—Are there extant any records of a grant made to Bishop Bedell of houses or tenements in the city of Dublin ? Was one of these the ancient mayoralty house, formerly situated in Pill Lane, a back street near the Law Courts, since pulled down ? This became the property of the Stanford family from Belturbet, county of Cavan, supposed to be descended from the bishop.   AIKEN IRVINE.

Kilbride, Bray.

CARFAX.—Passing through Horsham, in Sussex, a few days ago, I observed the name of Carfax given to a turning. I had not heard of the name except at Oxford, and I should be glad if any of your readers can tell me its meaning in this case. The explanation given of the Oxford Carfax (*Quatre voies*) cannot apply, as the Sussex one is a piece of ground of somewhat triangular shape, with two entrances at the west end, and one at the east, thus bearing no resemblance to the spot so well known to University men. F.

ANNUAL SERMON ON CENSORIOUSNESS.—I have a manuscript sermon in my possession, from the text " Judge not, that ye be not judged," and for genealogical reasons I am anxious to discover who was the writer of it. From memoranda on its covers I learn that it was preached " at ye Minster, May 16, 1714, upon Mrs Clerke's account."
" Vpon ye same acct at ye Minster, Whitsunday, 1721."
" Vpon ye same account at ye Minster, Whitsunday, 1759, by L. B. Junr for Mrs Cook of the Pool."
A note on the margin runs thus: —

" Endeavour to be as suitable to ye occasion as I can, in order to answer ye good intentions of a certain pious person, who, to express her detestation to censorious proceed. has occasion'd an annual disc. agn it to be transmitted to posterity."

Perhaps some of your readers may be able to inform me, at what " Minster " an annual sermon on this subject is or was preached. In order not unnecessarily to take up space in your columns, I add my address. H. FISHWICK.
Carr Hill, near Rochdale.

THE DUBLIN "COMET" NEWSPAPER.—I am sure some Dublin correspondent can furnish information respecting a weekly newspaper that was published in Dublin, commencing per a s about 1830, and ending some time before the commencement of 1835. I know that a perfect copy was sold at the sale of the library of the " Repeal Association," after the death of the late Mr. O'Connell, and, as I have heard, a large figure was given for it. It was, perhaps, one of the most extraordinary and talented hebdomadal publications (as a newspaper) of the present century; and there was published (I do not know the date) by the writers of the *Comet*, two literary gems: *The Parson's Hornbook* and the *Valentine Post Bag*. I would give a reasonable price for any of the three publications, or for the lot. Information relative to those publications will be grateful to
S. REDMOND.
Liverpool.

EDWARD DYER OF BRENT, CO. SOMERSET.—A commission, dated 1644, was granted by Prince Charles to Edward Dyer, Esq., to raise a regiment of foot in the hundred of Brent, co. Somerset, and to be Colonel thereof. I should be much in—, to any one who would enable me to con—— with the family of Dyer, which had long

been settled in that county, and would acquaint me with the names of his descendants, if any.
C. H. M.
The Union, Oxford.

FOREIGN DRAMATIC BIBLIOGRAPHY.—Is there any bibliographical catalogue of dramatic works written by—1. Dutch authors; 2. Danish (including Norwegian) authors; 3. Swedish authors? Where and at what price could I obtain any volumes of the description indicated above?
R. I.

KING'S LYNN.—In *A General History of the County of Norfolk*, 8vo, Norwich, 1829, i. 465, is mentioned " an old book," entitled *Lennæ Rediviua, or a Description of King's Lynn in Norfolk*, &c., by Ben Adam. The work is said to be in verse, and to consist of 214 MS. pages. A long extract from it is also said to be contained in a *Catalogue of Seals presented to the Norwich Museum by Richard Taylor, Esq.* This *Catalogue* is still in the Norwich Museum, or, I should rather say, was there when I last visited it, about two years ago, but no trace is to be found of the " old book," or of the " extract " above alluded to. The present curator could give me no information, nor could another gentleman on the spot, who has been intimately connected with the Museum from its commencement. Can any Norwich or Lynn correspondent give any tidings of this " old book," which from the description and specimen given in the *History of Norfolk* must be a curiosity, as it is said to commence with A.D. 1, and end with the reign of Edward IV.? Is anything known of the existence of such a book, and of its author? The *Catalogue*, I may add, is a very thin folio, consisting of only a few leaves, and shows no trace of anything having been cut or torn out of it since it was bound. Q.

LADY BIRDS.—*The Daily News* of 18th April quotes an article from the *City Press*, recording that a portion of the income of the parish of St. Peter, Cornhill, arises from a rent charge on certain property, which is to be applied to the destruction of lady birds in the parish. In these days, the offence of being found in the parish of St. Peter, Cornhill, might be followed by a milder punishment, and the convict lady birds would pay the cost of their transportation to parishes where they could earn an honest livelihood by the destruction of aphides " and such small deer." Can any of your correspondents inform me of the date of this gift to the parish, and the name of the donor, and the purpose to which the gift is now applied? VRYAN RHEGED.

MERCER'S HOSPITAL, DUBLIN.—Five years ago the late Mr. Horatio Townsend published Part I. of *The History of Mercer's Charitable Hospital in Dublin*, pp. 54. A promise was given to publish

Part II. with as little delay as possible; but the author was not spared to fulfil his undertaking. May we hope that some one will be found to complete what has been so well begun? ABHBA.

PETER PELHAM THE ENGRAVER. — In a recent Dictionary of Painters, Engravers, &c., I find mention of "Peter Pelham an English Engraver, born about 1684, and died about 1738. He executed quite a number of portraits in mezzotinto; among them those of George I., George II., Oliver Cromwell, Lord Carteret, Rubens," &c. Also mention of J. C. Pelham, his son, born in 1721, who painted history and portraits, but of whom little is known. Can any of your readers furnish more particulars, and especially can they point out any connection between him and Peter Pelham, the first artist and engraver resident in New England?

This Peter came to Boston prior to 1727, but had lived in London, where he had a son Peter baptized at St. Paul's, Covent Garden, in 1721, and Charles baptised in 1723. Of his relations I have one trace hereinafter mentioned. Peter married, secondly, the widow of Richard Copley, and thus became stepfather to John Singleton Copley, the well known artist, the father of the late Lord Lyndhurst. Peter Pelham, of Boston, engraved several portraits in admirable style, and I think was also quite a painter. To his instruction Copley was indebted for his first knowledge of the art.

Our Peter had a sister Helen living in Chichester in 1762, and a letter from her mentions that her father lived to be over eighty. In 1748 her father was alive, and she orders her letters sent to her at the Hon. Mrs. Conway's in Green Street, near Grosvenor Square. Perhaps some one from these facts can tell us who Peter Pelham's father was?

One other note. Writing from Chichester in 1762, Helen Pelham says: —

"I saw in the papers you had a fine burial at Boston; poor General Whitmore; some of his troops are here. I think it was a sad accident he met with."

This was Major-General Edward Whitmore, concerning whom I ineffectually inquired (2nd S. xii. 88.) It would seem as if he might have belonged in Sussex, and the local papers in the first half of 1762, may tell something about him if any one have access to them.

W. H. WHITMORE.
Boston, U. S. A.

PETRUS DE ALVA ET ASTORGA.
"Peter d'Alva has published forty-eight folios on the *Mysteries of the Conception.*"

Where can this work be seen? I cannot trace it in Watt. F. C.

WILLIAM RANKINS'S "CONCEITE OF HELL." — In the Dedication of his *English Ape*, 1588, 4to,

to Sir Christopher Hatton, the author alludes to Hatton's acceptance of his *Roughcast Conceite of Hell.* Pray is any such performance known to be extant? The title is promising.
W. CAREW HAZLITT.

GUSTAVUS SCHWAB.—This German poet, who died in or about 1849, was the author of Romances, Lyrical Poems, translations from Lamartine, De Vigny, &c., &c. I think that there was a memoir of this poet published in Germany a few years ago. Can any of your readers in Germany who may have seen this memoir inform me whether Schwab was the author of any dramatic work either *unpublished*, or in his miscellaneous poems? R. I.

THE SEVEN BISHOPS.—Can any of your readers inform me if paintings of "The Seven Bishops," similar to one in my possession, are common? This painting (4 ft. 2 in. × 3 ft. 4 in.) has the portraits of the bishops in small medallions suspended upon the columns of a temple with an altar and seven candlesticks behind them, with the following inscriptions: —

"Qui vicerit faciam illum columna in Templo Dei mei."
And "Ecce tabernaculum Dei cum hominibus, et habitabit cum eis, et ipsi populus ejus erunt, et Deus eorum erit in æternum."

Upon close observation, within the medallion portrait of Sancroft—the centre in the upper tier—*an eye* is seen represented. I suppose that such paintings may have been multiplied soon after the Bishops'. Trial, and shall be obliged to be informed if there is any known history attaching to them. K. S.

SHERIFFS OF DUBLIN EXCOMMUNICATED. — In the *Liber Munerum Publicorum Hiberniæ*, part III. p. 146, the following entry occurs: —

"1765. Jan. 8. *George Robbins.*
Jan. 10. [Writ of excommunication against the Sheriffs of the city of Dublin]."

Will some reader who is acquainted with the Municipal Annals, Dublin, kindly inform me why this writ was issued, or refer me to some authorities on the subject? AIKEN IRVINE,
Kilbride, Bray.

TIP ME THE TRAVELLER.—

"'Mayhap thou wouldest rather see me dead,' answered the uncle, 'for then, my lad, there would be some picking. Aha! dost thou *tip me the traveller*, my boy?' Tom answered him, he scorned any such mercenary views."—Smollet's *Sir Launcelot Greaves*, i. ch. vi.

What is the meaning of the italicised phrase? CYRIL.

TYLER'S "LIFE OF HENRY OF MONMOUTH."—In a note at p. 5 of this book Mr. Tyler speaks of—"an order, dated June 6, 1372, to lodge two pipes of good wine in Kenilworth Priory, and to hasten with all speed Dame Ilote, the midwife, to the Queen Constance at Hertford, on horse or in carriage, as should be best for her case."

Can any one kindly give me the reference to this order? It is not on the Issue Rolls. There can, moreover, be little doubt that the date of the year, 1372, is a mistake. The Duchess Constance was married in the early part of that year; and the two following years are also out of the question, since the Princess Katherine was born in March, 1374 (not Feb., 1373, as stated in the same note by Mr. Tyler). See the Issue Roll, Mich. 47 Edw. III., Mar. 31.　　HERMENTRUDE.

Queries with Answers.

EDWARD VI.—I have just met with a reprint of a curious Latin tract, ascribed by the editor (J. P. Berjeau) to no less a person than Peter Martyr, touching the death of King Edward VI. by unfair means.

Is there any hint of foul play in any English work of the time?　　NEWINGTONENSIS.

[Sir John Hayward, in his *Life of Edward the Sixth*, has adopted the story that the king's death was hastened by poison, administered by the agents of Northumberland. "At the last (he says), a gentlewoman, unworthy to be named, but accounted to be a schoole-mistresse for the purpose, offered her service assuredly to cure him, in case he were committed wholly to her hand. Hereto the physicians would in no case afford their advice, because, as she could give no reason either of the nature of the disease, or of the part afflicted, so she would not declare the meanes whereby she intended to worke the cure. After some shew of deliberation among the councell, it was resolved that the physitians should be discharged, and the case committed to her alone. The apparent defect both of her judgement and experience, joyned to the weightiness of the adventure, caused many to marvell, and some deeply to suspect that she was but an instrument of mischife. This surmise was strongly confirmed within a very short time ensuing, when the king did fall into desperate extremities; his vitall parts were mortally stuffed, which brought him to a difficultie of speech and of breath, his legs swelled, his pulse failed, his skin changed colour, and many other horrid symptomes appeared. 'Then were the physicians called againe, who, espying him in that fearefull estate, departed from him with a sad silence, leaving him to the miserable mercy of neere approaching death. Some of these whispered among their private friends, that they were called for fashion only, but neither their advice nor appliances were any deale regarded, but the king had been ill dealt with more than once, and that when by the benefit both of his youth and of carefull meanes there was faire hope of his recovery he was againe more strongly overlaid."

In the *Zurich Letters*, the First Portion, published by the Parker Society, 1846, p. 365, is a letter from Julius Terentianus to John [ab Ulmis], dated Strasburgh, Nov.

20, 1553. The writer says "The most godly Josiah, our earthly hope, died on the sixth of July; of consumption, as the physicians assert; by poison, according to common report." To this passage is appended the following editorial note: "Osorius, Bishop of Sylva in Portugal, affirmed expressly, in a letter wrote to Queen Elizabeth, that King Edward was poisoned in his childhood. But Walter Haddon, who replied to that letter, esteemed this report to be but a fable, raised by idle people, and carried about by such as favoured popery.— See Strype, *Memor.* II. ii. 118."]

MELANTHE: a Latin play by S. Brooke (afterwards Archdeacon of Coventry) was acted before King James I. at Cambridge University in 1614. The Rev. Dr. Pegge, a well known antiquary of last century was, I believe, possessed of a copy of the play, in which the names of the performers were noted. Is this copy still existing? If any of your readers who are dramatic collectors, have got it, perhaps they would have the kindness to give the names of the actors in this academic play.　　R. I.

[We have not been able to trace Dr. Pegge's annotated copy of *Melanthe*, 4to, 1615, but the names of the performers occur in a letter from the Doctor to his friend Professor Ward of Gresham College (Addit. MS. 6211, p. 33, Brit. Mus.). He says, "With your leave I will here subjoin the Dramatis Personæ, with the names of the Cantabrigians that acted those parts placed opposite, as they are written with a pen in my copy:—

Palemon, *Summus sacerdos Dianæ*	. .	Mr. Cleark.
Serranus } *Inferiores sacerdotes*	{	D' Pierce.
Montanus,		— Holmes.
Melanthe, *Nympha, Alcini amasia*	. .	Mr. Darcye.
Alcinus, { *Pastor adolescens, amator Melanthes*	}	D' Stubbe.
Alteus, { *Pastor senex, pater Melidori creditus*	}	D' Wilson.
Melidorus { *Pastor adolescens, amator Sylveriæ*	}	Mr. Chappel.
Sylveria, *Nympha, amica Melidori*	. .	Thorndicke.
Nicander, { *Pastor adolescens subrusticior, amator Ermillæ*	}	Mr. Goldfinche.
Ermilla, *Nympha lepida*	. . . .	Peake.
Glaucus, *Satyrus senex*	. . . .	Symons.
Leoniscus, *Satyrus juvenis, Glauci filius*		Mr. Sleepe.
Cervinus, *Satyrus juvenis*	. . . .	Hackluit.
Eccho	. . . .	D' Warde.

Chorus, *Sacerdotum, Pastorum, Satyrorum. Scœna in Arcadia.*"]

"ALBANIA."—Who was the author of a poem bearing this title? It is a production of considerable merit, though "now neglected and unknown." It was originally published at London in the year 1737. Are there any later editions of it?

This work is quoted from by Dr. Beattie in his *Essay on Poetry and Music*, ii. 172, and by Dr. Nathaniel Drake in his *Literary Hours*, ii. 240.

GEORGE VICKERS.

Shimpling, Suffolk.

[The fate of this remarkable poem has been extremely unlucky, as the author and the original editor are equally unknown. It was reprinted in *Scotish Descriptive Poems*, 12mo, 1803, edited by J. Leyden.]

"THE WESTERN PROSPECT OF BEAR'S-DEN HALL IN CO. SURREY."—I have a curious satirical print with the above heading, and sundry references and explanations, as—A. The Den's Front; B. The Beare; II. [Two Crutches.] Supporters to the arms [a tree with C. T. and a tent]; the crest, two chins [a head of Janus]. [Underneath one] C. T. Crab Tree. [Underneath the other] N. Numps. [In the air a bird with] K. Crab-tree transmigrated.

At the bottom in Greek capitals ΑΤΞ ΚΟΝΟΙΣ. ΣΕΤΡΣ ΔΕ ΛΑ ΚΟΝΟΙΣΣΑΝΣ, and the Latin motto "Non sine socio."

I shall feel obliged to any of your readers who will give me an explanation of it. It has at the back in an old hand "No 5848," and I was told that it came from the Gulston Collection. CPL.

[This print by James Hill is a burlesque on Charles Christiern's villa, near Putney, *circa* 1720. Gough's *British Topography*, ii. 280.]

ST. AGNES AND HER LAMB. — Where is to be found full, and where the original, account of the following, which I extract from *Notes Ecclesiological and Historical, on the Holy Days in the Kalendar of the English Church*, republished from the *English Church Union Kalendar*, 1864 (London: The Church Press Company, 1864)? —

"Her sorrowing parents continued to visit her tomb in secret. One night they had a dream: they saw the blessed martyr coming to them, and a spotless lamb was at her side. She told them of the glory to which she had attained. This appearance is commemorated in the Latin Church on January 28 [21.]"

H. C.

[The legend of St. Agnes, one of the oldest in the Christian church, is printed in Mrs. Jameson's *Sacred and Legendary Art*, ii. 601—604, edit. 1857.]

BULL AGAINST MENDICANT FRIARS. — Among my MS. collections I have memorandum of a bull or breve of Pope John XXII. against some friars mendicant who preached sedition in Ireland. The breve was directed "to the Archbishops of Dublin and Cashel, and the Dean of the Church of Dublin," and appears to be dated in 1317. So far I glean from the memorandum in my possession. Where will I find the original?

AIKEN IRVINE.
Kilbride, Bray.

[This Bull is printed Rymer's *Fœdera*, edit. 1739, ii. 122, and is entitled " Bulla contra Fratres de Ordine Mendicantium, ad populum Hybernicum Rebellionem prædicantes," and is signed " Dat. Avinion. quarto. Idus Aprilis, Pontificatûs nostri anno primo, *i. e.* 1317."]

Replies.

CAPITAL PUNISHMENTS.

(3rd S. vii. 351.)

On 30th December, 1818, a man named Robert Johnston was executed in Edinburgh for highway robbery. The circumstances which attended his execution were striking and painful.

A wooden platform on which the gibbet stood was erected at the west end of St. Giles's Cathedral, and around its south and east side a space was railed in to leave room for the criminal and officers of justice to have free access from the Lock-up-House to the place of execution. What follows is abridged from a letter to the Magistrates of the City by " an Eye-Witness " :—

" About half-past two they came out, and Johnson walked steadily. I marked his countenance, but saw no change of features. He ascended the scaffold with unaltered visage, and merely gave a look to the apparatus such as a man would give who was determined not to shrink. His convulsed effort to appear composed when he submitted his neck to the noose was appalling. I turned my back, and was about to withdraw, when one who stood next me exclaimed, ' Good God! his feet are not off the scaffold;' and it was so. He stood on the platform; a partial compression of the windpipe, caused by the sudden jerk, insufficient to cause death but sufficient to produce exquisite agony, shook his whole frame, but did not appear to have suspended his mental powers, for thrice he bent his legs upwards, evidently on purpose to terminate his sufferings. Still he touched the platform. He made several unsuccessful attempts to assist in his own strangulation. During all these efforts, unutterably horrible, carpenters were brought to cut away the wood below the table; but for at least ten minutes, could make no impression on the machinery. He remained convulsed in every fibre, till the whole motion of his limbs attracted the notice and sympathy of the immense crowd, from whom, the moment they perceived the protracted torture, a spontaneous burst of indignation resounded, and then followed a pause, still as death, for a few seconds; but when they saw no attempts at relief, a shower of stones aimed at the scaffold, accompanied a second expression of their indignation. A gentleman who had observed his ineffectual struggles, sprang forward and relieved the feelings of the spectators by cutting the man down."

" The populace then," says another writer, " took possession of the scaffold, loosed the rope, and after some time succeeded in restoring him to his senses. They then tried to bear him off, and had proceeded some way down the High Street, when the officers of police, who had abandoned their post at the scaffold, proceeded with their bludgeons to assail them, and recovered possession of the culprit. A spectacle now presented itself equal in horror to anything in Paris during the Revolution. The unhappy man, half alive, stript of part of his clothes, and his shirt turned up, lay on the ground in the middle of the street. At last, some of the officers laid hold of him and dragged him along the ground for about twenty paces into the Police Office. He remained there for about half-an-hour, where he was bled in both arms and in the temporal vein by a surgeon, and his half-suspended animation restored; but he uttered not a word. Meantime, a military force came from the castle. The soldiers surrounded the place of execution; he was carried again to the scaffold; his clothes thrown about him so that he seemed half-naked, and they fell down in such a manner as to shock decency. While they were adjusting his clothes he was left vibrating, upheld partly by the rope and partly by his feet on the table. At last the table was removed, when, to the indescribable horror of the spectators, he was seen suspended with his face uncovered, and one of his hands loose from the cords. Cries were heard from every quarter. A chair was brought and the hand disengaged from the noose in which it had been twisted. The executioner descended, leaving the face still uncovered, exhibiting a spectacle too shocking to be described. This continued till twenty-three minutes past 4 o'clock, when the street lamps were lighted for the night, and the moon and stars distinctly visible."

This writer concludes : —

" The above is a true account by an eye-witness, taken down by him in writing during the same evening, as the writer hopes to see God in mercy."

The legality of this proceeding was much questioned at the time, and apparently with justice, for the criminal had been out of the power of the magistrates ; and though they recovered possession of his person, there was a want of judicial identification. In this respect the case differed from the late one at Leeds, which it exceeds much also in the horror of its incidents. G.
Edinburgh.

H. H. PRINCE FRANCIS RHODOCANAKIS.

(3rd S. iv. 453 ; vii. 267, 348.)

In reply to the query of your correspondent BREVIS, I have to say that Constantine Rhodocanakis, or in Latin Rhodocanaces (genitive case, Rhodocanacidis), was the younger son of Prince Demetrius and of Theodora, only daughter of Theodorus Palæologus, of the imperial house of that name, whose tomb exists till now in the parish church of Landulph, in the eastern extremity of Cornwall (see *Archæologia*, vol. xviii. p. 90, and " N. & Q.") from his first wife Eudoxia Comnéna; and consequently grandson of Prince Francis Rhodocanakis, Duke, &c., &c.

He was born on the 5th of December, 1635, in Rhodocanaki Castle, situated a few miles from the capital of the Isle of Chios, and built during the tenth century by his ancestor Andronicus, then Lord High Admiral of Romanus II., Emperor of the Byzantine Empire.

There he remained until the age of twenty, when he departed in company with his learned uncle Stephanus, under whose tuition he was, for Flanders and France, where he became acquainted with the exiled young monarch of England, Charles II., at whose restoration to the throne of his ancestors, he wrote in Greek a congratulatory poem, dedicated to his friend Sir William Seymour, Duke of Somerset, Marquis and Earl of Hertford, &c., and entitled —

Carmina Græca Rythmica gratulatoria de reditu Serenissimi Sacratissimi, et Theophylaktu Principis Caroli II. Magnæ Britanniæ, Galliæ et Hiberniæ Regis Com-

posita a Constantino Rhodocanacide Chiensi tunc commorante in celeberrima Academia Oxoniensi. Oxoniæ, A.D. 1660. Typis, A. & L. Lichfield, Academ. Typograph." [In small 8vo.]

During the year 1667, he returned to his native isle, Chios, where he married the Duchess Henrietta Koressy, his cousin, but whence he was obliged, a few months afterwards, by the Turkish Government, on account of his political and religious opinions, to depart, and return to London, where he remained many years, always honoured with the friendship of H. M. King Charles II.

He died, not in London during the great plague, as an eminent English novelist of our days erroneously stated in one of his romances, but in Amsterdam, the 13th of August, 1689, whence his mortal remains were a few years later exhumed by his nephew, Prince Francis and his only daughter, transported in the Isle of Chios, and buried in our family mausoleum near his ancestors.

I conclude, observing that all his published literary works are preserved in the Library of the British Museum except the two following ones, both written in English : —

1. " Infallible Remedy against the Plague, by Doctor Constantine Rhodocanaces, Byzantine Nobleman, and Honorary Physician to His Majesty King Charles II. London. Printed by R. D. in the year 1665." Small 4to.
2. " The Last of the Greek Emperors ; or, the Fall of Constantinople ; written by Konstantinos D. Rhodocanakis, Grecian of the Isle of Chios, &c., and dedicated to H. H. Prince Pantoleon D. Rhodocanakis, Duke, &c., &c. London : Printed by R. D. in the year 1670." In 4to.
RHODOCANAKIS.

Higher Broughton, near Manchester.

" LANG-NEBBED THINGS."

(3rd S. vii. 334.)

Shall I be wrong in identifying the goblin *whaap*, the long-billed monster, SIR J. EMERSON TENNENT is inquiring for, in the *bittern* ?

" This bird," says Bewick, " flies in the same heavy manner as the heron, and might be mistaken for the heron, were it not for the singular resounding cry which it utters from time to time when on the wing ; but this cry is feeble when compared to the *hollow booming* noise which it makes during the night from its swampy retreats : —

' The Bittern booms along the sounding marsh.' "

Compare Isaiah xiv. 23, when foreboding desolation, " I will also make it a possession for the *bittern* ; and I will sweep it with the besom of destruction, says the Lord of hosts." Again, at xxxiv. 11 : " The cormorant and the *bittern shall* possess it ; the owl and the raven shall dwell in it." This exactly corresponds with the words in Zephaniah ii. 14 : " The cormorant and the *bittern* shall lodge in the upper lintels of it ; their voices shall sing in the windows ; desolation shall be in the thresholds." All these prophetical passages are strictly in accordance with the descriptions in classical writers of *Nocturnæ Striges*, or ill-omened birds. The —

>   ". . . feralia bubo
>   Damna canens"

of Statius is none other than the screech owl of Virgil : —

>   "Ferali carmine bubo
>   Sæpe queri et longas in fletum ducere voces."

The *n. v.* bubo is translated "to cry like a bittern." The long ears of the horned owl, in the dim and dismal night, might easily have led superstitious rustics to class it among "lang-nebbit things." Superstition and alarm are the parents of much of our folk lore. The long and terrible beaks of birds of prey were constantly floating in the imagination of Celt or Saxon in bygone ages ; and the scream or croak from them added horror to the nervous feelings of a lonely churl crossing "Mucklestane" or any other dreary "Moor," more especially in the gloom of night. Yes, so it has ever been ! Hence —

>   ". . . rostroque immanis Vultur obunco
>   Immortale jecur tundens,"

that preyed upon the vitals of Tityon in the infernal regions, corresponds with the long-beaked monster astride St. Antony in his "Persecution," in the picture of Salvator Rosa. The ἴυγξ of Theocritus, a name, according to Aristotle from its cry or shriek, is the wash-dish, or rather wag-tail (*Motacilla*) in the West of England, where the peasantry to this day believe when it flaps against and strikes with its beak the cottage window, that the death of one of the inmates is at hand. The connection, then, of long-beaks with misty demons and incubi by artists from the eleventh to the eighteenth century, correctly represents the fearful superstition innate in the human mind; and from this only can we hope to find any elucidation of the legendary belief about grallatorial birds, *i. e.* Birds on Stilts.   QUEEN'S GARDENS.

In India there is a peculiar performance of jugglers and players, in which a man dressed in a cloak of feathers, with the mask of a bird with a *very long beak*, causes invariably much excitement amongst the native spectators.

Amongst the African negroes of the West Indies, a similar figure causes the like agitation, and in this latter case, I have been led to suppose that there may be some connection between it and the *feathers* which invariably enter into the composition of an Obeah ball, such as is placed near the person whose life is being practised on.

I might add a curious coincidence connected with such superstitions, but fear I should be transgressing the limits of the present subject.

                                              SPAL.

May I request Sir J. E. TENNENT to reconsider his assertion respecting the curlew ? he says : —

"Why, then, in the instance of the curlew, has the accident of the prolonged bill inspired a kindred dread, *there being nothing in the tone of its voice to give rise to terror?*"

The following passage from *Recollections of Edward Williams, or Iolo-Morganwg, B.B.D.,* by the (late) E. Waring, illustrates both the terror caused by the "lang-nebbed things" and the source of the nocturnal cries.

In discussing various Cambrian superstitions, Mr. Waring says : —

"The *Cwn Wybr,* Dogs of the Sky, otherwise called *Cwn Annwn,* Dogs of Hell (or of the Abyss), are imaginary spirits of the same family as the diabolical sky hunts of German demonology. They are heard in the deep gloom of night over some dreary mountain or moorland district, appalling the benighted traveller, or the lonely dwellers in those remote places, by baying or yelling in the most horrid chorus. They are not, however, accused of doing any harm beyond the torments they are supposed to inflict on disembodied spirits, abandoned to their mercy in the region of air, doubtless in retribution for some heinous sins committed on earth.

"It was after the bard's death that I asked the late ingenious and well-informed Mr. William Weston Young, then residing at Newton Nottage, in Glamorgan, and riding and walking in all directions indifferently by night or by day, whether he had ever heard the *Cwn Wybr* in his nocturnal travels ? He replied in the affirmative, and said the strange aërial noises had at first greatly startled and perplexed him. Mr. Young, however, was not superstitious, and being a good naturalist, was observant of the notes of birds, and of the remarkable variation between the diurnal and nocturnal note of the same species ; the latter often producing a supernatural effect when heard in darkness and solitude. He suspected these *Cwn Wybr* to be really some gregarious birds flying by night, and at length perfectly satisfied his own mind on the subject. In the course of his business as a land surveyor, he was on a pony one intensely dark night, crossing a desolate tract of mountains, when he heard the most extraordinary yelping and clamorous noises over his head, in various keys, not unlike the cries of hounds and huntsmen in full chase. He looked intently upwards, but the darkness was impenetrable. His quick ear, however, soon caught a rushing sound, which he knew was the *burr* of pinions against the air, and presently a large flight of curlews descended so near him, that some of their wings brushed his hat as they swept obliquely down to the heather. They had no sooner settled on their feet than the *Cwn Wybr* ceased to be heard. He then recollected having heard the same peculiar nocturnal cry from the curlew on former occasions, but had never before encountered such an overpowering orchestra of these wild serenaders upon the wing. Mr. Young admitted that nothing could be more natural than the terror of a superstitious or uninformed person at the strange aërial cries he had listened to that night, amidst mountain echoes, and in so desolate a spot." (Pp. 141, 142.)

In addition to the report of Mr. Waring, I may mention that more than thirty years ago the late Mr. W. W. Young gave me an exactly similar account of the manner in which he discovered that the nocturnal cry of the curlew is the cause of the fearful *Cwn Wybr.*

Are the "Dogs of Tregeagle," in some parts of Cornwall, the same?　　Lælius.

With reference to the popular superstition which associated "lang-nebbed things" with hags or witches, your learned correspondent, Sir J. Emerson Tennent, asks—"Is there any theory or conjecture to elucidate this legendary belief, or to account for the connexion of the *long bill* of the grallatorial birds with this midnight superstition?" In reply to this question I would venture to offer the following suggestions.

It is to be remarked in the first place that the "lang-nebbed things," though we find them mentioned in connexion with witches, do not appear to be identical with them, but to constitute a distinct class. They were, I would suggest, the imps or familiars, whom the hags were so often accused of suckling; and the lang neb, or long bill, was for the purpose of getting at the secret teat, which was supposed to be often placed at no very accessible part of the person.

The idea of suction, as connected with the Roman *striges, strigæ*, or *lamiæ*, is one which frequently occurs in Roman writers. But then it is the strix herself who sucks—not suckles: and the idea of the creature's having a neb or bill adapted to the purpose—though it had not yet decidedly taken the form of a *lang* neb—already began to make its appearance in classic times. Thus Ovid, *Fast.* vi. 131:—

"Grande caput, stantes oculi, *rostra apta rapinæ*."

So that, line 138,

". . . plenum *poto sanguine* guttur habent."

And Q. Serenus Sammonicus, who lived in the early part of the third century, towards the close of his medical poem comes still nearer to the idea of lang nebs:—

"Præterea si forte premit strix atra puellos,
　Virosa *immulgens exsertis* ubera *labris*."

Exsertis, put forth, drawn out. Thus the nebs began to grow. We shall presently see how in mediæval times they acquired their full length.

The mediæval witchfinders, in accusing their hapless victims of *giving* suck, had, as they supposed, a very high authority. In the Vulgate Version, the first part of Lam. iv. 3 is thus translated:—"Sed et lamiæ nudaverunt mammam, lactaverunt catulos suos;" quite sufficient authority for accusing an imaginary witch of suckling an imaginary imp or familiar.

But now, as to that special point, the said familiar's having a "lang neb," or a long bill. Reference has been made already to the out-of-the-way position of the supposed teat. The best explanation, however, is to be found in the old-fashioned notion that long-billed birds lived by suction. Thus, in the *Ornithologiæ Libri III.* 1676, edited by Ray on the basis of MS. left by F.

Willughby, we find the following heading, p. 213: "Aves aquaticæ *limosugæ, rostris* tenuibus *longissimis*, rectis;" under which head appear the *scolopax* (woodcock), *gallinago minor* (snipe), &c.

Here we have the lang neb evidently connected with suction; and though the above heading is modified in Ray's translation, published in 1678, he there, in describing the snipe, has added, as if *motu proprio*, "It lives especially on the fatty unctuous humour it *sucks* out of the earth." Indeed, the idea of sucking, as connected with the long-billed snipe, is still vernacular amongst us in country places; and if a patient is unable to take solid food, one may hear it said, "Why, you are like a snipe; you live by suction!"

From these premises we may easily understand how sucking imps were supposed to have long bills.　　Schin.

Portrait of Milton (3rd S. iv. 26.)—The "Onslow" portrait, inquired for by Mr. Scharf, has, I believe, not yet come to light. Can it be the same which I saw at Cambridge about five and twenty years ago, in the possession of a solicitor named Cannon, representing Milton as a *very young man?* The "Onslow" portrait, if I remember rightly, was made when he was about twenty. Mr. Cannon told me that he had bought the picture in bad condition, and without a frame, from some dealer, either at Ipswich or Bury St. Edmunds, I cannot now recollect which. When I saw it it had been restored and put into a decent frame. But where is it now? Soon after the appearance of Mr. Scharf's query I wrote to Cambridge, but unfortunately my correspondent could give me no information on the subject, and only knew that Mr. Cannon had been dead for some years, and that his effects had been sold by auction. Surely there can be no great difficulty in pushing the investigation, if it is worth while (and I confess that to me it seems so), beyond the point at which I leave it.　　Q.

Hackney Horses: Affri (3rd S. vii. 55.)—This is simply an attempt to Latinize the popular word for cattle, whether horses or oxen, employed in drawing carts or ploughs, and a word which is still in use in the North. It is "aver." The unsuccessful farmer in Scott's *Pirate* says of the produce of his farm, "the carles and cart-avers (*i. e.* the labourers and cattle employed) make it a'; and the carles and cart-avers eat it a'." The word is often found in old books.

May I ask what is its derivation? Du Cange thinks "averia" (the usual Low Latin word) to be derived from the Old French "avoir," to have, and that it simply means possession. In this he certainly is fortified by the Latin analogy, where "pecunia" is derived from "pecus," and from the Teutonic, where "feoh," which originally meant cattle, at last became to be considered a "fee" or freehold possession. Can your readers assist me to a conclusion?　　　　　　　　　　　A. A.

Poets' Corner.

MARTIAL'S EPIGRAM (3rd S. vii. 97, 148, 229.)—There is no doubt that the phrase, "duri ingeni," is to some extent depreciatory; but not to the degree of imputing ignorance, or foolishness. "Stupidus" and "stolidus" clearly have such a meaning. "Crassus" is supposed by some to have the same sense as our "thick-headed;" but though Horace (*Sat.* ii. 2) applies this phrase to Ofellus, "crassaque Minerva," it is clear he means nothing like stupidity, for in the very same line he calls him "sapiens."

With all respect for the great authorities against me—"pace tantorum virorum"—I still think that my notion of the meaning of the Latin word *durus* is exactly that of our English word *hard*. Of course, no scholar for one minute would translate "durus arator," "durus amor," by any word, however euphemized, that would indicate stupidity. The "pater durus" of Ovid (*Met.* xiv. 587) means, a *hard*-hearted parent—not one who lacks brain. And in the Oration of Cicero for Archias, which has been cited, it is not attempted for a moment to impute stupidity to Marius; but simply to say that the poet Archias, when a young man, was quicker in understanding the measures of the Cimbri than the old soldier Marius. This surely did not impute stupidity to the latter. Many an old general of the present day would be glad of the assistance of a subaltern in French, German, or Danish, or of a young *attaché*, as to the secrets of the various foreign courts.

The "os durum" (Ovid, *Met.* v. 457) is exactly our phrase, "hard-mouthed;" and no one who reads Juvenal, would ever interpret "durumque Catonem" as "stupid Cato."

Again, suppose we refer directly to the expression used as regards the fine arts. Pliny (xxxv. 40,) speaks of Mechophanes as "durus in coloribus et sile multus;" and from the same expression as to other painters—"Antidotus in coloribus severior," "Athenion austerior colore"—the meaning is not that Mechophanes was ignorant as to colouring, but that he painted in a low tone, using ochre instead of the brighter yellows.

I will not multiply examples; but still think the expression "duri ingeni" to be exactly our "hard-headed": not brilliant, but shrewd, clever, and business-like—exactly the qualities an architect ought to have.　　　　　　　　　A. A.

Poets' Corner.

POSTERITY OF KING HAROLD (3rd S. v. 35, 217; vi. 318, 436.)—The arms borne by the family of Muskett of Intwood are almost identical with those ascribed to King Harold : arg. between 2 bars gu. six leopards' faces of the second, 3, 2,

1. These arms were confirmed to the family in 1576 by Cooke, the then Clarencieux, in the following words:—

"And being required of Henry Muskett of Halston, in the county of Suffolk, Gent., to make serche in the registers and recordes of my office, for such armes and crest as he may lawfully have ; whereupon at his request I have made serche accordingly, and do find that he may lawfully have the arms and crest hereafter followinge, &c." (Hollingworthe's *Stowmarket,* p. 125, quoted from Harl. MS. 2146.)

The Musketts held the manor of Harleston or Harold'stown (*Herolestun* of Domesday), co. Suffolk, whither they are supposed to have migrated from Somersetshire and Dorsetshire, and their arms appear to have been originally three muschets (sparrow-hawks) in allusion to the name. Is it possible that Cooke merely adopted the arms of Harold to the family into whose hands certain of the lands of that prince had fallen?

　　　　　　　　　　　　　JAMES A. HEWITT.

Capetown, S.A.

ADVERBS IMPROPERLY USED (3rd S. vii. 363.) I am tempted to add a few more instances of strange uses of adverbs. In Norfolk, one often hears of a person unwell, that he is "very sadly;" and when his health is improved, we are told that he is "finely," or "good tidily." But many years ago I was amused at a speech in Gloucestershire. It is common in the Western counties to say that a person is "pure," to signify that he is pretty well in health. "How do you do, this morning?" "Pure, thank ye." So on one occasion which I remember, an honest farmer, intending to inquire in the most respectful manner after the health of a family inhabiting a mansion in the place, said without the least consciousness of any equivocal signification in his phraseology : "I hope, Sir, the ladies are all pure."　　　　　　　F. C. H.

There is in the use of the verb "to be" an ambiguity similar to that which I pointed out (p. 225) in the use of the verbs "to look," "to feel."

1. "To be" may be simply the copula, and if by means of it, as such, I wish to predicate a quality of any subject, I use an adjective, as "the rose is sweet."

2. "To be" may be the *verbum secundæ adjacentis*, as the scholastic logicians term it; in other words, it may of itself containing, that is, a predicate in itself, predicate *existence* of the subject—*e. g.* Deus est, God is.

If, then, I wish to qualify the existence thus expressed, to add its state and conditions, I employ an adverb to modify the force of the verb "to be". Hence I say "She is well, is poorly," &c., because I refer to the present conditions of her *being*.

Now to compare our usage with that of the Greek and Latin languages. Our phrases "It is well," "She is well," correspond exactly to the

Latin "Bene est," "Bene se habet," * "Bene valemus;" and to the Greek εὖ ἔχειν· εὖ διακεῖσθαι. They may imply a certain *activity* (cf. "agere vitam," and *perhaps* the connection between βίος, βία, vivo, vita, vis, vir), which is correctly qualified by an adverb. This activity is seen more plainly in two phrases which express the same meaning in different words. I mean the Greek εὖ πράττειν and our "He shall *do* well," "How do you *do*?" In Latin we find the phrase "Satine salve?" (e. g. Liv. i. 58), which is often written "Satine salvæ," the question arising whether the Roman meant to say, "Satine salve res se habet?" "Satine salve est—agitur?" or "Satine salvæ res sunt?" I have no doubt that the reading "salve" and the construction it involves is the more correct, especially since in the *Trinummus* of Plautus we have the inquiry "Satine salve? dic mihi," answered by an adverb "*Recte.*'

After all it is undeniable that such an expression as "She is nicely" does *sound* peculiar and even incorrect. I apprehend the reason to be this: the construction by which "is" is merely the copula, and an adjective is used to predicate a quality of the subject is so much simpler than the adverbial construction which I have attempted to explain, that long use of such adverbial phrases as "He is well," "He is poorly," &c., has made us regard the words "well," "poorly," as *adjectives.* It is only on examination that their true character appears. But in the phrase, "She is nicely," familiarity has not yet bred contempt for the character of the word "nicely." We realise its adverbial importance, and hesitate to use it because it is not an adjective, because, that is, it will not resign its adverbial pretensions to accommodate itself to a mistaken notion.   FABIUS OXONIENSIS.

MEANING OF ARBERY (3rd S. vii. 345.)—Perhaps your recent decision in "Notices to Correspondents," against receiving just now any more notes about Cold Harbour, will not forbid my saying just a word or two in reply to C. T. I have something of my own to say about Cold Harbour, but will not intrude it upon you at present. I make no motion; "I only rise to explain." C. T. says, "*Arbery* is an old English word for wood-fuel;" but his quotation from Mandeville does not warrant this assertion: "In that contree is but lyttil *arbery,* ne trees that beren fruite, ne othere." "Arbery" is here used in the sense of "wood"=*sylva, wald;* not "wood" = *lignum, holz.*   J. DIXON.

THE PHILIPS, EARLS OF PEMBROKE (3rd S. vii. 378.)—Your correspondent will find in Sir R. C. Hoare's *Wiltshire,* vol. ii. p. 144, that the first Philip, Earl of Pembroke, died 23rd January, 1650, and was buried in Salisbury Cathedral, where a splendid monument was designed to

---

perpetuate his memory, for which a statue of brass, of extraordinary size, was cast, representing him clothed in armour, but it was never erected." From the same writer he will learn (*ibid,* p. 147) that the second Philip died in 1669-70, and was buried in the family vault in Salisbury Cathedral.   T.

DALYELL'S "SCOTTISH POEMS" (3rd S. vii. 254.) *Half mark steikis.* This, I think, simply means *half-mark pieces;* i. e. pieces of money of half a mark each in value. The context is clearly to this effect —

   "Sn gat thair handfull of thir *half mark steikis.*"

That *steik* may mean a piece of money is evident from the use of the German *stück;* compare A.-S. *sticce.*

Tottis.—Compare Burns's use of *tawted* or *tautie* hair, meaning locks of hair *matted* (twisted?) together

Bedene.—Bidding, commandment, seems most likely.   W. W. SKEAT.
22, Regent Street, Cambridge.

THE LINCOLNSHIRE CHURCH-NOTES OF GERVASE HOLLES (3rd S. vii. 356, 389) have been partially published in several of the works that have treated of portions of that county. In "*An Account of the Churches of the Division of Holland, in the County of Lincoln,*" with sixty-nine Illustrations," published at Boston in 1843, they are given, and the following remarks are made in the Preface: —

   "The notes taken on these Churches by Col. Holles, immediately previous to the visits of the Parliamentary perpetrators of sacrilege, are especially valuable; and they show how much the deadly hatred of the Puritan faction robbed and pillaged our sacred edifices, after the 'superstitious furniture' had been removed. They also show that the parochial clergy were very liberal benefactors to the edifices under their charge, giving windows and sedilia, and sometimes even entire chancels, at their own cost."

In Creasey's *History of Sleaford,* and the neighbouring parishes, 8vo, Holles's Notes for several churches are also published; and so also, in Thompson's *Boston,* fol. 1856, pp. 191—194; and Weir's *Horncastle,* 4to, 1820, p. 31.   J. G. N.

ROYAL FRANKING (3rd S. vii. 279, 350, 385.)—The misapprehension as to H. R. H. the Duke of Kent having franked by his Christian name, "Edward," may have arisen from his having so written his name on the address of letters *not* sent by post. I believe autograph-collectors will say that such has been a frequent practice with members of the royal family. But in the case of the late Duke of Gloucester, I have now before me two actual franks (that have passed the post) dated in 1830 and 1833, on which his Royal Highness has signed, not Gloucester, but *William Frederick.*   J. G. N.

* Cf. the French "Il se porte bien."

Pagan Caricature (3rd S. vii. 330.) — Mr. Walford is quite correct in stating that the "quotation wanted" occurs in one of the early chapters of Tertullian's *Apology*, and I have pleasure in furnishing your readers with the passage : —

"Sed nova jam Dei nostri in istâ proxime civitate editio publicata est, ex quo quidam frustrandis bestiis mercenarius noxius picturam proposuit cum ejusmodi inscriptione, Deus Christianorum Onochoëtes. Is erat auribus asininis, altero pede ungulatus, librum gestans, et togatus. Risimus et nomen et formam."—Tertullian, *Apologeticus adversus Gentes*, § 16, p. 17 D, edit. Paris, 1641.

In the margin of my copy is the following manuscript note on the word *Onochœtes*, written in a beautiful, clear, upright hand of the seventeenth century : —

"Legendum est *Ononychotos*, quod reperitur in Vossii etymologico, et notat Asinum ungulatum, 'Ovos et 'Ovυξ, ungula. Vide *Bibl. Bremensem*, class. III. fasc. vi. pp. 1041, 1036.; et Heinii *Diss. Sacr.*, lib. ii. cap. 10, in *Bth.* [bibliotheca] *Germ.*, t. xl. p. 193."

There is a reference to the same caricature in another work of Tertullian, in which he retorts with stinging severity upon the polytheistic heathens. The following is the passage : —

"Nova jam de Deo nostro fama suggessit. Adeo nuper quidam perditissimus in istâ civitate, etiam suæ religionis desertor, solo detrimento cutis Judæus, utique magis post bestiarum morsus, ad quas se locando quotidie toto jam corpore decutit, cum incedit picturam in nos proposuit sub istâ proscriptione, Onochoëtes. Is erat auribus canteriorum, et in togâ, cum libro, altero pede ungulato ; et credidit vulgus Judæo. Quod enim aliud genus seminarium est infamiæ nostræ ? Itaque in totâ civitate *Onochoëtes* prædicatur. Sed et hoc tamque hesternum, et auctoritate temporis destitutum, et qualitate auctoris infirmum, libenter excipiam studio retorquendi. Videamus igitur, an hic quoque nobiscum deprehendamini. Neque enim interest quâ formâ, dum deformia simulacra curemus ? Sunt penes vos et canino capite, et leonino, et de bove, et de ariete et hirco, cornuti dii, caprigenæ, vel anguini, et alites plantâ fronte et tergo. Quid itaque nostrum unicum denotatis ? Plures *Onochoëtæ* penes vos deprehenduntur."—*Ad Nationes*, lib. i. § 14, p. 59 C, D.

H. W. T.

The third Plague of Egypt (3rd S. vii. 297, 365.) — There are only two kinds of insects, the louse and the gnat, on which we have to decide. The evidence on which this question rests, consists of, 1, the context; 2, parallel passages; 3, the ancient versions; and 4, the *rationale* of the case. 1. The context speaks of the insects being on or in man and beast; this applies to the louse, which, as Aristotle shews, is a parasite* on man and beast, and also on birds and fish (*Hist. An.*, v. 31) ; but does not so well apply to the gnat.

    * So לֵב, place or situation (Gen. xl. 13, xli. 13), a stand, base, or pedestal (Is. xxxiii. 23, 1 Kings vii. 31), which is the root of כֵּן ; for there is no proof of the latter being an Egyptian word, as Rosenmüller conjectures.

2. The only parallel passage to Exodus viii. is Psalm cv. 31, for the word כִּנִּים, *cinnim*, does not elsewhere occur; but as it merely refers to this insect being in all their coasts, borders, or territories, in terms of Exodus x. 14, furnishes no proof either way. 3. The ancient versions chiefly read the louse, but the Septuagint and Vulgate read the gnat, which shows that between the event of the plague, B.C. 1491, and the translation of the Septuagint, B.C. 277, an interval of twelve centuries, doubt had crept in as to the kind of insect. A still longer interval occurred before the Syriac, Arabic, Latin, and other ancient versions were made. 4. As to the *rationale* of the case, I may refer to the improbability of the gnat or mosquito, on the ground that such a plague was avoidable, either by ascending to an elevation, inasmuch as this insect does not fly high, or by a covering of a curtain or net, for even a fisherman's net will suffice to keep off the mosquito, although the meshes are large (Herod. ii. 95). There appears also to be a special reason for Moses creating this plague of the louse, where the Egyptian priests first failed in imitating the plague, because, according to Herodotus, such priests shaved, every third day, all hairs from every part of their bodies, expressly to prevent the louse or any dirt from accumulating on their skin (ii. 37, Philo, *De Circumcisione*, vol. ii. p. 211; Maimonides, *De Suppellectile Templi*, ix.; Schmidt, *De Sacerd. et Sacrif. Ægypt.*, p. 15, note ; and Larcher's note *in loco*). Those who have read modern works on Egypt, as Lane's, Mrs. Poole's, &c., or on the Hottentots of South Africa, will be aware that the louse is still an almost unavoidable plague. Up to the time of Bochart there was general uniformity of opinion amongst Hebraists, beginning with Josephus, as to the louse, but after the publication of Michaelis' *Vermischte Sammlungen aus der Naturkunde zur Erklärung der heiligen Schrift* (P. I. c. vi. p. 74-91), the gnat has been preferred by Rosenmüller and the German school (*Scholia in Ex.* viii. 18).

T. J. Buckton.

Lichfield.

Caraboo (3rd S. vii. 269, 310.) — This remarkable woman was born Nov. 11, 1792, at Witheridge, Devonshire, and was the second child of Thomas Willcocks, an honest hardworking man, by trade a cobbler, and of Mary his wife, a sober industrious woman, whose maiden name was Burgess. This daughter was named Mary, and was admitted into the Magdalen Hospital, London, under the feigned name of Anne Burgess, on Feb. 4, 1813, previously to which she had led a loose life for some years. One of the men with whom she cohabited, and to whom she stated she was married after two months' acquaintance by a Romish priest, was named Bakerstendht or Beckerstein, a foreigner, from whom doubtless she learnt the Malay language, and thus became acquainted with

Asiatic customs and idioms, so useful to her in practising her subsequent impositions. Anglicising his name, she changed hers from Mary Willcocks into that of Mary Baker; although, after the discovery of her imposture, we find her in 1817 entered as a passenger on board the Robert and Ann, Captain Robertson, for Philadelphia as "Mrs. Burgess." How long she remained in America I am unable exactly to ascertain, but believe about seven years; and she afterwards exhibited herself in London, which, however, gratified her overweening vanity only for a time, when she travelled on the continent, where she remained some years in the South of France and North of Spain.

I became acquainted with her in Bristol in December, 1849, when, after much reluctance, she gave me her signature as "Mary Baker." She then lived under Pyle Hill, Bedminster, and gained her livelihood as well as supported her daughter, still living, by selling leeches to our Infirmary Hospital, and to many of our druggists.

She avoided as much as possible any conversation with regard to her former career, of which I think she was much ashamed; and nothing annoyed her more than when a neighbour's child ventured to call after her "Caraboo!"

She died in December last year, but I have not yet been able to ascertain the exact date.

BRISTOLIENSIS.

CUISHA: CUISHEAG (3ʳᵈ S. vii. 338.)—*Cuisheag*, or *cuisheog*, is a diminutive, formed from *cos*, a stalk, or tendril—Irish and Gaelic. The Irish pronunciation is *cushogue*. I am not aware that it denotes any particular variety of grass. The word is used in the Ossianic poems for the grass swept by the wind over the tomb of the hero, &c. The cotton grass (*Eriophorum*, one of the sedges) also furnishes a comparison for the white bosoms of the Ossianic maidens, the seeds of that plant being furnished with a pencil of snow-white filaments. This is the *canach* (canach) of the Irish and Gaelic. *Cushag* (cushag) is the wild mustard plant.

J. L.

Dublin.

BENJAMIN FRANKLIN (3ʳᵈ S. vii. 356.)—The following extract is from *The Streets of London*, by J. T. Smith, 1854 (Richard Bentley), and refers to the query of S. W. P. in the last number:—

"Duke Street, Lincoln's Inn Fields is memorable as the scene of the early life of Franklin. His lodgings were in Duke Street, and he worked as a journeyman printer in the office of Mr. Watts in Great Wyld Street adjoining. He first of all worked for a twelve month at a printer's named Palmer, in Bartholomew Close; but he worked for Mr. Watts during the remainder of his stay in England. It was in 1725 that he took his lodgings, consisting of one room, at the house of a widow lady opposite the Catholic chapel, which he paid for at the rate of 3s. 6d. a week. The landlady was a clergyman's daughter; who, marrying a Catholic, had abjured Protest-

antism, and became acquainted with several distinguished families of that persuasion."

At that time Franklin was about nineteen years of age, and the house where he lived probably No. 8. Some time back, I made the following note in connection with Franklin:— Pursuant to an order of the Court of Chancery, dated the 8th August, 1772, made in the matter of the proprietors of the Pensylvania Land Company of London, a sum of money was directed to be paid to "Dr. John Fothergill, me Benjamin Franklin, and me David Barclay, as attorneys to the managers of the Pensylvania Hospital in Pensylvania." This sum of money was accordingly received on the 27th August, 1772, by B. Franklin and D. Barclay for themselves, and as attorneys for Dr. John Fothergill, the eminent Quaker physician.

ALBERT BUTTERY.

DESCENDANT OF SARSFIELD (3ʳᵈ S. vii. 378.)—I presume MR. REDMOND means the celebrated Patrick Sarsfield, Earl of Lucan. Irish pedigrees have generally an exceedingly uncertain notoriety, particularly among those who are best acquainted with genealogical difficulties and inquiries; but the following, having the sanction of a title, I am happy to give it to MR. REDMOND *quantum valeat*. Sir John Bingham, Bart., married Anne, daughter of Agmondesham Vesey, Esq., niece or grandniece of Patrick Sarsfield, Earl of Lucan. He died in 1749, and was succeeded by his eldest son, who, dying without issue in 1752, the baronetcy devolved upon his brother, Sir Charles Bingham, who was raised to the peerage in 1776 as Baron Lucan of Castlebar, and advanced to be Earl of Lucan, 1795. Any peerage will tell the rest.

WILLIAM PINKERTON.

THE O'CONNORS OF KERRY (3ʳᵈ S. vii. 280, 364.) I have pleasure in referring your correspondent for much interesting information to the *Kerry Magazine*, 1855, vol. ii. pp. 181-188.

ABHBA.

"WODROW'S PRIVATE LETTERS" (3ʳᵈ S. vii. 378.)—This was one of the many works issued by the late John Stevenson, bookseller, Edinburgh (Sir Walter Scott's "True Jock"). In the Preface thereto it is remarked that—

"Although the ensuing *Letters* are both curious and interesting, their peculiar and local nature renders them best suited for private circulation among those persons who think there is no very great harm in being diverted with such (antiquated) scandal as afforded amusement to a person so truly respectable and virtuous as MR. Robert Wodrow, Minister of the Gospel at Eastwood, to whom (with the exception of a very few) they are all addressed."

In Fraser's *London Magazine* for March, 1834, p. 326, there appeared a very clever and amusing review of this curious little volume, where it is asserted that it was the joint productions of the late celebrated facetious Peter, Lord Robertson, and a highly popular clergyman. The impression having been limited to some fifty or seventy copies, it is now entirely out of print, and consequently rare.　　　　　　　　　　　　　　　T. G. S.

Edinburgh.

THE IMMORTALITY OF THE BRUTE CREATION (3rd S. vi. 415; vii. 339, 385.) — Those who are interested in this question may consult the *Lettres de quelques Juifs à Voltaire*, tom. iii. p. 394; Carpenter's *Instinct in Animals*; Gregory's *Comparative View of Men and Animals*; Turner's *Sacred History of the World*;* Hume's *Essays*, vol. ii. pp. 111-117; Rowton's *Debater*, p. 243; Jesse's *Anecdotes of Dogs*, and *Gleanings in Natural History*; Waterton's *Essay on Natural History*; Aimé Martin, *On Education* (by Lee); *Vestiges of Natural History of Creation*, p. 333; Reid, *On the Mind*, p. 489; Fletcher, *On Cruelty to Animals*; Willis, *De Animâ Brutorum*.

Your correspondent's hint in p. 339 induces me to confine the above references to the works of *laymen* only. I avail myself of this opportunity to express my thanks for the varied information supplied by MR. WOODWARD, P.M., J. B. SHAW, F.P.L. (in whom I have the pleasure of recognising an old archæological friend), MR. W. D. HOYLE, R.I.F., and on several occasions by yourself.

　　　　　　　　　　　　　　　　　H. W. T.

MANETHO (3rd S. vii. 356, 389.) — As regards the credibility of the history circulated under Manetho's name, see Faber, *Horæ Mosaicæ*, i. 251; and Rawlinson's *Bampton Lectures*, p. 56, and note.　　　　　　　　　　　　　H. W. T.

Miscellaneous.

NOTES ON BOOKS, ETC.

Calendar of State Papers, Domestic Series of the Reign of Elizabeth, 1581-1590, preserved in Her Majesty's Record Office. Edited by Robert Lemon, Esq., F.S.A., under the Direction of the Master of the Rolls, &c. (Longman.)

Mr. Lemon has not done justice to himself or to the value of the present Calendar by omitting an introduction. But it is impossible to open the book at any page without perceiving at a glance how full of interest are the documents relating to this period of Elizabeth's reign which are preserved in the Record Office, and how carefully Mr. Lemon has calendered them. Thus at p. 209, while the majority of the documents recorded on it relate to the works then (1584) in hand at Dover Castle, we find the Queen thanking the Captains of the Trained Bands for the diligence they had shown; and Sir Christopher Hatton writing to Burghley of the "Illness of Her Majesty through eating for breakfast a confection of barley sodden with sugar and water, and made exceeding thick with bread."

The Pursuit of Knowledge under Difficulties. By George L. Craik, M.A. A New Edition revised and enlarged. (Bell & Daldy.)

This book, the object of which is so well conceived, and which has been as ably carried out by Mr. Craik; this

---

* I greatly regret not having any specific reference to vol. and page.

---

book so happily named by Lord Brougham; for, as we learn from the present edition, Lord Brougham suggested the alteration of the proposed title, *The Love of Knowledge overcoming Difficulties in the Pursuit*, into its present terser and better form, this book will ever be a favourite, and Messrs. Bell & Daldy have done wisely in adding portraits to it, and including it in Bohn's *Illustrated Library Series*.

Devotions before and after Holy Communion. (J. H. & J. Parker.)

The well-known initials T. K. will sufficiently explain how the author has drawn up this little manual, "in the true spirit of the Ancient Liturgies and of our own."

The Fortnightly Review. Edited by George Henry Lewes. No. 1. (Chapman & Hall.)

A new candidate for the favour of the periodical-reading public, based on the idea of the *Revue des Deux Mondes*, and intended to further the cause of progress. The first number exhibits a goodly array of contributors, and a pleasant variety of subjects treated by them.

Mr. J. Payne Collier five-and-forty years ago proved himself a diligent student of Early English Literature by his *Poetical Decameron*. Mr. Lilly is now about to publish a couple of octavo volumes, in which our old friend and correspondent, will give us the fruits of that additional forty-five years' study under the title of *A Bibliographical and Critical Account of the Rarest Books in the English Language*, alphabetically arranged, accompanied with Numerous Extracts, in Verse and Prose, and a very copious and useful Index, which during the last fifty years have come under the observation of J. Payne Collier, F.S.A.

BOOKS AND ODD VOLUMES
WANTED TO PURCHASE.

Notices to Correspondents.

LONDON, SATURDAY, MAY 27, 1865.

CONTENTS.—N° 178.

Notes.

THE ORIGIN OF SMITHFIELD CATTLE-MARKET.

The following "Orders in Council" (which I met with quite accidentally while searching for other matters), show conclusively that the Cattle Market in Smithfield was *not* established from "time immemorial," as was asserted by the opponents to its removal to Islington a few years since. It appears, from these documents:—

1st. That the Cattle Market was not held in Smithfield till the year 1631.

2nd. That it was established there "against all warrant of law, or intention of any particular charter" . . . "by a combination of the Butchers of London."

3rd. That the market had, theretofore, been held at *Chipping-Barnet.*

4th. That a *quo warranto* was directed to be issued in the King's Bench against the Charter of the Butchers' Company.

5th. That four Commissioners, Justices of the Peace for the County of Middlesex, were appointed "to take the same into serious consideration" . . . "and to find out the best and readiest means to be applied for remedy of the said abuses."

6th. That the Act of Incorporation of the [Butchers'] Company ordered, 11th July, 1637, was rescinded on the 31st March, 1639.

"ORDERS IN COUNCIL, IN RELATION TO SMITHFIELD CATTLE MARKET.

"At Whytehall, the 16th of February, 1630-1.

"Whereas, it hath beene lately represented to the Board, as well by the Peticion of the Inhabitants of Chipping Barnett, in the County of Hertford, as by Complaint otherwise on the behalfe of divers Counties northward, lying upon that Roade, consisting cheefely of grazeing and feedeing of Cattell, that they being heretofore accustomed to bring theire Cattell noe further then to the usuall Munday Markett at Barnett, where by reason that the London Butchers and Forraignors resorting thither to buye, had equall Priveledges and Imunities, they made theire Marketts at such rates as were reasonable and indifferent betweene Buyer and Seller. That now by suppression of the said Markett (wrought by the Combinacion of the Butchers of London) in erecting a new Munday Markett at West Smythfield, and by the said Butchers becomeing graziers themselves in hyreing all the best Marshes and feedeing grounds within five myles or more distant from London, wherby they are able to supply the Markett themselves, and by confederacie to raise or beate downe the same at theire pleasure, and to make all Forraignors to sell as they list. That by this means, as well noble men, Gent., and others of the said Counties Northward (whose lands consist cheefely in grazeing and feedeing Cattell as aforesaid), as the said towne of Barnett in particular, sustained much prejudice and damage in theire Estates. And, therefore, were humble Suitors to the Board for some course to be taken for Redresse and remeadie therof.

"Theire Lordshipps, after mature advise and deliberacion had therupon, being well inclyned to restore and uphold the said Markett, as a Remedie in some degree to the Greevances complayned of, and being satisfied as well upon severall Informacions heretofore given, as upon consideracion had of the Articles presented by the Peticioners that the Practizes and Combinacions of the Butchers of London in governing the Marketts there as they list, was greatly to the prejudice of the publique, and against all Warrant of Lawe, or intencion of any particular Charter to them granted, did thinke fitt and order that his Majesties Atturney-Generall be hereby required to take the same into Consideracion, as a business of more then ordenarie Consequence, and wherof this Board hath taken noe light impression; and that hee proceede with speede and effect, as well in the Examinacion of any such Combinacion and indirect Practizes, as are complayned of, as in adviseing of and provideing such Reamedie therin, either by Proceeding against those in an Exemplarie way who shalbe found offendors, or by questioning theire Charter (if there be Cause), or by such other fitt course, as the case shall require, and as to Justice and equitie shall appertaine. And to make Reporte to the Board of his doeings and proceedings theron with all convenient Expedicion."

"At Whitehall, the 4th of May, 1631.

"Mr. Attorney is required to Command the Butchers' Bookes of Common Acts, and other bookes which may anie way give Light what Practise, Combinacion, or Order, hath bin taken in that Companie to overthrow or hinder Barnett Markett.

"To enquire what Butchers of London use graseing about the Cittie, and what quantitie of Lands, or Marsh Grounds they have nere about London, and where.

"To enquire of the practises and abuses of Smythfield Monday Markett, to the prejudice of the Gent., Grasiers, and of all others repaireing to the said Markett to buy and sell Cattle, and of the Courses holden in ordering the Markett, takeing toll, governing the Prices, &c.

" To take anie other course he shall finde fitt by Wittnesses, or otherwise, for discovery by what meanes, and by colour of what Graunts, Charters, Ordinances, or Orders, theise things are practised."

" At Whytehall, the 15th of June, 1631.

" Upon consideracion this day had at the Board, of a Certificate made by his Majestie's Atturney-Generall, upon a former refferrence to him from theire Lordshipp's, concerning the overthrowing of Barnett Markett by undue practize and Combinacion of the Butchers of London, to the great prejudice of all Landlords and Graiziers dwelling northward from thence, and tending to the enhanceing of the Prizes of all sorts of Butcher's meate, to the Greate damage of his Majestie's Subjects in and neere the Citty of London. Theire Lordshipps being of opinion, that the overthrowe of the said Markett at Barnet, and the practize of the Butchers of London, becomeing Graiziers as well as Butchers, and hyreing to that purpose most of the Marshes and feeding grounds neere the Citty, are (amongst other things fitt alsoe to be considered of) the cheefe Causes of the aforesaid mischeefes and inconveniences, did thinke fitt and order that his Majestie's Atturney-Generall, calling unto him Mr. Serjant Barkley, should advise of a Proceeding to be had against the said Butchers, as well by a *Quo Warranto* in the King's Bench against the Charter, under which they are protected, as by Informacion in the Starr-Chamber for the discoverie of the indirect practizes and Combinacions amongst themselves, wherin especially for that informacion in Starr-Chamber theire Lordshipps expect the same should be hastened, to the end some farther Proceedings may be had therupon this Tearme."

" 1634. *Touching Barnet Market and the Butchers of London.*

" At Starr-Chamber, the 10th October, 1634.

" Upon consideracion this day had of severall former orders of the Board, concerning the combinacion of the Butchers of London, in the putting downe of Barnett Market, and theire practize in becomeing Graiziers, as well as Butchers, and hyreing to that purpose most of the Marshes and feeding Grounds neere London, which tend to the greate damage and Prejudice of all Landlords and Graiziers dwelling northward from thence, and the later of them tending to the Greate Prejudice of Noblemen, Gent., and other his Majestie's Servants and Subjects, liveing neere or resorting to London, by converting all those Grounds which formerly furnished the Citty with hay into Graizeing, and upon Consideracion in particular of an order of the 15th of June, 1631, with a Certificate of his Majestie's then Atturney-Generall concerning the same. Theire Lordshipps did thinke fitt and order, that the said order and certificate should be herewithall sent unto his Majestie's now Atturney-Generall. Praying and requireing him to cause a speedie and effectuall proceeding to be had according to the opinion delivered in the said Certificate, and the Direccions of the said order ; or in such other way as he shall think fittest for the discoverie and reformacion of the said abuse."

" 1635. *Touching London Butchers.*

" At Whytehall, the 26th of June, 1635.

" Wheras, a Peticion was this day presented to the Board by *Abraham Cornish* and others, Butchers of London, expressing the causes of the inhaunceing the prizes of all sorts of Butcher's meate, together with a list of the names of the principall offenders therin. Theire Lordshipps, upon consideracion had therof, as alsoe of severall former orders, one of the 15th of June, 1631, and th'other of the 10th of October last, made concerning the same; did now againe thinke fitte and order : That his Majestie's

Atturney-Generall should be hereby prayed and required, to cause such proceeding to be therein had, as by the said orders is directed, or as he shall conceive to be most effectuall for the discovery and reforming of the said abuses and practizes mencioned in the said orders and Peticion, and for the punishment of the said offendors."

" 1636. *Touching the Butchers of London turninge Graziers, and Barnett Markett.*

" At Whitehall, the 30th of March, 1636.;

" Upon serious consideracion of the many greate and growing mischiefs, as well to the Inhabitants in and neare the Citty of London as to forraigne Graziers and Landlords, by the indirect practises and combinacion of the Butchers of London, in becomeing Graziers, and in hiring of Grounds in and neare the said Citty to feed Cattle. Their Lordshipps did this day order, that the severall former orders of the Boord, hereunto annexed, should bee sent unto Sr Henry Spiller, Kt, Charles Harbert, Esqr, his Majestie's Surveyor-Generall, Lawrence Whitaker, Esq., Clerke of the Councell in extraordinary, and George Longe, Esq., being all Justices of the Peace in the County of Middlesex, requiring them or any two, three, or more of them, to take the same into serious consideracion, and calling before them as well such Butchers, Graziers, and others, as they shall thinke fitt, to examine them concerning the said businesse. And for their further informacion therein to viewe the Books and Common Acts of the Company of Butchers aforesaid : And likewise to consider of the consequence of the overthrow of Barnet Market. To recover, if it may bee, the certificate mencioned in the orders annexed, dated the 15th of June, 1631 ; and of the 10th of October, 1634. And to examine and performe whatsoever is by the said annexed orders directed to bee done, for better discovery not only of the said Combinacion and indirect Practizes of the said Butchers, and the inconveniences and manifold prejudices arising by the same to the publique, but also to discover and finde out the best and readiest meanes to bee applied for remedy of the said abuses. And of their proceedings and opinions in the premises to make Certificate to the Boord with all convenient expedicion.

(Signed) " Ew. Nicholas."

· [Clerk to the Privy Council.]

" 1637. *Concerning the Butchers' Patent for a Corporacion.*

" At the Starr-Chamber, the 11th of July, 1637.

" It was this day ordered that his Majestie's Attourney Generall should bee hereby prayed and required, in drawing up the Patent for the Corporacion of Butchers, to insert these Acts following, vizt : —

" 2 & 3 Edw. VI. Cap. 5. An act touching Victuallers and Handicraftsmen. [About setting of prices.]

" 24 Hen. VIII. [Cap.] 9. Butchers shall sell no Wainelings under the age of two yeares. ·

" 3 & 4 Edw. VI. Cap. 19. An act for the buying and selling of Rother [*Rother ? sic orig.*] Beasts and Cattell.

" Not to buy and sell at one and the same Markett ; nor to buy fatt Cattell and sell them alive.

" 51 Hen. III. That a Butcher shall not sell contagious flesh, or that dyed of the Murren.

" 1 Jac. 22 Cap. That Butchers shall not gash hydes ; nor shall kill any Calfe to sell under 5 weekes old.

" 6 Edw. VI. Cap. 14. An Act against Regrators, Forestallers, and Engrossers. That none shall buy oxen, sheepe, &c., liveing, and-sell the same againe, unlesse he keepe and feede them 5 weekes.

" All which Acts the said Corporacion and Members thereof, are to bee enjoyned by the said Patent to cause to bee duely observed, so farre forth as shall bee in their power."

" At Whytehall, the 30th of March, 1638.

" Things desired by the Citty to be granted, wherof some are newe, for strengthening of Government. Some Explanaturie of the matters contayned in the former Agreement, consented unto by the Lords and others appointed by his Majestie to treate with the Citty."

[Among numerous other matters, 23 Articles in all, is the following] : —

" *That noe Markett shall be granted, erected, or suffered within seaven myles of London.*"

" 1639. *About the Recalling of Certain Pattents and Comissions.*

" At Whitehall, the last of March, 1639.

" According to his Majestie's especiall direction, their Lordshipps having this day considered of divers Graunts, Lycenses, and Commissions, which have bene procured upon untrue Suggestions, or which upon experience doe proove very burdensome and grievous to the King's Subjects, and of other intended Graunts which have not as yett passed the Great Seale, have thought fitt and ordered that his Majestie's Attorney-Generall shall draw a Proclamation for their Lordshipps to signe for revocation of the Commissions, Lycences, Letters Pattents, and Intended Graunts following, or for the prohibition of the exequution of them, as the case shall require, which Declaration of his Majestie's Attorney-Generall is to proceed legally to revoke them. That is to say : —

" No. 18. 'Pettie Corporations to bee recalled, such as are not past the Great Seale, the rest to bee prohibited to bee exequuted, and declared that they shall bee proceeded agaynst by *Quo Warranto*. Combmakers, Hatbandmakers, Gutstring-makers, *Butchers*, Tobacco-pipe makers, Horners, Spectacle-makers.'"

[32 various Patents, &c., named in the list, of which the above forms No. 18.]

G. A.

Barnsbury.

CERVANTES AND LOPE DE VEGA.

It has been asserted by some English and even Spanish writers, that Cervantes treated his contemporary, Lope de Vega, with great contempt and injustice. This assertion, I believe, cannot be supported. It is indeed true, that the illustrious author of *Don Quixote* spoke of Lope de Vega's better judgment occasionally yielding to the temptation of securing immediate profit, by sacrificing his permanent fame to a fleeting popularity with the public. But this was a fact which Lope himself often acknowledged ; and while his admirers styled him the "Phœnix of Spain," Cervantes called him "a prodigy of Nature." Indeed Cervantes possessed too much generosity and nobleness of mind, not to acknowledge the merits and literary excellence of Lope de Vega. This he does in two passages—1. In his *Viage de Parnaso,* where the following lines are applied to his rival : —

" Poeta insigne, à cuyo verso o prosa,
Ninguno le aventaja, ni aun le llega." *

, 2. A remarkable testimony to his poetic merits

* " Distinguished bard, whom none of modern time
Can pass, or even reach, in prose or rhyme."

occurs also in a prologue to one of the plays. These are the words of Cervantes : —

" At last appeared that prodigy of nature, the *great Lope de Vega,* and established himself the monarch of the stage : he subjected it to his controul, and placed all its actors under his jurisdiction. He also filled the world with plays, written well and with much purity. The number amounted to so many, that they exceed eighteen hundred sheets of paper. But what is the most wonderful of all that can be said on the subject, every one of these plays I have either seen acted myself, or have heard of their being so from those who had seen them. And if any persons, of whom in truth there are not a few, desired to enter into competition with him and share the glory of his labours, all that they have done, when put together, would not equal the *half* of what has been done by him alone."—Quoted by Ticknor in his *History of Spanish Literature,* vol. ii. p. 85, ed. Lond. 1849.

In the original Spanish, the expression "El monstruo de naturaleza, el gran Lope de Vega," must mean "*the prodigy of Nature,* the great Lope de Vega," &c. But, in *Don Quixote* (Primera Parte, cap. 46), Cervantes makes use of the words, *monstruo de naturaleza,* in a bad sense : thus, "Vete de mi presencia, monstruo de naturaleza, depositario de mentiras," &c. The expression is, however, frequently used in a *complimentary* sense. Thus Lope de Vega, in his *Hermosa Ester* (Comedias, tom. xv., Madrid, 1621), near the end of the first act, makes Ashuerus exclaim in admiration of the fair Esther : —

. . . . "Tanta belleza,
Monstruo será de la naturaleza," &c.

Cervantes no doubt used the words " prodigy of nature," in admiration of the prodigious fertility of Lope's muse, of which Montalvan (*Parnaso Español*) gives us such wondrous accounts, and also Lord Holland in his *Life of Lope de Vega,* London, 1817; Appendix, No. 1, vol. i.

J. DALTON.

Norwich.

MASTER JOHN SCHORNE.

Happening to take up the May number of the *Gentleman's Magazine,* I found under the heading of " Minor Correspondence," an inquiry from CANON DALTON of Norwich, for any references to publications containing accounts of *Sir John Schorne.* As I have no doubt that he will see " N. &. Q.," I forward the following in reply to his inquiry. All that is known of this venerated person may be found in Ashmole's *History of Windsor,* Lipscombe's *Bucks,* and Lysons's *Magna Britannia.* Among the papers of the Norfolk and Norwich Archæological Society, there is a very interesting one on this subject by Rev. Jas. Bulwer, in vol. ii. p. 280. In Chambers' *Book of Days,* vol. i. p. 609, is given nearly all that is known of *Master John Schorne.* There was a painting of him in Marston church, but three panel paintings only now remain, representing him with the devil in a boot; one at Cawston, another at Gately (both in Norfolk), and a third exhibited in 1850 at Sudbury, supposed to have belonged to the rood-screen of a church in that town.

An interesting account of this panel painting may be seen in the *Literary Gazette* for Oct. 19, 1850. But we need not go beyond the universal repertory of "N. & Q." In the second vol. were several articles on *Master John Schorne*; one by the Editor at p. 387, another by Mr. Albert Way at p. 450, and two others at p. 520 by correspondents signed respectively W. H. K. and E. S. T. These communications indeed include nearly all that is left on record of *Sir John Schorne*. But curiosity will be disappointed if it expects much. It will learn little more than that he was rector of North, or Great Marston, Bucks; of which the church is a striking edifice, with a good sacristy containing a piscina, and a staircase to an upper room, with a fire-place and a small opening through a blank window into the chancel. The will of this *John Schorne* is dated May 8, 1308. His remains were removed to Windsor, but brought back afterwards to Great Marston, which became a famous place of pilgrimage. As to the origin of the devil in the boot, with which he is always represented, nothing can now be ascertained with anything like certainty. Indeed it is not clear whether he is confining the devil in a boot, or causing him to come out of it. It is known that he was invoked for the ague; and if for the gout also, it is not unlikely that this emblem may have been intended to represent cures of that excruciating malady, obtained by his intercession. This is mere conjecture; but it is perhaps worth quite as much as any other hazarded upon *Sir John Schorne's* devil and boot.

F. C. H.

UGRIANS IN BRITAIN.

The *-by* termination and the Klint hills of East Anglia are Danish; but just where the *-bys* lie thickest northward of Yarmouth, I think we find a hint of a more northern origin, suggesting a link in the Ugrian or Finn chain. There, on the edge of that wide spread marshland, where Flora gains no wreath but of cotton grass, bulrush, and nagwort; where the "Broads" tempt the ornithologist and fisherman, but repel the artist, we find the villages of east and west Somerton situated on a rather steep but short ascent; and on the edge of the higher ground which bounds the Maddiscoe marshes, we have a place called Somerleyton; while in Lincolnshire, among the *-bys* east of Louth, are north and south Somercote overlooking the Saltfleet marshes. Now, in Dr. Latham's *Native Races of Russia*, p. 75, is this sentence:—

"The native name for the Tavastrians and Karelians— Hamalaiset and Kirialaiset—collectively, is Suomalaiset; from whence *Suoma, marsh or fen; Suomalaiset, the people of the marsh, swamp.*"

The Tavastrians and the Karelians lie in the Grand Duchy of Finland, between the gulfs of Bothnia and Finland. By these, Dr. Latham, p. 115, thinks—

"It (Suoma) was applied to the country occupied by their Samoyed neighbours, and taken up from the Karelian or Siranian by the Russians, from whom it spread over the learned world of Europe at large. If this be true, it is the same root that appears in the name *Suomolaiset* and *Sabine, Fin* and *Lap.*"

Dr. Latham says, "How it came into our language is a difficult question." Let us turn to Herodotus, who declares himself unable to obtain any information respecting the Hyperboreans from the Scythians of Little Tartary; their neighbours, the Essedones, being the sole people who knew anything about them. Here we are reminded of the British war chariot, Essedon or Essedum, brought hither by the Belgæ. Connected with the Hyperboreans were the Arimaspians, whom the historian almost treats as fabulous. After giving his reasons for his opinion, Dr. Latham (p. 90) says, "At present I commit myself to the idea that, name for name, the modern word *Tsheremis* is the ancient word *Arimaspi.*"

These Tsheremis lie on the western bank of the Volga, in the Government of Viatka; the Essedones lay probably to the west of them, as that would be the direction of the Hyperborean country; but I find no means in Dr. Latham of fixing their station. I end with a suggestion—that it might be worth while to seek in the neighbourhood of the villages I have named for relics of our earliest ancestors, bone or flint. F. C. B.

IRISH BOOKS PRINTED AT HOME AND ABROAD.

Space having been courteously afforded to the notices which, from time to time, I have contributed on Irish manuscripts, and to my recent supplementary list of published Gaelic grammars, I am led to opine that this communication will also be honoured with a place in the imperishable collection of "N. & Q." With many others I regret that "untoward" events, most potential amongst them national prejudices and mistaken notions of policy, secular and religious, proscribed for many years both the literature and language of Keltic Ireland. To this state of things is attributable the limited list I send. Though few the books I note, I believe this list is the most replete which has appeared in print, or indeed has yet been made, of Irish books printed before the nineteenth century. One beneficial result I anticipate, that it will lead to the discovery of other publications in the Irish language. And here again I have to express my obligations for some additions to Mr. John Power, compiler of the *Bibliotheca Hibernica*, now in preparation.

Rev. James Dowling, Suim Bhunudhasach an Teaguieg Chriosduighe a Chrosagundhan, *i. e.*, the Sum and Substance of the Christian Doctrine, in Prose and Verse, 12°, Lovain, 1728.

Rev. John O'Kearnaigh, treasurer of St. Patrick's: An Exposition of the Christian Doctrine, Articles of Faith and Prayers; printed in Irish in Dublin at the expense of Mr. John Uiser (Ussher), Alderman, at the head of the bridge, on 20th June, 1571.—This is said to be "certainly the first book *printed* with a view to the instruction of the Native Irish." A copy in the British Museum. This gentleman declined the archbishoprick of Tuam.

Dr. Nehemias Donellan, Archbishop of Tuam: Communion Book and New Testament.—Anderson, in his "Native Irish," says, it appears by a Privy Seal, dated 24 May, 1595, that he (the Archbishop) had taken great pains in translating and putting to the press the abovementioned works in the Irish language, which Queen Elizabeth greatly approved of" (3rd edition, p. 32).

Dr. William O'Donnell, Archbishop of Tuam: The New Testament, 1603; The Book of Common Prayer, fol., 1608.

Hugh M°Aingil, Scathan Shacramuinte na haitrighe, ar na cuma don bhrathair bhocht d'ord. Froinsias, Lovain, 1608.

Rev. Bonaventura Hussey (Hosæus): Catechism, Louvain, 1608.—This is the first Irish book known to have been printed on the Continent, and is in the Irish character. It was reprinted at Antwerp, 1611, and again in 1618.

Rev. Hugh Mac Caghwell (Cavellus): Mirror of the Sacrament of Penance, 1618.

Rev. Florence Conry, or O'Mulconaire: Mirror of Religion, a Catechism in the Irish character, Louvain, 1626.

Rev. Florence Gray, Lecturer in the College of Louvain, wrote an Irish Grammar, supposed to have been printed about 1626.

Theobaldus Stapleton, *Sacerdos Hibernus*: Catechism in parallel columns, Latin and Irish; it is entitled "Catachismus, seu Doctrina Latino-Hibernica per modum dialogi inter magistrum et discipulum," 4°, Bruxellis, 1639. To this is appended, "Modus perutilis legendi linguam Hibernicam.—There is a copy in the British Museum, press mark 1353 b; another in Trinity College; and one in the Royal Irish Academy, Dublin.

Rev. Michael O'Clery: Sanasan Nuadh; a Dictionary of the most obsolete and difficult Irish words, 8°, Louvain, 1643.

F. C. (Mr. Daly): Expositor, in Irish Character, 1643.

Rev. Anthony Gearnon: Parrthas an Anma, or Paradise of the Soul, 1645.—Copies, though very scarce, are still in the possession of several Irish gentlemen.

Godfrey Daniel, printed in Dublin the following:—A Catechism, all with Scripture proofs, in Irish, 1652; Church Catechism, with the elements of the Irish language, 1680; The New Testament, 1681; The Old Testament, 4°, 1686.

Rev. Richard Mac Giolla-Cuddy, or Arsdekin: Essay on Miracles done by the Relics of St. Francis Xavier, in the Jesuit's College at Mechlin, 8°, Louvain, 1667.—This seems to have been the first book printed in Irish and English.

The Rev. Francis O'Molloy: Lochran an Chreidimhtagh — Lucerna Fidelium; Lamp of the Faithful, 12°, 1676.

F. (Mr. Collins): Christian Doctrine, in Irish. Rome, 1676.

I have some grounds for concluding that in the seventeenth century other Irish publications were produced on the Continent for the instruction of the Irish-speaking Roman Catholics. I was shown, some years ago, a small Irish Prayer Book, printed I think in Louvain; and of those above-mentioned the most, if not all, ran through two, three, or more editions.

The following issued from the press during the eighteenth century:—

Edward Lhuyd, M.A. Jesus College, Keeper of the Ashmolean Museum, Oxford: Fochloir Gaoidheilge-Shagsonach; No Bearladoir Scot-Sagsamhuil.—An Irish-English Dictionary, Tit. X.; Archæologia Britannica, pp. 310—434 (an Irish Grammar precedes it), folio, Oxford, 1707.—A copy in the British Museum.

The Rev. John Richardson, Réctor of Annagh or Belturbet, in the diocese of Kilmore, and the Rev. John Brady, of the same diocese:—

1. Sermons: Selections from Bishop Beveridge and others. 8vo, London, 1716.
2. Liturgy, with parallel columns in English, 6,000 copies, 1712.
3. Church Catechism, with Lewis's Scripture proofs, 6,000 copies.

A portion of both publications were distributed in the Highlands of Scotland.

The Church Catechism (English-Irish), Belfast, 1722.— A copy in the British Museum.

An Irish Almanack for the year of Christ 1724, &c. Dublin, 1724. A copy in the British Museum. — It contains examples in Irish of acquittances, general discharges, promissory notes, last wills, and bonds. It comprises 31 pages.

Dr. James Gallagher, Bishop of Raphoe: Sermons, seventeen in number, 1735 [this work, in 1846, had gone through eighteen editions]; Catechism, 1750.

Rev. Hugh M'Curtin: English-Irish Dictionary, 4°, Paris, 1732. — This was at least completed by the Rev. Connor Begley. A copy in the British Museum.

The Rev. Andrew Donlevy: The Christian Doctrine by way of Question and Answer, with corresponding pages in English, published with the approbation of Louis XV., 8°, pp. 574, Paris, 1742. A copy in the British Museum.

Dr. John O'Brien, Bishop of Cloyne: Irish-English Dictionary, Paris, 1768. A copy in the British Museum.

Miss Charlotte Brooke: Reliques of Irish Poetry, consisting of Heroic Poems, Odes, Elegies, Songs, translated into English verse, &c. The originals in the Irish character, 4°, Dublin, 1784. A copy in the British Museum.

A Catechism, &c., to which are prefixed, Brief and Plain Rules for Reading the Irish Language. London, printed by E. Everingham, at the Seven Stars in Ave-Maria Lane, near Ludgate Hill. No date (1712). 16 pages. A copy in the British Museum.

Coyle's (Rt. Rev. Dr., Bishop of Raphoe), Collectanea Sacra; or Pious Miscellany in Verse and Prose, containing the Life of St. Columbkille, St. Fiech's Hymn in Irish and English, Pedigree of the O'Reillys, &c. 2 vols. 8vo. Strabane, 1788.

A list of Irish Grammars having been already given, none of them finds a place in this contribution. In a future paper I will supply a list of Irish books, printed in the nineteenth century; and also, if acceptable, of the various editions of Irish Bibles; Selections of Holy Scriptures; Tracts, and other publications in that language.

Of the Sacred Scriptures I will now confine myself to the following observation on what I esteem good authority. Anderson (*Native Irish*) says that, independently of portions and editions with exposition, he had numbered 290 editions in the English language from 1700 to 1800. By this time there had been printed and circulated in Welsh not fewer than twelve editions of the Bible, and as many of the New Testament, separately amounting to at least 120,000; of which 3000 Bibles, and 32,000 Testaments, in Gaelic, had been printed during the same period. Even in Manx there had been thousands, and all this before the Bible Society had been thought of; while for the Native Irish there had not been printed, he assures us, one single copy during the whole century.

JOHN EUGENE O'CAVANAGH.
Lime Cottage, Walworth Common, London.

LITERARY FORGERIES. — The following extract from *Galignani's Messenger* may deserve recording in the pages of "N. & Q.": —

"MARIE-ANTOINETTE'S LETTERS. — In the German literary world a certain sensation has been created by an article of M. de Sybel, the historian of the French Revolution, Professor of the University of Bonn, and formerly member of the Prussian Chamber. It appears in the *Historical Review*, which comes out at Munich, and discusses the correspondence of the unfortunate Queen of France. It is known that unedited letters and documents of Marie-Antoinette have been successively published; first by the Count Hunolstein (Paris, Dentu, 1864), then by M. Feuillet de Conches (Paris, Plon, 1864), and lastly by a German writer, the Chevalier d'Arneth. This last work appeared, in the course of the year 1865, both at Paris (Hentzel), and at Vienna (Braunmuller). M. Arneth alone indicated the sources of all the letters and documents which he gave to the public. He copied them from the original letters of Marie-Antoinette as they exist in the archives of Vienna, and from the authentic copies of the letters of Maria Theresa, which are also preserved there. M. de Sybel proves that the letters published by MM. Hunolstein and Feuillet de Conches are almost all, if not entirely, apocryphal, and that the autographs obtained by M. Feuillet, and on which his publication is based, must be for the most part the work of a forger. M. de Sybel states that even the most superficial reader of the three collections must have been struck with the circumstance that of the German publication, which is necessarily authentic, as being compiled in the official archives of Vienna, one letter only is found in the French collections, while the ninety-one other letters were as unknown to the French editors as were the fifty of MM. d'Hunolstein and Feuillet to the archives of Vienna. Likewise, even so slight an examination proves that the letters of the French editors, in their style and manner of regarding facts and events, all bear the same stamp, and evidently proceed from the same. It is the same with the documents of the German edition, of which the authenticity is proved. Therefore, as the two publications are directly contrary and cannot be reconciled, grave presumptions must at once arise to the detriment of the authentic nature of the French editions. M. de Sybel is not content with these merely negative proofs. He has brought out the manifest contradictions which exist between the letters themselves. To cite only one example: the authentic letter of Marie-Antoinette of May 14, and the answer of Maria Theresa of May 30, 1774, prove that all the letters of Count Hunolstein, from April 30 to May 18, can never have existed, because Marie-Antoinette had written to her family, in the month of May, only one letter, that of May 14, the particulars contained in which it would be impossible to reconcile with the letters of the month of May in the Paris collection. It is the same with several other cases. The letters of the French edition are, at least one-fourth, apocryphal; the others, which resemble them in style, composition, and other epistolary character, are apparently arranged after the *Memoirs of Mme. Campan*, and some journals of that date. M. de Sybel places side by side the passages of these memoirs and those which correspond to them in the letters, and he comes to the conclusion that MM. de Hunolstein and Feuillet have been the victims of an audacious forger."

PHILIP S. KING.

DUC DE CHATELHERAULT. — I observe from a recent notice in the *Globe* newspaper, that there is now before the French courts a dispute between the Marquis of Abercorn and the Duke of Hamilton as to their respective rights to the title. Upon looking over a list of the various publications of the late Mr. W. B. D. D. Turnbull, advocate, I discover that he had reprinted, in 1843, through the medium of Mr. Stevenson, the bookseller, in Edinburgh, a rather curious and valuable paper, bearing upon that interesting subject, entitled,—

"Factum of the Earl of Arran touching the Restitution of the Duchy of Chatelherault, 1685. Edited, with a Notice, and an Appendix of curious Illustrative Documents."

Only sixty copies appear to have been printed, and in the Preface thereto Mr. Turnbull remarks,—

"It is of excessive rarity." And again, "I shall merely observe that, in so far as I can see, the Marquis of Abercorn is *alone* entitled to it, and that his Grace of Hamilton, being neither heir-male nor heir-female, has as much right to it as he has to the throne of China."

The knowledge of such a publication being in existence may be of use to the disputants on this occasion.

T. G. S.
Edinburgh.

INEDITED WORK BY SIR CHRISTOPHER HEYDON.—This gentleman, well known as the author of *A Defence of Judicial Astrologie*, 1603, of which John Gadbury speaks in very high terms in his *Nativity of the late King Charles*, 1659, 8vo, also wrote the following, which, so far as I know, has never been printed : —

"A Recitall of the Cælestiall Apparitions (*sic*) of this present Trigon now in being: written by Sr Christopher Heydon, Knight."

It is a curious narrative of the eclipses of 1603, 1604, 1605; of the comet of 1607, and of the three comets of 1618; and is contained on fourteen leaves, small 4to, beautifully written in a handwriting of the time. I presume it to be Heydon's autograph MS. prepared for the press. See Evelyn's *Diary*, anno 1624.

W. CAREW HAZLITT.

WHETSTONE'S "CENSURE OF A LOYALL SUBJECT." — Of this tract there were two issues in 1587; one, I think, at the close of January, the other probably about the middle of February. The later impression contains a short account of the execution of Mary Stuart, which occurred Feb. 8, 1586-7, and will be found reprinted in MR. COLLIER'S *Illustrations of Early English Popular Literature*. Of the January issue, a copy with uncut leaves, as published, is now before me. On the top of the title-page is this memorandum by the original purchaser: " 27° Jan.r 7, 1586, pret° 4d," and lower down, above the imprint is written in the same hand, " Rob: ," with the motto or legend " 1 vite 5 mors 8 via 6."

W. CAREW HAZLITT.

GIBBON'S AUTOBIOGRAPHY: HERALDIC TERM MISUSED. — In the last number of the *Edinburgh Review* (April, 1865, p. 336), in an article headed "Heraldic Manuals," the following passage occurs: —

" As we come down to later times, commemorative augmentations were freely granted, and symbolisms, often of a ludicrous kind, used in granting and differencing coats. An amusing example is mentioned in Gibbon's autobiography :—' My family arms,' says the historian, ' are the same which are borne by the Gibbons of Kent, ... a lion rampant gardant between three scallop shells argent, on a field azure . . . . About the reign of James I. the three harmless scallop shells were changed by Edward Gibbon, Esq., into three ogresses, or female cannibals, with a design of stigmatising three ladies, his kinswomen, who had provoked him by an unjust lawsuit. But this singular mode of revenge, for which he obtained the sanction of Sir William Segar, King-at-Arms, soon expired with its author ; and on his own monument, in the Temple Church, the monsters vanished, and the three scallop shells resumed their proper and hereditary place.' "

The reviewer, strange to say, makes no remark on this passage from Gibbon ; but surely the historian, not versed in heraldry, had been misled by the word "ogress," and, assuming it to mean "female cannibal," had accepted a story about unjust kinswomen, which had doubtless been invented as an explanation of the supposed change of armorial bearings. Persons familiar with heraldry are aware that an *ogress* is synonymous with a pellet, and is represented by a black disk. In tricking a coat of arms, a change from an *ogress* of this kind to a scallop shell, or *vice versâ*, might readily take place.   J. DIXON.

WILLIAM MOLYNEUX'S MONUMENT. — As is stated in Wills' useful and interesting biographical work, entitled *Lives of Illustrious and Distinguished Irishmen*, vol. iv. p. 43 (Dublin, 1842,) William Molyneux, who died in Dublin, October 11, 1698, was buried "in St. Andrew's church, where there is a monument and Latin inscription." Mr. Wills is generally very accurate; but here he has made a mistake, which, even at the eleventh hour, I think it well to correct. Molyneux was

not buried at St. Andrew's, and happily for sake of the monument; inasmuch, as the building and its contents were destroyed by fire on Sunday morning, January 8, 1860. He was buried in his family vault in the northern aisle of St. Audoen's church, Dublin. It may indeed be said that this is merely a typographical error; but if so, there is another mistake, which certainly cannot be laid to the charge of the printer. The monument in question was removed from St. Audoen's early in the present century by Sir Capel Molyneux, Bart., and for many years past has been safely lodged in St. Patrick's Cathedral, Armagh. A copy of the inscription may be found in Gilbert's *History of the City of Dublin*, vol. i. p. 283.

Sir Capel Molyneux was the editor of—

"Anecdotes of the Life of that celebrated Patriot and Philosopher Wm. Molyneux, author of .The Case of Ireland ; published from a Manuscript written by himself, Dublin, 1803."

ABHBA.

FAMILIES OF DANISH OR BRITISH DESCENT. — I see in a work lately published, called *The Great Governing Families of England*, that it is stated that no one can certainly prove their descent from a Danish or British origin. This is, I believe, altogether a mistake; and I should be much obliged if any of your correspondents would prove to the contrary. I am convinced, with a little trouble, that the family of Scarth could clearly show their descent from that Skarthi, to whom King Sweyn raised a stone in Brietrass, A.D. 990, with the accompanying inscription, which I inclose for the perusal of your archæological readers.

SUIN . KUNUKR . SATI . STIN .
OFTIR . SKARTHA . SIN . HIMTHIKA .
IAS . UAS . FARIN . UESTR .
ION . NU . UARTH . TAUTHR . AT .
HITHABU .

SWAIN, KING, SET [this] STONE
AFTER SKARTHI, SIN
HOME THIGGER [*i. e.* body guard]
AS WAS FAREN WEST
AN NOW WORTH DEAD AT
HEDEBY.

J. S. D.

HOITY-TOITY. — John Selden (*Table Talk*, ed. Chiswick, 1818, p. 77), describing the customs of the court, says how much the dancing was altered : —

" In Queen Elizabeth's time, gravity and state were kept up. In King James's time, things were pretty well. But in King Charles's time, there has been nothing but French-more, and the cushion dance, omnium gatherum, tolly-polly, *hoite-come-toite*."

Now this latter phrase in modern French is simply *haut comme toit*, high as the roof. Is not this the origin of our hoity-toity?   A. A.

Poets' Corner.

Queries.

BORWENS.—What is the meaning of, and whence derived, is this term as a local designation? Farms so called occur in Westmoreland, in the West and North Ridings of Yorkshire, and I believe elsewhere.   WM. MATTHEW.

"BONNIE DUNDEE."—The fifty-seventh song in the *Beggar's Opera*, beginning thus —

> "The charge is prepar'd, the lawyers are met,
> The judges all rang'd (a terrible show !),"—

is directed to be sung by Macheath, to the tune of "Bonnie Dundee." Is this the air which is now popular, and to which are set the words by Walter Scott, originally published, I believe, in one of the *Annuals* : —

> "To the Lords of Convention 'twas Clavers that spoke."

Gay's words will go to the same tune as Scott's, though not so flowingly. As I have never seen the *Beggar's Opera* on the stage, my knowledge of it is only got from Gay's *Works*. The copy now before me is dated 1760.

GEO. CHRISTIAN BRAUN.—This German author published in 1821, at Mayence, *A Proposal for the Union of all related in the Christian Religion.* Can any of your readers inform me whether this theologian was a Lutheran or Romanist? He was author of many other works, some of which were published at Halle, Leipsic, &c., &c.   R. I.

BULL OF CLEMENT VI. — Has the bull of this Pontiff, relating to the marriage of Sir Thomas Holland with the Princess Joan, ever been printed? There is a copy of it in Rymer's MSS., Sloane MS. 4586, where it is said to be taken from the Register of Islip.   HERMENTRUDE.

CANNEL COAL.—Can you give me any information as to the derivation of this term? A writer, in a recent number of Newton's *London Journal*, says that it was so called because it was brought to Manchester by the Duke of Bridgwater's Canal, which was completed about 1766 : —

> "At this time," he says, "the word 'kennel,' or 'kannel,' was generally employed in Lancashire and Cheshire to designate an artificial watercourse ; and even Brindley himself, in some of his letters, speaks of 'the Duke's kennel.'"

In this way the coal, brought by the Duke's Canal, came to be called "canal" or "cannel" coal. There are, however, two objections to this etymology : 1. Camden, who wrote in the sixteenth century, says, in his *Britannia* (Gough's edition, vol. iii. p. 390), when speaking of Haigh, near Wigan : —

> "This neighbourhood abounds with that fine species of coal called 'canal,' or 'candle.' It is curious and valuable ; and besides yielding a clear flame when burnt, and therefore used by the poor as candles, is wrought into candlesticks," &c.

2. The usual name amongst the lower classes for a canal, in the midland and northern districts, is "cut "—the term "canal" being, as a rule, used only by the better-educated classes. I am unable, however, to say when the term "cut" as synonymous with canal was introduced. It appears in Ash's *Dictionary* (1775), where it is defined as "a canal made by art."

Camden's etymology is not very satisfactory, since cannel coal will not give such a "clear flame when burnt" as to permit of being used instead of a candle. At all events, I can say that I have tried to make it burn in this manner, but have not succeeded. My conclusion is moreover strengthened by the opinion of a chemist, who has devoted particular attention to this subject. Perhaps some correspondent may be able to help me in this matter.   RICHARD H. PROSSER.

25, Southampton Buildings, W.C.

CARABOO. — To complete the history of this celebrated woman (*ante*, pp. 269, 310, 408), there is still required the date of her death, and the place of her sepulture, with the entries in the parish register.   INQUIRER.

THE DEVIL'S MUSIC.—Can any of your readers inform me of the origin of the saying, that "Whistling is the devil's music"? It is remarkable that wickedly disposed persons, when up to anything wrong and likely to be caught, begin to whistle a tune.   INQUIRER.

DRAGON IN HERALDRY.—Can any of your correspondents kindly inform me the origin of the heraldic dragon? Is it synonymous, or in any way derived from, the dragon so frequently mentioned in the Psalms? In Psalm lxxiii. 14, the Psalmist says :—

> "Thou didst crush the heads of the *dragons* in the waters."

In verse 14 of same psalm : —

> "Thou hast broken the *heads* of the *dragon* (Hydra ?). Thou hast given him to be meat to the Ethiopian people."

Giving one the idea that it signifies the Evil One. Yet, in Psalm cxlviii. 7, we read :—

> "Praise the Lord from the earth, ye *dragons* and all ye deeps."

BLAZON.

"THE BISHOP OF DUBLIN'S PROPHECY," ETC.— Within the last few days I have met with a copy of a strange little publication, entitled *The Bishop of Dublin's Prophecy*, Dublin, 1722, 12mo, pp. 8. As stated on the title-page, it was —

> "written by the Reverend Brandan Birr, a Prophet and Divinity Lecturer in the Academies of Ardmagh and Clonard, in the Year of Man's Salvation, 1089 ;" and was "found in the Walls of Merion Church [near Dublin] the 13th of February last, 1721-2, as appears by a Certificate Sworn [by Elizabeth Oge and James Orme] before

Alderman Thomas Quin, on Monday the 26th of February, which is annex'd to the Latin Original; of which this is a Translation, word by word."

The original was "to be seen by the curious, at the Sign of the George, in Christ-Church Yard." The letters "I. S." are appended to the address from "the Translator to the Reader." And the following recommendation may be found in p. 7 :—

"Examin'd and approv'd by the Most Reverend Father in God, Lawrence Toole, by Divine Providence second Lord Archbishop of Dublin, in the Year of Christ, 1162."

Any particulars regarding the authorship, &c., of this literary curiosity, which was "printed by Cor. Carter, in Fish-shamble-street," will be thankfully received.   ABHBA.

ECCLESIOLOGICAL DESTRUCTION OR DESECRATION. I should be very grateful for detailed and certain information of destruction, removal, or desecration of (1) stone or wood carvings; (2) furniture, or other articles of interest, either from an antiquarian or art point of view; which has taken place during the last fifteen years; with, in the case of "restoration," the name of the architect employed. Information as to the present fate of any of them would also be acceptable.

The cases would possibly be too numerous for your insertion. If so, direct communication with myself would be much valued.   JOHN C. JACKSON.

5. Chatham Place, East Hackney, N.E.

THE EXODUS OF THE ISRAELITES. — I propose two queries, which I am aware are very difficult to answer. The first is—In what year of the world did the Exodus take place? The second is— Under which Egyptian King did this event happen?

I find that Dr. Kalisch adopts a date different from that advanced by the generality of biblical scholars. He fixes the Exodus in the year of the world 2269. He also mentions, with regard to the second query that, according to the authority of Josephus, who appears to rely on a statement of Manetho, the Israelites left Egypt during the reign of King Ramses V., Amenophis, who was the last monarch of the XVIII. dynasty. (See Commentary on the Old Test. Exodus. Preface, xx.-xxii., London, 1855.)

I should be glad to be informed if this statement of Dr. Kalisch has met with the approval of any sound German scholar or English writer of eminence.   J. DALTON.

Norwich.

GERMAN DRAMA.—Can you inform me whether Gottsched's History of the German Theatre, in two vols., published in or about 1768, contains the titles of all plays by German authors published in Germany from 1450 to 1760? Kayser's Lexicon contains a pretty correct list of dramas

printed in Germany, German Switzerland, German provinces of Russia, &c. from 1750 to 1832. Where can I find a good bibliographic catalogue of German dramas published before 1750? If Gottsched's book contains the desired information, can you tell me what is the cost of the book in English money?   R. I.

HORSE: GRACE.—In the Second Series of Prof. Müller's Lectures on Language (I speak from memory), he represents the myth of the sun's chariot being drawn by horses, and of Apollo being attended by the Graces, as derived from the same fact and idea; e. g., the common Sanscrit root gha means, to shine: and thence the rays of the sun come to be pictured as horses, for fleetness and sleekness, or shiningness; from thence comes also the legend of the Graces attending on the sun, they likewise being shining or beautiful.

I now ask, do the words horse and grace (χάρις) come from the same root? Horse, of course, has a long genealogy; and comes to us directly from the German Ross. But has it an ultimate Sanscrit root, identical with the root of charis?

Will MR. HEWITT KEY, who so obligingly answered the query about "Disciple," think it worth his while to answer this?

What, moreover, is the root of ἵππος? And how does Iacchus become Bacchus?—the original form being evidently Iakh.   ALPHA BETA.

"JOURNEY THROUGH SWITZERLAND."—Who was the author of an 8vo, entitled Sketch of a Descriptive Journey through Switzerland, London, 1796? It appears to have been printed for private circulation; and in my copy the following words have been written: "From the Author, Mr. R. L. Jun'., October, 1796."   ABHBA.

EPIGRAMS BY W. S. LANDOR.—Where will be found Landor's epigrams upon Pitt, Castlereagh, Napoleon III., &c.? They probably first appeared in The Examiner newspaper.   X. Y. Z.

WILLIAM PENNOCK. — Where is an account to be found of the two persons who bore this name? and who are mentioned in the following rather surprising quotation from Kent's Banner Display'd (London, 1728), p. 780 :—

". . . William Pennock, who invented the Pendulum for Clocks; he lived in the Earl of Arundel's House till it was burnt down by that dreadful Fire in London, in the Year 1666; which afterwards was built into several Houses, and now goes by the Name of Tokenhouse-Yard, in Lothbury. Also . . . John Pennock of Jamaica, Goldsmith, the Son of the above William, and . . . William Pennock, who invented the Art of Engraving on Wood for the Use of Printing; this William is the Son of the above John of Jamaica."

JOHN WOODWARD.

SUNDRY QUERIES CONCERNING PROVERBS, ETC. Will some one expound the following proverbs culled from Ray's Compleat Collection (1768)?—

"Where the Turk's horse once treads, the grass never grows."

"Pill a fig for your friend, and a peach for your enemy."

"Building is sweet impoverishing. It is called *the Spanish plague.*"

"London bridge was made for wise men to pass over, and for fools to pass under."

"Parsley fried will bring a man to his saddle, a woman to her grave."

ST. SWITHIN.

JOHN RITCHIE, author of "*Beaux and Belles*, a Dramatic Tale of the Olden Time," 12mo, no date (about 1850), Slater, Oxford. Wanted, any information regarding the author, who is said to have written various other works. R. I.

SHAKSPEARE'S WORKS, 1800. — I have lately found among some old books an edition of Shakspeare in nine small 16mo vols. It was printed in 1800 at Berwick, by John Taylor. The title-page of the first volume is lost, but on all the others is a small vignette of Shakspeare, and the names of the plays in the volume. The type is miserable, and the paper of the coarsest kind. There are no notes whatever to the plays; they may, perhaps, have been in the last volume, which unfortunately is missing. Some of the acts are divided into as many as ten or twelve scenes. In the first volume is a life beginning : "It seems to be a kind respect due to the memory of excellent men," &c., in which the poet is styled *Mr.* Shakspeare.

I am anxious to ascertain who is the editor &c. of this edition, and should be much obliged if any of your correspondents would favour me with the required information. I may just add, as another distinctive mark, that in the opening of *Measure for Measure*, the Duke is made to say : —

> ". . . . . Then no more remains
> But that to your sufficiency *you join*
> *A will to serve us* as your worth is able,
> And let them work."

C. HARWAL PERROT.

Rotherham.

PROVINCIAL SYNOD OF DUBLIN, 1862. — The late Archbishop of Dublin (Dr. Whately) convened his provincial synod in 1862, the year of his last triennial visitation. Where will I get *any* record of this synod. I am acquainted with the form of citation, &c. AIKEN IRVINE.

TIP.—Is there any earlier instance of this slang phrase than the following ? —

"Point out the means of succeeding . . . . if a private *tip*, tell him where to apply it."—*Letter of Lord Chesterfield to Dayrolles*, 1749.

CYRIL.

TRAVELLING SCOTCHMEN.—In the north of England a large trade has been done by travelling dealers in tea, coffee, drapery, goods, &c., and this business is generally conducted by Scotchmen. The term "travelling Scotchmen" is applied in Lancashire to these house-to-house packmen, irrespective of the place of their nativity. Is the term derived from the nationality of the itinerant tradesmen, or is the packmen's popular style derived from the word "scot," a shot or share of a contribution of the reckoning—from the Anglo-Saxon *Scoat ?* And is it merely a singular coincidence, that so many of these *scots*-men are Scotchmen ?

Another trace of the same old word is in the phrase "scot and lot voters." PRESTONIENSIS.

WITCHES AND BROOMS.—Why are witches and brooms so constantly associated in popular legends ? CARILFORD.

Cape Town, S. A.

Queries with Answers.

MEMORIA TECHNICA. — What is the secret of the Memoria Technica made use of in Longfellow's *Kavanah* (c. xxvi.) by Mr. Churchill, who thus addresses his wife ?—

"'What day of the week is the first of December ? Let me see,—

"At Dover Dwells George Brown, Esquire,
   Good Christopher Finch And Daniel Friar."
Thursday.'

'I could have told you that,' said his wife, 'by a shorter process than your old rhyme. Thanksgiving Day always comes on Thursday.'"

ST. SWITHIN.

[In Rees's *Cyclopædia*, art. "Dominical Letter," is the following explanation of this well-known couplet : —' "When the dominical letter is known, the day of the week corresponding to any day of the month may be easily found by the following Canon : —

"'At Dover Dwells George Brown, Esquire,
   Good Christopher Finch And David Friar.'

"These words correspond to the twelve months of the year,' and the first letter of each word marks in the order of the dominical letters the first day of each month, whence any other day may be easily found, *e. g.* : Let it be required to find on what day of the week Christmas day, or the 25th of December, falls in the year 1808, the dominical, or Sunday letter, of which is B. Friar answers to December, and the first day is F, *i.e.* B. being Sunday, it is Thursday, and therefore Christmas-day is Sunday."]

"AN ESSAY TOWARDS AN HISTORY OF THE ENGLISH TONGUE." PART I. BY JOHN FREE, D.D. 1749.—This is a thin post 8vo pamphlet of 78 pages, with an Introduction of 7 pages. On the back of the fly-leaf at. the end is an advertisement stating that "the Second Part of this Essay will be published with all convenient speed." With reference to this pamphlet and its author, I wish to make the following inquiries, viz., 1. Was the second part promised in the advertisement ever published? If so, in what year? 2. Was the author the same person as the writer of that name mentioned by Watt and Darling, as the vicar of East Coker, Somersetshire?

　　　　　　　　　　　　　　　LLALLAWG.

[Dr. Free's *Essay on the English Tongue* was completed. The Fourth Edition with Additions was published in 1788, 8vo, pp. 148, with a Catalogue of his numerous productions. Dr. Free was presented to the vicarage of East Coker in 1756, and in 1768 was chosen lecturer of Newington in Surrey, and had also the Thursday lecture of St. Mary-at-Hill, founded by Sir J. Leman, Bart. He died at his Chambers in Lyon's Inn on Sept. 9, 1791. For particulars of him, consult the *Gentleman's Magazine*, lviii. (i.) 381 ; lxi. (ii.) 966, 1048.]

BOOKS ON MAGIC.—What may be the meaning of the following entry in *Watt* under the head of "Magic": "1715. Ancient and uncommon Books on Magic see Britton, Thomas, 1815"?

　　　　　　　　　　　　　　　A. CHALLSTETH.

[Watt's reference is to his Index of *Subjects*, article BRITTON (Thomas), where the very curious Catalogue of the library of the celebrated Small-coal Man is noticed, as containing a collection of every ancient and uncommon book in Divinity, History, Physic, Chemistry, *Magic*, &c. The date 1815 is clearly a misprint for 1715. Britton died in September, 1714, and his library was sold by Thomas Ballard at Paul's Coffee-house on the 24th of January, 1714-15. It may not be generally known that a portion of Britton's curious collection of books, from some cause or other, had previously been dispersed by John Bullord at Tom's Coffee-house, adjoining to Ludgate, on the 1st of Nov. 1694, of which a Catalogue in 4to is in the British Museum, pp. 40.]

CLOCKS, WATCHES, HOROLOGY, AND HOROLOGISTS.—I shall be glad to have information on any of the above subjects — their history, curiosities, &c. References to works treating thereon or relating thereto will be useful to me.

　　　　　　　　　　　　　　　EDWARD J. WOOD.
Myddelton House, Clerkenwell.

[For information on the above subjects, our correspondent may consult the articles Clock, Chronometer, Horology, and Watch, in Watt's *Bibliotheca Britannica*, Index of Subjects, and in Lowe's *British Catalogue*, Alphabet of Subjects, 1837-1857. We would also refer him to the same articles in Rees's *Cyclopædia* and the various works there cited. For later improvements in Horology, see the article "Clock and Watch Work" in the eighth edition of the *Encyclopædia Britannica*, vii. 2—38, and "N. & Q." 1st S. iv. 240, 356.]

"BIG-NOSED MEN."—It is a common tenet with physiognomists that a large nose indicates force of character. I know some remarkable instances to the contrary; but perhaps the rule, as a rule, may hold good. Whose saying was it that, on

an emergency, "the big-nosed men always stood by him?" Was this said by Collingwood, or Nelson, or by what other commander? And where is the saying recorded?　　　　D.

[It is narrated of Napoleon I. that he was a practical nasologist, and influenced in his choice of men by the size of their noses. "Give me," said he, "a man with a good allowance of nose. Strange as it may appear, when I want any good head-work done, I choose a man—provided his education has been suitable—with a long nose." *Notes on Noses*, p. 43, 1847, 12mo.]

BRIDGE INSCRIPTION.—On a rude bridge which crosses a mountain stream near Dublin is this inscription : DI SUORE AMABILI. Can any of the correspondents of "N. & Q." tell me what it means? The exact locality of the bridge is, I think, called Kelly's Glen; but of this I am not quite sure.　　　　　　　　　　ACHENDE.
Dublin.

[This Italian phrase is probably connected with some local legend or occurrence, in which must be sought the true import of the words as inscribed upon the bridge. The translation is "Of Lovely Sisters." It seems to be the remnant of some longer inscription.]

LEWIS. — What is the origin of this name for the clever contrivance used by masons in raising stones?　　　　　　　　　　　　　CPL.

[The word is no doubt derived from the old French *lévis*, any contrivance for lifting ; thus a draw-bridge is called *Pont-a-lévis*.

This contrivance was known to the Romans, and several have been found among the *débris* of old buildings, and are now in the Vatican. Our correspondent will find one figured in the Elzevir Vitruvius (fo. Amstel. 1649), page 207.]

Replies.

WILLIAM, SON OF KING STEPHEN.

(3rd S. vii. 201.)

King Stephen had a son William, who was Count of Boulogne. He had a son William who was Count of Mortain ; and he had a son William, who, in right of his wife, became Earl Warren and Earl of Surrey. And I think there can be no doubt that these three were all one and the same person. I am not aware of their identity having ever been disputed ; and if there were any question about it, the extract which I subjoin from Dugdale's *Baronage* would, as I conceive, be sufficient to settle the point : —

"This William stiled himself Earl of Bolein, Warren and Moreton, as that Charter of his manifesteth (*Monast. Anglic.* vol. i. 358, b. n. 10), whereby he confirmed to the monks of Eye, in Suffolk, the Lordships of Acolt and Stoke, which had been given to them by his ancestors."— *Baronage*, vol. i. p. 76.

The identity being established, we next come to the question of legitimacy.

HERMENTRUDE takes it for granted that William Count of Boulogne was the legitimate son of King Stephen and his wife Matilda; and I am at a loss to conceive on what other hypothesis to account for his succeeding to the County of Boulogne, which was of Matilda's inheritance.

The idea of his being illegitimate probably arose from his not having succeeded his father on the throne of England. It will be remembered that in 1153 an accommodation was settled, by which, to use the language of Hume—

"It was agreed that Stephen should possess the crown during his lifetime, that justice should be administered in his name even in the provinces which had submitted to Henry; and that this latter prince should, on Stephen's demise, succeed to the kingdom, and William, Stephen's son, to Boulogne and his patrimonial estate."

The clause which related to the succession to the throne was couched in the following terms:—

"Sciatis quod ego Rex Angliæ Stephanus Henricum ducem Normanniæ post me successorem Angliæ Regni, et hæredem meum jure hæreditario constitui, et sic ei et hæredibus suis regnum Angliæ donavi et confirmavi."— Fœdera, n. e. vol. i. p. 18.

Roger of Wendover, in giving an account of this treaty, represents it to have been as follows:—

"King Stephen, being destitute of heirs, except only Duke Henry, hereby recognizes, in full assembly of the Bishops and other Nobles of the Kingdom, the hereditary right which Duke Henry had to the Kingdom of England."— Dr. Giles's Translation, A.D. 1153.

It will be seen that Wendover's representation is incorrect. Stephen did not recognise the hereditary right of Henry: he did a very different thing. He gave him the kingdom after his death, and constituted him his heir. Nor did Stephen say anything about his being himself destitute of heirs; but having once so represented the matter, we cannot be surprised that Wendover should afterwards describe William, Earl of Moreton and Warenne, as "the illegitimate son of King Stephen," A.D. 1157. Sandford in his Genealogical History gives what I take to be a correct statement of the matter.

In enumerating the "children of King Stephen by Queen Maud of Bologne his wife," he makes mention of "William, Earl of Mortaigne and Bologne, Lord of the Honours of Eagle and of Pevensey, third and youngest son of King Stephen, who, in the right of Isabel his wife, was the fourth Earl Warren and Surrey" (p. 43); and in the next page, coming to the natural issue of King Stephen, he discriminates between William of Bologne and another William, whose real illegitimacy may have been a source of confusion:—

"William is mistaken of some to be the same William that was Earl of Bologne; others who knew that William Earl of Bologne was lawfully born, do think. his father

had no other son named William but himself; wherein let William Earl of Bologne be a lawful witness of himself, who, having best cause to know it, doth best prove it. And in an ancient Charter of his, being written in those days, and extant in these, he doth name him for a witness, and calleth him his Brother."—P. 44.

I hope that these somewhat hurried notes may be sufficient to satisfy HERMENTRUDE that the husband of Isabella de Warenne was no other than King Stephen's legitimate son William, who on the death of his brother Eustace, became Count of Boulogne.　　　　　　　　MELETES.

SHELVES IN WILTSHIRE.
(3rd S. vii. 241, 301, 330, 362.)

MR. IRVING's remarks on this subject exhibit a curious specimen of what, in Parliamentary slang, is termed "riding off" from a question; as he takes the rather curious mode of investigating Wiltshire shelves by going to look for ancient earthworks in Scotland; and probably we may soon hear of him exercising his hobby among geological phenomena, careering, for instance, along the parallel roads of Glenroy. He has given up the plough, however, and taken to the spade and "lazy bed" for their mode of formation, though as those appliances are used only in the cultivation of potatoes, the "lazy bed" terraces cannot be of a very ancient date. The soil on hill sides is not generally rich. It is mostly barren, and artificial manures being unknown in early times, the people must have been simply mad to endeavour to cultivate such places, when there were plenty of more fertile lands nearer home. "Artificial manures unknown!" Will MR. IRVING tell us how long natural manure has been employed in Scottish agricultural operations? I have somewhere read, that it was the general custom in Scotland, when the midden obstructed the entrance to a farmer's house, the proprietor would take heart of grace some frosty day, and move the manure away to the ice on some river, so that when a thaw came, he would get rid of the obstruction. I cannot quote my author, as I am from home at present, but I am pretty positive that at so late a period as when the first series of Sir John Sinclair's Statistical Account was written, manure was then got rid of, in some Scottish parishes, by moving it to the sea shore, and leaving it there, under high-water mark, as is related in that work. And, in my own memory, I well knew a Scottish farmer, who would not remove the manure heap in front of his house; although he admitted that manure was good enough for a "kail-yard," he considered its virtues lost when placed in a field.

　　　　　　　　WILLIAM PINKERTON.

FIRES HOW ANCIENTLY KINDLED.

(1st S. xii. 205, 272; 3rd S. vi. 472, 536; vii. 82, 296.)

In reply to the query respecting any passage in the classics bearing on this subject, the following extracts, none of which have hitherto been referred to, will perhaps be acceptable to your correspondent J. N., inasmuch as he will here find mentioned the use of both flint and steel: Cornelii Severi *Ætna*, v. 362. Scaliger adduces *in loco*, illustrations from Lucretius, lib. i. [v. 896], lib. v. [1095]; Thucydides, lib. ii. [77]; Pliny, *Hist. Nat.* lib. xvi. c. 40; Homer's *Hymn to Mercury* [v. 108]; Festus [*s. v.* Ignis]:—

" Ignis Vestæ siquando interstinctus esset, virgines verberibus afficiebantur a Pontifice: quibus mos erat tabulam [lignum quadratum] felicis materiæ tamdiu terebrare, quousque exceptum ignem cribro æneo virgo in ædem ferret."

Michael du Fay, the Delphin commentator on Lucretius, has the following note:—

Lib. v. 1095. Et ramosa tamen, &c.] " Non ex solis arboribus contritis elici potest ignis, sed ex rebus fere omnibus. Namque ut ait Manil. lib. i. v. 850—

" Sunt autem cunctis permixti partibus ignes;
Qui gravidas halitant fabricantes fulmina nubes:
Et penetrant terras, Ætnamque minantur Olympo,
Et calidas reddunt ipsis in fontibus undas:
Ac silice in dura, viridique in cortice sedem
Inveniunt, cum sylva sibi collisa crematur.
Ignibus usque adeo Natura est omnis abundans."

In Bacon's *Advancement of Learning* are some most interesting remarks on the inventions and originals of things:—

" If you like better the tradition of the Grecians, and ascribe the first inventions to men; yet you will rather believe that Prometheus first struck the flints, and marvelled at the spark, than that when he first struck the flints he expected the spark; and therefore the West-Indian Prometheus had no intelligence with the European, because of the rareness with them of flint, that gave the first occasion. Neither is the form of invention which Virgil describeth much other:—

" Ut varias usus meditando extunderet artes
Paulatim."

Cf. Scaliger, *ut ante*, and Darwin's *Economy of Vegetation*, v. 209. In *Researches into the Early History of Mankind, and the Development of Civilization*, by Edward Burnet Tylor, Lond. 1865,—

" There is an excellent essay on flints and celts, in which it is shown that the transition from implements of stone to those of metal took place in almost every part of the globe, and a progress from ruder to more perfect modes of making fire and boiling food is traced in many different countries."—*The Times*, April 21, 1865.

BIBLIOTHECAR. CHETHAM.

IGNITION OF WOOD BY FRICTION (3rd S. vii. 296, 368).—Talking lately to the parish schoolmaster, who is a native of the Highlands, of the etymology of the term Beltane, applied to the 1st May (see

Calendars in Oliver and Boyd's *Edinburgh Almanack*), which' he derived from the Gaelic *teine*, fire, *quasi* the fire of Bel or Baal,—*Bealltuin*, he mentioned another use of the word *teine* with reference to a curious custom, which he remembered when he was a boy. This was the kindling of a forced fire called *tein'-éiginn*, by the violent rubbing of two bits of wood together, to be employed in some superstitious ceremonies for preserving cattle from murrain. It occurs to me that this practice affords a reply to the query of J. H. whether there is any known instance in this country of success in the experiment of producing fire by rubbing one piece of wood against another, as practised by the South Sea Islanders? I have no doubt that the Highlanders were formerly expert at the process, although at present, in consequence of the advance of civilisation and the extensive changes among the Gaelic people, the custom has probably become obsolete.　　W. E.

MEN OF KENT AND KENTISH MEN.

(3rd S. vii. 324.)

If this matter had not been mooted afresh, I had intended to revive the question which was raised in " N. & Q." 1st S. v. 321, 615. For a man of (East) Kent had had the last say, and had pronounced against the claim of those in the Western parts of the country to the more honourable appellation. And I observe that his arguments in favour of the men of (East) Kent have been adopted as conclusive by " N. & Q." in answering the above new query about the women of the county. This was I suppose of course, as MR. SANDYS has never been gainsaid.

I am not now going to speak of my own knowledge on the subject, or to suppose anything by way of explanation; but as I know my father's opinion about it, and he used to assert it undoubtingly, and as he was an authority in our county history, I wish to say that I have always understood the men of Kent to be those *born in the Weald* of Kent. I believe it is no question of East and West Kent, no diocesan distinction—nothing to do with a rural residence as compared with a metropolitan neighbourhood. This is the generally received belief of my friends and relations besides those of my late father, the Rev. T. Streatfeild, of Chart's Edge, who certainly was opposed to the view taken by MR. SANDYS. To be sure, those I am quoting were born in the Weald of Kent, and I too, for the same reason, have claimed to be a man of Kent, but the distinction is not one recognised in the world in which we are living; and the tradition in my part of the county is too widely spread to be probably a fiction imagined by some antiquaries for their own benefit. MR. SANDYS supposes many reasons in favour of East Kent, but gives no satisfactory proof; and I hope this protest from one born (it is not a question of residence) at the other end of the county, may be published, though it does not decide the matter.

In *Consuetudines Kanciæ*, MR. SANDYS quotes from the *Saxon Chronicle*, among other passages relating to Kent, one which is apparently against his view : —

"A.D. 853. In the same year Ealhere, with the *men of Kent*, and Huda, with the men of Surry, fought in *Thanet* against the heathen army, &c."

Is it not probable that the "men of Surry" would join with those of their next county neighbours who were near to them. If the "men of Kent" in the above passage means the men of East Kent with the "men of Surry," where were the men of West Kent, who were in such a case between the two ? I will never believe the West Kent men were passive in such a struggle. But I dispute MR. SANDYS's claim, because my father would have thought him wrong, not for arguments of my own.

May I add to this an enquiry concerning a ballad, which says—

> "The men of Kent
> To battle went,
> So loyal, bold, and free."

I have heard so much of it quoted by my friends and relations in the Weald of Kent, certainly never doubting it was said of their own forefathers. Has the ballad been printed at length ? Is it a part of the same as that referred to by MR. SANDYS, "N. & Q." 1st S. v. 616 ?

J. F. S.

TRANSMUTATION OF METALS.

(3rd S. vii. 200.)

I recollect the paragraph referred to by MR. IRVINE going the round of the papers, but I could never ascertain that there was any truth in it. It is, however, an undoubted fact that about twelve or eighteen months ago bismuth rose in price from 2s. 9d. to 24s. per pound; but I believe the company said to have been formed for transmuting it into silver to be a myth. Perhaps the following facts may clear up the mystery. The chief supply of bismuth is derived from the Royal Saxon mines at Schneeberg, which are also worked for cobalt and nickel. The lode in which these metals occur crosses in one part of its course a thin lode of silver.

At the point of contact a small percentage of this metal is of course obtained; but for some time past it has been so small as not to be worth extracting, and the three metals have been sent together to this country. When the cobalt and nickel have been extracted, whatever trace of silver there may be remains in the bismuth. Possibly some one may have accidentally met with a specimen unusually rich in silver, and thence concluded that the extraction of the precious metal would turn out a profitable speculation. The Schneeberg mines are now only partially worked. A cheaper substitute for cobalt blue has been discovered, and supplies of nickel being obtained from other sources, the prices of both metals have declined. The importation of washed ore obtained from these mines used to be about 700,000 pounds per annum, but it has now fallen to about 50,000 pounds. The supply of bismuth is almost exclusively obtained from Schneeberg, and this falling off in the supply would almost of itself be sufficient to account for the rise in price of the metal. This, I think, satisfactorily disposes of the "Transmutation of Metals Company (Limited) ; " but I hope in a future communication to show that believers in a sort of modified alchemy are not by any means rare even in the nineteenth century.   RICHARD B. PROSSER.

25, Southampton Buildings, W.C.

CARY FAMILY (3rd S. vii. 117, 170.)—In reply to ABHBA, I beg to explain that my authority for stating that " in 1588 there was a Cary or Carey, Bishop of Killaloe," was a note to the *Letters of Sir Robert Cecil*, recently published by the Camden Society, p. 157, in which, *à-propos* of " Mr. Campbell, Deane of Lymbrycke," of whom mention is made in the text, the Editor expresses himself as follows : —

"Dennis Campbell, a native of Scotland, Rector of Dumcliffe in the Diocese of Killaloe. In 1588 he was appointed co-adjutor to his Diocesan, *Bishop Carey.*"

I have no means at hand of verifying the statement. It would, however, be very satisfactory if any of your correspondents could ascertain what was the name of the Bishop of Killaloe in 1588.*

I should also like very much to know where a niche in the pedigree is to be found for Mordecai Cary, Bishop of Killala. Who were his parents ? When and where was he born ? The Reverend Henry F. Cary, the translator of Dante, was a descendant of his, being, if I am not mistaken, the grandson of the Henry Cary who is mentioned by ABHBA as Archdeacon of Killala.

MELETES.

KONX OMPAX (3rd S. vi. 263, 296, 392.)—After all are these words in their origin anything more than an attempt at a phonetic imitation of the sound of the dicast's pebble striking against the urn. They do not ill represent the noise of a pebble falling, rebounding, and falling again, especially in an urn made of thin metal. I have

[* Maurice, or Murtogh O'Brien-arra, was Bishop of Killaloe, A.D. 1570-1612.—ED.]

been led to make this suggestion by the passage quoted in the last reference placed at the head of this note, from Hesychius. Surely βλοψ is nothing but the noise made by the cup of the clepsydra as it marks the time by sinking. I can testify at least from my own experience (for water-clocks are still commonly used in Upper India), that βλοψ does very closely represent the sound so made. If this be so, then may not the passage be wrongly punctuated, and should not a free translation run as follows:—"Konx ompax, a term (applied) to matters finally disposed of; the sound of the dicast's pebble, as the sound of the clepsydra, βλοψ, is similarly used among the Attics?" These two expressions therefore would be in fact equivalent to our own phrases—"The die is cast;" "Time is up," signifying that any matter in hand has been finally and irrevocably settled.

E. C. B.

Calcutta.

"MELANTHE" (3rd S. vii. 401.)—I see that R. I. inquires after a copy of *Melanthe*, with MS. notes by Dr. Pegge. I beg to inform R. I. that I have that copy, and shall be glad to show it to him if he will favour me with a call :—

"MELANTHE, Fabulæ Pastoralis, acta cum Jacobus Magnæ Brit. Rex, Cantabrigiam suam nuper inviseret, ibidemque Musarum atque animi gratiâ dies quinque commoraretur: egerunt Alumni Coll. San. et Individuæ Trinitatis, Cantabrigiæ, 4to. Brown calf, 1l. 11s. 6d. Cantab. 1615.

"This Latin pastoral, which was written by Dr. Brookes of Trinity College, Cambridge, is of very great rarity. The present copy belonged to Dr. Pegge, the antiquary, and is specially referred to in the *Gentleman's Magazine* for May, 1756. It bears on the title the autograph signature of Matthew Hutton, and has the names of the Masters of Arts, &c., who acted in it before King James on the 10th of March, 1614, written against the various characters on the back of the title. It was afterwards Mr. Bindley's, and has one leaf in MS., but is the only one that can be traced in any sale. See *MS. notes by Mr. Mitford*.

JOSEPH LILLY.

17—18, New Street, Covent Garden.

ROBERT CRANMER (3rd S. vii. 376.)—I believe he was the great-grandson of the archbishop. In some family papers I find as follows :—

"1562. *Thomas* Cranmer and others restored in blood. *John* Cranmer, son of said Thomas.

"May 1617. *Robert* Cranmer, son of *Thomas* Cranmer, of Paternoster Row, London, Mercer, baptised."

"The above paper was found among the effects, in the own handwriting of *Robert Cranmer* aforesaid, of Mitcham, in Surrey, Esq., great Grandson of the Archbishop, and great-grandfather of the Rev. Robert Cranmer, Rector of Nursling, Hants. The date accords with Strype in his *Life of Archbishop Cranmer*, who says at page 418 (in folio), 'He had children who survived him, for whose sake an Act of Parliament passed in the year 1562 to restore them in blood, their father having been condemned for treason in consenting to the Lady Jane's succession to the Crown, for which act he was pardoned by Queen Mary.'"

This was copied from a fly-leaf in the *Life of Cranmer*, by Gilpin, and the original was written by the aforesaid Rev. Robert Cranmer, whose mother was related to Thomas, Bishop of Winchester (who gave him the living of Nursling) and to the Ogles. Mrs. Cranmer's grandfather was brother to the "judicious" Hooker, and for some time was Receiver-General for the county of Hants, and lived at Worthing, near Winchester, which his son sold to Sir Chaloner Ogle. M. P.

WORDS USED IN DIFFERENT SENSES (3rd S. vii. 278, 367.)—*Insense* is an expression very commonly used in the north of England with the same meaning as given by your correspondent E. L. S. In the pronunciation of the word, emphasis is laid upon the last syllable. *Insensed* is also often used when the individual "is *insensed* with, or understands the whole matter." *Awful* is another word we frequently hear perverted. How common are such expressions as the following : — "She's an *awful* fine woman." "He turns out an *awful* swell;" and of a coat or some other article of dress, "It's an *awful* good fit," &c.   GIBSON.

Liverpool.

MAY-DAY SONGS (3rd S. vii. 373.) — A contributor of the well-known *nom de plume*, CUTHBERT BEDE, gives in "N. & Q." for May 13 a May-day song sung at Denton and Caldecote, in Huntingdonshire. It consists of five verses. Words differing but slightly from those of the third verse are sung at Combe, in Oxfordshire, by a troop of little girls, dressed up fantastically, and carrying sticks, to the tops of which are tied bunches of flowers. The following is their version of the four lines : —

"Gentlemen and ladies !
We wish you happy May ;
We're come to show our garlands,
Because it is May-day."

The same verse, substantially, is the May-day song at Wootton, an adjoining parish. It would seem to be intended for the mouth of a χορηγίς. The first line is better than those of the versions sung at Combe and at the two Huntingdonshire villages. The verse runs thus,—

"Good morning, merry gentlefolks !
I wish you happy May ;
I'm come to show my May-garland,
Because it is May-day."

The last two of the four lines are sometime as follows : —

"Come, kiss my face, and smell my mace,
And give the lord and lady something."

In this case the final line breaks away from the fetters of rhyme, but only to come to what is, in this prosaic age, the point of the whole custom.

J. H. A.

Combe Parsonage, Oxon.

FOXES OR SHEAVES (3rd S. vii. 338.)—I am not aware who first proposed to write *shĕ'alim* for *shŭ'alim* in Judg. xv. 4. Allow me, notwithstanding, to demur to such an alteration—(1) because *shĕ'alim* does not mean "sheaves" at all. The word signifies "the hollow of the hand" (Is. xl. 12), and then as much as could be contained in the hollow of the hand, "a handfull" (1 Kings, xx. 10; Ezek. xiii. 19); it occurs nowhere else in the Bible; (2) the change proposed in Judg. xv. 4, would do violence to the context; sheaves have not "tails," and could not do all that is recorded in verse 5; (3) Parkhurst observes that the practice of tying firebrands to foxes' tails is mentioned in the thirty-eighth fable of Aphthonius, and adds that Ovid (*Fasti,* iv. 681), speaks of a custom observed at Rome every year, about the middle of April, of turning out foxes into the circus with burning torches to their backs:—

"... missæ junctis ardentia tædis,
Terga ferunt vulpes."

The Hebrew word *shŭ'alim* (sing. *shŭ'al*) is the original source of our *jackal*, and perhaps jackals are meant in Judg. xv. 4, as Fürst and others have suggested. B. H. C.

ANSAYRI (3rd S. vii. 358.)—Your correspondent W. A. M. will find this Oriental sect described in the following publications in addition to those furnished immediately after his query: Maundrell's *Journey to Aleppo;* Pocock's *Travels;* Walpole's *Ansayrii,* passim; Lyde's *Asian Mystery;* Conder's *Syria,* p. 261; *North British Review,* Nov. 1860, p. 340. H. W. T.

JACK STONES (3rd S. vii. 34, 143.)—According to Brand (*Pop. Antiquit.* vol. ii. p. 165, edit. Bohn), General Vallancey traces this word to the Irish "Seic Seona," which (pronounced Shee Sheona), "Was readily turned into Jack Stones by an English ear, by which name this game is now known by the English in Ireland. It has another name among the vulgar, viz. Gob Stones." (*Collect. de Reb. Hib.*)

This game is played by the coloured people in different parts of this colony, and is by them termed "Klip Verlaten." It is played by three persons, each having *eight* stones; one of the players begins by throwing all the stones into the air, and catching as many as possible on the back of the hand and arm.

Dr. Clarke found a similar game among the Russians, played with the joint-bones of sheep (cockalls). "This game," he tells us, "is called 'Dibbs' by the English." (*Travels in Russia,* 1810, i. 177.) JAMES A. HEWITT.
Capetown, S.A.

MISTLETOE (3rd S. vii. 76, 157.)—

"As the common misseltoe and other *Lorantheæ* are destitute of any true root, they possess the property of penetrating through the bark of the trees to which they are attached, and of fixing the base of their stems into the wood beneath. *Thus they absorb the rising sap in its progress towards the leaf.*" (*Botany,* by Prof. Henslow, p. 237.)

It is most probably for this reason that Shakspeare applies the epithet "baleful" to the mistletoe; or can he be alluding to an idea that mistletoe was "that forbidden tree" in the midst of the garden,

"... whose mortal taste
Brought death into the world, and all our woe"?

"For in the Edda, the misseltoe is said to be Balder's death, who yet perished through blindness and a woman." (*Gent's Mag.* Feb. 1791.)

JAMES A. HEWITT.
Capetown, S.A.

ADVERBS IMPROPERLY USED (3rd S. vii. 152, &c.) I cannot agree that the words *are* improperly used. "To look merrily," is to look *as if* the person were merry, or like a merry person. "To be merry," is an absolute assertion of a fact. "Your offer is fair," is one proposition. "I think you mean fairly," is another. "He is bad in health," means he is really ill. "He feels badly," as if he were bad, or like a man who is bad—he may be well, it may be only his fancy.

Is not the termination *-ly,* directly the old Anglo-Saxon *-lic?* Thus *werlic,* is manly; *wiflic,* womanly; *Godlic,* godly; *eorðlic,* earthly. See Bosworth's *Dictionary,* 42 d. A. A.
Poets' Corner.

CHAP (3rd S. vii. 380.)—I imagine that neither your correspondent CYRIL, nor your own editorial note, has lighted upon the first use of this "favourite slang word" in its now common but very modern signification of "fellow." The quotations from Captain Carleton and from Steele, both present it to us as a mere diminutive of the old Saxon "chapman"—"ceapman," a buyer or customer: and in this sense only I find it in Bailey's *Dictionary,* edit. 1773. There is no doubt, I venture to assume, of the original identity of the verbs "to chap" and "to cheap" (or "cheapen"); and that a "chap" is, therefore, properly a "cheapener," or one who (as we now say) "haggles" over a bargain. Hence, I suppose, it has come about that, in these days of national shopkeeping and *amor nummi,* we are all of us "chapmen," and consequently, in our anxiety to save time as well as money, all of us "chaps." But like CYRIL, I too shall be interested, if "N. & Q." will execute on this word one of its most important functions, by telling posterity when and where this deformed offspring of the Saxon language was born?
R. C. L.

From the context, and the use of the phrases "bargain" and "sell," it would seem this phrase is merely an abbreviation of *chapman* (Anglo-Sax. *ceapman*), a market man, a buyer and seller. "If

you want to sell, here is your chap," *i. e.* chapman. The same idea is still in common use in the streets: "Come on, I'm your customer."   A. A.
Poets' Corner.

ASSUMPTION OF ARMS (3rd S. vii. 381.)—I think the author of the paper in question is unduly severe on the rich tradesman; who acquires, on retirement from business, a coat of arms by purchase.

I scarcely say too much, when I affirm, that a very large proportion of the nobility has sprung from trade; and that in many instances their paternal coats, as well as those which they quarter, have originally been granted to ambitious ancestors retired from business.

Very often we see the most intolerant, those who in reality should be least so. I know a gentleman who laughs at new coat armour, because he firmly believes that he himself has a right to one of great antiquity; and which he considers it a personal insult to question. Nevertheless, he has no real right to any coat of arms whatever; and as he won't purchase one, his posterity will be in the same fix!

One of the very worst errors of the present period of heraldry, is the unchecked liberty which is taken with inexorable truth, by some families "claiming" to bear this or that coat, or to represent this or that ancient family. Such "claims" appear on the face of numerous pedigrees, and seem to give them an undue importance. Moreover they are unfair to those who really do possess valid claims. I now propose that *no claim should ever be mentioned,*[*] *without a statement of the facts (with full references) on which it is founded; so that the public at large may judge for itself.*   S.

URICONIUM, OR WROXETER (3rd S. vii. 183, 349.)—How is it that no one has cited a—

" Guide to the Ruins of the Roman City of Uriconium, at Wroxeter, near Shrewsbury. By Thomas Wright, Esq., M.A., F.S.A., Shrewsbury, J. O. Sandford, 12mo, 1859, pp. 92, with twelve plates from drawings by Mr. Hillary Davies, of Shrewsbury " ?
    WILLIAM BATES.
Birmingham.

QUOTATION WANTED (3rd S. vii. 241, 328.) — Did not Christopher Love rather refer to one or more of the axioms of the learned Jenkins? As for instance: —

" Pœnæ sunt restringendæ."— *Cent.* 29.

With a recollection also of —

" Favores ampliandi sunt. Odia restringenda."
    Cent. 186.

These seem nearer the mark than the maxims cited by R. C. L.   WILLIAM BATES.
Birmingham.

_____

[*] This, of course, could only be brought about by a combination.

CORONETS (3rd S. vii. 54.)—The coronets of the Princes of Wales, the princes of the blood royal, and their descendants, and of barons, were ordered to these degrees by King Charles the Second. (Chamberlain, *Mag. Brit. Not.* i. 60, 165, thirty-eighth edit. 1755.)   JAMES A. HEWITT.
Capetown, S.A.

HOG'S PRAYER (3rd S. vii. 114.)—I have carefully inquired in Kent, and so have many of my friends, whether they ever heard of such a thing as "a Hog's Prayer." Nothing of the sort could be discovered; but the other day, near Tunbridge, inquiring of a very intelligent old farmer, he said at once, "It is all a blunder; they mean the *hag* prayer, or prayer to keep away the old witches or hags," and told me it is not uncommonly used by the superstitious to this day. It is the well-known rhyme—

" Matthew, Mark, Luke, and John,
  Bless the bed that I lay on;
  Four corners to my bed,
  Four angels round it spread;
  And if that death should chance to call,
  I hope our Lord will save us all."

This is a very old rhyme, and something like it is given in Sinclair's *Invisible World Discovered,* Relation 3, where he calls it the Black Paternoster, and says it was used in Scotland. If this information should prove correct, all I can say is, it is a pity to make a charge of such degrading superstition against the lower classes without being perfectly certain of its accuracy.   A. A.
Poets' Corner.

STICK (3rd S. vii. 290.)—The meaning here is clearly the *composing stick* — the implement in which the printer's type is set up. "Our author makes his first paragraph a compleat stick of Railing," that is, as much railing as the stick would hold, or a compositor set up at one bout without going to his galley.   A. A.
Poets' Corner.

NAVAL VICTORY OF JUNE, 1665 (3rd S. vii. 336.)—A friend has pointed out these mistakes in the above; for which, I have no doubt, my imperfect decyphering of the original has made me answerable. The Editor of "N. & Q." may be glad of the corrections: for Sir John *Pawson,* read Sir John Lawson; for "perished" read "persued." The writing is very indistinct.
    E. W.

CUE (3rd S. vii. 317.)—In France, at any opera, play, or other exhibition, the people range themselves in a line, following the order they arrive in, and pass quietly on, one after the other, taking their turn fairly, without that unmannerly pushing and crowding which I believe exists nowhere else but in England. This line they call the "queue," and if any one tries to get out of his place, the cry is "Suivez la queue," take your turn. Is not

this the origin of the phrase, "It is your cue," that is, "It is your turn to speak"? The phrase is clearly not confined to the *entrance* of an actor, for every separate speech has its cue. A. A.
Poets' Corner.

CLASSICAL WASHERWOMEN (3rd S. vii. 34.)— If your correspondent E. S. takes an interest in this subject, I would refer him to a beautiful passage in the *Odyssey* (ζ, the early part of the book), where the Princess Nausicaa goes down to the shore with her suite to wash the royal clothes. A. A.
Poets' Corner.

RUN THE GAUNTLET (3rd S. vii. 374.)— Probably after all this *is* the correct phrase, and might have been derived at the time when the culprit ran through the double line of men, and was struck by the fist with the gauntlet on, as in later days has been done with the stick. A. A.
Poets' Corner.

THEODOLITE (3rd S. vii. 337.)—The tradition among surveyors is, that land surveying was generally performed by the cross-staff at the date J. C. J. speaks of, 1685. This instrument was superseded by the circumferentor, an instrument much like a theodolite, but without the needle; the angles being taken from back-sights, as is the case with the sextant. The use of the needle in land-surveying is said to have been derived from the practice of mining surveyors. As late as 1760, in the *Dictionary of Arts and Sciences*, an instrument exactly on the same principle as the theodolite is called a *mining dial*, and the rules for its use are given under the article "Dialling."
In all probability the word is composed of θε, the ordinary abbreviation of the Greek θεάομαι, and ὁδός, a way; an instrument by means of which you could see, or find your way. A. A.
Poets' Corner.

MANETHO (3rd S. vii. 389.)—Your learned correspondent, T. J. BUCKTON, has, I think, quite mistaken the question connected with Manetho. My previous note on the subject (3rd S. vii. 357) did not imply an "attempt to disparage the authority of Manetho by Hengstenberg." The two points discussed by this writer are, (1), that Manetho never resided in Egypt; (2), that he did not live earlier than about the commencement of the vulgar era. I did not touch upon the *authority* or *authenticity* of the works of Manetho. The questions, therefore, still remain unanswered. Did Manetho ever reside in Egypt, and did he live B.C. 260? Hengstenberg replies in the negative. (*Die Bücher Moses und Ægypten*, p. 237— 245, 256.) Your correspondent replies, that Hengstenberg must have "confounded some other of that name." Surely, whatever weight MR. T. J. BUCKTON may attach to Heeren's *Manual of Ancient History*, the name of such a writer as

Hengstenberg ought to be mentioned with great deference.
Bunsen, speaking of Manetho, says: "He is known to the ancients as a priest of Sebennytus. . . . . . The title of high-priest, ascribed to the genuine Manetho, is probably fictitious," &c. (*Egypt's Place in Universal History*, vol. i. p. 58, ed. London, 1848.) Heeren, however, asserts that he was "High-Priest at Heliopolis." The fact is, we know next to nothing of the personal history of Manetho; and hence we should not speak too positively about him or his works on the complex subject of Egyptian Chronology.
J. DALTON.
Norwich.

TOADS IN STONE (3rd S. vii. 388.)—This interesting question might, I think, be finally settled if any scientific person resident at Bath would obtain the assistance of some of the numerous masons employed in excavating and dressing the freestone on Coombe Down, as when staying in that neighbourhood some five years ago I was informed by a relative that he had on several occasions seen blocks of stone sawn in half, the saw in the course accidentally marked out for it, completely bisecting both the reptile and the closely-fitting cavity in which he lay, the blocks having, as described by your correspondent, neither fissure, "vein, nor chink." E. JOHNSON.
Cambridge.

THE DUKE OF BRUNSWICK'S "FIFTY REASONS" (3rd S. vii. 68, 121.)—The title of my copy of this work differs in some respects from that given by F. C. H. My copy is styled:—

"Fifty Reasons, or Motives, why the Roman Catholic, Apostolic Religion ought to be preferred to all the Sects this Day in Christendom; and which induced his most Serene Highness Anthony Ulrick Duke of Brunswick and Lunenburg to abjure Lutheranism. To which are added Three Valuable Papers. Antwerp: printed in the year M.DCC.XLI."

Can F. C. H. tell me whether this edition is scarce? CARILFORD.
Cape Town, S.A.

"ON AN ALTAR ED [?]" (3rd S. vii. 352.)— Your fortunate correspondent, who fell in with upwards of fifty epigrams by Mr. Thomas Fuller, has favoured us with a very appetising, not to say tantalising, list, including most of their *subjects*. Among these is No. 9, "On an Altar Ed," to which your correspondent has annexed a note of interrogation. For the import of this title I would refer to Joshua xxii. 34 :—

"And the children of Reuben and the children of Gad called the altar Ed: for it shall be a witness between us that the Lord is God."

Our translators have here supplied the word Ed (witness) from verses 27, 28, where it occurs in the Hebrew. SOHIN.

"No Man is a Hero to his Valet-de-Chambre" (3rd S. vii. 150, 309.) — The passage in question occurs in one of the minor treatises of Plutarch, and is perhaps worth citation as indicating the peculiar office of the servant in whose apprehension his master would fail to preserve the heroic character. The words are, —

"Ἀντίγονος ὁ γέρων, Ἑρμοδότου τινὸς ἐν ποιήμασιν αὐτὸν ἡλίου παῖδα, καὶ θεὸν ἀναγορεύοντος, Οὐ τοιαῦτά μοι (εἶπεν) ὁ λασανόφορος σύνοιδεν."
De Iside et Osiride. Francof. 1620, p. 360.

But in no greater degree should a man be a hero to himself; and in those elevated positions in which he may feel tempted to raise himself above the level of surrounding humanity, he may be ingeniously reminded of the frailty and degeneration which he has in common with those who crawl before him, by being constituted his own valet, and publicly made to act the part, as it were, of λασανόφορος, to himself. Thus Platina would interpret a ceremony which the newly appointed Pope has to go through: —

"Sentio sedem illam ad id paratam esse, ut qui in tanto magistratu constituitur, sciat se non Deum sed hominem esse; et necessitatibus naturæ, utpote egerendi, subjectum esse, unde merito Stercoraria sedes vocatur." — *De Vit. Pontific.*, ed. 1664, p. 258.

Thus much our historian says in opposition to the other theory, which Butler seems to adopt. (*Hudibras*, part I. cant. iii. line 1249.) For a full discussion of this vexed question, the *curious* reader is referred to the *Histoire de la Papesse Jeanne, de Monsieur de Spanheim,* 12mo, Cologne, 1694, p. 105.

Since writing the above I have noticed the inquiry of J. M. K. The *Antigonus* to whom the saying is attributed, is the celebrated general, and supposed half brother of Alexander the Great. The authority, as above cited, is Plutarch.

WILLIAM BATES.
Birmingham.

Hog Feast (3rd S. vii. 364, &c.) —
"The Romans gave the offal and harslet to their slaves, but highly esteemed those portions of the animal which we throw away, or give to the dogs. Apicius cared little for pork as meat, but invented many sauces from various parts of the pig, which were so much the better relished when it was fatted to death," p. 17.—*Letter to Dr. W. King.* Dublin, 1711, pp. 108.

The author cites Pliny, Strabo, and Athenæus, at the foot of the page. Can any reader of "N. & Q." save me the trouble of searching through indexes. J. M. K.

"The Vampyre" (3rd S. vii. 201.)—Is there not an error in the statement that the name of Lord Byron appears as the author on the title-page of *The Vampyre,* 8vo, 1819? I do not find it on the title of my copy, which is *verbatim* as you give it, with the exception of the words "by the Right Hon. Lord Byron." The tale itself occupies 72 pages; and there is appended "Extract of a letter containing an account of Lord Byron's residence in the Island of Mitylene," increasing the book to 84 pages. This extract alludes to the poet in the third person, and the concluding sentence speaks of him in terms which would not have been employed if it had been wished to persuade the public that the tale was the work of the poet: —

"Lord Byron's character is worthy of his genius. To do good in secret, and shun the world's applause, is the surest testimony of a virtuous heart and self-approving conscience."

WILLIAM BATES.
Birmingham.

[The copy of *The Vampyre* we consulted has not only the name of Lord Byron printed on the title-page, but on the half-title preceding it. In every other respect it agrees with our correspondent's copy.—ED.]

Bishop Lindwood (3rd S. vii. 134, 266.)—I am now enabled to give the result of more close inquiry as to Bishop Lindwood's arms; and I must plead by way of excuse for any discrepancy between this and my previous letter, that I am writing without access to my own books or MSS. By the kindness of Sir F. Madden I have again examined his notes, and find my original statement to be accurate, that he had recorded Lindwood's arms as *a chevron* simply. His authority I am unable to give, but it is *not* the Bishop's Register, which only applies to the coat of Rodburn, the predecessor of Lindwood. My own note, *between three leaves,* is also without reference, but was made previous to the year 1858. No light is thrown upon Lindwood's arms by Browne Willis, but in his MS. collections in the Bodleian I find that the bishop in his will, dated Nov. 22, 1443, desires that he may be buried in St. Stephen's Chapel, Westminster, and leaves a legacy to his native parish of Linwood. I have been kindly furnished (by the rector) with a rubbing of the coat now remaining on the brass of John and Alice Lyndewode, at Linwood, and find it exactly in accordance with the description in the Lincoln Architectural Society's Report for 1862; *i. e.,* a chevron between three lime tree (or linden) leaves. Will your correspondent give me a reference to the edition and page of Guillim in which he finds the "fess crenellée between three fleur-de-lys," given as arms of Lindwood. I do not find it in any ordinary earlier than Edmondson.

W. K. RILAND BEDFORD.

"Roman Hand" (3rd S. vii. 338.) — Without being able to answer Y. X.'s query as to the "precise meaning" of this phrase, I would refer him to the earliest work in which I have met with it, Shakspeare's *Twelfth Night,* Act III. Sc. 4, where Malvolio says to Olivia, —

"I think we do know the sweet Roman Hand."

WM. DOBSON.
Preston.

DEMOSTHENES (2nd S. vi. 114.) — Thanking you for the reference you have been so kind as to give me, I would beg further to inquire whether the saying of Demosthenes, in which he is supposed to have spoken of action as the one thing necessary to make an orator, is to be found in the works of any Greek author who wrote before the time of Cicero. P. S. C.

CHARGES, AGAINST HUBERT DE BURGH (3rd S. vi. 415; vii. 385.)—Many thanks to MELETES for his kind information. I had already discovered the passage in the Additaments, and should have written to say so, had not press of business prevented me. A comparison of this passage with the testimony of the Chronicle of Dunstaple, leaves, I think, no doubt that Isabel *was* married to Hubert. HERMENTRUDE.

HERBERT KNOWLES (2nd S. viii. 28, 55, 79, 116, 153; ix. 94; x. 417.)—We find that he was admitted a sizar of St. John's College, Cambridge, Jan. 31, 1817. As he died on Feb. 17 following, he of course never resided in college.
C. H. & THOMPSON COOPER.
Cambridge.

LODOWICK BRYSKETT (2nd S. xii. 3.) — Some of your readers may be interested by being informed that this able writer was matriculated as a pensioner of Trinity College, Cambridge, May 27, 1559. He was living in 1611, and we propose to notice him in the third volume of *Athenæ Cantabrigiensis*. C. H. & THOMPSON COOPER.
Cambridge.

Miscellaneous.

NOTES ON BOOKS, ETC.

The Superstitions of Witchcraft. By Howard Williams, M.A. (Longman.)
The object of the present volume is "to exhibit a consecutive review of the characteristic forms, and facts of a creed which (if at present apparently dead, or at least harmless in Christendom,) in the seventeenth century was a living and lively faith, and caused thousands of victims to be sent to the torture-chamber, to the stake, and to the scaffold." The sketch—for it is a sketch only—is pleasantly written, and will furnish the thoughtful reader with matter for reflection and thankfulness. In these dull matter-of-fact days (in which the so-called Spiritualism forms the sole exception to the practical realistic tendency of all thought and action), it is difficult to conceive the influence which the belief in witchcraft formerly exercised over all classes of society. Those who desire to know how powerful this influence really was, will be pleasantly instructed by Mr. Williams's little volume.

Murray & Co.'s Book of Information for Railway Travellers and Railway Officials. Illustrated with Anecdotes, &c. By R. Bond. (Murray & Co.)
A little book full of practical and useful hints, which all intending railway travellers would do well to read at least; if not, to make the companion of their *Bradshaw*.

The History and Antiquities of the Parish of Wimbledon, Surrey; with Sketches of the Earlier Inhabitants. By William A. Bartlett, M.A., Senior Curate of Wimbledon. With Map and Illustrations. (Simpkin & Marshall.)
A pleasant little volume full of gossip of one of the prettiest spots in the neighbourhood of London. The inhabitants of Wimbledon owe their Senior Curate their best thanks for this judicious employment of his small leisure.

The Autographic Mirror. Parts XXIX., XXX., XXXI., and XXXII.
This cheap and instructive Collection of inedited Autographs of Illustrious and Distinguished Personages maintains its popularity and interest. The last two Parts (double Parts) contain facsimiles of some seventy Autographs of Sovereigns, Statesmen, Literati, Artists, Theatrical Celebrities, &c.

We see that Messrs. Sotheby announce for sale on Monday next and five following days, the curious Library of our late valued friend and Correspondent MR. MARKLAND. Many of the books are enriched with critical, bibliographical, and biographical notes by MR. MARKLAND. The same firm will also sell, in the course of the month of June, the Library of another gentleman, to whom the readers of "N. & Q." have been frequently indebted for much curious and valuable information — MR. GEORGE OFFOR. His Library is peculiarly rich in early editions of the Scriptures, the writings of the Reformers, and works of a similar character.

BOOKS AND ODD VOLUMES
WANTED TO PURCHASE.

STORIA DELLA GUERRA DELL' INDEPENDENZA DEGLI STATI UNITI D' AMERICA, by Carlo-Botta, 4 Vols, 8vo. Milano, 1819. In good condition.

*** Letters stating particulars and lowest price, carriage free, to be sent to MR. W. G. SMITH, Publisher of "NOTES & QUERIES," 32, Wellington Street, Strand, W.C.

Notices to Correspondents.

Among many other Papers of interest which are in type, and will appear in our next or the following number, are—
A Moral Satire by Daniel Defoe; A General Literary Index; Inedited Letter of Randle Cotgrave; Epitaphs Abroad; Notes from the Issue Rolls; The Search for the Lapis in 1863; Napoleon I. as Author and Student; Cotton's Editions of the English Bible; and many curious Shakspeare articles and Folk Lore Illustrations.
T. W. *The correct quotation from Rowe's* Fair Penitent *is —*
"Is this that gallant gay Lothario?"
K. (Conservative Club) *is probably referring to the case of Courvoisier, for whom Mr. Charles Phillips was counsel.*
TORCHLIGHT FUNERAL.—S. REDMOND and C. F. S. WARREN *are thankよd, but the query referred to a torchlight funeral in Westminster Abbey.*
P. Q. (Cowbridge) *is too political.*
ACHENDE. *The Hoax is unsuited for our columns.* Thanks for it.
A. C. *Where did the seal come from? The arms are "Three bendlets sinister surmounted by a bend," not any known English coat. It purports to be the seal of Bruer; but the general coat for Brewer is "gules, two bendlets wavy, or."*
J. G. C. (London). *Thomas Maynard was the last person executed for forgery, which took place at the Old Bailey on Dec. 31, 1829.*
E. L. (Bayswater). *For a list of works on the Grecian Oracles consult the article "Oracle" in Watt's Bibliotheca Britannica, Index of Subjects. Rees's Cyclopædia, and the Penny Cyclopædia, and the works cited in the latter. See also "N. & Q." 3rd S. ii. 419.*
H. L. (Macclesfield). *The inscription on the Legh family of Lyme is printed in Ormerod's Cheshire, iii. 367.*

A Reading Case for holding the weekly Nos. of "N. & Q." is now ready, and may be had of all Booksellers and Newsmen, price 1s. 6d.; or, free by post, direct from the publisher, for 1s. 8d.

"NOTES AND QUERIES" is published at noon on Friday, and is also issued in MONTHLY PARTS. The Subscription for STAMPED COPIES for Six Months forwarded direct from the Publisher (including the Half-yearly INDEX) is 11s. 4d., which may be paid by Post Office Order payable at the Strand Post Office, in favour of WILLIAM G. SMITH, 32, WELLINGTON STREET, STRAND, W.C., where also all COMMUNICATIONS FOR THE EDITOR should be addressed.

"NOTES & QUERIES" is registered for transmission abroad.

LONDON, SATURDAY, JUNE 3, 1865.

CONTENTS.—N° 179.

Notes.

A MORAL SATIRE, BY DANIEL DEFOE.

I duly placed to the credit of Defoe the compliments I received on account of his letter last published in "N. & Q." My manuscript of his hitherto unknown writings now fills many hundred pages of foolscap paper, and is increasing daily. I have no doubt the following Introductory Article, from *Applebee's Original Weekly Journal* of the 28th October, 1721, will be equally acceptable; and, if desired, I will afterwards send one or two articles containing my author's views on the Assassination of Rulers,—mournfully appropriate to the present time.*

"Mr. Applebee,—It is a long while ago that I wrote to you anything about Religion. I pray you, if it be in the Power of any of the Members of your Oracle, tell me what Religion are you Journal Writers of?

"I have heard it related, how true I know not, that when the Dutch Ships came to Japan, and the Merchants heard that the King of the Country had resolv'd to admit no Christians to Trade there, no not on pain of Death; they resolv'd, when the Question was ask'd them, not to say they were Christians, but to say they were Hollanders.

"Now, I think, when any Man asks, as above, what Religion you are of, that is, you of the Brotherhood, you should answer, not that you are Christians or Protestants, but that you are *Printers.*

"As St. James says, that out of the same Mouth comes Blessing and Cursing; so out of the same Printing House comes Prayers and Play Books, Bibles and Ballads; the same *Types*, or Letters, compose the Companion for the

[* Any communications illustrative of the life of Defoe will be acceptable.—ED.]

Altar, and a Companion for the Halter: One Day you print for King George, and another Day Treason against King George; one Day you print Devotion, and the next Day Blasphemy; one Day for the King, another for the Pretender; one Day for God, and the next Day for the Devil; and all is one to the Printer; he is a Printer still.

"Well, the Letters may be Tories, but the Press is always a Whig; for it lives by Liberty, and often times (like some Whigs too) it turns that Liberty into Licentiousness: Liberty of the Press may be the most needful Liberty, but it is the most abus'd Liberty in the World; and therefore it is that I argue, that you ought not to say you are of any Religion, but that you are *Printers*.

"And yet, after all, you may plead in your own Defence, that you have as much Religion as your Neighbours; for pray, if we come to argue upon the Square, let them tell us:—

"1. What Religion is a Bookseller? that sells you all you print, and puts the Money which he gets by Religious Books, or Blasphemous Books, Modest and Bawdy, Adorable and Horrible, all into one Pocket, and all the Men alive can't know the Shillings asunder.

"2. What Religion is a South Sea Director? who gives one Account in upon Oath, and swears 'tis true, *so help him God*; but when his Neck is ty'd to it, and he is to say, *May I be hang'd if it is not!* then gives another Oath, and another Account, perhaps double to the former?

"3. What Religion is a Statesman? who to-day serves one Prince, and to-morrow serves his Enemy; to-day swears to him, to-morrow fights against him; to-day wears his Badge, to-morrow affronts him: of such this Nation has had many. I do not say there have been any in this Age; and if there were, I am not talking about them!

"4. What Religion pray is a Modern Arian of? who prays to Christ Jesus, and denies him; worships him, and yet disowns his being a God; stands up at the Prayers, and sits down at the Doxology; stays in the church at the Psalm, but goes out at the *Gloria Patri!*

"Certainly these are Hereticks, they must not be call'd Christians: I could name you abundance of double-minded Christians of this kind, besides these; but, for the present, let these few serve, and when I can be inform'd what to call these People I may talk with you again.

"In a Word, Religion is so much lost among these Sorts of People, that if I were of their Council, they should be advised to talk no more of it in the World, or to separate it, at least, from all the rest of their Management, as a Thing they can as well do without; and thus, I think, I have made your Printers amends for enquiring after your Religion.

"There are some Exchange-Alley Men whose Religion it would be hard to determine; but as they belong to another Country, where that may be Honesty which is not Honesty in our Country; and where that may be Religion which is not Religion in our Church, I therefore leave them to be try'd by a Jury of Foreigners like themselves, and shall talk next Time to you of the Religion of another sort of Folks, who pretend to more Religion than other People, but really have as little as any Body: 'Tis a strange thing to say, but it is too evident, there are Hypocrites in Politicks as well as in Religion; and we see some of your Profession practising the Art of Daubing as well as other Painters; but of this more hereafter.

"I am, SIR, your Humble Servant,
                                       "SINCERITY."

I did not remark upon the beauties of the last letter forwarded. It is equally unnecessary to do so with the present, especially to the readers of "N. & Q."   W. LEE.

COTTON'S EDITIONS OF THE ENGLISH BIBLE.

May I be allowed to say a few words, though upon a subject which almost entirely concerns myself?

For some years past, many booksellers, when announcing in their sale-catalogues editions of the English Bible, Testament, or Psalms, have thought proper to add by way of recommendation, "unnoticed by Dr. Cotton," "unknown to Dr. Cotton." I am grateful for the compliment which these words convey; as implying that, if such a book is unknown to me, it must of necessity be rare. But I think that, in many cases, they are introduced in a way which is not quite fair either to me or to the public.

(?Within the last week I have received a catalogue, in which no fewer than *three* instances of this kind occur. One is, in the announcement of two editions of Sternhold's *Psalms* of the years 1735 and 1736, "neither mentioned by Dr. Cotton." The second, two other editions of *the same,* dated 1758 and 1763, "neither mentioned by Dr. Cotton." Now, to avoid the almost endless repetition of editions differing from each other in nothing except their *dates,* I gave the following notice under the year 1700 (*English Bibles,* p. 199) : —

"From this time no notice is taken of editions of Sternhold's version; which, soon after the appearance of that by Brady and Tate, became altered into the form and language in which it is printed to this day."

In vain, therefore, will anybody look in my work for notices of any edition of Sternhold printed in the eighteenth or nineteenth centuries.

The third case mentioned in that catalogue is a still more glaring instance of the compiler's misconception of my book, and consequent unintentional misleading of the public : —

"The Holy Bible [Authorised Version], &c., 4to, *Cambridge,* 1673. An edition of extreme rarity, not in Lea Wilson's Catalogue, nor is it described in any Bibliographical work. Dr. Cotton states that there was no edition in 1673," &c., &c.

But I had warned my readers [*English Bibles,* p. 60] at the year 1611 : —

"N.B. From this period, no editions of the Authorised Version are here noticed, *except for some peculiarity attached to any particular one.*"

So that when I say at the year 1673, "no edition," I do not mean to assert that no edition of *the Authorised Version* was printed in that year; but merely that, in 1852, when my book was published, I knew of no Bible, or part of the Bible, *or any other translation,* which might fairly find its place among those described by me.

I feel that this explanation is called for at my hands; and trust that it may be of service, both to booksellers and book-buyers. H. Cotton.

Thurles.

FOLK LORE.

A Modern Ballad.—The following modern "folk" ballad is the production of some Rossendale rhymester, whose name I am unable to furnish. The piece has peculiar significance in these days of Surat and short staples; and though little can be said in commendation of its language and rhythm, for it is rough and ready, yet I doubt not that it will come home to the heart of many a "Surat Weyvur." The composition is a great favourite amongst the old "Deyghn*.Layrocks," who sing it to one of their easy going psalm-tunes with much gusto.

If the piece affords half the amusement to the readers of "N. & Q." that it has to me, the space it will require might be less profitably occupied.

It has been named —

> "SURAT WARPS.
>
> "Come all ye Weyvurs old and young,
> It is to you I'll sing a song;
> And if I tell you my desire,
> You cannot say that I'm a liar.
>
> "I wish I had these Warpers, and
> All Sallywinders in a band,
> I'd make the whole of them to groan—
> I'd cudgel every one their bones.
>
> "Their knots when they come up to th' yealds,
> They sweep them down just like bumshells—
> They fly across the shed and breyk ;
> They sweep down all within their reyk.
>
> "I look at th' yealds, and there they stick,
> I ne'er seed th' like sin' I wur wick !
> What pity could befal a heart,
> To think about these hard sized warps.
>
> "'Twill make the Master for to stare
> To see his cloth so rough and bare,
> He turns it over, every plait,
> He turns it up, and cracks to bate.
>
> "So I mon at his table ston,
> And dare not stir one foot or hon ;
> To see him rip the piece to rags,
> Or give me the eternal bag !
>
> "Thus Weyvurs are brought in for all,
> Both cops, and bobbins, grease, and all ;
> Both Warpers, Winders, Spinners too,
> For all their faults they are put through.
>
> "Ah ! what a spot for Weyvurs here,
> It makes me shiver and go queer ;
> Yet for all this, I connod help :
> It makes me fit to hang myself !"

T. N.

Bacup, Rossendale.

Spitting.—A passage from Shakspeare's *Henry IV.* induces me to send this note. The commentators are quite at sea on the subject. In the Second Part of the play, Falstaff remarks to the Lord Chief Justice : —

"An' I brandish anything but a bottle, would I might never spit white again ! "

---

* Dean, in the forest of Rossendale.

Now in certain districts in the north, especially in the dales, not being able to spit white is looked upon as a sure sign of death: so that Falstaff, in effect says, " would I might never breathe more." Another curious tradition is, that every time one meets a white horse one must spit out in order to be lucky. This good old custom was well illustrated at a bazaar held recently in this neighbourhood; in which a young man, who happened to be very fortunate, attributed all his success to the rigid observance of it. A third, and I believe more widely practised superstition, is that all first receipts from your customers, when in business, must be turned over in the hand and spit upon, in order that the recipient may be fortunate.

J. WETHERELL.

THE WISE TREE. — I was talking to-day (April 29) with a Huntingdonshire cottager, and was saying how cold the day had been after our previous hot weather. " Yes," said my friend, " you mus'n't expect the summer to come all at once. The wise tree would have told you better than that. I was up agen the hall this morning, and saw those two wise trees that grow nigh to the fish-stews, and they had'nt put out a mossel o' show." " And what tree may the wise tree be ? " I asked. " It's what some folks call the mulberry," was the reply ; " but the wise tree is the name as I've always known it by ever since I was a child." " And why do you call it the wise tree ? " " Why, because it isn't silly like some trees as puts out their leaves early, and then gets nipped ; but the wise tree, on the contrairy, always waits till the frosses has gone right away, and aint to be deceived by a stroke o' fine weather coming early [in the season. But when it's sartin sure that it be fine weather and well settled, then it puts out its leaves. O yes, sir, you may rest content on the wise tree telling you when you may be safe against frosses."   CUTHBERT BEDE.

PROVERBS.—I send the two following for insertion, if you think proper : —
1. The marriage of first-cousins is said to prove "healthless, wealthless, or childless."
2. "Wine is the milk of old age."   M. D.

EASTER RHYME. — On Good Friday morning, when a light shower seemed likely to usher in a wet Easter-tide, I heard a peasant girl repeat the following rhyme, with which I was not previously acquainted : —
" If it rains on Good Friday and Easter Day,
There'll be plenty of grass, and a little good hay."
H. W. T.

RECIPE FOR THE CURE AND PREVENTION OF TOOTHACHE.—Pare your finger- and toe-nails, wrap the parings carefully up in a small piece of paper. Make a slit in the bark of an ash tree ; loosen the bark a little from the trunk, slip the small paper parcel under the bark, press the opening together again as closely as possible, and you will no more be troubled with tooth-ache !

The above is the recipe of an old Rossendale dame; who declares that, when a girl, being much troubled with the disease, she tried the experiment with the happiest effect—never since having known what it is to suffer a pang from this cause.

T. N. M

Bacup, Rossendale.

S. T. COLERIDGE.

I possess a small volume of Coleridge's MSS., formerly belonging to Mr. Cottle. It contains the printed sheets of " Religious Musings," and the " Ode to the Departing Year " (two copies), of the edition of 1796; and there are interleaves of plain paper, on which the poet has written voluminous notes and additions. A rather lengthy advertisement, prefixed I suppose to the edition of 1797, is here in MS.; and the first twenty-three lines of " Religious Musings " are also in MS. There is no title-page to the book, but there is an MS. index ; and the only other contents, besides the two poems above mentioned, are two series of printed notes, occupying forty-nine pages. Some of the leaves have been on the printer's file, which leads to the supposition that the book consists of corrected proofs bound together by Cottle for his own use ; but it is equally probable that the printed leaves, with the plain interleaves, were bound for the greater convenience of correction by Coleridge.

The fifth line of " Religious Musings ", reads thus in the collected edition : —
" Yet thou more bright than all the angel blaze."

In my MS. original, the word " blaze " has been struck out, and " Host," which seems a much better image, introduced.

Another line, altered for the worse, is the twenty-first of the same poem ; which, in the MS. of 1796, reads thus : —
" Imaged the unimaginable God.'

And in the collected edition has been frittered down to :—
" Imaged the supreme Beauty uncreate."

The paradox in the first reading forms, as in Ephesians 3rd and 19th, half its sublimity. A friend of mine humorously describes the last line as a sort of poetical crab-catching. This however, with all deference.

The lines, —
"   While as the Thousand Years
Lead up their mystic dance," &c., —
are accompanied by the following interesting note in MS. The note was probably included in the 1797 edition, but I will venture to transcribe it :—

"The Millenium: in which I suppose that man will continue to enjoy the highest glory of which his human nature is capable. That all who in past ages have endeavoured to ameliorate the state of man, will rise and enjoy the fruits and flowers, the imperceptible seeds of which they had sown in their former life: and that the wicked will during the same period be suffering the remedies adapted to their several bad habits. And I suppose that this period will be followed by the passing away of this earth, and by an entering on the state of pure intellect; when all creation shall rest from its labours."

The four lines in the collected edition, commencing —

" Ye sweep athwart my gaze, so heavenly bright,"—

read as follows in an MS. correction of the 1796 edition:—

" Ye sweep before me in as lovely hues
. As stream reflected from the veiling plumes
Of them, that aye before the jasper Throne
Adoring bend. Blest years ! ye too depart."

The correction was afterwards erased by a stroke of the pen.

In his directions to the printer, Coleridge seems to have shown considerable humour. For instance, in one place he has written : " Begin the page here ; it is absolutely cheating, to give such open print." And three times over on one page occurs this exclamation : " Good heavens ! what a gap !" On the blank page, in front of the Ode, he has written : " The motto ! where is the motto ? I would not have lost the motto for a kingdom ; 'twas the best part of the Ode." And again, in front of the second copy : " Motto ; I beseech you let the motto be printed, and printed accurately." The word "illumines," in the second strophe of the Ode, had been printed with an apostrophe, and the following note appears in the margin : —

" That villainous apostrophe belongs to the *genitive case of substantives* only. O that printers were wise ! O that they would read Bishop Lowth !"

In the last paragraph of the second epode (first copy), the line —

" Flap their lank pennons," &c.,—

was printed —

" Flap their *dark* pennons."

And Coleridge wrote beneath : —

" I suspect, almost suspect, that word 'dark' was *intentionally* substituted for 'lank.' If so, 'twas the most *tasteless* thing thou ever didst, dear Joseph ! "

In a note to the second copy, Cottle replied:—

" I cannot but think now, that you gave me direction to alter this, or I am unaccountably mistaken ; because I like 'lank' so much better than ' dark' myself."

G. COTTERELL.

Walsall.

MR. D'ALTON'S MS. COLLECTIONS.

Many years have now elapsed since I had the pleasure of seeing myself in print on the pages of your valuable periodical, but those years have so sensibly pressed upon me, that I have arrived at a resolution to break up my collection of MSS. Historical, Topographical, and Genealogical. They comprise —

Three volumes, Indexes, detailing references and trustworthy authorities for illustrating upwards of 2500 surnames of the British Empire.

Nine volumes, Indexes, furnishing similar references in aid of the history of all Irish Localities, Counties, Parishes, Cities, Castles, &c. &c.

One volume, thick octavo, affording directions to facilitate searches for Family Pedigrees, with a classification of the materials and authorities for the display of such through the various reigns of the English sovereigns, and during the Commonwealth. In it are likewise distinct classifications for the provincial pedigrees of Leinster, Ulster, Munster, and Connaught, as well as those of Scotland and Wales ; and, lastly, those of English descent through each respective county of England.

Nine volumes of Notes and Extracts from MSS. of rare access in England and Ireland.

Seventy volumes, Compilations of Annals, Records, &c., furnishing references to trustworthy authorities, chronologically set down for distinct histories of the several counties of Ireland.

One volume, octavo, Syllabus of selected pedigrees (160) wherein the origin of each of these families, their habitats, the periods when, and the places where, they severally existed are detailed.

Thirty-eight volumes, Notices of Families of Ireland, as well of the Native Septs as those of English Introduction.

One volume, folio, a full list of those outlawed for High Treason in Ireland, from 1640 to 1698, alphabetically arranged, and under four columnar subdivisions, headed respectively—1. Parties' Names; 2. Residences; 3. Dates of Outlawry ; 4. Places of ditto.

Twenty volumes, Miscellaneous Essays, Excursions in England, Wales, and Ireland.

Two volumes, Copies of Charters, Patents, &c. &c.

All the above manuscripts are open for inspection *here*, with a view to their immediate disposal.

JOHN D'ALTON.

48, Summer Hill, Dublin.

" WHO KILLED COCK ROBIN ? "

In the recent debate on Mr. Baines's Borough Franchise Bill, Mr. Disraeli alluded to Mr. Massey as the person who " killed Cock Robin " (the Reform Bill). This doubtless had reference to some impromptu lines written, it was understood, by an occasional correspondent of " N. & Q." From a copy which was immediately circulated in the body of the House, I made another copy, which I send you ; and perhaps you may think it worth a corner in " N. & Q."

" WHO KILLED THE REFORM BILL ?
A New Song to the tune of ' Cock Robin.'

" Who killed the Reform Bill ?
' I,' said Will Massey,
' For reform's now quite *passé*,
And I killed the Reform Bill.'

" Who helped to kill it ?
    'I,' said Mackinnon,
    'That boroughs may sin on ;
And I helped to kill it.'
" Who saw it die ?
    'I,' said Charles Wood ;
    'It did my heart good,
And I saw it die.'
" Who'll be chief mourner ?
    'I,' said Lord Pam,
    'Though my grief's all a flam ;
And I'll be chief mourner.'
" Who'll ring the bell?
    'I,' said John Bright,
    'While I cry out of spite,
And I'll ring the bell.'
" Who'll nail the coffin ?
    'I,' said Scotch Black,
    'Mon, I'll do't in a crack,
And I'll nail the coffin.'
" Who'll count the mourners ?
    'I,' said Hal Brand,
    'Just to keep in my hand,
And I'll count the mourners.'
" Who'll dig the grave ?
    'I,' said John Russell,
    'Though I'll have a hard tussle,
And I'll dig the grave.'
" Who'll write the epitaph ?
    'We,' say the members,
    ' " Peace to its embers,"
This be its epitaph.'
" Who'll draw a new bill ?
    Up spoke Edwin James,
    ' The next my clerk frames,
And he'll draw a new bill.' "
                                        A.

MIS-INFORMATION FOR THE PEOPLE. — An illustrated Almanac has just been published containing a number of such pieces of useful or useless knowledge as the following : —

" STABILITY OF THINGS IN ENGLAND.

" In one of his lectures, Mr. Emerson tells a story to
exemplify the stability of things in England. He says
that William of Wykeham, about the year 1050, endowed a house in the neighbourhood of Winchester, to
provide a measure of beer and a sufficiency of bread to
every one who asked it, for ever ; and when Mr. Emerson was in England, he was curious to test this good
man's credit ; and he knocked on the door, preferred his
request, received his measure of beer and quantum of
bread, though its owner had been dead 800 years."

" LEAP-YEAR.

" The ladies' leap-year privilege took its origin in the
following manner : By an ancient act of the Scottish Parliament, passed about the year 1228, it was ' ordonit that
during ye reign of her maist blessit Majestie Margaret,
ilka maiden ladee, of baith high and low estait, shall hae
liberty to speak ye man she likes. Gif he refuses to take
her to be his wife, he shall be mulct in the sum of an
hundrity pundis or less, as his estait may be, except and
always gif he can make it appear that he is betrothit to
anither woman, than he shall be free.' "

Now St. Cross, to which no doubt the writer
alludes, was not founded by Wykeham, but by

Henry de Blois, and that nearly 100 years later
than the date cited. Wykeham has not been dead
800 years, but about 450. Margaret of Scotland
reigned 1286-1290 : and the first Scottish Parliament was called at Scone by John Baliol, 1292.
I say nothing about the absurdity of supposing
such an act could be passed under any circumstances, but it certainly is to be regretted that
such statements should go forth to the world,
especially as a reference to books of very easy access would enable the author to verify or disprove
them.   A. A.
Poets' Corner.

A RELIC OF 1745.—Mr. Thomas Parker, an attorney of this town, has in his possession a cane
sword that belonged to his grandfather who was a
staunch royalist in 1745, and who used the weapon
in some skirmishes that took place about Preston,
in which locality Mr. Parker held considerable
landed property. He was a Roman Catholic,
and, contrary to the general proceedings of a numerous body of his co-religionists in the neighbourhood, he joined the royalist ranks, but was
most ungratefully treated subsequently. He lived
to be upwards of ninety years of age.
                                    S. REDMOND.
Liverpool.

WALLER THE POET. — None of the biographers
of Waller, I believe, has explained who the poet
intended to address in the letter which is found
prefixed to Mr. Robert Bell's edition. But in a
MS. of Waller's Poems, probably anterior to any
printed edition, I find this very letter with a
superscription : " To my Lady Sophia Bartie
[Bertie];" to which, in a different but cotemporary hand, is added : " yᵉ earle of Linsey's daughter." The text of the composition itself is much
more antiquated as to orthography than Mr.
Bell's. The subscription is — " Yoʳ Laᵖˢ most
humble seruant.   E. W."

But the most remarkable feature about the
present MS. is, that it contains an inedited Dedication to Queen Henrietta Maria at the commencement, before the Poems ; and at the conclusion of the said Dedication, there is the ensuing
memorandum : —   ·

" Thus I intended long since to haue presented to hir
Matᵉ those things which I had writtin of the King. But
besids that I held thame not worthie of hir, the Tymes
alsoe hath made this epistle vnseasonable."

The volume, which is a thin folio in the original
calf binding, excellently preserved, contains forty-
nine pieces, exclusively of the two dedications,
and of the translation of " Hero and Leander "
alluded to elsewhere.   W. CAREW HAZLITT.

MUSÆUS'S " HERO AND LEANDER." — It does
not appear to be known that the version of " Hero
and Leander " (from the Greek of Musæus, the
grammarian), which has come down to us from

the pens of Marlowe and Chapman, is only one of two which happen to have been preserved. In a MS., containing an early copy of Edmund Waller's *Poems*, supposed to be in his own hand-writing, with important variations, &c., from the printed editions, I find (but in a different hand) "A Translation out of the Greeke of Musæus by way of Paraphrase, by Mr. J. Jones." This gentleman was perhaps the same John Jones, of Hereford, a schoolmaster, who rendered into English Ovid's *Invective against Ibis*, 1658, 1667. Mr. Dyce, in his edition of Marlowe, 1850, was not aware, it may seem, that that writer and Chapman had a follower. It was one, I fear, of whom they had no great cause to be jealous. I give, however, the opening :—

    " Divine Calliope, doe mee that right,
      As but to giue the Taper light ;
      Let that immortall fire never fade
        Which was Leanders sun and shade ;
        Show how the water did obay
        The louely youth, and did convey
        Him to his hidden Loues that ne'er saw day.
        Tell Sistus, and Abidus tell,
        Where the faire Hero once did dwell,
         And where
       Leander and the torch I still doe heare."

                 W. CAREW HAZLITT.

LINES FROM THE PRESTWOLD REGISTER. — SIR THOMAS E. WINNINGTON's extract from the Droitwich parish register on p. 322, reminded me of some curious entries in the registers of Prestwold, Leicestershire, e. g. :—

"Matrimonee : a matter of money now-a-days."

"Deliberandum est diu quod statuendum est semel."

"Nescio quid sit amor, nec amo, nec amor, nec amavi,
  Sed scio quisquis amat tangitur igne gravi."

"Nascitur indignè per quem non nascitur alter ;
  Indignè et vivit, per quem non vivit et alter."

"Quod sibi quisque serit præsentis tempore vitæ,
  Hoc sibi messis erit, cum dicitur, Ite—Venite."

                   S. S. S.

VERSES BY ROGER NORTH. — In the Ellesmere copy of Chaucer's *Canterbury Tales*, which formerly belonged to Roger North, are the following verses, signed with his initials :—

        " DVRVM PATI.
" From Joue aboue a spendyng breath
Ys lent to vs to leade oure lyfe,
To lyue, to dye whan hatefull death
Shall rydd vs hense, and stynt oure stryfe.
My ynward mane to heauenly thyngs wold trade me,
And styll thys fleash doth euermore dyssuade me.
            " R. NORTH."

" Retaine, refuse, no frend, no foe
Condeme, alowe, no chance, no choice
Your fame, your life, shall end, shall growe
No badd, no good, shall pine, reioice
So helpe so hate, mistrust your frend
As blisfull daies your life may end.—R. N."

" Thes worldly ioies, that faier in sight apeares
Arr lvring baits, whereto oure minds we cast ;
Thrise blessed they that have repenting yeares
To hate their sinns, and leve their follies past ;
My inward mane, to hevenly things wold trade me,
But aye this flesh, doth still and still disswade me.
               " R. N."

" In triflieng tales, by poets told,
Whoe spends their time, and beats their braine,
And leves good bookes yt vertews hold,
Doth spare the strawe, and spoile the graine.
Sotch folke build vpp their howses in the sand
And leves godds trewth, by wh. we owght to stand.
             F. J. FURNIVALL.

DRYDEN'S "SIR MARTIN MAR-ALL" (Act V. Sc. 1.) :—

" *Warner.* There's nothing more distant than Wit and Folly ; yet, like East and West, they may meet in a point, and produce *actions that are but a hair's breadth from one another.*"

How much was the author of the "sublime to the ridiculous," if a modern, indebted to Sir Martin's serving man ?   J. A. G.

Queries.

HERALDIC QUERIES.

The monumental chantry of Sir John Speke (died A.D. 1518), near the eastern end of the north choir-aisle of Exeter Cathedral, is richly adorned with shields of arms and other heraldic insignia executed in relief. In their artistic character and treatment, these interesting examples are remarkable for their close resemblance to the armorial accessories and adornments of the chantry of Abbot Thomas Ramryge at St. Alban's. One of the shields in the Speke chantry bears, boldly carved : Three bars, between ten church-bells, four, three, two, and one. This shield is in excellent preservation, but it does not exhibit any traces of colour. Will any reader of "N. & Q." kindly inform me what are the tinctures of this shield, together with the name of the family or the individual whose arms it displays ?

The arms of Sir John Speke himself (an ancestor I believe of the Nile explorer) appear repeatedly in his chantry. They are : Argent, two bars azure, over all an eagle displayed with two heads gules. The bars in this shield are represented couped at their extremities, like the St. Alban's saltire of Abbot Ramryge. The shield of Sir John Speke is supported by two porcupines. A porcupine also appears at the feet of the good knight's effigy, and he bears the same animal passant as his crest.

In Burke's *Armory*, the arms of Speke, or Le Espek, of Devon and Somerset, are given as : "Barry of eight az. and arg., over all an eagle displayed with two heads gules." And for Speke of Cornwall : "Arg., three bars az., over all an eagle with two heads gules, armed or."

In the singularly beautiful and interesting heraldic chimney-piece of Bishop Courtenay (A.D. 1478—1487), now in the hall of the episcopal palace at Exeter, several badges are introduced with the shield of arms. The sickles and garbs of Hungerford and Peverel are there; and with them are associated the *tau-cross*, and this same tau-cross having depending from it a church-bell. By whom were these devices borne as badges?

In Exeter Cathedral, beneath the heads of two boldly carved crossed-legged effigies are large helms; and surmounting each of these helms is a ring erect, through which a flowing *contoise* is represented as having been drawn. Have any other examples of this early chivalrous distinction for the knightly helm been observed in monumental effigies in England?

Edmund Stafford, Bishop of Exeter (A.D. 1394—1419), bore the arms of his brother, the first Earl of Stafford, differenced by a bordure charged with mitres; and this shield appears repeatedly upon the fine monument to the bishop, and also elsewhere in his cathedral.

Henry le Despencer, Bishop of Norwich (A.D. 1370—1406), in like manner differenced the arms of Le Despencer with a bordure charged with mitres; and William Courtenay, Archbishop of Canterbury (A.D. 1381—1396), charged mitres upon his label. Some few other prelates, about the same period, introduced the mitre in other ways into the blazonry of their shields of arms. I beg to ask if any other examples of this episcopal bordure and label are known? Also, I shall be glad to hear of the existence of early examples of the arms of prelates, which bear the mitre as a charge.

The arms of the See of Exeter, as now borne by the Bishops of that see, are: Gules, a sword in pale proper, the hilt or, surmounting two keys in saltire gold. In Mr. King's *Handbook to the English Cathedrals*, published by Murray, it is stated (p. 198 of the notice of Exeter Cathedral) that "the arms of the see, as borne at present, were settled by Bishop Hugh Oldham," whose episcopate commenced in 1504, and ended in 1519. My query is, What evidence exists to show at what time, under what circumstances, and upon what heraldic principles, the arms of the See of Exeter were actually "settled"? I should also be thankful for information relative to the corresponding "settling" of the armorial insignia of other sees.

Mr. King adds, referring still to the arms of Exeter as he records them to have been "settled" by Bishop Oldham, that "earlier examples (of the arms of the same see) vary the position of the keys and sword." The keys in these arms, doubtless, are the ensigns which might have been expected to appear upon the shield of the see of St. Peter of Exeter. I am anxious to learn what led to the introduction of the sword into this same

shield. In various parts of the cathedral, the arms appear with the sword in pale interposed between the two keys, which are in saltire; or, the keys are addorsed and in bend, and the sword is interposed between them in bend sinister; or, the sword, surmounting a single key in bend sinister, forms a saltire; or, the two keys are in saltire, without any sword. In the early glass of the window at the easternmost end of the north aisle, the two keys appear addorsed and erect, their bows being interlaced. In like manner, two keys of precisely the same character are represented upon the right shoulder of the chesuble of Bishop Walter de Stapleton (A.D. 1306—1329), in his effigy. Upon the monument to Bishop Walter Bronscomb (A.D. 1258—1281), which was evidently constructed early in the fifteenth century, his effigy being of the period of his own decease, the arms of that prelate are blazoned as: Or, on a chevron sable, three quatrefoils gold, between two keys in chief and a sword in base all erect and of the second. Did Bishop Bronscomb take the keys and sword from his see, or did the see derive the sword from this bishop? In Bishop Oldham's own Chantry, the arms appear with the keys in saltire, and with the sword both in pale and in fesse.   CHARLES BOUTELL.

FROM THENCE *versus* FROM THERE.

Dr. Johnson says, that "*from thence* is a barbarous expression, implying the same as *thence*, yet wants not good authorities."

> "There plant eyes, all mist *from thence*
> Purge and disperse."—*Milton.*

He might, I think, have said, "all good authorities." It is an expression constantly made use of in the best written books of our language, as well as in our authorised version of the Bible, which is the work of different hands, and is acknowledged by all to be singularly free from grammatical error. Dr. Johnson also says: *From hence* is a vicious expression which crept into use even among good authorities, as the original force of the word *hence* was gradually forgotten." He here impliedly admits that the simple word *hence* wants force. Much more, then, does the word *thence* want it. It was doubtless for this reason that the proposition *from* is so constantly added to it for the sake of clearness as well as force.

With all due deference to so great an authority as Dr. J. is, there does not appear any reason why this word *from* may not be added in the present instance, as other words are oftentimes added for this sole purpose. Thus in John iii. 13, it is said: "No man hath ascended up to heaven, but he that came down from heaven." Will any one presume to say, that the word *up* is a barbarous addition because the simple word *ascended* implies the same thing? What rule of grammar is infringed by the addition of the word *up*, by way of giving force to the contrast between *ascending up*, and *coming down?* In Ephes. iv. 8—10 also, the word *up*, though not necessary to the sense, appears to be quite lawfully and most properly introduced. Unless, therefore, some other and better reason can be assigned for calling *from thence* a barbarous expression, than that the word *from* is not necessary, I do not see that any case is made out against it. At all events, the expression is so embedded in the whole English literature, and so universally used in colloquial talk, that like many other expressions which can hardly be explained upon the strict principles of grammar, it may justly be considered equally with them to be part and parcel of the English idiom. An attempt, however, has been made of late years to supersede this supposed barbarism by the new expression *from there*, for which the same excuses cannot be made, for it is neither idiomatic, nor is it analogous to our idiom, nor is the preposition *from* added to the adverb *there* to give force to it; but it is prefixed to it precisely in the same way as it is prefixed to a noun as an auxiliary to it, to denote its case. This, I believe, to be contrary to all the rules of general grammar, and that there is nothing like it in our own or in any other language. When a preposition is joined to a relative adverb, as in the case of *to where* or *from where*, the preposition does not govern it, for the expression is elliptical, and in full it would be " *to this or that place* where." This is quite a different thing from such expressions as *to there* or *from there*. There is a pretty large number of compound words, in which the words *there* and *here* are compounded with one or other of the whole complement of prepositions, as for instance, *thereabout, thereafter, thereat, thereby, therefore, therefrom*, &c. These are quite justifiable, for each of them is in reality one word, although it is compounded of two. Those persons, then, who fancy that they have invented a legitimate expression in the one, *from there*, which they think may supersede what they assume to be a barbarous one, should be prepared to maintain on the same grounds that a whole circle of expressions of a like kind are perfectly legitimate; and instead of the old expressions above named, if they will consistently carry out their own theories of language, they should be prepared to maintain that such expressions as *about there, after there, at there, by there, for there*, were as perfectly legitimate; and the genuine productions of the English language as that to which they have given birth—*from there*.

Man is a rational animal, who very soon acquires distinct ideas of the relative position of things, as well as in the course of time of other things, and hence arises his power of speech. There are no two ideas which a child sooner acquires, perhaps, than those of *here* and *there*. A very little child who can just run about says to his mother, I have lost my plaything, where is it? She answers, *There* it is at the other end of the room, and she points to the spot, or she says *Here* it is on my lap, or close by my feet. The child thus instinctively learns that *there* means at a distance from the speaker, and *here* close by him. *There* is always some particular point at a distance from the person to whom it refers, and *here* is always some particular spot near him. There seems, therefore, to be almost as much confusion of thought as there is of impropriety of speech in such expressions as *from there to there, from here to here*. What a strange jargon also would our language become if we could imagine such expressions to come into general use! Mr. A. came from Oxford to Torrington. Mr. B. meets him and says, " I did not know you were come *to here*. When did you go *from there?* I did not stop at Exeter, but went *through there* and came straight *to here*," &c. &c.

I have said that the expression *from thence* is constantly used in our Bible. Let me conclude this trivial discussion with one very serious quotation *from thence* : —

" And beside all this, between us and you there is a great gulph fixed : so that they which would pass *from hence* to you cannot ; neither can they pass to us, that would come *from thence*."—Luke xvi. 26.

Would this language, think you, be improved by simply saying *hence* and *thence?* or will the time ever come when our language will have undergone such a radical change, that in a new translation yet to be, our posterity will read it *from here—from there?*   C. E. P.

AMERICAN DRAMATISTS.—I would be obliged if any of your American readers could give me any account of two American dramatists, viz. : —

1. Robert W. Ewing, author of several dramas, published about forty years since : such as *The Highland Seer* ; *Quentin Durward, &c.* In Mr. Rees's *Dramatic Authors of America*, it is stated that " this gentleman is better known to the reading community as a theatrical critic, having established a reputation as a severe censor of the stage under the signature of 'Jacques' during the years 1825 and '26."

2. Manly B. Fowler, author of three plays: *The Prophecy* ; *Orlando* ; *Female Revenge*. Neither the date nor place of publication is given, but they were in existence *before* 1834.   R. I.

ANONYMOUS HYMNS.—I shall be very much indebted to any of your correspondents who will kindly inform me who are the authors or translators of the following hymns : —

· 1. All is o'er, the pain, the sorrow.
2. Before the ending of the day.
3. Christ will gather in His own.
[See *Lyra Germanica*, Second Series, 1858, p. 120, translated by Catherine Winkworth.]
4. For man the Saviour shed.
5. Forty days and forty nights.
6. In the hour of trial.
7. Jesu meek and gentle.
8. Jesu meek and lowly.
9. Let every heart exulting beat.
10. O come and mourn with me awhile.
[By Frederick Wm. Faber, D.D. See his *Hymns*, edit. 1842, p. 81.]
                                        CPL.

Who are authors of the following hymns, in *Hymns Ancient and Modern* ? —
1. Hymn 114. (Easter) Alleluia! Alleluia! Alleluia! The strife is o'er, the battle done.
2. Hymn 132. (Trinity Sunday.) All hail, adored Trinity.
3. Hymn 152. Jesu, meek and lowly.
4. Hymn 189. Jesu, meek and gentle.
5. Hymn 258. Disposer Supreme, and Judge of the earth.
6. Hymn 273. For thy dear saint, O Lord.
[By Isaac Williams, a translation.]
                                        R. I.

AUTHOR WANTED. — Who was the compiler of " *A New Complete English Dictionary*, containing a brief and clear Explication of most words in the English Language," Edinburgh, printed by David Paterson, 2nd edition, 1770 ? It seems to contain an answer to Col. George Greenwood's question, in the *Athenæum* of the 11th of March last : " Can any *dictionary* be shown, where 'to shed' means 'to divide' ? " Here we have " *To shed*, to separate."
                                        ST. TH.

COLD KITCHEN : GREAT DOODS. — On recently looking over the map of Surrey, I was struck by the name of a place I never heard of before, "Cold Kitchen," and which is situated near Leith Hill. Has this name any connection with that of "Cold Harbour," about which so much has been said in " N. & Q." ? I see there is also a "Cold Harbour" not far off. Another query I would put is as to the meaning of "Great Doods," the name of an estate at Reigate. The residence, apparently of the time of Anne, is close to the old church, the grounds containing some exceedingly fine trees, among others a tulip tree of very large growth.   PHILIP S. KING.

EUDOSIA COMNENA.—May I ask RHODOCANAKIS whether there is any authority for giving Theodore Palæologus, buried at Landulph, a first wife, Eudosia Comnena ? and how is it to be accounted for that this marriage and its offspring are not mentioned on the tombstone, when the second English marriage and offspring are so mentioned ?
                                    CHARLES F. S. WARREN.
C. College, Cambridge.

GENERAL DE MALET. Wanted, the name and volume of a periodical containing a portrait of General de Malet, who conspired against the first Napoleon. I remember that, in the same volume, there is a portrait of Vice-Chancellor Wigram.
                                        C. M. Q.

DONNE'S POEMS.—Several of these are addressed to his friends, whose initials only are given. Of these, doubtless, " C. B." and " S. B." are Christopher and Samuel Brook ; and " R. W." Rowland Woodward, " M. H." Magdalen Herbert. But can any of your readers identify " I. W.," " T. W.," " B. B.," " I. L.," and " I. P." (Donne's *Poems*, pp. 175—186, ed. 1635) ?   CPL.

"FRAY GERUNDIO." — In the English translation of Padre Isla's *Fray Gerundio*, published in the year 1772, the translator in the advertisement says, that—
"The Council of Castile suppressed the first volume," and that "the Father had a second volume ready, but the prohibition of the first put a stop to the publication of the second."—" The father presented his only copy of the second volume, partly written by an amanuensis and partly with his own hand, to the gentleman who gives this account, and who was pleased very obligingly to lend it to the translator."

It would thus appear that the MS. of the second volume was in the hands of some one in England about the year 1772.

When in Spain lately, I by chance at an obscure shop purchased a volume in MS. called *Historia del famoso Predicador Fray Gerundio de Campazas*, *&c.*, and one from which most probably the Spanish edition of the first volume was printed, as the dedicatory and complimentary epistles are dated in October, 1757 (the first Spanish edition was published in 1758). I am anxious to compare my MS. copy of the first volume with that second above alluded to—the more so, as the description of the second volume tallies with that of the first in my possession, mine being written partly in the clerkly hand of an amanuensis, but the greater portion in another hand, most probably that of Padre Isla ; but a comparison would settle that point. I therefore reluctantly ask for space for this communication, hoping that the owner of the MS. of volume the second may see it. F. W. C.
Clapham Park.

GALLOWS INSCRIPTION.—
    " Cresce diu, felix arbor, semperque vireto
        Frondibus, ut nobis talia poma feras."
The above couplet is said to have been inscribed upon a gallows in Scotland, on the occasion of the execution of some remarkable criminal. I should be glad to know the name of the executed person; also in what part of Scotland this occurrence took place ?   H. A. KENNEDY.

GENEALOGICAL QUERIES.—Wanted information respecting the families of Swan, living at Great

Coxwell, Berks, 1778; families of Morgan, Powell, Popkin, and Howell, living in Glamorganshire a few years anterior to the date. Also, particulars of the family of Wicks, living at Farringdon in 1800. Information to be addressed to "H. A. B., Mr. Roberts's, Stationer, Seymour Street, Saint Pancras, N.W."

CAPT. HAVILAND'S "CAVALRY."—I am anxious to find a work on "Cavalry," by Capt. Haviland, late Queen's Bays, 2nd Dragoon Guards. I believe it to have been published from fifteen to twenty years since. I cannot find it in the British Museum, nor at the library of the Royal United Service Institution. Can any of your correspondents inform me if, or where, a copy can be seen for reference, or purchased? W. R. L.

THE REV. GEORGE ITCHENER, of St. John's College, Oxford, B.C.L., Dec. 15, 1738, became vicar of Great Baddow, Essex, 1741-2, and published *Elegiac Tears* (a poetical translation of the Rev. J. D. Cotton's *Lachrymæ Elegiacæ*), Chelmsford, 4to, 1766. Information respecting him, especially the date of his decease, will oblige. S. Y. R.

JUBILEES OF THE ROMAN CATHOLIC CHURCH. Where shall I find a list of the jubilees that have been held by the Roman Catholic church? The first was proclaimed by Pope Boniface VIII. in 1299, the last by the present pope in 1854. On their first institution they were ordered to be celebrated once in a century, but in more recent days they have been held at much shorter intervals. A. O. V. P.

NEW STYLE.—The Act of Parliament, directing that the year should begin on the 1st of January, instead of on the 25th of March, was passed in 1751, and came into operation in 1752. Did any considerable section of the population anticipate the action of Parliament in this matter, &c., commence their year of account, &c., before the passing of the act in question? I have before me the diary of a Nonconformist minister, who appended to the entry for Dec. 31, 1729, the words: "Thus ended ye year 1729," &c. He then writes, "Diary for ye year, 1730," &c., &c.; "Begun on January the first, 1730." WM. DOBSON.
Preston.

THE OSTRICH FEATHER BADGE.—In the clerestory of the choir of Exeter Cathedral, in the head of the fifth window from the east, I lately observed an early example of the group of three white ostrich feathers, now the badge of the Prince of Wales. These feathers are charged upon a shield, the field of which is tinctured per pale azure and gules. They all stand erect, and are grouped together by a scroll bearing the motto *Ich Dien*, but there is no coronet. The tips of these feathers bend over slightly towards

the spectator, the tips of the two side feathers also inclining severally to the dexter and the sinister. I shall be very glad to see other early examples of this most interesting badge described in "N. & Q." Does any contributor remember any example of the three feathers encircled with the Garter of the Order, in addition to the one in the vaulting of the ascent to the Hall of Christchurch at Oxford? CHARLES BOUTELL.

THE ROMANCE OF "FLORICE AND BLANCHE-FLOUR."—I have been looking at the copy of *Floris and Blauncheflur* in the Cambridge University Library. There are apparently four known English texts of the poem, which all have different spellings of the two names, and none of them seem to be perfect copies. 1. The Cotton MS. Vitellius, D. III., nearly destroyed in the fire. 2. The Cambridge MS., Gg, 4, 27, 2, imperfect at the beginning. 3. The Auchinlech MS., in the Advocates' Library at Edinburgh, printed by David Laing for the Abbotsford Club, imperfect at the beginning, almost at the same point as the Cambridge University MS. 4. The Bridgewater MS. The Cambridge and Edinburgh MSS. seem to me different translations from the same original. What portion is wanting at the beginning? Where is a French original to be seen? I don't, of course, mean merely a French Romance of that name, but a copy of the French text of the story from which our English versions appear really to be derived. What portions, exactly, still remain in the Cotton MS.? What portion, exactly, remains of the Bridgewater MS.? To which version do the Cotton and Bridgewater copies bear respectively the most resemblance? Can any reader give me an answer to any of these queries? H. B.

ST. AUGUSTINE AND THE MYSTERY OF THE BLESSED TRINITY. — Where is to be found full, and where the original account of the following, which I extract from Dr. Stanley's *Sermons in the East?*

"He [St. Augustine] is most generally represented with a child or infant Jesus by his side, holding a shell or spoon, and sometimes filling a hole with water from it. This is an allusion to a vision which he himself relates as occurring to him. While he was walking one day on the seashore, meditating on the mystery of the Blessed Trinity, he saw a child filling a hole in the sand with water baled out of the sea in a shell. In answer to an enquiry from the Saint, the child replied, 'I wish to empty the sea into this hole;' and, as the Saint said, 'Child, it is impossible,' he answered, 'Not more impossible than to comprehend what you are now meditating upon,' and immediately vanished."

H. C.

"A SHORT HISTORY OF IRELAND." — To whom are we indebted for *A Short History of Ireland*, which was published anonymously in London, 1843? ABHBA.

TRINITY COLLEGE, DUBLIN.—Are the following documents printed? And if so, a reference to them will oblige.

A.D. 1591. The *First* Speech of Adam Loftus, Archbishop of Dublin, and Lord Chancellor to y* Mayor of Dublin, &c., to persuade them to Grant Land whereon to erect Trinity College.—The *Second* Speech of Archbishop Loftus on same subject.

Warrant for the foundation of Trinity College, and for granting the Termon Lands of Monaghan to Undertakers (A° 34 Elizabeth).

Patent of Queen Elizabeth: Pro fundando Collegium Sanctæ et Individuæ Trinitatis juxta Dublin. (R. C. H. 34 Eliz., Irrot. 37 Eliz.).

Concordatum for paying 40^lb a-year to the College of Dublin. (A° 42 Eliz.)

AIKEN IRVINE.

Kilbride, Bray.

WORDSWORTH.— Can any one tell me where the following quotation from the poet is to be found? I think perhaps in some letter to the Quillinans or Southey. It is not to be found in the last Edition of Wordsworth's *Works* : —

> " A gleam of sunshine, 'mid the hills,
> All islanded with shadow.
> A cowslip nodding, all alone,
> Upon a lake-side meadow.
> These tell of solitude indeed,
> But solitude and pleasant.
> They bring full many a gentle thought,
> To many a passing peasant."

I cannot help thinking there must be some error in the reduplication of the word "many."

WALTER THORNBURY.

JAS. WALLACE of Christ's College, Cambridge, published *Shakspearian Sketches*, 1795. Are these sketches poems, dramas, or literary essays? The volume appears to be somewhat scarce. I have noted the author as being the Rev. Jas. Wallace, of Christ's College (who died in 1829 ?). R. H.

JOHN YORKE, of the Yorke family of Erddig, co. Denbigh, was living in London in 1709. Any particulars as to his descendants would greatly oblige. CARILFORD.

Cape Town, S. A.

Queries with Answers.

MARKET HARBOROUGH.—I shall feel obliged if you can give me some account of the early history of Market Harborough, in Leicestershire, and the origin of the name. CLARICE.

[It has been conjectured, that as this town, in the ancient record of Testa de Nevil, is called *Haverburg*, from *Haver*, a term still used in the northern counties to signify oats, and *berg*, a hill, that the name was afterwards converted into Haverbrowe and Harborough. That ingenious antiquary, the late John Cade, Esq., of Gainford, Durham, however, deduces the name of Harborough from a Roman road, which he calls Hare-street, on which it stands. He says, " I purposed publishing some further

observations on the old Ryknild-street and Hare-street roads, whence your Harborough derives its name, but my infirmities will not permit." Harborough is a very great thoroughfare town, and as early as the time of King Edward III. 1327, obtained the liberty of holding a *market* twice a-week, on Wednesdays and Saturdays. For the early history of this town, our correspondent may consult Nichols's *Leicestershire*, vol. ii. pt. II. pp. 486 to 508 ; and Harrod's *History of Market Harborough*, 8vo, 1808.]

DUCHESS OF QUEENSBERRY.—I shall feel obliged to any of your readers that will tell me who was the author of the lines on the celebrated Duchess of Queensberry, the friend of Pope and Gay, descriptive of her appearance when far advanced in life, and where they are to be found ? If in Scott's edition of Swift, in what volume ? C. M. Q.

[One of the last and most elegant compliments which the Duchess of Queensberry received was from the amiable William Whitehead (*Works*, iii. 65), and which is probably the one inquired after by our correspondent. The duchess was of great age when this compliment was paid to her, which was singularly well adapted, as her Grace never changed her dress according to the fashion, but retained that which had been in vogue when she was a young beauty. The little poem thus commences : —

> " Say, shall a bard in these late times
> Dare to address his trivial rhymes
> To her, whom Prior, Pope, and Gay,
> And every bard, who breath'd a lay
> Of happier vein, was fond to choose
> The patroness of every Muse," &c.]

SALT'S SALE. — I shall be much obliged if any correspondent of " N. & Q.," having a priced Catalogue of Salt's sale (June, 1835,) of Egyptian antiquities, will inform me to whom and at what price the following lots were sold : 296, a tablet ; 81 and 82, vases ; 552, a vase ; 248, a lachrymatory. JOHN DAVIDSON.

[The highly interesting collection of Egyptian antiquities, the property of the late Henry Salt, Esq., consul-general in Egypt, was disposed of by Messrs. Sotheby & Son. The sale continued nine days, and produced 7,168*l*. 18*s*. 6*d*. The trustees of the British Museum laudably laid out above 4,500*l*. at this sale. The Catalogue, with the prices and the articles purchased by the British Museum denoted by an asterisk, is printed at the end of Giovanni D'Athanasi's *Brief Account of Researches in Egypt*, 8vo, Lond. 1836. Lot 296 was purchased by Blanshard, 1*l*. 4*s*. Lot 81 by Ewbank, 2*l*. 18*s*. Lot 82 by Hay, 1*l*. 10*s*. Lot 552 by Lord Mountmorres, 2*l*. 8*s*., and Lot 248, by Mr. Cureton, for the British Museum, 1*l*.]

TOISON D'OR.—I should be greatly obliged to any correspondent who would kindly refer to the splendid manuscript of the Chevaliers de la Toison d'Or. (Harl. MS. 6199.) I wish to know who are the first and last knights whose names, &c., are recorded in it. The last knight in my copy, of qu

Chifflet's *Insignia Gentilitia Equitum Velleris Aurei* (Antwerp, 1632), is No. CCCLXVIII. Count Esterhazy-Galantha. Was any later edition, or continuation, of Chifflet ever published?

J. WOODWARD.

[The first name recorded in the Harl. MS. is Messire Guillaume de Vienne, Seigneur de St. George et de St. Croix, and the last Messire Philippe d'Austrice, Conte de Charolois. The only edition of Chifflet's *Insignia* is that of 1632.]

HINGHAM BOXES.—What does Oliver Wendell Holmes mean by saying:—

"I am simply an outsider you know; only it does not do very well for a nest of Hingham boxes to talk too much about outsiders and insiders."—*The Professor at the Breakfast Table*, p. 261.

What are Hingham boxes? Some Bostonian reader may tell.   ERINENSIS.

[Hingham is a post village of Plymouth County, Mass., on the south side of Massachusetts's Bay, and on the South Shore railroad, seventeen miles S.S.W. from Boston. It is a favourite summer resort, and several packets communicate regularly with Boston, and a steam-boat daily in the summer season. The allusion is possibly to some vehicle of conveyance between Hingham and Boston.]

LATIN BIBLE.—Will you inform me the value of a Breeches Bible, in Latin, dated 1585?

SUBLIGACULUM.

[The Bible designated by our correspondent "a Breeches Bible, in Latin," is probably the version by Francis Junius and Immanuel Tremellius, the third London edition of 1585, 4to, in which the passage of Gen. iii. 7, is translated "consutisquè foliis ficus fecerunt sibi subligacula." The Duke of Sussex's copy, in excellent condition, and bound in russia, fetched 14s.]

Replies.

EPITAPHS ABROAD.

(3rd S. vii. 129.)

EPITAPHS IN THE ENGLISH COLLEGE AT ROME.

The same Rawlinson MS. which contains the epitaphs at Paris, printed pp. 129-131 of the present volume, contains also transcripts of the memorial inscriptions in the English, Scotch, and Irish colleges at Rome. Those copied from the English college amount to forty-one; and that most of these no longer exist *in situ* may be concluded from the fact, that only *four* of them are printed in a "Paper of Extracts from the Records of the College," by W. C. Trevelyan, printed in vol. v. of Nichols's *Collectanea Topographica*, p. 87, where also these four are only stated to have been in existence in 1785; and are prin ed from a copy which was in the possession of Cardinal Wiseman in 1836. Probably many of the inscriptions were

destroyed when the church of the college was desecrated by the French revolutionary army during their occupation of Rome in 1798.

Inscriptiones Sepulchrales in Capella Collegii Anglicani Romæ, ab ipsis Monumentis et saxis sepulchralibus erutæ, diebus 14 et 15 Jan., N.S., 3 et 4 V.S. M.D.CC.XXI.

On a marble in the north wall:—

"Decreto S. Congregationis visitationis Apostolicæ, edito de [die?] xxix Maii MDCLXIV. Oratorium S. Edmundi regis Angliæ, trans Tyberim olim positum, suppressum fuit, et obligatio illic celebrandi missas ad summum hujus templi altare translatum, aliis omnibus in pristino suo vigore juxta mentem S. M. Gregorii XIII. permanentibus."

In the chappell of our Lady on the south side of the altar.

On a white marble bearing the effigies of a bishop, in his pontificalibus, and under his feet this inscription in capitals:—

"Joanni Gilio, Lucen. Vigornien epō, ju. utr. consul, consumatæ virtutis viro, ser. Henrici VII. Angl. Regis apud Pont. Oratori, Silvester, regia liberalitate dignitatis successor, patrueli B.M. posuit. Obiit An. Sal. MCCCCIIC, mens. Aug. ætatis vero suæ lxiiii."

On a small white marble grave-stone near, in capitals, is this inscription:—

"D. O. M.
Dᵒ Richardo Haddoco Anglo, Sæ
Theologiæ doctori, qui Elisa-
betha Angliæ Regina Catholic-
os persequente, multorum annorum exilium pietatis causa sus-
tinuit, fratrem præclaro martyrio coronari vidit ac demum Romæ sancte pieque obiit, xiii
Julii, anno Dñi. MDCV.
Curatores posuerunt."

Under another gravestone bearing a person cutt thereon in a religious habit, in capitals, is this following inscription:—

"Ne moriare (*sic*) Britañe, precor, neve omina credas
Cum vidias (*sic*) civis tam procul ossa tui.
Sic felix (*sic*: felix) meliorque mei pars reddita cælo est,
Quod mortale fuit maxima Roma tenet.
Die xxxi. Jenuari (*sic*) M.DXVII.
Epitaphium D. T. Colmañi."

On the wall, on a small white marble tablet bearing the cutt effigies of a woman, with books and beads in her hands, on her knees, and the Virgin and our Saviour at a distance as in Heaven, and in capitals, is this inscription:—

"D. O. M.
Margeriæ Kibli Angliæ
Depositum.
Obiit prid. April, an. MDXLVIII."

On another white marble, under a person in a priest's habit, in capitals, is this inscription:—

"D. O. M.
Religioso viro d. Jo. Weddisburi, priori de Worce-
stur qui dum pia divi Jacobi ac Ltorum Pe. et Pauli
limia, Dñcum sepulcrum visurus, attigisset, anno æta-
tis suæ L. decessit.
R. P. Sil. eps Wigornien.
Apud Leo X. Pont. ærmi
Regis Angliæ Or, uti religime fŕ1
posuit xxiii. Agusti (*sic*)
M.D.XVIII."

On another white marble gravestone, in capitals, is this
following inscription :—

" D. O. M.
D. Thomæ Pordage,
armigero Anglo,
Cantiano.
Pie obiit xvi. Feb.
Anno M.D.CXCIX.
Requiescat in pace.
Carolus Hill amicissimus
posuit."

On a small gravestone, under a cross fleury in capitals,
is this inscription :—

" Religioso
Thome Cap°
P'dicti Póris."

On another white marble gravestone, in capitals, is the
following inscription : —

" D. O. M.
Gulielmo Gressopo, presby-
tero Anglo, doctrina singulari, vita, mori-
busque integerrimo
octo annis ob fi-
dem Catholicam pa-
tria exulanti,
Thomas Kirtonus Anglus amico
amantissimo posuit.
Vixit annis xxxiiii,
diebus xxi. obiit
MDLXIX.

On another white marble gravestone, in capitals, is this
inscription following :—

" D. O. M.
Katharinæ Weston
Comitis Portlandiæ Magni Angliæ
Thesaurarii filiæ, singulari pietate,
integritate, modestia præditæ,
quæ fidei Catholicæ causa Angliam
deserens cum viro et familia, tandem
Romam venit, ad post varias triennio
placidissime toleratas ærumnas, relictis
octo liberis, ad meliorem vitam abiit,
II. Cal. Nov. anni M.DCXLV, ætatis suæ xxxiix.
Richardus White, ex Albiorum Essexien.
antiqua stirpe, conjugi amantiss. posuit."

This lady was buried in the church of S. Maria ad
Nives, as I find in pag. iii. of Hobbes's Lyricks.

On another white marble, under a person in a priest's
habit, in capitals, is this inscription :—

" Hic jacet R. Pater
Guilelm. Shirwood,
decanus de Acland,
Dunelmensis dioce-
sis, qui obiit xi.
Octobris, anno
M.CCCC.XCVII."

On another white marble, in capitals, is this inscription :—

" Dominus Nicolaus
Saxton,
Theologie
Bacularius, (sic) Eora-
ceñ. diocesis a° M°
opocur iii Octobris."

On another under a cross fleury, in capitals, is this following inscription :—

" Depositus Johannis Gam,
sacerdotis Anglici, artium

medicinarumque interpretis
qui xxix Augusti
MDVII mundo mortuus,
cum Xr̃o vivat. Amen."

On a small white marble gravestone, in capitals, is the
following inscription : —

" D. O. M.
Georgio Whito, nobili
opt. spei adoles-
centi, Stephani (sic) frater
chariss. ponendum cu-
ravit. Obiit idibus Ju-
nii MDLV."

On another, under a person in a priest's habit in capitals, is this inscription :—

+ Hic jacet Pater
Thomas Cabold,
utriusque juris doct-
or, Papæ penitentiarii,
Norvicensis dio-
cesis, qui obiit die xx
Julii, 1502."

On another white marble gravestone, in capitals, is the
following inscription : —

" D. O. M.
Thomæ Kyrtono, Anglo, hujus
Xenodochii capellano, viro in fide
orthodoxa constanti, vitæ et
morum integritate conspicuo,
solertia et studio gratificandi
parato. Patriæ hereses
detestans Romam properavit.
ubi post novennium, febri occul.i
correptus, naturæ cessit,
annum agens xL.
Obiit viii. id. Aprilis,
MDLXXI.
Hunc locum vivens sibi delegit,
cujus voluntati amici curatores
ex testamento satisfecerunt,
Nicol° Mortonus, Gul. Gibletus,
Robertus Talcarnus."

On another white marble gravestone is this inscription :—

" Thomæ Knyght, monacho or.
S. Bene, et sacristæ ecclië
Cathedralis Scti Suythuni
Wynten., doctrina, moribus,
et omnium (sic) virtute prædito,
ejusdem Or. et Ecclië Prior
bene merenti
posuit
qui innocentissime de se
posteris suis desiderio
relicto, nemini molestus,
obiit M.CCCC.IC."

On a small white marble monument fixed to a pillar, in
capitals, is this inscription :—

" D. O. M.
D. Rogero Bainesio, nobili Anglo,
qui, anno MDXLVI. natus, patriam,
regnante cum Elizabetha
hæresi, deserens, Romam venit,
ubi a morte ill. Card. Alani cui
a secretis fuerat, privatam vitam
Deo, sibi et communi calamitosæ
patriæ bono agens,
cum xLIV in urbe explesset annos,
obdormivit in Domino,

vii. id. Octobris, An. Sal. MDCXXIII.
Ætatis suæ LXXVII, mens. VI.
Ex testamento centum montium
loca in pios usus reliquit, prout
ex actis D. Michælis Angeli Cesii,
notarii, constat."

On a white marble gravestone, in capitals, is this inscription : —

"Hoc tumulo corpus ve-
nlis viri magri Thomæ Pur-
veour,* Sacre Theologie
Professoris, ac Londonien.
Wellen. eccārum canonici et
minoris in basilica Principis
Aplorum de urbe S. D. N. PPe.
Obiit die v Octobris An. D. MCCCCLXVIIII, Roma."

On a white marble gravestone, under a person in a priest's habit, in capitals, is this inscription : —

"Hic jacet Thomas
Metcale, sacre pagine
doctor, Ebor. dioc. qui
obiit 26 Noveb. 1503."

On another small white marble gravestone, in capitals, is this following inscription : —

"Hic jacet frater Guliel*
Bacheler Anglicus, Prior
domus Charmelitarum,
Londini, vir singularis
probitatis et modestie, qui
obiit in hoc Hospᵗⁱˢ die XXX
mensis Julii, A.D. MDXV, cujus
aīe propicietur Deus."

On a small marble gravestone, in capitals : —

"D. O. M.
D. Rogerio Bainesio,
diocesis Covent.ᵈⁱˢ
M.D.CXXIII."

On another, above a cross fleury in the body, in capitals, is this following inscription : —

"D. O. M.
D. Henrico Story, Ang-
lico Pbrō, hujus Hos-
pitalis sacristano, qui
obiit anno MDXVIIII.
XXII. Julii, etatis sue
anno LVIII."

"On another white marble gravestone, in capitals, is this inscription following : —

"D. O. M.
Hic jacet
Joannes Wilfridus,
Anglus, Collegii Gregoriani
de Urbe
Ordinis S. Benedicti abbas.
Obiit pridie Kal. Junii,
A.S. MDCLIX. ætatis suæ LX."

(*To be continued.*)

W. D. MACRAY.

---

* Proctor at Oxford in 1460.

HUDIBRASTIC COUPLET.

(3rᵈ S. iv. p. 61.)

The famed couplet —

"For he who fights and runs away,
May live to fight another day,"—

which caused the wits of Brooks's Club, in 1784, to wrangle over their wine and to bet about its authorship, in consequence dooming Dodsley to a night's vain search through *Hudibras*, where, when called upon as arbiter, he had incautiously asserted that "every fool" knew it to be; and since that time, has given rise to the spending of much ink and paper in various magazines, as well as in many numbers of "N. & Q."— was by MR. YEOWELL, in the article referred to, confidently fathered upon Oliver Goldsmith; who is therein said to have "unwittingly penned these celebrated lines — the authorship of which, for eighty long years, has baffled the researches and puzzled the ingenuity of the whole literary brotherhood." The book in which they are stated to have *first* appeared being *The Art of Poetry on a New Plan,* published by Newbery in 1762. By that article of July, 1863, doubtless, many searchers have considered the question as finally settled; just as the writer there states that, since the publication of Lowndes' *Bibliographer's Manual* in 1834, "our literary antiquaries had comfortably consoled themselves with the idea that the lines appear in the *Musarum Deliciæ,* and that Sir John Dennis was the author of them." A statement repeated in the new edition of Lowndes. But that certainty of *first* appearance, or of authorship, was not arrived at in that article, is proved by the following accidental discovery made by me in a bookseller's shop, when turning over the leaves of Ray's *History of the Rebellion,* printed at Bristol in 1752; at p. 48, occur these lines : —

"He that fights and runs away,
May turn and fight another day :
But he that is in battle slain,
Will never rise to fight again."

Here then, *ten* years earlier than the first edition of Newbery's publication, we find the sentiment (itself as old as Demosthenes) expressed in *four* lines almost, but not quite, identical with those given in Newbery's book, which are :

"For he who fights and runs away,
May live to fight another day :
But he who is in battle slain,
Can never rise and fight again."

I do not pretend to decide upon their authorship; but it may be well to remark that, as Goldsmith did not arrive in London until 1756 — four years after the date of Ray's book — the improbability of his having been the *author* is very great.

Whether Ray, quoting the sentiment from *Hudibras,* unconsciously or purposely altered the words — or whether these words, or others nearly the same, occupy four lines in any unknown edition of *Hudibras*, or exist in some forgotten book—yet remains a query. Thinking this note may be interesting to your readers, as showing an earlier occurrence of the lines than any recorded in your pages, I add the full title of the book : —

"A Compleat History of the Rebellion, from its rise in 1745, to its total suppression at the Glorious Battle of Culloden in April 1746. By James Ray of Whitehaven. Volunteer under his Royal Highness the Duke of Cumberland. Bristol : Printed by S. Farley & Comp., 1752."

A. B. MIDDLETON.

The Close, Salisbury.

KING'S LYNN (3rd S. vii. 399.) — I am sorry I cannot give your correspondent Q. a satisfactory answer respecting the "old book" or a *Description of King's Lynn in Norfolk*, &c., by Ben Adam, consisting, it is said, of 214 MS. pages in verse. Both the present obliging Curator of the Norwich Museum, and the respected librarian of the Literary Institute assure me that no such MS. *ever* existed in the museum. The *Catalogue of Seals* presented to the Norwich Museum by Richard Taylor, Esq., in which "extracts" from the "old book" are given, is not now in the museum. It is not known what became of *this* catalogue, which your correspondent seems to have confounded with another *distinct* catalogue, entitled *A Catalogue of the Seals and Ancient Deeds in the Norfolk and Norwich Museum*, arranged by Captain J. C. Woollnough, R.N., 1830. This catalogue I have examined, but it contains not a single allusion to the MS. inquired after by Q.

Mr. John Chambers, the author of the work, *A General History of the County of Norfolk* (8vo, Norwich, 1826), mentions, in vol. i. p. 465, that only thirty pages of the MS. refer to Lynn in particular. Judging from the extract in this work taken from the "old book," the verses are far from being poetic; but whether the MS. itself is worth any further inquiries being made is very doubtful.

J. DALTON.

Norwich.

Your correspondent Q. states (3rd S. vii. 399), that when he visited Norwich about two years ago, there was then in the Museum *A Catalogue of Seals presented to the Norwich Museum by Richard Taylor, Esq.*, which is referred to by the Editor of *A General History of the County of Norfolk*, 8vo, Norwich, 1829, vol. i. p. 465, as containing a long extract from an old book, entitled, *Lennæ Rediviva; or, A Description of King's Lynn in Norfolk*, &c., by Ben Adam. I beg to say that in this he is in error. The book he saw is "*A Catalogue of the Seals and Ancient Deeds in the Norfolk and Norwich Museum*, arranged by Capt. J. C. Woollnough, R. N. 1830." This Catalogue was compiled *after* the publication of the *History*

of *Norfolk*, therefore cannot possibly be the one therein referred to. I regret to say that the original Catalogue of the Seals given by Richard Taylor, and which contains the extract in question, is not now in existence in the Norwich Museum, and no person now connected therewith has any knowledge of it—it has not been there during the last twenty years. The "old book" itself, that is the MS. of 214 pages by Ben Adam, was certainly never in the possession of the Museum at any time, and I regret I cannot render any information respecting it, but shall be very glad to learn that it has been heard of from some other source.

J. QUINTON, Assistant Secretary.

Norwich.

CHAINED LIBRARIES IN PARISH VESTRIES (3rd S. vii. 355.) — The vestry of Wimborne minster contains a chained library which now consists of two hundred and forty volumes. Its chains have not saved it from the spoiler, for twenty-five volumes are missing of those which were catalogued in 1765, and many of those which remain have fallen from want of care into a state of decay. From a catalogue prepared in 1863, by "W. G. W.," it appears that the titles of several of the missing books are such as depredators would be attracted by :—Markham's *Way to get Wealth, Period of Human Life;* Venner's *Via Recta ad Vitam Longam, Way to Health and Long Life*, &c. The principal donors to the library are the Rev. T. Ansty (1697), and the Rev. Sam. Conant. Nearly all the books were printed between 1520 and 1710, and there is a MS. dated 1343. Two of the books are in black letter. On the flyleaf of Chamberlayne's *State of England* (1670) is written in a very neat hand,—

"Anglica gens est optima fiens et pessima ridens."

JOB J. B. WORKARD.

NOËL (2nd S. xii. 503.) — Reading again the notice of this word quoted above, it occurs to me to ask whether the explanation given in the editorial note is not fairly susceptible of being carried a step further. If "Noël" was really a cry "used on festive and on solemn occasions as a cry of joy," may it not be a form of "Nouvelles, Nouvelles," equivalent to the heralds' cry of "Tidings, Tidings," by which they were wont to announce their advent? If so, the use of the word at, and its eventual application to, the season when the "herald angels" brought "good tidings of great joy," would be peculiarly appropriate. E. C. B.

IRISH POOR LAW (3rd S. vii. 10.) — I rather think that in the passage referred to by LORD LYTTELTON, Swift is to be understood, not as laying down what the law of *Ireland* was, but as stating, for the edification of his hearers, what the law of *England* was. I must admit that, if this was his meaning, it is not very clearly expressed. But it must be borne in mind that it is in a sermon that the passage occurs; and in a more business-like composition of his, *The Proposal for giving Badges to Beggars*, written in April, 1737, the Dean expresses himself in such a manner as to leave little doubt upon the point: —

"I never heard," he writes, "more than one objection against this expedient of badging the poor, and confining their walks to their several parishes. The objection was this: What shall we do with the foreign beggars? Must they be left to starve? No: but they must be driven or whipped out of town; and let the next country parish do as they please, or rather, after the practice in *England*, send them from one parish to another, until they reach their own homes. *By the old Laws of* England *still in force, every parish is bound to maintain its own poor.*"

What makes this quotation the more to the purpose is, that on examination it will be found that the *Proposal* evidently constituted the basis of the sermon. STAFFORD CAREY.

SURGEON EXECUTED FOR MURDER (3rd S. vii. 112, 170.) — T. B. may be glad to have the following extract from Dr. Trusler's *Tablet of Memory, or, Historian's Guide*, Dublin, 1782 (p. 10): —

"Audouin, surgeon, executed in Dublin for a murder; of which it appeared, some time after, he was innocent, 1728."

ABHBA.

EPISCOPAL BLAZON (3rd S. vii. 376.) — On the secretum of Henry de Spenser, Bishop of Norwich, the escutcheon is timbred with a helmet, surmounted by a mitre, out of which rises the crest of his house. (He was surnamed "The Warlike," and held the see from 1370 to 1406.)

The shield of the Bishops of Durham was ornamented by a coroneted and plumed mitre, which was sometimes placed upon a helmet.

In Germany crested helmets are very frequently used by archbishops and bishops, especially by those who are temporal seigneurs. The crests of bishoprics and of the seigneuries are thus used, as well as those belonging to the personal arms of their possessor. Indeed the mitre itself is frequently treated as a crest, and is placed on a helmet above the arms.

These facts have probably escaped the notice of those writers who dispute the right of ecclesiastics to use a crest, on the ground that they could not use a helmet to support it. J. WOODWARD.
New-Shoreham.

HORSES FRIGHTENED AT THE SIGHT OF A CAMEL (2nd S. viii. 354, 406; 3rd S. i. 459, 496; v. 387.) I make no doubt the hump-backed culprit of the following is the same that frightened my father-in-law's horse, as described in the last above-quoted page of "N. & Q.":

"DEATH FROM FRIGHT.—The death of a horse from fright has taken place near Bingham, Notts. Edmunds's menagerie left that town at an early hour, *en route* to Newark, where the annual 'May Fair' is about to be held. One of the caravans is drawn by a camel. This was met by a cart which was coming in the opposite direction, drawn by a horse belonging to Mr. Smith, farmer, of Flintham. The horse caught a sudden view of the strange beast of burden, gave a sort of snorting scream, plunged violently, and dropped down dead."

I have cut the above from the *Sheffield Daily Telegraph* of the 18th May, 1865. W. LEE.

TATTOO (3rd S. vii. 374.) — The sound of the drum is represented among the Latin races · by combinations of the syllables *rap, tap, tar, tan.* Thus we have, French *rat-a-plan;* Piedmontese, *tan-tan, tar-a-pat-a-pan, ta-rap-a-tan;* Ital. *para-pata-pan, pata-pata-pan* (Zalli, *Vocab. Piedm.*); Spanish, *tap-a-rap-a-tan, tap-a-tán;* ·Ital. *tappa-tá* (*Vocab. Milanese*). The last of which is manifestly identical with Dutch *taptoe*, the origin of our *tattoo*. H. W.

SPUR MONEY IN BELFRIES (3rd S. vii. 324.) — The following lines, in the church of All Saints, Hastings, may prove interesting to MR. H. FISHWICK and others; showing that, in addition to a fine for ringing the church bells in spurs, a like penalty was imposed for wearing a hat whilst so engaged: —

"This is a belfry that is free,
    For all those that civil be;
And if you please to chime or ring,
It is a very pleasant thing.

"There is no musick, played or sung,
Like unto bells when they're well rung.
Then ring your bells well, if you can;
Silence is best for every man.

"But if you ring in spur or hat,
Sixpence you pay, be sure of that.:
And if a bell you overthrow,
Pray pay a groat before you go.
            1756."
                                R. H. HILLS.
28, Chancery Lane.

DESCENDANT OF SARSFIELD (3rd S. vii. 378, 409.) — MR. PINKERTON, always courteous and interesting, is right in his surmise. It was General Patrick Sarsfield to whom I alluded. The gentleman of whom I speak, however, claims from a daughter of the general, and not through a niece or grandniece. Had the general a daughter? If so, to whom was she married? S. REDMOND.
Liverpool.

LE POER QUERIES (3rd S. vii. 377.) — An ancient branch of the Le Poer family was settled at an early period at a place called Poer Hayes, afterwards Duke's Hayes, an heiress of the first family, having carried it to the second, and now known as Haye's Farm, in the parish of Budleigh, co. Devon. It is here that Sir Walter Rawley was born. It now belongs, by purchase, to the representatives of the late Lord Rolle. In his *Monasticon of the Diocese of Exeter*, p. 248, the late Dr. Oliver remarks: —

" This family was of Breton origin, assuming the name of a place in Cornouaille, which became a Vicomte. The name was formally spelt (according to Maurice, Bretagne, Preuves, vol. i. *passim*) Poukaer, Pochaer, &c., probably a slight variation from Polcaer, in which form we should have no difficulty in discerning a Celtic origin."

According to a pedigree furnished me by the eldest representative of this family, the descent ran thus: — Sir Bartolemy Le Poer, Sir Roger, Sir Roger, Sir John, Sir Roger, Cecilia, d. and co-heiress, who carried Poer Hayes to her husband John Duke, of the adjoining parish of Otterton, *circa*, 1380. From them succeeded Richard Duke, Richard, Richard, (sheriff 1562), Henry (nephew of Richard), John, Richard, (see brass in Otterton Church), Richard (sheriff 1678), Robert (other brass), Thomas, George, of whom only two children, daughters, left issue, namely, Elizabeth, who m. Yonge, of Puslinch, near Yealmton, co. Dev., and Frances, who m. Taylor, whose d. married Coleridge of Ottery.

Sir William Pole, in his *Collections*, p. 153, speaks of Poer Hayes, and gives the descent, as thus: —

" Poerhayes (now Dukeshayes). This hath always contynewed in the name of Poer and Duke. Bartholemew Le Poer held it in Kinge Henry 2 tyme, whom have succeeded lineally Roger, Roger, John, John, and Roger Poer, whose daughtr Cicely was married unto Richard Duke [my version says John], a citisen of Exeter, and contynewed in his lyne unto George Duke, wch sold it unto his kinsman, Mr. Richard Duke of Otterton, about ye latter end of King Henry 8, wch Richard was sonne of Henry Duke, sonne of Richard Duke; and also father of the said George. It is now [circa 1630] thinheritance of Richard Duke, of Otterton, Esquier, sonne of Richard, nephew of Richard the purchaser."

I may remark that these statements of Sir William relative to the Duke family, are a mass of confusion. My version of the Le Poers tallies with his, except that where I give one John, he gives two. I have seen several charters in the Cartulary of Otterton Priory in which the name occurs. It is there spelt Poher. With respect to coat armour, Le Poer bore — Party per pale wavy, or and azure. There is a shield on the front of the house immediately on the north side of Otterton church, on which appear the arms of Duke and Le Poer, quartered, thus—for Duke 1 and 4, per fess, argent and azure, 3 chaplets counterchanged; 2 and 3, for Le Poer, per pale wavy, or and azure.

                                        P. Hutchinson.

CARABOO (3rd S. vii. 408.)—This lady seems to keep up her interest, so I send a squib which was handed about in Somersetshire after her detection. It is well enough for a local and temporary satire, written while the points were fresh. I know it to be by H. C. S., whose initials will be enough for many. The best claim to publication is its preserving what I well remember was a very common impression at the time, namely, that when

the woman walked into a house saying nothing but " Caraboo," she did not know what she was to do next, and acted on the hints which, she pretending not to know English, were plentifully thrown in her way. Some part of it would have been much better done but for the attempt at parallel which parody requires; but Lochinvar was then in every one's mouth.

" CARABOO (1815).

" Oh ! young Caraboo is come out of the West,
   In Frenchified tatters the damsel is drest ; .
   And, save one pair of worsted, she stockings had none,
   She tramped half unshod, and she walked all alone :
   But how to bamboozle the doxy well knew ;
   You ne'er heard of gypsey like young Caraboo.

" She staid not for river, she stopt not for stone,
   She swam in the Avon where ford there was none ;
   But when she alighted at W—— gate,
   The dame and the doctor received her in state.
   No longer a gypsey, the club of bas-bleu
   To a princess converted the young Caraboo.

" So boldly she entered the W—— hall,
   Amongst linguists, skull-feelers, bluestockings and all ;
   Then spake the sage doctor, profoundly absurd,
   While the sly Caraboo answered never a word :
   ' Art thou sprung from the Moon, or from far Javasoo,
   Or a mermaid just landed, thou bright Caraboo ?'

" To these questions sagacious she answer denied,
   Though hard was the struggle her laughter to hide :
   ' But since they decree me these titles so fine,
   I'll be silent, eat curry, and taste not their wine ;
   With this imposition I've nothing to do,
   These are fools ready made,' said the young Caraboo.

" She looked at a pigeon—the dame caught it up ;
   Caraboo had a mind on a pigeon to sup :
   She looked down to titter—she looked up so sly—
   With the bird in her hand, and the spit in her eye :
   She dressed it—she ate it—she called it Rampoo,
   ' This proves,' swore the doctor, ' she's Queen Caraboo.

" When she fenced with the doctor, so queer her grimace,
   Sure never a hall such a galliard did grace :
   But her host seemed to fret—though the Doctor did fume,
   Should any to question her titles presume.
   And 'twas currently whispered the best they could do,
   Was to send up to London the young Caraboo.

" The hint was enough ;—as it dropt on her ear,
   It ruined her hopes ; it awakened her fear :
   So swift to the quay the fair damsel she ran,
   ' Oh ! take me, dear Captain, away if you can.'
   She's aboard—they are off ; ' Farewell Doctor Rampoo !
   They'll have swift ships that follow,' quoth young Caraboo.

" There was bustling 'mong dames of the W—— clan,
   The blue stocking junto they rode and they ran,
   There was racing and chasing from Bath to the sea,
   But the bright Queen of Javasoo ne'er could they see.
   What a hoax on the doctor and club of bas-bleu,
   Did you e'er hear of gypsey like young Caraboo ? "
                                        M.

YOUR SOUL (3rd S. v. 378.)—The quotation is from *A Churchman's Second Epistle*, by the author of *Religio Clerici*, London, 1819, 8vo, pp. 85. From the reply to a query of mine (1st S. v. 29, 161), I much wished to read *Religio Clerici*, but failed in my attempt to buy or borrow a copy, and could not find one in the British Museum. I lately had the good luck to come upon a volume of pamphlets containing both "Epistles," with which I have been much pleased. They are not exactly poetry, but good sense and good taste in very fair verse. As nearly fifty years have passed since the publication of the first epistle, I do not think it intrusive to ask for the author's name if known.* Pamphlets, even when they have gone through several editions, are very difficult to procure when a few years out of print, so perhaps the description of a popular preacher of 1819 may be worth insertion:—

> "Lo! now the Preacher, first with due grimace,
> A long-protracted reverence hides his face;
> Deep on the cushion sinks his buried chin,
> His cheeks are lost, a handkerchief within.
> Next drawls he forth a strange impromtu prayer,
> Conned well at home, and writ with special care:
> Some now and then may use a book or note,
> More Evangelic he who learns by rote.
> Then comes the text in two divisions cleft,
> This edifies his right hand, that his left:
> His doctrines so by turns suit every state,
> And catch the little vulgar, or the great.
> Here he propounds the wounded spirit's styptic,
> In terms obscure and phrase apocalyptic:
> Huge, burly language, words too big for rhyme,
> And windy mouthings of the false sublime;
> Where in the dark his misty meaning gropes,
> Half smothered by a tympany of tropes.
> Soon as this works his tone is changed again,
> And slides adroitly to another strain;
> A pert, familiar, brisk, and easy chat,
> Mere Gospel gossip about this and that;
> As if instead of 'How d'ye do?' he'd say,
> 'Sweet Sir, or Madam, how's your soul to-day?'
> If fitting action could our ears engage
> No squirrel bustles blither in his cage;
> When he quotes Scripture, loose the cambric flies,
> His arms expanded, lifted are his eyes;
> One long forefinger, like an index shews
> Some fine-spun argument is near its close;
> And two, when struck upon the cushion tell,
> The word that follows must be Heaven or Hell."
> (Ll. 204, 235, p. 25-29.)

U. U. Club.　　　　　　　　　　　H. B. C.

The Court, 1730 (3rd S. vii. 356.)—I, like your correspondent P., have had in hand the investigation of a case of propinquity, wherein the discovery of the evidence of the birth of a child, at about the same date as that he mentions, was

[* These pamphlets are by the Rev. Edward Smedley, M.A., an able scholar and learned divine. He was admitted at Westminster school 1800; graduated at Trinity College, Cambridge; elected Fellow of Sidney; gained four of the Seatonian prizes for English poems, made prebendary of Lincoln 1829; and died June 29, 1836. He was editor of the Encyclopædia Metropolitana. A Memoir of him, prefixed to his Poems and Correspondence, was published in 1837, 8vo. Both the pamphlets noticed above are in the British Museum, entered in the new Catalogue under "Churchman."—Ed.]

desirable. In my case, the Gentleman's Magazine supplied the "missing link," the parish register being then unknown. In the reign of the first two Georges, "contraband" and runaway marriages were frequent, and probably the registration of births was irregular; and hence the perplexity experienced in the pursuit of genealogical enquiries relating to that period. In the instance to which I refer, the daughter of a nobleman is stated to have "died young," when the truth was, she lived to be the mother of a large family. She was, however, suppressed in the Peerages. From my examination of such works, I have come to the conclusion that they are, as a class, characterised by the suppressio veri and the suggestio falsi to a very large extent. They insert what is convenient, not what is true.

If your correspondent thinks I can be of service to him, I forward my address for private communication.　　　　　　　Genealogicus.

"The Christian Breadbasket" (3rd S. vii. 356, 359.)—Mr. Willey does not seem to be aware that the monthly of this name was incorporated with The Rays of Light, the property of Messrs. Adams & Gee, and published by Stephenson, I think. The Rays was originally a monthly sheet, after the manner of the Band of Hope Review, with these differences, that it was smaller and not illustrated. When the much-abused Breadbasket was declining, it was purchased by the proprietors of the Rays of Light, and the two together assumed the latter name and the shape and characteristics of the former. But a no better fate befell the incorporation. Its circulation, influence, and literary claim grew small by degrees, so that at the immature age of sixteen months it suddenly collapsed.　　　　　T. P. Skinner.
Islington.

The Charters of Holyrood (3rd S. vii. 375.) As the quotations given by T. G. S. seem still to leave it a little doubtful whether Herbergare is the infinitive of a verb, or the proper name of the Canongate, I quote as follows from the Cartulary of Coldingham as referred to by Sir David Dalrymple (Lord Hailes) in his Annals, vol. i. 97:—

"The true sense of the word is to be seen in a Grant by Malcolm IV. to the Prior and Monks of Coldingham: 'Ut secundum voluntatem suam adducent suos proprios homines ubicunque maneant in terra sua ad herbergandam Villam de Coldingham.'"

This, it is presumed, must put an end to further question.　　　　　　　　　　　G.
Edinburgh.

Who was Philalethes (3rd S. vii. 220, 328.) Mr. J. Coleman does not claim the above pseudonym as the exclusive designation of the Rev. Thomas Stackhouse; but as the matter now stands, it might be inferred, that to him there is some specialty in the appropriation. It is for the

credit of " N. & Q." to say, that the same signa-
ture was used in newspapers by Dr. Edward
Young, 1718-20; Gabriel Gerberon, *On the Je-
suits,* 1689; Chas. Leslie, *View of the Times,* 1708;
Arthur Ashley Sykes, *Moral Philosophy,* 1715;
T. Morgan on the same, 1738; R. Bentley, *On
Mathematics,* 1735; A Gentleman in the Navy,
On Gibraltar, 1725; Nathl. Lardner, *Biblical
Criticism;* Sir R. Hill, 1770; C. Fleming, *On
Church Establishment,* 1767; Wm. Goode, *On the
Church,* 1834; Sir R. J. W. Horton, *On Colonies,*
1839; and appears in some hundred works alto-
gether, on almost all subjects, during the last *two
hundred* years.   W. LEE.

SASH WINDOWS (2nd S. vi.* 147, 175.) — Your
esteemed correspondent A. A. proves the use of
this word as apparently *rare* in May, 1710. A reply to his note, suggested that the term was derived from the Old English word *sasse,* a sluice;
and *sas,* the Dutch, also for a sluice; the common
French term for such a window being *à la guillotine.* The following note is, I venture to suggest,
a very little, if at all known, assertion of the introduction of the window into France from England, and opens the question whether the invention was a Dutch or German one, and brought
over with paint for house work, and sundry other
building inventions, by the Dutch with William
III.: —

"De Lorge: We had the good fortune here to find the
Marshal himself. He showed us his great *Sash Windows;*
how easily they might be lifted up and down, and stood
at any height; which contrivance, he said, he had out of
England, by a small model brought on purpose from
thence, there being nothing of this *poise* in windows in
France before; the house was but building" and was
situate near Montmartre.— Lister, *Journey to Paris,* 8vo,
London, 1699.

WYATT PAPWORTH.

BISHOP BEDELL: HOUSES IN PILL LANE, DUB-
LIN (3rd S. vii. 398.) — Will the following be of
any use to the REV. MR. IRVINE in reference to
the above? On the east side of Pill Lane, near
the back entrance to the Four Courts, Dublin,
there were some houses occupied as warehouses
by Mr. S. Gatehill, an extensive hardware merchant and ironmonger, and these houses were
there as late as 1845 (I know not if they have
since been pulled down). These buildings were
evidently old, and on a stone near the top of the
front wall of four of these buildings was cut a monogram, in relief, which consisted of G. B., and the
dates 1691 and 1712; two houses having the first
date, and two others the latter. The houses may
be standing still.   S. REDMOND.
Liverpool.

MAY-DAY SONGS (3rd S. vii. 373, 425.) — Being
lately on a visit near the town of Bourton-on-the-
Hill, co. Gloucester, I remarked how extensively

* Not v. as in the General Index.

the observance of May-day is still carried on in
that neighbourhood. The children, dressed out
with flowers and ribbons, go from house to house,
each party carrying a doll, seated in a sort of cage
composed of flowers. Their song is in the following words: —

> " Round the May-pole,
>   Trit trit trot,
> See what a May-pole
>   We have got.
>   Fine and gay,
>   Trip away,
> Happy is our new May-day.
> " Gentlemen and ladies,
> I wish you happy May,
> We come to show the garland,
> For 't is the first of May."
>   G.

WILLIAM PENNOCK (3rd S. vii. 419.) — A complete pedigree of the Pinnock (not Pennock) family will appear in a forthcoming volume on the
Monumental Inscriptions of Jamaica.   SPAL.

DRAGON IN HERALDRY (3rd S. vii. 418.) — The
dragon is, I believe, supposed to be emblematical
of wisdom or astuteness in heraldry; but this is
probably an invention for want of something better
to say on the subject. It is very likely that the
dragon's head was simply a convenient finish for
a seal, and so became a crest, and that his wonderful attributes were found in his trail by the more
modern possessors of such relics.   SPAL.

SAMUEL HARTLIB (3rd S. vii. 398.) — The name
of Mr. Hartlib appears occasionally in the State
Papers, and DR. RIMBAULT may like to have the
following references to the Calendars in which it
occurs.

In Mr. Bruce's volume for 1633-1634 he is
mentioned five times (pp. 2, 17, 31, 68, 149); the
first four in letters from John Durie to Sir Thomas
Roe, and the last from Sir Thomas to the Archbishop of Canterbury, on which there is a marginal note— "Mr. Hartlib, a Prussian." They are
all dated between April 2 and July 20, 1633, and
have reference to negotiations with Chancellor
Oxenstiern in Sweden regarding the Reformed
churches.

In Mr. Bruce's volume for 1634-1635 Mr. Durie
refers to him in two letters dated June 22 and 28
(pp. 89, 96) on the same subject.

In Mrs. Green's volume for 1661-1662 there is
a letter from Sam. Hartlib to [Sec. Nicholas] in
p. 336, relative to a warrant for 1000l. to Robert
Shaw for special services; and a memorandum in
p. 602 that he had received a letter to Sir Humphrey Hooke about destroying tobacco in Gloucestershire, and apprehending the rioters there.
They are severally dated April 9 and Dec. 24,
1662. In Mrs. Green's next volume, under date
1663, there is a note (p. 412) as to Mr. Hartlib's
desiring some warrants for French wines to be retained.   D. S.

THE LINCOLNSHIRE CHURCH-NOTES OF GERVASE HOLLES (3rd S. vii. 356, 389, 407.) — Many of these notes, not hitherto published, have appeared since January, 1864, in the *Stamford Mercury* from MSS. (copied from the original in the British Museum) in the possession of Mr. G. A. Hansard, 33, Kenton Street, Brunswick Square, London.   STAMFORDIENSIS.

COSHERING (3rd S. vii.391.)—MR. O'CAVANAGH, I think, has answered his own note and query both learnedly and elaborately. "Coshering" is universally known in the country parts of Ireland to apply to little tea-parties amongst farmers' wives, from which men are rigidly excluded. Such parties are most frequent about the close of harvest time, and any one who has lived in a rural district of Ireland, about the time mentioned, must have heard of "coshering parties."

                                        S. REDMOND.
Liverpool.

Miscellaneous.

NOTES ON BOOKS, ETC.

Annales Monastici. Vol. II. Annales Monasterii de Wintonia (A.D. 519—1277). *Annales Monasterii de Waverleia* (A.D. 1—1291). *Edited by* Henry Richard Luard, M.A. (Longman.)

Mr. Luard is carrying on the good work entrusted him by the Master of the Rolls in a most satisfactory manner. The present volume contains the Annals written in the Monasteries of Winchester and Waverley: portions of which have indeed been previously published, but which now appear for the first time in their integrity. The Annals of Winchester, which are carried down to the year 1277, are printed from the Cotton MS., Domit. A. XIII.; and, as relating the events which chiefly concern Winchester, the city and the cathedral, and the changes in the cathedral and monasteries, it is especially valuable. The Annalist, by-the-bye, mentions a remarkable prophecy of the death of Richard I., said to have been current among the Norman girls some time previous to that event :—

    " In Limozin sagitta fabricatur,
    Qua tyrannus morti dabitur."

The Annals of Waverley, here reprinted from the only known MS. (Cotton Vespasian, A. XVI.), are carried down to the year 1291; and the editor shows that, well as these Annals have been known through Gale's edition, and frequent as are the references to them, the full amount of historical information to be found in them has by no means been drawn out. It will not be the fault of the present learned editor, if this can much longer be urged with justice against this valuable document.

The Herald and Genealogist. Edited by J. Gough Nichols, F.S.A. *Part XIV.* (Nichols.)

This new Part—full of interest to heraldic and genealogical inquirers—contains two papers which are of especial interest just now : "Anglo-American Genealogy—North and South," and "Popular Genealogists, or the Art of Pedigree Making."

Messrs. Longman's MONTHLY LIST furnishes strong evidence of the approach of the Holiday Season in the announcement of a new *Map of the Chain of Mont Blanc*, a new *Map of Switzerland*, on a scale of four miles to an inch, and *A Guide to Spain*, by Mr. O'Shea. The same publishers announce also, a third edition of Earl Russell's *Essay on the History of the English Government and Constitution* ; of a second edition, with the omission of the controversial part, of Dr. Newman's *History of my Religious Opinions* ; and also, of what we are very glad to see, a *People's Edition* of Mr. Maguire's *Life of Father Mathew.*

MESSRS. GROOMBRIDGE announce also a seasonable book, *Sea Fishing as a Sport;* being an account of the various kinds of Sea Fish ; How, When, and Where to Catch them in their Seasons and Localities. By Lambton J. H. Young.

EXHIBITION OF PORTRAIT MINIATURES AT SOUTH KENSINGTON MUSEUM.—All lovers of Art, students of History, and admirers of the Beautiful—will be delighted with the matchless collection of Portrait Miniatures now assembled at South Kensington, and which will be opened to the public this day. Those who remember what a striking feature the Miniatures formed, in the Loan Exhibition of last Year, will readily imagine what a treat is in store for them, when we tell them that the present Collection amounts to upwards of three thousand Miniatures from the time of Holbein to our own day, and will judge of the value as well as the extent of the Collection when we add that among them will be found upwards of one hundred undoubtedly genuine specimens of Petitot' matchless skill. Horace Walpole would have been beside himself with delight at such a sight as may now be seen at South Kensington, where, by-the-bye, almost all the fine Strawberry Hill Miniatures may now be seen once more assembled together.

BOOKS AND ODD VOLUMES
WANTED TO PURCHASE.

Particulars of price, &c., of the following book to be sent direct to the gentlemen by whom it is required, and whose names and address are given for that purpose :—
COLEBROOKE'S DIGEST OF HINDOO LAW. 8vo. Vol. I.
    Wanted by *Messrs.* WILLIS & SOTHERAN, 136, Strand.

Notices to Correspondents.

H. A. E. 1. *The charade has already appeared without eliciting any satisfactory reply.* 2. *We are not aware that any peculiar facilities are to be obtained at the Legacy Office, Somerset House, for literary researches.* 3. *Advertisements 6d. per line, two guineas a column,* 4. *The genealogical queries shall be inserted.*

L. F. H. *Thomas Harley was the ancestor of Harley, Earl of Oxford. See* Collins's Peerage (by Brydges), *vol. iii. pp. 55, et seq.*

SCRUTATOR'S *query in our next, with any information we can obtain.*

M. M. *The Royal Academy generally closes at the end of June.*

GEORGE SWIFT. *For the special duties of synods-men or sidesmen, see* "N. & Q." 3rd S. v. 34, 65, 81, 181.

J. G. (Ipswich.) *For the origin of the term Roundhead, see our* 3rd S. ii. 450.

*** *Cases for binding the volumes of* "N. & Q." *may be had of the Publisher, and of all Booksellers and Newsmen.*

A Reading Case for holding the weekly Nos. of "N. & Q." is now ready, and may be had of all Booksellers and Newsmen, price 1s. 6d. or, free by post, direct from the publisher, for 1s. 8d.

"NOTES AND QUERIES" *is published at noon on Friday, and is also issued in* MONTHLY PARTS. *The Subscription for* STAMPED COPIES *for Six Months forwarded direct from the Publisher (including the Half-yearly* INDEX) *is* 11s. 4d., *which may be paid by Post Office Order, payable at the Strand Post Office, in favour of* WILLIAM G. SMITH, 32, WELLINGTON STREET, STRAND, W.C., *where also all* COMMUNICATIONS FOR THE EDITOR *should be addressed.*

"NOTES & QUERIES" *is registered for transmission abroad.*

LONDON, SATURDAY, JUNE 10, 1865.

CONTENTS.— No 180.

Notes.

RESTORATION OF MONUMENTS.

I wish to record in the pages of "N. & Q." the "restoration" (!) of an early monument, as such a process is conducted in the year 1865; the subject being a work of not quite five centuries earlier — of the year 1377, that is, or of the year following.

In Murray's *Hand-Book of Exeter Cathedral* (p. 158), the author writes as follows:—

"On the south side of the nave, (beneath the sixth pier-arch from the west end,) is the high tomb, with much mutilated effigies of Hugh Courtenay (died 1377), second Earl of Devon of the house of Courtenay, and of his Countess Margaret (died 1391), daughter of Humphrey de Bohun, Earl of Hereford and Essex, by Elizabeth, daughter of Edward I. On the pavement beside this monument is the brass, still interesting, and once very fine, of their son Sir Peter Courtenay (died 1406), standard-bearer to Edward III., and distinguished in the French and Spanish wars under the Black Prince. These tombs were formerly inclosed within a chantry."

The chantry in question has totally disappeared. The brass (since the foregoing passage was written about five years ago) now lies in the pavement of the south aisle of the choir, where certainly it is more out of harm's way. The "high tomb" also has been removed; that is, the original tomb of the Earl of Devon, whose countess was a grand-daughter of Edward I., has been taken away from its original site; and, as it was indeed "much mutilated," a new structure is to represent it in the south transept. Upon this new structure, which I suppose will claim to be considered a "restoration" of the original monument, rest the "restored" effigies of the earl and countess. No traces do they now exhibit of their "much mutilated" condition in 1861. Both effigies are as fresh as if they had been ordered within the last six months at the most enterprising establishment in the New Road. Still these are not to be considered new effigies, for they have been formed from the original stone. Skilful chisels have *cut away* every vestige of the mutilations, and a judicious process of *cutting down* has brought out fresh effigies from beneath the dishonouring ravages of time and barbarism. To be sure, not a vestige remains of what the widowed countess placed within a chantry to the memory of her lord: so thoroughly are the effigies "restored," that the "chiselmanship" of to-day has superseded every touch of the sculptor of that dark period, the thirteenth century.

Without a doubt, this "restored" memorial will claim the date of the original monument itself, A.D. 1377, and not 1865. This is indeed quite a typical achievement of a thorough "restorer." What the originals perhaps might have been, has been reproduced with most pains-taking fidelity, while whatever lingering traces of the actual originals yet remained have been no less faithfully obliterated. Centuries will leave their marks on the hardest stones, and their capacity for mischief no one will refuse to concede to Puritans *et id genus omne:* all their doings, however, sink into insignificance when compared with the cool and ruthless destructiveness of a genuine "restorer."

By all means let faithfully studied *copies* of fine old monumental memorials be executed by able hands, at the cost of the living inheritors of the noble names of long past ages, or by whoever may please to commission them, whether to amateur or to professional sculptors. But I must plead for the jealous preservation of the original memorials themselves. They are chisel-written chronicles of the England of our ancestors, which we received from them in trust that they may be transmitted by us to our successors. We have no right to tamper with early historical monuments; we have no right to destroy them; least of all have we any right to work our destructive will upon them under the plea and pretence of "restoration."

However grievous the mutilation of the original Courtenay monument with its effigies, those relics were valuable in themselves, and possessed the strongest claims for respectful care. This "restoration" has destroyed them; and, in their stead, Exeter Cathedral has to submit to the degradation of containing a sham monument, and two effigial parodies.

I would conclude with the queries, How was it possible that such a thing as this could have been perpetrated? and why is this "restoration" permitted to remain in one of our cathedrals?— did I not prefer to express the hope that the existence of such a *warning* as this in such a position as the centre of the south transept at Exeter, may be effectually instrumental in saving our other "much mutilated" memorials from sharing in the destructive "restoration," which has fallen upon the once noble monument of Hugh Courtenay, Earl of Devon, and Margaret de Bohun his Countess. CHARLES BOUTELL.

𝕾𝖍𝖆𝖐𝖘𝖕𝖊𝖆𝖗𝖎𝖆𝖓𝖆.

NEW SHAKSPEARE EMENDATION.

(3rd S. vii. 315, 360.)

A word or two in reply to MR. HERAUD. The question as to the value of his new reading of the line (*Julius Cæsar*, Act II. Sc. 1) :—

"For if thou *pall* thy native semblance o'er,"—

seems to narrow itself into this : To what does the phrase "native semblance" apply? MR. HERAUD says it is to the conspirators, and he regards both Coleridge and myself as "mistaking the meaning" of the poet in declining to recognise the prosopopeia, which to his mind is so self-evident.

Now I am not prepared to deny that, by MR. HERAUD's genetic process, we get sense. His view of "native semblance" paves the way for his emendation, and the two in conjunction render the passage intelligible. But it is one of the first canons of Shakspearean criticism as regards amendments that, where we have *a* meaning, it is not permissible to alter the text so as to get *the* meaning we fancy we ought to have. This rule is most wholesome in practice; and, I think, applies to the case before us.

The text as it stands yields a meaning, and could one sanction the use of "path" as an adjective, there would be no occasion to disturb it. All that is wanted then is, either a precedent for this special use of "path," or an equivalent for it if so used. But MR. HERAUD asks us to take a bolder course. We are to admit *two* new words into the text; and to do so with a view of giving a special reading, not only to one line, but to the whole passage in which it occurs. I think I do not go too far in stating this.

Let us see. The poet means to say, we are told :—

"That the true mode of concealment is to let their (the conspirators') naked faces (their 'native semblance') be seen, and only to 'hide' the monstrous visage of conspiracy in 'smiles and affability.'"

Now, here is clearly *a* meaning, and a very ingenious one; but was it Shakspeare's? To induce us to believe that it was, we are asked to accept the poetic idealisation in which Brutus indulges, "as a slight elevation of the style and not intended for a perfect figure." But why? There is no necessity for us to take this view of the matter—except in order to meet MR. HERAUD's theory. In the text as it stands, the figure *is* perfect. Apostrophising the abstract Conspiracy, as idealised in his own mind, Brutus follows out a train of ideas (suggested by the words just addressed to him it is true), to a natural and perfect conclusion.

Of this soliloquy, which is in perfect keeping throughout, I have given a paraphrase; but a somewhat ampler one will bring out its proportions more clearly :—

"O Conspiracy! Dost thou fear to show thy brow by night? O then, by day, where wilt thou find a cavern dark enough to hide its monstrosity in? Seek none, but hide it in smiles and affability : for failing to do this, no cavern—not even Erebus itself—were dim enough to hide thee."

Surely here is a "perfect figure," as perfect as it is possible for it to be. And what are we asked to do with it, in order to afford scope for the new reading? Why, we are to suppose that Brutus first addresses the abstract Conspiracy; but that after "monstrous visage," though he still uses the word "conspiracy," he means "conspirators;" and clumsily deserts to the prosopopeia in the middle of his soliloquy without the slightest possible reason for so doing.

I cannot myself consent to believe that the poet intended to do this; and, therefore, cannot yield assent to MR. HERAUD's new reading, nor to his position that it does not materially alter the sense of the passage in which the line in dispute occurs. WILLIAM SAWYER.

Clements' Inn.

PASSAGE FROM "MACBETH" (3rd S. vii. 51, 176, 266, 316.) — The statement that *blonket* means directly a thunder-cloud must be admitted to be probably an error, as, after much search, no confirmation of that sense can at present be found.

Blonket, blonquet, or *blunket,* adj. (obsolete) meaning grey or pale blue, appears in many dictionaries, the earliest notice of the word being in 1617. It is spelt *blunket* in Phillips's *Dictionary,* 1696; *blonket* is in Bailey, 1735, but not in subsequent editions. It is in the first edition of Johnson, and is continued through a number of more recent dictionaries.

In Spenser's *Shepherd's Kal.* May, v. 5, is —

"Our blonquet livery's been all too sad For thilke same season."

"I have not met the word elsewhere than in Spenser." Nares's *Glossary.*

If it be taken as an emendation of the text, it will become a substantive.

"Cibber, in his *Lives of the Poets* (that of Davenant), reminds us that in Shakspere's time *blanket* was a good and local image in the theatre. There being then no painted scenery, a blanket was used as the curtain."— Nares.

In old fashioned theatres there was a slit-hole in the curtain for the manager to peep through, to watch the entrance of the audience. In former times similar images were not unusual. There is an analogous expression in Drayton —

"The sullen'night in misty rug is wrapt."

The checked blanket on the table of the Court of Exchequer has always been considered a stately appliance. B. T.
New Club, Edinburgh.

Passage in "Othello," Act I. Sc. 1.—

"For-sooth, a great Arithmatician,
One Michaell Cassio, a Florentine
(A Fellow almost damn'd in a faire Wife),
That neuer set a Squadron in the Field,
Nor the deuision of a Battaile knowes
More then a Spinster . . . ."

Tyrwhitt, "faire life;" Dyce (few remarks), and Grant White, "fair wise;" Sidney Walker, as Tyrwhitt, "life." "Wise," in the sense of "way," occurs only once in Shakspeare (*Pericles*, Act V. Sc. 2); but if it were used twenty times I should not understand what it could mean here. It is nearly as unintelligible as "a fair life"—the life of a man, "of whom all men speak well!"

What has the "fair life" to do with the Arithmetician, with the Florentine, and with the man, who never set squadron in the field?

Iago intends to say that Othello has made a very bad choice in making a man his lieutenant, who is no man, who has only to do with theories, who never has met with a shower of bullets, who knows the division of a battle just so as a spinster does; in short —

"A fellow, almost damn'd in a *faint* wife."

F. A. Leo.
Berlin.

DEGENERATION OF WORDS.

It is in the nature of things that words should degenerate. Words, like any other implements, wear off their edges by much using. The more popular the word the oftener it passes the lips and the quill-nibs of common-place talkers and writers; and therefore the more quickly it vulgarises itself down to its lowest and most limited representative value. The scruples about calling a spade a spade, and the delicacies of allusive euphemism are mere offshoots from this radical tendency in words to blunt themselves by coarse application. Reek and stench have gone to the bad mainly, if not only, because they have been more used than odour and perfume, of which they are originally synonyms. A smell has rather the

disadvantage than the benefit of a doubt whether it be sweet or unsavory. Scent is pretty fairly balanced between sport and perfumery.

"Pretty" "fair"! Here are two words still in a transition state, though they have been rather slow travellers on the downward slant. Fair once meant beautiful: it now means tolerable, average, impartial. Pretty is not near so ancient a word in our language, but it has seen changes, and is visibly declining in value. Peart (probably a corruption of *peritus*, accomplished), is still provincially used in its original sense; a "peart" workman implies none of the bumptious self-sufficiency which attaches to the degenerate "pert."

"I am peartly" means I am in thoroughly ship-shape condition as to my corporeal vessel. Pretty is said to be the corruption of peartly, and probably meant very much the same thing. A "pretty fellow," before the phrase became ironical, no doubt implied an accomplished member of society.

A pretty woman does not mean so much as it did. The word "pretty" expresses the minor and more insignificant grades of good looks in woman, as the word "clever" does of ability in men. It is a bad compliment to a really beautiful woman to call her pretty, just as it is derogatory to a really able statesman to call him clever. In America the word clever had degenerated to mean merely good humoured. For our clever they use "smart," and for our able, "talented."

It is very difficult to invent new words, and their tendency to sink implies a power in words, so sinking, to displace material from the lower levels of language; and this naturally accounts for the rise of slang and obsolete terms. "Swell" and "prig" from meaning respectively a shabby and gorgeously attired thief have come colloquially to signify, without any imputation of dishonesty, persons distinguished by education and fashion from more ignorant and vulgar specimens of a low intellectual grade.

Political and theological denomination rise rapidly, and cannot be expected to wear well. A Puseyite is nearly as obsolete as a Lollard; Whig and Tory are but little less palæontological than Cavalier and Roundhead; Liberal and Conservative have run their *hues* and cries into a neutral tint and a *vox ambigua*. The head of the subtle race of Gladstone a few weeks back wished to give over even the perennially brazen word "Reformer" to a reprobate mind. But surely his substitute "Improver" was both weaker and more pretentious. Considering the proclivity of institutions as well as terms to warp themselves, by corrupt uses, out of their original shapes and intentions, Reform (in the sense of restoration to original meaning and purpose) is not inconsistent with the true spirit of intelligent Conservatism. What should we think of a surgeon, however his

patients might be encumbered with wens and undermined with ulcers, who should style himself " an improver of the human body " ?

A Conservative Reformer.

NAPOLEON I. AS AN AUTHOR AND A STUDENT.

The present Emperor Napoleon III. is the author of several works. Can you inform me, if there be extant any list of works composed by Napoleon I.? I have somewhere read that, as early as 1791, Napoleon published a pamphlet entitled *Lettre à Matteo Buttafuoco*. It was written in Corsica, but printed at Dôle. I believe he also wrote a brief *History of Corsica*, published about the year 1790. There are two French writers whose works I have seen quoted on this subject, *viz.*: (1) Nasica, *Mémoires sur la Jeunesse de Napoléon;* (2) M. Libri, *Souvenirs de la Jeunesse de Napoléon.*

Napoleon, before he left France for Egypt, drew up with his own hand a plan for a Travelling Library. It consisted of about three hundred and sixty volumes; more than half of which are historical, and nearly all in French. The ancient historians, comprised in the list, are: Thucydides, Plutarch, Polybius, Arrian, Tacitus, Livy, and Justinian. The poets are: Homer, Virgil, Tasso, Ariosto, Fenelon's *Télémaque*, Voltaire's *Henriade*, Ossian, and La Fontaine. Amongst the works of prose fiction are, *English Novelists in Forty Volumes.* These were, of course, translations. The list includes likewise the Bible, together with the Koran and the Vedas! (*Correspondance de Napoléon Ier*, iv. 37—38. See also Edwards' *Libraries and Founders of Libraries*, p. 130, London, 1864.)

A literary anecdote connected with Napoleon, while he resided in the island of Elba, is mentioned by Mr. Edward Edwards in the work mentioned above (p. 136). The story is worth quoting. It is this:—On one occasion, when Napoleon was speaking to Colonel Campbell about the battle of Austerlitz, he said "that a particular disposition of his artillery, which had a decisive effect in winning the battle, was suggested to his mind by the recollection of these lines in Milton's *Paradise Lost* (book vi.) : —

'.   .   .   .   . In hollow cube
Training his devilish engin'ry, impal'd
On every side *with shadowing squadrons deep*
To hide *the fraud.*'"

It may be as well to mention, that Mr. Edwards tells us he has no better authority for the story than a MS. note on the fly-leaf of a copy of Symmon's *Life of Milton*, signed by some unknown "J. Brown."   J. Dalton.

Norwich.

[* Mr. Edwards has quoted this anecdote from " N. & Q." 1st S. xii. 361, where will be found some detailed particulars of the volume containing the MS. note.—Ed.]

THE SEARCH FOR THE LAPIS IN 1865.

Let those who believe that the hope of transmuting the baser metals into gold expired with the last century, shrinking from the glare of light which in this boasted age dispels all idle dreams, read the following advertisement which appeared in the *Times* of April 4th, 1865 : —

" To Students in Alchymy.—Any gentleman who may require an Assistant can be recommended to an industrious foreigner, who has studied the books of the Alchymists for the last 15 years, and is a good experimentalist. He is now in Transylvania, but every information will be given by applying to Chas. F. Zimpel, M.D. 182, Marylebone-road."

Nor is the search now-a-days confined to laboratory experiments. Rumour asserts that an extraordinary rise in the price of bismuth which occurred last year was caused by the purchases of a Joint Stock Company, established for the purpose of carrying out on a large scale the discoveries of a gentleman who, it was understood, had succeeded in perfecting the preparation of the " Stomach of Anthion," or the " Sharpness of the Eagle," or whatever may be the name of the needful Alkahest. Had these modern patrons followed the example of the shrewd Medici, who sent Augurellus of Rimini an empty purse, they had contented themselves with the purchase of an iron safe. They did more. *Their* " Subtle" did not profess to turn *all* metals into gold; their spits and pans and andirons were not available; no use to strip the churches of their coverings. They bought bismuth. Did their imagination, I wonder, like Sir Epicure's in the play, run riot among pictures such " as Tiberius took from Elephantis," among mistresses " with great smooth marbly limbs," among mists of perfume, and baths "from whence we will come forth and roll us dry in gossamer and roses;" did they surround themselves with poets and flatterers, " the pure and gravest of divines," dream of Apician dainties served ".in Indian shells, and dishes of agate set in gold," and of raiment " such as might provoke the Persian " ?

" This day . . . ingots, and to-morrow
Give lords th' affront."

To-morrow came and with it : —

" Is all lost, Lungs ? will nothing be preserved
Of all our cost ? "—" Faith, very little, Sir;
A peck of coals or so ! "

In this instance, however, the result was not quite so lachrymose. Still — even counting the " cure for the itch " off " the scraped shards "—a *fiasco.*

There is time enough yet, however, in this nineteenth century for the fulfilment of the prophecy made by the eminent Göttingen professor, Dr. Christopher Girtanner, in his memoir on Azote in the *Annales de Chimie*, No. 100, that this century will assuredly give birth to the transmutation of metals, when every chemist and every artist will make gold; when kitchen utensils will be made of silver, and even of gold, which will contribute more than anything else to prolong life, poisoned at present by the oxides of copper, lead, and iron that we daily swallow with our food. (*Pettigrew.*) This is a prosaic, but eminently practical way of looking at the rejuvenescent power of the wonderful Elixir, and one likely to prove more efficacious, I take it, in retarding the advances of old age, than that method to which is attached the name of the unknown Hermippus—*puellarum anhelitu.*　　　　A. CHALLSTETH.

A GENERAL LITERARY INDEX: INDEX OF AUTHORS.*

The *Victoria et Triumphus de impia et multiplici Exsecrabilium Massalianorum Secta*, referred to by your correspondent H. B. C. (3rd S. iv. 458), is a kind of appendix to the *Panoplia* of Euthymius, the contents of which are here given. The former I propose to notice in a separate article on *Manicheism and the Origin of Evil* (1st S. iv. 346; 2nd S. iv. 199).

Euthymius Zigabenus (or Zygadenus), a Greek monk of the Order of St. Basil, flourished in the beginning of the twelfth century under the Emperor Alexius Comnenus; by whom he was highly esteemed for his learning and piety, and by whose command he compiled the *Panoplia*, as we learn from the *Alexiad* of the Princess Anna Comnena, p. 490.

Dupin never saw the Greek text of this work. The various editions of the Latin Version by Petrus Franciscus Zinus are given by him in his *History of Ecclesiastical Writers*, by Oudin and Fabricius. MSS. of his works are enumerated by Lambecius and Possevinus In the edition of 1714, the Patriarch Chrysanthus being apprehensive of the same cruelty from the Turks which they had exercised against Cyril Lucaris (see Smith's *Account of the Greek Church, &c.*, 1680; Aymon, *Monumens Authentiques de la Religion des Grecs*, 4to, 1708; and Mosheim's *Institutes*, cent. xvi. sect. 3, and cent. xvii. sect. 2, ch. ii., omitted the chapter against the Saracens, and what relates to the doctrine of the Trinity; neither is the Latin Version complete, *e. g.* the extract from Photius *concerning the procession of the Holy Spirit* is omitted (tit. xiii. in the Greek MSS.). The separate treatise on this subject differs but little, according to Dupin, from this portion of the *Panoplia;* but of Dupin's account of Euthymius's which, Simon (*Critique de la Bibliothèque*, p. 318) remarks: "Quot verba, tot errata." This, no

doubt, arose from his not having seen the Greek text:—

"Though Euthymius Zigabenus is a writer well known to scholars, his *Panoplia Dogmatica*, in many respects the most valuable of his works, is I believe an exceedingly rare book. The only printed edition of the original text appeared at Tergovist, in Wallachia, in the year 1710 ... and very few copies seem to have found their way to the west of Europe. The copy which was used by Fabricius (*Bibl. Græca*, vol. vii. p. 461) had been given to his friend Michael Eneman in the East by the Patriarch of Jerusalem. It is not in the Bodleian, nor in the British Museum;* and the only copy I ever saw was in the King's library at Paris, till a few months ago I purchased one from a bookseller in London. My good fortune in meeting with so rare a work would be more interesting to the members of certain clubs, which have now passed their hey-day, than to the readers of the *British Magazine*."—Vol. xiv. p. 287.

The Elenchus Sententiarum, or Contents, are as follow:—Contra Epicureos. On Epicurean Atheism, or Democritic Fate, the reader may consult Boyle's *Works* (Index, *s. v.* Epicureans, Epicurus). Cudworth's *Intellectual System*. H. More's *Letters to Des Cartes*. Stillingfleet's *Origines Sacræ*. Bentley's *Boyle Sermons* against Atheism. Dutens' *Origin of Discoveries*. Tit. i. De Deo uno, Filium, et Spiritum S. habente. Tit. ii. De Patre et Filio et Spiritu Sancto; see S. Maximi *Dialogi de Trinitate*, vol. ii.; and Photii Dissert. 4 (Canisii *Thesaur. Monum.*, t. ii. part 2). Tit. iii. De Deo communiter; tres hypostases declarantur, cf. Maximus, vol. ii. cap. 20, 22, and Petavii *Theologia Dogmatica*, vol. i. pp. 170—5, 261, 293, 301, 368, 372, in all which passages are references to Maximus and Euthymius. Tit. iv. Divinam naturam comprehendi non posse. Compare Mansel's *Bampton Lectures*, l. vi.; Cudworth's *Intellectual System*, 1845, vol. ii. p. 343. Tit. v. De Divina appellatione. On the works of Dionysius Areopagita, see Possevinus, *Appar. Sacer.*, pp. 469-74. Tit. vi. De opificio Dei, cf. Petavii *Theol. Dogmat.*, lib. yi. c. v.; De origine mali, Cudworth's *Treatise of Free-will*. Tit. vii. De divina humanæ carnis assumptione; cf. Radcliffe on the Athanasian Creed. Tit. viii. p. 49 *seq.* Contra. Hebræos; cf. Canisii *Thesaur. Monum.*, t. iv. pp. 256-7; Smith's *Scripture Testimony to the Messiah*. Tit. ix. 57. Adversus Simonem Samarensem et Marcionem Ponticum et Manetem Persicum et Manicheos, see Tit. xxi. *infrà*. Tit. x. Adversus Sabellium, see Mosheim's *Inst.;* Clinton's *Epitome of Chronology of Rome, &c.*, p. 385. Tit. xi. p. 61. In Arrianos et Eunomianos, see Clinton's *Fasti Romani*, vol. ii. pp. 434, 435. Tit. xii. De Spiritu Sancto, see Fabricii *Bibl. Gr.*, lib. v. c. ii. Tit. xiii. Adversus Apollinarium, see Clinton's *Epitome of the Chronology of Rome, &c.*, p. 395; Bayle's *Dictionary*. Tit. xiv. Adversus Nestorianos, see Clinton's *Chronology*, pp. 174, 175; and *Fasti Romani*,

[* A copy of the *Panoplia Dogmatica* is now in the British Museum.—ED.]

vol. i. p. 611.; also Theodoret, *Hæret. Fab.* xii. Tit. xv. Adversus Eutychianos et Monophysitas, see Mosheim's *Institutes.* Tit. xvi. Adversus Aphthardocitas, see Mosheim, cent. vi. part ii. ch. 5; and Clinton, *s. v.* Julianus Halicarn. Ep. Tit. xvii. Adversus Theopaschitas, see Mosheim, cent. v. part ii. ch. 5. Tit. xviii. Adversus Monotheletas, see *Encyclop. Metropol.*, vol. xi. p. 425. A copious account of the Monothelite Heresy is contained in the works of Johannes Damascenus in a *Treatise on the Two Wills,* and in his books on the *Orthodox Faith* (in Euthym., pp. 181—184). Tit. xix. Adversus imaginum oppugnatores. On the three famous orations of Damascenus, see Milman's *Latin Christianity.* Tit. xx. Adversus Armenios. Aphthartodocitarum simul et Theopaschitarum morbo insaniunt; see Vincentii *Bellovac.*, lib. xxx. c. 98; *Centuriæ Magdeburg.*, cent. 13. p. 562; Combefis, *Nov. Auctar.*, t. ii. p. 287. On the claims of the Armenian Church to orthodoxy, see Neale's *Hist. of the H. Eastern Church.* The Agnœtæ (see Lambecius, lib. iii. p. 168, who mentions them as the subject of one of the MSS. of Euthymius,) maintained the Monophysite or Eutychian doctrine: their heresy is refuted by Forbes in his elaborate work, *Instructiones Historico-Theologica,* lib. iii. c. 19. (The principle of equivocation is here discussed and exhausted.) Cf. the Treatise of Athanasius *Against Arianism,* Disc. iii. p. 470 (*Libr. of the Fathers*), and the editor's note; Theodoret, *Anath.*, t. v. p. 23, edit. Schutze, edit. Sirmondi, 1642, vol. iv. 712—714. Tit. xxi. Adversus Paulicianos, ex scriptis Photii Patriarchæ Constantinopolitani. Tit. xxii. Adversus Massalianos. Tit. xxiii. Adversus Bogomilos. An account of these heretics, by Euthymius and others, will be given under the art. "Manicheism and the Origin of Evil. Tit. xxiv. Contra Saracenos. This, which is wanting in the Greek edition, was published in Greek and Latin by Sylburgius, 1595, 8vo, and inserted in the *Biblioth. Græco-Latina,* Paris, 1624, vol. ii. pp. 292—312, and other collections: the translation [*Bibl. Patr.*, vol. xix.] was by J. J. Beurer. Lambecius (lib. iv. p. 206) describes a MS., entitled Euth. Zig. Monachi Græci *Disputatio cum Saraceno quodam Philosopho de Fide, &c.* : —

"It is a calumny that the Mahometans believe God to be corporeal. And yet Pope Pius the Second wrote so in in a *Letter to Morbisanus* (or *Mahomet II.*), tho' he is reckoned very honest and candid by those of his own party; but this is a matter of fact. . . . Euthymius Zigabenus, in *Panoplia Dogmatica,* hath fall'n into the same mistake, when writing of Mahomet, he says (p. 229) : 'That God is spherical. Now this is the figure of a Body, and signifies Body, as much as thick and compact. Since, therefore, according to him God is a corporeal Sphere, it will follow that he can neither hear nor see.' . . . This mistake hath sprung from the ambiguous signification of a word we translate Sphere, which also signifies Eternal; and in this sense it is rightly affirmed of God." — Reland, *Of the Mahometan Religion* (in *Four Treatises concerning the Doctrine, Discipline, and Worship of the Mahometans*), 1712.

"The Mahometans believe God to be the Author of Evil, if we trust Cedrenus. . . . . Euthymius Zigabenus, in *Panoplia Dogmat.*, insisting upon the same calumny, endeavours to demonstrate what he advances upon this head, out of the Alcoran. . . . . The Mahometans are unjustly charged with this opinion ; with which all who maintain the absolute Providence of God, and his independent Right in all things, are wont to be charged."— Reland, pp. 55, 56.

Bibl. ibid. Cf. Petavii *Theolog. Dogm.*, vol. i.; "N. & Q.," 2nd S. i. 301. With reference to Mahomet's Manicheism, see Wolfius, p. 246.

"Euthym. Zigaben., in *Panoplia,* writes that the Arabs were given to the worship of Venus; and he is cited by Selden *De Dis Syris,* p. 216. I wish this great man had bestow'd some strokes of his pen upon the words of Euthymius as being contrary to manifest truth; but Selden passes them over without any judgment upon them, and seems to be of the same mind with Euthymius, &c. . . . . Damascenus says more justly of the Arabians: 'They indeed worship'd the Images of the Star Lucifer, and of Venus, which in their own tongue they call Chabar, till the time of Heraclius. For when Mahomet arose he banished all worship of Idols.'"

Thus far Reland, who has himself made a great mistake, for Euthymius himself writes: " Saraceni *usque ad tempora Heraclii Imperatoris* colebant Idola, Luciferumque et Venerem . . . Tunc autem surrexit Moameth," &c.—P. 228.

Euthym. Zigab., in *Panoplia,* affirms the same thing (that the Mahometans worship all created beings), and endeavours to demonstrate it in these words (*Bibl. Patr.*, p. 230 E.) : " Mahomet swears by the Sun, Moon, Stars, &c. . . . He that sweareth, uses to swear by that which is greater than himself." As if the Jews, who swear by the Temple, by Jerusalem, by their head, should therefore be said to worship their head and the Holy City as gods (p. 59).

"Till the time," says Euthymius, "of the Emperor Heraclius, the Saracens served Idols and worshipped the Morning Star and Venus; by them called Chabar 'in their tongue, a word that signifies Great. Those are the words of Euthymius, in which he distinguishes Venus from the Morning Star; nor is it to be wondered at that the Jews, being neighbours to the Arabians, borrow'd of 'em this Idolatry."—Jurieu's *Critical History of the Doctrines and Worship of the Church,* p. 206.

Cf. Kircheri *Œdipus Ægyptiacus,* tom. i. p. 352, and "N. & Q.," 1st S. x. 190.

Appendix: Photii Patriarchæ Constantinopolitani ex epistola ad Michaelem Bulgariæ Principem de septem Conciliis Œcumenicis. The original "Opusculum," &c., is printed in Greek and Latin in Justelli *Bibl. Juris Can.*, tom. ii. p. 1141; and in Canisii *Thesaurus Monumentorum,* tom. ii. part ii. p. 382. See Lambecius, lib. iii. p. 161 *sqq.*, and Mich. Le Quien, *Contra Schisma Græcorum,* p. 174.

His other works are *Commentarii in Psalmos,* pp. 235—461: for other editions, see *Bibliotheca*

Bodleiana, Cantica et Orationes, pp. 461-74. *Commentarii in quatuor Evangelia*, pp. 475—728: for other editions, Bibl. Bodl. Walchii *Bibl. Theologica;* Fabricii *Bibl. Græca*, vol. viii. p. 328, &c. (or vol. vii. p. 474); Cave, *Hist. Lit.*, vol. i. p. 646.   BIBLIOTHECAR. CHETHAM.

DANTE AND HERALDRY.—In the various discussions on the early use of coat armour which have recently come before the public, reference has been freely made to rolls of arms, seals, &c. But I have nowhere noticed the interesting fact that, not only are heraldic insignia familiarly blazoned in Dante's great poem, but in certain passages of his work, the personages whom he commemorates are defined by these insignia alone. Hence an acquaintance with the distinctive devices which characterised Italian families in the thirteenth century must have been very general at the time when Dante wrote to insure such a result, as that the mere blazoning of their armorial ensigns in a poem should be sufficient to identify the historic personages so depicted.

The subjoined passage from the 17th canto of the *Inferno* may suffice as an example:—

"   .   .   .   io mi accorsi
Che dal collo a ciascun pendea una tasca,
Che avea certo colore, e certo segno.

.   .   .   .   .   .
In una borsa gialla vidi azzurro
Che di un lione avea faccia e contegno.
Poi procedendo di mio sguardo il curro,
Vidine un' altra, come sangue rossa,
Mostrare una oca bianca più che burro.
Ed un, che di una scrofa azzurra e grossa
Segnato avea lo suo sacchetto bianco
Mi disse : ' Che fai tu in questa fossa ? '

.   .   .   vegna il cavalier sovrano,
Che recherà la tasca coi tre becchi."

Here we have in succession the arms of the Gianfigliacci (or Gianfigliazzi) of Florence, of the Ubbriachi of the same city, and of the Scrovigni of Padua. While the last, "tre becchi," three goats (not three birds' beaks, as it is explained in an edition now before me, published by Fleischer of Leipsic in 1826, and edited by Adolph Wagner), was the bearing of the notorious usurer Giovanni Bujamonte of Florence.   H. W. T.

ORIGIN OF GODFREY'S CORDIAL. — The following advertisement is in Read's *Weekly Journal or British Gazetteer*, Feb. 17, 1722:—

"To all Retailers and others. The General Cordial formerly Sold by Mr. THO.GODFREY, of Hunsdon in Hertfordshire, deceas'd, is now Prepar'd according to a Receipt written by his own Hand, and by him given to my Wife, his Relation ; is now Sold by me THO. HUMPHREYS of Ware, in the said county, Surgeon, or at John Humphreys' at the Hand and Sheers in Jewin Street, near Cripplegate, London : Also may be furnished with Arca-

nums, or Vomits, &c. and will be allow'd the same for selling as formerly.
                                                    "THO. HUMPHREYS, Surgeon."

Let the world know through "N. & Q." to whom it is indebted for a mixture which all who have paid attention to Vital Statistics know to be, at this time, the cause of probably one-fourth of the infantile mortality in the manufacturing counties of York, Lancaster, and Chester; and in all England upwards of one-tenth.   W. LEE.

SIR HENRY RAEBURN. — In a work on *Scottish Worthies*, published some time since, this well-known artist is described as having met the charming young daughter of Mr. Peter Edgar, during one of his woodland walks, and then, after a short and pleasant courtship, married the young lady, and so acquired an ample fortune. The absurdity of this will be apparent when it is remembered that Miss Edgar was the eldest of a large family, and acquired her property by her first marriage with James Leslie, Esq., of Deanhaugh, whose only daughter, Jacobina, was the first wife of the last Vere of Stonebyres.   JHLA.

A COINCIDENCE. — The second volume of the *Monthly Review* for 1795 contains in its Index the following item:—

"*Little*, Captain ; see *Moore*"—

reminding us of the same conjunction of names in the case of a certain wild and witty Irish writer, whose brochure, under the pseudonyme of Little, was published a very few years afterwards, gaining its author More notoriety than credit.
                                                    HIBERNUS.

THE GREAT BELL OF WESTMINSTER.—
Claus. 35 *Hen. III. Memb.* 19.—" Mandatum est Edwardo de Westmon. sicut Rex alias mandavit, quod fieri faciat unam campanam quæ respondeat magnæ Campanæ Westmon., et quæ non sit ejusdem magnitudinis dum tamen convenienter ei per consilium magistri in sono respondeat. Magnam etiam Crucem collocari faciat in navi ecclesiæ Westmon., et ornet duos angelos in modum Cherubyn, utraque parte illius crucis collocandos. T. R. apud Westm. 4 die Febr."—Ashmole MS. (Bodl. Libr.) 860, pp. 86-7.

Warrants were also issued to the same Edward of Westminster to make standards, a crown to be offered to St. Edward, a stole with sapphires and pearls of the value of fifteen or twenty marks, and other ornaments.   W. D. MACRAY.

SHOEING THE GOOSE.—At p. 90 of Mr. Wright's charming work, entitled a *History of Caricature and Grotesque in Literature and Art*, I find that he alludes to the Shoeing of the Goose in the following words.   (N.B. The italics are my own):—

" In a cleverly sculptured ornament in Beverley Minster, represented in our cut, No. 57, the goose herself is represented in a grotesque situation, which might almost give her a place in ' the World turned upside down,' *although it is a mere burlesque without any apparent satirical meaning.*"

` It may be interesting to some of your readers to, know that there is another example of this strange shoeing in the parish church of Whalley in Lancashire. It occurs there under the seat of one of the stalls in the chancel, supposed to have been the Abbott's Stall, in the old Abbey of Whalley. There is an inscription beneath it, as follows : —

> " Whoso melles of wat men dos,
> Let hym cum hier and shoe the ghos."

A writer whose name I cannot remember, rendered the inscription thus, keeping, as he thought, the spirit of the original : —

> " That fool to shoe a goose should try,
> Who pokes his nose in each man's pie."

Is is right, therefore, to say that the carving in question has no satirical meaning? and are there any other examples known? 　　　**L. H. M.**

THE FRENCH AND SCOTTISH LANGUAGES. — Some of your readers may care to have another philological relic of our ancient connection with France.

The ordinary Scotch word for a draughtboard is *dambrod*. In Strutt's *Sports and Pastimes*, Hone's edition, p. 316, I find the following : — " The draughtman is called in French, *dame*." It would be interesting were some of your contributors to make a list of the words which have found their way into the Scottish language from the French. Here are three as a beginning : — *Ashet* for *assiette*. *Bonnet* in both languages is used for a man's cap. The *birretta* for ecclesiastics was in the French church called bonnet. *Design* for picture evidently has something to do with *dessein*. 　　　**WM. HUMPHREY.**

Cove, near Aberdeen.

JUSTICES' GRAMMAR. — On the sands at Scullercoats, near Tynemouth, a board has been fixed on which is inscribed the following notice : —

" Any persons passing beyond this point will be drowned, by order of the magistrates."

The old Northumbrian barons claimed the power of execution " fossa et furca." I suppose, however, the present threat to be a slip of the pen.

　　　J. F.

Clapham.

Queries.

EXHIBITION OF PORTRAIT MINIATURES, SOUTH KENSINGTON MUSEUM.

I shall be glad if any of your readers can enlighten me on the following points : —

1. *Minatures on Ivory.* — When did miniature painting on ivory first come into use? Can any one adduce a well authenticated instance before 1670?

2. *Mourning Costume.* — There are two curious portraits in Lord Spencer's collection, numbered 937, 939 in the catalogue. The gentleman is dressed in a white linen habit, with a black cloak thrown over the left shoulder and under the right arm; the lady is in a tight-fitting white habit, with long hair hanging loose down her back Is this the mourning-dress of the period? The two portraits I refer to are evidently in the costume of the end of the sixteenth century or the commencement of the seventeenth. A similarly costumed portrait, but fifty years later, is No. 349 in Mr. John Berners's collection. Can any of your readers enlighten me on this point?

3. *Sally of Salisbury.* — Who was Sally of Salisbury? There are two enamels of her and her daughter exhibited by Mr. William Meyer, casé G. Nos. 663–664, apparently of the first half of the seventeenth century. 　　**JAMES BECK, M.A.**

The Cottage, Storrington, Sussex.

ABRAHAM'S CONVERSION. — Where is to be found the first account of the following, which I extract from Dr. A. P. Stanley's *Sermons in the East* (London, Murray, 1863), p. 124 : —

" There is an ancient tradition that Abraham, as he stood on the hills above Damascus, was converted to the true faith in one God, from the worship of the heavenly. bodies, by observing that the stars, the moon, and the sun, however bright and glorious, at last sank and were succeeded by others. ' I like not,' he said, ' those that set :' and so turned to the one unchangeable Lord and Maker of all."

　　　H. C.

BEEST. — The milk given by a cow, for a few days after calving, is of a rich quality; and, in Lancashire, is called " beest " or " beast." Whence the name? 　　　**PRESTONIENSIS.**

" BIBLIOPHOBIA." — In a book written in 1832 by Mercurius Rusticus, there are several pseudonyms denoting celebrated Roxburghers. Can any venerable Roxburgher give me the *real* names of them? First, the author, Mercurius Rusticus; who was he? [*]

Some of the others I know, but with the following I am at fault : — Licius[†], Philelphus, Crassus, Decius, Philander, Portius, Marcus and M. R. the annotator. The book was printed by Henry Bohn, 4, York Street. 　SCRUTATOR.

BUNYAN DRAMATISED. — In *The Critic* (London literary journal) of June 1, 1855, there is a short paragraph stating that Bunyan's *Pilgrim's Progress* has found its way on to the boards of the Chesnut Theatre, Philadelphia. Who was the adapter of this dramatic version of Bunyan, and was it printed? Is there any notice of it in F. C. Wemyss's *History of the American Stage*, published in 1852 or 1853? 　　　**R. I.**

[* The Rev. Dr. Dibdin. 　† Sir Francis Freeling.— ED.]

Cock's Feather. — I am curious to know why Mephistopheles and other stage representatives of evil incarnate wear a cock's feather?

ST. SWITHIN.

THE REV. JOHN DANIEL COTTON.—This gentleman, who was vicar of Good Easter, Essex, published *Lachrymæ Elegiacæ sive Querelæ Epistolares*, 1765. When did he die?

S. Y. R.

EPISCOPAL RINGS. — In the effigy of Bishop Oldham (died A.D. 1519), in Exeter Cathedral, the uplifted hands of the recumbent figure, which are pressed together, are adorned with no less than seven large rings worn on the fingers: three being on the right, and four on the left hand. And, in addition to these, a single signet-ring of extraordinary size is represented as *worn over both the thumbs*. Can any reader of "N. & Q." kindly refer me to another example of an episcopal thumb-ring worn upon both the thumbs at the same time?

CHARLES BOUTELL.

FAMILY NAMES LOST.—Have any of our English family names ever became entirely extinct? In an assessment of the ward of Walbrook, made in 1635, I find the following names: —" Steven Wanspeire, Thomas Totty, Arthur Mousse, Henry Pitchforke, Richard Doelitell." Do these names still exist among us? I know, of course, that the race of the Dolittles is not extinct; but what about the name?

BENJ. CHR. OU.

REV. EDWARD FORD, F.T.C.D. — In Dr. Trusler's *Tablet of Memory; or, Historian's Guide*, Dublin, 1782, p. 176, there is the following entry: —

"1734, Feb. 7. Mr. Ford, one of the fellows of Trinity College, Dublin, was shot by one of the scholars."

In the *Dublin University Calendar*, 1865, p. 276, Mr. Ford is said to have been "killed by a shot fired from the College Park, March 8, 1734." A few years ago I read a very interesting article in a leading periodical, founded on the sad occurrence. I am desirous of reading it again; but I do not know what periodical to consult. Will you kindly aid me in the matter?

ABHBA.

INFANT-MORTALITY, OR INFANTILE MORTALITY? I shall be glad of an opinion as to which of the above is the more correct expression. I always use the first as I prefer it. These are my reasons for doing so: the compound word "infant-mortality" seems to express the sense intended — namely, the deaths of infants; that is to say, a positive unalterable fact is understood by the term "mortality," irrespective of the word going before. But when the adjective "infantile" precedes the noun, it implies something peculiar to infancy, as for instance, "infantile play," "infantile talk," "infantile disorders," &c.; but "infantile mortality" seems to me nonsense, because death is the same in young and old; while "infant-mortality" means death at an early age. This is my

idea of the matter. I shall, however, be greatly obliged if any of your readers will afford some information on the subject, as I find the majority of educated writers adopt the other term, of which the daily press and other publications afford ample proof.

M. A. B.

INFLUENZA.—Is this word of modern origin? I mean within the last fifty years or less. What is it derived from? I have almost answered my own query, for opening the first volume of the *European Magazine* for June, 1782, I came upon the following piece of poetry: —

"*Influenza:* a Glee.

"SET BY MR. BARTHELEMON.

" Influenza! haste away!
    Cease thy baneful empire here!
    Boast no longer of thy sway!
    Cease dominion o'er the year.
    Radiant Sun, exert thy pow'r,
    On the wings of Zephyr come,
    Dart thy beams and rule the hour!
    Health and Beauty then shall bloom! "

The word *influenza* is, however, not in the folio edition, 1765, of Johnson's *Dictionary*.

W. P.

IN TWO PLACES AT ONCE LIKE A BIRD.—At page 126 of a little book called *The Book-Hunter*, by Mr. Burton, published in 1862, I find the following foot-note : —

" I have doubts whether the saying attributed to Sir Boyle Roche, about being in two places at once *like a bird*, is the genuine article. I happened to discover that it is of earlier date than Sir Boyle's day, having found when rummaging in an old house among some Jacobite manuscripts; one from Robertson of Strowan, the warrior poet, in which he says about two contradictory military instructions, 'It seems a difficult point for me to put both orders in execution, unless, as the man said, I can be in two places at once, like a bird.' A few copies of these letters were printed for the use of the Abbotsford Club. This letter of Strowan's occurs in page 92."

Can any one throw any more light on the origin or antiquity of this expression? I have been unable to find Robertson's letter.

WORKWORTH.

WILLIAM ITCHENER, D.D., was of Corpus Christi College, Oxford, B.A., Feb. 13, 1695; M.A. July 8, 1698; D.D. by diploma, May 6, 1729. He published *A Defence of the Canon of the Old Testament*, Lond. 8vo, 1723, being then rector of Christian Malford, in Wilts. I am desirous of knowing when he died.

S. Y. R.

"LIBER FAMELICUS."—I was looking the other day through the publications of the Camden Society, and among others of that valuable series, I was attracted by a book with the curious title of *Liber Famelicus*. It is an interesting Diary kept by Sir James Whitelocke, the Judge of the King's Bench in the reigns of James I. and Charles I.; and the father of the more renowned Bulstrode Whitelocke, Cromwell's chancellor, whose *Memorials of the Rebellion* are oftener quoted than any work on the subject, and still retain their popularity.

I am puzzled about the meaning of the title; for the judge, who was a well-educated and very learned person, and withal thirty-nine years of age when he began the book, must have had some reason for so christening it. The word "Famelicus" is used by Pliny, Seneca, and Plautus, in the sense of hungry and famished, which would not be appropriate to Sir James, who was by no means a half-starved lawyer at the time, but rejoiced in a flourishing practice. Was it a hasty and mistaken idea of the judge, that the word was derived from "Familia"? I cannot otherwise account for its use. Perhaps some of your ingenious correspondents may suggest another interpretation. PHILOLOGUS.

MILTON.'— What crest and motto did the poet Milton bear? CARILFORD.
Cape Town, S. A.

NETTLES PROOFS OF HABITATION.—The British camp of Worlebury, on the hill above Weston-super-Mare, contains within its area many circular pits, from five to six feet in depth. These are the foundations of ancient dwellings, and human remains have been found in some of them. In many of these pits nettles are growing. None are to be found outside them, even where the area of the camp is covered with brushwood and coppice. It has been said more than once that nettles are a sure indication of ancient habitation. I have found them (although rarely) among the granite of hut circles on Dartmoor; and last autumn I saw them growing thickly about the pits of an ancient settlement on the side of Roseberry Topping in Yorkshire. They are found, also, I believe, on the sites of British villages which have lately been discovered on the Cheviots. I wish to ask whether there is sufficient proof that the presence of nettles is in such cases, a result of the former presence of man? and if so, what reason can be given for it? R. J. KING.

OATH OF THE ROMANS.—
"A Highlander, when sworn on the gospels or the cross, cares little for his oath, but will keep it if sworn on the point of his dirk. The degenerate Romans of the Lower Empire avowed, that it was better to break an oath to God than one by the head of the Emperor, for the mercy of God might forgive offences to himself, but not those to the Emperor: but when the Emperor changed his views, their casuistry argued that false swearing was not perjury," p. 15.—A Plea against the needless Multiplication of Oaths, by John Owen, Minister of Salem Chapel, Deptford, 8vo, London, 1789, pp. 32.

The pamphlet is an exposure of the oaths-of-course administered at the Custom House, and on affidavits before magistrates. The casuistry of the Romans is strange, but I have no doubt there is some authority for the statement, though I cannot find, and shall be glad to be, referred to one. J. M. K.

QUOTATION. — The following is in an old common-place book. Can any of your readers tell me whence it was taken? —

" . . . . Mollis
Qualis anas, quam pura beat piscinula, præceps
Conditur, accipiter rapidis ubi desilit alis:
Qui superas indigna ferent, se tollit in auras." *
P. H.

SIR WALTER SCOTT.—Is the following scrap of old Scotch ballad, met with in some stray letter of Sir Walter's, still current in Fifeshire? —

"There's as mony fish in Anster Bay
As there are lairds in Fife.
O! in that bonny kingdom
Lives mony a fisher-wife."
WALTER THORNBURY.

"THE SYNAGOGUE OF THE LIBERTINES."— In the Acts of the Apostles (chap. vi. 9) occur the following words: —

'Ἀνέστησαν δέ τινες τῶν ἐκ τῆς συναγωγῆς τῆς λεγομένης Λυβερτίνων, κ.τ.λ.

My query is, what particular synagogue is meant by the expression "the synagogue of the Libertines"? I am aware that several explanations are given; but those which I have seen do not appear to be satisfactory. Schleusner (sub voce Λυβερτῖνοι) mentions, that some writers suppose there was a town in Africa Proper named Libertus, or Libertina, whence a certain class of Jews came to Jerusalem and there established a synagogue. There is a monthly Bulletin published in Rome by the celebrated Cavaliere de Rossi, entitled Bulletino di Archeologia Cristiana. I understand that the discovery, on the walls of a house in Pompeii, of an electioneering appeal in favour of one Cuspius Pansa, who is recommended to the office of ædile by Fabius Eupor, Princeps Libertinorum, gives occasion to the learned archæologist for a valuable historical investigation into the meaning of this title. His remarks, I believe, throw great light on the expression under consideration, viz., " the synagogue of the Libertines." The article appeared in one of the late numbers of the Bulletin. Can any of your correspondents or readers refer me to the particular number? J. DALTON.
St. John's, Norwich.

THE TRINE BENEDICTION. — I have always understood the Roman Catholic sign of benediction, perpetually pictured in the old masters, of three fingers held up, to signify blessing in the name of the Holy Trinity; but to-day I meet with a reference to Lavater as an authority for that interpretation, and something more. My author says:—

"Three fingers [men] do oft lift up, and hold down two, to signify, saith Lavater, that God, who is Three in One, hath prepared a place in heaven for such as swear

[* Sic in the copy.—ED.]

rightly; but will thrust down to hell those that forswear themselves."

Where does Lavater thus interpret the sign?

QUERE.

ZINC SPIRES.—While recently on a visit to my old friend the rector of Ilford, in Essex, I was struck with the alterations already commenced on the very unsightly church, erected there early in the present century. It is sufficient to state that the designs are the work of that distinguished architect Mr. Ashpitel, without calling attention to their merits; but the admirable effect of the zinc spire and its comparative cheapness leads me to inquire whether such structures have stood the test of time, or are quite novel in this country. Are any medieval examples known? In Bohemia and the Tyrol I believe they are common.

THOMAS E. WINNINGTON.

Queries with Answers.

GEORGE CHAPMAN.—Can any of your correspondents obligingly inform me of any particulars of the life of George Chapman, the translator of Homer? The place of his birth seems unknown, and the account given in the *Athenæ* refers almost entirely to his works. Warton says, upon the authority of Francis Wise, that he passed two years in Trinity College, Oxford. The authority is a good one; but unfortunately, owing to both the university and college registers being incomplete or lost about that period, there is no opportunity of confirming it. Of his latter days in London we cannot expect to hear much.　　W.

[In Kippis's *Biographia Britannica*, iii. 436, will be found an excellent account of George Chapman. Consult also Edward Phillips's *Theatrum Poetarum*, by Brydges, edit. 1800, p. 250—258, and Dodsley's *Old Plays*, edit. 1825, iv. 101—106. In Nichols's *Select Poets*, i. 271, as well as in Collier's *History of Dramatic Poetry*, iii. 257, it is stated that Chapman was born about 1557, and that his family seems to have been respectably settled at Hitchin, in Hertfordshire. One member of it, Thomas Chapman, in 1619, petitioned Prince Charles for the Bailiwick of Hitchin, which the petitioner had formerly possessed under the Exchequer Seal, but of which the Earl of Salisbury had deprived him; and, on the 30th of November of that year, the claim was referred to the commissioners of the revenue of the Prince of Wales (*Vide* Harl. MS. 781). It would also seem, from an early portion of his poem *Enthymiæ Raptus: or the Teares of Peace*, 4to, 1609, that Chapman had been occupied in his Homeric labour near Hitchin, in Herts. The shade of Homer is supposed to answer the poet's inquiry, " What **may** I reckon thee, **whose** heavenly look showes not, nor **voice** sounds, man?"

" **I am** (sayd he) that spirit Elysian, **That in** thy native ayre, and on the Hill **Next Hitchin's** left hand, did thy bosome fill

With such a flood of soule, that thou wert faine (With acclamations of her rapture then) To vent it to the echoes of the vale; When meditating of me, a sweet gale Brought me upon thee; and thou didst inherit My true sense (for the time then) in my spirit : And I, invisible, went prompting thee To those fayre greenes, where thou didst English me."

That Hertfordshire has a better claim to the honour of Chapman's birth than Stone Castle in Kent (as conjectured by Wood) is further confirmed by his friend and contemporary William Browne in his *Britannia's Pastorals* (book i. song 1), where he styles him—" The learned shepherd on fair Hitching Hill."

Inigo Jones, at his own expense, erected an altar-tomb to the memory of George Chapman in the old church of St. Giles-in-the-Fields, London. It was repaired in 1827 by the Rev. James Endell Tyler, the rector, and is now fixed against the south wall of the church on the outside. The monument part alone is old; the inscription is a copy of all that remained visible.]

ELECTRIC TELEGRAPH FORESHADOWED.—

" They who spread positive and confident aspersions . . . are great advancers of defamatory designs than the very first contrivers. . . . What the others are fain to whisper, they proclame : like *our new Engine*, which pretends to convey a whisper many miles off. So that as in the case of Stealing, 'tis proverbially said, that if there were no receivers there would be no thieves : so in this of slander, if there were fewer spreaders, there would be fewer forgers of Libels ; the manufacture would be discouraged, if it had not these retailers to put off the wares."— *The Government of the Tongue*, by the author of *The Whole Duty of Man*, Oxford, 1675, p. 53.

What was the engine here referred to? Has any light been lately thrown on the authorship of *The Whole Duty of Man?* Is any particular person now generally admitted to have been the author? And if so, on what evidence does the conclusion rest?　　D.

[When the above passage was written the author may have been thinking either of Lord Bacon's " engine houses, where we prepare engines and instruments for all sorts of motions " (*New Atlantis*, p. 303, Bohn's edition), or to Glanville's remarkable prediction of the discovery and general adoption of the electric telegraph, in his *Scepsis Scientifica*, 1665, 4to, p. 134, where he writes : "I doubt not but posterity will find many things that are now but rumours, verified into practical realities, and to confer at the distance of the Indies by sympathetick conveyances, may be as usual to future times as to us in a literary correspondence."—No additional light has been thrown on the authorship of *The Whole Duty of Man* since the Rev. W. B. Hawkins wrote his valuable Preface in 1842. See the articles in our present volume, pp. 9, 57, 106, 124, 290, and 328.]

FRISIANS.—In a magazine, entitled *The Monthly Literary and Scientific Lecturer* for June, 1851, there is a report of a " Course of Lectures on 'The Ethnology of the British Colonies and Dependencies,' by Dr. R. G. Latham, F.R.S." Lect. 1 says:

"As early as the time of Archbishop Ussher, the probability, and something more, of Frisians making part and parcel of the Anglo-Saxon invasion was indicated."

Where is the statement referred to by Dr. Latham to be found? I have looked in Chalmers's *Biographical Dictionary*, and I do not find that Archbishop Ussher wrote any book on ethnology.

E. A.

[In the lecture as published by Dr. Latham in his *Ethnology of the British Colonies*, 1851, p. 15, the passage reads as follows: "The opinion, I believe, indicated by Archbishop Ussher, and recommended to further consideration by Mr. Kemble, that the Frisians took an important part in the Anglo-Saxon invasion of Great Britain, is gaining ground." The work most likely to contain a notice of the Frisians, is that great treasury of historical research, Ussher's *Britannicarum Ecclesiarum Antiquitates*, which comes down to the close of the seventh century.]

NURSERY RHYME. — I remember an amusing nursery rhyme commencing with the following words. Can the whole of the song be recovered ?—

"The Queen of Hearts
She made some tarts," &c.

W. P.

[We give the version printed in Halliwell's *Nursery Rhymes*, edit. 1846, p. 39 : —

"The Queen of Hearts
She made some tarts,
 All on a summer's day :
The Knave of Hearts
He stole the tarts,
 And took them clean away.

"The King of Hearts
Call'd for the tarts,
 And beat the Knave full sore :·
The Knave of Hearts
Brought back the tarts,
 And vow'd he'd steal no more."

Consult also "N. & Q.," 3rd S. i. 423.]

Replies.

SAVANNAH.

(3rd S. vii. 128.)

Allow me to sacrifice uniformity of reference, by altering your correspondent's spelling; which, being certainly wrong, it seems a pity to preserve. Common usage has settled the orthography as given above; and if worth while, any number of proofs might be offered, as the maps of James Cook in 1771, and of Henry Mouzon in 1775, and every official act relating to the city since, and indeed for a long time before—but this is of small moment. The query put is very hard to answer: Who gave name to Hutchinson's Island, opposite

the town? I find it so called in 1733. Francis Moore writes in 1735 : —

"I took a view of the town of Savannah . . . eastward you see the river increased by the northern branch which runs round Hutchinson's Island, and the Carolina shore beyond it, and the woody islands at the sea which close the prospect at ten or twelve miles' distance : over against it is Hutchinson's Island, great part of which is open ground, where they mow hay for the Trust's horses and cattle. The rest is woods, in which there are many bay trees eighty foot high" (*Georgia Hist. Collect.*, p. 94)—

which agrees well enough with your correspondent's account of his print, taken at about the same period. In 1787 its northern side was declared a part of the line of navigation, thereafter to be equally free to Carolinians and Georgians; but it has figured but little in history, saving the honour of causing the grounding of the ship Hinchinbroke in 1776, during the first battle in Georgia in the revolutionary war; in which vessel, says Dr. Stevens (now Assistant-Bishop of Pennsylvania) in his *History of Georgia*, vol. ii. p. 133, Lords Nelson and Collingwood were made post-captains. As to the nomenclator, we must look for him between the years 1660 and 1733, unless an earlier occurrence of the name than the latter date can be found. Between 1660 and 1670, some few English went from Virginia to Carolina, previous to which time perhaps no Europeans had visited it, at least the south-western part (now Georgia), for nearly one hundred years; that is, since the French and Spanish expeditions. If, as seems most likely, the island took its name from some person of consideration, would it not be worth while to look over the names of those gentlemen in Barbadoes who made proposals to settle in Carolina in 1663; and some of whom, I think, did actually go over shortly thereafter? These proposals are in the State Paper Office. Amongst the emigrants from the Barbadoes and St. Christopher's in 1635, who had "taken the oaths of Allegeance and Supremacie, as also being 'conformable to the order and discipline of the Church of England and no Subsedy men," was one Clement Hutchinson; but of what rank in life, I have no means of knowing. (*New England Genealog. Reg.*, vol. xiv. p. 351.) In the same year two Jo. Hutchinsons, aged respectively twenty-two and forty-seven, and a Michell Hutchinson, were passengers from Gravesend to Virginia (*Id.* vol. ii. p. 113; vol. xv. pp. 144, 145). But the records of Georgia proper are very imperfect, even more so than those of the Carolinas. It was emphatically, as Mr. Whitmore remarks in a late essay, a pauper settlement. And as to Carolina itself, Governor Glen, in 1751, reports to the Lords Commissioners of Trade, in reply to their Lordships' letter, requesting an account of the boundaries of Carolina, &c., that —

"in a general way, the settlers of a new county are agriculturists, mechanics, or artificers ; but as among the settlers of this province there existed many gentlemen, it was probable many interesting facts and observations might have been committed to writing, which would have enabled the writer to answer their Lordships' expectations; had not an unlucky fire, which took place about forty or fifty years ago, consumed one of the public offices, wherein were many papers."

It is very unlikely that the island was named from any one of the distinguished New England family; from which, I presume, your correspondent is descended. The migration from New England to Georgia did not take place until about 1752; and there is no historical event within my knowledge, previous to 1733 (when we know the island to have had its present name), which would have induced the colonists to have looked to distant Massachusetts for a local name. I do not infer from your correspondent's note, that there was any relationship between the family of Col. Hutchinson the Regicide and that of the celebrated Governor of Massachusetts Bay. The latter expressly denies it in a letter to the Hon. J. H. Hutchinson, in 1772, preserved in the *New England Register*, before referred to, at p. 302 of vol. i. It appears to have been a grandson, and not a son of Col. Hutchinson, who was said to have "emigrated to the West Indies or America." See the Preface to Bohn's edition, 1848, of *Memoirs of Col. Hutchinson*.

There was a Mr. Hutchinson living at Savannah before the late Southern rebellion; and if this should meet his eye, or that of some member of the Historical Society of Georgia, an answer may be obtained.

Who was Archibald *Hutchison*, who had a good deal to say about the government of Carolina in 1730, or thereabout? Let me add another query: Is Savannah really an Indian name?—

"On this hill they marked out a town, and from the *Indian* name of the river which ran past it, called it Savanna."—*Hist. Col. of South Carolina, New York*, 1836, vol. i. p. 290.

ST. TH.

SHELVES IN WILTSHIRE.

(3ʳᵈ S. vii. 241, 308, 330, 362, 422.)

MR. WILLIAM PINKERTON has accused me of "riding off" from the question. Had he a full knowledge of what is required in the scientific investigation of earthworks, he would know that it is only by comparing similar types in different localities that one can arrive at even an approximate idea of their period or purpose. If I have erred in comparing the shelves of Wiltshire with the terraces of Scotland, I have done so in good company. In the first volume of the *Proceedings of the Antiquaries of Scotland*, p. 127, MR. PINKERTON will find an article by Robert Chambers, in which, as illustrating our Scottish terraces, reference is most properly made to similar works in

England, France, Germany, Hungary, Peru, and Palestine.

MR. PINKERTON's expectation that I will be careering over the roads of Glenroy shows a very imperfect acquaintance with the subject on which he is writing. The very word *parallel* which he uses should have shown him the difference between such geological features and terraces, which are not parallel to the horizon, but sweep round the hill at varying angles.

MR. PINKERTON has, in his concluding observations, totally mistaken my meaning. I in no way connected the plough with the terraces, but only referred to the height at which it had been used on our hills at a remote period. In many cases the terraces, which are always formed on the most fertile land, have been obscured by its action. So far from giving up the plough, I have no doubt that many of those terraces were worked, where the breadth admitted, by the rude ploughs of the period.

"Lazy beds," although in modern times confined to potatoes, were formerly a means for cultivation of many other crops.

As to MR. PINKERTON's question, "How long natural manure has been employed in Scottish agricultural operations?" I would simply remind him that *south* of the Firths of Forth and Clyde the Romans occupied the country, and refer him to the Georgics for *their* knowledge of the use of manure.   GEORGE VERE IRVING.

Culter Mains, May 31st, 1865.

THE ORIGIN OF SMITHFIELD MARKET.

(3ʳᵈ S. vii. 411.)

Your correspondent G. A. draws important conclusions from small evidence when he asserts, that the cattle market was not held in Smithfield until the year 1631. If he had continued his researches he would have been convinced that this market was established from "time immemorial."

1253. In this year, it was enacted by the community, that no one of the franchise of the city should in future pay scavage for his beasts sold on the field of Smethefeld, as before they had been wont.

1266. 50 Henry III. *The Customs of Smythfelde.*—For every cow or ox sold that is full grown, one penny. For every dozen of sheep, one penny. If foreign dealers bring oxen, cows, sheep, or swine between the feast of St. Martin and Christmas, they shall give unto the bailiff the third best beast after the first two best.

1468. 8 Edward IV., April 9, a proclamation was made for Butchers Freemen to begin the market in Smithfield, concerning the buying of beasts and cattle, from seven o'clock in the morning till eleven, at which hour the bell shall be rung, then all foreigners shall begin their market, and so continue for one hour and no longer.

In 1576, 18 Elizabeth, Sep. 28, an order was passed to facilitate the trade of the market. He will also find in the first edition of Stow's *London*, 1798, allusions to the *pens* or *sheepe foldes* used on market days as well as to the cattle market.

1613, 10 James I., Dec. 17, a proclamation was made for the market to be held on every Monday instead of Wednesday and Friday : —

"In consequence of the confluence of People from all parts of this Kingdome to this City of London as of strangers from partes beyond the seas repairing and exercising in this City ; and the number of Citizens and Inhabitants also are farr more and greater than have been in former ages, and therefore the like proportions of provisions of victuals cannot nowe suffice to supply a place growne soe greate and so populous as the same City now is ; besides the places adjoyning, which be not of the liberties nor within the Government of the same, be it therefore enacted that in future the Market be held on a Monday, the bell to be rung at the opening of the same at 9 o'clock, and that it shall remain open until one."

Your correspondent will also find that by the charter granted to the city (1 Edw. III. sect. 12, March 6, 1327,) it is declared that no market shall be granted by the crown to be holden within seven miles all round about the city. This was confirmed by charter 14, Charles I., sect. 14, Oct. 14, 1638. I would also recommend him to read the several Parliamentary Papers referring to this subject before writing the history of the market, from which he will obtain much valuable information. W. H. OVERALL.

THE EXODUS OF THE ISRAELITES.
(3rd S. vii. 419, 428.)

" A date given in terms of "the year of the world," does not convey a distinct meaning, unless it be stated what mode of computation is used. The first year of the Christian era is the 3761st year of the world according to the modern Jewish calendar, and the 6310th according to Panvinius. There are ten intermediate systems of this early chronology, supported by great names, besides many theories of less note.

I am in possession of a restoration of the sacred reckoning, which has stood every test that I have yet been able to apply, and which has appeared to me to solve many chronological difficulties. According to this scheme, the Exodus took place in the year 3269 of the era of Adam, being the year 1541 before Christ.

According to the corrected Egyptian chronology of Brugsch, Amenophis III., the ninth king of the eighteenth dynasty, acceded in the year 1546 B.C. ; and would thus be the reigning monarch at the time of the Exodus. Josephus accuses Manetho of citing a fictitious King Ameno-

phis as then on the throne ; but modern discovery tends to confirm the testimony of the Egyptian historian in this particular.

In the Armenian Chronicle of Eusebius it is stated, under the ninth king of the eighteenth dynasty : "hujus ætate Magus Judæorum ex Egypto egressus dux fuit."

The Exodus has been referred by Sir J. G. Wilkinson to the reign of Thothmes III.—the predecessor by three reigns of Amenophis III. More bricks bear the name of this king than that of any other monarch ; and it is in a monument of his that "the curious process of brick-making is represented, which tallies so exactly with that described in the Exodus." Sir Gardner, in his note on Egyptian history, in Rawlinson's Herodotus, inclines indeed to a later date ; but he says : —

"The sending of the leprous persons to the sulphur springs on the east bank of the Nile, is also a misrepresentation of some real event ; and that it was not a mere fable, is proved by the recent discovery of these springs at Helwàn."

The name of Ramses is characteristic of the nineteenth and twentieth dynasties ; and the sixty-six years of the reign of the famous Ramses Miamoun, to which the Exodus has by some writers been referred, closed exactly 200 years later than the date above cited for the Exodus.

It may be added that the passage of Josephus, as to the employment of Moses in the Ethiopian war before his flight from Egypt, is perfectly consistent with what is known of the history of the eighteenth dynasty. And the disturbance and decadence of this great dynasty, on the death of Amenophis III., might be explained by the death of the first-born of the Pharaoh that sat on the throne. F. R. CONDER.

The Rev. Joseph Reeve, in his beautiful and instructive *History of the Holy Bible*, places the passage of the Red Sea A.M. 2513 and A.C. 1487. He does not quote any authority ; but, if I might venture an assertion, I believe he is borne out by ancient chronologists as regards the time. Who was the King of Egypt at that period, may probably be traced from the sacred text itself. S. REDMOND.

Liverpool.

Mr. Osburn, in his *Monumental History of Egypt*, makes the Exodus of the Israelites to have taken place under Sethos II. of the nineteenth dynasty. The whole account, both of the Exodus and of the antecedent events, is very interesting. It is contained in the 2nd volume, pp. 572—609.

CANON. DALTON will find Manetho's story given at length at pp. 606—608.

Osburn (vol. i. p. 181) confesses his inability to join in the "unbounded eulogy" heaped upon

Manetho's personal character by Bunsen and Lepsius. Bunsen's praise was founded on the favourable opinion entertained of Manetho by Syncellus, who lived a thousand years after Manetho.

JOHN WOODWARD.

New-Shoreham.

"BONNIE DUNDEE" (3rd S. vii. 418.) — The words Gay has assigned to Captain Macheath are not sung to the tune to which Scott's song is allied. In the latter case it is the song, and not the tune which bears the title of "Bonnie Dundee." "Bonnie Dundee" is a fine air of slow time, and very appropriate to the sentiment expressed by Macheath; which would not be the case with the other tune, it being one of a sprightly character, ill suited to express the feelings excited by the "terrible show" which Macheath is about to confront. Macneil's beautiful ballad—"Saw ye my wee thing?"—is sung to the tune introduced into the *Beggar's Opera.*   C. ROSS.

The tune of "Bonnie Dundee" in the *Beggar's Opera* is not the same to which Sir Walter Scott's words are sung. Scott writes of Claverhouse, Viscount Dundee, but the old ballad refers to the town, "Jockey's escape from Dundee," &c. The words of this will be found in the three volumes of *Old Ballads,* 8vo, published in the first quarter of the last century. They are not such as could be reprinted in the present day.

W. CHAPPELL.

"THAT'S THE CHEESE" (3rd S. vii. 397.)—The late David Rees, an eminent comedian, well known in London and Dublin, was celebrated for original *bon mots* on the stage. The above phrase was first introduced to Dublin by him, in a piece called *The Evil Eye,* the scene of which was laid in the Morea. The phrase became very popular, and was used when a person wanted to impress on another that something very important had been said or done in reference to something in hand. I have a clear recollection of having asked Mr. Rees what was the origin of the term, and he replied it arose in consequence of a half-witted boy having eaten a piece of soap and then told his grandmother what a nice piece of cheese he had devoured. "It was soap," cried the old lady. "Oh, no," shouted the boy, "that was the cheese." Such is the story as it was told to me.

S. REDMOND.

Liverpool.

In reference to the note by MR. TRENCH as to the origin of the phrase "That's the cheese," I may say that an old friend of mine, now dead, who was very fond of tracing the history of slang phrases, told me a very simple story as to how "That's the cheese" originated. The story was as follows:— In the north of Ireland there lived an old woman

with a grandson of some eight years of age, and the youth had an appetite that was considered voracious. This was a subject of remark amongst the neighbours; and the old woman on one occasion, when speaking to one of the neighbours, gave the following illustration of her grandson's readiness to eat anything without regard to taste or smell. She had purchased a piece of brown soap, and placed it in the bottom of the window. Some hours afterward, when she was about to commence washing, she said, "Paddy, where's the soap?" "What soap?" said Paddy. "Why," replied the old woman, "the soap that was in the window." "Oh! granny," says he, "that was the cheese!" Paddy had eaten the soap believing it to be cheese.

The story was made a standing joke against Paddy ever afterwards; and by degrees it got circulation, and came to be applied to anything that suited the taste of the party making use of the expression. It is easy to understand in these days, when people are anxious to appear witty, how this should come to be generally used amongst those who use slang for wit; and those who wish to appear more witty than their neighbours use instead, "That's the Stilton," "That's the Cheshire," &c.   J. S. GLASS.

Liverpool.

ST. AGNES AND HER LAMB (3rd S. vii. 402.) — The account, of which H. C. enquires, is found in most old books of Lives of Saints. I translate it as given in the old German work, *Passionael efte dat levent der hyllighen to dude uth dem Latina mit velen nyen hystorien unde leren.* Lubeck, 1507 : —

"Now the friends of St. Agnes were much oppressed with grief for her; and they bewailed her for eight days with great affliction; and watched all night, and wept by her sepulchre. On the eighth night, they saw several beautiful virgins near the sepulchre, who were clothed in rich attire. And on the right hand stood one virgin with a beautiful white lamb. At this sight they were very glad; and Saint Agnes comforted her friends who bewailed her, and spoke thus to them: 'You must not bewail me as among the dead, for I am with these virgins in everlasting bliss: there we have joy infinite and eternal.'"

This vision is inserted in the Roman Breviary on January 28, on which a second feast is kept, or rather a commemoration made of St. Agnes.

F. C. H.

SCARLETT FAMILY (3rd S. vii. 43.) — I am informed by GAMMA that I am "mistaken in regard to Christiana Scarlett's marriage into the family of the Gordons of Earlston." If he will turn to the genealogy of the Gordons of Earlston in Burke's *Peerage and Baronetage,* he will see that James Gordon of Jamaica, the son of Sir Thomas (of Earlston), third baronet, married in 1779, Christiana, daughter of James Scarlett, Esq., and died in 1794, having had issue by her, Sir John, fifth baronet, &c.

The James Scarlett above mentioned, a landed proprietor in Jamaica, was the grandfather of the first Lord Abinger, Chief Baron of the Exchequer, and of Sir William Anglin Scarlett his brother, who was Chief Justice of Jamaica.

A GENEALOGIST.

BEAR'S DEN HALL (3rd S. vii. 402.) — This house was situated on Putney Heath, and was the residence of Charles Christiern Reisen, seal engraver and painter, and —— Skelton, upholsterer. It was kept at their *joint expense!* I cannot learn any particulars of these eccentrics, but from the print it would appear that they pigged together in filth and wretchedness. Their armorials are a crab-tree and a tent; the supporters, a crutch and a walking-stick, intimate infirmity. The very small amount of "Smoak, by Chance," indicates poverty or parsimony. The bear and the crab-tree intimate that their discomforts were not alleviated by cheerfulness and good temper. A kite pouncing upon small birds is called "Crabtree transmigrated," not indicative of amiability. (See Walpole's *Painters.*)

E. H.

TRAVELLING SCOTCHMEN (3rd S. vii. 420.) — In this town there are a vast number of these persons engaged in the drapery business. The trade is carried on with dock-labourers, mechanics, and very humble people; yet it is most extensive, as the "Scotchmen" supply goods almost to any-one, and to any amount, taking weekly payments at one shilling in the pound. And when the bargain is faithfully kept by the purchaser, the profits, as any one acquainted with figures and interest tables can determine, become truly enormous. There is a special day set apart in the monthly sittings of the Liverpool County Court, which is devoted solely to hearing claims of these travelling drapers against defaulting debtors. The people of this town (particularly drapers) look on these "Scotchmen" as an extensive nuisance. With the needy and the honest customer they are well spoken of; for they supply goods not at an extravagant price, and those persons, whose income is weekly, and who are punctual in their engagements, find them a convenient and desirable sort of shopkeepers.

S. REDMOND.

Liverpool.

BISHOP LINDWOOD (3rd S. vii. 429.)—I have to thank MR. BEDFORD for the trouble he has taken to assist in the investigation as to the true arms of Bishop Lindwood. As Sir F. Madden's notes were not based upon the Bishop's Register, it is possible that, while the armorial bearings on the brass at Linwood were those of the Bishop's family, previous to his elevation to the offices of Dean of Arches, Keeper of the Privy Seal, and Bishop of St. David's, the coat which appears in the title-page of the *Provinciale* may be arms assigned to him for special distinction. Can anything be

learned from the Records of the Heralds' College on this point? I exceedingly regret that I cannot furnish MR. BEDFORD with a reference to Guillim, as I have no note of it. My memorandum was made many years ago, before the importance of such minutiæ had been so strongly impressed upon readers, as it has been since the publication of "N. & Q."

H. W. T.

TOASTS (3rd S. vii. 397.) — The toast attributed by CYRIL to Dr. Enfield, has been given to the celebrated Tom Sheridan when he contested the shoemaking borough of Stafford : "May the trade of Stafford be trampled under foot by all the world." The story adds, that it was misunderstood by the electors, and the wit was obliged to explain.

C. T.

MEANING OF ARBERY (3rd S. vii. 345, 407.) — MR. DIXON omits half of my quotation from Mandeville, which is important in fixing the meaning of the word "arbery": for, after mentioning the scarcity of "*arbery*, in that contree," he says: "thei brennen the dong of bestes for defaute of wood." Clearly showing that wood for fuel was included in his term *arbery*. It was a general term, which included "trees that beren fruite," as well as "othere," which were devoted to the fire.

C. T.

"COMPLAYNT" OF SIR DAVID LINDSAY (3rd S. vii. 78.)—L. will find that his explanation of the words "Pa Da Lyn" is considered by Lord Lindsay to be the correct one, by referring to *Lives of the Lindsays*, in the chapter treating of Sir David Lindsay's *Works*. Not having the work by me, I cannot give the number of the volume and page. The work was published in 1849.

SCOTUS.

DRAGON (3rd S. vii. 418.)—If BLAZON will refer to Mr. Lower's amusing *Curiosities of Heraldry* (London, 1845,) he will find in chapter iv., on the chimerical figures (pp. 92—97), an account of the dragon which will, I think, interest him.

J. WOODWARD.

CARY FAMILY: BISHOPRIC OF KILLALOE (3rd S. vii. 117, 170, 424.)—I regret that the typographical error of a letter on p. 157 of the *Letters of Sir Robert Cecil*, which I edited for the Camden Society, and which error escaped notice in revising the proofs, should have given so much trouble. The prelate intended to be referred to, was William *Casey* not *Carey.*

William Casey was Rector of Kilcornan, in the diocese of Limerick, and was advanced to the see of Killaloe by King Edward VI., by a mandate dated Oct. 23. Among the Pat.-Rolls, 4th Edward VI., is a letter of the Lord Protector and Council in behalf of the Earl of Desmond for conferring the bishopric, when it shall be void, to "such a man as shall for his literature and life be meet for the same." In pursuance of the terms of this letter, the bishopric was granted to William Casey, anno 5°.

He was consecrated at Dublin on Oct. 23 (Pat.-Rolls) by the Archbishop of Dublin, assisted by the Bishops of Kildare, Leighlin and Ferns. Queen Mary deprived him by a Commission, issued in 1556; but in 1571, he was restored by Queen Elizabeth. When he became aged and infirm, Dennis Campbell, Dean of Limerick, was appointed his coadjutor in 1588; and in 1591 he died, having been a bishop forty years.

                        JOHN MACLEAN.
Hammersmith.

I can explain how MELETES has fallen into the error of supposing that there was a Cary, Bishop of Killaloe. The authority quoted states that Dennis Campbell, Dean of Limerick and Rector of Drumcliffe, in the diocese of Killaloe, was, in 1588, appointed " coadjutor to his diocesan, Bishop Carey." MELETES overlooked the fact that Campbell had two diocesans, and, on referring to Archdeacon Cotton's *Fasti Ecclesiæ Hibernicæ*, it will be found that the bishop to whom he was appointed coadjutor was William *Casey*, Bishop of Limerick; not Carey, as misprinted in the passage cited from *Sir Robert Cecil's Letters.*

  Your correspondent will find a valuable contribution to the history of the Cary family·in Part XIII. of the *Herald and Genealogist.*

              JOHN RIBTON GARSTIN, M.R.I.A.
Dublin.

HAG'S PRAYER (3rd S. vii. 114, 427.) — The Hag's Prayer is well known in Lancashire, and is still repeated by boys and girls " in country places" *after* the Lord's Prayer on retiring to rest. Its terms, however, are somewhat different from those given by A. A. In a series of papers which I read before the Lancashire and Cheshire Historic Society, during the years 1859, 1860, and 1861, which are printed in vols. xi., xii., and xiii. of their *Transactions*, I have entered at length into our local superstitions, and have given the *Hag's Prayer* as follows :—

> " Matthew, Mark, Luke, and John,
>   Bless the bed which I lie on ;
>   There are four corners to my bed,
>   Which *four* angels overspread,
>   *Two* at the feet, *two* at the head.

> " If any ill thing me betide,
>   Beneath your wings my body hide.
>   Matthew, Mark, Luke, and John,
>   Bless the bed that I lie on. Amen."

The Rev. William Thornber notices the same custom in his *History of Blackpool*, p. 99, as still existing in the Fylde district; and my friend, the late Rev. James Dugan, M.A., T.C.D., informed me that the Irish midwives in Ulster use a similar formula when visiting their patients. He said that they first mark each corner of the house with

the sign of the cross, and on entering the house repeat the following words : —

> " Here are four corners to her bed,
>   Four angels at her head.
>   Matthew, Mark, Luke, and John,
>   God bless the bed that she lies on.
>   New moon, new moon, God bless me,
>   God bless this house and family."

The whole prayer appears to me to be simply a *Christianised* relic of the old Scandinavian faith. This is more particularly the case with the Ulster form, which exhibits the formula in its *transition* state. A Westmoreland friend of mine used to repeat the Lancashire form every night until some one persuaded his mother that it was a *Popish* invocation, and then he was ordered to discontinue it as something too impious to be uttered by a Protestant !   T. T. WILKINSON, F.R.A.S., &c.
Burnley, Lancashire.

ROMAN HAND (3rd S. vii. 338, 429.)—The saying, " Roman hand," no doubt, is derived from the passage cited from *Twelfth Night*, in which place, doubtless, it refers to the style of handwriting which Maria had learnt to imitate so well (Act V. Sc. 1, towards the end),—

> " Alas ! Malvolio, this is not my writing,
>   Though I confess much like the character ;
>   But out of question 'tis Maria's hand."

The fair Roman hand in fashion at the time (and beautiful it was) may be seen in examples at the British Museum. The term now generally refers rather to a bold style of *composition*, by which the writer can easily be detected, though he does not write under his own name. J. C. J.

THEODOLITE (3rd S. iv. 51, 135, 217.) — You now have had as etymological explanations of the word Theodolite, — θέα-δηλόω — θεάομαι — θεῶ*-δῆλος-ἴτυς, and θεάομαι ὁδός. The only one worth a moment's consideration is the last, and that is entitled to notice simply because more generally received, especially by professional men. Your valued correspondent, A. A., to whose opinion on a point simply professional one would have great hesitation in offering an objection, says that θε is " the ordinary abbreviation of the Greek θεάομαι." This is not so. There is not *a single word* in English with this abbreviation, nor is there either in Greek or Latin. I will go further, and say that there could be no such word. For the verbal would come last, as in telegraph, semaphore, monogram, viaduct, &c. ; and the verb † could not have been simple, but of a verbal form, and so that θε could be no abbreviation of it. A. A.'s objection as to date also falls to the ground, for the word Theodolite, *i. e.* " Theodelite, or a topographical glasse," occurs, as has already

---

   * There is no such word.
   † Greek verbs are never compounded except with prepositions.

been shown as early as 1611 in a book printed by A. Hopton, and in the same also occurs the word "circumferentor." So that neither of these words are modern as is set down by the "tradition among surveyors." This early date (1611) makes it also all but impossible that the word Theodolite was taken from the name of the person to whom the book I mentioned in my last was dedicated; but nearly certain that the name was borrowed from one of his family.   J. C. J.

THE DUKE OF BRUNSWICK'S "FIFTY REASONS" (3rd S. vii. 68, 121, 428.)—The title given by CARILFORD of the copy of the above work in his possession, is the original title under which it was published in English; and which it bore, I believe, till the new edition was published by Keating & Brown in 1822, of which copies used to be very common; but the work has now quite disappeared from our catalogues. The first edition must have been published towards the end of the seventeenth century, or early in the eighteenth. For I find it in the—

"Catalogue of Books sold by Tho. Meighan, Bookseller, in Drury Lane, where gentlemen may be furnished with all sorts of new books that come out; and have ready money for any library, in what language soever."

This Catalogue is appended to a very scarce book, *The Primer, or Office of the B. Virgin Mary*, printed in the year 1717.

CARILFORD enquires if his edition of 1741 is scarce. Certainly it is; and I fear that the same is to be said now of the edition even of 1822, the last with which I am acquainted. In the Catalogue of J. P. Coghlan for 1793, the work appears with its full title, thus:—

"Fifty reasons or motives why the Roman Catholic Apostolic religion ought to be preferred to all the sects this day in Christendom, and which induced his most serene Highness Anthony Ulrick, Duke of Brunswick and Lunenburgh, to abjure Lutheranism. To which is (sic) added, three valuable papers. I. The decision of the Protestant university of Helmstadt in favour of the Roman Catholic religion. II. Copies of two papers written by the late Charles II. King of Great Britain. III. And of a paper written by the late Duchess of York, spouse of James, afterwards the second king of that name. Price 1s. stitched in blue."

All these are included in the edition of 1822, but the title has been abbreviated. · F. C. H.

IRISH BOOKS AND MSS. (3rd S. vii. 414.) — MR. EUGENE O'CAVANAGH's enumeration of Irish publications will be serviceable in directing attention to the yet extant literature of the most ancient of European languages and races. If the catalogue was extended to MSS. likewise, it would assuredly lead to the discovery of many, especially those in possession of private persons, which have been jealously withheld from public ken, lest a *loan might become an appropriation*, or lest the prized documents should be marred, or

remodelled, in course of transcribing. Within the last fifty years, many such MSS. have been irrevocably lost; but numbers still are to be found, even among humble families (of ancient lineage, however), in the S. and W. of Ireland. These chiefly relate to genealogical and personal annals, and are dashed with a colouring of romance; but a vein of authentic history is traceable through them all.

In enumerating Irish versions of the Scriptures, I venture to call the attention of collectors to the Irish New Testament (Munster dialect) by Robert Keane, of Eccles Street, Dublin — or, as he subscribes on the title-page, adopting his ancient tribal surname O'Catain. Only a few score copies of this uncommonly beautiful edition were printed, the expense being considerable, and no encouragement manifest for sale of a large issue. It is a small 4to on good paper of even quality, substantially bound, and printed by Gill of Trinity College, Dublin, in Irish type, the clearest and *easiest to the eye* I have ever seen. The soundest guarantee for the correctness of this version is the reputation of the translator, whose unobtrusive disposition cannot altogether conceal from a large circle of friends his accurate and comprehensive acquaintance with the classical and Celtic languages.   J. L.
Dublin.

"PISCIS FLOTANS" (3rd S. vii. 55, 124, 288, 384.)—The query—"What was *piscis flotans*?"—has elicited an answer from MR. BINGHAM, a reply from the original querist P. S. C., and a rejoinder by the former which is evidently very far from the mark: inasmuch as the holibut (the fish suggested by him) is an inhabitant of the northern seas, rarely met with in the British Channel, and quite unknown in the island of Guernsey. Five minutes conversation with an intelligent and experienced fisherman of that island, Pierre le Noury (well known to the readers of *The Field*), has I believe put me in the way of giving a satisfactory solution of the difficulty. He tells me that the fishermen here make a distinction between "poisson du fond" and "poisson du flot." Among the former are included all sorts of flat fish, as well as congers; which last, it will, be remembered, was the staple fishery of the island. These are never taken except in deep water, and close to the bottom. The "poisson du flot" includes mackerel, pilchards, gar-fish, whiting, mullets, bream, and all other sorts of fish which swim near the surface of the water. "Piscis flotans" we may, therefore, conclude to be synonymous with "poisson du flot." I must however remark that, in a copy of the document referred to by P. S. C., to be found among the MSS. of the Harleian Collection (No. 1617), the sentence stands thus: "Omne batellum portans piscem. *flotans* in Normanniam." . This reading makes "flotans" refer to the boat, not to the fish carried in it; but as the copy appears to be inaccurate in other particulars, no great stress can be laid on this variation.   E. M'C.

Guernsey.

ASSUMPTION OF ARMS (3rd S. vii. 427.) — I have read with much pleasure the observations of your correspondents upon this subject. None of them have, however, suggested any practical remedy, such as would render it impossible for seal engravers and heraldic swindlers to practise on the vanity and credulity of would-be bearers of coats of arms. A catalogue of persons whose arms or pedigrees are registered in the College of Arms would do very much to mitigate the evil. It should be formed by one of the members of the College. A work of this kind was published for the Heralds' Office, Ireland, by William Skey, A.M., F.S.A., St. Patrick Pursuivant and Registrar of the Heralds' Office, in Ireland, under the following title : —

"*The Heraldic Calendar*, a List of the Nobility and Gentry whose Arms are registered and Pedigrees recorded in the Heralds' Office, Ireland. Dublin: 1846. 8vo."

Such a book would be the best means of informing us who the British gentry really are, would be of infinite use to the genealogist, and would no doubt prove remunerative to the compiler.   GEORGE W. MARSHALL.

KEY TO THE CHALDEE MANUSCRIPT (3rd S. v. 314-317.) — Looking over some old papers lately, I found among them the accompanying "Key," which I send as supplementary to MR. BATES's communication. I may add that the paper from which I copy is dated "Glasgow, 12th Nov. 1818," and was written by myself at that time.

Chapter I. verse 3. Blackwood; 4. Pringle and Cleghorn; 16. Constable; 17. *Edinburgh Review*; 39. Henry Mackenzie (Author of *The Man of Feeling*); 44. Walter Scott; 49. Professor Jameson; 53. Dr. Brewster; 55. P. H. Tytler; 56. A. Henderson (General Post Office); 57. R. P. Gillies; 58. C. Mackenzie; 62. Shairp of Hoddam. Chapter II. verse 2, Editor; 10. J. Wilson, J. of P.; 11. Author of *The White Cottage*; 12. Rev. A. Thomson; 13. James Hogg; 14. Dr. Mc Rie; 17. Mr. Riddell; 18. M'Culloch and Galloway (qy. *of Galloway ?*); 22. Dr. Gordon. Chapter III. v. 14. Mr. Jeffrey; 21. Prof. Leslie; 22. Prof. Playfair; 35. J. G. Dalzell; 45. Hugh Murray. Chapter IV. v. 1. Macvey Napier; 6. Jamieson, Register Office; 8. Neill, the printer; 18. Gray, High School; 19. S. M'Cormick; 20. John Ballantyne; 21. James Graham; 23. Principal Baird; 24. D. Bridges; 25. Dr. Duncan; 26. Ja. Baxter; 27. P. Gibson; 28. S. Anderson, Master of St. Luke's Hospital.

J. MACRAY.

Oxford.

PETRUS DE ALVA ET ASTORGA (3rd S. vii. 400.) The British Museum printed Catalogue contains two works by this author : —

"*Armamentarium seraphicum, et regestum universale sub titulo immaculatæ conceptionis.*"—*Matritii*, 1649, fol.

"*Sol veritatis, cum ventilabro seraphico, pro candida Aurora Maria, &c.*"—*Matritii*, 1660, fol.

His name does not appear in the Bodleian Catalogue, nor in Reading's Catalogue of Sion College. Græsse, in his *Trésor de Livres rares et précieux*, says that all the works of this Franciscan are rare and curious. In one of them he gives 4000 coincidences between St. Francis and Jesus Christ. No. 78 of these tells us that "the Saviour was nine months in his mother's womb, and so was St. Francis."   R. B. PROSSER.

25, Southampton Buildings, W.C.

THE WORD "MON" (3rd S. vii. 435.) — In the impromptu lines here given, the word "mon" is put into the mouth of a Scotch M.P. as meaning the English "man."

This is a very common supposition, made by Englishmen as to the Scotch mode of pronouncing the word, but it is a total mistake; and I use the freedom to quote as follows from the Preface to the abridged edition of Dr. Jamieson's *Dictionary* :

"*A* in *Man*, &c. has nearly the same sound in Scotch as in English. Vulgar English writers who use 'mon' for 'man,' 'hond' for 'hand,' &c., believing that this is pure Scottish, show that they have studied the works of Ramsay and Burns to little purpose. The rhymes to such words occurring in Scottish poems will at once point out the true pronunciation, as for example : —

'Then gently *scan* your brother *man*.'
         Address to the unco Guid.

'Untie these *bands* from off my *hands*.'
         Macpherson's Farewell."

Edinburgh.   G.

KONX OMPAX (3rd S. vi. 263; vii. 424.) — Can these mystical words have any connexion with the temple of Kom Ombos in Egypt? We know most of the mysterious rites originated in that country. The temple bears the cartouche of Thothmes III., B.C. 1600. See Roberts's *Egypt*, vol. i. 18.   A. A.

Poets' Corner.

TO OBJECT (3rd S. vi. 367.) — *To object* is now commonly used as a verb neuter, but if your correspondent will refer to the *Dictionary of the English Language* by Dr. Samuel Johnson, he will find that it there appears only as a verb active, and in one of the passages quoted from Pope, it is used nearly in the same manner as in the extract given from Farindon's *Sermons:* —

"... Pallas to their eyes
The mist objected."

MELETES.

TOADS IN STONE (3rd S. vii. 388, 428.) — The two halves of a block of stone in which a living toad had been found, were shown in Hyde Park at the Exhibition of 1851—"the stone without fissure, chink, or vein." The toad was alive during the earlier part of the Exhibition, but died before its close.   W. CHAPPELL.

TRINITY COLLEGE, DUBLIN (3rd S. vii. 441.)—
A speech of Archbishop Loftus made publicly in
the Tholsell soon after the Quarter Sessions of
St. John the Baptist to the Mayor and Aldermen
of Dublin, proposing to them the making of a
grant to be made from the city of Dublin of the
lands of Allhallows for the building of Trinity
College in Dublin, is printed in *Camdeni Annales*,
ed. Hearne, p. lvii. (See *Athen. Cantab.* ii. 405.)

C. H. & THOMPSON COOPER.
Cambridge.

WORDS USED IN DIFFERENT SENSES: KICK
(3rd S. vii. 278, 367, 425.)—In many parts of
Lancashire the word *kick* is used to signify ask or
beg. Its use in this sense is limited to the operatives, and generally forms part of a request for
beer. A man who having (if I may use the expression) "wet one eye," and not having money
enough to continue the process to his own satisfaction, seeing a gentleman coming along the
road, would say, "Here comes Mr. ——; I'll *kick*
him for a pint." H. FISHWICK.

COUPLETS (3rd S. vii. 398.)—It should not be
overlooked that the Greek couplet quoted, by
MR. TRENCH is an epigram of Plato on Aristophanes, transferred to Sir William Jones by the
change of name. C. G. PROWETT.

CHAP (3rd S. vii. 380.)—In the instances quoted,
the word "chap" is used in its proper and not its
slang meaning. It denotes a buyer or seller, and
is still used in the same way by old-fashioned
marketers. The slang use transfers it from this
special relation to a general purpose; so with the
word "party," which in slang means anybody,
but in legitimate English is restricted to the *parties* to a legal contract. C. G. P.

Miscellaneous.

NOTES ON BOOKS, ETC.

*Pre-Historic Times, as illustrated by ancient Remains and
the Manners and Customs of Modern Savages.* By
John Lubbock, F.R.S. (Williams & Norgate.)

It requires little acumen to discover the great value of
the present contribution to ethnological science. When
a gentleman of Mr. Lubbock's attainments devotes years
to the study of such a subject, and not content with
visiting all the great national museums in which collections
of primæval remains are to be found, examines for himself on the spot, and in the company of those who have
made these objects their especial study, the localities
where they were deposited, the result could not fail to be
a work rich in facts and in legitimate deductions from
those facts. The book may therefore be considered as a
repertory of all that has yet been ascertained with regard
to Tumuli or Burial Mounds, Peat Bogs, Shell Mounds,
Lake Inhabitations, Bone Caves, Riverdrift, Gravels, and
in short as a most valuable text-book for the study of
Pre-historic Times. We ought to add that it contains
upwards of one hundred and fifty illustrations.

*The New Testament for English Readers: containing the
Authorised Version; with a revised English Text, Mar-
ginal References, and a Critical and Explanatory Com-
mentary.* By Henry Alford, D.D., Dean of Canterbury.
*In Two Volumes. Vol. II. Part I. The Epistles of
St. Paul.* (Rivingtons.)

The readers of the first volume of Dean Alford's valuable edition of the New Testament will not be surprised
to find that the Epistles receive a somewhat different form
of illustration from that with which the learned editor
accompanied the Four Gospels and the Acts of the Apostles;
and that the number of corrections necessary to bring
out the readings and renderings is so great, that, instead of confining himself to noting these below the
text, the editor has found it unavoidable that a *Revised
Text* should be published; which is here accordingly
printed side by side with the *Authorised Version*. The
rendering in the subjoined notes is not always identical
with that in the Revised Text; but is usually rougher
and more literal, thus affording additional illustration of
the meaning. The Dean's valuable and learned Introductions to the several Epistles, in which he examines their
authorship and authenticity—the objects for which, and
the time when, and places where they were written—
occupies nearly one hundred and fifty pages; and abounds
with information calculated to make still more intelligible
to mere English readers, this important division of the
Holy Scriptures.

*Moxon's Miniature Poets. A Selection from the Works
of* Frederick Locker. *With Illustrations by* Richard
Doyle. (Moxon & Co.)

The second volume of Mr. Moxon's dainty series of
Miniature Poets is occupied with the effusions of Mr.
Locker, who obviously asks with Horace—

" . . ridentem dicere verum
Quid vetat ? "

and who masks many a deep thought and much true
poetic feeling under the quips and cranks and wreathed
smiles of a wearer of motley. Many of Mr. Locker's
graceful and touching little poems are as gracefully illustrated by Richard Doyle.

The Anti-Teapot Review. Nos. I. to V. (Houlston &
Wright.)

These are the literary effusions of a Club (mostly of
young Oxford men) which rejoices in the name of " Ye
Red Club"—a Club which when it meets, as we guess—

" May sometimes counsel take — but never tea."

If our readers would fain know what " Anti-Teapotism "
is, against which the Review declares war, we must refer
them to the Review itself.

Notices to Correspondents.

B. J. *For some account of the last wolf in Scotland see* "N. & Q."
2nd S. viii. 296, 402.

WM. BLOOM. "The Stars and the Angels" *was published in* 1858, *by*
*Hamilton, Adams & Co., London; Menzies, Edinburgh; and M'Glashan
& Gill, Dublin.*

FRANKS. *Will* "H. F.," *who wishes to exchange franks, furnish us
with his address.*

Answers to other Correspondents in our next.

∗∗∗ *Cases for binding the volumes of* "N. & Q." *may be had of the
Publisher, and of all Booksellers and Newsmen.*

A Reading Case for holding the weekly Nos. of "N. & Q." is now
ready, and may be had of all Booksellers and Newsmen, price 1s. 6d.;
or, free by post, direct from the publisher, for 1s. 8d.

"NOTES AND QUERIES" *is published at noon on* Friday, *and is also
issued in* MONTHLY PARTS. *The Subscription for* STAMPED COPIES *for
Six Months forwarded direct from the Publisher (including the Half-
yearly* INDEX) *is* 11s. 4d., *which may be paid by Post Office Order,
payable at the Strand Post Office, in favour of* WILLIAM G. SMITH, 32,
WELLINGTON STREET, STRAND, W.C. *where also all* COMMUNICATIONS
FOR THE EDITOR *should be addressed.*

"NOTES & QUERIES" *is registered for transmission abroad.*

LONDON, SATURDAY, JUNE 17, 1865.

CONTENTS.—N° 181.

Notes.

NOTES FROM THE ISSUE ROLLS.

In recently examining a quantity of the Issue Rolls for the reigns of Edward III. and Richard II., I met with various curious entries, of which I "made notes," thinking that they might be worth the attention of "N. & Q." They are mostly genealogical: —

"Die Martis, xiiij die Junii.—Rīco de Tempest, Custodi Ville Berewyci Ville Berewyci Tweadam, denar' sibi liber' p man' Joħis Wyclif, sup eadem custodia, etc., cxxv ħ." — (Exitus, Pasch. 36 Ed. III.)

Can this be the great reformer or any immediate relative?

Oct. 7, 41 Ed. III. [1367.] News brought to the king by Ludovico de Colonia of the birth of a son of the empress. [Sigismond, afterwards emperor.] He is rewarded with ten pounds. (Exitus, Mich. 41 Ed. III.)

Same date. News of the birth of a daughter of the Duchess of Barre, brought by Francisco, her messenger, who receives five pounds.

Oct. 29. News of the birth of a daughter of the King of France. [This must be Jeanne, the date of whose birth is, however, given by Moreri as June 7, 1366; she died, according to the same authority, Dec. 21, 1366. The three eldest daughters of Charles V. all died in 1366, and the fifth, Marie, was not born until 1370.]

Feb. 3, 42 Ed. III. [1368.] News of the birth of a son of the Duchess of Berry. [She had three sons, Charles, Jean, and Louis.] (Exitus, Mich. 41 Ed. III.)

Oct. 18, 22 Ric. II. [1398.] News of the birth of a son of the King of France. [Jean, afterwards dauphin, born Aug. 31, 1398.] (Exitus, Mich. 22, Rich. II.)

"Thos. Swynford, militi [legitimate son of Katherine Swynford], et Johanne Crophull uxi ejus."—Exitus, Mich. 19 Rich. II.

June 6. Payments for the burial of Thomas, late Earl of Kent [the king's half brother] in the church of the blessed Peter, Westminster, at the king's cost. (Fragment of Exitus Roll, qu. Pasch. 20 Rich. II.)

But the most remarkable entry of all is to come, and I should be glad to receive a good opinion upon its meaning. On July 7, 39 Ed. III. [1365], 66*l.* 13*s.* 4*d.* is paid to William de Harplo, valet of the Lord Prince of Aquitaine [Edward the Black Prince] bringing letters to Philippa, Queen of England, from the said Prince, concerning the birth of a son of the said prince. This was Prince Edward born at Angoulême in the previous February. On Tuesday, Feb. 25, 40 Ed. III [1366], 16*l.* 13*s.* 4*d.* was paid to a valet of the Lord Prince of Wales, coming from Aquitaine with news (*rumoribus*), *not* letters, to the king of the birth of a son of the said prince. This was Richard II., born at Bordeaux, Jan. 6, 1366. But on the third of May, 41 Ed. III. [1367], occurs the following entry, which I give verbatim that no mistake may appear: —

"Stepħo Rummelowe, vall'to Dħi Principis Vasconū, venienti cum l'ris directis Dño R. et Dñe Reᵑᵉ de natimitate filij. Principisse Vasconū; in denar' sibi lib' vidᵹ. de dono Dħi R. c. l'i., et de dono Dñe Reᵑᵉ c. mqᵹ. ꝑ l're de p'uaᵗᵒ sigillo de hoc P'rnčo."

Is there any question that "the Prince of Gascony" denotes the Black Prince? Or is there any probability that this letter was the *official* intimation of the birth of Richard II., then sixteen months old? If not so, and I can scarcely think either of these suppositions probable, we have here *a third and hitherto unknown son of the Black Prince.* According to Froissart, the prince quitted Aquitaine for his Spanish campaign in January, 1367, not returning until the early part of 1368. This extract from the Issue Rolls would seem to infer that he was in Aquitaine in April, 1367, as otherwise the valet would have been said to come from Spain bearing his letters. On Feb. 17, 1368, Geoffrey de Stynecle was despatched on an embassy to the prince *to Spain.* Froissart, be it remembered, places the birth of Richard II. in 1367; but even if his reckoning be adopted (and the general consent of historians seems against it), who then was the prince of whose birth news was brought to King Edward on Feb. 25, 1366?

Another awkward date is that of the battle of Navaretta, which, according to Froissart, was fought on April 3, 1367. But Sir John so rarely gives a date at all, and is so frequently wrong when he does give one, that his testimony is of little weight when it comes in competition with that of the Rotuli.   HERMENTRUDE.

LONGEVITY.

[The following articles have been in type for some time. Their publication has been delayed in order that they might appear in connection with a series of Papers on *Longevity* now preparing for these pages. As from the nature, extent, and difficulties of the inquiries connected with these Papers, some weeks may elapse before they can be ready, it has been thought advisable not to delay any longer the following communications from our correspondents. The note in which E. H. A. so candidly points out the error "of 21 years" in the instance formerly adduced, shows how necessary it is to receive with caution the statements of longevity which are so often and so readily advanced, without any evidence in support of them.—ED. "N. & Q."]

The interesting correspondence on longevity, which was lately carried on in *The Times*, has come to an abrupt termination, and as the parliamentary session has now begun, we cannot expect, as A DOUBTER truly observes, that the correspondence will be renewed. The subject is, I think, exactly suited for discussion in the columns of "N. & Q.," always supposing that correspondents would avoid accumulating instances of longevity picked up by hearsay, or extracted from works devoid of all critical tone, such as the *Annual Register*. Every parish has its stories of centenarians, and they appear in provincial newspapers as part of the regular stock in trade, along with toads in rocks, showers of fish and frogs, singing mice, living snakes in men's stomachs, year-long fasts, the sea-serpent, &c. What we want is a series of carefully investigated cases, where the centenarian's baptismal entry and course of life have been investigated, and with complete identification at the time of death. A great number of cases are to be found in a volume by Easton,—

"Human Longevity, recording the Name, Age, Place of Residence, and Year of the Decease, of 1712 Persons, who attained a Century and upwards, from A.D. 66 to 1799."

The work, however, displays no spirit of criticism. If we dismiss as altogether absurd and incredible, the stories of the Countess of Desmond, Old Parr, and Henry Jenkins, who are said to have reached the ages of 145, 159, and 169 years, there yet remains several cases of extreme longevity, in which the dates of baptism and burial appear to have been ascertained with precision. Two remarkable instances are those of Robert Bowman and Mary Noble, both natives of Cum-

berland. They were personally examined by Dr. Barnes, who reported their cases in the fourth and tenth volumes of the *Edinburgh Philosophical Journal*. The doctor himself searched the parish register of Hayton, and found the entry of Bowman's baptism in 1705; he was still living in 1820, having completed his 115th year. In 1823 Dr. Barnes saw a copy (not the original) of Mary Noble's baptismal certificate, dated Sept. 17, 1716. She was accordingly in her 107th year at the time of his visit to her.

On Jan. 10, 1864, Mr. Robert Chapman died at Rosherville, in Kent, in his 102nd year. He was born at Whitby, Oct. 12, 1762, and, belonging to one of the oldest and most respected families of the town, his whole career was well known. A friend of mine, now far on among the eighties, dined with Mr. Chapman on the occasion of his 100th birth day.   JAYDEE.

Having in 1st S. v. 356 adduced as an instance of remarkable longevity Patrick Machylwian, a Scotchman, vicar of Lesbury, in Northumberland, stated to have lived to the age of 112 years, and to have died in 1659, I think myself bound to notice the fact, that the said old gentleman did, in the year 1634, when on examination as a witness in the Ecclesiastical Court at Durham, state his age to be then only threescore and six, so that supposing him to have died in 1659 he would fall short of his reputed age of 112 by 21 years. See the *Proceedings in High Court of Commission for Durham and Northumberland*, edited by Mr. Longstaffe for the Surtees Society, case of Brandling.
E. H. A.

The paragraph below would be interesting if any of your American correspondents could authenticate the dates:—

"THE OLDEST MAN IN THE WORLD.—A Wisconsin paper says that the oldest man in the world is now living in Caledonia, in that state. His name is Joseph Crele, and his age is one hundred and thirty-nine years. He has lived in Wisconsin more than a century, and was first married in New Orleans one hundred and nine years ago. Some years afterwards he settled at Prairie du Chien, while Wisconsin was yet a province of France. Before the Revolutionary war he was employed to carry letters between Prairie du Chien and Green Bay. It is but a few years ago that he was called as a witness in the Circuit Court, in a case involving the title to certain real estates at Prairie du Chien, to give testimony in relation to events that transpired eighty years before. He now resides with a daughter by his third wife, who is over seventy years of age."
PERCY B. ST. JOHN.

Allow me to draw the attention of inquirers interested in this subject to an extract from a Diary of Dr. Thomas Raffles of Liverpool, pubin his *Life* by his son (8vo, London, 1864, p. 123.) It runs as follows : —

"July 22nd, 1814. Rode with Mr. Mather to Todmorden in the centre of the beautiful vale of that name. On our way called on Mr. Marden, near Bacup, where I saw and conversed with Mary Harrison, aged 104. She had been in the family ever since she was twelve years old, and is in full possession of every faculty except that of hearing."

Perhaps some correspondent can inform you when this exemplar of "the constant service of the antique world" died, and in what manner her death was registered.　　L. A. B.

BAGMAN.

In the latest edition of Mr. Hotten's *Slang Dictionary*, "Bagman" is said to be "a commercial traveller;" but no explanation is given as to the origin or derivation of the word. I venture to suggest that it took its rise in the saddle-bags in which the commercial traveller of the past century carried his patterns and goods; which saddle-bags, being of larger dimensions than those usually carried by travellers on horseback, would designate the commercial traveller, *par excellence*, as the Bag-man. I find from the recollections and traditionary belief of those who were acquainted with the pre-railway days of the Great North Road between Alconbury-hill and Wansford, that the commercial travellers usually dispensed with vehicles, and made their journeys on horseback — a system which permitted them to get at the remote villages, and along "droves," "bullock roads," and rough lanes whose rude state of nature would have made (and often now does make) them to be impracticable for carriages on springs. The horses of these commercial travellers were so laden with distended saddle-bags, that their riders were sometimes half hidden in them, and were hoisted into their seats with no little difficulty.

Among other tales that are told of the doings of the highwaymen near to Alconbury Hill is one in which a Bagman figures as the unheroic hero. This Bagman had turned off from the Great North Road, and was riding towards Huntingdon when he was stopped by a highwayman. By clapping spurs to his horse, however, he contrived to make his escape from the thief's clutches, though with some difficulty. He had not gone far when he overtook a decent-looking man riding in the same direction as himself. Now the Bagman was not over bold, and his saddle-bags were well filled, so he thought it prudent to ask the traveller to allow him to ride in his company; but, to his surprise, the stranger gave him no answer. He again repeated his request with a similar result, the stranger all the time watching him earnestly but suspiciously. For the third time the Bagman addressed the stranger, who thereupon turned his horse across the road and pulled up to arrest the Bagman's progress, at the same time thrusting his right hand into his coat pocket. The Bagman only paused long enough to catch sight of the gleam of a barrel, when, spurring his horse, he dashed past that of the traveller, and galloped away towards Huntingdon, expecting every moment to hear the clatter of pursuing hoofs and the report of a pistol. The Bagman reached Huntingdon in hot haste, and summoned the *posse comitatus* to sally back with him and make a capture of the highwayman. A strong party was formed, and, under the Bagman's guidance, started in pursuit. They had not gone very far when the Bagman cried, "There he is!" and pointed to a horseman approaching them at a sober jog-trot. "There he is! that's the highwayman; don't let him escape." That a highwayman!" cried his companions; "why, it's our Mayor. That's the Mayor of Huntingdon!" "Impossible!" said the incredulous Bagman. "But it's true," they rejoined, as the horseman drew nearer; "you can ask him for yourself." "Mayor or no mayor," said the Bagman stoutly, "he reined up his horse, and, without saying a word, pulled out a pistol upon me; and I might have been murdered and robbed, if I had not gallopped off." "What sort of a pistol was it?" said his companions with a grin. "Not one to be laughed at," said the indignant Bagman. "It was a very large pistol." "Well, we'll ask him to show it to us. Here the gentleman is. Good morning, Mr. Mayor." The horseman thus addressed reined up his steed, and thrusting his hand into his coat pocket, pulled out something without saying a word. "There's the pistol," said the Bagman, as he caught sight of the gleam of a barrel. His companions burst into a roar of derisive laughter; as well they might, for, to his great astonishment, the Bagman saw the horseman raise the weapon deliberately and place it to his own ear, where it resolved itself to a no more formidable weapon than an ear-trumpet. It is needless to add that the horseman, who was indeed the Mayor of Huntingdon, was not only very deaf, but was as honest a man as the Bagman, who now apologised to him for the mistake that he had made.　　Cuthbert Bede.

A Chichester Epigram.—Perceiving that you have recently, among other rich seasonings in your miscellany of what I would term, if I might coin a word, condimental literature, opened compartments for uncirculated epigrams, and for curious conjunctions of significant names (see the No. for April 22, p. 322), I beg leave to offer a notice which may perhaps be considered to combine both characters.

In the south-eastern outlet of the city of Chichester, called the Harnet, there was for many years until very lately a pawnbroker's shop, kept by Messrs. Need & Ransome. But the latter, and more eligible name for such an establishment, has, I believe, within a few years past disappeared from the front of the house. This extremely curious nominal coincidence has been thus versified rather than epigrammatised; for these having been, as I have every reason to conclude, the actual names of the two partners, constituted themselves a prosaic and suggestive epigram : —

On Messrs. Need & Ransome's Pawnbroker's Shop, Harnet, Chichester.

" Observe beneath those three gilt balls
Implied assurance handsome ;
That where the fond pledge *Need* enthrals,
Is always found a *Ransome*."

T. A. H.

DUFFER.—This word is an example of those which continue for almost an indefinite period in use, without attaining to reputable use. The *Oxford Journal* of Saturday, May 25, 1765, under the head of " Thursday's Post," has the following, which might have been written almost verbatim in 1865 : —

" Yesterday an East India *Duffer*, or fellow who pretends to sell ignorant people very great bargains of smuggled goods, accosted a well-looking man in Holborn with the usual address, at the same time showing some samples of his merchandise from under his great coat, and enjoining secrecy—all which was promised ; but the supposed countryman asking if he had no tea, was carried to a house in St. Giles's : where, in quality of his commission as a Custom-house officer, he seized some dozen of flimsy French silk stockings, a quantity of adulterated Dutch tea, and other goods, to the amount of sixty pounds."

H. B. C.

THE LAST MEMBER OF THE IRISH PARLIAMENT. Your correspondent MR. H. LOFTUS TOTTENHAM having supplied a copy of a curious document relative to Irish Parliamentary Representation (3rd S. vii. 375), I am induced to send you the following cutting from the *Daily Express*, May 15, 1865, for preservation in " N. & Q." : —

" We regret to announce the death of Sir Thomas Staples, which took place at his residence, 11, Merrion Square, East [Dublin], shortly before seven o'clock last evening. The deceased baronet, who was the father of the Irish Bar, had nearly completed his 90th year. He was the last Member of the Irish Parliament, in which assembly he sat for the borough of Coleraine, and subsequently for Knocktopher, county Kilkenny. He was one of the independent members who voted against the Act of Union."

The late Earl of Charlemont, who died in December, 1863, had also been a Member of the Irish Parliament. ABHBA.

PASSAGE IN PLAUTUS.—

" Duæ *maniculæ* connexæ."
Rudens, Act IV. Sc. 4, line 125.

There is a passage in Plautus's *Rudens* which has given me some trouble to understand ; but of

which I feel sure I have hit upon the right meaning at last. In the discovery scene, Palæstra describes, among other *crepundia* : —

" *Pal.* Post est situla argentea et duæ connexæ maniculæ et
Sucula."

The dictionaries citing this passage give, some of them, " manicula," a little hand ; others, a plough handle. Both of these interpretations are utterly unsatisfactory. " Connexæ maniculæ " would be a ridiculous way of expressing a toy-plough : and two little hands, joined together, would be no better. The real meaning of the passage is explained by poor Gripus's exclamation in the next line, when he wishes Palæstra may go and hang herself with her " situla et porculis," making no mention of the " maniculæ." " Maniculæ " means *handles*, not only of a plough. If we grant this, all is easy. The articles in question are a child's pail, with two ears rivetted or soldered separately ; and they were " connexæ " by the handle, which worked in them—just as is the case in all old examples of the " situla." Any one who collects Roman or Greek curiosities from London, and other excavations, must know how frequently these ears (" maniculæ "), and the handle which binds them together, are found still connected, though the pail itself has perished. Gripus, then, only mentions the pail and piggies ; because the " maniculæ connexæ " were part of the former. J. C. J.

NANKEEN.—The following note may be useful to some of your readers : —

" *Yellow Cotton.*—A new species of cotton, called Nankeen, of a bright yellow color, and fine texture, is now raised in the United States. The seed was furnished by Mr. Crawford, Secretary of the Treasury, and procured from Sicily." 1823.

W. P.

A FOURTH PARALLEL PROVERB. —To the three proverbs in different languages, lately published in " N. & Q." cautioning against the too early adoption of a summer dress, I can now add another : —

" Hasta el cuarenta de Mayo,
No te quites el sayo."

Literally, Till the fortieth of May do not strip yourself of the wrap. This proverb, I am told, is common in the north of Spain, but, as might be inferred from so late a day as the 9th of June, is unknown in the Centre and South. The odd way of negativing any change in May, puts one in mind of Greek Kalends. The word *sayo* is, I believe, of Oriental origin, and is identical with sash.

K.

OBJECTIVE.—It is generally supposed that what may be termed the German meaning of the words *objective* and *subjective*, is quite modern ; dating no further back, so far as we are concerned, than

Coleridge, who was much given to the use of the words in his philosophical monologues. But is this really the case? Does not the following extract from an old author go to prove the contrary; at least, so far as "objective" is concerned? —

"The last chapter having designed that idol-worship (as the Devil is therein proposed *objectively* to be adored) is not only a great countenance, but leads vastly to the promotion of diabolical confederacies." — *Pandæmonium, or the Devil's Cloyster*, by Richard Bovet, Gent., London, 1684.

Sir Walter Scott has used this book in his work on *Demonology.*   W. S.

Queries.

"LILLIBULLERO."

Can any of your correspondents state the exact meaning of the burden of the well-known song of "Lilliburlero," which had such an effect that, as Bishop Burnet says —

"It made an impression on the King's army that cannot be imagined by those that saw it not. The whole army, and at last the people, both of city and country, were singing it perpetually."

The bishop suggests that the burden was said to be Irish words. Given at length these apparently absurd words are —

> "Lilliburlero, Bullen-a-lah !
> Lero, lero, lilliburlero, lero, lero,
>   Bullen a lah ! '"

It is true that the word "lero" is to be found in the burdens of some Irish songs, as for example, in one common in the county of Clare, where a popular air is known by the title of "Lura, lura, no da. lura ;" but in another version the burden given is — *Meilso lero, is im bo ban*, rendered in English, "Mallo, lero, audeembo bawn."

In looking over a manuscript volume of music of the time of Queen Elizabeth, in lute tablature, I happened to find the word "lero" or "leerow" repeated more than once, seemingly as a direction for the mode in which an air was to be played ; as, for example, "a paven, leerow way ;" and sometimes spelled "lerrow." On another page occur the words "for the. leero," and "for the leerow."

This book contains a variety of airs, to which the title, "a galliard, a taranto, a pavin, an allemand," &c., are prefixed ; and the names of a few composers of the day, Edward Persé (Percy), John Jhonson, Daniel Batcheler, and Dowland occur in it.

I have, further, some faint recollection of having met elsewhere, but have lost the reference, some ancient airs "set for the leerow viol." If I am accurate in this, we have here the name of some species of instrument, different, doubtless, in

some degree from the viol de gamba, and others of the same class.

I should expect that some of your correspondents, who have engaged in studies similar to those of Dr. Rimbault, Mr. Chappell, or Mr. Rolfe, may be familiar with the word, and so readily supply the required information. If I am correct in my supposition, the word will be found to be of English or foreign origin, not Irish. Although Bishop Percy states that "Lillibullero" and "Bullena lah !" were said to have been the words of distinction used among the Irish Papists in their massacre of the Protestants in 1641.

Hume thought the popularity of the song was rather due to Purcell, the original composer of it, than to Lord Wharton, who is stated in a pamphlet of 1712, to have been the author of the words. A modern writer on musical composition, Mr. J. Curwen, in 1852, seeking for the source of the power of ridicule in the tune, seems to give it as his opinion that "FA, the fourth on the scale, recurring, with cold sarcasm, here lies the power."

J. Huband Smith, M.R.I.A.

Dublin.

J. L. Armstrong. — I have a copy of a little book, entitled —

"Heart Pearles ; or, Buds of Early Promise. A pleasant Fire-side or Home Companion. Forming a suitable Christmas or New Year's Present for young Readers of both Sexes. By their friend, the Editor, James Leslie Armstrong. London : Printed by William Jones, Duke Street, 1852."

This small volume contains many short poems, sonnets, ballads, &c., and also a drama, "John of Gischala." I believe that the "editor" and the author are one and the same person. Can any reader of "N. & Q." give me any information regarding the author? There was a book called *Scenes from Craven*, published at York in 1835, by Mr. J. L. Armstrong.   R. I.

Lord Aston of Forfar. — The casual mention of this nobleman's name, in a recent number of "N. & Q.," reminded me that I wished to put some queries concerning him to your readers.

It appears that, on the death of James, fifth baron, in 1751, without male issue, the title devolved upon Philip Aston — a very distant relation : that he died unmarried in 1755, and was succeeded by his brother Walter, who also died without male issue in 1763 ; when the honours descended to (the son of his uncle Edward) Walter Aston, father of the late Right Hon. and Rev. Lord Aston, Vicar of Tardebigge, in Worcestershire.

One of these noblemen was a cook in the employ of Sir —— Mordaunt, Bart., and another was a watchmaker. May I ask which was the cook, and which the watchmaker?

As the family is now extinct, or presumed to be

so, there can be no impropriety in my putting these questions:—

It appears, from the *Gentleman's Magazine* (1839, April, p. 377), that—

" The Rev. Walter Hutchinson Aston, Clerk, presented a petition claiming to be Baron Aston of Forfar, but no case was printed."

Was his right to so style himself ever allowed?

There is a pedigree of the family in Berry's *Hertfordshire Pedigrees,* deducing the descent of the late reverend peer from Wm. Aston of Milwich, in remainder to whose posterity the original patent was framed; but it does not show the extinction of the male descendants of an elder son, some generations before the late lord's line branched off.　　　　　　　　　　H. S. G.

CAWNPORE QUERIES.—I have just risen from the perusal of " *Cawnpore,* by G. O. Trevelyan," and wish to ask through your columns the following questions:—

1. Where did the author learn that a Ghazee was a " member of a class of religious enthusiasts," " *probably* hostile to our religion?"—P. 109.

2. Whence did he manage to procure the exclusive information that the infamous Nana Sahib, a Brahmin, was the adopted son of the Rajah of Sattarah, a Mahratta?—P. 57.

3. How came it to pass that Sir Henry Havelock, who did not enter the army till some years after the battle of Waterloo, was in a position to show to our Spanish allies in 1813 that an English s eed could clear a French breastwork?—P. 339.

By way of *Notes,* I take the liberty of mentioning—

1. That a Ghazee is not a Mahomedan Brother Ignatius, but a martial and bloodthirsty fanatic, armed to the teeth, and vowed to wage war to the knife against all infidels, which, in the Indian Mutiny, meant English women and children.

2. That Nana Sahib was as much related to the Rajah of Sattarah as Richard Cromwell to Charles Stuart. The Rajah was the lineal descendant of Seevajee, the founder of the Mahratta Empire, and Nana Sahib, the representative of the Peishwas or Brahmin Mayors of the Palace, who had supplanted their masters upon the throne.

3. El Chico Blanco, immortalised by Napier in his *Peninsular War,* was not Henry Havelock, but his elder brother William Havelock, who fell at the head of the Fourteenth Light Dragoons in the first battle of the last Sikh war.

　　　　　　　　　　　　　CHITTELDROOG.

EDWARD CROKE. — Any information respecting Mr. Edward Croke, who was governor of Fort St. David's on the Coromandel Coast, and died in February, 1769, will be acceptable.　　M. .P.

EXCHEQUER RECORDS. — The following transcript, which I have made from one of the mutilated Exchequer documents, appears to me well worth preserving in " N. & Q." Perhaps some of your readers may be able to tell us something of the parties who were so heavily fined:—

" Elias Best, fined 100l. for drinkeing a health to the pious memmory of Stephen Collidg.

" Thomas Swaden, a Collectour of Chimny mony, fined 100l. for not returneing 3 chimnys.

" David Bennables, a gold Smith, fined 500l. for selling little bawbleing things at faires that was not sterling.

" Isack Simbell fined 100l. for barratry."

　　　　　　　　　　　　　　　W. H. D.

FOSTER OF LEICESTER GRANGE, WARWICKSHIRE, AND OF CO. LEICESTER. — What were the arms of this family. The pedigree is given in Nichols's *Leicestershire,* but the arms are not given.

　　　　　　　　　　　　　　　H. S. G.

FUN.—In the ballad of the " Battle of Harlaw" (3rd S. vii. 394), this word occurs twice. It is not in the dictionaries of Skinner, Junius, Minshull, nor even so late as that of Elisha Cole, 1724. The earliest mention I can find is in Nathan Bailey. What is the derivation of " fun," and its earliest use? How could it have got into the ballad, or is the latter of recent date?

　　　　　　　　　　　　　　　A. A.

Poets' Corner.

SIR RICHARD HARDRES, BART. — This gentleman, who was the eldest son of Sir Thomas Hardres, Knight, of Upper Hardres, in Kent, by Eleanor, daughter of Henry Thoresby, Esq., Master in Chancery, was created a baronet, June 3, 1642. About Oct. 1660, he presented to Charles II. a petition, of which the following is an abstract:—

" Sir Rich. Hardres, Bart. of Great Hardres, co. Kent, servant to his late Majesty. Set on foot the Kentish petition in 1648, for preservation of the late King; led 2300 horse in Kent, reduced Sandwich, and seized the mock prince set up to represent His Majesty's person; suffered three long imprisonments, and high sequestration, to the loss of 7000l.; spent 500l. for plate, bedding, &c., for His Majesty, and though permitted to reclaim them, allowed them to remain on Prince Rupert's complaining of the injury to the service that their withdrawal would cause; hazarded his life by conveying information to His Majesty when in the Downs," &c.—Green's *Cal. Dom. State Papers, Charles II.* i. 332.

I desire to know when this loyal baronet died.

　　　　　　　　　　　　　　　S. Y. R.

KILPECK. — Can you refer me to any historical account of Kilpeck Castle?　　　P. S. C.

LOCAL NAMES. — The other day being in the north of London, I was much struck with the names of the following places:—Ball's Pond, Ponder's End, Potter's Bar.

Now my queries are—Who was Ball, and where

was his Pond? * Who was Ponder, and what
was his End? Where did Potter reside, and by
what right did he put up a Bar?
· Ignorantia Loci.

Marcolphus.—
"Marcolphus will not lightly find a fit tree to hang
himself on."—*Jewel*, iv. 124.
Who was Marcolphus, and what does Jewel
refer to? I cannot find any explanatory note
elucidating the allusion. F. C.

Marriage Customs.—In the year 1476, a certificate was made by the clergy and six parishioners of Ufford, in the county of Suffolk, to the
effect that:—
"Robert Hatchet, late a neighbour and parishioner of
the said town of Hufford, buried his wife Anne Hatchet
in the said parish, the next day after Saint Mark the
Evangelist, A.D. 1476; and we aforesaid testify and bear
true witness that we nor none of our neighbours never
knew unto this day that since the said Anne's decease,
that the said Robert was 'trowhplyht' to any woman by
the tityl of matrimony, but that the said Robert may take
him a lawful woman unto wife in any town of Yng-
land."

Can any of your readers inform me whether
such certificates were common, or was this a special
case?
In one of the old register books of the seventeenth century belonging to the parish of Clare,
Suffolk, is the following singular memorandum:—
"Memorandum, that I, Susan Ward of Clare, doe resigne all my right in John Manson to Susan ffrost, so that
they proceed to marriage, in witness of the truth herof I
the said Susan Ward have set my hand this the 5 of
Januarie. "The Mark of
"Witness, Susan + Ward.
"John Prentice."

Do you know of the existence of any similar
memorandums, and can you give an explanation of
such a singular entry? J. G.

"The Metropolitan Magazine."—Can any
one inform me who was editor of a periodical
called *The Metropolitan* [*Quarterly*] *Magazine*,
1826? The magazine only existed for about a
year. Are the names of any of the contributors
known? R. I.

· Miniature.—Mr. Fairholt, in his *Dictionary of
Terms of Art*, supposes this term to be derived
from the practice of writing the rubrics and initial
letters of manuscripts with red-lead, or *minium*—
the name given to vermilion by the ancients.

[* Ball's-pond, in the parish of Islington, derives its
name from one John Ball, who kept a house of entertainment here about the middle of the seventeenth century,
having for its sign "The Salutation." A large pond,
which remained till the commencement of the present
century, was probably in his day frequented by duck-
hunters, and by them coupled with the name of their host.
A token issued by him bears the inscription, "John Ball,
at the Boarded House neere Newington Green." — Lewis's
Islington, p. 360.—Ed.]

This is indeed the derivation which etymologists
follow each other in assigning to the term: Blount
(1670), Coles (1700), *Gloss. Angl. Nova* (1707),
&c. Kersey (1715), simply defines it "a drawing
of pictures in little." I do not find the word in
Cotgrave (1650), or remember meeting with it in
French treatises on painting earlier than this; but
his successor Guy Miege, in his *Great French Dictionary* (folio, 1688), has it immediately following, as if derived from the words "Mignardise,"
"Mignardes,". "Mignard," spelling it "Migna-
ture;" and explaining it—"*Miniature*, a sort of
painting in small, and in water-colours." I rather
fancy this derivation; but do not know how it
will fit in with the Italian "miniatori caligrafi," or
rubric penmen; whose labours, together with
those of the "illuminatori," produced the manuscripts and missals which have descended to us
from the pre-typographic ages.
· William Bates.
Birmingham.

An old Prophecy from Nostradamus.—I
cut the following from the *New York Times*, of
April 4, 1865. You may consider it of sufficient
interest to give to your readers.
"An old Prophecy. From the *Richmond Whig*,
March 30. By request, we publish the following extracts
from the *Prophéties et Vaticinations* of Nostradamus,
vol. ii. of 1609:—
"'About that time (1861), a great quarrel and contest
will arise in a country beyond the seas—America. Many
poor devils will be hung, and many poor devils will be
killed by a punishment other than a cord. Upon my
faith you may believe me. The war will not cease for
four years, at which none should be surprised, for there
will be no want of hatred and obstinacy in it. At the
end of that time, prostrate and almost ruined, the people
will re-embrace each other in great joy and love.'"
G. W.

Polygamy.—The late eminent prelate, Archbishop Whately, would have permitted polygamy
in the case of polygamous converts, rather than
have the wives in excess of one dismissed to their
great injury; the youngest probably being retained by the convert, if he were obliged to select
one; and the only true wife—the oldest and first—
being as probably amongst the rejected. This I
report *meipso teste*. It was said to me long before
Dr. Colenso came to the same conclusion, in presence of the same missionary difficulty.
Bishops Burnet and Berkeley are said to have
viewed favourably the principle of polygamy. Is
it so? Give chapter and verse—so to speak.*
Sir William Capell Brooke, in his *Sketches in
Spain and Morocco*, 1831, is further said to have
recommended the practice which even unchristian
nations are gradually coming to renounce.
I have not seen his book; nor Madan's extraordinary one of the last century. A Clergyman.

[* Bishop Burnet's work on *Polygamy* is noticed in
"N. & Q.," 2nd S. ii. 131.—Ed.]

COMPUTATIONS OF REGNAL YEARS. — Edward III. (as any History of England will inform its reader), began to reign Jan. 25, 1327, and died on June 21, 1377. I am but a poor arithmetician, but I think I shall not commit any great error in adding that this reign thereby extended over fifty years and five months, minus a few days. How, then, comes King Edward to possess an issue roll for the *Michaelmas* term of his fifty-first year, extending to the following Easter?

Moreover, Edward the Black Prince died June 8, 1376. What then mean the following entries on the Michaelmas Issue Roll for his father's fiftieth year? —

" Dec. 22. To Edward Prince of Wales, by the hands of William de Fulborne, his clerk, &c. 400*l*."

" To Edward Prince of Wales, by the hands of John Dony, mercer, of London, 240*l*."

" Mar. 8. To Edward Prince of Wales, &c. 266*l*. 13. 4."

Again, according to a Wardrobe Roll for 38 Edw. III., Elizabeth Duchess of Clarence was buried March 11, anno 38, the expenses for the transmission of her corpse to England commencing on the 31st of January previous. Yet the first part of these expenses are repaid only on Jan. 31, anno 39; appearing in the Michaelmas Issue Roll for 38 Edw. III.

Is it possible that the Michaelmas Roll takes its name from the year in which it closes, and should be reckoned *before* the Easter Roll of each year? *i. e.* does the Michaelmas Roll intitled anno 38 contain the Michaelmas term for anno 37, and the Hilary term for anno 38? or does it, as certainly seems more natural, contain the Michaelmas term for anno 38, and the Hilary term for anno 39?

This is an important question for the correct chronology of the reign. Will PROFESSOR DE MORGAN, who is learned in things in general, and ciphers in particular, or some other archæological and arithmetical authority, condescend to help me out of the Slough of Despond wherein I am floundering? HERMENTRUDE.

P.S. The dates of the Easter Rolls of Richard II., who commenced his reign in June, are in the same predicament.

SAGO AND PORT WINE.—When a boy, this aliment was fashionable with invalids. At that time sago was about four shillings a pound. I shall be obliged for information when, and by whom, it was introduced? While writing I may state, that a decoction of pearled barley, or Emden groats, with or without port wine, according to circumstances, offers the most nutritious food for invalids, more so than jellies or beef-tea; especially to those of the upper and middle classes, who, when in health, feed on animal diet.

A. P.

Canonbury.

STILTS.—In Marlowe's drama of *The Jew of Malta*, one of the characters is made to say: —

" Once at Jerusalem, where the pilgrims kneel'd,
I strewed powder on the marble stones,
And wherewithal their knees would rankle so,
That I have laugh'd a-good to see the cripples
Go limping home to Christendom on *stilts*."

By " stilts," in this passage, is evidently meant *crutches*. Was this its original meaning?

H. FISHWICK.

WILLIAM EARL OF ULSTER. — Can somebody kindly tell me the date of the death of this nobleman, the father of Elizabeth Duchess of Clarence? I should be glad to ascertain, if possible, the month as well as the year in which it occurred. For the date of his daughter's birth, if given by any trustworthy authority, I should also be greatly obliged. HERMENTRUDE.

VOSSIUS DE THEOLOGIA GENTILI. — Brunet, *Manuel du Libraire*, t. v. p. 1373, says: —

" De Theologia Gentili et Physiologia Christiana, lib. ix. sive de origine et progressu idolatriæ, éd. 2ª, Amstelodami 1668, 2 vol. in fol. L'édition d'Amsterdam, 1641, 3 vol. in 4to, est moins complète."

I have three quarto volumes, which I supposed were odd ones, but I find that the only copy in the British Museum is exactly like mine. Attention is directed to the peculiarity in the catalogue. The title-page of the first volume says: " Editio tertia priori longé auctior et correctior, Francofurti ad Mœnum, 1675." The second is Amsterdam, 1675; and the third Amsterdam, 1669. In vols. i. and ii., the pagination and register are continuous. Prefixed to vol. iii. is an imperial privilege, giving John Blaeu the exclusive right of printing the last five books for six years, and a like Saxon privilege for ten years. The former dated 1668, the latter, 1669.

I cannot find any notice of this edition. Has Brunet mistaken it for a folio? Gerard John Voss died in 1649. His prefaces, dated 1641 and 1645, are reprinted; and there is no indication of an editor to make the third edition, " auctior et emendatior." Should any reader of " N. & Q." know more about these curious title-pages, or have an opportunity of consulting the folio edition of Vossius's complete *Works*, Amsterdam, 1695—1701, information thereon will oblige H. B. C.

U. U. Club.

WORCESTERSHIRE FAMILIES.—Can any reader of " N. & Q." oblige me with the armorial bearings of the following Worcestershire families?—

Prattinton, a family long resident at Bewdley, of which the late Worcestershire antiquary, Dr. Prattinton, was a member.

Penn of Harborough Hall. This family was of Harborough in the fifteenth century. The last of the race, who was uncle to the poet Shenstone, died issueless in 1731.

Bland of Ham Court.
Ramell, Lord, of Great and Little Hampton.
Purcell of Purcell Hall.
Tristram of Moor Hall, in Belbroughton.
Lea of the Hill ; sheriff, 1816.
Ballard of Evesham.
Newce of Rock : co-heiress, married Cornwallis and Partinton.
Zachary, representing Mucklow of Arley.
Timbrell of Bradforton.
Holberrow of Wolverley.
Andrewes of Synton. (Arms were granted to Richard Andrewes, of Synton, in 1529.)
Hodges of Broadway. (John Hodges, of Broadway, had his arms confirmed, and a crest granted in 1610.)	H. S. G.

Queries with Answers.

WHIT-SUNDAY, WHITSUNDAY, OR WHITSUN DAY ? — In the *Churchman's Almanack* for the present year, published by the S. P. C. K., the compiler has called June 4, " Whitsun Day." What authority is there for this ? In the Prayer-book the day is called "Whit-Sunday." It is frequently , however, written "Whitsunday," as in Wheatly and the *Christian Year*. So that here are three ways of writing the word or words. Which is the right way ?	CUTHBERT BEDE.

[Whit-Sunday, Whit-Monday, and Whit-Tuesday, are ecclesiastical barbarisms. White-Sunday, or Huit-Sunday, as vulgar etymologies, are also utterly indefensible. Whitsun-day, or rather Whitson-day, from wit (mind, or understanding) is nothing more nor less than a corruption of Pentecost day, as is shown by the comparison of the corresponding names of Whitsun-day in foreign languages. (See "N. & Q." 2nd S. ii. 154.) The analogy of Easter favours this orthography. It is Easter Day, not Easter Sunday ; therefore it is Whitsun Day, not Whit Sunday. Easter Eve, Easter Monday, Easter Tuesday, have in like manner their parallels in Whitsun Eve, Whitsun Monday, and Whitsun Tuesday. The Book of Common Prayer says Monday and Tuesday in "Whitsun week." Until of late years the word was printed in one—Whitsunday, not Whit-Sunday. In the *Anglo-Saxon Chronicle* we have—

" A.D. 1067.—On thisan Eastron com se kyng to Wincestre, and tha wæron Eastra on x. kl. Apr., and sona æfter tham com Mathild seo hlæfdie hider to lande, and Ealdred arceb' hig gehalgode to cwene on Westmystre on hwitan sunnan dæg.

" This Easter came the King to Winchester ; and Easter was then on the 10th before the calends of April. Soon after this came the lady Matilda hither to this land ; and Archbishop Eldred hallowed her to queen at Westminster on Whitsunday."—*Saxon Chronicle*, ed. Ingram, p. 268.

The *Paston Letters* and Wickliffe spell it Whitsontide, the Bible of 1551 Wytsontyde, Chaucer, Whitsondaie, Sir Thomas More, Whytsontyde, Sidney, Whitsontide, William de Worde, Wytson.]

FIVE MINIATURES. — I have lately seen five miniatures, set as a group in one frame. The subjects are all men of middle age, or rather past it. Each man has a rope round his neck, with a knife plunged into the middle of the body, as if they had all suffered for treason. To four of them the names are given underneath, with the addition " passus," with the date. The names are Cooke, Heath, Ward, and Holland. The fifth has no name : he is in a dress apparently of a Roman Catholic priest, with his head shaved, and out of his mouth proceeds a legend with the inscription " Have mercy, Jesus." The dates are all from 1641 to 1646 ; no two in the same year. Can any of your correspondents inform me who these men can be ? The mode of death seems to point distinctly to the English punishment for treason ; and the names are unquestionably English, and the costume that of England at that period. But what trials for treason could have occurred during the Civil Wars ?	J. C. M.

[William Ward, whose true name was Webster, suffered at Tyburn on July 26, 1641 : see Dodd's *Church History*, iii. 95, fol. and *Memoirs of Missionary Priests*, Part II. pp. 155-171.—Thomas Holland, *alias* Sanderson, also suffered at Tyburn, Dec. 12, 1642 : see *Memoirs of Missionary Priests*, Pt. II. pp. 237-243, and Oliver's *Biography of Members of the Society of Jesus*, p. 117. There is a portrait of him in the *Certamen Triplex*.—Henry Heath, otherwise called Paulus de Sancta Magdalena, suffered at Tyburn on April 17 [or 27], 1643 : see Dodd's *Church History*, iii. 119, and *Memoirs of Missionary Priests*, Pt. II. pp. 243-256. We cannot throw any light on the other two miniatures.]

" SERMONS TO ASSES."—The above is the title of a small book published in 1768 (London), and followed in a year or two by a second series. It is dedicated " To the very excellent and reverend Messrs. G. W., J. W., W. R., and M. M.,"—some of whom (the dedication tells us), " have preached for many years to the members of the congregation that these sermons are designed for." We are also informed that " These Sermons should have been dedicated to the A—b—s, B—s, and their C—y, but the author was afraid of offending their modesty." I am anxious to learn who was the author, and to whom each of the above initials respectively refers.	R. C. L.

[This singular production is from the pen of James Murray, late pastor of the Scotch Presbyterian meeting-house, High Bridge, Newcastle, who died on January 28, 1782, in the fiftieth year of his age. The initials of the Dedication are intended for the following popular preachers of that time, namely, George Whitfield, John Wesley, William Romaine, and Martin Madan. Murray's *Sermons to Asses* was followed by *New Sermons to Asses*, also *Sermons to Doctors in Divinity*, *Sermons to Ministers of State*, and *Lectures to Lords Spiritual*. These have since been collected into an octavo volume, and published by William Hone in 1819, with a short biographical notice and portrait of the author. The best account, however, of this eccentric preacher, together with a list of his numerous works, will be found in Mackenzie's *History of Newcastle-upon-Tyne*, edit. 1827, vol. i. pp. 387-389.]

A JACOBUS PIECE OF GOLD.—In the will of a Mrs. Barbara Young, dated 27th of August, 1730, and proved at Armagh, 16th December, 1743, frequent mention is made of a Jacobus piece of gold; as, for example, in the following bequest:—"I leave and bequeath to my grandson, Latham Blacker, three hundred pounds and a Jacobus pees [*sic*] of gold." What may have been the meaning of leaving this piece of gold in addition to the sum of 300*l.*?   ABHBA.

[The Jacobus, or touch-piece, was hung round the neck of the individual afflicted with the Evil when the King touched for it : the latest are of James II., Anne, and the Pretenders. The sovereign power of the gold piece was distinctly admitted, as the disease is reported to have returned in some cases upon the medal being lost, and of being again subdued upon the presentation of a second piece. *Vide* Pettigrew's *Superstitions connected with Medicine and Surgery*. 8vo, 1844, p. 144.]

MOTHER-IN-LAW.—Edward Dennis in his Will (1708) leaves a legacy to his "Honoured Mother-in-law Elizabeth Dennis." Can a man's second wife be correctly called his children's mother-in-law? I should mention that Edward Dennis never married, as far as I can ascertain.
                                        SAMUEL TUCKER.
20, Doughty Street, Mecklenburgh Square.

[Wharton in his *Law Lexicon*, ed. 1860, says that a Mother-in-law is the mother of one's wife or husband (p. 496), whereas a Step-mother (*noverca*, Lat.) is the wife of one's father, who is not one's mother, p. 697.]

PARK.—How came the word Park to be applied to artillery?   G. S. D.

[A park, as Blackstone remarks, properly signifies any enclosure; hence a "park of artillery" is surrounded with a rope. In Scotland, any enclosure of considerable extent, whether by means of stone walls or fences, used as grazing ground for domesticated animals, for corn or grass crops, is termed a *park*.]

MUNDUNGUS.—Can any etymologist tell me the derivation of this cacophonous synonym for bad tobacco? I cannot find the word in any book earlier than the reign of Charles II. Is it Dutch?
                                        WALTER THORNBURY.

[Mundungus, trashy tobacco, is from the Spanish Mondóngo, paunch, tripes, black pudding. *Vide* Neuman and Baretti's *Spanish Dictionary*.]

Replies.

FACTITIOUS PEDIGREES: WILLIAM SIDNEY SPENCE.

(1st S. ix. 221, 275; 2nd S. x. 106.)

At the present moment, when attention is being so generally and so properly drawn to the many factitious pedigrees now put forth in books having the semblance of authority, the following particulars of a kind-hearted gentleman, who was ever ready to help pedigree-hunters out of their difficulties, will probably interest many readers of "N. & Q."

Good Mr. Spence having, I presume, heard that the late Mr. St. Barbe was engaged in collecting materials for a history of his family, addressed the following letter to that gentleman:—

"4 Feb. 1846.

"Having been engaged by the Widow of the late Sir John Cotgreave, of Netherleigh House, near Chester, to inspect and arrange the Title-deeds and other documents in her Ladyship's possession, I find a very ancient pedigree of the Cotgreaves de Hargrave in the co. of Chester, which family became extinct in the direct male line in the year 1724, but which was represented thro' females by the late Sir John Cotgreave. It is the work of Randle Holme, anno 1672, from the documents compiled by the learned William Camden in 1598, and contains the descents of three generations of the St. Barbes de South, Brent, Somerset, and Congleton in Cheshire, with their intermarriages and armorial bearings emblazoned, commencing with Robert St. Barbe de So. Brent and Congleton, living *temp.* Henry I. whose grandson Sir Robert flourished in the reign of Richard Cœur de Lion, and embraced the Cross, accompanied that Monarch to the Holy Land, and fought under him at the Battle of Ascalon against Sultan Saladin; presuming that you are of the same family, I will transmit you extracts from the pedigree as far as relates to your distinguished family, conditionally that you remunerate me for the information and definition of the armorial bearings, there being 3 shields containing 12 quarterings connected with the St. Barbes, and embracing the Ensigns of Hugh Lupus, the first Norman Earl of Chester, Eustace de Montalt, Lord Hawarden, Fitzhugh, Pole, Vernon, and other ancient families. Lady Cotgreave will allow me to make the extracts and has kindly consented to attest the same. The arms of St. Barbe are given chequy of 12 ar. and sab.
                          "Yours, &c.
                              "W. S. SPENCE.
"Grange Street, Birkenhead."

Like the late Lord Monson, Mr. Evelyn Shirley, and several other correspondents to whom this worthy addressed his liberal offer of service, Mr.

St. Barbe knew his own pedigree better than his correspondent. Determined, however, to find out the facts of the case, he put himself in communication with his friend, the Rev. H. Jones, who brought the matter under the notice of Mr. Davies, a resident at Birkenhead, and the results of whose inquiries are furnished in the following amusing letters:—

" 27 Feb. 1846.

" I scribble this after a fruitless attempt to see Mr. Spence. I went to Grange Street, and no one could or would tell me anything about him.

" I suspected he was known there, and so I got hold of a woman living in a cellar and tried her; she acknowledged at length that she knew him, but that he had removed. I followed her directions, and was told that he had again removed. I still kept on the chase, and again found myself with the old woman in the cellar, having been told that she knew more of him than any one else. She seemed surprised that I was so determined. In course of conversation I found she was Welsh. I spoke to her in the ancient British tongue, and it acted like magic. She now, as I was a Welshman, told me all about him, speaking Welsh all the while. It appears he is very poor, and she suspected I was after him for money or with a writ, or something of the sort. He will not make his appearance, being so shabbily dressed. I am afraid I shall find some difficulty in catching him, but to-morrow I shall seize him as he is going to his dinner at the same old woman's cellar, and try and make something of him.

" This morning she told me he was quite drunk before 11 o'clock, and I suspect he is accustomed to it. She also said that he is in the habit of sending a great number of letters off to noblemen and gentlemen of ancient pedigree, offering to furnish information, and that he seldom gets less than 3l. to 5l. for his trouble. If I find on questioning him to-morrow that he knows only what Mr. St. Barbe is already acquainted with, I should advise having nothing to do with him."

" 28 Feb. 1846.

" This morning I again visited the old woman's cellar, and witnessed a scene quite unique in its way. By the fire sat a stout good-looking man, just finishing his dinner, whom I suspected at once to be the identical person I was in search of, but lo! and behold, when I questioned him he said, ' I am not the person you want—it's a cousin of mine.' In a moment I knew this was a barefaced falsehood, but I did not allow him to think so. I sat down and entered into conversation with him, and was satisfied that he was the identical individual I was in search of. You would have been amused to have heard our conversation; having studied the subject before hand, I completely bothered him, and he was obliged to admit that the information he could give would not be of much importance, as Mr. St. Barbe's pedigree is registered from the time of the Conqueror at the Heralds' College. He was anxious to know whether " *his cousin* " might emblazon the shield of arms, saying that as it would take him a long time, he would expect to be remunerated accordingly; but I told him all that was required was the extract of the three descents with the intermarriages, as stated in the Cotgreave paper, and he promised to write to his Cousin to ask whether he would accept the proffered remuneration of the 1l. for the trouble, *and his cousin*, for which read *himself*, is to write to you. I therefore enclose Mr. St. Barbe's letter, as well as the one written by this extraordinary man, and I hope you may get the information you want for your friend; at any rate you will be able to deal with him as you like, now you know what sort of a being he is.

" I did not for a moment permit him to think I knew all about him; but in going away I was told, *sub rosâ*, by the old woman, in Welsh, that he was the real Simon Pure, and had no cousin that she ever heard of. He evidently wished to preserve the strictest incognito, and I am only surprised that he could so barefacedly tell the glaring falsehoods he attempted to make me believe."

This worthy is no longer in the flesh, but his mantle has fallen on shoulders quite as unscrupulous. Let the readers of " N. & Q." beware of them.   M. S.

SALLY SALISBURY.

(3rd S. vii. 458.)

Sarah Prydden was the name of this celebrated courtezan, who was the great toast of her day in dissolute circles. This very beautiful, but abandoned woman, is said to have possessed the form of an angel with the disposition of a fiend. Like Congreve's Doris, she always forgot, or affected to forget, the liberality of her gallants; and if released when arrested, she expelled from her breast all ideas of gratitude. At Bath she appeared in all the elegance of fashion, and was attended in public by men of aristocratic rank. Miss Prydden's tirewoman, when dressing her hair, having flatteringly said, that if she had not been with her at the time, she should have taken her for Lady Salisbury, who had just passed by, induced this vain woman to adopt or usurp the name of Salisbury.

She was indicted at the Old Bailey for an assault, with an intent to murder, the Hon. John Finch, son of Daniel, Earl of Winchelsea, of which she was found guilty on April 24, 1723, and sentenced to pay a fine of one hundred pounds, to suffer one month's imprisonment, and to find security for her good behaviour for two years more. Jealousy of her sister seems to have been the cause of her crime, without any intention of taking away the life of her honourable paramour. Such was the little restriction over prisoners at this period, that it was a raging fashion with the rakes of her day to dine and sup in her cell. Tom Hearne has several notices of her in his *Diary*; among others the following entry : —

"Oct. 12, 1724. Mr. Murray, being in Oxford, told me, that he happened once, with two or three gentlemen, to see the celebrated Sally Salisbury, while she was under confinement, being the only time he saw her. They found her with two or three others drinking a bowle of punch, of about fifteen or sixteen shillings. Mr. Murray and his companions sate at another table. But Mr. Murray being a great lover of punch, and expressing himself as if he desired to taste of it, he was very civilly accommodated. He said, she seemed to him to be about forty years of age, though she must be less, if, according to her life, she was born about 1690, or 1691. He said, she dressed plain but neat ; that she had the finest hand his eyes ever beheld, and that she had been most certainly a compleat beauty."

She died in Newgate, after ten months' imprisonment, on Feb. 11, 1723-4, and on the 14th of the same month was buried at St. Andrew's, Holborn. Some wag finding Sally's coffin was placed next to that of the celebrated Dr. Sacheverel in the vaults of the church, has left on record the following epigram : —

"Lo! to one grave consign'd, of rival fame,
A rev'rend Doctor, and a wanton Dame ;
Well for the world they did to rest retire,
For each, while living, set mankind on fire."

The trial of Sally Salisbury is printed in the *Select Trials at the Sessions-house in the Old Bailey*, i. 336-343, edit. 1742. Consult also Noble's *History of England*, iii. 476. There are at least four separate works containing " A complete History " of this unfortunate female, and two engraved portraits of her, one by Smith, after Kneller, fol., 1724; another by Faber, 4to, 1725. It does not appear that she ever had a daughter, so that the other miniature, in the South Kensington Museum, may be that of a younger sister.   J. Y.
Barnsbury.

HORSE: GRACE.
(3rd S. vii. 419.)

Your correspondent, ALPHA BETA, referring to Max Müller's second series of *Lectures on the Science of Language* (p. 369), in which the myth of the horses of the sun and that of Apollo attended by the Graces, are referred to the same original, wishes to know whether " the words *horse* and *grace* (χάρις) come from the same root." Following the most searching analytical inquiry, the conclusion is that they do not. Our word *horse*, A. S. *hors*, in its earliest Teutonic form *hros*, is closely connected with O. G. *horse*, alacer, celer, volucer, from which the Ger. *rasch*, and Eng. *rash*,

are derived. Bopp (*Gloss. Sans.*, 406) derives *horse* from Sans. इष्, *hresh*, hinnire. Pictet (*Origines Indo-Europ.*, i. 340) derives it from रसिक, *rasika*, one of the Sanskrit terms for a horse, from the root रस, *rasa*, spirited, impassioned. The derivation, after all, is very uncertain. As the Teutonic word begins with an aspirate we should look for a Sanskrit root commencing with *k*. The nearest approach in this direction is कर, *kara*, action, from कृ, *kri*, facio. As the word *rasika* is employed both for horse and elephant, and as *karaka* is also used for elephant, it is possible that the latter may have been employed also as a term for the horse.

The Greek χάρις is usually connected with the Sanskrit घृ, *ghri*, or *ghar* (there is no Sanskrit root *gha*) which means to shine, but there is considerable doubt on the subject. The Greek χάριτες were the goddesses who conferred all favours. We are referred for the derivation to the verb χαίρω, which originally signified parting, dismissing, taking away, and then by metonymy, dismissing with favours. We must then look for a root which has this primary signification, and which we find in Sansk. ह, *hri*, or *har*, the Sanskrit aspirate corresponding with the Greek χ. It will therefore be evident that *horse* and *charis* have no connection in their etymology.

The Greek ἱππος, originally ικϝος, Latin *equ-a*, or *equ-us*, are equivalent to Sansk. अश्व, *aswa*, the Sansk. *s* being the representative, in many cases, of the Greek and Latin gutturals. *Aswa* for *horse* does not appear to be a radical, but there does not exist any root to which it can be satisfactorily referred. अश्, *as*, means to enjoy. Probably the above hints may suffice for your correspondent's inquiries, unless a better solution be afforded.
                                                      J. A. P.
Wavertree, near Liverpool.

Your correspondent ALPHA BETA may rest assured that *horse* and χάρις are not connected with one another. The initial *h* of the Low German *horse*, *hors*, *hross*, &c. would require a corresponding κ in Greek. Χάρις, as Prof. Max Müller has pointed out, is referable to the root *ghar* (whence English *greedy*), while *horse*, Icelandic *hross* or *ross*, claims kinship with the Icelandic *ras*, English *rush*, *ride*, Swedish *rida*, &c. Symeon Magister (*Script. post Theoph.* ed. Paris, p. 490) says, οἱ Ῥῶς οἱ καὶ

Δρομεται λεγόμενοι, and the root is to be found in the Sanskrit *śrí*, whence Latin *currere, cursus,* &c.

Ἵππος is the Latin *equus*, Zend *aspa*, Sanskrit *aśwa*, *q* and *p* being interchanged as in *ἕπομαι* and *sequor*, σκῦλον and *spolia*, κώληψ and *poples*. The radix is *aś*, whence *aśus, aśan,* ὠκύς, ἀκίς, *acer, acus,* &c., containing the idea of "sharpness" or "swiftness."

As to Βάκχος and Ἴακχος, it is usual to connect them by assuming a change of *i* into *y* after the initial digamma, which we know from such passages as *Od.* iv. 454, *Il.* xi. 453, to have originally belonged to the simple verb. It is better, however, to regard the two words as severally derived from ἠχέω or ἀχέω and ἰάχω; the latter being merely correlative imitations of the same sound. A. SAYCE.

GIBBON'S AUTOBIOGRAPHY: OGRESSES.
(3rd S. vii. 417.)

I have not Gibbon's Autobiography at hand, but I suppose his authority for the statement in which he made so amusing a blunder was the quaint *Introductio ad Latinam Blazoniam* of his namesake, John Gibbon, Blue-Mantle Pursuivant. (London, 1682.) If MR. DIXON has not this curious book, he may be interested in the following extract from pp. 160, 161 of it, since it shows the real existence of the "unjust kinswomen":—

"The said author is guilty of another inadvertency (p. 296) in saying, Sir *William Segar* granted to this Family A LYON RAMPANT BETWEEN THREE OGRESSES. Now this was granted only to *Edmond Gibbon* (his Father always sealed with a LYON RAMPANT GARDANT BETWEEN THREE SCHALLOPS). But himself assumed a new Coat out of distaste against three Ladies his Kinswomen, Daughters of *Gervase Gibbon* of the Pump. *Frances*, married to Sir *Robert Point*, Knight of the Bath, *Ellinor* married to Sir *John Crook*: and *Grizeld* married to Sir *John Lawrence*, Knight and Baronet, who lyes buried at *Chelsy* in MIDDLESEX, in a Chapel belonging to (and re-edified by) her-self, with a fair Mural Monumental remembrance. The falling out was about the will of *Edmund Gibbon*, Founder of the Free-School in *Benenden*, the next parish to *Rolveden* aforesaid. As for *Edmund* aforesaid, he lyes buried in the *Temple* Church, LONDON (in the Walks or Western part) with a fair Monument against a Pillar, with a quartered Coat, that of the SCHALLOPS being placed *in prima Quadra*. (Mention is made of him *pag.* 38 foregoing.) I will only mysteriously add, *Deus sit Susceptor Meus*."

Gibbon appears to have made another mistake in making the Christian name of his ancestor Edward, whereas by the foregoing extract it was Edmund.

I conclude with two queries: First, Where was "the Pump" alluded to above? Secondly, What did Gibbon mean by the sentence he so "mysteriously" added? JOHN WOODWARD.

New Shoreham.

Your correspondent is surely in error in fancying that Gibbon, in the passage quoted, was so ignorant of heraldry as to suppose that the ogresses were actual representations of female cannibals. Heraldic writers in general give no explanation of the origin of the term *ogress*, synonymous with *pellet*, as applied to roundles sable; but it was exactly in the spirit of the heraldic conceits and puns of the seventeenth century, in which every charge had some fanciful meaning assigned to it, to fix on ogresses as appropriate emblems of the three litigious ladies. The historian's account of this matter receives a certain amount of confirmation from Guillim's *Display of Heraldry*, where "Sable a lyon rampant, guardant crowned or between three escallop shells argent" is given as the coat of the Gibbons of Dorchester; while it is also stated that—

"Or a lyon rampant sable between three pellets was borne by the name of Gibbon, and was confirmed to Edmund Gibbon, son and heir of Thomas Gibbon of Rolvenden, *alias* Rowenden, gentleman, by Sir William Segar the 6th of April, 1629, in the 5th year of the reign of King Charles the First."

G. B.

COLD OR COLE HARBOUR.
(3rd S. vii. 253, 302, 344, 407.)

In reading Miss Strickland's *Lives of the Queens of England*, vol. ii. p. 421, I have lighted on the following foot-note explanatory of the above designation, as applied to a dilapidated city palace, in which the Lady Margaret Douglas, Countess of Lennox, was imprisoned by Queen Elizabeth. The learned authoress would appear not to have been troubled with any doubts as to the true derivation of the name, such as have lately exercised the critical ingenuity of some of your contributors.

"There were two palaces belonging to the crown which claimed this name of Cold or Cole Harbour, both situated on little harbour creeks of the Thames, where doubtless crafts of coals put in for the supply of the metropolis and its environs. The easternmost Cole Harbour was situated on the spot where now is the West India Dock Basin. The name remains with some traditions, and that unfailing adjunct to a suburban royal demain, a Robin Hood Lane or Gateway — a remarkable place, modern corruption being grafted upon its primitive lack of civilisation. There were lately some antique mulberry trees braced with iron lingering in the adjoining gardens. It was the palace of George of Clarence, very conveniently situated across the Thames, opposite the Greenwich Palace. Margaret Duchess of Burgundy resided there on her visit to Edward IV., as Sir Harry Nicolas proves from their compotus. The other Cole Harbour, likewise in possession of the crown, built by a citizen is best known. All Hallow's church, Thames Street, was, in Stowe's time, originally part of its gateway. It does not appear which Cole Harbour was occupied by the Countess of Lennox."

In your issue (No. 170) DR. HAHN speaks of the name as being given to places, farms, lanes, &c., in different parts of England, Ireland, and America. Among the numerous inlets on the Atlantic coast of Nova Scotia there is one known as *Cole* Harbour, but why so called I have not at present the means of ascertaining. In connexion with this locality, I have heard of the following lines as current among the rough-and-ready class of the population in answer to inquiries about the news :—

> " Some say the devil's dead,
> And buried in Cole Harbour ;
> Some say he's rose again,
> And prenticed to a barber."

X.

Mr. Hartshorne has given a very copious list of Cold Harbours in England; this I greatly extended, and included the Cold Harbours abroad, and also gave a list of Harbours, Bowers, and Windy Harbours. The Kalterherberg of Dr. Hahn, four German miles south of Aix-la-Chapelle, I believe to be one recorded by me as near Treves, but the Kalterherberg in Baden and near Lörrach, are extensions of the list. I have no doubt but that the list of Cold Harbours in the Netherlands and Germany must be much more copious. The features I have remarked are, first, in confirmation of other observers, that the situation of Cold Harbours is near a Roman road. Second, that the word is Cold and not Coal, or Coluber, or any one of the meanings, Celtic or Latin, other than Cold, that have been attributed. This is proved by the various linguistic forms of the word Cold, Koude, Kalte; and by the use of synonyms, as wind and windy. How the word Cold comes to be applied to these stations I cannot satisfactorily see. Third, that Harbour is distinctly Harborough, meaning a military fort, and not a coal depot or sheepcot, as has been surmised. Fourth, that the term Cold Harbour is one of the class of terms applied by the Germanic natives to Roman establishments. As these conclusions rest upon a number of facts, and not upon theory, all that remains to be done is to find a meaning for Cold in conformity with the facts.

I may note for the guidance of those who are engaged in the investigation of the Anglo-Saxon nomenclature of the Roman establishments in Britain (that is to say the Germanic nomenclature) with that adopted by the Turks in Asia Minor. Where a Greek population was left, as on the coast, we find Greek names; where the Greek population was extirpated we find the Hissars, Kalehs, &c., answering to the Chesters, Boroughs, &c. In England, where a Celtic population remained, as in Wales, the Welsh border, and Cornwall, we find Welsh names; but in the main portion of the country we find Anglo-Saxon names.

Setting aside other evidence, we have here a strong analogous example from comparative his-

tory that the Anglo-Saxons extirpated the Celts in England, as the Turks did the Greeks in the main part of Anatolia.   Hyde Clarke.
Smyrna, May 27, 1865.

RHYMES TO DICKENS AND THACKERAY.

(3rd S. iv. 207, 277, 318.)

When the original verses on these two great names appeared in " N. & Q.," with a proposal that other contributors should send lines, " with the same rhyme-words, addressed to the strong points of the two," I felt, as I have no doubt others did, that while the former triplet merely touched one point in the " mannerism" of Dickens, the lines on Thackeray went entirely, without a word of reservation, to blacken his social, moral, and religious character. M. stated that he had heard the words repeated, but without the name of the author. We are required to believe him ignorant of the authorship; and, therefore, nothing personal can be intended in the remark, that whatever cynicism existed in the character of Thackeray, the writer of the satire is not without the same weakness.

The challenge was taken up by C., and again by your able correspondent J. J. B. Workard; but neither of them alluded to the " Satyr with the poison tooth." The difficulty of constructing verses indicative of the characters of two men of remarkable genius, within so brief a compass, and fettered by given rhyme words, is undoubtedly great; and it is no discredit to C. that his lines are lame, and limp. I prefer those by Mr. Workard.

Three months after the satire first appeared in " N. & Q.," I saw the earthly remains of Thackeray consigned to their quiet grave at Kensal Green, amidst the tears of a thousand representatives of unnumbered myriads of absent mourners; and, on my way home, composed the following reply to the challenge of M., taking only the liberty of adding an additional line :—

> " Intensely human is thy soul, Charles Dickens !
> Moral and social good to life it quickens !
> The bond of common blood and nature thickens
> In lordly halls,—and where the poor man sickens.
>
> " Who does not mourn departed Thackeray ?
> And feel—though hid by clouds in black array—
> His ' silver lined' genius shall ne'er lack a ray ? "

This I immediately forwarded to " N. & Q." with a remark that, if the early and sudden death of Thackeray could have been anticipated, I am sure the satire would not have been sent, or if sent, inserted. My manuscript was mislaid and lost, amongst others of perhaps as little value. The draft of the lines has, however, turned up among my own papers; and, if worth printing, is at the service of your readers.   W. Lee.

CANNEL COAL.

(3rd S. vii. 418.)

The writer in Newton's *Journal of Arts* for April upon "The true Origin of the Name now applied to this kind of Coal," asserts that Brindley's Canal from Worsley to Manchester, projected in 1758, originated the term "cannel" to designate a peculiar and well known kind of coal. Furthermore, the writer goes on to say that—

"This word has indeed been lately written 'cannel' in this country, and some ingenious persons finding themselves quite at a loss to discover the source of such a name, have come to the conclusion that it is derived from the word candle."

That the Duke of Bridgwater's Canal did not bring into existence the word "cannel," and also that word has not been *lately* written "cannel" in this country, the following will show:—

"Wigan is famous for fuel, especially for the choicest coal in England called *cannell*."—R. Blome's *Britania*, 1673.

"Firstly, I have sometimes seen native vitriol in these mines; secondly, by distillation, as more particularly in the *Kennel* near Haigh; from which by distillation in a retort, will come over a very austere vitriolic water."—Leigh's *Lancashire and Cheshire*, 1700.

"g. 10. Coal, very black, fine, and hard. This is the *Ampelites* of the shops, the *Lapis obsidianus* of some late writers, and is called *Canal Coal* at Haigh in Lancashire." J. Woodward, M.D., *Fossils of England* (1729), part I. vol. i. p. 165.

"d. 2. Another sort of canal coal, from the same pit. The lower part of the same stratum is of common coal."—Woodward, vol. ii. p. 17.

In Bailey's *Dict.* by J. Nicol Scott, M.D., 1755, it is called "Cannel or Canob Coal," and in Johnson's, 3rd edition, 1765, "Cannel or Canole Cole." Anent the derivation of the word "cannel." It is certain that an artificial watercourse has nothing whatever to do with it. The coal is so called "cannel" to distinguish it from the ordinary or common coal. Its properties are bituminous, easy of ignition, and burns with a continual flame: hence the term "cannel," kennel, kindle, or kendle. The verb to *kendle*, to set on fire, to make to burn, may be found in Rider's *Dict.* by Francis Holyoke, 1617. Kendle-coal or Kindling-coal is no doubt synonymous with "Cannel-coal."

Another derivation of the word "cannel" may be offered. In the Welsh language "cynnew" means to kindle; "cynnud" is fuel; and "cynneuawl" (pronounced kennoyol) is ignitible. "Cynneuawl-glo" is a common expression with the Welsh when they speak of coal that burns well. Your correspondent R. H. Prosser is right when he says that the term "cut" is used for canal. In Lancashire the latter word is seldom if ever used by the operatives on or in the neighbourhood of the canal: it is either "up th' cut," "down th' cut," or "through th' cut."

In Bailey's *Dict.* 1755, there is a quotation from "Knolles," a writer of the early part of the seventeenth century. He says that—

"This great *cut* or ditch, Sesostris, and long after him Ptolemeus Philadelphus, purposed to have made a great deal wider."

Liverpool.   GIBSON.

———

MR. PROSSER is mistaken in supposing that the mineral in question cannot be used as a substitute for a candle. I can well remember when almost every cottage in the Upper Ward of Lanarkshire had a piece of iron in the form of a horse-shoe fixed on the upper bar of the kitchen grate for the purpose of burning cannel coal in the long winter evenings instead of using candles. Indeed I have often used it in my own dining-room after dinner, and a very pleasant light it gave. At the time to which I refer, carters, at the close of autumn, made a regular trade of traversing the higher districts of the country with loads of this coal from the Duke of Hamilton's well known mines, which they sold to the cottagers in quantities of from one to two cwt. This traffic has now fallen off, I believe, in consequence of the great demand by gas works having raised the prices. The same demand has led to coals only partially possessing the qualities of cannel being classed as such, which may account for the failure of MR. PROSSER's experiments.

I may add that "cannel," pronounced with the broad *a*, is the common Scotch expression for candle.   GEORGE VERE IRVING.

———

The Camden quotation in MR. PROSSER's query is probably only from Gough's *Augmentations* (1789). It is not to be found in Holland's translation of the *Britannia* of 1610, but the following occurs at p. 735:—

"If the stone called *Obsidianus* be in our country, I should take that to be it which is commonly called *Canole Cole*: for it is hard, bright, light, and somewhat easie to be cloven peece meale into flakes, and being once kindled it burneth very quickly."

Dr. John Campbell, in his *Political Survey of Britain*, 1774, vol. ii. p. 29, observes in a note:—

"The learned Dr. Davies in his *Dictionary* (1632?), says 'It receives its name from *Canwyl*, which in the old British language signifies a candle, the want of which the bright flame from this coal supplies.'"

Here we have the name more than a century before either the Douglas Navigation at Wigan, or the Duke of Bridgewater's "Kennel" or "Cut" were made; so the *Canal* theory will not hold water.

Being somewhat of the nature of jet, it has been cut into ornaments, and possibly, as Gough says, into candlesticks: but excepting the allusion above, I have nowhere seen that it has been "used by the poor as candles;" and its name in all probability arises from the mere similarity of its flame to that of a candle. Thus Kirwan (*Elements of Mineralogy*, 1810, vol. ii. p. 45), says: "Its proper name is candle coal, as it burns like a candle;" and again (p. 454) "It easily kindles without melting, and burns with a large bright flame, but of short duration." Professor John Phillips, in a "Treatise on Geology," reprinted from the *Encyclopædia Britannica*, seventh edition, says: "The cannel coal of Lancashire and Yorkshire, which blazes like a candle, contains nearly half its weight of gaseous matter."

S. H. H.

CHEVISAUNCE (3rd S. vii. 114, 189.) — In the glossary appended to Speght's *Chaucer*, this word is defined: "Merchandise, devise, a bargain." In that at the end of the third volume of the *Roman de la Rose* (Amst., 1735), we get the following meanings: "expédient pour sortir—issuë de quelque affaire," and also "pour *chevance*, biens, richesses." The obsolete word *chevir*, from which it in all probability is derived, is defined "sortir d'une affaire; vient à bout; finir."

It is likely the word afterwards became *achever*. If so, *chevisaunce* might mean an "achievement"— any thing *finished*, or *completed*; and afterwards an *heroic deed*: which, in fact, is the explanation of the word in the glossary to Spenser (8vo, London, 1845). In the sense of *completion* it might mean a *bargain*, as that is a contract completed; and in the sense of *enterprise* it would certainly have an analogy with *imperatoria*, a master work.

A. A.

Poets' Corner.

DE LA TOUR D'AUVERGNE (3rd S. iv. 474.)—Information and references, on the point in question, will be found in *Biographie Universelle*, tom. xlvi. p. 349, *sub voce* "Tour D'Auvergne-Couet" (Théophile Malo de la). O. W.

KING'S LYNN: CHAUCER (3rd S. vii. 399, 445.) My thanks are due to the REV. J. DALTON and to MR. QUINTON for their obliging replies to my query, by which they have not only corrected the error I committed in confounding the "Catalogue" now in the Norwich Museum with the one referred to in the *General History of Norfolk*, but have at the same time confirmed the suspicion I had already entertained that the "extract from the old book" had never been between the covers of the present catalogue. I must, therefore, honestly confess that I (somewhat hastily, perhaps,) gave credit to the compiler of the *History* for a blunder which now turns out to be one of my own.

The "old book," it is to be observed, is not stated to have been in the museum; but only the "extract;" and, judging from MR. DALTON's con-

cluding remark, I am inclined to think that he and I shall not differ much in our estimate of the loss the world has sustained by its disappearance. Nor should I have troubled myself about the matter but for the sole purpose of ascertaining on what authority "Ben Adam" states that "Lynn had the honour to present the world with GEOFFERY CHAUCER, Capgrave," &c. This appears to me a question worth inquiring into.

F. NORGATE.

PHILIPS EARLS OF PEMBROKE (3rd S. vii. 378, 407.)—There were in the seventeenth century three Earls of Pembroke of the name of Philip. Those mentioned by M. P. are Philip the fourth Earl, and Philip the fifth Earl. Besides these, there was Philip the seventh Earl, who died August 29th, 1683, and he also lies buried at Salisbury. See Collins's *Peerage* (1812), vol. iii. p. 140. Probably all three died at Wilton. At all events, this is the first place to search in. The death of Philip the fifth Earl is stated by Collins to have occurred December 11th, 1669.

MELETES.

NEW STYLE (3rd S. vii. 440.) — Though the statute of 24 George II. fixed the commencement of the legal year to be on the 1st of January, that commencement had been anticipated by a considerable section of the population, for a very long period. It was generally understood to be the *historical* commencement of the year, while from about the end of the thirteenth century the 25th of March was the commencement of the *legal* year. MR. DOBSON must have seen many records of facts occurring between January 1st and March 25th in any year previous to 1750 mentioned with a double date, thus: January 14th, 1648-9, thus giving both the historical and legal date, the last figure indicating the year according to our present computation. Sir Harris Nicolas, in his excellent little work, called *The Chronology of History*, very clearly explains the various changes in the style.

D. S.

"RELIGIO CLERICI," ETC. (3rd S. vii. 448.)—Your correspondent, who so fully appreciates the wit and learning of Mr. Smedley's tracts, may be pleased to be referred to another by this gentleman, in which the same qualities will be found to exist. It is entitled—

"Lux Renata: a Protestant's Epistle, with Notes by the Author of Religio Clerici," 8vo, London, 1827, pp. 63.

This pamphlet, as the author tells us, was suggested in great measure by a perusal of Southey's *Book of the Church*; and he adds that, "he gladly embraces the opportunity of adding his testimony, such as it is, to the entire accuracy and fidelity of Mr. Southey's representations."

I am a little puzzled by one thing. Your correspondent speaks of "A Churchman's Second Epistle," *by the author* of "Religio Clerici." But these, as it appears to me, form simply a double title of one and the same book. The title of my copy, which is a later edition than the one cited, is —

"Religio Clerici : Two Epistles by a Churchman, with Notes. To which is now added, by the same author, a Parson's Choice of Town or Country ; an Epistle to a Young Divine." London, 8vo, 1821, pp. 149.

In the latter of these epistles occurs the passage transcribed by H. B. C., and this strengthens my belief that "Religio Clerici" is but a general or second title of the *Two Epistles*. Is this not the case ? *

Who is the author of the following poem, somewhat similar in character to those above-named ? —

"Ecclesia Dei : A Vision of the Church, with a Preface, Notes and Illustrations," 8vo. London, 1848. †

WILLIAM BATES.

Birmingham.

SASH WINDOWS (3rd S. vii. 449.) — The subject of sash windows may be trivial, but, as it is launched in your pages, it is probable any of the fast-fading anecdotes of their early locality may be acceptable. A personal acquaintance with an octagenarian, who has passed away at least thirty years, and who, I well remember, delighted in repeating anecdotes of his early life, more than once told me he well remembered being taken when a child to see the new house building at the "Deal Tree," by Mr. Seaborne, because he had put in windows never before seen in Wymondham. These were the first sash windows ever seen in that locality. H. D'AVENEY.

ADVERBS IMPROPERLY USED (3rd S. vii. 152, 363, 406.) — Bishop Blomfield, in his preface to his brother's translation of Matthiæ's *Greek Grammar*, has the following passage at p. xii. : —

"Our own language furnishes us with several instances, where the predicate is expressed by an adverb, *he is finely, the horse is well enough !*"

If such phrases as *he is finely* are admitted to be proper, I should like to know how it is possible for an adverb to be used improperly ? P. S. C.

ORIGIN OF THE WORD SUPERSTITION (3rd S. vii. 360.) — Notwithstanding the authority of Cicero (*De Naturâ Deorum*, ii. 28), a most fanciful etymologist as we all know, I cannot believe that *superstitio* has anything to do with *superstes* in the sense of "survivor." Is it not more likely to be derived from a general idea of reverence for that which *stands above* us, according to the notion suggested by the fine passage in Lucretius ? —

[* Our correspondent is correct in his conjecture. The first part was entitled *Religio Clerici, a Churchman's Epistle*, 8vo, 1818 ; the second, *A Churchman's Second Epistle*, by the author of *Religio Clerici*, 8vo, 1819. In the edition of 1821, both parts had the general title of *Religio Clerici*.]

[† By the Rev. William J. Blew, M.A.—ED.]

"Humana ante oculos fede quom vita jaceret
In terris, obpressa gravi sub Religione :
Quæ caput à cœli regionibus ostendebat
Horribili super adspectu mortalibus instans."

If this be so one would expect that the oldest meaning of the word would have indicated a righteous reverence, and that it would afterwards (like *religio* itself) have been degraded to denote an erroneous reverence. In Cicero, I believe, the words *superstitio* and *superstitiosus* are always used in a derogatory sense. But when Plautus says in the *Curculio* —

"Superstitiosus hic est : vera prædicat,"

he means to say "the man has something *supernatural* about him." The word is used in the same way in the *Rudens*, iv. 4, 95. Virgil probably directs us to the older use of the word when he says of the Styx (*Æn*. xii. 817) —

"Una superstitio superis quæ reddita Divis."

The chronicle of the changes which have from time to time passed on such words as *superstitio, religio*, &c., might (if we could authentically trace them) furnish a chapter for a work like Mr. Lecky's *History of Rationalism*.

C. G. PROWETT.

Garrick Club.

ANONYMOUS HYMNS (3rd S. vii. 438.)—A series of papers entitled "Hymns and their Authors," is now in course of publication in the *Penny Post*,— a most useful church organ issued by Messrs. J. H. & J. Parker. This is the source from whence I draw the following information for the use of CPL. and R. I. I wish it were more complete : —

"Before the ending of the day." Latin Hymn, *Te lucis ante terminum*, S. Ambrose, A.D. 374, translated by J. M. Neale.

"Let every heart exulting beat." Sarum Breviary, *Agnoscat omne sæculum*, translated by J. M. Neale.

"O come and mourn with me awhile." Latin hymn, *Venite et ploremus*, translated by . . . . .

"Disposer Supreme and Judge of the earth." Latin Hymn, Paris Breviary, *Supreme quales Arbiter*, translated by I. Williams, 1839.

"For Thy dear saints, O Lord," Rt. Rev. Richard Mant, D.D. Lord Bishop of Down and Connor.

"All hail adored Trinity !" Latin Hymn.

"Christ will gather in His own," Chr. Gregor, 1778. Translated by Miss Winkworth.

"Jesus meek and lowly." From *Hymns for Missions*.

ST. SWITHIN.

HOYLE FAMILY (2nd S. vii. 270.) — It is a pet theory amongst some members of the Hoyle family that they are rather of British than of Flemish origin, being the descendants of the ancient dynasty of Hoel, the brightest name being that of Hoël Dha, whose descendants are said to have settled in the neighbourhood of Harrington, whence they spread over the mountain-district of north-west Yorkshire, until they finally settled in the neighbourhood of Huddersfield. Can any of your readers furnish me with the knowledge of how much truth there is in this, and, if there be any in it, does the legend in Hoel Dha's coat-of-arms give title to the name, or does the name give the legend?

I believe that there is a memorial window in Gisborough church relative to the Hoyles; what is its subject, and why was it erected? Any information will be most welcome to

WILLIAM HOYLE.

HINGHAM BOXES (3rd S. vii. 442.) — I have always understood *a nest* of boxes to mean a set of boxes, the one fitting inside the other, just as we speak of a nest of weights when we want to describe the old-fashioned packages of weights ranging from a quarter of an ounce to half a pound, once in common use in druggists' shops and farm house kitchens. Nests of twelve boxes of this kind used to be sent over from Germany to Hull in large quantities. The largest of the set was usually about ten inches long, the smallest about one inch. A. O. V. P.

HENRY MARTEN (3rd S. vii. 114, 389.) — Your correspondent P. wished to know the arms of Marten the regicide, to which, as an answer, another correspondent, L. C. R., favours us with the arms of a certain Colonel Francis Martyn, on a monument in Ewelme church, Oxon, who is assumed to have been a relation of Henry Marten: why, except the similarity of the names, does not appear. The regicide wrote his name Marten, as appears by the epitaph written by himself on his tombstone, in Chepstow church, the arms on which are 2 bars. The tinctures are not shown, but, among the fifty or sixty arms under the name of Marten, Martin, or Martyn, given by Burke, there appear two or three families who bear argent two bars gules, in Dorset and Exeter, to one of which the regicide probably belonged. The tombstone was originally in the chancel of Chepstow church, from whence it was removed by an over zealous royalist vicar into the middle aisle. Some few years since the church was Vandalized in the worst possible taste, and I know not what has become of the stone.

The regicide was the son of Sir Henry Martin, Doctor of Laws, Judge of the Admiralty, Dean of the Arches, and Judge of the Prerogative Court, who was buried in Longworth church in Berkshire, where he resided, and where, if his family monument still exists, no doubt the arms are shown. T. W.

ABRAHAM'S CONVERSION (3rd S. vii. 458.) — The story of Abraham's conversion from the worship of the heavenly bodies to that of their creator, is related by Josephus (*Ant.* i. 6, 1); and the tradition is given in greater detail in the *Koran* (vi. 76),

" And when the night overshadowed him, he saw a star, and he said, This is my Lord; but when it set, he said, I like not [gods] which set ";

and so on in respect of the moon and sun. The Jews have preserved a like tradition. (R. Bechai, in Midrash, *Bartolocc. Bibl. Rabb.*, pt. i. p. 640.)

T. J. BUCKTON.

Let the inquirer for " the first account of " the tradition on this subject, which is mentioned in Dr. A. P. Stanley's *Sermons in the East* (p. 124), " try (as the saying is) a hair of the same dog's tail." Let him peruse the *Lectures on the Jewish Church, from Abraham to Samuel*, which were delivered by Dr. A. P. Stanley (now Dean of Westminster), as Regius Professor of Ecclesiastical History in the University of Oxford. He will find ample references on the subject of his inquiry.

J. H. A.

" THE ANTI-TEAPOT REVIEW " (3rd S. vii. 470.) In reply to your strictures, I beg to inform you that the " Anti-Teapot Society," and " Ye Red Club," are distinct Societies, and in no way connected. There is, I believe, one member of " Ye Red Club " who occasionally writes in the *Anti-Teapot Review*; but " Ye Red Club " is open only to members of this University, whereas the " Anti-Teapot Society " includes members of the Universities of Oxford, Cambridge, Paris, Dublin, and Edinburgh.

THE PRESIDENT OF " YE RED CLUB."
Oxford.

SPUR MONEY IN BELFRIES (3rd S. vii. 324, 446.) The following lines in the belfry of the church at Cardington, near Church Stretton, will, perhaps, add to the proof that fines were inflicted for ringing church bells in spurs. The custom appears to bear the stamp of age, as the " laws " are described as " old," and the lines are dated upwards of a century ago : —

" If to ring you do come here,
    You must Ring well with hand and ear ;
    And if a bell you chance to throw,
    Fourpence to pay before you go.
    And if you Ring with Spur or Hat
    Sixpence in Ale to pay for that.
    And if you either Swear or Curse,
    Twelvepence to pay, pull out yᵉ purse.
    Our laws are old, they are not new,
    Yᵉ Clerk and Ringers claim their due.
" Febʳ yᵉ 14th, 1755-6."

CHAS. P. FLECK.

EPISCOPAL BORDURE, LABEL, ETC. (3rd S. vii. 436.) — The following information, extracted chiefly from Mr. Bedford's *Blazon of Episcopacy*, may be of use to my friend, MR. BOUTELL, as a partial reply to the queries growing out of his interesting notes on Exeter Cathedral. First, with regard to the " Episcopal Bordure," another instance occurs among the Bishops of Exeter; for Henry Marshall (1194-1206) is said, on the authority of Harl. MS. 5827, to have borne or a lion ramp. gu., within a bord. az. entoyre of mitres of the first.

Wm. Heiworth, Bishop of Lichfield and Coventry (1420-1427) bore, az., a saltire or., on a bord. gu. nine mitres of the second. Thomas de Blundeville, Bishop of Norwich (1226-1236) bore, quarterly per fess indented or and az., a bend gu., all within a bord. of the second, entoyre of mitres of the first.

William, of St. Mary's Church, Bishop of London (1199-1221), is also said to have borne, or, a lion ramp. az., armed and langued arg., a bord. of the second, entoyre of mitres of the first.

Secondly, with regard to the label, — Peter Courtenay, Bishop of Exeter (1478-1487), afterwards translated to Winchester, appears to have used a similar label to that with which William Courtenay, Archbishop of Canterbury (1381-1396), differenced his arms. (See also Moule's *Heraldry of Fish,* p. 19.)

Thirdly, the mitre appears as a charge in the arms of nearly twenty bishops, for the most part of the fifteenth century. The arms of Simon de Apulia, Bishop of Exeter (1214-1223), are az. three mitres or. John de Keton, Bishop of Ely (1310-1316), bore, sa. three mitres or. Robert Mascall, Bishop of Hereford (1404-1416), is said to have used the same arms.

The present arms of the see of Gloucester are, az., two keys in saltire, but I am nearly certain that, in more instances than one, in Gloucester cathedral, a sword in pale appears as an additional charge. If I recollect rightly, a shield so charged is sculptured upon the north porch of the cathedral.   JOHN WOODWARD.
New-Shoreham.

QUOTATION WANTED (3rd S. vii. 241, 328, 427.) I am much obliged by the information given by several correspondents in answer to my inquiry about the maxim quoted by Christopher Love. The passages quoted by R. C. L. from the *Digest* seem to contain the germ of the idea. In the passage quoted by F. C. H. from the Canon Law, we can trace something of the expression. But the axiom quoted by MR. BATES from Jenkins, gives us the very phrase itself: — *Favores ampliandi sunt.* This would be of itself sufficient to show that if Love's quotation was made from memory, at all events it was not inaccurate. But in point of fact the phrase occurs elsewhere, and it seems to have been in the seventeenth century a commonly received maxim. But what was the origin of it? The word *ampliandi* is there used in a sense that, to the best of my knowledge, was never attached to it in the Latin language, at least to the time of Justinian. Where then did this ▓ of the word come from, and how did Jenkins ▓ it? May I hope for further assistance from ▓ATES?   MELETES.

LUNATIC LITERATURE (3rd S. vii. 120, 188.) — The most extraordinary production of this kind is

said to have been by a very celebrated naturalist, who went out of his mind, and fancied he had been taken up to heaven; and on his return, was directed to write the *Flora* and *Fauna* of Paradise. I was informed by a very competent judge that this was a most curious work, everything being described in the most scientific way. Can any of your readers recall the name, and state whether any part of the MS. is yet extant?   A. A.
Poets' Corner.

LIMEHOUSE (3rd S. vii. 35, 121, 190.) — It does not at all seem likely this word was originally Lime*hurst,* as the whole tract of land has been originally under high water-mark; and, like all the vale of the Lea till we get high up into Hertfordshire, is all marsh, without any *hurst* or wood for many miles.   A. A.
Poets' Corner.

SPITTING (3rd S. vii. 432.) — Notwithstanding MR. WETHERELL's ingenious elucidations of the fat knight's imprecation, I am inclined to think it admits of a simpler explanation. Thirst causes an inclination to spit. At such a time, the saliva is white and viscid. In the north I have heard the expression, "spitting sixpences," used as synonymous with thirst. Falstaff's exclamation I take it, therefore, means "May I never thirst again."
                                         W. E.

Surely Falstaff's spitting white is what, in Lancashire low life, is called "spitting feathers," *i. e.* suffering from the effects of a debauch. The lower classes now indulge in spitting; perhaps their betters did in Shakspeare's time. A man who has been drinking is feverish, his mouth is dry, and his *saliva white*: hence he is sarcastically said to be "spitting feathers." Therefore, Falstaff's meaning would be *not* "May I die," but "May I never have a drinking bout again." So, at least, I have always understood the passage.
                                         P. P.

BALLAD: "THE BATTLE OF HARLAW" (3rd S. vii. 393.) — This ballad is printed in Aytoun's *Ballads of Scotland,* 1859. MR. FERGUSON's version is almost the same as Professor Aytoun's, but not so complete. The latter has certainly been current, in the same form, for the last forty years (to my knowledge) in the district in which the field of Harlaw is situated. MR. FERGUSON's verse in which "Seggat's-land" is mentioned is incorrect. It ought to run: —

" And they buried him in *Leggatt's-den,*
   A large mile frae Harlaw."

"Leggat's-den" being a small ravine about that distance west from the battle field (in "lang Scots miles"), and crossed by the old road from Aberdeen to the north, by which line the Highland army retreated. Some years' ago a stone tomb, or cist (one of those well-known relics of the primitive inhabitants of our island), was discovered in or close to "Leggatt's-den," and was accepted by the neighbourhood as proving the truth of the tradition that "Donald of the Isles" was there entombed. The tomb was certainly there many centuries before Harlaw was fought, and history tells us that "Donald" survived that bloody field for several years. C. E. D.

DR. CARABOO (3rd S. vii. 447.) — There was a learned M.D. in Bath who was so beguiled by this arch-impostor, openly avowing his conviction of her real character as assumed, that he received the universal *sobriquet* of Dr. Caraboo. This gentleman, now deceased, was Dr. Wilkinson, of Pulteney Street. NICKNAME.

Miscellaneous.

NOTES ON BOOKS, ETC.

The Works of William Shakespeare. Edited by William George Clark, M.A., &c., *and* William Aldis Wright, M.A. *Volume VI.* (Macmillan.)

This sixth volume of the *Cambridge Shakespeare* contains *King Henry the Eighth*, which was printed for the first time in the Folio of 1623 ; *Troilus and Cressida*, first printed in 1609. The remarkable discrepancies between the Quarto and the Folio texts of this play are all pointed out : the more important at the end of the play, and all the others in the foot-notes. The next play here printed is *Coriolanus*, which was first published in the Folio of 1623. This is followed by the *Titus Andronicus*, published for the first time in the year 1600 in quarto. In the Folio, 1623, there is a whole scene (Act III. Sc. 2) not found in any of the Quartos ; but agreeing too closely in style with the main portion of the play, to allow of the supposition that it is due to a different author. *Romeo and Juliet*, including a Reprint of the Quarto of 1597, was to have formed a portion of this volume, but it was found that it would make it too unwieldy, and that play has consequently been reserved for Volume the seventh. The editors announce therefore that the work will now consist of nine volumes instead of eight. Every additional volume which we receive of this *Cambridge Edition* confirms our estimate of its value for all students of Shakespeare.

Romance of London : Strange Stories, Scenes, and Remarkable Persons of the Great Town. By John Timbs, F.S.A. *In three Volumes.* (Bentley.)

When closing the third of these chatty volumes, we felt inclined to parody the old Epigram on the word *Finis*, and say —

"Finis, an error or a lie my friend ;
In writing Books on London there's no end."

And when we cast our eyes over the vast range of London Books—from Stow to Strype, from Pennant down to Timbs, we feel disposed to ask, What more can the most ingenious writer have to tell us new about London ? "What !" replies Mr. Timbs, in the three volumes of gossip now before us, "much that you will find very amusing in Historical Sketches ; Notices of Remarkable Duels ; Pictures of Notorious Highwaymen ; Recitals of great Crimes, Rogueries, and Punishments ; Stories of Love and Marriage ; Ghost and other Supernatural Stories ; Descriptions of the various Sights of the Metropolis, and lastly,

Anecdotes of Remarkable Persons, their strange Adventures and Catastrophes."

THE HANDEL FESTIVAL.—The musical arrangements for the Great Handel Festival at the Crystal Palace may now be said to be complete ; and some idea of the extent of the arrangements which have been made to give effect to the masterpieces of the great composer may be formed from the fact that in the Orchestra there will be upwards of 400 performers on stringed instruments alone, including 75 double basses.

There will be a Grand Rehearsal on Friday, the 23rd inst. This will include both solos and choruses, and the pieces selected will present great variety as well as popularity, the object being to make the Rehearsal Day an epitome of the three days of the Festival. The first day of the Festival will be Monday, the 26th, the "Messiah ;" the second, on Wednesday, the 28th, will comprise a Selection from Handel's best known and most popular works ; and the third, on Friday, the 30th, will be "Israel in Egypt."

Permission has been graciously accorded for the exhibition at the Crystal Palace, during the Festival, of Handel's own MS. Score of the "Messiah," from the Royal Library, at Buckingham Palace ; and connected with this will be a very curious and interesting collection of the numerous printed editions of the Sacred Oratorio. It may be well to remind our readers that no more than the four days' performances can possibly be given ; and that the Rehearsal on the 23rd, and the performances of "Messiah" on the 26th, the Selection on the 28th, and "Israel in Egypt" on the 30th inst., are, therefore, the only occasions on which this unparalleled assemblage of musical ability can be heard this year, probably for many years.

BOOKS AND ODD VOLUMES
WANTED TO PURCHASE.

Particulars of Price, &c., of the following Books to be sent direct to the gentlemen by whom they are required, and whose names and addresses are given for that purpose:—

GLOSSARY OF ARCHITECTURE. Vol. I., in exchange for a volume, or to purchase.
Pompeii : Library of Entertaining Knowledge.
Wanted by *Bell & Daldy*, 186, Fleet Street.

DODSLEY'S COLLECTION OF POEMS. Vol. VI. Large copy.
MISSALE SPECIALE. Early editions.
Wanted by *Rev. J. C. Jackson*, 3, Chatham Place East, Hackney, N.E.

Notices to Correspondents.

MISS MARY BILLINGE. *We have received an interesting article on this lady, but which reached us unfortunately after the present number was made up. It shall appear in our next.*
FRANKS. *Mr. Waller*, 58, Fleet Street, *would probably do what is wished.*
ALBUM GRÆCUM *is described in Hooper's Medical Dictionary as the dung of dogs, which from exposure to the air, becomes white like chalk. It consists chiefly of phosphate of lime, and was formerly applied to the inside of the throat in quinsies, being first mixed with honey. There were formerly many medicines of this kind, but they have long since justly fallen into disuse.*

ERRATA.—3rd S. vii. p. 458, col. ii. line 17, *for* "seventeenth" *read* "eighteenth;" p. 468, col. ii. line 15, *for* "surname O'Catain" *read* "surname, O'Cahain."

*** Cases for binding the volumes of "N. & Q." may be had of the Publisher, and of all Booksellers and Newsmen.

A Reading Case for holding the weekly Nos. of "N. & Q." is now ready, and may be had of all Booksellers and Newsmen, price 1s. 6d., or, free by post, direct from the publisher, for 1s. 8d.

"NOTES AND QUERIES" is published at noon on Friday, and is also issued in MONTHLY PARTS. The Subscription for STAMPED COPIES for Six Months forwarded direct from the Publisher (including the Half-yearly INDEX) is 11s. 4d., which may be paid by Post Office Order, payable at the Strand Post Office, in favour of WILLIAM G. SMITH, 32. WELLINGTON STREET, STRAND, W.C., where also all COMMUNICATIONS FOR THE EDITOR should be addressed.

"NOTES & QUERIES" is registered for transmission abroad.

LONDON, SATURDAY, JUNE 24, 1865.

CONTENTS.—No 182.

Notes.

THE LATE DUKE OF DEVONSHIRE AND SIR JOSEPH PAXTON.

About twenty years ago, by the direction of the late Duke of Devonshire, I copied the following from the original in his Grace's handwriting : —

"Joseph Paxton was born the 3rd of August, 1803. I made his acquaintance at the Horticultural Society's Garden at Chiswick, where he was placed in 1823. He was chiefly employed then in training the creepers and newly introduced plants on the walls there, which first excited my attention; and being in want of a gardener at Chatsworth, I asked Mr. Sabine, who was then at the head of the establishment, whether he thought that young man would do ? He said, ' Young and untried,' but spoke so favourably that I had no doubt.

"The young man had made a large lake in 1822 at Sir Gregory Page Turner's place near Woburn. He came to Chatsworth in 1826. You shall have it in his own words : ' I left London by the Comet coach for Chesterfield, and arrived at Chatsworth at half-past four o'clock in the morning of the 9th of May, 1826. As no person was to be seen at that early hour I got over the greenhouse gate by the old covered way, explored the pleasure-grounds, and looked round the outside of

the house. I then went down to the kitchen garden, scaled the outside wall, and saw the whole of the place, set the men to work there at six o'clock; then returned to Chatsworth, and got Thomas Weldon to play me the waterworks, and afterwards went to breakfast with poor dear Mrs. Gregory and her niece : the latter fell in love with me, and I with her, and thus completed my first morning's work, at Chatsworth before nine o'clock.'

"He married Miss Sarah Bown in 1827. In a very short time a great change appeared in pleasure-ground and garden : vegetables of which there had been none, fruit in perfection, and flowers. Twelve men with brooms in their hands on the lawn began to sweep, the labourers to work with activity. The kitchen garden was so low and exposed to floods from the river, that I supposed the first wish of the new gardener would be to remove it to some other place, but he made it answer. In 1829 the management of the woods was entrusted to him, and gradually they were rescued from a prospect of destruction. Not till 1832 did I take to caring for my plants in earnest. The old greenhouse was converted into a stove, the greenhouse at the gardens was built, the Arboretum was invented and formed. Then started up Orchidaceæ, and three successive houses were built to receive the increasing numbers.

"In 1835 the intelligent gardener John Gibson was despatched to India to obtain the Amherstia nobilis, and other treasures of the East. The colossal new Conservatory was invented and begun in 1836; the following year Baron Ludwig was so charmed with its conception, that he stripped his garden at the Cape of the rarest produce of Africa. Paxton had now been employed in the superintendence and formation of my roads : he made one tour with me to the West of England, and in 1838 contrived to accompany me for an entire year abroad, in which time, having gone through Switzerland and Italy, he trod in Greece, Turkey, Asia Minor, Malta, Spain and Portugal. In absence he managed that no progress should be checked at home. A great calamity ruined the expedition he had set on foot to California; the unfortunate Wallace and Banks, young gardeners from Chatsworth, having been drowned in Columbia river. He went with me in 1840 to Lismore, and in that year the Conservatory was finished. The village of Edensor was new-modelled and rebuilt between 1839 and 1841, and the crowning works have been the fountains and the rock-garden."

After I had copied what precedes, I inquired of the Duke if he knew the amount of wages Paxton was receiving from the Horticultural Society in 1823 ? the answer was, "Only 18s. a-week, as I was informed by Mr. Sabine." As I knew that the Duke of Devonshire (by whom I had been most kindly aided for the last eighteen years) would not be offended by the question, I asked what wages he had himself given the " young and untried " gardener in the first instance? and his reply was, " I think 25s. a-week, and a cottage." Of course, his Grace afterwards rapidly advanced Paxton's wages; and eight or ten years subsequently, the young labourer of 18s. a-week, and the new gardener of 25s. a week, was often seen dining at the Duke's table.

J. PAYNE COLLIER.

GONZALES DE ANDIA: HEREDITARY KNIGHTS OF THE GARTER.

Finding myself for reasons of health in the Basque Provinces of Spain, I was induced to examine the documents appertaining to this town, which is in fact the old capital, although the modern governor resides at St. Sebastian. I have found an historical "Note and Query," which I think will be not uninteresting to your readers.

It is stated that a certain Gonzalez de Andia, a native of Tolosa, who lived in the reigns of John II. and Henry IV. (of Spain), commanded the military contingent of Guipuzcoa when, in the year 1471, it was sent into France to assist Edward IV. of England in a war against Louis XI. It is further stated that on account of his good services he was named a Knight of the Garter, *the dignity to descend in his family from male to male in order of primogeniture,* as testified by the following diploma: —

" Edward, by the Grace of God King of England and France, and Lord of Ireland, to all who the present may see health and greeting. As among the best merits of Princes there is none better than to appreciate the deeds of brave men, and to reward them according to their deserts, we make known that taking into especial consideration the nobility, valour, and prudence of our well-beloved Domingo Gonzalez de Andia, a native of Spain, from which country he has been highly recommended to us, we confer upon him the Insignia of our Collar for himself and his successors, let it be understood, for the eldest son in all legitimate descendance, that he and they may hereafter perpetually wear this order in the same way as it is worn by the Knights in this country, in testimony of which we have hereto affixed our Privy Seal. Given in our Castle of Windsor the 20th of August, in the year of our Lord 1471 in the eleventh year of our reign.—EDWARD."

It is then stated that this Gonzalez de Andia went to England in the year 1481, to frame a treaty of peace and commerce, which was signed the following year in London. He died in the year 1489. As in transcribing this document I have translated it from the Spanish, into which, of course, it must have been previously translated from the English, no weight can be attached to anything regarding its phraseology. The original diploma is said to be in the hands of the family, but the name has merged into others,

and I have been unable to make any further researches. As I (perhaps ignorantly) never heard of any instance where the Order of the Garter was conferred as an hereditary honour, I take the liberty of inserting this "Note" in your periodical, with the "Query" whether there is any other example of the sort?   HOWDEN.

Tolosa de Guipuzcoa, June 15, 1865.

NOTES FROM THE ISSUE ROLLS.—No. II.

Oct. 21, 49 Edw. III. To Robert de Merton, by his own hands, for the support of the children of Charles de Blois, in his custody, in the Castle of Nottingham, 183l. (Issue Roll, Mich. 49 Edw. III.)

Friar John Woodroue, Confessor of the King. (*Ib.* Mich. 50 Edw. III., and many others.)

June 3, 51 Edw. III. To Katherine, daughter of William, Duke of Bruxcella, and Henry Estor, Knt., son of the said Katherine, by the hands of the said Henry, &c., 16l. 13s. 4d. (*Ib.* Pasch. 51 Edw. III.)

June 20, 51 Edw. III. To Philippa Chaucer, by the hands of Roger de Trumpyngton, Knight, 66s. 8d. (*Ib.*)

Nov. 15, 51 Edw. III. To Blanche, Lady de Wake, for the support of two daughters of the late John, Lord de Moubray, in the custody of the King, and in the suite of the said Lady, 33l. 6s. 8d. (*Ib.* Mich. 51 Edw. III.)

To Philippa Chaucer, one of the damsels of the chamber of Philippa, late Queen of England, to whom the King assigned 10 marks per annum for her life, by the hands of Geoffrey Chaucer, 66s. 8d. (*Ib.*)

Dec. 16, 51 Edw. III. To Collardo Daubrichecôt, Armig., constable of the town and castle of Nottingham, for the support of the children of Charles de Blois, in his custody, &c., 24l. (*Ib.*)

Dec. 23. To John de Burlee, Knight, sent in secret negociations of the King, 13l. 6s. 8d. ' (*Ib.*)

——— To Geoffrey Chaucer, Armig., sent by precept of the King in the retinue of the said John, on the same secret negociations, 6l. 13s. 4d.

Jan. 21. To Walter of Leicester, and John Asshwell, serving the King at arms, sent by precept of the Council to the Castle of Nottingham, for the two sons of Charles de Blois, being in the said castle; for conducting them safely and securely to the Castle of Devises, in the custody of Reginald de Bello Campo, Knight, 6l. 13s. 4d. (*Ib.*)

For the expenses of the said sons, and the lodging of horses, from Nottingham to Dyvises, 10l. (*Ib.*)

To Philippa Pycard, damsel of the late Philippa, Queen of England, by the hands of Adam de Rumesey, valet of the Lord Prince, 100s.

The above entries suggest a few remarks, and one or two queries: —

1. Who was Katherine, "daughter of William, Duke of Bruxcella"?

2. Who was Blanche, Lady Wake? Blanche of Lancaster, widow of Thomas, Lord Wake, is said by Burke to have died in 1349 (*Extinct Peerage*, p. 551). The Princess of Wales bore the title (in right of her mother) in 1377.

3. Philippa Chaucer and Philippa Pycard are generally considered the same person. The manner of the appearance of their names on the Rolls leads me to doubt this.   HERMENTRUDE.

THE NEWNHAM STATE SWORD.

After the account given in your columns of the sale of the mace of Kinsale, which I hope has at length found a permanent resting place, permit me to send you a cutting from *The Standard*, June 1, 1865, respecting the contemplated sale of the sword of Newnham. It will show the manner in which relics of local interest are even now disposed of on occasion. I may add, that when at that town, I have made ineffectual attempts to see it, but have reason to believe it to be of later date than the reign of King John, though an object of great interest.

"(Before Sir W. PAGE WOOD.)

"THE ATTORNEY-GENERAL v. WASBROUGH.—THE NEWN-HAM STATE SWORD.

"This was an information by the Attorney-General on the relation of the churchwardens of Newnham, in the county of Gloucester, and Mr. E. Owen Jones, a justice of the peace for the county of Gloucester, against the trustees of the will of the late Mr. John James, the late lord of the manor of Newnham. The information prayed for an ex-parte injunction to restrain the defendants till the hearing of the cause from selling a certain sword, which it was alleged was the town sword of Newnham.

"Mr. Rolt, Q.C., and Mr. Winterbotham were the counsel engaged.

"The facts were shortly as follows:—Newnham, in Gloucestershire, is an ancient borough, and the manor of Newnham, which is co-extensive but distinct from the borough, was anciently part of the king's demesne. The manor was granted at intervals to various persons, but it reverted from time to time to the king, by forfeiture and otherwise, and in the reign of King John it was in the king's possession, and that monarch then presented to the borough of Newnham a charter, which has been lost, and with the charter a sword of state, made of steel finely wrought, and six feet in length. The privileges of the town have long since been lost, and the election of a mayor has not taken place for some time. This being the case the town sword was deposited, first in the parish church, and then in an ancient inn at Newnham, called the Bear Inn, where, there being, till lately, no town-hall, public meetings of the inhabitants were held from time to time. In the year 1554, A.D., the manor of Newnham was granted to Lord Stafford, and from him, through descent, and finally by purchase, it came, in the year 1850, into the possession of Mr. John James, who a short time after also purchased the Bear Inn, Newnham. In July, 1852, Mr. James held a leet court, and at this court he produced the state sword in question; the sword was removed the same day to Mr. James's house at Newnham,

where it still remains. In 1855, Mr. James died, after making a will by which he left all his property to the defendants in trust for sale, and in May of this year the defendants advertised their intention to sell by public auctions, in five lots, all the property so devised. The fifth lot was described as follows:—'The manor of Newnham, with the tolls, fishery, and appurtenances. With the manor of Newnham will be sold the sword of state, presented with the charter to Newnham by King John. The sword of state given with the charter by King John is of steel finely polished and ornamented with curious workmanship. Its whole length is six feet, the length of blade is four feet four inches; on the latter is this curious inscription:—

'John Morse being Maier,
This sworde did repaier—1584.'

See Rudder's *History of Gloucestershire*.' Upon this advertisement appearing, a meeting of the inhabitants of Newnham was at once called, and at this meeting it was resolved 'That the trustees of the late John James, Esq., be respectfully requested to place the sword of state given with the charter to Newnham by King John, in the town hall of Newnham, in order that it may be vested in the local board of Newnham, the ancient local magistracy having ceased to exist.' The trustees having refused to act in accordance with the above resolution, the present proceedings were taken to enforce compliance.

"Mr. Rolt, Q.C., after stating the facts as above, now applied for an immediate injunction, as the sale was to take place to-morrow (this day.)

"The Vice-Chancellor granted the injunction required, on the applicants giving an undertaking to abide by any order as to damage which might accrue in consequence; the injunction was to be in force up to next Thursday week.

"Mr. Rolt, Q.C., expressed a hope that some amicable arrangement would be come to in the meantime."

W. J. BERNHARD SMITH.

Temple.

THE FYLFOT.—In the monument of Bishop Walter Bronscomb (died 1281), now standing in the westernmost bay of the south side of the Lady Chapel of Exeter Cathedral, the upper cushion that supports the head of the recumbent effigy is diapered with fylfots of a more elaborate form than is commonly seen: they are coloured quarterly or and gules, the heraldic metal and colour alternating. This diaper was, doubtless, executed when the effigy was removed and placed on the altar-tomb in its present position, probably about the year 1420.   CHARLES BOUTELL.

DAY FOR MARRYING.—I have cut the following from one of our newspapers. I have frequently heard of this custom when I have been in Scotland, but never could find in what it originated. Perhaps some of your readers may be able to give us a fuller account of it:—

"There is a remarkable peculiarity in the Scottish people, says the Registrar-General—their fondness for marrying on the last day of the year. There are more marriages in Scotland on that day than in any week of the year; excepting, of course, the week in which that day occurs. The detailed returns for 1861 have just been issued, and the number of marriages in the eight principal towns would average some 25 a-day—that is to say, a work-day, for marrying is one of the things not to be done in Scotland on Sunday—but the Registrar-General states that, in fact, there are between 400 and 500 marriages in those towns on the 31st of December. By another curious usage, a large proportion of these marriages are not registered until January, making that appear a favourite month for marriage, which it is not."

T. B.

MANUSCRIPT POEM.—The following cutting from Mr. John Salkeld's *Catalogue of Second-hand Books* (No. 9), is worth preserving among your fly-leaf scribblings. The verses are stated to be contained in a volume of tracts of the earlier part of the eighteenth century :—

"410. TRACTS.—Proceedings of the House of Peers on the Public Accounts, with their Address to His Majesty, &c., 1702—Proceedings of the Lords in relation to the Occasional Conformity Bill, 1702—The Bill, or Act, for preventing Occasional Conformity, with Reports of the Conference, &c., 1702—An Account of the Trials of Benbow's Cowardly Captain, 1703—Some Weighty Considerations relating to the Duke of York, with the Answer, 1680—Articles of Peace between William III. and Lewis XIV., 1697—A Collection of Addresses concerning the Conception and Birth of the pretended Prince of Wales, 1690—The Pamphleteers, a Satyr, 1703, in 1 vol., folio, calf, 6s. 6d.

"Contains the following, in MS. :—

'ON THE QUEEN'S MESSAGE TO THE COMMONS.

'The Queen a message to the Senate sent,
To beg her Duke a boone in Parliament.
After a warm debate the House grew bold
And bid her pay her Duke in Vigo gold,
Tho' this was thought confounded hard by some,
To give to one what t'other Duke brought home.
Bulk broke, it did appeare, upon plain prooff,
The gold galloon had not brought wealth enough ;
At which her Grace and Majy. tooke snuffe.'"

A. O. V. P.

CURIOUS CHRISTIAN NAMES.—The famous Lord Collingwood had a brother named Winefred who commanded the Rattler. In searching the registers of Bobbington parish, I have found the very uncommon Christian name of Wylgeforde given to a daughter in two different families in 1582 and 1584. Two relatives of my own have borne the baptismal name of Polexena.

There was a Baroness Lyttleton of revered memory named Apphia, to whom a print of Malvern abbey church was inscribed. H. W. T.

A MATCH FOUND FOR A COMMON SAYING.—It is sometimes remarked of an uneducated, or stupid man—"He does not know B from a bull's foot." A quotation from Mrs. Everett Green's *Calendar of State Papers*, 1666-67, which is given in the *Saturday Review*, No. 500, furnishes us with a companion picture of ignorance: "Some of the captains know not to distinguish a horse's head from a Roman S in their demands." The phrase occurs in a letter, written from Portsmouth to Samuel Pepys by Commissioner Middleton.

ST. SWITHIN.

DOUBLE ACROSTIC.—When and by whom was this exercise of the ingenuity invented, which has now become the rage in the fashionable circles?

A. A.

Poets' Corner.

BASTILE ARCHIVES.—Can any of your readers refer me to any of the compilations from Bastile archives indicated in Carlyle's *French Revolution*, vol. i. p. 291, edit. 1837, or to any kindred source of information? B. D.

CLARET.—In some accounts for the year 1729, I find a payment for a pint of claret. Was the wine, then so called, of the same kind as that we now call claret? PRESTONIENSIS.

TO CLEAR THE GLASS.—Preparatory to starting on his third voyage, in search of a north-west passage to the east, Frobisher drew up a code of instructions to be observed by the fleet; the first article of which ran as follows :—

"*Imprimis.* To banishe swearing, dice, card playing, and all filthie talk, and to serve God twice adaie, with the ordinarie service, usuall in the Churche of Englande; *and to cleare the glasse everie night, according to the oulde order of England.*"

What is the meaning of "clearing the glass every night"? W. W. W.

COUTANCES : THE DIOCESE OF WINCHESTER.—The Bishop of Winchester, speaking in Convocation a week or two ago, upon the extent of his diocese, is reported to have said that besides extending over the Channel Islands, he was not sure that it did not also include Coutances in Normandy. Is there any ground for the supposition that Coutances was ever included in the diocese of Winchester? Perhaps it was meant that the Channel Islands were formerly in the diocese of Coutances. This seems more probable, but was it the case? J. WOODWARD.

DUMBLE.—I should be glad if any of your numerous readers could inform me what is the exact meaning and derivation of the word *dumble*. It is a term applied in the southern parts of Nottinghamshire to a narrow valley or small ravine, I believe, with a watercourse which is supplied only with an intermittent stream. It appears to be a word used only in a very limited district of Notts—namely, a locality of some six or eight miles diameter, between Nottingham and Southwell, on the south-east confines of old Sherwood Forest, where we have Lambley Dumble, Woodborough Dumble, Efferston Dumble, Oxton Dumble, Halloughton Dumble, Thurgarton Dumble, &c.; but no such term, as far as I am aware, is used in any other part of the county, nor in any other place that I am acquainted with. I find no explanation of the word in any of the dictionaries, and shall be glad if any of your readers can throw any light on the subject.   J. S.

FUNERAL PLUME OF FEATHERS.—Could any of your correspondents inform me the meaning of the plume of feathers attached to a board, and which are used at a funeral and carried on the head of some one in front of the hearse. Has it any reference to a banner, insignia, or armorial bearing supposed to belong to the deceased, or what?   ALEX. MOULTON.

GONZAGAS OF MANTUA: SACK OF FONDI. —
1. What is the best history of the Gonzagas of Mantua?
2. Did the sack of Fondi by the pirate Horuc of Mitelene (the younger of the two brothers surnamed in turn Barbarossa) occur in the spring or autumn of the year 1535?
3. Is the event and its attendant circumstances related in detail, or related at all, by Muratori?
4. From what writers do we glean most on the subject?   A STUDENT.

HERALDIC.—On visiting St. Patrick's Cathedral, Dublin, lately, I was much astonished to find that the Prince of Wales takes his place among the Knights of St. Patrick *not* as Prince of Wales but as Duke of Saxony, the arms on his banner being thus blazoned: Quarterly, 1st and 4th Saxony; second and third quarterly 1st and 4th England; second Scotland; third Ireland, with a label of 3 points. Perhaps Sir B. Burke, Ulster-King-at-Arms, could inform us why they are so blazoned, instead of quarterly England, Scotland, Ireland, differenced by a label of three points and an escutcheon of pretence for Saxony, as they are blazoned in England. I had hitherto supposed that Prince of Wales was a higher title than Duke of Saxony; but perhaps it is not so in Ireland.   CYWRM.
Porth yr Aur, Carnarvon.

"IL Y A FAGOTS ET FAGOTS."—Are we indebted to this discovery of Sganarelle (*Le Médecin Malgré Lui*, Acte I. Scène 6) for the numerous comparisons after the same pattern which abound in novels of the present day?   ST. SWITHIN.

"JOSEPH AND HIS BRETHREN."—In December, 1864, a sacred drama on this subject was performed at Burslem, for the benefit (I think) of the Ragged Schools of that town. Can any of your correspondents in that town inform me if this drama was printed, and also the name of the author?   R. I.

KALEYARD GATE.—I was surprised to notice the name "Kaleyard Gate" on the page of references to a plan of the fortifications of the city of Chester, an. 1643, inserted at page 26 of a reprint of King's *Vale Royal of England*, London, J. G.

Bell, 1852. Kale or Kailyard was, I thought, thoroughly Scotch. Is it common in England?   S. M.

N. D., A MINIATURE PAINTER. —There are several miniatures in the collection at the South Kensington Museum, signed with these initials, about the latter half of the seventeenth century. Who was this artist, and is anything known of him?   JAMES BECK.

LORD NEWHAVEN. — Is there any portrait in existence of William Mayne, who was created Viscount Newhaven in 1776, and who died *s. p.* 1794?   F. M. S.
229, Clarendon Villas, Plumstead.

ABBEY OF ST. OUEN AT ROUEN. — Can any contributor furnish a list of the Abbesses of St. Ouen since the time of the Abbess Renée de Harlay, in 1686? There exists at Rouen, or existed in 1842, a book in an old ivory cover, called *Le Livre d'Yvoire*, which contains the oaths of obedience taken by the abbés and abbesses of St. Ouen to the archbishop of Rouen, and a reference to this book would give an answer to the query.
The abbey was one of the most important pieces of ecclesiastical preferment in France. Sully had a charge on its revenues, and the abbé was for a long period a member of the royal family.   F. R. C.

QUOTATION. — The motto adopted in the title-page of Finlay's *History of Greece* is,—

'Ὄλβιος ὅστις τῆς ἱστορίας
Ἔσχε μάθησιν.

"Blest is he who possesses a knowledge of history."

From what author is this taken?   F.

SIR JOSHUA REYNOLDS' SURVIVING SITTERS. —
Reading the *Life and Times of Sir Joshua Reynolds*, I think it worthy of a note that the Dowager Countess of Shaftesbury, whose portrait forms so beautiful a feature of Sir Joshua's noble picture of the Marlborough family, which was painted in 1777, is still living (born Nov. 5, 1773). To my note I add a query: Is any other person alive who sat to Sir Joshua?   E. S. S. W.

[When the "Puck" was sold a few years since to the late Lord Fitzwilliam, who himself had been one of the sitters, it was said that the "model" from whom the "Puck" was painted, was in the auction room at the time of the sale. He was, we believe, many years ago, a gate-keeper at Elliot's brewery, at Pimlico.—ED. "N. & Q."]

"THOUGHTFUL MOLL." — The young people about me are always pressing me to tell them the story of "Thoughtful Moll," which they declare they have heard is very interesting. But both I and my "old Missus" are obliged to acknowledge our ignorance, though we too have heard it spoken of as notorious in every county. I at first thought it had appeared in one of your early volumes, but on looking at the Indexes I found myself mistaken. And yet I have no doubt you, Mr. Editor—for like all Editors you are most likely an old fogey, and have lots of little ones scrambling about your knees —must be perfectly competent to amuse your infantine mob with this sensational (I adopt the modern term) narrative; and I take it for granted will enable your antiquarian readers (I use the epithet in a double sense) to retail this little bit of Folk lore. If I give you credit for too much knowledge, perhaps some of your learned correspondents will supply your deficiency, or, at all events, tell where the veritable history is to be found. AVUNCULUS.

VOLTAIRE: DIOCLETIAN. — I have more than once in "N. & Q." * asked for a verification of sayings ascribed to Voltaire. My queries are unanswered. I try one more : —

" Nearly a century ago, Voltaire wrote : ' I am sick of hearing that twelve unlettered men established Christianity. I will show that one man can destroy it.' "— *Morning Advertiser*, June 14, 1865.

I do not remember the passage, and shall be glad to know in which of Voltaire's works it is.

In the same article it is said : —

" Diocletian declared his intention of abolishing the Christian name. So terrible was the persecution, that its authors declared they had succeeded in their object, and pillars of remembrance were raised in various parts of the Roman world to record the fact ' that the very name of Christianity had been rooted out.' "

Gibbon narrates the persecution, but omits the pillars. Where were they erected? How long did any of them remain? By what authors are they mentioned? and what was the inscription in the original language? FITZHOPKINS. Garrick Club.

Queries with Answers.

COACHMAKERS' COMPANY. — In Boswell's *Life of Johnson* (edit. 1835, vol. viii. p. 69), I find the following :—

" I mentioned a kind of religious Robin-Hood Society, which met every Sunday evening at Coachmakers' Hall for free debate,"&c.

Is this Coachmakers' Hall the parent and corrupted sponsor of the existing Cogers' Hall? If not, where was Coachmakers' Hall; and was the Society of Coachmakers one of the ancient guilds? A. F.

[The Company of Coachmakers was incorporated by Charles II. in 1671, and styled by letters-patent, "The Master, Wardens, Assistants, and Commonalty of the Company of Coach and Coach-harness Makers of London." The fraternity is governed by a Master, three Wardens, and twenty-three Assistants, their motto being " Surgit

* 2nd S. ix. 306 ; 3rd S. vii. 211.

post nubila Phœbus." Coachmakers' Hall is in Noble Street, Foster Lane, and was formerly the hall of the Scriveners. The building was once famed for the meeting of societies and clubs within its walls. Here the Protestant Association assembled, and here originated the riots of the year 1780, headed by Lord George Gordon.— The Society of Cogers, founded in 1755, is nothing more nor less than a political debating club, meeting sometimes in one place, and sometimes in another. Its present Discussion Hall is at Mr. G. Walter's house of refreshment in Shoe Lane, Fleet Street.]

"EPISCOPACY": HENRY SWINBURNE. — I have an old book in my possession, entitled *Episcopacy not prejudicial to Regal Power*, which wants the title-page. I presume that it was published by one Robert Pawlet : inasmuch as I find at the end of the work a "Catalogue of Books, printed for and sold by Robert Pawlet, at the sign of the Bible in Chancery Lane, near Fleet Street." And from its appearance, I think it was published somewhere between 1666 and 1680. Can you favour me with the author's name, and date of publication?

Further, can any of your readers acquaint me with the date of the death of the "late famous, learned, and ingenious Mr. Henry Swinburne, author of the *Treatise on Last Wills and Testaments;* whose *Treatise on Spousals* was posthumously published by "Robert Clavell," at the Peacock in St. Paul's Churchyard, 1686."

J. R. PHILLIPS.
Cardigan.

[The work possessed by our correspondent is from the pen of that learned prelate and distinguished casuist, Dr. Sanderson, whose Life was written by Izaak Walton in the eighty-fifth year of his age—which he states was "a pleasant toil," and modestly adds, " I seriously wish, both for the reader's and Dr. Sanderson's sake, that posterity had known his great learning and virtue by a better pen; by such a pen as could have made his life as immortal as his learning and merits ought to be." The work is entitled, "Episcopacy (as Established by Law in England) not Prejudicial to Regal Power. Written in the time of the Long Parliament by the special command of the late King. By the Right Reverend Father in God Robert Sanderson, late Lord Bishop of Lincoln. London, Printed for Robert Pawlet, at the Bible in Chancery Lane, near Fleet Street, 1678." Prefixed is the " Vera Effigies Reverendi in Christe Patris Dñi : Roberti Sanderson, Episcopi Lincolniensis."

There is no record extant giving the exact date of the birth or death of Henry Swinburne, the civilian ; but as his will, dated May 30, 1623 (the codicil July 15, 1623), was proved June 12, 1624, we may presume he died about that time. He was buried in the north aisle of York cathedral, where there is a monument of him in a civilian's gown kneeling before a desk. See an engraving of it in Drake's *Eboracum*, fol. 1736, p. 377.]

JUDICIAL.—What is the origin and significancy of the term *judicial*, applied to astrology? And what is its force when prefixed to the word *blindness*?   T.

[We are indebted to a correspondent who has read much on these matters for a solution to the first question; the second we derive from theological writers:—

"*Judicial* astrology is so called, because its professors deliver *judgments*, or opinions as to what in their *judgment* the events will be, which will follow certain configurations of the heavenly bodies: opinions based on the past experience of ages. Wherever the planets have been conjoined with each other in any peculiar way, either as regards general questions, or in private nativities, the results have been handed down by the professors to their successors as rules for future forecasts. The true astrologer never becomes the fortune-teller. All he says is this: 'From the position of those bodies, which the Great Ruler of the Universe has placed for signs and for seasons, I should infer these signs will be followed by war, peace, prosperity, ill-fortune, &c., as the significators may be.'"

Judicial blindness is a phrase used to signify that moral blindness, or obstinate refusal to see and pursue what is right, that has been inflicted by Providence on men or on nations as a *judgment*. Thus, the wilful blindness of Pharaoh to the miracles of Moses, and that of the Jews to those of the Messiah, are all instances of judicial blindness."]

MR. FORTESCUE'S ELMS.—I have read, in some work on Devonshire, I believe, an account of an avenue of elms planted by a Mr. Fortescue, who directed that when grown, the trees should be cut down and given to the poor of the parish. Where is the account to be found?   KAPPA.

[Near the churchyard of Brixton, co. Devon, is a fine grove of elms planted in the year 1677 by Mr. Fortescue of Spridlestone and other parishioners, for the express purpose of being sold, when at a proper growth, to raise a fund for the benefit of the poor: a singular instance of prudent foresight, and well worthy of imitation, there being many parishes in which small wastes might most beneficially be thus planted. Sixteen were cut down during the winter of 1819, and produced the sum of 92l. 2s. There is a stone on the spot with the following inscription: "This colony of elms, regularly disposed into walks, was planted in November, 1677, by Edward Fortescue, of Spridlestone, Esq., churchwarden, with the approbation and contribution of the majority of estated parishioners, to the intent that, when perfect in growth and sold, lands may be purchased with the money for relief of the poor of this parish, and that posterity, reaping the advantage of our benefaction, may be encouraged to provide for more succession, by substituting others in the room of these."

As land cannot legally be purchased, the proceeds are funded for the benefit of the poor.—Lysons's *Devonshire*, Part II. p. 75.]

Replies.

ALBINI BRITO: THE HERALDIC PUZZLE.
(3rd S. vi. 13, 113, 174, 255.)

I suppose D. P. is satisfied that the armorial bearings of De Todeni, otherwise D'Albini, of Belvoir, have been at last ascertained, since WATERBOUGET (going to original sources) has fished up out of the Exeter archives a thirteenth century seal of William Albini of Belvoir. (See Peck's *Stamford*, lib. viii. p. 27.) He blazons it, two chevronels within a bordure. This seems conclusive. WATERBOUGET however, I am sorry to say, seems abominably stingy. He keeps too much in his bucket for his own private drinking, instead of slaking the thirst of the readers of "N. & Q." Otherwise he would have told us that the chevrons do not stand alone in Albini's seal, but that a cross, a rose, and a sprig of broom, are emblazoned with them; not indeed within the shield, but, thirteenth century fashion, arranged around it. Now these were, and are to this day, royal national ensigns; and the same may perhaps be said of the chevrons, for they are the ancient bearings of the De Clares, who were of the royal house. Thus the whole seal displays the relationship with that house, which we otherwise know to exist. It is worthy of remark, that the lords of Stafford and of Belvoir both descended from Todeni, and both used substantially the same bearings; whence D. P. may fairly infer, if he likes, that they must have been borne by the common ancestor, however remote. A like remark may be made of several other houses; and I should be glad if any of the more sceptical antiquaries would give us a note of what he conceives is a more probable hypothesis than the above to account for the facts.

Further, stingy WATERBOUGET has not told us that the above forms only the privy, or counterseal, of W. d'Albini. His great seal—the quaintest I think I have chanced to see—has the following device:—A square tower (each of the two upper stories enriched with a row of Norman arches), surrounded by an embattled wall. On the summit a two-forked pennon; and two human heads, facing each other from the opposite sides, apparently gazing at the prospect. Clearly what we now call a "bellevue," for Belvoir. Thus we get at the territorial arms of Belvoir. They seem to be compound ones: for we learn from a Trentham deed cited by Eyton (*Antiquities of Shropshire*, vol. ii. p. 124), that, as early as A.D. 1210, the Trusbuts bore on their seal a human head within a tressure; and thus, also, we find the alliance with Trusbut displayed on the Belvoir seal.

The eagle within a bordure, we need have little doubt, was a fancy coat assigned to Robert de Todeni by the later heralds (as they were fond of

doing to the more ancient worthies); and, based perhaps upon the eagles borne by the De Tonies, another line descended from the Norman standard-bearer.

Combining this with what WATERBOUGET has pointed out, viz. that it is a mistake to look for the shield of Valoines among the quarterings under examination, MR. STAFFORD CAREY's solution of the heraldic puzzle appears verified: for the fourth coat may be safely assumed to be meant for Trusbut's—so we have in due sequence Trusbut, Albini, Todeni, and no further difficulty remains.

L. P.

SHAKESPEAR FAMILY.

(3rd S. vii. 175.)

Lieut.-Col. J. D. Shakespear, R.A., of Richmond, Surrey, claims descent from our great poet, and this interesting question was first raised by him in the *Times* of the 13th June, 1864.

The Shakespear tomb is in Stepney Churchyard, and records the death of Arthur Shakespear, Ropemaker, May 9, 1749, aged fifty years; Bennet Shakespear, Nov. 10, 1756, aged forty-nine; Jonathan Shakespear, Feb. 16, 1768, aged fifty-eight; and Alderman John Shakespear, May 19, 1775, aged 56. These four were brothers. Also Mrs. Elizabeth Shakespear * (widow of the alderman), Feb. 15, 1807, aged eighty.; Arthur Shakespeare (eldest son of the alderman), M.P. for Richmond, Yorkshire, June 12, 1818, aged seventy; his wife Jane (daughter of Matthew Ridley, and sister of Sir M. W. Ridley, Bart.), January 30, 1805, aged fifty-five; John Matthew Shakespear (son of the last named Arthur), April 2, 1844, aged sixty-six, and several children who died young.

Alderman Shakespear, of Billiter Square and Mile End, was originally a member of the Broderers' Company, but was translated from that guild to the Ironmongers', Friday, Sept. 23, 1768, as agreed to by the Court of Aldermen on the Tuesday previous. He was Master of the Ironmongers' Company, 1769, and died 1775, leaving a widow and eleven children, viz. five sons and six daughters.

As Jonathan Shakespear and his son, the alderman, were both members of the Broderers' Company, I naturally applied to the Clerk of that guild, Mr. Charles E. Freeman, of 11, Bucklersbury, to kindly help me by throwing some light on this subject by aid of the company's books. It was not till I wrote a second time he deigned to give me a reply, and then briefly stated his terms were three guineas for searching prior to 1728, and

* She was Elizabeth Currie, of the family of Bush-hill, Bankers of London. Her mother was Anne Campbell, of the House of Argyll and Eglinstoun.

10s. 6d. after that period. Lieut.-Col. Shakespear did not fare so well. Far different was the answer I received from John Nicholl, Esq., F.S.A., of Canonbury, author of a privately printed *History of the Ironmongers' Company* (of which he has been master), and whose elaborate and beautiful MS. history of the same guild was so much admired at the Society of Antiquaries' exhibition, June 21, 1860, and the Ironmongers' Hall Exhibition, May 1861. He took some trouble in the matter, and informed me the Ironmongers' books could not throw any light on the subject. He recommended a search in the Shadwell registers (which some of your correspondents may have spare time for); accounted for the alderman's coat of arms being the same as the poet's, as there is but *one* coat known of the name; and concluded by noticing the Shakespears of Essex, which included Thomas Shakspere, priest, 1557; Joseph Shakspere of Havering, 1640; Samuel Shakspere of Hornchurch; Samuel Shakspere of Romford, 1707; William Shakspere, whose sons were John (of Rawreth, 1723), Joseph and William.

The Rope Factory belonging originally to the family, and which to present knowledge dates back to 1660, is in Love Lane, Shadwell (Reed & Co.), and thirty years since the firm was Reed, Shakespear & Co. "Shakespear's Walk," 47, High Street, Shadwell, is named after the family, and the house, 47, is a curious weather-boarded two storey building of ancient date.

In a letter to Lieut.-Col. Shakspear, MR. HALLIWELL mentions he never heard of the Shadwell Shakespears till lately. They were wealthy folk in their day.

G. R. French, Esq., writing to me says:—

"I had the pleasure of first pointing out to Lieut.-Col. Shakspear his connection with the Ironmongers' Company (to which I belong) through his great-grandfather, the Alderman, whose father was Jonathan Shakespear, ob. April 1735, and he was son of John Shakespear, of the Rope Walk, Shadwell, born in 1612, and died Sept. 1689. The name of his father is not known, but he would be coeval with the poet, and Lieut.-Col. Shakespear fondly hopes that his ancestor was the Poet's brother Gilbert, who was living at Stratford in 1609, but nothing is known of his after history. My own impression is, that Lieut.-Col. Shakespear may be descended from a brother of the Poet's father. The Shakespears are found in Warwickshire registers in the 1st of Henry VI., and the name exists in some of the towns of that county to the present time."

Mr. Nicholl justly adds, that whether the Essex and Warwickshire families are of the same stock, remains to be proved; "it is a very interesting question."

Now the real question is, who was the father of John Shakespear, of Rope Walk, born 1612; married, July 14, 1654, Martha Seeley, aged nineteen, and died Sept. 1689? He had issue, Martha, Samuel, Benjamin, Mary, John, and Jonathan (born Feb. 6, 1670, and died 1735.) These names

·savour strongly of Puritanism, and it is known ·that the poet's relations were staunch Puritans, ,and this probably caused all relating to him to *i*be destroyed. But this, however (as Mr. French surmises) may have been but common at that :day : —

" John, the Poet's father, had two daughters, called Joan, which was. evidently a cherished name, and no doubt had been in the family for previous generations; his father was Richard, a name which John Shakespear gave to a younger son, of whom nothing is known except that he died in 1613."

T. C. N.

MILTON AND HIS ILLUSTRATOR.
(3rd S. vii. 150.)

The lines from Shakespeare — "Gives not the hawthorn bush a sweeter shade," &c., quoted by LORD LYTTELTON, partly furnishes a reply to the inquiry of another correspondent — "What propriety is there in making a shepherd count his sheep under a hawthorn rather than under any other tree?" The thorn, with its numerous and closely-placed branches, shooting out at no great distance from the ground, forms a good shelter ·from sun, storm, and night dews, and sheep and cattle resort to it on that account. Walking in pastures where the thorn is preserved any one may perceive unmistakeable evidence of the preference which the animals in question have for that tree.

A shepherd, if "stirring with the lark," would, in all probability, find his flock assembled under a thorn ready to be told. If those who hesitate to accept the verb to tell in the sense of counting would only pay a visit to the Commons and see Mr. Brand tell his tale, and never did rustic swain watch over his sheep with more tender solicitude than is shown by the indefatigable and amiable parliamentary shepherd for the flock under his charge, his scepticism would vanish. Mr. Speaker's "Tellers may proceed to tell" is decisive upon the point.

The word is used in the same sense not only in the provinces but also in London, more frequently than is supposed. At landing wharves, merchandise in the form of packets, barrels, &c., is, when counted, referred to as "told off." The ·word was, and I doubt not still is, used in that way at billiard and cricket matches. Devout .Catholics, I presume, continue to tell their beads. Miss Edgeworth's rendering of "tale" by "tally" makes what is plain somewhat obscure. The meaning of the word is shown in the following passages :

" And the tale of bricks, which they did make heretofore, ye shall lay upon them; ye shall not diminish ought thereof, &c.
"Go therefore now, and work; for there shall no straw be given you, yet shall ye deliver the tale of bricks," &c. *Exodus* v. 8 and 18.

· "Wherefore David arose and. went, he and his men, and slew of the Philistines two hundred men ; and David brought their foreskins, and they gave them in full tale to the king, that he might be the king's son in law." — 1 *Samuel* xviii. 27.

Before quitting the subject allow me to observe that break of day is not the usual period of rustic courtship. At that time each person hastens to his allotted duties, as Milton in his poem has described them. The ploughman " whistles o'er the furrowed land," the milkmaid "singeth blythe," the mower "whets his scythe" —

" And *every* shepherd tells his tale,
Under the hawthorn in the dale."

The word which I have marked in italics seems to 'set all doubt at rest. It is the duty of every shepherd to count his sheep in the morning; but it is beyond the bounds of probability that every shepherd should be able to find a sweetheart to talk to at that very uncomfortable hour for love-making.

C. ROSS.

That the shepherd's tale was one of sheep, not of love, is to my mind so evident, that I am surprised to find it still doubted by your correspondent D. (3rd S. vii. 210.) Milton is describing how all nature rouses up to activity with the break of day. To be sure the milkmaid is only spoken of as "singing blithe," and the ploughman as "whistling o'er the furrowed land," but no doubt they were both *at their work* just as much as the mower "whetting his scythe." In the midst of all this industry how inconsistent to make a single exception in favour of the shepherd, whose office demands such peculiar watchfulness and care! While all around are beginning the labours of the day, he alone is to be neglecting his flock, and making love under a bush. The word *every* would render this view still more absurd; *all* the shepherds are to be love-making in this fashion.   J. DIXON.

ST. AUGUSTINE AND THE MYSTERY OF THE BLESSED TRINITY.
(3rd S. vii. 440.)

The vision of St. Augustine, beautiful and instructive as it is, must, I fear, be ranked among the many traditional stories or legends of the olden times. Though Dr. Stanley, in the extract given, asserts that the saint himself relates it, I have never found it in his writings. It occurs, however, in. all the old books of legendary lore; and the following is one of the best readings of it : —

" Once upon a time as St. Augustine was walking by the sea shore, and considering very earnestly how he should best explain the doctrine of the Holy Trinity, saw a little child sitting on the sand, who kept lading water out of the sea with a little spoon into a small hole on the shore. Thereupon he spoke thus to the child :

'What are you trying to do?' The child answered: 'I want to lade the great sea into a small hole.' Then said he: 'My child, you cannot do that, for it is a thing impossible.' Then said the child: 'It is more easy to do than what you are thinking of.' With this the child disappeared: and St. Augustine well understood that he was our Lord himself."

The incident is said to have occurred at *Centum Cellæ*, now Civita Vecchia. F. C. H.

The passage in Dean Stanley's sermon must be a direct citation from some well known author, as I have before me some notes on the *Calendar* (published in 1860), in which it is given without inverted commas in precisely the same words as in *Sermons in the East*. In Dr. Husenbeth's edition of Butler's *Lives* there is an engraving of the Vision, which professes to be taken from a painting by Garofalo: it is, however, left unexplained by the text. I advise your correspondent to consult Parker's *Anglican Calendar*, and Jameson's *Legends of the Monastic Orders*. St. Swithin.

Leigh, *Body of Divinity* (p. 252), says:—

" A studious Father meditating on the mystery of the Trinity, there appeared unto him a childe with a shell lading the sea into a little hole; he demanding what the child did, 'I intend,' said the child, 'to empty the ocean into this pit.' 'It is impossible,' said the Father. 'As possible,' said the child, 'as for thee to comprehend this profound mystery in thy shallow capacity.'"

The margin has "Par. on Rom. ii. 23." The preceding reference is to "Petav. de Trin." This "Petav." may be Petavius, born 1583: a Jesuit, celebrated for chronology. With Scaliger, Salmasius, and Casaubon, he is said to have had controversies.

The foregoing is perhaps as "full" an account as may otherwise be met with. But it may be said that, as to the "original account," the extract given seems to afford it when it states: "This is in allusion to a vision, which he himself relates as occurring to him."

This appears to indicate, clearly, that St. Augustine was the original narrator. Anon.

Your correspondent H. C. is mistaken as to the origin of the legend he names. It is not told of St. Augustine; but I think it is St. Augustine who tells it of a learned convert to Christianity, who lived in the fifth or sixth century. His name was Alanus, and, from being born in an island, was surnamed De Insula. He went to Paris and studied divinity, &c., and returned to his native land (some part of Africa). He had attained so great a name from his sermons, that he at last determined upon expounding the mystery of the Trinity. And it was while walking on the sands, preparing this sermon, that an angel is said to have appeared to him in the form of a child, who told him he was trying to empty the sea with a ladle; and when Alanus replied it was not possible, gave the answer quoted by your correspondent. Not having books, or any facilities by me, I cannot give dates and authorities as I should wish; but these I know to be the main facts. It is sad to end by saying that Alanus de Insula, the most learned man perhaps of his day, returned to, and I believe died in, heathenism. A. T. T.

GALLOWS INSCRIPTION.

(3rd S. vii. 439.)

"The name of the executed person," or, properly speaking, the name of the person upon whom a sentence of death was executed, was John Hamilton, Archbishop of St. Andrews, and natural brother to James Hamilton, Regent of Scotland. The "part of Scotland" was Stirling Castle, the date about 1571. I believe Hamilton was the only bishop ever hanged in Scotland, though subsequently, in the same country, a band of base ruffians cruelly assassinated a venerable prelate in presence of his daughter.

There is a curious, though doubtful, astrological story told relating to the death of Hamilton. Some years previous the archbishop gave Jerome Cardan the princely fee of 1800 gold crowns, with other presents, for coming to Scotland and attending him as a physician. Before leaving, Cardan calculated his horoscope, and declared that he would die of *passio cordis*; the horoscope is in Latin, and may be found in Cardan's *Geniturarum Exemplar*. Now *passio cordis* might be translated disease of the heart, or it might typify suffering by the cord, the latter actually being the *disease* which caused Hamilton's death.

It was the *odium theologicum* of the reforming party that threw such a sting into the inscription; and thus I am reminded of another not unworthy of a place here, that derives its punning satire from the same source. Lord Moore, in defiance of a cessation of hostilities, attacked Owen (Latinised Eugenius) Roe O'Neill commanding the Irish Confederate forces about the beginning of 1643. O'Neill, who had been a general officer in the Spanish service, was too old a soldier to be taken by surprise, and repulsed his enemy, Moore himself being killed by a cannon ball. Upon which, a Romanist chaplain, in the Irish camp, wrote the following epigram:—

" Contra Romanos mores, res mira, Dynasta
Morus ab Eugenio *cannonizatus* erat."

William Pinkerton.

It was on the execution of Hamilton, Bishop of St. Andrews, who was captured in Dumbarton Castle in 1571 by the party of the Regent Lennox, that the lines—

"Cresce diu felix arbor, semperque vireto
  Frondibus, ut nobis talia poma feras,"
were affixed to the gibbet. Queen Mary's party
replied by affixing the following couplet: —
"Infelix pereas arbor! si forte virebis,
  Imprimis utinam carminis author eas."
Hist. of King James the Sext. (Banna-
tyne Club edit.), p. 72.

G. E.

TOASTS.

(3rd S. vii. 397.)

The first toast cited by CYRIL embodies a *mot*
in vogue in France during the latter half of the
last century. I do not know who first used it;
but Voltaire adopts the *formula* in a letter to
Helvetius, of May 11, 1761: —

"Les jansénistes, les convulsionnaires, gouvernent donc
Paris! C'est bien pis que le règne des jésuites: il y avait
des accommodemens avec le ciel du temps qu'ils avaient
du crédit; mais les jansénistes sont impitoyables. Est-ce
que la proposition honnête et modeste d'étrangler le dernier jésuite avec les boyaux du dernier janséniste ne
pourrait amener les choses à quelque conciliation?"

The same thought has been paraphrased by
Diderot, in a distich which has been well styled
"atrocement energique": —

"Et ses mains ourdiraient les entrailles du prêtre,
  A défaut d'un cordon pour étrangler les rois."

The toast attributed to Henry Erskine I have
seen in an amplified form: —

"Dam the canals, sink the coal-pits, blast the minerals,
consume the manufactures, disperse the commerce of
Great Britain and Ireland."

And I have somewhere read that it is appropriately
given at every anniversary dinner of an association of civil engineers, called the Smeatonian
Club, from the illustrious engineer who founded
it, and to whom is attributed the characteristic
"sentiment."

The substance of another of these toasts is sometimes given in a metrical form (into which, indeed, as a mnemonic aid I should recommend
diners-out to convert, if they can, that which
follows it): —

"Here's a health to all those that I love,
  Here's a health to all those that love me;
Here's a health to all those that love those that I love,
  And to those that love them that love me."

This reminds me of another doggrel toast: —

"Here's a health to me and mine,
  Not forgetting thee and thine;
And when thee and thine,
  Come to see me and mine;
May me and mine,
  Make thee and thine,
As welcome as thee and thine,
  Have ever made me and mine."

I transcribe the following, which is styled "The
Climax of Toasts," from the *Anecdote Library*,
London, 1822: —

"When Lord Stair was ambassador in Holland, he
made frequent entertainments, to which the foreign ministers were constantly invited; not excepting the ambassador of France, with whose nation we were then on
the point of breaking. In return, the Abbé de Ville, the
French ambassador, as constantly invited the English and
Austrian ambassadors, upon the like occasions. The Abbé
was a man of vivacity, and fond of punning. Agreeable to
this humour, he one day proposed a health in these terms:
'The rising sun, my master,' alluding to the device and motto
of Louis XV.; which was pledged by the whole company.
It came then to the Baron de Reisbach's turn to give a
toast; and he, to countenance the Abbé, proposed the
moon, in compliment to the empress queen, which was
greatly applauded. The turn then came to the Earl of
Stair, on whom all eyes were fastened; but that nobleman, whose presence of mind never forsook him, drank
his master King William by the name of Joshua, the son
of Nun, who made the sun and moon stand still."—P. 37.

The toast given by Campbell at, I think, a Literary Fund dinner, has often been cited. The poet
proposed the health of Napoleon Buonaparte, con-
necting him with the business of the day by
stating in explanation that he had "shot a publisher,"—alluding to the execution of the German
bookseller Palm, for the publication of the *Geist
der Zeit*. See " N. & Q.," July 30, 1853, p. 107.

WILLIAM BATES.
Birmingham.

CYRIL has missed the rhythm of his second
toast. I have generally heard it as —.

"Here's to those that love them that love us.
Here's to those that love those that love us.
Here's to those that love them, that love them that love
  those,
That love those that love them that love us."

It goes to a tune.   P. P.

IN TWO PLACES AT ONCE LIKE A BIRD.

(3rd S. vii. 459.)

This very-often-quoted expression, attributable
to the celebrated Sir Boyle Roche, has been so mis-
quoted that it has assumed its present form, which
is not the shape or form that Sir Boyle used.
When I was a schoolboy in Dublin I made the
acquaintance of Mr. John Ryder, a gentleman of
education and great information, who resided in
Upper Baggot Street, then (1829-30) a suburb of
the city, and he used to take much pleasure in
relating to myself and other juvenile friends
stories and anecdotes of the old Irish House of
Commons, where for many years he had spent his
evenings during the parliamentary sessions, having
an *entrée* to a private box near the Speaker's
chair, as a friend of his was an official of the
House, and procured him that favour. I have
memorandums of many of his remembrances of
the "Old House in College Green," and as few,
if indeed any of these recollections have ever been
printed, I may at some leisure time put them in

shape for type. The two seasons previous to the Union with England were peculiarly rich, and produced duels almost daily. During that period Mr. Ryder told me that he saw twenty-one duels, and out of that number nineteen were either killed or wounded. He was present at the duel between Henry Grattan and Sir Isaac Corry, when Grattan's pistol ball lodged in Corry's watch, but did no further damage. But I have wandered from my text. Mr. Ryder told often and often that he was in the House on the night that Sir Boyle made use of the expression, which, in its transmission to the present generation, has been twisted out of all propriety by the carriage. Sir Boyle was in the habit of saying witty things, but generally there was an absurdity about his mots, that used to set the House in a roar.* In some debate that took place, Sir Boyle, in illustrating an argument, remarked that " The honourable gentleman opposite might as well say (as the man·said once) that if he, the honourable gentleman opposite, was a bird, he could be in two places at one time."

It will be observed by this that Sir Boyle quoted from some one, and that the expression was not one of his own, as appears from·his observation, "as the man said once." Mr. Ryder was a man of accurate truthfulness ; and with this I leave the case for judgment.   S. Redmond.
Liverpool. ·

THE EXODUS OF THE ISRAELITES.
(3rd S. vii. 419, 428, 464.)

If Canon Dalton will again refer to Kalisch, he will see that the Doctor has fixed a date for the Exodus in consonance with that which is generally adopted by biblical scholars, being B.C. 1491, which is·in conformity with·Ussher. The corresponding year A.M., as Kalisch shows, is 2269 according to the Jewish reckoning, which together makes 3760 years, the interval from the creation to the birth of Jesus Christ being 244 years less than we compute it, but which may make our era suspicious to some minds as partly .astronomical (La Place, Mec. Cel. iii. 113.) Kalisch has also shown of Germans and others on the date of the Exodus different opinions, which, from one extreme to the other, vary 553 years. And he might have shown various opinions between the limits of 6984 and 3483 years, or 3501 years.

With respect to the Egyptian king, under whom the Exodus was made, Kalisch has adopted the name from Champollion, who states that " the captivity continued during the 18th dynasty and

* He proposed that every *quart* bottle should hold a *quart*—a proposition that at this day would not be out of place, for bottles now are called quarts, when, in point of fact, they hold little more than a pint.   .

that it was under Rameses ·V. or [meaning *the same* as] Amenophis, at the beginning of the fifteenth century, that Moses delivered the Hebrews." Rosellini also makes Rameses III. (= Rameses V.), the reigning Pharaoh at the Exodus (*Mon. Stor.* i. 299.)

The ·following .table is compiled on the assumption that the list of the 18th dynasty, given by Josephus from Manetho, is the correct one ; and that the date of the Exodus was 1491 B.C. The succession of Pharaohs in this list is confirmed, in part, by four distinct monuments—namely, the table of Abydos, the procession in the Ramesseion, the tomb of Gurnah at Thebes, and the procession of Medinet-Abou (Rosellini, i. 205) : —

	Began to Reign B.C.*
1. Amos [a] (=Tethmosis) . . .	1824
2. Chebros	1799
3. Amenophis . . .	1786
4. Amesis (Queen)	1765
5. Mephres	1743
.6. Mephramouthosis . . .	1730
7. Tethmosis	1704
8. Amenophis . . .	1694
9. Horus	1664
10. Acenchres [b] (Queen) . .	1628
11. Ratholis . . .	1616
12. Acenchres . . .	1608
13. Acenchres (another) . .	1595
14. Armais	1582
15. Ramesses . . .	1578
16. Armessis Miamoun [c] . .	1577
·17· Amenophis [d] . . .	1511
Sethosis, first of the 19th dynasty .	1491

·ᴬ The Exodus was in this reign according to Ptolemy and Julius Africanus.

[b] In this reign according to Eusebius ; but the monarch was a queen !

[c] In this reign (but B.C. 1474) according to Rosellini, being his Ramesses III. = Sesostris and Sesoösis.

[d] In this reign according to Champollion (being his Ramesses V. = Menaphthah III.) and Wilkinson (being his Pthamen, having given up Tethmosis III., No. 7 in this list); also according to Prudhoe, Bunsen, Levi, &c.

The dates in this table are proved by the synchronism of Egyptian and Sacred History in the reigns of Shishak (=Sheshank I.), and Rehoboam and Jeroboam (1 Kings xi. 40; xii. 2; xiv. 25-28 ; 2 Chr. xii.), when Judea was invaded and Jerusalem plundered in 971 B.C. This Pharaoh is the first of Manetho's 22nd dynasty, from whose chronology, as extracted by Eusebius, according to Syncellus, confirmed by the Armenian version, we find the duration of the 19th dynasty 194 years; of the 20th, 178 ; and of the 21st, 130; to which add the reign of Shishak, 21 ; together, 523 years, which, deducted from 1491, the Exodus, gives 968 B.C., the time of his death, just three years

* Two years earlier than Champollion and Rosellini fix it.

after the plunder of Jerusalem. The fore-court of Karnach confirms this invasion of Judea in his reign (Bunsen's *Egypt's Place*, iii. 241.)

T. J. BUCKTON.

Lichfield.

ZINC SPIRES.

(3rd S. vii. 461.)

Having had perhaps more to do with the use of this metal than many architects, I beg to say that these spires are not only very common on the continent but also in America and Canada. The only one I know of in England is that at Ripple, near Walmer.

With regard to the question as to the use of zinc in mediæval times, I believe we have no testimony of the use of copper, tin, or zinc as roof coverings; though the former most probably was used in Cornwall in parts where that metal abounds, and lead is scarce. The "Italia" of Naples, as cited in the *Moniteur* of Feb. 15th last, describes the discovery of a large fountain at Pompeii with a handsome front decorated with shell work, and "the upper part covered with zinc." This curious discovery shows the use of this metal to be known to the ancients.

The reports of the various commissions to foreign governments, and the results of observation in this country prove — 1. That sheet zinc is very durable if used of sufficient thickness; 2. That it must be laid so as to be quite free to contract and expand with change of temperature. Lead itself will not stand if too thin, and if it has not sufficient rolls and flashings. Zinc will, however, stand well at about one-fifth the thickness required for lead.

Objection has been taken as to smoky atmospheres, but this is a mistake. Liége is a great manufacturing town where nothing but coal is consumed. It is the Birmingham of the continent, and like that town its locality is called "the black land" from the abundance of smoke and soot. Here the use of zinc for house coverings is almost universal. One roof, fifty-five years old; another, covering some furnace-houses where volumes of smoke have been pouring out day and night, and which has been built about thirty years, were examined among many others and found perfect. When zinc is first put up it oxidises, and the coating thus formed is insoluble and protects the metal. Of course if it be rolled too thin, the oxide penetrates too deep, and the metal goes in holes on being walked over.

JAMES EDMESTON, Architect.

Crown Court, Old Broad Street.

Zinc, as covering for roofs, louvres, &c., if of the best quality, will last from twenty to thirty years. It is about the same in point of durability with slates of a fair quality. It is in nowise comparable to lead, in colour, durability, or capabilities of any kind. For an ordinary country spire it falls immeasurably short of the old shingle covering, now so seldom used. There is an active stir being made to extend the use of this metal. I, for one, hope that it will never be extensively used for church purposes; being very perishable under certain conditions of atmosphere, and the like. It is also hard and stubborn, and is scarcely applicable artistically; but above all its colour is, in my opinion, as bad as possible. Age has no softening or toning effect upon it. It is as neat and tasteless as a Quaker's coat. Slates are bad enough, but zinc is worse.

As to durability: The spire of St. Philip's, Dalston, which was built in 1841, had to be fresh covered about seven years ago.   J. C. J.

LONGEVITY.

(3rd S. vii. 154.)

MISS MARY BILLINGE. — I am now in a condition to furnish satisfactory information on the subject of the age of the supposed centenarian, Miss Billinge; and I will in a few words describe the process by which I have arrived at it.

On application to Mr. Newton, surgeon, I was furnished with a copy of the certificate of baptism of "Mary, daughter of William Billinge, farmer, and Lidia his wife; born 24th May, 1751, and christened the 5th of June." This was assumed to be the Mary Billinge recently deceased. The question thus became one of identity. After some inquiry, I found Miss Billinge had a brother and sister buried in Everton churchyard. I have extracted the inscriptions on their tombstones as follows: —

"William Billinge, obt. 7th May, 1817, aged 46.
"Anne Billinge, died 9th Feby., 1832, aged 59."

I have also seen a mourning ring which belonged to the late Miss Billinge, in memory of her brother, which confirms the above date of his death. It is clear, therefore, that William and Anne were the brother and sister of the late Mary Billinge.

The next point was to ascertain the parentage of William and Anne. I went over to Prescot church, and found the parish clerk — himself a relic of antiquity, ninety years of age, and still doing duty. He made a search for me, and found the registers of both: —

William in 1771, son of Charles and Margaret Billinge.

Anne in 1773, daughter of the same.

It was clear then that William and Anne, children of Charles and Margaret Billinge, could not be brother and sister of Mary, the daughter of William and Lidia Billinge.

To put the matter beyond a doubt, I persevered in the search, and found :

" Mary, daughter of Charles and Margaret Billinge, born 6th November, 1772, christened 23rd December."

The identity is here complete. The old lady was, therefore, in her ninety-first year, not in her 112th when she died. I suspect that most of the supposed instances of centenarianism will turn out to be cases of mistaken identity.   J. A. P.

Sandyknowe, Wavertree, Liverpool.

[We feel sure that in thanking our valued correspondent J. A. P. for the ingenuity and perseverance he has displayed in ascertaining the precise age of Miss Mary Billinge, we are only expressing the feeling of all those who take an interest in the question of CENTENARIANISM, which is now attracting such general attention. — ED. "N. & Q."]

MILTON (3rd S. vii. 460.) — In vol. vi. p. 199, of the *Journal of the Archæological Institute,* there are woodcuts of a small silver seal, the property of Mr. Disney ; and of the impress of this seal, which has been —

" well authenticated as having been used by Milton. The impress is a coat of arms, a double-headed eagle displayed. The shield is surmounted by a helm, lambrequins, and crest—which appears to be a lion's gamb grasping the head of an eagle by the neck, erased. This valuable little memorial had been in the possession of Mr. John Payne, on the death of Thomas Foster ; who had married Elizabeth Clarke, daughter of Deborah, Milton's youngest daughter, and wife of Abraham Clarke, a weaver in Spital Fields. Mr. Payne sold it to Mr. Thomas Hollis, in 1761 : on his death, 1774, it came into the possession of Mr. Thomas Brand Hollis, and then became part of the collection, inherited in 1804 by Mr. Disney's father."

The Rev. Joseph Hunter is recorded to have made " some interesting observations in reference to this seal," and to have remarked that the armorial bearings were certainly those which were borne by the great puritan poet. Mr. Hunter is also said to have traced out a connection between Milton and Thame in Oxfordshire. In his *Armory,* Sir Bernard Burke gives, for " *Milton,* of Milton, near Thame, co. Oxford, as borne by *John Milton,* the poet : Arg , an eagle displayed with two heads gu., beaked and legged sa." The crest is not given ; but for another Milton there is blazoned this crest : " A lion's gamb erect arg. grasping an eagle's head erased gu." I regret being unable to reply to the inquiry of CARILFORD concerning the motto of Milton.   CHARLES BOUTELL.

RASSELAS : DINARBAS (3rd S. vii. 199.) — In your number for 11th of March last, ABHBA inquires for the name of the author of *Second Part of the History of Rasselas, Prince of Abyssinia.* I do not remember *that* title, but was lately favoured with the loan of a book called *Dinarbas,* which is perhaps the same work. At any rate it raised the identical question as to authorship. Towards the solution of that question I found nothing, except

the following which was written inside the binding of the first volume of *Rasselas* (3rd edition, 1760) —

. " An ingenious continuation of Dr. Johnson's *Rasselas,* entitled *Dinarbas,* said to be wrote by Miss Knight, the author of *Marcus Flaminius.*—M.R., October, 1792, pages 164-169."

The writing is that of Mr. Samuel Maude, then of this town, whose turn towards such notanda appears constantly throughout his library, and affords a good guarantee for his accuracy.
                                J. M. O.

Sunderland.

THE ORIGIN OF INFIRMARIES IN ENGLAND (3rd S. vii. 176.) — In the Life of the Rev. Samuel Wesley, A.M., Jun., prefixed to his *Poems* (Simpkin, Marshall, & Co. 1862), it is recorded that when he resided at Westminster in 1715, " with limited means, by steadily active benevolence he effected an almost incredible amount of good. The establishment and success of the first infirmary in Westminster (now St. George's Hospital, Hyde Park Corner) were in a great measure due to our poet."

Mr. William Nichols, of 46, Hoxton Square, the writer of the *Life of Mr. S. Wesley,* could inform MR. LEE whether the handwriting in his pamphlet is that of Mr. Wesley. The Rev. S. Wesley was the elder brother of the celebrated Rev. John Wesley.   ELIJAH HOOLE, D.D.

8, Myddelton Square, Pentonville.

REV. EDWARD FORD (3rd S. vii. 459.) — I met the following memorandum amongst a large collection of family documents lately entrusted to me for historical purposes : —

" The King against Wm Crosbie, James Cotter, James Scholes, Charles Boyle.

" At a commission of Oyer and Terminer for ye County of ye City of Dublin, held ye 24th day of March, 1733. The deft Cotter was indicted for ye murder of ye Revd Edwd Ford, one of ye Fellows of Trinity College, Dublin, by firing, &c., whereof he died on ye 8 day of March last, and ye deft Crosbie, Scholes, and Boyle as accessarys to ye sd murder against ye form, &c.

" At an ajournment of ye commission ye 25th day of March, 1733, ye defts being arraigned on this indictment severally pleaded not guilty.

" At an ajournment ye 24 April, 1734. The defts being brought to ye Bar then moved by their counsel to bailed alledging their ill state of health, and ye closeness of ye prison where they were confined, but ye motion being opposed by ye Attorney-General was denyed by ye Court.

" 28 May, 1734. At an adjournment of ye commission of Oyer and Terminer.

" Commissioners present : — Lord Mayor, Earl of Ross, Earl of Meath, Lord Sautry, Justice Ward, Sergeant Betesworth, Sergeant Purdon, Mr. Le Hunt, Lord Chief Justice Reynolds.

" The Attorney-General moved to put off ye defts tryall yt Tisdall and Pain, two material witnesses for ye King, were not to be found, which affs were read. The defts being called upon by ye Court to know what they had (sic) object against putting off their tryal, and desired to be heard by their counsel, who were Mr Malone, Senr,

Mr Callaghan, Mr Daly, Mr Wall, Mr Parkinson, Mr Malone, Junr, who urged yo danger and ill consequence of keeping ye prisoners in gaol till another adjournment, which perhaps might be a long time, when they were ready to take their tryal, which they therefore had a right to, for it was ye libertie of ye subject, and that ye reasons now offered might hold for ever; and ye defts never have an opportunity to show their innocence, and to acquit themselves from so heavy an accusation.

"Lord Chief Justice Reynolds said, that this motion to put off ye tryall, was ye common practice of ye circuits, from one assize to another which was longer than until ye next adjournment of ye sessions, therefore on the authoritie of that practice, he was of opinion ye motion of Mr Attorney ought to be granted.

"Mr Justice Ward said, yt it appearing two material witnesses could not then be had, he was of opinion ye tryal ought to be put off."

I may mention that the family documents abovementioned are the property of the descendants of one of the defendants.   R. C.

Royal Institution, Cork.

I remember reading a novel (called *Recollections of Trinity College, Dublin*, or by some similar title,) in which the incident of Mr. Ford's murder is introduced; but how far the account agrees with what actually happened I do not know.

CHAS. F. S. WARREN.

Cor. C. Col. Cambridge.

THE SYNAGOGUE OF THE LIBERTINES (3rd S. vii. 460.) — If CANON DALTON does not, as he owns, find the several explanations he has seen of the above expression satisfactory, I can hardly hope to please him. But I will mention that the opinion of those who suppose these *Libertines* to have come from *Libya*, derives considerable probability from the remarkable coincidence of expression in Acts ii. 10, where we read of men from the *parts of Lybia about Cyrene.* Now in the passage under consideration, Acts vi. 9, we find these two places recurring in similar juxta-position, *the synagogue of the Libertines, and of the Cyrenians.* It seems to me that this is almost decisive in favour of the interpretation that the *Libertines* came from *Libya.* St. Luke would probably have written Ἀπελευθέρων, or Ἐξελευθέρων, instead of Λιβερτίνων, if these had been men liberated from slavery. The proper Greek derivative word from Libya would be Λιβυστίνων, but it has been surmised that this word might easily have been corrupted with Λιβερτίνων.

F. C. H.

Although Schleusner, as well as Kuinoel, gives the various interpretations, both concur in that of Chrysostom, — Λιβερτίνοι δὲ, οἱ Ῥωμαίων ἀπελεύθεροι οὕτω καλοῦνται. Ὥσπερ δὲ ᾤκουν ἐκεῖ πολλοὶ ξένοι οὕτω καὶ συναγωγὰς εἶχον ἔνθα ἔδει τὸν νόμον ἀναγινώσκεσθαι καὶ εὐχὰς γίνεσθαι. (*Acts* vii.; *Hom.* xv., vol. ix. p. 139.)

"The emancipated slaves of the Romans are called Libertines. As many strangers lived there, they required synagogues for the reading of the law and for prayer."

The word is therefore Latin, adopted into the Greek of the New Testament, as *census* and *centurio.* (See Justinian's *Institutes,* I. v.) I know nothing of the periodical in which De Rossi has referred to this subject.   T. J. BUCKTON.

"THAT'S THE CHEESE" (3rd S. vii. 397, 465.) The Hindostani word signifying *thing,* is pronounced cheese, and not chiz, as your correspondent supposes, and is therefore without any alteration of sound identical with the slang word in question; which, by the way, albeit a novelty in England, I remember to have heard used as a cant term in India thirty years ago. The English gipsy possesses several Hindostani words in his cant vocabulary, as for instance, *choori,* a knife, which is pure Oordoo, I believe. This, however, is not to be wondered at, there being gipsies in the East as well as in Europe, and as these nomads are known to have means of extensive intercommunication, the existence of Eastern words in the dialect of the English Bohemian, may be accounted for without much difficulty. There is, however, an Oriental word, the importation of which into our land has always puzzled me. I allude to the Persian noun, *tawziāndá,* signifying stripes, from which it would seem that the word *tawse,* the designation for a schoolmaster's *flagellum* in Scotland, must be derived. Possibly, however, this may be only a curious coincidence in sound and meaning between two words of different languages, such as may perhaps exist between the Syriac word, *tanfa,* and the Italian word, *tanfa,* both of which signify impure or unclean.   H. A. KENNEDY.

Gay Street, Bath.

I think your correspondent need not travel so far as India for the origin of this phrase; surely it is more probably derived from the French "*C'est la chose.*" Many of our popular slang phrases are mere corruptions of French words, *e. g.* "That's the ticket," from "*C'est l'étiquette,*" &c.

ARTHUR SHUTE.

HOG FEAST (3rd S. vii. 420.) —

Οὐ μὴν ἀλλ' εἰ καὶ ἀδύνατον, ἢ διὰ τὴν συνήθειαν τὸ ἀναμάρτητον αἰσχυνόμενοι, τῷ ἁμαρτάνοντι χρησώμεθα διὰ τὸν λόγον, ἐδόμεθα σάρκας, ἀλλὰ πεινῶντες, οὐ τρυφῶντες· ἀναιρήσωμεν ζῷον, ἀλλ' οἰκτείροντες καὶ ἀλγοῦντες, οὐχ ὑβρίζοντες οὐδὲ βασανίζοντες· οἷα νῦν πολλὰ δρῶσιν, οἱ μὲν εἰς σφαγὴν ὑῶν ὑθοῦντες ὀβελοὺς διαπύρους ἵνα τῇ βαφῇ τοῦ σιδήρου περισβεννύμενον τὸ αἷμα καὶ διαχεόμενον, τὴν σάρκα θρύψῃ καὶ μαλάξῃ· οἱ δὲ οὔθασι συῶν ἐπιτόκων ἐναλλόμενοι καὶ λακτίζοντες, ἵνα αἷμα καὶ γάλα καὶ λύθρον ἐμβρύων ὁμοῦ συμφθαρέντων ἐν ὠδίσιν ἀναδεύσαντες, ὦ Ζεῦ καθάρσιε, φάγωσι τοῦ ζῴου τὸ μάλιστα φλεγμαῖνον· ἄλλοι γεράνων ὄμματα καὶ κύκνων ἀπορράψαντες καὶ ἀποκλείσαντες ἐν σκότει πιαίνουσιν, ἀλλοκότοις μίγμασι καὶ καρυκείαις τισὶν αὐτῶν τὴν σάρκα ὀψοποιοῦντες. (Plutarchi *De Esu Carnium,* Or. ii. c. i. t. ix. p. 54, ed. Wyttenbach, Oxon, 1800.)

"Adhibetur et ars jecori feminarum, sicut anserum, inventum M. Apicii, fico arida saginatis ac satie, necatis repente mulsi potu dato. Neque alio ex animali numerosior materia gáneæ; quinquaginta prope sapores, cum cæteris singuli. Hinc Censoriarum legum paginæ, interdictaque cœnis abdomina, glandia, testiculi, vulvæ, sincipita verrina, ut tamen Publii mimorum poetæ cœna, postquam servitutem exuerat, nulla memoretur sine abdomine etiam vocabulo suminis ab eo imposito." (Plinii *Nat. Hist.*, lib. viii. c. 51, t. iii. p. 530, ed. Paris, 1771.)

There is much desultory conversation in Athenæus, lib. iii. c. 21, *et seq.*, on the μήτρα ὑεία, and citations from the comic poets on such matters.

"Non hercule miror,
Aiebat, si qui comedunt bona, quum sit obeso
Nil melius turdo, nil vulva pulchrius ampla."
Hor., 1 *Epist.* xv. 39.

Smart oddly reads "ursa," and translates:—
"While they fat thrushes could prepare;
And feast upon a banging bear."

"That which smokes in the middle is a sow's stomach filled with a composition of minced pork, hog's brains, eggs, pepper, cloves, garlick, aniseed, rue, ginger, oil, wine and pickle. On the right-hand side are the teats and belly of a sow, just farrowed, fried with sweet wine, oil, lovage, and pepper."—*Peregrine Pickle*, c. xliv.

The pig-question is fully investigated in sec. xx. of *The Heathen rejection of Christianity in the First Ages considered,* by Thomas Comber. London, 1747.

Garrick Club.   FITZHOPKINS.

INFLUENZA (3rd S. vii. 459.) — The word is in Foote's *Lame Lover*, acted 1770. Sir Luke Limp, who has just promised to dine with Alderman Inkle, receives an invitation from Sir Gregory Goose, and says:—

"George, give my compliments to Sir Gregory, and I'll certainly come and dine there. Order Joe to run to Alderman Inkle's in Threadneedle Street; sorry can't wait upon him, but confined to bed two days with the new influenza."— Act.I. vol. ii. p. 65. *Dramatic Works,* London, 1797.

Garrick Club.   FITZHOPKINS.

CLOVIS (2nd S. ix. 373.)—Since stating all that I could find about the poem of *Clovis* and its author, I have met with a short notice in De Bachaumont's *Mémoires Secrets*, Londres, 1777, t. i. p. 308:—

" 20 Septembre, 1763. *Clovis, poëme.* C'est le même plan de Desmarets, allongé de plusieurs chants: il est en vers de dix syllabes. On sent qu'il est traité d'un façon moins grave. *L'Orlando Furioso* paroit avoir été le modèle de l'auteur, modèle qu'il n'a pas attrapé à beaucoup près. Il a parodié Desmarets, comme Voltaire a parodié Chapelain. Il n'est pas plus heureux dans cette imitation. Il y a pourtant de la facilité et du pittoresque dans sa versification."

I ask insertion of the above less for its own importance than in the hope of reviving the question and learning something about Le Jeune.

                                                H. B. C.
U. U. Club.

EUDOXIA COMNENA (3rd S. vii. 439.) — According to the biographical work of Ignatius Mindonius, a native of the Isle of Chios, and a monk of the order of Saint Basil, printed in Paris (sm. 4to), in the year 1699, and entitled,— Βιογραφίαι τῶν κατὰ τὸν ιζ΄ καὶ ιη΄ αἰῶνα ἐν τῇ Ἑσπερίᾳ Εὐρώπῃ ἀκμασάντων λογίων εὐγενῶν. Χίων, &c., and to various original documents preserved in the archives of our family, and partly published sixty years ago in Amsterdam (4to) by my paternal grandfather, Prince Demetrius Rhodokanakis, at the end of his book,—

"Précis historique de la Maison royale des Rhodocanakis, &c., &c., le tout démontré par des preuves juridiques, accompagné d'une traduction Grecque et de plusieurs Documents très authentiques, qui servent à," &c.,

Eudoxia Comnena, third daughter of Alexius Comnenus and Helen Cantacuzene, was born in Constantinople, August 12, 1575, and married to Theodore Palæologus, July 6, 1593, in the Isle of Chios, where she died the same day three years later, in giving birth to her daughter, Theodora, the future wife of Prince Demetrius Rhodocanakis, and mother of Dr. Constantine.

Theodore Palæologus, in remarrying with a lady of an inferior social position to his own, and not belonging to the Greek church, displeased grievously his son-in-law and the rest of his family, who *never* recognised this marriage. Very probably for this reason the new English relatives of Theodore, who, doubtless, erected over his mortal remains the still extant brass tablet, did not inscribe on it either the name of his first wife or that of his daughter.   RHODOCANAKIS.

SIGNIFICANT NAMES (3rd S. vii. 322.) — These may be found to be more numerous than your columns will admit of. We have Blood, Wolfe, and Co., in this town; and Blood, Fury, and Death, were seen together in a market town in Ireland. There has been a Blood a surgeon, and a Blood who led with success a forlorn hope. "Blood and Thunder," so often on the lips in the heat of a *mêlée* at an Irish pattern or a wake, were to be seen at one period on the plates of two hall doors adjoining each other in Gloucester Street, Dublin: Blood on one, and Thunder on the other. In this town also we have Dodge and Wynne, attorneys at law; a Sheepwash for hair dressing; and a Halfpenny who carried parcels once for one penny. In Bristol there was once a Rod that kept a school.   W. B.
Liverpool.

DR. CARABOO (3rd S. vii. 490.) — Allow me to say that Dr. C. H. Wilkinson did not "receive the universal sobriquet of Dr. Caraboo." Vulgar persons, who can only see one side of anything, might have so called him. I knew him from my very childhood, and I now count threescore years: more than that, he himself took me to Bristol to see the pretended Indian lady, but something, I forget what, prevented my seeing her. He was accustomed, when I was just of an age to appreciate such things, to give very interesting and exceedingly well illustrated lectures on natural philosophy, and I hope there are many survivors of those days as well as myself who are willing to speak of him in terms of respect, affection, and esteem. He was taken in, as regarded the silly affair, hardly in itself worth remembering, from yielding to the kindness of his own character. He died at a very advanced age.   T. F.

CLENT HILLS (3rd S. vii. 365.)—In reference to this subject, I extract the following from a little work published at Halesowen, entitled *Clentine Rambles:* —

"There are four stones on the summit of Clent Hill erected by George, Lord Lyttleton, in imitation of a Druidical monument."

It would be pleasing to know that these stones have a claim to greater antiquity than this. Can any of your correspondents furnish additions to the following bibliography of this most lovely and interesting spot, besides what may be found in Plot's *Staffordshire* or Nash's *Worcestershire*, and similar works; or in the very interesting works published a very few years ago by Mr. Noake?—

Clentine Rambles. By William Harris. Halesowen. 1845.

Letters on the Beauties of Hagley, Euville, and the Leasowes, &c. By Joseph Heely. 2 vols. 12mo. London, 1777.

A Description of Hagley Park. By the Author of "Letters," &c. London, 1830.

Companion to Leasowes, Hagley, and Euville; with a Sketch of Fisherwick. 8vo. 1830.

Local and Literary Account of Leamington, Stratford, Coventry, Warwick, Hagley, and the Leasowes, &c. By Mr. Pratt. Birmingham, 1814.

Description of Hagley, Euville, and the Leasowes; wherein all the Latin Inscriptions are translated, and every particular beauty described. Birmingham, N.D.

Guide to the Clent Hills. By Mr. Limings.

History and Antiquities of St. Kenelm's. By Mr. Limings.

The two latter, which are mentioned in *The Antiquities of Worcestershire*, by Jabez Allies, I have not met with. A few particulars may be found in Thurstone's *Works* as well.

A. H. BATES.

Edgbaston.

BEEST (3rd S. vii. 458.) — This word is by no means confined to Lancashire, it is an abbreviated form of *beestings*, or *biestings*. In a Latin dictionary, dated 1664, I find it defined as — "The first milk that cometh in teats after the birth of anything, be it in women or beasts." It is probably derived from the Saxon word *byst*. Its German equivalent is *biestmilch*.   H. FISHWICK.

PRESTONIENSIS will find an explanation of the term, with reference to authorities, in v. "Beast-

lings," in Halliwell's *Dictionary of Archaisms, &c.* The derivation of the word is not from the Anglo-Saxon, but from Scandinavian; though the terminal syllable -*ling* or -*ing* denotes, in the former tongue, the young offspring. It is called *beastlings* in the East Riding of Yorkshire. In South Lancashire it is a custom, in country places, for the milk-venders to send to their customers a gift of *beastlings*, of which a light custard-like pudding is made.   CRUX.

"CHRISTIAN BREADBASKET" (3rd S. vii. 356, 389, 448.)—Under this head it may be well to give, for those who are not acquainted with it, the opening sentence of a sermon preached in the sixteenth century before the University of Oxford. The University pulpit was on this occasion occupied by a layman. The preacher was Sir Richard Tavernor, of Wood Eaton, sheriff of Oxfordshire. He had obtained a license to preach, under favour of the Protector Somerset. Wearing his sword and chain of office, he thus addressed the learned audience : —

"Arriving at the Mount of St. Mary's, in the stony stage where I now stand, I have brought you some fine biscuits, baked in the oven of charity, carefully conserved for the chickens of the church, the sparrows of the spirit, and the sweet swallows of salvation."

May be this sentence is the matrix of such tract-titles as *The Christian Breadbasket;* and, I may add, *Crumbs of Comfort for Chickens of Grace.*   J. H. A.

COCK'S FEATHER (3rd S. vii. 459.)—In reply to your correspondent's inquiry — "Why Mephistopheles, and other stage representatives of evil incarnate, wear a cock's feather?"—I would venture to suggest, so far at least as concerns the Mephistopheles of Goethe's *Faust*, that he wears the feather as appertaining to a youth of high degree, "edler Junker." So it is represented by Goethe himself : —

"Bin ich, als edler Junker hier,

Die Hahnenfeder auf dem Hut."

["Here I am, a youth of condition . . . with a cock's feather in my hat."]

Mephistopheles, in the same speech, advises Faust to don the same costume : —

"Und rathe nun dir, kurz und gut, Dergleichen gleichfalls anzulegen."

And it will accordingly be remarked that, in Retsch's engravings, Faust as well as Mephistopheles appears wearing a feather.

If "other stage representatives of evil incarnate" wear the feather as well as Mephistopheles, may they not have adopted it from him?

Dr. Zerffi tells us that German superstition frequently made the devil appear as a dashing young man, a fop; and that he was, therefore, spoken of as "Schönhans," or "Fine Johnny."

It must not, however, be forgotten that a far more profound explanation of the cock's feather, than that now offered from Goethe himself, is suggested by a learned critic : —

"Mephistopheles calls himself the Spirit of Negation, or he that denies—and adopts for his crest the cock's feather : the allusion is to the cock that crew when Peter denied." — *Faust*, translated by Birch, 1839, Part I., p. 266."

By those who prefer the recondite to the obvious, this may be deemed the better explanation.
　　　　　　　　　　　　　　　　Schin.

"THE DUBLIN LETTER" (2nd S. vi. 230.)—I am happy to state that the *Dublin Letter*, which I inquired for some years since, has at last turned up; and Dr. Reeves, who found it in the Archiepiscopal Library of Armagh, describes it as follows. Its title is —

"The Popish Doctrine of Transubstantiation. Not agreeable to the Opinion of the Primitive Fathers. Shewed in a Letter to a Friend." Pp. 8. No title-page. Ad calcem, "*Dulibn*, Printedy b '*sic*) *Jo. Ray* at *Colledg.* green, and are to be sold by most Booksellers."

The pamphlet is bound in a volume in this library, in the department Popish Controversy, vol. xxxii. No. 7.　　　BIBLIOTHECAR. CHETHAM.

CAVALIER (3rd S. vii. 179.) — "CAVALIER, in fortification, is a work generally raised within the body of the place, ten or twelve feet higher than the rest of the works." — Charles JAMES, 1805. "CAVALLIERE à CAVALLO, is a high mount or platforme of earth, raised very high so that the artillery upon the same may shoote over the walles and bulwarkes to scoure and cleare the fields all about." — Robert BARRET, 1598. As Barret had passed much time "in the profession of armes, and that among forraine nations" his information cannot be doubted. The famous sir Roger Williams, writing about ten years before Barret, thus maintains the necessity of using the foreign terms of war: "If I should call a Cavilere a mount, divers would aske — What to do? to place windmills?"　　　　　　　　BOLTON CORNEY.

CHARTULARY OF WHALLEY ABBEY (3rd S. vii. 371.)—Your correspondent, MONASTICUS, quotes a passage in a charter in the *Whalley Abbey Coucher Book*, vol. i. p. 95, in which occur the words *actionibus de dolo et in factum*, and inquires what is the proper reading instead of *in factum*, which he asserts is a misreading on the part of the editor, and that it is plainly a noun in the dative case, such as *infirmationi*, or *infractioni*, but that he cannot hit upon the right word. I beg, though no lawyer, to assure your correspondent that the words *in factum*, as given by the editor, are perfectly correct, and that the supposed mistake is merely in his own imagination; the words *actio in factum* being one of the ancient forms of representing the action on the case, in support of which

I need only quote the following passage from Cowell's *Interpreter*, 1658, folio, s. v. Actio : —

"Where you have any occasion of sute, that neither hath a fit name, nor certain form already prescribed, there the clerks of the Chancery in antient time conceived a fit form of action for the fact in question, which the civilians call *actionem in factum*, and our common lawyers action upon the case. *In factum actiones dicuntur ideo, quia quod nomine non possunt exprimere negotium, id rei gestæ declarant citra formulam ac solennitatem ullam.—Cuiacius et Gothofredus ad Rubricam de præscriptis verbis*."

With regard to his general charge that "this Chartulary is full of editor's blunders," although I will not pretend to assert that in four volumes, comprising 1314 pages, some errors have not crept in, yet I feel warranted in observing there are few similar publications that are more entitled to the praise of accuracy than this work. The transcript from the original (the latter is beautifully distinct, see Introduction, p. xi.), was very carefully made by the editor himself, and when it was committed to the press the proof sheets were also examined with the original volume.

　　　　　　　　　BIBLIOTHECAR. CHETHAM.

KING'S LYNN : CAPGRAVE (3rd S. vii. 486.) — "Ben Adam" is quite correct in stating "that Lynn had the honour of presenting the world with Capgrave." If MR. F. NORGATE consults *The Chronicle of England*, by John Capgrave, edited by Rev. F. C. Hingeston, M.A. (London : Longman & Co. 1858), he will see in Appendix III. p. 353, that Capgrave himself mentions in his metrical prologue to the *Life of St. Katharine*, that he was born in Lynn. These are his words : —

"If ye wil wete what that I am,
　Myn cuntre is Northfolk, of the toune of Lynne," &c.

He also states in his *Chronicle* that he was born on the 21st of April, 1393.

With regard to Chaucer being a native of Lynn, here I think "Ben Adam" is incorrect; for though the history of Chaucer is still involved in considerable obscurity; yet I have read in one of his biographies that in his *Testament of Love* he calls himself a *Londoner*. In the inscription on his tombstone, the date of his birth is mentioned as 1328. Is this correct? I understand that the accuracy of Nicholas Brigham, who placed this date on the tomb in 1556, has been called in question.　　　　　　　　　　　J. DALTON.
St. John's, Norwich.

SASH WINDOW (3rd S. vii. 449.) — These windows may be called *à la guillotine* occasionally in France, but this could not have been their original name, that instrument only having been first used in 1792. The word *chassis*, in its primary use, signifies any wood frame, particularly one that is moveable. Tarver's, which is I believe the best phraseological dictionary, says, *levez—baissez le chassis*, lift up — pull down the sash ; *chassis à coulisse*, a sliding sash ; *chassis dormant*, a fixed

sash, &c., &c. It still appears the most probable etymology of the word sash.   A. A.
Poets' Corner.

The first sash windows made in Swalcliffe and its vicinity, Oxon, were to a stone house built for Mr. John Hopkins at Sileford-Gower, which has the date of 1728 in the dovecote, erected at the same time as the house, and tradition states attracted as much notice from their novelty as at Wymondham. The stone built dovecote has the following inscription from the eighth elegy of the first book of Ovid's *Tristia:* —

  " Aspicis, ut veniant ad candida tecta columbæ;
  Accipiat nullas sordida turris aves."

  D. D. H.

EDWARD KIRKE, THE COMMENTATOR ON SPENSER'S SHEPHEARD'S CALENDAR (1st S. x. 204; 2nd S. ix. 42.)—We are glad to be able to furnish the following particulars respecting Edward Kirke, in addition to those contained in *Athenæ Cantabrigienses*, ii. 244. On 26 May, 1580, he was instituted, on the presentation of Sir Thomas Kytson, to the rectory of Risby, Suffolk, as he was on 31 August, 1587, to the rectory of the adjacent parish of Lackford on the same patron's presentation. He died 10 November, 1613, aged sixty, and was buried in the chancel at Risby, where he is commemorated by an inscription. By his will, which bears date three days before his death, he gave 30l. to the poor of Lackford. It is observable that his patron, Sir Thomas Kytson, in his account-book under date of April 1583, has the following entry: "For a shepard's calendar, ijs."

  C. H. & THOMPSON COOPER.
Cambridge.

Miscellaneous.

NOTES ON BOOKS, ETC.

The Natural History, Ancient and Modern, of Precious Stones and Gems, and of the Precious Metals. By C. W. King, M.A., &c. (Bell & Daldy.)

Those who are acquainted with Mr. King's *Antique Gems*, and his work on *The Gnostics and their Remains*, will be quite prepared to believe with how much learning and curious research he has illustrated the volume before us, which may indeed be considered as the filling up of the outline sketched out in the first section of his *Antique Gems*. One remarkable feature of the present work is Mr. King's illustration of gems as magical and medicinal agents; perhaps the most important of their characteristics in later antiquity, as it certainly was throughout the whole of the Middle Ages, when the beauty or rarity of a stone went for infinitely less in the estimation of its value than its reputed virtue in the Pharmacopœia. This portion of Mr. King's book will be found especially interesting, and is made the more valuable by his translation of "Orpheus on Stones"—the great storehouse of Chaldaic lore upon this subject. To practical men, the work will recommend itself in this age of British gold-mining, by its details on the operations of the ancients in the same art: especially as we are now

re-opening the *placers* anciently worked by the Roman masters of North Wales according to the very methods so fully specified by Mr. King's authorities. The ascertained weights of celebrated diamonds, and many authentic descriptions of noteworthy jewels and of celebrated gems, will also be found in this very amusing and instructive volume.

Ballads and Songs of Lancashire, chiefly older than the Nineteenth Century. Collected, compiled, and edited, with Notes, by John Harland, F.S.A. (Whittaker & Co.)

This handsomely printed little volume, containing upwards of sixty of the ballads and songs of Lancashire, will be welcome to all who take an interest in the County Palatine. Many curious snatches of family history, many interesting traces of bygone names and families, are scattered through the volume; which has been carefully and judiciously edited by Mr. Harland.

The Lady Ina, and other Poems. By R. F. H. (Virtue Brothers.)

It needs no ghost come from the grave to tell us that, the many graceful and touching little poems found in this volume, come from the pen of a lady. The strong feeling of affection for home and household which breathes through many of the smaller pieces could only spring from a wife and a mother.

Outlines of Norwegian Grammar, with Exercises; being a Help towards acquiring a Practical Knowledge of the Language. By J. Y. Sargent, M.A. (Rivingtons.)

A very useful little grammar to all intending visitors to Norway—which is so like Danish, that he who knows the one will find it only differs in dialect and pronunciation from the other.

Notices to Correspondents.

This being the last number of the present volume, We have been desirous to include in it as many Replies as possible, and have therefore to request the indulgence of some of our Querists and Note Makers for the postponement of their communications.

"N. & Q." *of Saturday next, the first number of our new volume, and following numbers, will contain, among other papers of interest* :—
  Literary Inquiries and the Court of Probate.
  The Academy of Paris, *by J. G. Nichols.*
  Purcell Papers, *by A. Roffe.*
  Daniel Defoe on the Assassination of Rulers.
  Luis de Leon, *by Canon Dalton.*
  Chaucer's Canterbury Tales.
  Inedited Letter of Randle Cotgrave.
  Bishop and Lord Chancellor Thomas Goodrich.
  Shakspeare Emendations.;
  General Literary Index.
  Duel of Junius, &c.

AMPHITRYON. *We have received a letter headed thus, and asking for the origin of the word. This is all that can be deciphered, although we have put the letter into several hands. Even the signature is wholly illegible. The word is spelt wrong. It should be* Amphitryon. *It is in all probability derived from ἀμφί, about, around, and τρύω, to wear, harass, or distress; as a predatory warrior does. Of course a complete history of this mythical hero may be found in Dr. W. Smith's Dictionary. The origin of the word as applied to the host at a dinner is from Molière's comedy, based on the old play of Plautus. When Sosia is puzzled to decide which of the two is the true Amphitryon, he gives his opinion in favour of* "l'Amphitryon chez qui l'on dîne."

TRAVIS. *We do not agree with Sheridan. The correct pronunciation is* "pro-pish-i-a-shun."

LOCKYER'S POEMS.—In the Advertisement in last week's "N. & Q." the price—"10s. 6d." was inadvertently omitted.

ERRATUM.— 3rd S, vii. p. 449, col. 1. line 14 from bottom, *for* "Gatehill" *read* "Gatchell."

*** Cases for binding the volumes of "N. & Q." may be had of the Publisher, and of all Booksellers and Newsmen.

A Reading Case for holding the weekly Nos. of "N. & Q." is now ready, and may be had of all Booksellers and Newsmen, price 1s. 6d.; or, free by post, direct from the publisher, for 1s. 8d.

"NOTES AND QUERIES" *is published at noon on Friday, and is also issued in* MONTHLY PARTS. *The Subscription for* STAMPED COPIES *for Six Months forwarded direct from the Publisher (including the Halfyearly* INDEX) *is 11s. 4d., which may be paid by Post Office Order, payable at the Strand Post Office, in favour of* WILLIAM G. SMITH, 32, WELLINGTON STREET, STRAND, W.C.; *where also all* COMMUNICATIONS FOR THE EDITOR *should be addressed.*

* NOTES & QUERIES" is registered for transmission abroad.

INDEX.

THIRD SERIES.—VOL. VI·I.

[For classified articles, see Anonymous Works, Books recently Published, Epigrams, Epitaphs, Folk Lore Proverbs and Phrases, Quotations, Shaksperiana, and Songs and Ballads.]

St. T. on Smith (R.), author of "A Wonder of Wonders," 155
. Stick, its obsolete meaning, 200
St. Th. on American depreciation of currency, 286
 Author wanted, 439
 Barcroft (John), 328
 Bookbinding, 329
 Massachusetts stone, 286
 Sancroft (Abp.), his sisters, 289
 Savannah, 462
St. Thomas's Hospital founded, 8, 9
Salisbury (Sally), courtesan, 458, 481
Salmon, its price in 1832, 322
Salt (Henry), sale of his antiquities, 441
Salt spilling alluded to by classic writers, 282, 348, 367, 385
Sancroft (Abp.), his sisters, 289
Sandes (Bp. Stephen C.), his seal, 376
Sanderson (Bp. Robert), work on "Episcopacy," 496
Sarsen stones, 43
Sarsfield (Gen.), descendant, 378, 409, 446
Sash windows, their origin, 449, 487, 508
Satan and hell, works on, 144, 220, 266
"Satirist, or Monthly Meteor," 223, 289
Savannah, old engraving of the city, 128, 462
Sawyer (Wm.) on a new Shakspeare emendation, 315, 452
Saxon topography, 65
Sayce (A.) on Horse: Grace, 482
Sayings, incongruous, 150
S. (B.) on Spencer's letter to R. B. Sheridan, 235
S. (C.) on medal of 1601, 114
Scarlett family, 43, 251, 465
Scarth family descent, 417
Schin on cock's feather, 507
 Lang-nebbed things, 405
 On an altar Ed, 428
 Palestine exploration fund, 354
 Sobriquets of regiments, 120
School Calendar, 48
Schorne (Master John), noticed, 413
Schwab (Gustavus), Memoir, 400
Scotch peers, A.D. 1713–14, 395
Scotchmen, travelling, 420, 466
Scotland, motto of the arms, 282; restoration of its ecclesiastical buildings, 47
Scots, Society of Ancient, 341
Scott (Rev. James) of Perth, his death, 223
Scott (Sir Walter) at Melrose Abbey by moonlight, 156, 211, 230; "Ivanhoe," dramatised, 242; his mottoes, 243, 329; Scotch ballad, 460
Scottish historical gossip, 3
"Scottish Monasticon and Episcopal Chronicle," in preparation, 298
S. (D.) on Samuel Hartlib, 449
 New style, 486
S. (E.) on Bernardino, a poet, 9
. Hunt (Leigh), "Description of a Classical Washerwoman," 34
 Milton (John) and Charles II., 35
Sea-serpent again, 178, 250
Seal of the provost of St. Quiricus at Asti, 150
Sebastopol, history of its defence, 86
Secker (Rev. George), D.D., noticed, 157
Sects, religious statistics of, 77
Sedes stercoraria, 102, 271

S. (E. L.) on epigrams, 264, 375
 Homer, translations of, 32
 "Macbeth," passage in, 176
 "Malbrough," a ballad, 262
 Vallancey (General), 26
 Words used in different senses, 367
Senescens on "Hymns Ancient and Modern," 379
"Sentimental and Masonic Magazine," 298
Sermon, a metrical one, 76, 143, 209, 308
Sermons, anecdote on short, 339, 385
Sermons, temp. the Civil War, in MS., 152
Seventh-day Baptists, 97
Sewell (S. C.), M.D., on Hengist and Horsa, 10
Seymour (Robert), "Survey of London," &c., its authorship, 233, 235
S. (F. M.) on John Anderson of Dumbarton, 97
 Anderson (Patrick), 202
 Duncanson family of Cantire, 96
 Fraser epitaphs, 34
 Lee (Principal), manuscripts, 356
 Macaulay (Lord), ancestry, 154
 Mackenzie, Earl of Cromarty, 78
 "Memoirs of the Life of Lord Lovat," 35
 Mount Athos libraries, 199
 Newhaven (Lord), his portrait, 495
 Shaw family of Saughie and Grenock, 299
 Wodrow's Private Letters, 378
 Wyvil of Constable Burton, 257
Shakspear (Arthur) on Shakspeare family, 175
Shakspeare family in Wiltshire, 151; in Rope Walk, Shadwell, 175, 498
Shakspeare (William), indenture of sale of a house in Blackfriars, 181; ode to, 357
Shakspeare's Editors and Commentators, 332
 Plays, Upcott's revision of 1808 of the first folio, 139; Keightley's Shakspeare's Expositor, 175, 207; edition of 1800, 420
Shakspeare and Samuel Daniel, parallel passages, 337

Shaksperiana:—
 Antony and Cleopatra, Act V. Sc. 2: "And never palates more the dung," 395
 Hamlet, Act I. Sc. 1: "The sleaded pollax," 21; Act III. Sc. 2: "A very piaock," 51; Act V. Sc. 2: "He is fat and scant of breath," 52
 Julius Cæsar, Act II. Sc. 1: "For if thou path thy native semblance on," 315, 360, 452
 King Henry the Fourth, Pt. I. Act II. Sc. 1: ' I am stung like a tench," 51; Part II. Act V. Sc. 3: "A dish of carraways," 316
 Macbeth, Act I. Sc. 5: "Blanket of the dark," 51, 176, 266, 316, 452; Act I. Sc. 2: "That do cling together," 175
 Much Ado about Nothing, Act V. Sc. 1: "And sorrow wag," 176
 Othello, Act I. Sc. 1: "A fellow almost damned in a fair wife," 453
 Pericles, Act III. Sc. 1: "The air-remaining lamps," 236, 316, 350
 Twelfth Night, Act II. Sc. 3: "Call me cut," 317
Shaksperiana from 1564 to 1864, 332; sold with Isaac Reed's library, 297, 317
Sharpset (Sam), inquired after, 155, 211
Shaw family of Saughie and Greenock, 299
Shaw (John B.) on "Watte vocat," &c., 366
Shaw (Samuel) on dragon in Herefordshire, 211

END OF THE SEVENTH VOLUME—THIRD SERIES.

Printed by GEORGE ANDREW SPOTTISWOODE, at 5 New-street Square, in the Parish of St. Bride, in the County of Middlesex;
and Published by WILLIAM GREIG SMITH, of 32 Wellington Street, Strand, in the said County.—*Saturday, July* 15, 1865.